# HANDBOOK

## OF THE

# LAW OF WILLS

## AND OTHER PRINCIPLES OF SUCCESSION INCLUDING INTESTACY AND ADMINISTRATION OF DECEDENTS' ESTATES

By
THOMAS E. ATKINSON
LATE PROFESSOR OF LAW, NEW YORK UNIVERSITY

SECOND EDITION

HORNBOOK SERIES

WEST GROUP

Bancroft-Whitney • Clark Boardman Callaghan
Lawyers Cooperative Publishing • WESTLAW® • West Publishing

*For Customer Assistance Call 1-800-328-4880*

610 Opperman Drive
P.O. Box 64526
St. Paul, MN 55164–0526
1–800–328–9352

**ISBN** 0–314–28333-1

*TEXT IS PRINTED ON 10% POST CONSUMER RECYCLED PAPER*

30th Reprint — 2004

To the memory of

WILLARD BARBOUR

under whose guidance the author
did his first legal writing

*

# PREFACE TO FIRST EDITION

This book has been prepared primarily for the use of law students. Hence, instead of confining the discussion entirely to points of law, there are occasional suggestions of a practical nature in connection with the drafting and execution of wills and certain matters relative to the administration of decedents' estates. Descent and distribution and the procedure of administration have been given equal prominence with the substantive law of wills, both because the latter should not be isolated from the other branches of the law of succession and for the reason that the former are left practically untouched in law school courses and handbooks except those entitled wills. A treatment of all topics which may arise in the preparation or construction of wills would necessitate the inclusion of most of the law of trusts and future interests. This has not been attempted. However such parts of these fields, as well as those of property, insurance, taxation, conflict of laws and others as are necessary to present a fair picture of the law of succession have been touched on briefly.

While differing in both approach and scope from Gardner on Wills, the present volume has benefited in many ways from the example of its predecessor in the Hornbook series. Of course any one working in the field is conscious of the influence of the scholarly treatises of Woerner on Administration and Page on Wills. A peculiar obligation must be acknowledged to Professor Percy Bordwell for his accurate and thorough study of the statute law of wills. If similar treatments of the legislation concerning intestacy and administration had been existent, the author's labors would have been greatly lightened and the quality of this volume considerably improved. Effort has been made to cite generally the recent law review notes and comments appertaining to the subject-matter. These critical studies by able law students, usually writing under professorial guidance, have been the source of much assistance in the preparation of the book. Finally acknowledgment must be made of the help received from many articles appearing in the legal periodicals. Their influence upon the book has been great, and only consideration of space dissuades the author from here recounting the names of all the monograph writers whose works are cited in the footnotes. By virtue of both the quality and the quantity of their production of these materials, Professor Joseph Warren, Dean Alvin E. Evans and Professor Philip Mechem deserve particular mention.

To the latter must be acknowledged a deep obligation for assistance and inspiration beyond his published writings. Many ideas, assimilated by the author during a happy association with Professor Mechem, have found their way into the following pages, and it is impossible to accredit them by footnote. Finally, appreciation is expressed for the aid rendered by Professor Robert E. Mathews, who read the book in manuscript and offered many constructive suggestions, most of which have been adopted in the final text.

T. E. A.

University of Missouri,
February 1, 1937.

# PREFACE TO SECOND EDITION

While there have been only minor alterations in arrangement in this edition, there has been a great deal of change in the treatment of particular matters. In part the changes are quite aside from the developments of the past sixteen years. Due to current trends some topics have demanded expansion; to keep the work within reasonable compass others have been condensed. Every section has been brought down to date; many have been largely or entirely rewritten.

The rise of estate planning and the appearance of the Model Probate Code stand out as the major recent events in the field of succession. The first of these has not been disregarded herein, but in the main a book of this character must be content with explanation of basic principles which estate planning takes for granted and upon which it builds. The present edition often reflects the position of the Model Probate Code which the author regards as an influence for elucidation as well as reform. He is proud of his association in the formation of the Code and takes this occasion to express his appreciation and regard for the principal co-laborers upon the project: Professor Lewis M. Simes, Professor Paul E. Basye, and R. G. Patton, Esq.

T. E. A.

New York University
February 2, 1953

# SUMMARY OF CONTENTS


| Chapter | | Page |
|---|---|---|
| 1. | Introduction | 1 |
| 2. | Intestacy | 37 |
| 3. | Limitations Upon Succession | 101 |
| 4. | Testamentary Character and Will Substitutes | 159 |
| 5. | Testamentary Capacity | 228 |
| 6. | Undue Influence, Fraud and Mistake | 253 |
| 7. | Execution of Ordinary Wills | 291 |
| 8. | Special Types of Wills | 355 |
| 9. | Integration, Reference and Condition | 380 |
| 10. | Revocation and Revival | 419 |
| 11. | Probate and Contest of Wills | 480 |
| 12. | Grant of Administration | 561 |
| 13. | Collection and Management of Estate | 629 |
| 14. | Distribution and Settlement of Estate | 716 |
| 15. | Construction and Drafting of Wills | 804 |
| Table of Cases | | 837 |
| Index | | 921 |


*

# TABLE OF CONTENTS

## Chapter 1. Introduction


| Sec. | | Page |
|---|---|---|
| 1. | Terminology | 1 |
| 2. | History of Succession—The Ancient World | 6 |
| 3. | History of Succession—England | 11 |
| 4. | History of Succession—United States | 23 |
| 5. | Social and Economic Bases of Succession | 30 |


## Chapter 2. Intestacy

### England


| | | |
|---|---|---|
| 6. | Descent of Realty | 37 |
| 7. | The Statute of Distribution | 41 |
| 8. | Half-Blood | 50 |
| 9. | Posthumous Heirs | 52 |
| 10. | Aliens | 53 |
| 11. | Felons | 54 |
| 12. | Escheats | 56 |
| 13. | The Modern Law of Succession | 57 |


### United States


| | | |
|---|---|---|
| 14. | General Plan of Descent and Distribution | 60 |
| 15. | The Surviving Spouse's Share | 61 |
| 16. | Descendants' Shares | 64 |
| 17. | Parents' and Their Issue's Shares | 66 |
| 18. | Next of Kin | 68 |
| 19. | Half-Blood | 74 |
| 20. | Posthumous Heirs | 75 |
| 21. | Ancestral Property | 77 |
| 22. | Illegitimates | 81 |
| 23. | Adopted Children | 86 |
| 24. | Aliens | 93 |
| 25. | Convicts | 95 |
| 26. | Escheats | 97 |

## Chapter 3. Limitations upon Succession


| Sec. | | Page |
|---|---|---|
| 27. | Property Interests Which May Pass by Succession | 101 |
| 28. | Property Interests Not Passing by Succession | 103 |
| 29. | Dower and Curtesy | 104 |
| 30. | Statutory Dower | 107 |
| 31. | Antenuptial and Postnuptial Settlements | 110 |
| 32. | Fraud on Spouse's Share | 111 |
| 33. | The Spouse's Election | 118 |
| 34. | Homesteads, Exemptions and Family Allowances | 125 |
| 35. | Charitable Devises | 135 |
| 36. | Protection of Children | 138 |
| 37. | Unworthy Heirs | 147 |


## Chapter 4. Testamentary Character and Will Substitutes


| | | |
|---|---|---|
| 38. | Extra-Legal Devises | 159 |
| 39. | Life Insurance | 161 |
| 40. | Survivorship Interests | 164 |
| 41. | Bank Account Trusts | 173 |
| 42. | Living Trusts | 177 |
| 43. | Deeds | 183 |
| 44. | Contractual Instruments | 193 |
| 45. | Gifts | 199 |
| 46. | Sham Wills | 205 |
| 47. | Letters as Wills | 207 |
| 48. | Contracts to Make Wills | 210 |
| 49. | Joint and Mutual Wills | 222 |


## Chapter 5. Testamentary Capacity


| | | |
|---|---|---|
| 50. | Status and Age | 228 |
| 51. | Mental Capacity—General Requirements | 232 |
| 52. | Insane Delusions | 242 |
| 53. | Moral, Educational and Physical Factors | 249 |


## Chapter 6. Undue Influence, Fraud and Mistake


| | | |
|---|---|---|
| 54. | Sources and Relationship of Rules | 253 |
| 55. | Undue Influence | 235 |
| 56. | Fraud | 263 |
| 57. | Remedies for Fraud and Duress | 270 |
| 58. | Mistake as to the Document Signed, Contents, and Legal Effect | 273 |
| 59. | Mistake in Inducement | 278 |

Sec. Page
60. Mistake in Description of Beneficiary or Property 281
61. Partial Invalidity of a Will 289

Chapter 7. Execution of Ordinary Wills

62. Statutory Sources of the Rules 291
63. Writing 294
64. Testator's Signature 297
65. Witnesses—Number and Competency 308
66. Making or Acknowledging Signature Before Witnesses 321
67. Testator's Request to Witnesses 325
68. Publication 327
69. Animus Attestandi 330
70. Witnesses' Signatures 333
71. Order of Signing 337
72. "In the Presence of" 339
73. Attestation Clause 346
74. Practical Hints Regarding Execution 348

Chapter 8. Special Types of Wills

75. Holographic Wills 355
76. Nuncupative Wills 363
77. Soldiers' and Sailors' Wills 368
78. Wills in Louisiana 375

Chapter 9. Integration, Reference and Condition

79. Integration of Wills 380
80. Incorporation by Reference 385
81. Reference to Acts 394
82. Conditional Devises and Bequests 401
83. Conditional Wills 416

Chapter 10. Revocation and Revival

84. Revocation—Concept and Methods in General 419
85. Revocation by Operation of Law 422
86. Revocation by Physical Act to Will 436
87. Revocation by Subsequent Instrument 446
88. Dependent Relative Revocation 452
89. Re-execution 464
90. Republication by Subsequent Instrument 466
91. Consequences of Republication by Codicil 468

## Chapter 11. Probate and Contest of Wills

| Sec. | | Page |
|---|---|---|
| 92. | Revival by Revocation of Revoking Will | 474 |
| 93. | Probate and Courts of Probate | 480 |
| 94. | Limitations upon Probate | 484 |
| 95. | Procedure in Probate of Will | 491 |
| 96. | Effect and Necessity of Probate | 499 |
| 97. | Probate of Lost or Destroyed Wills | 506 |
| 98. | General Nature of Will Contests | 514 |
| 99. | Parties to Will Contests | 518 |
| 100. | Procedure and Evidence in Will Contests | 531 |
| 101. | Burden of Proof and Presumptions | 541 |
| 102. | Costs and Attorney Fees | 555 |

## Chapter 12. Grant of Administration

| | | |
|---|---|---|
| 103. | Functions and Necessity of Administration | 561 |
| 104. | The Office of Personal Representative | 576 |
| 105. | Joint Representatives | 582 |
| 106. | Ancillary Representatives | 585 |
| 107. | Jurisdiction over Administration | 594 |
| 108. | Appointment of Executors | 602 |
| 109. | Right to Administer | 606 |
| 110. | Disqualifications for Office of Administrator | 612 |
| 111. | Acceptance and Renunciation by Personal Representative | 616 |
| 112. | Proceedings for Appointment | 618 |
| 113. | Bond of Personal Representative | 621 |
| 114. | Revocation of Letters, Removal, and Resignation | 624 |

## Chapter 13. Collection and Management of Estate

| | | |
|---|---|---|
| 115. | Inventory and Appraisal | 629 |
| 116. | Assets—What Are | 635 |
| 117. | Collection and Care of Assets | 645 |
| 118. | Torts of Personal Representatives | 649 |
| 119. | Contracts of Personal Representatives | 650 |
| 120. | Performance of Deceased's Contracts | 657 |
| 121. | Continuation of Deceased's Business | 660 |
| 122. | Sales of Personal Property | 664 |
| 123. | Sales of Realty | 668 |
| 124. | Investment of Assets | 677 |

| Sec. | | Page |
|---|---|---|
| 125. | Payment of Taxes | 680 |
| 126. | Survival of Claims Against Estate | 683 |
| 127. | Enforcement of Claims | 687 |
| 128. | Priority of Claims in Insolvent Estates | 708 |

**Chapter 14. Distribution and Settlement of Estate**

| | | |
|---|---|---|
| 129. | Advancements | 716 |
| 130. | Release of Expectancy | 725 |
| 131. | Transfer of Expectancy | 729 |
| 132. | Classes of Legacies and Devises | 731 |
| 133. | Satisfaction | 737 |
| 134. | Ademption | 741 |
| 135. | Increase and Interest | 749 |
| 136. | Abatement and Charges | 754 |
| 137. | Exoneration | 764 |
| 138. | Election | 767 |
| 139. | Renunciation | 774 |
| 140. | Lapse | 777 |
| 141. | Retainer for Debts of Beneficiaries | 787 |
| 142. | Accounting | 792 |
| 143. | Decree of Distribution | 796 |
| 144. | Refunding | 800 |

**Chapter 15. Construction and Drafting of Wills**

| | | |
|---|---|---|
| 145. | Jurisdiction of Courts | 804 |
| 146. | Construction of Wills | 807 |
| 147. | Suggestions Regarding Drafting of Wills | 817 |

Table of Cases ........ 837

Index ........ 921

# HANDBOOK
## ON
# THE LAW OF WILLS

---

## CHAPTER 1
## INTRODUCTION



### TERMINOLOGY

**1. A will is a person's declaration of what is to be done after his death, which declaration is (1) revocable during his lifetime, (2) operative for no purpose until his death, and (3) applicable to the situation which exists at his death. Usually a will relates to the disposition of the maker's property.**

**The Anglo-American law of succession is burdened with a complicated terminology due to the peculiarities of its historical growth, and particularly because of the distinction drawn between real and personal property.**

As indicated by the title page this book deals with the law of succession to property upon the owner's death. Succession is a broader field than the wills, which is the principal title of the work. Thus the narrower term predominates over the broader. This rather illogical choice of the main title is justified on the ground of traditional usage and because the law of wills probably exceeds in volume and practical importance the rest of the law of succession.

There is often false security in attempts at precise definitions. Still some knowledge of the terminology of the law of succession is advisable at the start. We commence with inquiry into the concept of a will.

Swinburne, one of the earliest English writers on the subject, says "A will is a lawful disposition of that which any would have done after his death." [1] Much later Blackstone defines the will as: "The legal declaration of a man's intention which he wills to be performed after his death." [2] Both of these definitions were suggested by the civil law.[3] They are subject to the possible objection that they may include certain transactions which are not testamentary, such as a present transfer of an interest to commence in enjoyment on the death of the maker.[4]

The celebrated nineteenth century English writer Jarman says: "A will is an instrument by which a person makes a disposition of his property to take effect after his decease, and which is in its nature ambulatory and revocable during his lifetime." [5] This definition properly calls attention to the two principal characteristics of wills, that they are revocable and ambulatory. Ambulatory is sometimes used to denote the quality of being inoperative until death.[6] At other times it is employed to indicate the feature of being capable of dealing with the situation at the time of the maker's death, e. g. by passing property then owned though not acquired until after the will was made.[7] The modern will is ambulatory in both respects, and is revocable as well.

However, Jarman's definition is inadequate in certain other respects. A will is not always a written instrument; there may be oral wills which are valid under some circumstances.[8] In addition, while wills usually dispose of property, this is not necessarily true; for example a duly executed instrument which mere-

1 Testaments and Last Wills, 1640, pt. 1, § 4.

2 2 Bl.Com. 499.

3 See Swinburne, supra note 1, pt. 1, § 2; 2 Bl.Com. 499.

4 See infra § 43.

5 1 Wills, 8th Ed. 1951, 26.

6 Nichols v. Emery, 109 Cal. 323, 329, 41 P. 1089, 50 Am.St.Rep. 43, 1895; Innis v. Michigan Trust Co., 238 Mich. 282, 213 N.W. 85, 1927; Starks v. Lincoln, 316 Mo. 483, 291 S.W. 132, 1927; Gridley v. Gates, 228 App.Div. 579, 240 N.Y.S. 260, 1930.

7 2 Pollock and Maitland, History of English Law, 1895, p. 313. And see Matter of Cutler's Will, 114 Misc. 203, 186 N.Y.S. 271, 1921; Matter of Snowden's Estate, 137 Misc. 56, 245 N.Y.S. 204, 1930; In re Hall's Estate, 159 Wash. 236, 292 P. 401, 1930.

8 See infra §§ 76, 77.

ly appoints a person to have charge of the property after the death is a will, although it contain no direction as to whom the decedent's property passes.[9] Again a will may simply appoint a guardian for the maker's children,[10] or merely revoke former wills.[11] Instruments which have been intended to have testamentary effect have been considered to be wills though they make no effective disposition of property.[12]

While the courts often declared that an instrument invalid for want of proper execution or for lack of capacity of the maker is not the latter's will,[13] it is preferable to use "will" as a colorless expression.[14] Thus there is certainly usage for the expression "invalid will" and that term is sometimes employed in this work.

Formerly the word "will" was used only in connection with real property. If the disposition related to personal property the term "testament" was employed. Often the same instrument disposed of both real and personal property and the term "last will and testament" came into common use. It is still employed, particularly in the instrument itself, but "will" is now ordinarily used to describe a testamentary disposition of either or both sorts of property.

*Other Terminology in the Law of Succession*

When a person leaves a will he is said to have died testate. The person making a will is referred to as the "testator," although in the case of females the expression "testatrix" is often employed. Formerly the expression "devisor" was used to apply to persons making wills of real property; and this is sometimes still done, although "testator" commonly designates the maker of the will regardless of the nature of property of which disposition is

9 Fontaine v. Fontaine, 169 Ark. 1077, 277 S.W. 867, 1925; Reeves v. Duke, 192 Okl. 519, 137 P.2d 897, 147 A.L.R. 634, 1943; In re Douglas' Estate, 303 Pa. 227, 154 A. 376, 1931. But see In re Campia's Estate, 161 S. W.2d 164, Tex.Civ.App.1942 (appointment of beneficiary to fraternal society death benefit not a will).

10 Matter of Meyer, 72 Misc. 566, 131 N.Y.S. 27, 1911; see In re Seymour's Will, 184 N.C. 418, 114 S.E. 626, 1922. But see Williams v. Noland, 10 Tex.Civ.App. 629, 32 S.W. 328, 1895.

11 In re Peirce's Estate, 63 Wash. 437, 115 P. 835, 1911; see infra § 87. But see Coffman v. Coffman, 85 Va. 459, 8 S.E. 672, 2 L.R.A. 848, 17 Am.St.Rep. 69, 1888.

12 Thomas v. Timonds, 179 Iowa 509, 159 N.W. 881, 1917; In re Douglas' Estate, supra note 9. Cf. In re Seymour's Estate, supra note 10. See Annotation, 147 A.L.R. 536.

13 These of course are the issues determined upon probate, and formerly under devisavit vel non. See infra §§ 93, 98.

14 Cf. Restatement, Property § 12.

made. The person to whom real property is given by a will is commonly called a "devisee" and the disposition itself is denominated a "devise." Money passing under a will is properly called a "legacy," and the person to whom it is given is designated as a "legatee." The term "bequest" includes any form of personalty passing under a will, and hence is technically broader than "legacy." Strictly speaking 'to devise" means to pass realty by testamentary act, while one "bequeaths" only personal property. However, the terms devise, bequest, bequeath, etc., are often used interchangeably without difference in legal effect,[15] though if it appears that the expressions are employed understandingly, their precise technical meanings may be applied.[16]

When a person, whether male or female, dies without leaving a will, he is called an "intestate." In such case the law determines the manner in which his property is divided. The persons entitled to an intestate's realty are called his "heirs," while those succeeding to the personalty are referred to as "distributees," or as "next of kin." [17] To considerable extent the term "heir" is now used to describe the successors of either the real or the personal property of an intestate.[18] This usage will be followed frequently in the present work. Indeed, in popular language the word "heir" is sometimes used to describe any successor to the property of a decedent whether the property passed under intestate laws or by virtue of a will. The intestate laws of a state are frequently called "statutes of descent and distribution." "Descent" applies only to real property, which passes at once from the intestate to the heir upon the former's death.[19] On the other hand, personalty is said to be "distributed" to the next of kin because it vests in the "personal representative," [20] who pays the debts and allots the remaining property among the persons entitled thereto.[21] In case of intestacy the personal representative

15 Miller v. Bower, 260 Pa. 349, 103 A. 727, 1918; Rumel v. Solomon, 54 Utah 25, 180 P. 419, 1919. Throughout the Model Probate Code "devise" includes a disposition of real or personal property or both, while legacy relates only to personalty. Ibid. § 3(c) (d) (e) (n) (*o*).

16 Moore v. Dick, 208 Iowa 693, 225 N.W. 845, 1929; Fleck v. Harmstad, 304 Pa. 302, 155 A. 875, 77 A.L.R. 874, 1931.

17 See N.Y. Decedent Estate Law § 83. Cf. Model Probate Code § 3 (f).

18 See Model Probate Code § 3(j).

19 See N.Y. Decedent Estate Law § 83 and infra §§ 6, 14, 103, 116.

20 This term includes "administrator" and executor. See Model Probate Code § 3(u) and infra this section.

21 See N.Y. Decedent Estate Law § 83 and infra §§ 7, 14, 103, 116.

is appointed by the court and is called the "administrator." If an administrator commences to act and later dies or is removed, his successor is called "administrator de bonis non," or, of the goods not administered, commonly abbreviated, d.b.n.

To revert again to testate estates, the real property devised generally passes directly to the devisee. On the other hand, the testate personalty passes to the personal representative and is by him distributed to the persons entitled thereto under the will.

The person who is named by the will as the one to have charge of the matter of the distribution of the personalty is called the "executor." He may have certain powers with reference to the realty also, either by virtue of the terms of the will or some statutory provision. In case the testator nominates no executor, or if for any reason the person nominated does not act, the court will appoint some one to perform the same functions; such a person is called an "administrator cum testamento annexo," or, with the will annexed, which is commonly abbreviated c.t.a. If an executor dies or is otherwise removed after partially completing the matters of administration, a successor must be appointed to complete the matter of administration, and he is called an "administrator c.t.a., d.b.n." The same cumbersome title would apply to one who succeeded to the duties of an administration c.t.a. In case that a personal representative is a female, the terms "executrix" and "administratrix" are often applied.

Technically the word "probate" denotes the proving of the will before a suitable court, together with the approbation thereof by that tribunal.[22] "Administration" signifies the process by which the personal representative collects the assets, pays the debts and distributes the surplus under supervision of the appropriate court.[23] According to orthodox concepts administration related only to personal property since the realty passed directly to the heirs or devisees,[24] but, with the present extensive powers which the personal representative has over the decedent's realty in many jurisdictions,[25] it is now permissible to speak of administration of both kinds of property. In popular language probate sometimes includes both technical probate and administration, or in other words everything that is done by the personal representative or the court with reference to a decedent's estate. The term probate code is often used to include the entire written law of decedent's estates, substantive as well as proce-

22 See infra § 93.

23 See infra § 103.

24 Ibid.

25 See infra §§ 103, 123.

dural,[26] and probate law ordinarily includes the case law as well as the statutes and is thus practically synonymous with the law of succession.

## HISTORY OF SUCCESSION—THE ANCIENT WORLD

**2. While intestate succession preceded disposition by will, there are evidences of testation before the time of the Romans, who developed a modern and complete theory of testation.**

We are told that family ownership preceded individual ownership.[1] In case of the former there was scarcely need for a system of succession to property because the family continued to exist, although its head had died. As rights and duties concerning property were attached to the group, laws and customs defining the scope and organization of the family took care of the situation. But even at this stage there was room for inheritance of status by individuals.[2] With the recognition of individual as distinguished from family property, rules of succession became necessary. Naturally these followed the earlier rules as to inheritance of status, which in turn depended upon the family or clan structure. It is a mistake to believe that relationship or inheritance was always reckoned on the present basis of kinship to both parents. On the contrary in many older civilizations and in some primitive people today relationship and inheritance are traced through the mother alone, and in others through the father.[3] The latter, sometimes called the agnatic system, prevailed in early Roman society; it finally gave way under change in the form of family organization.[4]

It has been said that intestate succession is much older than disposition by will.[5] Maine contends that the true power of tes-

26 E. g., Cal.Probate Code; Model Probate Code.

1 Maine, Ancient Law, 177 et seq.; Holmes, The Common Law, 1881, 342. Cf. Beaglehole, Ownership and Inheritance in an American Indian Tribe, 20 Ia.L.R. 304.

2 Hoebel, The Anthropology of Inheritance, in 1 Social Meaning of Legal Concepts 5, 20.

3 Adam, Inheritance Law in Primitive Culture, 20 Ia.L.R. 760; Beaglehole, supra note 1; Hoebel, supra note 2 at 16; Radcliffe-Brown, Patrilineal and Matrilineal Succession, 20 Ia.L.R. 286.

4 Radin, Roman Law, 1927, 456–459.

5 Maine, supra note 1 at 189; Beaglehole, supra note 1 at 307. Tacitus, writing in the first century, declares that the will was unknown to the Germans. Germania, c. 20. See also Huebner, History of Germanic Private Law, § 112, (Continental Legal History Series) 749 et seq.

tation was first known to Roman society.[6] However, there are certainly traces of the will in older civilizations.

*Wills in the Egyptian, Assyrian and Jewish Civilizations*

From the Fourth Egyptian Dynasty (2900–2750 B.C.) comes what appears to be a testamentary enactment of an unknown official establishing the endowment of his tomb.[7] In 2548 B.C. we find an Egyptian executing an instrument on papyrus, witnessed by two scribes, settling certain property upon his wife, and appointing a guardian for his infant children. The document, particularly its attestation clause, seems to be in phraseology which might almost be used in a will at the present time.[8] The ancient Code of Hammurabi (cir. 2100 B.C.) makes no mention of wills, except possibly for the provision[9] permitting the father by sealed deed to favor his first born son, in which case it is said that the latter should take the present over and above an equal share with his brothers. Whether this gift to the eldest son was one in præsenti, or whether the "sealed deed" was ambulatory and in the nature of a modern will, is problematical. Apparently the disinheritance of a son could be accomplished only through a judicial proceeding in the lifetime of the father.[10] The Assyrian monarch Sennacherib, who died in 681 B.C., left an instrument naming one of his sons as his successor and bequeathing to him a vast treasure.[11]

The rules regarding succession were a part of the religious code of the ancient Jews. In the Book of Genesis there are several signs of testamentary distribution,[12] but the text does not enable us to decide whether these arrangements were fully testamentary according to modern concepts.[13] At any rate the

6 Maine, supra note 1 at 190. For a study of testation among primitive people, see Cairns, The Explanatory Process in the Field of Inheritance, 20 Ia.L.R. 266, 279-285.

7 Kocourek and Wigmore, Evolution of Law Series, vol. 1, p. 665.

8 24 Irish Law Times, 223.

9 Johns, The Oldest Code of Laws, § 165.

10 Ibid., §§ 168, 169.

11 See Kocourek and Wigmore, Evolution of Law Series, vol. 1, p. 702, where the translated text is set forth. And see Harris, Ancient, Curious and Famous Wills 13. It should be noticed that the verb used in the instrument is in the perfect tense, "have given," instead of the present tense which would be customary today. From the fact that we find a sovereign making a will, we cannot necessarily infer that a subject would be permitted to do so.

12 Genesis, xv, 2–5; xxi, 10–15; xlviii, 21, 22.

13 Maine denies that the early Jews had the institution of testation. Ancient Law, 191.

early Hebrews did not seem to develop the idea of the will to any great extent, and only in default of heirs of the body did the later rabbinical jurisprudence allow testation.[14]

*Greek and Roman Wills*

Among the Greeks a somewhat qualified privilege of testamentary disposition was introduced by Solon.[15] The wills of Plato and Aristotle have been preserved.[16] In Rome the Twelve Tables (cir. 450 B.C.) declared that the head of a household might dispose of his estate, and that this bestowal should have the force and effect of law.[17] Anciently the will was made in the presence of the patrician assemblage, or comitia colata.[18] It is probable that at first the consent of this body was necessary for the validity of the arrangement, but by the time of the Twelve Tables the official audience was required only for reasons of publicity. Probably a plebian desiring to make a will would hesitate to go before the patrician assemblage for that purpose. In addition, the comitia colata met only twice a year. For these reasons, and perhaps others, a more convenient form of will-making was devised. This was the testament "with the copper and the scales" from which has come the modern concept of testamentary disposition.

Originally the testament "with the copper and the scales" was in form and in effect a sale by the owner to his intended successor in the presence of five witnesses and a balance holder to weigh the price paid by the grantee to the grantor.[19] At this time, the transaction differed widely from the present day will, because the transfer took effect immediately and not on the owner's death. In addition, the features of revocability and secrecy were not present. One part of the transaction, however, had in it the germ from which grew the modern concept of the will. This was the nuncupatio, or publication by the grantor. It was originally oral and formal; later it became written, and its terms

14 Maine, supra note 1 at 191; Kent's Commentaries (12th Ed., by O. W. Holmes, Jr.) vol. 4, p. *502, note (a).

15 Maine, supra note 1 at 190, 191; Kent's Commentaries, vol. 4, p. *502.

16 Translated and set forth in Harris, Ancient, Curious and Famous Wills 14–16.

17 Table V, 1; 1 Scott, The Civil Law 66.

18 Gaius, 103–108 (1 Scott, supra note 17 at 124, 125); Ulpian XX, 2 et seq. (Scott, supra note 17 at 239–241); Buckland, The Comitial Will, 32 L.Q.R. 97.

19 See authorities supra note 18.

were binding on the grantee, who no longer needed to be the successor, but who might be a disinterested trustee, and who finally became merely one of the seven witnesses to the civil law will along with the balance holder and the original five witnesses.[20] The history of this development is long, detailed and somewhat obscure, but it is sufficient for present purposes to notice that the change was effected by minimizing the originally important feature of mancipation, or sale, and emphasizing the nuncupatio feature. In this process there gradually evolved the Roman will, revocable, ambulatory and secret. About the only feature of the original testament "with the copper and the scales" which has been preserved is that of the seven witnesses who in later times were required to sign and seal the instrument.

At the time of the Twelve Tables the testator could entirely disinherit his children or other relatives. This led to troublesome attempts to set aside wills, and was followed by a series of enactments curtailing the freedom of testation. In 40 B.C. the Lex Falcidia provided that the person named in the will as the testator's heres, or successor, could not be deprived of more than three-fourths of the estate by legacies to others.[21] Later it was recognized that the testator could not cut off his immediate relatives from more than three-fourths of the estate by excessive legacies or by the naming of a stranger as the heres.[22] The one-fourth part over which the testator had no control was called the "portio legitima" and the share was increased by Justinian to one-third if the testator left four or less children, and one-half if the number exceeded four.[23] The principle of the legitima is found in most modern civil law codes.

As will appear hereafter, the English law received the Roman law concept of a will,[24] and indeed for several centuries the principle of the Roman legitima in the distribution of personal property.[25] On the other hand the Anglo-American law did not accept the basic Roman law theory of universal succession.[26] The latter was the concept that upon the death of the head of the family his personality, including his rights and obligations, con-

20 Radin, Roman Law 401, 402.

21 Ibid., 439, 440.

22 Ibid., 441–443.

23 Ibid., 444. See also Dainow, The Early Sources of Forced Heirship; Its History in Texas and Louisiana, 4 La.L.R. 42; infra § 36.

24 See infra § 3 at notes 32, 33, 57, 58, 76, 83.

25 See infra § 3 at note 38 et seq.

26 But cf. Atkinson, Brief History of Testamentary Jurisdiction, 8 Mo. L.R. 107, 111.

tinued in his heir. At the moment of death, the estates of both ancestor and heir, including their rights and obligations, were merged in the heir.[27] The latter might disclaim if he thought the succession would be burdensome to him, but if he accepted he was obliged to pay the hereditary debts even though they exceeded the value of the property coming from the ancestor. Under the Justinian law [28] this was modified by providing that the heir might take "with benefit of inventory," so as to restrict his liability to the extent of the assets received and recorded. If a will were made, that instrument appointed or instituted the heir or the heirs, for heirship might be plural. Usually the instituted heir would be among the testator's beneficiaries, but his beneficial interest might be reduced by legacies or by the legitima.[29] Indeed he might have no beneficial interest, in which case his function was simply to administer the estate. However, it is a mistake to regard him as the equivalent of the common-law executor or administrator, who took only the personalty of his decedent and even that was not merged with his own property. Likewise the civil law heir is distinguished from the English heir whose common-law liability for debts was limited and who took only the real property and even that by separate parcels.[30] If we could conceive of the English personal representative and English heir as a composite figure, he would be a different and somewhat lesser personage than the Roman universal heir. Universal succession is still basic in the civil law countries which have patterned their jurisprudence after Roman law.

27 Radin, Roman Law § 146.

28 Codex 6, 30, 22.

29 Radin, Roman Law §§ 164, 165.

30 Rheinstein, European Methods for the Liquidation of the Debts of Deceased Persons, 20 Ia.L.R. 431. See also note 26 supra.

## HISTORY OF SUCCESSION—ENGLAND

**3. The primitive law of succession among the Anglo-Saxons was supplanted after the Conquest by the principles that real property passed directly to the heir, while personal property went to the personal representative for administration and distribution among the next of kin. There were marked distinctions in many respects as to the passage of the two types of property upon death. Legislation in the 19th and 20th centuries has practically obliterated these distinctions and has placed succession upon a more rational basis.**

### *The Anglo-Saxon Era*

Pollock and Maitland declare that there is no record of family ownership among the Anglo-Saxons and that the indications are against it.[1] Rules of intestate succession existed although apparently the same scheme did not apply to all sorts of property.[2] Thus folkland might pass in a certain way and bookland in quite another. There are traces of primogeniture among the humbler folk but it certainly did not come into full operation until after the Conquest.[3] It is possible that distinction was drawn between property inherited from the father's and the mother's families. Different rules governed the succession of chattels from those appertaining to land, and distinction may have been made between various kinds of personalty. For example, a man's armor and the wife's effects probably went to different persons.

As in Rome, the modern concept of the will—revocable, ambulatory, and secret—was slow in developing. The chief struggle of the Anglo-Saxon period was over the question whether a man could deprive his heirs of his property by any form of transfer, regardless of whether it took effect in the lifetime or at the death of the owner. In the case of chattels there was considerable freedom of disposal, largely through the influence of the church, which hoped to gain thereby.[4] With respect to folkland, the fact

1 2 History of English Law, 1895, 248.

2 Ibid. 257.

3 Ibid. 261; Bigelow, The Rise of the English Will, 18 Harv.L.R. 69, 79. Tacitus says that the Germans preferred males to females in succession. Germania c. 20. See also Lex Salica, 59; 2 Pollock and Maitland 248. The Saxon law shows traces of the German scheme. 2 Pollock and Maitland, c. 6, § 1; Rightmire, Law of England at the Norman Conquest, 1932, 147, note.

4 2 Pollock and Maitland, 317. It has been suggested that as in twelfth and thirteenth century in England the power of free disposition may have been limited to a portion of the

that the heir ordinarily joined in the conveyance may be taken as an indication that one could not freely dispose of this species of property.[5] In the case of bookland, however, the owner could apparently give the property to whom he pleased.[6] We find that land was commonly transferred by post obit gift. By reserving a life estate in the realty, the owner retained the right of enjoyment until his death, when it passed to the donee.[7] There was also the deathbed disposition, usually made under the supervision of the priest in connection with the last confession.[8] The dying man gave his chattels and perhaps his land to some friend to be divided in accordance with verbal instructions. The transaction was a present transfer, accompanied by a delivery in so far as the situation permitted one. From the practical standpoint the fact that the gift took effect immediately was not objectionable because the donor was in extremis.

Neither the post obit gift nor the deathbed distribution had the characteristics of secrecy, revocability, or ambulatoriness, though they did perform imperfectly the functions of the modern will. In the ninth, tenth, and eleventh centuries these two forms of disposition seem to merge into the Anglo-Saxon cwide, a written statement directing the manner in which property should be disposed of after death.[9] The traditional view [10] that wills were permitted among the Anglo-Saxons doubtless was based on this form of instrument. Pollock and Maitland regard the cwides as special privileges of great personages, and they doubt whether these instruments were fully testamentary in nature.[11] Page, after a review of the preserved documents, tends toward the traditional view.[12]

*From the Conquest to 1540*

With the Conquest came two important factors which have shaped the English law of succession. One is the Norman brand of feudalism; its influence upon the land law is universally ap-

owner's property. 2 Holdsworth, History of English Law, 1927, 94. See note 39 infra.

5 2 Holdsworth, 94; see Rightmire, Law of England at the Norman Conquest 147, n. 97.

6 2 Holdsworth 94, 95.

7 2 Pollock and Maitland 315.

8 2 Pollock and Maitland 316, 317.

9 Ibid.

10 Reeves, History of the English Law, 1792 Dublin Ed., 11. See also Bigelow, The Rise of the English Will, 18 Harv.L.R. 69.

11 2 Pollock and Maitland 317, 318.

12 Wills, 1941, § 13.

preciated.[13] The other is the separation of the lay and ecclesiastical courts by royal ordinance of William the Conqueror.[14] The significance of this decree is great. As the result, the law of succession to land was moulded by the tough judgments of the royal courts, while succession to chattels came under the jurisdiction of the church courts, which developed an ecclesiastical pattern based on the canon and the Roman law and retained their testamentary powers, with some diminution toward the end, for almost eight centuries.[15] Different courts, different influences, different law. Hence the distinction between succession to real and personal property, a bother which continues in American law, though the English have dealt with it by modern forthright legislation.

*Same—Land*

After momentary wavering as to whether Norman feudal principles would permit inheritance of land at all,[16] the general principle of primogeniture or succession to the freehold by the eldest son was recognized.[17] Primogeniture was not the only precept of the law of descent of land but it was the most important one. Most of the basic principles were settled by the time of Henry III.[18] As the result of somewhat later developments it was established that neither the heir nor the land were liable for payment of the ancestor's debts except in case of sealed obligations by which the ancestor expressly bound his heir.[19]

The heir's position was thus an enviable one; moreover it became established that the ancestor could not defeat his interest by devise to another. While the Conquest did not result in any sudden change in the Saxon law and customs regarding testation,[20] Glanville, writing about 1180, said that God alone, and not man, can make an heir.[21] He declares that one might give away all his purchased land in his lifetime, but that wills and even deathbed gifts of realty were forbidden.[22] A case decided a few

13 Holdsworth, Historical Introduction to the Land Law 26.

14 Stubbs, Select Charters, 9th ed. 1913, 19.

15 Atkinson, Brief History of English Testamentary Jurisdiction, 8 Mo. L.R. 107, 109 and passim.

16 2 Pollock and Maitland 264.

17 Ibid. 257–272.

18 Ibid. 257. For details see infra § 6.

19 Ibid. 345.

20 2 Pollock and Maitland 321; Reeves, supra note 10 at 29, 30.

21 VII, 1.

22 VII, 1, 5.

years after Glanville supports his statement as to deathbed gifts.[23] Some authorities[24] place the judicial condemnation of wills devising land at a century later than Glanville. There can be no doubt, however, but that at least at the end of the thirteenth century the courts had firmly established the rule. This position was taken doubtless in part to strengthen the institution of feudalism, and in part to protect the heir against dissipation of the inheritance by the ancestor. Theoretical justification for the prohibition of devises can be found in the doctrine of the time, that land could be transferred only by livery of seisin. Certain interests in land were excepted from the rigor of the common law rule. Thus, leaseholds were regarded as personalty and might pass by will.[25]

Barred of the privilege of devising their freehold lands to younger sons or others, important landowners often escaped this common-law disability by making feoffments to uses. If A conveyed land to B to the use of C, courts of law recognized B as the owner and would not compel him to perform the use. Chancery, however, would intervene and require B to account to C in accordance with the terms of the use. By the latter part of the fourteenth century it came to be the practice for A to enfeoff B for the use of such person as A might appoint.[26] The instrument of appointment, enforceable in equity, performed the function of a will. This method of dealing with land continued until the passage of the Statute of Uses, 1535,[27] which abolished the use and declared that the legal title was in the person for whom the use was created. The gentry demanded some means through which they might make a post mortem disposition of land.[28] This request was fulfilled by the enactment of the Statute of Wills, 1540.[29]

23 2 Pollock and Maitland 325.

24 3 Holdsworth 75. His opinion is based upon fluctuating opinions by Bracton, who wrote about 1258. Maitland expressed the belief that the power to devise was almost won in the middle of the thirteenth century through the per formam doni (language contained in the grant which purported to give the donee the power to devise). A Conveyancer in the Thirteenth Century, 7 Law.Q.R. 63, 67, 68.

25 2 Pollock and Maitland, 115, 329.

26 4 Holdsworth 420, 422.

27 27 Hen. VIII, c. 10.

28 4 Holdsworth 464, 465.

29 32 Hen. VIII, c. 1. See infra note 56 et seq.

### *Same—Chattels*

It was in the realm of personalty that the modern concept of testation developed in England. Soon after the Conquest the church courts were allowed supervision over testamentary matters concerning chattels,[30] and in the thirteenth century they obtained exclusive jurisdiction in this field.[31] Borrowing the Roman law theory of the will, the ecclesiastical courts made testation popular.[32] At least by this time there was in England a revocable and ambulatory instrument, which, while it applied only to personalty, was well understood and enforced. Secrecy might be obtained through a writing, though the testament of this period might be wholly or partially oral.[33] The institution of the executor became firmly established,[34] though the origin of this office goes back to the Anglo-Saxon distributor of deathbed gifts, and perhaps to even more remote Germanic influences.[35] The church taught that intestacy was a horror to be avoided if humanly possible.[36] Dying without a will was regarded much the same as dying unconfessed, and in early times the prelates undertook to distribute the intestate's goods for the welfare of his soul.[37]

A testator, however, was not allowed freedom to dispose of all his chattels to whom he pleased. Something like the Roman legitima was recognized in the early Norman period, if indeed there was not a similar customary law among the Anglo-Saxons.[38] Liberty of testation was given only with respect to one-third of the chattels if the owner left a wife and children, and concerning half if either spouse or issue survived.[39] Only in

30 See infra note 31 and supra notes 14, 15.

31 2 Pollock and Maitland 330 332; Reeves, supra note 10 at p. 307; Reppy and Tompkins, History of Wills 4; Bordwell, Introduction to Wills and Administration, 14 Minn.L.R. 1, 4, 5. For an account of how equity later took over most of the functions of administration after probate and appointment of the personal representative, see Langdell, A Brief Survey of Equity Jurisdiction, arts. 6, 7, reprinted from 4 Harv.L.R. 99–127, 5 Harv.L.R. 101–138; Bordwell, supra at 8–10.

32 But see Lee, The Evolution of the Modern Will, 46 Am.L.Rev. 641.

33 3 Holdsworth 537–539.

34 2 Pollock and Maitland 332.

35 Ibid. 333 et seq. But see Holmes, The Common Law, p. 344.

36 2 Pollock and Maitland 354.

37 Ibid. 358. The widow's and children's shares were mentioned in Magna Charta, c. 18.

38 See Dainow, Limitations on Testamentary Freedom in England, 25 Corn.L.R. 337, 339.

39 Glanville, VII, 5; Bracton, De Legibus, f. 60b, 61; 2 Pollock and Maitland 347.

case one left neither wife nor children could he dispose of his entire personalty by testament. These rules were recognized in both the king's courts and the ecclesiastical tribunals.[40] An early common law writ called "de rationabili parte bonorum" existed by which the wife and children could obtain their shares.[41] In the fourteenth century the legitima principle tended to disappear from the general law of the land.[42] Although the system of forced shares based upon family ties continued to be recognized for many years thereafter in some places as a matter of local custom, freedom of testation became the norm of the English law with respect to personalty.[43]

Our knowledge of the manner of distribution of an intestate's chattels in the middle ages is far from complete, and the law itself seems to have been vague and fluctuating. Taken by and large the subject was not of great importance. The value of chattel interests was then comparatively small. Furthermore if a person died, confessed, he usually made a will.[44] Still, one might die possessed of tangible personalty of more than negligible value, and intestacy because of sudden death without the benefit of a priest was far from rare.[45] Three forces laid claim to the intestate's goods: (1) The king or the lord; (2) the church; (3) the family or next of kin.[46] It was not until comparatively late that the matter was settled in favor of the latter, subject to being worked out under the auspices of the church courts.

Glanville states that an intestate's chattels were understood to belong to his lord,[47] though perhaps the latter customarily gave the widow and children their reasonable shares of which the deceased could not have disposed by will. Magna Charta [48] provided that an intestate's chattels were distributed by his near kinsmen by view of the church, saving the debts due from the deceased,

40 2 Pollock and Maitland 350, 351; 3 Holdsworth 550.

41 The writ is given by Glanville, Bk. VII, 7.

42 3 Holdsworth 552.

43 The system of forced shares to the widow and children remained in York until it was abolished by 4, 5 Wm. & Mary, c. 2, 1692; in Wales by 7, 8 Wm. III, c. 38, 1696; in London by 11 Geo. I, c. 18, 1724. Moreover the old scheme remained the rule of intestate succession in these places until 19 & 20 Victoria, c. 94, 1856.

44 2 Pollock and Maitland 312, 354.

45 Cf. 2 Pollock and Maitland 358, with Gross, The Medieval Law of Intestacy, 18 Harv.L.R. 120, 121.

46 Gross, ibid.; 2 Pollock and Maitland 354–361; 161 L.T. 241.

47 The Laws and Customs of England, VII, 16

48 C. 27, 1215.

but this provision was not included in the later confirmations of the charter.[49] Bracton says that in case of sudden death the lord should not seize the chattels but these should go to his friends and the church.[50] The lord was losing the battle, and we know that the church was asserting the right to administer the chattels, since the Statute of Westminster II, 1285, provided that the ordinary (judge of the ecclesiastical court) must pay the intestate's debts in the same manner as executors were bound to pay their testator's debts.[51] Probably in most instances the church retained only the share of which the deceased could dispose by will, and allowed the widow and children their customary portions.[52]

The arrangement of administration by the ordinary proved unsatisfactory. In 1357 another statute declared that the later should depute the next and most lawful friends of the intestate to administer his goods.[53] This originated the offices of the administrator whose powers and duties were equivalent to those of the executor. Now there is a personal representative in intestate as well as testate estates. He gets his authority from the probate of the will or the grant of administration by the church courts, which supervise his handling of the chattels. He is the one who sues to collect the assets and is sued on account of the decedent's debts. True, these actions are in the king's courts, but the latter recognize his authority and the jurisdiction of the church courts over his appointment.[54]

At this stage there was one great deficiency in the law. It was not clear how the surplus should be divided after payment of the intestate's debts. The church once claimed the dead man's part over which he had power of testation, leaving to the widow and children only their reasonable portions. Probably the church was often satisfied with less, particularly if the estate was small and the family poor. But the church courts ordered distribution according to loose and uncertain practices, which were not solidified into a definite pattern until the seventeenth century.[55]

49 Gross, supra note 45; McKechnie, Magna Carta, 1914, 326–329.

50 Bracton, f. 60b.

51 13 Edw. I, st. 1, c. 19, 1285.

52 3 Holdsworth 550–554; 2 Pollock and Maitland, 359, 360, showing letters of administration of 1313, which follow this scheme of intestate succession.

53 31 Edw. III, st. 1, c. 11.

54 Atkinson, Brief History of Testamentary Jurisdiction, 8 Mo.L.R. 107, 112–114.

55 Ibid. at 114. See also note 52 supra; infra notes 63–66.

*1540 to 1776*

Five years after an effective substitute for the power to devise land had been cut off by the Statute of Uses, 1535, Parliament passed the Statute of Wills, 1540.[56] The latter permitted a devise of land by an instrument in writing. No attesting witnesses were necessary and the will was not required to be signed by the testator or written in his hand. The instrument was testamentary in the sense that it was revocable and inoperative until death, but it could not operate upon property which testator had acquired after execution of the will.[57] Hence wills under this statute were not fully testamentary in contrast with the testaments which the church courts had conceived for chattels according to Roman law patterns.[58]

At the commencement of this period the church courts' jurisdiction over decedent's personalty was in its heyday. While referred to as "testamentary jurisdiction" it included not only probate of wills but also grant of letters of administration, and supervision over and litigation concerning inventories and the payment of legacies and distributive shares.[59] But the ecclesiastical jurisdiction never extended to hearing a plea of debt in favor of or against decedent, nor over any matter concerning his freehold.[60]

After the reign of Elizabeth the prestige of the courts Christian declined. This was due in part to weaknesses in these courts, including their unwillingness to enforce their decrees except by threat of excommunication or less stringent ecclesiastical sanctions. Then, too, the courts of law began to issue writs of prohibition against the exercise of certain parts of the earlier testamentary jurisdiction.[61] Even more important was the competition of the Court of Chancery, which, through its machinery to enforce discovery and accounting, was better fitted to settle the controversies in an involved estate than the church courts ever were.[62]

56 32 Hen. VIII, c. 1, 1540. This law gave power to devise all socage land and two-thirds of that held in military tenure. With the abolition of military tenure by 12 Car. II c. 24, 1660, one could thereafter devise all his land.

57 See 2 Pollock and Maitland 313.

58 See supra at note 30 et seq.

59 Atkinson, Brief Summary of Ecclesiastical Jurisdiction, 8 Mo.L.R. 107, 115–117.

60 Ibid. at 113.

61 Ibid. at 117–118.

62 See Langdell, A Brief Survey of Equity Jurisdiction, arts. 6, 7, reprinted from 4 Harv.L.R. 99–127, 5 ibid. 101–138.

The Statute of Distribution, 1670,[63] was an attempt to bolster up the waning testamentary jurisdiction of the church courts. It required administrators to give bond to secure performance of their duties, forbade distribution until a year after the intestate's death, and brought the latter's advancements to his children into hotchpot in order to equalize their shares. Even more important was the enactment of a definite scheme of ultimate distribution of chattels between the widow and the children, or the next of kin. This clarified the prior loose practice,[64] and with little alteration[65] remained the plan of succession to personalty for more than two and a half centuries.[66] As the result of these provisions the church courts retained their powers to probate testaments of personalty and to grant administration of intestate until 1857.[67] They also exercised some of the other phases of their earlier jurisdiction if called on and permitted to do so.[68] But this was indeed a "lame jurisdiction",[69] overshadowed by equity and to some extent by the courts of the common law.

Several sections of the Statute of Frauds, 1677,[70] dealt with the formalities of wills and testaments. Prior to this statute testaments of personalty might be oral, though in practice they were usually in writing unless the testator was in extremis.[71] Section 19 specified a writing as a general requirement for testaments, although it did not require testator's signature or attesting witnesses. However, a testator in his last sickness was ex-

63 22 & 23 Car. II c. 10.

64 See supra at notes 52, 55.

65 The act was originally experimental and by its terms remained in force for only seven years. However, it was continued indefinitely with a single change by 1 James II, c. 17, § 7, 1685. Section iv of the original act provided that the rules of succession should not apply to London, York or other places having peculiar customs. See note 43 supra. According to section 8 of 1 James II, c. 17, 1685, the dead man's part which had formerly been claimed by the administrator thereafter passed according to the Statute of Distribution even in London and York. See 2 Bl.Com. 518.

66 See infra note 89.

67 See infra note 86.

68 It is a mistake to believe that the church courts' testamentary jurisdiction, aside from probate and grant of administration, became obsolete prior to 1857. On the contrary we find them entertaining litigation regarding inventories and accounts, legacies and similar matters down to the very last. Atkinson, Brief Summary of Testamentary Jurisdiction, 8 Mo.L.R. 107, 121, 123–124.

69 Matthews v. Newby, 1 Vern. 133, 23 Eng.Rep. 368, 1682.

70 29 Car. II, c. 3, xii.

71 Swinburne, Testaments and Last Wills, 1640, pt. 1, § 12.

pressly permitted to make an oral will of his chattels in the presence of three witnesses though no testimony was admissible to prove such disposition after six months unless the testimony was reduced to writing within six days after making of the oral will.[72] Moreover, no writing at all was required for dispositions of chattels under thirty pounds, nor if the testator were a soldier in military service or a mariner at sea.[73]

Section 5 of the statute increased the formalities required for devises of land by providing that they "shall be in writing, and signed by the party so devising the same, or by other person in his presence and by his express directions, and shall be attested and subscribed, in the presence of the said devisor by three or four credible witnesses." As a result, a will and testament disposing of both real and personal property was required to comply with the more stringent requirements of the fifth section. It was customary for a single instrument to dispose of both species of property, but two important distinctions were maintained. First it was necessary to secure probate by the church court so as to establish the disposition of the personalty but this probate had no effect as to devises made in the same instrument.[74] The validity of a devise was ordinarily tested in a common-law action of ejectment brought by the heir against the devisee or vice versa.[75] The second distinction was that after-acquired personalty might pass by the instrument but, in accordance with the earlier rule, devises were limited in their operation to land owned by the testator at the time of execution.[76]

As in the earlier law neither the heir nor the land were liable for the ancestor's debts except those which were created by instrument under seal and expressly made binding on the heir. Indeed the ancestor could defeat even his bond creditors by devising his land.[77] To remedy this situation Parliament passes the Statute of Fraudulent Devises, 1691,[78] extending the remedy of the testator's specialty creditor to the devisee of the land. The same act also provided that an heir who alienated the land should

[72] 29 Car. II, c. 3, §§ xix, xx.

[73] Ibid., § xxiii.

[74] See Ash v. Calvert, 2 Camp. 387, 170 Eng.Rep. 1193, 1810.

[75] Ibid. See infra § 93.

[76] Wright v. Hall, Fort. 182, 92 Eng.Rep. 810, 1725; Bunker v. Cooke, Fitz. 225, 94 Eng.Rep. 730, 1731. See 2 Pollock and Maitland 313; 7 Holdsworth, 364–366; infra §§ 85, 91.

[77] Muldoon v. Moore, 55 N.J.L. 410, 26 A. 892, 21 L.R.A. 89, 1893; 2 Bl. Com. 378.

[78] 3 Wm. & Mary, c. 14, made perpetual by 6 & 7 Wm. III, c. 14, 1695.

be liable on a specialty claim to the extent of the value received, but neither the grantee nor the land were liable for the debt.

Here is the broad picture of the law of succession in the mother country at the time of the separation of the American colonies. Land and personalty go their separate ways, the former to the heir or devisee and the latter to the administrator or executor. While the heir of the land is a distributee of the personalty he must usually share the property with other distributees. Land is devisable but there are important distinctions between the operation of wills of land and of personalty. There are also other distinctions in the manner of succession of land and of chattels, largely the result of the Norman differentiation of court jurisdiction over succession to the two species of property.

*After 1776*

What happened in England after the Revolution is not a part of the American heritage. But it has had influence upon our legislation and case law and doubtless will continue to do so. The younger nation cannot overlook the success of the mother country in simplifying and modernizing her law of succession.

The first half century after 1776 brought about little change in that law. Reform was in the air, however, and in 1832 and 1833 two royal commissions brought in reports. One suggested a reorganization of the church courts and the other the vesting of their testamentary jurisdiction in a new tribunal. Both urged uniform formalities for wills of realty and personalty and that probate should be equally effective as to each.[79]

In 1833 it was provided by statute that a decedent's land should be liable for all debts.[80] The Wills Act, 1837,[81] made uniform rules for the execution, revocation, revival and construction of wills of realty and personalty. The act provided that the will must be signed at the end thereof by the testator or by some other person in his presence and by his direction, and be attested and signed by two or more witnesses in his presence.[82] The old rule preventing the devise of after-acquired land was abolished by the provision that all wills shall be construed with reference

[79] See Atkinson, Brief Survey of Equity Jurisdiction, 8 Mo.L.R. 107, 122–123.

[80] 3 & 4 Wm. IV, c. 104. By 47 Geo. III, stat. 2, c. 74, 1807, the lands of deceased traders had been made liable for their debts generally.

[81] 7 Wm. IV and I Vict., c. 26, iii.

[82] See § ix. By § xl the pre-existing right of soldiers and sailors to dispose of their personalty by informal wills was continued. This privilege was extended to their realty by 7 & 8 Geo. V, c. 58, 1918.

to all property as to speak and take effect immediately before the death of the testator unless a contrary intention appears.[83] With some amendments this act is still in force in England.[84]

The ecclesiastical courts and their practitioners put up a determined battle against the abolition of their testamentary jurisdiction.[85] It was a losing fight for in 1857 Parliament passed the Court of Probate Act[86] which vested jurisdiction to probate wills and grant administrations in a new Court of Probate, although the Court of Chancery retained its power to administer estates of decedents, a jurisdiction which it had in practice largely obtained more than two centuries before. The act also made the probate of wills disposing of realty and personalty effective as to both species of property.[87]

An important provision of the Land Transfer Act, 1897,[88] vested both real and personal property in the personal representative, with the result that a decedent's land passed to his heir or devisee only upon assent or conveyance of the administrator or executor. In other words the statute applied the existing rule as to personalty to realty as well.

It remained for the Administration of Estates Act, 1925,[89] to abolish primogeniture and to enact a single uniform table for the intestate succession of all property, real and personal. A companion act put the procedural law of succession upon a rational uniform basis in many other respects, and also repealed or codified many old statutes, some of them of many centuries standing.[90]

The final important step was the passage of the Inheritance (Family Provision) Act, 1938,[91] which limited the principle of testamentary freedom by authorizing substantial judicial allowances for the benefit of the surviving spouse and children if the testator neglected to provide for them in his will.

83 7 Wm. IV & 1 Vict., c. 26, § iii. See also §§ xxiv, xxv.

84 See Lord St. Leonards' Act (Wills Amendment Act, 1852) 15 & 16 Vict. c. 24.

85 Atkinson, Brief History of Testamentary Jurisdiction, 8 Mo.L.R. 107, 123, 124.

86 20 & 21 Vict. c. 77.

87 Ibid. § 62.

88 60 & 61 Vict. c. 65 § 1(1). By § 1(3) probate is made effective as to wills which disposed of lands alone. See supra note 87.

89 15 Geo. V, c. 23 § 45 et seq. The original reform by the Law of Property Act, 1922, 12 & 13 Geo. V, c. 16 Part VII, was repealed except for § 152 regarding revocation of wills by marriage.

90 Supreme Court of Judicature (Consolidation) Act, 1925, 15 Geo. V. c. 49.

91 1 & 2 Geo. VI, c. 45. See infra § 5 at notes 33, 34.

As a result, the English statutory law of succession can now be found in a few well-considered statutes. The historical anomalies arising out of the distinction of real and personal are practically gone. It is true that court jurisdiction is divided; the Probate, Divorce and Admiralty Division grants probates and letters; the Chancery Division entertains judicial administration of estates; the King's Bench Division has jurisdiction over various types of litigations by and against personal representatives. Still all three divisions are parts of the single High Court of Justice. Moreover, the typical English estate is administered without judicial action after grant of probate and letters. Voluntary settlement is possible because the law is certain and the rights of the parties are usually apparent. Disputes are usually settled without litigation or judicial administration, although if the latter is demanded there are effective, though expensive, methods of adjudication.[92]

## HISTORY OF SUCCESSION—UNITED STATES

**4. While the basic pattern of the American substantive law of succession was derived from the English, there was considerable deviation from the very start and important American innovations in procedural and administrative aspects. Testamentary jurisdiction has been vested in the American probate courts which have exercised closer judicial supervision over decedents' estates than the English courts.**

America was spared many of the problems of succession which had already been settled by the English. Before colonization land had become devisable and the legitima was no longer the rule applied to personal property.[1] While the colonial charters enjoined the colonists to follow the law of England they did not always do so with regard to matters of succession; indeed, in certain respects they could not observe the system of the mother country. There were no bishops of the established church here, and hence no ecclesiastical courts to exercise testamentary jurisdiction. Then, too, social and economic conditions were different in the new land. For one thing land was plentiful and regarded as a commodity rather than a birthright.[2]

92 Atkinson, Brief History of Testamentary Jurisdiction, 8 Mo.L.R. 107, 125–127; Simes and Basye, The Organization of the Probate Courts in America, 42 Mich.L.R. 965, 974.

1 See supra § 3 at notes 42, 43, 56.

2 See Haskins, The Beginnings of

*Massachusetts*

Here the early divergence from the law of England was more marked than in the middle and southern colonies.[3] The independent spirit of the people was demonstrated by the way in which a decedent's land and goods passed in Plymouth and Massachusetts Bay. Primogeniture was usually disregarded.[4] Early laws called for the same division of both realty and personalty aside from the complications of dower and the share of the surviving spouse.[5] There was flexibility too, and the court was known to award the overplus of the goods to the lame daughter.[6] Land was liable for debts generally and was usually included in the inventory.[7] During the earlier part of the seventeenth century land and chattels seemed to pass as one conglomerate mass.[8] Perhaps the colonists did not know the law of England in this respect, or did not care, or both. This practice gave way in the eighteenth century to the orthodoxy of land passing to the heirs or devisees and of personalty vesting in the personal representatives.[9] But probate established devises as well as bequests.[10] A single table of descent and distribution remained.[11] In 1696 the liability of decedent's land for payment of his debts was implemented by a statute permitting a sale by the personal representative acting under court order.[12]

In both Plymouth and Massachusetts Bay testamentary jurisdiction was exercised first in the General Court or the Court of the Assistants; later in the county courts.[13] When these colonies were united as the Province of Massachusetts in 1691, the

Partible Inheritance in the American Colonies, 51 Yale L.J. 1280, passim.

3 See infra notes 4, 19–21.

4 Atkinson, The Development of the Massachusetts Probate System, 42 Mich.L.R. 425, 430. Until 1789 the eldest son was given a double portion. Ibid. 430, 437, 438, 443–444, 448. A like result obtained in Connecticut though there the struggle was more bitter. Andrews, The Influence of Colonial Conditions as Illustrated in the Connecticut Intestacy Laws, 3 Yale L. J. 261, reprinted in 1 Select Essays in Anglo-American Legal History, 431; Haskins, supra note 2. However, in Rhode Island, New York, Maryland, Virginia, the Carolinas and Georgia primogeniture was in force until after the American Revolution. Morris, Primogeniture and Entailment of Estates in America, 27 Col.L.R. 24, 25.

5 Atkinson, supra note 4 at 430, 439, 443–444, 448.

6 Ibid. 434, 437.

7 Ibid. 427, 428, 430, 433, 434, 439, 445, 451.

8 Ibid. 437, 443.

9 Ibid. 445, 447, 448, 449.

10 Ibid. 448.

11 Ibid. 443–444, 448.

12 Ibid. 445, 448, 450.

13 Ibid. 427, 431, 432–444.

new charter provided that the royal Governor should be the Supreme Court of Probate. The Governor appointed deputies known as judges of probate for each county, and provincial legislation granted these judges extensive testamentary jurisdiction. Chancery administration of decedents' estates never became established in Massachusetts. Courts of probate were established in 1784 and were vested with the prior powers of the judges of probate.[14] They became courts of record in 1862 and their procedure was improved and their jurisdiction extended from time to time.[15] Finally, their prestige was fully established by provision in 1932 that appeals from their decrees went to the full Supreme Judicial Court in the first instance.[16]

Dower, which of course is closely related to succession, has always existed in Massachusetts.[17] In its early maturity the commonwealth adopted many common-law principles of wills and intestacy which had been overlooked or rejected in colonial days. Still Massachusetts never became a total adherent to the English substantive law of succession; and in matters of procedure and court organization it moulded an American way of dealing with probate and administration by close court supervision of every step in the proceedings. This, sometimes indirectly through the other New England systems, became a model for other states, particularly those of the middle west.[18]

*New York*

Here and in the colonies to the south, the English law of succession was more closely followed than in New England.[19] The rules in force under the Dutch were rapidly swept away when the British took over. Under the Duke's laws the statutory order of succession related only to personalty and common-law principles determined who should inherit land in the colony.[20] Primogeniture was not abolished until 1786.[21]

14 Ibid. 441–447.

15 Ibid. 449–450.

16 Mass.Gen.Laws, 1932, c. 215 § 9 et seq.

17 Atkinson, supra note 4 at 430, 433–434, 444, 451.

18 Ibid. 450–452.

19 See supra note 4, 5. In Virginia the administrator still has nothing to do with land and the remedy of the decedent's creditor is to sue the heir. Peirce v. Graham, 85 Va. 227, 7 S.E. 189, 1888; Catron v. Bostic, 123 Va. 355, 96 S.E. 845, 1918.

20 Atkinson, Codification of Probate Law, in Field Centenary Essays 177, 187. As late as 1893 the Canons of Descent were applied to exclude great-aunts in favor of great-uncles in a case unprovided for by statute. Hunt v. Kingston, 3 Misc. 309, 23 N.Y.S. 352, 1893.

21 See supra note 4.

The rules for descent of land were reduced to statutory form in early statehood but they continued to be separate and different from the provisions for distribution of personalty until 1930.[22] David Dudley Field's proposed Civil Code would have codified the entire substantive law of succession. It would have practically abolished the distinction between the passage of real and personal property upon death, for there was not only a uniform table of descent and distribution but also a provision that all property passed to the personal representative. But the Field code was rejected in its entirety in New York.[23]

An incidental and unfortunate result of Field's work was that it led to the present New York separation of the statutory law of succession into the Surrogates' Court Act (principally procedural law) and the Decedent Estate Law (mainly substantive).[24] Indeed the situation is worse than that, for, due to mechanical reasons of statutory organization, important parts of the law of succession are scattered in various parts of the Consolidated Laws of New York.[25]

Testamentary jurisdiction is lodged in the Surrogate's Courts, a traditional name which indicates that these powers were exercised by deputation of the royal governors and shows the early influence of the English ecclesiastical practice.[26] The Surrogate's Courts have long been courts of record and their prestige is demonstrated by the fact that their decrees are reviewable directly by the Appellate Division of the Supreme Court. The New York case and statute law of succession has had great influence in other jurisdictions. However, there are some spots of unfortunate conservativism, and the scattering of the statutory provisions leaves much to be desired.

### *California*

Even apart from its many excellent provisions, the California testamentary system deserves attention on account of the considerable group of western states which have followed it.[27] Its origins were comparatively late and there was a Spanish-Mexican legal background. Both of these factors influenced the law of succession in California. The community property system [28]

22 N.Y.Decedent Estate Law § 83.

23 Atkinson, supra note 20 at 188–189.

24 Ibid. 190–192.

25 Ibid. 193.

26 See Brick's Estate, 15 Abb.Prac., N.Y., 12, 1862, for the early history of testamentary jurisdiction in New York.

27 Atkinson, supra note 20 at 196.

28 See infra §§ 15, 30.

gave to the surviving spouse the protection which the common law supplied inadequately through dower. The holographic will,[29] entirely in the testator's hand but unattested and unwitnessed, is also of civil law origin. Both of these institutions are still prominent in the law of the state. The pioneer legislation relating to succession was supplanted in 1872 by provisions of the Civil Code, borrowed very largely from the Field code which failed of enactment in New York. Thus, as did Field's code, the original California Civil Code vested intestate real and personal property in the personal representative for purposes of administration. However, this was amended two years later so that both realty and personalty were declared to pass to the heirs subject to control of the court and the possession of the personal representative for the purposes of administration.[30] Perhaps there was the thought that administration could be avoided in some cases by this half-hearted bow to universal succession. This principle remains to this day, but it is modified so as to extend also to testate property and to *require* the personal representative to take possession of real as well as personal property.[31]

Under the revision of 1872 the procedural provisions regarding succession were contained in the new Code of Civil Procedure. In 1931 all statutory provisions of wills, intestacy, probate and administration were removed from their respective places and included in a new Probate Code. This general scheme of interlarding substantive provisions with the implementing matters of practice is adopted in most states, although often the resultant is merely a part or several successive parts of the statutory revision or compilation, and is not called a probate code.

*General Tendencies*

Some of the colonial assemblies enacted the testamentary provisions of the Statute of Frauds, 1677, with the result that only devises of land required attesting witnesses. This differentiation continued in a few American jurisdictions until well into the present century, but today has totally disappeared.[32] Separate tables

29 See infra § 75.

30 Atkinson, supra note 20 at 196–197.

31 Cal.Probate Code §§ 300, 571.

32 Florida and Tennessee were the last states where the statutes provided less formality for wills of personalty than for wills of realty. Many states provide for informal soldiers' wills of personalty or informal bequests of personalty in small amounts. See infra §§ 76, 77. In a few states the testator's age requirement is lower for wills of personalty than in the case of realty. See infra § 50.

for the descent of land and the distribution of personalty in the case of intestacy were common in the nineteenth century, but at present most states have a single scheme for both land and personalty and in most of the minority group there is differentiation only as to the share of the surviving spouse.[33] The orthodox rule that probate is effective only as to personalty seems never to have been observed in some jurisdictions and today it has disappeared almost entirely.[34] However, the principles that real property descends directly to the heirs or devisees while personalty vests in the personal representative are still basic in most jurisdictions,[35] though almost everywhere the former is modified by statutory provisions giving the personal representative statutory powers and duties with respect to the decedent's realty.[36] As a whole it is a fair generalization that, while particular aspects of unified treatment of realty and personalty become general in America before these reforms were adopted in England, the recent complete English abolition of the distinction [37] has no counterpart in most of our states.

*Judicial Supervision of Decedents' Estates*

A striking feature in the American development has been the extent to which the administration of the decedent's property goes forward under court supervision. It is largely a routine supervision, not dependent upon controversy or litigation. This is accounted for by the invention of a number of statutory devices to promote efficiency and security in the settlement of estates. One of these is the special statute of nonclaim which bars claims after a designated lapse of time, for the benefit of the personal representative and in most states for the beneficiaries as well.[38] Another is the sale of the decedent's land under court order for the payment of decedent's debts.[39] A third is the provision, adopted in an increasing number of jurisdictions, that the final decree in the administration operates as a muniment of

33 See Report of Commission to Investigate Defects in the Law of Estates, New York Legislative Document No. 69, 304, 1930.

34 See infra § 103; Model Probate Code §§ 62, 81, 85; Simes, The Administration of a Decedent's Estate as a Proceeding in Rem, 43 Mich.L. R. 675, 678–679.

35 See infra § 103. Cf. Model Probate Code § 124 and comment.

36 See infra §§ 103, 123.

37 See supra § 3 at notes 88, 89.

38 See infra § 127; Model Probate Code § 135.

39 See infra § 123; Model Probate Code §§ 152, 161–167.

the title as to realty and is an adjudication of the right to succeed to all types of property.[40]

*Courts of Probate*

Testamentary jurisdiction in the colonies was lodged in the ordinary courts, the legislative assemblies, the governor or his council; this differed according to place and time.[41] From these beginnings there emerged in most states a special tribunal, usually known as the Probate Court, but called in some localities Surrogate's Courts, Orphans' Courts or Courts of Ordinary. In a few states the jurisdiction is vested in County Courts or Superior Courts [42] which also have general or at least some other jurisdiction; in some of these the clerk has power to perform routine functions in connection with probate and administration.[43]

Courts of probate are close to the people; one can be found in every county, and in Connecticut at practically every crossroad.[44] This is a public convenience, especially when we consider the detailed court supervision which our system contemplates. But it has had certain ill effects. While courts of probate are now courts of record in most, if not all, states, they often have had a relatively small amount of business in the rural areas. On this account the legislatures were often unwilling to provide suitable compensation and clerical assistance for probate judges, or to require that they be legally trained. Naturally the court business has not always been well handled, and distrust of the judges' abilities has been indicated by curtailing powers to pass on questions regarding realty, by requiring or allowing litigation over wills and claims to be conducted in other courts, and by providing that appeals are by way of trial de novo in the courts of general trial jurisdiction. These badges of inferiority have been removed entirely in some states where courts of probate are suitably staffed and duly empowered to pass on virtually all the difficult and financially important matters which may arise in connection with the administration of decedents' estates.[45] Wheth-

40 See infra § 143; Model Probate Code § 183; Generally, see Simes, Ten Probate Codes, 50 Mich.L.R. 1245.

41 See supra notes 13, 14, 26; Simes and Basye, The Organization of the Probate Court in America, 42 Mich. L.R. 965, 977–978.

42 It is so in California. See Simes and Basye, supra note 41, at p. 996.

43 See generally Simes and Basye, supra note 41.

44 See Clark and Clark, Court Integration in Connecticut, 59 Yale L.J. 1395, 1409; Mignone, A Colonial Court Today: Connecticut's Probate Court System, 37 A.B.A.J. 337.

45 See Atkinson, Organization of Probate Courts and Qualifications of Probate Judges, 23 J.Am.Jud.Soc. 93.

er this jurisdiction should be exercised in a separate court of probate or in a division of the ordinary trial court of general jurisdiction is not a vital matter; its solution depends on factors of geography, population and tradition in the various states.[46]

## SOCIAL AND ECONOMIC BASES OF SUCCESSION

**5. While the Constitution does not guarantee the right of inheritance, and estate taxes in effect limit it to considerable extent, there are adequate social justifications for the institution. The power of testation, while not so obvious as the right of the intestate's family to take upon his death, is a desirable part of any system of succession, though absolute freedom of testation should be limited in the interest of the surviving spouse and perhaps other members of the testator's family.**

The present work of course assumes general institution of inheritance. Since we find it among primitive peoples, ancient civilizations and in all present-day legal systems[1] including that of Russia,[2] inquiry here into the social and economic bases of succession to property on death might be considered a waste of time. Still the fact that an institution is generally recognized is not necessarily conclusive that it should or always will be. Witness earlier attitudes toward interest and usury and toward polygamy. It seems too clear for argument that there must be a law of torts,[3] and, unless an unthinkable system of regimentation is imposed, a law of contracts and of property as well. However, the necessity of a system of private inheritance is not quite so obvious.

It would be theoretically possible that ownership of lands and goods would be considered vacant upon the decedent's death and capable of being asserted by the first comer. However, this

46 Cf. Model Probate Code. p. 15, § 6 and comment thereto; Simes and Basye, The Organization of the Probate Court in America, 44 Mich.L.R. 113, 150–154.

1 See supra §§ 2 to 4.

2 In Russia both testate and intestate succession is permitted. Holman, The Law of Succession in Soviet Jurisprudence since 1922, 20 Ia.L.R. 389; Holman, The Law of Succession in Soviet Jurisprudence—A Survey, 21 Ia.L.R. 487; Gsovski, Soviet Law of Inheritance, 45 Mich.L.R. 291, 445; Soloreitchik, Family Law and Inheritance Law in U.S.S.R., 15 U. of K.C.L.R. 83.

3 The necessity for compensatory relief is perhaps not quite as obvious as preventative sanctions.

would lead to confusion and strife beyond toleration,[4] and would not be acceptable among any people who had progressed beyond the brute stage.

Not quiet so absurd would be a system wherein the state would succeed to the property of the decedent, though so far as history shows there never has been a time or place where this principle was applied to all species of property. However, it should be noticed that if a system of state or common ownership is desired, the abolition of inheritance would be a very effective device in the accomplishment of a socialistic scheme.[5] Except for the possibility of gifts in the owner's lifetime, all private ownership in land and the bulk of other private wealth would soon disappear. It would probably be constitutionally possible to repeal all laws of private inheritance and to provide that the state shall succeed to decedent's property. Though naturally they have not been confronted with the problem specifically, our courts are practically unanimous in their expressions that said legislation would not violate American constitutional principles.[6]

A hundred per cent tax on decedents' estate would have the effect of abolishing inheritance, and if coupled with a curtailment of inter vivos gifts, would result in the virtual end of private property. Our system of graduated succession taxes not only raises revenue, it also restricts private inheritance.[7] If further control upon accumulated wealth is desired this can be accom-

[4] The consequences of such a plan are elaborated in 2 Bl.Com. 10 and Bigelow, Theory of Post-Mortem Disposition: Rise of the English Will, 11 Harv.L.R. 69, and reprinted in 3 Select Essays in Anglo-American Legal History 770.

[5] Cole, 8 Encyclopedia of Social Sciences 35–43; Ely, 1 Property and Contract in Their Relation to the Distribution of Wealth 425.

[6] See Irving Trust Co. v. Day, 314 U.S. 556, 62 S.Ct. 398, 86 L.Ed. 1734, 137 A.L.R. 1093, 1942; note, 15 Bost. U.L.R. 205. The view expressed in Nunnemacher v. State, 129 Wis. 190, 108 N.W. 627, 9 L.R.A.,N.S., 121, 9 Ann.Cas. 711, 1906, to the effect that inheritance is a privilege protected by the Constitution, is said by the note writer in 9 L.R.A.,N.S., 121 to be "opposed to the views of all historians of law, and of all economic writers." But cf. Mill, Political Economy, Bk. 2, c. 2, § 4. The viewpoint of the court in the Nunnemacher Case persists in later Wisconsin decisions. In re Will of Rice, 150 Wis. 401, 136 N.W. 956, 137 N.W. 778, 1912; In re Wilkins' Estate, 192 Wis. 111, 211 N.W. 652, 51 A.L.R. 1106, 1927. See also Connor, The Nature of Succession, 8 Fordham L.R. 151.

[7] See Cahn, Federal Regulation of Inheritance, 88 U. of Pa.L.R. 297, also infra § 125, and infra § 147, note 8 et seq. For a plan under which each inheritance would be taxed at progressively higher rates, see Rignano, The Social Significance of the Inheritance Tax (Shultz ed. 1924) 19–24; Stamp, Some Economic Factors in Modern Life, 1929, c. 2; Wedgwood, The Economics of Inheritance, 1929, c. xi.

plished by raising the rates and decreasing the exemptions. Of course from the standpoint of future revenues this may be killing the goose that lays the golden egg, although from the standpoint of total revenues succession taxes are not particularly important contributors.[8]

When the matter is critically examined the conclusions reached are generally favorable to private inheritance. A recent study[9] of the subject by four social scientists is illuminating, although their views may not be shared by all co-workers in their respective fields. The anthropologist[10] shows that private property and inheritance are more important in primitive societies than is generally believed; that it is a myth, as contended by the Morgan-Marx-Engels school, that the emergence of inheritance and a money economy destroyed the "democratic" clan, or that the state was invented to secure the newly acquired riches to private individuals. The economist[11] finds that inheritance now plays a smaller part in the general economy than is generally supposed, and that it will be of decreasing importance in our future economy. The sociologist[12] finds that the existing law of inheritance implements fairly well the current social ideas of the family, although he believes that the children should have a forced share in the parent's estate. The last essay by a scholar[13] in the field of ethics, after finding that inheritance has ethical value, concludes that the adverse considerations should prevail. He points out that the great majority of people have no prospect of passing on sustained property benefits to their families, and that the testamentary power of the relatively few fortunate individuals enables them to exercise a tyranny over their children. A thoughtful recent study[14] by a banker, concluding that inheritance is a basic personal freedom, might well be considered in connection with this symposium.

Intestate succession is older and more basic than succession by will.[15] If we are to have inheritance at all we could scarcely get

[8] See Osgood, The Case against Estate Tax Increases, 88 Trusts and Estates 770, showing that in spite of high rates federal estate and gift taxes yield only two per cent of the federal tax revenues, and suggesting that these forms of taxation might well be reserved for the states.

[9] Inheritance of Property and the Power of Testamentary Disposition in 1 Social Meaning of Legal Concepts.

[10] Hoebel, supra note 9 at 5–26.

[11] Friedrich, supra note 9 at 27–53.

[12] Tappan, supra note 10 at 54–73.

[13] Nathanson, supra note 10 at 74–90.

[14] Headey, Inheritance—A Basic Personal Freedom, 88 Trusts and Estates 24.

[15] See supra §§ 2, 3.

along without rules which dictate what relatives of the decedent shall inherit and in what proportion. There are other possible bases to determine the path of inheritance than those of blood or marriage, such as dependency, age, household connection, friendship, etc.[16] These are so indefinite, however, that they would be difficult to apply and would lead to uncertainty and consequent litigation. As a practical matter we are driven to a system of intestate succession based upon consanguinity or affinity to the decedent, even if we might desire some other basis for determining heirship.[17]

As to the details of the intestate plan it is now almost universally agreed that the children should receive equal shares regardless of age and sex. Primogeniture, long sustained in the English law as sort of a feudal relic, has practically no present adherents except in some of the Asiatic countries. Equality among children is justified simply because no other plan has any just or rational basis today.[18] Aside from the children's shares there is considerable divergence between American jurisdictions as to the order and manner of succession among relatives.[19] It is universally agreed that the spouse should receive a portion, though this may come in part at least through dower or community property which do not technically amount to succession.[20] In the past it has been the general rule that the closest blood relatives may take (subject to the share of the spouse) no matter how remote their relationship to the intestate, though some recent statutes provide that collateral relatives beyond a certain degree cannot inherit.[21] The latter position is to eliminate "the laughing heir"[22] who has no ties of friendship with the intestate, is not dependent

16 Ely, supra note 5, at 422.

17 See infra c. 2.

18 But the Germans in 1933 enacted a law passing middle-sized farms to the eldest son or some single substitute, in order to prevent the breaking up of farms into small tracts and to insure the existence of a peasant class. See Kaden, The Peasant Inheritance Law in Germany, 20 Ia.L.R. 350. See infra note 28.

19 See infra §§ 15–18.

20 See infra § 15.

21 See infra §§ 13, 26. There have long been limitations on intestate inheritance in most of the European countries. See Meyers, Limits of Inheritance in the Laws of Europe, 20 Ia.L.R. 341; Dainow, Forced Heirship in French Law, 2 La.L.R. 669; Dainow, The Early Sources of Forced Heirship: Its History in Texas and Louisiana, 4 La.L.R. 42, 54 (Spanish law).

22 See Ely supra note 5 at 422; Atkinson, Succession among Collaterals, 20 Ia.L.R. 185, 192–197; Cavers, Change in the American Family and the "Laughing Heir," 20 Ia.L.R. 203.

upon him, and whose identity is sometimes ascertained only after extensive search and prolonged litigation.[23]

Should intestacy be the exclusive scheme of succession? May the decedent in his lifetime appoint the person or persons to whom he wishes his property to go after his death? There are certainly arguments in favor of the principle that the owner should not be allowed to disturb the course of inheritance which the law has provided. It is somewhat shocking to permit a man to will his property entirely away from his dependent family. When indulged in, this practice would tend to break down the institution of the family, and impose the burden of support upon society.[24] In addition, freedom of testation may tend toward great accumulations of wealth in the individuals, or the institutions favored by decedents. The scheme is also productive of litigation, involving the validity of the plan of succession contrived by the decedent. On the other hand, there are grave disadvantages to a rule which would forbid an owner any freedom of determining where his property shall go upon his death. Psychologically a forced arbitrary division thwarts the property instinct.[25] One obtains property in his lifetime and may do with it as he pleases—why should he not be permitted to appoint his successors? Akin to this is the argument that a plan of forced inheritance might discourage individual initiative and thrift.[26] Such a scheme would also tend to destroy parental control, and thus render family relations unwholesome. The testator would have no protection which would enable him to reward kindness or punish cruelty.[27] In addition, there is the economic argument that a system of forced division would lead to the breaking up of tracts of land into such small portions that it would become valueless.[28] This tendency has been felt in France, where the decedent's power to appoint his successors has been limited by the leg-

23 See Matter of Wendel's Estate, 143 Misc. 480, 257 N.Y.S. 87, 1932, where over 1600 claimants appeared.

24 Hegel, Philosophy of Right (translation by Dych) §§ 178–180.

25 Miraglia, Comparative Legal Philosophy (translation by John Lisle and published in the Modern Legal Philosophy Series) 749, 750.

26 2 Bl.Com. 11. But see Jenks, English Civil Law, 30 Harv.L.Rev. 109, 119, 120.

27 Bentham, Theory of Legislation (reprinted in Rational Basis of Legal Institutions) 420–423; Stamp, Some Economic Factors in Modern Life, 1929, c. 2 passim.

28 Charmont, Changes in Family Law (1912) in Progress of Continental Law in the 19th Century (vol. 11 of Continental Legal History Series) pp. 147, 160, and reprinted in Rational Basis of Legal Institutions 431–444. See also supra note 18.

itime. The typical small farmer in France does not own a single tract of land, but several tiny tracts as the result of frequent divisions among the heirs in earlier generations. Such a situation leads to many inconveniences. For example, the land is more difficult to cultivate because of the impracticability of using modern machinery.

As a matter of fact, the situation calls for some compromise. Freedom of testation is demanded to some extent. On the other hand, there should be limitations placed upon it.[29] In different nations the manner of solution has varied widely. In the continental countries the children, and generally the spouse and parents, have forced shares of which they may not ordinarily be deprived.[30] There the decedent can dispose of only a portion of his property by will if he leaves an immediate family. On the other hand, in England and in America, except in Louisiana, the decedent is generally given more freedom. Under earlier schemes the surviving spouse was provided for by the institutions of dower and curtesy. In addition to this, our laws provide for certain family allowances. In many jurisdictions dower and curtesy have been abolished in favor of a forced share passing by succession to the surviving spouse.[31]

Children, on the other hand, are not so protected in the Anglo-American legal systems. A decedent may disinherit his offspring, except as the latter may benefit from the homestead or family allowances allowed by law. This principle may be somewhat alleviated by the tendency of juries to disallow wills disinheriting children upon the ground of lack of mental capacity of the testator, or fraud, or undue influence practised upon him.[32]

The traditional means of limiting testamentary freedom are subject to certain criticisms. Our protection of the spouse and the civil law legitime usually give the same proportion of the estate to the spouse and children regardless of the size of the estate, the dependency of the members of the family, or other considerations. In response to this objection New Zealand in 1900

29 See a scholarly summary of this subject by Dean McMurray, Liberty of Testation and Some Modern Limitations Thereon, 14 Ill.L.Rev. 96; Nussbaum, Liberty of Testation, 23 A.B.A.J. 183.

30 But in Mexico and a few other Latin-American countries the civil law legitime has been abolished. Eder, Anglo-American and Latin-American Law, 128.

31 See infra §§ 30, 32–33.

32 A realistic study of this matter has been made by Professor Laube, The Right of a Testator to Pauperize His Helpless Dependents, 13 Corn.L.Q. 559. See infra § 36.

enacted a law authorizing the court to make reasonable provision for the dependent family when the testator's will did not make adequate provision for their maintenance.[33] Less than two per cent of all wills are contested under this law. Its principles have been enacted by most of the Australian states and Canadian provinces, and finally in England by the passage of the Inheritance (Family Provision) Act, 1938.[34] In some of our states pecuniary allowances may be made to the family, but these are limited to provisions for support during the administration of the estate.[35]

33 See Dainow, Restricted Testation in New Zealand, Australia and Canada, 36 Mich.L.R. 1107; Kennedy, Testator's Dependents Relief Legislation, 20 Ia.L.R. 317 and infra note 34. As to application of the law in the widow's favor in case of intestacy, see note, 27 Can.B.R. 228. The 1951 proposed draft of the Israeli Code of Succession applies the principle to cases of intestacy as well as testacy.

34 1 & 2 Geo. VI, c. 45; see Dainow, Limitations on Testamentary Freedom in England, 25 Corn.L.Q. 337; notes, 1 Mod.L.R. 296, 53 Harv. L.R. 465; supra note 33; infra § 13, note 18. The English Intestates' Act, 1952 extends the principle by allowing the court to depart from the normal intestate division in case of need by some of the heirs. See note, 102 LawJ. 648, 650.

35 See infra § 34.

# CHAPTER 2

# INTESTACY


ENGLAND

Sec.

6. Descent of Realty.
7. The Statute of Distribution.
8. Half-Blood.
9. Posthumous Heirs.
10. Aliens.
11. Felons.
12. Escheats.
13. The Modern Law of Succession.

UNITED STATES

14. General Plan of Descent and Distribution.
15. The Surviving Spouse's Share.
16. Descendants' Shares.
17. Parents' and Their Issue's Shares.
18. Next of Kin.
19. Half-Blood.
20. Posthumous Heirs.
21. Ancestral Property.
22. Illegitimates.
23. Adopted Children.
24. Aliens.
25. Convicts.
26. Escheats.


## DESCENT OF REALTY—ENGLAND

**6. Under the influence of feudalism, a system of rules was evolved for the descent of land which included the principles of preference of males over females, primogeniture, ancestral property, and the exclusion of lineal ancestors and the half-blood. Most of these doctrines were abolished during the nineteenth century and the remainder fell in 1925.**

*The Development of the Canons of Descent*

After the Conquest the law of descent of land was influenced by feudalism.[1] In harmony with that institution, primogeniture,

[1] See supra § 4.

or the right of the eldest son to inherit to the exclusion of his sisters and younger brothers, became established.[2] The social, economic and political philosophy of the times led to other developments [3] in the law of inheritance. The main principles of this branch of the common law had become established by the end of the reign of Henry III (1216–1272).[4] Several questions, however, were not decided until much later.[5] In 1713 Sir Matthew Hale described the course of descent by enunciating seven principal precepts with illustrations and subsidiary rules under each.[6] About half a century later, Blackstone in his famous Commentaries [7] announced his Canons of Descent, also seven in number. These were different in form, in order, and to some extent in substance from Hale's. The canons of Blackstone are the better known of the two. Minus the illustrations and explanatory clauses they read as follows:

I. Inheritances shall lineally descend to the issue of the person who last died actually seised in infinitum; but shall never lineally ascend.

II. The male issue shall be admitted before the female.

III. Where there are two or more males in equal degree. the eldest only shall inherit; but the females all together.

IV. The lineal descendants in infinitum of any person deceased shall represent their ancestor; that is, shall stand in the same place as the person himself would have done, had he been living.[8]

[2] 2 Pollock and Maitland 257–272. Cf. Cairns, The Explanatory Process in the Field of Inheritance, 20 Ia.L.R. 266, 268–279.

[3] Viz., exclusion of the ascendant and the half-blood. See Canons of Descent in text infra, this section.

[4] 2 Pollock and Maitland 257.

[5] E. g., the question of preference between the brothers or sisters of the paternal grandmother over the brothers or sisters of the paternal grandfather's mother. The former was preferred according to dicta in Clere v. Brook, 2 Plowden 442, 75 Eng.Rep. 663, 1573, and this was accepted as law. This position was criticized in 2 Bl.Com. 238–240, as being illogical in the light of the constant preference of the male stock. Blackstone's argument lead to a change by act of Parliament. 3 & 4 Wm. IV, c. 106, § 8, 1833. See infra note 8.

[6] History of the Common Law, c. 11.

[7] Bk. 2, c. 14. For comments of Blackstone and others on the Canons, see Rollison, Principles of the Law of Succession to Intestate Property, 11 Notre Dame Lawyer 14, 121, 339.

[8] This principle applied to descent by collateral relatives. See Canon V. Thus, male or female descendants of brothers or sisters, however remote, were preferred to uncles and aunts and their descendants. This is

V. On failure of lineal descendants or issue of the person last seised, the inheritance shall descend to his collateral relations being of the blood of the first purchaser [9]; subject to the three preceding rules.

VI. The collateral heir of the person last seised must be his next collateral kinsman of the whole blood.

VII. In collateral inheritance the male stock shall be preferred to the female, unless where the lands have in fact descended from a female.

Thus all of intestate's realty descended to his eldest son. If the eldest son predeceased the intestate, leaving no issue, the second son took and so on. In case deceased left daughters and no sons or issue of sons, the daughters took the land together as coparceners in preference to intestate's brothers, uncles, nephews or other collateral kindred. If the eldest son predeceased the intestate leaving issue, this issue male or female according to the above rules would inherit to the exclusion of younger sons of the intestate. If deceased left no descendants, his father could not inherit from him, but the land went to the deceased's oldest brother or his issue. If deceased left no brothers, his sisters took as coparceners as in the case of daughters. If there were no brothers or sisters or their issue the land went to the deceased's oldest paternal uncle or his issue and so on. Assuming that the deceased obtained the land by purchase, even the closest collateral on the mother's side would be postponed to the entire paternal line including females.[10]

the parentelic system of determining descent which exhausts the line of the closest common ancestor of intestate and claimant before admitting other claimants related through a more remote line. See 2 Pollock and Maitland 294 et seq. But within the closest line the principles of primogeniture and coparcency among females were observed. See again Canon V which refers to Canons II and III.

9 One was deemed to be a purchaser of land if he obtained it by deed, will or any other manner except by descent. Rollison, supra note 7 at 14–16. Under Canon V if the intestate died without descendants and owned land inherited from his mother, the first purchaser, this land descended to collaterals of intestate on his mother's side; upon absence of these the property would escheat rather than pass to collaterals upon his father's side. See infra § 21.

10 See the anomalous rule with respect to preference between certain classes of collaterals, supra note 5.

*Illegitimates*

One born out of wedlock was deemed to be filius nullius and could not inherit from anyone.[11] Likewise his collateral relatives could not inherit from him,[12] though his legitimate children or their legitimate descendants could do so.[13]

*Spouse*

The surviving spouse, as such, was never heir to the land of the decedent spouse. The widower was entitled to curtesy and the widow to dower but these marital estates did not pass to them by inheritance. Though enjoyment was postponed until the death of the spouse who owned the land, these interests were regarded as existing in inchoate form during the latter's lifetime.[14]

*Modern Changes in Descent*

The common-law scheme remained intact in England until the Inheritance Act, 1833.[15] This statute abolished the principle of noninheritance by parents and other lineal ancestors and thereafter the following order of preference prevailed: (1) Descendants; (2) parents; (3) brothers and sisters and their issue; (4) grandparents; (5) uncles and aunts, etc. Preference for the father, his ancestors and their descendants continued to be given over the line of the mother. The rule announced in Canon I requiring seisin was abolished, as was the rule excluding the half-blood. The latter were entitled to take next after relatives of the whole blood of the same degree when the common ancestor was a male and next after the common ancestor when the latter was a female. Certain changes were also made in the law of inheritance by collaterals.[16] Later legislation further altered the common-law rules.[17] But primogeniture remained until the whole matter of descent was modernized by the Administration of Es-

[11] 1 Bl.Com. 459, 2 id. 247. The principle of the second clause of Canon I by itself prevented his inheritance from his own descendants.

[12] Ibid.; see also 2 Bl.Com. 505. Of course Canon I forbade inheritance of land by a lineal ancestor regardless of legitimacy.

[13] Ibid.

[14] For a historical treatment of curtesy and dower, see 3 Holdsworth, 185–197. By the Dower Act, 3 & 4 Wm. IV, c. 105, 1833, a widow could only claim dower in land belonging to her husband at his death and of which he had made no disposition by will. See Holdsworth, Historical Introduction to the Land Law 87–89. See infra §§ 39, 45.

[15] 3 & 4 Wm. IV, c. 106.

[16] See note 5 supra.

[17] E. g. 33 Vict. c. 14, § 2, 1870.

tates Act, 1925, under which the persons who succeed to the realty of an intestate are the same as those who succeed to the personalty.[18]

## THE STATUTE OF DISTRIBUTION—ENGLAND

**7. After a period of uncertainty as to who was entitled to the personalty of the intestate, parliament passed the Statute of Distribution, 1670, which commanded the administrator to distribute the property after payment of debts:**

**(a) One-third to the widow and two-thirds to the children or their issue if both widow and children or issue survived;**

**(b) All to the children or their issue if the widow did not survive;**

**(c) Half to the widow and half to the next of kin if there were no issue;**

**(d) All to the next of kin if neither widow nor issue survived.**

**In case of collateral relatives and lineal ancestors, next of kin were computed by counting the number of steps from the claimant to the closest common ancestor of intestate and the claimant and adding the number of steps from the common ancestor to intestate. Claimants who were by this calculation closest related to the intestate were entitled to the personalty. Representation, or the right to stand in the place of one's predeceased parent, was permitted in case of nieces and nephews.**

### *Early Law of Succession to Chattels*

For centuries after the Conquest, intestacy as to chattels was the exception, and the chief interest revolved around the question as to what portion of a testator's estate was subject to his free testamentary disposition. In case of intestacy it became clear that the wife and children were entitled to their reasonable portions but there was controversy as to whether the law, the church or the kindred were entitled to the dead man's part of which he might dispose by will. The lord lost his claim at an early date, but the struggle between the church and the family remained and there was much temporizing of result. There was the further problem of preventing administrators from appropriating the intestate's goods to their own uses.[1]

18 See infra § 13.

1 See supra § 3 at notes 36–55 and 61–69.

*The Statute of Distribution, 1670*

The testamentary jurisdiction of the ecclesiastical courts was threatened by their inability to deal with the situation. In 1670, church court lawyers sponsored the Statute of Distribution [2] to avoid annihilation of this jurisdiction. Accordingly, the act required the administrator to give a bond to make distribution of the estate among those entitled thereto. A scheme of succession was provided by which the widow was entitled to a third of the husband's personalty if there were children or representatives of children surviving, and half if there was no such issue. The children or their representatives took two-thirds in case there was a widow and the entire personal estate if there was not. The next of kin took the entire estate if neither widow nor children nor the latter's representatives survived and half if the widow alone survived. The statute did not contemplate the situation of intestacy in case of a married woman because all her personalty became her husband's upon marriage.[3] In case of the death of a widow or single woman intestate, the above scheme applied so far as pertinent.

*Children and Their Descendants*

In case the intestate left a widow and children, the latter divided their two-thirds equally by express provision of the statute. Though the statute says "children," it was decided that a single child would take the entire two-thirds portion.[4] Grandchildren had no interest in the estate if their parent who was the child of intestate also survived the intestate.[5] However, in case that intestate's child should predecease him leaving issue, the grandchildren who were the issue of the predeceased child, divided the latter's share equally as his "legal representatives." Thus, suppose that the intestate had two sons, James and John. If both of the latter survived the deceased, they each took half of the two-thirds going to children (intestate's widow taking the other third). The children of James and John took nothing from the

[2] 22 & 23 Car. II, c. 10. See infra note 13.

[3] This was decided in the early Year Book period. See 3 Holdsworth 526, 527; cf. id. 561.

[4] See Brown v. Farndell, Carth. 51, 90 Eng.Reprint, 634, 1689. And see note 9 infra.

[5] This is practically a universal rule under all systems of succession. However, it was not always true in the case of inheritance by collaterals under the Canons of Descent because of the fact that the rule forbidding inheritance by a direct ancestor was entitled to priority over the rule excluding the issue of a living ancestor.

intestate in this situation. But if John died before the intestate, leaving two children, Mary and Thomas, the division would be to James, one-third, to Mary and Thomas, each one-sixth.[6]

Now let us assume that James also predeceased the intestate leaving a single child, Peter. It is obvious that two-thirds of the personalty would be divided between Peter, Mary, and Thomas; but what would be their respective shares? If the succession was per stirpes, or by stocks, Peter would take his father's share, or one-third, while Mary and Thomas would each take a sixth. On the other hand, the three grandchildren were all equally related to their grandfather so that the issue's share of property might reasonably be divided per capita, or per head, into three equal parts. Arguments might be made in favor of either view. For the per stirpes position it might be said that normally it might be expected that both James and John would have survived their parent and that their children would have survived them, so that, presuming that the patrimony was preserved, Peter would ultimately receive one-third and Mary and Thomas each one-sixth. Thus to adopt the per stirpes division would be to reach the same result as if the deaths of the succeeding generations had occurred in their usual order.

On the other hand, arguing for the per capita plan, it might be answered that the normal situation did not occur and that reasonable consequences should follow from the facts which actually happened. If a grandfather had made a will after the death of his two sons, probably he would have divided the property equally between the grandchildren. Possibly a mechanically minded grandparent might follow the per stirpes plan in his will, as well as one whose affections for his children greatly exceeded those for his grandchildren. It is likely that there is now and always has been more demonstrative affection for grandchildren than for children. Especially where the latter were dead, the ties of affection are usually direct ones between the survivors, the grandparent and the grandchildren. Most testators would be inclined to treat the grandchildren as individuals rather than collectively as the offspring of predeceased children. The point was not determined until a fairly late date. However, in 1741 the Lord Chancellor expressed the opinion, though he did not actually decide, that the grandchildren would take per stirpes

6 Williams on Executors (11th Ed.) 1239.

and not per capita.[7] The point was later actually settled in favor of the per stirpes position.[8]

Any descendant of a child no matter how remote represented the child in taking from the intestate father.[9] By this process of representation the closest living descendants of a predeceased child were, in effect, moved up into the latter's position, and took what would have been the latter's share. Thus intestate's great-grandchild was preferred to intestate's father, brother or other collateral relative or ancestor. This was because the Statute of Distribution specifies "the legal representatives" of children. Hence the courts did not apply the rules of degrees of relationship which were employed in the case of intestate's ancestors and collaterals. The persons who legally represented the children of an intestate were their descendants.[10]

In case the deceased left no widow but only children, the latter divided the entire personalty by the express terms of the statute. A single child would take all the chattels.[11] Of course the same scheme of representation applied in the case of remote descendants as it did if the intestate's widow survived. When the intestate was survived by a widow but not by children or any other descendants, the widow took half of the personalty. The remaining moiety went to the "next of kindred of the intestate who are in equal degree and those who legally represent them," as did the entire personal estate in case that there were neither widow nor issue.

### *Next of Kin*

Next of kin were not determined by the Canons of Descent which were applicable only to the descent of real property. The principles of primogeniture and preference of males over females had no application in the distribution of intestate's goods. Likewise a third rule of feudal origin, the noninheritance by the direct ascending ancestor, was not invoked. Moreover, the theory of computing next of kin was quite different from determining the heir at law of land. For example, according to the Canons of Descent in absence of descendants and brothers and sisters,

7 Lockyer v. Vade, Barn.Chan. 444, 27 Eng.Rep. 713, 1741.

8 In re Ross's Trusts, L.R. 13 Eq. 286, 1871; In re Natt, 37 Chan.Div. 517, 1888. See critical comment on these decisions in Williams on Executors (11th Ed.) 1238.

9 See Carter v. Crawley, T.Raym. 496, 500, 83 Eng.Rep. 259, 262, 1681.

10 See infra note 41.

11 Palmer v. Garrard, Prec.Ch. 21, 24 Eng.Rep. 11, 1690.

an uncle's descendants, however remote, would be preferred to a great uncle. The closest stocks were exhausted before one would pass to a more remote stock.[12]

On the other hand, in the case of personalty under the Statute next of kin were determined by the method of the civil law which was to ascertain the closest common ancestor of intestate and claimant and then count the steps from the intestate to the common ancestor and also the steps from the common ancestor to the claimant. The sum of the two figures represented the degree of relationship between the claimant and the intestate.[13] Of course, as so computed, the claimant who stood in the smallest numerical degree of relationship to the intestate took his personalty.[14] When claimants were in equal degrees of relationship to the intestate they shared the chattels equally.

There was another method of ascertaining kinship, namely, the method of the canon law which was used by the church to determine what marriages between relatives were forbidden.[15] According to the canon law the steps from the common ancestor to each of the persons involved were counted as in the case of the civil law. However, instead of taking the sum of these two figures, only the larger was taken. This represented the degree of relationship according to the canon law. The common law adopted this method of computation for the purpose of limiting the number of successive donees in frankmarriage.[16] The canon or common-law manner of determining kinship was never applied in England under the Statute of Distribution. It should be understood, however, as a few American jurisdictions adopt the plan.

12 See the Canons of Descent, especially IV, V, supra § 6. And see Rollison, Principles of the Law of Succession to Intestate Property, 11 Notre Dame Lawyer, 14, 121.

13 Carter v. Crawley, T.Raym. 496, 506, 83 Eng.Rep. 259, 264, 1681; Mentney v. Petty, Prec.Ch. 593, 24 Eng.Rep. 266, 1722. The reason for the adoption of the civil law method of computation is that the Statute of Distribution was drafted by a learned civilian lawyer, Sir Walter Walker, who left clear indication of the origin by including in section VII the civil law rule that representation should not be admitted among collaterals after brother's and sister's children. See Pett v. Pett, 1 Ld. Raym. 571, 574, 91 Eng.Rep. 1281, 1283, 1700.

Cf. the parentelic system employed in determining the collateral descent to land under the Canons of Descent. Supra § 6 note 8. In effect, this method was used to prefer brothers and sisters to grandparents under the Statute of Distribution—see infra notes 25, 26—but was not applied generally under the Statute.

14 This was subject to certain exceptions. See notes 25, 28, 29 infra.

15 See Mentney v. Petty, supra note 13; Co.Litt.Bk. 1, c. 2, § 20.

16 Co.Litt., supra note 15.

It may be helpful to an understanding of the situation to study the following chart of one's ancestors and collateral relatives.[17]

| | | | |
|---|---|---|---|
| | | | Great-grandfather III (3) |
| Great-uncle IV (3)............ | ............ | ............ | Grandfather II (2) |
| Great-uncle's Child V (3)[18] | Uncle III (2)............ | ............ | Father I (1) |
| Second Cousin VI (3) | First Cousin IV (2) | Brother II (1)... | Decedent |
| Second Cousin once removed VII (4) | First Cousin once removed V (3) | Nephew III (2) | |
| Second Cousin twice removed VIII (5) | First Cousin twice removed VI (4) | Grandnephew IV (3) | |

The Roman figure after each of the kindred represents the degree of relationship of that person to the deceased according to the civil law, while the Arabic figures in parentheses indicate the degree according to the canon or common-law rule. Let us consider a case where the deceased left no widow or lineal descendants. If he left a father his personalty would pass to him,[19] because he stands in the first degree of relationship according to the civil law rule. No other person except the mother is as close. It should be noticed that according to the Canons of Descent, the father could not take being the direct ancestor.[20] According to the canon law method of computation the brothers and sisters also are in the first degree of relationship. Indeed, the mother, according to the civil law rule, would seem to share equally with the father, but as the common law gave the wife's

17 Charts of this nature may be misleading in that they are an over-simplification of the true situation. Thus one may have several brothers and sisters, and other collateral relatives in the same class rather than one as is shown by this chart. In addition, and more important, everyone has two parents, four grandparents, eight great-grandparents and so on. When the twentieth previous generation is reached, one would have theoretically over a million ancestors of that generation. See 2 Bl.Com. 205. As a practical matter, intermarriage of relatives—near or remote—reduces this figure enormously.

18 The decedent is the first cousin once removed of the great-uncle's child, and the latter is sometimes referred to as the decedent's second cousin once removed in the ascendancy. Sometimes the first cousin once removed is called the second cousin and so on. Funk and Wagnalls New Standard Dictionary tit. cousin. It will be observed that the first cousin once removed is in the same degree of relationship to the deceased as the second cousin according to the canon law rule but not according to the civil law rule. See annotation, 99 A.L.R. 672.

19 See Blackborough v. Davis, 1 P. Wms. 41, 48, 24 Eng.Rep. 285, 288, 1701; Lewin v. Lewin, 36 N.B. 365, 1 Brit.Rul.Cas. 556, 1904.

20 See Canon V, supra § 6.

personalty to the husband,[21] she was excluded if both mother and father survived the deceased. If the father was dead and the mother alone survived the intestate, she took all the chattels of her child in preference to the latter's brothers and sisters. This result of the Statute of Distribution was thought to be unsatisfactory,[22] and in 1685, Parliament provided [23] "that if after the death of a father any of his children shall die intestate without wife or child, in the lifetime of the mother, every brother and sister, and the representatives of them shall have an equal share with her." [24]

In case neither parent survived, the brothers and sisters of the intestate stood in second degree of relationship, as did also the grandparents according to the civil law rule. Yet it was decided that brothers and sisters take the entire estate in preference to the grandfather.[25] This position was not a true application of the civil law method of computation, unless it was based upon the reasoning that the brothers and sisters were permitted to take by representation of the father who would be related in the first degree. However, the result was founded upon arguments of justice, convenience, and a prior existing practice of long standing.[26]

As the civil law rule prevailed under the Statute of Distribution, brothers and sisters were clearly preferred to uncles and aunts, being one degree of relationship closer. When there were brothers and also children of deceased brothers and sisters, under Section 7 the latter were permitted to represent their parents and a per stirpes division was made.[27] When the next of kin were all children of brothers and sisters the division among them was

21 See Madden on Domestic Relations §§ 28 and 29.

22 Because the mother might marry again and her second husband would thereby become the owner of her personalty and it would then go to his kindred upon his death. See Blackborough v. Davis, 1 P.Wms. 41, 49, 24 Eng.Rep. 285, 288, 1701.

23 1 James II, c. 17 § 7.

24 It was later decided that when both wife and mother and sisters and brothers or their children survived the deceased, the mother divided equally with the brothers and sisters, and the latter's children by representation. Keylway v. Keylway, 2 P. Wms. 344, 24 Eng.Rep. 758, 1726; Stanley v. Stanley, 1 Atk. 455, 26 Eng.Rep. 289, 1739

25 Winchelsea v. Norcliff, 2 Freem. 95, 22 Eng.Rep. 1080, 1686; Evelyn v. Evelyn, 3 Atk. 762, 26 Eng.Rep. 1237, 1754.

26 See Evelyn v. Evelyn, supra note 25; Williams on Executors (11th Ed.) 1250.

27 2 Bl.Com. 517.

per capita.[28] However, if no brothers and sisters survived, nephews and nieces took per capita with uncles and aunts, all being related in the third degree.[29] Representation permitted nephews and nieces, where their parent was dead, to draw themselves up in order to take with intestate's living brothers and sisters; but in absence of the latter representation could not be employed to supplant uncles and aunts who were deemed to be of equal degree though of a more remote line.[30] In theory this position is inconsistent with the one which preferred brothers and sisters to grandparents.[31]

Section 7 of the statute expressly declared that representation was not permitted beyond the children of brothers and sisters.[32] Thus grandnephews and grandnieces, whose parent and grandparent of the blood of intestate were dead, did not take any share with the surviving brothers, sisters, nephews, and nieces of the intestate.[33] Indeed, a grandnephew would be postponed to an uncle and would take equally with a first cousin. A grandparent would take before an uncle or aunt.[34] The latter shared equally with a nephew or a niece,[35] and with a great-grandparent,[36] and was preferred to a first cousin.[37] Great-great-grandparents, great-uncles, first cousins, and grandnephews were next in line, all being related in the fourth degree. The statute forbade representation in the case of cousins or grandnephews so they were excluded in favor of earlier generations of their own line. Theoret-

28 Walsh v. Walsh, Prec.Chan. 54, 24 Eng.Rep. 27, 1695, the reason assigned being that they all stand in equal degrees of relationship and hence do not take by representation. Accord: Davers v. Dewes, 3 P.Wms. 40, 24 Eng.Rep. 961, 1730. Cf. the case of direct descendants supra notes 7, 8.

29 Durant v. Prestwood, 1 Atk. 455, 26 Eng.Rep. 289, 1739; Lloyd v. Tench, 2 Ves.Sr. 213, 28 Eng.Rep. 138, 1750; Girardot Buissieres v. Albert, 2 Lee 51, 161 Eng.Rep. 260, 1754.

30 Lloyd v. Tench, supra note 29.

31 See notes, 25, 26 supra.

32 It was decided that this means brothers and sisters of the intestate and not those of his next of kin. See Pett v. Pett, infra note 33.

33 Caldicot v. Smith, 2 Show.K.B. 286, 89 Eng.Rep. 943, 1683; Pett v. Pett, 1 Ld.Raym. 571, 91 Eng.Rep. 1281, s.c. 1 Salk. 250, 91 Eng.Rep. 220, s.c. 1 P.Wms. 25, 24 Eng.Rep. 280, 1700.

34 Blackborough v. Davis, supra note 22; Woodroff v. Wicksworth, Prec.Ch. 527, 24 Eng.Rep. 236, 1719.

35 In case no brothers and sisters survived. See notes 27–29 supra.

36 See Mentney v. Petty, Prec.Ch. 593, 594, 24 Eng.Rep. 266, 1722; Lloyd v. Tench, 2 Ves.Sr. 214, 215, 28 Eng.Rep. 138, 139, 1750.

37 Carter v. Crawley, T.Raym. 496, 83 Eng.Rep. 259, 1681; Bowers v. Littlewood, 1 P.Wms. 594, 24 Eng.Rep. 531, 1719.

ically this classification could go on indefinitely, though as a practical matter there would be little likelihood of inheritance by the extremely remote generations because they were apt to be dead or unborn. One would be much more apt to be survived by a second cousin than by his great-great-great-great-grandparent or the grandchild of a grandnephew, though if he were, they would take equally being all related in the sixth degree. Apparently all relatives of the more remote degrees would take in strict accordance with the civil law rules. It should be remembered that all collaterals more remote than nephews and nieces took per capita if they took at all.[38]

*Source of Intestate's Title*

Unlike the case of the descent of land which the intestate had obtained by descent,[39] the source of the intestate's title had no effect upon the question of who was entitled to his personalty upon his death. This is true because of the language of the Statute of Distribution which says nothing of the matter in providing for its scheme of distribution. In providing an absolute share for the widow the Statute rejects the firm principle of the Canons of Descent that the claimant must be of the blood of the ancestor from whom the intestate obtained the property. Furthermore, any application of the ancestral property doctrine to personalty would result in much practical difficulty because the origin of the title to chattel interests is often difficult to trace.[40]

*Relatives by Marriage*

Aside from the surviving spouse no one was a distributee unless he was related to the intestate by blood. Under the Statute the spouse of a deceased child was not the legal representative of the latter and took no interest in the estate of the latter's parent.[41] One's parents-in-law were never his distributees,[42] nor were the spouses of his collateral relatives. Likewise stepchildren, stepparents, stepbrothers and stepsisters took nothing un-

[38] This follows from the provision forbidding representation beyond the children of brothers and sisters. See note 33 supra.

[39] See supra § 6 at note 9

[40] See infra § 21.

[41] See Price v. Strange, 6 Madd. 159, 161, 162, 56 Eng.Rep. 1052, 1053, 1820; Bridge v. Abbot, 3 Bro.C.C. 224, 226, 29 Eng.Rep. 502, 503, 1791.

[42] See Rutland v. Rutland, 2 P. Wms. 210, 216, 24 Eng.Rep. 703, 705, 1723.

der the Statute.[43] The English common law did not recognize adoption and hence there was no inheritance by a foster child.[44]

*Illegitimacy*

As in case of the descent of land,[45] illegitimacy was a bar to the intestate succession to personalty. Although the Statute of Distribution makes no mention of the matter it was clear that when it speaks of "children" or "next of kin" it meant those who were born in lawful wedlock. The Roman law considered a child legitimate if his parents married after his death,[46] but the common law did not grant this indulgence.[47]

A bastard could not inherit the personalty of his parents, other ancestors or collateral relatives and conversely they could not inherit from him.[48] However, his spouse or legitimate children or their legitimate descendants could claim under the Statute and he might succeed to their property.[49] If he left no wife or descendants his property went to the crown.[50] When an illegitimate left a wife but no descendants the widow took her portion of the intestate personalty under the Statute but the balance escheated.[51]

## HALF-BLOOD—ENGLAND

**8. Collateral relatives of the half-blood shared the personalty equally with those of the whole blood of the same degree and were preferred to all relatives of a more remote degree. However, the half-blood was excluded altogether in case of the descent of land.**

As used in the law of inheritance, half-blood refers to the degree of relationship between two individuals who have the same mother or the same father but not both parents in common. The position of relatives of the half-blood gave rise to considerable difficulty. Of course there can be no such things as direct an-

43 Halsbury, Laws of England, 1910, vol. 11, p. 22, tit. Descent and Distribution, § 41.

44 See infra § 13 at notes 14, 15.

45 See supra § 6 at notes 11 to 13.

46 Co.Litt. 123a; 1 Bl.Com. 454.

47 See infra § 22 at note 18.

48 See supra § 6 at notes 11 to 13.

49 Cf. supra § 6, note 13.

50 Jones v. Goodchild, 3 P.Wms. 33, 24 Eng.Rep. 958, 1729; Rutherford v. Maule, 4 Hagg.Eccl. 213, 162 Eng.Rep. 1424, 1832; Manning v. Napp, 1 Salk. 37, 91 Eng.Rep. 38, 1693.

51 Cave v. Roberts, 8 Sim. 214, 59 Eng.Rep. 86, 1836.

cestors or direct descendants of the half-blood. Each person is as much of the blood of one parent as he is of the other parent, and any child is as much of his parent's blood as any other child.[1] In the case of collaterals the half-blood frequently appears. Paul may be Henry's full brother, both having the same father and mother. Peter may have the same father as Paul and Henry but a different mother, as the result of a prior or subsequent marriage of the father. Peter is Paul's and Henry's half-brother. Likewise one may have half-uncles, half-cousins, and the like. The Canons of Descent exclude the half-blood entirely from the inheritance of land.[2] The Statute of Distribution does not mention the half-blood, but says that the property should go to "the next of kindred in equal degree of or unto the intestate."

There are several possible decisions as to what should be done with reference to the half-blood. Those [3] which concerned the English law were: (1) To exclude the half-blood entirely as did the Canons of Descent; (2) to give the half-blood a half share; [4] (3) to give the half-blood a full share. The third view was taken [5] in interpreting the statute, since the half-blood is as

1 Of course stepchildren are not of any blood of the stepparent and hence do not inherit from the latter, or vice versa. It is possible that a person should marry a relative of one of his parents. This would make the grandchildren of that marriage related by more ties to that grandparent than in the case of a grandchild of a different child who did not marry a relative. Apparently there are no cases upon this point, but it can be safely said that the grandchild as the result of the intermarriage would be entitled to no preference. Similar cases of double relationship might exist in case of collaterals. Thus one might be both a cousin and half-brother of the deceased if the latter's father had married his deceased wife's sister. Here again there are no English cases, but it seems apparent that such a person would take by the closer of the two relationships. But if both relationships were the same, would he take a double share? Probably he would not under the per capita division which prevailed among the only classes of collaterals where this might occur. See infra § 23, note 14. A marriage between parent and child might result in one being both the nephew and the brother of a child of the first marriage. But marriage between a parent and his own offspring has always been forbidden.

2 See Canon VI, § 6 supra. See 2 Bl.Com. 227. The rule was altered in 1833. See text supra § 6, just after note 15.

3 For others see infra § 19.

4 This is the rule in Scotland (see Crooke v. Watt, 2 Vern. 124, 126, 23 Eng.Rep. 689, 690, 1690). It is the present English statute rule. See infra § 13.

5 Smith v. Tracy, 1 Mod. 209, 86 Eng.Rep. 833, 1673; Id., T.Jones 94, 84 Eng.Rep. 1163, 1673; Crooke v. Watt, supra note 4; Id., Show.P.C. 108, 1 Eng.Rep. 74, 1690; Brown v. Farndell, Carth. 51, 90 Eng.Rep. 634, 1689. A half-brother may share equally with the whole brother and

closely related *in degree,* viz., number of steps in tracing relationship, as the whole blood, although not as completely related from the standpoint of common ties of ancestry. No doubt the fact that the civil law gave the half-blood an equal share was also an influencing factor.

## POSTHUMOUS HEIRS—ENGLAND

**9. Posthumous relatives of the intestate succeeded to the chattels if they were in embryo at the time of intestate's death; otherwise they took no share of the estate. However, in case of inheritance of land by collaterals the estate might shift to afterborn heirs, though born long after intestate's death.**

The case of the posthumous child presented little difficulty in the case of direct descendants. It is unlikely that a woman will have a posthumous child.[1] A man's posthumous child must be born within nine months of his decease. The same period of time represents the limit for the birth of any posthumous grandchild or more remote descendant who might take an intestate's property. Of course grandchildren might be born years after the death of the grandparent, but in case of these, the child would have inherited, unless he died within nine months before the birth of the grandchild. Inasmuch as the descendants must have been in embyro at the time of the ancestor's death in order to be entitled to the estate, the law considered him as in being though actually born after the intestate's death. A posthumous child would take the personalty just as if he had been born in the father's lifetime.[2] This resulted in no inconvenience, as the child must have been born within the year after intestate's death which was allowed for distribution of the estate by the personal representative.[3]

The same rule applied to posthumous brothers or half-brothers,[4] who were in embyro at the time of the death of intestate. They would take as if they were in esse. If they were not in esse

the mother in case that intestate died without issue, wife or father surviving. Jessop v. Watson, 1 My. & K. 665, 39 Eng.Rep. 832, 1833.

1 It might be possible for a child to be born alive within a short period after his mother's death. See Clendening, Behind the Doctor, 1923, 126.

2 See Wallis v. Hodson, Barn.Ch. 272, 27 Eng.Rep. 642, 1740; Id., 2 Atk. 114, 26 Eng.Rep. 472, 1740.

3 Cf. notes 8, 9 infra.

4 Wallis v. Hodson, supra note 2; Burnet v. Mann, 1 Ves.Sr. 156, 27 Eng.Rep. 953, 1748.

at the time, they would not ordinarily be entitled, for the parent of the claimant would then have survived the intestate and such parent would take under the Statute of Distribution. To this there was one exception as the mother of an intestate did not exclude the brothers and sisters.[5] If the mother married again, she might have a child who would be a half-brother of the intestate and born years after the latter's death and after the distribution of his estate. Could such a half-brother call his mother and surviving brothers and sisters to account and require a redistribution? Very likely he could not in the case of personalty.

In the case of the descent of land under the Canons of Descent, the following situation sometimes occurred: A man might die without issue leaving parents and two sisters but no brothers. The parents would be excluded by virtue of the rule concerning lineal ancestors.[6] The sisters would take as coparceners.[7] If a son was born to the decedent's parents three years after the decedent's death, the law declared that the land shifted to the afterborn son upon the principle of primogeniture.[8]

This doctrine of shifting estates seems not to have been applied to personalty in the single situation which might give a chance for it to operate.[9] Rather clearly one's next of kindred for the purpose of succession to personalty are confined to those who are born or in embyro at the time of intestate's death.

## ALIENS—ENGLAND

**10. At common law a friendly alien could pass or take personalty by will or intestacy, but similar privileges were not given in case of land. The latter restrictions have been removed by statute, but inheritance by alien enemies is a matter of grace.**

At common law a friendly alien could own personalty.[1] There might be succession to the alien's personalty upon his death, but the persons entitled thereto were determined by the law of decedent's domicile and not by the English law.[2] While an alien might purchase land, he could not hold it against the king, who

[5] See supra § 7, notes 22–24.

[6] See Canon V, § 6 supra.

[7] See Canon III, § 6 supra.

[8] 2 Bl.Com. 208; Co.Litt. 11b.

[9] Viz., the one mentioned supra note 5.

[1] 1 Bl.Com. 372.

[2] Enohin v. Wylie, 10 H.C.L. 1, 13, 11 Eng.Rep. 924, 929, 1862.

was entitled to it by his prerogative.[3] As an incident of this royal privilege, it was considered that even if the land so purchased was not taken by the king in the alien's lifetime, the latter could pass no title thereto by descent. It was said that the alien had no heritable blood. This doctrine was carried to the extent that land could not pass by descent from a British subject to his brother who was also a subject, if the father was an alien.[4] This particular view, however, was later abandoned.[5]

If a person entitled to the succession to personalty under a will or the Statute of Distribution were a friendly alien, he was not thereby disqualified.[6] He could not, however, take land by devise or descent.[7] This feature of the law was changed by the British Nationality and Status of Aliens Act, 1914,[8] which declared that an alien might own any species of real and personal property except a British ship. With the single exception noted, property can now pass by succession from and to aliens. No rights whatever were recognized in alien enemies; consequently succession by or through them was allowed solely by grace.[9]

## FELONS—ENGLAND

**11. By the ancient doctrines of forfeiture and escheat, the lands and goods of a convicted or outlawed felon passed to the king or the overlord. Legislation has greatly liberalized the old law.**

At common law one who fled after committing treason or felony was outlawed. If he was apprehended and found guilty, he was sentenced to death. Upon either outlawry or sentence, such a person was deemed attainted and neither his lands nor his chattels passed to the heir or distributees.[1] Two principles were involved in this interruption of the normal course of suc-

[3] And this rule was extended to leaseholds. 1 Bl.Com. 372; Co.Litt. 2b..

[4] Co.Litt. 129.

[5] Collingwood v. Pace, 1 Vent. 413, 86 Eng.Rep. 262, 1674.

[6] 1 Bl.Com. 372; Wells v. Williams, 1 Lut. 34, 125 Eng.Rep. 18, 1698.

[7] 2 Bl.Com. 249.

[8] 4 & 5 Geo. V. c. 17.

[9] See Halsbury's Laws of England, 2d Ed. 1931, vol. 1, pp. 455–457.

[1] See 3 Holdsworth 604–607. But attaint did not divest a person of his lands; this was done through a later inquisition known as "office found"; meanwhile the felon could will or deed the land subject to the rights of the king and the lord. 2 Bl.Com. 251; 4 Bl.Com. 380.

cession.[2] The first and more ancient was that of forfeiture, which was of Anglo-Saxon origin. This doctrine was that the king should be entitled forever to the lands of an attainted traitor but only for a year and a day in the case of other felons. Goods and chattels were also forfeited to the crown absolutely, not only for felonies but also many other offenses.[3] The second consequence of the attainder was the escheat, which was a product of feudalism. For any felony by the tenant, the fief was deemed at an end and the land escheated to the lord. Escheat, being of later origin, was subject to forfeiture. Thus, in case of treason the king took all the lands of the traitor so that there was nothing upon which the escheat could operate. In case of other felonies, the forfeiture to the king was only for a year and a day, and after that time the lord was entitled to the land by escheat. As the king was often the lord, the two principles were sometimes confused.

So far as forfeiture was concerned it stopped with divesting the property of the felon. His chattels went to the king and hence could not go to the distributees. But nothing prevented one brother from succeeding to the chattels of another, though the father was attainted. The forfeiture principle did not work corruption of blood, and escheat had no application to personalty. The doctrine of escheat, however, pursued the matter further in the case of land. Thus, if a son was attainted and the father died, the latter's land did not descend to the attainted son nor to any child of the latter but escheated to the lord.[4] Furthermore, if the father was attainted, land could not pass by descent from one brother to another as the succession was traced through the father whose blood was corrupted.[5] A series of statutes[6] alleviated the situation to some extent, and finally escheats and forfeitures for crime were practically abolished by the Forfeiture Act, 1870.[7]

2 2 Bl.Com. 251; 4 Bl.Com. 381.

3 2 Bl.Com. 420.

4 2 Bl.Com. 253.

5 Co.Litt. 8, 391, 392.

6 7 Ann. c. 21, 1708; 17 Geo. II, c. 39, 1744; 3 & 4 Wm. IV, c. 106, § 10, 1691.

7 33 & 34 Vict. c. 23.

## ESCHEATS—ENGLAND

**12. When no heirs were found for intestate, his realty passed to the overlord or to the crown by escheat, and his personalty went to the crown.**

If no person could claim the lands of a decedent under a will, or under the Canons of Descent, the property would escheat to the lord.[1] This was true even if the lands were held by the decedent in fee simple,[2] if the lord could be located. However, often there was no record of mesne tenure as subinfeudation had been forbidden by the Statute Quia Emptores, 1290, and the crown took as lord paramount.[3] Less frequently no successor would be found for the chattels of an intestate under the Statute of Distribution. With respect to this species of property, a proper distributee would be more apt to exist because of the inapplicability to personalty of the rules of ancestral property, of non-inheritance by lineal ancestors, exclusion of the half-blood, lack of heritable blood by aliens, and perhaps others. However, if no claimant appeared such goods were deemed to be bona vacantia, to which the crown was entitled by virtue of his prerogative.[4] Letters of administration were issued for the benefit of the crown, and the administrator accounted to the crown for the residue after payment of the decedent's debts.[5] Under the present law the matter is simplified by placing the crown at the end of the list of persons entitled to take by intestate succession.[6]

1 Glanville, Bk. 7, c. 17.

2 The possibility of an escheat is not regarded as a reversion. See 3 Holdsworth 133.

3 See Hardman, The Law of Escheat, 4 Law Q.R. 318.

4 Dyke v. Walford, 5 Moo.P.C. 434, 13 Eng.Rep. 557, 1846. See supra § 7, notes 50, 51. As to crown liability to creditors, see note, 27 Can.B.R. 592.

5 Megit v. Johnson, 2 Doug. 542, 99 Eng.Rep. 344, 1780.

6 See infra § 13.

## THE MODERN LAW OF SUCCESSION—ENGLAND

**13. Under the statute of 1925, there is no distinction in the succession based on the nature of the property nor on the age or sex of the surviving relatives. The table of inheritance favors first the surviving spouse and descendants, and in absence of these, the property passes to designated ancestors and collateral relatives. Great-grandparents or their descendants may not take intestate's property, which in absence of closer kin passes to the crown. The half-blood takes only in absence of whole blood of equal degree.**

The Inheritance Act, 1833,[1] was the first of a number of statutes which wrought great changes in the law of devolution of property. Important among these was the Married Women's Property Act, 1882,[2] which permitted a married woman to own, acquire, and dispose of by will or otherwise any personal property as if she were a feme sole. However, this act did not affect the husband's right to claim her intestate personalty.[3] By the Intestate Act, 1890, it was provided that when a man died without issue his widow was entitled to the first 500 pounds of his personalty and half of the residue.[4]

The culmination of this series of reforms is the current Administration of Estates Act, 1925[5] which consolidated the law of intestate succession and made sweeping alterations in accordance with modern social and economic concepts and conditions. This act provides that both real and personal property shall pass to the administrator,[6] upon trust to sell and to pay the debts and

1 See § 6 at notes 15–17 supra.

2 45 & 46 Vict. c. 75.

3 Re Lambert's Estate, 39 Ch.Div. 626, 1888.

4 53 & 54 Vict. c. 29. As to modern legislation regarding aliens, felons & escheats, see supra §§ 10, 11, 12.

5 15 Geo. V, c. 23. This is an adjunct to the Law of Property Act, 1925, 15 Geo. V, c. 20. The property law of England was covered by the Law of Property Act, 1922, 12 & 13 Geo. V, c. 16, which by its terms went into effect at the beginning of 1925. However, the operation was postponed, and new acts were passed in 1925 which made some new alterations. The 1925 acts went into effect January 1, 1926. See Warren, The Law of Property Act, 1922, 21 Mich.L.Rev. 245; Peake, The Law of Intestacy, 1927, 1.

6 This is not an innovation, for the Land Transfer Act, 1897, 60 & 61 Vict. c. 65, provided that land as well as chattels passed to the personal representative. As early as 1879, a unified system of succession for both realty and personalty was advocated by Maitland. See 1 Collected Papers 170–201 passim.

expenses, and distribute the residue. There is no difference between realty and personalty as to the persons entitled to succeed thereto. The rules of descent and the rights of dower, curtesy, and escheat to the mesne lord are abolished. No distinction is made between the estates of males and females, and no preference is given to male over female heirs.

The surviving spouse, whether male or female, is entitled to the "personal" chattels [7] absolutely and to the first thousand pounds of the residue.[8] The balance of the residue also goes to the surviving spouse for life if there is no issue. If there be a surviving spouse and also issue, the former is entitled to one half of the balance for life and the issue to the remaining half upon statutory trusts. If there be issue but no surviving spouse, the issue takes the whole upon statutory trusts.[9] The statutory trusts in favor of issue provide for a per stirpes division among the descendants whose intervening ancestors predeceased the intestate. Until majority or marriage of the issue so entitled, their shares are held, and do not vest until that time.[10] Ample power is given to make advancements for support during the period of minority and use of the personal chattels is permitted with the consent of the personal representatives.

In absence of issue and subject to the above-mentioned share of the surviving spouse, the following take in the order named in the absence of persons in the preceding classes: (1) Parents equally or the whole to the surviving parent; (2) brothers and sisters of the whole blood; (3) brothers and sisters of the half-blood; (4) surviving grandparents equally; (5) uncles and aunts of the whole blood; (6) uncles and aunts of the half-blood; (7) the surviving spouse absolutely; (8) the crown. When the succession falls to members of the second, third, fifth or sixth class, it goes upon statutory trusts for the survivors of the class and the representatives of the deceased members upon a per stirpes

7 These are defined by § 55x of the act and include furniture, household effects, and vehicles, but not chattels used in business, nor money or securities.

8 Since the above was written the spouse's share has been increased, so that he or she takes the first 5000 pounds if there is issue, the first 20,000 pounds if there is no issue, and the entire estate if there is no issue, parent or issue of parent. Intestate's Act, 1952.

9 The act does not provide for the termination of the trusts, but under the English law the beneficiary of the corpus of a trust can demand the principal sum at any time. Saunders v. Vautier, 4 Beav. 115, 49 Eng.Rep. 282, 1841.

10 This avoids the necessity of an

basis, as is provided in the case of the issue of the intestate.[11] Beyond the issue of uncles and aunts there is no succession to an intestate's property. Second cousins cannot take under the statute; if there are no closer relatives, the estate will go to the crown. The order of succession was drafted after the examination of many wills and as far as possible conforms to the division by the average testator.[12] It has been said [13] that while the plan is admirable in cases of persons of moderate wealth, it is not so suitable for very poor or very rich intestates because in the first case the one thousand pounds going to the widow will exhaust the entire estate, while in the latter case if there are no issue the widow can scarcely spend the income to which she is entitled.

By express terms of the act, issue en ventre sa mere at the time of intestate's death are considered living at that time. The Adoption Act, 1926,[14] recognized adoption but declared that the child may inherit from his natural parent and not from the adopter. However, under the Adoption of Children Act, 1940, the child may inherit from his adoptive parents.[15] Legitimation may now be accomplished by marriage of the parents after the child's birth.[16] Furthermore, the mother of illegitimate children may succeed to their intestate property, and if the mother leaves no legitimate issue, her illegitimate children or their issue may inherit from her.[17]

With the abolition of curtesy and dower an English testator had complete power to dispose of his property by will so as to deprive his family of all interest therein. There was considerable agitation for legislation for the benefit of the dependent family.[18] This resulted in the passage of the Inheritance (Family Provision) Act, 1938 [19] which authorized judicial allowance from the estate to members of the family when the testator did not make adequate provision for them.

administration and added death duty if the heir dies during his minority.

11 See 170 L.T. 311.

12 See Warren, supra note 5 at 265, 266; 161 L.T. 241.

13 167 L.T. 307.

14 16 & 17 Geo. V, c. 29. See Humphrys v. Polak, [1901] 2 K.B. 385, 163 L.T. 46.

15 See 94 Sol.J. 173.

16 Legitimacy Act, 1926, 16 & 17 Geo. V, c. 60.

17 Ibid.

18 Keeton and Gower, Freedom of Testation in English Law, 20 Ia.L.R. 326; 165 L.T. 451; note, 44 L.Q.Rev. 281; Parliamentary Debates, House of Lords, vol. 71 (1928) cols. 38–61.

19 1 & 2 Geo. VI, c. 45. See supra § 5 at notes 33, 34.

## GENERAL PLAN OF DESCENT AND DISTRIBUTION—UNITED STATES

**14. Most of the principles peculiar to the English Canons of Descent have disappeared from our law, and statutes in most jurisdictions now provide that the same relatives shall succeed to both realty and personalty. The inheritance tables of the various states differ from each other in many respects, but most follow in a general way the scheme of the English Statute of Distribution.**

The development of the English law of intestacy has been treated at some length for two reasons. First, many of our concepts and indeed of our positive rules of law are directly traceable to the mother country. In addition, the alterations of earlier British concepts are illustrative of what has taken place in America or what may be expected within the lifetime of the readers of this book. It can probably be said that few of our states have a system as advanced or as rational as now found in England.[1] On the other hand many of the forward steps were reached in this country long before Parliament had taken an enlightened position.[2]

For the most part there was an early American rejection of the principles of the Canons of Descent such as primogeniture, disinheritance of ancestors and of the half-blood and the like. Descent of land as well as distribution of personalty has long been governed by statute. Moreover, the legislative tendency has been to have a common scheme of proportional inheritance regardless of whether the property is real or personal.[3] Heirs and distributees are entitled to the same proportion of both in the great majority of states, and even in those jurisdictions where differences still exist they arise chiefly out of the surviving spouse's shares, which there continue to be diverse as to the two kinds of property.[4] In a general way the statutory provisions usually follow the plan of the English Statute of Distribution,

1 See supra § 13.

2 Thus, in the nineteenth century and up to 1925 America led generally in such respects as a common scheme of succession for both real and personal property and protection of the surviving spouse against testamentary disposition to others. Cf. § 4 and § 13 supra, with the remainder of this chapter and § 30 infra.

3 See supra § 4, note 33.

4 See infra § 15.

1670—at least in result.[5] The rights of the blood relatives do not depend upon their age or sex.[6]

Chancellor Kent observed in his Commentaries on American Law that each state had different rules of intestate succession.[7] This is almost as true under present statutes. However, in many respects some states may be grouped together and there are many other common principles in legislative provisions and in the decisions of the courts interpreting them. An attempt will be made to describe these, but considerations of space forbid a detailed description or even a summary of the law in each of the forty-eight states.[8]

## THE SURVIVING SPOUSE'S SHARE—UNITED STATES

**15. Typically the surviving husband or wife takes a half or third interest, which is often increased if the decedent left no issue or other designated relatives. However, there are numerous divergences from this plan in many states and provisions for the surviving spouse differ in plan and detail more than intestate provisions for blood relatives.**

At common law the surviving spouse was entitled to a life estate of curtesy or dower in the land of the deceased spouse but under no circumstances was he or she the heir of the deceased

[5] See infra §§ 15 to 18. For general discussions and summaries of American intestate laws, see Eagleton, Introduction to the Intestacy Act and Dower Rights Act, 20 Ia.L.R. 241; McCall and Langston, A New Intestate Succession Statute for North Carolina, 11 N.C.L.R. 266; Noyes, The Descent and Distribution of Real and Personal Property in Kentucky, 34 Ky.L.J. 268; Rollison, Principles of Succession to Intestate Property, 11 Notre Dame Lawyer 14, 121, 339. See also Oppenheim, The Fundamentals of Louisiana Succession Law—Part I, The Intestate Succession, 23 Tulane L.R. 305.

[6] But in some states provisions for the widow and for the widower are not the same. See infra § 15. And in a few states the father excludes the mother as heir. See infra § 17.

[7] Kent's Com. pt. 6, lec. 65, p. 374; Kent's Com. pt. 5, lec. 37, p. 427.

[8] A set of Canons attempting to describe the rules of general application for the descent of land was attempted by Kent in his Commentaries, pt. 6, lec. 65, p. 375 et seq. He was obliged to note many exceptions and qualifications of local nature, and the note writers of the later editions were forced to acknowledge many more. At the present time the task seems impractical in view of the larger number of jurisdictions and the still greater diversities in their statutes and decisions. For a proposed uniform statute of descent and distribution, see Eagleton, supra note 5; Model Probate Code § 22 et seq.

spouse.[1] The survivor could not be deprived of curtesy or dower by will.[2] Under the Statute of Distribution, 1670, the widow took a third of the personalty if intestate left descendants and half if he did not,[3] but by will in favor of others the husband could defeat the widow's intestate share of the personalty.[4]

American legislation has greatly altered this situation.[5] In most jurisdictions dower and curtesy have been abolished or greatly changed.[6] Usually the spouse takes a share of both realty and personalty by intestacy, and part or all of this share is secure against testamentary disposition. Only the spouse's intestate shares are considered in this section; the problems of what rights may be asserted against the will of the deceased spouse are reserved for later consideration.[7]

There is more diversity regarding the intestate share of the surviving spouse in the various states than with respect to the shares of blood relatives among themselves. This is because the spouse is a special case and consequently there is legislative disagreement as to how the various factors mentioned below should influence the result. There is one point of agreement: the spouse's case is so strong that all blood relatives take subject to the spouse's share—whatever that may be in the particular jurisdiction. In a few states the husband's share is not as favorable as the wife's, probably on the ground that he is not normally financially dependent upon her,[8] but usually the intestate shares of the surviving husband and wife are the same.

If there are no children or if the surviving spouse remarries the property inherited by the surviving spouse is likely to pass ultimately to the survivor's family rather than to the kindred of the spouse who was the original owner. This is an argument for confining the spouse's interest to a life estate by way of dower, curtesy or some statutory substitute therefor. However, there are practical reasons against creating a statutory life estate in personal property and hence some states have given the spouse

1 See supra § 6 at note 14.

2 See infra § 29.

3 See supra § 7 at note 2.

4 See supra § 3 at notes 42, 43.

5 For a detailed summary, see 3 Vernier, American Family Laws § 227. See also articles cited supra § 14, note 5.

6 See infra § 30.

7 See infra §§ 32, 33.

8 Yet the husband's curtesy amounted to a life estate in all the wife's land while the latter's dower was a life interest in only a third of her husband's land. See infra § 29.

an absolute interest in the personal property but merely a dower or other life interest in realty.[9] Under this plan the blood relatives take different ultimate interests in the real and in the personal property, and the real property in which the spouse takes a life interest may be unmarketable in the latter's lifetime. Then, too, a life interest is often an inadequate provision for the spouse. For these reasons most jurisdictions give the spouse an identical absolute share in fee in both species of property.

Typically the spouse is entitled to a third or half of both real and personal property, though in some jurisdictions the share is dependent on the number of children and in a few the spouse counts as a child and gets a child's share.[10] Frequently the spouse takes an increased interest or even the entire estate when the decedent left no issue, or neither issue nor certain other enumerated relatives.[11] Even a fixed fractional share in absolute ownership is inadequate for the spouse when the estate is small and must be shared by others. Accordingly a number of American jurisdictions have provided that the surviving spouse takes the entire estate up to a certain fixed amount if there is no issue,[12] but they do not go as far as the present English act.[13]

The Model Probate Code's provision [14] for the surviving spouse probably exemplifies the typical American position upon the subject. It gives the spouse half of the estate if issue survives; the first $5000 and half the remainder if there is no issue, and parents or their issue survive; the entire estate in other cases.

There is also the case of the exceedingly large estate where the surviving spouse's share may greatly exceed the needs of, and even become burdensome to, the recipient. In an exceedingly thoughtful article, Professor Paul L. Sayre has advocated legislation, classifying estates as to amount and making different provisions for the surviving spouse in each classification.[15]

In the community property states the separate property and the community property frequently do not pass alike. Thus, in

9 See supra note 5.

10 Ibid. See Leffler v. Leffler, 151 Fla. 455, 10 So.2d 799, 1942, sustaining a statute limiting the spouse to dower or a child's share where the decedent is survived by issue who are not the issue of the surviving spouse.

11 See infra §§ 17, 18.

12 E. g. N.Y. Decedent Estate Law § 83; 20 P.S. (Pa.) § 12. The American provisions apply only in absence of issue.

13 See supra § 13, note 8.

14 § 22(a).

15 Husband and Wife as Statutory Heirs, 42 Harv.L.R. 330.

California the surviving spouse is entitled absolutely to his half of the community and also the other half if there is no testamentary disposition thereof.[16] In the case of separate property, the surviving spouse shares with children, their descendants and other close relatives.[17] As the community property schemes differ in the eight states which have the system, it is impossible to attempt to describe them within brief compass. It is sufficient to notice here that community property rules are so devised as to provide for the surviving spouse in the same general way that dower, curtesy, and their statutory substitutes do in other jurisdictions.

## DESCENDANTS' SHARES—UNITED STATES

**16. Children of the intestate inherit the latter's property subject to the interests of the surviving spouse. They take equally regardless of sex or age, and the issue of predeceased children take in place of their parents. Descendants, however remote, take in preference to all other blood relatives.**

There is considerable uniformity regarding the shares of children or other descendants of an intestate.[1] Of course they take subject to, or along with, the surviving spouse. If there is no surviving spouse, the issue divide the entire estate. No distinction is made between issue on account of sex or order of birth. All

16 Probate Code § 201. In California, formerly at least, the wife was deemed to take community property by succession on the husband's death, but the surviving husband took under the orthodox theory elsewhere that he became the absolute owner of his part of the community by its dissolution upon death of the wife. Cf. Burdick's Estate, 112 Cal. 387, 44 P. 734, 1896, with Fields v. Michael, 91 Cal.App.2d 443, 205 P.2d 402, 1949. See Kirkwood, Ownership of Community Property in California, 7 So.Cal.L.R. 1; Simmons, The Interest of a Wife in California Community Property, 22 Cal.L.R. 404; Daggett, The Modern Problem of the Nature of the Wife's Interest in Community Property—A Comparative Study, 19 Cal.L.R. 567; Oppenheim, The Inheritance of the Surviving Spouse—Article 915, Louisiana Civil Code of 1870, 21 Tulane L.R. 54. For the general theory of community property in the various jurisdictions, see Evans, The Ownership of Community Property, 35 Harv.L.R. 47; note, 32 Ky.L.J. 63. As to the specific provisions for the disposition on the death of one spouse, see 3 Vernier, American Family Laws § 178; Vernier and Hurlbut, Descent and Succession under the Community Property System, 20 Ia.L.R. 232.

17 Probate Code §§ 220–229.

1 The statutory provisions are collected in 4 Vernier, American Family Laws § 239. See also articles cited supra § 14 note 5.

of the decedent's sons and daughters take equally, and the issue of a predeceased child will take the latter's share. If the predeceased child left several children (the intestate's grandchildren) the latter divide their parent's share, regardless of sex or order of birth. In no case does a grandchild take a share of the intestate's estate, if the grandchild's parent, the child of the intestate, survives. This scheme of succession continues through all generations of descendants.[2] Parents or other relatives of the intestate can claim no share as long as there are issue, however remote. It should be observed that the agreement in the various jurisdictions are due primarily to similarity of statutory provisions, since the whole matter of intestate succession is one of legislative enactment.

So far, the rules with respect to heirship by descendants are identical with those which were laid down in the interpretations of the English Statute of Distribution, 1670. But there is one situation in which the decisions in most American jurisdictions differ from those under the English statute. This is the problem of how to divide the property when all of the decedent's children die in his lifetime, leaving only grandchildren among whom the grandparent's property is to be divided. Should the division be per stirpes, according to the number of decedent's children, or per capita according to the number of grandchildren? It will be recalled that the English courts decided in favor of the per stirpes plan.[3] The statutory language in some [4] of our states indicates a per capita division in this case. Even when the statutory language is almost identical with the English statute, it has been held that the grandchildren take per capita,[5] though the per stirpes plan has been followed where a clear provision requires it.[6] When the survivors are children and grandchildren, issue of two or more deceased children, the division is per stirpes throughout though much can be said for legislation dividing the total grandchildren's shares per capita between them.[7]

2 Godden v. Long, 104 Neb. 13, 175 N.W. 655, 1919.

3 See supra § 7, note 8. For general discussions, see Page, Descent Per Stirpes and Per Capita, [1946] Wis.L.R. 3; White, Per Stirpes or Per Capita, 13 U. of Cin.L.R. 298.

4 Supra note 1. See also Cox v. Cox, 44 Ind. 368, 1873; notes, 10 Tulane L.R. 613, 616, 12 Am.St.Rep. 404.

5 In re Martin's Estate, 96 Vt. 455, 120 A. 862, 1923. See Person's Appeal, 74 Pa. 121, 1873.

6 Crump v. Faucett, 70 N.C. 345, 1874. See also Maud v. Catherwood, 67 Cal.App.2d 636, 155 P.2d 111, 1945, noted, 33 Cal.L.R. 324, where the court strains for a per stirpes distribution.

7 See McCall and Langston, A New Intestate Succession Statute for North Carolina, 11 N.C.L.R. 266 and infra § 18, note 6.

## PARENTS' AND THEIR ISSUE'S SHARES—UNITED STATES

**17. In most states parents take in absence of descendants, subject to the share of the surviving spouse; brothers and sisters take next after parents though in some states they share with parents. Nephews and nieces are permitted to take the share of their predeceased parent if other brothers and sisters survive; but if nephews and nieces are the sole survivors they usually take equally, or per capita.**

These persons take only in total absence of issue of the intestate and always subject ot the share of the surviving spouse. The English Statute of Distribution, 1670, made no special mention of parents or brothers and sisters and hence they took under the classification of next of kin.[1] American intestate statutes expressly provide for parents and usually for their issue as taking in absence of descendants of the intestate.[2] As a consequence there is no occasion for determining whether parents—or to the extent of specific statutory mention, the issue of parents—are next of kin because they take under the prior and more particular terms of the statute.[3]

No jurisdiction follows the common-law doctrine which forbade lineal ancestors from inheriting land. Indeed if the intestate leaves no issue his parents usually take the entire estate, subject to the share of the surviving spouse. Thus, when both parents survive and there are no brothers and sisters or issue thereof the parents divide the property equally in almost every jurisdiction, though in a very few the father takes it all. If only one parent survives he usually takes the entire estate.[4]

When brothers and sisters also survive, the parents are preferred in a majority of the states if both parents survive, and in a somewhat smaller majority a single surviving parent takes the entire estate. However, brothers and sisters share the estate with both parents in some jurisdictions and in others they take with the surviving parent if only one parent survives. In some of the minority of states where parents and brothers and sisters

1 However, an amendment in 1685 provided that the mother must share with brothers and sisters. See supra § 7 notes 23, 24.

2 For a summary of the provisions, see 4 Vernier, American Family Laws § 239. See also articles cited supra § 14 note 5. Cf. Model Probate Code § 22(b).

3 See Snodgrass v. Bedell, 134 Ohio St. 311, 16 N.E.2d 463, 1938.

4 Consult local statutes and see supra note 2.

share, it is provided that all share equally; in others the parents or the surviving parent take half the estate; still elsewhere a surviving parent is given a double share.[5]

In absence of descendants and parents, brothers and sisters are everywhere next in order of intestate succession. They take regardless of age or sex. If there are children of deceased brothers and sisters together with surviving brothers and sisters, the nephews and nieces take the share that their predeceased parent would have taken if he had survived the intestate.[6] This is a stirptual division, the number of stocks being the number of living brothers and sisters plus the number of predeceased brothers and sisters who left a child or children. The latter take their parent's share by representation, and in some jurisdictions the statutes extend the right of representation to grandchildren or to any descendants of brothers and sisters.

If intestate left no surviving brothers and sisters but only nephews and nieces of different predeceased parents, in most jurisdictions the nephews and nieces take per capita or equally among themselves and not according to the shares that their parents would have taken had they survived the intestate.[7] The preponderance of jurisdictions in favor of the per capita position is stronger here than in case of a division between grandchildren of the intestate when none of his children survive.[8] However, some statutes require that there be a stirptual division between nephews and nieces.[9]

Where the claimants were living nephews and nieces and the issue of predeceased nephews and nieces, it is usually held that the estate must be divided into the number of shares of nephews and nieces who survived or left issue, and that the issue take the

5 Ibid.

6 The argument that the children of several deceased brothers and sisters should take per capita inter se in a case where two sisters also survived was rejected in favor of a division per stirpes throughout. In re Estate of Poindexter, 221 N.C. 246, 20 S.E.2d 49, 140 A.L.R. 1138, 1942, discussed in 1942 Ann.Surv. Am.L. 685. Cf. supra § 16 note 7.

7 In re Reil's Estate, 70 Idaho 64, 211 P.2d 407, 19 A.L.R.2d 186, 1949; Nichols v. Shephard, 63 N.H. 391, 1885; Fisk v. Fisk, 60 N.J.Eq. 195, 46 A. 538, 1900; Peters v. Clancy, 192 S.W.2d 937, Tex.Civ.App.1946; Davis v. Rowe, 6 Rand. (Va.) 355, 1828. See Kales in 3 Ill.L.R. 74 and 5 Ill. L.Rev. 450; notes, 8 Fordham L.R. 425, [1940] Wis.L.R. 590.

8 See supra § 16 notes 3 to 6.

9 Swenson v. Lewison, 135 Minn. 145, 160 N.W. 253, 1916; In re Yong's Estate, 115 Utah 292, 204 P.2d 452, 1949.

predeceased parents' shares.[10] This might be called a per capita division with representation.[11] Of course the result would be otherwise in the jurisdictions where the statute indicates a stirptual division; there the primary division would be according to the number of brothers and sisters who left issue.[12] Of course all this assumes that the statute permits representation beyond brothers' and sister's children; if it does not the property would be divided among the living nephews and nieces, either according to the majority per capita or minority per stirpes rules as the case may be, and the grandnephews and grandnieces would be totally excluded. This is the consequence of denying them the right of representation.[13]

## NEXT OF KIN—UNITED STATES

**18. When none of the relatives specifically enumerated in the statute survive the intestate, his property usually goes to his next of kin computed by the method of the civil law.**

**Representation, or the right to stand in the place of one's predeceased ancestor, is generally confined to the children or descendants of brothers and sisters; but the principle is extended in some states to the issue of other relatives. Some states allow universal representation through adoption of a statutory formula which is based on the parentelic scheme and avoids use of the next of kin concept.**

The most usual type of statute of descent and distribution specifies the order in which certain designated classes of relatives shall take and then provides for the remaining cases by declaring that the property goes to the next of kin. In some states brothers and sisters and their issue are not expressly mentioned in the law,[1] but usually the statutes enumerate them and often also provide in their absence for grandparents and their issue.[2]

10 Garrett v. Bean, 51 Ark. 52, 9 S.W. 435, 1888; Williams v. Trust Co. of Georgia, 185 Ga. 643, 196 S.E. 74, 1938. See also authorities supra note 7.

11 See Eagleton, Introduction to the Intestacy Act and the Dower Rights Act, 20 Ia.L.R. 241, 244–249, 251; Model Probate Code § 22.

12 See Cook v. Catlin, 25 Conn. 387, 1856, and authorities supra note 9.

13 For further discussion regarding representation and the contest between the nephew and the uncle, see infra § 18.

1 So in In re Estate of Poindexter, cited supra § 17 note 6.

2 Ohio Gen.Code, Page, 1937, § 10503–4. Cf. infra notes 22 to 24.

When a person claims by virtue of being the relative designated by the statute, or as coming within the statutory designation of children, issue descendants or representatives of the named relatives, there is no occasion for determining whether he is next of kin. Such person takes by the specific provisions of the statute and the problem of next of kin is not reached.[3] It is only when no claimant falls within the specially provided classes that it is necessary to determine who is next of kin or closest related by degree to the claimant.[4]

Some statutes provide that next of kin shall be computed according to the rule of the civil law, in which the degree of relationship is determined by counting the number of steps from the claimant to the closest common ancestor of the claimant and the intestate and then adding the number of steps from this common ancestor to the intestate.[5] The sum of these two counts is the degree of relationship of claimant to intestate; the claimant related in the lowest degree takes as next of kin; if several claimants are related in equal degree they are all next of kin and share equally. The civil law method is also applied when the statute is silent as to the manner of determining next of kin.[6] A few statutes expressly declare that the computation shall be by the common-law method in which case the degree of relationship is the number of steps in the longer of the two lines from the common ancestor to the intestate and to the claimant, instead of the sum of both.[7]

*Representation*

The foregoing must be modified by the provisions in most statutes which allow children or other descendants of certain relatives to represent their predeceased ancestor in taking as next of kin. Some statutes provide for representation only in favor of children of intestate's brothers and sisters, others include grandchildren or all descendants of brothers and sisters, and still others extend representation to the descendants of other or

3 Hoffman v. Watson, 109 Md. 532, 72 A. 479, 1909; Snodgrass v. Bedell, 134 Ohio St. 311, 16 N.E.2d 463, 1938.

4 As to statutes which make no provision for next of kin see infra, note 22 et seq.

5 See supra § 7; Simonton v. Edmunds, 202 S.C. 397, 25 S.E.2d 284, 1943; McDowell v. Addams, 45 Pa. 430, 1863.

6 Thomas v. Marriott, 154 Md. 107, 140 A. 91, 1928; Taylor v. Bray, 32 N.J.L. 182, 1867; Toomey v. Turner, 184 Miss. 831, 186 So. 301, 1939.

7 See Wetter v. Habersham, 60 Ga. 193, 1878.

all collaterals.[8] Representation has several aspects. In the first place there is the matter of who takes by representation. Of course if representation is not allowed in his particular case the claimant cannot be moved up in degree to that of his predeceased ancestor who would have taken had he survived; hence such claimant fails if some living person is related in a closer degree than this claimant is.[9] On the affirmative side of this problem two different statutory situations should be noted. If the statutory grant is directly to the representatives of designated relatives, persons coming within the class of permissible representatives take regardless of whether they are next of kin.[10] For example if the statute provides for brothers and sisters and their representatives and then for next of kin, the intestate's nephew as a representative of a deceased brother or sister comes within the prior class and hence is preferred to the intestate's uncle who can claim only as next of kin.[11] However, if the statute makes no grant to the representatives of brothers and sisters but simply allows representation in case of brothers' and sisters' children the result may be different. Here the nephew as well as the uncle must claim as next of kin. Under the English law, while representation by the children of predeceased brothers and sisters of the intestate permitted them to take with the intestate's living brothers and sisters, intestate's nephew would not displace intestate's uncle by representation; both were related in the third degree and hence shared equally.[12] This exact problem will not arise under most American statutes,[13] though when it does it would seem that our courts *should* follow the English law. How-

8 The Statute of Distribution, 1670, stated the matter negatively "that there be no representations admitted among collateral after brothers' and sisters' children." 22 & 23 Car. II, c. 10, § VII. Cf. N.Y. Decedent Estate Law § 83(10) which is the same except that last word is "descendants." See Barnes v. Redmond, 127 Tenn. 45, 152 S.W. 1035, 1912 (universal representation, realty). It is clear that the statutes refer to brothers and sisters of the intestate and not to brothers and sisters of his collaterals. Draper v. Draper, 174 Tenn. 394, 126 S.W.2d 307, 1939. See supra § 7, notes 32, 33.

9 Wetter v. Habersham, 60 Ga. 193, 1878; Jahnke v. Selle, 368 Ill. 268, 13 N.E.2d 980, 1938; In re Fretheim's Estate, 156 Minn. 366, 194 N.W. 766, 1923; In re Downings' Estates, 146 Wash. 154, 262 P. 235, 1927.

10 See supra note 3.

11 Hoffman v. Watson, supra note 3.

12 Supra § 7 notes 29, 30.

13 Because nephews and nieces are expressly mentioned in many states and need not claim as next of kin. See note 3 supra. In addition some statutes prefer one claiming under the closest common ancestor. See Minot v. Harris, 132 Mass. 528, 1882; cf. infra notes 22–25.

ever, they have usually declined to do so and although all claim as next of kin it has been held that one entitled to representation may thereby displace another in a more remote line, who, but for the representation principle, would be in an equal or closer degree to the intestate.[14]

The second problem of representation is: assuming that a person is permitted to take under this principle, how will his share be computed? In this regard it is not important whether the statutory grant is *to* the representatives, or simply allows representation in the case at hand. The matter has already been explained with reference to nephews and nieces claiming under express designation of the statute,[15] and the situation is similar when they or other collaterals are claiming as next of kin. Thus, if the intestate had two brothers, one of whom predeceased him leaving six children, the latter will each take a twelfth of the estate and the surviving brother a half, assuming that there were no closer relatives and the statute allows representation in this case as it usually does. Let us suppose, however, that the intestate had two brothers, both of whom predeceased him, one leaving six children and the other a single child. Applying the rule of representation to its logical conclusion, the latter would take one half of the estate while the six nephews and nieces would each take a twelfth. The language of the statutes in some jurisdictions requires that this result should be reached.[16] Sometimes, however, the statute provides a general rule that when those entitled are related to the intestate in an equal degree of kindred, they will share equally.[17] Under such a provision the estate would of course be divided into seven equal parts. Where the language of the statute is indefinite the courts favor equality of shares as between collaterals equally related to the intestate.[18]

14 See Wetter v. Habersham, 60 Ga. 193, 1878; Caldwell v. Cowan, 60 N.C. 639, 1864. Cf. Matter of Davenport, 172 N.Y. 454, 65 N.E. 275, 1902, with Matter of Butterfield, 211 N.Y. 395, 105 N.E. 830, 1914. But see In re Fisher's Estate, 17 N.J.Super. 207, 85 A.2d 562, 1952.

15 See supra § 17 notes 6 to 12.

16 Harrell v. Storey, 175 Ga. 569, 165 S.E. 554, 1932. See also supra § 17 note 9.

17 See In re Samson's Will, 257 N.Y. 358, 178 N.E. 557, 1931.

18 Broward v. Broward, 96 Fla. 131, 117 So. 691, 1928; Blake v. Blake, 85 Ind. 65, 1882; In re Miller's Estate, 103 N.J.Eq. 86, 141 A. 676, affirmed 104 N.J.Eq. 491, 146 A. 915, 1929; Davis v. Rowe, 6 Rand. (Va.) 355, 1828; Overton v. Heckathorn, 81 W.Va. 640, 95 S.E. 82, 1918; Schneider v. Payne, 205 Wis. 235, 237 N.W. 103, 1931. And see supra § 17, notes 9, 10. See generally, Eagleton, Introduction to the Intestacy Act and the Dower Rights Act, 20 Ia.L.R. 241, 244–249; Page, Descent Per Capita and Per Stirpes [1946] Wis.L.R. 34;

Those who are closest related to the deceased take per capita and in their own right, while descendants of predeceased persons of this class take the latter's share per stirpes. Thus, where the closest surviving relatives are first cousins and there are also descendants of predeceased first cousins, the first cousins take per capita regardless of the derivation of their stocks, and if representation is allowed in their case, the descendants of each predeceased first cousin will take the latter's share. Here representation is often forbidden, in which case the living first cousins share the estate to the exclusion of the issue of the predeceased first cousins.

There is a third aspect of representation, namely, assuming that representation exists in the first sense, do the parties so represented take through their predeceased ancestor or do they take directly from the intestate? This may become important where third persons have judgment liens against the intermediate ancestor, or where the latter was indebted to the intestate.[19] It has even been questioned whether representation will be permitted when the claimant's immediate ancestor died testate.[20] In general, the courts have not been inclined to recognize representation in this sense and the parties, though taking by representation, do not take *from* their immediate ancestor but directly from intestate.[21]

*Statutes Not Mentioning Next of Kin*

Some states avoid use of the expression next of kin in their intestate statutes. One type sets forth the manner of distribution in case of the survival of parents or their issue, and in absence of these provides for grandparents and their issue and finally furnishes the rule for more remote generations by a clause such as "and so on in other cases, without end passing to the lineal ancestors and their children, and their descendants in equal parts." [22] Some of these statutes provide that if there are no parents or issue of parents, the estate is divided into equal

Ritchie, Methods of Intestate Succession, 14 U. of Cin.L.R. 508; White, Per Capita or Per Stirpes, 13 U. of Cin.L.R. 298.

19 In re Rees' Estate, 204 Iowa 610, 215 N.W. 726, 1927; Johnson v. Huntley, infra note 21.

20 Hayes' Adm'r v. Matlock, 27 Ind. 49, 1866.

21 Russell v. Bulliner, 370 Ill. 260, 18 N.E.2d 879, 1938; Harle v. Harle, 109 Tex. 214, 204 S.W. 317, 15 A.L.R. 1261, 1918 (adopted child of deceased parent does not inherit from grandparent); Johnson v. Huntley, 39 Wash.2d 499, 236 P.2d 776, 1951.

22 Missouri—V.A.M.S. § 468.010.

moieties, one going to each set of grandparents and their descendants and so on.[23]

This is a version of the parentelic scheme. The same is true of the statutes of Iowa and New Mexico. After providing for surviving spouses, descendants and parents, these declare that "if both parents are dead, the portion which would have fallen to their share by the above rules shall be disposed of in the same manner as if they had outlived the intestate and died in the possession and ownership of the portion thus falling to their share, and so on, through ascending ancestors and their issue." [24] Though some controversies have arisen under the statutes,[25] they have the advantage of stating the rule applicable to all situations of lineal ascendants and collaterals in a single sentence. Under them, the division would always be per stirpes and never per capita, and representation would be permitted in all generations no matter how remote. This is subject to the objection that the estate may be divided into many small fragments in cases where there are distant relatives only. The situation is similar to that in other jurisdictions which permit extensive representation.

*Relatives by Marriage*

In most states intestate's relatives by marriage other than his surviving spouse [26] do not take his property by intestacy. Intestate's stepchildren are not his children for purposes of the statute,[27] nephews and nieces of his spouse are never his next of kin,[28] and the spouse of his predeceased child is not a representative of the latter.[29] Aside from special statutory provisions

23 See Estes v. Nicholson, 39 Fla. 759, 23 So. 490, 1897. Cf. Florida—F.S.A. § 731.23; White, Ohio's "Half and Half" Inheritance Statute, 15 U. of Cin.L.R. 401.

24 Iowa—I.C.A. § 636.40; New Mex. § 31-114; cf. Kan.Gen.Stat.1949, § 59-508; Texas—Vernon's Ann.Civ.St. art. 2570. See note, 20 Ia.L.R. 626. One of the curious results of these statutes may be the inheritance by the stepmother. See also § 19, note 3.

25 It makes no difference which of deceased's parents or more remote ancestors survived the other for the purpose of determining the interest of their descendants. Lawley v. Keyes, 172 Iowa, 575, 154 N.W. 940, 1915; Sparks v. Bodensick, 72 Kan. 5, 82 P. 463. 1905. Cf. Russell v. Hallett, 23 Kan. 276, 1880.

26 See supra § 15.

27 Cf. note 24 supra and note 31 infra.

28 Fedi v. Ryan, 118 N.J.L. 516, 193 A. 801, 1937.

29 Morris v. First Nat. Bank of Atlanta, 202 Ga. 51, 42 S.E.2d 215, 1941; In re Estate of Vigil, 38 N.M. 383, 34 P.2d 667, 93 A.L.R. 1506, 1934 ("heir").

the property will escheat rather than pass to such persons.[30] However, in several jurisdictions there are express provisions that children or other relatives of intestate's spouse will inherit if there are no other takers.[31]

## HALF-BLOOD—UNITED STATES

**19. In most jurisdictions the half-blood shares equally with the whole blood of the same degree, though in some states the half-blood takes a smaller portion, or is postponed to whole blood of equal degree.**

As has already been explained,[1] there is no problem of half-blood until we reach the classes of collateral relatives. In most American jurisdictions the half-blood inherit equally with the whole blood.[2] In several states the statute expressly provides that the half-blood takes only a half portion. Another variation results from the application of the rule of inheritance of the Iowa and New Mexico statutes. In these jurisdictions a single half-brother will take one-fourth of the estate,[3] while a single full brother takes the other three-fourths as against a one-third and two-thirds division under statutes of the type just previously mentioned. Several jurisdictions have statutes that provide that relatives of the whole blood are preferred to those of the half-blood of equal degree and that the latter take only in the absence of the former.[4] No state absolutely excludes the half-blood as did the common law Canons of Descent.

[30] In re Roberts' Estate, 85 Cal. App.2d 609, 194 P.2d 28, 1948; Center v. Kramer, 112 Ohio St. 269, 147 N.E. 602, 1925.

[31] Hagedorn v. Reiser, 310 Ky. 657, 221 S.W.2d 633, 1949; In re McGraff's Estate, 83 N.E.2d 427, Ohio Prob.1948 (though intestate and his spouse were divorced). See also In re Abdale's Estate, 28 Cal.2d 587, 170 P.2d 918, 1945, construing statute passing separate property inherited from deceased spouse to the latter's heirs rather than to intestate's heirs.

[1] See supra, § 8. Nevertheless some American statutes speak of "children of the half blood." Wyo.Comp.Stat. 1945, § 6–2503. This has been interpreted as meaning kindred in Finley v. Abner, 129 F. 734, C.C.A.Ind.T. 1904. Cf. Genschorck v. Blumer, 136 Kan. 228, 14 P.2d 722, 1932.

[2] Comment, 42 Yale L.J. 101, 104–105. And see Atkinson, Succession among Collaterals, 20 Ia.L.R. 185, 197–202; Eagleton, Introduction to the Intestacy Act and the Dower Rights Act, 20 Ia.L.R. 241, 256; Model Probate Code § 24. Where the statute is silent, it has been held that the half blood inherits land equally with the whole blood. Gradwohl v. Campagna, 46 A.2d 850, Del.Ch.1946.

[3] See Tays v. Robinson, 68 Kan. 53, 74 P. 623, 1903.

[4] See Hughett v. Hughett, 29 Tenn. App. 366, 196 S.W.2d 720, 1946, and infra § 21, especially at note 9 et seq.

## POSTHUMOUS HEIRS—UNITED STATES

**20. Posthumous descendants of the intestate succeed to his property just as if they were born in his lifetime, and the same is generally true of posthumous collateral relatives if they are in embryo at the time of intestate's death. No other posthumous relatives may succeed to decedent's property.**

An intestate's posthumous child is considered in being and will inherit just as if he had been born in the intestate's lifetime. This rule is generally provided by statute,[1] but if not, the same conclusion is reached for this was the common-law rule with respect to both realty and personalty.[2] It has been held that a posthumous child may recover his share of the father's land from a bona fide purchaser obtaining title through a judicial partition sale.[3] In absence of statutory provision to the contrary the same rule applies to posthumous collaterals who are in embryo at the time of the intestate's death.[4] However, some statutes limit the taking to posthumous children; others declare that the doctrine only applies to lineal descendants.[5] We have seen, how in the case of grandchildren or more remote descendants, issue born after intestate's death must have been in embryo at the time of the intestate's death, or they would not have been entitled to succeed to intestate's property.[6] If one were neither

1 Vernier, American Family Laws § 239; see Model Probate Code, § 25. Sometimes statutes provide that the child must be born within ten months. See Cole v. Lewis, 159 Ky. 747, 169 S. W. 490, 1914.

2 Bishop's Heirs v. Hampton, 11 Ala. 254, 1847; Morrow v. Scott, 7 Ga. 535, 1849; Hall v. Hancock, 15 Pick.(Mass.) 255, 26 Am.Dec. 598, 1834; Deal v. Sexton, 144 N.C. 157, 56 S.E. 691, 119 Am.St.Rep. 943, 1907. See Cole v. Lewis, 159 Ky. 747, 169 S.W. 490, 1914. Cf. Boal v. Wood, 70 W.Va. 383, 73 S.E. 978, 42 L.R.A.,N.S., 439, 1912; In re Sankey's Estate, 199 Cal. 391, 249 P. 517, 1926 (involving the question of whether such child is bound by a decree probating his father's will.)

3 Deal v. Sexton, 144 N.C. 157, 56 S.E. 691, 119 Am.St.Rep. 943, 1907.

4 Harper v. Archer, 4 Smedes & M. (Miss.) 99, 43 Am.Dec. 472, 1845. See Melton v. Davidson, 86 Tenn. 129, 5 S.W. 530, 1887.

5 Vernier, American Statute Laws § 239; 1 Woerner on Administration, 225. See Shriver v. Reister, 65 Md. 278, 4 A. 679, 1886; Gibson v. Villines, 148 Okl. 262, 298 P. 592, 1931.

6 Supra § 9. The recent perfection of a method of freezing spermatozoa so that children can be born years after the father's death might, in theory, have ramifications in the law of succession, but in practice this manner of procreation is not apt to become popular enough to give much concern.

born nor in embryo at intestate's death, his parent would have survived the intestate and succeeded to the property.

In the case of collaterals, however, it was possible that a relative may be born long after the intestate's death, who would have been entitled to succeed to property if he had been born before intestate died. Such person could not succeed to the personalty in England and the same has been held in America.[7] But the English courts allowed him to take land by descent, giving rise to the possibility of shifting estates, which vested long after the intestate died.[8] This situation would not occur as often in America today because our laws do not recognize primogeniture and also permit a direct ascending ancestor to take. However, a situation permitting the application of shifting estates might occur in the states where parents share intestate's land with brothers and sisters.[9] Some early American decisions recognized the doctrine of shifting estates in land,[10] but later cases have denied that it will ever be applied.[11] The fact that most jurisdictions provide that both land and chattels shall go to the same persons is an additional reason for not applying the doctrine, as it was never recognized in the case of personalty. If rules of succession should follow the probable desires of the deceased owner, there is no reason for favoring a person born long after his death. Moreover, it is unfair to the person who apparently is entitled to the property to have it later pass from him. Knowledge of this possibility would often discourage the improvement of the realty and make it virtually unsalable.

7 Supra § 9; Grant v. Bustin, 21 N.C. 77, 1835.

8 Supra § 9, note 8.

9 See supra § 17.

10 Cutlar v. Cutlar, 9 N.C. 324, 1823; Caldwell v. Black, 27 N.C. 463, 1845; Baker v. Heiskell, 1 Cold. (Tenn.) 641, 1860. See note 11 infra.

11 Bates v. Brown, 72 U.S.(5 Wall.) 710, 18 L.Ed. 535, 1866; Drake v. Rogers, 13 Ohio St. 21, 1861; Melton v. Davidson, 86 Tenn. 129, 5 S.W. 530, 1887, overruling Baker v. Heiskell, supra note 10. The rule in North Carolina has been changed by statute. N.C.G.S. § 29-1, rule 7.

## ANCESTRAL PROPERTY—UNITED STATES

**21. The doctrine of ancestral property, or favoring the branch of the intestate's family from whom the realty was inherited, has been abolished in most jurisdictions though it still prevails elsewhere particularly so as to exclude the half-blood who is not of the blood of the ancestor. It is seldom applicable to personalty.**

When descendants or surviving spouse succeed to the property of intestate, there is no necessity for inquiry into the ancestral character of the property. Any descendants would be of the blood of the ancestor, while the surviving spouse ordinarily would not be of the blood of the husband or of his ancestor. In case that intestate's successors are his ancestors or collaterals the question arises as to whether ancestral property should go only to those who were of the blood of the ancestor. It will be recalled that at common law persons who were not of the blood of the first purchaser were excluded from the inheritance of land.[1] This principle was feudal in its origin and was not applied to personalty by the English courts.[2] Under the Statute of Distribution, 1670, the personalty went to next of kin regardless of its ancestral origin. In America where the statutes provide a table for succession but make no mention of ancestral property, that doctrine is deemed abolished.[3] A fortiori the principle is not applied to personalty in such jurisdictions.[4] Most states now make no general distinction between ancestral and non-ancestral property.

However a number of jurisdictions continue the principle by express statutory provision. In one respect American statutes often extend the principle by providing that it applies to cases where the property was obtained by devise or gift from the ancestor as well as when received by descent.[5] According to the common-law doctrine, when property passed by devise or gift inter vivos, the descent was deemed broken and the lands passed

[1] Supra § 6, note 9.

[2] Supra § 7, note 40.

[3] Toomey v. Turner, 184 Miss. 831, 186 So. 301, 1939; Smallman v. Powell, 18 Or. 367, 23 P. 249, 17 Am. St.Rep. 742, 1890. See Model Probate Code § 22, comment.

[4] Pierson, The Ancestral Status of Personal Property, 16 Georgetown L. J. 341; and infra note 14.

[5] Woerner on Administration, 222; annotation, 122 A.L.R. 820. But see Jones v. Jones, 227 N.C. 424, 42 S.E. 2d 620, 1947.

as if they were purchased by the devisee or grantee.[6] One exception to the latter statement was the case where the devise was of the same interest as would have been obtained by descent. In this case the devisee-heir was deemed to take by the "worthier title" of descent so that the ancestral property doctrine would apply.[7]

In most jurisdictions which adopt the ancestral property doctrine, there is a statute which permits the next of kin who are not of the blood of the ancestor to take in total absence of kin of the blood of the ancestor.[8] In a number of states the only statutory provision is that kindred of the half-blood inherit equally with the whole blood unless the inheritance comes from intestate by descent, devise or gift from an ancestor, in which case all those not of the blood of the ancestor must be excluded.[9] Under these statutes half-brothers and half-sisters take equally with full brothers and sisters if all are of the blood of the ancestor from whom the property was obtained by intestate, but they cannot take any share as against full brothers and sisters if the former are not of the blood of the ancestor. As to whether the half-blooded brothers and sisters not of the blood of the ancestor should take in preference to the more remote collaterals who are of the blood of the ancestor, there is a conflict under these statutes.[10] When the statute itself furnishes no clue as to whether the doctrine of ancestral property or the doctrine of

6 Latrobe v. Carter, 83 Md. 279, 34 A. 472, 1896; Bell v. Scammon, 15 N.H. 381, 41 Am.Dec. 706, 1844. See infra § 6, note 9.

7 Thompson v. Turner, 173 Ind. 593, 89 N.E. 314, Ann.Cas.1912A, 740, 1909. See Harper and Heckel, The Doctrine of Worthier Title, 24 Ill.L.R. 627; note, 46 Harv.L.R. 993.

8 See annotation, L.R.A.1916C, 903.

9 So in Alabama, California, Idaho, Michigan, Minnesota, Montana, Nebraska, Nevada, North Dakota, Oklahoma, South Dakota, Utah, and Wisconsin. See excellent note, Statutory Treatment of Ancestral Estate and the Half Blood in Intestate Succession, 42 Yale L.J. 101, 104, and annotation, 141 A.L.R. 976. Under these statutes the general doctrine of ancestral property would seem to have no application, being confined to cases when there are relatives of the half-blood who are not of the blood of the ancestor. Cf. Estate of Smith, 131 Cal. 433, 63 P. 729, 1901 (rival claimant was intestate's spouse). Most of these statutes apply apparently to personal as well as real property.

10 Half-blood not of the blood of the ancestor preferred to more remote kindred of the blood of the ancestor. In re Belshaw's Estate, 190 Cal. 278, 212 P. 13, 1923; Pond v. Irwin, 113 Ind. 243, 15 N.E. 272, 1888; Ryan v. Andrews, 21 Mich. 229, 1870; Cox v. Clark, 93 Ala. 400, 9 So. 457, 1891 (express statutory provision). Contra: Thompson v. Smith, 102 Okl. 150, 227 P. 77, 1924; Perkins v. Simonds, 28 Wis. 90, 1871. See notes, 29 Cal.L.R. 77, 27 Minn.L.R. 313.

inheritance by the closest of kin should be given the major emphasis, it would seem that the former should give way as less in accord with modern social concepts. Another class of statutes provides for the doctrine of ancestral property if an infant dies unmarried and without issue. Under this type of statute a surviving parent cannot inherit his child's land which descended from the other parent.[11]

Some statutes specifically state that the ancestral property principle is limited to realty.[12] Often the legislation is not clear on this point. In this situation most courts have held that the doctrine does not apply to personalty.[13] This position seems sound because: (1) The statutory expressions, inheritance, descent, devise, deed, etc., indicate realty; (2) the doctrine did not apply to personalty at common law; (3) personal property is difficult to trace; and (4) the entire principle is out of harmony with present conditions. Only a few jurisdictions have held that the statutory provisions are applicable to personal, as well as real, property.[14]

When realty has been sold and the proceeds invested in other lands, the latter do not partake of the nature of ancestral land.[15] The same is held with respect to personalty in the jurisdictions which apply the ancestral doctrine to chattels.[16] A conveyance

11 Tillinghast v. Coggeshall, 7 R.I. 383, 1863. See note 41 Harv.L.R. 919; Annotation, L.R.A.1916C, 926–930.

12 E. g., R.I.Gen.Laws, 1938, c. 567, § 6.

13 Estate of Ryan, 21 Cal.2d 498, 133 P.2d 626, 1943, noted, 31 Cal.L.R. 334, 41 Mich.L.R. 1200; Guier v. Bridges, 114 Ky. 148, 70 S.W. 288, 1902; In re Kirkendall's Estate, 43 Wis. 167, 1877. See Pierson, supra note 4; L.R.A.1916C, 935.

14 Purcell v. Sewell, 223 Ala. 73, 134 So. 476, 1931; Rountree v. Pursell, 11 Ind.App. 522, 39 N.E. 747, 1895; see Pierson, supra note 4; note, L.R.A.1916C, 936. But see supra note 9.

15 Armington v. Armington, 28 Ind. 74, 1867. And so even if the exchange has been made by the guardian of an infant heir. Terry's Appeal, 28 Conn. 339, 1859; Watson v. Thompson, 12 R.I. 466, 1879. Even where the ancestor directed a conversion of the lands which was done after the testator's death, the lands are robbed of their ancestral character. Burr v. Sim, 1 Whart.(Pa.) 252, 29 Am.Dec. 48, 1836. As to the effect of partition of ancestral land, see notes, 17 Tenn.L.R. 775, 103 A.L.R. 231.

16 Rountree v. Pursell, 11 Ind.App. 522, 39 N.E. 747, 1895 (change by guardian of intestate). Cf. Gray v. Swerer, 47 Ind.App. 381, 94 N.E. 725, 1911 (change by administrator of intestate does not change ancestral character). See, also, Stevenson v. Gray, 46 Ind.App. 412, 89 N.E. 509, 1909 (deposit of insurance funds in bank and subsequent loan and repayment does not alter ancestral character).

of the property by the intestate upon trust to reconvey destroys the ancestral character of the lands.[17] Lands obtained by purchase from the ancestor are not deemed ancestral lands.[18] Even when the deed from the ancestor is gratuitous, if it recitcs consideration, the doctrine has no application.[19] If the intestate receives the equitable title from the ancestor, but the legal title from another source, the doctrine has been held not to apply.[20] However, the placing of a charge upon land devised will not rob the realty of ancestral character.[21]

Under most American statutes the claimant must only be of the blood of the immediate ancestor from whom the intestate obtained the property.[22] Some jurisdictions, however, adopt the common-law rule that claimant must be of the blood of the first purchaser in order to inherit.[23] When a statute says property obtained from an ancestor, it is not generally restricted to that coming from lineal ascendants. Any relative including a collateral or a descendant is deemed an ancestor for the purpose.[24] Even the deceased spouse has been held to constitute an ancestor so that property obtained from that source goes entirely to children of the blood of this deceased spouse and no part to children of other marriages of the intestate.[25] A number of

17 Nesbitt v. Trindle, 64 Ind. 183, 1878; Holme v. Shinn, 62 N.J.Eq. 1, 49 A. 151, 1901; Kihlken v. Kihlken, 59 Ohio St. 106, 51 N.E. 969, 1898. But see Dudrow v. King, 117 Md. 182, 83 A. 34, 39 L.R.A.,N.S., 955, Ann.Cas. 1913E, 1258, 1912, noted, 12 Col.L.R. 625.

18 McElwee v. McElwee, 142 Ark. 560, 219 S.W. 30, 1920.

19 Gardner v. Kern, 115 Ohio St. 575, 155 N.E. 134, 1926. Cf. Morris v. Ward, 36 N.Y. 587, 1867; In re Lynch's Estate, 220 Pa. 14, 69 A. 290, 1908.

20 Earl v. Earl, 145 Ark. 559, 225 S.W. 289, 1920; Higgins v. Higgins, 57 Ohio St. 239, 48 N.E. 943, 1897. Cf. Bruer v. Johnson, 64 Ohio St. 7, 59 N.E. 741, 1901 (personalty). See R.I. Gen.Laws, 1938, c. 567 § 6.

21 Drake v. Knouff, 121 Ohio St. 535, 170 N.E. 170, 67 A.L.R. 1160, 1930.

22 Daly v. Connolly, 159 A. 314, 10 N.J.Misc. 407, 1932; Lincoln v. Herndon, 141 Okl. 212, 285 P. 120, 1930; Arnold v. O'Connor, 37 R.I. 557, 94 A. 145, L.R.A.1916C, 902, 1915.

23 Poisson v. Pettaway, 159 N.C. 650, 75 S.E. 930, 1912. See Reed v. Geddes, 287 Pa. 274, 135 A. 232, 1926 (gift by husband to wife who died leaving daughter as heir who then died—father takes in preference to maternal heirs of daughter); In re Knight's Estate, 57 Cal.App.2d 1010, 136 P.2d 68, 1943.

24 Purcell v. Sewell, 223 Ala. 73, 134 So. 476, 1931; Greenlee v. Davis, 19 Ind. 60, 1862. Cf. Penniman Bro. v. Francisco, 1 Heisk.(Tenn.) 511, 1870.

25 Cornett v. Hough, 136 Ind. 387, 35 N.E. 699, 1893. But see Brower v. Hunt, 18 Ohio St. 311, 1868. See notes, 16 Cal.L.Rev. 162, 110 A.L.R. 1014.

American statutes however restrict the application of the ancestral doctrine to cases where the property was obtained from "intestate's father" or "mother" or "parents." [26]

The ancestral property doctrine is a waning one. For example New York, which was formerly in the group which combined half-blood and ancestral problems,[27] has now abolished the doctrine altogether.[28] In Ohio where the doctrine was formerly very involved [29] the doctrine is now generally abolished,[30] though there is a special provision for inheritance of property coming from the surviving spouse.[31] Furthermore, the courts are inclined to limit rather than to extend the principle.

## ILLEGITIMATES—UNITED STATES

**22. While the spouse or the legitimate issue of a bastard may inherit from him or he from them, illegitimacy is otherwise a bar to intestate succession unless legislation provides otherwise. However, by statute in almost all states a bastard may inherit from his mother, and in the majority from her kindred as well. Quite generally legitimation by subsequent marriage of the parents permits inheritance from or through either parent. Usually if a bastard could inherit from certain relatives they are permitted to inherit from him.**

When a bastard marries he stands in lawful relationship with his spouse and with issue born of the marriage, and as to them he is said to establish a new line of descent. For the purpose of mutual inheritance these persons come within the general provisions of the statutes of descent and distribution; they may inherit from him [1] and conversely he from them.[2] However, in ac-

[26] See Turner's Trustee v. Washburn, 80 S.W. 400, 25 Ky.Law Rep. 2198, 1904; Whitten v. Davis, 18 N.H. 88, 1845.

[27] See supra note 9.

[28] Matter of Costello's Estate, 147 Misc. 629, 265 N.Y.S. 905, 1933.

[29] Simes, Ancestral and Non-Ancestral Realty under the Ohio Statutes of Descent, 2 U. of Cin.L.R. 387.

[30] Ohio Gen.Code § 10503—1.

[31] Ibid. § 10503—5. See supra § 18, note 31; White, Ohio's "Half and Half" Inheritance Statute, 5 U. of Cin.L.R. 401.

[1] Sutton v. Sutton, 87 Ky. 216, 8 S.W. 337, 12 Am.St.Rep. 476, 1888; Northrop v. Hale, 76 Me. 306, 49 Am.Rep. 615, 1884; Goodell v. Yezerski, 170 Mich. 578, 136 N.W. 451, 40 L.R.A.,N.S., 516, 1912.

[2] Statutory provisions for inheritance from an illegitimate by his mother (see infra note 15) would apply only in absence of lawful spouse or legitimate issue of the illegitimate.

cordance with the common-law rule,[3] there can be no inheritance through ties of illegitimacy unless the rule has been changed by statute. Terms such as "child", "descendant," "issue," parent," "brother" or "next of kin," as used in intestacy laws, refer to persons related by legitimate ties of blood except where the legislation shows a contrary intent.[4]

The rigor of the common-law rule has been alleviated by statute in every American jurisdiction.[5] Although many states do not go as far, Section 26 of the Model Probate Code represents a typical legislative provision. It provides that for the purpose of inheritance by, through, and from, an illegitimate he shall be considered as the legitimate child of his mother, and if his parents intermarry after his birth as the legitimate child of both parents. Statutes almost everywhere permit a bastard to inherit from his mother.[6] Where the legislation goes no further the cases are conflicting as to whether he may inherit from the kindred of his mother.[7] Some statutes expressly provide that he may not un-

[3] See supra § 6, notes 11 to 13; § 7, notes 45 to 51. As to the civil law, see note, 4 La.L.R. 147.

[4] Truelove v. Truelove, 172 Ind. 441, 86 N.E. 1018, transferred 172 Ind. 441, 88 N.E. 516, 1909; In re Shriver's Estate, 159 Pa.Super. 314, 48 A.2d 52, 1946. But see Heath v. White, 5 Conn. 228, 1824, holding that "child" in the statute of descent permits inheritance by an illegitimate at least from his mother. As to the right to take under such designation in a will, see In re Ellis' Estate, 225 Iowa 1279, 282 N.W. 758, 120 A.L.R. 975, 1938; Fiduciary Trust Co. v. Michou, 73 R.I. 190, 54 A.2d 421, 1947; 45 Harv.L.R. 890. As to tax exemptions and rates, see Whorff v. Johnson, 143 Me. 198, 58 A.2d 553, 3 A.L.R.2d 160, 1948, and cf. infra § 23, note 12. See also notes, 29 Cal.L.R. 185, 84 U. of Pa.L.R. 531. A child born in wedlock is legitimate, though conceived three months before the marriage. Hegarty v. Curtis, 121 Ind. App. 74, 95 N.E.2d 706, 1950. For a comparative study of the laws of different nations see Robbins and Deak, Familiar Property Rights of Illegitimate Children, 30 Col.L.R. 308. As to the legitimacy of "test-tube babies," see Ploscowe, Sex and the Law 113–118.

[5] See infra note 6.

[6] 3 Vernier, American Family Laws § 249; Vernier and Churchill, Inheritance by and from Bastards, 20 Ia.L.R. 216.

[7] That he may: In re Crapa's Estate, 344 Ill.App. 503, 101 N.E.2d 611, 1951; McGuire v. Brown, 41 Iowa 650, 1875; Smith v. Smith, 105 Kan. 294, 182 P. 338, 1919; State v. Chavez, 42 N.M. 569, 89 P.2d 900, 1938. That he may not: Burris v. Burgett, 16 Del.Ch. 10, 139 A. 454, 1927; Reynolds v. Hitchcock, 72 N.H. 340, 56 A. 745, 1903 (under former statute), with which compare Young v. Bridges, 86 N.H. 135, 165 A. 272, 1933; Matter of Cady's Estate, 257 App.Div. 129, 12 N.Y.S.2d 750, affirmed 281 N.Y. 688, 23 N.E.2d 18, 1939, noted, 9 Fordham L.R. 121. See infra notes 21 to 24.

less legitimated,[8] while others declare that he may although a few states limit this to certain of the mother's relatives.[9] Where an illegitimate would be entitled to inherit from his mother or her kindred, his legitimate children should likewise be permitted to inherit from them if he is dead.[10]

In a few states an illegitimate may also inherit generally from his father or the latter's kindred.[11] Sometimes he may inherit from his father provided the relationship was established in his father's lifetime,[12] or more often if the father acknowledged the child in his lifetime.[13] Quite generally children are legitimated by the subsequent intermarriage of the parents, in which case inheritance is permitted from the father as well as the mother.[14]

Both statute and case law are usually to the effect that if a bastard may inherit from his parents, other ancestors or collaterals they may inherit from him,[15] but this is not always the

8 Supra note 6.

9 Ibid.

10 Foster v. Lee, 172 Ala. 32, 55 So. 125, Ann.Cas.1913C, 1335, 1911; In re Magee's Estate, 63 Cal. 414, 1883; Bales v. Elder, 118 Ill. 436, 11 N.E. 421, 1887; McKellar v. Harkins, 183 Iowa 1030, 166 N.W. 1061, 1918; Sutton v. Sutton, 87 Ky. 216, 8 S.W. 337, 12 Am.St.Rep. 476, 1888; In re Cameron's Estate, 170 Mich. 578, 136 N.W. 451, 40 L.R.A.,N.S., 516, 1912; Contra: Curtis v. Hewins, 11 Metc. (Mass.) 294, 1846.

11 See In re Estate of Berg, 72 N.D. 52, 4 N.W.2d 575, 140 A.L.R. 1312, 1942 (but applies only to children born before statute). See also Ariz. Code 1949, § 27-401.

12 See Milis' Estate, 212 Wis. 283, 249 N.W. 282, 1933.

13 3 Vernier, American Family Laws, § 244. Jurisdictions differ as to whether the recognition or acknowledgment must be in writing and as to the required form thereof. Miller v. Pennington, 218 Ill. 220, 75 N.E. 919, 1 L.R.A.,N.S., 773, 1905; Diver v. Fourth Nat. Bank of Wichita, 132 Kan. 36, 294 P. 924, 1931; Houghton v. Dickinson, 196 Mass. 389, 82 N.E. 481, 1907; In re Snethun's Estate, 180 Minn. 202, 230 N.W. 483, 1930. See Thomas v. Thomas' Estate, 64 Neb. 581, 90 N.W. 630, 1902; Sanchez v. Torres, 35 N.M. 383, 298 P. 408, 1931; Kelly v. Scott, 125 Okl. 208, 257 P. 303, 1927. In most jurisdictions the statute applies although the father also has legitimate issue. Hall v. Gabbert, 213 Ill. 208, 72 N.E. 806, 1904; Alston v. Alston, 114 Iowa 29, 86 N.W. 55, 1901; Caldwell v. Miller, 44 Kan. 12, 23 P. 946, 1890; Ex parte Wallace, 26 N.M. 181, 190 P. 1020, 1920. Contra: Wilson v. Bass, 70 Ind.App. 116, 118 N.E. 379, 1918; Jones v. Hunter, 2 La.Ann. 254, 1847 (express statutory provision).

See infra notes 22–24.

14 3 Vernier, American Family Laws § 156. In some states, acknowledgment of the child by the father is necessary in addition to marriage. See Kimmel v. Williams, 217 Ky. 671, 290 S.W. 483, 1927, and supra note 13, and infra at note 18 et seq.

15 In the following cases inheritance was allowed: In re Paterson's Estate, 34 Cal.App.2d 305, 93 P.2d

case.[16] It is provided almost everywhere that the mother at least may inherit from her illegitimate child, and quite generally her kindred may do so if she is predeceased.[17]

*Legitimation*

The law recognizes certain acts on the part of the parents as a legitimation of a child born out of wedlock. Legitimation by subsequent marriage [18] is usually effective only if the marriage is a valid one.[19] However, statutes in some states declare that children of void marriages are legitimate.[20] Where the child had been legitimated under the statute, the courts usually permit him to inherit from collaterals and remote ancestors.[21] Some

825, 1939; Henson v. Johnson, 117 Okl. 87, 246 P. 868, 1926 (sister); Darrough v. Davis, 135 Okl. 263, 275 P. 309, 1929 (maternal grandmother); In re Olson's Estate, 54 S.D. 184, 223 N.W. 41, 1929 (illegitimate's maternal nephew preferred to illegitimate's illegitimate grandchild). See note, 24 A.L.R. 592–595. The following decisions denied inheritance: Hardesty v. Mitchell, 302 Ill. 369, 134 N.E. 745, 24 A.L.R. 565, 1922 (mother may not inherit from descendants of her bastard child); Jones v. James, 12 La. App. 224, 125 So. 761, 1930; Sharpe v. Carson, 204 N.C. 513, 168 S.E. 829, 1933 (brothers and sisters); Gibson v. Rikard, 143 S.C. 402, 141 S.E. 726, 1928 (children of brother of mother of intestate).

16 Cf. note 8 supra with note 17 infra. Also cf. N.Y. Decedent Estate Law § 83(7) with id. § 83(13).

17 See supra notes 2, 6.

18 See supra note 14.

19 Greenhow v. James' Ex'x, 80 Va. 636, 56 Am.Rep. 603, 1885 (miscegenous marriage); In re Moncrief's Will, 235 N.Y. 390, 139 N.E. 550, 27 A.L.R. 1117, 1923 (marriage under duress); Helm v. Goin, 227 Ky. 773, 14 S.W.2d 183, 1929 (common law marriage); see Adams v. Adams, 154 Mass. 290, 28 N.E. 260, 13 L.R.A. 275, 1891. Contra: Goodman v. Goodman, 150 Va. 42, 142 S.E. 412, 1928 (bigamous marriage—a statute of the type mentioned in note 20, infra, also existed in this jurisdiction.

20 See 1 Vernier, American Family Laws § 48. The cases are collected in a note to Evatt v. Miller, 114 Ark. 84, 169 S.W. 817, L.R.A.1916C, 759, 1914. See, also, annotation, 84 A.L.R. 499. Such statutes have been held to apply to the issue of a miscegenous marriage. In re Atkins' Estate, 151 Okl. 294, 3 P.2d 682, 84 A.L.R. 491, 1931; Jones v. Hyndman, 160 Okl. 61, 15 P.2d 582, 1932. See notes, 45 Harv.L.R. 933, 56 Harv.L.R. 624, 32 Mich.L.R. 792. Such a statute has been held to apply to a child born before the statute was passed. Taliaferro v. Rogers, 248 S.W.2d 835, Tenn. App., 1952.

21 Wolf v. Gall, 32 Cal.App. 286, 163 P. 346, 350, 1917; Jackson's Adm'rs v. Moore, 38 Ky. (8 Dana) 170, 1839; Brewer v. Hamor, 83 Me. 251, 22 A. 161, 1891; James v. James, 253 S.W. 1112, Tex.Civ.App. 1923; note, 23 N.C.L.R. 54. Contra: In re Wallace's Estate, 197 N.C. 334, 148 S.E. 456, 64 A.L.R. 1121, 1929, criticized, 29 Col.L.R. 1153, and 15 St. Louis L.R. 198. See Bernheimer v. First Nat. Bank of Kansas City, 359

courts regard the statutory acknowledgment by the father as a species of legitimation and do not permit the relationship to be thereafter denied.[22] As to rights of inheritance in this situation it seems that a distinction may be taken between two types of statutes. If the statute merely declares that the child shall inherit from the father as if legitimate, there may be no reciprocal right permitting the father to inherit from the child and no right to inherit by, from or through other ancestors or collaterals.[23] On the other hand if the statute declares generally that the acknowledged child is legitimated, the child seems to be brought within the provision of the statute of descent and distribution for all purposes.[24]

While reform legislation with reference to inheritance as affected by illegitimacy has made considerable inroad upon the common-law doctrine, most states have not reached the advanced position which removes the ancient bar altogether.[25] Difficulty in proof of paternity is the main drawback here. At any rate there is every reason why the courts should construe existing statutes broadly in favor of the unfortunate child.[26]

Mo. 1119, 225 S.W.2d 745, 1949 (legitimated child of void marriage takes as "lawful issue of the body" of his father).

22 Binns v. Dazey, 147 Ind. 536, 44 N.E. 644, 1896; In re Forney's Estate, 43 Nev. 227, 184 P. 206, 186 P. 678, 24 A.L.R. 553, 1919; Bowman v. Howard, 182 N.C. 662, 110 S.E. 98, 1921. It would seem from these decisions that an acknowledged child born out of wedlock may be in a more favorable position than a child born to a married mother. And see In re Dexheimer's Estate, 197 Wis. 145, 221 N.W. 737, 1928, holding that not only recognition but actual fatherhood must be shown.

See also supra note 13.

23 Phillips v. Townsend, 223 Ind. 561, 62 N.E.2d 860, 1946, noted, 44 Mich.L.R. 661, denying inheritance from sister of father of illegitimate acknowledged child; Blackwell v. Bowman, 150 Ohio St. 34, 80 N.E. 2d 493, 1948. But see Moore v. Moore, 169 Mo. 432, 69 S.W. 278, 58 L.R.A. 451, 1902.

24 See Pfeifer v. Wright, 41 F.2d 464, 73 A.L.R. 932, C.C.A.Okl., 1930; In re Garcia's Estate, 34 Cal.2d 419, 210 P.2d 841, 1949, noted, 30 Cal.L.R. 322, 2 Stanford L.R. 577 (legitimated child inherits from paternal kindred though his parents never intermarried); In re Ruff's Estate, 159 Fla. 777, 32 So.2d 840, 175 A.L.R. 370, 1947, and cases supra note 21.

25 See supra note 11.

26 Morin v. Holliday, 39 Ind.App. 201, 7 N.E. 861, 1906; Matter of Hoagland's Estate, 125 Misc. 376, 211 N.Y.S. 629, 1925; Goodman v Goodman, 150 Va. 42, 142 S.E. 412, 1928. See also State v. Chavez, 42 N.M. 569, 82 P.2d 900, 1938; Taliaferro v. Rogers, supra note 20.

## ADOPTED CHILDREN—UNITED STATES

**23. Statutes usually make provisions for inheritance in case of adoption though they are often not explicit as to some fact situations. Quite generally inheritance is permitted by the adopted child from the adoptive parents, but in other situations most courts have recognized blood rather than adoptive ties in the inheritance process when the statutes do not provide otherwise. The legislative tendency seems to be to make adoption the equivalent of natural birth for purposes of inheritance.**

The Hebrews, Romans and other ancient civilizations recognized adoption and laid stress upon the religious aspect of providing an heir for a childless man.[1] On the other hand adoption was unknown to the English common law.[2] However, starting with a Massachusetts statute in 1851,[3] legislation in all of our states has recognized the institution and emphasis has been upon the welfare of the adopted child.[4] Formerly adoption could often be accomplished by contract or deed, but judicial proceedings are now usually necessary.

There is probably more activity in the case and statutory law and in the writing upon the subject of inheritance by reason of adoption than in any other aspect of the law of intestacy. Statutory provisions are more apt to be found in separate adoption legislation than in the statutes of descent and distribution. Provisions regarding inheritance are diverse in the various jurisdictions and as to many of the fact situations the legislation is not explicit.[5] In most states it is expressly provided that the child may inherit from the adoptor, though in a few this depends on the terms of the adoption decree. A majority of statutes permit the adoptor to inherit from the adoptee, though in a number of these this is dependent on the source of the property. Others are not explicit on this subject and a few deny inheritance by the adoptor. Most states have no provision regarding inheritance by the adopted child from his natural parents, though some ex-

1 See Hockaday v. Lynn, 200 Mo. 456, 98 S.W. 585, 8 L.R.A.,N.S., 117, 118 Am.St.Rep. 672, 9 Ann.Cas. 775, 1906.

2 See supra § 13, notes 14, 15.

3 Mass.Acts & Resolves, 1851, c. 324.

4 For classification of legislation, see Vernier, American Family Laws, §§ 262, 263; Kuhlman, Intestate Succession by and from the Adopted Child, 28 Wash.U.L.Q. 221; Fairley, Inheritance Rights Consequent to Adoptions, 29 N.C.L.R. 227.

5 Ibid.

pressly permit and a few deny inheritance in this case. Many states have no provision regarding inheritance by the natural parents, and in others this is denied or limited to shares not taken by adoptive parents or other adoptive relatives. The statutes are very often silent as to inheritance between the adoptee and relatives of the adoptor, but some statutes permit this in some or all cases. The most advanced type of legislation, in force in a few states, declares that the adopted child shall be treated for purpose of inheritance as the natural born child of the adoptor and thus allows inheritance by, from and through the adopted parents and cuts off inheritance by, from and through the natural parents.[6]

*In Absence of Specific Inheritance Provision*

Where the legislation is not explicit as to inheritance rights in case of adoption there are two distinct approaches taken by the courts. The first is that of strict construction which follows the principle of inheritance by blood relationship and hence denies inheritance by reason of adoption in doubtful cases. The second is permeated by the desire to foster adoption as a social institution, and strives to give it legal effect in the law of inheritance. Strangely enough the majority views in particular fact situations have sometimes been dictated by the first and sometimes by the second of these two attitudes.[7]

The statutes are construed liberally in favor of the adopted child with respect to his right to share his adopted parent's estate.[8] Although the adoption statute may not mention inheritance particularly, it gives an enlarged definition of child with reference to the parent's estate. Thus, the adoption of a child may decrease the share of the surviving spouse.[9] The adopted

[6] See St. Louis Union Trust Co. v. Hill, 336 Mo. 17, 76 S.W.2d 685, 1934; In re Estate of Enyart, 116 Neb. 450, 218 N.W. 89, 1928.

[7] See articles by Kuhlman and Fairley, supra note 4.

[8] Bilderback v. Clark, 106 Kan. 737, 189 P. 977, 9 A.L.R. 1622, 1920 (in spite of deceased's agreement with child's father that the child should not inherit); Cooley v. Powers, 63 Ind.App. 59, 113 N.E. 382, 1916; In re Pepin's Estate, 53 Mont. 240, 163 P. 104, 1917; Cochrel v. Robinson, 113 Ohio St. 526, 149 N.E. 871, 1925; Hoch v. Hoch, 162 S.W.2d 433, Tex.Civ.App.1942. See infra notes 20, 21.

[9] Markover v. Krauss, 132 Ind. 294, 31 N.E. 1047, 17 L.R.A. 806, 1892; Atchison v. Atchison's Ex'rs, 89 Ky. 488, 12 S.W. 942, 1890; Buckley v. Frasier, 153 Mass. 525, 27 N.E. 768, 1891; Moran v. Stewart, 122 Mo. 295, 26 S.W. 962, 1894. Contra: Stanley v. Chandler, 53 Vt. 619, 1881. Even a second wife takes subject to the intestate rights of the adopted child. Ansley v. Ansley, 154 Ga. 357,

child may often take his intestate share against the adoptive parent's pre-existing will,[10] and an adopted child omitted from the will of the adoptive parent may claim the same interest as a natural child.[11] On the other hand, an adopted child is not usually permitted to take a child's exemption or pay a child's rate in inheritance taxation.[12] Here the state is concerned, and a different construction might lead to adoption for the purpose of reducing the tax in large estates.

When an adopted child dies, his children usually inherit their parent's share in the estate of the latter's adoptive parent.[13] A curious situation arises when a grandparent adopts his grandchild after the death of the latter's parent who was the child of the adopter. Does such person inherit a child's share, a grandchild's share, or both? By the better view it would seem that he should take a child's share—the larger of the two if there is any difference—and not inherit in both relationships.[14] Children

114 S.E. 182, 1922 (in spite of husband's representation that child was not adopted); Lee v. Bermingham, 199 Ill.App. 497, 1916.

10 Hopkins v. Gifford, 309 Ill. 363, 141 N.E. 178, 1923; In re Alter's Will, 92 N.J.Eq. 415, 112 A. 483, 1921; Bourne v. Dorney, 184 App.Div. 476, 171 N.Y.S. 264, affirmed, 227 N.Y. 641, 126 N.E. 901, 1919; Sandon v. Sandon, 123 Wis. 603, 101 N.W. 1089, 1905. The decisions are rather remarkable because they result in holding that a child adopted is equivalent to a "child born to the testator," the latter being the customary statutory language. See also Thornton v. Anderson, 207 Ga. 714, 64 S.E.2d 186, 24 A.L.R.2d 1079, 1951 (revocation "by birth of a child"); infra § 36.

11 James v. Helmich, 186 Ark. 1053, 57 S.W.2d 829, 1933; Bakke v. Bakke, 175 Minn. 193, 220 N.W. 601, 1928; Alexander v. Samuels, 177 Okl. 323, 58 P.2d 878, 105 A.L.R. 1171, 1936; In re Hebb's Estate, 134 Wash. 424, 235 P. 974, 1925 (adopted child of predeceased son omitted from the will).

12 Matter of Miller's Estate, 110 N.Y. 216, 18 N.E. 139, 1888; Commonwealth v. Nancrede, 32 Pa. 389, 1859. Cf. State ex rel. Walton v. Yturria, 109 Tex. 220, 204 S.W. 315, L.R.A. 1918F, 1079, 1918 (adopted children of testator are entitled to exemption under statute making them his heir, but this is not extended to children of the testator's adopted child). Some taxation statutes expressly favor the adopted as well as the natural children, e. g., Kan.Gen.Stat.1949, § 79—1501.

13 Pace v. Klink, 51 Ga. 220, 1874; Wilcox v. Sams, 213 Ky. 696, 281 S.W. 832, 1926; Williams v. Weber, 271 Mo. 150, 195 S.W. 1009, 1917; Kroff v. Amrhein, 5 Ohio App. 37, affirmed 94 Ohio St. 282, 114 N.E. 267, 1916; In re Webb's Estate, 250 Pa. 179, 95 A. 419, 1915; Meriwether v. Fourth & First Bank & Trust Co., 153 Tenn. 696, 285 S.W. 34, 1926. Contra: Harle v. Harle, 109 Tex. 214, 204 S.W. 317, 15 A.L.R. 1261, 1918.

14 Billings v. Head, 184 Ind. 361, 111 N.E. 177, 1916; Head v. Leak, 61 Ind.App. 253, 111 N.E. 952, 1916; Delano v. Bruerton, 148 Mass. 619, 20

who have been adopted several times are usually permitted to take from all the adoptive parents.[15] Unless the statute indicates the contrary, one may inherit from his natural parents, or their kindred as well as from his adoptive parents.[16]

Most courts have not been so liberal to the adopted child with respect to his inheritance from the ancestors or collateral kin of the predeceased adoptive parent. Thus, when intestate left a niece of the blood of one brother and a nephew by adoption of another brother, the latter took no interest in the estate.[17] The theory of this decision is that while one may make a child his own by adoption, he cannot make him the relative of other persons by the same process. No doubt this is the prevailing view,[18] though

N.E. 308, 2 L.R.A. 698, 1889; Mississippi Valley Trust Co. v. Walsh, 360 Mo. 610, 229 S.W.2d 675, 1950. Contra: Wagner v. Varner, 50 Iowa 532, 1879; Bartram v. Holcomb, 109 Kan. 87, 198 P. 192, 1921; In re Benner's Estate, 109 Utah 172, 166 P.2d 257, 1946. Cf. supra § 8, note 1.

15 Hawkins v. Hawkins, 218 Ark. 423, 236 S.W. 733, 1951; Holmes v. Curl, 189 Iowa 246, 178 N.W. 406, 1920, noted, 6 Ia.L.Bull. 60 (inherits from first adoptive parents, though readopted by natural parents); Dreyer v. Schrick, 105 Kan. 495, 185 P. 30, 1919; In re Egley's Estate, 16 Wash.2d 681, 134 P.2d 943, 145 A.L.R. 821, 1943. But see In re Klapp's Estate, 197 Mich. 615, 164 N.W. 381, L.R.A.1918A, 818, 1917, noted, 31 Harv.L.Rev. 488 (on theory that second adoption annuls the first); In re Talley's Estate, 188 Okl. 338, 109 P.2d 495, 132 A.L.R. 773, 1941.

16 In re Sauer's Estate, 216 Wis. 289, 257 N.W. 28, 1934; Roberts v. Roberts, 160 Minn. 140, 199 N.W. 581, 1924; Sledge v. Floyd, 139 Miss. 398, 104 So. 163, 1925; Sorenson v. Churchill, 51 S.D. 113, 212 N.W. 488, 1927; In re Roderick's Estate, 158 Wash. 377, 291 P. 325, 80 A.L.R. 1398, 1930. Contra: In re Hunsicker's Estate, 65 Cal.App. 114, 223 P. 411, 1923 (though adoptive parents are dead). But see In re Pillsbury's Estate, 175 Cal. 454, 166 P. 11, 3 A.L.R. 1396, 1917 (adoption after death of natural parents has no effect on heirship from natural parent); and In re Darling's Estate, 173 Cal. 221, 159 P. 606, 1916 (grandchild may inherit from natural grandfather though adopted by third persons). See suggested statute that he should inherit from his natural parent only in total absence of other next of kin of the latter. McCall and Langston, A New Intestate Succession Statute for North Carolina, 11 No. Car.L.R. 266, 295.

17 In re Bradley's Estate, 185 Wis. 393, 201 N.W. 973, 38 A.L.R. 1, 1925, noted, 38 Harv.L.Rev. 976, 3 Wis. L.Rev. 233; In re Harrington's Estate, 96 Utah 252, 85 P.2d 630, 120 A.L.R. 830, 1938.

18 In re Estate of Pence, 117 Cal. App. 323, 4 P.2d 202, 1931, noted, 20 Cal.L.Rev. 327; Hockaday v. Lynn, 200 Mo. 456, 98 S.W. 585, 8 L.R.A., N.S., 117, 118 Am.St.Rep. 672, 9 Ann.Cas. 775, 1906; Matter of Hall's Estate, 234 App.Div. 151, 254 N.Y.S. 564, 1931, noted, 18 Va.Law.Rev. 677; Mott v. National Bank of Commerce, 190 Va. 1006, 59 S.E.2d 97, 1950; Shoemaker v. Newman, 62 App.D.C.

a few courts have indicated their thorough approval of the institution of adoption by allowing inheritance by an adopted child from the ancestors or collateral relatives of the child's predeceased adoptive parent.[19] Sometimes the adopted child takes a legacy to his adoptive parent under statutes providing that the "child" of a predeceased legatee may be substituted for the latter.[20] Frequently the adopted child takes under provision of a will, settlement or insurance policy in favor of the "child," "heir" or "issue" of the adoptive parent.[21]

In absence of spouse or descendants of an adopted child, his property generally goes to his natural parents or their kindred and the adoptive parent cannot take unless the statute indicates otherwise.[22] Possibly this position may have been taken to re-

120, 65 F.2d 208, 89 A.L.R. 1034, 1933.

19 McCune v. Oldham, 213 Iowa 1221, 240 N.W. 678, 1932; Denton v. Miller, 110 Kan. 292, 203 P. 693, 1922. Sometimes the statute provides specifically for inheritance in these situations. Minnesota—M.S.A. § 259.07 (generally); Mass.Gen. Laws Ann. c. 210, § 7 (as to descendants of adopting parents but to no others).

20 In re Tibbetts' Estate, 48 Cal. App.2d 177, 119 P.2d 368, 1941; Warren v. Prescott, 84 Me. 483, 24 A. 948, 17 L.R.A. 435, 30 Am.St.Rep. 370, 1892. Contra: Phillips v. McConica, 59 Ohio St. 1, 51 N.E. 445, 69 Am.St.Rep. 753, 1898; In re Russell's Estate, 284 Pa. 164, 130 A. 319, 1925, with which compare In re Cryan's Estate, 301 Pa. 386, 152 A. 675, 71 A.L.R. 1417, 1930 (testatrix' adopted child may take estate of testatrix's brother who died intestate after testatrix). See infra § 140.

21 Mesecher v. Leir, 241 Iowa 818, 43 N.W. 2d 149, 1950; Isaacs v. Manning, 312 Ky. 326, 227 S.W.2d 418, 1950, noted in 39 Ky.L.J. 335; In re Upjohn's Will, 304 N.Y. 366, 107 N.E. 2d 492, 1952; see annotation, 98 A.L.R. 190.

The courts are more apt to allow the adopted child to take where the will being construed is that of the adoptive parent. See Madden, Domestic Relations, 364; Munie v. Gruenewald, 289 Ill. 468, 124 N.E. 605, 1919 (children); Young v. Stearns, 234 Mass. 540, 125 N.E. 697, 8 A.L.R. 1010, 1920 (my lawful heirs). It is said that the intention of the testator should govern and the adopted child frequently is held not to come within the language used. Moffet v. Cash, 346 Ill. 287, 178 N.E. 658, 1931; Id., 346 Ill. 311, 179 N.E. 186, 1931, noted, 12 Bost.U.L.R. 347 (adoption after testator's death); Russell v. Musson, 240 Mich. 631, 216 N.W. 428, 1927, noted 26 Mich.L.Rev. 588 (adoption being after will was made and while testator was incompetent); In re Puterbaugh's Estate, 261 Pa. 235, 104 A. 601, 5 A.L.R. 1277, 1918. Adoption by another does not prevent one from taking as issue or descendant of the natural parent. Amoskeag Trust Co. v. Haskell, 96 N.H. 89, 70 A.2d 210, 1950; Taylor Estate, 357 Pa. 120, 53 A.2d 136, 1947.

22 Russell v. Jordan, 58 Colo. 445, 147 P. 693, Ann.Cas.1916C, 760, 1915; Baker v. Clowser, 158 Iowa 156, 138 N.W. 837, 43 L.R.A.,N.S., 1056, 1912; In re Simmons, 121 Me. 97, 115 A. 765, 1922; Dodson v Ward, 31 N.M.

move temptation to adopt a child in the hope of inheriting from him. Some courts have given the estate to the adoptive parents,[23] though this is generally by virtue of express statute. One court divided the property equally between the surviving natural and adoptive parents.[24]

As adoption is only permitted by virtue of legislation, no rights of inheritance exist unless there have been proceedings in strict compliance with the statutory provisions.[25] However, when there is an agreement to adopt and at the same time a promise that the child shall inherit from his proposed foster parents, the latter promise is usually enforceable against the promisor's estate even though the adoption was never validly consummated.[26]

54, 240 P. 991, 42 A.L.R. 521, 1925; see In re Estate of Frazier, 180 Or. 232, 177 P.2d 254, 170 A.L.R. 729, 1947 (escheat rather than go to later wife of adopted father).

23 In re Jobson's Estate, 164 Cal. 312, 128 P. 938, 43 L.R.A.,N.S., 1062, 1912; Alexander v. Lamar, 188 Ga. 273, 3 S.E.2d 656, 123 A.L.R. 1032, 1939. For cases under statutes which declare that property inherited from an adoptive parent goes to the latter's kin, see MacMaster v. Fobes, 226 Mass. 396, 115 N.E. 487, 1917; In re Schultz's Estate, 212 Mich. 682, 180 N.W. 460, 1920. See proposal to this effect in McCall and Langston, A New Intestate Succession Statute for North Carolina, 11 No.Car.L.R. 266, 295. This result was reached without aid of specific statutory provision in Shepherd v. Murphy, 332 Mo. 1176, 61 S.W.2d 746, 1933.

24 In re Yates' Estate, 108 Kan. 721, 196 P. 1077, 1921. In a supplementary opinion of the same case reported in Baird v. Yates, 200 P. 280, 1921, the property was divided one-third each to the adoptive mother and father and the natural mother, the natural father being dead. But see Alexander v. Lamar, supra note 23.

25 Succession of Brand, 162 La. 880, 111 So. 267, 1927; Besche v. Murphy, 190 Md. 539, 59 A.2d 499, 1948; Wiseman v. Guernsey, 107 Neb. 647, 187 N.W. 55, 1922; Hatchell v. Norton, 170 S.C. 272, 170 S.E. 341, 1933; Clarkson v. Bliley, 185 Va. 82, 38 S.E.2d 21, 171 A.L.R. 1308, 1946; Wasmund v. Wasmund, 145 Wash. 394, 260 P. 259, 1927. Cf. McCary v. McCary, 239 S.W. 848, Mo. 1922 (informal adoption of one's illegitimate child is sufficient recognition to permit the child to inherit as a recognized illegitimate child). Under many modern statutes, adoption is effected by decree of a court, after certain procedural steps have been taken. The courts have been inclined to hold that the preliminary matters are "jurisdictional" and if not strictly complied with, subject the decree to collateral attack. Keal v. Rhydderck, 317 Ill. 231, 148 N.E. 53, 1925; Carter v. Capshaw, 249 Ky. 483, 60 S.W.2d 959, 1933; In re Mathews' Will, 198 Wis. 128, 223 N.W. 434, 1929, criticized, 38 Yale L.J. 984. Cf. Greene v. Fitzpatrick, 220 Ky. 590, 295 S.W. 896, 1927 (blood relatives may attack adoption for undue influence or fraud on adoptive parent).

26 Prince v. Prince, 194 Ala. 455, 69 So. 906, 1915; Chamblee v. Wayman, 167 Ga. 821, 146 S.E. 851, 1929 (in spite of fact that the children neglected filial duties to the foster

The individual courts vary a great deal in the willingness to enforce such agreements. Some go so far as to imply from a promise to adopt, that there is also an enforceable promise that the child should inherit, though there was a failure to carry out a legal adoption.[27] It would seem that the courts should not enforce loose or indefinitely implied contracts of heirship in connection with invalid adoptions. One may disinherit his natural child, or his validly adopted child.[28] At least, where the foster parent has left a will,[29] the foster child's claim of a contract that he should inherit should be subject to closest scrutiny. Otherwise in point of fact, a foster child may be in a more advantageous position than a child of the parent's body.

The law in force at the time of the death generally governs the inheritance rights of adopted persons.[30] Where there is a difference in the shares received under the law of the place governing the inheritance and under the law of the place where the adoption occurred, the better view is to follow the former.[31]

mother); Parks v. Burney, 103 Neb. 572, 173 N.W. 478, 1919; Wooley v. Shell Petroleum Corp., 39 N.M. 256, 45 P.2d 927, 1935, noted, 49 Harv.L. Rev. 644; Jones v. Guy, 135 Tex. 398, 143 S.W.2d 906, 142 A.L.R. 77, 1940 (estopped). See infra § 48, notes 6, 58.

27 Crawford v. Wilson, 139 Ga. 654, 78 S.E. 30, 44 L.R.A.,N.S., 773, 1913; Hickox v. Johnston, 113 Kan. 99, 213 P. 1060, 27 A.L.R. 1322, 1923. Other courts have reached the same result by declaring that they are specifically enforcing the agreement to adopt with the incidental right of inheritance. In re Biehn's Estate, 41 Ariz. 403, 18 P.2d 1112, 1933; Winkelmann v. Winkelmann, 345 Ill. 566, 178 N.E. 118, 1931, noted, 16 Minn. L.Rev. 578; Taylor v. Coberly, 327 Mo. 940, 38 S.W.2d 1055, 1931. But see Morris v. Trotter, 202 Iowa 232, 210 N.W. 131, 1926; Sisson v. Irish, 23 Ohio App. 462, 155 N.E. 168, 1926; Hatchell v. Norton, 170 S.C. 272, 170 S.E. 341, 1933; Wall v. McEnnery's Estate, 105 Wash. 445, 178 P. 631, 1919. But see Clarkson v. Biley, supra note 25.

28 Brown v. Blesch, 270 Mich. 576, 259 N.W. 331, 97 A.L.R. 1012, 1935; Odenbreit v. Utheim, 131 Minn. 56, 154 N.W. 741, L.R.A.1916D, 421, 1915; McLean v. McAllum, 131 Miss. 234, 95 So. 309, 1923; Pohle v. Nelson, 108 Neb. 220, 187 N.W. 772, 1922; Forsyth v. Heward, 41 Nev. 305, 170 P. 21, 1918. Cf. In re Schmidt's Estate, 85 Colo. 28, 273 P. 21, 1928 (decree made upon condition not to disinherit). The foregoing cases deal with disinheritance of adopted children; as to natural children, see § 36, infra.

29 See Wasmund v. Wasmund, 90 Wash. 274, 156 P. 3, 1916. Cf. In re Biehn's Estate, supra note 27.

30 In re Hack's Estate, 166 Minn. 35, 207 N.W. 17, 1926; In re Hagar's Estate, 98 Vt. 235, 126 A. 507, 1924; In re Hood's Estate, 206 Wis. 227, 239 N.W. 448, 1931. But see Wilson v. Anderson, 232 N.C. 212, 59 S.E.2d 836, 18 A.L.R.2d 951, 1950.

31 Anderson v. French, 77 N.H. 509, 93 A. 1042, L.R.A.1916A, 660, Ann. Cas.1916B, 89, 1915; Keegan v. Geraghty, 101 Ill. 26, 1881; Goodrich,

## ALIENS—UNITED STATES

**24. The alien's common-law ability to take or transmit personalty by succession and his disability to so take or transmit realty prevail in absence of legislation. The latter disability is often removed either by Federal treaties or state statutes.**

In absence of express provision to the contrary an alien may own personalty and take or transmit the same by succession.[1] The English common-law disability of the alien to hold realty against the state or to pass or take lands by descent applies in absence of statute or treaty.[2] However, most states have passed liberal legislation upon the subject. This frequently allows aliens the same privileges as citizens; sometimes it so favors resident aliens only; elsewhere it gives the alien a limited time to dispose of the realty coming to him by devise or descent.[3] In some states there have been legislative reactions against all or certain kinds of aliens.[4] Recent legislation making inheritance dependent on a reciprocal right to American citizens has been upheld.[5] There are also state statutes forbidding transmission of an inheritance to a foreigner unless there is reasonable assurance that he will be permitted to enjoy the benefits thereof.[6]

However, all state limitations upon transmission of property by or to aliens must fall when the Federal government has recognized broader inheritance provisions by treaties. The treaty-making power is superior to the rights of the various states to fix the property and inheritance rights of aliens by statute or court decision. The courts are bound to respect rights accruing under treaties though the contrary result would be reached un-

Conflict of Laws, 3d ed. § 147. But the law of the domicile governs the validity of the adoption. Barrett v. Delmore, 143 Ohio St. 203, 54 N.E.2d 789, 153 A.L.R. 192, 1944.

1 Fergus v. Tomlinson, 126 Kan. 427, 268 P. 849, 1928. See supra § 10.

2 Ripley v. Von Zedtwitz, 201 Ky. 513, 256 S.W. 1106, 1923; Mork v. Mellett, 62 Mont. 477, 205 P. 664, 1922; Techt v. Hughes, 229 N.Y. 222, 128 N.E. 185, 11 A.L.R. 166, 1920.

3 5 Vernier, American Family Laws §§ 288–293; see Model Probate Code § 30.

4 There has been legislation in Pacific coast states concerning aliens who are ineligible to become citizens of the United States. See 5 Vernier, American Family Laws § 289.

5 Clark v. Allen, 331 U.S. 503, 67 S.Ct. 1431, 91 L.Ed. 1633, 170 A.L.R. 953, 1947. See notes. 21 So.Cal.L.R. 14, 109; 22 id. 194.

6 In re Geffen's Estate, 199 Misc. 756, 104 N.Y.S.2d 490, 1951.

der the state law.[7] There is no escheat because of absolute incapacity of the nearest relative's alienage—the property will go to the heirs next in line.[8] Most jurisdictions follow the common-law distinction between descent and devise; that an alien can take nothing by descent, but in case of devise, he can hold even against the state until "office found." [9] The latter is a judicial proceeding to declare an escheat.

*Alien Enemies*

The right of inheritance by alien enemies became involved in many cases during World War I. In the leading case of Techt v. Hughes,[10] the intestate died in 1917 leaving two daughters one of whom was an alien by virtue of her marriage to an Austrian subject. Both she and her husband continued to live in this country after the war. Upon her suit for partition of her late father's property, the New York Court of Appeals held that she was an "alien enemy" and hence not entitled to the property under the state statute which provided only for inheritance by "alien friends." However, the treaty between United States and Austria contained no such restriction, and it was held that she took under the treaty which was not deemed abrogated by the war. This spirit permeated subsequent cases upon the subject.[11]

[7] Santovincenzo v. Egan, 248 U.S. 30, 52 S.Ct. 81, 76 L.Ed. 151, 1931; Techt v. Hughes, supra note 2; Goos v. Brocks, 117 Neb. 750, 223 N.W. 13, 1929.

[8] Mork v. Mellett, supra note 2; Ripley v. Von Zedtwitz, supra note 2; State v. Toop, 107 Neb. 391, 186 N.W. 371, 1919 (statute).

[9] Ripley v. Von Zedtwitz, supra note 2 (devise); Ripley v. Sutherland, 59 App.D.C. 273, 40 F.2d 785, 1930 (devise); Larkin v. Washington Loan & Trust Co., 58 App.D.C. 391, 31 F.2d 635, 1929 (devise to alien not open to attack by lineal descendants). See Techt v. Hughes, supra, notes 2, 10; (descent); but compare Dutton v. Donahue, 44 Wyo. 52, 8 P.2d 90, 79 A.L.R. 1355, 1932. See annotation, 23 A.L.R. 1244.

[10] 229 N.Y. 222, 128 N.E. 185, 11 A.L.R. 166, 1920, noted, 34 Harv.L.R. 776, 15 Ill.L.R. 459, 19 Mich.L.R. 104, 5 Minn.L.R. 373, 30 Yale L.J. 176.

[11] State v. Reardon, 120 Kan. 614, 245 P. 158, 47 A.L.R. 452, 1926; Goos v. Brocks, 117 Neb. 750, 223 N.W. 13, 1929. As to devises to alien enemies the same liberal attitude is manifested by the courts. In re Kielsmark's Will, 188 Iowa 1378, 177 N.W. 690, 11 A.L.R. 156, 1920; Ripley v. Von Zedtwitz, supra, note 2; In re Rahn's Estate, 316 Mo. 492, 291 S.W. 120, 51 A.L.R. 877, 1926; Ripley v. Sutherland, supra, note 9. Another point adjudged in the Techt Case was that there was no prohibition to the descent because of the Trading with the Enemy Act (50 U.S.C.A.Appendix, § 1 et seq.). The Kielsmark and Rahn Cases are in accord on this point as is In re Shafer's Estate, 50 S.D. 232, 209 N.W. 355, 1926.

Congress [12] created the office of Alien Property Custodian to preserve the interests of enemy aliens who owned or became entitled to property in this country. Under this act the property which an alien enemy took by succession was turned over to the Custodian until peace was declared.[13] The office was again established in 1942.[14]

## CONVICTS—UNITED STATES

**25. A felon's property is not forfeited to the state by his conviction. The heirs of a life convict do not succeed to his property until his natural death, even under statutes declaring life convicts to be civilly dead.**

The common-law consequences of conviction of felony [1] have been greatly altered by constitutional or statutory prohibitions of corruption of blood, forfeiture of estates, and escheat for felony.[2] For this reason the courts can scarcely recognize any common-law principle which has the effect of vesting the state with title to the felon's property.[3] Nevertheless, problems still occur as to what should be done with a convict's property during the period of his confinement. Obviously he cannot enjoy it for the time being, and some statutes provide for the appointment of a trustee for the care and preservation of the property and the satisfaction of the prisoner's legal obligations.[4]

### *Life Convicts*

In absence of statute the property of one sentenced to life imprisonment does not pass at once to his heirs.[5] However, stat-

12 Trading with the Enemy Act, 50 U.S.C.A.Appendix §§ 6, 7.

13 In re Gregg's Estate, 266 Pa. 189, 109 A. 777, certiorari denied Gregg v. Garvan, 252 U.S. 588, 40 S.Ct. 396, 64 L.Ed. 730, 1920. See Matter of Roeck's Estate, 119 Misc. 190, 195 N.Y.S. 505, affirmed 206 App.Div. 753, 200 N.Y.S. 917, 1923; Keppelmann v. Keppelmann, 89 N.J.Eq. 390, 105 A. 140, 1918; In re Muller's Estate, 199 Misc. 745, 104 N.Y.S.2d 133, 1951.

14 See Exec. Order 9193, July 6, 1942; Exec. Order 9788, Oct. 14, 1946; Exec. Order 9989, Aug. 20, 1948.

1 See supra § 11.

2 Bordwell, Statute Law of Wills, 14 Ia.L.R. 182.

3 See Collins v. Metropolitan Life Ins. Co., 232 Ill. 37, 83 N.E. 542, 14 L.R.A.,N.S., 356, 122 Am.St.Rep. 54, 13 Ann.Cas. 129, 1907; Grooms v. Thomas, 93 Okl. 87, 219 P. 700, 1923.

4 See Haynes v. Peterson, 125 Va. 730, 100 S.E. 471, 6 A.L.R. 1456, 1919; Martin v. Long, 92 W.Va. 624, 115 S.E. 791, 1923. Such a statute does not apply when the prisoner has been released on parole. Ward v. Morton, 294 Mo. 408, 242 S.W. 966, 1922.

5 Davis v. Laning, 85 Tex. 39, 19 S.W. 846, 18 L.R.A. 82, 34 Am.St.Rep.

utes sometimes provide that such a convict is deemed civilly dead.[6] In such cases should the property of a life convict be divided among his heirs as if he were actually dead? One court has adopted this construction,[7] though most courts have declined to do so, holding that the "civil death" contemplated refers only to a loss of contractual and civic rights and the capacity to sue or be sued.[8] The possibility of a pardon or commutation of sentence is doubtless a factor in these decisions.

Statutes in some jurisdictions specifically provide that the property of the life convict should be administered and disposed of in all respects as if he were naturally dead. Even under such a statute it has been held that land did not go to the heirs but that the intention was only to pass the personalty to an administrator for the protection of the convict's creditors.[9]

There is a dearth of authority upon the proposition as to whether loss of civil rights results in incapacity of the convict to take by will or inheritance. The better view would seem to allow this,[10] except in cases where the convicted person has unlawfully killed the person from whom the inheritance came.[11]

784, 1892; Frazer v. Fulcher, 17 Ohio, 260, 1848. See generally, American Law of Property § 14.5.

6 See notes, 50 Harv.L.R. 968, 48 Yale L.J. 912 and cases infra notes 7 to 10.

7 Holmes v. King, 216 Ala. 412, 113 So. 274, 1927. But see opinion of Simpson, J., in Graham v. Graham, 251 Ala. 124, 36 So.2d 316, 1948, urging repeal of the civil death statute.

8 Hall v. Crook, 144 Minn. 82, 174 N.W. 519, 1919 (pardon). See Avery v. Everett and other cases note 10 infra. Cf. In re Lindewall, 287 N.Y. 347, 39 N.E.2d 907, 139 A.L.R. 1301, 1942, noted, 42 Col.L.R. 1208, 27 Corn. L.Q. 562, 17 St. John's L.R. 46 (civil death of life convict prevents him from electing statutory share in estate of deceased wife).

9 Smith v. Becker, 62 Kan. 541, 64 P. 70, 53 L.R.A. 141, 1901 (here the court was influenced by the fact that life imprisonment had been commuted to a term of forty years before decision in the case). See also, Sullivan v. Prudential Ins. Co. of America, 131 Me. 228, 160 A. 777, 1932 (convict's life insurance policy); Wamsley v. Snow, 331 Mo. 261, 53 S.W.2d 258, 1932; American Law of Property § 14.5.

10 Avery v. Everett, 110 N.Y. 317, 18 N.E. 148, 1 L.R.A. 264, 6 Am.St. Rep. 368, 1888 (under civil death statute); La Chapelle v. Burpee, 69 Hun 436, 23 N.Y.S. 453, 1893 (convict imprisoned for less than life may take conditional devise); Hine v. Simon, 95 Okl. 86, 218 P. 1072, 1923 (no civil death statute); Grooms v. Thomas, 93 Okl. 87, 219 P. 700, 1923 (under civil death statute); notes, 39 Geo.L.J. 349, 20 St. John's L.R. 49. Contra: In re Estate of Donnelly, 125 Cal. 417, 58 P. 61, 73 Am.St.Rep. 62, 1899 (under civil death statute).

11 See infra § 37.

## ESCHEATS—UNITED STATES

**26. Under the usual rule an intestate's property escheats if there is no spouse or blood relatives. Most jurisdictions provide a long period during which the heirs may claim the property before the escheat becomes final.**

It is generally provided that in absence of heirs capable of taking, intestate property goes to the state or some public fund by escheat.[1] Sometimes this is part of the intestate statute, though there are often separate legislative provisions. Probably escheat would be recognized upon a common-law basis even if there were no statutory mention thereof. It has a broader and partly different connotation than in the early English law.[2] Thus, with us personal as well as real property may escheat; [3] and it is considered that the state takes as ultimate heir rather than as an incident of tenure.[4]

Escheat is not as apt to occur as it did at common law. This is because of our recognition of the eligibility of the half-blood, the adopted child, the lineal ancestor, the issue of a felon, the surviving spouse, and to some extent other relatives by marriage, and illegitimate children. However, in a few jurisdictions modern legislation has cut off intestate succession with the issue of grandparents so that the state takes if the only relatives are more remote.[5] The Model Probate Code [6] so provides, and other states will probably follow suit for it is increasingly felt that the state has a better claim than the "laughing heir." [7]

[1] Woerner on Administration §§ 131–135. Sometimes there is an escheat under the statute though decedent left some heirs. In re Roberts' Estate, 85 Cal.App.2d 609, 194 P.2d 28, 1948 (no spouse to take community property) with which compare In re Tripp's Estate, 239 Iowa 1370, 35 N.W.2d 20, 1948 (unclaimed legacy).

[2] See supra §§ 11, 12.

[3] In re Lindquist's Estate, 25 Cal. 2d 697, 154 P.2d 879, 1944. See infra note 17.

[4] See In re Lindquist's Estate, supra note 3; and infra note 17. But see In re O'Connor's Estate, 126 Neb. 182, 252 N.W. 826, 1934, noted, 48 Harv.L.R. 129, 20 Va.L. 913.

[5] Kan.Gen.Stat., Supp.1943, § 59–509; 20 P.S.(Pa.) § 1.3. See supra § 13. Maryland has long restricted intestate succession to relatives of the fifth degree, counting downward from the common ancestor to the more remote. Md.Code, 1939, arts. 93 & 143. See Dombrovski v. Mayor and City Council of Baltimore, 141 Md. 422, 118 A. 861, 1922. See also D.C.Code, 1940, § 18–717.

[6] § 22(b).

[7] See supra § 5, notes 21 to 23.

A recent case upheld the escheat of unpaid corporate dividends upon published notice when the only connection with the state was that the company was incorporated there; [8] a fortiori, the location of realty or tangible personalty within the state is sufficient basis of jurisdiction to escheat.[9]

Legislative protection for possible heirs is liberal—five to thirty years being frequently given within which they may appear and assert their claims.[10] The state has the burden of establishing the want of lawful heirs.[11] In most jurisdictions escheated estates are administered as ordinary estates, the state taking as ultimate heir, but in some states this authority is vested in a designated official who acts as escheator.[12] The practice of consolidation of escheat proceedings with petitions of the persons claiming to be heirs is a reasonable and timesaving one.[13]

The question as to whether a judicial proceeding is necessary in order to vest property in the state by escheat is an extremely confused one. This is due in part to a lack of understanding of the historical aspects of the subject, in part to the legislative provision in various jurisdictions, and also to the desire to protect the persons claiming an interest in the property in the particular case. The common-law rule seems to have been to require no inquest of office in the case that an alien owner died, as such person had no inheritable blood.[14] Nor was "office found" neces-

[8] Standard Oil Co. v. New Jersey, 341 U.S. 428, 71 S.Ct. 822, 95 L.Ed. 1078, 1951.

[9] Ibid; see also In re Rapoport's Estate, 317 Mich. 291, 26 N.W.2d 777, 1947.

[10] Woerner on Administration § 134. See McKeown v. Morrow, 183 Iowa 454, 167 N.W. 193, 1918 (successful claimant can also recover actual income on escheated property but not interest at legal rate).

[11] United States Fidelity & Guaranty Co. v. Dempster, 150 Md. 235, 133 A. 723, 1926 (state's claim for issuance of a patent denied because of inability to show that intestate, dying in 1807, left no heirs capable of taking); In re O'Connor's Estate, 117 Neb. 636, 222 N.W. 57, 1928. Cf. statutory rebuttable presumption sustained in Anderson Nat. Bank v. Luckett, 321 U.S. 233, 64 S.Ct. 599, 88 L.Ed. 692, 151 A.L.R. 824, 1944 (unclaimed bank deposits). See note, 1 Rutgers U.L.R. 314.

[12] Woerner on Administration § 135.

[13] In re O'Connor's Estate, 117 Neb. 636, 222 N.W. 57, 1928; In re Percival's Estate, 108 S.C. 39, 93 S.E. 243, 1917; Dutton v. Donahue, 44 Wyo. 52, 8 P.2d 90, 79 A.L.R. 1355, 1932. See also, State v. Kearns, 79 Mont. 299, 257 P. 1002, 1927, and In re French's Estate, 64 Utah 66, 228 P. 194, 1924, permitting state to appear or intervene in administration proceedings.

[14] Co.Litt. 2b; Etheridge v. Doe ex dem. Malempre, 18 Ala. 565, 1851; Reid v. State ex rel. Thompson, 74 Ind. 252, 1881 (sale for taxes after

sary in case the heirs were all aliens.[15] However, the older authorities declared that escheat for want of heirs remained inchoate or imperfect until judicial proceedings declared the property in the lord or in the sovereign as lord paramount.[16] Judge Cardozo in a characteristic opinion [17] declared that if judicial proceedings were ever necessary to vest title in the sovereign, they should not be required under modern concepts of land tenures and present day relations between the state and the people. This view has considerable support in the later cases.[18] Some recent cases take the opposite position out of desire to protect the interests of individuals against the state.[19]

death of alien is void). However, inquest of office or its equivalent were necessary to divest an alien of lands during his lifetime. Co.Litt. 2b; supra § 24 note 9.

15 Ettenheimer v. Heffernan, 66 Barb.(N.Y.) 374, 1873; Montgomery v. Dorion, 7 N.H. 475, 1835.

16 Doe v. Redfern, 12 East 96, 104 Eng.Rep. 39, 1810 (based in part on early English Statutes). These statutes have been held to be a part of our common law. Wilbur v. Tobey, 16 Pick.(Mass.) 177, 1834. But see Hardman, The Law of Escheat, 4 Law Q. R. 318, 336, asserting that inquest of office was only necessary to ascertain title to be in the crown and was not required for vesting title therein.

17 In re Melrose Avenue in Borough of the Bronx, 234 N.Y. 48, 136 N.E. 235, 23 A.L.R. 1233, 1922, noted, 7 Minn.L.Rev. 168 (holding that the state was entitled to recover from the city an award in a condemnation proceeding for a right of way across the lands of an heirless intestate without paying city taxes assessed against the lands after intestate's death but before the state asserted its claim).

18 Arizona Land & Stock Co. v. Markus, 37 Ariz. 530, 296 P. 251, 1931; In re Ohlsen's Estate, 158 Or. 197, 75 P.2d 6, 1938; State v. Unknown Heirs of Goldberg, 113 Tenn. 298, 86 S.W. 717, 1904 (state entitled to rent after death and before adjudication of escheat). See annotation, 23 A.L.R. 1237. In In re Clark's Estate, 271 App.Div. 691, 68 N.Y.S.2d 487, 1947, it was held that a sale for distribution could not be ordered in case of an heirless person. Cf. Standard Oil Co. of New Jersey v. Perkins, 29 So.2d 502, La.App.1947 (sale necessary under statute).

19 Puyoulet v. Gehrke, 143 La. 315, 78 So. 571, 1918 (purchaser at tax sale has valid title); State v. Kearns, 79 Mont. 299, 257 P. 1002, 1927; In re French's Estate, 64 Utah 66, 228 P 194, 1924; Dutton v. Donahue, 44 Wyo. 52, 8 P.2d 90, 79 A.L.R. 1355, 1932. Cf. Wallahan v. Ingersoll, 117 Ill. 123, 7 N.E. 519, 1886 (record of proceeding is only way to prove an escheat).

# CHAPTER 3

## LIMITATIONS UPON SUCCESSION

**Sec.**
27. Property Interests Which May Pass by Succession.
28. Property Interests Not Passing by Succession.
29. Dower and Curtesy.
30. Statutory Dower.
31. Antenuptial and Postnuptial Settlements.
32. Fraud on Spouse's Share.
33. The Spouse's Election.
34. Homesteads, Exemptions and Family Allowances.
35. Charitable Devises.
36. Protection of Children.
37. Unworthy Heirs.

*Forecast*

In general, one's property passes by succession upon his death. If he wishes, he can provide by will for the disposition thereof—otherwise the intestate laws govern. However, the claims of decedent's creditors are superior to those of his devisees, legatees, heirs and distributees. The persons designated by the intestate laws may be defeated by the provisions of a will, and neither they nor the testamentary beneficiaries are entitled to property which is necessary to pay decedent's debts. In this aspect the law respects the following interests in order: (1) Creditors; (2) devisees and legatees; (3) heirs at law and distributees.

These are the broad prevailing principles, but the statements must be qualified in order to present an accurate picture of American legal systems. Certain property interests do not pass by devise or by descent. While we are committed in the main to the policy of testamentary freedom, every jurisdiction imposes some limitations for the benefit of the widow. Most legislatures have been so solicitous for the welfare of the family that they have made provisions for the home and limited support which cannot be defeated by the will of the deceased nor even by his ordinary creditors. Finally in certain extreme cases succession is denied because of the unworthiness of the successors. This chapter will describe the types of limitations upon testate and intestate succession and the main problems arising in connection therewith.

## PROPERTY INTERESTS WHICH MAY PASS BY SUCCESSION

**27. Ordinarily one's property, whether equitable or legal, passes to the beneficiaries named in his will, or to the persons designated by the intestate laws if there is no valid testamentary disposition, both interests being subject to the claims of deceased's creditors.**

**Future interests should be descendable and devisable as freely as are interests in possession, but some courts hold to the contrary in case of a possibility of reverter or a power of termination.**

### *Equitable Interests*

Equitable as well as legal interests may be transmitted by will and under intestate laws.[1] It is important to distinguish between the situation in which the decedent has a mere expectancy of succeeding another, from that in which the deceased has a vested interest though he has not yet obtained legal title. Thus, if B is A's heir or distributee but B dies before A, B's heirs and distributees do not take A's property unless they are also A's lawful successors. On the other hand, if A dies and thereafter B dies before distribution of A's estate, B's distributees will succeed to B's interests in A's personalty though they are not the distributees of A and though legal title to B's share was never vested in him. Under the intestate laws there is frequently no difference in result between the two situations for B's distributees often are also A's distributees in the absence of B. However, in case that B is the spouse of A or if B's distributee is B's spouse, and in some other cases of intestacy, the fact of whether A or B died first would be vital.[2] The same would be true in case that either A or B left a will.

[1] Williams v. Cordingly, 46 Nev. 313, 213 P. 105, 1923 (unpatented mining claim); Spofford v. Rose, 145 Tenn. 583, 237 S.W. 68, 1922 (beneficial interest in trust property); Maudru v. Humphreys, 83 W.Va. 307, 98 S.E. 259, 1919. Life insurance payable to the insured's estate may be disposed of by will. Miller v. Miller, 200 Iowa 1070, 205 N.W. 870, 43 A.L.R. 567, 1925. Though contrary to the prevailing view, it has been held that the beneficiary named in the policy can be changed by will even if the policy states that a change may be made only by endorsement thereon. Pedron v. Olds, 193 Ark. 1026, 105 S.W.2d 70, 1937, noted, 2 Ark.L.R. 236.

[2] As to the situation where it is impossible to show survivorship, see infra § 107, note 23; § 140, note 25, § 147, note 40.

*Future Interests*

When a future interest continues after the owner's death it should pass by descent or by will in the same way as interests in possession of the same sort of property.[3] The common-law doctrine was that a reversion or remainder could be transferred by deed or will, but that if the owner thereof died before the future interest became possessory he could not become a new stock of descent. One who claimed a reversion by descent was obliged to show himself to be the heir of the person last seised of the land, and one claiming a remainder was required to show himself to be the heir of the person who last took such interest by purchase.[4] This doctrine is now obsolete as to reversions and remainders, and these future interests pass by descent just as if they were possessory estates.[5] However, in cases of possibilities of revester and powers of termination some courts have retained the common-law doctrine,[6] and it has also been held that these interests are not devisable.[7] There is no reason for the retention of such vestiges of the old rules based upon the ancient doctrine of seisin.

3 Restatement, Property §§ 164, 165; Simes, Future Interests, 1951, §§ 34, 35.

4 Co.Litt. 15a; 4 Kent. Com. 387. See supra § 6.

5 Abrahams v. Abrahams, 219 Ala. 533, 122 So. 625, 1929; Epperson v. Bennett, 161 Kan. 298, 167 P.2d 606, 166 A.L.R. 816, 1946; Copenhaver v. Pendleton, 155 Va. 463, 155 S.E. 802, 77 A.L.R. 324, 1930. See also Perkins v. Inglehart, 183 Md. 520, 39 A.2d 672, 1944 (statute) and supra note 3.

6 Upington v. Corrigan, 151 N.Y. 143, 45 N.E. 359, 37 L.R.A. 794, 1896; Elmore v. Austin, 232 N.C. 13, 59 S.E.2d 205, 1950. Contra: Russell v. Pagan, 167 Ark. 143, 267 S.W. 573, 1921; Reichard v. Chicago, B. & Q. R. Co., 231 Iowa 563, 1 N.W.2d 721, 1942; see Copenhaver v. Pendleton, supra note 5.

7 Puffer v. Clark, 202 Mich. 169, 168 N.W. 471, 1918; Upington v. Corrigan, supra note 6. Contra: Johnston v. City of Los Angeles, 176 Cal. 479, 168 P. 1047, 1917; Jones v. Lewis, 70 Ohio App. 17, 44 N.E.2d 735, 1941; Ball v. Milliken, 31 R.I. 36, 76 A. 789, 37 L.R.A.,N.S., 623, Ann. Cas.1912B, 30, 1910. See also Ledbetter v. Ledbetter, 188 Tenn. 4, 216 S.W.2d 718, 1949.

## PROPERTY INTERESTS NOT PASSING BY SUCCESSION

**28. Some property interests do not pass by succession although complete enjoyment of them is postponed until death of another who held a concurrent or prior interest. This is true in case of interests of the surviving joint tenant, the remainderman after a life estate, the issue in fee tail estates, and those entitled to dower or curtesy.**

### *Joint Tenancy and Life Estates*

The surviving joint tenant takes the enlarged interest by the terms of the original grant creating the joint tenancy, and not by succession from the deceased life tenant.[1] By reason of the latter's death, the property which had been held by both together is held solely by the survivor who need share it with no one. There is nothing to pass to the heirs or devisees of the joint tenant who died first. An ordinary life interest [2] ceases on the death of the life tenant and likewise there is nothing to pass from him by succession. The same is true if one's interest is contingent upon his survival of another. The remainderman after a life estate takes by terms of the grant and not by inheritance from the life tenant.

### *Estates Tail*

At common law a grant to A and the heirs of his body created an estate in fee simple conditional; after the Statute De Donis, 1285, it resulted in an estate tail.[3] Several American jurisdictions give one or the other effect to such a grant, with the result that, while A may convey to B so as to bar A's issue,[4] A may not devise the property,[5] but upon his death it goes to his issue or in absence thereof to the one holding possibility of reverter or the remainderman or reversioner.[6] Thus, nothing can pass from

1 See Oleff v. Hodapp, 129 Ohio St. 432, 195 N.E. 838, 98 A.L.R. 764, 1935; Matthew v. Moncrief, 77 U.S.App.D.C. 221, 135 F.2d 645, 149 A.L.R. 856, 1943.

2 An estate to A for the life of B is devisable by A if B survives A. Folwell v. Folwell, 65 N.J.Eq. 526, 56 A. 117, 1903. If A made no devise of this interest the Statute of Frauds, 29 Car. II c. 3 § 12, provided that it should pass to his personal representative. See Restatement, Property § 151.

3 Simes, Future Interests, 1951, 10–11.

4 Restatement, Property §§ 69, 70, 79, 80. For a classification of statutes, see ibid., Introductory Note to Ch. 5.

5 Ibid. §§ 71, 81.

6 Ibid. §§ 76, 85.

A by succession and this is also true in the states where the grant creates an estate tail in the first taker only,[7] or a life estate in the first taker with a remainder in fee simple absolute.[8] However, statutes in many states either prohibit the estate tail or convert it into a fee simple absolute in the first taker. In these jurisdictions the estate can pass by devise or descent from A.[9]

*Dower and Curtesy*

These are life estates in the real property of a married person in favor of his surviving spouse. It is the law which gives dower and curtesy; they exist in inchoate form even before the death of the owner spouse. While full enjoyment is postponed until the latter's death the interests are not inherited from him.[10]

## DOWER AND CURTESY

**29. At common law the widow was entitled to a life interest in one-third of the lands which her husband owned during coverture. She took this interest under the law and not by succession from him. It was not liable for his debts nor could he deprive her of it by deed or will.**

**Curtesy was a somewhat similar interest of the husband in the wife's land, except that it was dependent upon birth of issue and entitled the husband to a life interest in all of his wife's lands.**

While doctrinally the estates of dower and curtesy do not pass by succession from the deceased spouse,[1] they constitute important limitations on the interests of the heirs and are functionally closely related to the process of succession.

*Dower*

At common law the widow was never the heir of her husband's land,[2] but she was entitled to her dower which was a life estate in a third of the lands of which her husband was seised during coverture.[3] While she did not come into enjoyment thereof until

[7] Ibid. §§ 90, 94.

[8] Ibid. § 100.

[9] Ibid. §§ 102, 104, 105.

[10] Reese v. Stires, 87 N.J.Eq. 32, 103 A. 679, 1917; see infra § 29.

[1] See supra § 28, note 10.

[2] See supra § 6 at note 14.

[3] 2 Bl.Com. 129. By divorce she lost dower. Ibid. 130; and see 23 Chi-Kent L.R. 313.

the husband's death, she had an inchoate interest in the property from the time of the marriage, or of his acquisition of the lands after marriage. Inchoate dower amounted to an encumbrance which prevented the husband from defeating the interest by his alienation [4] or devise [5] of the land to others, since his grantee or devisee took subject to the wife's dower rights. Furthermore, dower was not subject to the husband's debts, either in his lifetime, or after his death.[6] The wife might be barred of dower by jointure,[7] or under the modern American law by joining in her husband's deed to others.[8] Thus, a woman's dower interest was secure in that she could not lose it by his act without her consent.

Dower extended only to real property. While the wife took an interest in intestate personalty under the Statute of Distribution, 1670,[9] there was nothing to prevent the husband from giving away or bequeathing all his personalty to others.[10] Furthermore, his entire personalty was subject to his debts and the widow's share therein was computed only upon the net estate after payment of debts.

*Curtesy*

At common law the husband was entitled to the possession or the rents and profits of all of the lands of which his wife was seised during the marriage as long as the marriage continued and before the birth of issue alive.[11] This was known as the estate by the marital right. The modern married women's property acts, which provide that the wife's property is free of her husband's control, have abolished this interest to all intents and purposes.[12]

In case of a marriage followed by birth of issue the husband was entitled to the estate "by the curtesy of England" which was an estate for his life in all of the lands of his wife.[13] Curtesy did

4 3 Vernier, American Family Laws § 200.

5 Ibid. § 199.

6 Spyer v. Hyatt, 20 Beav. 621, 52 Eng.Rep. 743, 1855.

7 See infra § 31 at note 1 et seq.; 2 Bl.Com. 137; 3 Vernier, American Family Laws § 196.

8 Ibid. § 200.

9 See supra § 7 at note 2.

10 See supra § 3 at notes 38–43. See Perkins v. Little, 1 Me. 148, 1820.

11 Haskins, The Estate by the Marital Right, 79 U. of Pa.L.R. 345.

12 Ibid. 352.

13 2 Bl.Com. 126; Farrer, Tenant by the Curtesy of England, 43 L.Q.R. 87; Haskins, Curtesy at Common Law: Historical Development, 29 B.U.L.R. 228.

not cease with death of the child nor with death of the wife, but it was known as curtesy initiate while she continued to live, and curtesy consummate thereafter during his life. His interest was little if any different after her death than in their joint lifetimes. At common law the wife could not transfer her property inter vivos unless her husband joined in the conveyance [14] and she also lacked the capacity to devise.[15] Hence she was unable to defeat the estates by the marital right or of curtesy by her sole act. In some states the married women's property acts have been held to abolish curtesy initiate as well as the estate by the marital right, so that the husband's entire curtesy interest may be defeated by the wife's deed or devise,[16] while elsewhere it has been held that the husband's curtesy interest is protected in the same manner as inchoate dower.[17]

At common law there was no problem concerning the wife's personalty since it became her husband's upon the marriage and she had nothing to dispose of inter vivos or by will.[18] When the married women's acts gave her the right to own, control and dispose of her property the situation became the same as in case of the husband's personalty; she could give or bequeath all her personalty to others,[19] except insofar as modern statutes have permitted a surviving spouse to take a share against the will of the deceased spouse.[20]

14 3 Vernier, American Family Laws §§ 183, 220.

15 Ibid. §§ 181, 215.

16 Brook v. Barker, 287 Mo. 13, 228 S.W. 805, 14 A.L.R. 347, 1921.

17 Wilmington Trust Co. v. Boden, 38 A.2d 168, Del.Ch.1944 (not subject to wife's debts); Hackensack Trust Co. v. Tracy, 86 N.J.Eq. 301, 99 A. 846, 1917; see Schaffler v. Handwerker, 152 Tenn. 329, 278 S.W. 967, 1926; Gilkison v. Gore, 79 W.Va. 549, 91 S.E. 395, 1917 (curtesy not subject to wife's general debts); Kemph v. Belknap, 15 Ind.App. 77, 43 N.E. 891, 1895 (same).

18 See supra § 7 at note 3.

19 See supra note 10.

20 See infra § 30 at note 14 et seq. and § 32.

## STATUTORY DOWER

**30. While a number of states preserve dower in its essential common-law form, some of these give the surviving wife an alternative by way of a fractional interest in fee in both realty and personalty which she may take against the husband's will but which is subject to his debts and free disposition in his lifetime. The most advanced type of legislation abolishes dower entirely and instead provides a share in the husband's net estate which is secure to the wife against his testamentary disposition.**

**Common-law curtesy is abolished or greatly modified in most jurisdictions. Modern legislation tends to give the same rights to the surviving husband as are provided for the surviving wife.**

In 1833 an English statute [1] restricted dower to lands of which the husband died seised, and the Administration of Estates Act, 1925,[2] abolished dower and curtesy generally. Dower essentially as at common law still exists in a substantial number of American jurisdictions.[3] The same is true of curtesy in a smaller group of states though this estate is usually reduced to dower proportions (life estate in a third instead of all of wife's lands), and has generally assumed the characteristics of the widow's dower.[4]

*Objections to Dower*

So far as they go dower and curtesy are excellent devices for the protection of the surviving spouse. He or she is protected against the conveyance, the will, and the debts of the other spouse.[5] But there are a number of serious objections [6] to the dower device, particularly if it is the sole measure for the protection of the surviving spouse. While dower may have worked fairly well in cases of the more fortunate families in agrarian society, it is not usually adequate in the present condition of urban living in which the average person owns nothing except personalty and perhaps a single residence. Even where the husband owns income-producing realty, a life interest in one-third is often insufficient for his widow's support. Then, too, the existence of

1 3 & 4 Wm. IV c. 105.

2 15 Geo. V c. 23 § 45(1) (b) and (c).

3 3 Vernier, American Family Laws, § 189.

4 Ibid. § 216.

5 See supra §§ 6, 15.

6 Cf. supra § 15 at note 8 et seq.

dower impedes the ready transfer of real property, for the wife may be unwilling, or unable on account of incompetency, to join in the husband's conveyance. Furthermore, after dower has become consummate the heirs of the land may be unable to find a purchaser who will pay a reasonable price due to the uncertainties of the life duration of the doweress. In addition the protection given against debts may be unfair to the husband's creditors.

*Community Property*

Some of these objections point to different and indeed inconsistent solutions than do the others. It is not surprising that legislation designed to remedy the situation has taken a variety of courses. In the community property states [7] dower does not exist and the surviving spouse is entitled to half of the community property, not by way of inheritance from the deceased spouse,[8] but simply because the community has been dissolved by death and the survivor is entitled to half [9] of the property which he or she once owned together with his deceased spouse. Over the other half of the community property and all of his separate property, the spouse who dies first has full power of testamentary disposition.

*Statutory Substitutes for Dower*

North Dakota and South Dakota have gone the extreme in favor of the principle of testamentary freedom. They have not only abolished dower and curtesy, but have set up nothing in the place thereof for the protection of the surviving spouse against inter vivos transfers or wills in favor of others, except liberal rights of homestead and family allowances out of the decedent's estate.[10]

In some states, dower and modified curtesy are still the only measures of protection for the surviving spouse; in other words the protection is limited to a life estate in one-third of the spouse's realty and the owner spouse has free power of disposition over his entire personalty.[11] However, in a majority of states includ-

7 Arizona, California, Idaho, Louisiana, Nevada, New Mexico, Texas and Washington. See supra § 15 at notes 16, 17.

8 As to the situation in California, see supra § 15 at note 16.

9 But in Nevada and New Mexico on death of the wife the entire community property belongs to the surviving husband. See Vernier, American Family Laws § 178; note, 2 Okl.L.R. 228.

10 See infra § 34.

11 3 Vernier, American Family Laws, § 189.

ing some of the states which preserve dower, the surviving wife is entitled to take a share of the personalty against the will, although this is subject to debts and frequently is smaller than the intestate share.[12] A somewhat smaller group makes similar provisions for the surviving husband.[13] A number of the dower states permit the surviving spouse to elect in lieu of dower or curtesy a fractional fee interest in the entire estate subject to debts.[14] This fractional share is sometimes the intestate share but it is often less; the proportion may be dependent on the number of children or the existence of other surviving blood relatives of the decedent spouse.

Finally a number of states have abolished dower and curtesy altogether,[15] and have guaranteed the surviving spouse an interest in both realty and personalty, similar to the alternative to dower provisions just mentioned, subject to debts, and usually to inter vivos disposition by the owner spouse.[16] Perhaps the trend of legislation is in this direction, though certainly there is no stampede.[17] In New York, which falls in this general group, the surviving spouse can elect one-third of the net estate if issue survive, otherwise one-half, but the decedent may satisfy the statutory provision by willing to his spouse $2500 in cash and the remainder of the elective share by way of a life interest.[18] It can readily be seen that the minimum provision for the widow under this statute may be inadequate for her support, even though the testator is of considerable means.[19]

12 Ibid.

13 Ibid. § 216.

14 Ibid. §§ 189, 216.

15 Ibid. Cf. Model Probate Code §§ 31, 32; Eagleton, Introduction to the Intestacy Act and the Dower Rights Act, 20 Iowa L.R. 241, 249, 261; Laube, The Revision of the New York Law of Estates, 14 Corn. L.Q. 461.

16 Provision in some of these states that the owner's spouse must join in his conveyance of real estate is of course a limitation upon power to defeat the spouse by inter vivos act.

17 See Cahn, Restraints on Disinheritance, 85 U. of Pa.L.R. 139; Sullivan, Passing of Dower and Curtesy, 19 Geo.L.J. 306; Sayre, Husband and Wife as Statutory Heirs, 42 Harv.L.R. 330, 359–361, and supra note 15. Cf. Herriott, Should the Estates of Dower and Curtesy be abolished in Wisconsin? [1948] Wis.L.R. 433.

18 New York Decedent Estate Law §§ 18, 83. See infra § 33, notes 4, 12.

19 Thus, if the widow and children survive, a testator leaving a $100,000 estate can satisfy his legal obligation to his family by leaving the spouse $2,500 and a life interest in the remainder of one-third of his net estate, which would amount to about $1,000. per year. The testator can totally disinherit his children by will —see infra § 36. Ironically enough where the couple has no children the

## ANTENUPTIAL AND POSTNUPTIAL SETTLEMENTS

**31. By the terms of an antenuptial, and with little dissent a postnuptial, agreement, the spouse may be barred of dower or other statutory rights, provided that the arrangement was made fairly and after full disclosure of the relevant facts.**

### *Jointure and Antenuptial Settlement*

At common law a woman could not be barred of her dower by reason of contract or settlement prior to marriage, but under the Statute of Uses it was provided that a woman having a jointure (joint estate with her husband) of part of husband's lands should not have dower in the residue.[1] There were several requirements for legal jointure under the Statute, but even if these requirements were not met, equitable jointure sufficient to bar dower was recognized on the basis of contract or estoppel.[2]

Statutes in a large number of states provide for bar of dower or curtesy by jointure, but these are often inadequate in that they do not provide for settlement of non-dower claims.[3] In a few states there is legislation expressly permitting antenuptial settlements to govern property rights on death.[4] However, even in absence of statute of the latter type and though archaic jointure statutes are still on the statute books, the courts generally enforce antenuptial settlements on the basis of the contractual principles which were the foundation of equitable jointure.[5] Indeed such agreements are judicially favored [6] but the courts insist that the consideration be adequate, and that the contract be fair and

widow's minimum share is greater (life income in half the estate) than if there were several dependent children. See generally 1950 Annual Surv.Am.L. 680; Sayre, Husband and Wife as Statutory Heirs, 42 Harv.L.R. 330, 360–361.

1 27 Hen. VIII, c. 10, § 6, 1535. See 2 Bl.Com. 137.

2 Druey v. Druey, 2 Eden 39, 28 Eng.Rep. 810, 1762 (infant wife). See 3 Vernier, American Family Laws § 196; 2 Tiffany, Law of Real Property, 3d ed., § 527.

3 3 Vernier, American Family Laws §§ 196, 220.

4 N.Y. Decedent Estate Law § 18 (9); Model Probate Code, § 39.

5 Barth v. Lines, 118 Ill. 374, 7 N.E. 679, 59 Am.Rep. 374, 1886; Hockenberry v. Donovan, 170 Mich. 370, 136 N.W. 389, 1912; see infra note 6. Cf. Broyles v. Magee, 71 S.W.2d 149, Mo.App.1934; Talley v. Harris, 199 Okl. 47, 182 P.2d 765, 1947. See Evans, Concerted Wills—A Possible Device for Avoiding the Widow's Privilege of Renunciation, 33 Ky.L.J. 79, and note, 33 Ky.L.J. 197.

6 Johnston v. Spicer, 107 N.Y. 185, 13 N.E. 753, 1887; Stilley v. Folger, 14 Ohio 610, 1846. See Ronken,

made after disclosure of the full facts.[7] Furthermore the agreement must be definite.[8] A spouse is not precluded by antenuptial agreement from also taking under will of the deceased spouse.[9] Under typical provisions the agreement must be in writing.[10]

*Postnuptial Settlement*

At common law a wife lacked general power to contract—a fortiori, to enter into a contract with her husband.[11] The Statute of Uses permitted jointure after marriage but allowed the widow to elect between the jointure property and her dower.[12] This provision is included in many of the American statutes relating to dower.[13] However, as the married women's property acts permit the wife to contract,[14] the great majority of states now give effect to a postnuptial agreement whereby the husband or wife surrenders the right of curtesy, dower or other marital portion,[15] provided that the contract is fair and not made under

Antenuptial Contracts: Their Origin and Nature, 24 Yale L.J. 65; annotation, 1 A.L.R.2d 1260. Cf. Seuss v. Schukat, 358 Ill. 27, 192 N.E. 668, 95 A.L.R. 1461, 1934 (agreement inoperative after divorce and remarriage). Cf. In re Phillips' Estate, 293 N.Y. 483, 58 N.E.2d 504, 1944 (fraud not presumed); In re McClellan's Estate, 365 Pa. 401, 75 A.2d 595, 1950, noted, 12 U. of Pitt.L.R. 317.

7 Denison v. Dawes, 121 Me. 402, 117 A. 314, 1922 declaring: "The burden is not upon her to inquire but upon him to inform;" Jones v. McGonigle, 327 Mo. 457, 37 S.W.2d 892, 74 A.L.R. 550, 1931; Juhasz v. Juhasz, 134 Ohio St. 257, 16 N.E.2d 328, 117 A.L.R. 993, 1938; note, 41 Mich.L.R. 1133.

8 In re Friese's Estate, 336 Pa. 241, 9 A.2d 401, 125 A.L.R. 1016, 1939.

9 In re Paulson's Will, 254 Wis. 258, 36 N.W.2d 95, 1949; see also In re Crane's Estate, 6 Cal.2d 218, 57 P.2d 476, 104 A.L.R. 1101, 1936 (postnuptial settlement).

10 In re Peterson's Estate, 55 S.D. 457, 226 N.W. 641, 1929; see also Smith v. Farrington, 139 Me. 241, 29 A.2d 163, 1942; Irving Trust Co. v. Day, 314 U.S. 556, 62 S.Ct. 398, 86 L.Ed. 1734, 137 A.L.R. 1093, 1942.

11 3 Vernier, American Family Laws §§ 152, 156.

12 27 Hen. VIII c. 10 § 9, 1535.

13 3 Vernier, American Family Laws §§ 196, 198. See Land v. Shipp, 98 Va. 284, 36 S.E. 391, 50 L.R.A. 560, 1900.

14 Supra note 11.

15 Rash v. Bogart, 226 Ala. 284, 146 So. 814, 1933; Matassa v. Matassa, 86 Cal.App.2d 206, 196 P.2d 599, 1948; Kohler v. Kohler, 316 Ill. 33, 146 N.E. 476, 1925; Keller v. Keller, 121 Kan. 520, 247 P. 433, 49 A.L.R. 113, 1926; Aitchison v. Chamberlain, 243 Mass. 16, 136 N.E. 818, 1922 (intervention of trustee); In re Prudenzano's Will, 116 Vt. 55, 68 A.2d 704, 1949; In re Cortte's Estate, 230 Wis. 103, 283 N.W. 336, 1939. See also, N.Y. Decedent Estate Law § 18(9), and note, 22 St. John's L.R. 170. Cf. 2 Tiffany, Law of Real Property, 3d ed., § 513. An agreement to release dower and curtesy will not be construed as a waiver of other marital shares. In

duress.[16] It is no objection that the agreement was made as part of a separation agreement.[17] The contrary position has been taken in a few states based largely upon express statutes,[18] although even here the releasing spouse may be bound upon principles of estoppel,[19] or be obliged to return the consideration received.[20]

## FRAUD ON SPOUSE'S SHARE

**32. A transfer of land prior to marriage will be set aside pro tanto upon proof that it was made fraudulently with intent to defeat dower, and there have even been similar holdings in case of transfers of personalty in fraud of the spouse's forced share.**

**In some jurisdictions an inter vivos transfer after marriage is ineffective to deprive the surviving spouse of his forced share if made with intent to deprive him thereof. Other courts have rejected this fraud test and recently some have applied the test as to whether the transfer is real or illusory. The present state of the law in this regard is largely unsatisfactory, and judicial or legislative developments may be expected to be forthcoming.**

### *Transfer before Marriage*

While a wife generally has no rights in land which her husband conveyed to others prior to the marriage,[1] there is an exception

re Colaci's Estate, 288 N.Y. 158, 42 N.E.2d 466, 1942.

16 See Rash v. Bogart, Matassa v. Matassa and In re Prudenzano's Will, all supra note 15; also Campbell v. Prater, 64 Wyo. 293, 191 P. 2d 160, 1948; Gaines v. California Trust Co., 48 Cal.App.2d 709, 121 P. 2d 28, 1942 (community property).

17 Kaiser's Estate, 199 Pa. 269, 49 A. 79, 85 Am.St.Rep. 785, 1901 and authorities supra note 16. See annotations, 35 A.L.R. 1505, 81 A.L.R. 693.

18 In re Kennedy's Estate, 154 Iowa 460, 135 N.W. 53, 1912; Pinkham v. Pinkham, 95 Me. 71, 49 A. 48, 85 Am.St.Rep. 392, 1901; House v. Fowle, 20 Or. 163, 25 P. 376, 1890, s. c. 22 Or. 303, 29 P. 890, 1892; In re Blaydes' Estate, 202 Okl. 558, 216 P.2d 277, 1950.

19 Woods v. Woods, 77 Me. 434, 1 A. 193, 1885. But see In re Kennedy's Estate, supra note 18. Cf. Merchants Nat. Bank v. Hubbard, 222 Ala. 518, 133 So. 723, 74 A.L.R. 646, 1931; Pinkham v. Pinkham, supra note 18 (mutual releases); Ireland v. Ireland, 43 N.J.Eq. 311, 12 A. 184, 1887 (no consideration).

20 Lively v. Paschal, 35 Ga. 218, 89 Am.Dec. 282, 1866.

1 Loeser v. Loeser, 88 Ind.App. 150, 163 N.E. 540, 1928; McLawhorn v. Smith, 211 N.C. 513, 191 S.E. 35, 110 A.L.R 980, 1937 (conveyed in fraud of creditors); Ballard v. Ballard, 230 N.C. 629, 55 S.E.2d 316, 1949. See infra note 5.

in case that the transfer was made fraudulently for the purpose of defeating her dower rights.[2] It has even been held that the spouse is entitled to the statutory marital interest in personalty transferred before marriage in fraud of such rights.[3] These decisions go a long way toward granting dower out of personal property, although the statutes upon which they are based are designed merely to give protection against the exclusion of the spouse by testamentary disposition.[4]

*Transfers after Marriage*

Even a bona fide purchaser of land from the husband takes it subject to his wife's dower.[5] When the surviving spouse's interest is nothing more than an intestate share, it seems that he has no right to set aside inter vivos transfers though made solely to defeat inheritance by him; here disinheritance could be accomplished even by will. Otherwise any heir or distributee could claim similar rights. A closer question is presented when the surviving spouse is entitled by statute to a designated share of the estate against the will of the deceased spouse. Here there are no general limitations on inter vivos transfers,[6] and obviously the survivor cannot be protected to the same degree as in the case of dower. However, the courts have groped for some solution which will permit alienation to others in good faith and

2 Barnett v. Barnett, 209 Ark. 973, 193 S.W.2d 319, 1946; Granger v. Granger, 296 Mich. 357, 296 N.W. 288, 1941. Cf. Knights v. Knights, 300 Ill. 618, 133 N.E. 377, 1921; Smigell v. Brod, 366 Pa. 612, 79 A.2d 411, 1951 (distinguishing between conveyance before and after engagement). But the courts are strict regarding proof of fraud. Bozarth v. Bozarth, 399 Ill. 259, 74 N.E.2d 658, 1948; In re Mann's Estate, 201 Iowa 878, 208 N.W. 310, 1926; Overbeck v. McHale, 354 Pa. 177, 47 A.2d 142, 1946. See Bregy and Wilkinson, Antenuptial Transfers as Frauds on Marital Rights in Pennsylvania, 90 U. of Pa. L.R. 62; notes, 14 U. of Cin.L.R. 451, 40 Mich.L.R. 300.

3 Martin v. Martin, 282 Ky. 411, 138 S.W.2d 509, 1940, noted, 54 Harv. L.R. 336, 30 Ky.L.J. 124. See also Le Strange v. Le Strange, 242 App.Div. 74, 273 N.Y.S. 21, 1934, noted, 35 Col.L.R. 115, 20 Corn.L.Q. 381. Cf. note 8 infra.

4 These cases apparently give a greater advantage than the spouse could assert against the will because that right would be subject to reasonable diminution of property during the marriage.

5 Williams v. Lambe, 3 Bro.Chan. 264, 29 Eng.Rep. 526, 1791; Clifford v. Kampfe, 147 N.Y. 383, 42 N.E. 1, 1895. See supra § 29. A wife was held entitled to dower in land purchased by her husband who caused title to be taken in his sister's name to defeat his creditors, though his heirs could not claim an interest in the land. Pope v. Bain, 6 N.J. 351, 78 A.2d 820, 1951.

6 See supra § 30, notes 14, 16.

at the same time give protection against gratuitous inter vivos transfers employed to accomplish a result which the law forbids to be done by will. Obviously the problem is not solved by determining whether the spouse's interest is a "property right," "expectancy," "contingency" or the like; if anything, such denomination is a mere statement of result reached.[7]

Some courts have held that the spouse will be protected as to his expectant interest if the transfer was made to deprive him of that interest.[8] This doctrine commonly called the fraud test [9] is rejected by other courts upon the ground that motive or intent is an unsatisfactory test of the validity of a transfer of property.[10]

In the leading case of Newman v. Dore [11] the New York Court of Appeals rejected the fraud test and declared that the matter depends upon whether "the conveyance is illusory, intended only as a mask for the effective retention by the settlor of the property which in form he had conveyed." The opinion is not definitive as to what constitutes an "illusory" transfer. In that case three days before his death the husband transferred all his estate to trustees and retained the income for life, the power of revocation, and the right to control the trustees in the administration of the trust. Although the court is careful not to decide the matter, this trust was probably invalid altogether except as an agency which would not survive the settlor's death,[12] and upon that event would become part of his estate in which the widow would be entitled to her statutory share. Apparently the court was of the

[7] But cf. note, 16 Brooklyn L.R. 229 and see Newman v. Dore, infra note 10.

[8] Payne v. Tatem, 236 Ky. 306, 33 S.W.2d 2, 1930; Mushaw v. Mushaw, 183 Md. 511, 39 A.2d 465, 1944; Wanstrath v. Kappel, 356 Mo. 210, 201 S.W.2d 327, 1947; Ibey v. Ibey, 93 N.H. 434, 43 A.2d 157, 1945, s. c., 94 N.H. 425, 55 A.2d 872, 1947. Cf. Nichols v. Nichols, 61 Vt. 426, 18 A. 153, 1880 with Patch v. Squires, 105 Vt. 405, 165 A. 919, 1933. See Smith v. Northern Trust Co., infra note 13; Model Probate Code § 33. Cf. Norris v. Barbour, 188 Va. 723, 51 S.E.2d 334, 1949, where testator unsuccessfully attempted to defeat his wife's share by gratuitous execution of a bond payable after his death. See annotation, 79 A.L.R. 377 as to taking of life interest as fraud on the spouse.

[9] The element of reliance distinguishes the cases of transfers before and after marriage. Technically a transfer after marriage is not fraud.

[10] Kerwin v. Donaghy, 317 Mass. 559, 59 N.E.2d 299, 1945; Newman v. Dore, 275 N.Y. 371, 9 N.E.2d 966, 112 A.L.R. 643, 1937; Potter Title & Trust Co. v. Braum, 294 Pa. 482, 144 A. 401, 64 A.L.R. 463, 1928 and cf. Cancilla v. Bondy, 353 Pa. 249, 44 A.2d 586, 1946.

[11] Supra note 10.

[12] See infra § 42.

opinion that some transfers might be "illusory" as to the surviving spouse without being invalid altogether. This distinction has been borne out by decisions in other states.[13]

However, a recent New York decision [14] went a long way toward denying that a transfer could be subject to the elective rights of the surviving spouse but be otherwise valid. That case involved Totten or tenative bank account trusts, created by establishing a bank account in the name of the depositor in trust for another. The case upheld the effectiveness of these trusts to vest the accounts in the beneficiary on the depositor's death, if not revoked by him or necessary for payment of his debts. In other words these trusts operate as effective transfers inter vivos although they have significant testamentary characteristics. The majority opinion denied that the widow was entitled to her elective share in the trusts and declared that the transaction could not be illusory and hence ineffective as to the spouse's rights, and at the same time valid in other respects. An earlier Court of Appeals decision held that a deposit in the name of the depositor and another, payable to either in their joint life-times or to the survivor on the death of one, was not illusory for the purpose of election by the depositor's surviving spouse,[15] and a like decision was reached in case of a deed reserving a life estate in the grantor spouse.[16] In part the New York cases deal with the general problem, though the local statutes have considerable bearing upon the decisions.[17] Cases in other jurisdictions which

13 Smith v. Northern Trust Co., 322 Ill.App. 168, 54 N.E.2d 75, 1944; Mushaw v. Mushaw, supra note 8; Bolles v. Toledo Trust Co., 144 Ohio St. 195, 58 N.E.2d 381, 157 A.L.R. 1164, 1944; Harris v. Harris, 147 Ohio 437, 72 N.E.2d 378, 1947; but cf. Kerwin v. Donaghy, supra note 10; Rose v. Rose, 300 Mich. 73, 1 N.W.2d 458, 1942. See Goldman, Rights of the Spouse and the Creditor in Inter Vivos Trusts, 17 U. of Cin.L.R. 1; King, A Reappraisal of the Revocable Trust, 19 Ry.Mt.L.R. 1; note, 34 Ky.L.J. 296.

14 In re Halpern's Estate, 303 N.Y. 33, 100 N.E.2d 120, 1951; cf. Krause v. Krause, 285 N.Y. 27, 32 N.E.2d 779, 1941; Mushaw v. Mushaw, supra note 8. For a discussion of Totten trusts, see infra § 41. See notes, 65 Harv.L.R. 512, 50 Mich.L.R. 783, 3 Syracuse L.R. 129. And for broader discussions, see notes, 40 Geo.L.R. 109, 17 Mo.L.R. 348, 27 N.Y.U.L.R. 306.

15 Inda v. Inda, 288 N.Y. 315, 43 N.E.2d 59, 1942.

16 Krause v. Krause, supra note 14.

17 There was basis for the belief that the spouse could claim a share in property transferred by illusory transfer when the decedent spouse left no will, although the statutory basis of this claim is not clear. Burns v. Turnbull, 294 N.Y. 889, 62 N.E.2d 785, 1945, affirming 266 App. Div. 779, 41 N.Y.S.2d 448, 1943, re-

purport to apply the test of illusory transfer show similar difficulty in protecting the surviving spouse.[18] It has been intimated that a satisfactory solution can be reached only through legislation.[19]

There is another facet of the problem which may arise under the illusory test, or indeed quite independent of it. Suppose that the spouse transfers property to a third person by an absolute and formally perfect transfer, but with the private understanding that the donor may obtain or control the property at any time. Here the donor spouse will have actual control as long as his donee is willing to comply with his wishes, though possibly neither the donor nor his personal representative can assert any legal right in the property. While cases are few,[20] it is compatible with the rule laid down in Newman v. Dore that this transfer is illusory as being only "a mask for the effective retention" of the property, notwithstanding that the contention will be decided by the same sort of intangible evidence on account of which the court rejects the fraud test.[21]

There are several conceivable solutions for this mooted problem. On the one hand any transfer by a married person might be subject to his spouse's forced share interest, except transfers that are made for fair consideration. This position might interfere with the practice of public and private charity. It would be unthinkable to extend the full dower principle to personal property. At the other extreme it would be possible to take the position that any inter vivos transfer should be effective so as to deprive the spouse and that restrictions should be solely upon

versing 37 N.Y.S.2d 380, 1942. See Schneider and Landesman, "Life, Liberty—and Dower" Disherison of the Spouse in New York, 19 N.Y.U. L.Q.R. 343, 355, 361, 366; note, 52 Yale L.J. 656. But the Halpern case, supra note 14 ends this possibility under present New York statutes.

18 See note, 44 Mich.L.R. 151 and cases supra note 13.

19 See In re Halpern's Estate, supra note 14; 1949–1950 Annual Surv.N.Y.Law in 25 N.Y.U.L.R. 1179 et seq.; infra last paragraph of the present section. For an example of legislation, see In re McKean's Trust Estate, 366 Pa. 192, 77 A.2d 447, 1951.

20 Kratli v. Booth, 99 Ind.App. 178, 191 N.E. 180, 1934; Cochran v. Cochran, 273 Ky. 1, 115 S.W.2d 376, 1938; Leonard v. Leonard, 181 Mass. 458, 63 N.E. 1068, 92 Am.St.Rep. 426, 1902; In re Halpern's Estate, supra note 14. Cf. Wilson v. Findley, 223 Iowa 1281, 275 N.W. 47, 1937. Some decisions have stressed the point that the transfer was made in contemplation of death. See Wanstrath v. Kappel, supra note 8; Cancilla v. Bondy, supra note 10. Generally, see Cahn, Restraints on Disinheritance, 85 U. of Pa.L.R. 139, 151.

21 See supra note 10.

testamentary disposition. In the majority of cases self interest of the owner spouse will probably be sufficient protection for the surviving spouse, but death-bed dispositions, revocable transfers, and various types of connivance occur often enough to present a real problem. The "fraud" and the "illusory" tests are attempts to strike a golden mean. The former has been thought objectionable because it is dependent on a state of mind, and because it may interfere with free alienation since prospective purchasers may fear that after the vendor's death a jury will find the transaction fraudulent as to his spouse. The illusory test is itself illusory. It has been suggested that the provisions of the Federal Estate Tax Law, wherein certain interests held by the decedent in his lifetime but which do not pass from him by succession are deemed part of his gross estate for tax purposes, provide an analogy for the solution of the present problem. Thus, it could be provided by statute that the surviving spouse should be entitled to his share in all property in which the deceased spouse once held an absolute interest but had transferred so as to retain a power of revocation, a joint interest, or even an ordinary life estate.[22] More complete protection would result if to these categories were added all transfers made to defeat the spouse,[23] though some persons would object to this upon the grounds stated above. The solution of this important problem deserves, and ultimately must receive, more attention than has been given to it in the past.

22 Cahn, supra note 20 at 152–153; Niles, book review, 45 Mich.L.R. 321, 331; Mechem, Why Not a Modern Wills Act? 33 Iowa L.R. 501; note, 27 N.Y.U.L.R. 306, 312.

23 Cahn, supra note 20 at 153; 1950 Annual Surv.Am.L. 755. See also supra note 8.

## THE SPOUSE'S ELECTION

**33. The surviving spouse must elect between testamentary provisions for him and dower or statutory forced share when it was intended that he should not have both. At common law it was presumed that devises and bequests to the spouse were in addition to dower, but statutes in many jurisdictions reverse this presumption.**

**Ordinarily the election must be exercised by the spouse personally in the manner and within the time prescribed by statute. Moreover, he may be precluded, by agreement or conduct, from dissenting from the will. An election once made is normally final though retraction is permitted if it was made as the result of fraud or misapprehension.**

**Some courts hold that in order to satisfy the spouse's elective share the shares of beneficiaries under the will are taken in the order of abatement for payment of debts, viz., residuary, then general, and finally specific gifts; other courts abate all legacies proportionately, regardless of their class. All this may be modified by the doctrine of acceleration of remainders when the spouse renounces a prior life interest, or by doctrine of sequestration under which the renounced interest is used to compensate disappointed legatees or devisees.**

The surviving spouse may be confronted with several sorts of choices between alternatives with respect to the property left by the deceased spouse. Different principles may be applicable in case of the various types of election. Even when the problem is the same the nomenclature employed differs between the several states.[1] A surviving spouse, like any other devisee, may be obliged to elect between the provisions of the will in his favor and other testamentary provisions which purport to give the survivor's own property to others.[2] A will may expressly put the spouse to an election, or an election may be otherwise necessary, between taking a devise under the will or common-law dower against it.[3] Sometimes the survivor is obliged to elect between a statutory forced share and the provisions of the will and in some

1 While most statutes relative to dower or other forced shares provide that the spouse may "elect," others say "dissent from," "renounce," "waive," "relinquish," "refuse," or "accept" the provisions made for him. 3 Vernier, American Family Law § 205.

2 See infra § 138.

3 See infra note 6 et seq.

jurisdictions there is also the third possibility of claiming common-law dower.[4] Even if there is no will, an election may be required in some states between common-law and statutory dower.[5]

*Necessity for Election*

While the husband cannot deprive his wife of dower by will[6] he can require her to elect between dower and some testamentary provision in her favor. Of course express language can require an election, and the terms of the will may otherwise indicate an intent to bar dower.[7] An election may also be required if the provisions for the widow are inconsistent with her claim of dower.[8] But at common law unless it is clear that the gift is in lieu of dower, the widow is entitled to both.[9] In most jurisdictions this presumption is reversed by statutes providing that the spouse is not entitled to dower or other forced share and also the testamentary provision for him, unless the contrary intention is expressed, or clearly appears, in the will.[10] These statutes usually provide that the spouse takes under the will unless he elects to take under the law, but it is often provided that the spouse takes his share under the law without an election if there is no testamentary provision for him.[11] In some jurisdictions

4 See supra § 30; 3 Vernier, American Family Laws § 205. As to whether the spouse's elective share is before or after taxes, cf. Miller v. Hammond, 156 Ohio St. 475, 104 N.E.2d 9, 1952 with In re Ryan's Estate, 280 App. Div. 410, 114 N.Y.S.2d 1, 1952 and see Jessee, Spouses' Rights and Marital Deduction, 91 Trusts & Estates 768; note 27 N.Y.U.L.R. 875.

5 Vernier, supra note 4; see Phelps, The Widow's Right of Election in the Estate of Her Husband, 37 Mich.L. R. 236, 244. For a discussion of the right of election under the community property system, see note, 19 So.Cal. L.R. 39.

6 See supra § 29.

7 Atkinson v. Sutton, 23 W.Va. 197, 1883; annotations, 22 A.L.R. 437, 68 id. 507, 171 id. 649.

8 Chalmers v. Storil, 2 Ves. & B. 222, 35 Eng.Rep. 303, 1813, (devise of all estate to wife and children); references supra note 7; note, 23 Harv. L.R. 138.

9 Brown v. Parry, Dick. 685, 21 Eng. Rep. 438, 1787. This rule is still followed in absence of statutes mentioned infra note 10. In re Gorden's Estate, 172 N.Y. 25, 64 N.E. 753, 92 Am.St.Rep. 689, 1902; Bomar v. Wilkins, 154 S.C. 64, 151 S.E. 110, 68 A. L.R. 501, 1930.

10 3 Vernier, American Family Laws § 199. See United States Nat. Bank v. Daniels, 180 Or. 356, 177 P. 2d 246, 171 A.L.R. 644, 1947; Willey v. Lewis, 113 Wis. 618, 88 N.W. 1021, 1902; cf. Wilson v. Fisher, 298 Ky. 790, 184 S.W.2d 104, 1944, noted, 43 Mich.L.R. 997 (can take both despite statute).

11 3 Vernier, American Family Laws § 205. Cf. Seaton v. Seaton, 184 Va. 180, 34 S.E.2d 236, 1945 (void devise of homestead to widow).

there is no right to elect against the will if it leaves to the spouse a prescribed share of the property.[12]

*Who May Elect*

In general the right to elect is personal to the surviving spouse. However, if he is a minor or is mentally incompetent, an election may be made by the court having jurisdiction over his estate in accordance with the best interests of the survivor.[13] The election cannot be made by his guardian,[14] unless legislation so provides.[15] If the surviving spouse dies without making an election the right to elect is gone and cannot be exercised by his personal representative.[16] It has been held, however, that where a treaty gives a foreign consul full authority to act upon behalf of his nationals in estate matters, he may exercise the right of election though he was not in fact authorized to do so by the surviving spouse.[17]

*Time and Manner*

Statutes commonly provide the period within which the election must be made, sometimes running from death, sometimes from probate or grant of letters, sometimes from the time within

[12] N. Y. Decedent Estate Law § 18, discussed supra § 30 at note 18. But a testator cannot prevent an election by providing that if his wife's right to elect should prevail, he gives to a trustee the minimum amount to pay her the income for life. In re Filor's Will, 267 App.Div. 269, 45 N.Y.S.2d 376, 1943. Likewise a trust for her until she remarries is insufficient to prevent an election. In re Byrnes' Estate, 260 N.Y. 465, 184 N.E. 56, 87 A.L.R. 223, 1933. When she elects she takes a fee interest in a third or half of the estate, dependent on the existence of children. Cases supra this note.

[13] Mead v. Phillips, 78 U.S.App.D. C. 365, 135 F.2d 819, 147 A.L.R. 322, 1943; In re Kees' Estate, 239 Iowa 287, 31 N.W.2d 380, 1948 (statute); Ambrose v. Rugg, 123 Ohio St. 433, 175 N.E. 691, 74 A.L.R. 449, 1931. See Model Probate Code § 37. As to the consideration of the spouse's best interest, see In re Harris' Estate, 351 Pa. 368, 41 A.2d 715, 1945, and Hogan v. Roche, 95 N.H. 368, 63 A.2d 794, 1949.

[14] Mead v. Phillips, supra note 13.

[15] Gowing v. Laing, 96 N.H. 364, 77 A.2d 32, 1950; Mead v. Phillips, supra note 13. Several states have statutes permitting the guardian to elect. 3 Vernier, American Family Laws § 207. See Hogan v. Roche, supra note 13.

[16] Eckert v. Givan, 298 Ky. 621, 183 S.W.2d 809, 1944; Vanderlinde v. Bankers Trust Co., 270 Mich. 599, 259 N.W. 337, 1935; Gowing v. Laing, supra note 15. Cf. Raleigh v. Raleigh, 153 Ohio St. 160, 91 N.E.2d 241, 1950. A few states by statute permit an election by the personal representative of the surviving spouse. 3 Vernier, American Family Laws § 207.

[17] In re Zalewski's Estate, 292 N. Y. 332, 55 N.E.2d 184, 157 A.L.R. 87, 1944. See supra § 24.

which claims must be presented.[18] The latter is the best type, for until the condition of the estate is known the spouse may be unable to determine the desirability of electing for or against the will.[19] When the statutes do not provide for an extension of the time, it is usually held that the court may not grant an extension,[20] even if the surviving spouse is incompetent.[21]

Usually there must be strict compliance with the statutory provisions as to the form and manner of exercising the right to claim against the will.[22] In addition, the survivor may be precluded from so electing because of an antenuptial or postnuptial settlement.[23] The same is true of acts in pais by which the spouse recognizes the will as binding,[24] although the courts are not inclined to construe doubtful or ambiguous acts as an election to take under the will.[25]

*Retraction of Election*

It is frequently stated that in order to be binding upon the spouse, the choice must be with full knowledge of the essential facts and of his legal rights. Where he has acted upon some

18 3 Vernier, American Family Laws § 205.

19 Model Probate Code § 35, also allowing an extension if the estate is involved in litigation.

20 Moise v. Moise's Ex'r, 302 Ky. 843, 196 S.W.2d 607, 1946; Barrett v. Clark, 189 Md. 116, 54 A.2d 128, 173 A.L.R. 988, 1947; In re Paskievitz' Estate, 184 Misc. 320, 55 N.Y.S.2d 595, 1944. But see Raleigh v. Raleigh, supra note 16.

21 First Nat. Bank of Kansas City v. Schaake, 240 Mo.App. 217, 203 S.W.2d 611, 1947, noted, 13 Mo.L.R. 120. But see Ambrose v. Rugg, supra note 13.

22 In re Slawson's Estate, 41 So.2d 324, Fla.1949. In re Zweig's Will, 145 Misc. 839, 261 N.Y.S. 400, 1932, noted, 42 Yale L.J. 1138. But this is not true where the statute provides that the will cannot affect the spouse's statutory share unless she consents thereto. Hahn v. Dunn, 211 Iowa 678, 234 N.W. 247, 82 A.L.R. 1503, 1931. For statutory provisions, see 3 Vernier, American Family Laws § 205; Model Probate Code § 36.

23 In re Sturmer's Estate, 303 N.Y. 98, 100 N.E.2d 155, 1951; cf. In re Blaydes' Estate, 202 Okl. 558, 216 P.2d 277, 1950. See supra § 31.

24 In re Anderson's Estate, 159 Kan. 512, 156 P.2d 860, 1945; In re Schaech's Will, 252 Wis. 299, 33 N.W.2d 319, 1948. See annotations, 82 A.L.R. 1509, 166 id. 316.

25 Hahn v. Dunn, supra note 22 (expressing satisfaction with will), with which compare Craig v. Walthall, 55 Va. (14 Gratt.) 518, 1858; Schaffenacker v. Beil, 320 Ill. 31, 150 N.E. 333, 1925 (acceptance of rent), with which compare Wilson v. Wilson, 145 Ind. 659, 44 N.E. 665, 1896; Pace v. Pace, 271 Ill. 114, 110 N.E. 878, 1915 (acting as executrix), with which compare McEachin v. People's Nat. Bank, 191 Ark. 544, 87 S.W.2d 12, 1935. See infra § 138.

real misapprehension, ne may change the decision upon discovery of the true facts if the rights of third parties have not intervened.[26] Particularly where the choice was brought about through fraud or undue influence, it may be withdrawn or set aside.[27] On the other hand, once having made an election with a full understanding of the law and the facts and without pressure by others, the spouse is bound even though the choice proves to be disadvantageous.[28]

### *Effect on Spouse's Share*

A spouse who elects to take under the will and gives up dower should be entitled to priority over other legacies if the existence of debts prevents the payment of all legacies in full.[29] Curious results have been reached in case of election where part of the decedent's property does not pass under the will. There is little express legislation as to the spouse's share in the intestate property in this event [30] though statutes under which a testamentary provision is deemed in lieu of dower have been thought to have a bearing upon the matter and of course the provisions of particular wills may be of vital consideration.[31] Some cases take the position that the spouse who elects to take under the will is not

26 Gaines v. California Trust Co., 48 Cal.App.2d 709, 121 P.2d 28, 1942; Nick v. Nick, 195 Iowa 351, 189 N.W. 829, 1922 (aged widow making election soon after husband's death); Dick v. Taylor, 124 Kan. 646, 261 P. 579, 1927 (misapprehension due to court's failure to make explanation required by statute); Ohio Merchants' Trust Co. v. Conrad, 42 Ohio App. 150, 181 N.E. 274, 1931 (failure of administrator to fully advise widow); Woodburn's Estate, 138 Pa. 606, 21 A. 16, 21 Am.St.Rep. 932, 1891. See Williams v. Sechler, 127 Kan. 314, 273 P. 447, 1929 (consent to will in husband's lifetime); Merchants' Nat. Bank v. Hubbard, 222 Ala. 518, 133 So. 723, 74 A.L.R. 646, 1931 (same). See Town of Raymond v. Goodrich, 80 N.H. 215, 116 A. 38, 1921.

27 See Nick v. Nick, supra note 26.

28 In re Bergren's Estate, 154 Neb. 289, 47 N.W.2d 582, 1951; Rau v. Krepps, 101 W.Va. 344, 133 S.E. 508, 1931. See also In re Daub's Estate, 305 Pa. 446, 157 A. 908, 81 A.L.R. 735, 1931. Cf. Model Probate Code, § 38.

29 See infra § 136. As to whether election to take under the will prevents claiming family allowance, see infra § 34 at note 29 et seq. Usually an election at the domicile is binding as the property in all states. Griley v. Griley, 43 So.2d 350, Fla.1949.

30 See 3 Vernier, American Family Laws § 207. Cf. Model Probate Code § 40.

31 For full discussions see Phelps, supra note 5 and Sayre, Husband and Wife as Statutory Heirs, 42 Harv.L. R. 330. See also note [1950] Wis.L. R. 182. As to the importance of the language of the will, see In re Hills' Will, 264 N.Y. 349, 191 N.E. 12, 93 A. L.R. 1380, 1934.

permitted to share in the intestate property,[32] while if he elects to defeat the will he gets his full intestate share of the intestate property.[33] Both of these positions are unjust and the situation should be just reversed. Holding that the spouse who supports the will is deprived of his intestate share is often based upon a too literal interpretation of the election statutes and is directly in the face of the statutes of descent and distribution which cover all cases of intestacy—partial as well as entire. If the spouse elects to take against the will he should take only his dower or forced share of the intestate property because that is the interest which the law gives him if he elects to take against the will.

*Effect on Shares of Others*

Renunciation of the spouse's will does not render the estate intestate.[34] Upon election against the will, the spouse is entitled to the dower or other forced share; but though the shares of other beneficiaries undergo some change and diminution, the provisions of the will are given effect in so far as it is possible to do so.[35] The courts declare that they try to conform with the probable intention of the testator in the necessary readjustment; but seldom does the will indicate that the testator contemplated his spouse's renunciation, much less what should be done in that event. Usually the question is simply one of seeking an equitable adjustment of the estate.[36] When the testator indicates no

32 Huxley v. Security Trust Co. 27 Del.Ch. 206, 33 A.2d 679, 1943; Bunker v. Bunker, 130 Me. 103, 154 A. 73, 1933; Trafton v. Trafton, 96 N.H. 188, 72 A.2d 457, 1950. Contra: Tilton v. Tilton, 382 Ill. 426, 47 N.E.2d 454, 1943; Mathews v. Krisher, 59 Ohio St. 562, 53 N.E. 52, 1899, but cf. Ohio Gen.Code § 10501-61.

33 Cain v. Barnwell, 125 Miss. 123, 87 So. 481, 1921. See Gamble v. Rooney, 192 Ind. 454, 134 N.E. 199, 1922. Contra: In re Noble's Estate, 194 Iowa 733, 190 N.W. 511, 26 A.L.R. 86, 1922; Harris v. Harris, 139 Md. 187, 114 A. 909, 1921.

34 Bank of Statesboro v. Futch, 164 Ga. 181, 138 S.E. 60, 1927; Davis v. Mather, 309 Ill. 284, 141 N.E. 209, 1923; Gamble v. Rooney, 192 Ind. 454, 134 N.E. 199, 1922; In re Grobe's Estate, 101 Neb. 786, 165 N.W. 252, 1917. But see Fennell v. Fennell, 80 Kan. 730, 106 P. 1038, 18 Ann.Cas. 471, 1909, s. c., 81 Kan. 642, 106 P. 1038, 1040, 1910.

35 Farmers' Loan & Trust Co. v. McCarty, 100 Conn. 367, 124 A. 40, 1924; Mercantile Trust Co. v. Schloss, 165 Md. 18, 166 A. 599, 1933; In re Lonergan's Estate, 303 Pa. 142, 154 A. 387, 1931, noted, 80 U. of Pa. L.R. 454.

36 Binkley v. Switzer, 69 Colo. 176, 192 P. 500, 1920; Farmers' Loan & Trust Co. v. McCarty, supra note 35, where widow electing to take a statutory life interest in one-third instead of a life interest in one-fourth under the will resulted in the life interests

contrary intent, most courts hold that, in accordance with the order in which property abates for payment of debts,[37] the loss due to the election must be borne by the residuary beneficiaries, and only if this is insufficient will general and then specific gifts be taken.[38] Some jurisdictions follow a more equitable rule of abating pro rata all devises and bequests regardless of their nature.[39] The application of one or the other of these rules determines many controversies as to the effect of the spouse's election upon the shares of other beneficiaries.[40]

However, when the testamentary interest which the spouse renounces is a life interest the results above indicated are often modified by application of the doctrines of *acceleration* and *sequestration*. If the spouse elects to take a fee interest in the entire estate instead of the life interest given by the will, the courts commonly accelerate the remaindermen's shares.[41] In

in the trust after depletion by the widow's election being divided into three parts instead of four; Ladd v. Baptist Church of East Randolph, Vt., 124 Me. 386, 130 A. 177, 1925; Levin v. Safe Deposit & Trust Co., 167 Md. 41, 172 A. 605, 1934, noted, 29 Ill.L.R. 541; In re Grobe's Estate, supra note 42; Alexander v. McAdams, 163 Tenn. 11, 40 S.W.2d 407, 1931 (an excellent case of abatement of legacies proportionately by reason of the widow's dissent to will). Cf. Crocker v. Crocker, 230 Mass. 478, 120 N.E. 110, 5 A.L.R. 1617, 1918, where the court said: "It is not for the court to speculate as to what the testator might have done if the exact situation which has arisen had in truth been in his mind when making his will." See, also, to the same effect, note, 43 Yale L.J. 655.

37 See infra § 136.

38 Lewis v. Sedgwick, 223 Ill. 213, 79 N.E. 14, 1906; Crocker v. Crocker, supra note 36; In re Lonergan's Estate, supra note 35. See Model Probate Code § 184.

39 Povey v. Povey, 271 Mich. 627, 261 N.W. 98, 99 A.L.R. 1183, 1935. Statutes play a part in some states. Gowling v. Gowling, 405 Ill. 165, 90 N.E.2d 188, 1950; cf. Lewis v. Sedgwick, supra note 38; In re Byrnes' Estate, 149 Misc. 449, 267 N.Y.S. 627, 1933, noted, 47 Harv.L.R. 889, 43 Yale L.J. 655; Bening v. Eischeid, 240 Iowa 1294, 39 N.W.2d 299, 1949.

40 This would be apt to be true if the will gave the spouse nothing or if there were no life estates involved. Of course the matter turns upon what property spouse takes by the election. See note, 24 Iowa L.R. 714, 716–722, and infra note 47. For statutes regarding assignment of dower, see 3 Vernier, American Family Laws §§ 208, 210, 211.

41 Union Trust Co. v. Rossi, 180 Ark. 552, 22 S.W.2d 370, 1929; Lowrimore v. First Savings & Trust Co. of Tampa, 102 Fla. 740, 140 So. 887, 891, 1931; Sherman v. Flack, 283 Ill. 457, 119 N.E. 293, 5 A.L.R. 456, 1918; Rench v. Rench, 184 Iowa 1372, 169 N.W. 667, 1918; Davis v. Hilliard, 129 Md. 348, 99 A. 420, 1916; Thomsen v. Thomsen, 196 Okl. 539, 166 P.2d 417, 166 A.L.R. 1426, 1946; American National Bank v. Chapin, 130 Va. 1, 107 S.E. 636, 17 A.L.R. 304, 1921; In re McIlhattan's Will, 194 Wis. 113, 216 N.W. 130, 1927. Contra: In re

other words the latter take immediately what remains after the spouse's election instead of a larger share after the spouse's death. It is said that in case of election to take against the will the rest of the estate is distributed as if the electing spouse were dead.[42] However, some courts refuse to accelerate if the interest is contingent,[43] or if acceleration will work inequitably as when the remaindermen have lost comparatively less than other beneficiaries by the election,[44] or if the will indicates that the property is not to be distributed until the spouse's actual death.[45] In such situations the courts may give the renounced life interest to the residuary beneficiaries or even treat it as intestate property.[46]

Sequestration is the process of giving the renounced portion to other beneficiaries disappointed by the spouse's election to compensate for their loss. While most of the cases using this device are ones in which the renounced interest is a life estate there is no reason why the doctrine should be confined to this situation.[47] Neither the judicial basis for the doctrine nor the instances in which it will be applied are as clear as in case of

Arms' Estate, 186 Cal. 554, 199 P. 1053, 1921. And see generally Simes, The Acceleration of Future Interests, 41 Yale L.J. 659; Restatement, Property §§ 231–233.

42 In re Dulles' Estate, 156 Pa. Super. 405, 41 A.2d 52, 1945.

43 Schaffenacker v. Beil, 320 Ill. 31, 150 N.E. 333, 1925; Brandenburg v. Thorndike, 139 Mass. 102, 28 N.E. 575, 1885. For special treatment of contingent remainders, see In re Byrnes supra note 39; United States Trust Co. of New York v. Douglass, 143 Me. 150, 56 A.2d 633, 1948. Allowing acceleration in case of contingent remainders: Decker v. Decker, 251 Ala. 278, 37 So.2d 204, 1948; Thomsen v. Thomsen, supra note 41; Disston's Estate, 257 Pa. 537, 101 A. 804, L.R.A. 1918B, 62, 1917. Cf. Restatement, Property §§ 231–233; Simes, Future Interests, 1951, § 95; and see annotation, 164 A.L.R. 1297.

44 Sellick v. Sellick, 207 Mich. 194, 173 N.W. 609, 5 A.L.R. 1621, 1919.

45 Farmers' Loan & Trust Co. v. McCarty, supra note 35; Foreman Trust & Savings Bank v. Seelenfreund, 329 Ill. 546, 161 N.E. 88, 62 A.L.R. 201, 1928; Windsor v. Barnett, 201 Iowa 1226, 207 N.W. 362, 1926; Rose v. Rose, 126 Miss. 114, 88 So. 513, 1921; Crossan v. Crossan, 303 Mo. 572, 262 S.W. 701, 1924; Stevens v. Stevens, 121 Ohio St. 490, 169 N.E. 570, 1930; In re France's Estate, 352 Pa. 522, 43 A.2d 139, 1945. And see Trustees of Kenyon College v. Cleveland Trust Co., 130 Ohio St. 107, 196 N.E. 784, 99 A.L.R. 224, 1935; Povey v. Povey, 271 Mich. 627, 261 N.W. 98, 99 A.L.R. 1183, 1935.

46 See supra notes 43 to 45. Cf. Bening v. Eischeid, supra note 39.

47 Thus, if the will gave all the personalty to the widow and all the realty to A, and the widow elected to take common-law dower, should not the personalty go to A as compensation for his loss, rather than to testator's distributees?

acceleration.[48] Of course, if the remainder is accelerated there is no reason to sequester the life interest. However, when acceleration is denied or is impossible, the courts have applied the doctrine of sequestration where the spouse's election has produced substantial distortion of the testator's plan and sequestration will ameliorate this result.[49] It is often impossible or impractical to work an exact proportional readjustment through sequestration; indeed, the doctrine is sometimes applied without attempt to reach mathematical accuracy in result. Sequestration has been refused altogether when it would work inequitably,[50] or where the will indicates that it would be contrary to the testator's desires.[51]

## HOMESTEADS, EXEMPTIONS AND FAMILY ALLOWANCES

**34. Most American jurisdictions have statutory provisions that the homestead, and often specified chattels, pass to the family of the deceased head. In addition the family is often given an allowance of money from the estate for support during the period of administration. These provisions are not subject to be defeated by will, nor by the non-lien creditors of the decedent.**

The various laws respecting homestead and personal property exemptions, and widow's or family allowances create limitation upon freedom of a testator as well as limited protection against the claims of decedent's creditors. The entire matter is statutory, and, while every state has provisions for at least one of these protective devices, the statutes vary greatly from state to state.[1]

[48] Compare note, 61 Harv.L.R. 850, 854, with Restatement, Property § 234 and Monograph on Aspects of the Law of Acceleration and Sequestration, Appendix ibid. pp. 44–54.

[49] Adams v. Legroo, 111 Me. 302, 89 A. 63, 1913; Dowell v. Dowell, 177 Md. 370, 9 A.2d 593, 125 A.L.R. 1008, 1939; Sellick v. Sellick, 207 Mich. 194, 173 N.W. 609, 5 A.L.R. 1621, 1919; Kenyon College v. Cleveland Trust Co., supra note 45. See Restatement, Property, §§ 234, 235. For operation of sequestration in favor of contingent beneficiaries, see Campbell v. Campbell, 380 Ill. 22, 42 N.E.2d 547, 1942.

[50] See Povey v. Povey, supra note 45.

[51] Crocker v. Crocker, 230 Mass. 478, 120 N.E. 110, 5 A.L.R. 1617, 1918; Hillman v. McLeod, 239 Wis. 162, 300 N.W. 157, 1941, noted [1942] Wis.L.R. 312.

[1] See 3 Vernier, American Family Laws § 228; Model Probate Code §§ 42–44.

*Homestead*

The exemption principle is of American origin,[2] and may be attributed to the feeling of a pioneer society that the family should be protected against the economic misfortunes and follies of the head of the family. Certain real and personal property is freed from the claims of creditors in order to prevent the family of the unfortunate debtor from being cast out into the world as objects of charity. The Republic of Texas is said to be the first to adopt homestead exemption laws, and the principle was imbedded in the constitution when Texas became a state.[3] Most American jurisdictions have followed the lead of Texas and have legislative, and frequently constitutional, provisions for a general homestead exemption.

One can readily see the importance of continuing the exemption after the death of the head of the family for the benefit of the widow and minor children. Accordingly in most states, legislation has assured the surviving members of the family the enjoyment of the home place against both the testamentary caprices of the deceased husband[4] and the demands of his creditors.[5] Statutes generally limit in size or value or both the tract which may be so claimed. In some jurisdictions the assertion of a homestead in particular land must be filed with a designated public officer in the lifetime of the head of the family, but more often the claim can be made by him as occasion requires, or by his family after his decease.[6] Homesteads are liable for taxes, for debts created in the purchase and erection of the homes, and for mortgages given by both husband and wife, but generally not for other forms of indebtedness. The authorities are not harmonious as to whether the widow may sell the homestead,[7] but it is clear that when the homestead has been granted to the children on the family, the widow's transfer cannot effect the

[2] Vance, Homestead Exemption Laws in Encyclopaedia of the Social Sciences, vol. 8, p. 441; Woerner on Administration § 94.

[3] See Roco v. Green, 50 Tex. 483, 1878, and references supra note 2.

[4] See In re Carother's Estate, 196 Okl. 640, 167 P.2d 899, 1946; cf. In re Fawcett's Estate, 163 Kan. 448, 183 P.2d 403, 1947 (written consent to will devising homestead). See generally Haskins, Homestead Rights of a Surviving Spouse, 37 Ia.L.R. 36.

[5] The decree of a probate court for the sale of homestead in order to pay ordinary creditors is void. Cline v. Niblo, 117 Tex. 474, 8 S.W.2d 633, 66 A.L.R. 916, 1928.

[6] See note, 26 Cal.L.R. 241.

[7] See Kemp v. Turnbull, 198 Okl. 27, 174 P.2d 384, 1946. As to the effect of remarriage of the widow, see note, 6 Mo.L.R. 80.

children's interest.[8] Sometimes she is compelled to elect between homestead, dower rights, and testamentary provisions in her favor. There is much divergence as to whether homestead comes out of dower or intestate shares, or is in addition thereto.

In some states the homestead passes in fee to the beneficiaries thereof, but more frequently the benefits continue for a period of the widow's lifetime or the children's minority or both. In jurisdictions of the latter sort, creditors and devisees may assert their interests upon termination of the exemption period. These and other problems are answered differently in the various states, and the mass of local statutes and decisions preclude further treatment here.[9] In some jurisdictions the legislation is framed so as to permit abuses,[10] and provisions designed for a rural society are often illy adapted to our present conditions. However, in the main, homestead laws have proved wholesome and beneficial—so much so that the principle has spread to Canada, Australia, South America and even continental Europe.[11]

*Family Allowances*

In addition to the homestead provisions, there are various types of statutory allowances of personalty for the benefit of the family of the deceased. Two concepts coalesce in the modern legislation in this field. The first is the quarantine of dower mentioned in Magna Charta which gave the widow the privilege of occupying the principal house of her deceased husband for forty days, presumably while her dower was being assigned.[12] Thus even the

[8] As to rights to the proceeds in case of sale, see annotation, 6 A.L.R. 2d 515.

[9] For an excellent treatment see Woerner, supra note 2, §§ 94–104. See also notes, 20 B.U.L.R. 81, 25 Minn.L.R. 66.

[10] In re Estate of Levy, 141 Cal. 646, 75 P. 301, 99 Am.St.Rep. 92, 1904, where premises consisting of three flats in one building of a value of $17,500 was a proper homestead and creditors and devisees were subordinated to the family as to the entire property.

[11] See Vance, supra note 2, at 443.

[12] Several jurisdictions retain, in addition to homestead rights, a statutory quarantine in favor of the widow until dower is assigned. Rash v. Bogart, 226 Ala. 284, 146 So. 814, 1929; Bowen v. Black, 170 Ark. 237, 279 S.W. 782, 1926; Hall v. Meriden Trust & Safe Deposit Co., 103 Conn. 226, 130 A. 157, 1925 (to family, until house is sold); Mullan v. Bank of Pasco County, 101 Fla. 1097, 133 So. 323, 1926; Jaster v. Spikings, 312 Ill. 170, 143 N.E. 393, 1924; Moore v. Hoffman, 327 Mo. 852, 39 S.W.2d 339, 75 A.L.R. 135, 1931; Gamble v. Fulton, 166 Tenn. 66, 59 S.W.2d 504, 1933 (until sold for debts); Amiss v. Hiteshew, 106 W.Va. 703, 147 S.E. 26, 1929 (excellent historical discussion—holds widower entitled to quarantine). As to alienability, see note, 18 N.C.L.R. 243.

ancients provided the widow and minor children with the necessary temporary shelter and sustenance. Likewise under modern conditions it is imperative that the dependent family of the deceased should receive money or other personalty for their support during the period of administration for they receive their share of the estate only when the estate is closed. Even if a sum sufficient for this purpose will exhaust the entire estate, it can be used more advantageously during the period of the family's economic readjustment than at a later time.

There are various kinds of statutory allowances. Some, as suggested above, create exemptions of particular articles while others give a specific amount in either goods or money. In many jurisdictions it is provided that if the estate does not exceed a certain value, the widow or the children, either or both, are entitled to everything. Frequently the court of probate is given power to fix a lump sum, or a monthly allowance for a designated period or during settlement of the estate. There are various other minor devices found in some states. A single jurisdiction may have two or even more statutory schemes to provide the deceased's family with temporary support.[13]

The other idea behind the statutory family allowances is that of carrying over the personal property exemptions of a householder in his lifetime,[14] for the benefit of his family after his death. Laws which are primarily motivated by this consideration are apt to set aside to the widow or to the family the deceased's clothing, furniture, supplies, tools, implements, animals and the like of a specific number or value.[15] The injustice which may result to creditors is generally slight compared with the benefit received by the family. However, many of such provisions are obsolete with regard to the sort of property designated. The more modern type of statute exempts a specified amount of money or goods of a certain value.

*Persons Entitled to Allowances*

In some states the provision is in favor of the widow, elsewhere it is for the widow and children, sometimes for the widow and her family or simply the family. Some states give the widower the same allowance from the estate of his wife as is granted to the

13 See supra note 1.

14 These exemptions are older than the homestead exemption. See Citizens' Nat. Bank v. Green, 78 N.C. 220, 1878, showing that they existed as early as 1773 in that state.

15 See In re Bosse's Estate, 247 Wis. 44, 18 N.W.2d 335, 158 A.L.R. 311, 1945; In re Pengelly's Estate, 247 Wis. 616, 20 N.W.2d 558, 1945.

widow in the husband's estate.[16] The courts have usually held that the widower is not entitled to an allowance under a statute granting one to the widow "for the support of the family." [17] The widow without children is within the scope of most statutes, even constituting a "family" where the statute does not expressly mention her.[18] A woman bigamously married to the testator is not his widow for the purpose of taking the widow's allowance.[19] Whether the right to the allowance survives the death of the widow seems to depend upon the character of the statutory grant.[20]

When the term "family" is used, the courts have been obliged to decide what individuals may be included therein. Of course, minor children living with the decedent at the time of his death are covered. The following have also been held to be embraced by the term, viz., minor children not living with decedent,[21] adult children living with decedent,[22] stepchildren,[23] and even servants.[24] When the statute uses the expression "children" and contains no reference to "family" the recipients of the allowance are a much more restrictive class. Under such legislation, adult children,[25] stepchildren,[26] and grandchildren,[27] have been held not entitled to the benefits of the allowance.

16 Nidy v. Rice, 226 Mo.App. 610, 44 S.W.2d 196, 1931; In re Jarrett's Estate, 138 Wash. 404, 244 P. 694, 1926; Jackson v. Hubert, 149 Tex. 451, 234 S.W.2d 414, 1950.

17 Hills v. Superior Court of Los Angeles County, 207 Cal. 666, 279 P. 805, 65 A.L.R. 273, 1929, noted 3 So.Cal.L.R. 226; Appeal of Rourke, 91 Conn. 76, 98 A. 718, 1916; Stuart v. Schoonover, 104 Okl. 28, 229 P. 812, 1924.

18 In re Hooper's Estate, 117 Wash. 463, 201 P. 740, 1921. See, also, In re Walley's Estate, 11 Nev. 260, 1876.

19 In re Jones' Estate, 195 Okl. 168, 155 P.2d 980, 1945. The right to allowances may be lost by agreement or improper conduct. In re Brooks' Estate, 28 Cal.2d 748, 171 P.2d 724, 1946. See infra § 37 at notes 18, 19, 30.

20 See In re Samson's Estate, 142 Neb. 556, 7 N.W.2d 60, 144 A.L.R. 264, 1942; In re Croke's Estate, 155 Ohio St. 434, 99 N.E.2d 483, 1951; State ex rel. Case v. Superior Court, 23 Wash.2d 250, 160 P.2d 606, 1945, noted, 20 Wash.L.R. 231. See also note, 20 U. of Cin.L.R. 134.

21 In re Van Duyn's Estate, 129 Wash. 528, 225 P. 446, 1924; Re Foster, 47 Nev. 297, 220 P. 734, 1923.

22 In re Rash's Estate, 256 S.W. 525, Mo.App.1923.

23 Sanderlin v. Sanderlin's Adm'r, 1 Swan (Tenn.) 441, 1852.

24 Strawn v. Strawn, 53 Ill. 263, 1870. Probably most courts would not give the term "family" such a broad meaning. See Whaley v. Whaley, 50 Mo. 577, 1872.

25 Quattlebaum v. Triplett, 69 Ark. 91, 61 S.W. 162, 1901.

26 Howland's Adm'r v. Harr, 123 Ky. 732, 97 S.W. 358, 1906.

27 Herring v. Elliott, 218 Ala. 203, 118 So. 391, 1928; Ross v. Martin,

*Effect of Will—Election*

The testator cannot defeat the allowances by specific bequest of the property necessary for their satisfaction.[28] As the statutory purpose is to allow support to the family during the period of administration, the courts are loathe to require an election between the allowances and the ultimate benefits contemplated under the will. The situation is distinguishable from that involving an election between common-law or statutory dower and testamentary provisions, as both of these are in the nature of permanent advantages to the widow. Unless the will clearly indicates that the devises and bequests are in lieu of allowances, the widow or family are entitled to both.[29] Under this rule it has been held that if a will states that the provisions thereof are "in lieu of all other demands against my estate," the widow may claim allowance for support in addition to the benefits conferred by the will.[30] According to the great weight of authority however, a clear testamentary stipulation may require an election between the will and the statutory allowances.[31] Much can be said in favor

104 Tex. 558, 140 S.W. 432, 141 S. W. 518, 1911. Contra: Succession of Durkin, 30 La.Ann. 669, 1878. See In re Braunstein's Will, 113 N.J.Eq. 473, 167 A. 222, 1933, holding that under statute expressly mentioning grandchildren, a grandchild of decedent is entitled to an allowance although not related to the widow who was the second wife of decedent.

28 In re Whitney's Estate, 171 Cal. 750, 154 P. 855, 1916; In re Miller's Estate, 158 Cal. 420, 111 P. 255, 1910; In re Fleshman's Estate, 51 Idaho 312, 5 P.2d 727, 1931; Lemp v. Lemp, 32 Idaho 397, 184 P. 222, 1919; Baker v. Baker, 57 Wis. 382, 15 N.W. 425, 1883. Cf. Hilt v. Ward, 128 Me. 191, 146 A. 439, 1929 (property specifically bequeathed should not be taken to satisfy allowance if there is other property from which allowance can be made).

29 Crownover v. Crownover, 216 Ala. 286, 113 So. 42, 1927; In re Cowell's Estate, 164 Cal. 636, 130 P. 209, 1917; Chambliss v. Bolton, 146 Ga. 734, 92 S.E. 204, 1917; In re Frick's Estate, 192 Iowa 75, 182 N.W. 790, 1921; Peugh v. McKinney, 211 S.W. 83, Mo.App.1919. But see Shaw's Guardian v. Grimes, 187 Ky. 250, 218 S.W. 447, 1920; In re Rosenthal's Estate, 141 Misc. 404, 252 N.Y.S. 596, 1931.

30 Hill v. Kalamazoo Probate Judge, 128 Mich. 77, 87 N.W. 113, 1909; Andros v. Flournoy, 22 N.M. 582, 166 P. 1173, 4 A.L.R. 387, 1917. But see In re Lufkin's Estate, 131 Cal. 291, 63 P. 469, 1901; Langley v. Mayhew, 107 Ind. 198, 6 N.E. 317, 8 N.E. 157, 1886, in which cases similar language was held to require an election. A post-nuptial settlement releasing all rights in husband's estate does not prevent claim of homestead and year's support as these are not parts of the estate. Hobbs v. Hobbs, 179 Tenn. 1, 162 S.W.2d 394, 1942.

31 See authorities in notes 29, 30, supra, and also those collected in 4 A.L.R. 391, 140 id. 1220. When the will devised everything to the widow and children, she was held obliged to

of the minority position,[32] which prevents the testator from requiring an election by any means. At least it seems that even in case of a clear testamentary provision for an election, the court should be able to make an allowance for temporary support to be deducted from the ultimate testamentary share of the estate going to the recipients of the allowance.

*Property Subject to Allowance*

Of course the allowances can be made only out of property which deceased owned at the time of his death.[33] Usually the widow or family takes subject to the liens which were binding upon the deceased husband.[34] Sometimes the allowance is also subordinate to the last illness, funeral and administration expenses.[35] With these exceptions, the awards for temporary support are superior to creditor's claims.[36] Hence they are important in intestate estates as well as where there is a will. It has been declared that the recipients do not take their exemption

elect between homestead and allowances on the one hand and her share under the will on the other. Miller v. Miller, 149 Tex. 543, 235 S.W.2d 624, 1951, noted in 29 Tex.L.R. 977.

32 Collier v. Collier's Ex'rs, 3 Ohio St. 369, 1854 (cf. Ohio Gen. Code, § 10504-61); In re O'Shea's Estate, 85 Neb. 156, 122 N.W. 881, 1909; Peebles' Estate, 157 Pa. 605, 27 A. 792, 1893 (but see Snider's Estate, 174 Pa. 620, 34 A. 318, 1896). See Industrial Trust Co. v. Dean, 68 R.I. 43, 26 A.2d 482, 140 A.L.R. 1213, 1942 (at least widow cannot waive as far as the children are concerned).

33 Plowden v. Plowden, 47 Ga.App. 751, 171 S.E. 388, 1933; Watson v. Wagner, 202 Mich. 397, 168 N.W. 428, 1918. It has been held that the allowance is payable out of the husband's separate property rather than community property. In re Crane's Estate, 201 Okl. 354, 206 P.2d 726, 9 A.L.R.2d 524, 1949.

34 Ingram v. Dowling, 11 S.W.2d 325, Tex.Civ.App.1928; Woerner on Administration § 85. In a few jurisdictions the statutes have been construed to render the allowance superior to certain liens. Cole v. Elfe, 23 Ga. 235, 1857 (mortgage lien); Commercial Bank of Augusta v. Burckhalter, 98 Ga. 736, 25 S.E. 917, 1896 (judgment lien); Gleason v. Traynham, 111 Ga. 887, 36 S.E. 969, 1900 (mechanic's lien); Kauffman's Appeal, 112 Pa. 645, 4 A. 20, 1886 (judgment and mortgage lien); In re Farmer's Estate, 17 Utah 80, 53 P. 972, 1898 (vendor's lien).

35 Eisenberg v. Reininger, 90 Colo. 511, 10 P.2d 945, 1932; Carlson v. Layman, 214 Iowa 114, 241 N.W. 457, 1932; Pace v. Eoff, 48 S.W.2d 956, Tex.Com.App.1932. Generally, however, the allowance is superior to claims of this sort. Woerner on Administration § 86.

36 Bank of Hampton v. Smith, 177 Ga. 532, 170 S.E. 508, 1933; Taylor v. Whitcomb, 192 Mass. 555, 78 N.E. 536, 1906. Hence a creditor may question the award. In re Pompal's Estate, 150 Wash. 242, 272 P. 980. As to creditors of the widow, see Rimes v. Graham, 199 Ga. 406, 34 S.E.2d 443, 1945.

or allowances by succession or inheritance.[37] When the estate consists of no more than is required for the statutory exemptions and allowances, there is no need for administration—or for further administration in case the fact appears after some proceedings have been taken. Some statutes expressly so declare.[38] On the other hand the probate court has always power to set apart the exemptions and allowances.[39] This judicial power is imperative when the allowance is in money and must be separated from the balance of the estate.

While the statutes sometimes provide otherwise as to certain types of exemptions or allowances, they are usually held to be in addition to the spouse's share under the will or the intestate laws and not by way of advances on such shares.[40]

*Amount of Allowance*

As family allowances are superior to the claims of creditors, insolvency of the estate is no ground for denial of an award.[41] On the other hand, the fact that an estate is solvent and that the widow and family will ultimately receive a substantial sum therefrom is no reason why allowances for temporary support should be denied.[42]

However, the questions of solvency and net worth of the estate are considerations which are important in determining the size of family allowances in those cases where the probate court has discretion to fix the amount.[43] Other factors which influence the

37 In re Myer's Estate, 115 Cal.App. 443, 1 P.2d 1013, 1931; In re Metcalf's Estate, 93 Mont. 542, 19 P.2d 905, 1933; Stauffer's Estate, 89 Pa. Super. 531, 1927. See supra note 30.

38 Woerner on Administration §§ 83, 202; 3 Vernier, American Family Laws § 228; Model Probate Code §§ 88, 92.

39 Gray v. Weatherford, 227 Ala. 324, 149 So. 819, 1933.

40 Davidson v. Miners' & Mechanics' Sav. & Trust Co., 129 Ohio St. 418, 195 N.E. 845, 98 A.L.R. 1318, 1935; cf. Jackson v. Wilson, 117 Ala. 432, 23 So. 521, 1898. See supra, notes 28–32.

41 Tetzloff v. May, 172 Iowa 617, 154 N.W. 905, 1915; Taylor v. Whitcomb, 192 Mass. 555, 78 N.E. 536, 1906; Barnhard v. Barnhard, 109 W.Va. 375, 154 S.E. 874, 1930.

42 In re Mays' Estate, 43 S.W.2d 306, Tex.Civ.App.1931.

43 In re Nelson's Estate, 167 Cal. 321, 139 P. 692, 1914; In re McClellan's Estate, 187 Iowa 866, 174 N.W. 691, 1919; Glover v. Glover, 215 Mass. 576, 102 N.E. 945, 1913; Hooker v. Porter, 273 Mass. 316, 173 N.E. 588, 1930; Strauch v. Uhler, 95 Minn. 304, 104 N.W. 535, 1905; In re Frizzell's Estate, 95 Or. 681, 188 P. 707, 1920; In re Pugsley's Estate, 27 Utah 489, 76 P. 560, 1904; Griesemer v. Boyer and Rex, 13 Wash. 171, 43 P. 17, 1896.

amount of the award are the age, health and earning capacity of members of the family, the amount of their separate estates and their scale of living in decedent's lifetime.[44] In the estate of William Randolph Hearst the widow was allowed $10,000 a month for eighteen months.[45] However, allowances should not ordinarily be set at such a high figure that they will disrupt testamentary plans.[46]

Usually the probate court has power to increase or decrease the allowances, if it had discretion in the first instance in fixing the amount,[47] but these changes cannot be made retroactive.[48] In a few jurisdictions the orders of allowance are not appealable upon the theory that to make them so would interfere with the object of temporary support.[49] Usually the appellate courts may pass upon the question of the amount of the award,[50] though ordinarily the trial court's discretion is not disturbed on appeal.[51]

44 See authorities, supra, note 43. Cf. Succession of Hawk, 9 La.App. 211, 120 So. 93, 1928, where the Code provided for an allowance to widows in necessitous circumstances—held that financial means rather than health and ability to earn money should govern. See also Malone v. Cannon, 215 La. 939, 41 So.2d 837, 1949.

45 N. Y. Times, Feb. 26, 1952, p. 29, col. 5; see also In re Lux's Estate, 114 Cal. 73, 45 P. 1028, 1896 ($2500 per month).

46 Dorsey v. Georgia R. Bank & Trust Co., 82 Ga.App. 237, 60 S.E.2d 828, 1950.

47 In re Crouse's Estate, 208 Iowa 333, 223 N.W. 510, 1929; In re Boselly's Estate, 179 Cal. 218, 176 P. 45, 1918. Cf. In re Fritch's Estate, 179 Mo.App. 434, 164 S.W. 659, 1914; Cummings v. Allen, 34 N.H. 194, 1856 (second order made without notice).

48 In re Houston's Estate, 205 Cal. 276, 270 P. 939, 60 A.L.R. 730, 1928; Ford v. Ford, 80 Wis. 565, 50 N.W. 409, 1892. The change may date from the filing and service of the motion to alter the allowance. In re Boselly's Estate, supra, note 47.

49 In re Koch's Estate, 121 Mich. 667, 80 N.W. 641, 1899; Leach v. Leach's Executor, 51 Vt. 440, 1878. See Model Probate Code § 20(b).

50 See cases supra note 43. See note, 30 Col.L.R. 571.

51 In re Nelson's Estate, 167 Cal. 321, 139 P. 692, 1914; In re Crouse's Estate, 208 Iowa 333, 223 N.W. 510, 1929; Moseley v. Harper, 202 Miss. 442, 32 So.2d 192, 1947; Drewry v. Raleigh Savings Bank & Trust Co., 173 N.C. 664, 92 S.E. 593, 1917; In re Crane's Estate, supra note 33; In re Pugsley's Estate, 27 Utah 489, 76 P. 560, 1904.

## CHARITABLE DEVISES

**35. Some jurisdictions by statute limit charitable and religious devises and bequests. These stipulations take the form of:**

**(1) Stipulations that such testamentary gifts are invalid unless the will is executed a specified time before testator's death,**

**(2) Limitations of the proportion of the entire estate which may be devoted to these purposes.**

**Frequently a state has provisos of both types. Generally these limitations have no effect unless the testator is survived by specified classes of close relatives, who alone may object to the excessive charitable devises.**

In general, anyone is entitled to receive property by will. Except for statutory provisions occasionally found, the beneficiary may be a business corporation,[1] the state or national government,[2] a convict,[3] an alien,[4] the testator's paramour, or his illegitimate child.[5] In the United States there are now no general mortmain statutes voiding all charitable or religious devises,[6] but a dozen jurisdictions have statutes which either: (1) declare charitable gifts invalid unless the will is executed more than a designated time before the testator's death, (2) limit the

1 McMillan v. St. Louis Union Trust Co., 358 Mo. 1215, 219 S.W.2d 364, 8 A.L.R.2d 449, 1949.

2 Mississippi Valley Trust Co. v. Ruhland, 359 Mo. 616, 222 S.W.2d 750, 1949; In re Moore's Estate, 190 Or. 63, 223 P.2d 393, 1950 (United States). But see In re Burnison's Estate, 33 Cal.2d 638, 204 P.2d 330, 1949, affirmed sub nom. United States v. Burnison, 339 U.S. 87, 70 S.Ct. 503, 94 L.Ed. 675, 1950, noted, 59 Yale L.J. 793. A later statute permitted the United States to take as devisee. Cal.Laws 1951, c. 223.

3 See supra § 25 at note 10.

4 See supra § 24.

5 By statute in South Carolina devises to testator's mistress or illegitimate children in excess of one-fourth of his estate are void at the election of his wife or legitimate children. Gore v. Clarke, 37 S.C. 537, 16 S.E. 614, 20 L.R.A. 465, 1892; White v. White, 212 S.C. 440, 48 S.E.2d 189, 1948. Similar but more comprehensive provisions are found in Louisiana—LSA–C.C. arts. 1481, 1483, 1486. See note, 12 Tulane L.R. 447. Cf. Lee v. Hunter, 208 La. 248, 23 So.2d 61, 1945 (devise to children of bastard son valid); Texada v. Spence, 166 La. 1020, 118 So. 120, 62 A.L.R. 281, 1928.

6 Formerly Mississippi forbade all charitable and religious devises of land and also limited bequests of personalty of this nature, but these restrictions were changed in 1940 to the more limited type described infra in this section. See Bell v. Mississippi Orphans Home, 192 Miss. 205, 5 So. 2d 214, 1941; cf. Gardner v. McNeal, 117 Md. 27, 82 A. 988, 40 L.R.A.,N.S., 553, Ann.Cas.1914A, 119, 1912.

proportion of the estate which can be devised for charitable purposes,[7] or both.[8]

*Limitations of Time*

The policy of the statutes which invalidate charitable gifts unless the will is executed before a specified time before the testator's death is to prevent the testator from being unduly influenced while under fear of impending death. This period varies between the states from thirty days to one year.[9] A will made at four p. m. on October eight was held invalid when the testator died at seven p. m. November eight.[10] There had been more than thirty days of elapsed time, but, for the benefit of the heirs the computation was made by excluding the day of making the will though including the day upon which the testator died. For purposes of the statute, the date of the will is the date of the acknowledgment before witnesses, and not the prior date upon which it is signed by the testator.[11] Sometimes the question arises as to the effect of a codicil executed within the statutory period, upon a will made prior to the period. Though made within the prohibited time, a codicil which reduces bequests to charities is valid,[12] as is one which leaves them unchanged,[13] or merely contains administrative provisions with respect to the gifts.[14] If such a codicil revokes certain bequests which would normally fall into residue to charities, the latter may not take the additional amount.[15]

7 As to what institutions come within the prohibition of the statutes, see In re Coleman's Estate, 66 Idaho 567, 163 P.2d 847, 1945; annotation, 111 A.L.R. 525.

8 Iowa and New York have the first type of limitation; District of Columbia, Florida, Montana, Ohio and Pennsylvania have the second; California, Georgia, Idaho, and Mississippi have both. See note, 50 Col.L.R. 94.

9 See supra note 8.

10 In re Gregg's Estate, 213 Pa. 260, 62 A. 856, 1906.

11 Gray's Estate, 147 Pa. 67, 23 A. 205, 1892.

12 In re McDole's Estate, 215 Cal. 328, 10 P.2d 75, 1932; In re Bingaman's Estate, 281 Pa. 497, 127 A. 73, 1924. See generally infra § 91.

13 In re Pence's Estate, 117 Cal.App. 323, 4 P.2d 202, 1931.

14 In re Darlington's Estate, 289 Pa. 297, 137 A. 268, 1927.

15 Lightner's Appeal, 57 Pa.Super. 469, 1914. Cf. Ruple v. Hiram College, 35 Ohio App. 8, 171 N.E. 417, 1928, where the revoked bequest was not in favor of a relative for whose protection the statute was designed. Cf. infra § 88, note 49.

*Limitation of Amount*

Five of the states which have time limitations also restrict the proportion of the estate which can be willed to charity, and two others have restrictions only of the latter sort.[16] This proportion is typically one-third, though it is one-fourth in Iowa and one-half in New York.[17] In California it has been held that the amount which may be given to charity is one-third of the estate after payment of debts and administration expenses, and that the valuation should be determined at the date of distribution.[18] The New York courts hold that the value is to be determined as of the date of death after the deduction of debts,[19] though the charity may share in the increase in value after death.[20] Somewhat complicated formulae are necessary to determine the amount of the excess when the will leaves life estates to relatives with remainders to charity.[21]

*Who May Object*

Some of the statutes described in this section make no requirement that the testator be survived by relatives in order for the legislation to operate in limiting charitable devises.[22] Most of the statutes, however, make the invalidity of the charitable gift dependent on the survival of designated relatives, e. g., the spouse, children or other descendants, or parents.[23] Under legislation of this type only the designated relatives can object to the devise,[24] and they may waive the objection.[25]

A little testamentary manipulation can nullify the effect of the statutory limitations on charitable devises when only designated relatives can object. Thus, if the charitable gifts are

16 See supra note 8.

17 Ibid.

18 In re Campbell's Estate, 175 Cal. 345, 165 P. 931, 1917.

19 In re Seymour's Will, 239 N.Y. 259, 146 N.E. 372, 1925.

20 Will of Opdyke, 255 N.Y. 255, 174 N.E. 646, 74 A.L.R. 641, 1931.

21 In re Mayer's Will, 299 N.Y. 388, 87 N.E.2d 422, 11 A.L.R.2d 1136, 1949, noted, 1 Syracuse L.R. 321.

22 In re Garthwaite's Estate, 131 Cal.App. 321, 21 P.2d 465, 1933 (will within 30 days of death). See notes, 31 Cal.L.R. 118, 50 Col.L.R. 94.

23 Ibid.

24 Karolusson v. Paonessa, 207 Iowa 127, 222 N.W. 431, 1928; In re Tone's Will, 186 App.Div. 361, 174 N.Y.S. 391, affirmed 226 N.Y. 696, 123 N.E. 892, 1919.

25 Taylor v. Payne, 154 Fla. 359, 17 So.2d 615, 154 A.L.R. 677, 1944; see Matter of Plaster, 266 App.Div. 439, 43 N.Y.S.2d 1, 1943, affirmed 293 N.Y. 822, 59 N.E.2d 181, 1944; Deeds v. Deeds, infra note 26.

specific or pecuniary and the will provides that the residue goes to individual non-relatives,[26] and particularly if the will provides for a gift over to non-relatives if the charitable devise or bequest should fail,[27] the latter cannot be contested for there is no person with sufficient interest to object. Of course, the result is otherwise if the charitable gift is residuary and there is no gift over,[28] and the entire matter depends somewhat upon the particular statutory provisions.[29] However, since the legislation has been designed for the protection of specific relatives and not for the purpose of disfavoring charitable gifts it is often possible to circumvent the statutes. The only certain way of preventing this is amendatory legislation adopting the old mortmain principle of declaring the excessive or untimely charitable gifts altogether void.[30]

## PROTECTION OF CHILDREN

**36. In all states except Louisiana a parent has the power to disinherit his children by willing his property to other persons.**

**This power is qualified by the already noticed provisions for homestead and family allowances and for limitations on charitable devises. Certain legal principles or other factors also operate to curb disinheritance of children. Of major importance are statutes in almost every state permitting the afterborn child, and in many states the omitted child living at the time of the parent's will, to take his intestate share against the will unless the omission appears to be intentional.**

By the time of Charles I the children of an English testator had generally lost the right to claim a share of his personalty against the will. The American jurisdictions which have the common-law system of jurisprudence have followed the principle of testamentary freedom, except as concerns the surviving spouse.

26 See Deeds v. Deeds, 94 N.E.2d 232, Ohio Prob.1950; but see Matter of Smallman, 141 Misc. 796, 253 N.Y.S. 628, 1931. See supra note 15.

27 Estate of Davis, 74 Cal.App.2d 357, 168 P.2d 789, 1946; Estate of Haines, 76 Cal.App.2d 673, 173 P.2d 693, noted, 45 Mich.L.R. 776; In re Davison's Estate, 96 Cal.App.2d 263, 215 P.2d 504, 1950.

28 Of course the designated heirs may object to a forbidden residuary gift to charity. In re Coleman's Estate, 66 Idaho 567, 163 P.2d 847, 1945; see Estate of Randall, 86 Cal.App.2d 422, 194 P.2d 709, 1948.

29 See notes, 31 Col.L.R. 118, 41 Yale L.J. 771 and cf. infra note 30.

30 Compare notes, 50 Col.L.R. 94, 25 N.Y.U.L.R. 144. See supra note 22.

With the exception of the latter, a testator may generally disinherit all his relatives, even his dependent children. However, in Louisiana the civil law principle of the legitime is in effect. There the testator can dispose of only one-third of his estate if he leaves three or more children, one-half if he leaves two, and two-thirds if he leaves but one child.[1] The descendants of a predeceased child are entitled to the latter's share and each child, or group of descendants of a child, is entitled to an equal share of the non-disposable portion. Only for certain enumerated sorts of misconduct may a child or descendant be disinherited in Louisiana.[2]

*Disallowance of Wills Disinheriting Children*

While freedom of testation is the accepted norm in the remaining states,[3] there are certain limitations which must be considered. Some of these are legal principles invoked by statutes described in the two preceding sections, while others are factors of an extra-legal and hazy nature. There is no legal objection to wills on the ground that they fail to provide substantially for testator's children.[4] However, such wills are often contested because of the testator's incompetency or for alleged fraud or undue influence practiced upon him. When juries pass upon these issues, they doubtless let the unnatural provisions of the will influence their decision.[5] Sympathy for the children may

[1] Louisiana—LSA–C.C. art. 1493. See Walet v. Darby, 167 La. 1095, 120 So. 869, 1929. Nor can he dispose of more than two-thirds of his estate in case he leaves a surviving parent, ibid., art. 1494. The same limitation is put upon gifts inter vivos. Ibid art. 1227 et seq.

[2] Louisiana—LSA–C.C. arts. 1617–1622. And so also as to disinherison of parents, ibid., art. 1623. In all cases the cause of the disinherison must be expressed in the will, ibid., art. 1624.

[3] In Idaho there is a limitation against willing descendant's share of community property to others than children, grandchildren or parents of either spouse and further prohibition against willing more than half of the testator's share to parents. Idaho Code, 1948, § 14-113. See also Leffler v. Leffler, 151 Fla. 455, 10 So.2d 799, 1942, for application of the Florida "Stepmother" Act limiting the amount willed to a second wife, when testator left children by a prior marriage.

[4] Lepper v. Knox, 179 Iowa 419, 161 N.W. 454, L.R.A.1918A, 43, 1917 (acknowledged illegitimate child); In re Bliss' Estate, 247 Mich. 389, 225 N.W. 576, 1929; Smith v. Smith, 48 N.J.Eq. 566, 25 A. 11, 1891; In re Moore's Estate, 114 Or. 444, 236 P. 265, 1925; In re Ford's Estate, 70 Utah 456, 261 P. 15, 1927; In re Golz's Will, 190 Wis. 524, 209 N.W. 704, 1926. See infra §§ 51, 55.

[5] Lehman v. Lindenmeyer, 48 Colo. 305, 109 P. 956, 1910; Maroncelli v. Starkweather, 104 Conn. 419, 133 A. 209, 1926; Newman v. Smith, 77 Fla. 633, 82 So. 236, 1918; Bradley v. Onstott, 180 Ind. 687, 103 N.E. 798, 1914; Gott v. Dennis, 296 Mo. 66, 246 S.W.

interfere with an impartial verdict. Even trial judges may be somewhat influenced by these considerations.[6] Legislatures and appellate courts assert stoutly the principle of testamentary freedom and text-writers repeat it in the clearest language, but trial courts and particularly juries continue to deny it in their decisions. This is a factor not capable of measurement but almost everyone is realist enough to recognize its existence and importance.[7]

### *Effect of Failure to Mention Living Children*

The idea that a child could not be effectively disinherited unless he was given something was current among laymen at least as early as Blackstone's time. From this we have the expression of "cutting off the heir with a shilling." Blackstone[8] speaks of the concept as a groundless vulgar error and attributes it to the Roman law principle that an ancestor could not totally pass by the heir without assigning a reason therefor. While the common law has no such doctrine, it is highly desirable that the testator should at least mention his children in his will. Failure to do so may be material upon the issue of whether the testator has the required mental capacity—more particularly whether he is able to recognize the persons who are the natural objects of his bounty.[9]

218, 1922; In re Gunderman's Estate, 102 Neb. 590, 168 N.W. 359, 1918; In re Hinton's Will, 180 N.C. 206, 104 S.E. 341, 1920; Campbell v. Campbell, 215 S.W. 134, Tex.Civ.App.1919. But see De Crow v. Harkness, 100 Kan. 144, 163 P. 630, 1917. There must be other evidence of mental incapacity or undue influence in order to submit the matter to the jury. Frye v. Frye, 17 Ohio App. 246, 1922. See, also, Erickson v. Lundgren, 37 S.W.2d 629, Mo.1931; In re Ehle's Estate, 115 Cal. App. 656, 2 P.2d 398, 1931.

6 Weston v. Hanson, 212 Mo. 248, 111 S.W. 44, 1908; In re Barney's Will, 70 Vt. 352, 40 A. 1027, 1898; Deans v. Deans, 166 Ga. 555, 144 S.E. 116, 1928 (statute). Cf. In re Budlong's Will, 126 N.Y. 423, 27 N.E. 945, 1891; Seaman v. Husband, 256 Pa. 571, 100 A. 941, 1917 (on issue of genuineness of will and due execution). But see In re Martin's Estate, 170 Cal. 657, 151 P. 138, 1915 (no presumption of insanity from disinheritance of wife and children).

7 For a forceful treatment of this matter, see Laube, The Right of a Testator to Pauperize His Helpless Dependents, 13 Corn.L.Q. 559.

8 2 Bl.Com. 503. See also In re Newlin's Estate, 209 Pa. 456, 58 A. 846, 68 L.R.A. 464, 1904.

9 In re Burns' Will, 121 N.C. 336, 28 S.E. 519, 1897 (children not mentioned). As to inequality generally, see supra note 5.

*Pretermitted Children Statutes*

By virtue of statutory provisions in almost every state a child omitted from his parent's will may, under some circumstances, take his intestate share of the parent's estate.[10] These statutes are based upon the presumption that the parent did not wish to disinherit his children. They do not forbid disinheritance; indeed they are premised upon the proposition that this is permissible if the omission is intentional. Except in Wyoming, a child born after execution of the will is entitled to his intestate share unless it appears that he is intentionally omitted from the will or is otherwise provided for. Moreover, in about half of the states the same privilege is granted to the omitted child living at the time of execution of the will. In some of the latter there are separate statutes for the afterborn and for the omitted living child, while elsewhere a single statute does duty for both cases. Some states have variations as to the effect of the presence or absence of living children, upon the rights of the afterborn, as to children reported dead, or as to those born posthumously. There are other differences in detail, but in all there is a case of similarity in that protection is given only upon the basis that the omission was unintentional.

There are different types of statutory provisions with reference to how the fact of intentional or unintentional omission must appear. The Missouri type makes its provision for children "not named or provided" for in the will. The Massachusetts type permits the child to take his intestate share "unless it appears that the omission was intentional and not occasioned by accident or mistake." A variant of the latter appears in Michigan and some other states; it simply reverses the presumption and declares that the child takes only "if it appears that such omission was not intentional but was made by accident or mistake." These variations are found in statutes applicable to both after-born

10 See Bordwell, Statute Law of Wills, 14 Ia.L.R. 174–177, 290 et seq.; Mathews, Pretermitted Heirs: An Analysis of Statutes, 29 Col.L.R. 748; Mathews, Trends in the Power to Disinherit Children (1930) 16 Am.Bar Ass'n J. 293; King, Statutory Status of Pretermitted Heirs, 13 B.U.L.R. 672; Evans, Should Pretermitted Issue Be Entitled to Inherit, 31 Cal.L.R. 263; Dainow, Inheritance by Pretermitted Children, 32 Ill.L.R. 1.

Except in the case of a few statutes making special provision for the situation where no children were living at the time of execution of the will, the statutes do not speak of revocation of the will by reason of the child's subsequent birth. See infra note 29. To the extent that a jurisdiction preserves the common-law rule that marriage and birth of issue revokes a pre-existing will—see infra § 85—a child takes his intestate share by virtue of the revocation.

and omitted living children.[11] Many statutes also state that a provision or settlement outside the will prevents the child from taking his intestate share.[12]

A testamentary provision, however slight, for a child is usually sufficient to prevent him from taking under the statute.[13] Any mention of him by name in the will has the same effect under any type of statute.[14] The chief controversy occurs in the cases where it is claimed that mention of or nominal provision for one's "heirs", "children" or the contestants of his will prevents a taking under the statute.[15] This is a matter which depends upon several factors, including the type of statute, the other provisions of the will, and the admissibility of evidence outside the will to show whether the omission of the child was intentional.

Under the Missouri type of statute parol evidence is not admissible to show that the testator had not forgotten his omitted child—the question is simply whether the child was named or provided for in the will, and if not he takes his intestate share

[11] As to the effect of this type of statute upon the decisions, see Goff v. Goff, 352 Mo. 809, 179 S.W.2d 707, 152 A.L.R. 717, 1944.

[12] See Hale's Estate, 75 Cal.App.2d 227, 170 P.2d 961, 1946; In re Curry's Will, 21 N.Y.S.2d 544, 1940. But the following have been held not to be settlements. In re Griffin's Will, 159 Misc. 12, 287 N.Y.S. 514, 1936 ($7.13 in baby's bank); In re Robinson's Estate, 188 Misc. 720, 66 N.Y.S.2d 705, 1946 (insurance, savings bonds, and bank account after will); Williamson v. Williamson, 232 N.C. 54, 59 S.E.2d 214, 1950 noted, 29 N.C.L.R. 218 (life insurance).

[13] Walker v. Case, 211 Ark. 1091, 204 S.W.2d 543, 173 A.L.R. 1000, 1947; In re Benolken's Estate, 122 Mont. 425, 205 P.2d 1141, 1949; McLean v. McLean, 207 N.Y. 365, 101 N.E. 178, 1913; Allison v. Allison's Ex'rs, 101 Va. 537, 44 S.E. 904, 63 L.R.A. 920, 1903. But see In re Ridgway's Estate, 33 Wash.2d 249, 205 P.2d 360, 1949, noted, 26 Wash.L.R. 64 (contingent interest). A devise to an adopted child by name without stating the relationship prevents application of the statute. Mares v. Martinez, 54 N.M. 1, 212 P.2d 772, 1949, noted, 49 Mich.L.R. 152.

[14] See Boucher v. Lizotte, 85 N.H. 514, 161 A. 213, 1932 (use of son's name in describing his wife is sufficient reference to son to disinherit him); Kinnear v. Langley, 209 Ark. 878, 192 S.W.2d 978, 1946, noted, 45 Mich.L.R. 242 (child named in husband's will incorporated by reference); Culp v. Culp, 206 Ark. 875, 178 S.W.2d 52, 1944. As to mention of future children, see York v. York, 60 N.E.2d 70, Ohio App.1944, and annotation, 126 A.L.R. 750.

[15] See Boman v. Boman, 49 F. 329 C.C.A. 9, C.C.A.Wash.1892 ("to each of my heirs at law the sum of one dollar" is not sufficient because heirs are not named). See also Goff v. Goff, supra note 11; In re Ridgway's Estate, supra note 13; In re Fell's Estate, infra note 18; In re Ray's Estate, 245 P.2d 990, Nev.1952. But cf. Walker v. Case, In re Benolken's Estate, both supra note 13.

under the statute.[16] Certain other statutes expressly provide that the child takes unless it appears *by the will* that testator intended to disinherit the child.[17] However, in the jurisdictions where the statute provides that the child takes unless it appears that the omission was intentional, parol evidence is usually admissible to show that intent.[18]

Grandchildren are usually within the express provisions of the statute if their parent is predeceased,[19] but even if the statute provides only for afterborn children an omitted grandchild has been permitted to take his intestate share.[20] When there is a testamentary provision for a child who predeceases the testator, and the child's issue takes the legacy under the anti-lapse statute,[21] the issue are "provided for" and hence cannot claim under the statute for pretermitted children.[22] If there is no benefit to the grandchild under the anti-lapse statute or if his parent is merely mentioned, the holdings are in conflict as to whether the unmentioned grandchild can take his intestate share.[23]

16 Yeates v. Yeates, 179 Ark. 543, 16 S.W.2d 996, 65 A.L.R. 466, 1929; Goff v. Goff, supra note 11; Wadsworth v. Brigham, 125 Or. 428, 259 P. 299, affirmed 129 Or. 428, 266 P. 875, 1928.

17 Hedlund v. Miner, 395 Ill. 217, 69 N.E.2d 862, 170 A.L.R. 1306, 1946, holding, however, that the surrounding circumstances at time of execution are admissible; to the same effect, see Marshall v. Marshall, 25 Tenn.App. 309, 156 S.W.2d 449, 1941, noted, 17 Tenn.L.R. 405, under a statute similar to that of Missouri. Cf. Spaniard v. Tantom, infra note 18.

18 Appeal of Ingraham, 118 Me. 67, 105 A. 812, 1919; O'Neall v. Her, 254 Mich. 631, 236 N.W. 890, 1931; In re Estate of Peterson, 49 Mont. 96, 140 P. 237, Ann.Cas.1916A, 716, 1914; In re Parrott's Estate, 45 Nev. 318, 203 P. 258, 1922; Hedderich v. Hedderich, 18 N.D. 488, 123 N.W. 276, 1909; Scott v. Nolan, 53 R.I. 89, 164 A. 193, 1933; In re Swenson's Estate, 57 S.D. 90, 230 N.W. 884, 1930; In re Newell's Estate, 78 Utah 463, 5 P.2d 230, 1931. Contra: In re Estate of Trickett, 197 Cal. 20, 239 P. 406, 1925; Spaniard v. Tantom, 131 Okl. 75, 267 P. 623, 1928 (surrounding circumstances excluded); In re Fell's Estate, 70 Idaho 399, 219 P.2d 941, 1950.

19 See In re Fell's Estate, supra note 18; In re Goff's Estate, supra note 11; In re Benolken's Estate, supra note 13; note, 44 Yale L.J. 841.

20 Matter of Horst, 264 N.Y. 236, 190 N.E. 475, 1934; but see Alburger's Estate, 274 Pa. 101, 117 A. 450, 1922.

21 See infra § 140.

22 Miller v. Aven, 327 Mo. 20, 34 S.W.2d 116, 1930. This is the only argument for a legacy of a nominal sum to the child instead of merely mentioning him. Most skilled draftsmen prefer to take care of the grandchild problem in other ways.

23 That he may take: In re Ross' Estate, 140 Cal. 282, 73 P. 976, 1930; Riley v. Collier, 111 Okl. 130, 238 P. 491, 1925. Contra: In re Newell's Estate, 78 Utah 463, 5 P.2d 230, 1931; In re Phillips' Estate, 193 Wash. 194, 74 P.2d 1015, 1938, noted, 13 Wash.L.R. 337; see also Miller v. Aven, su-

The share which an omitted child or grandchild takes under the state is the share he would have taken if testator had died intestate, which of course depends upon the existence of a surviving spouse and other issue.[24] If the omitted child is the only issue he takes the entire estate, subject to the spouse's share.[25] When one child is merely mentioned or provided for by a nominal legacy and another child is entirely omitted, the statutes often give the latter an unfair advantage over the former.[26] Much can be said of a provision which would make the statute inapplicable when the will leaves the entire estate to his surviving spouse.[27]

When the omitted child is not the only heir there is the problem as to how the interests of the legatees and devisees will be affected in making up his share. Typically the statutes provide that all must contribute proportionately out of the parts devised or bequeathed to them, but some statutes declare that intestate property or the residuary estate must be taken first, and others provide that pro rata abatement should not be employed to defeat the testator's intent.[28] The omitted child does not assert his rights by contest of the will but rather by claiming his intestate share at the time of distribution in an appropriate proceeding.[29]

In the drafting of a will it is desirable that all the heirs at law be mentioned. This is true even in those jurisdictions which have no statutory provision in favor of the omitted child living at the time of the will. Everywhere failure to mention a child would

pra note 22. The latter view seems preferable, especially when the statute provides that the matter turns on intent to exclude.

24 D'Arcangelo v. D'Arcangelo, 137 N.J.Eq. 63, 43 A.2d 169, 1945.

25 In re Hatfield's Estate, 153 Fla. 817, 16 So.2d 57, 1943; In re Wurmbrand, 194 Misc. 203, 86 N.Y.S.2d 705, 1949, affirmed 275 App.Div. 915, 90 N.Y.S.2d 686, 1949. But see In re Vicedomini's Estate, 195 Misc. 1057, 91 N.Y.S.2d 472, 1949, noted, 14 Albany L.R. 109, 19 Fordham L.R. 232, 63 Harv.L.R. 703, 25 N.Y.U.L.R. 177.

26 As to this problem see Mathews, supra note 10 at 753–763.

27 See Model Probate Code § 41 based upon the Texas statute, as to which see note, 1 Baylor L.R. 511. See also note, 10 U. of Pitt.L.R. 219 for commentary on recent Pennsylvania amendment.

28 Bordwell, supra note 10 and 297; Mathews, supra note 10 at 774. See also supra note 27. As to abatement generally, see infra § 136.

29 In re Philippi's Estate, 71 Cal. App.2d 127, 161 P.2d 1006, 1945 (omitted children claimed entire estate); Story v. Story, 188 Mo. 110, 86 S.W. 225, 1905; see Toomer v. Van Antwerp Realty Corp., 238 Ala. 87, 189 So. 549, 123 A.L.R. 1063, 1939. But see Newman v. Waterman, 63 Wis. 612, 23 N.W. 696, 53 Am.Rep. 310, 1885. See supra note 10; infra §§ 85, 98.

be a circumstance which would be material upon the question of mental capacity and would sometimes lead to the setting aside of the whole will. In most jurisdictions it is possible by apt language to mention or make provision for after-born children and grandchildren so as to prevent statutes of that type from operating. However, it is highly desirable that a new will should be drawn whenever a testator has acquired a new heir.

*Express Disinheritance of Heirs*

There is another principle which sometimes serves as a practical limitation upon the right to disinherit a child or other heir. A testator may not cut off his heir simply by declaring the intention to do so in the will—it is necessary that he should also give the property to someone else.[30] Thus if the testator has a son John and a nephew Henry, and wishes to disinherit the former, his will which merely says, "I hereby declare that my son John shall receive none of my estate," would not have the effect of giving the property to Henry who is next in the line of kinship after John. The theory is that such a will is ineffective as it does not dispose of testator's property, which passes to John under the intestate laws in spite of the owner's direction in the instrument. In order to disinherit John, it would be necessary to direct that the property go to Henry or to some other person. However, it would also be highly desirable—and indeed imperative in many jurisdictions—to mention John or to make some provision for him in the will in order to show that testator intended to omit him.

*Claims for Support of Minor Children*

Generally there is a legal duty upon the father to support his minor child. This obligation can be asserted by the child in a civil action against the father in a few states, though usually it can be enforced only through criminal proceedings.[31] Does the duty of support continue after the parent's death, so that the

30 In re Fritze's Estate, 85 Cal.App. 500, 259 P. 992, 1927; Dailey v. Dailey, 224 Ill.App. 17, 1922; Jones v. Warren, 124 Me. 282, 128 A. 1, 1925; Nagle v. Conard, 79 N.J.Eq. 124, 81 A. 841, 1911. See In re Stephan's Estate, 142 Fla. 88, 194 So. 343, 128 A.L.R. 440, 1940. The principle operates most often when a part of the property is intestate because of a lapsed gift. The heirs who are expressly "disinherited" are not prevented from sharing the intestate property. In re Martz' Estate, 318 Mich. 293, 28 N.W.2d 108, 1947.

31 Madden, Domestic Relations § 112; 3 Vernier, American Family Laws § 234.

child may assert a claim against the estate? The question arises most frequently where the spouses have been divorced or separated. A number of decisions have sustained the child's claim against the father's estate when based upon a support provision in a divorce decree.[32] In absence of such a decree, a few decisions and much dicta refuse recovery to the infant.[33] It seems unjust to permit a parent to pauperize his helpless dependent children.[34] On the other hand it is doubtful if we should establish a universal principle that a child may claim support money from his father's estate. Such a doctrine would interfere with the testamentary plan wherein a husband leaves everything to his widow, trusting her to care for the child so far as the property permits. The law should not prevent the carrying out of such an arrangement which is often the most socially and economically desirable scheme that the situation allows.

A much better solution is that of England and some of the dominions where the court is authorized to make such allowances for the spouse or children as seems proper when it appears that the testator has not made adequate provision for their support.[35] The chief recommendation for this scheme is its humanity and its flexibility. As Professor Mathews has pointed out in his excellent study of the subject of pretermitted heirs, this is far superior to our provisions for the omitted or afterborn child, described in the previous pages.[36]

[32] Miller v. Miller, 64 Me. 484, 1874; Creyts v. Creyts, 143 Mich. 375, 106 N.W. 1111, 114 Am.St.Rep. 656, 1906; Smith v. Funk, 141 Okl. 188, 284 P. 638, 1930; Mansfield v. Hill, 56 Or. 400, 107 P. 471, 108 P. 1007, 1910; Murphy v. Moyle, 17 Utah, 113, 53 P. 1010, 70 Am.St.Rep. 767, 1898; Gainsburg v. Garbarsky, 157 Wash. 537, 289 P. 1000, 1930. Contra: Sandlin's Adm'r v. Allen, 262 Ky. 355, 90 S.W.2d 350, 1936; Blades v. Szatai, 151 Md. 644, 135 A. 841, 50 A.L.R. 232, 1927; Stone v. Duffy, 219 Mass. 178, 106 N.E. 595, 1914 (dicta); In re Moore's Estate, 34 Tenn.App. 131, 234 S.W.2d 847, 1950. Recovery by the child was denied in a case where he was sole legatee under the will. Schultze v. Schultze, 66 S.W. 56, Tex. Civ.App.1931. This seems reasonable as the only advantage he could gain would be at the expense of other creditors of an insolvent estate. For freedom of family allowance from claims of creditors, see § 34 supra.

[33] Rice v. Andrews, 127 Misc. 826, 217 N.Y.S. 528, 1926, noted, 25 Mich. L.R. 555 and 36 Yale L.J. 424; Carey v. Carey, 163 Tenn. 486, 43 S.W.2d 498, 1931; Cissna v. Beaton, 2 Wash. 2d 491, 98 P.2d 651, 1940.

[34] See Madden, supra note 31, § 115; Laube, supra note 7 at 575; note, 22 Cal.L.R. 79.

[35] See supra § 5 at notes 33, 34, and § 3 at note 91. Cf. § 34 supra.

[36] See Mathews, supra note 10 at 768.

## UNWORTHY HEIRS

**37. In general misconduct of an heir toward the decedent does not prevent the heir from taking under the latter's will or the intestate laws. Thus, a father may inherit from his child though the former has denied his paternity, or has abandoned the latter.**

**An ancient English statute barred a wife of her dower when she eloped and lived in adultery. This statute applies in some states and in others there is legislation denying dower or other statutory shares to a husband or wife who is guilty of bigamy, living in adultery, desertion, etc. In absence of applicable statutory principles some courts have barred the guilty spouse on account of certain types of marital misconduct, while others decline to apply principles of equitable estoppel on this account.**

**In absence of statute, most courts have held that a person wrongfully killing another may take the latter's property if otherwise entitled thereto by will or under the intestate laws. A minority of jurisdictions have held that the murderer is barred from inheriting from his victim. Decisions permitting the inheritance generally have resulted in legislation designed to alter the rule in such cases. These statutes have usually been construed narrowly so as to prohibit the inheritance only in the situations clearly covered by the statute.**

In a variety of situations the question is presented as to whether one who has wronged the decedent may take under his will or under the intestate laws. When a testamentary disposition is involved and the misconduct occurred before the execution of the will and was concealed from the testator, the question is apt to be decided upon the issue of fraud.[1] Where, however, the guilty claimant asserts a right to inherit under the intestate laws or when he claims under a will the execution of which preceded the misconduct, the courts are usually obliged to determine the matter on some other basis.

As a whole the courts are not inclined to bar a claimant because of his misconduct toward decedent. Controversy is confined chiefly to three general situations. These are: (1) Where the claimant has abandoned or denied the paternity of the decedent who is his child; (2) where the claimant has violated his marital obligations toward the decedent; (3) where the claimant

[1] See infra § 56

has feloniously killed the one from whom he seeks to inherit under a will or the intestate laws.

*Abandonment or Denial of Paternity of Child*

When a parent has abandoned his infant child and the latter dies intestate, it seems inequitable that the parent should inherit from the child. Nevertheless in the few cases of this nature that have come before the courts, it has been held that when the intestate laws make no exception because of the abandonment, none will be implied.[2] The parent is not estopped as the child was not induced to change his position because of the misconduct. The situation is a particularly hard one as the child is generally too young to make a will cutting off the offending parent. Here the courts have followed the statutes of descent and distribution literally. A few states have passed statutes barring the parent in such cases.[3]

*Violation of Marital Obligations toward Decedent—Elopement*

The famous Statute of Westminster II, 1285, contained a provision that if a woman left her husband and continued to live in adultery, she was barred of dower unless her husband voluntarily permitted her to return to his house.[4] In some American jurisdictions this clause was regarded as part of the common law of the state.[5] In others, similar statutes have been enacted.[6] Under the ancient English statute and those patterned after it, adultery while living with her husband and without desertion, elopement or cohabitation with another does not bar dower.[7] Likewise

[2] Files v. Green, 197 Iowa 1169, 196 N.W. 993, 33 A.L.R. 573, 1924, noted, 10 Va.L.R. 650; Avery v. Brantley, 191 N.C. 396, 131 S.E. 721, 1926, noted, 5 N.C.L.R. 72.

[3] The case of Avery v. Brantley, supra note 2, led to legislation designed to prevent inheritance by the abandoning parent, now contained in N.C.Gen.Stat., 1943, § 28–149–6. See note, 11 N.C.L.R. 296–297. See also Matter of Daniels' Estate, 193 Misc. 862, 83 N.Y.S.2d 752, 1948.

[4] 13 Edw. I, c. 34.

[5] Reel v. Elder, 62 Pa. 308, 1 Am. Rep. 414, 1869; Gogswell v. Tibbetts, 3 N.H. 41, 1824. See Schmeizl v. Schmeizl, 186 Md. 371, 46 A.2d 619, 1946; Keicher v. Mysinger, 184 Tenn. 226, 198 S.W.2d 330, 1946 (but not deprived of vested estate by entireties).

[6] Bell v. Nealy, 1 Bailey (17 S.C. Law) 312, 19 Am.Dec. 686, 1829 (English statute expressly made of force by South Carolina legislature); Morrello v. Cantalupo, 91 N.J.Eq. 415, 111 A. 255, 1920. See 3 Vernier, American Family Laws §§ 202, 221; Model Probate Code, appendix 263.

[7] Cogswell v. Tibbetts, supra note 5; Jarnigan v. Jarnigan, 12 Lea (Tenn.) 292, 1883; Sergent v. North Cumberland Mfg. Co., 112 Ky. 888, 66 S.W. 1036, 1902. But see Ferguson

under these statutes, the departure of the wife must be voluntary and when she leaves because of her husband's compulsion, cruelty and neglect, her subsequent adultery does not bar her.[8] However, it is generally held that where the parting was by agreement, or where she left voluntarily, and later committed adultery, she is barred although she did not elope with the paramour.[9]

In absence of statute some courts have refused to follow the Statute of Westminster.[10] Some of these decisions have argued that as adultery is ground for divorce,[11] and as divorce for the wife's fault will bar dower,[12] there is no reason for holding that adultery, which is not followed by divorce, results in loss of dower. This argument loses validity when the husband does not survive long enough to procure a divorce.

The Statute of Westminster II did not apply to curtesy. Hence the husband's living in adultery does not work a loss of his marital property rights in absence of statute.[13] However, under some statutes both spouses are put upon a parity and if the wife's conduct would bar her dower, similar acts by the husband will cause a loss of curtesy.[14]

v. Ferguson, 153 Ky. 742, 156 S.W. 413, 1913.

8 Heslop v. Heslop, 82 Pa. 537, 1876; Walters v. Jordan, 35 N.C. 361, 57 Am.Dec. 558, 1852 (though driven away for her adultery); Beaty v. Richardson, 56 S.C. 173, 34 S.E. 73, 46 L.R.A. 517, 1899 (here wife made unsuccessful attempt to win back deserting husband before herself going to live in adultery); Shaffer v. Richardson's Adm'r, 27 Ind. 122, 1866. But see Reynolds v. Reynolds, 24 Wend.(N.Y.) 193, 1840 (wife left because of adultery of her husband and later committed adultery herself); Phillips v. Wiseman, 131 N.C. 402, 42 S.E. 861, 1902 (woman abandoned by her husband later committed adultery). Where the husband deserts and the wife, believing him dead or divorced, marries again, she is not barred of dower. Payne v. Dotson, 81 Mo. 145, 51 Am.Rep. 225, 1883.

9 Hethrington v. Graham, 6 Bing 135, 130 Eng.Rep. 1231, 1829; McAlister v. Novenger, 54 Mo. 251, 1873; Wilson v. Craig, 175 Mo. 362, 75 S.W. 419, 1903. Cf. Reynolds v. Reynolds, supra note 8.

10 Grober v. Clements, 71 Ark. 565, 76 S.W. 555, 100 Am.St.Rep. 91, 1903; Smith v. Fuller, 138 Iowa 91, 115 N.W. 912, 16 L.R.A.,N.S., 98, 1917, semble; Littlefield v. Paul, 69 Me. 527, 1878; Lakin v. Lakin, 2 Allen (Mass.) 45, 1861; Bryan v. Batcheller, 6 R.I. 543, 78 Am.Dec. 454, 1860; Davis v. Davis' Estate, 167 Wis. 328, 167 N.W. 819, 1929.

11 Except in South Carolina.

12 See 2 Vernier, American Family Laws §§ 96, 99, 100; Dawson v. Mays, 159 Ark. 331, 252 S.W. 33, 30 A.L.R. 1463, 1923; Seuss v. Schukat, 358 Ill. 27, 192 N.E. 668, 95 A.L.R. 1461, 1934.

13 Wells v. Thompson, 13 Ala. 793, 48 Am.Dec. 76, 1848.

14 Stock v. Mitchell, 252 Ill. 530, 96 N.E. 1076, 1911; Landreth v. Casey,

Probably if the principles of the Statute of Westminster II are in force in the jurisdiction, they will apply to statutory dower as well as to common-law dower.[15] However, in absence of express statutory provision, a spouse who is guilty of living in adultery with another is not barred of his distributive share of the deceased spouse's personalty.[16] The same would probably be true with respect to interests in realty which are inherited from the other spouse, as distinct from that which is claimed by way of a forced interest.[17]

When a wife is living in adultery at the time of her husband's death, it would seem that she should not be entitled to a homestead. As homestead is for the preservation of the family, the better view would seem to be that where the family relationship has ceased because of fault of the wife she should not be entitled to the benefits.[18] Some decisions, influenced by the fact that the statute makes no exception, have granted homestead in this situation.[19]

*Bigamous Marriage*

What is the effect of a subsequent bigamous marriage of one spouse upon his right to inherit from his first and lawful spouse? Of course in the jurisdictions where living in adultery is recognized as a bar and applies to the particular property interest involved, there is no doubt but that the guilty spouse could not take. In other jurisdictions, and as to the property interests in which this ancient rule is not applied, the additional fact of the bigamous marriage has been enough to induce some courts to hold that the guilty spouse is barred.[20] The opposite result has

340 Ill. 519, 173 N.E. 84, 1931. See statutory references, supra note 6.

15 Daniels v. Taylor, 145 F. 169, C.C.A.Ind.T.1906.

16 Turner v. Cole, 24 Ala. 364, 1854; Nolen v. Doss, 133 Ala. 259, 31 So. 969, 1901; Mack v. Pairo, 136 Md. 179, 110 A. 198, 1920; Vreeland's Ex'rs v. Ryno's Ex'r, 26 N.J.Eq. 160, 1875.

17 Davis v. Davis' Estate, 167 Wis. 328, 167 N.W. 819, 1918. See Estes v. Merrill, 121 Ark. 361, 181 S.W. 136, 1915.

18 Somers v. Somers, 27 S.D. 500, 131 N.W. 1091, 36 L.R.A.,N.S., 1024, 1911; Keicher v. Mysinger, 184 Tenn. 226, 198 S.W.2d 330, 1947. Cf. In re Harrington's Estate, 140 Cal. 244, 73 P. 1000, 98 Am.St.Rep. 51, 1903; Id., 140 Cal. 294, 73 P. 1131, 74 P. 136, 1903; Id., 147 Cal. 124, 81 P. 546, 109 Am.St.Rep. 118, 1905. See infra note 30.

19 Duffy v. Harris, 65 Ark. 251, 45 S.W. 545, 40 L.R.A. 750, 67 Am.St. Rep. 925, 1898; Lyons v. Lyons, 101 Mo.App. 494, 74 S.W. 467, 1903.

20 Israel v. Arthur, 18 Colo. 158, 32 P. 68, 1893; Moore v. Robinson, 139 S.C. 393, 137 S.E. 697, 1927; Darrough v. Davis, 135 Okl. 263, 275 P.

also been reached.[21] If the spouse marries again honestly believing that the other spouse is dead or that a divorce has been obtained, it is generally held that he may inherit from his first spouse.[22]

Some of the cases in which the surviving spouse has lived in adultery or contracted a bigamous marriage speak of estoppel to assert the right of inheritance or marital property interest.[23] It seems clear that living in adultery or contracting of a bigamous marriage do not by themselves constitute true estoppels when no one has acted on these facts to his detriment.[24] The question of estoppel is sometimes raised in cases in which the lawful spouse is silent as to the first marriage or denies its validity by marrying another. Several decisions have enforced an estoppel against such spouse in favor of the other spouse's vendees who have relied upon the silence.[25] As against the marital rights of a person who has married the other spouse, the estoppel does not in general operate. In this situation the courts assert that one has no duty toward the party who attempts to marry his spouse to

309, 1929, noted, 43 Harv.L.R. 140; Walker v. Matthews, 191 Miss. 489, 3 So.2d 820, 1941.

21 In re Newman's Estate, 124 Cal. 688, 57 P. 686, 45 L.R.A. 780, 1899; Brown v. Parks, 169 Ga. 712, 151 S.E. 340, 71 A.L.R. 271, 1930; Cox v. Cox, 95 Okl. 14, 217 P. 493, 34 A.L.R. 432, 1923, noted, 8 Minn.L.R. 66, 33 Yale L.J. 878 (this case seems substantially overruled in Darrough v. Davis, supra note 20, but see United States v. McCarty, 144 F.2d 341, C.C.A.Okl., 1944).

22 Estes v. Merrill, 121 Ark. 361, 181 S.W. 136, 1915; Grober v. Clements, 71 Ark. 565, 76 S.W. 555, 100 Am.St. Rep. 91, 1903; Smith v. Fuller, 138 Iowa 91, 115 N.W. 912, 16 L.R.A.,N. S., 98, 1917.

23 See cases supra note 20, and infra note 28.

24 Smith v. Fuller, supra note 22; Grober v. Clements, supra note 22; Nolen v. Doss, 133 Ala. 259, 31 So. 969, 1901; Reel v. Elder, 62 Pa. 308, 1 Am.Rep. 414, 1869. See also cases supra note 21.

25 De France v. Johnson, 26 F. 891, C.C.Minn.1886; Gilbert v. Reynolds, 51 Ill. 513, 1869; Kantor v. Cohn, 181 App.Div. 400, 168 N.Y.S. 846, 1917; Edgar v. Richardson, 33 Ohio St. 581, 31 Am.Rep. 571, 1878; H. W. Wright Lumber Co. v. McCord, 145 Wis. 93, 128 N.W. 873, 34 L.R.A.,N.S., 762, Ann.Cas.1912B, 92, 1910. Cf. Reel v. Elder, supra note 24, where the purchaser did not rely upon the silence or declarations of the spouse claimed to be estopped. See, also, Dunn v. Portsmouth Sav. Bank, 103 Iowa 538, 72 N.W. 687, 1897; Smith v. Fuller, 138 Iowa 91, 115 N.W. 912, 16 L.R.A.,N.S., 98, 1908; Cazier v. Hinchey, 143 Mo. 203, 44 S.W. 1052, 1898; Norton v. Tufts, 19 Utah 470, 57 P. 409, 1899, where the court refused to find an estoppel in favor of purchasers either because the spouse was under no duty to speak or because no purchaser placed reliance upon the conduct.

break the silence and furthermore that such party has no marital property rights as the second marriage is invalid.[26]

*Abandonment and Separation*

In absence of statute, abandonment does not bar the spouse from dower [27] or the distributive share [28] of the estate. Of course the statute of Westminster II and laws patterned thereon have no bearing unless adultery has been committed. However, in several states statutes exist which declare that the deserting spouse loses dower, curtesy and the general right of inheritance.[29] Even in absence of statute, the better view would seem to be to deny homestead and family allowances to the deserting spouse upon the ground that these provisions for the preservation of the family unit should not be allowed where the family relationship has been discontinued through the fault of the claimant spouse.[30]

As may be inferred from the foregoing, a mere separation of the spouses by agreement does not bar the right to claim dower or to succeed to interests of the other's estate except possibly with regard to homesteads or family allowances. However, as

[26] De France v. Johnson, 26 F. 891, C.C.Minn.1886; Darrow v. Darrow, 201 Ala. 477, 78 So. 383, 1918; Payne v. Payne, 142 Tenn. 320, 219 S. W. 4, 1920. See, also, Reel v. Elder, supra note 24 and cases following it. But see Richardson's Estate, 132 Pa. 292, 19 A. 82, 1890.

[27] Wiseman v. Wiseman, 73 Ind. 112, 38 Am.Rep. 115, 1880; Nye's Appeal, 126 Pa. 341, 17 A. 618, 12 Am.St.Rep. 873, 1889; Newland v. Holland, 45 Tex. 588, 1876; Thayer v. Thayer, 14 Vt. 107, 39 Am.Dec. 211, 1842.

[28] Nolen v. Doss, 133 Ala. 259, 31 So. 969, 1901; Meyers' Adm'r v. Myers, 244 Ky. 248, 50 S.W.2d 81, 1932; In re Torres Estate, 61 Nev. 156, 120 P.2d 816, 139 A.L.R. 481, 1942.

[29] See statutory references supra note 6; In re Abila's Estate, 32 Cal. 2d 559, 197 P.2d 10, 1948; Kantor v. Bloom, 90 Conn. 210, 96 A. 974, 1916; In re Archer's Estate, 363 Pa. 534, 70 A.2d 857, 1950, noted 98 U. of Pa.L.R. 927; Edwards v. Cuthbert, 184 Va. 502, 36 S.E.2d 1, 1945. See also In re Rathschek's Estate, 300 N.Y. 346, 90 N.E.2d 887, 1950.

[30] Accord Homestead: Dickman v. Birkhauser, 16 Neb. 686, 21 N.W. 396, 1884; Newland v. Holland, 45 Tex. 588, 1876. Family allowances: In re Miller's Estate, 158 Cal. 420, 111 P. 255, 1910; Nye's Appeal, supra note 27; see note, 24 Tulane L.R. 151. Contra: Homestead: Coker v. Coker, 160 Ala. 269, 49 So. 684, 135 Am.St.Rep. 99, 1909; Lies v. De Diablar, 12 Cal. 327, 1859; Whitehead v. Tapp, 69 Mo. 415, 1879.

A wife living apart from her husband because of his cruelty is entitled to homestead. O'Neal v. Miller, 143 Fla. 171, 196 So. 478, 129 A. L.R. 295, 1940; Meech v. Grigsby, 153 Kan. 784, 113 P.2d 1091, 1941. Under these circumstances the husband is not entitled to homestead in his wife's property. Bydalek v. Bydalek, 396 Ill. 65, 71 N.E.2d 19, 1947.

has been seen,[31] if a valid separation agreement provides expressly that the spouse gives up these interests, the waiver will be given effect. As a general rule the contract of separation is deemed to be rescinded by reconciliation and resumption of the marital relation so far as the executory provisions are concerned.[32] This may not be true in case either the terms of the agreement,[33] or the circumstances and conduct of the parties [34] at the time of reconciliation, indicate a contrary intention.

*Murder of the Ancestor*

When an heir or a distributee feloniously kills the intestate, it seems shocking to allow the former to succeed to the latter's property. However, in absence of statute, the majority of cases have held that he may.[35] In at least one such decision it appeared that the slaying was for the purpose of obtaining the property. The chief reason assigned for this view is that as the

[31] See supra § 31.

[32] Sherman v. Sherman, 159 Ark. 364, 252 S.W. 27, 1923; Haile v. Hale, 40 Okl. 101, 135 P. 1143, 1913; Roberts v. Hardy, 89 Mo.App. 86, 1901. The agreement was held avoided by the reconciliation even if it continued for only a few weeks and was followed by another separation. Knapp v. Knapp, 95 Mich. 474, 55 N.W. 353, 1893. But mere agreement to live together in the future does not annul the property aspects of the separation agreement. Garrett v. Kirtley, 97 W.Va. 484, 125 S.E. 347, 40 A.L.R. 1222, 1924.

[33] Daniels v. Benedict, 97 F. 367, C.C.A.Colo.1899; Mach v. Baranowski, 152 Md. 53, 136 A. 34, 1927; Hagerty v. Union Guardian Trust Co., 258 Mich. 133, 242 N.W. 211, 85 A.L.R. 417, 1932.

[34] Hitner's Appeal, 54 Pa. 110, 1867; Hewett v. Gott, 132 Kan. 168, 294 P. 897, 1931.

[35] Hagan v. Cone, 21 Ga.App. 416, 94 S.E. 602, 1917; Wall v. Pfanschmidt, 265 Ill. 180, 106 N.E. 785, L.R.A.1915C, 828, Ann.Cas.1916A, 674, 1914; McAllister v. Fair, 72 Kan. 533, 84 P. 112, 3 L.R.A.,N.S., 726, 115 Am.St.Rep. 233, 7 Ann.Cas. 973, 1906 (here killing was for the purpose of obtaining the property); Eversole v. Eversole, 169 Ky. 793, 185 S.W. 487, L.R.A.1916E, 593, 1916; Gollnik v. Mengel, 112 Minn. 349, 128 N.W. 292, 1910; Shellenberger v. Ransom, 41 Neb. 631, 59 N.W. 935, 25 L.R.A. 564, 1894; Wilson v. Randolph, 50 Nev. 371, 261 P. 654, 1927; Owens v. Owens, 100 N.C. 240, 6 S.E. 794, 1888 (dower); Deem v. Millikin, 53 Ohio St. 668, 44 N.E. 1134, 1896; Holloway v. McCormick, 41 Okl. 1, 136 P. 1111, 50 L.R.A.,N.S., 536, 1913; Carpenter's Estate, 170 Pa. 203, 32 A. 637, 29 L.R.A. 145, 50 Am.St.Rep. 765, 1895; Murchison v. Murchison (Tex.Civ.App.) 203 S.W. 423, 1918; Johnston v. Metropolitan Life Ins. Co., 85 W.Va. 70, 100 S.E. 865, 7 A.L.R. 823, 1919; In re Duncan's Estates, 40 Wash.2d 850, 246 P.2d 445, 1952. However in most of these states legislation has been passed which changes the rule. See note 42, infra. For a historical discussion, see Reppy, The Slayer's Bounty—History of Problem in Anglo-American Law, 19 N.Y.U.L.Q.R. 229.

statutes of descent and distribution make no exception for the situation, the courts should not imply one. Some of the opinions also mention constitutional and statutory provisions forbidding forfeitures for crime.[36] There is a strong minority view,[37] denying recovery to one who has killed his ancestor, largely upon the broad ground that one should not be permitted to take advantage of his own wrong. Most of the recent cases take this position. Some of them proceed upon the theory that the murderer takes no legal title to the property,[38] while others assume that legal title passes to him but a trust ex maleficio will be impressed.[39] The procedure may differ according to which of these theories is adopted. However, this distinction ordinarily would make little difference in ultimate effect, except that under the trust theory an innocent purchaser from the murderer would be protected, which would not be true if no title passed to the slayer.

Theoretically it may be more justifiable to deny recovery to the legatee or devisee who has murdered the testator than in the case of the heir who has killed the intestate. It is conceivable that a court might imply a condition to the will, but refuse to create an exception to the intestate statute.[40] On the other hand

36 See supra §§ 11, 25.

37 Slocum v. Metropolitan Life Ins. Co., 245 Mass. 565, 139 N.E. 816, 27 A.L.R. 1517, 1923; Garwols v. Bankers Trust Co., 251 Mich. 420, 232 N.W. 239, 1930, noted, 8 N.Y.U.L.Q.R. 492; Perry v. Strawbridge, 209 Mo. 621, 108 S.W. 641, 16 L.R.A.,N.S., 244, 123 Am.St.Rep. 510, 14 Ann.Cas. 92, 1908; Van Alstyne v. Tuffy, 103 Misc. 455, 169 N.Y.S. 173, 1918; Parker v. Potter, 200 N.C. 348, 157 S.E. 68, 1931; De Zotell v. Mutual Life Ins. Co. of New York, 60 S.D. 532, 245 N.W. 58, 1932, noted, 19 Va.L.Rev. 518, 28 Ill.L.Rev. 127; In re Tyler's Estate, 140 Wash. 679, 250 P. 456, 51 A.L.R. 1088, 1926, noted, 2 Wash.L.R. 121; Re Medaini [1927] 4 D.L.R. 1137; In re Sigsworth [1934] 104 L.J.R. (Ch.Div.) 46, noted, 83 U. of Pa.L.R. 923. See Box v. Lanier, 112 Tenn. 393, 79 S.W. 1042, 64 L.R.A. 458, 1904; In re Pitts, [1931] 1 Ch. 546, noted, 47 Law Q.R. 320, 9 Can.Bar R. 504. See also cases infra notes 38, 39. As to the necessary intent to bar the killer, see notes, 40 Col.L.R. 327, 24 Wash.U.L.Q. 277.

38 Weaver v. Hollis, 247 Ala. 57, 22 So.2d 525, 1945; Price v. Hitaffer, 164 Md. 505, 165 A. 470, 1933. See also Perry v. Strawbridge and In re Tyler's Estate, both supra note 37.

39 Garner v. Phillips, 229 N.C. 160, 47 S.E.2d 845, 1948. See also Ellerson v. Westcott and Whitney v. Lott, both infra note 41; Van Alstyne v. Tuffy, supra note 37; Bryant v. Bryant, infra note 59. This view was developed by Ames, Lectures on Legal History, 1913, "Can a Murderer Acquire Title by His Crime and Keep it?" 310–322. See also Restatement, Restitution § 187; notes, 8 N.Y.U.L.Q.R. 492, 495, 29 Mich.L.R. 745, 751. Cf. Matter of Sparks, 172 Misc. 642, 15 N.Y.S.2d 926, 1939, discussed at length in Reppy, The Slayer's Bounty—in New York, 20 N.Y.U.L.Q.R. 270, 424.

40 Formerly Professor Page treated the subject on the chapter on Con-

the constructive trust doctrine seems equally applicable to the cases of both will and intestacy. In the few decided cases involving the will situation, it is held that the guilty beneficiary is not entitled to the testator's bounty.[41] It should be noticed, however, that these cases were not decided in jurisdictions which adhere to the majority rule in intestacy cases permitting the heir to take.

Public sentiment has not regarded with favor the decisions enabling the murderer to inherit his victim's property. A large number of states [42] have passed statutes to prevent this result. Much of this legislation was brought about by decisions permitting such an heir to take. Unfortunately many of these laws were framed with the facts of a single case in mind.[43] Thus, in some jurisdictions it is provided that the heir who "murders" his ancestor is barred. Under such a statute it has been held that one who is guilty of manslaughter only may take.[44] Again some of the statutes require conviction of the crime to work a forfeiture. In these jurisdictions it is held that if the murderer prevents conviction by suicide, his estate or his heirs are entitled to the property.[45] The statutes are also strictly construed with reference to the sorts of property interests which are forfeited. Unless

ditions. Page, Wills, 1926, § 1155. Cf. 1 Page, Wills, 3d ed. §§ 231, 232, and see Re Medaini, [1927] 4 D.L.R. 1137.

41 Riggs v. Palmer, 115 N.Y. 506, 22 N.E. 1888, 5 L.R.A. 340, 12 Am. St.Rep. 819, 1889; In re Wilkins' Estate, 192 Wis. 111, 211 N.W. 652, 51 A.L.R. 1106, 1927, noted, 26 Mich. L.R. 947, 11 Minn.L.Rev. 680; In re Hall, [1914] P. 1. The constructive trust theory has been applied in the testacy cases. Whitney v. Lott, 134 N.J.Eq. 586, 36 A.2d 888, 1944; Ellerson v. Westcott, 148 N.Y. 149, 42 N.E. 540, 1896. But In re Wilkins' Estate, supra, appears to assume that no title passes to the murderer. See Rasor v. Rasor, 173 S.C. 365, 175 S.E. 545, noted, 21 Va.L.R. 232 (statute).

42 See Bordwell, Statute Law of Wills, 14 Ia.L.R. 304, 305; Wade, Acquisition of Property by Wilfully Killing Another—A Statutory Solution, 49 Harv.L.R. 715; notes, 46 Dick.L.R. 99, 29 Mich.L.R. 745, 749, 22 Temple L.Q. 443, 43 Yale L.J. 164.

43 Cf. the carefully drafted provisions of a civil law code. Louisiana—LSA—C.C. arts. 966–975.

44 Re Estate of Kirby, 162 Cal. 91, 121 P. 370, 39 L.R.A.,N.S., 1088, 1912. Cf. Hamblin v. Marchant, 103 Kan. 508, 175 P. 678, 6 A.L.R. 1403, 1918; Id., 104 Kan. 689, 180 P. 811, 6 A.L.R. 1403, 1919 (under statute providing for conviction of the killing). See also In re Lysholm's Estate, 79 Cal.App.2d 467, 179 P.2d 833, 1947.

45 Bruns v. Cope, 182 Ind. 289, 105 N.E. 471, 1914; Hogg v. Whitham, 120 Kan. 341, 242 P. 1021, 1926; In re Tarlo's Estate, 315 Pa. 321, 172 A. 139, 1934, criticized, 33 Mich.L.R. 446 and also noted, 44 Yale L.J. 164, 20 Iowa L.R. 524, 83 U. of Pa.L.R. 97. See Smith v. Todd, 155 S.C. 323, 152 S.E. 506, 70 A.L.R. 1529, 1930.

the particular kind of interest comes clearly within the terms of the legislation the murderer is entitled thereto.[46]

When the murderer is denied the property of his victim, as is now usually the case either by statute or by decision, what becomes of the property? An Oregon case held that the murderer's child, who was the grandchild of the slain man, could not take as he was not the heir of his grandfather in the lifetime of the murderer.[47] Inconsistently the same court held later that the deceased's sister took in a contest with the state claiming by escheat.[48] In effect, these holdings work corruption of blood. A better result was reached in a Kentucky case which allowed the grandchild to take as if his parent, the slayer, were dead.[49] Of course the spouse of the murderer, or one who can claim only from the latter, has no right to the estate of the victim.[50]

*Murder of One Joint Tenant by Other Joint Tenant*

In case of a tenancy in common, the killer should neither lose his moiety, nor be entitled to the interest of the slain co-tenant by survivorship.[51] Where the tenancy is joint and there are rights of survivorship, the problem becomes acute. This question is not one of succession,[52] though it is reasonable to expect that a court will follow here its general position on the matter of the slayer's right to take by descent or will from his victim.[53] However, many of the statutes designed to deny the right in case

46 In re Mertes' Estate, 181 Ind. 478, 104 N.E. 753, 1914; Kuhn v. Kuhn, 125 Iowa, 449, 101 N.W. 151, 2 Ann.Cas. 657, 1904; In re Emerson's Estate, 191 Iowa 900, 183 N. W. 327, 1921; Beddingfield v. Estill & Newman, 118 Tenn. 39, 100 S.W. 108, 9 L.R.A.,N.S., 640, 11 Ann.Cas. 904, 1907. See, also, Harrison v. Moncravie, 264 F. 776, C.C.A.Okl. 1930, for another example of strict construction where the killing was in one state and the deceased's land was in another, both states having statutes forbidding the killer to take. Cf. Garner v. Phillips, supra note 39.

47 In re Norton's Estate, 175 Or. 115, 151 P.2d 719, 156 A.L.R. 617, 1944.

48 In re Norton's Estate, 177 Or. 342, 162 P.2d 379, 161 A.L.R. 439, 1945.

49 Bates v. Wilson, 313 Ky. 572, 232 S.W.2d 837, 1950. See also Ohio Gen. Code § 10503–17; Blanks v. Jiggetts, 192 Va. 337, 64 S.E.2d 809, 24 A.L.R.2d 1114, 1951; Restatement, Restitution § 187(b). But cf. note, 39 Ky.L.J. 496, favoring position of the Norton case, supra note 47.

50 Price v. Hitaffer, supra note 38; Perry v. Strawbridge, supra note 37.

51 Bierbrauer v. Moran, 244 App. Div. 87, 297 N.Y.S. 176, 1935.

52 See supra § 28.

53 The cases infra notes 55, 58–60 are in states, which, on non-statutory grounds, refuse to permit the slayer to take.

of succession do not cover the joint tenancy situation, in which case the question must be determined on a non-statutory basis.[54]

There is a conflict in the few cases dealing with an ordinary joint tenancy; it has been held that the murderer forfeits all interest to the representatives of the victim,[55] and on the other hand he has been given the entire interest as the survivor of the tenancy.[56] Most of the decisions involve a tenancy by the entireties, which cannot ordinarily be terminated by the sole act of either spouse and which under modern law entitles each spouse to half of the income during their joint lifetimes. A variety of results have been reached. It has been held that the murderer is entitled to the entire interest as the survivor,[57] while other cases have awarded half the property to the murderer and half to the heirs of his slain spouse.[58] Most of the entirety cases have applied the doctrine of constructive trust, however. In doing so the courts have usually presumed that the slain spouse would have been the survivor in normal course, or at least have treated the situation as if he would have survived.[59] A New York decision imposed a trust for the entire interest in favor of the representatives of the slain spouse,[60] but this is subject to the objection that his own vested life interest is forfeited for his crime. A more reasonable application of the constructive trust doctrine

54 Oleoff v. Hodnapp, infra note 56; Wenker v. Landon, 161 Or. 265, 88 P.2d 971, 1939, noted, 24 Minn.L.R. 430; Beddingfield v. Estill & Newman, 118 Tenn. 39, 100 S.W. 108, 109 L.R.A.,N.S., 640, 11 Ann.Cas. 904, 1906. Cf. Garner v. Phillips, 229 N.C. 160, 47 S.E.2d 845, 1948.

55 In re Santourian's Estate, 125 Misc. 668, 212 N.Y.S. 116, 1925, noted, 26 Col.L.R. 482. See infra note 60.

56 Oleff v. Hodapp, 129 Ohio St. 432, 195 N.E. 838, 98 A.L.R. 764, 1935, noted, 16 B.U.L.R. 248, 4 Fordham L.R. 510, 1 Ohio St.L.R. 131, 42 W.Va. L.Q. 241.

57 Wenker v. Landon and Beddingfield v. Estill & Newman, both supra note 54.

58 Barnett v. Couey, 224 Mo.App. 913, 27 S.W.2d 757, 1930, noted, 44 Harv.L.R. 125, 79 U. of Pa.L.R. 100, 43 Law Series, Mo.Bull. 31; Grose v. Holland, 357 Mo. 874, 211 S.W.2d 464, 1948, noted, 20 Tenn.L.R. 697, 27 Tex.L.R. 551.

59 See Colton v. Wade, 80 A.2d 923, Del.Ch.1951; Van Alstyne v. Tuffy, infra note 60, though victim was nine years older than the slayer; Bryant v. Bryant, 193 N.C. 372, 137 S.E. 188, 51 A.L.R. 1100 (victim younger); Neiman v. Hurff, 11 N.J. 55, 93 A.2d 345, 1952, in effect overruling Sherman v. Weber, 113 N.J. Eq. 451, 167 A. 517, 1933, where the victim was older the trust was made to terminate at end of victim's expectancy. See Ames, supra note 39 at 321; Restatement, Restitution § 188; notes, 44 Harv.L.R. 125, 8 N.Y. U.L.Q.R. 492.

60 Van Alstyne v. Tuffy, 103 Misc. 455, 169 N.Y.S. 173, 1918, noted, 16 Mich.L.R. 561, 27 Yale L.J. 964. See supra note 55.

would be to allow the slayer to retain a half interest for his life, free of the trust which is otherwise imposed in favor of the representatives of the slain spouse.[61]

*Murder of Insured by Beneficiary of Policy*

Both because of the policy against allowing one to take advantage of his own wrong, and because of the principle of insurance law that one cannot recover for a loss which he has intentionally caused, a beneficiary who has murdered the insured cannot recover on the policy.[62] Usually the insurer cannot defeat payment of the policy on this ground and the insured's personal representative can recover the full amount.[63] By the prevailing and better doctrine the guilty beneficiary is not entitled to share in the proceeds so recovered by the estate though he is one of the distributees.[64] However, there are some cases to the contrary.[65]

[61] See Colton v. Wade, supra note 59; Sherman v. Weber, supra note 59; In re King's Estate, 261 Wis. 266, 52 N.W.2d 885, 1952; Neiman v. Hurff, supra note 59. In Bryant v. Bryant, supra note 59, the husband was given a life estate in the entire property since under North Carolina law he was entitled to the entire rents and profits during the joint lifetimes of the spouses. See also Restatement, Restitution § 188.

[62] Beck v. West Coast Life Ins. Co., 38 Cal.2d 643, 241 P.2d 544, 26 A.L.R. 2d 979, 1952; Schmidt v. Northern Life Ass'n, 112 Iowa 41, 83 N.W. 800, 51 L.R.A. 141, 84 Am.St.Rep. 323, 1900; Smith v. Todd, 155 S.C. 323, 152 S.E. 506, 70 A.L.R. 1529, 1930; Johnston v. Metropolitan Life Insurance Co., 85 W.Va. 70, 100 S.E. 865, 7 A.L.R. 823, 1919, noted, 18 Mich. L.R. 430; Mutual Life Ins. Co. v. Armstrong, 117 U.S. 591, 6 S.Ct. 877, 29 L.Ed. 997, 1886; Cleaver v. Mutual Reserve Fund Life Ass'n [1892], 1 Q.B. 147. See generally Vance on Insurance, 3d ed., 1951, § 117.

[63] Cleaver v. Mutual Reserve Fund Life Ass'n, supra note 62; Slocum v. Metropolitan Life Ins. Co., 245 Mass. 565, 139 N.E. 816, 27 A.L.R. 1517, 1923; Moore v. Prudential Ins. Co. of America, 342 Pa. 570, 21 A.2d 42, 1941, noted, 8 Pitt.L.R. 128, 3 Wash. & L.L.R. 137. But see State v. Phoenix Mutual Life Ins. Co., 114 W.Va. 109, 170 S.E. 909, 91 A.L.R. 1482, 1933, noted, 2 U. of Chi.L.R. 148, 18 Minn.L.R. 599, 40 W.Va.L.R. 188.

[64] Illinois Bankers Life Ass'n v. Collins, 341 Ill. 548, 173 N.E. 465, 1931, noted, 9 N.Y.U.L.Q.R. 98; Slocum v. Metropolitan Life Ins. Co., supra note 63; De Zotell v. Mutual Life Ins. Co., supra note 37; Smith v. Todd, 155 S.C. 323, 152 S.E. 506, 70 A.L.R. 1529, 1930. See note, 17 Minn. L.R. 759.

Of course a state, in which the guilty distributee cannot share in other assets of the deceased, would deny participation in the proceeds of the insurance. See supra note 37–42. Even in other states the courts might well impose a constructive trust in order to carry out the principles stated supra at note 62.

[65] Moore v. Prudential Ins. Co. of America, supra note 63; Murcheson v. Murcheson, 203 S.W. 423, Tex Civ. App. 423, as to which see notes, 20 Tex.L.R. 237, 27 id. 551, 552.

# CHAPTER 4

# TESTAMENTARY CHARACTER AND WILL SUBSTITUTES

Sec.
38. Extra-Legal Devices.
39. Life Insurance.
40. Survivorship Interests.
41. Bank Account Trusts.
42. Living Trusts
43. Deeds.
44. Contractual Instruments.
45. Gifts.
46. Sham Wills.
47. Letters as Wills.
48. Contracts to Make Wills.
49. Joint and Mutual Wills.

## EXTRA-LEGAL DEVICES

**38. The extra-legal devices which are used to obviate the execution of a will or the judicial administration of one's estate frequently fail because the arrangement cannot be supported on any valid theory of law.**

If the provisions of the intestate laws coincide with one's desires as to who should share his property at his death, there is no purpose in making a will except to designate a particular person as personal representative, or perhaps to excuse the latter from giving a bond.[1] However, the owner of property often wishes to dispose of his property in some different manner from that provided in the statute of descent and distribution. This may be accomplished within the limitations suggested in the previous chapter, by the execution of a will in the manner prescribed by law. By so doing the owner may secure for his lifetime the advantages of secrecy of his plan of disposition, complete enjoyment of his property including freedom of alienation, and the privileges of revoking the will and setting up a new plan by later testamentary act.

Notwithstanding these benefits many persons do not believe in wills and avoid making them. A superstitious prejudice against wills is found in many persons past middle age. Ap-

[1] See infra § 147.

parently they think that testamentary preparation for disposition of their property at their death may somehow hasten their demise. While this attitude is a foolish one, it frequently cannot be altered by any amount of sound advice. Some of the dislike of wills is based upon the knowledge that expense and trouble are incurred in the process of probate and administration and that delays occur before the beneficiaries are permitted to enjoy the testator's bounty. It should be noticed that with the exceptions of the distractions connected with will contests, the same objections apply to intestate estates.[2] Property owners frequently believe that they can prevent the collection of their debts and inheritance taxes by neglecting to make wills and using certain devices to prevent administration under the intestate laws. The schemes are often without sound theoretical basis and frequently fail in practice. They may entail, because of litigation, a greater diminution of decedent's property than subjection to the ordinary course of testate or intestate succession. On the other hand, some of the devices used are well recognized in the law and may fit the needs and desires of the individual property owner, though most of them involve the surrender of some of the control that the owner could have retained in his lifetime had he chosen to allow his property to pass by testate or intestate succession.[3]

### *The Safe Deposit Device*

One scheme is to give the person desired to be benefited access to a safe deposit box containing money, jewels or negotiable securities. The plan is that upon the death of the owner, the other person will go to the box and take charge of the contents. This is an extra-legal, if not an illegal, method of procedure. If discovered, a personal representative may be appointed to administer the property for the benefit of creditors and distributees of the deceased. Severe penalties may be incurred for evasion of inheritance taxes. The transaction does not constitute a gift to the intended beneficiary as the required delivery is lacking. If

[2] A study in Wisconsin shows that there is little difference between testate and intestate estate in the costs of administration except in very small estates where the costs are smaller where there is a will. [1950] Wis.L.R. 393. This may be due to the fact that wills usually dispense with giving of a bond, the expense of which is always present in an intestate estate.

[3] For a functional study of the subject matter covered in the present chapter, see Gulliver and Tilson, Classification of Gratuitous Transfers, 51 Yale L.J. 1. See also note, 48 Dick.L.R. 22, for treatment of the Pennsylvania situation.

the box is rented by a contract between the deposit company and the decedent, any appointment by the latter of an agent to open the box is revoked by death of the principal.[4]

Even if the contract is a joint one, it is doubtful whether the deposit company is authorized to give access to the survivor though some states have passed legislation permitting this to be done.[5] Obviously this scheme can only be applied to certain non-bulky types of property and it is subject to the additional drawback of requiring absolute confidence in the intended beneficiary. Usually the box, whether in decedent's or in joint names, cannot be opened except in the presence of the state tax authorities.

## LIFE INSURANCE

**39. Both insurance policies upon one's life and insurance trusts of such policies are valid non-testamentary arrangements though the insured retains the right to change the beneficiary.**

By investing in life insurance policies payable to designated beneficiaries, one may reduce the amount of his estate which is subject to administration. This plan like the preceding one and most of those following does not entirely dispense with administration for ordinarily a person does not wish to, and indeed cannot, reduce his entire wealth to insurance. Within the limits of a feasible amount so invested, life insurance presents perhaps the most satisfactory method of limiting the estate which is subject to probate and administration. The insured may keep the amount and the beneficiaries secret from the world in general, can cash the policy or borrow against it or change the beneficiaries at will, and the latter come into enjoyment upon his death without court proceedings. Unless creditors can show fraud upon them, the proceeds cannot be reached in the hands of the beneficiary.[1] It is clear that the insurance policy is not

[4] Mitchell v. Weaver, 242 Mass. 331, 136 N.E. 166, 1922. See Clarke v. Commerce State & Savings Bank, 68 Colo. 401, 189 P. 842, 1920; In re Brown's Estate, 343 Pa. 230, 22 A.2d 821, 1941 (delivery of key to box).

[5] Louisiana—LSA–R.S. 6:33; Virginia Code, 1950 § 6–264. As to the possibility of creating a right to the contents in the survivor, see infra § 40, notes 17–22, § 44, notes 15–16.

[1] Gurnett v. Mutual Life Ins. Co. of New York, 356 Ill. 612, 191 N.E. 250, 1934, noted, 19 Minn.L.R. 135 (life insurance trust); Vance on Insurance, 3d Ed., §§ 108, 124; Hanna, Some Legal Aspects of Life Insurance Trusts, 78 U. of Pa.L.R. 346, 349–355. See Pierson, Recent Legislation Preserving Insurance Proceeds for Beneficiaries, 16 A.B.A.Jo. 23; note, 84 U. of Pa.L.R. 236; infra §

testamentary and does not require execution in the form of a will, or probate in order to be effective. The beneficiary obtains his interest upon the theory of a contract or a trust for his benefit.[2] However, insurance on the decedent's life payable to his estate, or to individual beneficiaries to the extent that it was paid for or owned by the decedent, is part of his gross estate for the purpose of the Federal Estate Tax.[3]

*Insurance Trusts*

In recent years insurance trusts have increased in popularity.[4] These are devices by which insurance policies are made payable to third parties or the insurers as trustees. The terms of the trust are expressed in the policy or in a separate instrument. Sometimes the settlement is funded by a transfer of sufficient property to the trustee to pay the premiums.[5] These arrangements have been sustained against various objections including the contention that they are in the nature of testamentary dispositions because the insured persons reserve many rights of control over the policies and the trusts. Insurance trusts seem no more objectionable than ordinary life insurance transactions in this regard. In both cases the insurance is not deemed to be an asset of the insured's estate unless it is payable to his estate. The same strong public policy of favoring dependent persons causes the courts to sustain both life insurance policies and insurance trusts as non-testamentary transactions. This factor leads the courts to draw a rather artificial distinction between the interests of the beneficiary or trustee which is regarded as a substantial one, and the shadowy hope which the legatee has in his

116. Cf. In re Kenin's Trust Estate, 343 Pa. 549, 23 A.2d 837, 1942.

2 Kansas City Life Ins. Co. v. Rainey, 353 Mo. 477, 182 S.W.2d 624, 155 A.L.R. 168, 1944 (though it was an "investment annuity policy" and insured was entitled to return of the sum in his lifetime). See also Mutual Benefit Life Ins. Co. v. Ellis, 125 F.2d 127, 138 A.L.R. 1478, C.C.A.N.Y.1942, and infra note 7; Toulouse v. New York Life Ins. Co., 40 Wash.2d 538, 245 P.2d 205, 1952. Cf. Hall v. Mutual Life Ins. Co., 201 Misc. 203, 109 N.Y.S.2d 646, 1952, noted, 21 U. of Cin.L.R. 320 (designation by beneficiary to take on his death held testamentary); see N.Y.Per.Prop.L. § 24a. The Hall case, supra, was reversed in 282 App.Div. 203, 122 N.Y.S. 2d 239, 1953.

3 26 U.S.C.A. § 811(g); see note, 34 Mich.L.R. 1207; infra §§ 125, 147.

4 Vance on Insurance, 3d Ed., § 119; see note, 50 Harv.L.R. 511.

5 Ibid.; Van Hecke, Insurance Trusts—the Insurer as Trustee, 7 N.C.L.R. 21; Fraser, Personal Life Insurance Trusts, 16 Corn.L.Q. 19.

testator's lifetime.[6] The former are not regarded as testamentary and accordingly judicial administration is not required.[7]

*Facility of Payment Clause*

One of the modern devices used to avoid administration of the estates of wage earners is the issuance of industrial life insurance policies containing a facility of payment clause. The latter generally provides that the insurer may discharge itself by paying the amount of the policy to any of the insured's relatives by blood or marriage or to other persons appearing equitably entitled thereto.[8] While the relatives have not generally been permitted to recover the amount of the policy by action,[9] and the option to make use of the clause has been held to be in the insurer, the latter usually exercises this option and much burdensome administration is thereby obviated.[10] However, the payee may be required to pay the amount over to the personal representative if one is appointed.[11]

6 Fidelity Trust Co. v. Union Nat. Bank of Pittsburgh, 313 Pa. 467, 169 A. 209, 1933. See Grahame, The Insurance Trust as Non-Testamentary Disposition, 18 Minn.L.R. 391; Fraser, Personal Life Insurance Trusts, 16 Corn.L.Q. 19, 30, 31; Phillips, The Testamentary Character of Personal Unfunded Life Insurance Trusts, 82 U. of Pa.L.R. 700; notes, 46 Harv.L.R. 818, 10 St. John's L.R. 291.

7 Sigal v. Hartford Nat. Bank & Trust Co., 119 Conn. 570, 177 A. 742, 1935; In re Albert Anderson Life Ins. Trust, 67 S.D. 393, 293 N.W. 527, 1940. See also Legrande v. Legrande, 178 S.C. 230, 182 S.E. 432, 102 A.L.R. 582, 1935 and authorities supra note 2.

8 See note, 32 Col.L.R. 1185; annotation, 166 A.L.R. 10.

9 Lewis v. Metropolitan Life Ins. Co., 178 Mass. 52, 59 N.E. 439, 86 Am. St.Rep. 463, 1901; Williard v. Prudential Ins. Co. of America, 276 Pa. 427, 120 A. 461, 28 A.L.R. 1348, 1923; Metropolitan Life Ins. Co. v. Chappell, 151 Tenn. 299, 269 S.W. 21, 1925. From these cases it appears that the personal representative has a right of action. But see Minuto v. Metropolitan Life Ins. Co., 58 R.I. 71, 191 A. 117, 135 A.L.R. 953, 1937.

10 See note, 32 Col.L.R. 1185; infra § 103.

11 Lutostanski v. Lutostanski, 120 Conn. 471, 181 A. 533, 1935; In re Caroleo's Estate, 103 N.Y.S.2d 776, Sur.1951. See annotation, 166 A.L.R. 78–85.

## SURVIVORSHIP INTERESTS

**40. Although joint estates are now disfavored they may often be created in both real and personal property, thereby permitting the surviving tenant to take without judicial administration of the property.**

**Bank accounts payable to the survivor of the depositor and another have been held to create joint estates on the theory of a gift, trust or contract. As all three justifications of a joint estate are somewhat inconsistent with the attempts to permit withdrawals by the depositor but not by the donee, it is preferable to disregard the joint property hypothesis and consider the matter from the standpoint of a contract between the depositor and the bank for the benefit of the donee as third party beneficiary in case he survives.**

Another means of dispensing with the necessity of a will and administration of the estate is to create some form of joint estate or right of survivorship between the intended beneficiary and the donor. Upon the death of the latter the former takes the joint property by operation of law without legal proceedings.[1] At common law a grant to two or more persons was presumed to create a joint estate with the right of survivorship.[2] This survivorship concept is not known to the civil law.[3] It has been recognized that the doctrine is a harsh one as applied to the heirs of the joint tenants, and that it often operates to evade the claims of creditors.[4] Statutes are frequently found, which reverse the common-law presumption that a joint estate rather than an estate in common is created, or deny the right of survivorship unless it is clearly expressed in the instrument, or purport to abolish the joint estate or the right of survivorship generally.[5] However, even under legislation of the latter type it is usually held that the right of survivorship can be created by contract.[6] Indeed in almost every jurisdiction the survivor-

[1] See supra § 28.

[2] 2 Bl.Com. 180.

[3] Amos and Walton, Introduction to French Laws 112.

[4] Martin v. Smith, 5 Bin.(Pa.) 16, 6 Am.Dec. 395, 1812; Noble v. Teeple, 58 Kan. 398, 49 P. 598, 1897; see notes, 23 Harv.L.Rev. 214, 22 Cal.L.R. 450, 23 Corn.L.Q. 598.

[5] Stephenson, Joint Ownership of Property, 25 Trust Bull. No. 1, 25.

[6] Shroff v. Deaton, 220 S.W.2d 489, Tex.Civ.App.1949; see Fawcett v. Fawcett, 191 N.C. 679, 132 S.E. 796, 1926; note, 18 Tex.L.R. 232.

ship feature can still be employed with reference to both real and personal property.[7]

About one-third of the states retain the common-law estate by the entireties as to real property and most of these as to personal property also.[8] This is a species of joint estate between husband and wife with right of survivorship and it secures to them many of the results gained by the execution of mutual wills without the accompanying necessity for probate and administration. From their standpoint there is the added advantage that the property so owned is not subject to the debts of the deceased tenant.[9] On the other hand this is an argument for the abolishment of the tenancy by the entireties; other objections to it are the uncertainties as to what language will create the estate and the indestructibility of the estate without mutual consent in the event of matrimonial discord.[10] These are valid reasons for denying to the spouses any special treatment not accorded to ordinary joint tenants but of course they must be addressed to the legislatures rather than the courts.

It is sometimes supposed that, in addition to the convenience of the full, immediate and automatic vesting of ownership in the survivor upon the death of the first tenant, there may be a tax saving on account of the joint tenancy arrangement. This is true under some inheritance tax laws of the early type.[11] However, there is no saving under the present Federal Estate Tax Law or under state laws patterned thereon for the reason that property which the decedent owns in joint tenancy with another is deemed part of his estate for estate tax purposes.[12] Indeed a

[7] Supra note 5.

[8] Supra note 5; Niles, Abolish Tenancy by the Entirety, 79 Trusts & Estates 366.

[9] Scrogin v. Dickison, 57 Ind.App. 353, 107 N.E. 86, 1930; Bloomfield v. Brown, 67 R.I. 452, 25 A.2d 354, 141 A.L.R. 170, 1942; Ritchie, Tenancies by the Entirety in Real Property with Particular Reference to the Law of Virginia, 28 Va.L.R. 608; notes, 29 Mich.L.R. 788, 89 A.L.R. 499. However, if it can be established that the estate was created in fraud of the husband's creditors the latter may subject the property to their claims. Splaine v. Morissey, 282 Mass. 217, 184 N.E. 670, 1933, noted, 13 B.U.L.R. 534; First State Bank of Milford v. Wallace, 201 Mich. 673, 167 N.W. 887, 1918.

[10] See Niles, supra note 8.

[11] Palmer v. Treasurer & Receiver General, 222 Mass. 263, 110 N.E. 283, L.R.A.1916C, 677, 1915.

[12] 26 U.S.C.A. § 811(e). As to gift tax liability, see Commissioner v. Hart, 100 F.2d 269, C.C.A. 10th, 1939; Gift Tax Regulation 108 § 86.2(a)4–6. See Rudick, Federal Tax Problems Relating to Property Owned in Joint Tenancy and Tenancy by the Entireties, 4 Tax L.R. 3; Marshall, Joint Tenancy, Taxwise and Otherwise, 40 Cal.L.R. 501; infra §§ 125, 147.

joint tenancy may increase tax liability in certain cases, either because a second tax may be payable upon the death of the survivor, or because if the tenant who contributes the subject matter of the joint tenancy happens to be the survivor the property will be deemed part of the estate of the other tenant for tax purpose unless the donor-survivor is able to offer satisfactory proof of his own contribution.[13] Of course when the total estates of the joint tenants are small, estate tax considerations are non-existent or negligible. A recent study shows a tendency to increase the use of joint estates and this is particularly true in case of persons of modest estates.[14]

### *Partnership Agreements*

When the members of a partnership so desire they may provide by the partnership agreement that upon the death of a member his interest shall become the property of the survivors. Such arrangements have usually been sustained as contractual dispositions and are not regarded as testamentary transactions requiring the formality and procedure of wills.[15] This result is possible because of the co-ownership of the partnership property by the members.

### *Joint Safe-deposit Box*

The fact that a safe deposit box is leased jointly to two or more persons or that the terms of the lease give them joint access does not constitute them joint owners of the contents.[16] Furthermore, even written evidence that the property was intended to belong to the survivor is not by itself effective for this purpose,[17] though some cases have held that the joint box arrangement is evidence

13 Robinson v. Commissioner, 63 F. 2d 652, C.C.A. 6th, 1933.

14 Supra note 5.

15 Hale v. Wilmarth, 274 Mass. 186, 174 N.E. 232, 73 A.L.R. 980, 1931; Green v. Whaley, 271 Mo. 636, 197 S. W. 355, 1917; In re Mildrum's Estate, 108 Misc. 114, 177 N.Y.S. 563, 1919. Cf. In re Eisenlohr's Estate, 258 Pa. 438, 102 A. 117, 1917. See note, 43 Col.L.R. 260. But see Gomez v. Higgins, 130 Ala. 493, 30 So. 417, 1901, where an agreement also attempting to designate the disposition of the property upon the death of the surviving partner was adjudged testamentary; In re Gardner's Will, 66 N.Y.S.2d 256, Sur.1946. And compare attempts to make this sort of an agreement when the parties are not partners, infra § 44, notes 15, 16.

16 California Trust Co. v. Bennett, 33 Cal.2d 694, 204 P.2d 324, 1949; Richards v. Richards, 141 N.J.Eq. 579, 58 A.2d 544, 1948; Wohleber's Estate, 320 Pa. 83, 181 A. 479, 101 A.L.R. 829, 1935.

17 In re Wilson's Estate, 404 Ill. 207, 88 N.E.2d 662, 14 A.L.R.2d 940, 1949; Trautz v. Lemp, 329 Mo. 580, 46 S.W.2d 135, 1932.

of a gift by the decedent to the surviving lessee.[18] Some rental agreements provide that the contents shall be the joint property of the lessees and there are cases which accept these arrangements at their face value.[19] This is a perilous doctrine for a momentary deposit in the "magic box" might make the object joint property. Furthermore, the rental agreement is usually prepared by the safe deposit-box company on its printed form and is designed for its protection; often it does not represent the true understanding of the lessees.[20] For these reasons, it is reasonable to deny that a joint tenancy can be created by this method.[21] At any rate it should be permissible to show that no joint tenancy of the contents was intended in the particular case.[22]

*Bank Accounts Payable to Survivor*

In most states there are statutes which facilitate the use of joint bank accounts in order to pass the account to survivor of the named persons.[23] This is ordinarily done through a deposit of the money in the name of the depositor, "and" or "or" the intended beneficiary, usually with words indicating an intention that the whole is payable to the survivor. Without the latter the beneficiary is usually denied the right to take,[24] but if the proper

18 Nelson v. Spotts, 114 Colo. 72, 162 P.2d 224, 1945; Lowry v. Florida Nat. Bank of Jacksonville, 42 So.2d 368, Fla.1949.

19 Brown v. Navarre, 64 Ariz. 262, 169 P.2d 85, 1946; In re Gaines' Estate, 15 Cal.2d 255, 100 P.2d 1055, 1940; Duling v. Duling's Estate, 211 Miss. 465, 50 So.2d 39, 1951.

20 See In re Horn's Estate, 102 Cal. App.2d 635, 228 P.2d 99, 1951.

21 See note, 32 Cal.L.R. 301; 1944 Annual Surv.Am.L. 849; 1949 id. 741.

22 Black v. Black, 199 Ark. 609, 135 S.W.2d 837, 1940; Clevidence v. Mercantile Home Bank & Trust Co., 355 Mo. 904, 199 S.W.2d 1, 1947.

23 See Stephenson, Joint Ownership of Property with Right of Survivorship, 25 Trust Bull. No. 1, 25, showing that some states also have statutes regarding joint ownership of stock and building and loan shares. See Gugle v. Gugle, 75 N.E.2d 808, Ohio Prob.1948; In re Vance's Estate, 149 Neb. 220, 30 N.W.2d 677, 1948 (no statute). Cf. Strout v. Burgess, 144 Me. 263, 68 A.2d 241, 12 A.L.R.2d 939, 1949, noted, 48 Mich.L.R. 1034. As to statutes regarding joint bank deposits, see also note, 32 Ill.L.R. 57, 63, and infra notes 39 to 42.

24 Denigan v. Hibernia Sav. & Loan Soc., 127 Cal. 137, 59 P. 389, 1899; Engelbrecht v. Engelbrecht, 323 Ill. 208, 153 N.E. 827, 1926; Brodrick v. O'Connor, 271 Mass. 240, 171 N.E. 479, 1930; Godwin v. Godwin, 141 Miss. 633, 107 So. 13, 1926; Commercial Trust Co. v. White, 99 N.J.Eq. 119, 132 A. 761, 1926; Daly v. Pacific Savings & Loan Ass'n, 154 Wash. 249, 282 P. 60, 1929. It has been held that where the parties are husband and wife words of survivorship are not necessary to create survivorship. First Nat. Bank of Birmingham v. Lawrence, 212 Ala. 45, 101 So. 663, 1924; Holyoke Nat. Bank v. Bailey,

precautions are taken the desired effect of survivorship can be obtained in most states even in absence of statutory authorization.[25] However, without implicit statutory provision it is necessary that the survivorship arrangement be established by some nontestamentary means known to the law. If the transaction creates no interest in the intended donee until the donor's death and is revocable by the latter until that time, it will be deemed testamentary.[26] In that event the instrument cannot be given effect unless it meets the formal requirements for a will and is probated.

In order to avoid probate and administration, it is often urged that a joint estate in the account has been created. The suggested justifications for this result are: (1) gift, (2) trust, (3) contract. There are serious objections to the gift theory, viz., that the facts do not indicate the intention or delivery requisites for a valid gift. Usually the donor has reserved sole, or at least joint, control over the deposit including the right of withdrawal by retaining possession of the bank book or by express stipulation. These things militate against the presence of the necessary elements of a gift. When the donee is given no control the courts usually refuse to sustain the transaction as a gift.[27] If the donee is given the right of withdrawal in the donor's lifetime, there is authority upholding the right of the surviving donee to take by survivorship upon the theory of a gift.[28]

273 Mass. 551, 174 N.E. 230, 1931, noted, 11 B.U.L.R. 423; In re Kane's Estate, 246 N.Y. 498, 159 N.E. 410, 1928. See also Burns v. Nolette, 83 N.H. 489, 144 A. 848, 67 A.L.R. 1051, 1929; note, 9 Corn.L.Q. 48; note 40 infra.

25 Beach v. Holland, 172 Or. 396, 142 P.2d 990, 149 A.L.R. 866, 1943; see Stephenson, supra note 23; note, 32 Ill.L.R. 57.

26 Onofrey v. Wolliver, 351 Pa. 18, 40 A.2d 35, 155 A.L.R. 1074, 1944; see also cases infra note 27.

27 Clark v. Bridges, 163 Ga. 542, 136 S.E. 444, 1927; Garland's Appeal, 126 Me. 84, 136 A. 459, 1927; McKenna v. McKenna, 260 Mass. 481, 157 N.E. 517, 1927; Dover Cooperative Bank v. Tobin's Estate, 86 N.H. 209, 166 A. 247, 1933; Marshall & Ilsley Bank v. Voigt, 214 Wis. 27, 252 N.W. 355, 1934. And see In re Crist's Estate, 106 Pa. Super. 571, 162 A. 478, 1932. Contra: First Nat. Bank v. Mulich, 83 Colo. 518, 266 P. 1110, 1928. See, also, Bedirian v. Zorian, 287 Mass. 191, 191 N.E. 448, 1936, noted, 48 Harv.L.R. 338, which involves the respective rights of the parties during their joint lifetimes where there had been no delivery of the bank book.

28 Mississippi Valley Trust Co. v. Smith, 320 Mo. 989, 9 S.W.2d 58, 1928 (statute); In re Johnson's Estate, 116 Neb. 686, 218 N.W. 739, 1928 (statute); Burns v. Nolette, 83 N.H. 489, 144 A. 848, 67 A.L.R. 1051, 1929; Mardis v. Steen, 293 Pa. 13, 141 A. 629, 1928; Beach v. Holland, supra note 25 (though donor retained passbook).

The application of the principle of a trust to the situation is more doubtful, for there is generally no express declaration of a trust nor any unequivocal act showing an intent to create one. A trust should not be enforced in case of an imperfect gift simply because there was donative intent.[29] The donor's ability to withdraw is inconsistent with regarding him as a trustee, and the bank cannot be a trustee of its own debt. In addition all rights which the donee has in the donor's lifetime seem to be legal rather than equitable.[30] For example, if the donee has the right of withdrawal, this is a legal claim which may be asserted against the bank. These objections are also pertinent if it is considered that there is a joint equitable estate created by the trust or that there is simply a trust for the donee conditioned upon his survivorship. In spite of all these objections, the courts of a few jurisdictions have upheld the survivorship in cases of deposits in joint names with words of survivorship added, upon the theory that the donor holds the account in trust during his lifetime, and upon his death the legal estate passes to the donee.[31]

A more reasonable ground of sustaining the right of survivorship in the donee is upon the basis of the creation of a joint estate by contract between the donor, the donee and the bank. When both the donor and the donee sign the deposit agreement there seems to be no legal objection to this theory.[32] Difficulty may be

29 Milroy v. Lord, 4 De G.F. & J 264, 45 Eng.Rep. 1185, 1862; Norway Sav. Bank v. Merriam, 88 Me. 146, 33 A. 840, 1895; McGillivray v. First Nat. Bank of Dickinson, 56 N.D. 152, 217 N.W. 150, 1927. In some states, however, the trust theory has been applied. Halstead v. First Savings Bank, 36 Cal.App. 500, 172 P. 613, 1918; Sturgis v. Citizens' Nat. Bank of Pocomoke, 152 Md. 654, 137 A. 378, 1927.

30 See note, 38 Harv.L.R. 243. Cf. Murray v. Gadsen, 197 F.2d 194, C.A. D.C.1952.

31 Halstead v. First Sav. Bank, 36 Cal.App. 500, 172 P. 613, 1918; Ladner v. Ladner, 128 Miss. 75, 90 So. 593, 1922. See note, 11 Cal.L.R. 192, 193. See also, McDevit v. Sponseller, 160 Md. 497, 154 A. 140, 1931 (express declaration of trust in depositor and donee subject to check of either and payable to survivor—survivorship upheld); Dyste v. Farmers & Mechanics Sav. Bank, 179 Minn. 430, 229 N.W. 865, 1930 (express declaration of trustee for donee, trust held valid). Cf. infra § 41.

32 See Cleveland Trust Co. v. Scobie, 114 Ohio St. 241, 151 N.E. 373, 48 A.L.R. 182, 1926; Holt v. Bayles, 85 Utah 364, 39 P.2d 715, 1934; Holyoke Nat. Bank v. Bailey, supra note 24; notes, 11 B.U.L.R. 423, 11 Cal.L.R. 192, 38 Harv.L.R. 243, 8 N.C.L.R. 73, 81 U. of Pa.L.R. 737, 745. Where both parties sign the deposit agreement it has been held that parol evidence is not admissible to show that survivorship was not intended. Matthew v. Moncrief, 77 U.S.App.D.C. 221, 135 F.2d 645, 149 A.L.R. 856, 1943, noted, 6 N.Y.U.Intermural L.R.

encountered where the donee has no part in the transaction. Yet even here the donee's right may be sustained upon the ground that he is a third party beneficiary.[33] However, some difficulty may be incurred in working out this theory where there is a presumption against joint estates and particularly where the latter have been abolished. As to the former, express words of survivorship would seem to dissipate the presumption.[34] Under statutes abolishing joint tenancies, transactions of this sort have been regarded as contractual arrangements not coming within the scope of the legislation.[35] An even more serious objection may be that the ordinary joint bank deposit arrangement differs from an ordinary joint tenancy in that either tenant may withdraw funds from the account.[36] This argument is an embarrassment to the application of the joint estate theory whether deemed created through gift, trust or contract. The joint tenancy must be regarded as a peculiar one, due to the terms of its creation which permit withdrawals by either tenant.[37]

There seems to be a better solution of these difficulties, viz., to consider the matter solely from the standpoint of contract, disregarding the property side of joint tenancy. The bank can be regarded as promising to pay the deposit to the survivor of the donor and the donee, with such right of withdrawal in either, both, or neither, as may be stipulated in the agreement. Some of the cases seem to proceed upon this basis.[38] It is often difficult

107. See also notes, 28 Cal.L.R. 224, 43 Ill.L.R. 872.

33 Reder v. Reder, 312 Ill. 209, 143 N.E. 418, 1925; Chippendale v. North Adams Sav. Bank, 222 Mass. 499, 111 N.E. 371, 1916. See First Nat. Bank v. Mulich, supra note 27. Cf. Reap v. Wyoming Valley Trust Co., 300 Pa. 156, 150 A. 465, 1930 (acceptance by donee of joint tenancy presumed).

34 See Burns v. Nolette, 83 N.H. 489, 144 A. 848, 67 A.L.R. 1051, 1929. But see Garland's Appeal, 126 Me. 84, 136 A. 459, 1927.

35 First Nat. Bank of Birmingham v. Lawrence, 212 Ala. 45, 101 So. 663, 1924; Erwin v. Felter, 283 Ill. 36, 119 N.E. 926, L.R.A.1918E, 776, 1918; Malone v. Sullivan, 136 Kan. 193, 14 P.2d 647, 85 A.L.R. 275, 1932; Foraker v. Kocks, 41 Ohio App. 210, 180 N.E. 743, 1932; Wisner v. Wisner, 82 W.Va. 9, 95 S.E. 802, 1918.

36 Garland's Appeal, 126 Me. 84, 136 A. 459, 1927; McLaughlin v. Cooper's Estate, 128 Conn. 557, 24 A.2d 502, 1942. But see Burns v. Nolette, 83 N.H. 489, 144 A. 848, 67 A.L.R. 1071, 1929. On the other hand a provision that only the depositor may draw has been held to make the transaction testamentary. Onofrey v. Wolliver, supra note 26.

37 See Beach v. Holland, supra note 25, where it is called "an estate analogous to a joint tenancy."

38 Chippendale v. North Adams Savings Bank, supra note 33; New Jersey Title Guarantee & Trust Co. v. Archibald, 91 N.J.Eq. 82, 108 A. 434,

to say whether a decision upholding the right of the survivor is based on this theory, or whether it is considered that a joint estate has been created by contract.

Statutes sometimes declare that a joint tenancy is created, at least presumptively, by the deposit in the names of two or more with right of survivorship stipulated.[39] More often the legislation simply authorizes the bank to pay such deposits to the survivor.[40] Statutes of the latter type are generally held to be for the protection of the bank and are not determinative of contests between the donor's personal representative and the surviving donee.[41] However, these statutes have had some influence in causing the courts to uphold the donee's rights upon the basis of survivorship.[42] Where such a statute exists, controversies do not usually arise between the survivor and the deceased tenant's estate.

Of course if the court refuses to recognize the interest of the surviving donee, the deposit becomes a part of the deceased donor's estate subject to the claims of his creditors. On the other hand, if the survivorship is recognized, the donor's creditors can not reach the fund unless they can show that deposit in the joint names was in fraud of creditors' rights.[43] Funds passing to the

1919; Reder v. Reder, supra note 33. Other cases go on the theory that a joint tenancy was created. Cleveland Trust Co. v. Scobie, 114 Ohio St. 241, 151 N.E. 373, 48 A.L.R. 183, 1926—or a tenancy by entireties. In re Sloan's Estate, 254 Pa. 346, 98 A. 966, 1916. See note 53 Col.L.R. 103, 109.

39 45 Bank Law J. 733, 813, 897. See Houle v. McMillan, 83 Colo. 210, 263 P. 409, 1928; Equitable & Central Trust Co. v. Zdziebko, 260 Mich. 366, 244 N.W. 505, 1932; Ball v. Mercantile Trust Co., 220 Mo.App. 1165, 297 S.W. 415, 1927; Moskowitz v. Marrow, 251 N.Y. 380, 167 N.E. 506, 66 A.L.R. 870, 1929; Winner v. Carroll, 169 Wash. 208, 13 P.2d 450, 1932. In New York the presumption of joint tenancy is conclusive after the death of the depositor. Moskowitz v. Marrow, supra. But see Matter of Yauch, 270 App.Div. 348, 59 N.Y.S.2d 642, 1946. Cf. note, 38 Mich. L.R. 710.

40 45 Bank.L.J. 733, 813, 897. In some jurisdictions the bank is protected even when words of survivorship are not employed in making the deposit. Ibid.

41 Portland Nat. Bank v. Brooks, 126 Me. 251, 137 A. 641, 1927; Godwin v. Godwin, 141 Miss. 633, 107 So. 13, 1926; Gordon v. Toler, 83 N.J. Eq. 25, 89 A. 1020, 1914; Marshall & Ilsley Bank v. Voigt, supra note 27.

42 In re Rehfeld's Estate, 198 Mich. 249, 164 N.W. 372, 1917; Dyste v. Farmers & Mechanics Sav. Bank, 179 Minn. 430, 229 N.W. 865, 1930; In re Johnson's Estate, 116 Neb. 686, 218 N.W. 739, 1928.

43 See Schnur v. Dunker, 38 S.W.2d 282, Mo.App.1931, and supra notes 4, 9. See infra § 116.

survivor are taxable under the Federal Estate Tax Law, and the same is true under the tax laws of some states.[44]

*War Savings Bonds*

The popular appeal of the survivorship arrangement doubtless underlies Treasury regulations under which bonds may be registered in: (1) the name of the purchaser and a co-owner, in which case the bonds are payable to either and at the death of either the survivor is considered the absolute owner, or (2) the name of the purchaser and a beneficiary so that if the purchaser dies survived by the beneficiary the latter is considered the absolute owner.[45] A divided court in the State of Washington held that the beneficiary must pay over the amount collected to the estate of the purchaser, absent circumstances establishing a gift of the bond or its proceeds to the beneficiary.[46] The prevailing view,[47] however, is that the regulations are not merely for the protection of the government in making the payment, but that the co-owner or beneficiary is absolutely entitled to the bond and its proceeds, either as a third party beneficiary,[48] or because the regulations have the effect of federal law, which here prevails over the state law.[49] It has also been held that the beneficiary prevails against the creditors of the deceased purchaser who was solvent at the time of the purchase but became insolvent thereafter.[50]

44 McLaughlin v. Cooper's Estate, 128 Conn. 557, 24 A.2d 502, 1942; Marble v. Treasurer & Receiver General, 245 Mass. 504, 139 N.E. 442, 1923; In re McKelway's Estate, 221 N.Y. 15, 116 N.E. 348, L.R.A.1917E, 1143, 1917, (jointly owned corporate bonds). See supra notes 11, 12.

45 See 1943 Annual Surv.Am.L. 605.

46 Decker v. Fowler, 199 Wash. 549, 92 P.2d 254, 131 A.L.R. 961, 1939, noted, 4 Mont.L.R. 61, 14 Wash.L.R. 312.

47 See annotation, 168 A.L.R. 245, 246–250.

48 Franklin Washington Trust Co. v. Beltram, 133 N.J.Eq. 11, 29 A.2d 854, 1943.

49 Harvey v. Rackliffe, 141 Me. 169, 41 A.2d 455, 161 A.L.R. 296, 1945; Reynolds v. Reynolds, 325 Mass. 257, 90 N.E.2d 338, 1950.

50 Application of Laundree, 277 App.Div. 994, 100 N.Y.S.2d 146, 1950.

## BANK ACCOUNT TRUSTS

**41. One may establish a valid trust in a bank account so as to pass it to the beneficiary on the depositor's death even if the latter retains the right to revoke. Beyond this there is an increasing tendency to sustain the New York tentative trust doctrine, whereby A's deposit, "A in trust for B," is revocable by A and subject only to his withdrawals in his lifetime, but otherwise entitles B to the account if B survives, subject to the rights of A's creditors.**

The trust device is frequently used in connection with bank accounts in order to pass the deposit to the beneficiary upon the depositor's death and thus avoid the trouble of executing a will and the expense and delay of probate and administration. The bank account trust cases usually arise when A deposits money in the style "A, in trust for B." The later ordinarily claims that this creates a trust in his favor, which terminates upon the trustee's death, entitling the beneficiary to receive the funds from the bank. Two legal obstacles must be overcome before this result can be reached: (1) Do the facts show that A intended a trust for B's benefit? (2) Is the arrangement in violation of the Statute of Wills?

It should be noticed that A may not have intended to create a trust at all. Other reasons may account for the use of this form of deposit. For example he may have wished merely to conceal his pecuniary condition from others, or to avoid taxation, or to evade bank rules limiting the amount of deposits or interest rates payable on larger accounts.[1] Most courts hold that this form of deposit is only evidence of a trust or, at best, merely creates the presumption of one.[2] Evidence is admissible to show the intention of A in this respect. Among the circumstances tending to establish a trust are delivery of the bank book to B and notice of the deposit to him or to a third person.[3] The Massachusetts rule

1 Schauberger v. Tafel, 202 Ky. 9, 258 S.W. 953, 1924; Austin v. Central Savings Bank of Baltimore, 126 Md. 139, 94 A. 520, 1915; Brabrook v. Boston Five Cents Sav. Bank, 104 Mass. 228, 6 Am.Rep. 222, 1870. See Beaver v. Beaver, 117 N.Y. 421, 22 N.E. 940, 6 L.R.A. 403, 15 Am.St.Rep. 531, 1889. See infra note 18.

2 Gaffney's Estate, 146 Pa. 49, 23 A. 163, 1892; Connecticut River Sav. Bank v. Albee's Estate, 64 Vt. 571, 25 A. 487, 33 Am.St.Rep. 944, 1892; Nicklas v. Parker, 69 N.J.Eq. 743, 61 A. 267, 1905 (revocable trust presumed); Cazallis v. Ingraham, 119 Me. 240, 110 A. 350 (irrevocable trust presumed). As to creation of a trust when the account is in ordinary individual form, see annotation, 168 A.L.R. 1273.

3 For discussion of the kinds of facts which are favorable or unfavorable for the finding of a trust, see

formerly required notice to B in order to create a valid trust,[4] but most courts hold that this is not imperative.[5] A trust may be found though A retains the bank book,[6] for while this is a factor unfavorable to the existence of a trust, it is not necessarily inconsistent therewith.

Assuming that a trust is intended, the further questions arise as to whether the trust is revocable and whether A retains the privilege of withdrawal from the account. Unless these matters are expressed in the terms of the deposit, they are questions of intention to be determined from the circumstances. These problems lead us into the second aspect of the question namely whether the transaction is invalid because in conflict with the Statute of Wills.

If an irrevocable trust is created, there is no violation of the Statute of Wills.[7] The beneficiary has an interest of which he may not be deprived by the depositor, though until the latter's death the beneficiary may not come into enjoyment of the funds. If the depositor withdraws from such an account, his estate and possibly the bank also are liable.[8] Furthermore, upon orthodox trust principles, the fact that the depositor reserves the right to receive the interest does not make the transaction testamentary.[9] Again upon strict trust principles the retention of the right to re-

Bogert, The Creation of Trusts by Means of Bank Deposits, 1 Corn.L.Q. 159.

4 Hogarth-Swann v. Steele, 294 Mass. 396, 2 N.E.2d 446, 1936; see Fleck v. Baldwin, 141 Tex. 340, 172 S.W.2d 975, 1943. But cf. Cohen v. Newton Savings Bank, infra note 6, holding that notice is not necessary when the form of deposit indicates the terms of the trust.

5 Cazallis v. Ingraham, supra note 2; Connecticut River Savings Bank v. Albee's Estate, supra note 2; Merigan v. McGonigle, 205 Pa. 321, 54 A. 994, 1903. See annotation, 157 A.L.R. 925.

6 Cohen v. Newton Savings Bank, 320 Mass. 90, 67 N.E.2d 748, 168 A.L.R. 1321, 1946; Baker v. Baker, 123 Md. 32, 90 A. 776, 1914; Merigan v. McGonigle, supra note 5; Connecticut River Savings Bank v. Albee's Estate, supra note 2. If a gift instead of a trust is claimed there must be some sort of delivery. See 81 U. of Pa.L.R. 737, 741, and, in general, Mechem, The Requirement of Delivery in Gifts, 21 Ill.L.R. 341, 457, 568; Moynihan, Trusts of Saving Deposits in Massachusetts, 22 B.U.L.R. 271.

7 Cazallis v. Ingraham, supra note 2. See also, cases infra notes 8–10.

8 Sayre v. Weil, 94 Ala. 466, 10 So. 546, 15 L.R.A. 544, 1892; Minor v. Rogers, 40 Conn. 512, 16 Am.Rep. 69, 1873.

9 Cazallis v. Ingraham, supra note 2. See, also, Hallowell Sav. Inst. v. Titcomb, 96 Me. 62, 51 A. 249, 1901; Smith v. Ossipee Valley Ten Cents Sav. Bank, 64 N.H. 228, 9 A. 792, 10 Am.St.Rep. 400, 1887. See infra § 42.

voke the entire trust does not defeat its validity,[10] though some courts have held that it does so upon the theory that such control by the depositor in his lifetime can be obtained only by means of a will.[11] When the depositor further retains the right to withdraw any part of the principal the orthodox view in the bank account cases is that the limits of a non-testamentary document have been exceeded and the trust is invalid.[12] It is difficult to explain the distinction between the effect of retention of the rights of revocation and that of withdrawal. Withdrawal of all seems equivalent to revocation, while withdrawal of part seems to be a pro tanto revocation. It can be argued that what is substantially the right of partial revocation should not make the transaction testamentary if the privilege of total revocation does not. However, if the depositor has the right of withdrawal of funds from time to time, he obtains greater freedom than when he merely has the right to total revocation. The former gives him privilege of dealing with the property as if it were his own, which is a characteristic inconsistent with a non-testamentary arrangement.

Most states have legislation authorizing such trust deposits to be paid to the beneficiary upon the death of the trustee if no notice to the contrary has been given to the bank.[13] However, most of these statutes are only for the protection of the bank and do not determine the respective rights of the trustee's estate and the surviving beneficiary.[14] Controversies between these parties may arise either before or after the bank has paid the account, and these statutes have little bearing upon decision of such cases.

*Tentative Trust Doctrine*

In order to permit the depositor trustee to withdraw the funds in his lifetime, and at the same time to allow the beneficiary to have the remainder of the funds at the depositor's death, New York established the tentative trust doctrine, in the leading case

10 Jones v. Old Colony Trust Co., 251 Mass. 309, 146 N.E. 716, 1925; Restatement, Trusts, § 57.

11 See Springvale Nat. Bank v. Ward, 122 Me. 227, 119 A. 529, 1923; Cazallis v. Ingraham, supra note 2; Nicklas v. Parker, 69 N.J.Eq. 743, 61 A. 267, 1905, affirmed 71 N.J.Eq. 777, 71 A. 1135, 14 Ann.Cas. 92, 1908.

12 Springvale Nat. Bank v. Ward, 122 Me. 227, 119 A. 529, 1923; Nutt v. Morse, 142 Mass. 1, 6 N.E. 763, 1886; Smith v. Speer, 34 N.J.Eq. 336, 1881. But see Booth v. Oakland Bank of Savings, 122 Cal. 19, 54 P. 370, 1898. See also notes 15–22 infra.

13 See 1 Bogert, Trusts and Trustees, 1951, 323.

14 Alger v. North End Sav. Bank, 146 Mass. 418, 15 N.E. 916, 4 Am. St.Rep. 331, 1888. See note, 11 B.U. L.R. 83, and supra § 40, notes 39–42.

of Matter of Totten.[15] The principle is well entrenched in that state and has considerable following elsewhere.[16] It is not entirely clear whether the trust arises only on the trustee's death or whether it is initiated upon the deposit subject to a condition subsequent.[17] At any rate the presumption is that the trust is revocable,[18] and subject to withdrawals by the depositor, and these features do not invalidate it as a trust. Predecease of the beneficiary revokes the trust [19] and it may be revoked by subsequent wills.[20] The concept has been criticized [21] as judicial legis-

15 179 N.Y. 112, 71 N.E. 748, 70 L.R.A. 711, 1 Ann.Cas. 900, 1904; see also In re Halpern's Estate, 303 N.Y. 33, 100 N.E.2d 120, 1951; Gulliver and Tilson, Classification of Gratuitous Transfers, 51 Yale L.J. 1, 32–39.

16 Katz v. Greeninger, 96 Cal.App. 2d 245, 215 P.2d 121, 1950; Wilder v. Howard, 188 Ga. 426, 4 S.E.2d 199, 1939; Hale v. Hale, 313 Ky. 344, 231 S.W.2d 2, Ky.1950; Dyste v. Farmers & Mechanics Sav. Bank of Minneapolis, 179 Minn. 430, 229 N.W. 865, 1930, noted, 14 Minn.L R. 701; Scanlon's Estate, 313 Pa. 424, 169 A. 106, 1933, noted, 82 U. of Pa.L.R. 413. See also Delaware Trust Co. v. Fitzmaurice, 27 Del.Ch. 101, 31 A.2d 383, 1943; Cohen v. Newton Sav. Bank, 320 Mass. 90, 67 N.E.2d 748, 168 A.L.R. 1321, 1946; notes, 28 Cal. L.R. 202, 48 Harv.L.R. 1168, 26 Wash. U.L.R. 286; Restatement, Trusts § 58.

Other states reject the tentative trust doctrine. Springvale Nat. Bank v. Ward, 122 Me. 227, 119 A. 529, 1923; Nicklas v. Parker, 69 N.J.Eq. 743, 61 A. 267, 1905, affirmed 71 N.J.Eq. 777, 71 A. 1135, 14 Ann.Cas. 921, 1907. Cf. Reynolds v. Reynolds, 325 Mass. 257, 90 N.E.2d 338, 1950, with Cohen v. Newton Savings Bank, supra note 6. See also Warner v. Burlington Federal Sav. & Loan Ass'n, 114 Vt. 463, 49 A.2d 93, 168 A.L.R. 1265, 1946, and note, 25 N.Y. U.L.R. 626, discussing the New Jersey cases and recent statute; supra note 12.

17 Cf. Scott, Trusts and the Statute of Wills, 43 Harv.L.R. 521, 542, 543; notes, 37 Yale L.J. 1133, 28 Mich. L.R. 603, 606.

18 Matter of Totten, supra note 15; In re Ingels' Estate, 92 A.2d 881, 372 Pa. 171, 1952. But if the depositor delivers the bank book to the beneficiary there is an irrevocable trust. In re Farrell, 298 N.Y. 129, 81 N.E.2d 51, 1948. Cf. Brucks v. Home Federal Sav. & Loan Ass'n, 36 Cal. 2d 845, 228 P.2d 545, 1951 (notice to beneficiary does not make trust revocable). It can be shown that no trust was intended. See In re Halpern's Estate, supra note 15; also supra notes 1, 2.

19 Hyman v. Tarplee, 64 Cal.App. 2d 805, 149 P.2d 453, 1944; Matter of United States Trust Co. of New York, 117 App.Div. 178, 102 N.Y.S. 271, 1907, affirmed 189 N.Y. 500, 81 N.E. 1177, 1907; Collopy's Estate, 33 D. & C. 169, Pa.1938. Cf. note, 7 So. Cal.L.R. 116. As to case of simultaneous deaths of depositor and beneficiary, see notes, 88 U. of Pa.L.R. 886, 7 U. of Pitt.L.R. 144. As to subsequent insanity of depositor, see annotation, 138 A.L.R. 1383.

20 Brucks v. Home Federal Sav. & Loan Ass'n, supra note 18; In re Scanlon's Estate, 313 Pa. 424, 169 A.

21 See Note 21 on following page.

lation because it allows complete control of the funds by the depositor in his lifetime and hence is in violation of the Statute of Wills. The substantial testamentary character of the arrangement is also recognized by holdings that the account is subject to the debts of the deceased depositor.[22] In spite of the inconsistencies, the result reached by this doctrine is socially desirable, for it enables people of limited means to obtain the advantages of a will without the expense and delay usually attending testamentary disposition and with little chance of fraud upon the heirs or creditors of the deceased.

## LIVING TRUSTS

**42. A person may convey realty and personalty upon a trust for the benefit of a third person upon the settlor's death. This arrangement may be a valid trust though it reserves the income to the settlor and gives him the right of withdrawal or is entirely revocable. However, an interest must be presently created so that if the settlor also retains an unlimited control over the administration of the property, the transaction will be deemed testamentary.**

In the so-called living trust, real or personal property is ordinarily transferred by the settlor to a third party trustee who acts in accordance with a written trust agreement or deed.[1] The

106, 1933, noted, 82 U. of Pa.L.R. 413; Matter of Murray's Estate, 143 Misc. 499, 256 N.Y.S. 815, 1932, noted, 42 Yale L.J. 141. But see Bradford v. Eutaw Sav. Bank of Baltimore City, 186 Md. 127, 46 A. 2d 284, 1946. Cf. Pozzuto's Estate, 124 Pa.Super. 93, 188 A. 209, 1936 (bequest of residue does not revoke the trust).

21 Larremore, Judicial Legislation in New York, 14 Yale L.J. 312, 315; notes, 81 U. of Pa.L.R. 737, 739; 28 Mich.L.R. 603, 606. But cf. Havighurst, Gifts of Bank Deposits, 14 N. C.L.R. 129.

22 Matter of Reich's Estate, 146 Misc. 616, 262 N.Y.S. 623, 1933, noted, 81 U. of Pa.L.R. 1011, 33 Col.L.R. 548, 42 Yale L.J. 1136 (funeral and administration expenses charged against the account, balance to go to the beneficiary of the trust account). Likewise the depositor's creditors can reach the account in his lifetime. Banca D'Italia & Trust Co. v. Giordano, 154 Pa.Super. 452, 36 A.2d 242, 1944. As to whether the account is part of the depositor's estate for the purpose of determining the share of his surviving spouse, see supra § 32, note 14.

1 See Scott, Trusts and The Statute of Wills, 43 Harv.L.R. 521; Leaphart, The Trust as a Substitute for a Will, 78 U. of Pa.L.R. 626; Seftenberg, The Borderline of Agency, Living Trusts and Testamentary Disposition, 5 Wis.L.R. 321; Rowley, Living Testamentary Dispositions and the Hawkins Case, 3 U. of Cin. L.R. 361; King, A Reappraisal of the Revocable Trust, 19 Ry.Mt.L.R. 1.

transaction is valid as an inter vivos transfer if a beneficial interest passes to the beneficiary at once, or during the settlor's lifetime. On the other hand if the whole beneficial interest remains in the settlor until his death, the instrument is testamentary in character and to be valid must be executed with the formalities required of a will, followed by probate thereof and judicial administration of the property. An instrument is not considered testamentary because it reserves the income to the settlor for life,[2] nor because it provides that the settlor may have as much of the principal as is necessary for his support [3] or even as much as he demands.[4] A trust is not revocable unless this privilege is expressly reserved,[5] but the retention of the privilege of revocation either in whole,[6] or in part,[7] does not invalidate the

The living or inter vivos trust is distinguished from the testamentary trust which is created by will leaving property to trustees to be administered in accordance with the terms of the trust as set forth in the will. As to the possibility of devising or "pouring over" property by will in accordance with the terms of an existing living trust, see infra § 81.

2 Patterson v. McClenathan, 296 Ill. 475, 129 N.E. 767, 1921; Harrod v. McComas, 78 Kan. 407, 96 P. 484, 1908; Brown v. Mercantile Trust & Deposit Co., 87 Md. 377, 40 A. 256, 1898; Gilman v. McArdle, 99 N.Y. 451, 2 N.E. 464, 52 Am.Rep. 41, 1885; Hall v. Hall, 109 Va. 117, 63 S.E. 420, 21 L.R.A.,N.S., 533, 1909; Spangler v. Vermillion, 80 W.Va. 75, 92 S.E. 449, 1917.

3 Cramer v. Hartford-Connecticut Trust Co., 110 Conn. 22, 147 A. 139, 73 A.L.R. 201, 1929; Spangler v. Vermillion, supra note 2; Harrod v. McComas, supra note 2; Lovett v. Farnham, 169 Mass. 1, 47 N.E. 246, 1897. In the first two cases the determination of the amount was left to the trustee but in the others to the settlor himself. See also case infra note 4.

4 In re Shapley's Deed of Trust, 353 Pa. 499, 46 A.2d 227, 164 A.L.R. 877, 1946; see Cleveland Trust Co. v. White, 134 Ohio St. 1, 15 N.E.2d 627, 118 A.L.R. 475, 1938. Contra: Warsco v. Oshkosh Sav. & Trust Co., 183 Wis. 156, 196 N.W. 829, 1924, though the result would now be otherwise under Wis.Stat. § 231.205; McEvoy v. Boston Five Cents Sav. Bank, 201 Mass. 50, 87 N.E. 465, 1909, but this case is expressly overruled in National Shawmut Bank v. Joy, 315 Mass. 457, 53 N.E.2d 113, 1944.

5 Reddy v. Graham, 110 Kan. 753, 205 P. 362, 1922; Price v. Price, 162 Md. 656, 161 A. 2, 1889, noted 17 Minn.L.R. 232; Ewing v. Warner, 47 Minn. 446, 50 N.W. 603, 1891. But see Cal.Civ.Code § 2280.

6 Cramer v. Hartford-Connecticut Trust Co., supra note 3; Keck v. McKinstry, 204 Iowa 487, 215 N.W. 497, 1927; Id., 206 Iowa 1121, 221 N.W. 851, 1928; Roche v. Brickley, 254 Mass. 584, 150 N.E. 866, 1926; National Newark & Essex Banking Co. v. Rosahl, 97 N.J.Eq. 74, 128 A. 586, 1925. But see Union Trust Co. v. Hawkins, 121 Ohio St. 159, 167 N.E. 389, 73 A.L.R. 190, 1929 (statute—the court indicating that in absence thereof the right to alter, amend or revoke makes the instrument testamentary). See also cases

7 See Note 7 on following page.

trust as an inter vivos transaction. Furthermore the settlor may retain the privilege to change the beneficiaries.[8] Living trusts have also been sustained although it is provided that the settlor's debts and funeral expenses shall be paid out of the corpus if his other property is inadequate.[9]

Probably all of the foregoing reservations could be included in a single trust instrument without fatal effect. Theoretically if one purports presently to give an interest to the beneficiary though it be a future one and subject to be defeated or controlled by all sorts of acts by the settlor, there may be a valid inter vivos trust. Apparently the distinction between a will and a trust is a very fine one. If one studies the attitude of the courts, however, there appear to be limitations upon the degree of control which may be retained safely by the settlor. When in addition to the powers mentioned in the previous paragraph the settlor reserves an unlimited right to control the details of the administration of the trust, it will be considered testamentary.[10] In such cases the transaction is a mere agency, terminated by the principal's death.[11] Either of these positions is fatal to the success of the arrangement as a trust. However it has been held that the settlor may reserve the right of possession of the property during his lifetime without destroying the trust character.[12] Control over the investments,[13] and voting of the stock [14] have

notes 3, 4 supra. As to revocation by will of a living trust, see Leahy v. Old Colony Trust Co., 326 Mass. 49, 93 N.E.2d 238, 18 A.L.R.2d 1006, 1950.

7 Bear v. Millikin Trust Co., 336 Ill. 366, 168 N.E. 349, 73 A.L.R. 173, 1929; Windolph v. Girard Trust Co., 245 Pa. 349, 91 A. 634, 1914.

8 Bear v. Millikin Trust Co., supra note 7; Keck v. McKinstry, supra note 6; Talbot v. Talbot, 32 R.I. 72, 78 A. 535, Ann.Cas.1912C, 1221, 1911.

9 Cramer v. Hartford-Connecticut Trust Co., supra note 3; Bear v. Millikin Trust Co., supra note 7.

10 Atlantic Nat. Bank of Jacksonville v. St. Louis Union Trust Co., 357 Mo. 770, 211 S.W.2d 2, 1948; see Russell v. Webster, 213 Mass. 491, 100 N.E. 637, 1913; Restatement, Trusts § 57(2).

11 See Union Trust Co. v. Hawkins, supra note 6; Warsco v. Oshkosh Sav. & T. Co., supra note 4; Restatement, Trusts § 57, comment g.

12 Keck v. McKinstry, 206 Iowa 1121, 221 N.W. 851, 1928.

13 Windolph v. Girard Trust Co., 245 Pa. 349, 91 A. 634, 1914; see Adams v. Hagerott, 34 F.2d 899, C.C.A.N.D.1929. See Goodrich v. City Nat. Bank & Trust Co. of Battle Creek, 270 Mich. 222, 258 N.W. 253, 1935, where the right to control investments coupled with reservation of power to change the beneficiary, to revoke, and to withdraw all or part of the principal was not fatal to a valid trust. See also National Shawmut Bank v. Joy, supra note 4.

14 Bear v. Millikin Trust Co., 336 Ill. 366, 168 N.E. 349, 73 A.L.R. 173,

also been permitted, particularly when the settlor does not also reserve the right of revocation.[15] As a whole the more dominion which the settlor retains, the more apt the intended trust is to be held invalid. There is not general agreement as to the exact degree of control which is permitted. Frequently there appear to be inconsistencies in the cases decided by a single jurisdiction.

In the living trust cases, almost all courts permit the settlor to retain substantially the same dominion over the property that the depositor has in the trust bank account cases according to the tentative trust doctrine and much greater control than the depositor has according to the orthodox position in the trust bank account cases. The distinction which is apparently made by the courts retaining the latter theory may result from the fear that the bank account trusts are dangerous because the terms are seldom expressed completely in writing. It may also be noticed that in the bank account cases the settlor is also the trustee, which fact, if coupled with the right of revocation and particularly of withdrawal, gives him substantially all the advantages of complete ownership. In inter vivos trusts the legal title is ordinarily in a third party fiduciary who also has powers and duties of the administration of the trust. The Restatement of Trusts declares that, aside from the tentative bank account trusts, a trust is testamentary if the settlor is himself the trustee and retains the right to deal with the property as he likes.[16]

The fact that the settlor establishes the trust in lieu of making a will, or to avoid executing one, or even to evade the Statute of Wills is not material on the question of testamentary character if the trust is otherwise valid.[17] A draftsman wishing to create a trust inter vivos should take care that the wording of an instrument indicates an intention to create presently an interest in the beneficiary and not merely upon the death of the settlor. There is little or no difference in substance between using terms

1929; Newland v. McNeill, 277 Ky. 245, 126 S.W.2d 127, 1939.

15 Reinecke v. Northern Trust Co., 278 U.S. 339, 49 S.Ct. 123, 73 L.Ed. 410, 66 A.L.R. 397, 1929 (taxation case); Forney v. Remey, 77 Iowa 549, 42 N.W. 439, 1889.

16 § 57(3). See McGillivary v. First Nat. Bank, 56 N.D. 152, 217 N.W. 150, 1927; note, 47 Mich.L.R. 907. But there can be a valid trust though the settlor-trustee retains the privilege of revocation. Robb v. Washington & Jefferson College, 185 N.Y. 485, 78 N.E. 359, 1906.

17 Patterson v. McClenathan, 296 Ill. 475, 129 N.E. 767, 1921; National Shawmut Bank v. Joy, supra note 4; Newman v. Dore, 275 N.Y. 371, 9 N.E.2d 966, 112 A.L.R. 643, 1937. But cf. Jones v. Old Colony Trust Co., 251 Mass. 309, 146 N.E. 716, 1925.

of revocation rather than directions that the trustee shall pay the settlor on demand, but the latter form suggests an agency rather than a trust.[18] Language directing the trustee to pay the beneficiary or deliver the property to him is more appropriate to a trust document than the expression that the property shall go to the beneficiary on the settlor's death.[19] A formally executed trust deed is more apt to be sustained as such than a more informal instrument containing the same essential provisions. If the document intended to create a trust is testamentary, it may be probated as a will if executed with the formalities required of the latter.[20] Therefore, it may be advisable to so execute the instrument that if it fails as a trust, it can be used as a will. However, employment of an ordinary attestation clause would scarcely be wise, since the court might seize upon its presence as an indication that the instrument was intended as a will.[21]

*Estate Taxes and Creditors*

The right of the settlor's surviving spouse to an elective share in the subject matter of a living trust which is revocable or subject to other controls by the settlor has already been treated.[22] Most living trusts would be included within the settlor's gross estate for Federal estate tax purposes, either as transfers in contemplation of or taking effect at death, or because they are revocable;[23] and even if they did not they would be subject to the gift tax.[24] It has been held that while the initial duty to pay estate taxes is on the executors, the ultimate burden falls on the recipients of the taxed property, i. e. the beneficiary of the inter

18 Warsco v. Oshkosh Savings & Trust Company, supra note 4.

19 See Union Trust Co. v. Hawkins, supra note 6; Restatement, Trusts § 57, comment g; Goldman & DeCamp, When Is a Trust Not a Trust, 16 U. of Cin.L.R. 191, 215.

20 In re Bybee's Estate, 179 Iowa 1089, 160 N.W. 900, 1917 (deed, invalid as such because not to take effect until death). See Scott, supra note 1 at 534, 535; Goldman & DeCamp, supra note 19 at 214.

21 In the states which require testator to publish his will to the witnesses, there would be further practical difficulty. See infra § 68. If the testator expressly declared the instrument to be his will, the case for the preferred result of a living trust would be seriously jeopardized. Perhaps the settlor should make no declaration as to the nature of the instrument, and merely call on persons learned in the law, who had read the instrument, to witness it.

22 See supra § 32, especially at note 11.

23 Int.Rev.Code § 811(c), (d).

24 Int.Rev.Code § 1000.

vivos trust.[25] Even if the residuary beneficiaries of the settlor's estate should be obliged to bear the burden of the tax imposed by virtue of the inter vivos trust,[26] it would seem that in case of an insolvent estate, the executors should pay the debts first and look to the trustee of the inter vivos trust to satisfy the unpaid amount of the estate tax attributable to the trust.[27] Since the government could go against the trust estate,[28] it is reasonable that the trust rather than the decedent's creditors should bear the burden of the tax attributable to the trust.

There is authority for the view that in the settlor's lifetime his creditors cannot reach the trust property though the right of revocation has been retained.[29] This result is reached upon the ground that the privilege of revocation is personal to the settlor and cannot be exercised by others. There is a contrary line of cases decided upon the basis that the settlor is the substantial owner of the property and should not be permitted to play fast and loose with his creditors.[30] The latter position seems equitable, and in case of a spendthrift trust the creditors of the settlor may reach his interest in trust corpus though he retained no right of revocation and had no intent to defeat his creditors.[31] Even in case claims are asserted after the settlor's death and his power to revoke has of course ceased, it would seem that upon broad

25 McLaughlin v. Green, 136 Conn. 138, 69 A.2d 289, 15 A.L.R.2d 1210, 1949 (unless the will clearly indicates that the tax burden falls on the residuary estate). But cf. Goldman v. Goldman, 2 N.J.Super. 412, 64 A.2d 251, 1949. See also annotation, 128 A.L.R. 123; infra § 147.

26 See Goldman v. Goldman, supra note 25. State apportionment statutes often provide that the tax burden falls proportionately on all the beneficiaries unless the will directs otherwise. See N.Y.Decedent Estate Law § 124.

27 Alexander, Certain Problems Confronting Creditors when a Revocable Trust Accomplishes Testamentary Succession, 31 Mich.L.R. 449.

28 See annotation, 144 A.L.R. 702.

29 Jones v. Clifton, 101 U.S. 225, 25 L.Ed. 908, 1879; Hill v. Cornwall & Bro.'s Assignee, 95 Ky. 512, 26 S.W. 540, 1894; Murphey v. C. I. T. Corporation, 347 Pa. 591, 33 A.2d 16, 1943. See Restatement, Trusts § 330, comment o; annotation, 93 A.L.R. 1211.

30 First Wisconsin Nat. Bank of Milwaukee v. Schwab, 141 Fla. 748, 194 So. 307, 1950; Herd v. Chambers, 158 Kan. 614, 149 P.2d 583, 1944; Scott v. Keane, 87 Md. 709, 40 A. 1070, 42 L.R.A. 359, 1898; Schofield v. Cleveland Trust Co., 135 Ohio St. 328, 21 N.E.2d 119, 1939 (statute). See Alexander, supra note 27 at 462 et seq.; supra § 41, note 22.

31 McColgan v. Walter Magee, Inc., 172 Cal. 182, 155 P. 995, Ann.Cas. 1917D, 1050, 1916. Cf. In re Watland, 211 Minn. 84, 300 N.W. 195, 1941.

general principles the creditors should prevail.[32] Of course if the trust is created to defraud either present or future creditors of the settlor, they may attack the transfer and obtain satisfaction of their claims.[33]

## DEEDS

**43. In order to be valid as a deed the instrument must take effect upon delivery though the grantee need not come into enjoyment until the grantor's death. The courts are in conflict as to whether an instrument in the general form of a deed is testamentary because it contains provisions of the following types:**

**(1) By the better view, a condition that the grantee survive the grantor does not make the instrument testamentary.**

**(2) Most courts uphold provisions in a deed that the conveyance has no effect until the grantor's death.**

**(3) If the instrument is revocable by its terms, it is generally held testamentary.**

**(4) The same result usually obtains if the document purports to pass all the property which the maker may own at his death.**

**An instrument in the general form of a deed and invalid as such because of testamentary provisions contained therein or because of lack of delivery may be sustained as a will if testamentary intent and essentials of form are present.**

**Delivery in the grantor's lifetime is necessary for the validity of a deed, but delivery may be to a third person with instructions to give it to the grantee upon the grantor's death. The grantor must give up all control over the instrument in order to have a valid delivery.**

Theoretically the distinction between a will and a deed is a simple one. A will passes no interest until the death of the testator and up to that time it is freely revocable. A deed, on the other hand, passes an interest in the property to the grantee in the grantor's lifetime, and the latter ordinarily has no privilege of revocation. At early common law a grant of land could not reserve a life interest in the grantor because the freehold was con-

[32] Coston v. Portland Trust Co., 131 Or. 71, 278 P. 586, rehearing denied 131 Or. 71, 282 P. 442, 1929. But see Schofield v. Cleveland Trust Co., supra note 30, and cases supra note 29.

[33] Petree v. Brotherton, 133 Ind. 692, 32 N.E. 300, 1892; Abramson v. Horner, 115 Md. 232, 80 A. 907, 1911; Sovell v. Lincoln County, 129 Minn. 356, 152 N.W. 727, 1915. See infra § 116.

veyed by livery of seisin, which must pass a present estate.[1] This ancient handicap was nullified under the Statutes of Uses by deeds of bargain and sale, and covenants to stand seised.[2] Under modern American systems of land transfer there is nothing to prevent a grantor from deeding his land to another while reserving a life estate for himself.[3] Such estates may also be created in personal property.[4] If the grantor continues to be satisfied with the arrangement throughout his lifetime this is a simple will substitute. However, the unalterable consequences of the use of this device must be appreciated. The grantor has the right to possess and enjoy the land as long as he lives, and he may sell or mortgage this life interest. He is not privileged to dispose of the remainder nor to revoke the transfer. He may persuade the grantee to reconvey the property if unforeseen emergency arises, but the latter is under no legal obligation to do so. If the grantee dies before the grantor, the former's successors and not the latter's are entitled to the remainder.

*Conditions Expressed in Deeds*

Not every instrument in the general form of a deed will be considered as such by the courts. Often they are held to be testamentary and invalid as deeds for the reason that they create no interest presently but only upon the maker's death. Whether

1 2 Bl.Com. 166, 314. See Carter v. Madgwick, 3 Lev. 339, 83 Eng.Rep. 719, 1693 (grantee takes property immediately and grantor's life estate is ineffective in order to prevent entire conveyance from being void under the above rule).

2 2 Bl.Com. 332, 338. See Bunch v. Nicks, 50 Ark. 367, 7 S.W. 563, 1888; Dennett v. Dennett, 40 N.H. 498, 1860.

3 Bunch v. Nicks, supra note 2; Shornick v. Shornick, 25 Ariz. 563, 220 P. 397, 31 A.L.R. 159, 1923; Latimer v Latimer, 174 Ill. 418, 51 N.E. 548, 1898; O'Day v. Meadows, 194 Mo. 588, 92 S.W. 637, 112 Am.St.Rep. 542, 1906; McLain v. Garrison, 39 Tex.Civ.App. 431, 88 S.W. 484, 89 S.W. 284, 1905; Gorham v. Daniels, 23 Vt. 600, 1851. The foregoing cases are based upon statutes abolishing livery of seisin or providing other form of conveyance. The same result has been reached in absence of such statutes. See Chandler v. Chandler, 55 Cal. 267, 1880; Fish v. Sawyer, 11 Conn. 545, 1836; Puukaiakea v. Hiaa, 5 Hawaii, 484, 1885; Savage v. Lee, 90 N.C. 320, 47 Am.Rep. 523, 1884; Ferguson v. Mason, 60 Wis. 377, 19 N.W. 420, 1884.

4 Banks' Adm'r v. Marksberry, 3 Litt.(Ky.) 275, 1823; Wall v. Wall, 30 Miss. 91, 64 Am.Dec. 147, 1855; Nalley v. First National Bank of Medford, 135 Or. 409, 293 P. 721, 296 P. 61, 76 A.L.R. 625, 1930; Jaggers v. Estes, 2 Strob.Eq.(S.C.) 343, 49 Am. Dec. 674, 1848; Caines v. Marley, 2 Yerg.(Tenn.) 582, 1831. But see Ingram v. Porter, 4 McCord (S.C.) 198, 1827. Cf. Peterson v. Weiner, 71 S.W.2d 544, Tex.Civ.App.1934, noted, 13 Tex.L.R. 234 (gift invalid for lack of valid delivery). See infra § 45, notes 3, 12.

a certain paper will be considered a will or a deed is a difficult and important field of the law.[5] Controversies may arise either in proceedings to probate the instrument as a will or in actions at law or in equity where a party relies upon the document as a deed. The question of testamentary character is also presented in cases where the maker asserts the right to revoke the instrument in his lifetime, or where his heirs or devisees claim that he revoked it by subsequent will, or disposed of the property by a later deed.

Broadly speaking the question is one of the maker's intention. Where there is nothing on the face of the document to raise doubt as to its character, parol evidence is not ordinarily admissible to determine the intention.[6] But when the instrument itself suggests uncertainty in this respect, parol evidence may be received of all facts and circumstances which shed light upon the problem of what was intended.[7] These include the family relations of the decedent,[8] instructions given the draftsman as to the nature of the paper to be prepared,[9] and the maker's conduct in permitting the instrument to be recorded or the land sold.[10]

Use of the designation and general form of a deed is some evidence of intent to create a present interest,[11] but is not con-

5 See Ballantine, When are Deeds Testamentary? 18 Mich.L.R. 470; Keegan, Deeds in Lieu of Wills, 16 A.B.A.J. 779; notes, 4 Wis.L.R. 56, 60, 32 Va.L.R. 148; annotations, 11 A.L.R. 23, 76 A.L.R. 636.

6 Wilenou v. Handlon, 207 Ill. 104, 69 N.E. 892, 1904; Noble v. Fickes, 230 Ill. 595, 82 N.E. 950, 13 L.R.A.,N.S., 1203, 12 Ann.Cas. 282, 1907; Bardsley v. Spencer, 215 Iowa 616, 244 N.W. 275, 1932; Clay v. Layton, 134 Mich. 317, 96 N.W. 458, 1903; Cox v. Reed, 113 Miss. 488, 74 So. 330, 11 A.L.R. 5, 1917; Dexter v. Witte, 138 Wis. 74, 119 N.W. 891. But see Wilcox v. Wilcox, 283 Mich. 313, 278 N.W. 79, 1938, where deed was set aside because grantor wanted a will. See also note, 25 Ia.L.R. 161, and infra § 46.

7 Seay v. Huggins, 194 Ala. 496, 70 So. 113, 1915; Trumbauer v. Rust, 36 S.D. 301, 154 N.W. 801, 11 A.L.R. 10, 1915. See also Benton Harbor Federation of Women's Clubs v. Nelson, 301 Mich. 465, 3 N.W.2d 844, 1942.

8 Sharp v. Hall, 86 Ala. 110, 5 So. 497, 11 Am.St.Rep. 28, 1889.

9 Marsh v. Rogers, 205 Ala. 106, 87 So. 700, 1920.

10 Wilson v. Carrico, 140 Ind. 533, 40 N.E. 50, 49 Am.St.Rep. 213, 1895.

11 Pass v. Stephens, 22 Ariz. 461, 198 P. 712, 1921; Beck v. Belcher, 172 Ga. 491, 157 S.E. 678, 1931; Saunders v. Saunders, 115 Iowa 275, 88 N.W. 329, 1901; Trumbauer v. Rust, supra note 7; Lauck v. Logan, 45 W.Va. 251, 31 S.E. 986, 1898. But cf. Crocker v. Smith, 94 Ala. 295, 10 So. 258, 16 L.R.A. 576, 1891; Knight v. Knight, 133 Miss. 74, 97 So. 481, 1923.

clusive.[12] It is not so much what the maker called it or whether he thought or spoke of it as a will or a deed, but rather what is its force in law? [13] The facts that the instrument is delivered, recorded, acknowledged, or was not witnessed, evidence, though not decisively, that a deed was intended.[14] The primary determining factor of the problem under discussion is the language and the terms of the instrument. It is agreed that a deed in usual form except for the fact that it reserves a life estate to the grantor is a valid conveyance and not testamentary.[15] At the other extreme an instrument was held testamentary when it purported to transfer all of the grantor's property and contained all of the following provisions: (1) That the transfer was upon the condition that the grantee survive the grantor; (2) that the conveyance was to take effect only upon the grantor's death; (3) that the instrument was revocable upon the part of the grantor.[16]

There is a decided split of authority as to the effect of each one of these provisions taken singly. No difficulty should be encountered in upholding the provision that the transfer was conditional upon survival by the grantee. "It is simply a question of springing use. It is sufficient that the deed creates an irrevocable possibility or executory interest in the grantee, which renders the title of the grantor subject to be drawn out of him at a future time and gives the grantee a right which will vest in the event

12 Seay v. Huggins, 194 Ala. 496, 70 So. 113, 1915; Cunningham v. Davis, 62 Miss. 366, 1884; Lauck v. Logan, supra note 11.

13 Lauck v. Logan, supra note 11.

14 Abney v. Moore, 106 Ala. 131, 18 So. 60, 1895 (lack of attestation); Wilson v. Carrico, 140 Ind. 533, 40 N.E. 50, 49 Am.St.Rep. 213, 1898 (recording); Pentico v. Hays, 75 Kan. 76, 88 P. 738, 9 L.R.A.,N.S., 224, 1907 (recording); Ferguson v. Ferguson, 27 Tex. 339, 1864 (delivery). As a corollary, lack of these formalities and presence of attestation is evidence that a will was intended. Leonard v. Leonard, 145 Mich. 563, 108 N.W. 985, 1906 (lack of delivery); Jones v. Lingo, 120 Ga. 693, 48 S.E. 190, 1904 (attestation). Cf. Willis v. Fiveash, 297 S.W. 509, Tex.Civ.App.1927 (pointing out that deeds are frequently witnessed—indeed, this is required in some jurisdictions).

15 Johnson v. Lavene, 196 Iowa 471, 192 N.W. 885, 1923; Bowen v. Bowen, 120 Kan. 545, 246 P. 992, 1926. See, also, authorities supra note 3. In Young v. Payne, 283 Ill. 649, 119 N.E. 612, 1918, it was pointed out that the reservation of a life interest is a strong indication that a deed is intended for if it were a will, the reservation would be useless. As to reservations in favor of grantor's spouse, see notes, 129 A.L.R. 310, 7 U. of Chi.L.R. 559.

16 Butler v. Sherwood, 196 App.Div. 603, 188 N.Y.S. 242, 1921, affirmed memorandum decision, 233 N.Y. 655, 135 N.E. 957, 1922, noted, 31 Yale L. J. 106.

designated according to the terms of the deed." [17] This should be particularly so if the grantor also expressly reserved a life interest in the property. However, the authorities are divided, some recognizing that a present contingent interest is created sufficient to sustain the instrument as a deed,[18] while others declare that there is no present passing of any interest and that the paper is testamentary.[19]

Literally the provision that the instrument shall not take effect, or that title shall not pass, until the maker's death sounds testamentary. This language is suggestive of the ambulatory concept of a will and in it may lurk the idea that it is revocable by the maker. Probably most courts [20] give these instruments the more liberal construction of immediately passing the fee subject to a life estate in the maker. While this seems contrary to the intent revealed by these provisions alone, it is a reasonable interpretation when the other language of the instrument contains words of present grant. The fact of delivery is another argument in favor of the liberal view.

When the maker reserves the right of revocation in an instrument having the general form of a deed, most courts probably declare it testamentary, though some courts have refused to do so.[21] Here again the language suggests a will. Theoretically if

17 Ballantine, supra note 5, at 480.

18 Abbott v. Holway, 72 Me. 298, 1881; Thomas v. Williams, 105 Minn. 88, 117 N.W. 155, 1908.

19 Chaplin v. Chaplin, 105 Kan. 481, 184 P. 984, 1919; Aldridge v. Aldridge, 202 Mo. 565, 101 S.W. 42, 1907; Swann v. Housman, 90 Va. 816, 20 S.E. 830, 1894; Young v. O'Donnell, 129 Wash. 219, 224 P. 682, 1924.

20 White v. Smith, 388 Ill. 23, 169 N.E. 817, 1930; Shaull v. Shaull, 182 Iowa 770, 166 N.W. 301, 11 A.L.R. 15, 1918; Jennings v. Jennings, 173 Ga. 428, 160 S.E. 405, 1931; Nalley v. First Nat. Bank of Medford, 135 Or. 409, 293 P. 721, rehearing denied 135 Or. 409, 296 P. 61, 76 A.L.R. 625, 1930; Trumbauer v. Rust, supra note 7; Turner v. Montgomery, 293 S.W. 815, Tex.Com.App.1927. Contra: Cox v. Reed, 113 Miss. 488, 74 So. 330, 11 A.L.R. 5, 1917; Goodale v. Evans, 263 Mo. 219, 172 S.W. 370, 1914; but see Wimpey v. Ledford, 177 S.W. 302, Mo.1915; Herren v. Herren, 152 Okl. 281, 4 P.2d 92, 1931. See Benton Harbor Federation of Women's Clubs v. Nelson, supra note 7; Coulter v. Carter, 200 Miss. 135, 26 So.2d 344, 1946.

21 That the instrument is testamentary is held in: Cunningham v. Davis, 62 Miss. 366, 1884; Wren v. Coffey, 26 S.W. 142, Tex.Civ.App. 1894; Roberts v. Coleman, 37 W.Va. 143, 16 S.E. 482, 1892; Warsco v. Oshkosh Savings & Trust Co., 183 Wis. 156, 196 N.W. 829, 1924. See Lacy v. Comstock, 55 Kan. 86, 39 P. 1024, 1895, but cf. Durand v. Higgins, 67 Kan. 110, 72 P. 567, 1903. That it is a valid deed is held in: Mays v. Burleson, 180 Ala. 396, 61 So. 75, 1913; Tennant v. John Tennant Memorial Home, 167 Cal. 570, 140 P. 242, 1914; Smith v. Smith, 167

an interest is intended to pass presently, it would seem that such provision is no more fatal to the validity of a deed than it is in case of a living trust.[22] A liberal court will seize upon the general deed character of the instrument, the delivery and extrinsic evidence of the maker's intention in order to uphold the transaction as a conveyance when it would fail as a will because of lack of proper execution.

Whether one of these provisions taken alone will cause the instrument to be regarded as testamentary depends upon the position taken in the particular state. There is considerable confusion even within a single jurisdiction since few cases arise upon exactly the same language and practically none upon identical facts outside the instrument. If two or more of the provisions mentioned above are included in the document, the chances for sustaining it as a deed are diminished. When an instrument purports to pass all property which the maker owns at his death, the courts usually hold that it is testamentary.[23]

*Probate of Deeds as Wills*

A single instrument may be regarded in part as a deed or contract and in part as testamentary.[24] Usually the beneficiary of the instrument wishes, if possible, to sustain it as a deed. If he is able to do so, he is not put to the trouble and expense of probate proceedings, and also he ordinarily runs no risk of an attempted revocation. He is also in a more advantageous position with respect to creditors of the donor. If the document is regarded as a deed, it may fail through lack of proper delivery.[25] Some courts

Ga. 368, 145 S.E. 661, 1928. And see Campbell v. Campbell, 207 Ky. 17, 268 S.W. 588, 1925.

22 See supra § 42. Deeds of property in trust fall under the scope of that section.

23 Poore v. Poore, 55 Kan. 687, 41 P. 973, 1895; Ison v. Halcomb, 136 Ky. 523, 124 S.W. 813, 1924; Evans v. Evans, 69 Misc. 86, 125 N.Y.S. 960, 1924; Watkins v. Dean, 10 Yerg. (Tenn.) 321, 31 Am.Dec. 583, 1837. But see Youngblood v. Youngblood, 74 Ga. 614, 1885; McAlister v. Pritchard, 287 Mo. 494, 230 S.W. 66, 1921; Glocksen v. Holmes, 299 Ky. 626, 186 S.W.2d 634, 1945.

24 Kinnebrew's Distributees v. Kinnebrew's Adm'rs, 35 Ala. 628, 1860; Taylor v. Wilder, 63 Colo. 282, 165 P. 766, 1917; Robinson v. Schly, 6 Ga. 515, 1849; Powers v. Scharling, 64 Kan. 339, 67 P. 820, 1902. But see Merrill v. Boal, 47 R.I. 274, 132 A. 721, 45 A.L.R. 830, 1926. See infra § 44, note 3.

25 Noble v. Fickes, 230 Ill. 594, 82 N.E. 950, 13 L.R.A.,N.S., 1203, 12 Ann.Cas. 282, 1907; Lowry v. Lowry, 160 Kan. 11, 159 P.2d 411, 1945 (written provision for delivery on grantor's death ineffective).

have declared that if a paper cannot operate as a will, but may as a deed, it should be pronounced to be the latter if possible.[26] The corollary of this proposition has also been asserted in case of lack of delivery,[27] or some other reason rendering the paper ineffectual as a deed.[28] The latter rule would be particularly applicable in jurisdictions where deeds are required to be attested; otherwise an instrument in the form of a deed is not apt to be witnessed. This rule is not carried to the extent of holding that a document containing no language of a testamentary nature may be considered as a will simply because it would otherwise fail. Thus, where a paper is in the usual form of a deed and contains no ambiguous provisions, but fails as a deed because of nondelivery, it cannot be regarded as a will simply because it is attested by two witnesses.[29]

*Delivery upon Grantor's Death*

Another use of the deed as a will substitute is by manipulating the delivery of an ordinary conveyance so that it does not operate to entitle the grantee to possession until after the grantor's death. The courts recognize the validity of a transaction wherein the grantor delivers the deed to a third person with instructions to give it to the grantee upon the grantor's death.[30] In many states this is deemed to pass the fee to the grantee at once, subject to a life estate reserved by implication in the grantor.[31] Elsewhere

[26] Clark v. Boaler's Estate, 62 Colo. 465, 163 P. 965, 1917; Collier v. Carter, 146 Ga. 476, 91 S.E. 551, 11 A.L.R. 1, 1917; Turner v. Montgomery, 293 S.W. 815, Tex.Com.App. 1927.

[27] Sharp v. Hall, 86 Ala. 110, 5 So. 107, 11 Am.St.Rep. 28, 1889.

[28] Heaston v. Krieg, 167 Ind. 101, 77 N.E. 805, 119 Am.St.Rep. 475, 1910; McKinley v. McKinley, 286 Ky. 484, 151 S.W.2d 392, 1941, noted, 26 Minn.L.R. 417; In re Wnuk's Will, 256 Wis. 360, 41 N.W.2d 294, 1950, noted, [1952] Wis.L.R. 181. But see Palmer v. Riggs, 209 Miss. 127, 46 So.2d 86, 1950, where a testamentary deed by husband and wife was denied probate because it provided that it was not effective until death of the survivor of the grantors.

[29] Noble v. Fickes, supra note 25.

[30] Reynolds v. Balding, 183 Ark. 397, 36 S.W.2d 402, 1931; Thurston v. Tubbs, 257 Ill. 465, 100 N.E. 947, 1913; Mason's Guardian v. Soaper, 232 Ky. 525, 23 S.W.2d 956, 1930; Wilson v. Jones, 280 Mass. 488, 182 N.E. 917, 1932; Noah v. Noah, 246 Mich. 324, 224 N.W. 611, 1929; Southern v. Southern, 52 S.W.2d 868, Mo.1932; Horn v. Horn, 118 Neb. 364, 224 N.W. 857, 1929; Stalting v. Stalting, 52 S.D. 309, 217 N.W. 386, 1928. See annotation, 52 A.L.R. 1222; note, 6 Brooklyn L.R. 79.

[31] Mason's Guardian v. Soaper, supra note 30; Wilson v. Jones, supra note 30; Noah v. Noah, supra, note 30; Blackiston v. Russell, 328 Mo. 1164, 44 S.W.2d 22, 1931; Stalting v.

it does not operate as a present complete transfer but only as an escrow to pass title upon the grantor's death.[32]

Whatever the proper theory may be, there must be delivery in order to validate the deed. An undelivered deed has no effect as a conveyance and vests the grantee with no title either before or after the grantor's death.[33] Unless the grantor gives up dominion over the instrument at the time of handing it to the third party there is no delivery, and the transaction is ineffectual as one inter vivos.[34] The courts do not presume that the grantor intended to give up control over the deed but require affirmative proof of this fact.[35] Naturally the question of whether there was delivery cannot be determined from the face of the instrument; usually the grantor's acts must be shown by oral evidence, and his intention must be determined from his declarations and the surrounding circumstances. It is the intention at the time which governs; hence where there has been unqualified delivery to a third person, the grantor's later wrongful obtaining of the deed does not nullify its effect.[36]

Stalting, supra, note 30. See Bigelow, Conditional Deliveries of Deeds of Land, 26 Harv.L.R. 565, 575; Ballantine, When are Deeds Testamentary, 18 Mich.L.R. 470; note, 15 N.Y.U.L. Q.R. 463.

32 Kirkwood v. Smith, 212 Ill. 395, 72 N.E. 427, 1904; Stephens v. Rinehart, 72 Pa. 434, 1872. See Gridley v. Home Ins. Co., 226 App.Div. 593, 236 N.Y.S. 205, 1929. This position is criticized by Bigelow, supra note 31 at 578.

33 Hardin v. Russell, 175 Ark. 30, 298 S.W. 481, 1927; Anderson v. Larson, 177 Minn. 606, 225 N.W. 902, 1929; Allenbach v. Ridenour, 51 Nev. 437, 279 P. 32, 1929; Thomas v. Conyers, 198 N.C. 229, 151 S.E. 270, 1930 (left in grantor's safe-deposit box). See annotation, 129 A.L.R. 11.

34 Hardin v. Russell, supra note 33; Northern California Conference Ass'n v. Smith, 209 Cal. 26, 285 P. 314, 1930; Hudemann v. Dodson, 215 Cal. 3, 7 P.2d 997, 1932; Eddy v. Pinder, 131 Me. 139, 159 A. 727, 1932. Contra: Davis v. John E. Brown College of Siloam Springs, Ark., 208 Iowa 480, 222 N.W. 858, 1929. Cf. with later case where deed was delivered for safekeeping only. Keating v. Augustine, 213 Iowa 1336, 241 N.W. 429, 1932.

35 Williams v. Kidd, 170 Cal. 631, 151 P. 1, Ann.Cas.1916E, 703, 1915; Johnson v. Fleming, 301 Ill. 139, 133 N.E. 667, 1911; Eddy v. Pinder, supra note 34; Anderson v. Larson, 177 Minn. 606, 225 N.W. 902, 1929. See Snodgrass v. Snodgrass, 107 Okl. 140, 231 P. 237, 52 A.L.R. 1213, 1925. Cf. Stalting v. Stalting, 52 S.D. 309, 217 N.W. 386, 1923. See notes, 124 A.L.R. 462, 34 Cal.L.R. 437.

36 Boicelli v. Giannini, 65 Cal.App. 601, 224 P. 777, 1924; Selby v. Smith, 301 Ill. 554, 134 N.E. 109, 1922; Johnson v. Cooper, 123 Kan. 487, 255 P. 1112, 1927. See Trumbull v. Hale, 250 Mich. 117, 229 N.W. 414, 1930. Cf. Saltzsieder v. Saltzsieder, 219 N.Y. 523, 114 N.E. 856, 1916, recognizing the above rule, but also declaring that subsequent acts inconsistent with delivery are evidential that

*Other Conditions to Delivery*

When a grantor delivers a deed to a third person with instructions that it is to become effective only upon the survival of the grantee over the grantor, or some other uncertain event not within the control of the grantor, it is generally held that the grantee is not entitled to the property even if the contingency occurs.[37] Most courts label this a testamentary transaction which can only be effectuated by a duly executed will. Their reason seems to be that no title can be regarded as passing until the event takes place. This, however, should not be fatal for there may be valid delivery though title does not pass at that time. Possibly the courts have been misled into believing that the condition, though the grantor has no control over the events, makes the situation the same as where the right to revoke has been retained.[38] Quite inconsistently the majority of the cases hold that delivery to a third person to be effective only upon performance of a condition to be performed by the grantee after the grantor's death, such as payment of burial expense or the support of a third person, is valid.[39] This view can be justified upon the ground that upon delivery to the third person title passes to the grantee at once, subject to both a life estate in the grantor and to the further condition subsequent.

If the delivery to the third person is subject to the right of revocation by the grantor, the great weight of authority is to hold that the transaction is testamentary and the deed, as such, invalid.[40] Iowa formerly held the delivery good if the grantor does

the grantor never intended a complete delivery.

37 Conditional on survivorship of grantee by grantor: Stone v. Daily, 181 Cal. 571, 185 P. 665, 1919; Weber v. Brak, 289 Ill. 564, 124 N.E. 654, 1919; Stanforth v. Bailey, 344 Ill. 38, 175 N.E. 784, 1931; Dunlap v. Marnell, 95 Neb. 535, 145 N.W. 1017, 1914; Bloor v. Bloor, 105 Wash. 110, 177 P. 722, 1919. See Long v. Ryan, 166 Cal. 442, 137 P. 29, 1914. Conditional upon nonrecovery of health by grantor. Seeley v. Curts, 180 Ala. 445, 61 So. 807, Ann.Cas. 1915C, 381, 1913; Moore v. Trott, 156 Cal. 353, 104 P. 578, 134 Am.St.Rep. 131, 1909; Williams v. Daubner, 103 Wis. 521, 79 N.W. 748, 74 Am.St.Rep. 902, 1899.

38 See Ballantine, supra note 31 at 476–479.

39 Rust v. Rutherford, 95 Kan. 152, 147 P. 805, 1915 (where the condition was included in the language of the deed); Stockwell v. Shalit, 204 Mass. 270, 90 N.E. 570, 571, 1910; Plymale v. Keene, 76 Mont. 403, 247 P. 554, 555, 1926; Jackson v. Jackson, 67 Or. 44, 135 P. 201, Ann.Cas.1915C, 373, 1913. Contra: Taft v. Taft, 59 Mich. 185, 26 N.W. 426, 60 Am. Rep. 291, 1886.

40 In re Sweitzer's Estate, 215 Cal. 489, 11 P.2d 633, 1932; Linn v. Linn,

not exercise the right of recall.[41] This transaction has surely a testamentary flavor but no more so than where the deed is by its terms revocable,[42] nor than in the savings bank trust [43] and living trust cases.[44] In the latter, the arrangement is fully disclosed in a formal document and there is little danger of fraud. To a lesser degree the same distinction exists between the other two cases and an oral reservation of revocation. It must also be remembered that there is a conflict of authority as to the effect of retaining the right to revoke by express provision in deeds and in the savings bank trust cases.

261 Ill. 606, 104 N.E. 229, 1914; Kirby v. Hulette, 174 Ky. 257, 192 S.W. 63, 1917; Padden v. Padden, 171 Wis. 212, 177 N.W. 22, 1920. See, also, cases note 34 supra. Cf. Kokomo Trust Co. v. Hiller, 67 Ind.App. 611, 116 N.E. 332, 1917 (where the right reserved in the deed to sell the property did not affect the delivery to third person). But see In re Smith's Estate, 162 Kan. 215, 174 P.2d 1012, 1946.

In Larson v. Johnson, 53 S.D. 299, 220 N.W. 500, 1928, where the deed was delivered to third person to be delivered upon grantor's death with understanding that the grantor might have the deed redelivered in her lifetime, which was done, the delivery was held valid. The fact that the escrow agent would have returned the deed to the grantor if the latter called for it is not fatal to delivery. Stalting v. Stalting, 52 S.D. 309, 217 N.W. 386, 1927.

41 Lippold v. Lippold, 112 Iowa 134, 83 N.W. 809, 84 Am.St.Rep. 331, 1900; Davis v. John E. Brown College of Siloam Springs, Ark., 208 Iowa 480, 222 N.W. 858, 1929. But see Smith v. Fay, 228 Iowa 868, 293 N.W. 497, 1940. See Eckert v. Stewart, 207 S.W. 317, Tex.Civ.App. 1918; Morse v. Slason, 13 Vt. 296, 1841.

42 See supra notes 21, 22.

43 See supra § 41.

44 See supra § 42.

## CONTRACTUAL INSTRUMENTS

**44. A document in the general form of a contract, assignment, negotiable instrument or the like may be considered testamentary if its terms indicate an intention to create no present interest but merely direct what should be done after maker's death. If so, the instrument has no legal effect unless it is executed in the form of a will and is probated as such. If not, the instrument may be asserted as a contractual claim against the maker's estate, or in certain cases against a third person who has engaged to pay the claimant as third party beneficiary. The fact that the obligation is due at the maker's death does not by itself make the instrument testamentary.**

The upholding of life insurance policies [1] and survivorship interests [2] upon the basis of contract, as against the claim that the arrangement is testamentary has already been treated. Similar problems in connection with other types of contracts will be considered in the present section.

In most cases instruments in the form of leases, contracts, releases, assignments, bills of sale, notes, bonds, etc., are not testamentary. They have been sometimes so regarded by the courts, and very close questions arise when they direct something to be done at or after the maker's death. In general the test of testamentary character is the same as in the situations discussed heretofore, viz., does the paper presently create an interest in another though enjoyment is postponed, or does it create no such interest but merely direct what shall be done after the maker's death, being entirely ambulatory until that time? This is frequently a fine and difficult distinction to draw, but it is often vital to the success of the instrument. Thus, if the court decides that the document is testamentary, it can be valid only as a will and if it lacks the required formalities of the latter, it will be of no effect. On the other hand, if the instrument is nontestamentary in character, its execution with testamentary formalities will not sustain it, but it is invalid for all purposes unless it has all the requirements necessary for some sort of inter vivos transaction.[3] A given transaction may be invalid as a gift through lack of de-

1 Supra § 39.

2 Supra § 40.

3 But the fact that an instrument is partly contractual in character does not prevent its operation as a valid will. In re Koellen's Estate, 162 Kan. 395, 176 P.2d 544, 1947. Cf. In re Boucher's Estate, 329 Mich. 569, 46 N.W.2d 577, 1951. See supra, § 43, note 24.

livery, and as a contract because of absence of consideration, and also ineffective as a will because of lack of either testamentary formality or intent. This branch of the law can be best understood by consideration of a number of specific examples.

*Leases*

A lease for the owner's life to his wife executed contemporaneously with a deed to his daughter to be delivered upon his death and a mortgage by the daughter to the wife does not constitute a testamentary transaction, as the instruments take effect at once.[4] A lease for the lessor's life with the option to buy at or after his death is not testamentary,[5] even if the lessor reserves the right to avoid the lease upon certain conditions.[6] On the other hand, the provision that if the lessor dies before the expiration of the lease, the lessee is to pay the rent to the lessor's wife has been held testamentary.[7] It would seem that the opposite result might well be reached, and the latter provisions sustained as a contract for the benefit of a third person.[8]

*Contracts*

The mere fact that a promise to pay money is to be performed at or after the promisor's death does not make the instrument testamentary. This has been held in the case of charitable subscriptions,[9] marriage property contracts [10] and other agreements.[11]

4 Johnson v. Becker, 251 Mich. 132, 231 N.W. 96, 1930.

5 In re Specht's Estate, 268 Pa. 384, 112 A. 92, 1921. But see In re Murphy's Estate, 193 Wash. 400, 75 P.2d 916, 1938, noted, 37 Mich.L.R. 167, 23 Minn.L.R. 112, 86 U. of Pa.L.R. 792.

6 In re Estate of Ogle, 97 Wis. 56, 72 N.W. 389, 1897.

7 Murray v. Cazier, 23 Ind.App. 600, 53 N.E. 476, 55 N.E. 880, 1900; Priester v. Hohloch, 70 App.Div. 256, 75 N.Y.S. 405, 1902.

8 See Wilson v. Wilson, 211 Ark. 1030, 204 S.W.2d 479, 1947.

9 Transylvania University v. Rees, 297 Ky. 246, 179 S.W.2d 890, 1944; In re Griswold's Estate, 113 Neb. 256, 202 N.W. 609, 38 A.L.R. 858, 1925. But see American University v. Conover, 115 N.J.L. 468, 180 A. 830, 1935, criticized, 16 B.U.L.R. 269, 36 Col.L.R. 834; American University v. Collins, 190 Md. 688, 59 A.2d 333, 1948, noted, 17 Fordham L.R. 271.

10 Norton v. Norton's Estate, 41 Cal.App. 614, 183 P. 214, 1919; Johnston v. Spicer, 107 N.Y. 185, 13 N.E. 753, 1887.

Probate of such an instrument was granted in Re Heuler's Estate, 207 Cal. 391, 278 P. 1031, 1929, where the instrument though signed by both spouses and called a marriage contract contained language usually

11 See Note 11 on following page.

An agreement on the part of the creditor that the balance owing at the creditor's death is considered paid or shall not be collected is usually upheld if it is part of the original loan agreement.[12] Likewise a provision in a land contract that the balance of the purchase price unpaid at the vendor's death is forgiven has usually been upheld on a contractual basis,[13] though some cases have held that such provisions are testamentary.[14] When two persons, who were not partners, jointly bought a safe and each put certain securities therein, agreeing that the safe and contents should become the property of the survivor, the executor of the one who died first was held entitled to recover his testator's property by replevin from the survivor.[15] Of course no title passed to the survivor by way of trust or gift, though possibly the contract might be enforceable as a claim against the decedent's estate.[16]

In the well-known case of McCarthy v. Pieret,[17] it was held that a provision in an extension of a mortgage to the effect that any unpaid balance at the mortgagee's death should be paid to designated persons was testamentary. The court declared that no present interest was transferred to the beneficiaries and that the mortgagee intended to retain control until his death; further that contracts for the benefit of a third person were recognized only where the promisee is unable to revoke, or to control the

found in a will. The court makes no reference to In re Lowe's Estate, 178 Cal. 111, 172 P. 583, 1918, a somewhat similar case wherein probate was denied.

11 In re McIntosh's Estate, 182 Iowa 23, 159 N.W. 223, 1916. See also, In re Beyschlag's Estate, 201 Wis. 613, 231 N.W. 165, 1931, noted, 3 Dak.L.R. 277; In re Howe's Estate, 31 Cal.2d 395, 189 P.2d 5, 1 A.L.R.2d 1171, 1948 (contract for services providing that employee should have the business at employer's death, though agreement could be terminated on 90 days' notice by either).

12 Church of Jesus Christ of Latter Day Saints v. Scarborough, 189 F.2d 800, C.A.Utah, 1951; Miller v. Allen, 339 Ill.App. 471, 90 N.E.2d 251, 1950, noted, 29 Chi-Kent L.R. 194.

13 Daugherty v. Preuitt, 113 Okl. 66, 242 P. 529, 1925; In re Lewis' Estate, 2 Wash.2d 458, 98 P.2d 654, 127 A.L.R. 628, 1940.

14 Juneau v. Dethgens, 200 Wis. 360, 228 N.W. 496, 1930.

15 Thomas v. Byrd, 112 Miss. 692, 73 So. 725, 1916; United States Trust Co. of Paterson v. Giveans, 97 N.J. L. 265, 117 A. 46, 1922. Cf. partnership cases, supra § 40, note 15; see also supra § 38.

16 See Fawcett v. Fawcett, 191 N.C. 679, 132 S.E. 796, 1926.

17 281 N.Y. 407, 24 N.E.2d 102, 1939, noted, 18 Chi-Kent L.R. 417, 26 Corn.L.Q. 130, 53 Harv.L.R. 1060, 38 Mich.L.R. 900, 24 Minn.L.R. 109.

promisor in the fulfillment of the promise. It is not apparent how the mortgagee had control over payments not due in his lifetime, and the underlying rationale seems to be that the arrangement is bad simply because it was used as a substitute for a will. The same result has been reached without noticing the possibilities of third party beneficiary,[18] but other cases have sustained similar transactions upon the latter basis, at least so far as the sum was not payable and could not be demanded by the creditor.[19] However, an order by a bank depositor to the bank to pay another on the depositor's death was held to be testamentary since the depositor undoubtedly intended to retain the right to withdraw and thus control the account of his lifetime.[20]

While the retention of control by the creditor or owner is an important factor in holding that attempted contractual devices are testamentary, it cannot be said that some control is necessarily fatal to sustaining the transaction as a contract. Thus, it has been held that the person named in an employee's stock purchase plan as the beneficiary in case of death of the employee-purchaser is entitled to the stock as against the latter's administrator.[21] In holding that this stipulation was not testamentary the court emphasizes that the stock did not belong to the employee in her lifetime because she died before the time set for delivery, although she could have withdrawn the amount paid with interest at any time.[22] In other words the employee's interest and the beneficiary's were not the same. Another factor in the decision may have been that there was a degree of formality in connection with the agreement, which formality is a guar-

18 Sliney v. Cormier, 49 R.I. 74, 139 A. 665, 1928.

19 Robinson's Women's Apparel v. Union Bank & Trust Co., 67 F.Supp. 395, D.C.N.Y.1946; Kansas City Life Ins. Co. v. Rainey, 353 Mo. 477, 182 S.W.2d 624, 155 A.L.R. 168, 1944. See infra note 21.

20 Tucker v. Simrow, 248 Wis. 143, 21 N.W.2d 252, 1946. See also In re Brown's Estate, 343 Pa. 230, 22 A.2d 821, 1941.

21 In re Koss' Estate, 106 N.J.Eq. 323, 150 A. 360, 1930, reversing 105 N.J.Eq. 29, 146 A. 471, 1929. See also, Siter v. Hall, 220 Ky. 43, 294 S.W. 767, 1927, sustaining the transaction as a declaration of trust. But see Tensfield v. Magnolia Petroleum Co., 134 Okl. 38, 272 P. 404, 1928. A custodian account agreement that the bank would hold the securities upon a designated trust on depositor's death was held to be testamentary as a mere agency. Matter of Ihmsen's Estate, 253 App.Div. 472, 3 N.Y.S. 2d 125, 1938.

22 The court distinguishes Stevenson v. Earl, 65 N.J.Eq. 721, 55 A. 1091, 103 Am.St.Rep. 790, 1 Ann.Cas. 49, 1903, where a savings fund was involved, upon which the depositor might draw. See, also, Trenton Savings Fund Soc. v. Wythman, 104 N.J. Eq. 271, 145 A. 462, 1929.

antee against the dangers that the naming of the beneficiary was the result of over-reaching or a momentary whim. The same can be said of life insurance policies wherein the insured retains considerable control.[23] But the courts are chary of informal arrangements, which, under the guise of contracts, attempt to have all the advantages of a will without compliance with the formal requirements of testamentary succession.[24]

*Releases and Bills of Sale*

An instrument which releases an obligation is not testamentary,[25] but one which directs that a credit should be charged against a daughter as an advancement is, and if properly executed, is provable as a will.[26] A bill of sale in ordinary language cannot be probated as a will, and extrinsic facts cannot be shown to indicate testamentary intent.[27] But a bill of sale which states that the property is to pass at the death of the maker has been held testamentary,[28] as was one which purported to pass all the personalty owned by him at his death.[29]

*Assignments*

The question sometimes arises as to whether an instrument more or less in the form of an assignment should be regarded as a will. When the transfer is gratuitous and is stated to take effect upon the assignor's death it has been held testamentary.[30] The fact that a document executed with the form and language of a will is prefaced "assignment, will, and testament," does not af-

23 See supra § 39.

24 Imthurn v. Martin, 150 Kan. 906, 96 P.2d 860, 1939; Lakin v. Blum, 43 S.W.2d 853, Mo.App.1931. See supra note 21.

25 Jones v. Jones, 163 Tenn. 237, 43 S.W.2d 205, 1931; Condry v. Coffey, 163 Tenn. 508, 43 S.W.2d 928, 1931.

26 Condry v. Coffey, supra note 25.

27 In re Lloyd's Estate, 256 Mich. 305, 239 N.W. 390, 391, 1931. But see Clarke v. Commerce State & Savings Bank, 68 Colo. 401, 189 P. 842, 1920.

28 Taylor v. Wilder, 63 Colo. 282, 165 P. 766, 1917.

29 In re Salzwedel's Estate, 171 Wis. 441, 177 N.W. 586, 1920; see Todd v. Williams' Adm'x, 264 Ky. 788, 95 S.W.2d 593, 1936.

30 In re Thompson's Will, 196 N.C. 271, 145 S.E. 393, 62 A.L.R. 288, 1928 (assignment probated as holographic codicil); Knoll v. Hart, 308 Pa. 223, 162 A. 228, 1932 (assignment held invalid as transfer inter vivos). And see Paine v. Paine, 28 R.I. 307, 67 A. 127, 12 L.R.A.,N.S., 547, 1907, where the assignment was to the assignor as attorney for the assignee and assignor gave up no control during his lifetime—held testamentary. Cf. McCloskey v. Tierney, 141 Cal. 101, 74 P. 699, 99 Am.St.Rep. 33, 1904, where word "leave" instead of "assign" was not fatal to a present assignment.

fect its validity as a will.[31] When the language of an assignment indicates a present transfer, it is not invalid as such merely because it contains a provision that it is not to be recorded until assignor's death.[32] An instrument addressed to a life insurance company naming a beneficiary to a policy may not be probated as a will, though subscribed by sufficient witnesses.[33]

*Notes, etc.*

An instrument stating that deceased wanted his daughter to receive $1,000 for her services was considered to be testamentary and not contractual and hence unable to support a claim against the estate.[34] While perhaps there was consideration to sustain a contract, the language of the paper indicated testamentary intent. In this case the decision was not fatal as the paper was witnessed and could be proved as a will. A promissory note, or an order for the executor to pay, is valid as such if supported by consideration and is not rendered testamentary because payable at or after the maker's death.[35] The same is true of a covenant to pay after death when the language indicates that the maker is presently bound.[36] Where however, such an instrument merely directs the executor to pay a sum at the maker's death, and

31 Noel v. Noel, 109 Kan. 440, 199 P. 459, 1921.

32 Burkett v. Doty, 32 Cal.App. 337, 162 P. 1042, 1917.

33 In re Wheatley's Estate, 184 Cal. 399, 193 P. 934, 1920. See, also, Southern Mut. Life Ins. Ass'n v. Durdin, 132 Ga. 495, 64 S.E. 264, 131 Am. St.Rep. 210, 1909. Cf. where assignment was to the trustee named in deceased's will; held testamentary and invalid because not executed as a will. Frost v. Frost, 202 Mass. 100, 88 N.E. 446, 447, 27 L.R.A.,N.S., 184, 132 Am.St.Rep. 476, 1909; In re Kenin's Estate, 343 Pa. 549, 23 A.2d 837, 1942. See Gulliver and Tilson, Classification of Gratuitous Transfers, 51 Yale L.J. 1, 24.

34 Lakin v. Blum, 43 S.W.2d 853, Mo.App.1931. Evidently the testamentary language contained therein distinguishes this case from those cited in note 35 infra. See also In re Gibson's Estate, 128 Pa.Super. 44, 193 A. 302, 1937.

35 University of Southern California v. Bryson, 103 Cal.App. 39, 283 P. 949, 1930; Lawrence v. Scurry, 187 Iowa 1055, 175 N.W. 22, 1920; Miller v. McClune, 88 Pa.Super. 128, 1907; Gostina v. Whitham, 148 Wash. 72, 268 P. 132, 1928; Sheldon v. Blackman, 188 Wis. 4, 205 N.W. 486, 1925; In re Sense's Will, 206 Wis. 89, 238 N.W. 811, 1931. See supra notes 9–11. It has been held that where the instrument recited consideration and there was a statutory presumption of consideration from the writing, it is enforceable as a contract. Patterson v. Chapman, 179 Cal. 203, 176 P. 37, 2 A.L.R. 1467, 1918.

36 Krell v. Codman, 154 Mass. 454, 28 N.E. 578, 14 L.R.A. 860, 26 Am.St. Rep. 260, 1891. See In re Eisenlohr's Estate, 258 Pa. 438, 102 A. 117, 1917; note, 25 Corn.L.R. 119.

there is no consideration therefor, it is testamentary and will not support a claim against the estate.[37] If such an instrument is executed with the formalities of a will, it can be probated and enforced as such.[38] A check payable at or after the drawer's death if given without consideration is invalid as an assignment or gift and if not executed with testamentary formalities, it is invalid for any purpose.[39]

## GIFTS

**45. A gift may be made of a chattel if there is donative intent and sufficient delivery. While delivery to a third person to be handed over on the donor's death may be a valid gift, a gift inter vivos may not be revocable or conditional.**

**However, if a person is in apprehension of impending death, he may make a gift causa mortis, which is revocable and also subject to the claims of donor's creditors without proof of intent to defraud them.**

Of course an owner of personalty may make an outright gift in lieu of disposing of it by will, or of permitting it to pass under the intestate laws. If he wishes to make a present donation and is willing to be bound by the finality of the gift, this is an appropriate manner of disposition. However, a person in good health seldom desires to make a gift of all his property, although some rich men give a considerable portion of their property to members of their families paying the gift tax which is smaller than the tax on decedent's estates. The desire to retain one's property for his own use, or the hope of controlling the conduct of the intended beneficiary, prompts most owners to use some other device than the simple gift. To a limited degree these objections to gifts may be avoided by delivery of the chattel to a third person with instructions to give to the donee upon the donor's death, as in the case of deeds of land.[1] Such transactions are valid if the donor reserves no right to recall the property,[2] even if he re-

[37] Cover v. Stein, 67 Md. 449, 10 A. 231, 1 Am.St.Rep. 406, 1887. See Hydrick v. Hydrick, 142 S.C. 531, 141 S.E. 150, 1927; Roberts v. Coleman, 37 W.Va. 143, 16 S.E. 482, 1892, where a bond directed the maker's executor to convey land unless conveyed by maker in his lifetime—held testamentary.

[38] Little's Adm'r v. Sizemore, 208 Ky. 135, 270 S.W. 729, 1925. See Lakin v. Blum, supra note 34.

[39] In re Knapp's Estate, 197 Iowa 166, 197 N.W. 22, 1924; Graham v. Hoke, 219 N.C. 755, 14 S.E.2d 790, 1941. See infra § 45, notes 29–31.

[1] Supra § 43, note 30.

[2] Pyle v. East, 173 Iowa 165, 155 N.W. 283, 3 A.L.R. 885, 1915; Innes

tains a life income.[3] It is well established that a gift inter vivos is not, and cannot be made, revocable or conditional.[4] Furthermore the owner may not play fast and loose so as to obtain the advantages of a gift by way of avoiding making a will and judicial administration of the property after his death, and at the time reserve control by retaining possession of the chattel. Delivery is necessary for a valid gift, and many cases occur in which the personalty passes to the personal representative because of the owner's attempts to retain physical control during his lifetime.[5] However, an "affirmation of gift" which gives all of testator's property to her brothers was effective as a will when it was duly attested.[6]

*Gift Causa Mortis*

This form of gift is subject to revocation by the donor.[7] It is limited to cases when the donor is in apprehension of impending death,[8] though he need not be in extremis.[9] If a gift is made un-

v. Potter, 130 Minn. 320, 153 N.W. 604, 3 A.L.R. 896, 1915; Payne v. Tobacco Trading Corp., 179 Va. 156, 18 S.E.2d 281, 1942. Cf. Baugh v. Howze, 211 Ark. 222, 199 S.W.2d 940, 1947; Hill v. Hill, 144 Me. 224, 67 A. 2d 533, 1949.

3 Novak v. Reeson, 110 Neb. 229, 193 N.W. 348, 1923; In re Chapple's Estate, 332 Pa.St. 168, 2 A.2d 719, 121 A.L.R. 422, 1938.

4 Moore v. Layton, 147 Md. 244, 127 A. 756, 1925; Matter of Van Wert, 193 Misc. 165, 83 N.Y.S.2d 92, 1948. In both cases death of donor was the condition. See also Baugh v. Howze, supra note 2.

5 See e. g., Trautz v. Lemp, 329 Mo. 580, 46 S.W.2d 135, 1932, where corporate stock was transferred to donees' names and placed in a safe to which donor and donees had access—delivery held insufficient; Geisel v. Burg, 283 Mich. 73, 276 N.W. 904, 1937 (undelivered certificates of deposit endorsed to another in event of owner's death). See annotations, on various problems of delivery: 126 A. L.R. 924, 127 id. 780, 145 id. 1386, 152 id. 427. Generally, see Mechem, infra note 20.

6 In re Mathew's Estate, 234 Iowa 188, 12 N.W.2d 162, 1943.

7 Regarding the history of gifts causa mortis, see notes, 59 U. of Pa. L.R. 95, 96, 32 Col.L.R. 702, 704. The English and American concept of this device was probably more influenced by the Roman law than other matters of succession. See also note, 7 N.Y.U.Intermural L.R. 139.

8 This is ordinarily a question for the jury. Castle v. Persons, 117 F. 835, C.C.A.Minn.1902; McCoy v. Shawnee Building & Loan Ass'n, 122 Kan. 38, 251 P. 194, 49 A.L.R. 1441, 1927. Gifts causa mortis have been sustained where the donor did not die until a year after the transaction. Moore v. Shifflett, 187 Ky. 7, 216 S. W. 614, 1920. On the condition of health, compare: Taylor v. Harmison, 79 Ill.App. 380, 1898; Johnson v. Grice, 140 Miss. 562, 106 So. 271, 1925; Butler v. Sherwood, 114 Misc. 483, 186 N.Y.S. 712, 1921; Simpkins v. Old Colony Trust Co., 254 Mass. 576, 151 N.E. 87, 1926; Kennedy v.

9 See Note 9 on following page.

der these circumstances the right of revocation is ordinarily implied,[10] but this presumption may be rebutted by proof that the donor intended an absolute gift. In other words it can be shown that the gift was inter vivos though made on the deathbed.[11] Though under the circumstances a donor would not be apt to retain a life income in the property, this provision is not fatal to a gift causa mortis.[12]

Some difference of opinion exists as to whether the gift causa mortis is effective at once but subject to defeasance by revocation,[13] or whether it operates only upon the donor's death.[14] According to the latter view the gift causa mortis would be regarded as a specie of testamentary succession, but the former is the position taken by most courts. This is principally a doctrinal difference which does not seem to affect the holdings of the cases [15] though the point would be material if the donee transferred to a bona fide purchaser and later the donor revoked the gift. The transaction may be, and ordinarily is, entirely oral. As in gifts inter vivos, there may be donations causa mortis of choses in action as well as of money or tangible chattels.[16] The doctrine of gifts causa mortis has no application to real

Nelson, 125 Neb. 185, 249 N.W. 546, 1933. By the prevailing view one about to participate in a war is not in sufficient apprehension of death to make a valid gift causa mortis. Reedy v. Kelley, 206 Ala. 132, 89 So. 275, 1921; Stradcutter v. Stradcutter, 151 Minn. 80, 185 N.W. 1016, 1921. Contra: Virgin v. Gaither, 42 Ill. 39, 1866. Contemplated suicide though not carried out for over two months was held sufficient in a case which must be regarded as an extreme one. In re Van Wormer's Estate, 255 Mich. 399, 238 N.W. 210, 1931. Se excellent note, 32 Col.L.R. 702, 706, et seq.

9 Weiss v. Fenwick, 111 N.J.Eq. 385, 162 A. 609, 1932; Begovich v. Kruljac, 38 Wyo. 365, 267 P. 426, 60 A.L.R. 1046, 1928. See also cases cited supra note 8; Braun v. Brown, 14 Cal.2d 346, 94 P.2d 348, 127 A.L.R. 773, 1939, where donor hoped to recover.

10 Harmon v. Harmon, 131 Ark. 501, 199 S.W. 553, 1917. See Allen v. Hendrick, 104 Or. 202, 206 P. 733, 1922.

11 Grand Rapids Trust Co. v. Bellows, 224 Mich. 504, 195 N.W. 66, 1923; Williams v. Finnigan, 185 S.W. 1165, Mo.App.1916; Harriman v. Bunker, 79 N.H. 127, 106 A. 499, 1919.

12 Fender v. Foust, 82 Mont. 73, 265 P. 15, 1928.

13 Emery v. Clough, 63 N.H. 552, 4 A. 796, 56 Am.Rep. 543, 1886; Nicholas v. Adams, 2 Whart.(Pa.) 17, 1836; Basket v. Hassell, 107 U.S. 602, 2 S.Ct. 415, 27 L.Ed. 500, 1882.

14 Hatcher v. Buford, 60 Ark. 169, 29 S.W. 641, 27 L.R.A. 507, 1895; Stagg v. Stagg, 90 Mont. 180, 300 P. 539, 543, 1931 (statute). See Bordwell, Testamentary Dispositions, 19 Ky.L.J. 283, 286–289.

15 See In re Nols' Estate, 251 Wis. 90, 28 N.W.2d 360, 1947.

16 See infra notes 21–28.

property,[17] though one may probably dispose of his entire personal estate in this manner.[18]

### *Delivery*

Delivery is as essential to a gift causa mortis as it is to a gift inter vivos.[19] In general, the acts which would not suffice for delivery of a gift inter vivos are not sufficient to sustain a donation causa mortis.[20] It is clear that any set of facts which would constitute good delivery for a gift inter vivos will satisfy this requirement of a gift causa mortis. Thus, delivery to a third person to be given to the donee at the donor's death is good.[21] While acceptance is necessary it will be presumed if the transaction is beneficial to the donee.[22] The delivery may be symbolic,[23] as well as of the thing itself. The handing over of savings bank

[17] Wentworth v. Shibles, 89 Me. 167, 36 A. 108, 1897; In re Reh's Estate, 196 Mich. 210, 162 N.W. 978, 1917 (lease of years). Cf. Davie v. Davie, 47 Wash. 231, 91 P. 950, 1907 (vendor's interest in lands sold on contract; gift causa mortis good).

[18] In re Elliott's Estate, 312 Pa. 493, 167 A. 289, 90 A.L.R. 360, 1933, noted, 33 Mich.L.R. 307. See Quarles v. Fowlkes, 147 Va. 493, 137 S.E. 365, 1927.

[19] Szabo v. Speckman, 73 Fla. 374, 74 So. 411, L.R.A.1917D, 357, 1917; Drake v. Security Trust Co., 203 Ky. 733, 263 S.W. 4, 1924; In re Tart, 180 N.C. 105, 104 S.E. 65, 1920; McHale v. Toole, 258 Pa. 293, 101 A. 988, 1917. Return to donor is fatal to gift. Genteman v. Sutter, 215 S.W. 2d 477, Mo.1948.

[20] The cases generally bear this out. See authorities cited infra notes 21 to 28. See, also, Mechem, Delivery in Gifts of Chattels, 21 Ill.L.R. 341, 356, 357. But cf. note, 59 U. of Pa.L.R. 95, 98, urging that the law should be more lenient as to what constitutes delivery in the case of gifts causa mortis because of the necessities of the situation.

[21] Williams v. Letton, 228 Ky. 371, 15 S.W.2d 296, 1929; Stagg v. Stagg, 90 Mont. 180, 300 P. 539, 1931; Emery v. Clough, 63 N.H. 552, 4 A. 796, 56 Am.Rep. 543, 1886; Rosenau v. Merchants Bank, 56 N.D. 123, 216 N.W. 335, 1927; Sharpe v. Sharpe, 105 S. C. 459, 90 S.E. 34, 3 A.L.R. 891, 1916; Begovich v. Kruljac, 38 Wyo. 365, 267 P. 426, 60 A.L.R. 1046, 1928. See annotations, 3 A.L.R. 902, 60 A.L.R. 1054.

[22] Williams v. Letton, supra note 21; Varley v. Sims, 100 Minn. 331, 111 N.W. 269, 8 L.R.A.,N.S., 828, 117 Am.St.Rep. 694, 10 Ann.Cas. 473, 1907; Stagg v. Stagg, supra, note 21.

[23] In re Escolle's Estate, 134 Cal. App. 473, 25 P.2d 860, 1933 (key); Rule v. Fleming, 85 Ind.App. 487, 152 N.E. 181, 1926 (duplicate key); In re Elliott's Estate, 312 Pa. 493, 167 A. 289, 90 A.L.R. 360, 1914 (key); for an extreme case placed in this category, see Pushcash v. Dry Dock Sav. Inst., 140 Misc. 579, 251 N.Y.S. 184, 1931, criticized, 11 B.U.L.R. 597. Cf. In re Tart, supra, note 19. See also Scherzinger v. Scherzinger, 280 Ky. 44, 132 S.W.2d 537, 1939 (adding donee's name to checking account, though donor had right to draw).

books,[24] written obligations of third persons,[25] policies of life insurance,[26] and certificates of stock,[27] may constitute delivery in case of gifts causa mortis, though there is no written assignment or endorsement thereof. On the other hand a chose in action which is not represented by a writing cannot pass without a documentary assignment.[28] When the transaction is gratuitous, delivery by a drawer of his personal check does not constitute a gift either inter vivos or causa mortis of the amount of the check, as the order on the bank is considered revoked by the donor's death,[29] except where the check is cashed before the death, in which case the gift is valid.[30] Some courts hold that if the check is for the drawer's entire balance, it may operate as an assignment and be considered valid though not presented until after his death.[31] There must either be delivery of the thing itself or something which stands in its stead by way of a symbol or evidence. A gift causa mortis is not perfected by the preparation

24 Brooks v. Mitchell, 163 Md. 1, 161 A. 261, 84 A.L.R. 547, 1932; Pierce v. Boston Five Cents Sav. Bank, 129 Mass. 425, 37 Am.Rep. 371, 1880. See annotations, 40 A.L.R. 1249, 84 A.L.R. 558; Fender v. Foust, 82 Mont. 73, 265 P. 15, 1928; Snidow v. Brotherton, 140 Va. 187, 124 S.E. 182, 40 A.L.R. 1246, 1924. The contrary is held in Pennsylvania. Grigonis' Estate, 307 Pa. 183, 160 A. 706, 1932, criticized, 81 U. of Pa.L.R. 224.

25 Simpson v. Heberlein, 259 Ill. App. 579; Baker v. Moran, 67 Or. 386, 136 P. 30, 1913; Veal v. Veal, 27 Beav. 303, 54 Eng.Rep. 118, 1859; or of the donee's obligations, Hoks v. Wollenberg, 209 Wis. 276, 243 N.W. 219, rehearing denied 209 Wis. 276, 245 N.W. 128, 1932. See annotation, 25 A.L.R. 660. Delivery of Postal Savings Certificate was held effective, though it was not transferable. Blair v. Kirchner, 319 Ill.App. 348, 49 N.E. 2d 292, 1943.

26 Hani v. Germania Life Ins. Co., 197 Pa. 276, 47 A. 200, 80 Am.St.Rep. 819, 1900. See annotation, 47 A.L.R. 738.

27 Grimes v. Barndollar, 58 Colo. 421, 148 P. 256, 1915; Grymes v. Hone, 49 N.Y. 17, 10 Am.Rep. 313, 1872.

28 Adams v. Merced Stone Co., 176 Cal. 415, 178 P. 498, 3 A.L.R. 928, 1919; Hawn v. Stoler, 208 Pa. 610, 57 A. 1115, 65 L.R.A. 813, 1922. See annotation, 3 A.L.R. 933.

29 Pullen v. Placer County Bank, 138 Cal. 169, 66 P. 740, 71 P. 83, 94 Am.St.Rep. 19, 1903; Weiss v. Fenwick, 111 N.J.Eq. 385, 162 A. 609, 1932; Burrows v. Burrows, 240 Mass. 485, 137 N.E. 923, 20 A.L.R. 175, 1922. See Tate v. Hilbert, 2 Ves.Jr. 111, 30 Eng.Rep. 548, 1793. See annotations, 20 A.L.R. 177, 44 A.L.R. 625, 53 A.L.R. 1119.

30 Conners v. Murphy, 100 N.J.Eq. 280, 134 A. 681, 53 A.L.R. 1115, 1926.

31 Varley v. Sims, 100 Minn. 331, 111 N.W. 269, 8 L.R.A.,N.S., 828, 117 Am.St.Rep. 694, 10 Ann.Cas. 473, 1907. Cf. In re Campbell's Estate, 274 Pa. 546, 118 A. 547, 1922. Contra: Burrows v. Burrows, supra note 29.

and handing over of a mere memorandum indicating a present gift.[32]

*Compared with Wills*

The revocability of gifts causa mortis is the chief feature which distinguishes them from gifts inter vivos. In this respect gifts causa mortis are like wills; indeed they are revocable not only by the donor's express act but also by his recovery from the illness or passing of the danger as well, and probably also by the donor's survival of the donee.[33] Another characteristic of gifts causa mortis which is in common with testate and intestate succession is that the property is liable for the debts of the donor.[34] The law does not permit one to give away his property in this manner to the prejudice of his creditors. In case of insolvency of the donor's estate his personal representative is entitled to recover gifts causa mortis to the extent necessary to satisfy creditors. This is in contrast with gifts inter vivos which cannot be so recovered except upon proving an intent to defraud the creditors. Probably a gift causa mortis made with design of depriving the donor's spouse of the statutory share would not be permitted to stand,[35] though a gift inter vivos made with this intention would be valid.[36] On the other hand there are several

[32] Eschen v. Steers, 10 F.2d 739, C.C.A.Mo.1926; Garde v. Goldsmith, 204 Cal. 166, 267 P. 104, 1928; Howard v. Williams, 228 Ky. 259, 14 S.W.2d 1096, 1929; McGillivray v. First Nat. Bank of Dickinson, 56 N.D. 152, 217 N.W. 150, 1928; Garde v. Goldsmith, 131 Or. 481, 283 P. 39, 1930; Steuer v. Lang, 145 Wash. 271, 259 P. 722, 1927, noted, 5 Wash.L.R. 56. But see Scott v. Union & Planters' Bank & Trust Co., 123 Tenn. 258, 130 S.W. 757, 1910.

[33] See Conser v. Snowden, 54 Md. 175, 39 Am.Rep. 368, 1880; Allen v. Hendrick, 104 Or. 202, 206 P. 733, 1922. A gift causa mortis is not revoked by birth of issue to the donor, though the circumstances would cause revocation of a will. McCoy v. Shawnee Bldg. & Loan Ass'n, 122 Kan. 38, 251 P. 194, 49 A.L.R. 1441, 1926; but see Bloomer v. Bloomer, 2 Bradf.(N.Y.) 339, 1853.

[34] Chase v. Redding, 13 Gray (Mass.) 418, 1859; see Rosenau v. Merchants' Nat. Bank of Dickinson, 56 N.D. 123, 216 N.W. 335, 60 A.L.R. 1040, 1927. But the personal representative can recover the goods only if other assets are insufficient to pay debts. Virgin v. Gaither, 42 Ill. 39, 1866; see Hoks v. Wollenberg, 209 Wis. 276, 243 N.W. 219, 245 N.W. 128, 1932. See infra § 116.

[35] Hatcher v. Buford, 60 Ark. 169, 29 S.W. 641, 27 L.R.A. 507, 1895; Crawfordsville Trust Co. v. Ramsey, 55 Ind.App. 40, 100 N.E. 1049, 102 N.E. 282, 1913; Dunn v. German-American Bank, 109 Mo. 90, 18 S.W. 1139, 1892. But see Marshall v. Berry, 13 Allen (Mass.) 43, 1866.

[36] Potter Title & Trust Co. v. Braum, 294 Pa. 482, 144 A. 401, 64 A.L.R. 463, 1929. See annotation, 64 A.L.R. 466. See supra § 32.

important distinctions between testamentary disposition and donations causa mortis.[37] The former must ordinarily be in writing,[38] while the latter need not be. Delivery to the donee is required in the case of gifts, but not in the case of legacies or bequests. While a will is ordinarily made in general prospect of death a gift causa mortis requires a more immediate apprehension of this nature. Finally land can be disposed of by will but not by gift causa mortis. Upon analysis the gift causa mortis appears to be a sort of a hybrid species of transfer. Within the narrow field in which it may operate the property owner can secure most of the advantages of both the will and the ordinary gift.

## SHAM WILLS

**46. Upon clear proof that an instrument in the form of a will was intended as a joke or a sham, the instrument will be denied probate and all testamentary effect. Parol evidence is not usually admitted to show that an instrument apparently in final form was intended only as a specimen, though the contrary is true if the appearance or contents indicate an incomplete or tentative document.**

Considerable difficulty occurs in the situation where one has executed a document in regular testamentary language and form but there is an attempt to show that he did not intend it as his will. Of course it is permissible to show mental incapacity, undue influence and to some extent fraud and mistake to prove lack of testamentary intent.[1] Aside from these matters, can one show that testamentary intent was not present? Here one is confronted with the parol evidence rule with its policy of rejecting testimony to contradict the plain import of a written instrument. It is true that wills are unilateral so that there is no reliance upon the instrument by others at the time of execution as in case of contracts. From this it might be argued that the parol evidence rule should not be applied. However, there is a counteracting element in that when the alleged testator is dead he should not be at the mercy of oral evidence to the effect that he did not mean what he solemnly declared in writing. If proof of this kind

[37] See Smith v. Eshelman, 235 Ala. 588, 180 So. 313, 1938; Johnson v. Hilliard, 113 Colo. 548, 160 P.2d 386, 1945. See note, 34 Ky.L.J. 69 as to use of memorandum in lieu of delivery.

[38] And indeed also be attested, except in the jurisdictions allowing holographic wills. See infra c. 7. Cf. infra § 76.

[1] See infra §§ 51, 55, 56.

is permitted, it should be clear and positive in order to upset the will.

There is a group of cases which involve the question of whether it may be shown that a will, though regular on its face, was intended as a mere sham or jest. The leading case is that of Lister v. Smith,[2] where a testator was shown to have executed a codicil to induce a member of his family to surrender a house which she then occupied. Evidence that this was the sole purpose of making the codicil and that there was no intention of having it stand was held admissible. Furthermore, this was deemed a sufficient showing of absence of testamentary intent and the will was denied probate. On the question of admissibility of evidence, the American cases have followed this decision in the main,[3] though they have manifested some reluctance to permit an apparently genuine will to be overthrown by testimony of this sort.[4]

A degree of the Masonic order requires, or at least has required in recent years, the candidate to make a will as part of the initiation ceremony. If it can be shown that the candidate did not intend the instrument to be his will but merely executed it as a necessary part of the initiation, it should not be admitted to probate. On the other hand, if he did regard the instrument as his will, though motivated in part by the requirements of the initiation, it may be probated if it conforms with other requirements for a will. His intent is a difficult question to determine after the death, and naturally different conclusions have been reached in the cases.[5] Lodge wills have also presented other serious problems.[6] It seems very unwise to indulge in ritualistic forms which

2 3 Sw. & Tr. 280, 164 Eng.Rep. 1282, 1864.

3 In re Siemer's Estate, 202 Cal. 424, 261 P. 298, 1935; Fleming v. Morrison, 187 Mass. 120, 72 N.E. 499, 105 Am.St.Rep. 386, 1904; Clark v. Hugo, 130 Va. 99, 107 S.E. 730, 1921. But see Brown v. Avery, 63 Fla. 355, 58 So. 34, Ann.Cas.1914A, 90, 1912; In re Kennedy's Estate, 159 Mich. 548, 124 N.W. 516, 28 L.R.A.,N.S., 417, 134 Am.St.Rep. 743, 18 Ann.Cas. 892, 1910; In re Smith's Estate, 308 Mich. 518, 14 N.W.2d 71, 1944, noted, 8 U. of Detroit L.J. 49.

4 See Fleming v. Morrison and Clark v. Hugo, both supra note 3. Wigmore suggests that it should be permissible to show that the maker's pretense was a justifiable one as to calm a lunatic or console a dying person but not where it is morally beyond sanction. Evidence, § 2406.

5 Vickery v. Vickery, 126 Fla. 294, 170 So. 745, 1936; In re Sharp's Estate, 133 Fla. 802, 183 So. 470, 1938; Shiels v. Shiels, 109 S.W.2d 1112, Tex.Civ.App.1937; In re Watkins' Estate, 116 Wash. 190, 198 P. 721, 17 A.L.R. 372, 1921. See notes, 20 Mich.L.R. 722, 16 N.Y.U.L.Q.R. 323, 31 Yale L.J. 334.

6 See Succession of Torlage, 202 La. 693, 12 So.2d 683, 1943; Gooch v. Gooch, 134 Va. 21, 113 S.E. 873, 1922.

are so apt to result in controversy and litigation over the exercise of the testamentary power.

*Specimen Wills*

Much the same question is involved in the cases where it was claimed that the instrument, though in the usual form of a will, was meant only as a specimen or a guide. Perhaps evidence of this kind is even more dangerous because it is less capable of verification by surrounding circumstances. At any rate the American authorities have held generally that if there is nothing in the writing to indicate that it was intended as a mere specimen, parol evidence is not admissible to show that fact.[7] On the other hand where the instrument was written with pencil, lack of a present testamentary intent can be shown.[8] A writing which is apparently incomplete and states that further matters are to be arranged later should be denied probate.[9] However, intent to use the present instrument as a stopgap will is good enough, and in such cases probate is proper though the testator intended to execute a more formal or perfect instrument later.[10]

## LETTERS AS WILLS

**47. Letters may operate as holographic or soldiers' wills if the instrument indicates that it should have dispositive effect but casual expressions of a desire as to how one's property should go or information as to what future wills shall contain are usually held not to amount to wills.**

If the required formalities are observed, it is universally agreed that a letter may operate as a will. To be sustained as ordinary wills, letters must be attested by the required number of wit-

[7] Barnewall v. Murrell, 108 Ala. 366, 18 So. 831, 1895; Toebbe v. Williams, 80 Ky. 661, 1883; Douglass v. Harkrender, 3 Baxt. (Tenn.) 114, 1873.

[8] Smith v. Smith, 33 Tenn.App. 507, 232 S.W.2d 338, 1949, noted, 21 Tenn.L.R. 337; Brackenridge v. Roberts, 114 Tex. 418, 267 S.W. 244, 270 S.W. 1001, 1925.

[9] In re Barber's Will, 92 Hun 489, 37 N.Y.S. 235, 1896; In re Taylor's Will, 220 N.C. 524, 17 S.E.2d 654, 1941 (letter). See also Langehennig v. Hohmann, 139 Tex. 452, 163 S.W.2d 402, 1942; Wayman v. Miller, 195 Wash. 457, 81 P.2d 501, 1938; Harlan v. Anderson's Ex'r, 267 Ky. 779, 103 S.W.2d 310, 1937.

[10] In re Kemp's Will, 37 Del. (7 W.W.Harr.) 514, 186 A. 890, 1936; Parrott v. Parrott's Adm'x, 270 Ky. 544, 110 S.W.2d 272, 1937; In re Cosgrove's Estate, 290 Mich. 258, 287 N.W. 456, 125 A.L.R. 410, 1939; Richberg v. Robbins, 33 Tenn.App. 66, 228 S.W.2d 1019, 1950.

nesses.[1] Or course, this happens comparatively seldom.[2] However, where attesting witnesses are not required, as in the case of holographic and soldiers' wills,[3] the requirements of execution are often met by a letter. Not every letter which speaks of a disposition of the writer's property can be given the effect of a will. Testamentary intent must be manifested or the letter will not be given testamentary effect; though as shown subsequently in this section the courts sometimes find testamentary intent in a letter primarily written for another reason.[4]

A letter of instructions to one's attorney regarding the drafting of a will,[5] a casual remark that a certain person should have the property,[6] mere precatory language that the heir should make a certain disposition of the heritage,[7] statements of an intention to make one his heir or devisee at some future time,[8] declarations indicating a present donation,[9] or information as to how the

[1] Orth v. Orth, 145 Ind. 184, 42 N.E. 277, 44 N.E. 17, 32 L.R.A. 298, 57 Am.St.Rep. 185, 1896; Gibson v. Van Syckle, 47 Mich. 439, 11 N.W. 261, 1882; Magoohan's Appeal, 117 Pa. 238, 14 A. 816, 2 Am.St.Rep. 660, 1888.

[2] This occurred, however, in Ellison v. Clayton, 164 Md. 35, 163 A. 695, 1933; In re Tollefson's Estate, 198 Wis. 538, 224 N.W. 739, 1929. And cf. In re Henry's Estate, infra note 5, where the letter was witnessed but held to lack testamentary intent. See also In re Purcell's Estate, 198 Okl. 166, 176 P.2d 986, 1947.

[3] See infra §§ 75, 77.

[4] See infra notes 14 to 17.

[5] In re Grobe's Estate, 96 Cal.App. 2d 70, 214 P.2d 535, 1950; In re Henry's Estate, 263 Mich. 410, 248 N.W. 853, reversing, 259 Mich. 499, 244 N.W. 141, 1932, noted, 19 Corn.L.Q. 345. Cf. Scott's Estate, 147 Pa. 89, 23 A. 212, 30 Am.St.Rep. 713, 1892.

[6] In re Branick's Estate, 172 Cal. 482, 157 P. 238, 1916; In re Henning's Estate, 186 Cal. 307, 199 P. 39, 1921; In re Spencer's Estate, 87 Cal.App.2d 591, 197 P.2d 351, 1948; Craig v. McVey, 200 Okl. 434, 195 P.2d 753, 1948. But see Alston v. Davis, 118 N.C. 202, 24 S.E. 15, 1896.

[7] Garde v. Goldsmith, 204 Cal. 166, 267 P. 104, 1928; Thruston's Adm'r v. Prather, 77 S.W. 354, 25 Ky.Law Rep. 1137, 1903; In re Jamison's Estate, 253 Pa. 284, 98 A. 565, 1916. But there may be a valid disposition though in form of a request. Knox's Estate, 131 Pa. 220, 18 A. 1021, 6 L.R.A. 353, 17 Am.St.Rep. 798, 1890.

[8] In re Kelleher's Estate, 202 Cal. 124, 259 P. 437, 54 A.L.R. 913, 1927; In re Major's Estate, 89 Cal.App. 238, 264 P. 542, 1928; In re Bennett's Will, 180 N.C. 5, 103 S.E. 917, 1920; In re Zech's Estate, 70 S.D. 622, 20 N.W.2d 229, 1945; In re Jensen's Estate, 37 Utah 428, 108 P. 927, 1910. Cf. Milam v. Stanley, 33 Ky. Law Rep. 783, 111 S.W. 296, 17 L.R.A.,N.S., 1126, 1908.

[9] In re Kauffman's Estate, 283 Pa. 375, 129 A. 98, 1925. See In re Wheatley's Estate, 184 Cal. 399, 193 P. 934, 1920. Cf. Adams v. Maris, 213 S.W. 622, Tex.Com.App.1919; Estes v. Estes, infra note 14.

writer has decided to leave his property,[10] have been held to show no testamentary intent, and hence result in denial of probate of the instrument as a will. On the other hand, a letter expressing the desire that it should be regarded as a will is testamentary,[11] as is correspondence indicating the person is entitled to property at the writer's death.[12] A letter indicating the disposition desired until a formal will was prepared has been considered a valid testamentary instrument.[13] Even in absence of such expressions, letters have been probated as wills where testamentary intent was found to be present.[14] Although a letter was written primarily for a nontestamentary purpose, the court may find a "double intent" sufficient to consider the dispositive part as a will.[15] The courts are quite liberal in admitting evidence of the surrounding circumstances to show testamentary intent, when the language is ambiguous.[16] If a letter indicates that the writer wishes it to operate as a disposition to become effective on his

10 In re Pagel's Estate, 52 Cal.App. 2d 38, 125 P.2d 2, 853, 1942; In re Watt's Estate, 117 Mont. 505, 160 P. 2d 492, 1945; Early v. Arnold, 119 Va. 500, 89 S.E. 900, 1916; Thompkins v. Randall, 153 Va. 530, 150 S.E. 249, 1929, noted, 16 Va.L.R. 410; In the Estate of Beech, [1923] Prob. 46.

11 Sneed v. Reynolds, 166 Ark. 581, 266 S.W. 686, 1924; Estate of Richardson, 94 Cal. 63, 29 P. 484, 15 L. R.A. 635, 1892; In re Billis' Will, 122 La. 539, 47 So. 884, 129 Am.St.Rep. 355, 1908; In re Straulina's Estate, 134 A. 88, 4 N.J.Misc. 599, 1926.

12 De Lapp v. Anderson, 305 Ky. 333, 203 S.W.2d 388, 1947, noted, 46 Mich.L.R. 578; In re Mey's Estate, 200 Miss. 548, 28 So.2d 125, 1946; In re Kimmel's Estate, 278 Pa. 435, 123 A. 405, 31 A.L.R. 678, 1924.

13 Nelson v. Nelson, 235 Ky. 189, 30 S.W.2d 893, 1930, noted, 30 Col.L. R. 1217. See supra § 46, note 10.

14 In re Smilie's Estate, 99 Cal.App. 794, 222 P.2d 692, 1950; Estes v. Estes, 200 Miss. 541, 27 So.2d 854; In re Glass' Estate, 331 Pa. 561, 1 A. 2d 239, 117 A.L.R. 1322, 1938, noted, 5 U. of Pitt.L.R. 60, 13 Temple L.R. 136 (direction to deliver securities); In re McKean's Estate, 159 Pa.Super. 409, 48 A.2d 74, 1946 (direction to destroy notes of heirs). The courts sometimes are particularly liberal in finding testamentary intent in case of soldiers. Gattward v. Knee, [1902] P. 99. But cf. Estate of Beech, supra note 10.

15 In re Skerrett's Estate, 67 Cal. 585, 8 P. 181, 1885. See cases cited supra note 14 and infra note 16; also In re Estate of Dimmitt, 141 Neb. 413, 3 N.W.2d 752, 144 A.L.R. 704, 1942, noted, 37 Ill.L.R. 425, 41 Mich. L.R. 751, 22 Tex.L.R. 87, and supra § 46, note 5.

16 In re Sargavak's Estate, 35 Cal. 2d 93, 216 P.2d 850, 1950; Ellison v. Clayton, 104 Md. 35, 163 A. 695, 1933; In re Noyes' Estate, 40 Mont. 231, 106 P. 355, 1910; Hooker v. Bodine, 232 S.W.2d 371, Tex.Civ. App.1950; but cf. In re Golder's Estate, 31 Cal.2d 848, 193 P.2d 465, 1948; Maxey v. Queen, 206 S.W.2d 114, Tex.Civ.App.1947.

death and to be entirely revocable until that time, and if the testamentary requirements of execution are met, it should be admitted to probate though he did not consider it in terms as a will.[17]

The problem of whether a letter discloses testamentary intent is a difficult and elusive one and it is hard to reconcile all the cases or even to classify them. The civil law codes sometimes declare that a letter cannot constitute a holographic testament.[18] There is considerable justification for such provisions, even though they limit the testamentary power and may involve the further question as to what constitutes a letter.

## CONTRACTS TO MAKE WILLS

**48. A contract to make a will is not required to be executed with the formalities necessary for a will. Its essential and formal validity is determined by the law of contracts. Even if such an agreement is witnessed, it cannot be probated as a will for lack of testamentary character. If duly established, it may be enforced in law or equity against the promisor's estate.**

The general distinction between wills and contracts has already been discussed.[1] It may be a close question to determine whether a given document is a will, or a contract to make a will.[2] Important consequences hinge upon this decision. If the instrument is a will and lacks the requisites of a contract, it may be revoked by the testator in his lifetime, but if not revoked it is entitled to probate upon his death. Such a document does not give rise to a claim against the estate of the decedent. On the other hand, a contract to make a will cannot be probated. If valid as a contract it may be enforced against the estate of the promisor, who may not repudiate it except upon grounds which are sufficient for the avoidance of contracts. Such agreements are valid if, and

17 Barnes v. Horne, 233 S.W. 859, Tex.Civ.App.1921; Rice v. Freeland, 131 Va. 298, 109 S.E. 186, 1921; Langfitt v. Langfitt, 108 W.Va. 466, 151 S.E. 715, 1930; In re Tollefson's Estate, 198 Wis. 538, 224 N.W. 739, 1929. See Henderson v. Henderson, 183 Va. 663, 33 S.E.2d 181, 1945.

18 Argentine Civ.Code, Joanni, 1917, § 3682.

1 Supra § 44.

2 See In re Heuler's Estate, 207 Cal. 391, 278 P. 1031, 1929; Buehrle v. Buehrle, 291 Ill. 589, 126 N.E. 539, 1920; Matter of Hill's Estate, 126 Misc. 768, 215 N.Y.S. 655, 1926. See note, 16 B.U.L.R. 269. A testamentary instrument which fails as a will cannot be enforced as a contract. Spinks v. Rice, 187 Va. 730, 47 S.E.2d 424, 1948, noted 34 Va.L.R. 741.

only if, they meet the legal requirements of contracts in general. Of course an instrument may be both a contract and a will; this is frequently the contention in case of joint or mutual wills.[3]

*Terms*

As in the case of contracts generally, contracts to make wills must be certain in their terms. The agreement must be definite on both sides and must disclose what was to be left by the promisor's will and also what the promisee undertook to do in return. The latter phase has to do with the sufficiency of the consideration for the promise to leave one's property and will be discussed presently.[4]

The promise may be too general or indefinite to be recognized as creating a legal obligation. Thus a promise to devise "something" to the plaintiff is unenforceable.[5] An agreement upon adopting a child to treat him as promisor's own is not one to will property because a parent may disinherit a child of his own blood by will.[6] A promise to an employee to leave him as much as he would lose by declining another position was deemed too indefinite.[7] The latter holding seems overly strict. Somewhat inconsistent with it are the cases which hold valid agreements to leave promisee enough so that she would not have to work,[8] or sufficient to live in comfort as theretofore enjoyed.[9] It is enough that the property to be left is ascertained at the time of promisor's death. Hence promises to leave all or a specified fractional share of that which one owns at his death are sufficiently definite,[10] as is one to devise a child's share.[11] The agreement need

3 In re Stuart's Estate, 97 Cal. App.2d 218, 217 P.2d 723, 1950. See infra § 49.

4 Infra notes 13–26.

5 Richardson v. Cade, 150 Ga. 535, 104 S.E. 207, 1920.

6 Baumann v. Kusian, 164 Cal. 582, 129 P. 986, 44 L.R.A.,N.S., 756, 1913; Fowler v. Lowe, 241 Iowa 1093, 42 N.W.2d 516, 1950; Clarkson v. Bliley, 185 Va. 82, 38 S.E.2d 22, 171 A.L.R. 1308, 1946. But see Jones v. Guy, 135 Tex. 398, 143 S.W.2d 906, 142 A.L.R. 77, 1940. Cf. note 11 infra. See generally, supra § 23, note 25 et seq.

7 Russell v. Agar, 121 Cal. 396, 53 P. 926, 66 Am.St.Rep. 35, 1898.

8 Thompson v. Stevens, 71 Pa. 161, 1872.

9 Thompson v. Tucker-Osborn, 111 Mich. 470, 69 N.W. 730, 1897.

10 Howe v. Watson, 179 Mass. 30, 60 N.E. 415, 1901; Svanburg v. Fosseen, 75 Minn. 350, 78 N.W. 4, 43 L.R.A. 427, 74 Am.St.Rep. 490, 1899; Kofka v. Rosicky, 41 Neb. 328, 59 N.W. 788, 25 L.R.A. 207, 43 Am.St. Rep. 685, 1894; Popejoy v. Boynton, 112 Or. 646, 655, 229 P. 370, 230 P. 1016, 1925. Cf. Beaver v. Crump, 76 Miss. 34, 23 So. 432, 1898, promise to devise all property not willed to others is too uncertain.

11 Healy v. Healy, 55 App.Div. 315, 66 N.Y.S. 927, 1900, affirmed 166 N.Y.

not provide expressly for the making of a will, and a promise to leave or give property to the promisee on promisor's death is certain enough.[12]

*Consideration*

There must be consideration for the promisor's agreement to make a will. A mere promise to leave one's property to a certain person, unsupported by any consideration, is not enforceable. A type of consideration often met is that of a promise to furnish services, care, support or a home to the promisor. An agreement to live with the latter is sufficiently descriptive of the services to be performed to support the contract to make a will.[13] Unless the plaintiff was already legally bound to furnish the services or support,[14] the promise constitutes valid consideration.[15] The same is generally true of the surrender of a child for adoption by the promisor in return for the latter's agreement to leave property to the child.[16] Another frequent type of consideration is a promise to make a particular will in exchange for the promisor's like promise.[17] Many other varieties of consideration have been held sufficient such as marriage,[18] conveyance of property,[19] payment of an annuity,[20] improvement of promisor's property,[21] or forbearance of a law suit.[22] But payment of an existing debt is not good consideration for a contract to make a will.[23] When

624, 60 N.E. 1112, 1901. See also In re Krause's Estate, 173 Wash. 1, 21 P.2d 268, 1933 (promise not to make a new will).

12 Owens v. McNally, 113 Cal. 444, 45 P. 710, 33 L.R.A. 369, 1896; Svanburg v. Fosseen, supra note 10. See also Brunk v. Merchants Nat. Bank, 217 Ark. 499, 230 S.W.2d 932, 1950.

13 Jefferson v. Simpson, 83 W.Va. 274, 98 S.E. 212, 1919.

14 Bagley v. Bagley, 110 Or. 368, 222 P. 722, 1924.

15 Dalby v. Maxfield, 244 Ill. 214, 91 N.E. 420, 135 Am.St.Rep. 312, 1910; Emery v. Darling, 50 Ohio St. 160, 33 N.E. 715, 1893.

16 Oles v. Wilson, 57 Colo. 246, 141 P. 489, 1914; White v. Smith, 43 Idaho 354, 253 P. 849, 1927; Jones v. Bean, 136 Ill.App. 545, 1908; Bassett v. American Baptist Publication Soc., 215 Mich. 126, 183 N.W. 747, 15 A.L.R. 213, 1921. Cf. Baumann v. Kusian, 164 Cal. 582, 129 P. 986, 44 L.R.A.,N.S., 756, 1913.

17 See infra § 49.

18 Sarasohn v. Kamaiky, 193 N.Y. 203, 86 N.E. 20, 1908.

19 Manchester v. Loomis, 191 Iowa 554, 181 N.W. 415, 1921; Riley v. Allen, 54 N.J.Eq. 495, 35 A. 654, 1896.

20 Garard v. Yeager, 154 Ind. 253, 56 N.E. 237, 1900.

21 Osborn v. Hoyt, 181 Cal. 336, 184 P. 854, 1919.

22 Kundinger v. Kundinger, 150 Mich. 630, 114 N.W. 408, 1908.

23 Dawson v. Corbett, 71 S.D. 106, 21 N.W.2d 758, 1946. Attaching a

the consideration is unlawful sexual intercourse, it is illegal and the promise is unenforceable.[24] As in contracts generally, the disproportionate amount of the consideration does not affect the validity of the contract.[25] In equity, however, it has sometimes been held that the plaintiff will be relegated to damages in a court of law if the consideration furnished is grossly inadequate for the property promised to be left by will.[26]

In most jurisdictions a third person may sue upon a contract to make a will in his favor.[27] The courts which disfavor third party beneficiary agreements generally are more strict; but even they will allow a moral obligation of the promisee to the third party to support the latter's right to sue upon a promise to make a will.[28] The third party beneficiary doctrine seems particularly necessary to do justice in cases of agreements to leave property to an adopted child as the child is generally too young at the time of the adoption to be regarded as a party to the contract. One court, which was committed by prior decisions to deny the right of third party beneficiaries, went to the extreme length of holding that the child had become a party to the contract though he was only seven years old at the time.[29] Such decisions impress one that the recognition of the third party's right by the majority of the courts is desirable.

*Statute of Frauds*

Contracts to make wills are not within the Statute of Wills and do not require execution in testamentary form. Some states, however, have special statutes requiring all such contracts to

seal to the will is without effect. Kessler v. Olen, 228 Wis. 662, 281 N.W. 691, 1938.

24 Drennan v. Douglass, 102 Ill. 341, 40 Am.Rep. 595, 1882.

25 Lovett v. Lovett, 87 Ind.App. 42, 155 N.E. 528, rehearing denied 87 Ind. App. 42, 157 N.E. 104, 1927; Watkins v. Covington Trust & Banking Co., 303 Ky. 644, 198 S.W.2d 964, 1947.

26 Kurtz v. De Johnson, 42 Cal.App. 221, 183 P. 588, 1919; Richardson v. Orth, 40 Or. 252, 66 P. 925; Id., 40 Or. 252, 69 P. 455, 1902. See also In re Johnson's Estate, 233 Iowa 782, 10 N.W.2d 664, 148 A.L.R. 748, 1943, noted, 29 Iowa L.R. 130.

27 In re Edmundson's Estate, 259 Pa. 429, 103 A. 277, 2 A.L.R. 1150, 1918; Stevens v. Myers, 91 Or. 114, 177 P. 37, 2 A.L.R. 1155, 1919; Smith v. Thompson, 250 Mich. 302, 230 N. W. 156, 73 A.L.R. 1389, 1930. See infra § 49, note 6.

28 Seaver v. Ransom, 224 N.Y. 233, 120 N.E. 639, 2 A.L.R. 1187, 1918; Morgan v. Sanborn, 225 N.Y. 454, 122 N.E. 696, 1919.

29 Bassett v. American Baptist Publication Soc., supra note 16.

be proved by writing.[30] These promises are not within the clause of the Statute of Frauds referring to contracts not to be performed within one year.[31] As the promisor may die within a year, the contract may be fully performed within that time so that an oral agreement does not offend this provision. If the promise is to bequeath personalty it does not generally come within the sales of goods section of the Statute of Frauds.[32] This seems a sound conclusion for even if the promised legacy or bequest is regarded as a sale it is not such a one as is contemplated by the section which speaks of part delivery and part payment. Neither of the latter are appropriate to this type of transaction. Accordingly the oral character of a promise to will personalty does not make it unenforceable, unless the promise is given in consideration of marriage in which case it comes within the Statute.[33]

By the great weight of authority promises to devise realty are within the clause of the Statute of Frauds which relates to sales of land.[34] A devise when given for consideration is considered a sale. There is no provision in this section for part payment or part delivery to indicate its inapplicability to contracts to leave land. However, a strong argument can be made for the minority position, particularly if the promise is to will all or a fractional part of the estate which may consist wholly of personalty at the

30 Cal.Civ.Code § 1624; Mass.Laws Ann. c. 259, § 5; Ohio Gen.Code § 10504-3a; see note, 16 U. of Cin.L.R. 166.

31 Appleby v. Noble, 101 Conn. 54, 124 A. 717, 1924; Wellington v. Apthorp, 145 Mass. 69, 13 N.E. 10, 1887; Carlin v. Bacon, 322 Mo. 435, 16 S.W. 2d 46, 69 A.L.R. 1, 1929; Updike v. Ten Broeck, 32 N.J.L. 105, 1866. For general treatment, see Peterson, Effect of Statute of Frauds on Contracts for Testamentary Disposition, 17 Ind.L.J. 399; Schnebly, infra note 36.

32 Hull v. Thoms, 82 Conn. 647, 74 A. 925, 1910; King's Ex'rs v. Hanna, 9 B.Mon.(Ky.) 369, 1849; Wellington v. Apthorp, supra note 31; Day v. Washburn, 76 N.H. 203, 81 A. 474, 1911. Contra: Ohlendiek v. Schuler, 30 F.2d 5, C.C.A Ohio, 1925, criticized, 38 Yale L.J. 997. But see Maloney v. Maloney, 258 Ky. 567, 80 S.W.2d 611, 1935, noted, 20 Minn.L.R. 238.

33 Mallett v. Grunke, 107 Neb. 173, 185 N.W. 310, 1921; Watkins v. Watkins, 82 N.J.Eq. 483, 89 A. 253, 1913, affirmed 85 N.J.Eq. 217, 95 A. 1079, 1915; Hunt v. Hunt, 171 N.Y. 396, 64 N.E. 159, 59 L.R.A. 306, 1902; Rogers v. Joughin, 152 Wash. 448, 277 P. 988, 1929.

34 Allen v. Bromberg, 163 Ala. 620, 50 So. 884, 1909; Hoopeston Public Library v. Eaton, 283 Ill. 449, 119 N. E. 647, 1909; Hirschberg v. Horowitz, 105 N.J.L. 210, 143 A. 351, 1928; Loper v. Estate of Sheldon, 120 Wis. 26, 97 N.W. 524, 1903. But see Stahl v. Stevenson, 102 Kan. 447, 171 P. 1164, 1918; Id., 102 Kan. 844, 171 P. 1164, 1918; Woods v. Dunn, 81 Or. 457, 159 P. 1158, 1916. And see note 8 U. of Cin.L.R. 215.

time of promisor's death. When the property consists of both realty and personalty the prevailing view is that the whole promise is unenforceable and is not separable as to the personalty.[35] This position has been ably criticized.[36] There is a conflict as to whether a contract to die intestate or to refrain from making a will is within the Statute.[37] It would seem sound to refuse to apply the Statute of Frauds in all cases of doubt as to its applicability; otherwise there may be more injustice than prevention of fraud.[38] Seemingly the courts in general are somewhat of this mind for they often allow relief in equity in cases of performance by the promisee,[39] and at law they generally permit recovery upon a quantum meruit for the value of the consideration furnished.[40]

Interesting questions arise as to whether a revoked will may be regarded as sufficient memorandum of a contract to make a will to satisfy the Statute of Frauds. Generally the point must be answered in the negative,[41] because no promise appears on the face of the will and none should be implied merely from the execution of the testamentary instrument. In a few cases the promise appears in the language of the will, in which case the Statute is satisfied.[42] It should also be noticed that the contract need not be evidenced by a single writing. Sometimes the will may be used in connection with other documents to satisfy the Statute.[43]

35 Ohlendiek v. Schuler, 30 F.2d 5, C.C.A.Ohio, 1929, noted, 38 Yale L.J. 997. But see Mayfield v. Cook, 201 Ala. 187, 77 So. 713, 1918; Id., 203 Ala. 49, 82 So. 9.

36 Schnebly, Contracts to Make Testamentary Dispositions as Affected by the Statute of Frauds, 24 Mich.L.R. 749, 767.

37 That it is: Dicken v. McKinlay, 163 Ill. 318, 45 N.E. 134, 54 Am.St. Rep. 471, 1896; Wright v. Green, 67 Ind.App. 433, 199 N.E. 379, 1918. That it is not: Stahl v. Stevenson, supra note 34; Cleaves v. Kenney, 63 F.2d 682, C.C.A.Mass.1933.

38 See Schnebly, supra note 36.

39 See infra notes 83–86.

40 See infra note 69.

41 Holsz v. Stephen, 362 Ill. 527, 200 N.E. 601, 106 A.L.R. 737, 1936; White v. McKnight, 146 S.C. 59, 143 S.E. 552, 59 A.L.R. 1297, 1928; Canada v. Ihmsen, 33 Wyo. 439, 240 P. 927, 43 A.L.R. 1010, 1925. See note, 20 Cal.L.R. 654. But see Johnston v. Tomme, 199 Miss. 337, 24 So.2d 730, 1946, noted, 18 Miss.L.J. 328; Harris v. Morgan, 157 Tenn. 140, 7 S.W.2d 53, 1928 (four mutual wills.)

42 Woods v. Dunn, 81 Or. 457, 159 P. 1158, 1916. And see In re McLean's Estate, 219 Wis. 222, 262 N.W. 707, 709, 1935, noted, 21 Ia.L.R. 653.

43 See Johnson v. McCue, 34 Pa. 180, 1859.

*Conditions and Breach*

In order to recover upon a promise to make a will, the promisee must perform all conditions precedent. Thus, failure to furnish the agreed care, support or services to the promisor discharges the latter if he so elects.[44] But if the promisor fails to treat such conduct as a breach in his lifetime, the successors to his estate may not.[45] Furthermore if the conduct of the promisor is the cause of the promisee's failure to perform, the non-performance is not regarded as a discharge.[46] Even if certain acts would constitute a breach of conditions to be performed by the promisee, they are not ground for contesting the will which promisor made in pursuance of such contract.[47]

The contract to will property is ordinarily breached either by failure to execute any will,[48] or by leaving one contrary to the terms of the agreement.[49] It is sometimes said that the contract cannot be regarded as broken until testator's death, as up to that time the promisor may comply with the contract and die with the agreed testamentary arrangement.[50] Even if this is true of contracts to leave one's entire estate, it appears that an agreement to leave particular property may be breached in promisor's lifetime by a conveyance to another.[51] Moreover if the promisor renounces the contract in his lifetime there is no reason why the ordinary rules of anticipatory breach should not apply. In such cases some jurisdictions give an action for damages to the promisee.[52] Equitable relief has also been

44 Tussey v. Owen, 139 N.C. 457, 52 S.E. 128, 1905; Mathews v. Tobias, 126 Or. 358, 268 P. 988, 1928; Wall v. McEnnery's Estate, 105 Wash. 445, 178 P. 631, 1919.

45 Gravelin v. Porier, 77 Mont. 260, 250 P. 823, 1926; Tuttle v. Winchell, 104 Neb. 750, 178 N.W. 755, 11 A.L.R. 814, 1920.

46 Brandes v. Brandes, 129 Iowa 351, 105 N.W. 499, 1906; Bruce v. Moon, 57 S.C. 60, 35 S.E. 415, 1900.

47 Weathers v. McFarland, 97 Ga. 266, 22 S.E. 988, 1895; see In re Massey's Estate, 187 Or. 40, 208 P.2d 341, 1949.

48 Mills v. Smith, 193 Mass. 11, 78 N.E. 765, 6 L.R.A.,N.S., 865, 1906.

49 Phalen v. United States Trust Co., 186 N.Y. 178, 78 N.E. 943, 7 L.R.A.,N.S., 734, 9 Ann.Cas. 595, 1906; Clark v. West, 96 Tex. 437, 73 S.W. 797, 1903.

50 Skinner v. Rasche, 165 Ky. 108, 176 S.W. 942, 1915; Lawson v. Mullinix, 104 Md. 156, 64 A. 938, 1906; Warden v. Hinds, 163 F. 201, 25 L.R.A.,N.S., 529, C.C.A.Va.1908.

51 Evans v. Cole, 225 Iowa 756, 281 N.W. 230, 1938, noted, 24 Ia.L.R. 390. But see Ohms v. Church of the Nazarene, 64 Idaho 262, 130 P.2d 679, 1942, criticized, 1942 Annual Surv.Am. L. 668–670. See also annotation, 108 A.L.R. 867.

52 Stone v. Burgeson, 215 Ala. 23, 109 So. 155, 1926 (declining equitable

granted in the promisor's lifetime by way of establishment of a trust,[53] injunction to prevent interference with compliance by the promisor,[54] injunction against an inconsistent conveyance,[55] declaration of a lien upon promisor's land for improvements,[56] rescission of the promisor's inconsistent conveyance,[57] and even a decree that an adopted child should be defendant's heir.[58] One court went so far as to enjoin the revocation of a will made in accordance with contract.[59] This holding seems inconsistent in principle with the general view that equity will not order promisor to execute a will in accordance with the contract.[60] The reason generally assigned for the latter holding is that the testator can undo the matter by revoking the will in secret.

*Remedies*

Generally the enforcement of a contract to make, or to refrain from making, a will comes after the death of the promisor. Of course the probate of the contract is not the proper procedure. Even if the contract is executed with the formalities required for a will, the document usually lacks testamentary intent as it merely looks forward to the making of a future will. Likewise, when the promisor makes a will in accordance with his contract and later revokes it, by the prevailing view the contract cannot be used to defeat the probate of a subsequent inconsistent will.[61]

relief in promisor's lifetime); Mug v. Ostendorf, 49 Ind.App. 71, 96 N.E. 780, 1911; Carter v. Witherspoon, 156 Miss. 597, 126 So. 388, 1930. Contra: Warden v. Hinds, supra note 50; Henson v. Neumann, 286 Ill.App. 197, 3 N.E.2d 110, 1936.

53 Hayes v. Moffatt, 83 Mont. 214, 271 P. 433, 1928; Duvale v. Duvale, 56 N.J.Eq. 375, 39 A. 687, 40 A. 440, 1898; Brackenbury v. Hodgkin, 116 Me. 399, 102 A. 106, 1917.

54 White v. Massee, 202 Iowa 1304, 211 N.W. 839, 66 A.L.R. 1434, 1927.

55 Pflugar v. Pultz, 43 N.J.Eq. 440, 11 A. 123, 1887.

56 Soho v. Wimbrough, 145 Md. 498, 125 A. 767, 1924 (specific performance denied).

57 Brackenbury v. Hodgkin, 116 Me. 399, 102 A. 106, 1917; Bird v. Pope, 73 Mich. 483, 41 N.W. 514, 1889.

58 Wold v. Wold, 138 Minn. 409, 165 N.W. 229, 1917.

59 Lovett v. Lovett, 87 Ind.App. 42, 155 N.E. 528, 157 N.E. 104, 1927, noted, 26 Mich.L.R. 464.

60 Maud v. Maud, 33 Ohio St. 147, 1877; Stone v. Burgeson, 215 Ala. 23, 109 So. 155, 1926, holding only action for damages could be brought in promisor's lifetime; Van Meter v. Norris, 318 Pa. 137, 177 A. 799, 1935. See also Watson v. Hobson, 401 Ill. 191, 81 N.E.2d 885, 7 A.L.R.2d 1156, 1948, declining specific performance because of inability of the court to order performance of the plaintiff's personal service contract.

61 Sumner v. Crane, 155 Mass. 483, 29 N.E. 1151, 15 L.R.A. 447, 1892;

A will is a revocable instrument, and a contract not to dispose of one's property contrary to its terms does not make it any the less so. The promisee's remedy is rather against the promisor's estate or his successors in interest. There is some authority to the effect that a will made in accordance with a contract is irrevocable and that probate of a later testament should be refused.[62] Superficially this decision seems desirable as a short-cut method of giving effect to the contractual rights which must ultimately prevail. Upon analysis this position seems unsound because it results in the probate court passing on the question of the validity of the contract, a jurisdiction which some probate courts lack, which is limited to certain types of contracts in other states, and which everywhere comes at an inappropriate stage of the probate proceedings.[63]

At law, the promisee has two remedies if the promisor does not make the disposition which he had agreed to provide. First, the promisee may sue the personal representative for damages for the breach of promisor's agreement.[64] Ordinarily the measure of damages here is the value of the property which was to come to the promisee.[65] The alternative remedy at law is that of quantum meruit to recover the value of the services or other consideration furnished by the promisee.[66] This relief is not

Matter of Martin's Will, 128 Misc. 659, 220 N.Y.S. 398, 1927; In re Lieurance's Estate, 181 Or. 646, 182 P.2d 969, 185 P.2d 575, 1947; Pohlman v. Untzellman, 2 Lee Ecc. 319, 161 Eng.Rep. 355, 1756. See infra § 49, note 7; § 84, note 2.

62 Walker v. Yarbrough, 200 Ala. 458, 76 So. 390, 1917, noted, 16 Mich. L.R. 59, 27 Yale L.J. 542; In re Englé's Estate, 129 Or. 77, 276 P. 270, 1929. Cf. In re Schmidt's Estate, 85 Colo. 28, 273 P. 21, 1929. See Cobb v. Hanford, 88 Hun (N.Y.) 21, 34 N.Y. S. 511, 1895 (probate of inconsistent will enjoined); Johnson v. Tomme, supra note 41; In re Wentworth's Will, 272 App.Div. 974, 71 N.Y.S.2d 542, 1947.

63 See In re Adkins Estate, 161 Kan. 239, 167 P.2d 618, 1946; In re Gudewicz' Will, 72 N.Y.S.2d 838, Sur. 1947; In re Lieurance's Estate, 181 Or. 646, 182 P.2d 969, 1947, and infra § 96.

64 Roy v. Pos, 183 Cal. 359, 191 P. 542, 1920; Hotsinpiller v. Hotsinpiller, 72 W.Va. 823, 79 S.E. 936, 1913; McNaughton v. McClure, 169 Wis. 288, 171 N.W. 936, 1919.

65 Strakosch v. Connecticut Trust & Safe Deposit Co., 96 Conn. 471, 114 A. 660, 1921; Jefferson v. Simpson, 83 W.Va. 274, 98 S.E. 212, 1919. But see Frieders v. Estate of Frieders, 180 Wis. 430, 193 N.W. 77, 31 A.L.R. 118, 1923; In re Stichler's Estate, 359 Pa. 262, 59 A.2d 51, 1948.

66 Morrison v. Land, 169 Cal. 580, 147 P. 259, 1915; Hankins v. Young, 174 Iowa 383, 156 N.W. 380, 1916; Pancoast v. Eldridge, 134 Okl. 247, 273 P. 255, 1929. See Struble v. Struble, 42 Ohio App. 353, 182 N.E. 48, 1932.

generally as advantageous to the promisee as that of the first type because it can not exceed the value of the property promised,[67] and may be much less. Indeed in many cases no recovery could be had on this theory, as in case that the consideration for the deceased's promise was a promise to execute a will in deceased's favor. Often, however, a quantum meruit will be the only form of recovery possible, as in case that action on the contract is impossible because of uncertainty of the agreement,[68] or because the Statute of Frauds has not been satisfied.[69] In addition, some courts allow recovery in quantum meruit where the promisee has performed part of the conditions precedent but is in default as to the remaining ones.[70]

Of course strictly speaking equity does not decree specific performance of a contract to make a will. It will not do so in the promisor's lifetime, for he can at once undo the relief by revocation of the will. Naturally also the court cannot compel a dead man to make a will, nor can it compel the personal representative or other successors to do so for him. Nevertheless the courts frequently purport to grant specific performance of such contracts.[71] What is meant is that they will compel the successors to transfer the property to the promisee in accordance with the deceased's agreement.[72] The promisor's pretermitted children [73]

67 Hull v. Thoms, 82 Conn. 647, 74 A. 925, 1910; Boldwin v. Lay, 226 S.W. 602, Mo.App.1920. However, any other basis of recovery may give rise to a claim that an estate tax is forthcoming. See notes, 34 Va.L.R. 590, 596–598, 61 Harv.L.R. 675, 685.

68 Schmetzer v. Broegler, 92 N.J.L. 88, 105 A. 450, 1919; Collier v. Rutledge, 136 N.Y. 621, 32 N.E. 626, 1892.

69 Hensley v. Hilton, 191 Ind. 309, 131 N.E. 38, 1921; Hirschberg v. Horowitz, 105 N.J.L. 210, 143 A. 351, 1928; Kling v. Bordner, 65 Ohio St. 86, 61 N.E. 148, 1901; Laughnan v. Laughnan's Estate, 165 Wis. 348, 162 N.W. 169, 1917.

70 Hodgson v. Martin, 90 Or. 105, 166 P. 929, 175 P. 671, 1918. Contra: Roberts v. Johnson, 152 Ga. 746, 111 S.E. 194, 1922; Tussey v. Owen, 139 N.C. 457, 52 S.E. 128, 1905.

71 Bolman v. Overall, 80 Ala. 451, 2 So. 624, 60 Am.Rep. 107, 1887; Andrews v. Aikens, 44 Idaho 797, 260 P. 423, 69 A.L.R. 8, 1927; Hanson v. Fiesler, 49 S.D. 442, 207 N.W. 449, 1926; Burdine v. Burdine's Ex'r, 98 Va. 515, 36 S.E. 992, 81 Am.St.Rep. 741, 1900. See also annotation, 69 A.L.R. 26.

72 See Costigan, Constructive Trusts Based on Promises Made to Secure Bequests, Devises or Intestate Succession, 28 Harv.L.R. 237, 244, 245.

73 Worden v. Worden, 96 Wash. 592, 165 P. 501, 1917; In re McLean's Estate, 219 Wis. 222, 262 N.W. 707, 1935, noted, 21 Iowa L.R. 653. But see Burkhart v. Rogers, 134 Okl. 219, 273 P. 246, 1928, noted, 42 Harv.L.R. 966.

and probably his surviving spouse [74] take subject to his contract to leave his property to others. Frequently it is said, that the courts will impress a constructive trust upon the successors.[75] This language has been criticized because the recovery is of the thing promised rather than the value of the thing given by the promisee in return, as is the general situation in case of constructive trusts.[76] Perhaps the terms quasi specific performance,[77] or relief in the nature of specific performance [78] are more suitable designations of the remedy which equity gives in this situation.

Equitable relief is not given in every case of contracts to will property. If the contract is to leave a legacy the remedy at law is adequate so that chancery will decline to act unless there is an independent ground for its jurisdiction.[79] This point is seldom noticed since the amount of recovery is the same in both law and equity.[80] It might become important where separate courts are maintained, or if jury trial is demanded. If the contract is to devise land the uniqueness of the subject matter is ground for specific relief upon the same basis as in ordinary contracts of sale of realty.[81]

Soon after the passage of the Statute of Frauds it was decided that equity would decree specific performance of an oral contract for the sale of land when possession thereof had been delivered by the promisor.[82] It is difficult to justify the decision

[74] Baker v. Syfritt, 147 Iowa 49, 125 N.W. 998, 1910; Lewis v. Lewis, 104 Kan. 269, 178 P. 421, 1919; Harris v. Harris, 130 W.Va. 100, 43 S.E.2d 225, 1947. But see Wides v. Wides' Ex'r, 299 Ky. 103, 184 S.W.2d 579, 1945; In re Arland's Estate, 131 Wash. 297, 230 P. 157, 1924. Cf. In re Massey's Estate, 187 Or. 40, 208 P. 2d 341, 1949. See Evans, Concerted Wills—A Possible Device for Avoiding the Widow's Privilege of Renunciation, 33 Ky.L.J. 79; note, 34 Va. L.R. 590, 595.

[75] Carstairs v. Bomar, 119 Tex. 364, 29 S.W.2d 334, 1930.

[76] Costigan, supra note 72 at 244.

[77] Costigan, supra note 76.

[78] Page on Wills, 3d Ed. § 1736.

[79] Costigan, supra note 72 at 242.

[80] But see Downing v. Maag, 215 Minn. 506, 10 N.W.2d 778, 1943.

[81] Bolman v. Overall, 80 Ala. 451, 2 So. 624, 60 Am.Rep. 107, 1887; Oswald v. Nehls, 233 Ill. 438, 84 N.E. 619, 1908; Brickley v. Leonard, 129 Me. 94, 149 A. 833, 1930. Some courts refuse to grant specific performance unless the consideration furnished by the plaintiff was of a unique character. Hoyt v. Thomas, 58 Cal.App. 14, 207 P. 1038, 1922, criticized, 23 Col. L.R. 313. For a case in which specific performance was refused on the ground of superior equities of a third person, see In re Arland's Estate, 131 Wash. 297, 230 P. 157, 1924, noted, 38 Harv.L.R. 696.

[82] Butcher v. Stapely, 1 Vern. 363, 23 Eng.Rep. 524, 1685.

upon the basis of the language of the statute but equity came to this view in order to prevent the statute from becoming an instrument of injustice and fraud. This position has been generally recognized in cases of contracts to devise.[83] A few jurisdictions hold that no other type of part performance takes the case out of the Statute of Frauds.[84] Others also allow the giving up of a child for adoption to suffice since no pecuniary compensation can make up for loss of the child.[85] The prevailing view allows the rendering of services which are of such character as not to permit a fair valuation in money to satisfy the Statute in equity cases.[86] It is more problematical whether the making of a mutual will in the promisor's favor is sufficient part performance.[87] It should be noticed that it is in equity alone that part performance may satisfy the Statute of Frauds; the doctrine does not apply in legal actions for damages.

*Statute of Limitations*

Usually the promisor has his entire lifetime to comply with the contract which is not breached until his death, so that the Statute of Limitations does not begin to run until that time.[88] When the agreement is renounced by the promisor in his lifetime, some cases assert that the cause of action is then mature so that

[83] Warren v. Warren, 105 Ill. 568, 1883; Van Natta v. Heywood, 57 Utah 376, 195 P. 192, 1921; Whitney v. Hay, 181 U.S. 77, 21 S.Ct. 537, 45 L.Ed. 758, 1901.

[84] Wallace v. Long, 105 Ind. 522, 5 N.E. 666, 55 Am.Rep. 222, 1886; Rodman v. Rodman, 112 Wis. 378, 88 N.W. 218, 1901.

[85] Bassett v. American Baptist Publication Soc., supra note 16; Odenbreit v. Utheim, 131 Minn. 56, 154 N.W. 741, L.R.A.1916D, 421, 1915; Nowack v. Berger, 133 Mo. 24, 34 S.W. 489, 31 L.R.A. 810, 54 Am.St.Rep. 663, 1896. Contra: Synder v. French, 272 Ill. 43, 111 N.E. 489, 1916; Wallace v. Long, 105 Ind. 522, 5 N.E. 666, 55 Am.Rep. 222, 1886.

[86] West v. Sims, 153 Kan. 248, 109 P.2d 479, 1941, noted, 40 Mich.L.R. 328; Kelley v. Devin, 65 Or. 211, 132 P. 535, 1913; Worden v. Worden, 96 Wash. 592, 165 P. 501, 1917. Cf. Brennen v. Derby, 124 Or. 574, 265 P. 425, 1928; Weeks v. Lund, 69 N.H. 78, 45 A. 249, 1900, where the services were regarded as of the character which could be compensated in money. And see Holsz v. Stephen, 362 Ill. 527, 200 N.E. 601, 106 A.L.R. 737, 1936.

[87] That it is: Brown v. Webster, 90 Neb. 591, 134 N.W. 185, 37 L.R.A.,N.S., 1196, 1912. That it is not: Burt v. McKibbin, 188 S.W. 187, Mo. 1916; McClanahan v. McClanahan, 77 Wash. 138, 137 P. 479, Ann.Cas. 1915D, 253, 1914. See infra § 49 note 22.

[88] Hull v. Thoms, 82 Conn. 647, 74 A. 925, 1910; Sturgeon's Adm'r v. McCorkle, 163 Ky. 8, 173 S.W. 149, 1915; Kent v. Kent, 62 N.Y. 560, 20 Am.Rep. 502, 1875.

the statute will run,[89] while others hold that the promisee is not obliged to treat the declaration as a breach.[90] The latter is probably the prevailing and also the better rule, particularly if the renunciation is secret. In case of a quantum meruit action where there is an oral agreement which cannot be relied upon because of the Statute of Frauds, there are two views as to when the statute starts to run. It has been suggested that the position taken depends upon whether the statute makes the contract void or merely unenforceable. If the contract is void it is said that the claim for quantum meruit accrues when the services are rendered, while if it is merely unenforceable the statute does not commence to run until the date of performance which is that of the promisor's death.[91] When the cause of action at law has been barred by the Statute of Limitations, it has been held that this is a ground for equity to intervene by way of granting specific performance.[92]

## JOINT AND MUTUAL WILLS

**49. A joint will is one in which the same paper is executed by two persons as their respective wills. Mutual wills are the separate testaments of two persons, more or less reciprocal in their provisions.**

**These instruments may or may not be accompanied by a contract not to revoke them, though some courts imply this in case of joint wills. If a contract not to revoke is found, some courts admit the will to probate although it has been revoked in defiance of the agreement. By the better view this breach can be asserted only as a claim against the heirs or the estate of the revoking testator.**

When two or more persons execute the same instrument as their respective wills the result is ordinarily called a joint will; if they executed separate wills which are, in part at least, reciprocal or identical in their provisions as the result of some preconcerted plan, the term mutual wills is applied. If this usage[1] is

[89] Paul v. Snyder, 52 Ind.App. 291, 100 N.E. 571, 1913, noted, 13 Col.L.R. 441; Englebrecht v. Herrington, 101 Kan. 720, 172 P. 715, L.R.A.1918E, 785, 1918.

[90] Wold v. Wold, 138 Minn. 409, 165 N.W. 229, 1917; Ga Nun v. Palmer, 202 N.Y. 483, 96 N.E. 99, 36 L.R.A., N.S., 922, 1911.

[91] See Page on Wills, 3d Ed. § 1744.

[92] Warren v. Warren, 105 Ill. 568, 1883; Winfield v. Bowen, 65 N.J.Eq. 636, 56 A. 728, 1903.

[1] There has been great confusion by the courts with reference to definition of joint wills and mutual wills. See Goddard, Mutual Wills, 17 Mich.L.R.

accepted it is obviously impossible to have wills which are both joint and mutual. Yet the expression joint and mutual wills is often used in case of an instrument or instruments wherein the respective testators leave some interest to their co-testators or to the same third persons or to both. A joint will may dispose of property owned jointly by the co-testators or that held by them separately. Often a joint will is in favor of the same beneficiaries in case of each of the co-testators. Some mutual wills leave the entire interest to the co-testator, while in others only a life interest is so given. In the latter case, the remainders are usually the same in the case of both testators, but this is not necessarily so.

Most of the early cases declared that a joint will was invalid.[2] The probable basis of these decisions was the idea that the will was a single instrument not to become effective until the death of both joint testators, and hence could not be said to be the will of the one first dying as it was not effective on his death. Even today a joint will which expressly or impliedly does not become effective until the death of the survivor is invalid.[3] However, in the absence of this factor, there is no reason why the joint will cannot be regarded as the will of each co-testator and probated twice, once at the death of each. This is the modern and generally recognized view.[4]

If the provisions of reciprocal wills—whether joint or separate—are solely in favor of the co-testator, the survivor takes all and he may then make any will he wishes or may die intestate.[5] Where the surviving co-testator receives only a life interest and the remainder goes to a third person, some question has been raised as to whether the third person may assert

677; Partridge, The Revocability of Mutual or Reciprocal Wills, 77 U. of Pa.L.R. 357, 358; Eagleton, Joint & Mutual Wills, 15 Corn.L.Q. 358, 361; Evans, Concerted Wills, 33 Ky.L.J. 79; notes, 61 Harv.L.R. 675, 35 Ky. L.J. 214, 19 Minn. L.R. 95; annotation, 169 A.L.R. 9.

2 Clayton v. Liverman, 19 N.C. 558, 1837; Walker v. Walker, 14 Ohio St. 157, 82 Am.Dec. 474, 1862; Darlington v. Pulteney, 1 Cowp. 260, 98 Eng. Rep. 1075, 1775.

3 Hershy v. Clark, 35 Ark. 17, 37 Am.Rep. 1, 1879; Epperson v. White, 156 Tenn. 155, 299 S.W. 812, 57 A.L. R. 601, 1927; Richmond v. Richmond, 189 Tenn. 625, 227 S.W.2d 4, 1950.

4 George v. Smith, 216 Ark. 896, 227 S.W.2d 952, 1950; American Trust & Safe Deposit Co. v. Eckhardt, 331 Ill. 261, 162 N.E. 843, 1928, noted, 27 Mich.L.R. 356; Anderson v. Anderson, 181 Iowa 578, 164 N.W. 1042, 1917. Louisiana forbids joint wills. LSA–C.C. art. 1572.

5 In re Pennington's Estate, 158 Kan. 495, 148 P.2d 516, 1944. See note, 36 Col.L.R. 1013.

the right to the remainder under a contract not to revoke the will found to have been made for his benefit. This is now permitted in accordance with the general law of third party beneficiary.[6]

*Revocability*

Frequently joint or mutual wills are made in pursuance of an agreement or compact not to revoke them. Here it is important to distinguish between the concept of wills and that of contracts. Our law has no separate concept of "will made in pursuance of contract;" we must treat the will part as a will and the contract part as a contract. Viewed in the aspect of a will, such instruments do not differ from other wills. In order to be effective, they must be admitted to probate and they are revocable although there has been an agreement not to revoke. The matter of the contractual aspect does not properly arise upon probate, but only when the agreement is sought to be established as a claim against the estate, or in a proceeding against the successors of the decedent. This is the sound and orthodox treatment of the question.[7] Some cases hold, however, that the contract not to revoke may be used as a basis for admitting the joint or mutual will to probate in spite of its revocation, or of refusing to probate later revoking wills.[8] These short-cut methods are subject to objections already noticed.[9]

[6] Smith v. Thompson, 250 Mich. 302, 230 N.W. 156, 73 A.L.R. 1389, 1930; Stevens v. Myers, 91 Or. 114, 177 P. 37, 2 A.L.R. 1155, 1919; Doyle v. Fischer, 183 Wis. 599, 198 N.W. 763, 33 A.L.R. 733, 1923. But cf. Rose v. Southern Michigan Nat. Bank of Coldwater, 328 Mich. 639, 44 N.W.2d 192, 1950. Most recent cases assume this without discussion. Tutunjian v. Vetzigian, 299 N.Y. 315, 87 N.E.2d 275, 1949, noted, 1 Syracuse L.R. 480; Nye v. Bradford, 144 Tex. 618, 193 S.W. 2d 165, 169 A.L.R. 1, 1946. See supra § 48 at notes 27–29.

For an anomalous holding that the beneficiary takes a vested interest upon the death of the first testator, see Chadwick v. Bristow, 204 S.W.2d 65, Tex.Civ.App.1947, noted, 48 Col.L. R. 288, 46 Mich.L.R. 1005, 1 Vanderbilt L.R. 157. Cf. Berry v. Berry's Estate, 168 Kan. 253, 212 P.2d 283, 1950.

[7] Houck v. Anderson, 14 Ariz. 502, 131 P. 975, 1913; Rolls v. Allen, 204 Cal. 604, 269 P. 450, 1928 (statute); Sumner v. Crane, 155 Mass. 483, 29 N. E. 1151, 15 L.R.A. 447, 1892; In re Burke's Estate, 66 Or. 252, 134 P. 11, 1913; Williams v. Williams, 123 Va. 643, 96 S.E. 749, 1918; Doyle v. Fischer, 183 Wis. 599, 198 N.W. 763, 33 A.L.R. 733, 1924. See supra § 48, note 61; infra § 84, note 2.

[8] Warwick v. Zimmerman, 126 Kan. 619, 270 P. 612, 1928; In re McGinley's Estate, 257 Pa. 478, 101 A. 807, 1917; cf. In re Adkins' Estate, 161 Kan. 239, 167 P.2d 618, 1946.

[9] See supra § 48, note 63; cf. Goddard, supra note 1, at 686. See Eagleton, supra note 1, at 386, 387.

In the English case of Stone v. Hoskins,[10] it was held that where there was an agreement not to revoke mutual wills, the surviving co-testator could not complain of the revocation by the one who died first. The reason assigned was that the survivor may then alter his will. By way of dicta the case declared that the survivor is bound not to depart from the arrangement if the other had complied therewith. Some American decisions [11] have also asserted that all makers of mutual wills are privileged to revoke them in the joint lifetimes of the co-testators, especially if notice is given to the other.[12] To declare this as a flat proposition seems unsound.[13] Whether the parties should be entitled to revoke during their joint lifetimes should depend upon the contract which was made. Conceivably the agreement may be that the parties may revoke in their joint lifetimes but that the survivor may not, or vice versa, or that neither may revoke at any time. If evidence of the terms of the agreement is lacking or the agreement appears to be indefinite and hazy, each party should be allowed to revoke his will at any time, whether in the lifetime of the co-testator or thereafter.

Many questions arise concerning the proof of contracts to leave one's property in accordance with the terms of joint or mutual wills. It is important to distinguish between a mere agreement to make a will and one not to revoke the same. Sometimes, though not often, there is a separate written contract to the latter effect.[14] The wills themselves may recite the agreement which is made.[15] It is generally held that the mere making of mutual separate wills is not sufficient evidence of a contract not to revoke.[16] While their form and content often indicate that each testator knew about the other's will and it may even be

10 [1905] P. 194.

11 Peoria Humane Soc. v. McMurtrie, 229 Ill. 519, 82 N.E. 319, 1907.

12 Frazier v. Patterson, 243 Ill. 80, 90 N.E. 216, 27 L.R.A.,N.S., 508, 17 Ann.Cas. 1003, 1909; Lally v. Cronen, 247 N.Y. 58, 159 N.E. 723, Id., 247 N.Y. 575, 161 N.E. 188, 1928; McClanahan v. McClanahan, 77 Wash. 138, 137 P. 479, Ann.Cas.1915A, 461, 1914. In the following case no notice of revocation was given and specific performance was decreed. Wright v. Wright, 215 Ky. 394, 285 S.W. 188, 1926.

13 Eagleton, supra note 1, at 383–385; note, 39 Harv.L.R. 663.

14 Buehrle v. Buehrle, 291 Ill. 589, 126 N.E. 539, 1920; In re Krause's Estate, 173 Wash. 1, 21 P.2d 268, 1933 (contract providing that either party might make a new will). See also Tutunjian v. Vetzigian, supra note 6.

15 See Warwick v. Zimmerman, 126 Kan. 619, 270 P. 612, 1928.

16 Monninger v. Koob, 405 Ill. 417, 91 N.E.2d 411, 1950; Wanger v. Marr, 257 Mo. 482, 165 S.W. 1027, 1914; Knox v. Perkins, 86 N.H. 66, 163 A. 497, 1933; Matter of Rosenblath's Es-

inferred that there was concert in making them, we should not infer a contract not to revoke without further proof. In the case of a joint will however, some courts have indicated that the will by itself permits the inference of an agreement not to revoke.[17] Possibly the execution of a joint will has more of a tendency to indicate a contract not to revoke than in the case of mutual separate wills.[18] But the better view is that the proof of the execution of a joint will without further evidence is not sufficient proof of a contract not to revoke.[19]

Two recent cases refused to enforce an agreement disclosed on the face of a joint will invalidly executed by the survivor who had accepted the benefits from the will of the co-testator; this was put upon the tenuous ground that since it was not the survivor's will it was not binding upon him as a contract or declaration of trust.[20] Ordinarily the survivor who has taken under a will should be estopped to deny an agreement recited in the instrument.[21] Indeed probate of the will by the survivor and acceptance of the benefits has been held to amount to part performance sufficient to take an oral agreement out of the Statute of Frauds.[22] Whether the survivor, who has agreed to devise his property to a certain person, may convey to another seems to depend upon a construction of the agreement and upon the intent

tate, 146 Misc. 424, 263 N.Y.S. 303, 1933; In re Weir's Estate, 134 Wash. 560, 236 P. 285, 1925; Canada v. Ihmsen, 33 Wyo. 439, 240 P. 927, 43 A.L.R. 1010, 1925. But see Trindle v. Zimmerman, 115 Colo. 323, 172 P.2d 676, 1946; note, 21 Miss.L.J. 179.

17 Frazier v. Patterson, 243 Ill. 80, 90 N.E. 216, 27 L.R.A.,N.S., 508, 17 Ann.Cas. 1003, 1909; Rastetter v. Hoenninger, 214 N.Y. 66, 108 N.E. 210 (relying on joint language of the dispositions). See, also, Larrabee v. Porter, 166 S.W. 395, Tex.Civ.App. 1914; Curry v. Cotton, 356 Ill. 538, 191 N.E. 307, 1934, noted, 29 Ill.L.R. 1090; Culver v. Hess, 234 Iowa 877, 14 N.W.2d 692, 1944; Tutunjian v. Vetzigian, supra note 6.

18 See Wanger v. Marr, supra note 16; Eagleton, supra note 1, at 374, 375.

19 Rolls v. Allen, 204 Cal. 604, 269 P. 450, 1928; Jacoby v. Jacoby, 342 Ill.App. 277, 96 N.E.2d 362, 1951; Menke v. Duwe, 117 Kan. 207, 230 P. 1065, 1925; In re Rhodes' Estate, 277 Pa. 450, 121 A. 327, 1923; Beveridge v. Bailey, 53 S.D. 98, 220 N.W. 462, 60 A.L.R. 619, 1918. And see Wanger v. Marr, supra note 16.

20 Ireland v. Jacobs, 114 Colo. 168, 163 P.2d 203, 161 A.L.R. 1413, 1945; Graser v. Graser, 147 Tex. 404, 215 S.W.2d 867, 1949. For criticisms, see Sears, Joint and Mutual Wills, 18 Ry. Mt.L.R. 365; Dean Evans in 35 Ky. L.J. 214, 217; 1949 Annual Surv.Am. L. 841.

21 McGinn v. Gilroy, 178 Or. 24, 165 P.2d 73, 1946.

22 Estate of Doerfer, 100 Colo. 304, 67 P.2d 492, 1937; O'Connor v. Immele, 77 N.D. 346, 43 N.W.2d 649, 1950. Cf. Shaw v. Hamilton, 346 Mo. 366, 141 S.W.2d 817. See supra § 48.

with which the conveyance was made.[23] Surely a contract to leave all or a fractional part of one's property does not ordinarily mean that the promisor may not change his investments or use his property for the necessaries or comforts of life. On the other hand, a gratuitous transfer to another may well violate the spirit of the particular contract to devise.

While there may be temptation to use a joint will to prevent suppression or revocation of the will by the survivor in violation of his agreement, the difficulties of execution and draftsmanship are arguments against the joint will. Then, too, there may be problems of probate as the survivor's will, especially if the survivor dies domiciled in a different jurisdiction from that of the first probate. Separate mutual wills are better devices from the practical standpoint, but in all cases there should be explicit understanding as to whether or not the respective testators are privileged to revoke either in their joint lifetimes or after the death of one. This agreement should be set forth in the wills and probably in a separate contract as well. In most situations it would be advisable to provide that each will is freely revocable at any time. Many later conditions, brought about by death, birth, marriage, divorce, wealth, health or emnity, may make any present plan a most unreasonable one after these events have occurred. In other words, one should be cautious in the use of contractual wills, or wills which are open to the claim that they are contractual.

23 Compare Nye v. Bradford, supra note 6, with Harrell v. Hickman, 147 Tex. 396, 215 S.W.2d 876, 1950. See also Sample v. Butler University, 211 Ind. 122, 4 N.E.2d 545, 108 A.L.R. 857, rehearing denied and modified 211 Ind. 122, 5 N.E.2d 888, 108 A.L.R. 857, 1936, and supra § 48 at note 51 et seq.

# CHAPTER 5

## TESTAMENTARY CAPACITY



### STATUS AND AGE

**50. The common law testamentary disability of married women has now completely disappeared, and, except for minor exceptions in a few jurisdictions, there is no longer disability on account of conviction of crime or alienage.**

**Testamentary age is now fixed by statute in all states; the most usual age is twenty-one, though a number of jurisdictions deviate from this figure, either generally, or on the basis of sex, marital status, or nature of the property involved. The age requirement must be met at the time of execution of the will.**

*Married Women*

The original Wills Act, 1540, provided that "any and every person" might devise his lands,[1] but the act passed three years later provided that the devise of a married woman should not be good or effectual.[2] Hence her will was not good as to land even with her husband's consent.[3] Her incapacity to bequeath personalty followed largely from the principle that by marriage her husband acquired title to all her personalty except her paraphernalia,[4] though she might bequeath her personalty with her husband's consent.[5] Her will was also good to exercise a power of appoint-

[1] 32 Hen. VIII, c. 1.

[2] 34 and 35 Hen. VIII, c. 5. § 14.

[3] See Osgood v. Breed, 12 Mass. 525, 1815.

[4] Madden, Persons and Domestic Relations §§ 28–30.

[5] Marston v. Norton, 5 N.H. 205, 1830; Williford v. Phelan, 120 Tenn. 589, 113 S.W. 365, 1908. But the husband could revoke his consent at any time until probate. Van Winkle v. Schoonmaker, 15 N.J.Eq. 384, 1862.

ment which she possessed [6] and likewise in equity to pass property settled upon her separately.[7]

Her incapacity has been entirely removed in every state by the married women's acts or other statutory provisions so that she can make a valid will as freely as a man or a single woman.[8] Of course both husband and wife are usually limited in their power to deprive the surviving spouse by will, but these restrictions are not due to lack of testamentary capacity.

*Aliens, Convicts, Indians*

The ancient disability of aliens [9] and convicts [10] has likewise largely disappeared. In order to protect them against fraud and overreaching, Congress has placed limitations upon the testamentary power of Indians.[11] This power has not been exercised to its fullest extent. Congress has provided, however,[12] that allotment property held under trusts or restrictions may not be disposed of by will unless the same is approved by the Secretary of Interior. This approval can be given either before or after the death, and is subject to be set aside within one year for fraud. Except insofar as Congress has imposed restrictions, an Indian may will his property under the state law as in case of other persons.[13]

*Age Capacity—English Law*

The civil law rule was that males of fourteen and females of twelve had the age capacity to make a will. Above these years persons had testamentary powers provided they had sufficient mental capacity. Below these ages no degree of mental maturity and soundness would suffice. The ecclesiastical courts adopted the civil law rule when called upon to probate testaments of personalty. As this was a matter within the recognized jurisdiction of the ecclesiastical courts, the common-law courts did not inter-

[6] Anderson v. Miller, 6 J.J.Marsh. (Ky.) 568, 1831; Dunn's Appeal, 85 Pa. 94, 1877.

[7] Tappenden v. Walsh, 1 Phill.Ecc. 352, 161 Eng.Rep. 1008, 1811; Caldwell v. Renfrew, 33 Vt. 213, 1860.

[8] See Bordwell, Statute Law of Wills, 14 Ia.L.R. 179–181; Vernier, American Family Laws § 186. Cf. supra § 30.

[9] Bordwell, supra note 8 at 183; see supra § 24.

[10] Bordwell, supra note 8 at 182; see supra § 25.

[11] Taylor v. Johnson, 92 Okl. 145, 218 P. 1095, 1923.

[12] 25 U.S.C.A. § 373. See also Long v. Darks, 184 Okl. 449, 87 P.2d 972, 1939.

[13] Hanson v. Hoffman, 150 Kan. 121, 91 P.2d 31, 1939; see Long v. Darks, supra note 12.

fere but indeed recognized the holdings of the church tribunals.[14] This was the law of England as to wills of personalty until 1837.

The original Statute of Wills, 1540, literally permitted a devise of land by minors,[15] but within three years an amendment declared that the devises should not be good unless the testator was twenty-one years of age.[16] This has been the English rule ever since as to wills of realty, and after the Wills Act, 1837, as to the testaments of personalty as well.[17]

*Age Capacity in the United States*

Until comparatively recently a few states had no statutory provisions as to testamentary age. Here the courts followed the English rule at the time of separation from the mother country.[18]

In every American jurisdiction the testamentary age is now fixed by statute. Some states merely provide that the testator must be of full or lawful age. In such cases reference must be made to general statutes fixing the age of majority. In other jurisdictions the wills' statutes themselves fix the age at which one may make a will. This may, or may not, be different from the general age of majority for other purposes.

Most often we find the age fixed at twenty-one years, though there are many deviations from this figure.[19] In a considerable group of states the age is eighteen, and other figures are found elsewhere. Certain jurisdictions permit females to make wills at a lower age than males. Often personalty can be bequeathed at a lower age than that at which realty can be devised. In some states married persons can will their property, though an unmarried person of the same years may not.

14 Hyde v. Hyde, Pre.Ch. 316, 24 Eng.Rep. 148, 1711; Smallwood v. Brickhouse, 2 Mod. 315, 86 Eng.Rep. 1095, 1694; 2 Bl.Com. 497; Swinburne on Testaments, pt. 2, § 2.

15 See supra note 1.

16 See supra note 2.

17 1 Vict. c. 26, 7.

18 Holzman v. Wager, 114 Md. 322, 79 A. 205, Ann.Cas.1912A, 619, 1911 (personalty); Campbell v. Browder, 7 Lea (Tenn.) 240, 1881.

19 The rules in the various states are collected in Bordwell, Statute Law of Wills, 14 Ia.L.R. 177–179. As to whether a soldier under the general statutory age may make a military will, see annotation, 137 A.L.R. 1311, infra § 77.

*Computation of Age*

The age requirement must be met at the time of execution of the will.[20] The law considered that one obtained his majority on the day preceding his twenty-first birthday.[21] This resulted from the common-law maxim that the law would not regard the fractional parts of a day. Conceivably the disability due to nonage may be removed in a little less than forty-eight hours before one has lived a full twenty-one years. Thus, if one was born at eleven o'clock in the night of February first, his will made at one o'clock in the morning of the last of January in his twenty-first year would be valid.[22]

*Different Rules for Personalty and Realty*

In jurisdictions which fix a greater age for the disposition of real than for personal property, it is possible that the will may be valid as to the personalty but not as to the realty.[23] One who has passed the years required for wills of personalty may dispose of a leasehold interest, though he has not attained the age required for devises of land.[24] A legacy by such person must be paid out of his personal estate and cannot be charged upon his realty.[25]

[20] Dallett v. Taggart, 223 Pa. 180, 72 A. 380, 1908. As to ratification of a will made during minority after one has attained full age, see generally infra § 90.

[21] 1 Bl.Com. 463.

[22] Anon., 1 Salk. 44, 91 Eng.Rep. 44, 1705.

[23] Early v. Arnold, 119 Va. 500, 89 S.E. 900, 1916.

[24] Holzman v. Wager, supra note 18.

[25] Banks v. Sherrod, 52 Ala. 267, 1875.

## MENTAL CAPACITY—GENERAL REQUIREMENTS

**51. To make a valid will one must be of sound mind though he need not possess superior or even average mentality. One is of sound mind for testamentary purposes only when he can understand and carry in his mind in a general way:**

**(1) The nature and extent of his property,**

**(2) The persons who are the natural objects of his bounty, and**

**(3) The disposition which he is making of his property.**

**He must also be capable of:**

**(4) Appreciating these elements in relation to each other, and**

**(5) Forming an orderly desire as to the disposition of his property.**

**As shown above, testamentary capacity is determined according to one's mental ability to make a will; one may have testamentary capacity though he is under guardianship or lacks the ability to make a contract or transact other business.**

### *Character of Will*

While the character and provisions of the testator's will, as well as of his former wills, may be considered in determining mental capacity,[1] the fact that the disposition is unjust or unnatural does not by itself establish testamentary disability.[2] Thus, one who has capacity may make a good will although the terms are "as eccentric, as injudicious or as unjust as caprice, frivolity or revenge can dictate."[3] On the other hand the will

[1] In re Jensen's Estate, 185 Minn. 284, 240 N.W. 656, 1932; Norris v. Bristow, 358 Mo. 1177, 219 S.W.2d 367, 11 A.L.R.2d 725, 1949, and authorities note 2 infra. See Galloway v. Hogg, 167 Ga. 502, 146 S.E. 156, 1928; Laube, The Right of a Testator to Pauperize His Helpless Dependents, 13 Corn.L.Q. 559, 568; supra § 36, notes 5–7 and infra § 100. As to other wills as bearing on question of capacity, see note, 6 N.C.L.R. 318.

[2] Abrahams v. Woolley, 243 Ill. 365, 90 N.E. 667, 1909; Mileham v. Montagne, 148 Iowa 476, 125 N.W. 664, 1910; Smith v. Shuppner, 125 Md. 409, 93 A. 514, 1915; Old Colony Trust Co. v. Di Cola, 233 Mass. 119, 123 N.E. 454, 1919; Kaechelen v. Barringer, 19 S.W.2d 1033, Mo.1929. Cf. In re Lawrence's Estate, 286 Pa. 58, 132 A. 786, 1926. See Green, Proof of Mental Incompetency and the Unexpressed Major Premise, 53 Yale L.J. 271, 298 et seq.

[3] Schneider v. Vosburgh, 143 Mich. 476, 106 N.W. 1129, 1906. See generally, Hibschman, Whimsies of Will-Makers, 66 U.S.L.R. 362, and infra § 52.

of a person whose mind is unsound for testamentary purposes is not valid, though the provisions are the same as he would likely have made if he had possessed capacity.[4] The ultimate question is that of the rational character of testator's mind rather than the objective reasonableness of the will itself.

### *General Policy Regarding Mental Capacity*

It is just conceivable that the law should not make any particular requirement of mental capacity for testamentary purposes. This would be carrying the conception of freedom of testation to its fullest extent. But it would be socially undesirable to give this power to one who is so deficient or unbalanced mentally that he does not appreciate the significance of the disposition. It is better to distribute the property according to intestate laws than according to the caprice of an unsound mind. Furthermore, it is a traditional common-law attitude that the title to property should not be affected except by operation of law or act of the owner. In the latter case an attitude of consent is essential and this presupposes some degree of mental capacity.[5]

On the other hand, it is conceivable that the position should be taken that will-making should be permitted only when the person is of high, or at least average, intelligence. The objection to this attitude is that one whose mind is in a somewhat weakened condition due to old age or sickness often needs the will-making power to induce others to render him assistance. In addition almost everyone has peculiarities and eccentricities, which, if the standard of mentality for will-making were very high, might be seized upon by juries sympathetic to disinherited relatives.

Any standard analogous to the ordinary careful and prudent man test in the law of negligence would not be feasible in connection with capacity to make a will. It has been judicially declared that the testator need not be possessed of average mentality, for that requirement would incapacitate practically half of the people from making wills.[6] Courts have also said that no particular degree of mentality is required,[7] or that each case

4 Shirley v. Ezell, 180 Ala. 352, 60 So. 905, 1913.

5 See Green, Public Policy Underlying the Law of Mental Incompetency, 38 Mich.L.R. 1189, 1217.

6 In re Whitworth's Estate, 110 Cal. App. 526, 294 P. 84, 86, 1931; Hoban v. Piquette, 52 Mich. 346, 361, 17 N.W. 797, 804, 1884.

7 In re Whitworth's Estate, supra note 6; In re Loomis' Will, 133 Me. 81, 174 A. 38, 1934; Crum v. Crum, 231 Mo. 626, 132 S.W. 1070, 1073, 1910; In re Riggs' Estate, 120 Or. 38, 241 P. 70, 250 P. 753, 755, 1926; Wampler v. Harrell, 112 Va. 635, 72 S.E. 135, 138, 1911.

must be determined upon its own facts and circumstances.[8] One can appreciate the realistic wisdom of the latter statement when the many divergent fact situations are noted in the multitude of cases which have been before the courts. However, as a practical matter, trial courts need a test or formula by means of which juries can be instructed in will contests. The law has wavered between the imposition of high[9] and low[10] standards. The courts now substantially agree upon the compromise position stated in the black letter text.

### *Deficient and Deranged Minds Distinguished*

There are two types of persons who are deemed mentally incompetent to make a will. The first is the class which is mentally *deficient,* that is, lacking in the qualities of mind and memory as to the matters which are important in making a will. This condition may be a congenital one or it may be produced through age, sickness, injury or other causes. The second sort of incapacitated persons are those who are quite capable of understanding the disposition that they are making, the nature and extent of the property and the natural objects of their bounty, but whose minds are so warped and *deranged* that they are unable to form a rational testamentary plan. Such persons are said to have insane delusions; when the delusions are on a single subject the term monomania was formerly applied. Of course some individuals fall in both classes; others in one only. While in either case the will is invalid for want of mental capacity, the case of the deluded or deranged mind calls for special consideration and is treated in the following section. The distinction between minds which are deficient and those which are distorted is also recognized in medical science.[11]

8 In re Riggs' Estate, supra note 7; Crum v. Crum, supra note 7. Cf. In re Vaughn's Estate, 137 Wash. 512, 242 P. 1094, 1095, 1926: "Any definition of testamentary capacity is more or less arbitrary and subject to revision or modification as new combinations of fact arise."

9 See Waring v. Waring, 6 Moore P.C. 341, 13 Eng.Rep. 715, 1848. Cf. Banks v. Goodfellow, L.R. 5 Q.B. 549, 1870, which represents the present English view.

10 The majority opinion in Stewart's Executor v. Lispenard, 26 Wend.(N.Y.) 255, 1841, declares at page 303: "weak minds differ from strong ones only in the extent and power of their faculties; but unless they betray a total loss of understanding, or idiocy or delusion, they cannot properly be considered unsound." This case was overruled in Delafield v. Parish, 25 N.Y. 9, 1862, which however lays down no definite test.

11 See Menninger, The Human Mind, 1930, 162, 163. Cf. Singer & Krohn, Insanity and Law, 1924, 328; Green, supra note 2.

If the testator is under a doctor's care it is often advisable to consult with him and perhaps with the nurses to ascertain their opinion of the patient's mental condition. Furthermore, it may be wise to have them act as attesting witnesses to the will in order "to hold them in line" in case that the question of incapacity is raised later. However, the latter precaution is occasionally a two-edged sword, for it may indicate consciousness that the situation is a marginal one, and these witnesses may even prove later to be unfavorable to the establishment of the will.

*Medical Classifications*

If a person has a mental deficiency or derangement, its exact medical nature is not particularly important from the testamentary standpoint. The vital matter is whether the testator's mind meets the pragmatic requirements which the law demands. However, the medical classifications are of some benefit in recognizing the mental condition of the prospective testator, and in determining whether he has testamentary capacity. The deficient types of mentality range from idiocy ("lack of brains"), through imbecility (knowledge of physical wants only) and moronity to subnormality. The fact that one is subnormal in mental power, or even is a moron (these do much of our hard work), does not prove lack of capacity to make a simple will. On the other hand, persons classified as idiots and imbeciles would not possess testamentary power.

Among the many forms of mental derangement, as distinguished from the gradations of deficiency of mind, perhaps four are of especial significance in connection with the determination of testamentary capacity. Paranoia is a condition manifested by delusions of persecutions and extreme jealousy. The victim is apt to retaliate by engaging in elaborate conspiracies against the objects of his distrust. There may be little general intellectual impairment for many years, yet it may readily be seen that testamentary incapacity may result from this disorder while the person is still leading a useful life. Paresis results from syphilis of the brain, quite generally unaccompanied by skin eruptions or other physical indications which are discernible to laymen. Sufferers from this disease often have delusions of grandeur and pretend great wealth, strength, or mentality, or intimate acquaintanceship with celebrated people. Sometimes they engage in extreme tirades against persons or causes. They frequently retain considerable purely intellectual power but are extremely flighty and irresponsible.

Two sorts of mental disease occur in old age. One is senile dementia which is a progressive mental enfeeblement and hence more in the nature of a deficiency than a derangement. Persons so afflicted lose their power of concentration and often manifest little or no interest in things around them. They often become slovenly about their personal appearance and disregard the ordinary rules of sanitation. Older persons suffering from senile psychosis, on the other hand, are extremely active, irritable, and at times depressed. With it all they are apt to be forgetful of such common facts as where they live, or whether they are married. Naturally these combinations of characteristics often lead to testamentary incapacity.

Of course an attorney should not prepare a will for a person whom he strongly suspects to be mentally incapacitated. However, a word of warning must accompany this brief description of mental diseases and their symptoms. Some of the foregoing attributes can be discovered in persons of undoubted capacity. The mere fact that these traits are observed does not mean that the person is lacking in testamentary power, or is a proper subject for a doctor's, or an institution's, care. Mental derangements are probably nothing more than extreme cases of the personality traits found in normal persons. Only instances of excessive deviation and actual disease are of importance from the testamentary standpoint.

*Statutory Provisions*

The only English statute declared that idiots and persons not of sane memory could not make valid wills.[12] Somewhat similar language is found in the wills' statutes of a few of our states,[13] but the great majority merely provide that the testator must be of sound mind.[14] A few jurisdictions have no statutory language indicating the mental capacity required to make a will. It is not believed that these legislative differences are important. Even in absence of statutory provision, a court will require sound mind for a valid will.[15] What constitutes sound mind is almost [16] everywhere a matter for the courts to determine.

12 34 & 35 Hen. VIII, c. 5, § XIV, 1542.

13 See New York Decedent Estate Law §§ 10, 15.

14 See Bordwell, Statute Law of Wills, 14 Ia.L.R. 181.

15 See Horne v. Horne, 31 N.C. 99, 1848; Ford v. Ford, 7 Humph.(Tenn.) 92, 1846.

16 Georgia has more specific provisions as to mental capacity. Ga.Code Ann. § 113–201 et seq. See Deans v. Deans, 166 Ga. 555, 144 S.E. 116, 1928,

*Derivation of the Test*

The general test of mental capacity to make a will can be gleaned from the hundreds of appellate cases approving or disapproving instructions to juries in will contests, or considering whether there is evidence to sustain the verdict or the court's finding. Expressions vary from case to case. In some opinions the rule is stated in briefer form than in the black letter text while in others it is more elaborately explained. However, a complete examination of the opinions in any jurisdiction would show that the black-letter text contains the generally approved ideas.[17] Often some one or more of the five requirements are not mentioned in a particular opinion for the reason that the point is not in controversy in the trial or appeal of the case.

*Ability Rather Than Actual Understanding*

It is not necessary that the testator should actually understand or remember the nature and extent of his property and the other elements mentioned above in order to have testamentary capacity. It is enough if he has the ability to understand or comprehend them.[18] Thus, where a woman with this ability left her residuary estate to a college thinking that it was about $500, when in truth it was many times that sum, her will was valid.[19] A person with a memory somewhat impaired may still have testamentary capacity.[20]

for application thereof in a case involving a will disinheriting an only child.

17 Banks v. Goodfellow, supra note 9; Am.Digest System, tit. Wills § 50; Green, Judicial Tests of Mental Incompetency, 6 Mo.L.R. 141; notes, 27 Ky.L.J. 224, 3 Ohio St.U.L.R. 108; annotation, 155 A.L.R. 281; cf. note, 11 Tulane L.R. 429. See Macveigh, Appeal of, 141 Me. 260, 42 A.2d 903, 1945, where it is said that "intelligence which belongs to the weakest class of sound minds is enough." The question as to who are the natural objects of the testator's bounty depends upon the circumstances of the particular case. Norris v. Bristow, supra note 1.

See Stephens and Hulbert, Probate Psychiatry, 25 Ill.L.R. 276, 288, for a discussion of the feasibility of a psychiatrist acting as a subscribing witness to a will, with a view of testifying as to the capacity of the testator. And see generally Wood-Renton, Testamentary Capacity in Mental Disease, 4 L.Q.R. 442.

18 Emerich v. Arendt, 179 Ark. 186, 14 S.W.2d 547, 1929; Roller v. Kling, 150 Ind. 159, 49 N.E. 948, 1898; Holmes v. Campbell College, 87 Kan. 597, 125 P. 25, 41 L.R.A.,N.S., 1126, Ann.Cas.1914A, 475, 1912.

19 Holmes v. Campbell College, supra note 18.

20 Bishop v. Scharf, 214 Iowa 644, 241 N.W. 3, 1932; Mecutchen v. Gigous, 150 Md. 79, 132 A. 425, 1926; McLoughlin v. Sheehan, 250 Mass. 132, 145 N.E. 259, 1924; where it is

Many cases declare that the testator should understand the business in which he is engaged.[21] Of course the courts are here referring to the business of making a will. It is not clear whether actual understanding that one is making his will is necessary or whether mere ability to so understand is sufficient. This particular distinction is not of much practical importance, for one can scarcely have the present ability at the time to realize that he is executing his will, if he does not in fact realize that he is so doing. It is not necessary that the testator should be able to grasp the meaning of the technical legal terms used by his lawyer in the instrument,[22] nor that he understand the exact details of a complicated arrangement.[23] Often lawyers and learned judges differ as to the construction to be given to a will. Of course exact comprehension concerning such matters will not be required of the testator.

*Complexity of the Estate*

The language of some of the opinions indicates that mental capacity to make a will is a general one and that the size and the intricacy of the estate are not important in this regard.[24] Surely one may possess mentality enough to deal with a simple disposition of his property, when he would be baffled and quite at sea in considering complicated testamentary matters. The question of capacity should be to make the will in hand and not to make any will whatever. This position has been taken by the better considered cases.[25]

said that the testatrix must be able "to grasp the relationship of all who might reasonably be regarded by a person in her situation as natural objects of her remembrance."

21 Byars v. Smith, 203 Ala. 66, 82 So. 26, 1919; Maroncelli v. Starkweather, 104 Conn. 419, 133 A. 209, 1926; Chaney v. Baker, 304 Ill. 362, 136 N.E. 804, 1922. Wampler v. Harrell, 112 Va. 635, 72 S.E. 135, 1911; In re Seattle's Estate, 138 Wash. 656, 244 P. 964, 1926. And see Johnson v. Farrell, 215 Ill. 542, 74 N.E. 760, 1905.

22 Havens v. Mason, 78 Conn. 410, 62 A. 615, 3 L.R.A.,N.S., 172, 1906; O'Brien v. Spalding, 102 Ga. 490, 31 S.E. 100, 66 Am.St.Rep. 202, 1898; Dunham v. Holmes, 225 Mass. 68, 113 N.E. 845, 1916.

23 Ditton v. Hart, 175 Ind. 181, 93 N.E. 961, 1910; Young v. Ridenbaugh, 67 Mo. 574, 1878.

24 Appeal of Rogers, 126 Me. 267, 138 A. 59, 1927; Delafield v. Parish, 25 N.Y. 9, 97, 1862; Matheson v. Matheson, 125 S.C. 165, 118 S.E. 312, 1923.

25 Drum v. Capps, 240 Ill. 524, 88 N.E. 1020, 1909; In re Weber's Estate, 201 Mich. 477, 167 N.W. 937, 1918; Clifton v. Clifton, 47 N.J.Eq. 227, 21 A. 333, 1891. See Hedin v. Westdala Lutheran Church, 59 Idaho 241, 81 P.2d 741, 1938.

*Insanity an Ambiguous Term*

It is sometimes said that the will of an insane man is not valid, or, that unless the testator is insane he has the mental capacity to make a will.[26] There is of course a grain of truth in these assertions. However, they are very apt to be misleading. Insanity is a general term which connotes some marked deviation from the normal mental equipment. There is no legal or medical definition of insanity, the application of which would divide all people into the two classes of the sane and the insane. Whenever the classification is profitably made, it is made with some particular purpose in mind. Thus a doctor will ordinarily place a patient in one category or the other for the purpose of deciding whether a particular form of treatment would be beneficial. Similarly the law is always interested in some particular problem, such as one's mental capacity to make a deed, a contract, or a will, or to be chargeable with crime, or to be confined to an insane hospital, or to be placed under guardianship either as to his person or his property.

Undoubtedly the majority of people fall in the "sane" class for all of these purposes. On the other hand an unfortunate few are clearly "insane" for all purposes. There is however a third group of persons whom the law considers sane for some purposes and insane for other purposes. Litigation frequently results over the capacities of this type of person. Thus, one may be so mentally incapacitated that he is unable to take active charge of his possessions so that the court will appoint a guardian for the property. The same individual, however, might have the mental capacity to make a will.[27] It is not profitable to determine whether

26 Kuehmsted v. Turnwall, 115 Fla. 692, 155 So. 847, 1934; Eggers v. Eggers, 57 Ind. 461, 1877; Bounds v. Johnson, 192 S.W. 972, Mo.1917. For a sounder treatment, see In re Greene's Estate, 40 Ariz. 274, 11 P.2d 947, 1932; In re Wasserman's Estate, 170 Cal. 101, 148 P. 931, 1915; In re Sexton's Estate, 199 Cal. 759, 251 P. 778, 1927; In re Carroll's Estate, 59 Mont. 403, 196 P. 996, 1921.

27 Estate of Wornall, 53 Cal.App.2d 243, 127 P.2d 593, 1942 (statute), noted, 16 So.Cal.L.R. 355; Nichols v. Wentz, 78 Conn. 429, 62 A. 610, 1905; Pendarvis v. Gibb, 328 Ill. 282, 159 N.E. 353, 1928; Reeves v. Hunter, 185 Iowa 958, 171 N.W. 567, 1919; Collins v. Long, 95 Or. 63, 186 P. 1038, 8 A.L.R. 1370, 1920; Clement v. Rainey, 50 S.W.2d 359, Tex.Civ.App.1932. Hence a legatee participating in a guardianship proceeding is not estopped to assert testamentary capacity. In re Powers' Estate, 81 Cal. App.2d 480, 184 P.2d 319, 1947. See Green, The Operative Effect of Mental Incompetency on Agreements and Wills, 21 Tex.L.R. 554, 584; note, 18 Tulane L.R. 620. But see Kuehmsted v. Turnwall, supra note 26. In addition to the question of insanity being different for testamentary and guardianship purposes, it is possible

such a person is sane or insane. The purpose of the inquiry is of vital importance, and the law has laid down for each purpose different tests, which are designed to produce socially desirable results in the decision of the problem in hand.

*Ability to Make Contracts Compared*

The statement is sometimes made that it takes less mental capacity to make a will than to enter into a contract.[28] There is a semblance of truth in this declaration. The performance of a one-party act such as testament-making needs less strength of mind than a transaction that requires bargaining with another person. In the case of an agreement, the other contracting party must be dealt with, while in the execution of a will the testator can be removed from the influence of opposing minds. This distinction however has more to do with the subject of undue influence than with mental capacity. The statement is misleading in that it does not take into consideration the fact that individual wills may require far greater mental capacity than certain simple contracts.[29] One who has the necessary degree of intelligence to purchase a cake of soap might lack the judgment to dispose of a large estate by means of a complicated will.

*Ability to Transact Business Compared*

Ordinarily, less mental ability is required to make a will than to conduct regular business affairs.[30] Therefore, it is true in general that one who may do the latter should be permitted to make

that, though under guardianship, the testator may have made the will during a lucid interval. In re Brennan's Estate, 312 Pa. 335, 168 A. 25, 1933. See note 33 infra. Evidence of adjudication of incompetency in a guardianship proceeding is usually admissible, however, to show testamentary incapacity. See infra § 100, notes 63, 64.

28 In re Weedman's Estate, 254 Ill. 504, 98 N.E. 956, 1912; Bishop v. Scharf, 214 Iowa 644, 241 N.W. 3, 1932; In re Weber's Estate, 201 Mich. 477, 167 N.W. 937, 1918. See In re Whitmarsh's Estate, 133 Misc. 858, 234 N.Y.S. 505, 1929, declaring that less mental capacity is required for a will than for any other legal instrument. Cf. Coleman v. Robertson's Executors, 17 Ala. 84, 1849; Lyon v. Townsend, 124 Md. 163, 91 A. 704, 1914 (statute) and Gilliken v. Norcom, 197 N.C. 8, 147 S.E. 433, 1929, holding that the capacity required for making a contract or deed and a will are the same. See, also, Aubert v. Aubert, 6 La.Ann. 104, 1851, declaring that wills are more easily avoided than contracts for unsoundness of mind. The most reasonable attitude is that taken by Murphy v. Nett, infra note 29.

29 See Murphy v. Nett, 47 Mont. 38, 130 P. 451, 1913. See note, 27 Ky. L.J. 224, 226.

30 In re Sexton's Estate, 199 Cal. 759, 251 P. 778, 1927; Nichols v. Wentz, 78 Conn. 429, 62 A. 610, 1906;

a valid will. This is not true, however, where the person has insane delusions which are of such nature as to affect the testamentary disposition of his property but not the conduct of ordinary financial and commercial matters. The will of such an individual may be disallowed while his business transactions are perfectly valid.

*Time of Capacity*

Testamentary capacity must exist at the time of the execution of the will.[31] If there is then capacity, the will is valid; otherwise it is not, unless the will is republished by codicil [32] after capacity has been restored. If one is ordinarily incapacitated under the legal tests but makes the will in a lucid interval, it will be given effect.[33] Conversely, if the testator is usually of sound mind but executes the instrument when his mind is temporarily impaired so that he does not meet the established test, probate will be denied. These principles are applied in case of the use of liquor or drugs by the testator.[34]

Dowdey v. Palmer, 287 Ill. 42, 122 N.E. 102, 1919; Bishop v. Scharf, 214 Iowa 644, 241 N.W. 3, 1932. See Appeal of Rogers, 126 Me. 267, 138 A. 59, 1927; In re Chongas' Estate, 115 Utah 95, 202 P.2d 711, 1949.

31 In re Sexton's Estate, 199 Cal. 759, 251 P. 778, 1927; Bishop v. Scharf, 214 Iowa 644, 241 N.W. 3, 1932; Appeal of Rogers, 126 Me. 267, 138 A. 59, 1927; In re Estate of Wah-kon-tah-he-um-pah, 108 Okl. 1, 232 P. 46, 1925. As to admissibility of evidence of mental condition before and after the making of the will, see § 100, infra. It has been held in England that it was sufficient if the testator had mental capacity at the time of giving instructions for his will though not at the time of execution. Perera v. Perera [1901] A.C. 354. American authority is that capacity at the time of giving instructions is not sufficient. James White Memorial Home v. Haeg, 204 Ill. 422, 68 N.E. 568, 1903; In re Ross' Will, 182 N.C. 477, 109 S.E. 365, 1921. But see Weems v. Weems, 19 Md. 334, 1862.

32 See In re Journeay's Will, 162 N.Y. 611, 57 N.E. 1113, 1910; Brown v. Riggin, 94 Ill. 560, 1880; Green, supra note 27 at 582.

33 Dowdey v. Palmer, 287 Ill. 42, 122 N.E. 102, 1919; Succession of Connor, 165 La. 890, 116 So. 223, 1928; Daly v. Hussey, 275 Mass. 28, 174 N.E. 916, 1931; Snyder v. De Remer, 143 Or. 414, 22 P.2d 877, 1933.

34 In re Anderson's Estate, 142 Okl. 197, 286 P. 17, 1930 (drugs). Cf. Applehans v. Jurgenson, 336 Ill. 427, 168 N.E. 327, 67 A.L.R. 851, 1929.

## INSANE DELUSIONS

**52. An insane delusion is a false belief which is the product of a diseased mind and to which one adheres against evidence and reason. However, an insane delusion does not invalidate the will unless it affects the disposition.**

**Mere eccentricities, prejudices or unusual religious beliefs do not by themselves constitute insane delusions although these and other similar factors are of evidentiary value in determining whether testamentary capacity exists.**

As shown in the preceding section one may have *sufficient* mentality to make a will, but his mind may be so *deranged* that his will should not be permitted to stand. Such a person may possess some of the requisites of testamentary capacity yet lack the ability to make a rational selection of his beneficiaries and form an orderly desire as to the disposition of his property.[1] If so, he is said to be affected with insane delusions, or to use the older term, monomania.

### *Effect of Insane Delusions*

One may be able to transact complicated business dealings and yet the existence of insane delusions may deprive him of testamentary capacity.[2] However, an insane delusion may have no effect on the disposition for the testator's mind may be deranged upon a subject which has no connection with the will. Such partial insanity was once held in England to be fatal to testamentary capacity.[3] The reasoning was that a mind unsound on some subjects cannot be deemed sound upon others. While it is true that the mind is a unit and a maladjustment in one respect may affect the entire organism, it may still be capable of operating fairly well along certain lines. Perfect mental soundness is not a requirement of testamentary capacity.

The American authorities as well as the present English decisions declare that if the mind is not deficient, an insane delusion

1 See black-letter type to § 51 supra.

2 In re Lundquist's Will, 205 Wis. 667, 238 N.W. 861, 1931. In Harbison v. Beets, 84 Kan. 11, 113 P. 423, 1911, in holding will invalid it is said: "He (testator) knew what he was doing but he had an insane reason for doing it." A person having business dealings with testator is not estopped to assert that the will was due to insane delusions. Davis v. Aultman, 199 Ga. 129, 33 S.E.2d 317, 1945.

3 Waring v. Waring, 6 Moore P.C. 341, 13 Eng.Rep. 715, 1848. For the modern medical view see supra § 51 at note 11; also Renton, Legal Test of Lunacy, 6 L.Q.R. 317; note, 26 Ind.L.J. 291.

which does not affect the will does not result in testamentary incapacity.[4] A man may believe that he is the supreme ruler of the universe, and yet that delusion may not affect the will.[5] When a delusion merely moves testator to execute a will but does not influence the manner of the disposition, testamentary capacity is not destroyed.[6] However, if it appears that the derangement likely affected the disposition in the will, the latter cannot be sustained.[7] A modern English case holds that when the delusion affects only a part of the will the remainder may stand,[8] and there are American dicta to the same effect.[9]

*Definition of "Insane Delusion"*

An attack on a will because of insane delusions doubtless goes to the matter of testamentary capacity,[10] but in submitting the question to the jury it is necessary to charge specially upon the subject of delusions instead of leaving the matter under the general test of mental capacity.[11] Therefore it is necessary to define insane delusions.

However, it is not easy to frame a satisfactory definition. Literally a delusion is a false belief. In a sense the wisest and most

[4] In re Greene's Estate, 40 Ariz. 274, 11 P.2d 947, 1932; Rodney v. Burton, 4 Boyce (Del.) 171, 86 A. 826, 1913; Pendarvis v. Gibb, 328 Ill. 282, 159 N.E. 353, 1928, noted, 23 Ill.L.R. 299; Gallmeier v. Kaiser, 88 Ind.App. 161, 163 N.E. 533, 1928, noted, 3 Cin. L.R. 93; Brown v. Fidelity Trust Co., 126 Md. 175, 94 A. 523, 1915; In re McDowell's Estate, 137 A. 823, 5 N.J. Misc. 605, 1927; In re Heaton's Will, 224 N.Y. 22, 120 N.E. 83, 1918; In re Morley's Estate, 138 Or. 75, 5 P.2d 92, 1931; Banks v. Goodfellow, L.R. 5 Q.B. 549, 1870.

[5] Fraser v. Jennison, 42 Mich. 206, 3 N.W. 882, 900, 1880. And see In re Eveleth's Will, 177 Iowa 716, 157 N.W. 257, 1916, where the testator believed that his son was trying to kill him and yet left everything to the son. The court reasoned that if this delusion had any effect, it would be to disinherit the son.

[6] Spry v. Logansport Loan & Trust Co., 191 Ind. 522, 133 N.E. 827, 1922.

[7] Newman v. Smith, 77 Fla. 633, 667, 688, 82 So. 236, 1918; Power v. Overholt, 257 Pa. 254, 101 A. 733, 1917; Campbell v. Campbell, 215 S.W. 134, Tex.Civ.App.1919; In re Shanks' Will, 172 Wis. 621, 179 N.W. 747, 1920. See also in re Strittmater's Estate, 140 N.J.Eq. 94, 53 A.2d 205, 1947 (insane man-hater left property to National Women's Party).

[8] Bohrmann's Estate, [1938] 1 All E. R. 271, noted, 24 Iowa L.R. 630.

[9] Florey's Ex'rs v. Florey, 24 Ala. 241, 1854; Holmes v. Campbell College, 87 Kan. 597, 125 P. 25, 41 L.R. A.,N.S., 1126, Ann.Cas.1914A, 475, 1912.

[10] Galindo v. Garcia 145 Tex. 507, 199 S.W.2d 499, 1947.

[11] Rodgers v. Fleming, 3 S.W.2d 77, Tex.Com.App.1928. See Allman v. Malsbury, 244 Ind. 177, 65 N.E.2d 106, 1946 (inaccurate definition properly refused).

brilliant of men have delusions. An insane delusion must be one to which the testator adheres against evidence, argument, and reason.[12] It is a belief, due to mental disease, in a state of facts which does not exist and which no rational person would believe to exist.[13] It is not proper, however, to apply the test of whether an average or normal man would harbor the delusion. It is rather a question of whether the belief is so extravagant, fanciful or preposterous as to indicate mental disease. On the other hand, the belief need not be something impossible in the nature of things in order to constitute an insane delusion.[14]

In many cases the courts try the issue of testamentary capacity without a jury, and they also frequently take the matter out of the jury hands because there is no sufficient showing of insane delusions.[15] A definition of the term is not particularly important in these cases, and we turn to the decisions to determine what may or may not constitute insane delusions.

*Eccentricities*

Mere eccentricities do not constitute insane delusions.[16] A person may have testamentary capacity although his actions and views seem very unusual. Almost everyone has peculiarities. A testator was held competent although he permitted dogs and cats to eat at the same table with him.[17] Dirty habits,[18] or extreme

[12] In re Putnam's Estate, 1 Cal.2d 162, 34 P.2d 148, 1934; Jackman v. North, 398 Ill. 90, 75 N.E.2d 324, 175 A.L.R. 868, 1947; Robbins v. Fugit, 189 Ind. 165, 126 N.E. 321, 1920; Hall v. Mercantile Trust Co., 332 Mo. 802, 59 S.W.2d 664, 1933; Potter v. Jones, 20 Or. 239, 25 P. 769, 12 L.R.A. 161, 1891. Cf. Trustees of Epworth Memorial Methodist Church v. Overman, 185 Ky. 773, 215 S.W. 942, 1919. See Guadnola, Insane Delusions, 5 Notre Dame Lawyer 393.

[13] Batson v. Batson, 217 Ala. 450, 117 So. 10, 1928; Hooper v. Stokes, 107 Fla. 607, 145 So. 855, motion denied 107 Fla. 607, 146 So. 668, 1933; Jackman v. North, supra note 12; In re Doster's Estate, 271 Pa. 68, 113 A. 831, 1921.

[14] Medill v. Snyder, 61 Kan. 15, 58 P. 962, 78 Am.St.Rep. 307, 1899.

[15] No jury: Jorn v. Tallett, 341 Ill. App. 240, 93 N.E.2d 82, 1950; In re Millar's Estate, 167 Kan. 455, 207 P. 2d 483, 1949; In re Klein's Estate, 28 Wash.2d 456, 183 P.2d 518, 1947. Jury directed: Ahmann v. Elmore, 211 S.W.2d 480, Mo.1948. Most of the cases cited infra in this chapter involve no charge defining insane delusions.

[16] Morecraft v. Felgenhauer, 346 Ill. 415, 178 N.E. 877, 1932; Holladay v. Holladay, 294 Ky. 540, 172 S.W.2d 36, 1943; note, 46 Dick.L.R. 253.

[17] Bennett v. Hibbert, 88 Iowa 154, 55 N.W. 93, 1893.

[18] In re Collins' Estate, 174 Cal. 663, 164 P. 1110, 1917; Eddey's Appeal, 109 Pa. 406, 1 A. 425, 1885.

miserliness,[19] do not by themselves incapacitate one from the testamentary standpoint. While such conduct is admissible in evidence in determining mental capacity,[20] a will would undoubtedly be held valid if there was no further showing of testator's mental condition. Generally, the eccentricities of the nature mentioned above do not affect the disposition of the property, and, on that account also, would not invalidate the will.[21]

### *False Beliefs and Prejudices Regarding Family*

In many cases there are false beliefs or groundless prejudices entertained by testators with respect to their relatives. These, of course, often influence the disposition of the property. Generally, a false belief, however unfounded, if based on any evidence does not constitute an insane delusion.[22] In other words, to invalidate a will the mistake must be one which no rational man, putting himself in the testator's place, would entertain.[23] Thus, neither unwarranted grievances against one's wife,[24] children,[25] or other relatives,[26] nor disinheritance of a son by reason of rumors that he was not testator's child,[27] nor belief that her sister had tried to poison testatrix after being informed that the sister had administered a double dose of morphine to testatrix,[28] warrants a finding of incapacity because of delusions. Instinctive prejudices cannot be regarded as insane delusions.[29] A violent dislike of one's daughter-in-law and a stubborn resistance to her attempts at reconciliation are not sufficient to invalidate a will disinheriting her.[30]

19 Pendarvis v. Gibb, 328 Ill. 282, 159 N.E. 353, 1928; Eddey's Appeal, supra note 18.

20 See infra § 100.

21 See notes 4–6 supra.

22 For two recent extreme cases, see In re Millar's Estate, 167 Kan. 455, 207 P.2d 483, 1949; In re O'Neil's Estate, 35 Wash.2d 325, 212 P.2d 823, 1949. See infra notes 23 to 30.

23 In re Stephenson's Estate, 132 Or. 234, 285 P. 224, 1930.

24 In re Greene's Estate, 40 Ariz. 274, 11 P.2d 947, 1932; In re Thomson's Will, 4 N.J.Super. 150, 66 A.2d 540, 1949.

25 Davis v. Aultman, 199 Ga. 129, 33 S.E.2d 317, 1945; Jorn v. Tallett, 341 Ill.App. 240, 93 N.E.2d 82, 1950, and cases supra note 22.

26 Jackman v. North, supra note 12; In re Walter's Estate, 167 Kan. 627, 208 P.2d 262, 1949; Holladay v. Holladay, supra note 16.

27 In re Smith's Will, 24 N.Y.S. 928, 1893. Cf. infra note 32.

28 In re Kendrick's Estate, 130 Cal. 360, 62 P. 605, 1900.

29 In re Perkins' Estate, 195 Cal. 699, 235 P. 45, 1925; Farmer v. Davis, 289 Ill. 392, 124 N.E. 640, 1919; Newman v. Dixon Bank & Trust Co., 205 Ky. 31, 265 S.W. 456, 1923.

30 In re Spencer, 96 Cal. 448, 31 P. 453, 1892.

On the other hand there are cases where similar beliefs have been held to warrant the inference that they proceeded from the diseased condition of the testator's mind rather than mistake or prejudice on his part. Groundless belief in the spouse's infidelity, adhered to in spite of all arguments to the contrary, has been held to amount to an insane delusion.[31] The same has been ruled where the testator had an absurd belief that he was not the father of his child,[32] or that another was trying to kill him,[33] or to put him under guardianship.[34] The courts have considered that when possessed with these obsessions it is impossible for the testator to form a rational or orderly desire as to the disposition of his property. The nature of the belief is not necessarily the turning point, or even the apparent lack of a basis for such belief. Rather the question is whether, considering all the facts and circumstances, it is fairly shown that the will proceeded from and on account of a deranged mind.

*Supernatural Beliefs*

Numerous learned and brilliant men have believed in witchcraft. The list includes such imposing names as Blackstone, Coke, Hale, Sir Francis Bacon and John Wesley.[35] Generally, faith in witches has no effect upon the testamentary disposition of one's property and many cases have held that the will is not invalidated thereby.[36] However, one case intimated that the belief might indicate a derangement resulting in testamentary incapacity.[37]

In modern times, most people do not accept spiritualism or the possibility of communication with the dead. On the other hand,

31 Burkhart v. Gladish, 123 Ind. 337, 24 N.E. 118, 1890; In re Kaven's Estate, 279 Mich. 334, 272 N.W. 696, 1937.

32 In re Russell's Estate, 189 Cal. 759, 210 P. 249, 1922; Stephens v. Bonner, 174 Ga. 128, 162 S.E. 383, 1932; McGovern's Will, 241 Wis. 99, 3 N.W.2d 717, 1942 (baby had red hair). Cf. Ahmann v. Elmore, 211 S.W.2d 480, Mo.1948.

33 Fulleck v. Allison, 3 Hagg.Ecc. 527, 162 Eng.Rep. 1251, 1830; In re Klein's Estate, 28 Wash.2d 456, 183 P.2d 518, 1947. Cf. In re O'Neil's Estate, supra note 22.

34 Leedom Estate, 347 Pa. 180, 32 A.2d 3, 1943.

35 Singer and Krohn, Insanity and the Law, 327.

36 Carnahan v. Hamilton, 265 Ill. 508, 107 N.E. 210, Ann.Cas.1916C, 21, 1915; Kelly v. Miller, 39 Miss. 17, 1860; Fulbright v. Perry County, 145 Mo. 432, 46 S.W. 955, 1898; Van Guysling v. Van Kuren, 35 N.Y. 70, 1866; Chafin Will Case, 32 Wis. 557, 1873.

37 Addington v. Wilson, 5 Ind. 137, 61 Am.Dec. 81, 1854.

many distinguished men have declared their conviction that voices of deceased persons are accessible to the living.[38] The courts are practically unanimous that mere belief of this kind does not indicate mental incapacity.[39] Generally this credence on the part of the testator has no effect upon the provisions of his will so that, on principles already stated, there is no testamentary disqualification.[40] Even when belief in spiritualism is reflected in the terms of the will, the instrument should not necessarily be invalid because of insane delusions. Applying the general test of such matters, we cannot say that no rational person could entertain belief in spiritualism, when many persons, who exhibit shrewdness and leadership in the various affairs of life, assent to the doctrine.[41] Upon this basis the devise of an ardent spiritualist of a large part of his property to a spiritualist church was sustained against claims of testamentary incapacity.[42] However, the courts set limitations upon the degree of credence which one may rationally entertain. Thus, one's will made under the notion that spirits ordered him to make a certain disposition of his property was declared invalid for want of testamentary capacity.[43]

[38] See McCrocklin's Adm'r v. Lee, 247 Ky. 31, 56 S.W.2d 564, 566, 1933, for a list of leaders in modern politics, literature and science who have so declared. See, also, Menninger, The Human Mind 238.

[39] Steinkuehler v. Wempner, 169 Ind. 154, 81 N.E. 482, 15 L.R.A.,N.S., 673, 1907; In re Randall, 99 Me. 396, 59 A. 552, 1904; Mecutchen v. Gigous, 150 Md. 79, 132 A. 425, 1926; In re Saunders' Estate, 235 Mich. 342, 209 N.W. 75, 1926; McClary v. Stull, 44 Neb. 175, 62 N.W. 501, 1895; Keeler v. Keeler, 51 Hun 636, 3 N.Y.S. 629, 1889; Buchanan v. Pierie, 205 Pa. 123, 54 A. 583, 97 Am.St.Rep. 725, 1903; In re Hanson's Estate, 87 Wash. 113, 151 P. 264, 1915. See infra note 42 and Hibschman, Spooks and Wills, 64 U.S.L.R. 471.

[40] Reiche v. Williams, 183 S.W.2d 587, Tex.Civ.App.1944, error refused 143 Tex. 365, 185 S.W.2d 420.

[41] In re Randall, supra, note 39. See note 38 supra.

[42] Owen v. Crumbaugh, 228 Ill. 380, 81 N.E. 1044, 119 Am.St.Rep. 442, 10 Ann.Cas. 606, 1907; Crumbaugh v. Owen, 238 Ill. 497, 87 N.E. 312, 1909.

[43] Irwin v. Lattin, 29 S.D. 1, 135 N.W. 759, Ann.Cas.1914C, 1044, 1912. In this case there was no evidence of undue influence, unless it was that of the spirits. When in such cases there is some proof of undue influence by a designated person, courts are inclined to permit a jury to find insane delusions resulting in mental incapacity. Orchardson v. Cofield, 171 Ill. 14, 49 N.E. 197, 40 L.R.A. 256, 63 Am.St.Rep. 211, 1898; Steinkuehler v. Wempner, 169 Ind. 154, 81 N.E. 482, 15 L.R.A.,N.S., 673, 1907; McReynolds v. Smith, 172 Ind. 336, 86 N.E. 1009, 1909; O'Dell v. Goff, 149 Mich. 152, 112 N.W. 736, 10 L.R.A.,N.S., 989, 119 Am.St.Rep. 662, 1907. See, also, McClary v. Stull, 44 Neb. 175, 62 N.W. 501, 1895. It could be argued from these cases that belief in spiritualism which affects the will is regarded as an insane delusion. Quære,

*Peculiar Religious Beliefs*

One may have mental capacity to make a will although he is an atheist,[44] or adheres to one of the less common religious faiths such as Christian Science,[45] or Swedenborgianism.[46] Religion is a matter of such nature that we should not hold another to be irrational simply because we cannot agree with his religious beliefs. Even if it were not for the principle of religious freedom, it would be impossible to say that one is deranged because he accepts an uncommon creed rather than Catholicism or Methodism. Even when the unusual religious belief directly prompts a testamentary disposition, the latter is not invalid on that account.[47] However, belief that a certain living person is the Deity has been held to justify a finding of incapacity due to insane delusion, when the will was in that person's favor or according to his dictation.[48] Often the wills in these cases could be held invalid on the ground of undue influence,[49] and less difficulty would be encountered in so doing than in resting the decision upon the basis of testamentary incapacity.

should not the case be put upon the basis of undue influence? See infra, § 55, and Hibschman, Spooks and Wills, 64 U.S.L.R. 471, 476.

44 Woodruff's Ex'r v. Woodruff, 233 Ky. 744, 26 S.W.2d 751, 1930.

45 In re Brush's Will, 35 Misc. 689, 72 N.Y.S. 421, 1901 (bulk of property left to Christian Science Church).

46 Scott v. Scott, 212 Ill. 597, 72 N. E. 708, 1904 (large religious gift).

47 See supra notes 45, 46.

48 Ingersoll v. Gourley, 78 Wash. 406, 139 P. 207, Ann.Cas.1915D, 570, 1914; Smith v. Tebbitt, L.R. 1 P. & D. 398, 1867. See supra note 43.

49 See supra note 43; infra § 55, notes 19, 30.

## MORAL, EDUCATIONAL AND PHYSICAL FACTORS

**53. Moral depravity, illiteracy, extreme old age, great weakness and severe illness do not disqualify the testator, though the latter three elements sometimes prevent one from having the necessary mental capacity to make a will.**

**While a person is not disqualified from making a will by reason of being deaf, dumb, or blind, or even all three, one so afflicted from birth may lack testamentary capacity because his mind has not developed to sufficient understanding. Moreover, these afflictions, as well as other physical weakness or illiteracy, may call for special precautions in the execution of the will and increase the difficulty of proof thereof.**

### *Immorality and Illiteracy*

No degree of moral depravity, unless accompanied by mental incapacity, will result in testamentary incapacity.[1] The law's requirements are on the side of intellect and mind, rather than on the side of character and conduct. A thoroughly bad man may make a valid will.

Nor do the courts exact any educational standard of testators. An illiterate person may make an ordinary will,[2] though the ordinary presumption that the testator knows and approves of the contents of the will does not apply in the case of one who cannot read.[3]

### *Old Age*

Extreme old age does not disqualify one to make a will. The instrument has been held valid although the testator is over eighty,[4] ninety,[5] or even a hundred,[6] years of age. It has been

[1] Daugherty v. State Sav., Loan & Trust Co., 292 Ill. 147, 126 N.E. 545, 1920; Leach v. Alger, 302 Ky. 149, 194 S.W.2d 164, 1946.

[2] In re Shay's Estate, 196 Cal. 355, 237 P. 1079, 1925; Wood's Ex'rs v. Wood, 109 Va. 470, 63 S.E. 994, 1909; Cutler v. Cutler, 103 Wis. 258, 79 N.W. 240, 1899. It is not necessary that the will be read to the testator. Maxwell v. Hill, 89 Tenn. 584, 15 S.W. 253, 1890.

[3] See infra § 58.

[4] Farmer v. Davis, 289 Ill. 392, 124 N.E. 640, 1919; Gambill's Adm'r v. Gambill, 236 Ky. 491, 33 S.W.2d 325, 1930 (containing a list of historical figures who have accomplished great work at an advanced age); In re Carter's Will, 60 N.J.Eq. 338, 51 A. 65, 1900; In re Snelling's Estate, 136 N.Y. 515, 32 N.E. 1006, 1893.

[5] In re Koll's Estate, 200 Iowa 1122, 206 N.W. 40, 1926; Collins v. Townley, 21 N.J.Eq. 353, 1871; In re Brower's Will, 112 App.Div. 370, 98 N.Y.S. 438, 1906; Collins v. Long, 95 Or. 63, 186 P. 1038, 8 A.L.R. 1370, 1920.

[6] Wilson v. Mitchell, 101 Pa. 495, 1882.

judicially declared that the right to make a will should be carefully vouchsafed to elderly persons having testamentary capacity.[7] The fact that advanced years are accompanied by mental sluggishness, impairment of memory, childishness, eccentricities and physical infirmity does not show lack of testamentary capacity.[8] Even senile dementia, which is an ailment of old age causing, among other things, disintegration of mental faculties, does not necessarily invalidate a will.[9] This disease is progressive in nature and until it has reached the point where the mind is either deficient or deranged under the ordinary test of capacity, the testamentary disposition will be upheld.[10]

*Illness and Weakness*

One is not disqualified from making a will merely by reason of sickness, or bodily weakness.[11] As facetiously stated by a digester: "a man with a sore leg may make a will." [12] Even a person who is suffering great pain may be a competent testator.[13] Moreover, such diseases as tumors of the brain,[14] apoplexy,[15] softening of the brain,[16] and epilepsy [17] are compatible with testamentary capacity. The question in all the cases is the ability

7 McCrocklin's Adm'r v. Lee, 247 Ky. 31, 56 S.W.2d 564, 1933; In re Alvord's Estate, 258 Mich. 497, 243 N. W. 40, 1932.

8 Challiner v. Smith, 396 Ill. 106, 71 N.E.2d 324, 1947; Burgess v. Belford, 306 Ky. 711, 209 S.W.2d 90, 1948; Am.Dig.System, tit. Wills §§ 32, 45, 47.

9 Graham v. Deuterman, 244 Ill. 124, 91 N.E. 61, 1910; Byrne v. Fulkerson, 254 Mo. 97, 162 S.W. 171, 1914.

10 Byrne v. Fulkerson, supra note 9; see supra § 51.

11 Griffin v. Union Trust Co., 166 Ark. 347, 266 S.W. 289, 1924; In re Stump's Estate, 202 Cal. 308, 260 P. 543, 1927; Cookman v. Bateman, 210 Iowa 503, 231 N.W. 301, 1930; In re Brown's Estate, 55 S.D. 53, 224 N.W. 942, 1929; Tabb v. Willis, 155 Va. 836, 156 S.E. 556, 1913; Payne v. Payne, 97 W.Va. 627, 125 S.E. 818, 1910.

12 Mo.Dig. tit. Wills, ⚷45, digesting Thomas v. Stump, 62 Mo. 275, 1876.

13 Griffin v. Union Trust Co., 166 Ark. 347, 266 S.W. 289, 1924; Stevens v. Leonard, 154 Ind. 67, 56 N.E. 27, 77 Am.St.Rep. 446, 1900. Cf. Blake v. Rourke, 74 Iowa 519, 38 N.W. 392, 1888 (testator incompetent when in paroxysms of pain at time of execution).

14 In re Fricke, 64 Hun 639, 19 N. Y.S. 315, 1892.

15 Cheney v. Price, 90 Hun 238, 37 N.Y.S. 117, 1909. Cf. Lim v. Chinco, 55 Philippine 891, 1931 (testator in state of coma and unable to speak).

16 Parramore v. Taylor, 11 Grat. (Va.) 220, 1854; In re Silverthorn's Will, 68 Wis. 372, 32 N.W. 287, 1887.

17 Bodine v. Bodine, 241 Ky. 706, 44 S.W.2d 840, 1931; In re Derusseau's Will, 175 Wis. 140, 184 N.W. 705, 16 A.L.R. 1412, 1921.

of the individual testator to meet the mental requirements for making a will.[18] Sickness of almost any nature may so impair the mind that one or more of these essential mental abilities may be lacking. When the illness renders one incapable of understanding to a reasonable degree the effect of the will upon his property and those entitled to receive it, he is lacking in testamentary capacity.[19] However, capacity may exist while the testator is in a dying condition and even practically up to the moment of death.[20]

*Deaf and Dumb*

The older English writers classed deaf mutes with idiots, particularly if the sense of sight was also lacking and if these infirmities had existed since nativity. Coke[21] declared that one deaf, dumb, and blind since birth could not make a valid grant, though a person, who once possessed these senses but later lost them and who had understanding and ability to express his intention by signs, could enfeoff another. It was said by Blackstone[22] that there was testamentary incapacity in one born deaf, dumb, and blind. Swinburne,[23] the earliest English writer on wills, asserted that an individual who was deaf and dumb from birth, or one who afterward lost the senses of hearing and speech and could not write, was incapable of making a will unless it was shown that he understood his act.

Modern decisions indicate that one so afflicted may lack legal capacity because he is unable to comprehend the ordinary affairs of the world.[24] The sensory handicaps, particularly when existing from an early age, may prevent the mentality from evolving to the point of testamentary capacity. In other words, the mind may be in darkness when the law requires an understanding of human affairs. But this condition is not necessarily so, and wills

[18] Deery v. Hall, 96 Ind.App. 683, 175 N.E. 141, 1931; Chrisman v. Chrisman, 16 Or. 127, 18 P. 6, 1888. See supra §§ 51, 52.

[19] Hudson v. Hughan, 56 Kan. 152, 42 P. 701, 1895; Crum v. Crum, 231 Mo. 626, 132 S.W. 1070, 1910.

[20] In re Doolittle's Estate, 153 Cal. 29, 94 P. 240, 1908; Hall v. Hall, 18 Ga. 40, 1855; Bevelot v. Lestrade, 153 Ill. 625, 38 N.E. 1056, 1894; Gurley v. Park, 135 Ind. 440, 35 N.E. 279, 1893; In re Vesper's Estate, 4 N.J. Misc. 791, 134 A. 651, 1926.

[21] Co.Litt. 42b. See Yong v. Sant, 1 Dyer, 55b, 73 Eng.Rep. 123, 1547.

[22] 2 Bl.Com. 497.

[23] Testaments, pt. 2, § X.

[24] In the Goods of Owston, 2 Sw. & Tr. 461, 164 Eng.Rep. 1075, 1862. See Perrine's Case, 41 N.J.Eq. 409, 5 A. 579, 1886 (guardianship).

of deaf mutes have been sustained.[25] In olden times, before means of communication with, and education of, these persons were developed, it was natural that they should be regarded as stricken persons incapable of possessing mind sufficient for testamentary purposes. With the coming of modern methods of education, we know that this attitude is wrong. The case of Helen Keller who lost the ability to see, hear and smell in early infancy, yet possesses marvelous intelligence and creative power, illustrates the fallacy of the ancient view. At present there is not even a presumption that a deaf and dumb person lacks testamentary capacity.[26] Of course a blind person can make a valid will.[27]

*Difficulties of Execution*

While not going to the matter of testamentary capacity there are difficulties in execution of the will of a person who is unable to see or hear or speak.[28] These can be overcome in case of a deaf-mute who can write,[29] or express his intention by signs.[30] Care must be taken to guard against imposition upon a blind testator.[31] Formerly the ecclesiastical courts required that the instrument be read over to him,[32] but this is not now necessary if there is other proof of his knowledge of the contents.[33] However, the ordinary strong presumption that a testator knows the contents of his duly executed will does not apply in the case of a blind person,[34] nor in case of an illiterate or one in a greatly weakened condition.[35]

25 In the Goods of Geale, 3 Sw. & Tr. 431, 164 Eng.Rep. 1342, 1864; Bagtas v. Paguio, 22 Phillipine 227, 1912. See Potts v. House, 6 Ga. 324, 50 Am.Dec. 329, 1849.

26 See Potts v. House, 6 Ga. 324, 50 Am.Dec. 329, 1849. Cf. note 23 supra.

27 Goldsmith v. Gates, 205 Ala. 632, 88 So. 861, 1921; Collis v. Walker, 272 Mass. 46, 172 N.E. 228, 1930; Dabbs v. Richardson, 137 Miss. 789, 102 So. 769, 1925; In re Pickett's Will, 49 Or. 127, 89 P. 377, 1907; Wilson v. Mitchell, 101 Pa. 495, 1882 (deaf also); Edwards v. Fincham, 4 Moo.P.C. 198, 13 Eng.Rep. 277, 1842.

28 In re Eklund's Estate, 186 Minn. 129, 242 N.W. 467, 1932 (deaf). See infra note 31.

29 See note 23 supra.

30 In the Goods of Geale, 3 Sw. & Tr. 431, 164 Eng.Rep. 1342, 1864. Cf. In the Goods of Owston, 2 Sw. & Tr. 461, 164 Eng.Rep. 1075, 1862.

31 Collis v. Walker, 272 Mass. 46, 172 N.E. 228, 1930. See infra § 72.

32 Barton v. Robins, 3 Phil. 455, n. b., 161 Eng.Rep. 1382, 1778; Swinburne on Testaments, pt. 2, § 11.

33 Clifton v. Murray, 7 Ga. 564, 50 Am.Dec. 411, 1849; Edwards v. Fincham, 4 Moo.P.C. 198, 13 Eng.Rep. 277, 1842.

34 Day v. Day, 3 N.J.Eq. 549, 1836; annotations, 9 A.L.R. 1416, 37 A.L.R. 603. But see In re Bakke's Will, 160 Minn. 56, 199 N.W. 438, 37 A.L.R. 597, 1924.

35 See infra § 58.

# CHAPTER 6

# UNDUE INFLUENCE, FRAUD AND MISTAKE

Sec.
54. Sources and Relationship of Rules.
55. Undue Influence.
56. Fraud.
57. Remedies for Fraud and Duress.
58. Mistake as to the Document Signed, Contents, and Legal Effect.
59. Mistake in Inducement.
60. Mistake in Description of Beneficiary or Property.
61. Partial Invalidity of a Will.

## SOURCES AND RELATIONSHIP OF RULES

**54. The rules concerning undue influence, fraud and mistake have their basis almost entirely in the decisions rather than in statutes.**

**While each of these elements may be theoretically distinct from the others and from lack of mental capacity, there is a factual relationship between them.**

The statutes[1] of a few states declare that wills procured by means of fraud and undue influence are invalid. Legislation concerning mistake is occasionally found.[2] With the exception of certain provisions in Georgia as to mistake,[3] these pronouncements are general and intended as merely declarative of the common law. We look then to the decisions to discover what is meant by these terms, the effect of these matters upon wills and the relationship of each to the other and to the matter of mental capacity already discussed.

At the outset it is important to notice language which is sometimes found to the effect that undue influence, fraud and mistake presume a mentally competent testator.[4] It is true that if the testator is incompetent, the other elements may be con-

[1] See Bordwell, Statute Law of Wills, 14 Ia.L.R. 173. In general, see Cahn, Undue Influence and Captation—A Comparative Study, 8 Tulane L. R. 506.

[2] Bordwell, supra note 1 at 174; see infra § 60, note 20.

[3] Ga.Code Ann. § 113–210. See infra § 59, note 20; § 60, note 20.

[4] Johnson v. Shaver, 41 S.D. 585, 172 N.W. 676, 1919; Moore v. Horne, 136 S.W.2d 638, Tex.Civ.App.1940.

sidered immaterial, for his will is invalid for lack of testamentary capacity alone. However, many wills are contested both on the ground of incapacity and also because of undue influence, fraud, or mistake.[5] It has been held that a will may be invalid for both mental incapacity and undue influence,[6] and that the matters are so closely related that the courts will consider them together.[7] These grounds are not mutually inconsistent in the sense that proof of one disproves the others.

Theoretically, mental incapacity connotes a mind unable to make the disposition in question; undue influence refers to coercion of the testator's mind by some person; fraud includes the idea of another's deception of the testator; while mistake indicates the latter's self-induced error. Each concept points in a different direction; still they are somewhat overlapping and interrelated. Thus a mind which is weak, though of sufficient strength to have testamentary capacity, may be more susceptible to pressure and fraud than one of great vigor. Undue influence has a close relationship with fraud; [8] in fact, the terms are sometimes used interchangeably.[9] The subjective state of mind may be the same in case of a mistaken testator as in case of one defrauded, the only difference being in the objective cause of the error. While it is orthodox to say that contestant's evidence upon two or more of these issues does not have any more effect than the strongest case made on one of them, the fact that they can be made concurrently may permit some cumulative, though unconscious, effect on the minds of the triers. It has been sug-

5 Hays v. Bowden, 159 Ala. 600, 49 So. 122, 1909; McDonald v. McDonald, 142 Ind. 55, 41 N.E. 336, 1895. But see In re Hock's Will, 74 Misc. 15, 129 N.Y.S. 196, 1911.

6 Hoff v. Hoff, 106 Kan. 542, 189 P. 613, 1920.

7 Phillips v. Jones, 179 Ark. 877, 18 S.W.2d 352, 1929; In re Telsrow's Estate, 237 Iowa 672, 22 N.W.2d 792, 1946. See also infra notes 8, 9.

8 In re Pohlmann's Estate, 89 Cal. App.2d 563, 201 P.2d 446, 1949, noted, 10 U. of Pitt.L.R. 602; Allen v. Heys, 204 Ga. 635, 51 S.E.2d 417, 1949; Sweeney v. Vierbuchen, 224 Ind. 341, 66 N.E.2d 764, 1946; Klingner v. Dugacki, 356 Pa. 143, 51 A.2d 627, 1947; In re Jaaska's Estate, 27 Wash.2d 433, 178 P.2d 321, 1947.

9 Lavalleur v. Hahn, 152 Iowa 649, 132 N.W. 877, 39 L.R.A.,N.S., 24, 1911; Neill v. Brackett, 234 Mass. 367, 126 N.E. 93, 1920; Ball v. Boston, 153 Wis. 27, 141 N.W. 8, 1913. But the courts often insist that the two are distinct and should be considered separately: Ginter v. Ginter, 79 Kan. 721, 101 P. 634, 22 L.R.A.,N.S., 1024, 1909; Gockel v. Gockel, 66 S.W.2d 867, 92 A.L.R. 784, Mo.Sup.1933; In re Chinsky's Will, 150 Misc. 274, 268 N.Y.S. 719, 1934; note, 28 A.L.R. 787. Cf. In re Newhall's Estate, 190 Cal. 709, 214 P. 231, 28 A.L.R. 778, 1923.

gested that the courts have indicated a tendency to unite fractions of all these grounds to spell out a composite ground for avoiding the will.[10]

## UNDUE INFLUENCE

**55. A will is invalid if it is obtained through an influence which destroys the free agency of the testator and substitutes another's volition for his. Influence may be undue although it does not amount to physical coercion, but mere advice, persuasion or kindness does not constitute undue influence.**

It is difficult to put a realistic concept of undue influence into a capsule. Definitions in court opinions and in instructions to juries are not without value, but the gist of the matter cannot be understood without considering what the courts have held does or does not amount to proof of undue influence. As in case of mental capacity we are dealing largely with subjective elements. Furthermore any objective phases of undue influence are apt to be veiled in secrecy. Hence, proof of undue influence must be largely, or even entirely, circumstantial.

### *Character of the Will*

Just as in the case of mental capacity,[1] undue influence is not established by the inequality of the provisions of the will with respect to the natural objects of one's bounty, or by the injustice or unnaturalness of the will.[2] Hence, when there is no other evidence of undue influence, the provisions thereof should not be admissible to show this fact.[3] Any other position would interfere with the testator's right to dispose of his property as he pleases. Where there are other circumstances which indicate undue influence, the unjust character of the will is evidence upon this issue.[4] It is sometimes declared that an unjust will, taken in connection with other evidence, calls for an explanation and a

10 Green, Fraud, Undue Influence and Mental Incompetency, 43 Col.L.R. 176.

1 See supra § 51 at notes 1–4.

2 Cook v. Morton, 241 Ala. 188, 1 So.2d 890, 1941; In re Mazanec's Estate, 204 Minn. 406, 283 N.W. 745, 1939.

3 In re Hesse's Estate, 62 Ariz. 273, 157 P.2d 347, 1945; Jackson's Ex'r v. Semones, 266 Ky. 352, 98 S.W.2d 505, 1937; O'Brien v. Collins, 315 Mass. 429, 53 N.E.2d 222, 1944; Look v. French, 346 Mo. 972, 144 S.W.2d 128, 1940. But see Longanecker v. Sowers, 148 Md. 584, 129 A. 896, 1925.

4 In re Ruffino's Estate, 116 Cal. 304, 48 P. 127, 1897; Meier v. Buchter, 197 Mo. 68, 94 S.W. 883, 6 L.R.A., N.S., 202, 7 Ann.Cas. 887, 1906.

showing that undue influence did not produce it.[5] Perhaps even slighter corroborative evidence is necessary than where mental capacity is the issue, because direct outward manifestations of undue influence are seldom capable of proof.[6]

*The Nature of the Influence*

Every one is more or less swayed by his associations with other persons. Obviously the courts would not characterize all such environmental influence as undue. Some decisions declare that the presence or absence of undue influence must be determined by the facts of each case and decline to lay down any general test.[7] Other courts beg the question of what influence is undue by laying stress upon the four elements necessary to establish undue influence: (1) a testator subject to undue influence, (2) opportunity to exercise it, (3) disposition to exercise it, (4) a result appearing to be the effect thereof.[8] Often undue influence is defined as coercion of something that the testator did not desire to do.[9] The most usual language is that in order to constitute undue influence, the conduct of the other must be such as to destroy the free agency of the testator,[10] or substitute another's volition for his.[11] To be classed as undue, the influence must place the testator in the attitude of saying: "It is not my will but I must do it." [12] The question is subjective, viz., whether

[5] Franks' Ex'r v. Bates, 278 Ky. 337, 128 S.W.2d 739, 1939; see In re Bowman's Estate, 143 Neb. 440, 9 N.W.2d 801, 1943.

[6] Gardiner v. Goertner, 110 Fla. 377, 149 So. 186, 1933; Rollwagen v. Rollwagen, 63 N.Y. 504, 1875.

[7] Caldarone v. Caldarone, 48 R.I. 163, 136 A. 489, 1927; Reinhardt v. Nehring, 283 S.W. 347, Tex.Civ.App. 1926. See realistic discussion in note, 50 Mich.L.R. 748.

[8] In re Inda's Estate, 146 Neb. 179, 19 N.W.2d 37, 1945; In re Rowland's Estate, 70 S.D. 419, 18 N.W.2d 290, 1945; In re Faulk's Will, 246 Wis. 319, 17 N.W.2d 423, 1945, noted in 1945 Wis.L.R. 633. See also 1945 Annual Surv.Am.L. 1038; note, 30 Ia. L.R. 321.

[9] Workman v. Workman, 113 Ind. App. 245, 46 N.E.2d 718, 1943; In re Bottger's Estate, 14 Wash.2d 676, 129 P.2d 518, 1942; Wingrove v. Wingrove, 11 P.D. 81, 1885.

[10] In re Arnold's Estate, 16 Cal.2d 573, 107 P.2d 25, 1940; Griffin v. Barrett, 183 Ga. 152, 187 S.E. 828, 1936; In re Geske's Estate, 211 Minn. 447, 1 N.W.2d 423, 1942.

[11] Marston v. Churchill, 137 Fla. 154, 187 So. 762, 1939; Knudson v. Knudson, 382 Ill. 492, 46 N.E.2d 1011, 1943; Croft v. Snedow, 183 Va. 649, 33 S.E.2d 208, 1945. See also cases supra note 10.

[12] Ginter v. Ginter, 79 Kan. 721, 101 P. 634, 22 L.R.A.,N.S., 1024, 1909; Wingrove v. Wingrove, 11 P.D. 81, 1885. In general, see Gifford, Will or No Will, 20 Col.L.R. 862; Green, Fraud, Undue Influence and Mental Incompetency, 43 Col.L.R. 176; Hutton, Undue Influence and Fraud in

the desire of the testator was overcome, not whether an average testator's mind would have been coerced under the circumstances.

In the ordinary case of undue influence, the will is that of the testator in the sense that it is executed by him and he realizes this, but it is held invalid because it does not represent his true wish or desire. To say that the pressure must be absolutely irresistible is probably putting the matter too strongly; the influence is fatal to the will if it is such that the testator could not well resist. It is not necessary that the coercion be physical or that there be threats of violence in order to cause the courts to refuse probate on this ground.[13]

Threats of violence,[14] of litigation among the children,[15] of criminal prosecution of the testator,[16] or to leave a sick testator,[17] may constitute undue influence. Likewise creation of resentment toward a natural object of the testator's bounty by false statements, though not amounting to fraud, may invalidate the will.[18] A testator's religious belief may be used so artfully as to make a case of undue influence.[19] The ways and means of domination

Wills, 37 Dick.L.R. 16; King, Undue Influence in Wills in Illinois, 2 U.Chi. L.R. 457; Spracher, Undue Influence, 16 Marq.L.R. 130; Warren, Fraud, Undue Influence and Mistake in Wills, 41 Harv.L.R. 309, 326; Winder, Undue Influence and Coercion, 3 Mod.L.R. 97; note, 46 W.Va.L.R. 168.

13 In re Faust's Estates, 150 Kan. 784, 96 P.2d 680, 1940; In re Hinton's Will, 180 N.C. 206, 104 S.E. 341, 1920; In re Bryan's Estate, 82 Utah 390, 25 P.2d 602, 1933; Hall v. Hall, L.R. 1 P. & D. 481, 1868.

14 Gay v. Gillilan, 92 Mo. 250, 5 S. W. 7, 1 Am.St.Rep. 712, 1887.

15 Moore's Ex'rs v. Blauvelt, 15 N. J.Eq. 367, 1862.

16 In re Brunor, 21 App.Div. 259, 47 N.Y.S. 681, 1897. See also In re Pohlmann's Estate, 89 Cal.App.2d 563, 201 P.2d 446, 1949, noted, 10 U. of Pitt.L.R. 602.

17 In re Sickles' Will, 63 N.J.Eq. 233, 50 A. 577, affirmed 64 N.J.Eq. 791, 53 A. 1125, 1903.

18 In re Stoddart's Estate, 174 Cal. 606, 163 P. 1010, 1917; Friedersdorf v. Lacy, 173 Ind. 429, 90 N.E. 766, 1910; Spurr v. Spurr, 285 Mo. 163, 226 S.W. 35, 1920. See Duckett v. Duckett, 77 App.D.C. 303, 134 F.2d 527, 1943. Mere speaking unkind words to testator about contestant does not amount to undue influence. In re Klink's Estate, 210 Mich. 614, 178 N.W. 14, 1920. As to the necessity of the representation being false in order to constitute undue influence, see In re Corblis' Will, 52 A. 996, affirmed 65 N.J.Eq. 768, 55 A. 1132, 1903.

19 Orchardson v. Cofield, 171 Ill. 14, 49 N.E. 197, 40 L.R.A. 256, 63 Am.St. Rep. 211, 1897; In re Hanson's Estate, 87 Wash. 113, 151 P. 264, 1915; In re Bishop's Estate, 2 Cal.2d 132, 30 P.2d 201, 1934. See supra § 52, notes 43, 49. Cf. Minturn v. Conception Abbey, 227 Mo.App. 1179, 61 S.W. 2d 352, 1933 (influence of natural course of one's religious training will not be considered undue). See In re McIntyre's Estate, 193 Mich. 257, 159 N.W. 517, 1917.

over the testator's mind are innumerable. Though cases are rare, it is possible that excessive flattering attentions may cause disallowance of the will.[20]

General influence is not sufficient to invalidate the will.[21] Mere advice,[22] or persuasion,[23] does not constitute undue influence nor does kindness and assistance even by a stranger.[24] The fact that the testator made a disposition to obtain or preserve peace in his household does not by itself show undue influence.[25] Even the influence which results from immoral relationships to the testator is not undue if it springs from affection rather than domination of mind.[26] The influence of a mistress is not necessarily undue,[27] while that of a wife under certain circumstances may be so regarded.[28] The law does not condemn the gift merely be-

[20] See Keller v. Keller, 239 Pa. 467, 86 A. 1065, 1913. Cf. In re Faulk's Will, supra note 8. See note 24 infra.

[21] In re Hops' Will, 103 N.J.Eq. 11, 141 A. 771, 1928; Myers v. Myers, 130 Okl. 184, 266 P. 452, 1928; Decker v. Koenig, 37 S.W.2d 378, Tex.Civ. App.1931. The comparative rarity of undue influence is shown by the fact that in less than seven percent of the undue influence cases was the decree for contestants affirmed on this ground. See King, Undue Influence in Wills in Illinois, 2 U. of Chi.L.R. 457.

[22] Flanigon v. Smith, 337 Ill. 572, 169 N.E. 767, 1929; Greenlees v. Allen, 341 Ill. 262, 173 N.E. 121, 1930; Barbee v. Barbee, 134 Wash. 418, 235 P. 945, 1925 (suggestion).

[23] MacMillan v. Knost, 75 App.D.C. 261, 126 F.2d 235, 1942; In re Cookson's Estate, 325 Pa. 81, 188 A. 904, 1937.

[24] In re Goist's Estate, 146 Neb. 1, 18 N.W.2d 513, 1945. General flattery cannot be regarded as undue influence. Wellman v. Carter, 286 Mass. 237, 190 N.E. 493, 1934.

[25] Hale v. Cox, 222 Ala. 136, 131 So. 233, 1930; Warwick v. Zimmerman, 126 Kan. 619, 270 P. 612, 1928. But see Hacker v. Newborn, Style 427, 82 Eng.Rep. 834, 1654: "If a man makes his will in his sickness, by the overimportuning of his wife, to the end he may be quiet, this shall be said to be a will made by constraint, and shall not be a good will." Cf. Hall v. Hall, L.R. 1 P. & D. 481, 1868, to same general effect. And see Emery v. Emery, 222 Mass. 439, 111 N.E. 287, 1916, where impossibility of securing peace otherwise than by executing the will seems to be one of the evidences of coercion sufficient to invalidate the will.

[26] Glider v. Melinski, 238 Iowa 140, 25 N.W.2d 379, 1946; Faulkes v. Brummett's Adm'r, 305 Ky. 434, 204 S.W.2d 493, 1947; In re Swartz's Will, 79 Okl. 191, 192 P. 203, 16 A.L.R. 450, 1920 (testatrix and beneficiaries all inmates of house of prostitution); Farr v. O'Neall, 1 Rich.(S.C.) 80, 1844. See note, 21 Notre Dame Lawyer 116

[27] See Glider, Faulkes and Farr cases, supra note 26. It has been held that influence when exercised by a wife might be proper and the same influence when exercised by a mistress would be considered undue. Kessinger v. Kessinger, 37 Ind. 341, 1871.

[28] Street v. Street, 246 Ala. 683, 22 So.2d 35, 1945; Martin v. Martin, 267 Mass. 157, 166 N.E. 820, 1929. See

cause of immoral activities between the testator and the donee, nor is the disposition allowed to stand simply because their general association is one which is socially approved.

*The Person Exerting the Influence*

In order to invalidate the will, the influence must be that of some other person. Where the spell is cast by the workings of the testator's own mind and without pressure of another there cannot be said to be undue influence.[29] Thus when a will was made simply because the testator believed that spirit voices commanded the disposition the case should be decided on the basis of insane delusions rather than undue influence.[30] If, however, the belief in the existence of the voices was engendered by some living individual, a case of undue influence may be presented. Again, a desire to comply with the wishes of a deceased husband, fearing his displeasure in the next world, does not constitute undue influence.[31] When a wife makes a certain will because of fear for the peace of mind of her dying husband who was exercising no coercion, undue influence has not been established.[32]

It is said that influence in order to invalidate the will must be exercised with the object of procuring a particular will,[33] though it has been doubted whether this would be necessary in all cases.[34] Generally the undue influence is exerted by the beneficiary himself, but a will may be invalid though the beneficiary took no part in the activities,[35] and was even ignorant of the fact.[36] In the

also In re Teel's Estate, 25 Cal.2d 520, 154 P.2d 384, 1944 (husband). Cf. Latham v. Udell, 38 Mich. 238, 1878 (spouse may properly use her wifely influence).

29 See Mitchell v. Mitchell, 43 Minn. 73, 44 N.W. 885, 1890; In re White's Will, 121 N.Y. 406, 24 N.E. 935, 1890; Fox v. Martin, 104 Wis. 581, 80 N.W. 921, 1899.

30 See supra § 52, note 43.

31 Henderson v. Jackson (In re Powell), 138 Iowa 326, 111 N.W. 821, 26 L.R.A.,N.S., 479, 1907. See also In re Dillon's Will, 82 N.J.Eq. 322, 87 A. 161, 1913.

32 Warwick v. Zimmerman, 126 Kan. 619, 270 P. 612, 1928. But see Trust Co. of Georgia v. Ivey, 178 Ga. 629, 173 S.E. 648, 1934; noted 13 N.C.L.R. 268.

33 Milton v. Jeffers, 154 Ark. 516, 243 S.W. 60, 1922; Allmon v. Pigg, 82 Ill. 149, 25 Am.Rep. 303, 1876; In re Wallace's Will, 197 Wis. 323, 222 N.W. 255, 1928. When the influence merely caused the testator to make a will, leaving him free as to the provisions, it was not fatal to the will. Struth v. Decker, 100 Md. 368, 59 A. 727, 1904; In re Lowe's Will, 180 N.C. 140, 104 S.E. 143, 1920.

34 4 Page, Wills, 3d ed. § 186.

35 Little v. Sugg, 243 Ala. 196, 8 So. 2d 866, 1942; Gidley v. Gidley, 130 Neb. 419, 265 N.W. 245, 1936; In re Hanson's Estate, 169 Wash. 637, 14 P.

36 See Note 36 on following page.

case of gifts to associations or institutions it is surely sufficient that the person exercising control over the testator be one who is interested in the beneficiary.[37]

*The Causal Connection*

Finally, the disposition must be caused by the undue influence in order to hold it invalid on this ground. Thus, it must be shown that the pressure resulted in a will which the testator would not otherwise have made.[38] The influence must be operative at the time of execution of the will,[39] although it is not necessary that the overt acts should be done then,[40] or that the person exercising the pressure should be present.[41] If the mind of the testator, though once coerced, is free from the domination at the time of signing the will, the showing is insufficient to deny probate.

A will procured by undue influence does not become valid by reason of the fact that the testator acquiesced in it by allowing it to stand after the pressure has been removed.[42] However, if the

2d 702, 1932. See Minturn v. Conception Abbey, 227 Mo.App. 1179, 61 S.W.2d 352, 1933. Undue influence by one beneficiary operates against all. Synder v. Steele, 304 Ill. 387, 136 N.E. 649, 28 A.L.R. 1, 1922. Expressions can be found that undue influence must be by the beneficiary or those interested in him. Convey v. Murphy, 146 Iowa 154, 124 N.W. 1073, 1910 (semble); Stutiville's Ex'rs v. Wheeler, 187 Ky. 361, 219 S.W. 411, 1920. It should be noticed, however, that independent of this question the influence in the latter cases was not undue. And see Stege v. Stege's Trustee, 237 Ky. 197, 35 S.W.2d 324, 1931, which is in accord with the statement in the text above. See annotation, 96 A.L.R. 613.

36 Barr v. Sumner, 183 Ind. 402, 107 N.E. 675, 109 N.E. 193, 1915. See In re Erickson's Estate, 140 Cal.App. 520, 35 P.2d 628, 1934; noted, 48 Harv.L. R. 692.

37 In re Wilson's Estate, 223 Minn. 409, 27 N.W.2d 429, 1947; Clark v. Commerce Trust Co., 333 Mo. 243, 62 S.W.2d 874, 1933.

38 Bollinger v. Arkansas Val. Trust Co., 202 Ark. 525, 151 S.W.2d 675, 1941; Downey v. Lawley, 377 Ill. 298, 36 N.E.2d 344, 1941.

39 Boland v. Aycock, 191 Ga. 327, 12 S.E.2d 319, 1941 (statute); Downey v. Lawley, supra note 38.

40 Drury v. King, 182 Md. 64, 32 A. 2d 371, 1943; In re George's Estate, 100 Utah 230, 112 P.2d 498, 1941.

41 In re Pohlmann's Estate, 89 Cal. App.2d 563, 201 P.2d 446, 1949, noted, 10 U. of Pitt.L.R. 602 and 1949 Annual Surv.Am.L. 834; Minturn v. Conception Abbey, supra note 35.

42 Haines v. Hayden, 95 Mich. 332, 54 N.W. 911, 35 Am.St.Rep. 566, 1893 (ratification of will invalid because of fraud); In re Van Ness' Will, 78 Misc. 592, 139 N.Y.S. 485, 1912; Chaddick v. Haley, 81 Tex. 617, 17 S.W. 233, 1891. But see In re Reynold's Estate, 132 N.J.Eq. 141, 27 A.2d 226, 1942, affirmed 133 N.J.Eq. 344, 32 A. 2d 353, 1943. However, retention of the will after the alleged influence has ceased is evidence of absence of undue influence. In re Branther's

will is republished by codicil or otherwise, the material question is the presence or absence of undue influence at the time of this republication. In such a case undue influence at the time of the original execution is immaterial,[43] except for its possible evidential value upon the situation at the later time.[44]

*Wills Drawn by Beneficiaries*

According to the Roman law, a will written by the beneficiary was void.[45] The Anglo-American law is not so severe.[46] "When the beneficiary sustains confidential relations and drafts the will or controls its drafting, it is variously stated, the phraseology and perhaps the precise thought changing from case to case, with some attendant confusion of expression and meaning, that a presumption of undue influence arises, or that an inference to that effect may be drawn as a fact, or that the facts stated make a prima facie case, or that the case is one for scrutiny." [47] The foregoing quotation reflects the diverse and somewhat confused state of the authorities.[48] In case that the beneficiary is a close relative of the draftsman, a court normally takes the same position which it does when the draftsman is himself the benefici-

Estate, 115 Colo. 133, 169 P.2d 326, 1946. Cf. In re Wilson's Estate, 223 Minn. 409, 27 N.W.2d 429, 1947.

43 In re Horton's Estate, 128 Cal. App. 249, 17 P.2d 184, 1932.

44 See In re Horton's Estate, supra note 43; infra § 91.

45 Digest, Lib. 48, tit. 10, 15. See Graham v. Courtright, 180 Iowa 394, 161 N.W. 774, 1917; In re Nixon's Will, 136 N.J.Eq. 242, 41 A.2d 119, 1945; In re Lobb's Will, 173 Or. 414, 160 P.2d 295, 1945.

46 The nearest approach to the civil law rule is found in Kan.Gen.Stat. 1947 Supp. § 59–605. But the will is not invalid unless the *principal* beneficiary prepared the will; furthermore, if the testator knew the contents of the will and had independent advice with reference thereto, the will is valid. See Sellards v. Kirby, 82 Kan. 291, 108 P.73, 28 L.R.A.,N.S., 270, 136 Am.St.R. 110, 20 Ann.Cas. 214, 1910; Smith's Estate v. Davis, 168 Kan. 210, 212 P.2d 322, 1949 (token gift).

47 In re Simmons' Estate, 156 Minn. 144, 194 N.W. 330, 1923.

48 Zeigler v. Coffin, 219 Ala. 586, 123 So. 22, 63 A.L.R. 942, 1929 (presumption of undue influence created); In re Johnson's Estate, 85 Cal.App. 2d 760, 193 P.2d 782, 1948 (strong presumption); Cook v. Hollyday, 185 Md. 656, 45 A.2d 761, 1946 (attorney has burden); In re Putman's Will, 257 N.Y. 140, 177 N.E. 399, 79 A.L.R. 1423, 1931 (inference of undue influence justified); Graham v. Courtright, supra note 45 (suspicious circumstance); Caswell v. Lehrman, 85 Ohio App. 206, 88 N.E.2d 405, 1948, noted, 19 U. of Cin.L.R. 297 (no presumption). See also, Wunderlich v. Buerger, 287 Ill. 440, 122 N.E. 827, 1919, emphasizing that the presumption of undue influence arose from the fact that the draftsman was the beneficiary rather than from confidential relationship between the beneficiary and the testa-

ary.[49] Dependent upon the rule in the particular jurisdiction and the circumstances of the particular case, troublesome litigation, judicial criticism, and loss of the will's benefits may result from the lawyer's preparation of an instrument in which he or his relatives are beneficiaries, even though there was no actual overreaching on his part.[50]

"Attorneys for clients who intend to leave them or their families a bequest would do well to have the will drawn by some other lawyer." [51] Moreover, the employment of another attorney should be real and not a mere formal subterfuge, for one who participates in procuring the will is in the same position as the actual draftsman.[52] Even in absence of the element of confidential relationship, some cases cast doubt upon wills in which the draftsman is a legatee.[53] The same consequences do not follow in cases where the draftsman is merely executor or trustee under the will for the reason that the financial benefits are ordinarily small and the fees are earned and are not gratuitous.[54] However, questions of ethics may arise from combined relationships of this nature and some members of the bar avoid them entirely.

This topic is part of the subject of the effect of activity in procuring a will by a beneficiary who is in confidential relationship with the testator. The broader aspects are reserved for later consideration,[55] but the difficulties and embarrassments of the attorney-beneficiary situation warrant mention of this matter here in order to indicate the proper course of conduct to be observed in the process of drafting and execution of a will.

trix. In some states the rule is far from clear. Cf. In re Nixon's Will, supra note 45 with In re Heim's Will, 136 N.J.Eq. 138, 40 A.2d 651, 1945, and see Clapp, Presumption of Undue Influence, 67 N.J.L.J. 216. See generally note, 31 Corn.L.Q. 80.

49 Mackay v. Costigan, 179 F.2d 125, C.C.A.Ill., 1950; Sweeney v. Vierbuchen, 224 Ind. 341, 66 N.E.2d 764, 1946, noted, 22 Ind.L.J. 106.

50 See Graham v. Courtright, supra note 45.

51 In re Putman's Will, 257 N.Y. 140, 177 N.E. 399, 79 A.L.R. 1423, 1931. See also In re Nixon's Will supra note 45.

52 In re Lobb's Will, supra note 45.

53 Hughes v. Meredith, 25 Ga. 325, 71 Am.Dec. 127, 1858; England v. Fawbush, 204 Ill. 384, 68 N.E. 526, 1903.

54 Williams v. Ragland, 307 Ill. 386, 138 N.E. 599, 1923; Breadheft v. Cleveland, 184 Ind. 130, 108 N.E. 5, 1915, rehearing denied 110 N.E. 662; In re Heitholt's Estate, 202 Okl. 351, 213 P.2d 865, 1950. Cf. Zeigler v. Coffin, 219 Ala. 586, 123 So. 22, 63 A.L.R. 942, 1929 (large benefits as trustee). See also Questions, Committee on Professional Ethics, Association of the Bar of the City of New York, 1925–1930, No. 14.

55 See infra § 101.

## FRAUD

**56. A will is invalid if the testator has been wilfully deceived by the beneficiary as to the character or contents of the instrument, or as to extrinsic facts which are material to the disposition and in fact caused it. The elements of fraud are essentially those necessary to establish a deceit; hence innocent misrepresentation does not invalidate a will unless relief would be given on account of a simple mistake by the testator as to the same facts.**

Fraud and undue influence are often related in point of fact and the terms are sometimes used interchangeably.[1] Moreover, the effect of each upon the will is the same. Still there is a difference between the unduly influenced or coerced testator and the one who is defrauded or deceived. The courts distinguish between undue influence and fraud in obtaining a will if it is material to do so.[2] Thus, it is error to charge the jury that a will cannot be set aside for fraud unless the testator is coerced,[3] and it has been held that a will contest on the ground of undue influence cannot be amended to cover fraud after the time for contest has expired.[4]

There are no common or well established definitions of fraud as applied to wills, due perhaps to the comparative scarcity of contests on this ground. The writers show a tendency to discuss fraud without defining it.[5] However, one of them has declared that fraud in the execution or in the inducement of the will is a form of deceit.[6] The cases on fraud in the inducement indicate that the elements are similar to those in a tort action for deceit.[7] It has been also said that fraud necessary to invalidate a will does not differ from that which will vitiate a contract.[8] It is fairly

1 See supra § 54.

2 Wellman v. Carter, 286 Mass. 237, 190 N.E. 493, 1934; Gockel v. Gockel, 66 S.W.2d 867, 92 A.L.R. 784, Mo.1933, and see infra notes 3 and 4.

3 Councill v. Mayhew, 172 Ala. 295, 55 So. 314, 1911.

4 In re Wilson's Estate, 117 Cal. 262, 49 P. 172, 711, 1897.

5 Warren, Fraud, Undue Influence and Mistake in Wills, 41 Harv.L.R. 309. Cf. Green, Fraud, Undue Influence and Mental Incompetency, 43 Col.L.R. 176, 177–179.

6 Gifford, Will or No Will, 20 Col. L.R. 178, though he says that this is not true of "fraud in the effect," as to which see infra § 57. Cf. Green, supra note 5.

7 See infra notes 19–25.

8 In re Newhall's Estate, 190 Cal. 709, 214 P. 231, 28 A.L.R. 778, 1923; Knox v. Perkins, 86 N.H. 66, 163 A. 497, 1933. See Restatement, Con-

clear that there must be intent to deceive the testator and that innocent misrepresentation of the facts does not constitute fraud.[9]

The situations in case of fraud, innocent misrepresentation, and mistake are similar in that the testator acts upon false data. Subjectively his mind is the same in all three cases. The difference consists in the cause of the testator's error. In fraud it is the wilful result of another's conduct; in innocent misrepresentation the other person caused the error without intending to do so; in mistake the error is induced by the testator himself. Here is the basis of the distinction upon which the courts grant relief for fraud, although they would do nothing about the same sort of error induced by innocent misrepresentation or by the testator's own mistake.[10] Perhaps something may be said for planting this result upon the objective aspects of fraud. Undue influence likewise has objective manifestations while mistake is entirely in the testator's mind. However, this explanation falls when we consider that the same restrictive attitude found in the mistake cases is taken with regard to innocent misrepresentation, which has as many objective manifestations as fraud or undue influence. The true, or at least the main, reason for the distinction is the deep feeling that fraud should vitiate everything which it touches and that the conscious wrongdoer should not have advantage of his act. The courts are willing to embark upon an examination of the alleged fraud or undue influence because they believe that the enforcement of moral precepts are so important that they can afford to run the risk of inquiring into the testator's state of mind—an excursion which they will not usually take in case of innocent misrepresentation or simple mistake, where similar moral grounds do not exist. In the latter cases the desire to give final effect to the formal act of will-making often prevails over considerations of trying to rectify an error.[11]

*Fraud in the execution*

While there are no differences in the effect upon the will,[12] it is customary to give separate consideration to: (1) fraud in

tracts §§ 470–474; Restatement, Restitution § 8.

9 In re Newhall's Estate, supra note 8. See infra notes 24, 25.

10 See infra § 59.

11 Ibid.

12 In § 124 of the first edition of his work on Wills, Professor Page insisted that fraud in the inducement had no effect upon the validity of the will, unless it amounted to undue influence. See also note, 5 Minn.L.R. 403. This view was abandoned in 2d ed. § 186, 3d ed. § 181.

the execution, or misrepresentation as to the character or contents of the instrument; (2) fraud in the inducement, or falsification of facts dehors the instrument.

Although the instrument is duly executed in the form of a will, if the beneficiary induced the maker to sign it upon the representation that it was a document of a different and non-testamentary nature, it is invalid as a will.[13] The fraud, however, must be upon the testator; where the misrepresentation of the character of the paper is to the witnesses only, the will may be admitted to probate.[14] Even if the testator knew he was signing his will, if the contents are misrepresented to him, it is not valid.[15] When there is actual deceit as to either character or contents of the document, it is apparently immaterial whether the testator had an opportunity and ability to examine the instrument. Even the deceitful giving of advice as to the meaning of the terms of the will may constitute fraud.[16] However, misrepresentation of contents not induced by the beneficiary is not ground for judicial relief,[17] unless under the circumstances redress would be given for mistake alone.[18]

*Fraud in the Inducement*

The precedents as to fraud in the inducement are somewhat more numerous than those on fraud in execution. This gives a better opportunity for a survey of the essential elements to warrant rejection of the will upon this ground. On the whole the requirements are not different from the necessary ingredients of actions for deceit.[19] The representations must be made directly

13 Hildreth v. Marshall, 51 N.J.Eq. 241, 27 A. 465, 1893 (representation that instrument really a will was a burial permit). In this case the same result would probably follow where there was mere mistake and no fraud. See infra § 58; Warren, Fraud, Undue Influence, and Mistake in Wills, 41 Harv.L.R. 309, 324–326.

14 Slade v. Slade, 155 Ga. 851, 118 S.E. 645, 1923. Cf. infra §§ 68, 69.

15 Wombacher v. Barthelme, 194 Ill. 425, 62 N.E. 800, 1901; Rollwagen v. Rollwagen, 3 Hun (N.Y.) 121, 1874; Doe ex dem. Small v. Allen, 8 T.R. 147, 101 Eng.Rep. 1314, 1799.

16 Lyon v. Dada, 111 Mich. 340, 69 N.W. 654, 1896. See Reed v. Hollister, 44 Cal.App. 533, 186 P. 819, 1919 (constructive trust imposed). Cf. Leonard v. Stanton, 93 N.H. 113, 36 A.2d 271, 1944, noted, 43 Mich.L.R. 209.

17 Dye v. Parker, 108 Kan. 304, 194 P. 640, rehearing denied, 195 P. 599, 1921 (relief by way of reformation of will and constructive trust denied though husband of residuary beneficiary fraudulently induced testator to believe that will contained a certain devise.)

18 Cf. Leonard v. Stanton, supra note 16.

19 See Hopper v. Sellers, 91 Kan. 876, 139 P. 365, 1914; Gockel v. Gockel, 66 S.W.2d 867, 92 A.L.R. 784, Mo.

or indirectly to the testator,[20] apparently either by the person benefiting under the will, or at least by someone in his behalf.[21] The statements must be false,[22] although under some circumstances suppression of the facts may be sufficient.[23] Furthermore, the representation must be known to be false by the person making it.[24] Innocent misrepresentation does not invalidate the will.[25]

To invalidate the will, the fraud must be as to a material point.[26] This requirement probably eliminates a large number of situations where a prospective legatee puts his best foot forward in his relations with the testator or actually deceives the latter as to the former's character or conduct. Perhaps most of

1933; In re Bottger's Estate, 14 Wash.2d 676, 129 P.2d 518, 1942.

20 Sanger v. McDonald, 87 Ark. 148, 112 S.W. 365, 1908; Gockel v. Gockel, supra note 19. See Spurr v. Spurr, 285 Mo. 163, 226 S.W. 35, 1920, where part of representations were made to others with the intention that they should reach testator's ears.

21 Hopper v. Sellers, 91 Kan. 876, 139 P. 365, 1914; Ater v. Moore, 231 S.W. 457, Tex.Civ.App.1921; Anderson v. Berkley [1902] 1 Ch. 936, criticized, 16 Harv.L.R. 310. See infra, note 36. But see In re Roy's Estate, 113 Wash. 277, 193 P. 682, 1920; Davis v. Calvert, 5 Gill & J.(Md.) 269, 25 Am.Dec. 282, 1833; infra § 57 notes 9, 10.

22 In re Hollis' Estate, 234 Iowa 761, 12 N.W.2d 576, 1944; Knox v. Perkins, 86 N.H. 66, 163 A. 497, 1932; In re Janes, 87 Hun 57, 33 N.Y.S. 968, 1895.

23 In re Nutt's Estate, 181 Cal. 522, 185 P. 393, 1919. See In re Stirk's Estate, 232 Pa. 98, 81 A. 187, 1911.

24 Martindale v. Bridgforth, 210 Ala. 565, 98 So. 800, 1924; In re Petts, 27 Beav. 576, 54 Eng.Rep. 228, 1859. See also note 25, infra. Where the person has no knowledge of the truth of the testator's statement, his failure to contradict does not amount to fraud. In re Shay's Estate, 196 Cal. 355, 237 P. 1079, 1925.

25 In re Benton's Estate, 131 Cal. 472, 63 P. 775, 1901; In re Dries' Will, 69 N.J.Eq. 475, 55 A. 814, 1903; In re Roy's Estate, 113 Wash. 277, 193 P. 682, 1920. See Black v. Smith, 58 N.D. 109, 224 N.W. 915, 1929, where concealment of a fact for a good motive was held not to invalidate the will. Cf. In re Arnold's Estate, 147 Cal. 583, 82 P. 252, 1905, where the person believed only part of the representations, yet the will was held invalid for fraud.

26 See In re Janes, 87 Hun 57, 33 N.Y.S. 968, 1895; Weathers v. McFarland, 97 Ga. 266, 22 S.E. 988, 1895 (misrepresentation as to extent of the estate). With the latter case, compare however Reed v. Hollister, 44 Cal.App. 533, 186 P. 819, 1919. And see generally note 30 infra. Poisoning testator's mind regarding another may be considered material fraud. Spurr v. Spurr, 285 Mo. 163, 226 S.W. 35, 1920; In re Will of Budlong, 126 N.Y. 423, 27 N.E. 945, 1891. See, also, Gordon v. Burris, 153 Mo. 223, 54 S.W. 546, 1899 (agreement, by beneficiary who knew he was insolvent, to provide for another out of testator's property was deemed material fraud).

these cases could also be decided upon the ground that the will was not caused by the fraud. Though there is reason to doubt whether strict proofs will always be required, it has been declared that the deceit must have been practiced with the intention of procuring the will.[27]

It is necessary that the testator should have been deceived by the representations. Accordingly, when the testator entered into a purported marriage with his beneficiary, who was unable to marry because of some impediment, there was no fraud if the testator knew of this disability at the time of executing his will.[28] A representation made after the execution of the will does not affect the validity of the instrument.[29] Fraud which does not result in the making of the will is immaterial upon the question of whether the will should be admitted to probate.

The problem of causation is interrelated with some of the elements mentioned above. It is sometimes difficult to say whether the claim of fraud was unsuccessful because one other than the beneficiary made the misrepresentations, or because the statements were immaterial, or because they did not result in the disposition.[30] A test for causation is not easy to discover. Certainly we can reject the "but-for" rule which is so thoroughly rejected in the law of torts. To adopt this test would lead to serious consequences and even absurd results. For example, in one case a man having a prejudice against married females employed a woman upon her false representation that she was single and later left her a legacy. The gift was held valid,[31] yet "but for"

[27] In re Newhall's Estate, 190 Cal. 709, 214 P. 231, 28 A.L.R. 778, 1923. Cf. Smith v. Du Bose, 78 Ga. 413, 3 S.E. 309, 6 Am.St.Rep. 260, 1887, indicating that it is enough if the person made the representation "in bad faith." And see In re Carson's Estate, infra note 35, where in an otherwise fully considered case nothing is said as to whether the deceit must be practiced to procure the will as distinguished from other material advantages.

[28] Moore v. Heineke, 119 Ala. 627, 24 So. 374, 1898; McDole v. Thurm, 276 Ill. 200, 114 N.E. 542, L.R.A.1917B 1150, 1916; In re Donnely's Will, 68 Iowa 126, 26 N.W. 23, 1885; In re Wagstaff [1907] 2 Ch. 35, [1908] 1 Ch. 162. And so also in case of suspicion. Meluish v. Milton, L.R. 3 Ch.Div. 27, 1876.

[29] In re Rick's Estate, 160 Cal. 450, 117 P. 532, 1911; Montgomery v. Willbanks, 202 S.W.2d 851, Tex.Civ. App.1947.

[30] See Matter of Janes, 87 Hun 57, 33 N.Y.S. 968, 1895, affirmed 152 N.Y. 647, 46 N.E. 1148 (matter of materiality and causation); Wilkinson v. Joughin, L.R. 2 Eq. 319, 1866 (matters of fraud by third person and causation); Howell v. Troutman, 53 N.C.L. (8 Jones) 304, 1860 (same); Provenza v. Provenza, 201 Miss. 836, 29 So.2d 669, 1947 (same).

[31] Matter of Janes, supra note 30.

the fraud, undoubtedly she would not have secured the position, and in absence of the employment she would not have been remembered in the will. The decision seems just, for her faithful service rather than the fact that testator believed that she was unmarried was clearly the principal motivating force behind the gift.

The old English case of Kennell v. Abbott [32] states, unwittingly perhaps, two different tests of causation. According to the first-mentioned the gift is invalid if the testator would not have made the provision had he known the true facts.[33] Elsewhere in the same opinion it is said that the fraud must be the sole motive for the bounty in order to work this result. The difference in result of the two tests becomes apparent in situations where the fraud and some other reason both impelled the testator to make his will. Under the first of these rules the will might be invalid if the other reason was not sufficient by itself to have caused the legacy while under the second the will would be valid. Professor Warren [34] declared himself in favor of the first test. The authorities, while not explicit on the point, are consistent with his view.[35]

To illustrate the problem further let us consider the case of a testatrix who makes a will in favor of her assumed husband who falsely represented that he was single at the time of their marriage. The belief of the testatrix that the beneficiary was her lawful husband is only one of the causes of the gift—doubtless affection for him was also a considerable factor. Moreover, the element of affection played a large part in the purported marriage so that the fraud can not be said to be the sole basis of the gift. Under the second test the disposition would seem to be valid, yet we have an instinctive feeling that the "husband" should not take. This rule seems to go as far in one direction as the "but-for" test does in the other.

32 4 Ves.Jr. 803, 31 Eng.Rep. 416, 1797.

33 This is the civil law rule. Digest xxxv, 1, 72, 6.

34 Fraud, Undue Influence, and Mistake in Wills, 41 Harv.L.R. 309, 316, 317.

35 See Davis v. Calvert, 5 Gill & J. (Md.) 269, 309, 25 Am.Dec. 282, 1833; Knox v. Perkins, 86 N.H. 66, 163 A. 497, 1932; In re Carson's Estate, 184 Cal. 437, 194 P. 5, 17 A.L.R. 239, 1920. But cf. Rishton v. Cobb, 5 My. and Cr. 145, 150, 41 Eng.Rep. 326, 1839; Meluish v. Milton, 3 Ch.D. 27, 29, 1876; Smith v. Diggs, 128 Md. 394, 97 A. 712, 1916, when the language is consistent with the second test though the cases do not turn on the point. The ordinary tort cases for deceit declare that the representation need not be the sole cause of the loss. Addington v. Allen, 11 Wend.(N.Y.) 374, 375, 1833.

The courts have sustained the contest in cases of this nature.[36] This tends to support the validity of the first position. However, even under this test, if the marriage had preceded the making of the will by many years, the testatrix might have made the same will although she had known the true facts, because of affectionate associations extending over the long period.[37] It is true that this test requires some speculation on the part of the court or jury as to what the testatrix would have done had she known the true facts at the time of making the will. This seems unavoidable. Even the question of physical causation is so fraught with difficulty that it is not surprising that uncertainty is encountered when we consider human conduct. Apparently the subject is a matter for jury determination,[38] under control of the court, viz., the submission to the jury only of questions where there may be said to be reasonable doubt.[39]

In conclusion we should notice two classes of cases in which relief will be given though some of the elements of fraud enumerated in this section are not established. There are certain instances of innocent misrepresentation where the courts give relief because they would have done so even in case of a mere mistake induced by the testator himself.[40] There are also cases of constructive fraud, or "fraud in effect", wherein equity imposes a trust for mere breach of an agreement by the devisee to convey to another; here, however, the so-called fraud is no ground of contest of the will and relief must be obtained in equity.[41]

[36] In re Carson's Estate, supra note 35; Wilkinson v. Joughin, supra note 30; Kennell v. Abbott, supra note 32. But the mere fact that the survivor was married to another at the time of his marriage to the testatrix does not invalidate the will if there is no fraud. Wenning v. Teeple, infra note 39; see Stothers v. Flieger, 13 N.J. Super. 379, 80 A.2d 583, 1951 (construction case).

[37] In re Carson's Estate, supra note 95. And see Wilkinson v. Joughin, Howell v. Troutman, Provenza v. Provenza, all supra note 30, where affection for a child rather than the mother's misrepresentation as to facts concerning the paternity was deemed the cause or the possible cause of the legacy. See also Knox v. Perkins, supra note 22, where it was assumed that testator would have made the same disposition even if he had known the facts.

[38] See In re Carson's Estate, supra note 35; In re Newhall's Estate, 190 Cal. 709, 214 P. 231, 28 A.L.R. 778, 1923; Smith v. Diggs, 128 Md. 394, 97 A. 712, 1916; Diggs v. Smith, 130 Md. 101, 99 A. 952, 1917.

[39] See Wenning v. Teeple, 144 Ind. 189, 41 N.E. 600, 1895; Matter of Janes, supra note 30.

[40] This would apply, however, only if the misrepresentation were concerning the document signed or its contents. See infra §§ 58–60.

[41] See infra § 57 at note 15.

## REMEDIES FOR FRAUD AND DURESS

**57. Heirs at law, or devisees under a former will, can obtain relief against fraud or duress in the execution of a will only by contest of the will. However, where the testator was unlawfully prevented from making a will, the intended beneficiaries obtain their redress by the impression of a constructive trust or by a damage action against the wrongdoer.**

**When a devisee, or heir at law in case of intestacy, promises the owner to convey to or hold on trust for another and fails to perform, a trust will be imposed for the intended beneficiary although there was no actual fraud.**

*Contest of Will*

It is now agreed that a will procured through fraud or duress is void.[1] These issues are ordinarily litigated upon contest of the instrument. The probate court is the proper forum since it can give relief under the circumstances.[2] Indeed, if the matter can be determined by rejecting the will from probate, a court of equity has no jurisdiction.[3] Thus, a trust ex maleficio in favor of the heir will not be imposed upon one who has fraudulently obtained a devise or legacy, since the heir can obtain relief by contesting the provision in the probate court for fraud.[4]

*Equitable and Legal Relief*

In some cases of fraud or duress the machinery of the probate court is inadequate to give relief.[5] The latter tribunal cannot possibly probate a will which someone prevented the testator

[1] See supra §§ 55, 56.

[2] See infra note 3, and generally §§ 93, 96 infra.

[3] Allen v. M'Pherson, 5 Beav. 469, 1 Phillips 133, 1 H.L.Cas. 191, 49 Eng. Rep. 660, 41 Eng.Rep. 582, 9 Eng.Rep. 727, 1847; Broderick's Will, 21 Wall. 503, 22 L.Ed. 599, 1875 (forged will); Graham v. Graham, 175 Ark. 530, 1 S.W.2d 16, 1927. See also Petitt v. Morton, 28 Ohio App. 227, 162 N.E. 627, 1928, noted, 3 Cin.L.R. 107, 14 Corn.L.Q. 108, 27 Mich.L.R. 452 (forged will); Langdon v. Blackburn, 109 Cal. 19, 41 P. 814, 1895; Stowe v. Stowe, 140 Mo. 594, 41 S.W. 951, 1897. But see Seeds v. Seeds; 116 Ohio St. 144, 156 N.E. 193, 52 A.L.R. 761, 1927, where it is indicated that the test should be whether the probate court can give relief at the time the fraud was discovered, not at the time that will was originally offered for probate.

[4] Langdon v. Blackburn and Stowe v. Stowe, both supra note 3. See Axe v. Wilson, 150 Kan. 794, 96 P.2d 880, 1939 (damage action).

[5] See Page, of Forbidding or Hindring the Testator to Make Another Testament [1951] Wis.L.R. 474.

from executing.[6] As there is no adequate remedy in probate, equity will impress a constructive trust in favor of the intended beneficiary against the wrongdoer,[7] although equity has no jurisdiction to reform a will.[8] While there is authority to the contrary,[9] it is reasonable that a trust should be imposed even against an innocent heir or devisee if he would otherwise take by reason of the fraud of another.[10]

In the jurisdictions which do not impose a trust against the innocent heir or devisee, the intended beneficiary possibly has a remedy for damages against the one who interfered with the execution of the will in the plaintiff's favor. Indeed this should be a remedy alternative to the constructive trust. At any rate existence of a claim for damages should not prevent imposition of a trust, or vice versa. Damages have been denied on the ground that plaintiff did not allege and prove that testator would have executed and retained until his death a will in plaintiff's favor.[11] However, in both damages and constructive trust cases the plaintiff should not be held to an unreasonable degree of proof in this regard.[12] Courts of law and of equity should afford effective relief against fraud and duress in connection with wills when there is no remedy in probate. The damages cases are few in number but there is no reason why the courts should not grant damages as readily as equitable relief.

6 A parallel problem is the case of one who by fraud prevents the testator from revoking his will. Here the probate court is without power to deny probate and relief must be had in another forum. See infra § 84 at note 16.

7 Monach v. Koslowski, 322 Mass. 466, 78 N.E.2d 4, 1948; Latham v. Father Divine, 200 N.Y. 22, 85 N.E. 2d 168, 11 A.L.R.2d 802, 1949, noted, 48 Mich.L.R. 1058, 34 Minn.L.R. 80; Pope v. Garrett, 147 Tex. 18, 211 S.W. 2d 559, 1948.

8 Dye v. Parker, 108 Kan. 304, 194 P. 640, rehearing denied 195 P. 599, 1921.

9 Ibid.; see Lowe Foundation v. Northern Trust Co., 342 Ill.App. 379, 96 N.E.2d 831, 1951, supra § 56, note 21.

10 Pope v. Garrett, supra note 7; Restatement, Restitution § 184. See note, 26 Tex.L.R. 684.

11 Lewis v. Corbin, 195 Mass. 528, 81 N.E. 248, 1907. See also Cunningham v. Edward, 52 Ohio App. 61, 3 N.E.2d 58, 1936, noted, 21 Minn.L.R. 345, 23 Va.L.R. 220 (intended beneficiary has no property right).

12 See Manach v. Koslowski and Latham v. Father Divine, both supra note 7; Restatement, Torts § 870, comment (b)(3) and § 912, comment (f) (13). See Bohannon v. Wachovia Bank & Trust Co., 210 N.C. 679, 188 S. E. 390, 1936 ("cause of action may be difficult to prove") and its sequel Bohannon v. Trotman, 214 N.C. 706, 200 S.E. 852, 1939 (settlement). As to the cases of fraudulent suppression of a will see infra § 96, at notes 31, 32.

*Secret Trusts*

There is a class of will cases in which the terms "fraud in effect" or "constructive fraud" is used, but there is no actual fraud as in case of deceit. These are the secret trust cases where A, the devisee or heir of B, agrees with B to hold in trust for or to convey to C, property which A will receive by devise or descent from B. Of course if A did not intend to perform the promise at the time of making it, this is a case of actual fraud and a clear situation for declaring a constructive trust.[13] In absence of actual fraudulent intention at the time the will was made, some courts refuse to declare a constructive trust.[14] The view approved by most courts is that a trust should be imposed in favor of C regardless of the state of mind of A at the time of making his promise.[15] This has the advantage of carrying out the plan of the testator, but it has been criticized [16] as nullifying the provisions of the Statute of Wills and the Statute of Frauds which require written instruments for such arrangements. Because of this, some writers [17] would declare a trust in favor of the heir at law, thus preventing A from reaping any advantage and at the same time avoiding the objection of allowing an oral will in effect. The foregoing are cases where the devise to A was absolute on the face of the will; when the will discloses a trust

13 Vance v. Grow, 206 Ind. 614, 190 N.E. 747, 1934; Winder v. Scholey, 83 Ohio St. 204, 93 N.E. 1098, 33 L. R.A.,N.S., 995, 21 Ann.Cas. 1379, 1910; see Montgomery v. Willbanks, 202 S. W.2d 851, Tex.Civ.App.1947.

14 Brown v. Kausche, 98 Wash. 470, 167 P. 1075, 1917.

15 Caldwell v. Caldwell, 7 Bush (Ky.) 515; Strype v. Lewis, 352 Mo. 1004, 180 S.W.2d 688, 155 A.L.R. 99, 1944; Teuscher v. Gragg, 136 Okl. 129, 276 P. 753, 66 A.L.R. 143, 1929. See Gemmel v. Fletcher, 76 Kan. 577, 92 P. 713, rehearing denied 93 P. 339, 1907; Bogert, Trusts, 3d ed., § 85; Costigan, Constructive Trusts Based on Promises to Secure Bequests, Devises or Intestate Succession, 28 Harv.L.R. 237, 366; Restatement, Trusts § 55; Restatement, Restitution §§ 184, 186; infra note 16.

16 Gifford, Will or No Will?, 20 Col. L.R. 862, 867–874; Scott, Conveyances upon Trusts not Properly Declared, 37 Harv.L.R. 653, 672–682. Cf. Ames, Lectures on Legal History, 430, for the view that the trust violates the Statute of Frauds but not the Statute of Wills and hence would allow the trust in case of personalty only, as it is not covered by the former statute. Ibid.; Ames, Constructive Trusts Based upon Breach of an Express Oral Trust of Land, 20 Harv.L. R. 549, 554.

17 Gifford, supra note 16, at 871, 872; Scott, supra note 16, at 675, 676, 681, 682; Simpson, Constructive Trusts and the Statutes of Frauds and Wills, 11 Bost.U.L.R. 22; Lord and Van Hecke, Parol Trusts in North Carolina, 8 N.C.L.R. 152, 156.

but not the beneficiary or the terms, there are variant holdings as to whether C or B's heir or residuary legatee is entitled.[18]

## MISTAKE AS TO THE DOCUMENT SIGNED, CONTENTS, AND LEGAL EFFECT

**58. Probate will be denied when the testator through mistake executed the wrong document as his will.**

**No relief can be obtained on account of provisions omitted from a will by mistake. A will may be denied probate if the testator was ignorant as to its contents, but there is a strong presumption that an able-bodied testator knew the contents of his will. Provisions inserted by mistake may be omitted from probate, but the American courts do not reject words from probate so as to change the meaning of the remaining words.**

**No relief at probate will be granted for the testator's mistake as to the legal effect of the language used.**

### *Mistake as to Document Signed*

It is usually held that where the testator intended to execute his will, but by mistake signed the wrong document, the latter should be denied probate.[1] Mistakes of this nature are capable of satisfactory proof for the error generally appears upon the very face of the document signed, or in some other manner almost as conclusive.[2] The typical case is the situation where mutual wills are being executed and each testator signs the wrong instrument.[3] An error of signing the wrong document is a very serious one. It goes to the point that testamentary intent is entirely lacking for the instrument, and warrants rejection of the

[18] That C is: Blackwell v. Blackwell, L.R. [1929] A.C. 318. Cf. Olliffe v. Wells, 130 Mass. 221, 1881; Reynolds v. Reynolds, 224 N.Y. 429, 121 N.E. 61, 1918. And see Wagner v. Clauson, 399 Ill. 403, 78 N.E.2d 203, 3 A.L.R.2d 672, 1948 where A was described in the will as trustee for distribution in accordance with a memorandum which was not communicated until after B's death; trust for B's heir was imposed.

[1] In re Cutler's Will, 58 N.Y.S.2d 604, 1945; Alter's Appeal, 67 Pa. 341, 5 Am.Rep. 433, 1871; Goods of Nosworthy, 4 Swa. & Tr. 44, 164 Eng.Rep. 1431, 1865; Goods of Hunt, L.R. 3 P. & D. 250, 1875, In the Estate of Meyer [1908] Prob. 353, 3 B.R.C. 339.

[2] See Goods of Nosworthy, supra note 1, where two wills on the same sheet of paper were executed, the second of which was denied probate because it was signed upon the impression that it was a formal part of the first.

[3] The Cutler, Alter, Hunt and Meyer Cases, supra note 1, are of this nature.

will, although fraud is not shown.[4] The objection is litigated at probate or contest of the will.[5] While the unintended paper may be rejected, there is no basis for probating the intended paper if it was not duly executed.

*Mistake or Ignorance As to Contents*

A mistake as to contents may be one of omission, or inclusion, or both. For example, if the testator thought the will provided a gift of $1,000 to his cousin Charles, but there was no such provision, the error is one of omission. If he did not believe that the will contained such a provision but in fact it did so, there is a mistake of inclusion or commission. If the testator thought that the will contained a legacy of $1,000 to his cousin Charles and in fact it contained no such provision but did make a legacy of $1,000 to his cousin Charlotte, which testator had not intended, there are, in a sense, two mistakes, the omission of the gift to Charles and the inclusion of the gift to Charlotte. The latter example is in substance a case of incorrect designation of the beneficiary. Cases of combined errors of omission and inclusion are usually of this nature and will be considered later under the category of misdescription.[6]

Clearly, there is no remedy on probate for mistakes of omission. The terms of the will must be in writing, and the court cannot admit anything to probate which is not in the instrument.[7] Conceivably a court of equity might impose a constructive trust upon the person whose name was inserted by mistake for that of the intended beneficiary as is done often in cases of fraud. But there is no authority for the imposition of a constructive trust in case of mere mistake.[8] Equity has no jurisdiction to reform a will for mistake,[9] and an omitted devise cannot be supplied in

[4] See supra § 56 at notes 10, 11.

[5] See cases supra note 1.

[6] See infra § 60.

[7] Yates v. Cole, 54 N.C. 110, 59 Am. Dec. 602, 1853; Whitlock v. Wardlaw, 7 Rich.(S.C.) 453, 1854; Anonymous, Godb. 131, pl. 149, 78 Eng.Rep. 80, 1587; In the Goods of Schott, [1901] P. 190, disapproving In re Goods of Bushell, 13 P.D. 7, 1887. Cf. cases infra note 18.

[8] See Gray, Striking Words Out of a Will, 26 Harv.L.R. 212, 214; Warren, Fraud, Undue Influence, and Mistake in Wills, 41 Harv.L.R. 309, 329. But see Whitlock v. Wardlaw, 7 Rich.(S.C.) 453, 458. As to fraud, see supra § 57.

[9] Avery v. Chappel, 6 Conn. 270, 16 Am.Dec. 53, 1826; McAlister v. Butterfield, 31 Ind. 25, 1869; Sherwood v Sherwood, 45 Wis. 357, 30 Am.Rep. 757, 1875; In re Baylis' Will, 78 N.Y.S.2d 893, 1948. See Gray supra note 8 at 212, 213; Warren supra note 8. But see dicta in Martindale v. Bridgforth, 210 Ala. 565, 98 So. 800, 801, 1924.

the construction of the will.[10] Accordingly the intended beneficiary cannot obtain relief in any form of proceeding.

In the case of words included by mistake the probate court has the machinery to deny probate of the words or to reject the entire will. On the other hand there is the third possibility that the probate court will do nothing concerning the mistake but probate it as it is written. Certainly the spirit of the parol evidence rule points in this direction for the mistake is subjective and often, if not generally, the point is not capable of satisfactory proof after testator's death. When are we justified in finding mistake in the contents of the instrument which testator has solemnly declared to be his will?

There have been many cases where wills have been contested upon the ground that the testator was entirely ignorant of the contents of the instrument signed by him. In England it was laid down in the celebrated case of Guardhouse v. Blackburn [11] that "the fact that the will has been duly read over to a capable testator on the occasion of its execution or that its contents have been brought to his notice in any other way, should, when coupled with the execution thereof, be held conclusive evidence that he approved as well as knew the contents thereof." The English courts have receded from making this presumption conclusive.[12] In America this imperative doctrine of Guardhouse v. Blackburn is not accepted.[13] Particularly when the testator was ill, blind, feeble or lacking in education there should be no conclusive presumption.[14] Mere proof of execution of the will, however,

[10] In re De Moulin's Estate, 101 Cal.App.2d 221, 225 P.2d 303, 1951; Stearns v. Stearns, 103 Conn. 213, 130 A. 112, 1925; In re Wirsig's Estate, 128 Neb. 297, 258 N.W. 467, 1935. Cf. infra § 146; Blacker v. Thatcher, 145 F.2d 255, 158 A.L.R. 1, C.C.A.Mont., 1944.

[11] L.R. 1 P. & D. 109, 1866.

[12] Fulton v. Andrew, L.R. 7 H.L. 448, 1875. Cf. Gregson v. Taylor, [1917] Prob. 256 (very strong presumption when will has been read over to testator).

[13] Gaither v. Gaither, 20 Ga. 709, 1856; Ex parte King, 132 S.C. 63, 128 S.E. 850, 1925; Rutland v. Gleaves, 31 Tenn. (1 Swan) 198, 1851. See Ga.Code Ann. § 113–305, 3850. See note, 24 Mich.L.R. 178 and authorities note 17 infra. But see In re Gluckman's Will, 87 N.J.Eq. 638, 101 A. 295, L.R.A.1918D 742, 1917. Cf. Wigmore on Evidence, § 2421, evidently approving of this proposition of Guardhouse v. Blackburn. See also note, 8 U. of Det.L.J. 49.

[14] Even in the case of such a testator there is a rebuttal presumption that he knew and approved the contents of the will. Sansona v. Laraia, 88 Conn. 136, 90 A. 28, 1914 (foreign language testator); Riggs v. Safe Deposit & Trust Co., 186 Md. 54, 46 A. 2d 97, 1946 (weak); in re Bakke's Will, 160 Minn. 56, 199 N.W. 438, 37 A.L.R. 597, 1924 (blind); Lipphard v.

creates a presumption that the will contained the provisions intended by the testator.[15] The fact that the will was read by, or to, the testator is strong evidence that he had knowledge of the contents.[16] It is not conclusive, however, and particularly when it was not read, there may be denial of probate on the ground that the testator was mistaken as to its contents.[17] However, a mistake as to part of the contents does not invalidate the entire will.[18]

When a single entire provision of a will was included by mistake, there should be nothing to prevent the court from probating the will minus the portion in question. This would have no effect on the remaining provisions except to increase the residuary shares. American authority, though not abundant, follows this procedure.[19] The English practice goes beyond this. There, words are sometimes omitted from probate on the ground that

Humphrey, 209 U.S. 264, 28 S.Ct. 561, 52 L.Ed. 783, 14 Ann.Cas. 872, 1907 (illiterate). See also in re Gluckman's Will, supra note 13. Cf. Waite v. Frisbie, 45 Minn. 361, 47 N.W. 1069, 1891 (testatrix in dying condition, final form of will not read over to her, held invalid); Barber v. Barber, 362 Ill. 634, 1 N.E.2d 44, 1936.

15 Downey v. Lawley, 377 Ill. 298, 36 N.W.2d 344, 1941; In re Rowland's Estate, 70 S.D. 419, 18 N.W.2d 290, 1945. See cases supra note 14.

16 Hughes v. Meredith, 24 Ga. 325, 71 Am.Dec. 127, 1858; In re White, 121 N.Y. 406, 24 N.E. 935, 1890; Gregson v. Taylor [1917] Prob. 256. See notes 11–13 supra.

17 In re Kempthorne's Estate, 188 Iowa 70, 175 N.W. 857, 1920; Will of Jose Nadal, 2 Hawaii 400, 1861; Ford v. Jeane, 159 La. 1041, 106 So. 558, 1925 (will in English not properly read back to testator understanding French only); Waite v. Frisbie, 45 Minn. 361, 47 N.W. 1069, 1891; Bradford v. Blossom, 207 Mo. 177, 105 S.W. 289, 1907 (scrivener did not follow instructions, will not read by testator). Cf. Couch v. Eastham, 27 W.Va. 796, 55 Am.Rep. 346, 1886 (declarations of testator not admissible to show that will did not express his intent); Hogan v. Whittemore, 278 Mass. 573, 180 N.E. 526, 1932 (same). But see Iddings v. Iddings, 7 Serg. & R.(Pa.) 111, 10 Am.Dec. 450, 1821 (parol evidence not admissible to show mistake due to scrivener's ignorance of meaning of word "cancel" in will of ninety-two year old testator).

18 Comstock v. Hadlyme Ecclesiastical Society, 8 Conn. 254, 20 Am.Dec. 100, 1830 (legacies to grandchildren omitted); Campbell v. Campbell, 138 Ill. 612, 28 N.E. 1080, 1891 (mistake in description of land devised; Johnson v. Ramsey, 18 Ohio App. 321, 1923 (legatee's name omitted); Whitlock v. Wardlaw, 7 Rich.(S.C.) 453, 1854; Ex parte King, 132 S.C. 63, 128 S.E. 850, 1925 (misnomer and confusion regarding legatee, will admitted—difficulty reserved for construction of the will). Cf. In re Kempthorne's Estate, supra note 17.

19 Burger v. Hill, 1 Bradf.(N.Y.) 360, 1850, aff'd Hill v. Burger, 10 How.Prac. 264, 1854. See Sherwood v. Sherwood, 45 Wis. 357, 362, 30 Am. Rep. 757, 1878; O'Connell v. Dow, 182 Mass. 541, 66 N.E. 788, 1903 (fraud). Cf. Ex parte King, supra note 18.

they were included through mistake, when the effect of this omission is to alter the effect of the words of the provision remaining.[20] For example,[21] where a testator directed his solicitor to give all his shares in a company to a legatee and the solicitor by mistake inserted the word forty before the word shares, the probate court struck the word forty from the will in four places, so that the legatee took all the shares as testator intended. The English practice has been defended [22] upon the ground that the probate court deals with the words of the will rather than the effect of those words, and that if a word is included by mistake the probate court should omit it from probate regardless of the effect of so doing. It is said that no American case authorizes such action, though our courts sometimes disregard words in the process of construction.[23]

*Mistake As to Legal Effect*

When there is no mistake as to what the will contains but the testator merely misconceives the legal effect of the language used, this is not ground for the rejection of the will or any part thereof.[24] This is true even if the error was caused by incorrect legal advice.[25] However, to a limited extent errors as to legal effect may be rectified in the course of construction of the will.[26] By giving general relief for misapprehension of the will's provisions "we should upset half the wills in the country." [27] The evidence of the mistake would often be unsatisfactory and untrustworthy. The courts simply refuse to embark upon the inquiry where mistake alone is suggested, though relief may be granted if misapprehension as to legal effect was caused by fraud.[28]

20 Morrell v. Morrell, L.R. 7 P.D. 68, 1882; Brisco v. Hamilton, [1902] Prob. 234. And see Goods of Boehm, [1891] Prob. 247; Goods of Cooper, [1899] Prob. 193.

21 Morrell v. Morrell, supra note 20.

22 Gray, Striking Words Out of a Will, 26 Harv.L.R. 212, 231, 235. Cf. Warren, Fraud, Undue Influence, and Mistake in Wills, 41 Harv.L.R. 309, 333–339.

23 Cf. Burger v. Hill, supra note 19; Hudson Trust Co. v. Horwood, 124 N.J.Eq. 20, 199 A. 387, 1938. See infra § 146.

24 Munnikhuysen v. Magraw, 35 Md. 280, 1871; Elam v. Phariss, 289 Mo. 209, 232 S.W. 693, 1921; Leonard v. Stanton, 93 N.H. 113, 36 A.2d 271, 1944, noted, 43 Mich.L.R. 209; In re Gluckman's Will, 87 N.J.Eq. 638, 101 A. 295 L.R.A.1918D 742, 1917; Collins v. Elstone, [1893] Prob. 1. But see Snyder v. Raymond, 48 Idaho 810, 285 P. 478, 1930.

25 Elam v. Phariss, Leonard v. Stanton, In re Gluckman's Will, Collins v. Elstone, all supra note 38.

26 See infra §§ 60, 146. But cf. Mahoney v. Granger, 283 Mass. 189, 186 N.E. 86, 1933, noted, 19 Corn.L.Q. 154.

27 Foley, S. in In re Cotter's Estate, 180 Misc. 399, 40 N.Y.S.2d 93, 1943.

28 See supra § 56 at note 16.

## MISTAKE IN INDUCEMENT

**59. In absence of statute, relief will not be given for mistake in the inducement of the will except possibly in the rare case where the mistake and what the testator would have done but for the mistake both appear on the face of the instrument.**

A mistake in the inducement is an error as to facts outside the instrument itself. Common examples are the testator's misconceptions as to the nature, condition or extent of his property, or as to the conduct or status of the beneficiaries or of the persons who are the natural objects of testator's bounty. However freely the courts may decline probate because of mistake in the identity of the instrument signed, and for errors as to contents, they do not generally invalidate a will, or its provisions, because of mistake in the inducement. Almost every testator is mistaken about some of the collateral facts which enter into the making of his will. It would be intolerable to allow every such error to avoid the provisions of the will. If a line were attempted to be drawn between mistakes in inducement which should invalidate the provision and those which should not, it would doubtless be upon the basis of the extent that the mistake affected the provisions of the will. We would be thrust into the realm of speculation as to how far the mistake entered into the legacy or devise and what the testator would have done except for the mistake. The fact that the courts are willing to enter into this speculative field in the case of fraud may be accounted for by reason of the strong feeling that the wrongdoer should not prosper by reason of the wrong.[1]

Neither mistake as to the amount of loans and advancements to relatives,[2] nor as to the property which the relatives owned or had acquired from others,[3] nor as to the value of testator's property,[4] nor error in believing that a natural object of one's bounty is living,[5] or is dead,[6] is ground for refusing probate.

1 See supra § 56.

2 Watkins v. Jones, 184 Ga. 831, 193 S.E. 889, 1937; Hopper v. Sellers, 91 Kan. 876, 139 P. 365, 1914; In re Reidy's Will, 199 Misc. 311, 106 N.Y.S.2d 270, 1951; Wyatt v. Wyatt, 188 S.W.2d 685, Tex.Civ.App.1945. Cf. infra § 141, note 7.

3 Riley v. Casey, 185 Iowa 461, 170 N.W. 742, 1919.

4 Barker v. Comins, 110 Mass. 477, 1872; In re Jones' Will, 85 N.Y.S. 294, 1890.

5 In re Woods, 189 App.Div. 324, 178 N.Y.S. 573, 1919. Cf. Black v. Smith, 58 N.D. 109, 224 N.W. 915, 1929 (concealment of this fact).

6 In re Holmes Estate, 98 Colo. 360, 56 P.2d 1333, 1936; In re Tousey's Will, 34 Misc. 363, 69 N.Y.S. 846,

Likewise an incorrect notion as to the attitude or conduct of a relative toward the testator does not invalidate the will.[7] Probably the strongest case is where the testator is mistaken as to the relationship which a certain person bears to him. In case of misconception induced by fraud, the courts have held that false belief that the beneficiary was the lawful spouse of the testator avoids the gift.[8] But in cases where there is simple mistake as to such matters without fraud,[9] as well as in other cases of mistaken relationship,[10] the courts give no relief. There is very little authority[11] in absence of statute for avoiding a testamentary gift because of mistake in the inducement.

It is important to emphasize the difference between the effect of mistake in the inducement on the one hand and of insane delusions, undue influence and fraud on the other. The courts are generally unwilling to give relief against the will in case of mistake, though they will do so if insane delusions,[12] undue influence,[13] or fraud,[14] are established as to the same subject matter. In other words, if a contestant in trying to establish an insane delusion goes no further than to show that testator was mistaken, or had a sane delusion, the will is valid. One who fails in proof of the elements of insane delusions, undue influence or fraud, cannot fall back upon the fact that he has proven mistake in the inducement. This is true even if mistake was included in the grounds of contest, since mistake in the inducement does not invalidate the will, save perhaps in the exceptional case mentioned below.

1901; Bowerman v. Burris, 138 Tenn. 220, 197 S.W. 490, 1917. Cf. statutes infra note 22, covering the situation of a testator who erroneously believes that his child is dead at the time of making the will. And see Gifford v. Dyer, discussed infra note 15.

7 Davis v. Aultman, 199 Ga. 129, 33 S.E.2d 317, 1945; In re Bedlow, 67 Hun 408, 22 N.Y.S. 290, 1893.

8 See supra § 56.

9 In re Carson's Estate, 184 Cal. 437, 194 P. 5, 17 A.L.R. 239, 1920. In re Will of Donnely, 68 Iowa 126, 26 N.W. 23, 1885.

10 Martindale v. Bridgforth, 210 Ala. 565, 98 So. 800, 1924. See annotation 17 A.L.R. 247.

11 See Snyder v. Raymond, 48 Idaho 810, 285 P. 478, 1930; Armorer v. Case, 9 La.Ann. 288, 61 Am.Dec. 209, 1854. Cf. Texada v. Spence, 166 La. 1020, 118 So. 120, 62 A.L.R. 281, 1928. See also notes 21, 23 infra.

12 Riley v. Casey, supra note 3; Maynard v. Tyler, 168 Mass. 107, 46 N.E. 413, 1897; Matter of White, supra note 7.

13 Hopper v. Sellers, supra note 2; In re Bedlow, supra note 7.

14 See authorities cited notes 9, 10 supra.

*Mistake Appearing from the Will*

The leading case of Gifford v. Dyer[15] contains a suggestion which might afford relief in a few cases of mistake in the inducement. There the testatrix, believing her son to be dead, did not mention him in her will. As a matter of fact he was living. The court declined to set aside the will and said it would only have done so if it has appeared on the face of the will: (1) That she was mistaken,[16] and (2) what the testatrix would have done with her property if she had not been so mistaken. The case relies on an old English case of dependent relative revocation. This is a doctrine according to which the courts give relief against a revocation made through mistake under the guise that it was a conditional revocation.[17] But there is no authority, and little suggestion aside from Gifford v. Dyer, that this doctrine should apply to mistakes regarding the execution of wills. In a rare case there might be sufficient recitals in the will to warrant giving relief upon this theory.[18] Generally, however, in the cases where the doctrine is mentioned relief cannot be granted for the reason that the will does not show what the testator would have done had he not been mistaken.[19]

*Statutes*

In Georgia it is provided by statute[20] that "a will executed under a mistake of fact as to the existence of, or conduct of, the heirs at law of the testator is inoperative, so far as such heir at law is concerned, but the testator shall be deemed to have died intestate as to him." This legislation warrants relief for this type of mistake in the inducement.[21] In two or three states a child absent and erroneously reported dead, if not provided for in the will, takes the same share he would have received had testa-

15 2 R.I. 99, 57 Am.Dec. 708, 1852.

16 Of course literally this would never occur; what is meant is that it must appear on the will that she thought her son dead; if it did it would be permissible to show dehors the will that he was in fact alive.

17 See infra § 88.

18 Mordecai v. Boylan, 59 N.C. (6 Jones Eq.) 365, 1863 (a case, however, of construction of a will); Penick's Ex'r v. Walker, 125 Va. 274, 99 S.E. 559, 1919.

19 In re Tousey's Will, 34 Misc. 363, 69 N.Y.S. 846, 1901; Bowerman v. Burris, 138 Tenn. 220, 197 S.W. 490, 1917.

20 Ga.Code Ann. § 113–210.

21 For cases construing this statute, see Jones v. Grogan, 98 Ga. 552, 25 S.E. 590, 1896; Watkins v. Jones, supra note 2; Davis v. Aultman, supra note 7.

tor died intestate.[22] Relief for mistake could sometimes be afforded under other statutes providing that children omitted from the will may under certain circumstances take their intestate shares.[23] Except for these provisions there seems to be no legislation altering the common-law rule that mistake in the inducement does not invalidate a will.

## MISTAKE IN DESCRIPTION OF BENEFICIARY OR PROPERTY

**60. Upon construction of a will the court may reject erroneous parts of the description of the beneficiary or the property when the part which remains sufficiently describes the person or thing that testator must have intended.**

**When a description in a will applies accurately to a given person or thing, it cannot be shown that the testator intended some other person or thing which does not fit the description unless it can be proved that the testator customarily described the latter by the terms used in the will.**

**When a description applies in part to one and in part to another person or object, it may be shown by the surrounding circumstances, and according to the better view by the testator's express declarations, which was intended by him.**

**When a description in a will applies equally to two or more persons or things, it is permissible to show which of them was intended by the testator. Here it is clear that the testator's intention can be shown by his express declarations.**

Issues of the types of mistake already treated, as well as of undue influence and fraud, are ordinarily litigated at contest of the will, or, in certain situations, in a suit to impose a constructive trust or in an action for damages.[1] Usually these questions have been determined by probate and are not before the court in proceedings to construe the will.[2] On the other hand questions concerning misdescriptions of the beneficiary or of the property devised normally do not arise on probate but rather upon construction of the will, either in a separate suit for that purpose, or in the part of the administration process wherein the property is distributed or rights therein under the will are deter-

[22] Ohio Gen.Code § 10504–49; Ky. Rev.Stat.1948, § 394.390.

[23] See Bordwell, Statute Law of Wills, 14 Ia.L.R. 172, 174–177; Mathews, Pretermitted Heirs, 29 Col.L.R. 748; supra § 36.

[1] See supra §§ 57, 58.

[2] See supra § 58, notes 10, 26; but cf. § 58, note 23.

mined.[3] Occasionally the construing court may decide that the attempted devise must fail for indefiniteness.[4] Such a decision has the result of passing the property either under the residuary clause of the will or the intestate laws. While this has the same ultimate effect as rejecting the will from probate, the order admitting to probate is not disturbed and the failure of the gift proceeds on a different theory than that of denial or annulment of probate.

Misdescriptions of persons or things in wills occur in two different ways. First, the testator may have had the proper designation in mind, but through clerical error the description may not have appeared in the instrument as he intended. This is really a case of mistake in the contents of the will. As shown above,[5] this may be ground for rejecting the particular provision from probate, but if the mistake is merely a misdescription, the will is apt to be admitted to probate as it was written. Second are the cases in which the testator intended that the will should read as it did, but was in error as to the proper designation of the property or the beneficiary. This is not a mistake in contents and is not ground of rejection of the will or part thereof from probate. After probate, both sorts of misdescription are usually treated in the same way. The question is simply one of construction of the will to determine whether a certain person, or which of two rival claimants, shall be entitled to certain property. The question is not one of reforming the instrument,[6] but rather one of dealing with ambiguities or uncertainties when there is an attempt to apply the will to existing persons or things. The same is true when the description is incomplete rather than faulty.[7]

3 See infra §§ 143, 145. But see Hall v. Williams, 204 Okl. 308, 229 P.2d 584, 1951.

4 Grimes Ex'rs v. Harmon, infra note 6; Murphy v. McBride, 14 Del. Ch. 457, 130 A. 283, 1925. See Doe d. Hiscocks v. Hiscocks, 5 M. and W. 363, 151 Eng.Rep. 154, 1839; Drake v. Drake, 8 H.L.Cas. 172, 11 Eng.Rep. 392, 1860, infra § 146.

5 See supra § 58 at note 6 et seq.

6 Grimes' Ex'rs v. Harmon, 35 Ind. 198, 9 Am.Rep. 690, 1871; Chambers v. Watson, 56 Iowa 676, 10 N.W. 239, 1881; Gilmore v. Jenkins, 129 Iowa 686, 106 N.W. 193, 6 Ann.Cas. 1008, 1906; Burke v. Central Trust Co., 258 Mich. 588, 242 N.W. 760, 1932. See Succession of Rusha, 158 La. 74, 103 So. 515, 1925. Cf. note, 24 Mich. L.R. 84, arguing that there should be power to reform wills for mistake. And see note, 78 U. of Pa.L.R. 1035; supra § 58 at note 9.

7 See infra text following note 27, and generally § 146.

*Falsa Demonstratio Non Nocet*

There are many cases where it appears that the description of a person or thing mentioned in a will fits a certain person or thing in part but is incorrect in some respect. For example, a testatrix devised her seven houses on a certain street when she really owned eight houses there. The construing court inquired into the circumstances of the devise, decided that the testatrix meant to devise all of the eight, and, rejecting the word seven as a matter of erroneous description, held that all passed under the devise.[8] This was done in accordance with the ancient principle of "falsa demonstratio non nocet" [9]—a false description does not vitiate a document. The theory is that the false part of the description can be rejected if the part which is true describes the subject or object with reasonable certainty. Similarly, a devise to John William Halston, son of Israel Halston, was considered to apply to Israel's son, John Robert Halston upon proof that testator must have so intended.[10] All courts recognize the doctrine though there is some doubt as to the exact situations in which it will be employed. While it is generally agreed that the court may put itself into the situation of the testator to discover his intention,[11] the testator's direct declarations of intention are not admissible.[12] From the admissible evidence a court must be

8 Moore v. Moore, [1920] 1 Ir.R. 232. But cf. Mann v. Land, 177 Va. 509, 14 S.E.2d 341, 1941.

9 Cf. Institutes of Justinian, 2, 20, 30; "Falsa demonstratione legatur non perimitur"—a legacy will not fail from a false description. For an excellent treatment of this and kindred doctrines, see Warren, Interpretation of Wills—Recent Developments, 49 Harv.L.R. 689.

10 In re Halston, [1912] 1 Ch. 435. See also In re Price, [1932] 2 Ch. 54; In re Crawley: Robertson v. Flynn, [1920] 1 Ir.R. 78; Polsey v. Newton, 199 Mass. 450, 85 N.E. 574, 15 Ann. Cas. 139, 1908; Norton v. Jordan, 360 Ill. 419, 196 N.E. 475, 1935; McCall v. McCall, 4 Rich.Eq. (S.C.) 447, 57 Am.Dec. 733, 1852. American authorities which might be explained upon the falsa demonstratio doctrine though placed upon a somewhat broader basis are: Sadler v. Sadler, 107 Conn. 409, 140 A. 639, 1928; Elk Horn Coal Corp. v. Jacks Creek Coal Co., 240 Ky. 769, 43 S.W.2d 13, 1931; Farrell v. Sullivan, 49 R.I. 468, 144 A. 155, 1929, noted, 38 Yale L.J. 999; House of the Good Shepherd in Binghamton v. Rector, etc. of Church of Good Shepherd in City of Binghamton, 207 App.Div. 129, 201 N.Y.S. 796, 1923. See note, 21 Harv.L.R. 434. Cf. Newburgh v. Newburgh, 5 Mad. 364, 56 Eng.Rep. 934, 1820; Doe ex dem. Hubbard v. Hubbard, 15 Q.B. 227, 117 Eng.Rep. 445, 1850; and infra notes 18, 19, 22, 24.

11 Haddox v. Jordan, 36 Ohio App. 209, 173 N.E. 11, 1930; Parsons v. Fitchett, 148 Va. 322, 138 S.E. 491, 1927. See authorities cited supra notes 8, 10; Wigmore on Evidence, § 2470.

12 Doe ex dem. Hubbard v. Hubbard, supra note 10; Haddox v. Jordan, supra note 11; Wigmore on Evidence § 2471.

satisfied that application of the maxim would result in observation of testator's intent before it is justified in applying the doctrine.[13]

The application of the doctrine to certain cases of error in the description of lands has given rise to much controversy.[14] When testator devised "*my* lot number 6 in square 403" which he did not own, it was held permissible to show that he owned and intended to pass lot number 3 in square 406.[15] This decision was reached by rejecting for purposes of construction the erroneous numbers and considering that the remaining language sufficiently described the land which belonged to testator. However, when the testator devised "*the* south half of the east half of the south quarter of section 31," when he did not own this property but held the corresponding part of section 32, the devisee was not permitted to take in spite of the fact that the latter was testator's grandson and was a tenant on the land in section 32.[16] Probably most courts today would disagree with this decision upon the ground that a testator will be presumed to devise his own land and that the presence or absence of the word "my" does not really distinguish the cases.[17]

13 See Baker v. Hendricks, 240 Ala. 630, 200 So. 615, 1941; Mann v. Land, supra note 8; also cases infra note 22.

14 Horner in 2 Ill.L.Bull. 175, 286, 293; Kales, 2 Ill.L.Bull. 293; Wigmore, 15 Ill.L.R. 99; Betts, Misdescriptions in Wills, 7 Can.Bar. R. 579; Warren, Progress of the Law, 33 Harv.L.R. 556, 560–565; note, 78 U. of Pa.L.R. 1035.

15 Patch v. White, 117 U.S. 210, 6 S.Ct. 617, 710, 29 L.Ed. 860, 1886 (a five to four decision). In that case the reference to "my" property was not as clear as stated in the text above. Whether the particular will refers to property owned by the testator has been a source of much controversy. See, note 14 supra & notes 16, 17 infra.

16 Kurtz v. Hibner, 55 Ill. 514, 8 Am.Rep. 665, 1870. For more recent cases involving the general problem in Illinois, see Stevenson v. Stevenson, 285 Ill. 486, 121 N.E. 202, 1918; Brown v. Ray, 314 Ill. 570, 145 N.E. 676, 1924; Koelmel v. Kaelin, 374 Ill. 204, 29 N.E.2d 106, 1940; Appleton v. Rea, 389 Ill. 222, 58 N.E.2d 854, 1945 See also in re Lynch's Estate, 142 Cal 373, 75 P. 1086, 1904.

17 Wilmes v. Tiernay, 187 Iowa 390, 174 N.W. 271, 1919; Wiechert v. Wiechert, 317 Mo. 118, 294 S.W. 721, 1927. See Old Ladies Home v. Cooper, 206 Miss. 508, 40 So.2d 268, 1949; In re Murphy's Will, 67 N.Y.S.2d 641, 1946; Holmes v. Roddy, 176 Tenn. 624, 144 S.W.2d 788, 1940. Indeed the doctrine has undergone considerable liberalization in Illinois. See Smith v. Burt, 388 Ill. 162, 57 N.E.2d 493, 157 A.L.R. 1118, 1944 and the more recent cases cited supra note 16.

*Other Inaccurate Descriptions—Unusual Personal Usage*

There are many cases in which the courts disregard mistake in description of persons and things upon a broader basis. Typically there are no rival claimants, no plausible claim for a different construction, and the courts are convinced of what was intended. There are many holdings of this nature in case of a misnomer of charitable, religious, educational or public devises,[18] but mistakes in designation of private individuals are also disregarded in some cases without much discussion.[19] Statutes in California and some of the western states declare that such imperfect descriptions shall be corrected if the error appears from the context of the will or from extrinsic evidence, but that the testator's declarations of his intention shall not be received.[20] Roughly speaking, this is declaratory of the law generally.

Suppose, however, that the testator left property "to my cousin John", and he had a cousin John and also a cousin William, may William successfully claim the property as against John on the basis of intention and mistaken expression? It is commonly supposed that he can not.[21] Stating the problem in somewhat broader vein, when the testator accurately describes a person or thing it cannot usually be shown that he intended another which does not fit the description.[22] To hold otherwise would be

[18] Women's Foreign Missionary Society v. Mitchell, 93 Md. 199, 48 A. 737, 53 L.R.A. 711, 1901; Indianapolis Home, etc. v. Altenheim, 120 Ind.App. 595, 93 N.E.2d 203, 1950, noted 49 Mich.L.R. 1260; In re Peterson's Estate, 202 Minn. 31, 277 N.W. 529, 1938; Guaranty Trust Co. v. Catholic Charities, 141 N.J.Eq. 170, 56 A.2d 483, 1948; In re Stymus Will, 64 N.Y.S.2d 304, 1946; First Baptist Church in Exeter v. Soban, 77 R.I. 115, 73 A.2d 772, 1951; Reformed Presbyterian Church of North America v. McMillan, 31 Wash. 643, 72 P. 502, 1903.

[19] Borah v. Lincoln Hospital Assn., 153 Neb. 846, 46 N.W.2d 1951, noted, 49 Mich.L.R. 1262, 1950; In re Gerety's Estate, 354 Pa. 14, 46 A.2d 250, 1946. See also cases supra note 10.

[20] Cal.Prob.Code, § 105, derived from former Civ.Code §§ 1318, 1340. See In re DeMoulin's Estate, 101 Cal. App.2d 221, 225 P.2d 303, 1951. Montana, North Dakota, Oklahoma, South Dakota and Utah have like statutes, and Georgia and Louisiana also have liberal provisions in this regard. Bordwell, Statute Law of Wills, 14 Ia.L.R. 174.

[21] See In re Lepley's Estate, 235 Iowa 664, 17 N.W.2d 526, 530, 1945, and cases infra note 22; also infra § 146.

[22] Combs v. Combs, 172 Ark. 1073, 291 S.W. 818, 1927; National Society for the Prevention of Cruelty to Children v. Scottish National Society for the Prevention of Cruelty to Children, [1915] A.C. 207. See also Stearns v. Stearns, 103 Conn. 213, 130 A. 112, 1925 (cannot show intention to pass realty under disposition of "personal estate"), with which compare West v. West, 215 App.Div. 285, 213 N.Y.S.

considered to violate the statutory provision requiring that wills be in writing and also the parol evidence rule. The thought is sometimes expressed in the form of a rule which forbids the disturbing of the plain meaning of words. At any rate in these cases the testator's extrinsic declarations of intention are not admissible to show the mistake.[23]

Even in the cases last mentioned it has been held that it can be shown that the testator customarily used his expression to refer to a certain person or thing rather than to another which the term accurately describes. Thus, where a testator bequeathed $20,000 to Mrs. M, it was permissible to show that he was very slightly acquainted with the lady of that name, but always referred to his friend, Mrs. T, as Mrs. M, and the bequest was construed as one for Mrs. T.[24] As wills are unilateral and their dispositions gratuitous, a very plausible argument is presented for the acceptance of testator's individual usage of terms when it is established by the admissible evidence.

### *Description Applying in Part to One, and in Part to Another, Person or Object*

A somewhat different situation occurs when the language of the will applies in part to one person or object and in part to another but does not accurately describe either. For example, suppose that testator makes a provision for "my cousin John" and it turns out that he has no such relative but does have a cousin Joseph and also a nephew John. Here the construing court will look to the facts surrounding the testator to see which was intended.[25] They will hear evidence to the effect that tes-

480, 1926, noted, 74 U. of Pa.L.R. 854, and 12 Va.L.R. 598; Rodarmel v. Gwinnup, 92 Ind.App. 684, 173 N.E. 327, 1930, noted, 6 Ind.L.J. 459; Meglemry v. Meglemry, 222 Ala. 229, 131 So. 906, 1931; Mahoney v. Grainger, 283 Mass. 189, 186 N.E. 86, 1933; Appleton v. Rea, supra note 16, and cases supra note 13. Cf. Pawtuxet Baptist Society v. Pawtuxet Baptist Church and Society, 50 R.I. 200, 146 A. 762, 1929; Siegley v. Simpson, 73 Wash. 69, 131 P. 479, 47 L.R.A.,N.S., 514 Ann.Cas 1915B 63, 1913; Indianapolis Home, etc. v. Altenheim, supra note 18; In re Gerety's Estate, supra note 19; Northern Trust Co. v. Perry, 105 Vt. 524, 168 A. 710, 94 A.L.R. 7, 1933.

23 Wigmore, Evidence § 2471; Restatement, Property, § 242, comment j; Warren, Interpretation of Wills—Recent Developments, 49 Harv.L.R. 689, 707.

24 Moseley v. Goodman, 138 Tenn. 1, 195 S.W. 590, Ann.Cas.1918C 931, 1917. See In re Estate of Soper, 196 Minn. 60, 264 N.W. 427, 1935; Farrell v. Sullivan and Norton v. Jordan, both supra note 10 (no rival claimants); Restatement, Property § 242d (2)(4); note, 37 Col.L.R. 842, 849.

25 Bond v. Riley, 317 Mo. 594, 296 S.W. 401, 1927; Siegley v. Simpson, supra note 22. In re Crawley: Robertson v. Flynn, [1920] 1 Ir.R. 78;

tator had never heard of one of these persons, or was on good or bad terms with one or the other. Some courts have excluded evidence of testator's declarations of intention to benefit one of them,[26] though the better view is to receive this evidence.[27]

*Incomplete Descriptions—Latent and Patent Ambiguities*

There are many decisions in which the description given in the will may apply equally well to two or more persons or objects. For example, the testator may have left "$1000 to my nephew John" when he has two nephews of that name. Obviously there is no misdescription here; the fault is rather that the description is not complete enough to deal with the situation presented. This defect has been termed equivocation because on application to external objects it fits two or more equally. In the above example the ambiguity is latent and does not appear upon the examination of the instrument itself. From all that appears on the face of the will, it might have described only one person. It is not until application of the terms to a definite person is attempted that difficulty is encountered. In cases of this kind the court upon construction receives evidence freely as to which person or object was intended by the testator,[28] and admits express declarations of the testator's intention for this purpose.[29]

This doctrine has been applied even when the ambiguity appeared on the face of the will. Thus, where a will contained a legacy to "George Gord, the son of John Gord," and another to "George Gord, the son of George Gord," and also a devise to "George Gord, the son of Gord," it was permissible to show

Smalley v. Scotton, [1929] 2 Ch. 112, noted, 28 Mich.L.R. 781; In re Jackson [1933] Ch. 237. See In re Wolverton Mortgaged Estates, L.R. 7 Ch.D. 197, 1877.

26 Drake v. Drake, 8 H.L.Cas. 172, 11 Eng.Rep. 392, 1860; Doe d. Hiscocks v. Hiscocks, 5 M. & W. 363, 151 Eng.Rep. 154, 1839.

27 Willard v. Darrah, 168 Mo. 660, 68 S.W. 1023, 90 Am.St.R. 468; Wigmore on Evidence, § 2474. Cf. Warren, supra note 23, at 710–711.

28 De Mouy v. Jepson, 255 Ala. 337, 51 So.2d 506, 1951; Bodman v American Tract Society, 9 Allen(Mass.) 447, 1864; Tilton v. American Bible Society, 60 N.H. 377, 49 Am.Rep. 321, 1880; Nicholl v. Bergner, 76 Ohio App. 245, 63 N.E.2d 828, 1945. Doe d. Allen v. Allen, 12 Ad. & El. 451, 113 Eng.Rep. 882, 1840. See In re Gisler's Estate, 242 Iowa 933, 48 N.W.2d 866, 1951; Northern Trust Co. v. Perry, 105 Vt. 524, 168 A. 710, 94 A.L.R. 7, 1933.

29 De Mouy v. Jepson, Bodman v. American Tract Society, and Doe d. Allen v. Allen, all supra note 28; West v. Hardwick's Ex'r, 301 Ky. 312, 191 S.W.2d 385, 1946. See annotation, 94 A.L.R. 26, 95; note, 53 Harv. L.R. 1213. But cf. Doe ex dem. Hubbard v. Hubbard, supra note 10

testator's declarations as to which of the Georges was intended as devisee.[30] This is an ambiguity patent on the face of the will, but not such a one that the devise will fail.[31]

Some patent ambiguities, however, are of such nature that the devise must fail because of the imperfection in expression. Thus, a devise of 80 acres out of a tract to A and the remaining 135 acres to B is void if it were intended to give a particular 80 acres because it violates the principles that a will must be in writing and cannot be reformed.[32] However, such devises have been construed to vest title in A and B as tenants in common in proportion to the designated acreage.[33] A will which left A "one of my three houses" presents another situation. This may give A the right of election,[34] but unless this construction is adopted, the gift fails because evidence that testator intended to pass a particular house would be inadmissible.[35]

30 Doe d. George Gord v. Needs, 2 M. & W. 129, 150 Eng.Rep. 698, 1836. See also Von Fell v. Spirling, 96 N.J. Eq. 20, 124 A. 518, 1924, noted, 34 Yale L.J. 214. Cf. Chafee, Progress of the Law: Evidence, 35 Harv.L.R. 673, 679.

31 See also In re Arrington's Will, 200 Misc. 72, 104 N.Y.S.2d 55, 1951; Schlottman v. Hoffman, 73 Miss. 188, 18 So. 893, 55 Am.St.Rep. 527, 1895, where there were ambiguities as to the amount given.

32 See Jones v. Camak, 142 Ga. 278, 82 S.E. 626, 1914. Similarly a blank is not subject to construction. Hunt v. Hort, 3 Bro.Ch.Cas. 311, 29 Eng. Rep. 554, 1791; Asten v. Asten, [1894] 3 Ch. 260; Engelthaler v. Engelthaler, 196 Ill. 230, 63 N.E. 669, 1902; Wigmore on Evidence § 2474. Cf. Re Hubbuck, [1905] Prob. 129.

33 Smith v. Burt, 388 Ill. 162, 57 N.E.2d 493, 157 A.L.R. 1118, 1944 (no right of selection to A).

34 In re Turner's Will, 206 N.Y. 93, 99 N.E. 187, 41 L.R.A.,N.S., 1049, 1912. See infra § 138, note 2.

35 See Asten v. Asten, supra note 32; Wigmore on Evidence § 2474.

## PARTIAL INVALIDITY OF A WILL

**61. By the majority and better doctrine when only a part of a will is affected by undue influence, fraud, mistake or insane delusions, the remainder will be enforced unless the two portions are so interrelated that to give effect to one without the other would probably do violence to testator's intention, in which case the entire will should be denied probate.**

When the testator lacks general mental capacity to make a will,[1] or when by mistake he signs the wrong document,[2] the entire instrument must be denied probate. In cases of inclusion of provision through mistake,[3] and those of undue influence,[4] fraud,[5] and insane delusions,[6] most courts normally reject only the portions of the will which are affected and probate the remainder.

However, if the parts of the will which are tainted by these elements are so related to the remainder that to accept the latter without the former would probably do violence to the testator's intention, the whole instrument should be held invalid.[7] In a few jurisdictions, the courts have held that if any part of the will is invalid for undue influence, fraud, insane delusion or mistake as to contents, the entire will falls.[8] These decisions were based upon statutes which make the issue upon probate that of "will or

1 In re Baker's Estate, 176 Cal. 430, 168 P. 881, 1917; Hildreth v. Hildreth, 153 Ky. 597, 156 S.W. 144, 1913.

2 See supra § 58.

3 See supra § 58, note 18.

4 Zeigler v. Coffin, 219 Ala. 586, 123 So. 22, 63 A.L.R. 942, 1929; Morris v. Stokes, 21 Ga. 552, 1857 (express statute); In re Ankeny's Estate, 238 Iowa 754, 28 N.W.2d 414, 1947; In re Koller's Estate, 116 Neb. 764, 219 N.W. 4, 1928; Sumner v. Staton, 151 N.C. 198, 65 S.E. 902, 18 Ann.Cas. 802, 1909; In re Carother's Estate, 300 Pa. 185, 150 A. 585, 69 A.L.R. 1127, 1930. See infra § 95, note 67.

5 In re Carson's Estate, 184 Cal. 437, 194 P. 5, 17 A.L.R. 239, 1920; In re Hollis' Estate, 234 Iowa 761, 12 N.W.2d 576, 1944; Black v. Smith, 58 N.D. 109, 224 N.W. 915, 1929. See also In re Holmes' Estate, 98 Colo. 360, 56 P.2d 1333, 1936.

6 See supra § 52, note 9 and cf. cases note 1 supra, where general mental incapacity is involved.

7 In re Cooper's Will, 75 N.J.Eq. 177, 71 A. 676, aff'd Harrison v. Axtell, 76 N.J.Eq. 614, 75 A. 1100, 1909; Walker v. Irby, 238 S.W. 884, Tex. Com.App.1922. See also In re Carother's Estate, supra note 4.

8 Snyder v. Steele, 304 Ill. 387, 136 N.E. 649, 28 A.L.R. 1, 1922, criticized, note, 32 Yale L.J. 294; McCarthy v. Fidelity National Bank & Trust Co., 325 Mo. 727, 30 S.W.2d 19, 69 A.L.R. 1122, 1930, noted, 16 Ia.L.R. 119.

no will." Even where such legislation exists, to deny probate of the whole will merely because of fraud or undue influence as to part seems an unreasonably literal interpretation of the statutes. In the jurisdictions where there are no statutory provisions of this nature, the doctrine of partial invalidity is well established.

Atkinson Wills 2nd Ed. HB

# CHAPTER 7

## EXECUTION OF ORDINARY WILLS

**Sec.**
**62. Statutory Sources of the Rules.**
**63. Writing.**
**64. Testator's Signature.**
**65. Witnesses—Number and Competency.**
**66. Making or Acknowledging Signature Before Witnesses.**
**67. Testator's Request to Witnesses.**
**68. Publication.**
**69. Animus Attestandi.**
**70. Witnesses' Signatures.**
**71. Order of Signing.**
**72. "In the Presence of".**
**73. Attestation Clause.**
**74. Practical Hints Regarding Execution.**

### STATUTORY SOURCES OF THE RULES

**62. The formalities required for execution of wills are governed by statute. While some courts have held that the statutes in force at the time of execution govern and others that those at the time of testator's death control, the best view is that a will is valid if it meets the statutory requirements at either time. The courts insist upon at least substantial compliance with every statutory requisite but no additional formalities are necessary.**

*What Statutes Govern* [1]

In most jurisdictions there are one or more special types of wills, which will be discussed in the following chapter. The present chapter deals with the formalities for ordinary wills. These matters are governed by local statutes. There is a conflict as to whether the legislation in force at the time of the execution, or at the time of testator's death, should apply. There can be no objection to the validity of a statute which expressly makes the latter provision.[2] Moreover, a number of courts take

[1] As to whether execution is governed by the law of the testator's domicile, of the place of execution, or of the situs of the property, see infra § 94, notes 20, 21.

[2] Long v. Zook, 13 Pa. 400, 1850; Burford v. Burford, 29 Pa. 221, 1857. See infra note 3.

this view even in absence of special provision.[3] At least an equal number of courts have taken the more desirable position that the statutes prevailing at the time of execution should control.[4] The most reasonable position is that later statutes which increase the formalities should not be construed to impair wills already made, while those which are less stringent should aid wills which were defectively executed at the time they were made.[5] When there is any doubt, wills should be re-executed after a change in the law regarding testamentary execution. Changes in the law after testator's death cannot validate [6] nor invalidate [7] his will.

The provisions of the English Statute of Frauds, 1677, as to the execution of wills of land [8] constitute the basic pattern of the American legislation, although certain features of the Wills Act, 1837,[9] have had considerable adoption here, and there are also American innovations.[10] As will appear later in this chapter, there are numerous divergencies in the requirements as between the various states. However, every state now has the same provisions for wills of personalty as for wills of realty.[11] The last state to reach this goal was Tennessee, which in 1941 adopted the Model Execution of Wills Act.[12]

*Compliance with All Statutory Requirements*

The prescribed formalities of execution are the legislature's idea of safeguards necessary to prevent tentative, doubtful or

3 Learned's Estate, 70 Cal. 140, 11 P. 587, 1886; Sutton v. Chenault, 18 Ga. 1, 1855; Langley v. Langley, 18 R.I. 618, 30 A. 465, 1894.

4 Lane's Appeal, 57 Conn. 182, 17 A. 926, 4 L.R.A. 45, 14 Am.St.Rep. 94, 1889; Packer v. Packer, 179 Pa. 580, 36 A. 344, 57 Am.St.Rep. 615, 1897; Barker v. Hinton, 62 W.Va. 639, 59 S.E. 614, 13 Ann.Cas. 1150, 1907.

5 Hoffman v. Hoffman, 26 Ala. 535, 1855; Lawrence v. Hebbard, 1 Bradf. (N.Y.) 252, 1850; In re Thompson's Will, 191 Misc. 168, 76 N.Y.S.2d 742, 1948; In re Estate of Spain, 327 Pa. 226, 193 A. 262, 111 A.L.R. 902, 1937. As to law regarding other matters than execution, see annotation, 129 A.L.R. 859.

6 Greenough v. Greenough, 11 Pa. 489, 51 Am.Dec. 567, 1849.

7 Rowlett v. Moore, 252 Ill. 436, 96 N.E. 835, Ann.Cas.1912D 346, 1911.

8 See supra § 3 note 70 et seq.

9 Ibid., note 81 et seq.

10 Bordwell, Statute Law of Wills, 14 Ia.L.R. 1, 2, 4.

11 But nuncupative and soldiers wills usually can pass personalty only —see infra §§ 76, 77.

12 Tenn.Pub.Acts, 1941, c. 125; contained also in Model Probate Code §§ 45–50. See Blackard, The Effects of the Enactment of the 1941 Wills Act, 17 Tenn.L.R. 447.

coerced expressions of desire from governing succession to one's property.[13] The courts enforce the legislative safeguards. Hence, no will is valid unless there is compliance with all of the statutory requirements.[14] The fact that the testator intended to comply,[15] or that the will contained commendable provisions,[16] is not ground for relaxing the rule. The heirs at law are thus favored, although this is probably more of a by-product of the desire for certainty than of a policy to discourage free testation. The courts do not insist upon performance of the formalities in the most literal or exacting sense which construction of the statute permits. Substantial or reasonable compliance with each requirement should be enough.[17]

*No Added Requirements*

The courts do not require other formalities than those found in the statutes.[18] No present statute requires a seal in the case of ordinary wills, [19] and accordingly sealing is unnecessary.[20] Delivery of a will likewise is unnecessary.[21] While a well drafted will has an attestation clause, this formality can be omitted.[22] An ordinary will need not be dated.[23] A date may be inserted

13 See Gulliver and Tilson, Classification of Gratuitous Transfers, 51 Yale L.J. 1, 5–13. Cf. Fuller, Consideration and Form, 41 Col.L.R. 799, where emphasis is put on the "channeling function" of formalities, much as the stamp on a coin relieves us from the necessity of inquiring what it is.

14 In re Krause's Estate, 18 Cal.2d 623, 117 P.2d 1, 1941; Bowen v. Morgillo, 127 Conn. 161, 14 A.2d 724, 1940; Ball v. Miller, 31 Tenn.App. 271, 214 S.W.2d 446, 1948; McElroy v. Rolston, 184 Va. 77, 34 S.E.2d 241, 1945. See infra § 63 at note 18; cf. infra § 70, notes 14, 15.

15 In re Manchester's Estate, 174 Cal. 417, 163 P. 358, L.R.A.1917D 629, Ann.Cas.1918B 227, 1917; In re Steiner's Estate, 142 Misc. 710, 255 N.Y.S. 397, 1932; In re Taylor's Estate, 39 S.D. 608, 165 N.W. 1079, 1917.

16 See In re Flynn's Estate, 142 Misc. 7, 253 N.Y.S. 638, 1931.

17 Rybolt v. Futrell, 296 Ky. 158, 176 S.W.2d 269, 1944; In re Bragg's Estate, 106 Mont. 132, 76 P.2d 57, 1938; In re Free's Estate, 181 Okl. 564, 75 P.2d 476, 1938; In re Lagershausen's Estate, 224 Wis. 479, 272 N.W. 469, 1937. Cf. note, 34 Va.L.R. 726, 741. See also infra §§ 63–72.

18 Davis v. Davis, 45 S.W.2d 240, Tex.Civ.App.1931; In re Lagershausen's Estate, supra note 17; cf. infra § 67, note 5.

19 But sealing in the sense of closing is required for mystic wills in Louisiana; see infra § 78, note 12.

20 Kessler v. Olen, 228 Wis. 662, 281 N.W. 691, 1938.

21 In re Brackenridge's Estate, 245 S.W. 786, Tex.Civ.App.1922.

22 See infra §§ 73, 74.

23 In re Swan's Estate, 287 Mich. 662, 284 N.W. 599, 1939; Pulley v. Cartwright, 23 Tenn.App. 690, 137 S.W.2d 336, 1940. Cf. infra § 75.

after the execution of the will without destroying its effect,[24] and an erroneous date does not invalidate the instrument.[25] The date of the will may be shown by extrinsic evidence.[26] However, intestacy results if there are several undated wills, each of which expressly revoked all prior wills, and it is impossible to show which was the last.[27] It is always advisable that a will be dated.

No case is found holding that a will executed on Sunday is inoperative on that account. While to execute a will on the Sabbath might be courting difficulty, the terms of the Sunday laws do not generally forbid this form of activity.[28] Possibly it may be illegal under some statutes for a lawyer to draft a will on Sunday, even though its execution on that day would not affect the validity. A somewhat parallel situation is the case of a will which has been drafted by a layman in violation of a criminal statute; this violation does not invalidate the will.[29]

## WRITING

**63. Ordinary wills must be in writing but may be in any language and inscribed with any material or device on any substance which results in a readable and fairly permanent record.**

Every state now requires that wills must be in writing,[1] except in case of nuncupative or military testaments.[2] Unless coming within these special provisions, oral wills are invalid,[3] and a bequest to one to distribute it in accordance with oral instructions has no effect.[4] However, a will may be typewritten,[5] or written

24 Lange v. Wiegand, 125 Mich. 647, 85 N.W. 109, 1901.

25 In re Bates' Estate, 286 Pa. 583, 134 A. 513, 48 A.L.R. 294, 1926 (here the will bore a date five months after testator's death).

26 Cunningham v. Hallyburton, 342 Ill. 442, 174 N.E. 550, 1931.

27 Peace v. Edwards, 170 N.C. 64, 86 S.E. 807, Ann.Cas.1918A 778, 1915.

28 See Rapp v. Reehling, 124 Ind. 36, 23 N.E. 777, 7 L.R.A. 498, 1890; In re Ferguson's Estate, 295 Mich. 576, 295 N.W. 318, 1940.

29 In re Estate of Peterson, 230 Minn. 478, 42 N.W.2d 59, 18 A.L.R.2d 910, 1950. As to whether the drafting of wills constitutes practice of law, see annotation, 151 A.L.R. 781, 783.

1 Bordwell, Statute Law of Wills, 14 Ia.L.R. 1, 10. See supra § 62, note 12.

2 See infra §§ 76, 77.

3 See Soules v. Silver, 118 Or. 96, 245 P. 1069, 1926, and authorities note 4 infra.

4 Frazier v. Frazier, 83 Colo. 188, 263 P. 413, 1927; Rinker's Adm'r v. Simpson, 159 Va. 612, 166 S.E. 546, 1932; Porter v. Wolf, 272 Pa. 93, 116 A. 55, 1922. See also infra §§ 80, 81.

5 Statutes sometimes so provided. See note 1 supra; see also Stuck v.

with pencil,[6] or partly in ink and partly in pencil,[7] or partly printed on a legal blank.[8]

A lower court decision to the effect that a will written on a slate is invalid has been disapproved.[9] Probably the courts would insist upon some fairly permanent record—a will scratched on a cake of ice or moulded in the sand might not be allowed. A will chalked on a corncrib and one inscribed on a bed post are said to have been admitted to probate in England.[10] There is a recent case of a will scratched on the fender of a tractor,[11] and another of one written on a petticoat.[12] Reported cases show that a will written on an empty egg shell,[13] and a microscopic testament engraved on a navy identification disk have been sustained.[14] Newspaper reports carry stories of wills written on wrapping paper, and on a collar box.[15] No one has been able to find the decision approving a will written with chalk on the barn door, but the opinion seems to be that it should be probated.[16] Sir Rider Haggard wrote a fanciful tale of an attested will tatooed on a lady's back.[17] Either of the latter two cases would disturb the routine of the probate office—though probably the difficulties would be overcome if the actual case were presented.

Howard, 213 Ala. 184, 104 So. 500, 1925; Succession of Patterson, 22 So. 2d 214, La.App.1945 (carbon copy). Of course most wills today are typewritten. For the suggestion that a clause should be added in testator's own hand for the purpose of identification, see Osborne, Signing Wills and Other Documents, 7 A.B.A.J. 20; infra § 74.

6 Myers v. Vanderbelt, 84 Pa. 510, 24 Am.Rep. 227, 1877; Tomlinson's Estate, 133 Pa. 245, 19 A. 482, 19 Am. St.Rep. 637, 1890.

7 Musgrove v. Holt, 153 Ark. 355, 240 S.W. 1068, 1922; Paglia v. Messina, 270 Mass. 1, 169 N.E. 423, 1930. Cf. Stuck v. Howard, supra note 5 (partly written and partly typewritten). Cf. where the pencil part was partly erased and partly written over by ink writings. Matter of Adams, L. R. 2 P. & D. 367, 1872.

8 Sears v. Sears, 77 Ohio St. 104, 82 N.E. 1067, 17 L.R.A.,N.S., 353, 11 Ann. Cas. 1008, 1907; In re Murphy's Will, 48 App.Div. 211, 62 N.Y.S. 785, 1900; Matter of Adams, supra, note 7.

9 Reed v. Woodward, 11 Phila.(Pa.) 541, 1875.

10 Miller, Notes on Some Interesting Wills, 12 Mich.L.R. 467, 468.

11 See note, 26 Can.B.R. 1242. This and the cases infra notes 12–14 are of unattested wills.

12 28 J.Crim.L. & Crim. 106.

13 In the Goods of Barnes, 136 L.T. 380, 43 T.L.R. 71, 1926.

14 66 Sol.J. 638.

15 Harris, Ancient, Curious and Famous Wills, 168.

16 Harris, supra note 15, at 167. See also note, 100 Cent.L.J. 65.

17 "Mr. Meeson's Will." See Miller, supra note 10, at 468; Burger, The Tattooed Will, 14 Law Student 9.

Ingenious persons have conceived the notion that a valid will can be made by the manufacture of a phonographic record, or talking moving picture with the testator as the speaker or actor. No reported case seems to have passed upon the question but the situation raises the general problem of the attitude of the courts toward the observance of statutory formalities in the execution of a will. The arguments would doubtless be made that these devices are at least as good guarantees against fraud, coercion and fabrication as the ordinary written will, and that there is also a satisfactory degree of permanence in the memorial. These arguments alone hardly suffice because the courts do not allow substitutes for the safeguards which the legislature has prescribed.[18] The devices could not be sustained unless the courts are prepared to hold that the product is a "writing." The author hazards the view that it would be held that phonographic records or picture films were not writings and that authorization of them must come from express legislation. Even if these devices satisfy the requirement that the will must be in writing, there are added difficulties because of the requirements of signature, attesting witnesses and other elements of execution.

*Language*

A will may be written in any tongue,[19] although upon probate it is translated into the language of the court.[20] The language need not be the one understood by the testator,[21] provided that he understood what the contents were.[22] Probably a will written in some recognized system of shorthand would be valid.[23] If it were written in a private cipher code known only to the testator the validity would be more doubtful, though this is possible if he customarily used the code.[24] However, a key to a code which

18 See supra § 62.

19 Heupel v. Heupel, 197 Okl. 567, 174 P.2d 850, 1946; In re Cliff's Trusts, [1892], 2 Ch.Div. 229.

20 Heupel v. Heupel, supra note 19; Caulfield v. Sullivan, 85 N.Y. 153, 1881. See note, 74 Sol.J. 128.

21 In re Gluckman's Will, 87 N.J. Eq. 638, 101 A. 295, L.R.A.1918D, 742. 1917; In re Zych's Will, 251 Wis. 108, 28 N.W.2d 316, 1947; In re Knutson's Estate, 144 Minn. 111, 174 N.W. 617, 1919. Cf. Gonzales v. Gonzales, 13 La. 104, 1839; Acop v. Piraso, 52 Philippines 660, 1929, for the contrary rule by statute.

22 Miltenberger v. Miltenberger, 78 Mo. 27, 1883; Kittleson's Estate v. Kittleson, 42 S.D. 126, 173 N.W. 161, 1919. In re Zych's Will, supra note 21.

23 See note, 74 Sol.J. 128; also Kell v. Charmer, 23 Beav. 195, 53 Eng.Rep. 76, 1856 (amounts of bequests valid though written in shop code); Restatement, Property § 242(d)(3).

24 See supra § 60 at note 24.

testator used only in the making of the will is not admissible in evidence,[25] and, if without this the will is unintelligible, probate of the instrument would be an idle act.

## TESTATOR'S SIGNATURE

**64. A will must be signed by the testator, but he need not write his full or correct name, and even a mark or stamp is sufficient if that was the complete act with which testator intended to authenticate the instrument.**

**Most statutes permit the testator to sign by proxy, and if so the testator's name written by another at his direction and in his presence is sufficient signature.**

**Most states do not require that the will be signed at the end, so that the writing of the testator's name anywhere on the instrument is sufficient if he intended it to operate as his signature.**

**The statutes in a number of jurisdictions require that the will be signed at the end or subscribed by the testator. In such case if any dispositive portion of the will is below or after the signature at the time of execution the entire will is invalid.**

With a few trifling exceptions the statutes require that all wills should be signed by the testator.[1] However, the courts have been very liberal in their holdings as to what constitutes a sufficient signature. The signature is not invalid because of illegibility.[2] Misspelling of the testator's name does not vitiate his signature.[3] Wills have been sustained when signed "Father,"[4] "Aunt Nannie,"[5] or with the given name,[6] or nickname,[7] or ini-

[25] Clayton v. Lord Nugent, 13 M. & W. 200, 153 Eng.Rep. 83, 1844.

[1] See Bordwell, Statute Law of Wills, 14 Ia.L.R. 1, 11. Some of the cases cited herein are of holographic wills, as to which see infra § 75.

[2] In re Larson's Estate, 141 Minn. 373, 170 N.W. 348, 1919; In re Iverson's Estate, 39 Wyo. 482, 273 P. 684, 64 A.L.R. 203, 1929.

[3] Word v. Whipps, 28 S.W. 151, 16 Ky.Law Rep. 403, 1894; Succession of Bradford, 124 La. 44, 49 So. 972, 18 Ann.Cas. 766, 1909. Nor does using the maiden name by a married testatrix. In re Westerman's Will, 402 Ill. 489, 82 N.E.2d 474, 1948.

[4] In re Button's Estate, 209 Cal. 325, 287 P. 964, 1930; Kimmel's Estate, 278 Pa. 435, 123 A. 405, 31 A.L.R. 678, 1924.

[5] Wells v. Lewis, 190 Ky. 626, 228 S.W. 3, 1921.

[6] Knox's Estate, 131 Pa. 220, 18 A. 1021, 6 L.R.A. 353, 17 Am.St.Rep. 798, 1890.

[7] Cartwright v. Cartwright, 158 Ark. 278, 250 S.W. 11, 1923. Cf. Knapp v. Reilly, infra note 20.

tials,[8] if the respective designations were intended as signatures of the testator.

The signature may be in pencil,[9] or with an engraved or rubber stamp.[10] One case indicates that it would be sufficient if the signature on a previous will was cut out and pasted on the new one.[11] There is some doubt as to whether the affixing of a seal is sufficient signature,[12] but if it is so intended it has been held good, especially where the testator's initials were impressed upon the seal.[13] A typewritten signature has been sustained[14] as was the testator's fingerprint when intended as his signature.[15]

The testator's cross or mark may be regarded as his signature,[16] and this is generally true even if he has the educational and physical ability to write his name.[17] This is held even if the testator's name does not appear in the body of the instrument or in connection with the mark.[18] By the usual and better practice, the testator's name should be written by another either before, after, or around the mark. When the act is the voluntary

[8] Quimby v. Greenhawk, 166 Md. 335, 171 A. 59, 1934 (last name added by another); In re Shoemaker's Estate, 47 D. & C. 337, Pa.1943.

[9] Knox's Estate, supra note 7.

[10] Jenkins v. Gaisford, 3 Sw. & Tr. 93, 164 Eng.Rep. 1208, 1863 (testator's hand paralyzed).

[11] See Bennett v. Bennett's Ex'x, 303 Ky. 565, 198 S.W.2d 301, 1947.

[12] See Wright v. Wakeford, 17 Ves. Jr. 454, 34 Eng.Rep. 176, 1811.

[13] Warneford v. Warneford, 2 Str. 764, 93 Eng.Rep. 834, 1727; Goods of Emerson, L.R. 9 Ir. 443, 1882. See In re Severance's Will, 96 Misc. 384, 161 N.Y.S. 452, 1916 (testator's initials written on a Red Cross seal affixed to the will).

[14] Zaruba v. Schumaker, 178 S.W.2d 542, Tex.Civ.App.1944, noted, 43 Mich. L.R. 808.

[15] In re Romaniw's Will, 163 Misc. 481, 296 N.Y.S. 925, 1937.

[16] Ziegler v. Brown, 112 Fla. 421, 150 So. 608, 1933 (also signed per alium); Cunningham v. Hallyburton, 342 Ill. 442, 174 N.E. 550, 1930; Succession of Gauthreaux, 173 La. 993, 139 So. 322, 1932 (dicta limits this to one unable to write); In re Stegman's Estate, 133 Misc. 745, 234 N.Y.S. 239, 1929; Short v. Short, 67 S.W.2d 425, Tex.Civ.App.1933; In re Mueller's Will, 188 Wis. 183, 205 N.W. 814, 42 A.L.R. 951, 1934. See annotations, 31 A.L.R. 682, 114 A.L.R. 1110, and infra note 38. As to the Pennsylvania law and recent changes, see In re Zakatoff's Estate, 367 Pa. 542, 81 A.2d 430, 1951; notes, 90 Pa.L.R. 194, 52 Dick. L.R. 58.

[17] In re Stegman's Estate, supra note 16 (but this fact calls for close scrutiny); In re Mueller's Will, supra note 16; In re Canterbury's Estate, 198 Mich. 743, 165 N.W. 747, 1917. See note, 20 U. of Cin.L.R. 310. But see Succession of Gauthreaux, supra note 16, and Pennsylvania citations, supra note 16.

[18] Cunningham v. Hallyburton, supra note 16; In re Romaniw's Will, supra note 15.

one of the testator, the signature is valid though he was assisted to a considerable extent by another.[19]

In order to have a valid signature the mark or other writing by the testator must have been intended as his signature, and moreover it must be the whole act which he contemplated. If a testator starts to write his name and his strength fails after he has partly completed it, this will not be regarded as his signature.[20] There must be some physical act done to the instrument either by or for the testator.[21] If the testator is unable to make his mark or procure the assistance of someone to do this for him, he cannot make a will.[22] When the testator writes his name on a blank sheet of paper and his will is thereafter written above it, the signature will suffice if he afterward adopts it as such.[23]

*Per Alium*

In absence of statutory authorization the testator must sign the will personally.[24] However, in all but four [25] states there is legislation that another may sign for him at his direction or request or with his consent. The request or direction does not have to be express.[26] Gestures have been held sufficient,[27] but mere

19 In re Kehl's Estate, 397 Ill. 251, 73 N.E.2d 437, 1947; In re Cox' Will, 139 Me. 261, 29 A.2d 281, 1943; In re Lodge's Estate, 123 Neb. 531, 243 N.W. 781, 1932; In re Morley's Estate, 138 Or. 75, 5 P.2d 92, 1931; In re Carmello's Estate, 289 Pa. 554, 137 A. 734, 1927. See Faught, Assistance or Manual Aid in Signing or Affixing Mark to Wills in Pennsylvania, 77 U. of Pa.L.R. 741.

20 Knapp v. Reilly, 3 Dem.(N.Y.) 427, 1885 (testator wrote "Pat", the first syllable of his first name); Prescott's Estate, 20 Pa.D. 8 C. 232, 1934 (similar); Plate's Estate, 148 Pa. 55, 23 A. 1038, 33 Am.St.Rep. 805, 1892 (testator formed first stroke of his name). It should be noticed that if the testator intended to write no more than he did, the writings in these cases would have been valid signatures. See notes 7, 16 supra.

21 Catlett v. Catlett, 55 Mo. 330, 1874; In re Rand's Will, 120 Misc. 670, 200 N.Y.S. 334, 1923.

22 Stricker v. Groves, 5 Whart.(Pa.) 386, 1839.

23 In re Bullivant's Will, 82 N.J.Eq. 340, 88 A. 1093, 51 L.R.A.,N.S., 169, Ann.Cas.1915C, 72, 1913.

24 In re McElwaine's Will, 18 N.J. Eq. 499, 1867. Cf. infra note 32.

25 Connecticut, Louisiana, New Jersey and Utah. See Bordwell, Statute Law of Wills, 14 Ia.L.R. 1, 11.

26 Welch v. Kirby, 255 F. 451, C.C.A. Mo.1918 (blind testator); In re Cox' Will, supra note 19. Response to a question has been held sufficient direction. In re Mullin's Estate, 110 Cal. 252, 42 P. 645, 1895; Steele v. Marble, 221 Mass. 485, 109 N.E. 357, 1915.

27 Ziegler v. Brown, 112 Fla. 421, 150 So. 608, 1933. Cf. Waite v. Frisbie, 45 Minn. 361, 47 N.W. 1069, 1891.

28 Waite v. Frisbie, supra note 27; Murry v. Hennessey, 48 Neb. 608, 67

knowledge by the testator that another is signing for him has been held insufficient.[28] Almost everywhere,[29] the signing by another must be in the testator's presence. The requirement of presence raises the same problem as the provision that the witness must sign in the testator's presence.[30]

Generally the testator may sign by another although he has the educational and physical ability to sign personally.[31] In practice it is sometimes difficult to distinguish signatures by proxy from those where manual assistance is given to the testator.[32] Statutes often provide that the person signing the testator's name must also sign his own name, though they sometimes declare that failure to do so does not invalidate the will.[33] But if the provision for the form of the proxy signature is mandatory, failure to observe it invalidates the will.[34] The best form of signature by proxy is to write the testator's name "by ——— (the proxy)," and perhaps following this with a statement that it was written by testator's direction and in his presence.[35] However, many forms of signature by proxy have been upheld.[36]

When the testator signed by mark and someone writes his name opposite the mark,[37] this is regarded as a personal signa-

N.W. 470, 1896. But see In re Kelly's Estate, 306 Pa. 551, 160 A. 454, 1932.

29 Except in Arkansas and New York, and of course the jurisdictions noted supra note 25 which do not permit signature by proxy at all. See Bordwell, supra note 25. Of course a signature not made until after testator's death is insufficient. Shutz's Estate, 43 Pa.Co. 324, 1915.

30 See infra § 72; Ex parte Leonard, 39 S.C. 518, 18 S.E. 216, 22 L.R.A. 302, 1893; In re Silverman's Will, 198 Misc. 274, 97 N.Y.S.2d 490, 1950 (testator in oxygen tent).

31 In re Canterbury's Estate, 198 Mich. 743, 165 N.W. 747, 1917, and cases supra note 17. For the peculiar statutory provision in Pennsylvania and its interpretation, see In re Kelly's Estate, supra note 28.

32 See Goldsmith v. Gates, 205 Ala. 632, 88 So. 861, 1921, and cases cited supra note 19.

33 See Bordwell, supra note 25; In re Me-hun-kah's Will, 78 Okl. 214, 189 P. 867, 1920.

34 Graves v. Bowles, 193 Ark. 546, 101 S.W.2d 176, 1937; Wilson v. Craig, 86 Wash. 465, 150 P. 1179, Ann. Cas.1917B 871, 1915.

35 This was used in Abraham v. Wilkins, 17 Ark. 292, 1856. But this is not necessary, and proof may be supplied by oral evidence. In re Starke's Estate, 67 N.D. 178, 271 N.W. 131, 1937.

36 See Riley v. Riley, 36 Ala. 496, 1860; Vernon v. Kirk, 30 Pa. 218, 1858; In re Clark, 2 Curt. 329, 163 Eng.Rep. 428, 1836.

37 This is frequently the case. See Ziegler v. Brown, supra note 27; Ahnert v. Ahnert, 98 Kan. 768, 160 P. 201, 1916; Reed v. Hendrix's Ex'r, 180 Ky. 57, 201 S.W. 482, L.R.A.1918E 423, 1918; In re Canterbury's Estate, supra note 31.

ture rather than a signature by another.[38] In other words, the writing of the testator's name is regarded as being for identification of the mark merely and not as a signature. Hence the name may be writtên outside the testator's presence without invalidating the will. If the testator's name was written in his presence and at his request, it could be regarded as a signature in addition to the mark. The fact that one of these signatures is invalid for want of compliance with the statute should not effect the ability of the other to sustain the will.[39]

*Place of Signature Under Statutes Requiring Signing*

The English Statute of Frauds [40] merely provided that the will should be signed by the testator and contained no requirement as to the place of the signature. Under this statute, the leading case of Lemayne v. Stanley [41] held that when the testator wrote his own will which began, "I, John Stanley, make this my last will" the testator's name should be regarded as his signature. The decision declares that the signing could be at the top, bottom or margin of the will, but makes no mention of any requirement of an intention that the writing by the testator of his name should operate as his signature. The statutes in most American jurisdictions likewise make no mention of the place of the signature.[42] In these states the courts follow the doctrine of Lemayne v. Stanley to the extent that the signature need not appear at the end of the will,[43] but they generally insist that the intention

[38] See In re Wilcox's Will, 215 Wis. 341, 254 N.W. 529, 1934. But cf. Ahnert v. Ahnert, supra note 37.

[39] In re Dombrowski's Estate, 163 Cal. 290, 125 P. 233, 1912; Moreland v. Brady, 8 Or. 303, 34 Am.Rep. 581, 1880; Wilson v. Craig, supra note 34.

[40] 29 Car. II, c. 3, § V, 1677.

[41] 3 Lev. 1, 83 Eng.Rep. 545, 1681.

[42] Except in Arkansas, California, Florida, Idaho, Kansas, Montana, New York, North Dakota, Ohio, Oklahoma, Pennsylvania, South Dakota and Utah, which require that the will be signed at the end, and in Connecticut, Kentucky, where the testator must "subscribe" the will. See Bordwell, Statute Law of Wills, 14 Ia.L.R. 1, 12. Statutes sometimes provide that holographic wills must be "subscribed." See infra note 52, and infra § 75.

[43] Thrift Trust Co. v. White, 90 Ind.App. 116, 167 N.E. 141, 1929, rehearing denied 168 N.E. 250, noted, 3 Cin.L.R. 489, 5 Ind.L.R. 129, 25 Ill. L.R. 226 (top); In re Johnson's Estate, 209 Iowa 757, 229 N.W. 261 (top), 1930; Thomson v. Carruth, 218 Mass. 524, 106 N.E. 159, 1914 (margin); In re Thomas' Estate, 243 Mich. 566, 220 N.W. 764, 1928, noted, 14 Ia.L.R. 323, 365 (top); In re Cravens' Estate, 177 Minn. 437, 225 N.W. 398, 1929 (exordium); Potter v. Ritchardson, 360 Mo. 661, 230 S.W.2d 672, 1950 (exordium); In re Phelan's Estate, 82 N.J. Eq. 316, 87 A. 625, 1913, noted, 62 U. of Pa.L.R. 236 (attestation); In re McNair's Will, 72 S.D. 604, 38 N.W.

appear that the testator's name written elsewhere than at the end of the will should operate as his signature.[44] Virginia and West Virginia statutes declare that the will should be signed "in such manner as to make it manifest that the same is intended as a signature." [45] In some other jurisdictions the courts insist that the intention should be gathered from the form of the instrument itself,[46] but most permit evidence of the testator's declarations at the time for this purpose.[47] Wills not materially different from that in Lemayne v. Stanley have been held invalid for lack of showing of an intention that the name should operate as a signature.[48] On the other hand, some courts have gone to the extreme of holding that the testator may adopt as his signature his name written by another in some other place than the normal one.[49] After a critical review of the cases and the questions of policy involved, Professor Philip Mechem offers the suggestion that statutes might be framed to dispense with signing altogether as an absolute requirement, leaving only the question as to whether: (1) Testator made it clear to the witnesses that he adopted the instrument as his will, and (2) the witnesses attest this fact by writing their names on the will.[50]

2d 449, 1949; Murguiondo v. Nowland's Ex'r, 115 Va. 160, 78 S.E. 600, 1913; note, 17 N.D.Lawyer 270; annotation, 29 A.L.R. 891. See generally Evans, Incidents of Testamentary Execution, 16 Ky.L.J. 199, 205–207. For application of the doctrine of Lemayne v. Stanley to unwitnessed holographic wills, see infra § 75.

44 See generally authorities note 43 supra, and notes 45–48 infra.

45 See Bordwell, supra note 42 at 13. For interpretation of these statutes, see Hall v. Brigstocke, 190 Va. 459, 58 S.E.2d 529, 19 A.L.R.2d 921, 1950.

46 Matter of Will of Booth, 127 N.Y. 109, 27 N.E. 826, 12 L.R.A. 452, 24 Am.St.Rep. 429, 1891. And see Bamberger v. Barbour, infra note 48.

47 Armstrong's Ex'r v. Armstrong's Heirs, 29 Ala. 538, 1857; Meads v. Earle, 205 Mass. 553, 91 N.E. 916, 29 L.R.A.,N.S., 63, 1910; Stone v. Holden, 221 Mich. 430, 191 N.W. 238, 29 A.L.R. 884, 1922; Armstrong v. Walton, 105 Miss. 337, 62 So. 173, 46 L.R.A.,N.S., 552, Ann.Cas.1916E 137, 1913; In re Phelan's Estate, 82 N.J.Eq. 316, 87 A. 625, 1913.

48 Bamberger v. Barbour, 335 Ill. 458, 167 N.E. 122, 1929, noted, 25 Ill. L.R. 226, 28 Mich.L.R. 355.

49 Armstrong's Ex'r v. Armstrong's Heirs, 29 Ala. 538, 1857; Armstrong v. Walton, 105 Miss. 337, 62 So. 173, 46 L.R.A.,N.S., 552, Ann.Cas.1916E 137, 1913; In re Williams' Will, 234 N.C. 228, 66 S.E.2d 902, 1951. Cf. Catlett v. Catlett, 55 Mo. 330, 1874.

50 The Rule in Lemayne v. Stanley, 29 Mich.L.R. 685, 706.

### *Place of Signature Under Statutes Requiring Signature at the End*

In part to break away from the subjective subtleties which have followed in the wake of Lemayne v. Stanley and also to minimize the opportunities of subsequent additions to the will by the testator and others, the English Wills Act [51] and the statutes in some sixteen American jurisdictions,[52] require that the will be signed at the foot or end, or that the will be subscribed by the testator. These provisions no doubt have accomplished the above purposes, and in addition help to guarantee that the will was regarded by the testator as in final form.[53] On the debit side, these statutes have invalidated a number of otherwise unquestionable wills, and in addition have given rise to much litigation as to what is the end of a will.

Where is the end of a will? Quite obviously the expression refers to space and not to time. It attempts to tell where the will should be signed rather than when. The New York Court of Appeals once insisted that the end of a will means the physical end, or that part which is furthest from the beginning.[54] Usually the courts take a more liberal view and sustain the will if it is signed at the logical end.[55] To illustrate this difference in attitude, suppose that a will is written like many letters on a folded piece of paper. The letter writer often fills the first page and then skips to the third page and after completing the latter returns to the second page and signs underneath the last written

[51] 7 Wm. IV and 1 Vict. c. 26, 1837. See infra note 83.

[52] See note 42 supra. A statutory provision that testator must subscribe the will requires that he sign at the end. Baker v. Baker's Estate, 199 Miss. 388, 24 So.2d 841, 1946, noted, 18 Miss.L.J. 331.

[53] In re Seaman's Estate, 146 Cal. 455, 80 P. 700, 106 Am.St.Rep. 53, 2 Ann.Cas. 726, 1905; In re Knox's Estate, 131 Pa. 220, 18 A. 1021, 6 L.R.A. 353, 17 Am.St.Rep. 798, 1890.

[54] In re Andrews' Will, 162 N.Y. 1, 56 N.E. 529, 48 L.R.A. 662, 76 Am.St. Rep. 294, 1900; In re Whitney's Will, 153 N.Y. 259, 47 N.E. 272, 60 Am.St. Rep. 616, 1897; In re O'Neil's Will, 91 N.Y. 516, 1883. But see Matter of Field's Will, 204 N.Y. 448, 97 N.E. 881, 39 L.R.A.,N.S., 1060, Ann.Cas. 1913C 842, 1912, noted, 12 Col.L.R. 380; notes, 1 Corn.L.Q. 136, 6 Fordham L.R. 147.

[55] In re Chase's Estate, 51 Cal.App. 2d 353, 124 P.2d 895, 1942; In re Swire's Estate, 225 Pa. 188, 73 A. 1110, 1909; In re Stinson's Estate, 228 Pa. 475, 77 A. 807, 30 L.R.A.,N.S., 1173, 139 Am.St.Rep. 1014, 1910, noted, 12 Col.L.R. 182, 24 Harv.L.R. 247, 9 Mich.L.R. 342. And see Graham v. Edwards, 162 Ky. 771, 173 S.W. 127, 1915, noted, 13 Mich.L.R. 616, where testator completely filled the page and wrote his signature on the margin—held validly subscribed. And see generally Evans, Incidents of Testamentary Execution, 16 Ky.L.J. 199, 209–214.

part there. In the courts which recognize the "logical" end, this will is signed in the proper place,[56] though not under the view formerly taken in New York.[57]

It has been held that where the testator wrote a dispositive clause along the margin of the last page of his will, after he had written all of the other items and then signed under the body of the will, it was not signed at the end.[58] References to attached sheets,[59] or to writings on the reverse side of the document signed,[60] have prevented the will from being regarded as signed at the end. A mere fastening together of the pages arranged in improper order does not invalidate the will,[61] nor does pasting the paper on which the testator and the witnesses signed to the bottom of the will.[62] Of course if a dispositive provision is clearly below or after the testator's signature, the will is not signed at the end.[63]

There are cases in which the testator has left blank spaces in the body of his will, or after the dispositive part thereof and before the signature. A short space, though sufficient to permit a

[56] In re Stinson's Estate, supra note 55.

[57] See In re Andrews' Will, supra note 54; In re Schroeder's Will, 98 Mich. 92, 163 N.Y.S. 956, 1916. But see In re Reid's Will, 47 N.Y.S.2d 426, 1944; In re Golden's Will, 165 Misc. 205, 300 N.Y.S. 737, 1937.

[58] Irwin v. Jacques, 71 Ohio St. 395, 73 N.E. 683, 69 L.R.A. 422, 1904. But see In re Swire's Estate, supra note 55.

[59] In re Whitney's Will, 153 N.Y. 259, 47 N.E. 272, 60 Am.St.Rep. 616, 1897; Smith v. Ellis, 15 Ohio App. 38, 1921; In re Reilly's Will, 129 Misc. 77, 220 N.Y.S. 781, 1927. Conceivably these wills might be sustained upon the doctrine of incorporation by reference—see infra § 80—but the fact that the testator intended to make them an integral part of his will rather than merely to incorporate them would seem to forbid this.

[60] In re Conway, 124 N.Y. 455, 26 N.E. 1028, 11 L.R.A. 796, 1891; In re Ryan's Estate, 133 Misc. 174, 231 N.Y.S. 90, 1928, noted, 3 Cin.L.R. 91. Contra: Baker's Appeal, 107 Pa. 381, 52 Am.Rep. 478, 1884; In re Goods of Birt, L.R. 2 P. & D. 214, 1871 (statute—see note 83 infra).

[61] Chandler v. Dockman, 8 Ohio App. 113, 1917. Cf. Sellards v. Kirby, 82 Kan. 291, 108 P. 73, 28 L.R.A.,N.S., 270, 136 Am.St.Rep. 110, 20 Ann.Cas. 214, 1910; In re Goods of Madden [1905] 2 Ir. 612. The problems of loose sheets and signing on the envelope are considered in connection with integration. See infra § 79.

[62] Butler v. Moulton, 42 S.D. 410, 175 N.W. 701, 1920.

[63] Sisters of Charity of St. Vincent de Paul v. Kelly, 67 N.Y. 409, 1876; In re Coyne's Estate, 349 Pa. 331, 37 A.2d 509, 1944; In re Dietterich's Estate, 127 Pa.Super. 315, 193 A. 158, 1937 (signature on back). Cf. infra note 65. See Millward v. Buswell, 20 T.L.R. 714, 1904; In re Goods of Malen, 54 L.J.Prob. 91, 1885.

fraudulent addition, does not violate the statute.[64] A will was held to be signed at the end though there was a space of over twenty-three inches between the testimonium clause and the signature.[65] On the other hand, leaving an entire page between the written part and the signature was held not a signing at the end.[66]

That the signature follows the attestation clause instead of the testimonium clause does not invalidate the instrument.[67] If the testator signed in the body of the attestation clause, we sometimes have the problem of whether he intended that writing as the signature to his will.[68] Assuming that he did so intend, there is little doubt but that the signature can be regarded as at the end.[69]

Clauses which are merely formal in their nature do not invalidate a will, though they appear below the testator's signature. Thus, the addition of the date of the will,[70] or a map of the testator's property,[71] or even a revocatory clause which is immaterial

[64] Musgrove v. Holt, 153 Ark. 355, 240 S.W. 1068, 1922; In re Dutcher's Estate, 172 Cal. 488, 157 P. 242, 1916; Lucas v. Brown, 187 Ky. 502, 219 S.W. 796, 1920; In re Morrow's Estate, 204 Pa. 479, 54 A. 313, 1903.

[65] Mader v. Apple, 80 Ohio St. 691, 89 N.E. 37, 23 L.R.A.,N.S., 515, 131 Am.St.Rep. 719, 1909.

[66] In re Schroeder's Will, 98 Misc. 92, 163 N.Y.S. 956, 1916; In re Estate of Seaman, 146 Cal. 455, 80 P. 700, 106 Am.St.Rep. 53, 2 Ann.Cas. 726, 1905. And see Lucas v. Brown, supra note 64. Cf. In re Seiter's Estate, 265 Pa. 202, 108 A. 614, 1919 (four separate papers, one of which was signed, were held not signed at end where there was no physical or internal connection between them).

[67] In re Dutcher's Estate, supra note 64; McCue v. Turner, 252 Ky. 849, 68 S.W.2d 415, 1934; Matter of Laudy's Will, 161 N.Y. 429, 55 N.E. 914, 1900; Graham v. Tucker, 47 N.E. 2d 801, Ohio App.1942. Of course a signature immediately above the attestation clause is sufficient. In re Ellis' Estate, 168 Kan. 11, 210 P.2d 417, 1949; see Parrott v. Parrott's Adm'x, 270 Ky. 544, 110 S.W.2d 272, 1937.

[68] See Sears v. Sears, 77 Ohio St. 104, 82 N.E. 1067, 17 L.R.A.,N.S., 353, 11 Ann.Cas. 1008, 1907. Even if testator wrote his name at the very end, he may not have intended it as his signature. In re Bond's Estate, 159 Kan. 249, 153 P.2d 912, 1944 (ending "Will of H. G. Bond").

[69] In re Tonneson's Estate, 81 Cal. App.2d 703, 185 P.2d 78, 1947; In re Rudolph's Estate, 180 App.Div. 486, 167 N.Y.S. 760, 1917; In re Jarvis' Will, 124 Misc. 563, 208 N.Y.S. 796, 1925. But see In re Churchill's Estate, 260 Pa. 94, 103 A. 533, 1918.

[70] Flood v. Pragoff, 79 Ky. 607, 1881. See Wikoff's Appeal, 15 Pa. 281, 53 Am.Dec. 597, 1850; In re Giffith's Estate, 358 Pa. 474, 57 A.2d 893, 1948.

[71] Tonnele v. Hall, 4 N.Y. 140, 1850; In re Schmitt's Estate, 187 Misc. 203, 61 N.Y.S.2d 569, 1946.

because testator had disposed of all his property in the will,[72] do not effect the will. Provisions for the compensation of the executor,[73] or that he should serve without bond,[74] likewise have been held to be immaterial for this purpose, and do not invalidate the will by reason of appearing after the signature. There is a conflict as to whether the appointment of an executor following the signature invalidates the will.[75] It is true that the appointment is not necessary for the validity of the will and has no dispositive effect; yet a will may do no more than appoint the personal representative.[76] This is a material, and at times vital, part of the testamentary scheme[77] and the decisions which permit the will to stand in such cases seem to do violence to the statutory language. A clause giving the personal representative power of sale found after the testator's signature invalidates the will.[78] It has been intimated that the same would be true of a statement of suggestions or reasons for the disposition if they might effect the construction of the will.[79]

Of course the non-dispositive words following the signature cannot be given effect as part of the will. If the words in this position are dispositive, the American view is that the whole will is invalid.[80] This result is reached both because of the language of the statute which makes signing at the end or subscribing a requirement for the validity of the will, and because to hold that only the part after the signature is void would often interfere with the testamentary scheme so seriously as to render intestacy

72 In re Serveira's Will, 205 App. Div. 686, 200 N.Y.S. 464, 1923.

73 In re McConihe's Estate, 123 Misc. 318, 205 N.Y.S. 780, 1924. See Musgrove v. Holt, 153 Ark. 355, 240 S.W. 1068, 1922 (the provision was in the handwriting of another).

74 Baker v. Baker, 51 Ohio St. 217, 37 N.E. 125, 1894.

75 That it does: Sisters of Charity of St. Vincent de Paul v. Kelly, 67 N.Y. 409, 1876; In re Winters' Will, 302 N.Y. 666, 98 N.E.2d 477, 1951; Appeal of Wineland, 118 Pa. 37, 12 A. 301, 4 Am.St.Rep. 571, 1888. That it does not: Ward v. Putnam, 119 Ky. 889, 85 S.W. 179, 1905. See note, 21 Corn.L.Q. 351.

76 Fontaine v. Fontaine, 169 Ark. 1077, 277 S.W. 867, 1925; In re Hickman's Estate, 101 Cal. 609, 36 P. 118, 1894.

77 Sisters of Charity of St. Vincent de Paul v. Kelly, supra note 75.

78 In re Blair's Will, 84 Hun 581, 32 N.Y.S. 845, aff'd 152 N.Y. 645, 46 N.E. 1145, 1897.

79 See Baker v. Baker, 51 Ohio St. 217, 37 N.E. 125, 1894; Wikoff's Appeal, 15 Pa. 281, 53 Am.Dec. 597, 1850. Cf. In re Jordan's Estate, 81 Cal.App. 2d 419, 184 P.2d 165, 1947.

80 In re Estate of Seaman, supra note 66; In re Winters' Will, supra note 75; Appeal of Wineland, supra note 75. Cf. In re Frickey's Will, 198 Misc. 716, 96 N.Y.S.2d 825, 1950.

preferable.[81] This was the original English view; [82] but under the amendment of 1852, the courts hold that the part prior to the signature is valid and the remainder is invalid.[83]

*Words Added after Execution*

When words are added to the will below the testator's signature at some time after execution, they do not affect the validity of the will.[84] The addition of the words does not work a revocation,[85] and the part above the signature is valid, because the will was signed at its end at the time of execution. When a will is found with some independent disposition following the signature, it will be presumed that the latter was added after execution, thus giving effect to that which appears above the signature.[86] Of course the words which are written after execution, whether above or below the signature, constitute no part of the will, and if this is shown, the added provisions will be denied probate.[87] This is true in all jurisdictions, regardless of whether the statute provides that the will should be signed at the end. However, if the will with the added parts is re-executed with the signature at the end, the whole becomes valid.[88]

[81] See Evans, supra note 55 at 208.

[82] Sweetland v. Sweetland, 4 Sw. & Tr. 6, 164 Eng.Rep. 1416, 1864; Goods of Milward, 1 Curt. 912, 163 Eng.Rep. 315, 1838.

[83] Royle v. Harris, [1895] P. 163; Millward v. Buswell, 20 T.L.R. 714, 1904; Goods of Evans, 128 L.T.R. 669, 1923. This amendment reads: "No signature shall be operative to give effect to any disposition which is underneath or which follows it." 15 & 16 Vict. c. 24, § 1.

[84] Wikoff's Appeal, supra note 79; Parrott v. Parrott's Adm'r, 270 Ky. 544, 110 S.W.2d 272, 1937; In re Moller's Will, 61 N.Y.S.2d 638, 1946.

[85] Wikoff's Appeal, supra note 79. See note, 28 Cal.L.R. 413.

[86] In re Taylor's Estate, 230 Pa. 346, 79 A. 632, 36 L.R.A.,N.S., 66, 1911; Parrott v. Parrott's Adm'r, supra note 84.

[87] Wikoff's Appeal, supra note 79; Musgrove v. Holt, 153 Ark. 355, 240 S.W. 1068, 1922.

[88] Clark v. Carpenter, 14 Ohio App. 278, 1921; see infra § 89.

## WITNESSES—NUMBER AND COMPETENCY

**65. Most statutes require only two attesting witnesses but in a few states three are necessary.**

**The witnesses to a will must be competent to testify at the time of execution in a proceeding for the probate of the will. One who is then competent is a qualified attester regardless of later events and one incompetent at the time of execution cannot usually become a proper witness by any change of his situation.**

**In most jurisdictions the statute provides that a beneficiary under the will is a proper attester but that he is not permitted to take under the will unless he is also an heir at law in which case he may take up to his intestate share.**

In addition to the signature of the testator, the statutes require attesting witness for the validity of ordinary wills. Postponing for the moment the subject of the requisites of attestation, we will consider first the number and character of witnesses required.

### *Number of Witnesses*

The English Statute of Frauds required "three or four" witnesses for the validity of devises.[1] The English Wills Act, 1837,[2] requires "two or more" witnesses for all wills. In most American jurisdictions two are sufficient, though most of the New England States, Connecticut, Maine, Massachusetts, New Hampshire and Vermont, and two southern states, Georgia and South Carolina, all require three witnesses.[3] These provisions are mandatory and if the will has less than the statutory number of witnesses, it is invalid as an ordinary will.[4] A will is perfectly good though attested by an excessive number of witnesses.[5] The attestation by

1 29 Car. II c. 3, § v, 1677. The alternative is an absurdity, since it was certainly not intended to forbid the use of more than four witnesses. See infra note 5. Early drafts of the statute read "three or more." Hening, The Original Drafts of the Statute of Frauds (29 Car. II c. 3) and Their Authors, 61 U. of Pa.L.R. 283, 293, 298, 306. Probably the change in the final act was the result of carelessness, or of a hasty meaningless compromise.

2 7 Wm. IV and 1 Vict. c. 26.

3 See Bordwell, Statute Law of Wills, 14 Ia.L.R. 1, 16, 17. For the number of witnesses required in Louisiana, see infra § 78. As to the peculiar law as to witnesses in Pennsylvania, see infra § 70, note 2.

4 Johnson v. Hinton, 130 Ark. 394, 197 S.W. 706, 1917; Stuart v. Foutz, 185 Md. 401, 45 A.2d 98, 1946.

5 Jones v. Brooks, 184 Ala. 115, 63

a superfluous witness who is incompetent, or who does not attest in proper manner, does not affect the validity of a will properly attested by the requisite number of competent witnesses.[6] However, the signing by superfluous witnesses may necessitate the additional burden of producing or accounting for all of these persons upon probate.[7]

*The English Law*

The English Statute of Frauds provided that the witnesses to the will should be "credible." [8] Although there was some early difference of opinion as to the meaning of this word, it became established that credible witnesses were those who were competent to testify on behalf of the will.[9] This was rather alarming, for interest then disqualified a witness.[10] If the will was signed by a devisee, or even a creditor when the will charged the realty with payment of debts, the entire will was invalid.[11] Moreover, a release of the interest of the witness who was also a devisee or a creditor could not save the will because the witnesses were required to be competent at the time of the execution of the will.[12] This situation led to the enactment of the Statute of George II,[13] which provided that when a witness was also a legatee, devisee, or a creditor, he should lose all advantage of the provisions of the will. This had the effect of validating the will by nullifying the gift or charge in favor of the interested witness. But the spouse of an interested party was also incompetent to testify at common law,[14] and as the statute made no provision for avoidance of a legacy or devise when the husband or wife of the beneficiary was a witness, wills so attested were as invalid as one witnessed by the legatee or devisee before the statute.[15] To remedy this situation, the Wills Act, 1837,[16] also in-

So. 978, 1913; Ackless v. Seekright, Breese (Ill.) 76, 1823; Scattergood v. Kirk, 192 Pa. 263, 43 A. 1030, 1899.

6 In re Sizer's Will, 129 App.Div. 7, 113 N.Y.S. 210, aff'd 195 N.Y. 528, 88 N.E. 1132, 1909; Boone v. Lewis, 103 N.C. 40, 9 S.E. 644, 14 Am.St.Rep. 783, 1889; Scattergood v. Kirk, supra note 5.

7 See infra §§ 74, 95, 100.

8 29 Car. II, c. 3, § v, 1677.

9 Holdfast d. Anstey v. Dowsing, 2 Strange 1253, 93 Eng.Rep. 1164, 1746. But see Lord Mansfield in Windham v. Chetwynd, 1 Burr. 414, 97 Eng.Rep. 377, 1757.

10 See authorities cited note 9 supra, and Wigmore on Evidence, § 575.

11 Holdfast d. Anstey v. Dowsing, supra note 9.

12 Ibid. But cf. Windham v. Chetwynd, supra note 9.

13 25 Geo. II, c. 6, 1752.

14 Wigmore on Evidence, §§ 600–603.

15 Hatfield v. Thorp, 5 B. and Ald. 589, 106 Eng.Rep. 1305, 1822.

16 7 Wm. IV and 1 Vict. c. 26, § xv.

validated gifts to the spouse of an attesting witness, thus making the latter competent. Indeed, this statute declared that a will should never be invalid by reason of the incompetence of an attesting witness.[17]

*The American Law—In General*

Some American jurisdictions follow the Statute of Frauds in requiring that the attesters be credible, but a larger number declare that they should be competent.[18] This difference in phraseology is not material for our courts uniformly hold that credible means competent.[19] A will may be valid although an attesting witness is not a person of veracity or worthy of credit.[20] On the other hand, one is not a suitable attester unless he is competent to testify.[21] This refers to competency to testify as to the facts of execution of the will and as to the mental capacity of the testator, for these are the matters to which the witness attests or bears witness.[22]

It should be noticed that the requirement of attesting witnesses is a provision of the substantive law.[23] Without witnesses, the will is invalid. These provisions of the wills' statutes do not attempt to indicate the persons by whom the will must be proved. As a matter of fact, the attesters may or may not be the ones whose testimony establishes the will in the probate court. To think of the competency of the attesters to the will as a sub-

17 Ibid. § xiv.

18 Bordwell, Statute Law of Wills, 14 Ia.L.R. 1, 17, 18. As to competency of witnesses in Louisiana, see infra § 78, notes 16–18.

19 In re Noble, 124 Ill. 266, 15 N.E. 850, 1888; Hiatt v. McColley, 171 Ind. 91, 85 N.E. 772, 1908; Fuller v. Fuller, 83 Ky. 345, 1885; In re Look, 129 Me. 359, 152 A. 84, 1930; King v. King, 161 Miss. 51, 134 So. 827, 1931; Lord v. Lord, 58 N.H. 7, 42 Am.Rep. 565, 1876; Moos v. First State Bank, 60 S.W.2d 888, Tex.Civ.App.1933. See annotation, 18 Ann.Cas. 1091.

20 In re Noble, Fuller v. Fuller, King v. King, all supra note 19.

21 See Lord v. Lord, supra note 19.

22 In general it is held that the attesters should bear witness to the mental capacity of the testator as well as the facts of execution. Smith v. Young, 134 Miss. 738, 99 So. 370, 35 A.L.R. 69, 1924, and annotation, 35 A.L.R. 79. But it is somewhat difficult to see how this can apply in the jurisdictions where the witnesses attest merely the signature of the testator and may not know that it is a will. See infra, § 66. And see Dunkeson v. Williams, 242 S.W. 653, Mo.1922 (desirable that attesting witnesses of aged person's will should be acquainted with testator); In re Moxley's Will, 103 Vt. 100, 152 A. 713, 1930.

23 Evans, The Competency of Testamentary Witnesses, 25 Mich.L.R. 238; Wigmore on Evidence, § 582.

stantive requirement for the validity of wills is somewhat confusing for the test of the competency is their eligibility to give testimony in court. Nevertheless this frame of mind is necessary for an understanding of the matter. The statutes are unfortunate in using the word "witnesses." "Attesters" would have been a much better term.

Competence of the witnesses in the substantive law sense must exist at the time of the execution of the will.[24] If they are incompetent then but later become competent to testify, the will is invalid.[25] Conversely if they are competent at the time of making the will, their subsequent inability to testify does not invalidate the will.[26] The soundness of the general proposition cannot be doubted for the testator should not be obliged to take the risk of the attesters becoming incompetent or dying before his own death.

There is a further problem. Is the competence of the attester to be determined by the procedural law of competency of witnesses at the time of passage of the Statute of Frauds or the particular wills' statute, or at the time of the execution or probate of the will? This is a matter of some importance for many persons are competent to testify today who were not at the time of the enactment of the Statute of Frauds, or even of the wills' statutes of our various states.[27] Unfortunately the answer is not clear and most cases are not articulate upon this point.[28] When the matter is discussed in the authorities it is generally assumed that competence is to be tested by the procedural law in force at the time of execution of the will.[29] However, it is sometimes

24 See authorities, supra notes 9, 19. The statutes frequently so declare. Bordwell, supra note 18 at 19.

25 Britt v. Darnell, 315 Ill. 385, 146 N.E. 510, 1925; Giddings v. Turgeon, 58 Vt. 106, 4 A. 711, 1886 (change of law). Vrooman v. Powers, 47 Ohio St. 191, 24 N.E. 267, 8 L.R.A. 39, 1890 (release of interest). See infra notes 62–65.

26 In re Delavergne's Will, 259 Ill. 589, 102 N.E. 1081, 1913 (purchase of devisee's share); Thorpe v. Bestwick, 6 Q.B.D. 311, 1881 (subsequent marriage to devisee). See, also, Wisehart v. Applegate, 172 Ind. 313, 88 N.E. 501, 1909; Renwick v. Macomber, 233 Mass. 530, 124 N.E. 670, 1919.

27 See infra notes 33, 34, 77.

28 See infra notes 29, 30, 35, 36, 50 et seq.

29 See Kumpe v. Coons, 63 Ala. 448, 1879; White v. Bower, 56 Colo. 575, 136 P. 1053, Ann.Cas.1917A 835, 1913; Hudson v. Flood, 5 Boyce (Del.) 450, 94 A. 760, 1915, noted, 64 U. of Pa.L.R. 93; Elliot v. Brent, 17 D.C. (6 Mackey) 98, 1887; Kaufman v. Murray, 182 Ind. 372, 105 N.E. 466, Ann.Cas.1917A 832, 1914; Pfaffenberger v. Pfaffenberger, 189 Ind. 507, 127 N.E. 766, 1920; Calvert v. Calvert, 208 Ky.

inferred that the concept of who is a proper attesting witness has not kept pace with the changes in the procedural law. In other words the test of who is a competent attester may have solidified around the earlier rules of evidence. At least this is true to some extent in certain jurisdictions.[30] Therefore, in the selection of attesting witnesses it would be prudent to obtain persons who would qualify not only as witnesses in court at the present time but also would have been suitable to be sworn in upholding the will when the Statute of Frauds was enacted.

*Devisees and Legatees*

Application of the last-discussed problem is illustrated by the cases where a witness is named as devisee or legatee under the will. At the time of the passage of the Statute of Frauds, interest disqualified a witness to testify, so that a beneficiary under the will would not be a competent attester.[31] If competency of attesting witnesses is to be determined by the procedural law at the date of the Statute of Frauds,[32] a devisee-witness would not be a valid attesting witness to the will. On the other hand modern statutes have removed interest as a ground of disqualification to testify generally.[33] If it is the modern procedural law that determines the competency of attesters, then the devisee or legatee witness is competent, unless the situation comes within the statutory exception that the survivor of a transaction may not testify against the successors of the deceased party. Almost every jurisdiction [34] has a statute which retains this fragment of the old rule that interest disqualifies. These statutes are differently worded in the various jurisdictions and have received

760, 271 S.W. 1082, 1925; Leitch v. Leitch, 114 Md. 336, 79 A. 600, 1911; In re Wiese's Estate, 98 Neb. 463, 153 N.W. 556, L.R.A.1915E 832, 1915; Hayden v. Hayden, 107 Neb. 806, 186 N.W. 972, 25 A.L.R. 305, 1922; In re Estate of Charles, 118 Neb. 634, 225 N.W. 869, 64 A.L.R. 1299, 1929. See Foster, Interest as a Disqualification for Attesting Witnesses in Nebraska, 22 Neb.L.R. 103.

30 Caesar v. Burgess, 103 F.2d 503, C.C.A.Okl.1939; Jones v. Habersham, 63 Ga. 146, 1879; Smith v. Goodell, 258 Ill. 145, 101 N.E. 255; Scott v. O'Connor-Couch, 271 Ill. 395, 111 N.E. 272, L.R.A.1916D 179, 1915, noted, 29 Harv.L.R. 795, 11 Ill.L.R. 207; Miltenberger v. Miltenberger, 78 Mo. 27, 1883; Hodgman v. Kittredge, 67 N.H. 254, 32 A. 158, 68 Am.St.Rep. 661, 1892. And see Sparhawk v. Sparhawk, 10 Allen (Mass.) 155, 1865 (express statute that later procedural statutes do not affect). And see Bordwell, supra note 18 at 18.

31 See supra notes 10, 11.

32 See supra note 30.

33 Wigmore on Evidence, §§ 488, 576, 577.

34 Wigmore on Evidence, §§ 488, 578.

diverse constructions by the respective courts. In the majority of the states where the question has been passed upon, the so-called dead man's statutes have been held not to apply to the situation, so that the devisee or legatee witness is a competent one.[35] However, this whole question is often academic today under modern statutes which expressly invalidate legacies to attesters.[36] By force of this legislation the legatee-attester is clearly a competent attester under any procedural test since he loses his interest under the statute.

An indirect interest such as membership by the attester in a church,[37] or society,[38] which is benefited by the will, or the fact that he is a taxpayer,[39] in a municipality which is a devisee or legatee does not render him an improper attester. Even if interest is fatal, it must be a direct pecuniary one. Mere sharing in the general benefits of the gift to a town, club or church is not sufficient to disqualify. On the other hand, if the benefit is direct, though small, it makes the attester incompetent in those jurisdictions where interest disqualifies.[40] The fact that the benefici-

35 Kumpe v. Coons, 63 Ala. 448, 1879; Hudson v. Flood, 5 Boyce (28 Del.) 450, 94 A. 760, 1915, noted, 64 U. of Pa.L.R. 93; Hiatt v. McColley, 171 Ind. 91, 85 N.E. 772, 1908; Kaufman v. Murray, 182 Ind. 372, 105 N.E. 466, Ann.Cas.1917A 832, 1914; Pfaffenberger v. Pfaffenberger, 189 Ind. 507, 127 N.E. 766, 1920; In re Wiese's Estate, 98 Neb. 463, 153 N.W. 556, L.R.A.1915E, 832, 1915. Contra: In re Otting's Estate, 57 S.D. 420, 233 N.W. 274, 1930; Calvert v. Calvert, 208 Ky. 760, 271 S.W. 1082, 1925. See note, 23 Ry.Mt.L.R. 458.

36 See infra note 50 et seq.

37 Jones v. Habersham, 63 Ga. 146, 1879; Warren v. Baxter, 48 Me. 193, 1859; Conrades v. Heller, 119 Md. 448, 87 A. 28, 1859.

38 Appeal of Cox, 126 Me. 256, 137 A. 771, 53 A.L.R. 208, 1927; Jones v. Habersham, supra note 37; In re Ralston's Estate, 290 Pa. 374, 139 A. 129, 1927; Kennett v. Kidd, 87 Kan. 652, 125 P. 36, 44 L.R.A.,N.S., 544, Ann.Cas.1914A 592, 1912; Rockland Trust Co. v. Bixby, 247 Mass. 449, 142 N.E. 107, 1924; In re Channon's Estate, 266 Pa. 417, 109 A. 756, 1920. Statutes sometimes provide that the persons named in this and the preceding and subsequent note shall be competent attesters. Bordwell, Statute Law of Wills, 14 Ia.L.R. 1, 22. In Pennsylvania it is provided that the attesting witnesses to a charitable bequest or devise should not be interested in such religious or charitable use. See In re Kisner's Estate, 254 Pa. 597, 99 A. 168, 1916; In re Crozer's Estate, 296 Pa. 48, 145 A. 697, 1928, noted, 14 Minn.L.R. 197.

39 In re Marston, 79 Me. 25, 8 A. 87, 1887 (bequest to worthy poor of the town); Hawes v. Humphrey, 9 Pick.(Mass.) 350, 20 Am.Dec. 481, 1830 (money to establish public school); Hitchcock v. Shaw, 160 Mass. 140, 35 N.E. 671, 1893 (money for maintenance of public library); In re Potter's Will, 89 Vt. 361, 95 A. 646, 1915.

40 Crowell v. Tuttle, 218 Mass. 445, 105 N.E. 980, 1914 (attester being the guarantor of a note given by a church to whom a legacy of $300 was given);

ary's interest may depend upon the happening of a contingency prior to the testator's death will not render him a competent witness, even though the contingency does not occur.[41] One who is a direct beneficiary under a trust created by a will is disqualified as a witness by reason of his interest.[42]

*Executors and Trustees*

The prevailing rule is that the person named as executor, or an employee, officer or director of a corporate executor, is not disqualified from acting as a witness to the will.[43] This is based upon the theory that the personal representative does not receive his fees gratis, but earns them. The minority of jurisdictions, holding to the contrary, evidently proceed upon the basis that the chance to gain lucrative employment as executor is a substantial benefit amounting to a disqualifying interest.[44] The same difference of opinion is found in case that the attesting witness is a

In re Kelly's Estate, 236 Pa. 54, 84 A. 593, 1912. See Clark v. Johnson, 268 Ky. 591, 105 S.W.2d 576, 1937 (legacy of priest for saying masses); cf. In re Ainsworth's Estate, 102 Colo. 392, 79 P.2d 1045, 1938.

41 In re Trinitarian Congregational Church & Society of Castine, 91 Me. 416, 40 A. 325, 1898.

42 In re Fleetwood, L.R. 15 Ch.D. 594, 609, 1880.

43 Fontaine v. Fontaine, 169 Ark. 1077, 277 S.W. 867, 1925; In re Haupt's Estate, 200 Cal. 147, 252 P. 597, 1926; Farmers' Loan & Trust Co. of Columbia City v. Security Trust Co. of Indianapolis, 79 Ind. App. 537, 138 N.E. 97, 1923, noted, 23 Col.L.R. 599; Rockland Trust Co. v. Bixby, 247 Mass. 449, 142 N.E. 107, 1924; In re Ferguson's Estate, 295 Mich. 576, 295 N.W. 318, 1940; Geraghty v. Kilroy, 103 Minn. 286, 114 N. W. 838, 1908; Hayden v. Hayden, 107 Neb. 806, 186 N.W. 972, 25 A.L.R. 305, 1922; Stewart v. Harriman, 56 N.H. 25, 22 Am.Rep. 408, 1875; In re Archambault's Estate, 308 Pa. 549, 162 A. 801, 1932; Moos v. First State Bank, 60 S.W.2d 888, Tex.Civ.App.1933; State ex rel. Schirmer v. Superior Court for Spokane County, 143 Wash. 578, 255 P. 960, 1927. See annotations, 15 Ann.Cas. 789, L.R.A.1916D 185. And see in re Rehard's Estate, 163 Iowa 310, 143 N.W. 1106, 1913, where the testator provided that the person attesting should act as attorney for the executor. Statutes sometimes provide that the person named as executor is a proper attesting witness to the will. Bordwell, Statute Law of Wills, 14 Ia.L.R. 1, 21; Salyers v. Salyers, 186 Va. 927, 45 S.E.2d 481, 1947.

44 Allison's Ex'rs v. Allison, 11 N. N.C. 141, 1825; Smith v. Goodell, 258 Ill. 145, 101 N.E. 255, 1913. See note, 4 Ill.L.R. 427. By statute in Illinois the executor-attester now loses his appointment without affecting the validy of the will. Scott v. O'Connor-Couch, supra note 30; Olson v. Larson, 320 Ill. 50, 150 N.E. 337, 1926; Lawndale Nat. Bank of Chicago v. Kaspar Am. State Bank, 288 Ill.App. 555, 6 N.E.2d 670, 1937; cf. Auerbach v. Continental Illinois Nat. B. & T. Co., 340 Ill.App. 64, 91 N.E.2d 144, 1950 (attester was attorney for executor).

trustee under the will. The majority does not regard this as a disqualification.[45]

*Creditors*

One is no longer disqualified as an attesting witness by reason of being a creditor of the testator. At the present time testator's land is charged by law with the payment of his debts,[46] so that a creditor has the right to reach the real property regardless of any provision in the will to this effect.[47] Usually he is not interested in the sustaining of the will in order to obtain payment of his claim.

*Heirs*

If the attesting witness is also an heir at law of testator, he does not have a disqualifying interest unless the share which he takes by the will exceeds that which he would take in case of intestacy.[48] Indeed, if the testamentary gifts to the heir are less than his intestate share, his interest is against the establishment of the will. Statutes in many jurisdictions provide that the heir is a competent attester but can take no more than his intestate share.[49]

*Statutes Avoiding Interest*

One reason why we are unable to say with definiteness whether interest now prevents one from being a competent attester is that, as did the Statute of George II, legislation in most states de-

45 In re Haupt's Estate, supra note 43; Lord v. Miller, 277 Mass. 276, 178 N.E. 649, 1932; In re Baughman's Estate, 281 Pa. 23, 126 A. 58, 1924; In re Wiese's Estate, 98 Neb. 463, 153 N. W. 556, L.R.A.1915E 832, 1915, noted, 14 Mich.L.R. 84. But see Olson v. Larson, supra note 44 (appointment of trustee void but trust is enforceable); Lawndale Nat. Bank of Chicago v. Kaspar Am. State Bank, supra note 44.

46 See infra §§ 110, 127.

47 Yet statutes in some twenty-seven jurisdictions declare the creditor-witness is competent. Bordwell, Statute Law of Wills, 14 Ia.L.R. 1, 21. Such a statute can now have little meaning.

48 Smalley v. Smalley, 70 Me. 545, 35 Am.Rep. 353, 1880; Sparhawk v. Sparhawk, 10 Allen (Mass.) 155, 1865; Coffman v. Hedrick, 32 W.Va. 119, 9 S.E. 65, 1899; In re Hoppe's Will, 102 Wis. 54, 78 N.W. 183, 1899. See In re Charles' Estate, 118 Neb. 634, 225 N. W. 869, 64 A.L.R. 1299, 1929.

49 See Bordwell, Statute Law of Wills, 14 Ia.L.R. 24. In Re Knapp's Will, 102 Vt. 143, 146 A. 253, 1929, a curiously worded statute resulted in the heir-legatee losing his legacy if his spouse was an attesting witness, though if he had been the attesting witness he could have taken up to his intestate share.

clares that a legacy or bequest to an attesting witness is void.[50] In addition, it has been held that the Statute of George II, being passed before the separation with the mother country, applies in absence of state legislation on the subject.[51] To the extent that these statutes apply, they relieve all doubts as to the competency of the interested attesters. Even if interest would disqualify an attesting witness, the attester-legatee is competent since he cannot take his bequest. Most statutes are so worded as to render the gift to the attester invalid unless there are a sufficient number of other competent witnesses.[52] The effect is to render the legacy or bequest to the attesting witness ineffective but to sustain the will in other respects.[53] Under most statutes the legatee-attester loses his legacy regardless of whether or not under the existing procedural law he would otherwise be competent to give testimony in support of the will. Ordinarily then, the question of whether interest disqualifies an attester is never reached.

A number of states have statutes which provide for loss of the attester's legacies only if the will cannot be otherwise proved or established.[54] Such provisions have given rise to controversy in cases where the law permits probate of the will on the testimony of a single witness. The view has been taken that the attester loses his legacy by the very act of attesting since otherwise he would not be a competent attester and without him the will would lack the required number.[55] Motivated by the desire to uphold legacies wherever possible, other courts have held that if the will is probated without the testimony of the legatee witness he does not lose his legacy.[56] This position led to an unfortunate

50 See Bordwell, Statute Law of Wills, 14 Ia.L.R. 24.

51 Elliot v. Brent, 17 D.C.(6 Mackey) 98, 1887. But see Hudson v. Flood, 5 Boyce (Del.) 450, 94 A. 760, 1915.

52 See infra note 72 et seq.

53 In re Puckett's Estate, 240 Iowa 986, 38 N.W.2d 593, 1949; In re Knutson's Estate, 144 Minn. 111, 174 N.W. 617, 1919; State ex rel. Schirmer v. Superior Court for Spokane County, 143 Wash. 578, 255 P. 960, 1927; In re Johnson's Estate, 170 Wis. 436, 175 N.W. 917, 1920 (the fact that two other persons who did not subscribe as witnesses saw the execution does not prevent the loss of the legacy by the attester). See Williams v. Way, 135 Ga. 103, 68 S.E. 1023, 1910 (where all witnesses were legatees—their devises void and will otherwise valid).

54 Bordwell, supra note 50.

55 Wiley v. Gordan, 181 Ind. 252, 104 N.E. 500, 1914; Fowler v. Stagner, 55 Tex. 393, 1881; Scandurro v. Beto, 234 S.W.2d 695, Tex.Civ.App. 1950; Bruce v. Shuler, 108 Va. 670, 62 S.E. 973, 35 L.R.A.,N.S., 686, 15 Ann.Cas. 887, 1908.

56 Doyle v. Brady, 170 Ky. 316, 185 S.W. 1133, 1916; Matter of Walters, 285 N.Y. 158, 33 N.E.2d 72, 133 A.L.R.

result in a New York case where both witnesses were legatees; one testified and so lost his legacy; the other left the state and the will was probated without his testimony, with the uneven result that the latter was permitted to take.[57]

*The Spouse of the Beneficiary*

Following the English Wills Act, 1837, a number of our states invalidate testamentary gifts to the spouse of the attesting witness.[58] Under legislation of this sort, the attester is a proper one, though of course his spouse loses the legacy or devise.[59] In absence of statutes of this kind, three different positions have been taken as to the effect of a witness being the husband or wife of a devisee or legatee. Some courts, which adhere to the view that interest disqualifies, take the strict view that the witness is incompetent and the entire will fails.[60] If the disqualification is not removed by statutory provision taking away the interest, the logic seems unescapable, for at common law one spouse could not testify in behalf of the other. A second view is followed elsewhere, either upon the theory that the interest of his spouse no longer disqualifies the attester, or because the spouses are now regarded as separate entities for this purpose in the law.[61] Probably the modern tendency, as well as the weight of authority,

1283, 1941, noted, 20 Chi-Kent L.R. 109, 41 Col.L.R. 1130, 26 Corn.L.Q. 739, 53 Harv.L.R. 858, 27 Iowa L.R. 163, 18 N.Y.U.L.Q.R. 603, 50 Yale L. J. 701; Davis v. Davis, 43 W.Va. 300, 27 S.E. 323, 1897.

57 Matter of Walters, supra note 56. This decision led to an amendment of N. Y. Decedent Estate Law § 27 providing that an attesting witness cannot take a legacy unless there are two other disinterested witnesses. See note, 17 St. John's L.R. 50; cf. note, 53 Harv.L.R. 858.

58 See Bordwell, Statute Law of Wills, 14 Ia.L.R. 1, 23.

59 Rowlett v. Moore, 252 Ill. 436, 96 N.E. 835, Ann.Cas.1912D 346, 1911; Powers v. Codwise, 172 Mass. 425, 52 N.E. 525, 1898; Vester v. Collins, 101 N.C. 114, 7 S.E. 687, 1888.

60 Caesar v. Burgess, 103 F.2d 503, C.C.A.Okl.1939 (Oklahoma law); Fearn v. Postlethwaite, 240 Ill. 626, 88 N.E. 1057, 1909; In re Clark, 114 Me. 105, 95 A. 517, Ann.Cas.1917A 837, 1915; Sullivan v. Sullivan, 106 Mass. 478, 1871; Hodgman v. Kittredge, 67 N.H. 254, 32 A. 158, 68 Am.St.Rep. 661, 1892; Giddings v. Turgeon, 58 Vt. 106, 4 A. 711, 1886.

61 White v. Bower, 56 Colo. 575, 136 P. 1053, Ann.Cas.1917A 835, 1914; In re Williams' Estate, 158 Kan. 734, 150 P.2d 336, 1944; In re Holt's Will, 56 Minn. 33, 57 N.W. 219, 22 L.R.A. 481, 45 Am.St.Rep. 434, 1893, noted, 7 Harv.L.R. 500; Gore v. Dace, 157 Miss. 221, 127 So. 901, 1930; Hayden v. Hayden, 107 Neb. 806, 186 N.W. 972, 25 A.L.R. 305, 1922; Lippincott v. Wikoff, 54 N.J.Eq. 107, 33 A. 305, 1895; In re Otting's Estate, 57 S.D. 420, 233 N.W. 274, 1930; Gamble v. Butchee, 87 Tex. 643, 30 S.W. 861, 1895.

accepts this position which of course has the effect of sustaining both the will and the legacy or devise to the attester's spouse. A third view has also been taken: that the gift to the spouse of the witness is avoided but the will is otherwise valid.[62]

*Release of Interest*

In a few states the witness may become competent by releasing the interest under the will.[63] This view is, however, out of harmony with the general principle that competency must exist at the time of the execution of the will. The orthodox and the prevailing position is that release of interest by the attester cannot sustain a will which would otherwise be invalid.[64] Often the attester cannot release the interest effectively, as in case the gift is to his spouse or to a partnership or corporation in which he is interested.[65]

*The Spouse of Testator*

Because of the common-law fiction of legal identity, a wife was not a competent witness to her husband's will,[66] nor was a husband to his wife's will.[67] Probably these decisions would not be followed today under the modern legislation relating to husband and wife.[68] However, the witness spouse could not take more than his intestate share in most jurisdictions even if the will gave him more.[69]

[62] Kaufman v. Murray, 182 Ind. 372, 105 N.E. 466, Ann.Cas.1917A 832, 1914; Winslow v. Kimball, 25 Me. 493, 1846; Jackson ex dem. Cooder v. Woods, 1 Johns.Cas. (N.Y.) 163, 1799. This has been criticized as judicial legislation. Caesar v. Burgess, Sullivan v. Sullivan, Hodgman v. Kittredge, all supra note 60.

[63] Rockafellow v. Rockafellow, 192 Ark. 563, 93 S.W.2d 321, 1936; Grimm v. Tittman, 113 Mo. 56, 20 S.W. 664, 1892 (statute); Nixon v. Armstrong, 38 Tex. 296, 1873; see also Wehrkamp v. Burnett, 82 Colo. 5, 256 P. 630, 1927.

[64] Caesar v. Burgess, 103 F.2d 503, C.C.A.Okl.1939; Smith v. Goodell, supra note 61; In re Trinitarian Congregational Church & Society of Castine, 91 Me. 416, 40 A. 325, 1898; Allison's Ex'rs v. Allison, 11 N.C. 141, 1825; Vrooman v. Powers, 47 Ohio St. 191, 24 N.E. 267, 8 L.R.A. 39, 1890

[65] Smith v. Goodell, 258 Ill. 145, 101 N.E. 255, 1913.

[66] Pease v. Allis, 110 Mass. 157, 14 Am.Rep. 591, 1872.

[67] Dickinson v. Dickinson, 61 Pa. 401, 1869; Gump v. Gowans, 226 Ill. 635, 80 N.E. 1086, 117 Am St.Rep. 275, 1907; Smith v. Jones, 68 Vt. 132, 34 A. 424, 1896.

[68] Pritchard v. Pritchard, 93 Ind. App. 89, 177 N.E. 502, 1931, noted, 7 Ind.L.J. 327; West v. West, 131 Miss. 880, 95 So. 739, 29 A.L.R. 226, 1923.

[69] See supra note 49.

### *Heirs of Beneficiaries*

The fact that the attester is the heir of a beneficiary under the will has no effect either on the will or on the legacies or devises.[70] Such person takes nothing directly under the will. Aside from the husband or wife of an interested party, the common law did not disqualify relatives of interested parties.[71] Modern legislation, if it has any bearing, certainly does not render any one incompetent who was competent at common law. If anything, the present statutory law has the effect of increasing the classes of persons who are competent to testify, and hence to attest a will.

### *Supernumerary Witnesses*

In most states there is legislation providing that if there are sufficient other competent witnesses, the entire will, including gifts to supernumerary witness, is valid.[72] Possibly the same result would be reached in absence of statute, at the present time.[73] However, if two witnesses are necessary to the validity of a will and three persons sign as attesters two of whom are beneficiaries, it has been declared that both of the latter must lose their interest.[74] A different result has been reached by an early New York decision, invalidating the legacy to the first of the interested witnesses but sustaining the gift to the other.[75] It seems

[70] Speer v. Josenhans, 274 Ill. 237, 113 N.E. 622, 1916; Jones v. Tebetts, 57 Me. 572, 1870; Maxwell v. Hill, 89 Tenn. 584, 15 S.W. 253, 1891. Accord, though witness would take under anti-lapse statute due to death of the legatee. Matter of Ackerina, 195 Misc. 383, 90 N.Y.S.2d 794, 1949; cf. In re George's Estate, 175 Misc. 804, 25 N.Y.S.2d 333, 1940. The guardian of the beneficiary under the will is a competent witness. In re Look, 129 Me. 359, 152 A. 84, 1930. Possibly where common-law dower still exists, the wife of a devisee may be an incompetent witness. See Evans, Competency of Testamentary Witnesses, 25 Mich.L.R. 239, 249.

[71] Wigmore on Evidence, § 600. See In re Ferguson's Estate, 295 Mich. 576, 295 N.W. 318, 1940.

[72] Bordwell, Statute Law of Wills, 14 Ia.L.R. 1, 24. See Bruce v. Shuler, 108 Va. 670, 62 S.E. 973, 35 L.R.A., N.S., 686, 15 Ann.Cas. 887, 1908; Calvert v. Calvert, 208 Ky. 760, 271 S.W. 1082, 1925; Matter of Owen, 48 App. Div. 507, 62 N.Y.S. 919, 1900.

[73] See Wisehart v. Applegate, 172 Ind. 313, 88 N.E. 501, 1909; Caw v. Robertson, 5 N.Y. 125, 1851; Evans, The Competency of Testamentary Witnesses, 25 Mich.L.R. 238, 265. And see note, 9 Can.B.R. 47. But see the English cases cited ibid.; Patanska v. Kuznia, 102 N.J.Eq. 408, 141 A. 88, 1928, criticized, 77 U. of Pa.L.R. 142.

[74] Nixon v. Armstrong, 38 Tex. 296, 1873.

[75] Caw v. Robertson, 5 N.Y. 125, 1851, approved, 77 U. of Pa.L.R. 142. See supra note 57 as to present rule in New York.

artificial to favor one witness merely because he has signed after the other.

*Miscellaneous*

The competency of a person convicted of crime to act as an attesting witness seems to depend upon whether qualifications are tested by the earlier law, or by the present-day rules relating to testimony of witnesses. If the former, the convict would not be a proper witness,[76] while in the latter event he would be.[77] Of course on principles already announced,[78] conviction after the date of the execution should have no effect. A minor may be a good attester if he has the capacity to observe, remember and relate the facts concerning the execution of a will.[79] A person is not disqualified from acting as attesting witness by reason of being the probate judge,[80] the attorney drafting the will,[81] or the person who acts as proxy in signing testator's name to the will.[82]

[76] O'Connell v. Dow, 182 Mass. 541, 66 N.E. 788, 1903; Pendock v. Mackender, 2 Wils.K.B. 18, 95 Eng.Rep. 662, 1755.

[77] Few jurisdictions retain incompetency on account of conviction of crime. See Wigmore on Evidence, §§ 575, 595, 598, 603.

[78] See supra notes 24–26.

[79] Jones v. Tebbetts, 57 Me. 572, 1870; Collis v. Walker, 272 Mass. 46, 172 N.E. 228, 1930 (here the witnesses were husband, wife and their minor son); Spier v. Spier, 99 Neb. 853, 157 N.W. 1014, L.R.A.1916E, 692, 1916; Carlton v. Carlton, 40 N.H. 14, 1859. In Louisiana the statute provides the attesters must be at least sixteen, while in Arizona and Texas they must be fourteen or over. Bordwell, Statute Law of Wills, 14 Ia.L.R. 1, 22. See also infra § 78, notes 16–18 for qualification of witnesses in Louisiana.

[80] Patten v. Tallman, 27 Me. 17, 1847. Cf. Martin v. Long, 200 Ala. 210, 75 So. 968, 1917; Sullivan v. Brabason, 264 Mass. 276, 162 N.E. 312, 1928.

[81] In re Ferguson's Estate, 295 Mich. 576, 295 N.W. 318, 1940 (attorney-executor and his wife); In re Miller's Estate, 10 Wash.2d 258, 116 P.2d 526, 1941; In re Lane's Estate, 50 Wyo. 119, 58 P.2d 415, 1936.

[82] Van Meter v. Van Meter, 183 Md. 614, 39 A.2d 752, 1944; In re Mimey's Estate, 149 Okl. 85, 299 P. 199, 1927; Ex parte Leonard, 39 S.C. 518, 18 S.E. 216, 22 L.R.A. 302, 1893.

## MAKING OR ACKNOWLEDGING SIGNATURE BEFORE WITNESSES

**66. A few statutes require signing by the testator in the presence of the witnesses, but most jurisdictions also permit an acknowledgment to them of his signature as an alternative. In the states where the legislation follows the modern English Wills Act, there are no other alternatives and in case of an acknowledgment the testator's signature must be visible to the witnesses. In most other jurisdictions authentication by the testator may also be effected by acknowledgment of the instrument as a will, regardless of whether the witnesses see the testator's signature.**

Having seen the necessity and nature of the testator's signature,[1] the present section and those immediately following deal with the other aspects of execution—or what else must be done by the testator and what must be done by the witnesses. In almost all jurisdictions the statutes require that the witnesses must attest.[2] The present section deals with the concept of attestation and several specific matters that turn on this concept.

For this matter we go first to the statutes. While there are many individual peculiarities, a majority of our states follow the substance of the Statute of Frauds which provided that the will "shall be attested and subscribed in the presence of the said devisor by three or four credible witnesses." [3] Many of the statutes, however, are patterned after the English Act, 1837, which declared that "such signature shall be made or acknowledged by the testator in the presence of two or more witnesses present at the same time and such witnesses shall attest and shall subscribe the will in the presence of the testator." [4]

With few exceptions the American statutes require the witness to both attest and subscribe, but especially under laws such as the Statute of Frauds, it is not clear what constitutes the act of attestation.[5] While the word attestation is sometimes used to include the subscription of the witness's name, it is not so used in the English statutes. Surely to attest connotes more than merely to sign. Indeed the strict meaning of the two words is quite different. To attest means to bear witness, or to see and

1 See supra § 64.

2 Bordwell, Statute Law of Wills, 14 Ia.L.R. 1, 15.

3 Ibid. at 13, 15.

4 Ibid.

5 See also Model Probate Code §§ 46, 47. As to the mental aspects of attestation, see infra § 69. See also supra § 65, note 22.

hear as distinguished from signing. To what must the witness bear witness? The Statute of Frauds clearly indicates that it is the will which must be attested. It does not give any further clue, however, as to how this may be done. Possibly the English Wills Act also so intends, although it certainly is subject to the construction that it is the testator's signature rather than the will which is to be attested.[6] The latter statute makes up for the ambiguity in part by reciting certain details of the execution, which bear on the matter of attestation.[7]

*Signing in Witnesses' Presence*

When the will is signed by the testator in the presence of the witnesses, it has been held that they need not see him sign, as in case of inattention.[8] Nor is it necessary that they should actually see the signature if they saw testator in the act of writing it.[9] The question of what constitutes signing in the presence of the witnesses is identical with the problem of whether the witnesses have signed in testator's presence. These topics will be considered together later.[10]

*Acknowledgment Required?*

Under any statute, if the testator signs the will in the presence of the witnesses there need be no further authentication of his signature. Signing in the sight or presence of the witnesses is always sufficient.[11] Only in case that the testator has signed beforehand and outside of the witnesses' presence is there any need for considering the necessity for, and the sufficiency of, an acknowledgment.

*Acknowledgment Permitted?*

In a few states the statutes expressly provide that the witnesses must see the testator sign, or that the will must be signed in their presence.[12] These statutes are mandatory and do not permit ac-

[6] See infra note 21 et seq.

[7] Cf. Model Probate Code § 47.

[8] Peck v. Cary, 27 N.Y. 9, 84 Am. Dec. 220, 1863; Bullock v. Morehouse, 57 App.D.C. 231, 19 F.2d 705, 1927.

[9] Smith v. Smith, 1 P. & D. 143, 1866; Le Blanc v. Coombes, 325 Mass. 431, 91 N.E.2d 222, 1950.

[10] See infra § 72; also Green v. Davis, 228 Ala. 162, 153 So. 240, 1934; Wood v. Davis, 161 Ga. 690, 131 S.E. 885, 1926.

[11] Webster v. Yorty, 194 Ill. 408, 62 N.E. 907, 1902.

[12] So in Louisiana, New Mexico and Utah. See Bordwell, Statute Law of Wills, 14 Ia.L.R. 1, 13.

knowledgment of a prior signature by the testator.[13] Generally, however, the testator may either sign in the witnesses' presence or acknowledge his prior signature to them.

The acknowledgment by the testator of his signature was considered proper authentication by the testator under the Statute of Frauds.[14] American legislation of a similar kind has been likewise construed.[15] Of course this is expressly authorized by the English Wills Act, 1837, and the same is true of many American statutes.[16] Under statutes of the latter type there must be either a signing or acknowledgment of the signature before the witnesses.[17] The Statute of Frauds does not expressly require either, yet in some jurisdictions having provisions of this type one or the other has been regarded as mandatory.[18] Generally under similar legislation, neither is required and it is sufficient if the instrument is acknowledged as testator's will or as his act and deed.[19]

13 In re Alexander's Estate, 104 Utah 286, 139 P.2d 432, 1943, noted, 42 Mich.L.R. 940; see also In re Riedlinger's Will, 37 N.M. 18, 16 P.2d 549, 1932.

14 Ellis v. Smith, 1 Ves.Jr. 11, 30 Eng.Rep. 205, 1754 (overruling an earlier case to the contrary); White v. Trustees of British Museum, 6 Bing. 310, 130 Eng.Rep. 1299, 1829.

15 Massey v. Reynolds, 213 Ala. 178, 104 So. 494, 1925; Bullock v. Morehouse, 57 App.D.C. 231, 19 F.2d 705, 1927; Shewmake v. Shewmake, 144 Ga. 801, 87 S.E. 1046, 1916; Wersich v. Phelps, 186 Ind. 290, 116 N.E. 49, 1917; In re McElderry's Estate, 217 Iowa 268, 251 N.W. 610, 1934; Nunn v. Ehlert, 218 Mass. 471, 106 N.E. 163, L.R.A.1915B 87, 1914; In re Schneider's Will, 204 Wis. 94, 235 N.W. 412, 1931. But see a note by Professor Goodner indicating some doubt concerning whether acknowledgment is permitted under a statute similar to the Statute of Frauds, 6 Wash.L.R. 84.

16 In Arkansas, California, Colorado, Idaho, Montana, New Jersey, New York, North Dakota, Ohio, Oklahoma, Rhode Island and South Dakota the statutes provide for acknowledgment of the testator's signature as an alternative to signing by the testator in witnesses' presence. In Illinois, Kansas, Kentucky, Virginia and West Virginia the statutes specify acknowledgment of the will. See Bordwell, Statute Law of Wills, 14 Ia.L.R. 1, 14; Ohio Gen.Code, § 10504–3.

17 In re Halton's Estate, 111 N.J. Eq. 143, 161 A. 809, 1932; In re Redway's Will, 238 App.Div. 653, 265 N.Y.S. 848, 1933. An acknowledgment after an invalid execution is sufficient. In re Karrer's Will, 63 Misc. 174, 118 N.Y.S. 427, 1909.

18 Green v. Davis, 228 Ala. 162, 153 So. 240, 1934; Wood v. Davis, 161 Ga. 690, 131 S.E. 885, 1926; Nunn v. Ehlert, 218 Mass. 471, 106 N.E. 163, L.R.A.1915B 87, 1914; Tredick v. Bryant, 269 Mass. 50, 168 N.E. 162, 1929, noted, 28 Mich.L.R. 780. And see In re Droge's Will, 216 Iowa 331, 249 N.W. 209, 1933.

19 Betts v. Lonas, 84 U.S.App.D.C. 206, 172 F.2d 759, 1948; In re Carey's Estate, 56 Colo. 77, 136 P. 1175, 51 L.R.A.,N.S., 927, Ann.Cas.1915B 951,

### *Must See the Signature?*

Considerable controversy has centered around the question of whether the witnesses must see the testator's signature in case the will was not signed in testator's presence. Under the statutes of the type of the Wills Act, which expressly require one of these two alternatives, it is held that the acknowledgment is ineffective unless the testator's signature is visible to the witness.[20] This seems a sound construction of this legislation. On the other hand, this is unnecessary where the statute provides merely for acknowledgment of the will.[21] Under provisions such as contained in the Statute of Frauds, where the attestation of the will is the only thing called for, it should not be necessary for the witness to see the signature. This is the orthodox holding,[22] yet some courts, evidently influenced by decisions under legislation of the modern English Wills Act type, hold that there can be no sufficient acknowledgment unless the witnesses see the signature.[23]

### *What is Sufficient Acknowledgment?*

Where there must be acknowledgment of the signature, the production of the will by the testator with the signature in plain sight accompanied by a declaration that it is his will is sufficient.[24] Making a scroll after an existing signature has been held

1913; In re Dougherty's Estate, 168 Mich. 281, 134 N.W. 24, 38 L.R.A.,N.S., 161, Ann.Cas.1913B 1300, 1912; In re Johnston's Will, 225 Wis. 140, 273 N.W. 512, 1937; White v. Trustees of British Museum, 6 Bing. 310, 130 Eng.Rep. 1299, 1829; see In re Davis' Estate, 168 Kan. 314, 212 P.2d 343, 1949.

20 In re Keefe's Will, 155 App.Div. 575, 141 N.Y.S. 5, 1913, aff'd, 209 N.Y. 535, 102 N.E. 1104; In re Sage's Will, 90 N.J.Eq. 209, 107 A. 151, 1919, aff'd, 90 N.J.Eq. 580, 107 A. 445. But it has been held that it is enough if the witnesses are able to see the signature. Daintree v. Butcher and Fasulo, 13 P.D. 102, 1888; see Barber v. Henderson, 304 Mass. 3, 22 N.E.2d 620, 127 A.L.R. 382, 1939, noted, 25 Corn.L.Q. 469; note, 28 B.U.L.R. 73.

21 Hobart v. Hobart, 154 Ill. 610, 39 N.E. 581, 45 Am.St.Rep. 151, 1895; Robertson v. Robertson, 232 Ky. 572, 24 S.W.2d 282, 1930; and see cases supra note 19, and infra note 22.

22 Shewmake v. Shewmake, 144 Ga. 801, 87 S.E. 1046, 1916; Wersich v. Phelps, 186 Ind. 290, 116 N.E. 49, 1917; Lott v. Lott, 174 Minn. 13, 218 N.W. 447, 1928. See also cases notes 19, 21 supra.

23 In re Harter's Estate, 229 Iowa 238, 294 N.W. 357, 1940; Nunn v. Ehlert, 218 Mass. 471, 106 N.E. 163, L.R.A.1915B 87, 1914; Tredick v. Bryant, 269 Mass. 50, 168 N.E. 162, 1929, noted, 28 Mich.L.R. 780. Cf. Barber v. Henderson, supra note 20; Richardson v. Orth, 40 Or. 252, 66 P. 925, 69 P. 455, 1901.

24 In re Abbey's Estate, 183 Cal. 524, 191 P. 893, 1920; Appeal of Pope, 93 Conn. 53, 104 A. 241, noted, 27

a good acknowledgment thereof, though no words are spoken.[25] However, the bare presence of the testator when the witnesses sign is not an acknowledgment.[26] There must be something more than simple passivity.

## TESTATOR'S REQUEST TO WITNESSES

**67. Statutes in some states expressly require that the testator request the witnesses to act as such. Even in absence of such provision the courts make a similar requirement. However, a request is readily implied from the testator's acquiescence in the signing by the witnesses.**

### *Necessity of Request*

Statutes in a number of states expressly require that the testator should request that the witnesses attest and subscribe.[1] The purpose of this requirement is apparently that the testator should be privileged to choose, or at least assent to, the persons who act as witnesses to his will. Its function is to prevent bystanders from thrusting themselves forward at the time of the execution.[2] Probably most testators would not have desired that their wills should be invalid on this account. It is open to some question whether the enforcement of the principle may not cause more injustice than the evil at which the rule is aimed. In the liberal interpretation of what may be considered a request by the testator, the courts avoid much of the difficulty.[3]

In the majority of states there is no express requirement of a request,[4] but even here the courts usually declare that a request is necessary.[5] This is probably because acquiescence by the testator to the signing by the witnesses is a part of the attestation

Yale L.J. 847; Humphrey v. Wallace, 169 Kan. 58, 216 P.2d 781, 1950; In re Bragg's Estate, 106 Mont. 132, 76 P.2d 57, 1938. Cf. In re Redway's Will, 238 App.Div. 653, 265 N.Y.S. 848, 1933.

25 In re Halton's Estate, 111 N.J. Eq. 143, 161 A. 809, 1932. Cf. In re Dawley's Estate, 148 Misc. 828, 266 N.Y.S. 550, 1933.

26 In re Manners' Estate, 72 N.J.Eq. 854, 66 A. 583, 1907; Luper v. Werts, 19 Or. 122, 23 P. 850, 1890.

1 So in Arkansas, California, Idaho, Montana, New Mexico, New York, North Dakota, Oklahoma, South Dakota and Utah. See Bordwell, Statute Law of Wills, 14 Ia.L.R. 1, 16.

2 See Gilbert v. Knox, 52 N.Y. 125, 129, 1873.

3 See infra notes 8–11.

4 See Bordwell, supra note 1.

5 Huff v. Huff, 41 Ga. 696, 1871; In re Droge's Will, 216 Iowa 331, 249 N.W. 209, 1933; Moore v. Sanders,

and a concomitant of his acknowledgment of the instrument or of his signature. On the whole there is little difference between the two groups of states as to the language of the decisions on the point, or in the actual holdings.[6]

*Sufficiency of Request*

The courts agree that the request need not be an express oral one.[7] It may be implied from what the testator says or does.[8] A signing by the witnesses with the testator's consent,[9] or with his knowledge and approval may be considered to be with his implied request.[10] A request to the witnesses by the attorney who drew the will, or by some other person, acquiesced in by the testator is sufficient.[11] However, acquiescence amounting to a request was not implied when the testator was under the influence of drugs,[12] or when there was evidence of his mental incompetency.[13]

202 Ky. 286, 259 S.W. 361, 1924; Woodstock College of Baltimore County v. Farmers' & Mechanics' Nat. Bank of Frederick City, 129 Md. 675, 99 A. 962, 1917; In re Herring's Will, 152 N.C. 258, 67 S.E. 570, 1910. Cf. Burnham v. Grant, 24 Colo.App. 131, 134 P. 254, 1913; Thompson v. Thompson, 49 Neb. 157, 68 N.W. 372, 1896. Probably the court in the latter cases merely meant that an express request was not necessary. Cf. note, 32 Geo.L.R. 284. See also supra § 62.

6 See annotation, 125 A.L.R. 414 and notes 8–11 infra.

7 In re Johnson's Estate, 100 Cal. App. 676, 280 P. 987, 1908; Farmer's Ex'r v. Farmer's Ex'r, 213 Ky. 147, 280 S.W. 947, 1926; In re Silver's Estate, 98 Mont. 141, 38 P.2d 277, 1934; In re Heller's Will, 222 App. Div. 64, 225 N.Y.S. 244, 1927; In re Kelly's Will, 206 N.C. 551, 174 S.E. 453, 1934; In re Adam's Estate, 149 Okl. 90, 299 P. 226, 1931; In re Vaughn's Estate, 137 Wash. 512, 242 P. 1094, 1926. See infra § 68, note 10.

8 In re Davis' Will, 172 Or. 354, 142 P.2d 143, 1943 (handing pen to witness who signed and handed to second witness); and see cases supra note 7.

9 Ritchey v. Jones, 210 Ala. 204, 97 So. 736, 1923; see Burgan v. Kinnick, 225 Iowa 804, 281 N.W, 734, 1938.

10 In re Cosgrove's Estate, 290 Mich. 258, 287 N.W. 456, 125 A.L.R. 410, 1939; In re Lillibridge's Estate, 221 Pa. 5, 69 A. 1121, 128 Am.St.Rep. 723, 1908.

11 Ritchey v. Jones, supra note 9; In re Droge's Will, supra note 5; Green v. Pearson, 145 Miss. 23, 110 So. 862, 1927; Clark v. Crandall, 319 Mo. 87, 5 S.W.2d 383, 1928; In re Williams' Estate, 50 Mont. 142, 145 P. 957, 1915; Bouton v. Fleharty, 215 App.Div. 180, 213 N.Y.S. 455, 1926; aff'd 242 N.Y. 591, 152 N.E. 440; In re Miller's Estate, 146 Wash. 324, 262 P. 646, 1908.

12 In re Lyman's Will, 14 Misc. 352, 36 N.Y.S. 117, 1895.

13 In re Cummings' Estate, 92 Mont. 185, 11 P.2d 968, 1932.

## PUBLICATION

**68. Publication, or the signification by the testator to the witnesses that the instrument is his will, is not usually required in absence of express statutory provision. Only a minority of jurisdictions require publication and in no state is it necessary for the witnesses to know the contents of the will.**

### *Necessity of Publication*

Publication is the declaration or other manifestation by the testator to the witnesses that the instrument is his will. While the English Wills Act, 1837, does not require publication, most of the American jurisdictions which follow its general form have an express requirement of publication.[1] In several other American jurisdictions publication is also required.[2] Under provisions like the Statute of Frauds requiring the witnesses to attest and subscribe the will, it is arguable that publication is required. Conceivably one cannot bear witness to a will unless he knows that the instrument is a will. Early English cases took this view,[3] but it was later abandoned.[4] In America, publication is not generally required under legislation of this type.[5] This seems

[1] So in Arkansas, California, Colorado, Idaho, Montana, New Jersey, New York, North Dakota, Oklahoma, South Dakota, Tennessee, Utah, and also possibly New Mexico. See Bordwell, The Statute Law of Wills, 14 Ia.L.R. 1, 14; Model Probate Code § 47.

[2] In Kansas, Kentucky, Virginia, West Virginia the statute provides for acknowledgment of the will (as distinguished from the signature). See Bordwell, The Statute Law of Wills, 14 Ia.L.R. 1, 14. As acknowledgment of the will is substantially the same as publication, it would seem that there must be a publication in these jurisdictions if the witnesses did not see the testator sign. See Underwood v. Rutan, 101 Ohio St. 306, 128 N.E. 78, 1920, noted, 3 Cin.L.R. 191 (under former statute). Cf. Beane v. Yerby, 12 Grat. (Va.) 239, 1855. In Illinois, if the witnesses do not see the testator sign, the statute declares that the testator must acknowledge the instrument to be "his act and deed." Under this statute publication is unnecessary. Hoover v. Keller, 339 Ill. 126, 171 N.E. 163, 1930.

[3] Ross v. Ewer, 3 Atk. 156, 26 Eng. Rep. 892, 1744.

[4] Windham v. Chetwynd, 1 Burr. 414, 421, 97 Eng.Rep. 377, 381, 1757; Bond v. Seawell, 3 Burr. 1773, 1775, 97 Eng.Rep. 1092, 1093, 1765; Wright v. Wright, 7 Bing. 457, 131 Eng.Rep. 177, 1831. See, also, Daintree v. Fasulo, 13 P.D. 67, 1888, under the modern English Statute of Wills.

[5] Massey v. Reynolds, 213 Ala. 178, 104 So. 494, 1925; Slade v. Slade, 155 Ga. 851, 118 S.E. 645, 1923 (here testator deceived witnesses as to character of instrument—will held valid); In re Elkerton's Estate, 380 Ill. 394, 44 N.E.2d 148, 1942; In re Balk's Estate, 298 Mich. 303, 298 N.W. 779,

sound, for one may bear witness to a document which happens to be a will without knowing of its testamentary character. Moreover, even if the witnesses' knowledge of testamentary character were essential, this could be obtained from other sources than the testator's declaration.

If the question of the necessity of publication were one for judicial determination, it might be contended that publication would tend to fix the transaction in the witnesses' minds and to call their attention to the question of mental competency of the testator.[6] In reply to the latter argument it can be asserted that witnesses seldom think of this point—at least they could not be expected to have in mind the difference between the capacity required to make a will or another instrument. It is probably true that any advantage obtained by the fixation of the transaction in the witnesses' memory because of the publication is more than overcome by the undesirability of overturning a will because the testator has omitted to declare the testamentary character or because the witnesses fail to remember this.[7] Most jurisdictions have no legislative provision upon the subject and do not require publication.[8] However, in the states requiring publication, absence of this formality is fatal to the validity of the will.[9]

1941; Tyson v. Utterback, 154 Miss. 381, 122 So. 496, 63 A.L.R. 1188, 1929; Underwood v. Rutan, supra note 2 (when signed before witnesses); In re Neil's Estate, 111 Or. 282, 226 P. 439, 1924; In re Lillibridge's Estate, 221 Pa. 5, 69 A. 1121, 128 Am.St.Rep. 723, 1908; Long v. Mickler, 133 Tenn. 51, 179 S.W. 477, 1915; cf. Woodstock College of Baltimore County v. Hankey, 129 Md. 675, 99 A. 962, 1917. In Missouri, publication is evidently required though the statute does not so declare. Cone v. Donovan, 275 Mo. 557, 204 S.W. 1073, 1918. In a number of cases where the will was sustained, the court proceeds upon the theory that publication, or at least knowledge by the witnesses that the instrument is a will, is required though there is no express statutory requirement. Pope v. Rogers, 92 Conn. 248, 102 A. 583, 1917; In re Salmons' Will, 7 Boyce (Del.) 446, 108 A. 93, 1919; Leary v. Leary, 203 Ky. 344, 262 S.W. 293, 1924; Spier v. Spier, 99 Neb. 853, 157 N.W. 1014, L.R.A.1916E 692, 1914.

6 Fuller v. Williams, 125 Kan. 154, 264 P. 77, 1928 (the opinion here only insists that the witnesses have knowledge that the instrument is a will and does not in terms require publication).

7 Cf. supra § 67 following note 2.

8 See notes 1, 2, 5 supra.

9 In re Williams' Estate, 52 Mont. 192, 156 P. 1087, Ann.Cas.1917E 126, 1916; Hill v. Davis, 64 Okl. 253, 167 P. 465, L.R.A.1918B 687, 1917; In re Tiger's Will, 94 Okl. 103, 221 P. 441, 1923; In re Taylor's Estate, 39 S.D. 608, 165 N.W. 1079, 1917; In re Johnson's Estate, 115 N.J.Eq. 249, 171 A. 307, 1934.

*Sufficiency of Publication*

In point of fact, publication and request to witnesses are closely related. The same sentence may constitute both a declaration that the instrument is testator's will and also a request that the witnesses act as such.[10] There need be no express publication in the form of "this is my will."[11] Acts and signs may be sufficient.[12] Thus, the acquiescence of the testator in the statement of another that the document is testator's will is sufficient.[13] The witnesses must know that the instrument is testator's will;[14] furthermore he must know this from some word or act of the testator.[15] Knowledge from another source will not suffice.[16] Where the testator and one or more of the attesting witnesses do not speak the same language it would seem that the usual method of publication would be impossible.[17] When the witnesses have read the will or heard it read, and have seen the testator sign, this is the equivalent of a publication.[18] Publication does not require that the witnesses should know the contents of the will.[19] A valid publication may be before the testator signs, while

10 Coffin v. Coffin, 23 N.Y. 9, 80 Am. Dec. 235, 1861.

11 Aquilini v. Chamblin, 94 Colo. 367, 30 P.2d 325, 1934; In re Gordon's Estate, 48 Idaho 171, 279 P. 625, 1929; Pritchard v. Thomas, 192 S.W. 956, Mo.1917; In re Halton's Estate, 111 N.J.Eq. 143, 161 A. 809, 1932; Speaks v. Speaks, 98 Okl. 57, 224 P. 533, 1924; In re Taylor's Estate, supra note 9.

12 In re Gordon's Estate, supra note 11; Spier v. Spier, 99 Neb. 853, 157 N.W. 1014, L.R.A.1916E 692, 1914; In re Halton's Estate, supra note 11; Speaks v. Speaks, supra note 11; In re Taylor's Estate, supra note 9.

13 In re Cummings' Estate, 92 Mont. 185, 11 P.2d 968, 1932; Hildreth v. Marshall, 51 N.J.Eq. 241, 27 A. 465, 1893 (announcement to testator that witnesses were brought to witness his will).

14 In re Norswing's Estate, 47 Cal. App.2d 730, 118 P.2d 858, 1941; In re Dong Ling Hing's Estate, 78 Utah 324, 2 P.2d 902, 1931. See Robbins v. Robbins, 50 N.J.Eq. 742, 26 A. 673, 1893 (witness not paying attention).

15 In re Emden's Estate, 87 Cal. App.2d 115, 196 P.2d 627, 1948; In re Cummings' Estate, supra note 13.

16 In re Williams' Will, 50 Mont. 142, 145 P. 957, 1915; Gilbert v. Knox, 52 N.Y. 125, 1873; Hill v. Davis, 64 Okl. 253, 167 P. 465, L.R.A. 1918B 687, 1917, noted, 18 Col.L.R. 96, 66 U. of Pa.L.R. 89.

17 Hill v. Davis, supra note 16; In re Tiger's Will, 94 Okl. 103, 221 P. 441, 1923. See Kittleson's Estate, v. Kittleson, 42 S.D. 126, 173 N.W. 161, 1919. But see Hauer v. Hauer, 44 S.D. 375, 184 N.W. 1, 1921.

18 In re Salmons' Will, 7 Boyce (Del.) 446, 108 A. 93, 1919; In re Wilson's Will, 107 N.J.Eq. 604, 153 A. 107, 1931, affirmed, 110 N.J.Eq. 68, 158 A. 342; In re Clarke's Estate, 51 N.Y.S.2d 291, 1944.

19 Singleton v. Singleton, 269 Ky. 330, 107 S.W.2d 273, 1937; Redford v. Booker, 166 Va. 561, 185 S.E. 879, 1936.

he is in the act of signing, or even afterward if both are parts of the same transaction.[20] But if the declaration occurs on an occasion subsequent to the other acts of execution, it is ineffective,[21] though if the will is then before the parties it has been held sufficient.[22] When the testator has previously made an appointment for the witnesses to execute his will and presents a signed document at the time of the subsequent meeting, there need be no further publication.[23] A declaration while the witness has partially completed his signature is clearly in time.[24]

A mere request to the witnesses to sign the instrument is not a publication of it.[25] Acknowledgment of the signature does not constitute by itself publication of the will.[26] Nor does publication itself amount to an acknowledgment of the signature unless the latter is visible.[27] When the statute requires both, each must be done.

## ANIMUS ATTESTANDI

**69. The witnesses must sign with the intention of giving validity to the instrument as the act of the testator.**

The statutes in all jurisdictions require the witnesses to attest;[1] in most jurisdictions it is expressly provided that they must sign their names.[2] When only the word "attest" is used, it generally includes the idea of subscription.[3] Whether or not at-

[20] In re Gordon's Estate, supra note 11; In re Halton's Estate, supra note 11; In re Baldwin's Will, 67 Misc. 329, 124 N.Y.S. 612, 1910.

[21] In re Dale's Will, 56 Hun 169, 9 N.Y.S. 396, aff'd 134 N.Y. 614, 32 N.E. 649, 1892 (several weeks later). Cf. In re Baldwin's Will, supra note 20, where the declaration was made without separation as the parties were at luncheon together an hour later—will upheld.

[22] In re Meier's Will, 249 N.Y. 549, 164 N.E. 579, 1927.

[23] Robbins v. Robbins, 50 N.J.Eq. 742, 26 A. 673, 1893.

[24] In re Phillips' Will, 98 N.Y. 267, 1885.

[25] In re Delprat's Will, 27 Misc. 355, 58 N.Y.S. 768, 1899.

[26] See Ludlow v. Ludlow, 36 N.J.Eq. 597, 1883; In re Stover's Will, 104 Okl. 251, 231 P. 212, 1924; Moultrie v. Hunt, 23 N.Y. 394, 1861.

[27] See supra § 66.

[1] Bordwell, Statute Law of Wills, 14 Ia.L.R. 1, 15.

[2] Except in Illinois, Iowa, Mississippi, Pennsylvania and Wyoming. Ibid.

[3] International Trust Co. v. Anthony, 45 Colo. 474, 101 P. 781, 22 L.R.A.,N.S., 1002, 16 Ann.Cas. 1087, 1909; Sloan v. Sloan, 184 Ill. 579, 56 N.E. 952, 1907. The Pennsylvania statute has been construed not to require signing by witnesses except in the case of charitable gifts. See infra § 70, note 2.

testation includes the idea of subscription, it surely connotes something more than the physical acts of signing or seeing. Attestation is, in part at least, a state of mind. Whether the witnesses attest the instrument as the testator's will, or only as his act, or merely bear witness to the signature depends upon the individual statutes and their judicial construction.[4] Regardless of what it is that is attested, the witnesses must intend to act as witnesses, or the will is not valid. The mere presence of persons during the performance of the acts required by the statute, coupled with the fact that they sign the will, is not sufficient unless the witnesses have the requisite animus attestandi.[5]

This frame of mind may be satisfied though neither the persons signing the instrument nor the testator understand exactly the requirements of the law for a sufficient attestation. It is enough if the required number of persons sign for the purpose of validating the instrument. Thus, when one purports to take the acknowledgment of the testator or otherwise signs in the capacity of justice of the peace,[6] or notary,[7] or as executor,[8] the attestation has been held sufficient. A draftsman who subscribes his name "written by ———" has been held to be a proper wit-

4 See supra §§ 66, 68, also § 65 note 22.

5 In re Goods of Duggins, 22 L.T. N.S. 182, 1870; Baxter v. Bank of Belle of Belle Maries County, 340 Mo. 952, 104 S.W.2d 265, 1937, noted, 2 Mo.L.R. 532; and see infra notes 7, 12, 13.

6 Bolton v. Bolton, 107 Miss. 84, 64 So. 967, 1914; Tilton v. Daniels, 79 N.H. 368, 109 A. 145, 8 A.L.R. 1073, 1920. See, also, Franks v. Chapman, 64 Tex. 159 1885 (signed as county clerk); Keely v. Moore, 196 U.S. 38, 25 S.Ct. 169, 49 L.Ed. 376, 1904 (signed as vice consul).

7 Tyson v. Utterback, 154 Miss. 381, 122 So. 496, 63 A.L.R. 1183, 1929; Adams v. Norris, 23 How. 353, 16 L. Ed. 539, 1859; see also Gump v. Gowans, 226 Ill. 635, 80 N.E. 1086, 117 Am.St.Rep. 275, 1907; Ferguson v. Ferguson, 187 Va. 581, 47 S.E. 346, 1948. Cf. In re Hull's Will, 117 Iowa 738, 89 N.W. 979, 1902, where the certificate by the notary recited that the testator and two witnesses came before him and acknowledged the same to be their voluntary act and deed, this rebutted the inference that the notary acted animo attestandi. There is a line of cases holding that the notarial certificate is insufficient, based upon the notion that the notary signed only to give effect to an oath or acknowledgment. In re Montgomery's Estate, 89 Cal.App.2d 664, 201 P.2d 569, 1949; Baxter v. Bank of Belle of Belle Maries County, supra note 5; Matter of McDonough, 201 App.Div. 203, 193 N.Y.S. 734, 1922.

8 Griffiths v. Griffiths, L.R. 2 P. & D. 300, 1871. Cf. Snelgrove v. Snelgrove, 4 Desaus.(S.C.) 274, 1812, where the executor penned the will; held that the naming of himself as executor in the body of the will could not be deemed a signature as a witness, though he was present at the time of signing by the testator.

ness.[9] While the parties were evidently mistaken as to the necessity of the formality, the purporting to act in the official or other capacity is merely superfluous, as the parties do bear witness for the purpose of giving the will legal force and effect. In these cases, it may usually be said that the signers have a double intent, one of which is entirely unnecessary but the other is sufficient to validate the instrument.

A person who acting as proxy writes the testator's,[10] or witnesses',[11] names may also serve as a witness. But when he merely attaches his name for the purpose of indicating that he has signed the testator's,[12] or witnesses',[13] names, this is not animo attestandi. Likewise, a physician who signed a certificate of sound mind was not regarded as an attesting witness.[14]

The mental attitude of the purported witnesses, while not ordinarily drawn into question, may be a matter of great importance. Probably persons placing their names below that of the alleged testator at the latter's request, and upon his representation that the document was a political petition, would not be regarded as attesting witnesses if the instrument turned out to be one of testamentary character. However, it would seem improper to permit persons, who have seemingly complied with testator's request to act as witnesses to the will or the signature thereon, to declare later that they did so with a secret mental reservation that they did not intend to attest.[15] This would be a papable fraud on the testator; the spirit, at least, of the parol evidence rule would seem to call for the rejection of this testimony of private intention.[16]

9 Pollock v. Glassell, 2 Grat.(Va.) 439, 1846. Cf. infra notes 12–14.

10 Love v. Gibbs, 273 Ky. 775, 117 S.W.2d 987, 1938; Darnaby v. Halley's Ex'r, 306 Ky. 697, 208 S.W.2d 299, 1948; Van Meter v. Van Meter, 183 Md. 614, 39 A.2d 752, 1944. See also Ferguson v. Ferguson, supra note 7.

11 Smythe v. Irick, 46 S.C. 299, 24 S.E. 69, 32 L.R.A. 77, 57 Am.St.Rep. 684, 1896.

12 Cf. In re Rothstein's Estate, 133 Misc. 547, 233 N.Y.S. 235, 1929. But see Mortgage Bond Corp. of New York v. Haney, 105 S.W.2d 488, Tex. Civ.App.1937, and cases supra note 10.

13 In re Jones' Estate, 101 Wash. 128, 172 P. 206, 1918; In re Goods of Duggins, supra note 5.

14 Elston v. Price, 210 Ala. 579, 98 So. 573, 1923.

15 Love v. Gibbs, supra note 10; but see Fuller v. Williams, 125 Kan. 154, 264 P. 77, 1928, where the will was held invalid, partially because one of the witnesses testified that he signed merely in order to quiet the testator and not with the mind of attesting the will. This seems a very dangerous precedent.

16 Wigmore on Evidence, § 2414. See In re Paradis' Will, 87 A.2d 512, Me. 1952 (no attention to testator's mental state).

## WITNESSES' SIGNATURES

**70. The will must be signed by the witnesses though they need not sign their correct or full names. Signatures by mark or entirely by proxy are permitted as in case of testator's signature.**

**In all cases the witnesses must sign upon some paper attached to the will, though generally it need not be on any particular part thereof. Some statutes, however, require the witnesses' signatures to be at the end of the will.**

The most usual requirement for signature by witnesses is taken from the Statute of Frauds, that the will must be "attested and subscribed;" though a number of states require that each witness "shall sign his name as a witness".[1] A few statutes merely provided that the will be "attested" or "witnessed" but this has been held to require a signature by the witnesses.[2]

### *Sufficiency of Signature*

The general principles relative to what is sufficient in case of a testator's signature [3] apply to signature of the witnesses. A signature by initials has been held sufficient; [4] though if a witness wrote his first name and then desisted because of weakness, the will was held invalid as the intended act was not completed.[5] Use of an assumed name or other designation is not fatal.[6] Under a statute requiring a witness to sign his name, the writing by the witness of his own initials and the surname of the testator was held insufficient.[7] This opinion has been disapproved in an-

1 Bordwell, Statute Law of Wills, 14 Ia.L.R. 1, 16.

2 Ibid. at 15. See Sloan v. Sloan, 184 Ill. 579, 56 N.E. 952, 1900 (under statute requiring will to be "attested"); In re Irvine's Estate, 206 Pa. 1, 55 A. 795 (same—in case of charitable devises and bequests); In re Boyeus' Will, 23 Iowa 354, 1867 (statute requiring will to be witnessed). In Pennsylvania wills must be proved by witnesses, but except for charitable devises they need not sign the will. 20 P.S. §§ 180.2, 180.4. See Hutton, The Execution of Wills, 47 Dick.L.R. 23, 65 at 73; supra § 69, notes 1–3.

3 See supra § 64.

4 Lord v. Lord, 58 N.H. 7, 42 Am. Rep. 565, 1876.

5 Jackson ex dem. Van Dusen v. Van Dusen, 5 Johns. (N.Y.) 144, 4 Am. Dec. 330, 1809; Goods of Christian, 2 Rob. 110, 163 Eng.Rep. 1260, 1849.

6 In re Olliver, 2 Spinks Eccl. 57, 164 Eng.Rep. 305, 1854. Cf. In re Sperling, 3 Sw. & Tr. 272, 164 Eng. Rep. 1279, 1863, where witness simply signed "servant to Mr. Sperling". See Lord v. Lord, 58 N.H. 7, 42 Am. Rep. 565, 1876.

7 In re Walker's Estate, 110 Cal. 387, 42 P. 815, 1082, 30 L.R.A. 460, 52 Am.St.Rep. 104, 1895 (three judges dissenting).

other jurisdiction having an identical statute,[8] and doubtless it would not be followed in a jurisdiction which merely required the will to be signed or subscribed by the witness.[9]

While an attachment of a seal by the witness has been considered insufficient as a signature,[10] the witness' mark is sufficient.[11] It has been held a sufficient signature where the witness' hand was guided by another,[12] or even if he holds the top of the pen while another writes his name for him.[13] By the prevailing American rule the witnesses' names may be written entirely by another.[14] A different conclusion has been reached by some courts upon the ground that the statutes do not expressly authorize signature by another for the witnesses as they do in the case of the testator.[15] Moreover, there is not as much reason for the allowance of the signature by proxy in case of the witnesses as exists in case of the testator, because a witness is not unique and another can generally be obtained.

8 In re Jacobs' Will, 73 Misc. 162, 132 N.Y.S. 481, 1911.

9 Smith v. Buffum, 226 Mass. 400, 115 N.E. 669, L.R.A.1917D 897, 1917, noted, 17 Col.L.R. 571 (where witness copied another witness's surname instead of writing his own).

10 In re Byrd, 3 Curt.Eccl. 117, 163 Eng.Rep. 674, 1842.

11 Gillis v. Gillis, 96 Ga. 1, 23 S.E. 107, 30 L.R.A. 143, 51 Am.St.Rep. 121, 1895; Love v. Gibbs, 273 Ky. 775, 117 S.W.2d 987, 1938. But the mere retouching of the prior signature made outside of testator's presence by crossing an F in the testator's presence is not sufficient. Hindmarsh v. Chariton, 8 H.L.C. 160, 11 Eng.Rep. 388, 1861.

12 Campbell v. Logan, 2 Bradf.(N.Y.) 90, 1852; Harrison v. Elvin, 3 Q.B. 117, 1842. But see Dawkins v. Dawkins, 179 Ala. 666, 60 So. 289, 1912 (where testator's name also was signed by mark.)

13 Montgomery v. Perkins, 2 Metc. (Ky.) 448, 74 Am.Dec. 419, 1859; In re Pope's Will, 139 N.C. 484, 52 S.E. 235, 7 L.R.A.,N.S., 1193, 111 Am.St. Rep. 813, 4 Ann.Cas. 635, 1905 (even though the witness could write his own name), with which compare Riley v. Riley, 36 Ala. 496, 1860 (signature per alium of witness able to write, invalid).

14 Schnee v. Schnee, 61 Kan. 643, 60 P. 738, 1900; Lord v. Lord, 58 N.H. 7, 42 Am.Rep. 565, 1876; In re Humiston's Estate, 128 Misc. 71, 218 N.Y. S. 234, 1926; Wolber v. Rose, 92 Okl. 100, 218 P. 323, 1923; In re Crawford's Will, 46 S.C. 299, 24 S.E. 69, 32 L.R.A. 77, 57 A.S.R. 684, 1896; Jesse v. Parker's Adm'rs, 6 Grat.(Va.) 57, 52 Am.Dec. 102, 1849 (here the testator's name and those of all three witnesses were written by a single person).

15 Horton v. Johnson, 18 Ga. 396, 1855; Simmons v. Leonard, 91 Tenn. 183, 18 S.W. 280, 30 Am.St.Rep. 875, 1892. This seems to be the English rule. In re Goods of Duggins, 22 L.T. N.S. 182, 1870.

*Place of Signature*

If there is an attestation clause the normal place for witnesses to sign is below the clause; otherwise at the left of the testator's signature. However, in most jurisdictions their signatures at some other place is not fatal. Thus, signatures of witnesses in the attestation clause,[16] or above it,[17] have been held sufficient, as well as an attestation on the back of the will.[18] Even a signature in the margin opposite certain alterations has been held sufficient upon proof that the witnesses intended to bear witness to the whole will or to the testator's signature.[19] Without such explanation, however, a court might hold that this position of the signature shows an intent to bear witness merely to the alterations. Under somewhat similar circumstances wills have been held invalid on account of the unusual and unexplained position of witnesses' signatures.[20]

When the statute merely provides that the witnesses must subscribe the will, it is probably orthodox to consider that they must only set their hands to the will and hence need not sign at the end.[21] However, some courts construe such provisions to mean that the witnesses must write their names under the will, and so reach the result that they must sign at the end thereof.[22] Some of the statutes which require the testator to sign at the end also expressly demand the same of the witnesses.[23] Witnesses' signatures preceding dispositive portions of the will,[24] or the appointment of the executor,[25] or the giving of a power of sale to the latter,[26] have been held ineffective under these statutes.

16 Franks v. Chapman, 64 Tex. 159, 1885.

17 Moale v. Cutting, 59 Md. 510, 1882; In re Haber's Will, 118 Misc. 179, 192 N.Y.S. 616, 1922.

18 Murray v. Murphy, 39 Miss. 214, 1860. See Goods of Braddock, 1 P.D. 433, 1876.

19 Goods of Streatley, [1891] Prob. 172, 1891.

20 Phipps v. Hale, L.R. 3 P. & D. 166, 1874. See In re Rothstein's Estate, 133 Misc. 547, 233 N.Y.S. 235, 1929; In re Moro's Estate, 183 Cal. 29, 190 P. 168, 10 A.L.R. 422, 1920.

21 Hughes v. Merchants Nat. Bank of Mobile, 256 Ala. 88, 53 So.2d 386, 1951; Roberts v. Phillips, 4 El. & Bl. 450, 119 Eng.Rep. 162, 1855.

22 Owens v. Bennett, 5 Har.(Del.) 367, 1852; see Potter v. Ritchardson, 360 Mo. 661, 230 S.W.2d 672, 1950; annotation, 10 A.L.R. 429.

23 So in Arkansas, California, Idaho, Montana, New York, North Dakota, Oklahoma, South Dakota, and Utah. Bordwell, Statute Law of Wills, 14 Ia.L.R. 1, 16.

24 Owens v. Bennett, supra note 22; In re Murphy's Estate, 46 N.Y.S.2d 677, 1944.

25 In re Nies' Will, 13 N.Y.St.Rep. 756, 1887.

26 In re Blair's Will, 84 Hun 581, 32 N.Y.S. 845, 1885.

Some space may intervene between the conclusion of the will and the signatures of the witnesses,[27] though it has been held that a blank space of one or two pages invalidates the will.[28] Possibly the courts should be more liberal in their holdings regarding the position of the witnesses' signatures than with respect to that of the testator's, as a signing by the latter at an abnormal place offers better opportunity for fraudulent additions.

The witnesses must sign on some paper attached to the will. Thus, if the will is drawn in duplicate and the testator signs one copy and the witnesses the other, the will is invalid.[29] A signing by the witnesses on the envelope containing the will is not sufficient.[30] However, the mere folding of the paper signed by the witnesses with that signed by the testator was considered enough in a case where the two sheets were pasted together but failed to adhere to each other because of defective mucilage.[31] The attachment of the paper signed by the witnesses by a string,[32] pin,[33] staple,[34] or clipless fastener,[35] has been held sufficient. It is possible that this sort of physical attachment would not be effective in states requiring the witnesses to sign at the end.

27 In re Singer, 19 Misc. 679, 44 N.Y.S. 606, 1897 (two pages of blank space; will held valid). See In re Moro's Estate, 183 Cal. 29, 190 P. 168, 10 A.L.R. 422, 1920, where a blank space was left below testator's signature at the bottom of the page and the attestation clause and signatures of the witnesses appear on a fresh page stapled onto the first. And see accord, In re Dunlap's Will, 87 Okl. 95, 209 P. 651, 1922. See also authorities cited note 28 infra.

28 In re Seaman's Estate, 146 Cal. 455, 80 P. 700, 106 Am.St.Rep. 53, 2 Ann.Cas. 726, 1905; cf. In re Singer supra, note 27.

29 In re Goods of Hatton, L.R. 6 P.D. 204, 1881. And see In re Baldwin's Will, 146 N.C. 25, 59 S.E. 163, 125 Am.St.Rep. 466, 1907; In re Di Persia's Estate, 9 N.J.Super. 576, 75 A.2d 833, 1950.

30 Shane v. Wooley, 138 Md. 75, 113 A. 652, 1921 (sealed envelope); Vogel v. Lehritter, 139 N.Y. 223, 34 N.E. 914, 1893; In re Lee's Estate, 80 F.Supp. 293, D.C.D.C.1948, noted, 18 U. of Cin. L.R. 234, 37 Geo.L.J. 651, 20 Miss.L.J. 399.

31 Bolton v. Bolton, 107 Miss. 84, 64 So. 967, 1914. See infra § 79, note 2.

32 Goods of Horsford, L.R. 3 P. & D. 211, 1874.

33 Goods of Braddock, 1 P.D. 433, 1876.

34 In re Moro's Estate, supra note 27. See annotation, 10 A.L.R. 429.

35 In re Dunlap's Will, supra note 27.

## ORDER OF SIGNING

**71. The testator should sign the will before the witnesses subscribe, though it is usually held that the reverse order is permissible if all sign as part of a single transaction.**

The normal order of events is that the testator should sign the will before the witnesses do.[1] This seems especially appropriate under enactments like the English Wills Act, 1837, where it is provided that the testator shall make or acknowledge his signature in the presence of the attesting witnesses who shall subscribe the will. As the witnesses attest the signature, they can scarcely do so until the testator has signed. Even in case that the legislation, like the Statute of Frauds, provides that it is the will which is to be attested, it can be urged that the instrument is not a will until it has been signed by the testator and hence cannot be attested until that time. However, an appropriate answer to the latter argument is that the instrument is not a valid will until both testator and witnesses have signed, thus rendering the attestation of the will a theoretical impossibility in any case.[2]

It has also been suggested that the Statute of Frauds language merely requires attestation for the purpose of identifying the will as a document, as distinguished from an instrument having testamentary effect, thus permitting the signing by the witnesses to occur before the testator signs.[3] However, even under this type of statute it seems reasonable to regard the subscription by the witnesses as the final act of attestation, thus precluding them from attesting to anything thereafter.[4] At any rate, regardless of the type of wills' statute, it is agreed in general that a signature by the testator on a subsequent occasion to that upon which the will is signed by one or more of the witnesses is a fatal defect of execution.[5] Clearly if the testator subscribes after the wit-

1 See In re Halton's Estate, 111 N.J.Eq. 143, 161 A. 809, 1932: "Everything required to be done by the testator must precede, in point of time, the subscription of the testamentary witnesses."

2 Kaufman v. Caughman, 49 S.C. 159, 27 S.E. 16, 61 Am.St.Rep. 808, 1897.

3 Swift v. Wiley, 1 B.Mon.(Ky.) 114, 1840; see also Bloechle v. Davis, 132 Ohio St. 415, 8 N.E.2d 247, 1937, noted, 11 U. of Cin.L.R. 390, where the will was sustained though the testator signed in the witnesses' presence four days after they had signed. Cf. Limbach v. Bolin, 169 Ky. 204, 183 S.W. 495, L.R.A.1916D 1059, 1916, and see infra notes 7, 8.

4 See Evans, Incidents of Testamentary Execution, 16 Ky.L.J. 199, 204.

5 Duffie v. Corridon, 40 Ga. 122, 1869; Lacey v. Dobbs, 63 N.J.Eq. 325,

nesses sign and out of their presence, the will is invalid.[6] Even if the testator attaches his signature on an occasion subsequent to the signing by the witnesses, but in their presence, there is a fatal defect of execution.[7] The same would be clear if the testator signs after the witnesses in their absence and later acknowledges his signature to them.[8] The execution cannot be justified in either of these situations upon the ground that the witnesses have acknowledged their previously made signatures after testator has signed. Even if such acknowledgment is in fact made, the statutes do not authorize witnesses to acknowledge their signatures to the testator,[9] though usually a testator may acknowledge his pre-existing signature to the witnesses.[10]

There remains the situation where the witnesses sign before the testator does, but all acts are parts of a single continuous transaction. The English view [11] that this is fatal has some following in this country.[12] However, the prevailing American view and the modern tendency of our decisions is to uphold the exe-

50 A. 497, 55 L.R.A. 580, 92 Am.St. Rep. 667, 1901; Sisters of Charity of St. Vincent de Paul v. Kelly, 67 N.Y. 409, 1876; In re Irvine's Estate, 206 Pa. 1, 55 A. 795, 1903; Fowler v. Stagner, 55 Tex. 393, 1881; Hindmarsh v. Charlton, 8 H.L.Cas. 160, 11 Eng.Rep. 388, 1861; note, 173 L.T. 170; annotation, 39 A.L.R. 933. But see supra note 3. See Allen v. Griffin, 69 Wis. 529, 35 N.W. 21, 1887 (presumption, however, is that testator signed first).

6 Reynolds v. Massey, 219 Ala. 265, 122 So. 29, 1929; Reed v. Watson, 27 Ind. 443, 1867; Limbach v. Bolin, 169 Ky. 204, 183 S.W. 495, L.R.A.1916D 1059, 1916; In re Irvine's Estate, 206 Pa. 1, 55 A. 795, 1903. See In re Kahl's Estate, 278 Mich. 561, 270 N. W. 787, 1936.

7 Barnes v. Chase, 208 Mass. 490, 94 N.E. 694, 1911; Duffie v. Corridon, 40 Ga. 122, 1869 (here one additional witness signed). But see Bloechle v. Davis, supra note 3.

8 Hindmarsh v. Carlton, 8 H.L.Cas. 160, 11 Eng.Rep. 388, 1861.

9 Duffie v. Corridon, supra note 7; Pawtucket v. Ballou, 15 R.I. 58, 23 A. 43, 2 Am.St.Rep. 868, 1885; Hindmarsh v. Carlton, supra note 8. But see Cook v. Winchester, 81 Mich. 581, 46 N.W. 106, 8 L.R.A. 822, 1890; Cunningham v. Cunningham, 80 Minn. 180, 83 N.W. 58, 51 L.R.A. 642, 81 Am. St.Rep. 256, 1900; In re Karrer's Will, 63 Misc. 174, 118 N.Y.S. 427, 1909. See infra § 72, note 30 et seq.

10 See supra § 66.

11 Goods of Olding, 2 Curt. 865, 163 Eng.Rep. 611, 1841; Cooper v. Bockett, 3 Curt. 648, 163 Eng.Rep. 853, 1843; note, 173 L.T. 170.

12 Marshall v. Mason, 176 Mass. 216, 57 N.E. 340, 79 Am.St.Rep. 305, 1900; Jackson v. Jackson, 39 N.Y. 153, 1868. Cf. In re Haber's Will, 118 Misc. 179, 192 N.Y.S. 616, 1922; Matter of Jones' Estate, 157 Misc. 847, 285 N.Y.S. 894, 1936, noted, 21 Corn.L.Q.R. 674.

cution in cases of this kind.[13] This is a reasonable position for in acts substantially contemporaneous, it cannot be said that there is any real priority.

## "IN THE PRESENCE OF"

**72. The statutes almost universally require that the witnesses should sign the will in the presence of the testator but it is not necessary that the testator actually see the witnesses sign. The stricter courts insist that the testator should be in position to see the witnesses in the act of signing and also to see the will without material movement of his body. The more liberal view is to uphold the will though the signing was not within the range of testator's vision if it was close at hand and within his general cognizance.**

**Statutes in some states provide that the witnesses must sign in the presence of each other, while other statutes require that the testator must sign or acknowledge in the presence of witnesses present at the same time. However, in most jurisdictions neither of these is required.**

The English Statute of Frauds, the Wills Act, 1837, and almost all American wills' acts, require the will to be subscribed in the presence of the testator.[1] When the statute does not require signing by the witnesses in the testator's presence, there is no necessity that this be done.[2] Where the usual statutory provi-

13 In re Silva's Estate, 169 Cal. 116, 145 P. 1015, 1915; Re Shapter's Estate, 35 Colo. 578, 85 P. 688, 6 L.R.A., N.S., 575, 117 Am.St.Rep. 216, 1906; Gibson v. Nelson, 181 Ill. 122, 54 N.E. 901, 72 Am.St.Rep. 254, 1899; Robertson v. Robertson, 232 Ky. 572, 24 S.W.2d 282, 1926; Harmening v. Harmening, 84 Ind.App. 459, 150 N.E. 376, 1928; Sellers v. Hayden, 154 Md. 117, 140 A. 56, 57 A.L.R. 828, 1928; noted, 6 N.Y.U.L.R. 186, 37 Yale L.J. 1003; Horn's Estate v. Bartow, 161 Mich. 20, 125 N.W. 696, 26 L.R.A.,N.S., 1126, 20 Ann.Cas. 1364, 1910; Gordon v. Parker, 139 Miss. 334, 104 So. 77, 39 A.L.R. 931, 1925; Cutler v. Cutler, 130 N.C. 1, 40 S.E. 689, 57 L.R.A. 209, 89 Am.St.Rep. 854, 1902; Kaufman v. Caughman, supra note 2; Billings v. Woody, 167 F.2d 756, C.A.Dist.Col. 1948, noted, 1 Okl.L.R. 327; annotation, 39 A.L.R. 933, 935.

1 Bordwell, Statute Law of Wills, 14 Ia.L.R. 1, 15–16; Model Probate Code § 47. For exceptions, see infra note 2.

2 Lyon v. Smith, 11 Barb.(N.Y.) 124, 1851; see Matter of Martin, 270 App. Div. 875, 60 N.Y.S.2d 77, 1946. The same was formerly true in Arkansas —see Rogers v. Diamond, 13 Ark. 474, 1853. Ark.Acts 1949, No. 140 § 19, p. 304, now requires signing in testator's presence. The provision that the will be attested in testator's presence has been held to require signing in his presence. Calkins v. Calkins, 216 Ill. 458, 75 N.E. 182, 1 L.R.A.,N.S., 393, 108 Am.St.Rep. 233, 1905. The same has been indicated where the statute

sion exists, the question of whether, in the particular case, the signing by the witnesses was "in the presence of the testator" has given rise to much litigation. This expression is more uncertain and indefinite than most of the other provisions with regard to the execution of wills.

To say that W is in the presence of T connotes two related ideas: (1) That W is somewhere in the proximity of T; (2) that T is conscious of this fact. How close W must be to T in order to be in the latter's presence is a matter of degree. The same is true as to the kind and extent of physical barriers which may have existed between the two persons. In drawing the lines between that which is, and that which is not, presence, we should first inquire into the purpose of the statutory provision which makes this requirement.

*Purpose of the Provision*

It is frequently said that the requirement of signing in the presence of the testator is to prevent substitution of some other writing, or of making certain that the genuine will is the one which the witnesses sign.[3] As has been pointed out by Professor Page,[4] very little fraud is prevented by compliance with this particular provision. If the witnesses sign a substituted instrument outside of testator's presence, the signature of the testator must have been forged. In such case they would not be able to testify truthfully as to the testator's signature being made or acknowledged in their presence. If they were willing to perjure themselves concerning the latter, they would be just as ready to swear that they had signed in the testator's presence.[5]

It is sometimes assumed that the requirement is for the satisfaction of the testator himself.[6] If so, it is rather strange that the will should be held invalid for disregard of this provision,

simply requires that the will be witnessed. Burgan v. Kinnick, 235 Iowa 804, 281 N.W. 734, 1938; see note, 14 Iowa L.R. 560.

3 Dubach v. Jolly, 279 Ill. 530, 117 N.E. 77, 1917; Kitchell v. Bridgeman, 126 Kan. 145, 267 P. 26, 1928.

4 Wills, 3d Ed. § 353.

5 Professor Page mentions one instance where the requirement may prevent fraudulent substitution, viz., where the testator has signed two wills and desires to complete the execution of only one of them. Another possibility of fraud which may be avoided by the provision is that of the attesters procuring others to sign the attesters' names to the will in the absence of the testator, thus deceiving the latter into the belief that the witnesses he has chosen have signed the will.

6 See Welch v. Kirby, 255 F. 451, 9 A.L.R. 1409, C.C.A. 8th, 1918, noted, 17 Mich.L.R. 712.

especially if the testator has permitted the witnesses to sign outside of his presence. A more plausible reason for the provision is that it promotes compactness and solemnity of the execution ceremony. On the whole, there is not sufficient basis in policy for a strict construction of the provision.

*Consciousness of Testator*

Very little dispute has arisen over the element of conscious presence. It is not sufficient that the testator and the witnesses be together at the time when the latter sign, if the testator has not the physical or mental capacity to know that the act is being done. When the testator was insensible,[7] or in a dying stupor,[8] or dead,[9] at the time that witnesses signed, the will is invalid. The same is true if the will is signed in a clandestine manner,[10] though in the same room with the testator, or when signed in an adjoining room when he is not aware of the fact.[11] However, it is not necessary that the testator actually see the witnesses sign.[12] A will has been sustained though the testator was busily engaged in writing a letter at the time that the witnesses signed.[13]

*Physical Presence*

Although criticized by the writers,[14] the proximity element of the parties has generally turned upon the ability of the testator

7 Orndorff v. Hummer, 12 B.Mon. (Ky.) 619, 1851; Right v. Price, 1 Doug. 241, 99 Eng.Rep. 157, 1779.

8 Walters v. Walters, 89 Va. 849, 17 S.E. 515, 1881.

9 In re Cannock's Will, 81 N.Y.S.2d 42, 1948, noted, 37 Geo.L.J. 467, though statute did not require signing in testator's presence. See supra note 2.

10 See Longford v. Eyre, 1 P.Wms. 740, 24 Eng.Rep. 593, 1721.

11 Jenner v. Ffinch, L.R. 5 P.D. 106, 1879.

12 Mullis v. Phillips, 152 Ga. 811, 111 S.E. 400, 1922; Brittingham v. Brittingham, 147 Md. 153, 127 A. 737, 1925; In re Larson's Estate, 141 Minn. 373, 170 N.W. 348, 1919; In re Demaris' Estate, 166 Or. 36, 110 P.2d 571, 1941, noted, 13 Ry.Mt.L.R. 345. Will of Meurer, 44 Wis. 392, 28 Am.Rep. 591, 1878; Bullock v. Morehouse, 57 App.D.C. 231, 19 F.2d 705, 1927; Shires v. Glascock, 2 Salk. 688, 91 Eng.Rep. 584, 1687.

13 Dubach v. Jolly, 279 Ill. 530, 117 N.E. 77, 1917.

14 Evans, Incidents of Testamentary Execution, 16 Ky.L.J. 109, 200–203; Schouler, In Presence of a Testator, 26 Am.Law Rev. 857; note, 27 Ky.L.J. 447. Some cases, however, have insisted that presence may be satisfied by the ability to hear or through a general consciousness of events. In re Tracy's Estate, 80 Cal. App.2d 782, 182 P.2d 336, 1947; In re Demaris' Estate, supra note 12; Riggs v. Riggs, 135 Mass. 238, 46 Am. Rep. 464, 1883; In re Lane's Estate, 265 Mich. 539, 251 N.W. 590, 1933; In re Wilm's Estate, 182 Wis. 242, 196 N.W. 255, 1923. See infra note 21.

to see the witnesses subscribe. If the testator could see by doing no more than turning his head, this is sufficient if he was physically able to make the movement in question.[15] Some courts take the view that if the testator is unable to make the slight movement necessary for him to see, the will is not signed in his presence.[16] Others uphold the will of such a disabled testator.[17] Even if the witnesses signed outside the room, it is valid if the testator is able to see them sign.[18] Although neither presumption is conclusive, it is said that a signing in the same room with the testator is presumed to be in his presence, while if the will is signed outside the room, the contrary inference is indulged.[19]

If the testator would have had to make a substantial change in the position of his body in order to see the witnesses sign, the older view is that they did not sign in his presence.[20] There is,

[15] Brittingham v. Brittingham, In re Larson's Estate, both supra, note 12. The same has been held in case of a testator who could see by raising himself slightly in bed. Raymond v. Wagner, 178 Mass. 315, 59 N.E. 811, 1901. And likewise if the testator could see but for the bed curtain which he was able to move. Davy v. Smith, 3 Salk. 395, 91 Eng. Rep. 892, 1683; Newton v. Clarke, 2 Curt. 320, 163 Eng.Rep. 425, 1839. But the contrary was held if the testator is unable to move the obstruction. Tribe v. Tribe, 1 Rob. 775, 163 Eng. Rep. 1210, 1849; Reed v. Roberts, 26 Ga. 294, 71 Am.Dec. 210, 1858.

[16] Reed v. Roberts, supra note 15; Jones v. Tuck, 48 N.C. (3 Jones L.) 202, 1855 (in this case the testator was able to make the required movement but his doctor had forbidden it); Burney v. Allen, 125 N.C. 314, 34 S.E. 500, 74 Am.St.Rep. 637, 1899; In re Colman, 3 Curt. 118, 163 Eng.Rep. 674, 1842; Tribe v. Tribe, supra note 15.

[17] Cook v. Winchester, 81 Mich. 581, 46 N.W. 106, 8 L.R.A. 822, 1890; Riggs v. Riggs, 135 Mass. 238, 46 Am. Rep. 464, 1883; Sturdivant v. Birchett, 10 Grat.(Va.) 67, 1853.

[18] Casson v. Dade, 1 Bro.C.C. 99, 28 Eng.Rep. 1010, 1781; Shires v. Glascock, 2 Salk. 688, 91 Eng.Rep. 584, 1687. Cf. Kersey v. Lovell, 299 Ill. 611, 132 N.E. 763, 1921 (one witness signed within a latticed cashier's cage); In re Larson's Estate, 141 Minn. 373, 170 N.W. 348, 1919; In re Deyton's Will, 177 N.C. 494, 99 S.E. 424, 1919; Moore v. Glover, 196 Okl. 177, 163 P.2d 1003, 1945. But see Green v. Davis, 228 Ala. 162, 153 So. 240, 1934; Walker v. Walker, 342 Ill. 376, 174 N.E. 541, 1931, noted, 16 Ia. L.R. 560.

[19] McKee v. McKee's Ex'r, 155 Ky. 738, 160 S.W. 261, 1913, noted, 14 Col. L.R. 180; Jones v. Tuck, 48 N.C.(3 Jones' Law) 202, 1855; Neil v. Neil, 1 Leigh.(Va.) 6, 1829.

[20] Reed v. Roberts, 26 Ga. 294, 71 Am.Dec. 210, 1858; Clarkson v. Kirtright, 291 Ill. 609, 126 N.E. 541, 1920; McKee v. McKee's Ex'r, supra note 19; In re Beggans' Will, 68 N.J.Eq. 572, 59 A. 874, 1905, noted in 3 Mich. L.R. 591; In re Jones' Estate, 101 Wash. 128, 172 P. 206, 1918; Norton v. Bazett, Deane 259, 164 Eng.Rep. 569, 1856. See, Winston, Attestation in the Presence of the Testator, 2 Va. L.R. 403; notes, 10 Can.B.R. 55, 253; annotations, 6 Ann.Cas. 414; L.R.A. 1916C 950.

however, a more liberal view now being taken by many courts, which hold that if the witnesses sign close enough to the testator so that he comprehends the act, that is sufficient.[21] For the most part they also take the position that presence may turn upon the ability to hear or upon general consciousness as well as upon the sense of sight.[22]

*What Testator Must Be Able to See*

It is certainly not necessary that the testator must be able to distinguish the letters being formed by the pen of the witness.[23] A number of cases, however, have held that the testator must be able to see not only the witnesses while they are writing but their hands, the pen, and the will itself.[24] According to this position, if the bodies of the witnesses shield the actual writing operation from the testator's range of vision, their signatures are not made in his presence.[25]

This seems an unusually strict position, and other authorities declare that it is enough for the testator to be able to see the witness when he is in the act of signing, though his hand and the paper are shut off from testator's view.[26] In this regard, as in the case of other aspects of the presence requirement, a liberal viewpoint is warranted, as the requirement is not a substantial fraud preventative.

21 Kitchell v. Bridgeman, 126 Kan. 145, 267 P. 26, 1928; Cook v. Winchester, 81 Mich. 581, 46 N.W. 106, 8 L.R.A. 822, 1890; In re Lane's Estate, 265 Mich. 539, 251 N.W. 590, 1935, noted, 33 Mich.L.R. 465; Cunningham v. Cunningham, 80 Minn. 180, 83 N.W. 58, 51 L.R.A. 642, 81 Am.St.Rep. 256, 1900; Healey v. Bartlett, 73 N.H. 110, 59 A. 617, 6 Ann.Cas. 413, 1904; In re Demaris' Estate, 166 Or. 36, 110 P.2d 571, 1941, noted, 13 Ry. Mt.L.R. 345. In Cook v. Winchester and Cunningham v. Cunningham, both supra, the proponent's case was bolstered by the fact that the witnesses later acknowledged their signatures to the testator. See infra text at note 30 et seq.

22 See supra note 14.

23 Ayres v. Ayres, 43 N.J.Eq. 565, 12 A. 621, 1887.

24 Green v. Davis, 228 Ala. 162, 153 So. 240, 1934; Reed v. Roberts, 26 Ga. 294, 71 Am.Dec. 210, 1858; Walker v. Walker, 342 Ill. 376, 174 N.E. 541, 1931; Jones v. Tuck, 48 N.C.(3 Jones' Law) 202, 1855, with which compare Bynum v. Bynum, 33 N.C.(11 Ired. Law) 632, 1850.

25 Graham v. Graham, 32 N.C. 219, 1849. But see authorities cited infra note 26.

26 Riggs v. Riggs, 135 Mass. 238, 46 Am.Rep. 464, 1883; Earl v. Mundy, 227 S.W. 716, Tex.Civ.App.1921; Nock v. Nock's Ex'rs, 10 Grat.(Va.) 106, 1853. See In re Offill's Estate, 96 Cal. App. 640, 274 P. 623, 1929; Re Tobin, 196 Ill. 484, 63 N.E. 1021, 1902; Maynard v. Vinton, 59 Mich. 139, 26 N.W. 401, 60 Am.Rep. 276, 1886.

### *Blind Testators*

The problem of when the witnesses are deemed to sign the will in the presence of a blind testator puts to a test the general theory that testator should be in a position to see the witnesses. Some decisions adhere to the general rationale, and insist that the parties should have been so situated that testator could have seen if he had had vision.[27] Other cases go upon the theory that the other senses must act as a substitute for that of sight.[28] Obviously a court should not be too strict in this regard, for a blind testator can seldom be certain from his other senses that the witnesses he has chosen are signing his will.[29] Such a position would practically preclude a blind man from executing a will.

### *Effect of Acknowledgment by Witnesses*

Generally a subscription by a witness outside of the testator's presence, followed by the witnesses' acknowledgment of their signatures to the testator is not sufficient.[30] The statutes do not provide for such acknowledgment as they do in the case of testator's own signature. Retracing the signature with a dry pen in testator's presence is no more than an acknowledgment of the signature.[31] Some decisions, however, have attached considerable importance to an acknowledgment of witness' signature, though in these cases the signature was made very shortly before the acknowledgment and within close proximity of the testator and indeed in his presence according to the liberal rule.[32]

### *Mutual Presence of Witnesses*

While the requirements of attestation must be performed by all of the required number of witnesses, the majority of jurisdic-

27 Welch v. Kirby supra note 6; Piercy's Goods, 1 Rob. 278, 163 Eng. Rep. 1038, 1845.

28 Re Allred's Will, 170 N.C. 153, 86 S.E. 1047, L.R.A.1916C, 946, Ann.Cas. 1916D 788, 1915; Ray v. Hill, 34 S.C. L.(3 Strob.) 297, 49 Am.Dec. 647, 1848. See Riggs v. Riggs, 135 Mass. 238, 46 Am.Rep. 464, 1883; Arneson's Will, 128 Wis. 112, 107 N.W. 21, 1906; Professor Warren in 33 Harv.L.R. 556, 566.

29 See dissenting opinion in Welch v. Kirby, supra note 6.

30 Calkins v. Calkins, 216 Ill. 458, 75 N.E. 182, 1 L.R.A.,N.S., 393, 108 Am. St.Rep. 233, 1905, noted in 4 Mich.L. R. 246; Chase v. Kittredge, 11 Allen (Mass.) 49, 87 Am.Dec. 687, 1865; Pawtucket v. Ballou, 15 R.I. 58, 23 A. 43, 2 Am.St.Rep. 868, 1885. See supra § 71, note 9.

31 Playne v. Scriven, 1 Rob. 772, 163 Eng.Rep. 1209, 1849. Cf. Craig v. Wismar, 310 Ill. 262, 141 N.E. 766, 1923.

32 Cook v. Winchester and Cunningham v. Cunningham both supra note 21.

tions do not require that the witnesses sign in each others presence, or that all witnesses be present at the same time.[33] In these states neither is necessary.[34] Some statutes, however, expressly require that the witnesses must sign in the presence of each other.[35] What is presence as between the witnesses involves essentially the same problems as arise with regard to the provisions requiring witnesses to sign in the testator's presence. The witnesses need not actually see each other sign, but generally they must be in a position where they could have seen.[36]

A few other jurisdictions require that the signature or acknowledgment of the testator shall be made in the presence of witnesses present at the same time.[37] Such a statute does not require that the witnesses sign in each other's presence.[38] This provision does, however, prevent the testator from signing in the presence of one witness and acknowledging his prior signature to another.[39] Under the ordinary statute this method of execution is permissible.[40]

33 Bordwell, Statute Law of Wills, 14 Ia.L.R. 13, 14.

34 In re Dow's Estate, 181 Cal. 106, 183 P. 794, 1919, noted, 8 Cal.L.R. 124; Heavner v. Heavner, 342 Ill. 321, 174 N.E. 413, 1930; In re Hull's Will, 117 Iowa 738, 89 N.W. 979, 1902; In re Thomas' Estate, 243 Mich. 566, 220 N.W. 764, 1928; Willis v. Mott, 36 N.Y. 486, 1867; In re Shaff's Estate, 125 Or. 288, 266 P. 630, 1928; Moore v. Glover, 196 Okl. 177, 163 P. 2d 1003, 1945. See annotation, 99 A.L.R. 554. Cf. In re Emart's Estate, infra note 40.

35 So in Colorado, Louisiana, New Mexico, South Carolina, Tennessee, Utah, Vermont, West Virginia and Wisconsin. Bordwell, Statute Law of Wills, 14 Ia.L.R. 14, 16. A will which does not comply with such statute is invalid. Lane's Appeal, 57 Conn. 182, 17 A. 926, 4 L.R.A. 45, 14 Am.St.Rep. 94, 1889 (as indicated in the opinion this requirement has been abolished in this state); Roberts v. Welch, 46 Vt. 164, 1873.

36 In re Claflin's Will, 73 Vt. 129, 50 A. 815, 87 Am.St.Rep. 693, 1902; Nera v. Rimando, 18 Philippines 450, 1911. In Wade v. Wade, 119 W.Va. 596, 195 S.E. 339, 115 A.L.R. 686, 1938, it was held that one witness might acknowledge his signature to the other witness under provision requiring the witnesses to sign in the presence of each other. Contra: Eslick v. Wodicka, 31 Tenn.App. 333, 215 S.W.2d 12, 1948. See generally supra notes 7–26.

37 So in New Jersey, Rhode Island, Virginia, West Virginia and England. Bordwell, Statute Law of Wills, 14 Ia.L.R. 13, 14.

38 In re Cook's Estate, 118 N.J.Eq. 288, 179 A. 259, 99 A.L.R. 551, 1935; Parramore v. Taylor, 11 Grat.(Va.) 220, 1854.

39 In re Sutterlin's Will, 99 N.J.Eq. 363, 132 A. 115, overruling 98 N.J.Eq. 307, 128 A. 624, 1925.

40 In re Reycraft's Estate, 260 Mich. 40, 244 N.W. 221, 1867; Baskin v. Baskin, 36 N.Y. 416, 1932. But see In re Emart's Estate, 175 Cal. 238, 165 P. 707, L.R.A.1917F 866, 1917, under a peculiar statute. See note, 8 Cal.L.R. 124.

## ATTESTATION CLAUSE

**73. While an attestation clause is not required for the validity of a will, it is a valuable and desirable aid in the proof of the facts of execution.**

An attestation clause subscribed by the witnesses normally appears in the will following the testator's signature. It recites the observation of the formalities necessary for the due execution of the will. A common form of attestation clause, which recites all the formalities necessary in any state except Louisiana, is as follows:

"The foregoing instrument was at the date thereof signed, published, and declared by the said John Doe as and for his last will and testament in the joint presence of us, who, at his request and in his presence, and in the presence of each other, have subscribed our names as witnesses." [1]

It is fairly common to insert after the word "instrument" a general description of the instrument, such as "consisting of five pages including the page upon which this is written." Sometimes there is reference to the fact that the individual pages have been signed or initialed for identification by the testator, or by the testator and the witnesses. If alterations appear on the face of the instrument it is wise to refer to these in the attestation clause.[2] Of recent years many attorneys add the words "this clause having been first read aloud" at the end of the clause.[3] When the testator signs by mark, or perhaps when he is blind, there may well be a modification of the clause indicating the circumstances and the special precautions taken.

However, aside from the foregoing in the situations to which they apply, it is not desirable to over-elaborate the clause. It is better to adhere to a simple uncomplicated form and depart therefrom only under special circumstances. Occasionally attestation clauses recite the witnesses' belief that the testator is competent to make testamentary disposition of his property.[4]

1 Older forms commonly contained the word "sealed" after the words "signed," but sealing is not required in any jurisdiction. See supra § 62, notes 19, 20. Cf. Gest, Drawing Wills and Settlement of Estates in Pennsylvania, 49 (1909). Unless the testator actually affixes his seal as part of the execution ceremony there should be no recital of sealing in either the testimonium or attestation clauses. See infra § 74. For a series of forms, see Rollison, Will Clauses, Ann. Forms 49–61.

2 See infra § 74 at note 6.

3 Infra § 74.

This is not a desirable practice for it may be seized upon as an indication that the lawyer considered that there was doubt as to the matter; furthermore, a recalcitrant witness may be impeached even if there is no such recital.[5]

A will is perfectly valid though there is no attestation clause, and even though no words indicate the capacity in which the witnesses signed.[6] Even if the attestation clause omits some requirement of the statute, it can be shown that all necessary formalities were observed.[7]

However, the use of an attestation clause which recites all the required formalities may aid in the establishment of the will at probate or contest. If the person drafting the will also supervised the execution, an adequate attestation clause shows at least that he had in mind the statutory requirements.

While due execution of the will is evidenced by the mere fact that the witnesses have signed the same,[8] at least in some jurisdictions the presumption is much stronger if there is a proper attestation clause.[9] Moreover, the clause may serve as an aid

4 Rood, Wills, 2d ed. § 288. The opinion in Hoover v. Keller, 339 Ill. 126, 171 N.E. 163, 1911, speaks of this as a usual item of the attestation clause. The form books do not bear this out, and neither does the author's experience.

5 See Stevens v. Leonard, infra note 11.

6 In re Pitcairn's Estate, 6 Cal.2d 730, 59 P.2d 90, 1936; Wehrkamp v. Burnett, 82 Colo. 5, 256 P. 630, 1927; Cunningham v. Hallyburton, 342 Ill. 442, 174 N.E. 550, 1931 (no words); In re Serveira's Will, 205 App.Div. 686, 200 N.Y.S. 464, 1923; Maynard v. Jacobs, 49 R.I. 224, 141 A. 616, 1928. Failure of witnesses to read the clause is no worse than total absence of clause. In re Klein's Estate, 241 Iowa 1103, 42 N.W.2d 593, 1950.

7 Hoover v. Keller, 339 Ill. 126, 171 N.E. 163, 1911; In re Me-hun-kah's Will, 78 Okl. 214, 189 P. 867, 1920.

8 Reynolds v. Massey, 219 Ala. 265, 122 So. 29, 1929; Maynard v. Jacobs, 49 R.I. 224, 141 A. 616, 1928. See German Evangelical Bethel Church of Concordia v. Reith, 327 Mo. 1098, 39 S.W.2d 1057, 76 A.L.R. 604, 1931; Wigmore on Evidence, § 1512. Some cases assert that this creates a presumption of due execution. Leatherbee v. Leatherbee, 247 Mass. 138, 141 N.E. 669, 1923, noted, 22 Mich.L.R. 623; Carpenter v. Denoon, 29 Ohio St. 379, 1876. Cf. infra § 101, note 8 et seq.

9 Norton v. Goodwine, 310 Ill. 490, 142 N.E. 171, 1923; In re Repp's Estate, 241 Iowa 190, 40 N.W.2d 607, 1950; In re Johnson's Estate, 115 N.J.Eq. 249, 171 A. 307, 1934; In re Davis Estate, 172 Or. 354, 142 P.2d 143, 1943. See Moore v. Walton, 158 Ga. 408, 123 S.E. 812, 1924; Goff v. Knight, 201 Okl. 411, 206 P.2d 992, 1918 (witnesses unavailable). Cf. In re Pitcairn's Estate, supra note 6. But upon proof that the attestation clause was not read to or by the witnesses, its recitals are without weight. Kittleson's Estate v. Kittleson, 42 S.D. 126, 173 N.W. 161, 1919. See generally Severns, The True

when the witnesses fail to recall the events of execution.[10] The clause also tends to hold in line the attester who later becomes hostile to the will. Instruments have been admitted to probate upon the strength of an attestation clause and the surrounding circumstances though in direct contradiction to the testimony of the subscribing witnesses.[11] The attestation clause does not lose all its force by reason of the fact that it recites certain unnecessary formalities which were not in fact observed.[12] Of course the recitals of the attestation clause are not conclusive; wills have been held invalid for want of proper execution though they contained attestation clauses which recited the performance of all the requisites.[13]

## PRACTICAL HINTS REGARDING EXECUTION

**74. Extreme care should be taken in the supervision of the execution of the will to insure that all the recitals of the attestation clause as well as certain other precautions are observed, even though some of them may not be necessary for the validity of the instrument.**

To a considerable extent the present section merely puts in reverse the matters in the previous sections of this chapter. However, a brief positive treatment of the manner in which a will should be executed seems appropriate at this point.[1] Every lawyer should perfect and ordinarily follow a definite practice with

Function of the Attestation Clause in a Will, 11 Chi-Kent L.R. 11; note, 23 Corn.L.Q. 588; annotation, 76 A.L.R. 617.

10 Flynn v. Flynn, 283 Ill. 206, 119 N.E. 304, Ann.Cas.1918E 1034, 1918; see Van Meter v. Van Meter, 183 Md. 614, 39 A.2d 752, 1944.

11 Szarat v. Schuerr, 365 Ill. 323, 6 N.E.2d 625, 1937; In re Repp's Estate, supra note 9; German Evangelical Bethel Church of Concordia v. Reith, supra note 8; Lott v. Lott, 174 Minn. 13, 218 N.W. 447, 1928, noted, 12 Minn.L.R. 661; In re Estate of Shaff, 125 Or. 288, 266 P. 630, 1928.

So also when attesters testify that the testator was mentally incompetent, though perhaps the ruling would be the same if there was no attestation clause. Stevens v. Leonard, 154 Ind. 67, 56 N.E. 27, 1920. See annotations, 35 A.L.R. 79, 79 A.L.R. 399.

12 Craig v. Wismar, 310 Ill. 262, 141 N.E. 766, 1923; see Humphrey v. Wallace, 169 Kan. 58, 216 P.2d 781, 1950. However, it would seem unwise to recite the observation of some formality which was not done. See infra § 74.

13 Spangler v. Bell, 390 Ill. 152, 60 N.E.2d 864, 1944; In re Smith's Estate, 130 Neb. 739, 766 N.W. 611, 1936; Fann v. Fann, 186 Tenn. 127, 208 S.W.2d 542, 1948, noted, 20 Tenn.L.R. 396.

1 For suggestions on planning and drafting of wills see infra § 147.

regard to this, but still be flexible enough to depart from his usual technique in unusual situations. Lawyers of experience and distinction may differ as to some of the details treated herein. It remains for the individual to decide with what qualifications the following suggestions should be adopted.

*Wills or Part Thereof in Testator's Handwriting*

Usually lawyer-prepared wills are written entirely in typewriting except for the signatures and possibly the date. This facilitates the preservation of an exact carbon copy and avoids the dangers of illegibility which may result if the testator writes the will in his own hand. It also removes much of the temptation for small subsequent additions by the testator after execution and tends to avoid disputes as to when alterations were made.[2] Many testators would shirk the painstaking labor of penning their wills, particularly if the instrument is a lengthy one. These considerations in most cases outweigh the arguments [3] in favor of having the will copied entirely by the testator, viz., protection against forgery and fraudulent substitution of pages, use of the instrument as a holographic will if proof of due execution fails,[4] rebuttal of claims of undue influence, and proof of testator's knowledge of the contents of the will.

However, a master in the field of handwriting identification declares that a bare signature is sometimes difficult to identify, and for this reason a will should contain other specimens of the testator's own writing.[5] When any reasonable possibility of a claim of forgery is foreseen, it would be well to have the testator pen the testimonium, and perhaps also the exordium, clause of his will.

*Alterations*

All sorts of erasures, interlineations, and corrections on the face of the will should be avoided whenever humanly possible. This is much more important than in the drafting of a pleading or a bi-party instrument. Where an error in language occurs, the entire page should be recopied if time and circumstances permit. When use of an altered page is unavoidable, the testator should sign the margin opposite the change, indicating his approval of it. In addition the witnesses should sign at these places to indicate that the alteration was made prior to execution. An-

2 See supra § 64, note 87.

3 Rood on Wills, 2d Ed., § 318a.

4 See infra § 75 note 19.

5 Osborn, Signing Wills and Other Documents, 7 A.B.A.Jo. 20.

other means of identifying corrections is to mention them in the attestation clause.[6]

*Identification of Pages*

Certain precautions should be taken so that it will appear that the document presented for probate is the very instrument which was executed.[7] Of course there is ordinarily little doubt concerning the last page which is signed by the testator and the witnesses. There is much more chance of dispute concerning the other sheets. The practice in force in some of the civil law countries of writing the entire will on both sides of a long sheet of paper has something to recommend it. This method is not usual in the United States. At the every least, however, the pages of the will should be fastened together in some permanent form at the time of execution. The pages of some important wills are fastened together with a ribbon, the ends of which are placed under a wax seal on the signatory page. If this is not done, the testator and the witnesses may sign each page on the margin for the purpose of identification. The latter fact can be recited in the attestation clause, which, in any event, can well specify the number of pages contained in the instrument.

•*Number of Witnesses*

Wills executed in the seven states[8] which require three witnesses should of course have at least three attesters. Many lawyers in the two-witness states customarily use three witnesses. It has sometimes been thought that this is a wise precaution because the testator may own property, or indeed be domiciled, in a three-witness state at the time of his death. There is practically nothing to this thought because in all of the three-witness states statutes validate wills which were executed in accordance with the law of the place of execution. However, the practice has advantages where it turns out that one of the witnesses cannot be easily located or it is inconvenient for him to go to court,

6 Remsen, Preparation of Wills and Trusts, 403, 416; supra § 73.

7 See infra § 79.

8 Connecticut, Georgia, Maine, Massachusetts, New Hampshire, South Carolina and Vermont. Non-notarial wills in Louisiana require five, sometimes seven, witnesses. See infra § 78. Attorneys unskilled in the civil law should not attempt to execute wills for use in Louisiana or other civil law jurisdictions. In case of emergency a holographic instrument would be best for execution in Louisiana. See infra § 75. However, Louisiana and most other jurisdictions recognize wills which are executed according to the law of the place of execution.

and the law permits probate on the testimony of any two witnesses.[9] Carried to its logical conclusion perhaps there should be four, or possibly a dozen, attesters in these jurisdictions; but there are obviously practical limitations as to the number. In occasional cases it may be well to have doctors, nurses or others act as supernumerary witnesses with the idea of thus committing them to testify favorably as to testator's mental capacity, though there is substantial risk in asking unreliable or vacillating individuals to serve as attesters. Finally one witness may be incompetent for some reason unknown at the time of execution so that the will is invalidated unless there are enough others who are competent.

Something can be said against a practice which calls for employment of unnecessary witnesses in the ceremony of execution. Some jurisdictions require that all the available attesters, and not merely the number required to validate the will, must testify even upon uncontested probate.[10] In these states the employment of supernumerary witnesses increases the burden of securing probate. Here at least, the author suggests that ordinarily only the minimum number of witnesses should be used.

*Choice of Witnesses*

In the case of a testator in the prime of life, of undoubted mental competency, and not subject to undue influence, one need not be particularly concerned regarding the choice of attesting witnesses, especially if the provisions of the will are the ones which might normally be expected. In this case it would not be objectionable if the witnesses had no previous acquaintance with the testator. Such witnesses should be introduced to the testator by a common acquaintance, however, and the parties should be permitted to talk together for a few moments in order that the witnesses can throw some light upon the mental state of the testator. Of course one should not select a legatee or devisee or any one who might be considered financially interested in the will, including executors or trustees. It would not be advisable to choose an heir under any circumstances. Naturally, the witnesses should be sufficiently mature so that no question might arise on this score. It is desirable that the witnesses be younger than the testator so that they may be expected to outlive him, although of course a will is not invalid because some or even all

9 See infra § 95.

10 Ibid.

of the witnesses predecease the testator. They should be permanent residents of the locality so that they can be reached readily when needed. A witness who is deceased presents less of a problem upon probate than one who cannot be located. It is preferable not to have women act as a witnesses, particularly if they are unmarried, as their names may be changed by marriage, and they are consequently sometimes difficult to locate even when living in the same community.

When the testator is old or infirm, or if there are any possible circumstances upon which his competency might be questioned, it is advisable to choose the attesting witnesses from among the testator's closest acquaintances. While it might conceivably be somewhat of a two-edged sword, the testator's attending physician and nurse may be appropriate witnesses. All things considered, the attorney drafting the will is a desirable attester.[11] Business associates of the testator are likewise proper persons for this purpose. While care should be taken in making the selection, the whole matter is not one which should cause too much concern. The fact that a person has acted in the capacity of a witness will generally hold him in line to testify favorably on the subject of mental capacity, and a proper attestation clause normally commits him to the recited facts of the execution.[12]

*Attestation Clause and Compliance Therewith*

As indicated in the preceding section, every will should contain an attestation clause. The clause there set forth mentions all the formalities which are required in any of our states, except Louisiana. While one or more of the recited formalities may be unnecessary in your jurisdiction, all should be fully complied with, for the testator may remove to another state or acquire an interest in realty therein. An even more important consideration is that a clause which recites the performance of acts which were not actually done loses in large part of its effectiveness.

11 Choice of the attorney who drafted the will as a witness thereto constitutes a waiver by the testator of the attorney-client privilege. Wigmore on Evidence, § 2315. But this is probably what the testator would have desired so far as disclosure of facts relevant to the validity of the will. If there is litigation concerning the validity of the will, an attorney-witness may have precluded himself from acting as counsel in support of the will because of the ethical principle that one should not act both as witness and as counsel. However, this should not prevent the attorney from acting as attester, particularly if the client so desires. See Slater, Avoidance of Litigation as to Wills, 13 A.B.A.Jo. 43, 48.

12 See supra § 73.

That which is false in part may be considered untrue altogether. For this reason a sealing should not be mentioned either in the testimonium or attestation clauses unless the will is actually sealed. Some lawyers do employ the seal and even blue ribbons, but the main purpose of this seems to be to impress the client. The observance of such formalities makes the ceremony a little more impressive and thus promotes recollection by the witnesses. In addition, the unrequired formalities may be some indication that the actual requisites were performed.

*Details of Execution*

Prior to execution the testator should be acquainted with the instrument so as to make sure that it complies with his instructions and desires. Usually the witnesses are not present on this occasion. They need not know the contents of the will, and usually the testator prefers that the provisions are not disclosed to anyone unnecessarily.

When the will and the testator are in readiness for execution he and the witness should be brought together in a room—seated around a table if possible. It is advisable to take precautions against interruptions. The attorney acts as master of ceremonies and should warn the persons to follow his instructions and bear close attention to the transaction. He should then present the instrument to testator and ask him to examine it to make sure it is the paper he wants. If the individual pages are to be signed or initialed in the margin by the testator, or by the testator and the witnesses, for the purpose of identification, this should be done first and the process kept separate from the actual execution. Then the testator should be asked to sign if he so desires. He should sign, the witnesses being cautioned to observe him in the act of signing. Next the testator should be asked whether he declares the instrument to be his will and whether he requests the others—naming them—to act as attesting witnesses. Upon receiving an affirmative answer, it is advisable to read the attestation clause aloud to the witnesses, and perhaps also to allow them to read it for themselves.

In jurisdictions where the witnesses are obliged to see the testator's signature,[13] some attorneys have the witnesses sign twice, once directly to the left of the testator's signature and again following the attestation clause; this is particularly desirable when testator's signature is on the page preceding the attestation clause. The testator and the witnesses should be cautioned to

13 See supra § 66.

observe each witness in the act of signing and none should leave until all have signed. Each witness should write his complete address opposite his name; some statutes direct this.[14] If there is the slightest doubt about the legibility of the witnesses' signatures the names should be printed in ink immediately below. These precautions are important for the sake of locating the witnesses for purpose of probate, especially when the testator lives many years after execution of his will.

Some of these suggestions are not vital to the validity of the will and call for a little more formality than is usual. However, the matter is important enough to call for an impressive ceremony and it is wise to proceed with abundance of caution. Doing so results in peace of mind to the testator while he lives, serves to impress the transaction upon the memories of the witnesses, eases the burden of establishment of the will at the testator's death, and minimizes the chances that the will may be contested.

### *Custody of the Completed Will*

After all formalities are completed the instrument should be tendered to the testator. It is his will, and he should choose the manner of its custody. Some testators prefer to keep the document among their valuable papers. Statutes in some jurisdictions provide that the will may be delivered to the probate office for safekeeping until the testator's death unless he demands its return.[15] If so, this fact may be explained to the testator. Some testators wish their attorney to keep their wills and, if so, the document should be kept in a safe place in the lawyer's office. In any event, a copy of the will, complete with the testator's and witnesses' names and plainly marked "copy," should be retained in the attorney's private files. This conformed copy is not signed by the testator or witnesses themselves. Ordinarily it is used only for reference purpose though it may become invaluable if the original becomes lost.[16] Sometimes wills are completely executed in duplicate so that there are two originals, but as a whole this practice is undesirable for reasons to be explained hereafter.[17]

[14] Bordwell, Statute Law of Wills, 14 Ia.L.R. 1, 16. Most of the statutes expressly provide that failure of the witnesses to write their place of residence does not affect the validity of the will. See Wattenbarger v. Wattenbarger, 39 Okl. 531, 135 P. 1141, 1913. The New York statute provides a penalty of fifty dollars for failure to comply. Decedent Estate Law, § 22.

[15] See New York Decedent Estate Law, §§ 30 to 32; Model Probate Code § 59; infra § 94, note 5.

[16] See infra § 97.

[17] See infra § 86.

# CHAPTER 8

## SPECIAL TYPES OF WILLS



*Forecast*

In addition to ordinary wills described in the preceding chapter, most jurisdictions have one or more special types of wills which require less formality than ordinary wills. These are: holographic wills, or those written in the testator's hand; nuncupative, or oral, wills; and soldiers' and sailors' wills. In Louisiana where the civil law prevails the term nuncupative will is used to describe certain formal written wills, and in this state there is also a species known as sealed or mystic wills. All of these are described in the present chapter. Wills of these special categories differ from ordinary wills only in the manner and form of execution. Indeed some matters of execution such as what constitutes a writing or a signature are generally the same for all wills.

### HOLOGRAPHIC WILLS

**75. By statute in nineteen jurisdictions, holographic wills, or those written and signed in the testator's hand, are valid without formal attestation.**

**Some of these states require that the will should also be dated in the testator's hand, and in one state holographic wills must be found among the testator's valuable papers.**

Holographic (or olographic) wills are those which are wholly in the testator's handwriting. The fact that the instrument is holographic does not dispense with any of the formalities of execution except when so provided by statute.[1] Most jurisdictions have no such statutes so that the holographic character has no legal effect. In nineteen states the fact that the will is so written obviates the necessity of attesting witnesses. This result

1 Corcoran v. Williams, 271 Ill.App. 312, 1933; In re Turell's Will, 166 N.Y. 330, 59 N.E. 910, 1901; In re Brown's Estate, 101 Wash. 314, 172 P. 247, 1918.

comes about through two different types of statutory provisions. There is the Virginia type,[2] which exists also in Arizona, Arkansas, Kentucky, Mississippi, North Carolina, Tennessee, Texas and West Virginia, which does not create a new kind of will but merely dispenses with the necessity of witnesses if the instrument is in the handwriting of the testator. In these jurisdictions the term holographic is seldom found in the statutes. In addition there is the Louisiana type found also in California, Idaho, Montana, Nevada, North Dakota, Oklahoma, South Dakota, Utah and Wyoming, where following the civil law codes holographic wills are recognized as a distinct kind of will, which need not be witnessed.[3] Under statutes of the former kind, the requirements of execution of ordinary wills other than those of attestation would seem to apply. Furthermore, there are seldom any additional requirements for holographic wills except that they must be in the testator's handwriting.[4] When holographic wills are recognized as a distinct species of wills the formalities for ordinary wills do not apply at all, but generally there is the additional requirement that they be dated.[5]

The general rules regarding capacity are the same as for ordinary wills.[6] Likewise the same rules regarding testamentary intent govern both species of wills.[7] The holographic will may be informal, and letters have often been held sufficient.[8] It is frequently a troublesome question whether the decedent wrote the letter with testamentary intent, and the prohibition of the use

[2] See Bordwell, Statute Law of Wills, 14 Ia.L.R. 1, 25, 26. For a history of the Virginia statute, see Waller v. Waller, 1 Grat.(Va.) 454, 42 Am. Dec. 564, 1845. The Tennessee provision is § 5 of the Model Execution of Wills Act, also Model Probate Code § 48 which reads "No witness to a holographic will is necessary, but the signature and all its material provisions must be in the handwriting of the testator and his handwriting must be proved by two witnesses."

[3] Bordwell, supra note 2. For an historical and comparative study of holographic wills, see Lorenzen, Holographic Wills and Their Dating, 28 Yale L.J. 72; see also Parker, History of the Holographic Testament in the Civil Law, 3 Jurist 1.

[4] But see infra notes 47–50.

[5] Nevada and Wyoming lack a provision requiring dating. Bordwell, supra note 2.

[6] Scott v. Harkness, 6 Idaho 736, 59 P. 556, 1899. See supra chapter 5.

[7] In re Henning's Estate, 186 Cal. 307, 199 P. 39, 1921; Sullivan v. Jones, 130 Miss. 101, 93 So. 353, 1922; Howell v. Moore, 14 Tenn.App. 594, 1930.

[8] See supra § 47. As to endorsements on notes and bank books, see annotation, 62 A.L.R. 292 and cf. Succession of Knight, 158 So. 233, La. App., 1935 (forgiveness of note). A will written in a small memorandum book was held good. In re Lanart's Estate, 9 Alaska 535, 1941.

of letters as holographic wills by some civil law codes seems wise but for the fact that it involves the further question as to what is a letter.[9]

*Entirely in Testator's Hand*

Most of the statutes provide that an unattested holographic will must be entirely in the handwriting of the testator, although some omit the word "entirely." [10] A self typewritten testament is not sufficient though signed by the testator's hand.[11] This seems sound as the dispensation for this type of will is granted largely because the handwritten character is a guarantee of genuineness.

When the instrument contains any printed or typed matter or words in another's hand, two different theories have been taken as to the will's validity. The first has been called [12] the intent theory and the result turns upon whether the testator intended the nonholographic matter as part of his will. If not the will, without the nonholographic words, is valid. But if the testator intended these words to be part of his will the entire instrument is invalid even though the nonholographic matter was not necessary for an understanding of the will. The leading case is Estate of Thorn [13] where the testator devised "my country place *Cragthorn,"* the last word being inserted with a rubber stamp. The will was held invalid because it was not written entirely in the testator's hand. California and Utah have generally adhered to this position,[14] though recent cases have shown signs of relent-

9 See supra § 47, especially at note 18.

10 Cf. the Tennessee Statute, supra note 2. It is pointed out in Gulliver and Tilson, Classes of Gratuitous Transfer, 51 Yale L.J. 1, 13–14 that, while this requirement is an excellent precaution against forgery, holographic wills may be as easy to obtain as ransom notes, and furthermore their frequent casual character leaves doubt as to whether there was testamentary intent, as to which see supra notes 7–9; and § 47.

11 Estate of Dreyfus, 175 Cal. 417, 165 P. 941, L.R.A.1917F 391, 1917 noted, 5 Cal.L.R. 503; Adams' Ex'x v. Beaumont, 226 Ky. 311, 10 S.W.2d 1106, 1929, noted in 17 Ky.L.J. 412; Dean v. Dickey, 225 S.W.2d 999, Tex. Civ.App.1949.

12 See Mechem, Integration of Holographic Wills, 12 N.C.L.R. 213, 214–219.

13 183 Cal. 512, 192 P. 19, 1920.

14 See infra notes 17, 23. In 1931, § 53 was added to the California Probate Code providing that: "no address, date or other matter written, printed or stamped upon the document, which is not incorporated in the provisions which are in the handwriting of the decedent, shall be considered as any part of the will." This is probably merely declaratory of the

ing.[15] Objections to this theory are that it invalidates many wills and that it often involves a purely conjectural determination of the testator's intent. The obvious "out" from the rigor of this rule is to find that the testator did not intend the objectionable words to be a part of his will.

The rival doctrine may be called the surplusage theory. It disregards the nonholographic matter, provided that enough remains in the testator's hand to be given effect.[16] Cases have gone as far as holding that the testator's writing which filled in the blanks of a printed will form could be probated, though obviously he intended the printed words as part of his will.[17] The principal objections to this theory are that it makes hash of the statute, especially if it requires that the will be *entirely* in the handwriting of the testator, and that while the courts may carefully omit the nonholographic words on probate, they may be tempted to give them effect in the process of construction.

There are certain cases where the presence of nonholographic words on the paper would not invalidate the will under either the intent or surplusage theory. This is true in case of a printed place or heading unreferred to in the body of the will,[18] and prob-

pre-existing California law. See Estate of Towle, 14 Cal.2d 261, 93 P.2d 555, 124 A.L.R. 624, 1939, noted, 28 Cal.L.R. 413; Evans, Comments on the Probate Code of California, 19 Cal.L.R. 602, 609. In the Towle case, supra, it was held that subsequent changes made in the instrument by another with testator's consent vitiated the will entirely.

15 Estate of Durlewanger, 41 Cal. App.2d 750, 107 P.2d 477, 1941; In re Yowell's Estate, 75 Utah 312, 285 P. 285, 1930. See also infra notes 18, 19.

16 McMichael's Heirs v. Bankston, 24 La.Ann. 451, 1872; Baker v. Brown, 83 Miss. 793, 36 So. 539, 1 Ann.Cas. 371, 1903; Will of Lowrance, 199 N. C. 782, 155 S.E. 876, 1930. See Tennessee statute, supra note 2, and also infra notes 17, 18, 19, 23.

17 In re Will of Parsons, 207 N.C. 584, 178 S.E. 78, noted, 13 N.C.L.R. 524, 1935; Gooch v. Gooch, 134 Va. 21, 113 S.E. 873, 1922. Contra on intent theory: In re Bower's Estate, 11 Cal. 2d 180, 78 P.2d 1012, 1938; In re Wolcott's Estate, 54 Utah 165, 180 P. 169, 4 A.L.R. 727, 1919. Cf. Blankenship v. Blankenship, 276 Ky. 707, 124 S.W. 2d 1060, 1939; In re Bauer's Estate, 5 Wash.2d 165, 105 P.2d 11, 1940.

18 In re Oldhams' Estate, 203 Cal. 618, 265 P. 183, 1928; In re De Caccia's Estate, 205 Cal. 719, 273 P. 552, 61 A.L.R. 393, 1928, noted, 17 Cal.L.R. 297, 24 Ill.L.R. 723, 3 So.Cal.L.R. 67; Succession of Heinemann, 172 La. 1057, 136 So. 51, 1931. But where the testator incorporated this printed caption into his will, it was invalid. In re Bernard's Estate, 197 Cal. 36, 239 P. 404, 1925; see, however, cases supra notes 16, 17, and generally infra §§ 79, 80.

A second will or codicil written on an earlier typed will is usually sustained. In re Atkinson's Estate, 110 Cal.App. 499, 294 P. 425, 1930; Moon v. Norvell, 184 Va. 842, 36 S.E.2d 632, 1946. See In re Goodman's Will, 229

ably also in case that witnesses added their signatures at the end of the instrument.[19] But in many situations the validity of the will depends upon which theory is applied.

*Date*

In absence of express statutory provision there is no more necessity for a holographic will to be dated than in the case of other wills.[20] Some jurisdictions where holographic wills are most used require that they be dated,[21] and moreover that this be done in the testator's own hand.[22] Where this provision exists, the will must be dated wholly in the testator's hand, at least if the court is operating under the intent theory. There, if a part of the date is printed, as it sometimes is on correspondence paper, a filling in of the month and day and the completion of the year is insufficient, and the entire will is invalid.[23]

A will may be dated March 23, '34,[24] or even 3/23/34,[25] but the abbreviation 9/8/18 has been held insufficient because according to certain usage this would refer to September 8th and by other

N.C. 444, 50 S.E.2d 34, 1948, noted, 2 Vand.L.R. 496.

19 In re Morrison's Estate, 55 Ariz. 504, 103 P.2d 669, 1940; In re Clark's Estate, 55 Cal.App.2d 85, 129 P.2d 969, 1942; Succession of Eastman, 6 So.2d 788, La.App.1942. See also Jones v. Myers, 178 Tenn. 24, 154 S.W.2d 245, 1941, noted, 27 Wash.U.L.R. 293 (joint will also signed by testator's wife); cf. supra § 49, notes 2, 3, 20.

20 Sneed v. Reynolds, 166 Ark. 581, 266 S.W. 686, 1924; In re Lowrance's Will, 199 N.C. 782, 155 S.E. 876, 1930. See supra § 62, notes 23–27.

21 California, Idaho, Louisiana, Montana, North Dakota, Oklahoma, South Dakota and Utah.

22 Estate of Billings, 64 Cal. 427, 1 P. 701, 1884; Succession of Mathews, 158 So. 233, La.App.1935.

23 In re Estate of Francis, 191 Cal. 600, 217 P. 746, 1923; Succession of Robertson, 49 La.Ann. 868, 21 So. 586, 62 Am.St.Rep. 672, 1897; In re Noyes' Estate, 40 Mont. 190, 105 P. 1017, 26 L.R.A.,N.S., 1145, 20 Ann.Cas. 363, 1925. But see In re Durlewanger's Estate, supra note 15. Cf. In re Yowell's Estate, 75 Utah 312, 285 P. 285, 1930, where will was dated entirely in testator's hand in the body of the will; the partially printed date above was ignored, and the will upheld. Accord: In re Whitney's Estate, 103 Cal.App. 577, 284 P. 1067, 1930; Jones v. Kyle, 168 La. 728, 123 So. 306, 1929. In Will of Parsons, 207 N.C. 584, 178 S.E. 78, 1935, noted, 13 N.C.L.R. 524, it was held that the printed portion of the date might be disregarded in a jurisdiction which did not require dating. See also Will of Wallace, 227 N.C. 459, 42 S.E.2d 520, 1947.

24 Matter of Lakemeyer's Estate, 135 Cal. 28, 66 P. 961, 87 Am.St.Rep. 96, 1901; Succession of Wenling, 172 La. 673, 135 So. 21, 1931. See Succession of Caro, 175 La. 402, 143 So. 355, 1932, noted in 7 Tulane L.R. 270.

25 In re Olssen's Estate, 42 Cal.App. 656, 184 P. 22, 1919; Matter of Chev-

custom to August 9th.[26] Where either of the first two numbers exceeds twelve, this must refer to the day and there can be no ambiguity. It has been held that when the year is uncertain because of illegibility the will is invalid.[27]

A correct date is not required,[28] but if the date is incomplete the instrument is not valid.[29] The date may appear at any place on the document,[30] and probably it can even be added after the will has been otherwise completed.[31] The fact that the will is dated twice with different dates is not fatal as there is no requirement that the entire holographic will be written on a single day.[32]

*Signature*

All holographic wills' legislation requires that the instruments be signed by the testator. Some statutes require that the will be subscribed or signed at the end of the instrument,[33] though this

allier's Estate, 159 Cal. 161, 113 P. 130, 1911.

26 Succession of Beird, 145 La. 756, 82 So. 881, 6 A.L.R. 1452, 1919; Succession of Lasseigne, 181 So. 879, La. App.1938. But see in re Olssen's Estate, supra note 25. Cf. Matter of Chevallier's Estate, supra note 25, where a holographic will dated 4–14–07 was upheld.

27 Succession of Buck, 208 La. 556, 23 So.2d 215, 1945, containing a discussion of the French authorities.

28 In re Estate of Fay, 145 Cal. 82, 78 P. 340, 104 Am.St.Rep. 17, 1904. See Estate of Clisby, 145 Cal. 407, 78 P. 964, 104 Am.St.Rep. 58, 1904 (testator may adopt the date upon which the will was started and dated, though completed and signed on a later day).

29 In re Vance's Estate, 174 Cal. 122, 162 P. 103, L.R.A.1917C 479, 1916, where the testator wrote "in the year one thousand;" will held invalid; In re Anthony's Estate, 21 Cal.App. 157, 131 P. 96, 1913 (month omitted); In re Maguire's Estate, 14 Cal.App.2d 388, 58 P.2d 209. 1936 (no day); Succession of Swanson, 132 La. 606, 61 So. 685, 1913; Montague v. Street, 59 N.D. 618, 231 N.W. 728, 1930 (year only given—will invalid). But see In re Irvine's Estate, 114 Mont. 577, 139 P.2d 489, 147 A.L.R. 882, 1943, noted, 5 Mont.L.R. 82; cf. note 27 supra.

30 Jones v. Kyle, 168 La. 728, 123 So. 306, 1929. But the year cannot be supplied by testator's reference in the body to his 1935 La Salle though he died in 1935. In re Schiffman's Estate, 16 Cal.App.2d 650, 61 P.2d 331, 1936. See also In re Wunderle's Estate, 30 Cal.2d 274, 181 P.2d 874, 1947.

31 Jones v. Kyle, supra note 30.

32 Picard v. Succession of Picard, 179 La. 746, 155 So. 11, 1934; Jones v. Kyle, supra note 30. Cf. infra § 79 at notes 17, 18.

33 Borchers v. Borchers, 145 Ark. 426, 224 S.W. 729, 1920; Graham v. Edwards, 162 Ky. 771, 173 S.W. 127, 1915; Succession of Fitzhugh, 170 La. 122, 127 So. 386, 1930 (interpretation of French code); In re George's Estate, 208 Miss. 734, 45 So. 2d 571, 1950. As to statutes requiring will to be signed "in such manner as to make it manifest that the name was intended as a signature," cf. McElroy v. Rolston, 184 Va. 77, 34 S.E. 2d 241, 1945 with Hall v. Brigstocke,

provision has been liberally construed.[34] In most jurisdictions allowing holographic wills there is no statutory stipulation for signing at the end, and the signature if intended as such may be at any place on the instrument. If the court is convinced that the instrument is the complete will intended by the testator, the signature may be at the beginning of the will,[35] in the exordium clause,[36] in the body of the will,[37] or in the margin.[38] Where the will ends "last will of ——— (testator's name)" it was held sufficiently signed.[39] Signature on the envelope containing the will has been held insufficient,[40] and when the appearance of the document is such as to indicate that it was not complete, the testator's name appearing thereon will not be regarded as his signature.[41] The question resolves itself into that of whether the testator intended that his name should operate as his signature. This problem is particularly acute in the case of holographic wills since there are not attesting witnesses to whom the intention may be indicated. Aside from this, the problem is not different from that of ordinary wills where the testator's name is written in a place other than the normal one used for signatory purposes.[42]

190 Va. 459, 58 S.E. 529, 19 A.L.R.2d 921, 1950, noted, 2 Mercer L.R. 284, 37 Va.L.R. 348. See also Black v. Maxwell, 131 W.Va. 247, 46 S.E.2d 804, 1948.

34 Weems v. Smith, 218 Ark. 554, 237 S.W.2d 880, 1951; Graham v. Edwards, supra note 33 (signature on margin proper when page was entirely filled).

35 In re Morgan's Estate, 200 Cal. 400, 253 P. 702, 1027; In re England's Estate, 85 Cal.App. 486, 259 P. 956, 1927 (though there was no period at end of the will); Alexander v. Johnston, 171 N.C. 468, 88 S.E. 785, 1916; Dinning v. Dinning, 102 Va. 467, 46 S.E. 473, 1904.

36 In re Wallace's Estate, 100 Cal. App.2d 237, 223 P.2d 284, 1950; In re McNair's Estate, 72 S.D. 604, 38 N.W.2d 449, 1949, noted 48 Mich.L.R. 384, 98 U. of Pa.L.R. 272. But see In re Manchester's Estate, 174 Cal. 417, 163 P. 358, L.R.A.1917D 629, Ann.Cas. 1918B 227, 1917.

37 In re Harris' Estate, 38 Ariz. 1, 296 P. 267, 1931.

38 Forrest v. Turner, 146 Va. 734, 133 S.E. 69, 1926. See In re Button's Estate, 209 Cal. 325, 287 P. 964, 1930.

39 In re Brandow's Estate, 59 S.D. 364, 240 N.W. 323, 1932; cf. supra § 64, note 68; also infra note 41. And so also if the will commenced with a similar recital and the closing words recited that the will was signed. In re Estate of McMahon, 174 Cal. 423, 163 P. 669, L.R.A.1917D 778, 1917.

40 In re Tyrrell's Estate, 17 Ariz. 418, 153 P. 767, 1915; In re Manchester's Estate supra, note 36. As to integration of holographic wills, see infra § 79 at note 16.

41 In re Brooks' Estate, 214 Cal. 138, 4 P.2d 148, 1931.

42 See in general, Mechem, The Rule in Lemayne v. Stanley, 29 Mich. L.R. 685, 691 et seq.; note, 17 Cal.L.R. 297, 301. See supra § 64 at note 40 et seq.

While the testator cannot effectively sign his holographic will by a rubber stamp, or by proxy, he need not sign his full name. Letters have been sustained as holographic wills though signed with an abbreviation of the first name,[43] or initials.[44] Even letters signed "mother," [45] or with other familiar terms [46] have been held sufficient.

*Place of Deposit*

In North Carolina and formerly in Tennessee [47] the holographic will must have been found among the testator's valuable papers or effects, or have been given to another for safekeeping. This provision is intended to insure that the testator believed the paper to be sufficiently valuable to keep carefully and as sort of a guarantee of testamentary intent.[48] As a whole, the provision has been liberally construed with this purpose in mind.[49] Even in absence of such requirement the fact that a holographic will was preserved with valuables in a safe deposit box has been held to be a strong indication of testamentary intent.[50]

43 Cartwright v. Cartwright, 158 Ark. 278, 250 S.W. 11, 1923; Barnes v. Horne, 233 S.W. 859, Tex.Civ.App. 1921.

44 Pilcher v. Pilcher, 117 Va. 356, 84 S.E. 667, L.R.A.1915D 902, 1915.

45 In re Henderson's Estate, 196 Cal. 623, 238 P. 938, 1925; In re Southerland's Will, 188 N.C. 325, 124 S.E. 633, 1924. See supra § 64.

46 In re Button's Estate, 209 Cal. 325, 287 P. 964, 1930, ("Love from Muddy," near the end of a long letter only a small part of which dealt with property matter, was held sufficient signature). But see In re George's Estate, supra note 33.

47 See supra note 2; note, 19 Tenn. L.R. 856.

48 In re Williams' Will, 215 N.C. 259, 1 S.E.2d 857, 1939.

49 In re Will of Groce, 196 N.C. 373, 145 S.E. 689, 1928 (on person); In re Williams' Will, supra note 48; Pulley v. Cartwright, 23 Tenn.App. 690, 137 S.W.2d 336, 1940 (in pocketbook). Cf. Fransioli v. Podesta, 21 Tenn.App. 577, 113 S.W.2d 769, 1938; In re Bennett's Will, 180 N.C. 5, 103 S.E. 917, 1920 (sending letter is not equivalent of custody).

50 Tobin v. Nordness, 47 S.D. 255, 197 N.W. 783, 1924.

## NUNCUPATIVE WILLS

**76. The statutes of most states recognize the validity of oral wills of personalty, subject to some or all of the following restrictions:**

**(1) That the will was made during the testator's last sickness,**

**(2) at the home of the testator or in the house in which he died,**

**(3) that testator asked one or more of the required number of witnesses to bear witness to the will,**

**(4) provided that the testimony of the witnesses is reduced to writing within a designated number of days,**

**(5) and the will is offered for probate within a certain period, typically six months;**

**(6) usually the amount of property which may pass by oral will is limited.**

*Statutes—English and American*

Prior to the Statute of Frauds, oral wills of personalty were generally recognized.[1] Under this statute,[2] the unrestricted right to bequeath personalty by verbal will was confined to cases where the estate bequeathed did not exceed thirty pounds. Over that value the statute validated oral or nuncupative wills only in case: (1) That the oral will should be proved by the oaths of three witnesses present at the making thereof; (2) that the testator bid the persons present or some of them to bear witness that such was his will; (3) that the will should be made in the time of the last sickness of the deceased and in his house or where he had a residence for at least ten days before making the will except in case where a person was taken sick away from his home and died before he returned to his dwelling; (4) that after six months no testimony should be received to prove a nuncupative will except that which was committed to writing within six days after the making of the will. The statute expressly provided that soldiers' and mariners' wills did not come within the above restrictions.[3]

1 See supra § 3, note 33.

2 29 Car. II, c. 3, XIX, XX, 1677.

3 Ibid., § XXIII. See infra § 77. The Wills Act, 1837, provides in effect that no oral wills are good except in case of soldiers and sailors. 7 Wm. IV and 1 Vict., c. 26, §§ IX, XI.

While nuncupative wills in Louisiana and the civil law countries are formal and written,[4] the term is used in common law jurisdictions to denote oral wills. Statutes in the majority of our states allow oral will of personalty but as a whole under greater restrictions than under the English Statute of Frauds.[5] Only in Georgia can real property be so disposed of.[6] A number of states do not allow oral wills in any case, or permit them only in case of soldiers and sailors.[7]

*Condition of Testator*

California and a group of states following her code provisions allow oral wills only in case testator is in "expectation of immediate death from an injury received the same day." [8] Almost all the other statutes provide that the will must be made "in the last sickness." [9] There is authority holding that this means that the testator must be in extremis,[10] although other cases take the position that it is enough if he is in expectation of death from his present disability and does not in fact recover.[11] Some American statutes require that the will be made at testator's home or in the house in which he died, but this provision is often omitted.[12]

*Testamentary Intent and Rogatio Testium*

Testamentary intent is as necessary in the case of nuncupative wills as in the other types.[13] The testator must not only desire to make a will, but he must intend that the words themselves should operate as his will.[14] Thus, the giving of instructions for

4 See infra § 78.

5 Bordwell, Statute Law of Wills, 14 Ia.L.R. 1, 28–34; see Model Probate Code § 49.

6 Bordwell, supra note 5 at 30.

7 Ibid. at 28. As to military wills, see infra § 77.

8 Bordwell, supra note 5 at 29.

9 Ibid. at 32. As to the distinction between a nuncupative will and a gift causa mortis or inter vivos, see Starks v. Lincoln, 316 Mo. 483, 291 S.W. 132, 1927; Godard v. Conrad, 125 Mo.App. 165, 101 S.W. 1108, 1907. See supra § 45.

10 Schmitz v. Summers, 179 Miss. 260, 174 So. 569, 1937; In re McClellan's Estate, 325 Pa. 257, 189 A. 315, 1937; McClain v. Adams, 135 Tex. 627, 146 S.W.2d 373, 1941.

11 Baird v. Baird, 70 Kan. 564, 79 P. 163, 68 L.R.A. 627, 3 Ann.Cas. 312, 1905 (death not occurring until seventeen days thereafter); Godfrey v. Smith, 73 Neb. 756, 103 N.W. 450, 10 Ann.Cas. 1128, 1905; In re Miller's Estate, 47 Wash. 253, 91 P. 967, 13 L.R.A.,N.S., 1092, 125 Am.St.Rep. 904, 14 Ann.Cas. 1163, 1907.

12 Bordwell, supra note 5 at 33. See Nowlin's Adm'r v. Scott, 10 Grat. (Va.) 64, 1853.

13 See supra § 47.

14 In re Buehrer's Estate, 349 Pa. 353, 37 A.2d 587, 1944; Brown v.

a written will is not generally deemed to be a nuncupative one, even though the other circumstances were such that an oral will would have been valid.[15] Dictating a letter which document the testator conceives would be his will cannot be considered a nuncupative will.[16] An expressed desire to make a new will is not itself a nuncupative will.[17] The giving of checks and notes to another with directions for their use can only be sustained as an inter vivos transaction for testamentary intent is lacking.[18] However, no particular form of words is necessary for a nuncupative will [19]; the testator need not use the expression, "bequeath" or "will," as long as he, in effect, intended that the property should pass by testamentary succession as the result of the words.[20]

Most of the jurisdictions which have legislation allowing oral wills require the witnesses to bear witness that the declaration is testator's will.[21] The rogatio testium need not be in the statutory form; a request to inform the beneficiaries,[22] or to see that the will is carried out,[23] is sufficient. However, a mere declaration of how the testator wants his property to go is not sufficient.[24]

State, 87 Wash. 44, 151 P. 81, Ann. Cas.1917D 604, 1915. See also cases infra note 24.

15 Knox v. Richards, 110 Ga. 5, 35 S.E. 295, 1900; In re Male's Will, 49 N.J.Eq. 266, 24 A. 370, 1892; Brown v. State, 87 Wash. 44, 151 P. 81, Ann. Cas.1917D 604, 1915. Contra: In re Snelling's Estate, 113 Kan. 151, 213 P. 641, 1923. Cf. In re McClellan's Estate, 325 Pa. 257, 189 A. 315, 1937.

16 Lee v. Barrow, 156 Miss. 711, 126 So. 648, 1930 (defective also as a written will). See also In re Taylor's Estate, 56 Ariz. 211, 106 P.2d 492, 1940 (oral attempt to adopt written will).

17 In re Glebus' Estate, 267 Pa. 125, 110 A. 80, 1920.

18 Starks v. Lincoln, 316 Mo. 483, 291 S.W. 132, 1927. See supra § 44, note 39; § 45, notes 29–31.

19 Weir v. Chidester, 63 Ill. 453, 1872. It is no objection that questions were asked the testator in order to clarify his desires. In re Snelling's Estate, 113 Kan. 151, 213 P. 641, 1923.

20 Kellner v. Hagood, 39 Ohio App. 351, 177 N.E. 637, 1931. Cf. Robinson v. Jones, 167 Ga. 38, 144 S.E. 774.

21 See Bordwell, supra note 5 at 32. Under legislation following the language of the Statute of Frauds it is enough to call on a single person to bear witness, provided that this is in the hearing of the others. Jones v. Robinson, 169 Ga. 485, 151 S.E. 8, 1929. Under some statutes it is necessary that the required number of attestors each be called to bear witness that the declaration is testator's will. Dockum v. Robinson, 26 N.H. 372, 1853.

22 Gwin v. Wright, 8 Humph.(Tenn.) 639, 1848.

23 Baird v. Baird, 70 Kan. 564, 79 P. 163, 68 L.R.A. 627, 3 Ann.Cas. 312, 1905.

24 In re Wiley's Estate, 187 Pa. 82, 40 A. 980, 67 Am.St.Rep. 569, 1898; Scales v. Heirs at Law of Thornton, 118 Ga. 93, 44 S.E. 857, 1903.

*Witnesses*

As the statutes expressly provide, the required number of witnesses must be present at the same time.[25] There is every reason why this should be so, in spite of the usual rule to the contrary with regard to written wills.[26] In case of the nuncupative will the witnesses testify to the terms of the will as well as the facts of execution. In the written will the proof of testamentary intent also is preserved in permanent form as approved by the testator, which of course is not true of nuncupative wills. The larger functions and greater importance of witnesses to nuncupative wills justified strict enforcement of the requirement that all should testify to the same transaction.

Some states follow the Statute of Frauds in requiring three witnesses for oral wills; others require only two.[27] When the statute does not specify the number but uses the term "witnesses", two but no more are necessary.[28] An oral will cannot be proved by the testimony of a legatee.[29]

*Value of Property Bequeathed*

The Statute of Frauds requires the designated formalities only for bequests in excess of thirty pounds. If the property was below that amount it seems that the only requirements would be proof of terms and testamentary intent. Some of the American statutes have similar stipulations with varying amounts.[30]

There is another type of provision as to amount found in some of the American statutes, namely, a value above which nuncupative wills are not effective.[31] In other words a written will is required where the amount exceeds the fixed legislative limit. This

25 Wester v. Wester, 50 N.C. 95, 1857; In re Yarnall's Will, 4 Rawle (Pa.) 46, 26 Am.Dec. 115, 1833; Tally v. Butterworth, 10 Yerg.(Tenn.) 501, 1837. But see Portwood v. Hunter, 6 B.Mon.(Ky.) 538, 1846.

26 See supra § 72.

27 Bordwell, supra note 5 at 31.

28 Johnston v. Glasscock, 2 Ala. 218, 1841.

29 In re Repush's Will, 257 Wis. 528, 44 N.W.2d 240, 1950 (because of dead man's statute); see Godfrey v. Smith, 73 Neb. 756, 103 N.W. 450, 10 Ann.Cas. 1128, 1905; Vrooman v. Powers, 47 Ohio St. 191, 24 N.E. 267, 8 L.R.A. 39, 1890, pointing out that statutes invalidating gifts to witnesses and rendering them competent do not apply to oral wills; but cf. Denmark v. Rushing, 208 Ga. 557, 67 S.E.2d 766, 1951. See supra § 65.

30 Most states do not have any such minimum, and in these jurisdictions the statutory formalities for nuncupative wills must be observed regardless of the insignificance of the value of the property involved. See Bordwell, supra note 5 at 31.

31 Most jurisdictions have no such maximum amounts. Ibid.

has been construed to validate nuncupative wills up to the amount permitted by statute, but rendering them void as to the excess.[32]

*Reduction to Writing*

Most American jurisdictions which permit nuncupative wills have provisions similar to those of the Statute of Frauds,[33] regarding the reduction of the testimony to writing and probate within limited periods. Under provisions following the English statute the will need not be reduced to writing if probated within six months.[34] A number of our statutes are more stringent in their requirements, demanding both a reduction to writing within a designated number of days and also probate within a longer definite period, typically six months.[35] The respective provisions are mandatory and must be complied with, or the oral testament will be denied effect.[36]

*Attitude Toward Oral Wills*

In addition to the restrictions imposed by the legislatures, the courts have declared that nuncupative wills should be disfavored.[37] They are subject to the frailties of oral proof, are of inferior dignity,[38] and certainly do not now constitute an important legal category although they do breed a certain amount of litigation. Professor Rheinstein has declared that they are obsolete and should be entirely abolished.[39] His conclusions seem sound.[40]

32 Mulligan v. Leonard, 46 Iowa 692, 1877 (express statutory provision to this effect); Brown v. United States, 65 F.2d 65, C.C.A.9th, 1933 (under California law). But see Erwin v. Hammer, 27 Ala. 296, 1855 (will entirely void because it attempted to dispose of excessive property).

33 See supra text, subd. 4, after note 2.

34 American statutes following this type of language have been similarly construed. Johnston v. Glasscock, 2 Ala. 218, 1841; Walker v. Fields, 247 S.W. 272, Tex.Com.App.1923.

35 See Bordwell, supra note 5 at 33, 34; Felker v. Taylor, 162 Ga. 433. 134 S.E. 52, 1926, is an example of a case holding the will invalid under the more stringent type of statutory provision. Cf. Robinson v. Jones, 167 Ga. 38, 144 S.E. 774, 1928, overruling the Felker Case on its particular

36 Felker v. Taylor, supra note 35; Martinez v. De Martinez, 19 Tex.Civ. App. 661, 48 S.W. 532, 1898.

37 In re Tylor's Estate, 56 Ariz. 211, 106 P.2d 492, 1940; Cannon v. Seybolt, 55 Idaho 796, 48 P.2d 406, 1935; In re Male's Case, 49 N.J.Eq. 266, 24 A. 370, 1893; In re McClellan's Estate, 325 Pa. 257, 189 A. 315, 1937; Scales v. Heirs at Law of Thornton, supra note 24; see note, 1 Wash.L.R. 61.

38 A nuncupative will cannot revoke a prior written will. See infra § 87 at note 4. Cf. In re Grattan's Estate, 157 Kan. 116, 138 P.2d 497, 1943.

39 Rheinstein, The Model Probate Code: A Critique, 48 Col.L.R. 534, 550.

40 See 1948 Annual Surv.Am.L. 759.

## SOLDIERS' AND SAILORS' WILLS

**77. Testaments of soldiers in actual military service and of sailors at sea were excepted by the Statute of Frauds from the requirements of execution imposed generally in case of bequests of personalty. In most American jurisdictions wills of these persons are similarly privileged so that their verbal or unattested written wills are capable of passing personalty.**

Julius Caesar gave his soldiers the privilege of making wills without the formalities required for other persons; later this became a permanent part of the Roman law and was extended to those in the naval service.[1] A similar privilege to dispose of their personalty was said to exist for English soldiers under the early law,[2] although it is hard to see wherein soldiers could be privileged at a time when any person could make an oral or informal written testament.[3] The Statute of Frauds, after specifying the requirements for nuncupative wills in general, provided: "That notwithstanding this act, any soldier being in actual military service, or any mariner or seaman being at sea may dispose of his moveables, wages, and personal estate, as he or they might have done before the making of this act."[4] The English Wills Act, 1837, continued the exception of soldiers' and sailors' wills although otherwise prohibiting unwritten and unattested wills.[5]

In about one-fourth of our states there are no special privileges for the wills of soldiers and sailors, although most of these jurisdictions allow any persons to make holographic or nuncupative wills or both.[6] Statutes in the remaining states allow privileged military and maritime wills; many of them follow closely the language of the Statute of Frauds although there are frequent variations and restrictions.[7]

1 See Drummond v. Parish, 3 Curt. 522, 163 Eng.Rep. 812, 1843. For recent general treatments on the subject of this section, see infra notes 7, 61.

2 Swinburne, Testaments & Last Wills, 1635, pt. 1, § 14.

3 See supra § 3, note 33.

4 29 Car. II, c. 3, § xxiii, 1676.

5 7 Wm. IV and I Vict. c. 26, § xi. The phraseology is slightly changed from that used in the Statute of Frauds. The Wills (Soldiers' and Sailors') Act, 1918, 7, and 8 Geo. 5, c. 58, extends provision in favor of soldiers under 21, and includes members of the Air Forces and permits disposition of realty.

6 See supra §§ 75, 76.

7 See Weiss, The Formalities of Testamentary Execution by Service Personnel, 33 Ia.L.R. 48.

*Soldiers*

The dispensation for soldiers' wills applies to all rank and branches of the services.[8] According to the Roman law the privilege was granted only for soldiers "in expedition".[9] It has been declared that the expression "in actual military service" means the same thing as "in expedition." [10] In the leading English case of Drummond v. Parish,[11] a major general stationed in England in peace time was held not to come within the privilege. Since this case it has never been doubted but that war is necessary for operation of the soldier's privilege and that the testator must have some connection with the hostilities. The reason for the privilege is the difficulty in compliance with the ordinary requirements of execution in the emergency.

Changes in the nature of warfare have resulted in modification of the concept of "actual military service." Earlier English decisions indicated that a soldier in barracks could not make a military will,[12] though there were opinions to the contrary during the Boer and First World Wars if the soldier had received orders for embarkation.[13] During the Second World War, the British cases were even more liberal and held that wills of soldiers stationed in England were privileged.[14]

The early American cases were in accord with the older British decisions in this regard.[15] Still, it was never thought necessary

8 Leathers v. Greenacre, 53 Me. 561, 1866 (volunteer); In the Estate of Donaldson [1916] P. 192 (female nurse).

9 Digest, 6. 21. 17.

10 In re Dumont's Estate, 170 Misc. 100, 9 N.Y.S.2d 606, 1938; Leathers v. Greenacre, supra note 8; Drummond v. Parish, supra note 1.

11 3 Curt. 522, 163 Eng.Rep. 812, 1843. Cf. In re Rippon, [1943] P. 6 (privilege allowed after recall to service where there was a declaration of urgency though no declaration of war or general mobilization).

12 Matter of Hill, 1 Rob. 276, 163 Eng.Rep. 1038, 1845; White v. Repton, 3 Curt. 818, 163 Eng.Rep. 912, 1844. See Drummond v. Parish, supra note 1.

13 Goods of Hiscock, [1901] Prob. 78; Gattward v. Knee, [1902] Prob. 99. See Anderson's Estate [1916] Prob. 49.

14 In re Estate of Spark [1941] P. 115 (bombed in English camp); Doherty v. Mangan [1943] Ir.R. 78 (killed in aircraft accident in England); In re McLennan Estate, [1940] 1 West. Wkly.R. 465 (collapsed in drill parade in Canada). But the informal will of a dental officer, living at his home which was bombed, was held not privileged. In the Estate of Gibson [1941] P. 118. See generally Megarry, Actual Military Service and Soldiers' Privileged Wills, 57 L Q R. 481; notes, 60 ibid. 28; 64 ibid. 174, 65 ibid. 6, 299; 27 Can.B.R. 199.

15 Leathers v. Greenacre, 53 Me. 561, 1866; In re McGarry's Estate,

that the soldier be in fear or in the face of the enemy.[16] Later opinion was to the effect that wills of men stationed in training camps should be privileged,[17] but privilege was denied when the will was made while the soldier was out of camp and on inactive duty immediately after induction.[18] The privilege has been granted to American soldiers when they were prisoners of war.[19]

Although organized hostilities had ceased an officer serving in the war area and who was killed by a fanatic was held privileged.[20] On the other hand the oral will of American soldier who had returned from the war in Europe although he was still a member of the army was denied probate.[21] Like so many other legal matters, the concept of "actual military service" has undergone development and the exact extent of the change cannot be indicated with assurance.

*Sailors*

While the ancient Roman maritime privilege was restricted to members of the naval forces[22] and occasionally American statutes do likewise,[23] the Statute of Frauds also includes ship's personnel on all sorts of ocean craft, and in most of our states the same rule applies.[24] The Louisiana provision, like that in many other civil law codes, grants a privilege to all those on shipboard including passengers.[25]

242 Mich. 287, 218 N.W. 774, 1928; Van Deuzer v. Gordon's Estate, 39 Vt. 111, 1866.

16 Van Deuzer v. Gordon's Estate, supra note 15. Cf. Cal.Prob.Code § 54.

17 Matter of Mallery, 127 Misc. 784, 217 N.Y.S. 489, 1926, affirmed, 247 N.Y. 580, 161 N.E. 190, 1928; In re Miller's Will, 134 Misc. 671, 236 N.Y.S. 529, 1929; In re Straulina's Estate, 4 N.J.Misc. 599, 134 A. 88, 1926 (warned). See Summers, Wills of Soldiers and Seamen, 2 Minn.L.R. 261, 273.

18 In re Sheridan's Estate, 21 N.J. Misc. 473, 34 A.2d 654, 1943, noted, 30 Va.L.R. 481.

19 In re Kapp's Will, 191 Misc. 309, 77 N.Y.S.2d 922, 1947; see In re Thompson's Will, 191 Misc. 109, 76 N.Y.S.2d 742, 1948.

20 In re Limond [1915] 2 Ch. 240.

21 Matter of Dumont, 170 Misc. 100, 9 N.Y.S.2d 606, 1840, affirmed, 257 App.Div. 952, 13 N.Y.S.2d 289, affirmed, 282 N.Y. 606, 25 N.E.2d 388.

22 Digest, 37. 13. 1(1).

23 Md.Ann. Code art. 93 § 336, Supp. 1947. Cf. Cal.Prob. Code § 54.

24 Ex parte Thompson, 4 Brad. (N. Y.) 154 1856 (cook); Matter of O'Connor, 65 Misc. 403, 121 N.Y.S. 903, 1909 (engineer); In the Goods of Hale [1915] 2 Ir. 362 (female typist on liner). But a mariner travelling as a passenger is not privileged. Warren v. Harding, 2 R.I. 133, 1852.

25 La.Civ.Code, Dart 2d ed. § 1601. See French Civil Code, Wright 1908 §

The maritime privilege under legislation of the Statute of Frauds type is not limited to war times; [26] apparently the philosophy is that perils of the sea take the place of the dangers of war in case of military wills. The commandant of a gun boat operating on the Mississippi River was held not to be "at sea" because he was above the ebb and flow of the tide.[27] But one who has started a sea voyage may make a valid sailor's will although the boat has not yet reached the open seas.[28] A will made while a sea-going boat was at the wharf was held valid [29] even if there was no immediate intention of sailing.[30] Even a will made ashore at an intermediate port was sustained as a sailor's will,[31] but if the will was made at the sailor's home though on the eve of sailing it was held not to come within the statute.[32] The privilege has been declared inapplicable if the will was made while the sailor was ashore without leave.[33]

*Minors*

On the theory that soldiers' and sailors' wills were governed by the principles of the common law prior to the Statute of Frauds,[34] it was held in Eugland that a person otherwise qualified could make a will of personalty although he was under the age of twenty-one.[35] When this was later questioned during the first World War,[36] a statute was passed, expressly giving the privilege to minor soldiers.[37] In America the same principle has been de-

988; German Civil Code, Wang, 1907 § 2251; Ex parte Thompson, supra note 24.

26 See infra notes 28, 29.

27 In re Gwin's Will, 1 Tuck. (N.Y.) 44, 1865, criticized in Gardner on Wills, 2d Ed. 53, pointing out that the construction excludes mariners on the Great Lakes from making sailors' wills. The Michigan statute says "on shipboard." Mich.Stat.Ann. § 27, 3178 (75).

28 See Warren v. Harding, supra note 24.

29 Ex parte Thompson, supra note 24.

30 McMurdo's Goods, L.R. 1 P. & D. 540, 1867.

31 Ex parte Thompson, supra note 24.

32 Goods of Corby, 1 Spinks, 292, 164 Eng.Rep. 169, 1854; see In re Anderson's Estate, 180 Misc. 827, 46 N.Y.S.2d 128, 1944. But see Goods of Hale, [1915] 2 Ir. 362.

33 Matter of McDonald, 179 Misc. 284, 37 N.Y.S.2d 945, 1942.

34 See supra § 50 at note 14.

35 In re Farquhar, 4 Notes of Cases 651, 1846.

36 In re Wernher [1918] 1 Ch. 339; cf. s. c. [1918] 2 Ch. 82 (C.A.).

37 See supra note 5. Cf. Holt, Wills (Soldiers' and Sailors') Act, 1918, 30 Jurid. R. 335; Watt, Wills in Wartime, 4 Convey. (N.S.) 150.

clared,[38] although it has also been denied upon the theory that the general statute requiring testators to be of full age permitted no exceptions.[39]

*Property*

As in the case of nuncupative wills, soldiers' and sailors' wills ordinarily may dispose of personalty only. This is the rule followed in absence of statutory provision to the contrary.[40] In a few jurisdictions these wills may dispose of realty.[41]

*Form*

Under statutes similar to the Statute of Frauds, soldiers' or sailors' wills may be oral [42] or written.[43] If oral, it seems that one witness to the words is sufficient,[44] though the statutes in some jurisdictions have been held to require two.[45] The requirements for nuncupative wills do not apply to privileged oral wills.

[38] Henninger's Estate, 30 Pa.Dist. 413, 1921, and see 20 P.S.(Pa.) § 180.1.

[39] In re Evans' Will, 193 Iowa 1240, 188 N.W. 774, 1922; Goodell v. Pike, 40 Vt. 319, 1867; In re Knight's Estate, 19 N.J.Super. 47, 87 A.2d 778, 1952. See also notes, 31 Harv.L.R. 1022, 8 Mo.L.R. 59, 63, 49 W.Va.L.Q. 162.

[40] Pierce v. Pierce, 46 Ind. 86, 1874. It has been held that if the will purports to dispose of realty and personalty, both are void unless separable. Godman v. Godman [1920] P. 261 (C.A.); see In re Beck's Will, 142 N.J.Eq. 15, 58 A.2d 869, 1948. The recent Tennessee statute allowing nuncupative wills generally of personal property to $1,000, but up to $10,000 in case of soldiers and sailors was upheld in In re Holliday's Estate, 180 Tenn. 646, 177 S.W.2d 826, 1944.

[41] New York Decedent Estate Law § 16; N.C.Gen.Stat., 1950 § 31–26. See supra note 5.

[42] Hubbard v. Hubbard, 8 N.Y. 196, 1853 (will made orally in answer to questions); Matter of Mason's Will, 121 Misc. 142, 200 N.Y.S. 901, 1923; In re Stable, [1919] Prob. 7; Brown v. United States, 65 F.2d 65, C.C.A. Cal., 1933.

[43] Matter of Hickey's Estate, 113 Misc. 261, 184 N.Y.S. 399, 1920; May v. May, [1902] Prob. 103. See in the Estate of Beech, [1923] Prob. 46. Statutory complications are described in Weiss, supra note 7 at 68–72

[44] Gould v. Safford's Estate, 39 Vt. 498, 1866. See Hubbard v. Hubbard, supra note 42.

[45] So in New York at present. Decedent Estate Law § 16. Before 1942 New York statutes forbade probate of an unattested written soldier's will, although curiously enough his oral will could be probated. In re Zaiac's Will, 279 N.Y. 545, 18 N.E.2d 848, 1939. This anomalous situation was remedied by amendments to the above statute and to Surrogate's Court Act § 141 so that written unattested wills are probatable while oral ones are not unless proved by two witnesses. See Grant and Palmer, Soldiers' and Sailors' Wills in New York, 12 Albany L.R. 68, 13 ibid. 10; note, 12 Fordham L.R. 80.

Privileged written wills need not be witnessed, and letters or other unattested papers have been held sufficient.[46]

While the writing or the oral declaration must be with testamentary intent,[47] the courts have been somewhat liberal in attaching testamentary intent in the case of soldiers and sailors.[48] On the other hand, a letter which merely declared what the testator had already done was not deemed a testamentary disposition in accordance with the recital.[49] Likewise, the declaration of a seaman as to how he wanted his property divided was held ineffective in absence of proof that he wanted the words to operate as his will.[50]

*Duration and Revocation*

A valid will of a soldier or sailor does not lose effect by reason of the fact that he has returned to another occupation and has opportunity thereafter to make an ordinary will.[51] The privilege does not contemplate that the testator must die from the perils of war or of the sea in order for the will to be valid.[52] Occasionally the statutes provide that privileged wills shall be good only if the testator dies within the designated time.[53]

It seems clear that a privileged written will may revoke a prior formal will, and it is even possible that an oral privileged will may do so.[54] The statutes are silent as to how a privileged will may be revoked. Apparently the statutory provisions for revocation of wills in general apply. Thus, the change of status by marriage or birth of issue or both which revokes generally under the law of

[46] Warren v. Harding, 2 R.I. 133, 1852 (one attesting witness); Rice v. Freeland, 131 Va. 298, 109 S.E. 186, 1921, noted, 8 Va.L.R. 310; Goods of Hiscock, [1901] Prob. 78.

[47] In re Satar's Estate, 275 Pa. 420, 119 A. 478, 1923; In the Estate of Beech, [1923] Prob. 46.

[48] Phoenix Mut. Life Ins. Co. v. Cummings, 67 F.Supp. 159, D.C.Mo. 1946; Rice v. Freeland, supra note 46; Matter of Stein's Will, 119 Misc. 9, 194 N.Y.S. 909, 1922; In re Stable [1919] P. 7 ("if I stop a bullet everything of mine is yours"). Cf. infra note 50.

[49] See authorities cited supra note 47.

[50] In re Buehrer's Estate, 349 Pa. 353, 37 A.2d 587, 1944, noted, 43 Mich. L.R. 416; but cf. Rice v. Freeland, supra note 46. See supra § 47..

[51] See in the Estate of Beech, supra note 47, rejecting the Roman law limitation that the will became ineffective one year after discharge from the army. See note, 8 Mo.L.R. 59, 61.

[52] Hubbard v. Hubbard, 8 N.Y. 196, 1853 (here the testator died at sea from cholera); In re Beck's Will, 142 N.J.Eq. 15, 58 A.2d 869, 1948 (death shortly after discharge from army).

[53] See Weiss, supra note 7 at 76.

[54] Ibid. at 73–74.

the jurisdiction also revokes a soldiers' will.[55] Destruction or mutilation of a written military will doubtless may work a revocation,[56] though acquiescence in its accidental destruction does not.[57] Of course there may be revocation by a subsequent written will, including one coming within the privileged class.[58]

A recent amendment in Pennsylvania permits the revocation of privileged wills regardless of the continuation of this status of the testator as a soldier or sailor.[59] This is a wise provision for otherwise a soldier testator who was discharged when he was still a minor might be unable to rid himself of his will until he had attained his majority.

Soldiers' wills may be indeed a doubtful privilege.[60] What the soldier said, or is alleged to have said, to a companion in a foxhole or to a barmaid in an English pub might conceivably govern the disposition of his large estate when he dies many years later. Indeed ex-service people would be well advised to make formal wills, if only for the purpose of avoiding the consequences of the claim that they had made informal military wills, which would otherwise be unrevoked.

Since 1937 there have been only about a dozen reported American cases involving privileged military wills. This is probably accounted for by the collaboration of the bar in preparing the wills for service men before they left their homes, and of the armed services in providing facilities for the execution of attested wills after entrance into the service. Still, legislation should remove the objections and uncertainties which inhere in the law of privileged wills. There are certainly arguments for a Federal act upon the subject of service men's wills. It would constitute less of an encroachment upon the power of the states than some of the provisions of the Soldiers' and Sailors' Civil Relief Act. An even greater benefit which such an act might perform is to provide for deposit of the wills and an official certification which would establish a prima facie case for their probate.[61]

55 In the Estate of Wardrop [1917] P. 54. See infra § 85.

56 See infra § 86. Cf. the case of an oral will.

57 In re Booth [1926] P. 18.

58 In the Estate of Gossage [1921] P. 194 (C.A.).

59 20 P.S.(Pa.) § 180.1.

60 See notes, 65 L.Q.R. 6, 299.

61 See Atkinson, Soldiers' and Sailors' Wills, 28 A.B.A.J. 753, 757; Weiss, supra note 7 at 81-90; note, 15 U. of Chi.L.R. 702, 709-715.

## WILLS IN LOUISIANA

**78. A nuncupative will by public act is one dictated to a notary in the presence of three resident or five non-resident witnesses, is then read back by the notary, and finally is signed by the testator, the witnesses and the notary who mentions the performance of the formalities in his notarial act which is made part of the will.**

**A nuncupative act by private signature is similar, but it does not require the services of a notary. Five resident or seven non-resident witnesses are necessary, unless the will is executed in the country where three or five respectively are sufficient if more cannot be found.**

**A mystic or closed will is one signed and sealed up by the testator and presented to three witnesses and a notary with the testator's declaration that it is his last will. A written indorsement reciting the facts of execution must be made on the cover by the notary and signed by him, the testator, and the witnesses.**

Most civil law jurisdictions, including Louisiana, have three principal classes of wills: (1) holographic, (2) nuncupative or open, (3) mystic or sealed.[1] The second and third are formal and traditional instruments in the civil law. It is solely because we look at them from the eyes of the Anglo-American lawyer that we classify them here as special types of wills. These types vary in detail in the various civil law countries. Only a brief description of the Louisiana law is attempted here. For the most part these wills require participation of a notary. The notary in the civil law system is a far different person than in the United States generally. He is a skilled official who performs important legal functions and who is required to keep records of all of his transactions.[2] Hence it would be unthinkable to employ a notary in a common-law jurisdiction to participate in the execution of a civil law notarial will.[3]

A nuncupative will in the civil law is one that is orally and openly declared to the witnesses, but it is then reduced to writing with a very considerable formality. In Louisiana there may be nuncupative wills by public act, or by act under private signature.

1 Louisiana—LSA—C.C. art. 1574. As to holographic wills, see supra § 75.

2 See Eder, Anglo-American & Latin-American Law, 130.

3 See supra § 74, note 8.

*Nuncupative Will by Public Act*

This type must be "received" by a notary in the presence of three resident or five non-resident witnesses.[4] The code declares that the will must be dictated by the testator and written by the notary as dictated, and then must be read to the testator in the presence of the witnesses; all formalities must be fulfilled at one time without interruption.[5] The will must be signed by the testator if he is able to do so, and if not he must so declare and there must be express mention of his declaration and of the cause of his disability.[6] The will must be signed by the witnesses or by at least one of them if the others cannot write.[7] The will is invalid unless the notarial act is made part of the will and it recites that the will was written by the notary himself and that all of the code requirements were fulfilled.[8]

*Nuncupative Will under Private Signature*

This form does not require the presence of the notary. It must be written in by the testator himself, or by some other person from his dictation in the presence of five resident or seven non-resident witnesses, but it also suffices if in the presence of the witnesses the testator presents a paper which he has written or caused to be written, and declares to be his last will.[9] In either case the will must be read to all the witnesses by the testator or by one of the witnesses, and signed by the testator if he is able and by the witnesses, or at least two of them, the other witnesses affixing their mark.[10] In the country (rural districts) it is sufficient if there are three resident or five non-resident witnesses if more cannot be had.[11]

[4] A resident witness is one living in the house where the will was executed. Louisiana—LSA—C.C., art. 1594.

[5] Ibid. § 1578. See infra notes 8, 12, 15.

[6] Ibid. § 1579.

[7] Ibid. § 1580.

[8] Fakouri v. Cadais, 147 F.2d 667, rehearing denied 149 F.2d 321, C.C.A. La.1945. See Horton, Formalities of the Nuncupative Will by Public Act, 12 Tulane L.R. 439. One of the advantages of this type of will is the extent to which the will is proved by the notarial act, thus facilitating probate and practically eliminating contest on most of the common grounds. Fakouri v. Cadais, supra. Cf. infra § 98.

[9] Louisiana—LSA—C.C. art. 1581.

[10] Ibid. art 1582.

[11] Ibid. art. 1583.

*Mystic Wills*

It will be observed that in case of a nuncupative will the witnesses know the contents of the instrument from hearing it read. In mystic, sometimes called sealed or closed wills, they do not. Here the testator must sign the instrument which he has written or has caused to be written by another. This paper or the envelope containing it must be closed and sealed, and presented to the notary and three witnesses, or testator may cause it to be closed and sealed in their presence. Then he must declare to the notary in the presence of the witnesses that it contains his will signed by him. The notary then draws up the "act of superscription" upon the cover and the act must be signed by the testator, the notary and the witnesses.[12] All this must be done without interruption, and if the testator becomes unable to write so that he cannot sign the superscription, mention must be made of his declaration to that effect.[13] Those who cannot "write" or sign their names cannot make a valid mystic will.[14] The will must be signed by at least two witnesses and mention must be made in the superscription if there are any other witnesses who are unable to sign.[15]

*Witnesses*

The following persons are absolutely incapable of being witnesses in Louisiana: (1) children under 16, (2) the insane, deaf, dumb and blind, (3) persons whom the criminal laws declare incapable of exercising civil functions, (4) married women to the wills of their husbands,[16] (5) heirs or legatees of the testator.[17] A legatee is incompetent to act as notary to a nuncupative will by public act.[18]

*Choice of Type of Will—Alternatives*

Partly because of the civil law institution of the legitime which limits freedom of testator,[19] wills are not as frequent in Louisi-

12 Ibid. art. 1584. Probably a will is sufficiently closed and sealed if enclosed in an envelope with the flap adhering by mucilage. Saint v. Charity Hospital, 48 La.Ann. 236, 19 So. 275, 1896. Cf. Succession of Fertel, 209 La. 655, 25 So.2d 296, 1946.

13 Louisiana—LSA—C.C. art. 1581.

14 Ibid. art. 1586. As explained in the compiler's note, "write" probably should have been translated "read".

15 Ibid. art. 1587.

16 Ibid. art. 1591.

17 Ibid. art. 1592. But article 1593 excepts mystic will from the fifth prohibition.

18 See Succession of Purkert, 184 La. 791, 167 So. 444, 1936.

19 See supra § 36 at note 1.

ana and other civil law jurisdictions as in common-law states and countries. Furthermore, a civil law will is apt to be shorter and more simple in its provisions, and lawyers often prepare a draft which is copied by the client under the lawyer's supervision so as to comply with the requirements of a holographic will. However, nuncupative wills are frequently made and they are far more common than mystic wills. Where attempt to execute a nuncupative will by public act fails, it may still be good as a will by private signature.[20] A defectively executed mystic will has been held valid as a holographic testament,[21] and the same may be true in certain cases when a nuncupative will by private signature was intended.[22]

[20] Succession of Lombardo, 205 La. 261, 17 So.2d 303, 1944.

[21] Broutin v. Vassant, 5 Mart. (O. S.) 169, 1817; but only if the instrument was entirely in testator's hand and signed and dated by him.

[22] Succession of Sullivan, 178 La. 230, 151 So. 190, 1933. See supra note 21.

# CHAPTER 9

# INTEGRATION, REFERENCE AND CONDITION



## *Forecast*

In this chapter we start with the proposition that the will is restricted to the papers which were covered by the formalities of execution. The security thus afforded becomes somewhat illusive when we consider that the questions of what physically could be, and what were intended to be, integrated into the will may require resort to oral evidence. Furthermore, where the will itself refers to other documents, events or conditions we are confronted with the dilemma of whether the reference is to be denied effect for reasons of security or whether evidence aliunde is to be considered for the purpose of giving effect to the testator's intent. All this is functionally related to the matter of giving relief for fraud and mistake,[1] and to the broad subject of the admissibility of external evidence in the process of interpretation and construction of wills.[2] Doctrinally these matters are distinct, and each is traditionally approached in an entirely different manner. However, due to their realistic relationship it is not surprising to find some blurring of the various matters and doctrines.

1 See supra §§ 58–60.

2 See infra § 146.

## INTEGRATION OF WILLS

**79. A will may be written on several sheets of paper, provided that all are intended to operate as the will and are present at the time of execution. These facts may be presumed from physical connection of the sheets or coherence of the provisions and can also be established in other manners.**

**The problem of integration, or what may be regarded as the will so as to operate by force of a single act of execution, must be distinguished from problems of revocation and construction when the testator leaves several testamentary instruments, each of which is validly executed.**

The integration of a will is the process of embodying it in a written memorial which is validated by a single act of execution.[1] The authorities are clear that the will may be written upon several separate pages.[2] While it is good practice to have the testator sign each page for the purpose of identification,[3] this is not necessary.[4] However, all the parts of the will must be present at the time of execution.[5] One may not integrate a paper into

[1] See Evans, Incorporation by Reference, Integration and Non-Testamentary Act, 25 Col.L.R. 879, 888; Mechem, The Integration of Holographic Wills, 12 N.C.L.R. 213. When two or more papers are each validly executed the problem is not one of integration, but rather of revocation or construction. See infra at note 20 et seq.

[2] Kyle v. Jordan, 187 Ala. 355, 65 So. 522, 1914; Paglia v. Messina, 270 Mass. 1, 169 N.E. 423, 1930 (signatures of testator and witnesses on separate sheets); In re Cook's Estate, 113 N.J.Eq. 225, 166 A. 32, 1933; In re Deyton's Wills, 177 N.C. 494, 99 S.E. 424, 1919; Goethe v. Browning, 146 S.C. 7, 143 S.E. 362, 1928. Cf. Shane v. Wooley, 138 Md. 75, 113 A. 652, 1921, holding that witnesses must sign on the same sheet as testator, or on a sheet physically attached thereto, and that their signatures on a sealed envelope containing the will were insufficient. But see Johnston v. King, 250 Ala. 571, 35 So.2d 202, 1948, noted, 47 Mich.L.R. 440. In Bolton v. Bolton, 107 Miss. 84, 64 So. 967, 1921, the will was sustained though the mucilage failed to work in attaching the paper on which the witnesses signed. See supra § 70, note 29 et seq.

[3] Hathaway v. Warren, 277 Mass. 161, 178 N.E. 288, 1931; Dearing v. Dearing, 132 Va. 178, 111 S.E. 286, 1922. See supra § 74 at note 7.

[4] Goethe v. Browning, supra note 2; Hathaway v. Warren, supra note 3; Dearing v. Dearing, supra note 3.

[5] Re Sleeper, 129 Me. 194, 151 A. 150, 71 A.L.R. 518, 1930, noted, 17 Va.L.R. 69, 40 Yale L.J. 144, 11 Bost. U.L.R. 148. See Re Maginn's Estate, 281 Pa. 514, 127 A. 79, 1924; Id., 278 Pa. 89, 122 A. 264, 30 A.L.R. 418, 1923; Cole v. Webb, 220 Ky. 817, 295 S.W. 1035, 1927. A letter written after the execution of an attested will, explaining it, cannot be regarded as a part of the will. In re Johnson's Estate, 100 Or. 142, 196 P. 385, 1921;

a will which is not there at the time of execution. On the other hand, a paper present is not integrated into the will if not so intended.[6]

While there is much loose language to the effect that there must either be a physical connection between the various pages of the will or else a coherence of sense,[7] this is insisted upon more as a means of proof of integration rather than a requisite of the process. Thus, if it can be shown that testator intended to embody the pages offered for probate as his will, it is not necessary to prove physical or consensual connection.[8] If the pages are substantially fastened together, or if there is a connection of language carrying over from page to page, this is sufficient prima facie evidence of integration to admit the entire document to probate.[9] However, in absence of either proof by witnesses or by internal evidence establishing unity of the pages, probate will be denied.[10] Of course the contestant of the will may show a subsequent substitution of pages in any case.[11]

### *In Jurisdictions Where Will Must be Signed at End*

In the jurisdictions which require wills to be signed at the end, there are certain peculiar problems of integration. Here it may be true that unless there is a physical or consensual connection of

Bond v. Seawell, 3 Burr. 1773, 97 Eng. Rep. 1092, 1755; Gass' Heirs v. Gass' Ex'rs, 3 Humph.(Tenn.) 278, 1842.

6 In re Bryen's Estate, 328 Pa. 122, 195 A. 17, 1937 (loose sheet signed by mistake). Cf. In re Seymour's Will, 299 N.Y. 767, 87 N.E.2d 675, 1949.

7 See Sellards v. Kirby, 82 Kan. 291, 108 P. 73, 28 L.R.A.,N.S., 270, 136 Am.St.Rep. 110, 20 Ann.Cas. 214, 1910; Wikoff's Appeal, 15 Pa. 281, 53 Am.Dec. 597, 1850; Re Maginn's Estate, supra note 5; Seiter's Estate, 265 Pa. 202, 108 A. 614, 1919; In re Fisher's Estate, 283 Pa. 282, 129 A. 90, 1925.

8 Stanard v. Miller, 212 Ala. 605, 103 So. 594, 1925; Harp v. Parr, 168 Ill. 459, 48 N.E. 113, 1897; Palmer v. Owen, 229 Ill. 115, 82 N.E. 275, 1907; Cole v. Webb, supra note 5; Re Sleeper, supra note 5; Murphy v. Clancy, 177 Mo.App. 429, 163 S.W. 915, 1914; In re Cook's Estate, 113 N.J.Eq. 225, 166 A. 32, 1933.

9 Barnewall v. Murrell, 108 Ala. 366, 18 So. 831, 1895; Kyle v. Jordan, supra note 2; Ela v. Edwards, 16 Gray (Mass.) 91, 1860; Re Sleeper, supra note 5 ("fastening them together is, of course, the conventional method and is seldom questioned"); Johnson's Will, 80 N.J.Eq. 525, 85 A. 254, 1912; In re Swaim's Will, 162 N.C. 213, 78 S.E. 72, Ann.Cas.1915A 1207, 1913; In re Covington's Estate, 348 Pa. 1, 33 A.2d 235, 1943 (liberal application of coherence between pages).

10 In re Allen's Will, 282 N.Y. 402, 272 N.E.2d 22, 1940; In re Davis' Estate, 344 Pa. 520, 26 A.2d 339, 1942.

11 Varnon v. Varnon, 67 Mo.App. 534, 1896. See Hathaway v. Warren, 277 Mass. 161, 178 N.E. 288, 1931.

the pages, or a numbering thereof or something to indicate from the instrument itself what is the end of the will it may not be properly integrated.[12] Perhaps in such jurisdictions evidence aliunde the instrument should not be received for the purpose of showing that the testator had intended that the pages offered for probate were to be his will.[13] This is more for the satisfaction of the requirement of signing at the end than for the purpose of proof of integration proper. It is not clear, however, but that a temporary fastening may not be enough for satisfaction of this requirement. Thus if the papers in their proper order were held together by a pin, a removable clip, or even the testator's thumb, the rule of signing at the end may be satisfied.[14] But where the sheet which testator and the witnesses signed was on top of the remaining pages and merely clipped to it by a removable clip, the execution was held insufficient in a state requiring signing at the end.[15]

### *Integration of Holographic Wills*

Holographic wills present some troublesome questions of integration.[16] Unlike attested wills there is no ceremony performed at which witnesses, testator and will are necessarily together and where the testator expressly, or by implication, declares that these papers are his will, or at least, his act. While some cases seem to require that holographic wills should be written entirely as part of one transaction,[17] the better view seems to consider all the papers which the holographic testator intended as his will, to constitute the same, regardless of the time and place of making them.[18] One case sustained a holographic will which was signed only on the envelope containing the memoranda of dispositions.[19]

[12] In re Baldwin's Estate, 357 Pa. 432, 55 A.2d 263, 1947, noted, 9 U. of Pitt.L.R. 239; authorities noted supra note 7; note, 33 Harv.L.R. 989.

[13] Pennsylvania cases cited supra note 7.

[14] See Evans, supra note 1 at 890. Wills have been sustained where the signatures are on an envelope containing the disposing part. In re Nichols [1921] 2 Ch. 11. See notes, 11 Fordham L.R. 320, 59 L.Q.R. 20.

[15] Re Maginn's Estate, supra note 5.

[16] One aspect of their integration has already been treated supra § 75 at note 12 et seq.

[17] Lagrave v. Merle, 5 La.Ann. 278, 52 Am.Dec. 589, 1850. See Estate of Taylor, 126 Cal. 97, 58 P. 454, 1899. But see Succession of Cunningham, 142 La. 701, 77 So. 506, 1918; Succession of Guiraud, 164 La. 620, 114 So. 489, 1927, and California cases infra note 18.

[18] Estate of Skerrett, 67 Cal. 585, 8 P. 181, 1885; In re Dumas' Estate, 34

[19] See Note 19 on following page.

*Duplicate Wills*

Sometimes in order to minimize the risk of loss, two or more identical copies are each completely executed, but, since there is only one will in legal contemplation, only one copy is probated.[20] As a whole, duplicate wills are inadvisable because serious problems concerning revocation arise when all of the duplicates are not accounted for at probate.[21] When the testator signs one copy of his will and by mistake the witnesses sign another the two cannot be considered together as the will since the testator did not so intend.[22] However, if the copies are physically attached to each other it has been held that the will is validly executed.[23]

*Two or More Instruments as Single Will*

Separately executed instruments may together constitute the testator's will, and all be admitted to probate.[24] These cases involve no problem of integration though questions of revocation and construction may be presented.[25] If two inconsistent documents are executed simultaneously it has been held that neither should be probated.[26] Testators sometimes execute separate wills for property located in different jurisdictions. Ordinarily each

Cal.App.2d 406, 210 P.2d 697, 1949, noted, 24 Tulane L.R. 382, 3 Vand.L. R. 844; In re Morrison's Estate, 98 Cal.App.2d 380, 220 P.2d 413, 1950; Hays v. Marschall, 243 Ky. 392, 48 S. W.2d 540, 1932; Druen v. Hudson, 17 Tenn.App. 428, 68 S.W.2d 146, 1933. See In re Deyton's Wills, supra note 2. Cf. In re Fritz's Estate, 102 Cal. App.2d 385, 227 P.2d 539, 1951.

19 Alexander v. Johnston, 171 N.C. 468, 88 S.E. 785, 1916. But see In re Tyrrell's Estate, 17 Ariz. 418, 153 P. 767, 1915, noted, 14 Mich.L.R. 522. Cf. Mechem, supra note 1 at 224. A signed inscription on an envelope was held not to pass the contents thereof by succession. Hunt v. Furman, 52 S.E.2d 816, W.Va. 1949, noted, 2 Ala. L.R. 144. See also supra note 14.

20 Crossman v. Crossman, 95 N.Y. 145, 1884.

21 See infra § 86.

22 Baldwin's Will, 146 N.C. 25, 59 S.E. 163, 125 Am.St.Rep. 466, 1907; In re Goods of Hatton, L.R. 6 P.D. 204, 1881. But see In re Dawson's Estate, 277 Pa. 168, 120 A. 828, 1923, where signing by witnesses was not required under the statute.

23 In re Goettel's Will, 184 Misc. 155, 55 N.Y.S.2d 61, 1944.

24 In re Ballesio's Estate, 201 Cal. 357, 256 P. 1101, 1927 (on opposite sides of same paper); Whitney v. Hanington, 36 Colo. 407, 85 P. 84, 1906; Smith v. Gorham, 152 Ill.App. 125, 1909; Whittle v. Roper, 156 Va. 407, 157 S.E. 827, 1031 (both executed on the same day.)

25 See infra §§ 86, 146.

26 In re Love's Estate, 75 Utah 342, 285 P. 299, 1930. And see Whittle v. Roper, supra note 24.

such will should be probated in the appropriate place, and a court should not probate wills operating solely upon real property located elsewhere.[27]

[27] Parnell v. Thompson, 81 Kan. 119, 105 P. 502, 33 L.R.A.,N.S., 658, 1909; noted, 23 Harv.L.R. 467; In the Goods of Coode, 1 P. and D. 449, 1867; In the Goods of Murray, [1896] Prob. 65.

## INCORPORATION BY REFERENCE

**80. If a will, executed as required by statute, incorporates by reference any document or paper not so executed, whether the paper referred to be in the form of a will, codicil, deed, note or mere list or memorandum, the paper so referred to, if it was in existence at the time of the execution of the will, is referred to as being in existence, and is identified by satisfactory proof as the paper referred to, takes effect as part of the will in most jurisdictions.**

The process of integration just described, must be distinguished from the different, though somewhat related and overlapping, matter of incorporation by reference.[1] When papers are integrated into a will they must be present at the time of the execution and they become a part of the will in the fullest sense of the word. Unless lost, such papers must be probated. On the other hand, incorporation by reference is the doctrine by which a document is considered as part of the will for certain purposes only. Under this doctrine the paper need not be present at the time of execution,[2] and need not be probated with the will proper.[3] Yet if the document is incorporated by reference it will be considered as part of the will for the purpose of construction and application of the will's provisions to persons and things. The two doctrines may overlap in case that the document in question is present at the time of execution and is also referred to in the attested pages in the manner required for incorporation by reference.

The doctrine of incorporation by reference is recognized in England,[4] and in the great majority of American jurisdictions.[5]

1 See generally Dobie, Testamentary Incorporation by Reference, 3 Va.L.R. 583; Evans, Incorporation by Reference, Integration and Nontestamentary Act, 25 Col.L.R. 879; Evans, Nontestamentary Acts and Incorporation by Reference, 16 U. of Chi.L.R. 635; Rowley, A Relaxation of the Requirement of Self-sufficient Integration, 6 U. of Cin.L.R. 295; note, 46 Mich.L.R. 77.

2 If this were required, there would be no necessity for the doctrine of incorporation by reference, as there would be compliance with the requirements of integration. See § 79, supra.

3 In re Willey's Estate, 128 Cal. 1, 60 P. 471, 1900; Tuttle v. Berryman, 94 Ky. 553, 23 S.W. 345, 1893; Goods of Balme, [1897] P. 261 (bulky catalogue). Cf. Newton v. Seaman's Friend Society, 130 Mass. 91, 39 Am. Rep. 433, 1881, where the incorporated document was held properly probated. And see Merrill v. Boal, 47 R. I. 274, 132 A. 721, 45 A.L.R. 830, 1926.

4 Allen v. Maddock, 11 Moo.P.C. 427, 14 Eng.Rep. 757, 1858; In re Nicholls, [1921] 2 Ch. 11, 125 L.T.N.S.

Obviously an unrestricted recognition of incorporation of unattested papers into wills would open the door to fraud and in addition may be said to violate the spirit of the requirements of execution. For this reason, a minority of jurisdictions have refused general recognition of the doctrine.[6] In the remaining states the requirements suggested by the black letter text above have been laid down in order to keep the doctrine within due bounds, though there are occasional relaxations. When reference is made to an *act* of the testator or of another, different consid-

55, 11 B.R.C. 844. In the latter case the paper in question could have been given testamentary effect either on the ground that it was duly integrated into the will, or that it was incorporated therein by reference.

5 Estate of Atkinson, 110 Cal.App. 499, 294 P. 425, 1930; Eschmann v. Cawi, 357 Ill. 379, 192 N.E. 226, 1934; Fickle v. Snepp, 97 Ind. 289, 49 Am. Rep. 449, 1844; In re Cameron's Estate, 215 Iowa 63, 241 N.W. 458, 1932 (incorporation of a prior will which had been revoked); Shulsky v. Shulsky, 98 Kan. 69, 157 P. 407, 1916 (incorporation of invalid deed); Bemis v. Fletcher, 251 Mass. 178, 146 N.E. 277, 37 A.L.R. 1471, 1925; In re Bresler's Estate, 155 Mich. 567, 119 N.W. 1104, 1909 (books of account); Jennings v. Reeson, 200 Mich. 559, 166 N. W. 931, 1918 (undelivered deed); Ray v. Walker, 293 Mo. 447, 477, 240 S.W. 187, 1921; In re Estate of Hopper, 90 Neb. 622, 134 N.W. 237, 1912; Linney v. Cleveland Trust Co., 30 Ohio App. 345, 165 N.E. 101, 1928; Boehmer v. Silvestone, 95 Or. 154, 186 P. 26, 1920 (will of another); Clark v. Dennison, 283 Pa. 285, 129 A. 94, 1925 (same); Merrill v. Boal, 47 R.I. 274, 132 A. 721, 45 A.L.R. 830, 1926; and see O'Leary v. Lane, 149 Ark. 393, 232 S. W. 432, 1921; Hull's Estate, 164 Md. 39, 163 A. 819, 1933; Swetland v. Swetland, 100 N.J.Eq. 196, 134 A. 822, 1928; Watson v. Hinson, 162 N.C. 72, 77 S.E. 1089, Ann.Cas.1915A 870, 1913; Triplett's Ex'r v. Triplett, 161 Va. 906, 172 S.E. 162, 1934. For a long note on the doctrine in general, see 17 Minn.L.R. 527. See codification of the rule in Ohio Gen. Code § 10504-4.

6 Hatheway v. Smith, 79 Conn. 506, 65 A. 1058, 9 L.R.A.,N.S., 310, 9 Ann. Cas. 99, 1907; Succession of Ledet, 170 La. 449, 128 So. 273, 1930, but cf. Hessmer v. Edenborn, 196 La. 575, 199 So. 647, 1940, noted, 40 Mich.L. R. 492; Murray v. Lewis, 94 N.J.Eq. 681, 121 A. 525, 1923, but see Swetland v. Swetland, supra note 5 and First Mechanic's Nat. Bank of Trenton v. Norris, 134 N.J.Eq. 229, 34 A.2d 746, 1943; Booth v. Baptist Church of Christ, 126 N.Y. 215, 28 N.E. 238, 1891, with which compare Matter of Fowles, 222 N.Y. 222, 118 N.E. 611, Ann.Cas.1918D 834, 1918, and Matter of Rausch, 258 N.Y. 327, 179 N.E. 755; 80 A.L.R. 98, 1932, noted, 6 Cin.L.R. 295, 32 Col.L.R. 917, 17 Minn.L.R. 564, 9 N.Y.U.L.R. 507. The Fowles and Rausch cases have been regarded as recognizing the doctrine of incorporation by reference, but limited to cases of the will of another or of a trust deed, situations where there could be little chance of fraud or uncertainty. But the cases have also been explained upon the basis of reference to non-testamentary acts (infra § 81). See articles by Dean Evans, supra note 1; cf. note, 46 Mich.L.R. 77; Samuels, Incorporation by Reference in New York Wills, 19 N.Y.U.L.Q.R. 270.

erations apply, and the restrictions connected with incorporation by reference are not applicable.[7]

*Identification of the Writing*

This requirement has two aspects: (1) The will itself must refer to the writing to be incorporated, with reasonable certainty; (2) there must be a showing that the writing corresponds to the description in the will and is the one intended by the testator. The law does not require absolute certainty of description, for this would often be laying down a condition impossible of fulfillment.[8] Conceivably there might be two or more documents in existence which would answer to almost any description.

In a leading American case, instructions to pay legacies "according to the directions written in a book by Melvin W. Pierce, signed by me Alexander De Witt and witnessed by said Melvin W. Pierce," was held sufficient description.[9] Identification of deeds,[10] contracts,[11] or notes,[12] can be made by designation of date and parties. In the leading English case,[13] a statement that "this is a codicil to my last will and testament" was held definite enough to refer to a will improperly executed found in the possession of the testatrix, no other document answering to this description being found. A reference to the amount which a legatee may be owing "on my books" was held sufficient, there being only one set of accounts kept by the testator.[14] Reference to another paper "in my pocketbook" was held to incorporate the same.[15]

7 See infra § 81.

8 See Simon v. Grayson, 15 Cal.2d 531, 102 P.2d 1081, 1940. But cf. language in In re Young's Estate, 123 Cal. 337, 342, 55 P. 1011, 1012, 1899; Richardson v. Byrd, 166 S.C. 251, 256, 164 S.E. 643, 644, 1932.

9 Newton v. Seaman's Friend Society, 130 Mass. 91, 39 Am.Rep. 433, 1881.

10 Fesler v. Simpson, 58 Ind. 83, 1877; Bizzey v. Flight, L.R. 3 Ch.D. 269, 1876.

11 Allday v. Cage, 148 S.W. 838, Tex.Civ.App.1912.

12 Fickle v. Snepp, 97 Ind. 289, 49 Am.Rep. 449, 1884; Loring v. Summer, 23 Pick.(Mass.) 98, 1839.

13 Allen v. Maddock, 11 Moo.P.C. 427, 14 Eng.Rep. 757, 1858. See also Rogers v. Agricola, 176 Ark. 287, 3 S.W.2d 26, 1928; Derr v. Derr, 123 Kan. 681, 256 P. 800, 53 A.L.R. 515, 1927; Taft v. Stearns, 234 Mass. 273, 125 N.E. 570, 1920. Hughes v. Bent, 118 Ky. 609, 81 S.W. 931, 1904, is an unusually liberal case in which a devise "upon sacred trust" was held sufficient to incorporate an explanatory paper attached to the will. Cf. § 57 supra at note 18.

14 In re Bresler's Estate, 155 Mich. 567, 119 N.W. 1104, 1909.

15 In re Miller's Estate, 128 Cal. App. 176, 17 P.2d 181, 1932.

On the other hand, references to "a sealed letter which will be found with this will," [16] as well as to certain furniture "which she has got a list of," [17] were held insufficient. Likewise reference to a deed of gift without further description thereof was not enough.[18] These cases seem to take a stricter view than some of the decisions mentioned in the last paragraph.

All the cases upon sufficiency of description cannot be reconciled. The question is intimately tied up with the matters of whether the document was in existence at the time of the execution of the will, of whether the latter refers to the document as being in existence, and of whether there was intention to incorporate it. The decisions are also undoubtedly influenced by the attitude of the particular courts upon the general doctrine of incorporation by reference. Thus, while the New York Court of Appeals has declared that it will not recognize the principle,[19] it has held that where there was clear reference to an existing trust agreement, the effect of incorporation might be given.[20] In this case the description and the circumstances permit practically no chances of fraud or uncertainty so that even the New York court was unwilling to carry its hostility to incorporation by reference to a "dryly logical extreme."

*Reference to Document as Existing*

Not only must the document be in existence at the time of the execution of the will,[21] but it must normally be referred to as being then in existence.[22] This requirement is met if a codicil

[16] Bryan's Appeal, 77 Conn. 240, 58 A. 748, 68 L.R.A. 353, 107 Am.St.Rep. 34, 1 Ann.Cas. 393, 1904. Connecticut later rejected the doctrine of incorporation by reference altogether. See note 6 supra.

[17] In re Goods of Greves, 1 Sw. & Tr. 250, 164 Eng.Rep. 715, 1858.

[18] Brooker v. Brooker, 130 Tex. 27, 106 S.W.2d 247, 1937. See Bailey v. Bailey, 52 N.C. 44, 1859. And see also O'Leary v. Lane, supra note 5, where a reference to a deed to certain heirs in a specified safety box was held insufficient identity. But see Ray v. Walker, supra note 5, "the real estate I have this day deed to him." See infra notes 31, 32.

[19] Booth v. Baptist Church of Christ, supra note 6.

[20] Matter of Rausch, supra note 6; see also Matter of Fowles, supra note 6, where the reference was to the will of testator's wife. And see comment, supra note 6.

[21] Wagner v. Clauson, 399 Ill. 403, 78 N.E.2d 203, 3 A.L.R. 672, 1948; Daniel v. Tyler, 296 Ky. 808, 178 S.W.2d 411, 1944; Sleeper's Appeal, 129 Me. 194, 151 A. 71, 71 A.L.R. 518, 1930.

[22] In re Soher, 78 Cal. 477, 21 P. 8, 1889; Bryan's Appeal, supra note 16; Keeler v. Merchants' Loan & Trust Co., 253 Ill. 528, 97 N.E. 1061, 1912; Appeal of Sleeper, 129 Me. 194, 151 A.

refers to "my last will and testament," the latter being invalid for want of proper attestation,[23] or when a deed is specified as made.[24]

If the will speaks of an instrument "to be" prepared, the latter cannot be regarded as incorporated in the will and parol evidence is not admissible to show that it was then in existence.[25] Where a bequest refers to such personal property "as shall be ticketed or may be described on a paper in my own handwriting," [26] or to such articles "as are contained in the inventory signed by me and deposited herewith," [27] or to the purposes of a trust instrument "which will be found with this will," [28] the references were deemed to be insufficient compliance with this requirement. Some of these expressions may be said to be ambiguous for they might conceivably refer to either existing or future documents. When stated in such uncertain terms the will does not meet the requirements of incorporation by reference and the attempted devises or bequests ordinarily fail.[29]

### *Intention to Incorporate*

The will must not only mention the document so as to identify it as an existing document, but the will must also show an in-

150, 71 A.L.R. 518, 1930, noted, 11 Bost.U.L.R. 148; Newton v. Seaman's Friend Society, 130 Mass. 91, 39 Am. Rep. 433, 1881; Allen v. Boomer, 82 Wis. 364, 52 N.W. 426, 1892; Goods of Truro, L.R. 1 P. & D. 201, 1866; Ohio Gen.Code § 10504-4. Cf. note, 26 Harv.L.R. 278.

23 Allen v. Maddock, 11 Moo.P.C. 427, 14 Eng.Rep. 757, 1858.

24 Shulsky v. Shulsky, 98 Kan. 69, 157 P. 407, 1916; see note, 29 Cal.L.R. 94.

25 Keeler v. Merchants' Loan & Trust Co., supra note 22. See Lawless v. Lawless, 187 Va. 511, 47 S.E. 2d 431, 1948.

26 Goods of Sunderland, L.R. 1 P. & D. 198, 1866.

27 Goods of Truro, supra note 22.

28 Bryan's Appeal, supra note 16.

29 Goods of Sunderland, supra note 26. And see Magnus v. Magnus, 80 N.J.Eq. 346, 84 A. 705, 1912. For this reason it would seem that the doctrine of incorporation by reference would not apply to an ordinary reference in a will to words appearing below or on the reverse side of the page. But see In re Poole, [1929] 1 D.L.R. 418, noted, 42 Harv.L.R. 965, and Pallin v. Ponting, [1930] P. 185, criticized, 29 Mich.L.R. 956. However, it would be possible to hold that this matter is actually integrated into the will, and even in jurisdictions requiring the will to be signed at the end, to consider that the matter appears at the asterisk or place of reference. Baker's Appeal, 107 Pa. 381, 52 Am. Rep. 478, 1884; In re Goods of Birt, L.R. 2 P. & D. 214, 1871. Contra: In re Conway, 124 N.Y. 455, 26 N.E. 1028, 11 L.R.A. 796, 1891; In re Whitney's Will, 153 N.Y. 259, 47 N.E. 272, 60 Am. St.Rep. 616, 1897. See Dobie, Testamentary Incorporation by Reference, 3 Va.L.R. 583, 594.

tention to incorporate the instrument.[30] Mere reference to a deed, as if it were effective as such, is usually held insufficient to devise the property therein described when it turns out that the deed is ineffective as such.[31] Nor does the direction in a will to deliver certain deeds amount to an incorporation thereof into the will so as to work devises to the grantees.[32]

### *Proof of Existence*

Turning from the three requirements respecting the will itself necessary for successful application of the doctrine of incorporation by reference, we come to the things which must be proved with reference to the documents sought to be incorporated. We have seen how the will itself must refer to the document as being in existence. This recital or reference must be true; in other words, it must be shown that the document was in existence at the time of execution of the will.[33] Even if the will states that the document is in existence, it can be shown that the latter was written after the will.[34] However, if a will refers to a document as being in existence, though in fact it was not, and the will is republished by a codicil after execution of the specified document, the latter is incorporated.[35] The contrary

[30] Estate of McCurdy, 197 Cal. 276, 240 P. 498, 1925; Hunt ex rel. City of Streator v. Evans, 134 Ill. 496, 25 N.E. 579, 11 L.R.A. 185, 1890; Zimmerman v. Hafer, 81 Md. 347, 32 A. 316, 1895; Richardson v. Byrd, 166 S.C. 251, 164 S.E. 643, 1932. And see cases infra notes 31, 32.

[31] Noble v. Tipton, 219 Ill. 182, 76 N.E. 151, 3 L.R.A.,N.S., 645, 1905; In re Watts' Estate, 117 Mont. 505, 160 P.2d 492, 1945, noted, 7 Mont.L.R. 76; Allenbach v. Ridenour, 51 Nev. 437, 279 P. 32, 1929; Witham v. Witham, 156 Or. 59, 66 P.2d 281, 110 A.L.R. 253, 1937. Contra: In re Dimmitt's Estate, 141 Neb. 413, 3 N.W.2d 752, 144 A.L.R. 704, 1942, noted, 37 Ill. L.R. 425, 41 Mich.L.R. 751, and 22 Tex.L.R. 87. As the opinion and notes show the result could also be justified on the basis of a gift by implication. See also supra note 18; infra § 146.

[32] Bottrell v. Spengler, 343 Ill. 476, 175 N.E. 781, 1931. But see Arrington v. Brown, 235 Ala. 196, 178 So. 218, 1938.

[33] Shillaber's Estate, 74 Cal. 144, 15 P. 453, 5 Am.St.Rep. 433, 1887; Vestry of St. John's Parish v. Bostwick, 8 App.D.C. 452, 1896; Hunt ex rel. City of Streator v. Evans, 134 Ill. 496, 25 N.E. 579, 11 L.R.A. 185, 1890; Appeal of Sleeper, 129 Me. 194, 151 A. 150, 71 A.L.R. 518, 1930; Hull's Estate, 164 Md. 39, 163 A. 819, 1933.

[34] Shillaber's Estate, supra note 33. This case indicates that the after-written document cannot be incorporated though made as part of the same transaction Accepting this view is Dobie, Testamentary Incorporation by Reference, 3 Va.L.R. 583, 590. But see Hopper's Estate, 90 Neb. 622, 134 N.W. 237, 1912.

[35] In re Goods of Truro, L.R. 1 P. & D. 201, 1866; see Simon v. Grayson,

has been held however if the will referred to a document to be made later, though a codicil was executed after the document was made.[36]

The requirement that the incorporated document be in existence at the time of the execution of the incorporating will is doubtless made so as to meet the substance of the safeguards regarding execution. Otherwise the testator might incorporate future papers and change his will without compliance with the spirit of the wills' statute. In this respect the doctrine of incorporation by reference is just as strict as that of integration; the only difference being that an integrated paper must be present at the time of the execution, while the incorporated paper need not be present if it is in existence.[37] Obviously, oral instructions cannot be incorporated by reference; [38] to hold to the contrary would violate the whole spirit of the doctrine, as well as several of the specific requirements thereof.

*Proof of Identity*

Of course this problem is not reached unless the other essentials of incorporation by reference are met. However, if there is compliance with the other requirements, parol evidence is admissible to effect the identification.[39] For example, if a will refers to a paper of a certain date, parol evidence is admissible to show that there are no other papers of this date.[40] The mere possibility that there might have been two or more papers answering to the description in the will does not prevent application of the doctrine. However, testimony cannot be given to identify the document when it contradicts the description given in the will.[41]

15 Cal.2d 531, 102 P.2d 1081, 1940; infra §§ 90, 91.

36 In re Goods of Smart, [1902] P. 238. Cf. Simon v. Grayson, supra note 35.

37 In re Willey's Estate, 128 Cal. 1, 60 P. 471, 1900.

38 Wilcox v. Attorney-General, 207 Mass. 108, 93 N.E. 599, 1911; Kurtz v. Kurtz, 123 Ohio St. 425, 175 N.E. 694, 1931. But cf. the situation of the secret trust, supra § 57 at note 18; see note, 46 Mich.L.R. 77, 83-85.

39 In re Estate of Hopper, 90 Neb. 622, 134 N.W. 237, 1912; Baker's Appeal, 107 Pa. 381, 52 Am.Rep. 478, 1884; Allen v. Maddock, 11 Moo.P.C. 427, 14 Eng.Rep. 757, 1858. See supra note 8 et seq.

40 Allen v. Maddock, supra note 39.

41 Estate of Young, 123 Cal. 337, 55 P. 1011, 1899; Tuttle v. Berryman, 94 Ky. 553, 23 S.W. 345, 1893. See Schillinger v. Bawek, 135 Iowa 131, 112 N.W. 210, 1907.

*Nature of Document*

The doctrine of incorporation by reference is as applicable to holographic as to ordinary wills.[42] Even if the document sought to be incorporated is not wholly in the handwriting of the testator, the incorporation has been given effect.[43] This seems sound as a recognition of incorporation as a doctrine distinct from that of integration. Other cases hold to the contrary in this regard.[44] They evidently go upon the theory that an incorporated document is to be regarded as integrated, so that it must be wholly in the handwriting of the testator in case of an unattested will.

In general, the character of the document to be incorporated is immaterial.[45] It may be a dispositive instrument having independent legal effect,[46] or it may be non-dispositive and made only for the purpose of being incorporated.[47] The statute of distribution may be incorporated by apt reference,[48] though the same result would doubtless be reached even in jurisdictions not recognizing the doctrine.[49]

It often happens that a testator establishes an inter vivos trust and in his subsequent will desires to "pour over" part of

[42] Estate of Miller, 128 Cal.App. 176, 17 P.2d 181, 1932. For a discussion of the peculiar problems in this connection, see Mechem, Integration of Holographic Wills, 12 N.C.L.R. 212, 225; Malone, Incorporation by Reference of an Extrinsic Document into a Holographic Will, 16 Va.L.R. 571.

[43] Plumel's Estate, 151 Cal. 77, 90 P. 192, 121 Am.St.Rep. 100, 1907. See Rogers v. Agricola, 176 Ark. 287, 3 S.W.2d 26, 1928; Gooch v. Gooch, 134 Va. 21, 113 S.E. 873, 1922, noted, 21 Mich.L.R. 485. See notes, 40 Mich. L.R. 492, 16 Tenn.L.R. 741.

[44] Sharp v. Wallace, 83 Ky. 584, 1886; Hewes v. Hewes, 110 Miss. 826, 71 So. 4, 1939; In re Watts' Estate supra note 31. See also Scott v. Gastright, 305 Ky. 340, 204 S.W.2d 367, 173 A.L.R. 565, 1947. Professor Mechem, supra note 42 at 227 et seq., argues that the doctrine that printed matter invalidates a will on the integration theory is inconsistent with the theory that a document not wholly in the testator's hand may be incorporated by reference.

[45] See supra note 5.

[46] Bemis v. Fletcher, 251 Mass. 178, 146 N.E. 277, 37 A.L.R. 1471, 1925 (will of another); see infra note 50 et seq.

[47] Pickering v. Young, 282 Mass. 292, 184 N.E. 727, 1833, noted, 19 Iowa L.Rev. 487 (list); Allday v. Cage, 148 S.W. 838, Tex.Civ.App.1912.

[48] In re Estate of Smith, 16 Del. Chan. 272, 145 A. 671, 1929; Johnson v. Jacob, 11 Bush. (Ky.) 646, 1876.

[49] There is no chance of fraud here. See supra notes 7, 20, and infra note 52. It would be unthinkable to refuse to recognize the statute as a permissible source of reference.

his estate on his death to that trust.[50] Can he do so without repeating the detailed terms of the trust in the will by virtue of the doctrine of incorporation by reference? If the trust is nonrevocable and nonamendable, it seems clear that he may do so by apt reference to the trust instrument in the jurisdictions which recognize incorporation by reference; [51] even elsewhere it is possible that the transaction will be given effect because the formalities observed in connection with the creation of the trust afford little chance of fraud or uncertainty.[52] When the trust is amendable a variety of results have been reached. If the trust had not in fact been amended it has been considered that the attempted incorporation is invalid because of the possible shifting provision of the trust instrument.[53] Elsewhere the incorporation has been sustained in this situation.[54] When the testator has amended the trust there are added difficulties due to the fact that that trust instrument which was obviously intended was not in existence at the time of execution of the will. Several cases [55] favor the result of permitting incorporation of the trust as it existed at the time of execution of the will, but this is unsatisfactory because it was not in accord with the testator's intent. Other cases have denied in toto application of the doctrine here,[56]

[50] See Shattuck, An Estate Planner's Handbook, 1948, 83–90, 95–97; Lauritzen, Can a Revocable Trust Be Incorporated by Reference?, 45 Ill. L R. 583; Palmer, Testamentary Disposition to the Trustee of an Inter Vivos Trust 50 Mich.L.R. 33; Notes, 39 Col.L.R. 1256, 26 Corn.L.Q. 172, 25 Minn.L.R. 254, 50 Yale L.J. 342, 100 U. of Pa.L.R. 924; annotation, 21 A.L.R.2d 212.

[51] See infra notes 54, 55.

[52] See Matter of Rausch, supra note 6, which suggests that in case of formal trusts the courts may not insist on satisfaction of all the ordinary requirements of incorporation by reference; the same may be true of a reference to the duly executed will of another. See Matter of Fowles, supra note 7; Bemis v. Fletcher, supra note 46. Contra: Hatheway v. Smith, 79 Conn. 506, 65 A. 1058, 1907 (trust).

[53] Atwood v. Rhode Island Hospital Trust Co., 275 F. 513, C.C.A.R.I. 1921, with which cf. Merrill v. Boal, 47 R.I. 274, 132 A. 721, 45 A.L.R. 830, 1926; Matter of Jones, [1942] Ch. 328, [1942] 2 All.E. 642.

[54] Montgomery v. Blankenship, 217 Ark. 357, 230 S.W.2d 51, 1950; see In re York's Estate, 95 N.H. 435, 65 A.2d 282, 8 A.L.R.2d 611, 1949. And see cases infra note 55.

[55] See Old Colony Trust Co. v. Cleveland, 291 Mass. 380, 196 N.E. 920, 1935; Koeninger v. Toledo Trust Co., 49 Ohio App. 490, 197 N.E. 419, 1934; Bolles v. Toledo Trust Co., 144 Ohio St. 195, 58 N.E.2d 381, 157 A.L.R. 1104, 1944; Fifth Third Union Trust Co. v. Wilensky, 79 Ohio App. 73, 70 N.E.2d 920, 1946 (subsequent revocation of trust).

[56] President and Directors of Manhattan Co. v. Janowitz, 260 App.Div. 174, 21 N.Y.S.2d 232, 1940. See Sam-

though the possibility remains of sustaining the arrangement under the doctrine of reference to a non-testamentary act.[57]

## REFERENCE TO ACTS

**81. The will may provide for designation of the beneficiary or of the thing or amount given, by reference to an act of the testator, the beneficiary, or a third person, or any of these in combination, provided that the act is one which has ordinarily independent significance. If the act referred to is palpably specified for the purpose of allowing subsequent control through unattested act and has no other real significance, the gift is invalid.**

### *Future Acts of Testator*

It is permissible for a will to make the beneficiary or the thing given depend upon the testator's future acts. Clearly the bequest of "the automobile owned by me at the time of my death" is effective to pass the car which he then owned.[1] A devise "to the woman whom I may marry" is likewise effective,[2] as are bequests "to such persons as shall be in my employ at the time of my death," [3] or "to the person taking care of me at my death." [4] A similar situation is one in which the testator bequeaths property in a certain house, room or receptacle; this usually has the effect of passing the property so located at the time of testator's death.[5] It is true that by shifting the contents after execution of

uels, Incorporation by Reference in New York Wills, 19 N.Y.U.L.Q.R. 269, 287. Cf. Continental Illinois Nat. B. & T. Co. of Chicago v. Art Institute, 341 Ill.App. 624, 94 N.E.2d 602, 1950.

57 Cf. In re York's Estate, supra note 54, with President and Directors of Manhattan Co. v. Janowitz, supra note 56. And see citations supra note 50, and infra § 81 at note 9.

1 See infra § 134, notes 35–37. But cf. Matter of Gibbons' Estate, 139 Misc. 658, 249 N.Y.S. 753, 1931 (direction in will that outstanding check be paid held ineffective).

2 Brooke v. Kent, 3 Moo.P.C. 334, 13 Eng.Rep. 136, 1840.

3 Metcalf v. Sweeney, 17 R.I. 213, 21 A. 364, 33 Am.St.Rep. 864, 1891. See In re Hirshorn's Estate, 120 Colo. 294, 209 P.2d 543, 1949; Abbott v. Lewis, 77 N.H. 94, 88 A. 98, 1913 (gift to employees of a corporation controlled by testator); Stubbs v. Sargon, 3 Myl & C. 507, 40 Eng.Rep. 1022, 1838 (gift to partners at the time of testator's death); Reinheimer's Estate, 265 Pa. 185, 108 A. 412, 1919 (gift to person farming my land and taking care of me at the time of my death). Cf. Ireland v. Hudson, 96 Colo. 240, 41 P.2d 237, 1935 (gift of stock to employees of corporation at time of death of testator's wife).

4 See infra notes 7, 29.

5 Buchwald v. Buchwald, 175 Md. 103, 199 A. 795, 1938; Gaff v. Cornwallis, 219 Mass. 226, 106 N.E. 860, 1914; Creamer v. Harris, 90 Ohio St.

the will the testator may effect a change of disposition, and indeed it is just conceivable that the other aforementioned acts might have been done by the testator with the purpose of determining the passage of his property.[6] This point is seldom noticed in these cases, and apparently it makes no difference that the will was drafted with this in mind or that the future acts were performed for the purpose of affecting succession. The foregoing acts normally have significance independent of testamentary purpose, and this seems to be sufficient to meet the objection that the testator should not alter or implement his will by means other than a duly executed instrument.

Furthermore, the fact that a writing is somehow involved in the future act is not necessarily fatal to the reference to a nontestamentary act. Clearly the fact that a marriage certificate is a concomitant of a marriage and is used in proof thereof would be no reason for invalidating a devise "to the woman whom I may marry." Not so clear is the case [7] where the will left the entire estate to the person taking care of testatrix at the end of her life and further provided that this was conditional upon the person having a written statement to that effect. A post-testamentary letter by testatrix was held admissible to substantiate the claim in a decision which many—perhaps most—courts would label one essentially of incorporation by reference and which did not meet the requirements of that doctrine. Another marginal case admitted an envelope to identify the legatees under a bequest to the persons named on an envelope in the lockbox of the testatrix, although the requirements of incorporation were not met.[8]

160, 106 N.E. 967, L.R.A.1915C 653, Ann.Cas.1916C 1137, 1914; Appeal of Magoohan, 117 Pa. 238, 14 A. 816, 2 Am.St.Rep. 660, 1887. Also cases infra note 8. These authorities show that this problem is often overlooked in the contents cases, and the cases usually turn upon whether choses in action or other property "found" in the room or receptacle come within the description of the gift. In this connection, see also Succession of McBurney, 165 La. 357, 115 So. 618, 1928; Merrill v. Winchester, 120 Me. 263, 113 A. 261, 1921; Old Colony Trust Co. v. Hale, 302 Mass. 68, 18 N.E.2d 432, 120 A.L.R. 1207, 1939; Winkler v. Woodruff, 21 Del.Ch. 147, 182 A. 409, 1935.

[6] Noticing this argument is Hastings v. Bridge, 86 N.H. 172, 164 A. 906, 1933; S.C., 86 N.H. 247, 166 A. 273, 1933; Matter of Angle, infra note 8. See also In re Robson, [1891] 2 Ch. 559; Ragland, Administrator v. Wagener, infra note 15.

[7] Dennis v. Holsapple, 148 Ind. 297, 47 N.E. 631, 46 L.R.A. 168, 1897. See also Hessmer v. Edenborn, 196 La. 575, 199 So. 647, 1941, noted, 40 Mich. L.R. 492.

[8] Daniel v. Tyler's Executors, 296 Ky. 808, 178 S.W.2d 411, 1943; see also In re Le Collen's Will, 190 Misc. 272, 72 N.Y.S.2d 467, 1947, noted, 22 St. John's L.R. 299, with which cf.

There has been a similar blurring of the doctrines of incorporation by reference and of nontestamentary act in the cases in which the testator attempts to pour over property by will into an inter vivos trust, and the traditional requirements of incorporation by reference are not met or the jurisdiction does not recognize that doctrine.[9] The trust instrument is of course a document, but the setting up of the trust is also an act which normally has significance independent of testamentary purpose.[10] The view has been taken that the reference can be sustained upon the latter basis in cases where it is impossible to do so under the doctrine of incorporation by reference.[11] The form of the reference may be somewhat significant, i. e. whether it is to the instrument, or to the trust, although it seems somewhat artificial to have the result turn upon such a distinction.[12] The application of the doctrine of testamentary act is not firmly established in the case of the inter vivos trust; indeed at least in some jurisdictions it will take legislation to do so comprehensively.[13]

There are certain cases where it is clear that the attempt to govern the disposition by testator's future act will not be successful. Where the will provides that the beneficiary or the subject matter is to be determined by a future list or written instructions the devise or bequest fails.[14] The writing is clearly testamentary

Matter of Angle, 147 Misc. 445, 264 N.Y.S. 29, 1933. Cf. note 5 supra.

9 See supra § 80 at note 50 et seq.

10 Cf. the cases where the inter vivos trust contained little or no property and was created solely to be augmented by testamentary gift. Matter of Jones, [1942] Ch. 328, [1942] 1 All E.R. 642; Bolles v. Toledo Trust Co., 144 Ohio St. 195, 58 N.E.2d 381, 157 A.L.R. 1164, 1944.

11 In re York's Estate, 95 N.H. 435, 65 A.2d 282, 8 A.L.R.2d 611, 1949. For conflicting views of the writers, see supra § 80 at note 50; Evans, Incorporation by Reference, Integration and Nontestamentary Act, 25 Col.L.R. 879; Evans, Nontestamentary Acts, 16 U. of Chi.L.R. 635.

12 "Only a quibble will find a difference between a gift to a trust company *as* trustee under a deed and a gift to the same company with instructions to hold what is given in accordance with the deed." Cardozo, C. J., in Matter of Rausch, 258 N.Y. 327, 179 N.E. 755, 80 A.L.R. 98, 1932.

13 See Lauritzen, Can a Revocable Trust Be Incorporated by Reference? 45 Ill.L.R. 583, 613; Palmer, Testamentary Disposition to the Trustee of the Inter Vivos Trust, 50 Mich.L.R. 33, 67. Cf. Report of Law Revision Commission, New York, 1935, 431.

14 Hastings v. Bridge, 86 N.H. 172, 164 A. 976, 1933; S.C., 86 N.H. 247, 166 A. 273, 1933; Hartwell v. Martin, 71 N.J.Eq. 157, 63 A. 754, 1906; Rose v. Cunynghame, 12 Ves. 29, 33 Eng.Rep. 12, 1805; annotation, 3 A.L.R.2d 682; supra § 80 at note 21 et seq. And see Langdon v. Astor's Ex'rs, 16 N.Y. 9, 26, 1857. As to whether memorandum of this sort raises a trust, cf. In re Maddock,

and recognition of it would palpably be in disregard of the statutory requirements for execution of wills. In a Texas case,[15] a devise conditioned upon the testator's making a deed and placing it with the will was declared invalid as being dependent upon the future act of the testator. Likewise a court might well refuse to give effect to a bequest "to the persons with whom I shall eat dinner on next Christmas day," as the choice of a dinner partner might in the circumstances be solely for testamentary purposes and not parallel to the devise "to the woman whom I may marry."

Professor Scott has declared that the legacy or devise may depend upon testator's future act having independent significance,[16] while Dean Evans has used the term "nontestamentary act".[17] These are convenient tags but they do not indicate the extent and limitations of the doctrine. The latter are difficult to state, but a number of observations may be made with some assurance. As shown by the receptacle cases, the significance of the act need not be a legal one, and the act may be done with testamentary purpose or even in fulfillment of a prior testamentary plan. The existence of a writing as an accompaniment of the act, while not a favorable factor, is not necessarily fatal to the application of the doctrine. Probably application may be refused although the act is one which may have nontestamentary significance or perhaps none at all. It may be somewhat helpful to consider the doctrine as a partial escape device from the rigors of the incorporation by reference rule, and yet one which cannot be used to remove entirely the limitations which incorporation by reference has imposed.[18] It seems reasonable, and perhaps the courts have tacitly insisted, that: (1) there be some necessity or at least convenience, as distinguished from mere whimsy, for the testator's designation of his particular act as the one upon which the disposition of his property depends, (2) it must be relatively free of uncertainties and frauds to have the disposition of the property depend upon the designated future act.[19]

[1902] 2 Ch. 220, with Bryan v. Bigelow, 77 Conn. 604, 60 A. 266, 107 Am. St.Rep. 64, 1904, and see supra § 57 at note 18.

15 Ragland, Administrator v. Wagener, 142 Tex. 651, 180 S.W.2d 435, 152 A.L.R. 1232, 1944, noted in [1945] Wis.L.R. 116.

16 Trusts and the Statute of Wills, 43 Harv.L.R. 521, 546.

17 Incorporation by Reference, Integration and Non-Testamentary Act, 25 Col.L.R. 879, 891.

18 See supra § 80.

19 Cf. note, 46 Mich.L.R. 77, 89–92.

*Future Act of Third Persons*

A testator can provide that his bounty shall be determined by the future acts of another who is not the beneficiary. The same limitation applies as in case of future acts of the testator, viz., the act must have independent significance. If the act is such a one as would likely be done only to determine the amount or the beneficiary of the gift, it is open to the objection of alteration of the will by unattested act and also that the testamentary power is being delegated to another.

References to the will of a third person present varying possibilities. If the will of this person is in existence at the time of the execution of testator's will, and the other conditions of incorporation by reference are met, and the jurisdiction subscribes to that doctrine, the other's will may be said to be incorporated.[20] Of course this technique cannot be applied to future wills of others. However, a testator may give to another a power of appointment to be exercised by the latter's will. This would be perfectly valid if the donee survives the testator.[21] It is a permissible manner of delegation of will-making power, for the donee is considered to have a species of property upon the death of the testator. If the donee survives the testator, the power is deemed exercised though the donee's will is executed before testator's death,[22] or even before latter's will.[23] Nothing is better settled, however, than that the donee must survive the testator in order that there be a valid exercise of the power. There is still another workable theory which may be applied in lieu of the two just set forth. If the testator provides that the property shall go to the residuary devisees or legatees of another's will, the provision is given effect.[24] When the third person provides the way his own property goes, this is an act which has significance independent of the will-making of another testator. Further-

[20] See supra § 80. And see Nightingale v. Phillips, 29 R.I. 175, 72 A. 220, 1908.

[21] In re McCurdy's Estate, 197 Cal. 276, 240 P. 498, 1925; Columbia Trust Co. v. Christopher, 133 Ky. 335, 117 S.W. 943, 1909. A codicil providing that a person may change the will creates a power. In re Estate of McKallip, 324 Pa. 438, 188 A. 343, 108 A.L.R. 1095, 1936.

[22] Stone v. Forbes, 189 Mass. 163, 75 N.E. 141, 1905; Hirsch v. Bucki, 162 App.Div. 659, 148 N.Y.S. 214, 1914; Machir v. Funk, 90 Va. 284, 18 S.E. 197, 1893.

[23] Title Guarantee & Trust Co. v. Ebaugh, 184 N.Y.S. 351, 1920.

[24] Matter of Piffard, 111 N.Y. 410, 18 N.E. 718, 2 L.R.A. 193, 1888. And see Haskell v. Staples, 116 Me. 103, 100 A. 148, L.R.A.1917D 819, 1917; Buzzell v. Fogg, 120 Me. 158, 113 A. 50, 1921.

more, the property passes by the latter's will rather than by that of the third person, and hence the requirement of survivorship in the power of appointment cases has no application.

However, if the testator provides that his property shall go as shall be provided in the future will of a third person, this is not valid unless in the proper exercise of a power.[25] In that case the third person by providing how the testator's property shall go is not doing an act which has any significance apart from the passing of testator's property.[26]

There are other cases where the testator refers to future acts of third persons. If these may have a reasonable non-testamentary significance the gift is good. Thus, testamentary gifts to one who shall marry a certain other person are effective,[27] as are gifts to one's grandchildren living at the time of his death.[28]

*Future Acts of Beneficiary*

Where the gift is dependent upon the future non-testamentary acts of the beneficiary, the provision is valid. Thus a gift "to the person taking care of me at the time of my death" is a proper method of designation.[29] And gifts to the future wife of the testator,[30] or of another,[31] are likewise valid. In cases of this kind the qualification that the beneficiary's act should be non-testamentary seems superfluous. In fact, it would seem that any act by which the beneficiary puts himself within the class of persons designated would be sufficient. On the whole, when the act referred to in the will is that of a beneficiary, the problem is essentially that of condition,[32] and does not differ therefrom except possibly in form.

25 Curley v. Lynch, 206 Mass. 289, 92 N.E. 429, 1910. But see Condit v. De Hart, 62 N.J.Law, 78, 40 A. 776, 1888.

26 Cf. Evans, supra note 17, at 898–901, with Scott, supra note 16, at 551–553.

27 Knowles v. Knowles, 132 Ga. 806, 65 S.E. 128, 1909; Bate v. Amhert, 1 T.Raym. 82, 83 Eng.Rep. 45, 1675.

28 Merrill v. Winchester, 120 Me. 203, 113 A. 261, 1921.

29 Dennis v. Holsapple, 148 Ind. 297, 47 N.E. 631, 46 L.R.A. 168, 62 Am.St. Rep. 526, 1897; Lear v. Manser, 114 Me. 342, 96 A. 240, 1916; Moss v. Axford, 246 Mich. 288, 224 N.W. 425, 1929; Glasgow's Estate, 243 Pa. 613, 90 A. 332, 1914; Bosserman v. Burton, 137 Va. 502, 120 S.E. 261, 38 A.L.R. 767, 1923. Contra: In the Matter of Wilson's Estate, 143 Misc. 491, 256 N.Y.S. 813, 1932.

30 Van Brunt v. Van Brunt, 111 N.Y. 178, 19 N.E. 60, 1888; Brook v. Kent, 3 Moore P.C. 334, 13 Eng.Rep. 136, 1840.

31 See supra note 27.

32 See infra § 82.

It will be noticed that in some of the instances mentioned, the reference is to combined acts of two of the following: testator, beneficiary or a third person. This is true in the marriage,[33] employment,[34] and care,[35] cases. Probably the same could be said of the bequest of an eccentric Canadian millionaire who left the entire residue of his estate to the woman who should bear the most children during the period of ten years next after testator's death. This factor of joint activity does not alter the situation for the same test is applied to the acts of all three classes of individuals.

*Reference to Past Acts*

The determination of a testamentary gift according to the future act of the testator is subject to the objection that testator's will may be altered by his unattested act, but as we have seen from the foregoing this objection does not prevail when the act is one which normally has significance independent of testamentary purpose. When the reference is to past acts of the testator there is obviously no change in the will by reason of the act, and furthermore it is not likely that the past act was done for testamentary purpose. Of course, a reference to either future or past act makes the determination of persons or property depend upon something which is not in writing. That this objection is not necessarily fatal is shown by the fact that the courts do and indeed must admit oral evidence as to acts or facts in the outside world for the purpose of interpretation of the will or carrying it into effect, and indeed in certain cases even admit the testator's declarations in order to determine his intent.[36] While the provision would be unwise there could be no legal objection to a devise "to the person who ate dinner with me last Christmas day."

33 See supra notes 2, 27, 30, 31.

34 See supra note 3.

35 See supra notes 7, 29.

36 See supra §§ 60, 63; 81, and infra § 146; annotation, 94 A.L.R. 26.

## CONDITIONAL DEVISES AND BEQUESTS

**82. A conditional devise or bequest is one which takes effect, or continues in effect, according to the happening of some future event.**

**A condition precedent is one that must be fulfilled before the interest vests, while a condition subsequent is one in which the nonhappening or breach will defeat an estate already vested. The courts prefer to construe doubtful testamentary language as creating a condition subsequent rather than precedent.**

**A condition to a legacy or devise is invalid if it encourages conduct which is deemed contrary to public policy, but otherwise a gift may be subject to any definite condition. Thus, it is usually held that conditions in total restraint of a first marriage of the beneficiary or dependent upon his obtaining a divorce are invalid, while restraints upon the remarriage of testator's spouse or reasonable partial restraints upon marriage are valid.**

**A testamentary condition that a gift shall be void in case the beneficiary shall contest the will is valid, at least as to contests without probable cause.**

**If a condition subsequent is illegal or performance thereof is impossible, the gift becomes absolute and the condition is disregarded. Some decisions have taken the same position in case of conditions precedent, although here the traditional view is to declare that devises upon illegal or impossible conditions are entirely void, and likewise if the condition to a bequest is malum in se.**

In case of conditional devises and bequests the will specifies the beneficiary and the subject matter with certainty but makes the effectiveness of the gift depend upon some event. This event is ordinarily one which may be brought about by the beneficiary, though it may be within the control of a third person, or it may depend upon natural forces.[1] Ordinarily at least, it is not an event the happening of which is within the control of the testator. For these reasons, the matters treated in the last section are not usually discussed in the condition cases.

1 Carroll v. Carroll's Ex'r, 248 Ky. 386, 58 S.W.2d 670, 1933 (devise qualified by condition subsequent of survivorship); cf. Ross v. Clore, 225 Ind. 597, 76 N.E.2d 839, 1948 (same, condition precedent). See infra notes 64, 90.

The principal problems connected with conditions in wills are: (1) Whether a certain provision is to be regarded as a condition; (2) if so, whether it is precedent or subsequent; (3) the validity of various types of conditions; (4) excuses for nonperformance; and (5) the effect of an impossible or illegal condition.

Problems connected with the construction of limitations creating future interests dependent upon survival or upon death without issue or the like are outside the scope of this section and of this book.[2] The same is true of restrictions upon alienation, the rule against perpetuities and accumulations,[3] and limitations affecting the rights of creditors of the beneficiary.[4]

*What are Conditions?*

Usually if the language of the will and the nature of the subject-matter permit, the provision is not regarded as a condition.[5] Even where the words "upon condition" are used, a conditional estate is not necessarily created.[6] A devise upon the condition that the devisee pay testator's widow a certain sum was held merely to impose a charge upon the land and not to make the title conditional.[7] Where the testator devised his farm to his wife for life as a home for herself and children, her life interest was not regarded as conditional upon the occupancy of the farm as her home.[8] Similarly a devise of a house for a parsonage was held not to create a condition that it be so used.[9] So also a provision that all timber on devised land should be worked in accordance with an existing contract does not attach a condition to a devise in fee.[10] In the three preceding examples the pro-

[2] See Restatement, Property §§ 249–278; Simes on Future Interests §§ 81–89. Cf. infra note 5.

[3] See Restatement, Property §§ 370–423; Simes on Future Interests §§ 100 to 115.

[4] See Beals v. Croughwell, 140 Neb. 320, 299 N.W. 638, 138 A.L.R. 1330, 1941; Simes on Future Interests § 101; Bogert on Trusts, 3d ed. § 40; annotations, 119 A.L.R. 19, 138 id. 1319.

[5] Cook v. Sink, 190 N.C. 620, 130 S.E. 714, 1926; Bobblis v. Cupol, 297 Mass. 164, 7 N.E.2d 410, 1937. And see infra notes 6–10.

[6] Ditchey v. Lee, 167 Ind. 267, 78 N.E. 972, 1906; see In re Mead's Estate, 227 Wis. 311, 277 N.W. 694, 1938.

[7] Ditchey v. Lee, supra note 6; Matter of Watson's Estate, 149 Misc. 753, 269 N.Y.S. 67, 1934; Cook v. Sink, supra note 5. Contra: Crowley v. Nixon, 127 Kan. 178, 272 P. 104, 62 A.L.R. 585, 1928. The authorities are collected in 62 A.L.R. 589–620.

[8] Talbott v. Hamill, 151 Mo. 292, 52 S.W. 203, 1899.

[9] Whitmore v. First Congregational Parish, 121 Me. 391, 117 A. 469, 1922. And see In re Mead's Estate, supra note 6.

[10] Lambden v. West, 7 Del.Ch. 266, 44 A. 797, 1899.

vision was regarded simply as a statement of the testator's motive or inducement in making the gift. While a gift-over or a provision for forfeiture is not an absolute requirement for the creation of a condition,[11] the courts often seize upon the absence thereof to justify a holding that no condition was created.[12]

*Conditions Subsequent and Precedent*

In case that a condition is created, it often becomes important to determine whether the gift is upon condition precedent or condition subsequent. When the event upon which the estate depends must be performed before the estate can vest, the condition is precedent. If the estate vests upon the will becoming operative but subject to be divested upon the happening of a specified event, the condition is subsequent.[13] When property is devised to A upon a condition and then to B, the condition may be subsequent as to A but is clearly precedent as to B.

It is sometimes immaterial whether the condition is precedent or subsequent.[14] On the other hand, if the time for full performance has not passed, the right of the devisee or legatee to possession depends upon whether the condition is precedent or subsequent.[15] Decision of this problem may be also important in consideration of whether it is necessary to declare a forfeiture. Likewise if the condition is illegal or impossible of performance, there may be a marked difference of result in case of conditions precedent and of conditions subsequent.

Broadly speaking, the decision of this question depends upon the intention of the testator as it can be gleaned from the lan-

11 Matter of Mahlstedt's Estate, 140 Misc. 245, 250 N.Y.S. 628, 1931; Re Thompson's Estate, 304 Pa. 349, 155 A. 925, 76 A.L.R. 1339, 1931.

12 Whitmore v. First Congregational Parish, supra note 9; Matter of Watson's Estate, supra note 7; In re Mead's Estate, supra note 6. Indeed it is sometimes stated as a rule of law that the language cannot operate as a condition without a gift-over. Patterson v. Brandon, 226 N.C. 89, 36 S.E.2d 717, 163 A.L.R. 1150, 1946.

13 Carroll v. Carroll's Ex'r, supra note 1; Parmentier v. Pennsylvania Co. for the Ins. on Lives and Granting Annuities, 122 N.J.Eq. 25, 192 A. 62, affirmed, 124 N.J.Eq. 272, 1 A.2d 332, 1937; Matter of Mahlstedt's Estate, supra note 11; Winters Nat. Bank & Trust Co. of Dayton v. Cullen, 58 N.E.2d 702, Ohio App. 1945. See Sherrard v. Sloan, 117 Neb. 776, 223 N.W. 17, 1929, noted, 15 Iowa L.R. 229; Restatement, Property § 24. Cf. "A condition subsequent is an event which . . . must take place in order to prevent an interest from being divested," Simes, The Effect of Impossibility upon Conditions in Wills, 34 Mich.L.R. 909, 911.

14 Boggess v. Crail, 224 Ky. 97, 5 S.W.2d 906, 1928.

15 See Mountain Park Institute v. Lovill, 198 N.C. 642, 153 S.E. 114, 1930.

guage of the will in the light of his general situation.[16] The grammatical form of expression is not conclusive.[17] The same words may create a condition precedent in some cases and a condition subsequent in others.[18] The presumption is in favor of a condition subsequent rather than the condition precedent, based upon the law's preference for a vested estate.[19]

The logic of the situation is more important than the wording of the will. Thus, a legacy to be paid to the beneficiary at a certain time provided that he be a reformed man,[20] a bequest to one upon her marriage,[21] and a gift upon the formation of a partnership between the beneficiaries,[22] have been held to be conditions precedent. On the other hand, conditions subsequent were held to exist in case of a devise to hold during widowhood,[23] a bequest requiring the legatee to pay an annuity to the testator's wife,[24] one for the purpose of giving a youth a college education with limitation over should he fail to carry out this purpose,[25] and devise to an absent son with gift-over if he failed to return within ten years.[26] While testamentary conditions for the sup-

[16] See Colonial Trust Co. v. Waldron, 112 Conn. 216, 152 A. 69, 1930; Carroll v. Carroll's Ex'r, supra note 1; Bullard v. Village of Albion, 128 Misc. 292, 217 N.Y.S. 849, 1926.

[17] Winn v. Tabernacle Infirmary, 135 Ga. 380, 69 S.E. 557, 32 L.R.A., N.S., 512, 1910 (held a condition subsequent, though testator denominates it a condition precedent); Clausen v. Leary, 113 N.J.Eq. 324, 166 A. 623, 1933.

[18] Birmingham v. Lesan, 77 Me. 494, 1 A. 151, 1885; Merrill v. Wisconsin Female College, 74 Wis. 415, 43 N.W. 104, 1889. See Hoblit v. Howser, 338 Ill. 328, 170 N.E. 257, 71 A.L.R. 1046, 1930: "There is no technical form of words by which the condition of a devise is determined."

[19] Colonial Trust Co. v. Waldron, supra, note 16; Clausen v. Leary, supra, note 17; Mountain Park Institution v. Lovill, supra, note 15; Lafferty's Estate, 311 Pa. 455, 167 A. 44, 49, 1933. See infra § 147. But this doctrine will not be pushed to an unreasonable length where the language is clear. Kerens v. St. Louis Union Trust Co., 283 Mo. 601, 223 S.W. 645, 11 A.L.R. 288, 1920.

[20] Markham v. Hufford, 123 Mich. 505, 82 N.W. 222, 48 L.R.A. 580, 81 Am.St.Rep. 222, 1900; Kerens v. St. Louis Union Trust Co., supra note 19.

[21] McClelland's Ex'r v. McClelland, 132 Ky. 284, 116 S.W. 730, 1909; Stimpson v. Murch, 197 Mass. 381, 83 N.E. 1107, 1908.

[22] Re Thompson's Estate, 304 Pa. 349, 155 A. 925, 76 A.L.R. 1339, 1931.

[23] Chenault v. Scott, 66 S.W. 759, Ky. 1902.

[24] Sherman v. American Congregational Ass'n, 113 F. 609, C.C.A.Mass. 1902. And see infra note 27. But cf. In re Mahlstedt's Estate, 140 Misc. 245, 250 N.Y.S. 628, 1931.

[25] Ellicott v. Ellicott, 90 Md. 321, 45 A. 183, 48 L.R.A. 58, 1900.

[26] Connor v. Sheridan, 116 Wis. 666, 93 N.W. 835, 1903.

port of a third person are usually construed to be conditions subsequent,[27] if they are for the support of the testator they are obviously either conditions precedent or non-binding statements of motive.[28]

*Validity of Conditions Regarding Marriage and Divorce*

We start with the proposition that any condition is valid unless it is too indefinite or offends some statute or rule of public policy.[29] A large number of cases have dealt with conditions subsequent which tend to restrain marriage of the beneficiary. These decisions are more conflicting than is commonly thought. The confusion stemmed from the fact that the Roman law doctrine that these restraints were generally void was accepted by the English ecclesiastical courts which had jurisdiction over legacies of personalty, while the common-law judges took the general position that such conditions in a devise were valid. In the Court of Chancery, which had jurisdiction in case of both legacies and devises, different rules were sometimes announced for land and personalty,[30] but there were here attempts to make a unified compromise, either upon substantial distinctions such as between total and partial restraints on marriage or upon certain formal grounds. Thus, a difference was declared between a limitation of the estate until marriage (valid), and a condition terminating the general interest by condition subsequent (invalid). In addi-

[27] Cronin v. Cronin, 314 Ill. 345, 145 N.E. 619, 1924; Campbell v. Durant, 110 Kan. 30, 202 P. 841, 1921; Cf. Irvine v. Irvine, 15 S.W. 511, Ky. 1891, (condition precedent); Cook v. Sink, 190 N C. 620, 130 S.E. 714, 1926, (charge).

[28] Martin v. Martin, 131 Mass. 547, 1881 (mere motive).

[29] Clemenson v. Rebsamen, 205 Ark. 123, 168 S.W.2d 195, 1943; Greenwich Trust Co. v. Tyson, 129 Conn. 211, 27 A.2d 166, 1942; In re Irving Trust Co., 185 Misc. 866, 57 N.Y.S.2d 745, 1945. See note, 36 Col.L.R. 439. Gifts conditional on the donee's adherence to a certain religious faith are usually upheld. Delaware Trust Co. v. Fitzmaurice, 31 A.2d 383, Del.1943; see also Barnum v. Mayor, etc., of City of Baltimore, 62 Md. 275, 50 Am. Rep. 219, 1884. The same can be said of most conditions. See Browder, Illegal Conditions and Limitations; Miscellaneous Provisions, 1 Okl.L.R. 237; Restatement, Property §§ 433–437. But a condition that donees abstain from social and family intercourse with a brother and sister was declared void as against public policy and also for uncertainty. Girard Trust Co. v. Schmitz, 129 N.J.Eq. 444, 20 A.2d 21, 1941. See also Anonymous, 80 Misc. 10, 141 N.Y.S. 700, 1913 (condition that beneficiary set aside adoption of child held void).

[30] Thus, the "in terrorem" doctrine (infra) did not apply to devises, Williams v. Fry, 1 Mod. 86, 86 Eng.Rep. 752, 1670.

tion, there was the doctrine of in terrorem, sustaining the condition if there is a gift-over, but otherwise not.[31]

The latter distinctions have some basis in the matter of determining whether the testator intended the enjoyment of the property to depend upon marriage of the beneficiary,[32] but should have no validity otherwise, unless the solution of the matter is to depend upon whether the testator intended that the beneficiary should enjoy the property until marriage (valid), or that the estate should cease upon marriage (invalid). Though there is authority sustaining this position,[33] it is a mere quibble and involves the determination of a state of mind to no real purpose. The determining factor should be whether in the circumstances there is a restraint which is against public policy; in other words the important thing is the effect of the restraint rather than the intent of the testator to discourage marriage on the one hand, or to make provision until marriage on the other.[34]

It is orthodox to regard a condition in total restraint of a person's first marriage as void,[35] though the effect of the rule has been rendered largely nugatory in many jurisdictions by: (1) declaring that it does not apply to limitations as distinguished from conditions and holding that almost everything is a limitation,[36] or (2) holding that a condition is not effective unless there is a gift-over.[37] Much more honest is an early Pennsylvania decision which enforced the condition because it does not restrain marriage, since it "leaves the donee free as air to do anything,

[31] See Crowder, Conditions and Limitations in Restraint of Marriage, 39 Mich.L.R. 1288.

[32] See supra notes 6–12.

[33] See infra note 36, 37; Browder, supra note 31 at 1328–1331. Cf. Restatement, Property §§ 424e, 425g.

[34] See Knost v. Knost, 229 Mo. 170, 129 S.W. 665, 49 L.R.A.,N.S., 627, 1910.

[35] Knost v. Knost, supra note 34; Goffe v. Goffe, 37 R.I. 542, 94 A. 2, Ann.Cas.1916B 240, 1915; In re Liberman, 279 N.Y. 458, 18 N.E.2d 658, 122 A.L.R. 1, 1939; see Latorraca v. Latorraca, 132 N.J.Eq. 40, 26 A.2d 522, affirmed, 133 N.J.Eq. 298, 31 A. 2d 819, 1942.

[36] Bradford v. Culbreth, 1 Terry (Del.) 373, 10 A.2d 534, 1940, affirmed, 2 Terry (Del.) 167, 18 A.2d 143; Mann v. Jackson, 84 Me. 400, 24 A. 886, 16 L.R.A. 707, 30 Am.St.Rep. 358, 1892; Ijams v. Schapiro, 138 Md. 16, 113 A. 343, 1921. See also Cal.Civ.Code § 710; Ind.Stat.Ann., Burns 1933, § 7–704. For a criticism of the distinction, see In re Holbrook's Estate, 213 Pa. 93, 62 A. 368, 2 L.R.A.,N.S., 545, 110 Am.St.Rep. 537, 5 Ann.Cas. 137, 1905.

[37] Gard v. Mason, 169 N.C. 507, 86 S.E. 302, 1915. But see McCullough's Appeal, 12 Pa. 197, 1849, holding that the "in terrorem" doctrine does not apply to devises.

at pleasure." [38] Today there is no rational basis for different rules for devises and for bequests.[39]

It is generally recognized that conditions against the remarriage of the testator's widow [40] or of the widower of the testatrix are valid.[41] This view has been taken irrespective of whether or not there is a gift-over.[42] The cases are divided as to whether a testator may make a condition against the remarriage of a devisee or legatee other than his spouse. Where the provision has some reasonable basis it is usually sustained.[43]

Partial restraints are usually held valid unless they are unreasonable. However, a condition that the legacy should be forfeited if the legatee should cease to be a member of a certain religious sect was held invalid because the church forbade marriage outside its membership, and there were only a few unmarried persons of the opposite sex in the congregation.[44] Most partial restraints upon marriage have been held reasonable. In this class are conditions against the devisee's marrying one below her station,[45] or against marriage into a certain family,[46] or those restraining marriage before reaching the age of twenty-one,[47] or without the consent of certain persons interested in the

38 Commonwealth v. Stauffer, 10 Pa. 350, 355, 1849 (remarriage case, but decision placed on general grounds).

39 Cf. In re Holbrook's Estate, supra note 36, with McCullough's Appeal, supra note 37. See Restatement, Property, Introductory Note to Part III.

40 Wilmington Trust Co. v. Houlehan, 15 Del.Ch. 84, 131 A. 529, 1925; Glass v. Johnson, 297 Ill. 149, 130 N.E. 473, 1921; Latorraca v. Latorraca, supra note 35; Bryan v. Harper, 177 N.C. 308, 98 S.E. 822, 1919; Overton v. Lea, 108 Tenn. 505, 68 S.W. 250, 1902.

41 Bostick v. Blades, 59 Md. 231, 43 Am.Rep. 548, 1882. See Knost v. Knost, supra note 34.

42 Chapin v. Cooke, 73 Conn. 72, 46 A. 282, 84 Am.St.Rep. 139, 1900; Glass v. Johnson, supra note 40. But see Wilmington Trust Co. v. Houlehan, supra note 40.

43 Anderson v. Crawford, 202 Iowa 207, 207 N.W. 571, 45 A.L.R. 1216, 1926, noted, 11 Minn.L.R. 84; Wise v. Crandall, 215 S.W. 245, Mo.1919; Overton v. Lea, supra note 40. See Restatement, Property § 426; In re Liberman, supra note 35. But see Crawford v. Thompson, 91 Ind. 266, 46 Am.Rep. 598, 1883.

44 Maddox v. Maddox's Adm'r, 11 Grat.(Va.) 804, 1854.

45 Greene v. Kirkwood, [1895] 1 Ir. 130.

46 In re Seaman's Will, 218 N.Y. 77, 112 N.E. 576, L.R.A.1917A 40, Ann. Cas.1918B 1138, 1916; Phillips v. Ferguson, 85 Va. 509, 8 S.E. 241, 1 L.R.A. 837, 17 Am.St.Rep. 78, 1888; Turner v. Evans, 134 Md. 238, 106 A. 617, 1919 (though requiring a breach of promise).

47 Reuff v. Coleman, 30 W.Va. 171, 3 S.E. 597, 1887.

devisee's welfare.[48] Some cases, however, have held that legacies upon conditions subsequent of the latter type are not terminated unless there is a limitation over to another.[49]

Where a condition is such that it induces the divorce or separation of a married pair it is apt to be a condition precedent. Usually it is declared to be against public policy and void.[50] Some courts have held, however, that this does not apply to divorces to be procured in a legal manner, upon the ground that a divorce sanctioned by a court cannot be deemed against public policy.[51] Where the parties are already separated, or are contemplating a divorce, the condition for a divorce has been upheld.[52] Likewise a provision for a life income to testator's son with remainder to his widow other than his present wife was sustained since the son's interest was firm and there was no tendency to induce him to obtain a divorce.[53]

*Validity of Conditions Against Will Contests*

Frequently a will contains the provision that the testamentary gifts shall be void in case that the beneficiary disputes or contests the will. If the beneficiary successfully contests the will, this condition falls with the rest of the will, but in case of an unsuccessful contest there is the question as to whether there is a

[48] Collier v. Slaughter's Adm'r, 20 Ala. 263, 1852; Hogan v. Curtin, 88 N.Y. 162, 42 Am.Rep. 244, 1882 (assent after marriage is not sufficient); Pacholder v. Rosenheim, 129 Md. 455, 99 A. 672, L.R.A.1917D 464, 1916; but see In re Liberman, supra note 35.

[49] Hogan v. Curtin, supra note 48; Bostick v. Blades, 59 Md. 231, 43 Am. Rep. 548, 1882.

[50] Brizendine v. American Trust & Savings Bank, 211 Ala. 694, 101 So. 618, 1924; Tripp v. Payne, 339 Ill. 178, 171 N.E. 131, 1938; Hawke v. Euyart, 30 Neb. 149, 46 N.W. 422, 27 Am.St.Rep. 391, 1890; Re Haight, 51 App.Div. 310, 64 N.Y.S. 1029, 1900; Conrad v. Long, 33 Mich. 78, 1875; Wilkinson v. Wilkinson, L.R. 12 Eq. 604, 1871; Re Moore, L.R. 39 Ch.Div. 116, 1887.

[51] Born v. Horstmann, 80 Cal. 452, 22 P. 169, 338, 5 L.R.A. 577, 1899; Daboll v. Moon, 88 Conn. 387, 91 A. 646, L.R.A.1915A 311, Ann.Cas.1917B 164, 1914; Baker v. Hickman, 127 Kan. 340, 273 P. 480, 68 A.L.R. 743, 1929; Cowley v. Twombly, 173 Mass. 393, 53 N.E. 886, 46 L.R.A. 164, 1914; In re Tiemens' Estate, 152 Wash. 82, 277 P. 385, 68 A.L.R. 753, 1929, noted, 14 Minn.L.R. 104. See note, 28 Col. L.R. 792.

[52] Ransdell v. Boston, 172 Ill. 439, 50 N.E. 111, 43 L.R.A. 526, 1898; Dusbiber v. Melville, 178 Mich. 601, 146 N.W. 208, 51 L.R.A.,N.S., 367, 1914; Cooper v. Remsen, 5 Johns.Ch.(N.Y.) 459, 1821.

[53] In re Rothchild's Will, 271 App. Div. 582, 66 N.Y.S.2d 573, 1946, noted, 21 St. John's L.R. 240.

[54] See generally Browder, Testamentary Conditions Against Contest, 36 Mich.L.R. 1066; Browder, Testamentary Conditions Against Contest

forfeiture of devises or bequests to the contestants.[54] Of course there is nothing against public policy in the discouragement of unmeritorious litigation, and all courts will enforce the condition if the contest is without probable cause, at least if there is a gift-over.

The main dispute today is whether the courts will enforce the condition where the contest is upon probable cause. Some courts have held that there is forfeiture although the contest was upon probable cause.[55] Other courts have made an exception in the case there is probable cause.[56] This view protects the family of the testator in the litigation of a just cause and encourages exposure of frauds and forgeries.[57] In these jurisdictions the contestant has the burden of showing that he acted with probable cause,[58] and this is evidently a matter for the court rather than for the jury.[59]

Re-examined, 49 Col.L.R. 320, and infra note 57.

55 Re Miller's Estate, 156 Cal. 119, 103 P. 842, 23 L.R.A.,N.S., 868, 1909; Rudd v. Searles, 262 Mass. 490, 160 N.E. 882, 58 A.L.R. 1548, 1928, noted, 23 Ill.L.R. 405; Re Chambers' Estate, 322 Mo. 1086, 18 S.W.2d 30, 67 A.L.R. 41, 1929, noted, 41 Law Ser.Mo.Bull. 51; Burtman v. Butman, 97 N.H. 254, 85 A.2d 892, 1952; Bender v. Bateman, 33 Ohio App. 66, 168 N.E. 574, 1929; Barry v. American Security & Trust Co., 77 U.S.App.D.C. 351, 135 F.2d 470, 1943, noted, 22 Tex.L.R. 361, 30 Va.L.R. 184.

56 South Norwalk Trust Co. v. St. John, infra note 62; In re Cocklin's Estate, 236 Iowa 98, 17 N.W.2d 129, 157 A.L.R. 584, 1945, noted, 25 B.U. L.R. 152, 44 Mich.L.R. 172; Ryan v. Wachovia Bank & Trust Co., 235 N.C. 585, 70 S.E.2d 853, 1952; Friend's Estate, 209 Pa. 442, 58 A. 853, 68 L.R.A. 447, 1904; Tate v. Camp, 147 Tenn. 137, 245 S.W. 839, 26 A.L.R. 755, 1922; Calvery v. Calvery, 122 Tex. 204, 55 S.W.2d 527, 1932; Dutterer v. Logan, 103 W.Va. 216, 137 S.E. 1, 52 A.L.R. 83, 1927; Re Keenan's Will, 188 Wis. 163, 205 N.W. 1001, 42 A.L.R. 837, 1925, noted, 12 Va.L.R. 431.

Restatement, Property § 428 adopts the probable cause exception where the contest is based upon the ground of forgery or revocation by subsequent will, but otherwise accepts the position taken supra note 55, except that under § 429 attacks based upon the rule against perpetuities, mortmain statutes, etc., are invalid if the attack is successful or if unsuccessful when there was probable cause. See Burtman v. Butman, supra note 55; Kirkbride v. Hickok, 155 Ohio St. 293, 98 N.E.2d 815, 1951, noted, 50 Mich.L.R. 625. Ind.Ann.Stat. § 7-501, Burns, 1933, makes all non-contest provisions void; see also N.Y.Decedent Estate Law § 126 declaring that certain acts shall not work a forfeiture.

57 See Browder, supra note 54; Goddard, Forfeiture Conditions in Wills as Penalty for Contesting Probate, 81 U. of Pa.L.R. 267. Other articles on the subject are Keegan, Provisions in Wills Forfeiting Share of Contesting Beneficiary, 12 A.B.A. Jo. 236; Kenner, Non-Contesting Clauses in Wills, 3 Ind.L.Jo. 269; see notes 36 Col.L.R. 439, 25 Wash. U.L.Q. 483.

58 Friend's Estate, supra note 56.

59 See Dutterer v. Logan, supra note 56.

The English authorities [60] distinguished between bequests subject to this condition which were held void as being merely in terrorem if there was no gift-over, and devises where the validity of the condition was unaffected by the absence of a limitation over. Some American authority [61] has echoed this distinction, yet it seems that the differentiation is extremely artificial. Most modern cases have not deemed the character of the property important and have not insisted upon the gift-over in order to make the condition effective even in case of personalty.[62]

Some courts have held that the condition is inapplicable to contests on behalf of infants.[63] A provision for forfeiture in case of contest may, by its terms, be made to operate even against beneficiaries not participating in the contest and although the unsuccessful contestant was disinherited by the will.[64] This is due to the fact that the forfeiture is dependent upon the specified condition and not upon the doctrine of election by the legatees.[65]

*Performance or Breach*

If there is a condition precedent the burden is on the beneficiary to show performance before the estate may vest.[66] Strict

60 Morris v. Burroughs, 1 Atk. 399, 26 Eng.Rep. 253, 1737; Cooke v. Turner, 14 Sim. 493, 60 Eng.Rep. 449, 1846.

61 Wells v. Menn, 158 Fla. 228, 28 So.2d 881, 169 A.L.R. 892, 1946; see Smithsonian Institute v. Mead, 169 U.S. 398, 18 Sup.Ct. 396, 42 L.Ed. 793, 1898; Wright v. Cummins, 108 Kan. 667, 196 P. 246, 14 A.L.R. 604. See also In re Matchette's Estate, 183 Misc. 228, 49 N.Y.S.2d 561, 1944.

62 Re Hite's Estate, 155 Cal. 436, 101 P. 443, 21 L.R.A.,N.S., 953, 17 Ann.Cas. 993, 1909; South Norwalk Trust Co. v. St. John, 92 Conn. 168, 101 A. 961, Ann.Cas.1918E 1090, 1917; Bradford v. Bradford, 19 Ohio St. 546, 2 Am.Rep. 419, 1869.

63 Farr v. Whitfield, 322 Mich. 275, 33 N.W.2d 791, 1948, noted, 47 Mich. L.R. 728, 35 Va.L.R. 121; Bryant v. Thompson, 59 Hun 545, 14 N.Y.S. 28, affirmed 128 N.Y. 426, 28 N.E. 522, 13 L.R.A. 745, 1891; see also N.Y.Decedent Estate Law § 126. But see Moorman v. Louisville Trust Co., 181 Ky. 30, 203 S.W. 856, 1918; Old Colony Trust Co. v. Wolfman, 311 Mass. 614, 42 N.E.2d 574, 1942.

64 Alper v. Alper, 2 N.J. 105, 65 A.2d 737, 7 A.L.R.2d 1350, 1949, noted, 34 Minn.L.R. 169, 1949. Annual Surv. Am.L. 844. See also Perry v. Rogers, 52 Tex.Civ.App. 594, 114 S.W. 897, 1908; Restatement, Property § 428, h; notes, 97 U. of Pa.L.R. 574, 35 Va. L.R. 378. Cf. infra note 90.

65 However, it has been declared that the doctrine of estoppel to contest by acceptance of the bequest applies with special force when there is a no-contest clause in the will. Bender v. Bateman, 33 Ohio App. 66, 168 N.E. 574, 1929; Von Koenneritz v. Hardcastle, 231 S.W.2d 498, Tex.Civ. App.1950. Cf. Burtman v. Butman, supra note 55. See generally, annotation, 72 A.L.R. 1134.

66 See Sicourmat's Estate, 161 Wash. 406, 296 P. 1047, 1931.

performance is usually required,[67] though at least if there is no limitation over, substantial performance has been held sufficient when there is adequate reason for absence of full performance.[68] If performance is tendered and refused by the executor, there is no forfeiture of the gift.[69] Ordinarily if the will specifies a time for performance, the condition must be performed within that time.[70] This is true though the beneficiary was unaware of the condition until the time for performance had expired.[71] If no time is specified, performance must be within a reasonable period, to be determined by the circumstances of the particular case.[72]

When the condition is subsequent, failure to fulfill the condition causes the gift to fail. Here the burden of showing nonperformance or breach is upon the one attempting to establish the forfeiture.[73] In accordance with the judicial policy against declaring forfeitures, the courts are more willing to adhere to the doctrine of substantial performance, both as to the nature of the act,[74] and the time thereof,[75] than in the case of conditions precedent. Furthermore in case of condition precedent with respect to personalty with no limitation over to another, it has been held that the provision is in terrorem and that forfeiture will not be declared.[76] Other cases refuse to recognize this general doctrine,[77] and it has no application to devises of land.[78]

67 Maguire v. City of Macomb, 293 Ill. 441, 127 N.E. 682, 1920; Pacholder v. Rosenheim, 129 Md. 455, 99 A. 672, L.R.A.1917D 464, 1916; In re Thompson's Estate, 304 Pa. 349, 155 A. 925, 76 A.L.R. 1339, 1931.

68 Cantillon v. Walker, 78 A.2d 782, Me. 1951; Clausen v. Leary, 113 N.J. Eq. 324, 166 A. 623, 1933.

69 Will of Trybom, 277 N.Y. 106, 13 N.E.2d 596, 116 A.L.R. 359, 1938.

70 In re Thompson's Estate, supra note 67.

71 Fisher v. Fisher, 80 Neb. 145, 113 N.W. 1004, 1907; Powell v. Rawle, L. R. 18 Eq. 243, 1874. But cf. Morris v. Mull, 110 Ohio St. 623, 144 N.E. 436, 39 A.L.R. 323, 1924 (executor liable in damages for failure to notify legatee). And see Peek v. Woman's Home Missionary Society, 304 Ill. 427, 136 N.E. 772, 26 A.L.R. 917, 1922.

72 Campbell v. Durant, 110 Kan. 30, 202 P. 841, 1921 (erection of tombstone); Maguire v. City of Macomb, 293 Ill. 441, 127 N.E. 682, 1920.

73 Garman v. Glass, 197 Pa. 101, 46 A. 923, 1900.

74 Lobb v. Brown, 208 Cal. 476, 281 P. 1010, 1929; In re Feinson's Estate, 200 Misc. 858, 104 N.Y.S.2d 303, 1950.

75 See Treadwell v. Putman, 62 App.D.C. 156, 65 F.2d 604, 1933.

76 Green v. Old People's Home of Chicago, 269 Ill. 134, 109 N.E. 701, 1915; Sherman v. Richmond Hose Co. No. 2, 230 N.Y. 462, 130 N.E. 613, 1921; Stackpole v. Beaumont, 3 Ves. Jr. 89, 30 Eng.Rep. 909, 1796.

77 In re Peterson's Estate, 85 N.J. Eq. 135, 95 A. 613, 1915; Carr's Estate, 138 Pa. 352, 22 A. 18, 1890.

78 Bradford v. Bradford, 19 Ohio

Special problems occur with reference to what is a breach of a no-contest clause. Whether the conduct of the beneficiary constitutes a breach of the condition depends on the particular language used by the testator in his will.[79] The usual provision is for forfeiture for "contest" of the will; hence it must be decided what is a contest. Aiding the contestants has been held to be a breach of the condition,[80] as well as offering a later will known to be spurious for probate.[81] Claiming title to land,[82] or chattels,[83] which the testator gave by his will has been deemed to be a contest within the forfeiture clause. A suit to set aside the will because it violated the rule against perpetuities was deemed a contest,[84] though suits to construe wills are generally deemed not to be contests.[85] There is a conflict of authority as to whether proceedings to oppose wills, withdrawn before hearing, are within the particular forfeiture clause. In accordance with the principle of disfavoring forfeitures most courts have held they are not.[86] Objection to the jurisdiction of the probate court is

St. 546, 2 Am.Rep. 419, 1869; Phillips v. Ferguson, 85 Va. 509, 8 S.E. 241, 1 L.R.A. 837, 17 Am.St.Rep. 78, 1888; but see Wright v. Jenks, 124 Kan. 604, 261 P. 840, 1927.

79 For cases involving peculiarly expressed conditions, see Dutterer v. Logan, supra note 56, and Hickman's Estate, 308 Pa. 230, 162 A. 168, 1932. As to conditions against filing claims, see infra notes 89–95.

80 Donegan v. Wade, 70 Ala. 501, 1881; Kayhart v. Whitehead, 77 N.J. Eq. 12, 76 A. 241, affirmed 78 N.J.Eq. 580, 81 A. 1133, 1910; Re Stewart's Will, 1 Con. 412, 5 N.Y.S. 32, 1889. But cf. Haradon v. Clark, 190 Iowa 798, 180 N.W. 868, 1925; Richards v. Piefer, 229 Mich. 609, 201 N.W. 877, 1925; Lobb v. Brown, 208 Cal. 476, 281 P. 1010, 1929, noted, 19 Cal.L.R. 216, 4 So.Cal.L.R. 73.

81 Re Kirkholder's Estate, 171 App. Div. 153, 157 N.Y.S. 37, 1916. The contrary is held where the will is thought to be genuine. Re Bergland's Estate, 180 Cal. 629, 182 P. 277, 5 A.L.R. 1363, 1919.

82 Moran v. Moran, 144 Iowa 451, 123 N.W. 202, 30 L.R.A.,N.S., 898, 1909; see Smithsonian Institution v. Meech, 169 U.S. 398, 18 Sup.Ct. 396, 42 L.Ed. 793, 1898.

83 Re Bratt, 10 Misc. 491, 32 N.Y.S. 168, 1894; In re Howard's Estate, 68 Cal.App.2d 9, 155 P.2d 841, 1945.

84 South Norwalk Trust Co. v. St. John, supra note 56. However, no forfeiture was declared here because the contest was upon probable cause.

85 Black v. Herring, 79 Md. 146, 28 A. 1063, 1894; Morrison v. Reed, 6 N.J.Super. 598, 70 A.2d 799, 1950; Perry v. Perry, 175 N.C. 141, 95 S.E. 98, 1918. And see South Norwalk Trust Co. v. St. John, supra note 56. A fortiori, participation in a construction suit started by another is not a contest of the will. Griffin v. Sturges, 131 Conn. 471, 40 A.2d 758, 156 A.L.R. 972, 1944.

86 Ayers' Adm'r v. Ayers, 212 Ky. 400, 279 S.W. 647, 1926; Matter of Cronin's Estate, 143 Misc. 559, 257 N.Y.S. 496, 1931; McCahan's Estate, 221 Pa. 188, 70 A. 711, 1909. To the contrary, see Re Hite's Estate, 155 Cal. 436, 101 P. 443, 21 L.R.A.,N.S.,

not a contest,[87] nor is an attempt to obtain one's share under the will from the executor.[88]

Filing a claim as a creditor is scarcely a contest of the will,[89] but a different matter is presented if there is a provision for forfeiture of the gift if the beneficiary files a claim against testator's estate. Such conditions are generally valid,[90] but some courts have almost annihilated their effect by holding that the forfeiture does not apply if the claim was one which was barred,[91] or which the testator intended should be paid,[92] or where he was mistaken in his statement that he owed beneficiaries nothing,[93] or when there is no gift-over.[94] The forfeiture provision has been held not to apply to claims asserted in testator's lifetime.[95]

*Effect of Illegality and Impossibility*

If the condition is subsequent, the authorities seem to agree that impossibility or illegality of the condition simply causes the condition to be disregarded and the gift is valid.[96] This follows from the nature of the condition subsequent. As the condition

953, 17 Ann.Cas. 993, 1909; Kayhart v. Whitehead, supra note 80; Tate v. Camp, supra note 56.

87 Re Hill's Estate, 176 Cal. 619, 169 P. 371, 1917.

88 Estate of Seipel, 130 Cal.App. 273, 19 P.2d 808, 1933; Loyd v. Spillet, 3 P.Wms. 344, 24 Eng.Rep. 1094, 1734; Atty. Gen. v. Parkin, 1 Ambl. 566, 27 Eng.Rep. 365, 1769.

89 In re Madansky's Estate, 29 Cal. App.2d 685, 85 P.2d 576, 1938; Wright v. Cummins, 108 Kan. 667, 196 P. 246, 14 A.L.R. 604, 1921. See notes 90–95 infra.

90 Re Kitchen's Estate, 192 Cal. 384, 220 P. 301, 30 A.L.R. 1008, 1923, noted, 22 Mich.L.R. 741; Hapgood v. Houghton, 22 Pick.(Mass.) 480, 1839; Re Bratt, 10 Misc. 491, 32 N.Y.S. 168, 1894; Dunlap v. Ingram, 57 N.C. (4 Jones Eq.) 178, 1858; Berlin's Estate, 74 Pa.Super. 455, 1920; Rogers v. Law, 66 U.S. (1 Black) 253, 17 L.Ed. 58, 1862. But a forfeiture provision in case any of the beneficiary's relatives should file a claim was held invalid. Matter of Andrew's Estate, infra note 91; cf. supra note 64.

91 Matter of Andrews' Estate, 151 Misc. 361, 272 N.Y.S. 847, 1934.

92 Matter of Cronin's Estate, 143 Misc. 559, 257 N.Y.S. 496, 1932.

93 Re Vandervort's Estate, 62 Hun 612, 17 N.Y.S. 316, 1892.

94 Re Marshall's Estate, 119 Misc. 407, 196 N.Y.S. 330, 1922.

95 Snelling v. Darrell, 17 Ga. 141, 1855.

96 Keyser v. Calvary Brethren Church, 192 Md. 526, 64 A.2d 748, 1949; Conrad v. Long, 33 Mich. 78, 1875; Jones v. Jones, 223 Mo. 424, 123 S.W. 29, 25 L.R.A.,N.S., 424, 1909; Drace v. Klinedinst, 275 Pa. 266, 118 A. 907, 25 A.L.R. 1520, 1922; and see Taylor v. Mason, 22 U.S.(9 Wheat.) 325, 6 L.Ed. 101, Md. 1824. This has been held in the case of a devisee being unable to fulfill the condition because of insanity. Lynch v. Melton, 150 N.C. 595, 64 S.E. 497, 27 L. R.A.,N.S., 684, 1909.

cannot be fulfilled in the impossibility cases and as the law will not encourage the performance of an illegal act, forfeiture will not be declared. Since the court often has considerable leeway in holding a condition to be precedent or subsequent,[97] it often can, by the simple expedient of putting it in the latter category, reach a desired result by application of the simple rule as to conditions subsequent.

However, there are some cases where the condition is clearly precedent, and others which are marginal but where disregard of the condition will not reach a desirable result. When the condition is regarded as precedent, there has been great diversity of opinion as to the effect of illegality of the condition or impossibility of its performance. The orthodox view in the case of devises is that the gift must fail, as the condition of the gift has not been met.[98] In a masterful legalistic argument,[99] Dean Pound has contended that the same reasoning should apply to legacies upon condition precedent. However, there is both American,[100] and English authority,[101] following the civil law view that if the condition precedent is originally impossible, or is made so by the act or default of the testator, or is merely malum prohibitum, the bequest is absolute, but if the illegality involves malum in se both gift and condition are void. A third view has been taken making the gift valid generally in case of illegal or impossible condition precedent.[102] Of course it would be unthinkable to sustain the gift if and only if the illegal condition is performed, as this would nullify the effect of the illegality.

It seems extremely artificial to reach a different result in the case of devises and legacies on the same facts. The civil law test is unsatisfactory in that it calls for a distinction between

97 See supra note 17 et seq.

98 Carter's Heirs v. Carter's Administrators, 39 Ala. 579, 1865; Phillips v. Ferguson, 85 Va. 509, 8 S.E. 241, 1 L.R.A. 837, 1888; In re Turton, [1926] 1 Ch. 96; see Winterland v. Winterland, 389 Ill. 384, 59 N.E.2d 661, 1945; Girard Trust Co. v. Schmitz, 129 N.J. Eq. 444, 20 A.2d 21, 1941.

99 Legacies on Impossible or Illegal Conditions Precedent, 3 Ill.L.R. 1.

100 Matter of Haight, 51 App.Div. 310, 64 N.Y.S. 1029, 1900. See Hawke v. Euyart, 30 Neb. 149, 46 N.W. 422, 27 Am.St.Rep. 391, 1890; Cal.Civ. Code § 709.

101 Brown v. Peck, 1 Eden 140, 28 Eng.Rep. 637, 1798; see Patton v. Toronto General Trusts Corp., [1930] A.C. 629, noted, 31 Col.L.R. 334; 2 Jarman on Wills (7th Ed. 1930) 1443.

102 Brizendine v. American Trust & Savings Bank, 211 Ala. 694, 101 So. 618, 1924; and see Boggess v. Crail, 224 Ky. 97, 5 S.W.2d 906, 1928; Girard Trust Co. v. Schmitz, 129 N.J.Eq. 444, 20 A.2d 21, 1941; supra note 69; Succession of Reilly, 136 La. 347, 67 So. 27, 1914 (code provision).

malum prohibitum and malum in se which is extremely hazy,[103] and should be applied only if no other reasonable test can be suggested. On the other hand, we are scarcely prepared to go to the extreme of nullifying all illegal or impossible conditions precedent in order to sustain the gift. A gift to a woman upon condition of her continuance in immoral relations up to the time of testator's death should scarcely be sustained.

As in the first edition,[104] the author offers the following as a solution, regardless of the nature of the illegality or of the impossibility, or of whether a devise or bequest is involved, or of whether the condition is subsequent or precedent:[105] If the probable intention of the testator and the general policy of the law will be best promoted by overlooking the impossible or illegal condition, this should be done and the gift sustained; unless this is so, such conditional gift should fail entirely. It must be conceded that this is not a mechanical test, and its application may often give rise to differences of opinion. While no court seems to have taken this position expressly,[106] it has the support of the recent writers.[107]

103 For example, would a condition that one marry his first cousin be malum in se or merely malum prohibitum?

104 See Atkinson on Wills, 1937 p. 351.

105 However, in the application of the suggested test the fact that a condition was subsequent would tend to show that the testator would have preferred that the gift be sustained and the condition disregarded.

106 It is perhaps approached in Snorgrass v. Thomas, 166 Mo.App. 603, 150 S.W. 106, 1912, and In re Going, [1951] Ont.R. 147, noted, 29 Can.B.R. 434. See also cases supra note 96, 98; but see cases supra notes 100, 102.

107 Simes, The Effect of Impossible Conditions in Wills, 34 Mich.L.R. 909; Klockau, The Effect of Illegal Conditions Annexed to Dispositions of Property, 40 Ill.L.R. 464; Browder, Illegal Conditions and Limitations: Effect of Illegality, 47 Mich.L.R. 759. Restatement, Property § 438 adopts this test in case of impossibility, but in case of illegality (at least in restraints on marriage and no-contest clauses) announces that the condition should be disregarded in all cases, §§ 424d, 428*l*.

## CONDITIONAL WILLS

**83. By its terms, the entire will may operate as a will only if the stated event actually occurred. However, as far as possible, the courts should construe doubtful expressions as mere statements of the inducement in making the will, so that it becomes effective upon the testator's death regardless of the occurrence of the event referred to.**

In this section consideration is given to cases in which the alleged condition relates to the operation of the will as a whole, as distinguished from those just discussed where the condition refers only to particular devises or bequests in a will otherwise unconditional. The contingent character of a particular gift does not make the entire will conditional.[1]

Parol evidence is not admissible to show that a will absolute on its face was intended to be conditional.[2] A condition is not implied from indefinite language,[3] and in doubtful cases the courts favor the construction that the will is unconditional.[4] When the instrument is stated to be made in the light of a specified future event, the reference may be a condition precedent to the operation of the instrument as the testator's will, or it may be a mere statement of the motive which prompted its preparation and which was carelessly stated in language suggestive of a condition. If the former construction is adopted the instrument is not entitled to probate unless the condition is fulfilled,[5] while if the latter conclusion is reached, the will is effective upon the testator's death even though the event, the possibility of which appears to

1 Slaughter's Adm'r v. Wyman, 228 Ky. 226, 14 S.W.2d 777, 1929; Lee v. Kirby, 186 Ky. 603, 217 S.W. 895, 1920.

2 Sewell v. Slingluff, 57 Md. 537, 1882. Cf. Clark v. Hugo, 130 Va. 99, 107 S.E. 730, 1921. See also Barber v. Barber, 368 Ill. 215, 13 N.E.2d 257, 1938, noted, 16 Chi-Kent L.R. 303; In re Johnston's Estate, 186 Misc. 533, 53 N.Y.S.2d 212, 1945. And see supra § 46.

3 See Cartwright v. Cartwright, 158 Ark. 278, 250 S.W. 11, 1923; Barber v. Barber, supra note 2. But see Capps v. Richardson, 73 S.C. 586, 53 S.E.2d 876, 1949, noted, 2 S.C.L.R. 94.

4 Barber v. Barber, supra note 2; Succession of Gurganus, 206 La. 1012, 20 So.2d 296, 1945; see In re Morrison's Estate, infra note 6. See generally Evans, Conditional Wills, 35 Mich.L.R. 1049; Hutton, Conditional Wills and Wills with Conditions in Pennsylvania, 53 Dick.L.R. 258.

5 Wilson v. Higgason, 207 Ark. 32, 178 S.W.2d 855, 1944; Walker v. Hibbard, 185 Ky. 795, 215 S.W. 800, 11 A.L.R. 832, 1919; Ellison v. Smoot's Adm'r, 286 Ky. 768, 151 S.W.2d 1017.

have been the inducement for making the will, has never taken place.[6]

Typically the testator states that he is about to set out on a journey and makes the provisions in case he should not return, or declares that he disposes of his property if he does not recover from a contemplated surgical operation. A number of cases have held such wills conditional, and hence ineffective when death did not come from the stated hazard.[7] These cases can be matched by others which hold that similar language is merely a statement of the inducement for the execution of the will and that the will is effective in any event.[8] The latter conclusion is preferable whenever the wording of the will can reasonably bear this construction,[9] although the other provisions of the will and the circumstances surrounding the testator at the time of execution of the will may swing the result in the particular case.[10]

Of course the court is governed primarily by the language used by the testator. However, as in other cases of construc-

1941; Capps v. Richardson, supra note 3. See infra note 7.

6 In re Morrison's Estate, 361 Pa. 419, 65 A.2d 384, 1949. See infra note 8.

7 Re Cook's Estate, 173 Cal. 465, 160 P. 553, 1916 ("if I should die from the operation"); Dougherty v. Dougherty, 4 Metc.(Ky.) 25, 1860 ("I intend starting in a few days for the state of Missouri and should anything happen that I should not return alive"); Magee v. McNeil, 41 Miss. 17, 90 Am. Dec. 354, 1866; Robnett v. Ashlock, 49 Mo. 171, 1872; Goods of Winn, 2 Sw. & Tr. 147, 164 Eng.Rep. 949, 1861 ("in case of my decease during my absence"). See In re Young's Estate, 95 Okl. 205, 219 P. 100, 1923 (death before death of another); In re Poonarian's Will, 234 N.Y. 329, 137 N.E. 606, 1922; Bagnall v. Bagnall, 148 Tex. 423, 225 S.W.2d 401, 1949, noted, 4 Miami L.Q. 531, 4 S.W.L.J. 357; also cases supra note 5.

8 Re Tinsley's Will, 187 Iowa 23, 174 N.W. 4, 11 A.L.R. 826, 1919 ("in case of any serious accident, after my just debts are paid, I direct"); McMerriman v. Schiel, 108 Ohio St. 334, 140 N.E. 600, 1923; Ferguson v. Ferguson, 121 Tex. 119, 45 S.W.2d 1096, 79 A.L.R. 1163, 1931 ("I am going on a journey and I may never come back alive so I make this will, but I expect to make changes if I live"); Eaton v. Brown, 193 U.S. 411, 24 S.Ct. 487, 48 L.Ed. 730, 1904 ("I am going on a journey and may not ever return. And if I do not this is my last request").

See also Barber v. Barber, supra note 2; Watkins v. Watkins' Adm'r, 269 Ky. 246, 106 S.W.2d 975, 1917, noted, 3 Mo.L.R. 83; In re Moore's Estate, 332 Pa. 257, 2 A.2d 761, 1939.

9 American Trust and Safe Deposit Co. v. Eckhardt, 331 Ill. 261, 162 N.E. 843, 1928; Eaton v. Brown, Ferguson v. Ferguson, McMerriman v. Schiel, In re Moore's Estate, all supra note 8; Porter's Appeal, L.R. 2 Prob. & Div. 22, 1869. See note 4 supra.

10 See notes 12, 13 infra.

tion, the court should look to the entire will, place itself in the position of the testator, and consider all the surrounding circumstances.[11] It has been considered relevant that the testator preserved the will or instructed the beneficiary to take care of it, after the event in question had failed to occur.[12] However, too much weight should not be given to such circumstances for they bespeak mainly the intention at a time subsequent to execution. A later desire that a will once conditional should become absolute is ineffective without re-execution or republication of the will.[13]

[11] French v. French, 14 W.Va. 458, 1878; Eaton v. Brown, supra, note 8; Barber v. Barber, supra note 2; In re Poonarian's Will, supra note 7; Watkins v. Watkins' Adm'r, supra note 8. See infra § 146.

[12] Likefield v. Likefield, 82 Ky. 589, 56 Am.Rep. 908, 1885; National Bank of Commerce of Charlestown v. Wehrle, 124 W.Va. 268, 20 S.E.2d 112, 1942.

[13] When a conditional will is republished after the contingency mentioned has not occurred as contemplated, the will is absolute. In re Forquer's Estate, 216 Pa. 331, 66 A. 92, 8 Ann. Cas. 1146, 1907.

# CHAPTER 10

## REVOCATION AND REVIVAL



### REVOCATION—CONCEPT AND METHODS IN GENERAL

**84. Revocation is the termination of the potential capacity of the will to operate at testator's death, either by the latter's act or by operation of law.**

**A will can be revoked at the pleasure of the testator, even if he has contracted not to do so, though in the latter case appropriate remedy may be had against the estate upon a contractual basis.**

**The exclusive methods of revocation are:**

**(a) Certain well-defined changes in the circumstances of the testator from which a revocation will be implied by law.**

**(b) Physical acts done to the will, as prescribed by statute.**

**(c) A subsequent writing, in the form fixed by statute, either expressly or impliedly revoking the will.**

Revocability as above defined is one of the leading characteristics of a will. This is everywhere recognized though some statutes stress the idea particularly.[1] Even if the testator has contracted not to revoke his will, a revocation in the manner prescribed by law is effective for the purpose of denying probate,[2]

1 See Bordwell, Statute Law of Wills, 14 Ia.L.R. 284, 285.

2 In re Rolls' Estate, 193 Cal. 594, 226 P. 608, 1924; Menke v. Duwe, 117 Kan. 207, 230 P. 1065, 1924; In re Burke's Estate, 66 Or. 252, 134 P. 11, 1913. See Partridge, Revocability of Mutual or Reciprocal Wills, 77 U. of Pa.L.R. 357; note, 2 Cin.L.R. 435. Cf. Goddard, Mutual Wills, 17 Mich.L.Rev. 677, 686. See also supra §§ 48, 49; annotation, 43 A.L.R. 1025; note, 27 Yale L.J. 542; Doyle v. Fischer, 183 Wis. 599, 198 N.W. 763,

though the promisee or third party beneficiary may obtain legal or equitable relief against the estate upon the promise made.[3]

Prior to the Statute of Frauds a will could be revoked by oral declarations.[4] This obvious opportunity for fraud was precluded by provisions of that statute,[5] to the effect that no written will of personalty could be repealed or altered by oral words, and that no devise of realty should be revoked except by instrument executed with the formalities of the will or by burning, cancelling, tearing, or obliterating. By the Wills Act, 1837,[6] the language of the earlier provision as to revocation of wills of realty was altered but its substance retained and applied to wills of personalty as well. While the terms of the Statute of Frauds seemed to imply that no other manner of revocation is possible, the courts recognized revocation by operation of law in certain cases, such as the marriage and birth of issue to a male testator, or the marriage of a testatrix, but the Wills Act, 1837 made express exclusive provisions for revocation by operation of law.[7]

In the United States the statutes universally recognize revocation by subsequent instrument, and except in one state there is provision for revocation by physical act.[8] In addition, there is frequently specific provision for revocation by operation of law, and elsewhere that common-law doctrine is usually recognized.[9]

*Capacity, Form and Intent*

In general, the same degree of mental capacity is required for revocation of a will as for its execution.[10] Even by express pro-

33 A.L.R. 733, 1924. There is some authority to the contrary. McGinley's Estate, 257 Pa. 478, 101 A. 807, 1917; Sherman v. Goodson's Heirs, 219 S.W. 839, Tex.Civ.App.1920. And see Lovett v. Lovett, 87 Ind.App. 42, 155 N.E. 528, 157 N.E. 104, 1927, enjoining revocation of will. Cf. In re Smith's Will, 254 N.Y. 283, 172 N.E. 499, 72 A.L.R. 867, 1930, noted 16 Ia. L.R. 285.

3 Andrews v. Aikens, 44 Idaho 797, 260 P. 423, 69 A.L.R. 8, 1927; Padfield v. Padfield, 72 Ill. 322, 1874; Nelson v. Schoonover, 89 Kan. 388, 131 P. 147, 1912; Smith v. Thompson, 250 Mich. 302, 230 N.W. 156, 73 A.L.R. 1389, 1930; Huffine v. Lincoln, 52 Mont. 585, 160 P. 820, 1916. See annotations, 3 A.L.R. 172, 69 A.L.R. 14, 73 A.L.R. 1395.

4 Brooke v. Ward, Dyer 310 b, 73 Eng.Rep. 702, 1572.

5 29 Car. II, c. 3, § 22, 1677.

6 7 Wm. IV & 1 Vict. c. 26, § 20.

7 See infra § 85.

8 See Bordwell, Statute Law of Wills, 14 Ia.L.R. 284–290.

9 See infra § 85.

10 Tonnelier v. Tonnelier, 132 Fla. 194, 181 So. 150, 1938; In re Marsden's Estate, 217 Minn. 1, 13 N.W.2d 765, 1944 (undue influence); In re

vision in the will testator cannot effectively set up a method of revocation not permitted by law.[11]

An oral attempt to revoke a will is inoperative however unquestionable the intent may be, unless attended by the requisite statutory manifestations.[12] This position is indicated by the authorities holding that no revocation results where the testator's intention to revoke is thwarted by the fraud of a beneficiary. Thus where X brought a will to a blind testator at the latter's request who, after feeling of the seals of the envelope in which it was inclosed, requested X to throw it into the fire, and X pretended to do so, substituting however another paper for the will and calling the testator's attention to the odor and the crackling of the burning paper, in consequence of which the testator died in the belief that his will had been revoked, it was held that there was no sufficient revocation.[13]

"The law will not permit the formalities of the execution of a will to be dispensed with because of fraudulent interference, and the same rule must be applied in respect to the statutory requisites of revocation." [14] Revocation (except possibly revocation by operation of law) is simply a question of complying with the requirements of the statute. The few decisions [15] which have reached the opposite conclusion must be regarded as instances of judicial legislation.

There is no remedy for an intended but ineffective revocation except where it was prevented by fraud. Even in the latter case

Woehrle's Will, 53 N.Y.S.2d 412, 1945; Sutton v. Sutton, 222 N.C. 274, 22 S.E.2d 553, 1942; In re Bond's Estate, 172 Or. 509, 143 P.2d 244, 1943; Gregory v. Susong, 185 Tenn. 232, 205 S.W.2d 6, 1947. See supra § 51.

11 Ragland v. Wagener, 179 S.W.2d 380, Tex.Civ.App.1944, reversed on other grounds, 142 Tex. 651, 180 S.W. 2d 435, 152 A.L.R. 1232.

12 Aten v. Tobias, 114 Kan. 646, 220 P. 196, 1923; In re Watson's Will, 213 N.C. 309, 195 S.E. 772, 1938; Kent v. Mahaffey, 10 Ohio St. 204, 1859. A written will cannot be revoked by a subsequent nuncupative will. McCune's Devisees v. House, 8 Ohio 144, 31 Am.Dec. 438, 1837. Cf. In re Glebus' Estate, 267 Pa. 125, 110 A. 80, 1920.

13 Kent v. Mahaffey, 10 Ohio St. 204, 1859. And see Bohleber v. Rebstock, 255 Ill. 53, 99 N.E. 75, 41 L.R.A.,N.S., 105, Ann.Cas.1913D 307, 1912; Moneyham v. Hamilton, 124 Fla. 430, 168 So. 522, 1936; Trice v. Shipton, 113 Ky. 102, 67 S.W. 377, 101 Am St. Rep. 351, 1902; In re Winters' Will, 97 N.Y.S.2d 477, 198 Misc. 87, 1950; In re Silva's Estate, 169 Cal. 116, 145 P. 1015, 1915; Doe d. Perkes v. Perkes, 3 B. & Ald. 489, 106 Eng.Rep. 740, 1820.

14 Vanderburgh, J., in Graham v. Birch, 47 Minn. 171, 49 N.W. 697, 28 Am.St.Rep. 339, 1891.

15 Pryor v. Coggin, 17 Ga. 444, 1855; Ford v. Ford, 7 Humph.(Tenn.) 92, 1846.

the fraud is not ground for denial of probate. Relief is obtained by a suit asking that the beneficiary be decreed a constructive trustee for those losing by this act.[16]

## REVOCATION BY OPERATION OF LAW

**85. At common law, a woman's will was revoked by her subsequent marriage; that of a man, by marriage and birth of issue. Neither of these events, alone, affected a man's will.**

**In many jurisdictions the above rules have been materially modified by express statutory provisions, or by legislation altering the rules of descent and distribution, and the giving to married women the capacity to control and make testamentary disposition of their property.**

**In absence of express statute divorce alone does not revoke a will, but when coupled with a settlement of property rights between the parties, it is often deemed to revoke prior devises and bequests in favor of the divorced spouse.**

**At common law, the alienation of the subject matter of a devise or bequest was said to revoke the same, and some courts continue to so regard the matter though this problem should now be considered solely from the standpoint of ademption, or failure of the devise because the subject-matter is not owned by the testator at the time of his death.**

In spite of the fact that the Statute of Frauds, 1677, provided that no devise of land could be revoked except by duly attested instrument or by certain physical acts done to the instrument, and further emphasized this by adding "any former law or usage to the contrary notwithstanding,"[1] it was recognized that a man's will was revoked by his marriage and subsequent birth of issue,[2] and a woman's by her subsequent marriage.[3] In explana-

[16] That such remedy is available, see Brazil v. Silva, 181 Cal. 490, 185 P. 174, 1919; Trice v. Shipton, supra note 13; Latham v. Father Divine, 299 N.Y. 22, 85 N.E.2d 168, 11 A.L.R. 2d 802, 1949, noted, 48 Mich.L.R. 1018, 34 Minn.L.R. 80, see supra § 57. But in Kent v. Mahaffey, 10 Ohio St. 204, 220, 1859, it was said in answer to this suggestion: "The fraudulent prevention of its revocation could not well be tortured into a promise to hold for the heir at law; and to hold the legatee a trustee in such case would seem to nullify the statute prohibiting revocation except in a specified manner." And see Bohleber v. Rebstock, supra note 13. Cf. Moneyham v. Hamilton, supra note 13; Reiter v. Carroll, 210 Ark. 841, 198 S.W.2d 163, 1947.

[1] 29 Car. II, c. 3, § vi.

[2] See infra note 44.

[3] See infra note 24.

tion of these holdings it was declared that the statute dealt only with intentional revocations and not with cases of revocation by operation of law where the testator's intent is immaterial.[4] While this type of revocation is perhaps based in part, upon the thought that the average testator would have desired revocation in the circumstances,[5] the inquiry is merely what testators in general would have wished and not what the particular testator desired.[6] At any rate, revocation by operation of law in these two situations was well established in the English case law until the matter was altered by the Wills Act, 1837, which expressly provided for revocation by subsquent marriage and absolutely abolished all other sorts of revocation by change of circumstances.[7]

In some American jurisdictions the language of the Statute of Frauds is followed.[8] As would be expected in these states, the courts permit revocation by operation of law,[9] though literally the statutory wording seems to forbid it. In a number of other jurisdictions,[10] the language of the statutes is similar except that there is an express recognition of the general principle of revocation by operation of law. There seem to be few, if any, differences in the decisions on account of these two types of statutes. A third type of legislation like the present English statute does away with all but statutory revocations, and the jurisdictions adopting this form of provision usually provide for specified changes of conditions or circumstances of the testator which will work a revocation.[11] A few other states mention certain circumstances of this nature which will revoke a will,[12] and these specifications would seem to exclude all others.

4 See infra notes 6, 22.

5 See infra note 45.

6 Donaldson v. Hall, 106 Minn. 502, 119 N.W. 219, 20 L.R.A.,N.S., 1073, 130 Am.St.Rep. 621, 16 Ann.Cas. 541, 1909; In re Battis' Will, 143 Wis. 234, 126 N.W. 9, 139 Am.St.Rep. 1101, 1910; Marston v. Roe, 8 Ad. & E. 14, 112 Eng.Rep. 742, 1838. But see Del Genovese's Will, 169 App.Div. 140, 154 N.Y.S. 806, 1915.

7 7 Wm. IV & 1 Vict., c. 26, §§ xviii, xix.

8 Bordwell, Statute Law of Wills, 14 Ia.L.R. 305.

9 Baldwin v. Spriggs, 65 Md. 373, 5 A. 295, 1886; In re Teopfer's Estate, 12 N.M. 372, 78 P. 53, 67 L.R.A. 315, 1904; Pascucci v. Alsop, 79 App. D.C. 354, 147 F.2d 880, 1945. See Mersch, Implied Revocation of Wills Revived in the District of Columbia, 33 Geo.L.J. 182.

10 Bordwell, supra note 8 at 303. The rules of the common law must be applied in this situation. Herzog v. Trust Co., 67 Fla. 54, 64 So. 426, Ann. Cas.1917A, 201, 1914.

11 Bordwell, supra note 8 at 306.

12 Bordwell, supra note 8 at 306. For classifications of the statutes on

*A Man's Marriage*

At common law, marriage of a man did not revoke his will.[13] As applied to devises this seems sensible, since his wife obtained her dower in spite of the will and would be entitled to no more of the realty even if the will was revoked as she was never her husband's heir.[14]

Although the widow would profit with regard to personalty by a revocation of her husband's will made before the marriage[15] there was no revocation as to personalty; indeed the rule that a man's marriage did not revoke his will seems to have originated in the personalty cases and was later extended to devises of land.[16]

Today the widow is usually an heir to both lands and chattels. However, the argument that on this account the husband's will should now be deemed revoked by his marriage is weakened by the fact that she generally has a right to take a forced share against the will, although this share is often less than her intestate share.[17] Some modern cases have held that the husband's will is revoked upon the basis that he acquired a new heir by his marriage,[18] while others adhere to the common-law rule.[19]

There is a legislative tendency to depart from the old rule that a man's marriage does not revoke his pre-existing will. In a considerable number of jurisdictions,[20] it is now provided by statute

other bases, see Graunke & Beuscher, The Doctrine of Implied Revocation of Wills by Reason of Change in Domestic Relations of the Testator, 5 Wis.L.R. 387; Durfee, Revocation of Wills by Subsequent Change in Condition or Circumstances of the Testator, 40 Mich.L.R. 406; 1 Vernier, American Family Laws, pp. 299–305.

13 See infra notes 16, 19.

14 See supra §§ 6, 29.

15 Supra § 7.

16 See Graunke & Beuscher, supra note 12 at 389–392.

17 See supra § 30.

18 Brown v. Scherrer, 5 Colo.App. 255, 38 P. 427, 1895, affirmed 21 Colo. 481, 42 P. 668; Morgan v. Ireland, 1 Idaho 786, 1880; Tyler v. Tyler, 19 Ill. 151, 1857; In re Lewis' Will, 41 N.M. 522, 71 P.2d 1032, 1937. And see In re Teopfer's Estate, supra note 9.

19 Herzog v. Trust Co., 67 Fla. 54, 64 So. 426, Ann.Cas.1917A 201, 1914; Vanek v. Vanek, 104 Kan. 624, 180 P. 240, 1919; Hulett v. Carey, 66 Minn. 327, 69 N.W. 31, 34 L.R.A. 384, 61 Am.St.Rep. 419, 1896; Hoy v. Hoy, 93 Miss. 732, 48 So. 903, 25 L.R.A., N.S., 182, 136 Am.St.Rep. 548, 17 Ann. Cas. 1137, 1908; Hilton v. Johnson, 194 Miss. 671, 12 So.2d 524, 1943; In re Wehr's Will, 247 Wis. 98, 18 N.W. 2d 709, 1945, noted, 29 Marq.L.R. 122.

20 See Bordwell, supra note 8 at 298, 299. The statutory situation at the time of the testator's death, rather than at the time of the will or subsequent marriage ordinarily governs.

that a testator's marriage revokes his will either absolutely, or as to the spouse,[21] or unless it appears from the will that it was made in contemplation of the marriage,[22] or unless the wife was provided for in the will or otherwise mentioned therein so as to indicate an intention not to revoke.[23]

In re Derruau's Estate, 133 Cal.App. 769, 24 P.2d 865, 1933; cf. Re Goldberg, 275 N.Y. 186, 9 N.E.2d 829, 1937; see notes, 33 Col.L.Rev. 1078, 20 Va.L.Rev. 242. As to the law of what state governs, see In re Wehr's Will, supra note 19; In re Culley's Will, 182 Misc. 998, 48 N.Y.S.2d 216, 1944.

21 For typical decisions under statutes of this type, see In re Matteote's Estate, 59 Colo. 566, 151 P. 448, 1915 (will revoked by common-law marriage with divorced spouse); Lawman v. Murphy, 321 Ill. 421, 152 N.E. 220, 1926 (in spite of antenuptial release of the spouses); Shackelford v. Shackelford, 181 Va. 869, 27 S.E.2d 354, 1943; In re Kelly's Estate, 191 Minn. 280, 254 N.W. 437, 438, 92 A.L.R. 1007 1934 (same—woman's will); Moore v. Moore, 198 N.C. 510, 152 S.E. 391, 1930; Puckett's Ex'r v. Puckett, 305 Ky. 812, 205 S.W.2d 1016, 1947 (no revocation when will provided it became effective only on date of marriage); In re Goods of Cadywold, 1 Sw. & Tr. 34, 164 Eng.Rep. 617, 1858 (though will left major part of estate to the woman whom testator married later). The Law of Property Act, 1925, § 177, provides that there shall be no revocation by marriage of a will made in contemplation of the marriage. Cf. note 22 infra. See Gillmann v. Dressler, 300 Ill. 175, 133 N.E.2d 186, 1921, noted, 20 Mich.L.R. 921 and 31 Yale L.J. 673, where provision for the widow in the will prevented revocation though the statute made no such exception.

Under a statute providing that an unmarried person's will becomes void upon his marriage, the testator's will made during his first marriage was not revoked by his remarriage. Grave v. Kittle, 101 N.E.2d 830, Ind.App. 1951.

22 Sughrue v. Barlow, 233 Mass. 468, 124 N.E. 285, 1919 (revocation, though testator left everything to the woman he later married because the will did not show on its face the contemplated marriage); Levine v. Ramler, 325 Mass. 141, 89 N.E.2d 339, 1949 (cannot be revived by oral evidence of intent).

23 In re Appenfelder's Estate, 99 Cal.App. 330, 278 P. 473, 1929, noted, 18 Cal.L.R. 207 (same problem as in Sughrue v. Barlow, supra note 22—held no revocation). The revocation under this type of statute is usually total unless coming within the exceptions. In re Anderson's Estate, 14 Ariz. 502, 131 P. 975, 1913; In re Ryan's Estate, 191 Cal. 307, 216 P. 366, 1923; In re Larsen's Estate, 18 S.D. 335, 100 N.W. 738, 5 Ann.Cas. 794, 1904. But the present California statute provides for revocation only "as to the spouse." In re Piatt's Estate, 57 Cal.App.2d 211, 134 P.2d 321, 1943, noted, 31 Cal.L.R. 614. As to what constitutes "mention" in the will, see Estate of Axcelrod, 23 Cal.2d 761, 147 P.2d 1, 1944, noted, 32 Cal. L.R. 213, 42 Mich.L.R. 1132 (general disinheritance of all heirs is insufficient mention of husband married later); In re Hall's Estate, 159 Wash. 236, 292 P. 401, 1930, noted, 6 Wash. L.Rev. 36 (provision that in case of remarriage, spouse should take nothing was sufficient mention to prevent a revocation).

*A Woman's Marriage*

At common law, if a single woman made a will it was revoked by her subsequent marriage.[24] The chief reason for the holding was that marriage destroyed her testamentary capacity,[25] and she was incapable of making another will during coverture or of revoking her pre-marital will. It was thought that the intestate laws should govern the disposition of her property, rather than her will made prior to marriage. In addition, her husband acquired title to her personalty as well as certain control over her realty,[26] and these things were inconsistent with the potential operation of her prior will. However, a will operating as an appointment under a power was not revoked by the marriage, for such a will could be made or altered after coverture.[27] With this exception, marriage revoked a woman's will, and death of her husband did not revive it.[28]

Under modern legislation a married woman has power to make a valid will and her husband's control over her property is almost, if not entirely, abrogated.[29] As the reason for the old common-law rule has ceased to exist, it is not surprising that most modern decisions are to the effect that a woman's will is not revoked by her marriage, unless there is an express statutory provision to this effect.[30] However, the view has been taken that, while the removal of the married woman's common-law disabilities would seem an argument for the abolition of the common-law rule, the fact that she obtains in her husband a new heir un-

[24] Hodsden v. Lloyd, 2 Bro.C.C. 535, 29 Eng.Rep. 293, 1789. It has been declared that if an antenuptial agreement was made retaining control in the woman of her property, the marriage did not operate to revoke the will. Stewart v. Mulholland, 88 Ky. 38, 10 S.W. 125, 21 Am.St.Rep. 320, 1888; In re Carey's Estate, 49 Vt. 236, 24 Am.Rep. 133, 1876. See In re Kelly's Estate, 191 Minn. 280, 254 N.W. 437, 92 A.L.R. 1007, 1934. Cf. Taylor v. Rains, 7 Mod. 147, 87 Eng. Rep. 1155, 1702.

[25] See supra § 50.

[26] See supra §§ 7, 29.

[27] Rich v. Beaumont, 6 Bro.P.C. 152, 2 Eng.Rep. 994, 1727; see Ward's Will, 70 Wis. 251, 35 N.W. 731, 5 Am. St.Rep. 174, 1887. Cf. Yerxa v. Youngman, 241 Mass. 251, 135 N.E. 117, 922 (statute).

[28] Hodsden v. Lloyd, supra note 24; but cf. Forse v. Hembling, 4 Coke 60b, 76 Eng.Rep. 1022, 1588.

[29] See supra § 50.

[30] Hastings v. Day, 151 Iowa 39, 130 N.W. 134, 34 L.R.A.,N.S., 1021, Ann.Cas.1913A, 214, 1911; Emery, Appellant, 81 Me. 275, 17 A. 68, 1889; In re Hillaert's Estate, 313 Mich. 344, 21 N.W.2d 155, 1946; Lee v. Blewett, 116 Miss. 341, 77 So. 147, L.R.A.1918B 941, 1917; Kelly v. Stevenson, 85 Minn. 247, 88 N.W. 739, 56 L.R.A. 754, 89 Am.St.Rep. 545, 1902; In re Ward's Will, 70 Wis. 251, 35 N.W. 731, 5 Am.St.Rep. 174, 1887.

der the intestate laws should cause a revocation,[31] by the same philosophy that some courts now hold that a man's will is revoked by his marriage.[32]

Most of the statutes expressly providing that a testator's will is revoked by his marriage are equally applicable to the case of a testatrix,[33] and the decisions thereunder are parallel.[34] In a few states [35] it is provided that a woman's marriage revokes her will, though there is no corresponding provision in case of a man. This type of legislation is not repealed by implication upon the passage of legislation giving a married woman testamentary power and full property rights.[36]

*Birth of Issue*

In absence of statute it is orthodox to hold that a will made by a married man is not revoked by the subsequent birth of a child.[37] "Husbands are likely to foresee that they may become fathers. Particularly when the child is young and the estate small, husbands who are fathers often choose to leave all their property to their wives." [38] However, there is certainly substantial authority to the effect that birth of issue alone does revoke.[39] It is significant that in one of the few jurisdictions which have no statutory protection for the after-born child, birth of issue was held to revoke a will made by a married man.[40]

31 Colcord v. Conroy, 40 Fla. 97, 23 So. 561, 1898; In re Teopfer's Estate, 12 N.M. 372, 78 P. 53, 67 L.R.A. 315, 1904. See also Vandeveer v. Higgins, 59 Neb. 333, 80 N.W. 1043, 1899.

32 See supra note 18.

33 See supra notes 20–23.

34 With Grave v. Kittle, supra note 21, cf. Parker v. Foreman, 252 Ala. 77, 39 So.2d 574, 9 A.L.R.2d 505, 1949; with In re Goods of Cadywold, supra note 21, cf. In re Shepherd's Estate, 183 Or. 629, 194 P.2d 425, 1948. And see In re Kelly's Estate, supra note 21; Estate of Axcelrod, supra note 23.

35 See infra note 36.

36 Ward v. Pipkin, 180 Ark. 855, 22 S.W.2d 1011, 1930; Barnett v. Bellows, 315 Mo. 1100, 287 S.W. 604, 1926.

37 In re Hatfield's Estate, 153 Fla. 817, 16 So.2d 57, 1944; In re Rendell's Estate, 244 Mich. 197, 221 N.W. 116, 1928; Marshall v. Marshall, 25 Tenn. App. 309, 156 S.W.2d 449, 1942; Burns v. Burns, 67 Wyo. 314, 333, 224 P.2d 178, 185, 1950. As to the English authorities, see Graunke & Beuscher, supra note 12 at 396–397.

38 Edgerton, A. J., in Allen v. Heron, 81 App.D.C. 298, 157 F.2d 707, 1946, affirming In re Allen's Estate, 64 F.Supp. 107, D.C.D.C., 1946.

39 Negus v. Negus, 46 Iowa 487, 26 Am.Rep. 157, 1877; Karr v. Robinson, 167 Md. 375, 173 A. 584, 1934, noted, 35 Col.L.R. 787.

40 Karr v. Robinson, supra note 39; see Lenz, Revocation of a Will by Birth of a Child, 1 Md.L.R. 32.

Legislation for the protection of the after-born child naturally has considerable bearing upon the present problem. While statutes in a few states declared that the will is entirely revoked by the subsequent birth,[41] typically the provisions are not revocation statutes but merely permit the child to take his intestate share against the will.[42] This usually has the substantive effect of a pro tanto revocation, although the child does not assert his rights at probate of the will as in case of true revocation. Almost always provision for after-born children, and usually also mere mention of them in the will, prevents operation of the statutes in their favor.[43] Except to the extent that these statutes provide for total revocation, they are based upon the tacit assumption that, in accordance with the orthodox common-law position, the will is not revoked and is effective subject to the right of the afterborns.

*Marriage and Subsequent Birth of Issue*

While it was usually said that at common law neither a man's subsequent marriage, nor the subsequent birth of issue to him, revoked his existing will, if both the marriage and the birth occurred after execution of the will, it was entirely revoked.[44] This doctrine has been said to rest upon a presumed change of testamentary intent,[45] but a more tenable ground is that there is such a radical change in the testator's situation that the law should regard the will as revoked regardless of the wishes of the

[41] In some of these, there is total revocation only if there are no other children, or if the after-born children survive. See Bordwell, Statute Law of Wills, 14 Ia.L.R. 292. Under these statutes the will is entirely revoked. Strong v. Strong, 106 Conn. 76, 137 A. 17, 1927; Hughes v. Hughes, 37 Ind. 183, 1871; In re Patterson's Estate, 282 Pa. 396, 128 A. 100, 38 A.L.R. 1340, 1925.

[42] See Bordwell, Statute Law of Wills, 14 Ia.L.R. 290–298; Mathews, Pretermitted Heirs: An Analysis of Statutes, 29 Col.L.R. 748.

[43] See supra § 36; annotation, 127 A.L.R. 750.

[44] Pascucci v. Alsop, 79 App.D.C. 354, 147 F.2d 880, 1945; Shorten v. Judd, 60 Kan. 73, 55 P. 286, 1898; Brush v. Wilkins, 4 Johns.Ch. (N.Y.) 506, 1820; Glascott v. Bragg, 111 Wis. 605, 87 N.W. 853, 56 L.R.A. 258, 1901; Israell v. Redon, 2 Mo.P.C. 51, 12 Eng.Rep. 922, 1839 (through settlement made after the will for future wife and children); Marston v. Fox, 8 Ad. & E. 14, 112 Eng.Rep. 742, 1838. But if provision is made for both wife and children in the will, it has been held that there is no revocation. Morey v. Sohier, 63 N.H. 507, 3 A. 636, 56 Am.Rep. 538, 1886; Kenebel v. Scafton, 2 East 530, 102 Eng.Rep. 472, 1802; see Brady v. Cubitt, Dougl. 31, 99 Eng.Rep. 24, 1778.

[45] See Overbury v. Overbury, 2 Show. 242, 89 Eng.Rep. 915, 1682; Lugg v. Lugg, 2 Salk. 592, 91 Eng. Rep. 497, 1697.

individual testator. Accordingly, his intention is immaterial and parol evidence is inadmissible to show that testator did not intend that his will should be revoked by his marriage followed by birth of issue.[46]

In the absence of peremptory legislation abolishing revocation by operation of law in general,[47] a man's will is still usually regarded as revoked by marriage and birth of issue.[48] However, a recent case has held to the contrary because of the statutory provisions allowing the wife and children to take against a will which makes no provision for them.[49] Of course in those states where the will is revoked by marriage alone or by birth of issue, the present question does not arise.

At the common law, in case of women, it was immaterial whether marriage plus birth of issue would revoke a will, for the reason that marriage alone had that effect. Since the will was entirely revoked by marriage, the later birth of issue to the woman could have no further effect. As we have seen,[50] most courts hold that the old rule to the effect that a woman's will is revoked by her marriage is abrogated. If, then, her will is not revoked by her marriage alone, will it be revoked in case of subsequent marriage followed by birth of issue? Every argument, to the effect that these events caused revocation of a man's will, now applies equally to the case of a woman's will; accordingly it has been held that a woman's will is revoked by marriage plus birth of issue.[51]

*Illegitimate Children*

The effect of the birth of illegitimate children upon a prior will depends wholly upon their statutory status. If not legitimated, they do not inherit from their father in case of intestacy, and his will is not revoked, either totally or pro tanto as the case may be.[52] There is no reason in holding the will revoked, if the child for whose benefit the revocation would be declared can not in-

[46] Marston v. Fox, supra note 44; Hoitt v. Hoitt, 63 N.H. 475, 3 A. 604, 56 Am.Rep. 530, 1886.

[47] See supra notes 11, 12.

[48] See supra note 44.

[49] Appeal of De Mendoza, 141 Me. 299, 43 A.2d 816, 1945; but cf. Shorten v. Judd, supra note 44.

[50] See supra note 30.

[51] Durfee v. Risch, 142 Mich. 504, 105 N.W. 1114, 5 L.R.A.,N.S., 1084, 7 Ann.Cas. 785, 1905. And see Nutt v. Norton, 142 Mass. 242, 7 N.E. 720, 1886. But cf. supra note 49.

[52] Irving v. Irving, 152 Ga. 174, 108 S.E. 540, 18 A.L.R. 88, 1921; Sneed v. Ewing, 5 J.J.Marsh.(Ky.) 460, 22 Am.Dec. 41, 1831. See In re Estate of Loyd, 170 Cal. 85, 148 P. 522, 1915.

herit. If the child is legitimated by statute so as to become an heir of the father, the prior will should be revoked as and if it would be in the case of the birth of a legitimate child.[53] In the case of a mother's will, as her illegitimate child may generally inherit from her it would seem that her will should be revoked, to the same extent as if the child were born in wedlock.[54] Of course if the statute provides for revocation only on account of legitimate children, the birth of an illegitimate child, even though acknowledged, does not revoke the parent's will.[55]

*Adopted Children*

Whether the adoption of a child is attended with the same consequences as the birth of issue depends to some extent upon the language of the statutes respecting revocation of wills and the adoption of children. Some decisions have held that the adoption of a child does not meet the legislative requirement of birth of issue. Most modern authorities declare that adoption of a child has the same effect as natural birth,[56] being influenced by the terms of the adoption statutes declaring that adopted children shall have the full rights of children by birth. From a technical standpoint the cases could generally have been decided either way; the majority view is no doubt influenced by a judicial policy favoring the institution of adoption.

[53] Milburn v. Milburn, 60 Iowa 411, 14 N.W. 204, 1882. Cf. Appeal of McCulloch, 113 Pa. 247, 6 A. 253, 1886, where child was born before will and legitimated afterward. Held, no revocation.

[54] Bunce v. Bunce, 14 N.Y.S. 659, Sup., 1891; In re Patterson's Estate, 282 Pa. 396, 128 A. 100, 38 A.L.R. 1340, 1925. And see In re Wardell's Estate, 57 Cal. 484, 1881, with which compare Kent v. Barker, 2 Gray (Mass.) 535, 1854, and Mansfield v. Neff, 43 Utah, 258, 134 P. 1160, 1913.

[55] Eckart v. Eckart, 95 Ind.App. 148, 163 N.E. 288, 1928, noted, 38 Yale L.J. 552.

[56] Thornton v. Anderson, 207 Ga. 714, 64 S.E.2d 186, 24 A.L.R.2d 1079, 1951; Hilpire v. Claude, 109 Iowa 159, 80 N.W. 332, 46 L.R.A. 171, 77 Am.St.Rep. 524, 1899; Dreyer v. Schrick, 105 Kan. 495, 185 P. 30, 1919, noted, 33 Harv.L.R. 724; In re Rendell's Estate, 244 Mich. 197, 221 N.W. 116, 1928, noted, 27 Mich.L.R. 357; Remmers v. Remmers, 239 S.W. 509, Mo., 1922; In re Book's Will, 90 N.J. Eq. 549, 107 A. 435, 1919; Bourne v. Dorney, 184 App.Div. 476, 171 N.Y.S. 264, 1918; Surman v. Surman, 21 Ohio App. 434, 153 N.E. 873, 1916; In re Hebb's Estate, 134 Wash. 424, 235 P. 974, 1925. See Fulton Trust Co. v. Trowbridge, 126 Conn. 369, 11 A.2d 393, 127 A.L.R. 747, 1940. Contra: Davis v. Fogle, 124 Ind. 41, 23 N.E. 860, 7 L.R.A. 485, 1890; Succession of Carre, 212 La. 839, 33 So.2d 655, 1948, noted, 22 Tulane L.R. 661; In re Boyd's Estate, 270 Pa. 504, 113 A. 691, 1921. See Evans, Testamentary Revocation by Adoption of a Child, 22 Ky.L.J. 600.

*Divorce*

On account of the infrequency of divorce, there were no early English decisions on the question of whether a divorce revoked a testator's will. In absence of statute, it is generally agreed in this country that a divorce, unaccompanied by a property settlement, does not revoke the testator's will, nor the legacy in favor of the divorced spouse.[57] Where there is an agreement regarding property rights and the jurisdiction recognizes generally the doctrine of revocation by operation of law, it is usually held that there is revocation of the provisions in favor of the divorced spouse.[58] These decisions have the effect of adding another type of revocation by operation of law to those which were recognized at common law. Like the others, it is based upon the marked change of circumstances which probably would have caused the average testator to desire revocation. However, if the statutes enumerate the instances of revocation by operation of law and particularly if it is declared that there shall be no others, divorce and property settlement do not cause revocation.[59]

[57] Card v. Alexander, 48 Conn. 492, 40 Am.Rep. 187, 1881; Speroni v. Speroni, 406 Ill. 28, 92 N.E.2d 63, 1950; Murphy v. Markis, 98 N.J.Eq. 153, 130 A. 840, 841, 1925 (though described as "beloved husband"); In re Jones' Estate, 211 Pa. 364, 60 A. 915, 69 L.R.A. 940, 107 Am.St.Rep. 581, 3 Ann.Cas. 221, 1905. But see In re McGraw's Estate, 228 Mich. 1, 199 N.W. 686, 37 A.L.R. 308, 1924; Id., 233 Mich. 440, 207 N.W. 10, 42 A.L.R. 1283, 1926, criticized, 21 Ill.L.Rev. 282. See also note, 9 Minn.L.Rev. 169. And see Rogers v. Hollister, 156 Wis. 517, 146 N.W. 488, 1914 (express condition that devisee was to remain testator's wife was effective). See also Re Boddington, 25 Ch.Div. 685, 1884 (same). Cf. In re Blanchard's Estate, 267 Mich. 189, 255 N.W. 190, 1934, noted, 33 Mich.L.R. 637. In general, see Evans, Testamentary Revocation by Divorce, 24 Ky.L.J. 1.

[58] Lansing v. Haynes, 95 Mich. 16, 54 N.W. 699, 35 Am.St.Rep. 545, 1893; Donaldson v. Hall, 106 Minn. 502, 119 N.W. 219, 20 L.R.A.,N.S., 1073, 130 Am.St.Rep. 621, 16 Ann.Cas. 541, 1909; In re Bartlett's Estate, 108 Neb. 681, 189 N.W. 390, 25 A.L.R. 39, 1922, noted, 8 Ia.L.Bull. 281, 21 Mich. L.R. 357, 71 U. of Pa.L.R. 192, 32 Yale L.J. 32; In re Martin's Estate, 109 Neb. 289, 190 N.W. 872, 1922 (regardless of intention); Pardee v. Grubiss, 34 Ohio App. 474, 171 N.E. 375, 1929; In re Battis' Will, 143 Wis. 234, 126 N.W. 9, 139 Am.St.Rep. 1101, 1910. Contra: Hertrais v. Moore, 325 Mass. 57, 88 N.E.2d 909, 1949, noted, 30 B.U.L.R. 276, 50 Col.L.R. 531; see also In re Arnold's Estate, 60 Nev. 376, 110 P.2d 204, 1941; Codner v. Caldwell, 156 Ohio St. 197, 101 N.E.2d 901, 1951, noted, 21 U. of Cin. L.Rev. 212.

[59] Mosely v. Mosely, 217 Ark. 536, 231 S.W.2d 99, 18 A.L.R.2d 695, 1949; In re Patterson's Estate 64 Cal.App. 643, 222 P. 374, 1924; Ireland v. Terwilliger, 54 So.2d 52, Fla., 1951; Succession of Cunningham, 142 La. 701, 77 So. 506, 1918; Robertson v. Jones, 345 Mo. 828, 136 S.W.2d 278, 1940; In re Nenaber's Estate, 55 S.D. 257, 225 N.W. 719, 1929, noted, 5 Wis.L.R. 377.

Even here there are possibilities—largely unexplored—that the testamentary provision for the spouse may be regarded as satisfied by the settlement.[60] In an increasing number of states there is legislation providing that subsequent divorce revokes provisions in favor of the spouse.[61] In the light of present provisions allowing the spouse and after-born children to take against the will, divorce probably presents the strongest case today for revocation by operation of law.[62]

*Other Changes of Circumstances*

Other changes in the testator's situation than those already enumerated do not work an implied revocation of his will. Although much time elapsed after the execution of the will and before testator's death and meanwhile his estate increased greatly in value, his last testament must be given effect.[63] If the testator did not choose to change the provisions of his will on this account, the law will not do it for him. Even if the testator's feelings toward a child had greatly altered,[64] or if a principal beneficiary had died,[65] the will must be given effect to the extent that there is subject-matter on which it may act and beneficiaries alive who may take. The fact that the testator became insane before some of these changes occurred does not revoke the will which he had made while competent.[66] The revocation of one of two mutual wills by marriage of one testator does not revoke the other.[67]

60 See infra § 133.

61 See Moseley v. Moseley, supra note 59; Peiffer v. Old Nat. Bank & Union Trust Co., 166 Wash. 1, 6 P.2d 386, 1931, and infra note 62.

62 Model Probate Code § 53 provides that divorce is the only case of revocation by circumstances; see comment thereto.

63 Ater v. McClure, 329 Ill. 519, 161 N.E. 129, 1923; Aten v. Tobias, 114 Kan. 646, 220 P. 196, 1923; Warner v. Beach, 4 Gray (Mass.) 162, 1855; Hill v. Hill, 106 Neb. 17, 182 N.W. 578, 1921.

64 Aten v. Tobias, supra note 63.

65 Ater v. McClure, supra note 63; Warner v. Beach, supra note 63; Bennett v. Brown, 222 Mass. 283, 110 N.E. 266, 1915; Redwood v. Howison, 129 Md. 577, 99 A. 863, 1917 (death of wife). Cf. In re Strelow's Estate, 117 Neb. 168, 220 N.W. 251, 1928, where death of sole legatee and executor was held to leave the will without force or effect.

66 Warner v. Beach, supra note 63. And see World's Gospel Union v. Johnson, 162 Mich. 79, 127 N.W. 37, 1910. It might be contended that insanity should revoke a prior will upon the same basis that a woman's will at common law was revoked by her marriage. See text supra following note 24.

67 In re Massey's Estate, 187 Or. 40, 208 P.2d 341, 1949, noted, 29 Or.L.R. 57, 2 Stanford L.R. 431.

*Revocation by Alienation*

If testator wills Blackacre to A and later conveys it to B, A cannot take the land under the will. A sufficient explanation is that the will does not transfer the title until testator's death, and as the realty is not owned by testator at that time, the devise fails by necessity. This is a clear case of ademption and there seems to be no need to justify the result on the basis of revocation. However, from a very early time, the courts have spoken of the alienation of the subject-matter of devises and bequests—particularly the former—as revocations.[68]

Prior to the Statute of Frauds, no formalities were required for revocation;[69] any manifestation of intent to revoke was enough; ordinarily a conveyance of devised land showed an intent to revoke. Hence it was natural to speak of alienation as a revocation.[70] It was later held that a change in testator's estate was a revocation of his devise even though he did not intend to revoke.[71] When T made a devise, then conveyed the land and later received a reconveyance, it was held that the devise failed.[72] This was called a revocation, though at this time the doctrine that a will could not operate on after-acquired land[73] would have been sufficient explanation of the result.

The Statute of Frauds did not abolish revocation by alienation any more than it put an end to revocation by change of testator's family circumstances. Thus, there was revocation even if the conveyance was invalid,[74] or if the lands were reconveyed to testator and owned by him at his death.[75]

However, from the first, it was recognized that certain quantitative changes in the testator's estate did not revoke the entire devise. This was true in case of conveyance of part of the lands,[76] lease,[77] or mortgage[78] of the land, or even partition proceedings

68 See infra notes 70–75, 80.

69 See supra § 84.

70 Montague v. Jeofferevs, Moore K. B. 429, 72 Eng.Rep. 674, 1595.

71 Lutwich & Mitton, 1 Rolle Abr. 614, 0, 3, 1619.

72 See Putbury v. Tervilian, 2 Dyer 142a, 143, 73 Eng.Rep. 310, 1557.

73 See supra § 3 at notes 57, 76, 83.

74 See Beard v. Beard, 3 Atk. 72, 26 Eng.Rep. 844, 1774; see supra note 70. But see Eilbeck v. Wood, 1 Russ. 564, 38 Eng.Rep. 217, 1826.

75 See Grant v. Bridger, L.R. 3 Eq. 347, 1866.

76 Clark v. Berkeley, 2 Vern. 719, 23 Eng.Rep. 1073, 1716.

77 Lamb v. Parker, 2 Vern. 495, 23 Eng.Rep. 917, 1706.

78 Hall v. Dench, 1 Vern. 329, 23 Eng.Rep. 501, 1685.

unless the new estate in severalty was a different type of estate from that formerly held in common.[79]

Many American courts still talk of revocation by alienation;[80] indeed they are prompted to do so in some jurisdictions by certain statutory provisions.[81] There is no reason why we should think or legislate in these terms. At present in all states, a will may operate upon after-acquired property; in most states because of express statutes to that effect.[82] Accordingly most modern cases hold that devised property, which the testator later conveyed and which was still later reconveyed to him, may pass under the will.[83] It is generally recognized that an invalid or ineffective conveyance does not revoke a devise,[84] thus tending to show that the true basis of failure of the devise is not revocation by alienation but rather ademption or necessity.

79 Risley v. Dame Battingiass, Ld. Raym. 240, 83 Eng.Rep. 124, 1688. Cf. Attorney General v. Vigor, 8 Ves.Jr. 256, 32 Eng.Rep. 352, 1803.

80 In re Estate of Smith, 273 Ill. App. 332, 1934; Appeal of Hay, 233 Mich. 663, 208 N.W. 38, 1926; Laurain v. Ernst, 237 Mich. 252, 211 N.W. 623, 1927, noted, 26 Mich.L.R. 124 (revocation depends on testator's intent); In re O'Connor's Estate, 191 Minn. 34, 253 N.W. 18, 1934; Caine v. Barnwell, 120 Miss. 209, 82 So. 65, 1919 noted, in 29 Yale L.J. 469; Schwartz v. Gertwagen Realty Corp., 114 N.J.Eq. 428, 168 A. 820, 1933; In re Gensimore's Estate, 246 Pa. 216, 92 A. 134, 1914. Cf. Gregory v. Lansing, 115 Minn. 73, 131 N.W. 1010, 1911, pointing out that the conveyance constitutes an ademption rather than a revocation. And see Meyerovitz v. Jacobovitz, 263 Mass. 47, 160 N.E. 331, 1928; Brown v. Heller, 30 N.M. 1, 227 P. 594, 1924; Eddington v. Turner, 27 Del.Ch. 411, 38 A.2d 738, 155 A.L.R. 562, 1944 (option).

81 See infra notes 87, 89, 90.

82 See Bordwell, Statute Law of Wills, 14 Ia.L.R. 187 et seq.

83 Woolery v. Woolery, 48 Ind. 523, 1874; Matter of Bush's Estate, 134 Misc. 494, 236 N.Y.S. 331, 1929; Morey v. Sohier, 63 N.H. 507, 3 A. 636, 56 Am.Rep. 538, 1885; Ridenour v. Callahan, 19 Ohio Cir.Ct.R. 65, 1906. Contra: Phillippe v. Clevenger, 239 Ill. 117, 87 N.E. 858, 16 Ann.Cas. 207, 1909, criticized, 4 Ill.L.Rev. 350. And see Walton v. Walton, 7 Johns.Ch.(N.Y.) 258, 11 Am.Dec. 456, 1823. Cf. Eckardt v. Osborne, 338 Ill. 611, 170 N.E. 774, 75 A.L.R. 509, 1930 (testator's absolute interest in land passed though at time of execution of will he was mere joint tenant—Phillippe case not mentioned in the opinion); Strang v. Day, 362 Ill. 110, 199 N.E. 263, 103 A.L.R. 1215, 1935, noted, 3 U. of Chi.L.R. 679, 34 Mich.L.R. 1272, indicating that rule of Phillippe case does not extend to general devises.

84 Leach v. Burr, 17 App.D.C. 128, 1900 (deed not delivered); Yott v. Yott, 265 Ill. 364, 106 N.E. 959, 1914 (incapacity and undue influence); Graham v. Burch, 47 Minn. 171, 49 N.W. 697, 28 Am.St.Rep. 339, 1891 (fraud and undue influence); In re O'Connor's Estate, supra note 80 (invalidity of provision); Caine v. Barnwell, 120 Miss. 209, 82 So. 65, 1919, noted, 29 Yale L.J. 468 (deed lacked husband's signature); Brown v. Heller, supra note 80 (undue influence).

Of course, a conveyance which did not operate as a revocation at common law will not do so today. Thus, leases [85] and mortgages [86] do not nullify the devise in its entirety but only pro tanto, the devisee taking the land subject to the lease or mortgage existing at the time of the testator's death. Statutes [87] in a number of jurisdictions provide that devises and legacies shall pass subject to charges and incumbrances placed upon the property, but they are mainly if not entirely declaratory of pre-existing case law; [88] the fact that they are usually cast in terms of the incumbrance not being deemed a revocation is a confusing factor. The same is true of other legislation which declares that no conveyance shall prevent the operation of the will upon the property of which the testator has power of disposal at the time of his death.[89] Again cast in terms of negativing revocation are other statutes providing that if the testator sells the devised land on contract, the property passes to the devisee subject to the agreement.[90] These have been interpreted as entitling the devisee to the purchase money unpaid at the testator's death.[91] However, when the testator absolutely conveys the specifically devised property and obtains the total proceeds of the sale, the latter do not pass to the devisee even if the testator so intended at the time of the conveyance and up to his death.[92] By the prevailing view, even if the testator took back a mortgage upon

85 Brady v. Brady, 78 Md. 461, 28 A. 515, 1894 (99-year lease, renewable forever); In re Evans' Estate, 145 Minn. 252, 177 N.W. 126, 8 A.L.R. 1631, 1920, noted, 4 Minn.L.R. 548; Frame v. Whitaker, 7 S.W.2d 140, Tex.Civ.App.1928 (oil and gas lease). See also Murphy v. Boling, 273 Ky. 827, 117 S.W.2d 962, 117 A.L.R. 1373, 1938 (life estate).

86 In re Doughty's Will, 154 A. 871, 9 N.J.Misc. 149, affirmed 112 N.J.Eq. 320, 164 A. 279, 1933.

87 See Bordwell, supra note 82 at 303.

88 See supra notes 76, 77, 78, 85, 86.

89 See Bordwell, supra note 82 at 301-303.

90 Ibid. at 303.

91 Scarbrough v. Scarbrough, 176 Ala. 141, 57 So. 820, 1912; Washington Escrow Co. v. McKinnon, 40 Wash.2d 432, 243 P.2d 1044, 1952; Chadwick v. Tatem, 9 Mont. 354, 23 P. 729, 1890; Contra: Ostrander v. Davis, 191 F. 156, C.C.A.S.D., 1911. In absence of statute, the devise is deemed revoked by the contract and the devisee is not entitled to the unpaid proceeds of the sale. Walton v. Walton, supra, note 83 (even though the contract is later rescinded); Gale v. Gale, 21 Beav. 349, 52 Eng.Rep. 894, 1856. The doctrine of equitable conversion is involved here. McClintock, Equity, 2d Ed. §§ 106-108. See also infra § 134, notes 20, 21.

92 Lang v. Vaughn, 137 Ga. 671, 74 S.E. 270, 40 L.R.A.,N.S., 542, Ann. Cas.1913B, 52, 1912; Dunlap v. Hart, 274 Mo. 600, 204 S.W. 525, 3 A.L.R. 1493, 1918 (proceeds invested in other lands).

the devised land, the devisee does not obtain the proceeds nor the mortgage because these do not fit the description of a devise of specific lands.[93] These matters will be discussed in more detail under the topic of ademption.[94]

## REVOCATION BY PHYSICAL ACT TO WILL

**86. Revocation may be accomplished by some designated act of mutilation done either by the testator or by another in his presence and at his direction. The will need not be entirely destroyed, and the slightest burning or tearing of the instrument or the cancellation of any material part of the will is usually sufficient to work a revocation if the testator so intended.**

**Most statutes permit revocation of a part or clause of a will leaving the remainder unaffected. By the prevailing view, however, partial revocation is not recognized without statutory authorization.**

**While the mutilation of one copy of duplicate wills works a revocation, physical acts done to a codicil can not revoke a will and, by the better view, the act of destroying or mutilating a will does not revoke separate codicils.**

### *What Acts Are Sufficient*

In almost every state there is statutory provision for revocation by some physical act of the testator to the instrument.[1] Fifteen states [2] follow the language of the Statute of Frauds in providing for revocation by burning, cancelling, tearing, or obliterating. Other expressions often found in the statutes are destroying, mutilating and cutting. In the typical jurisdiction some three or four of these words are designated by the statute.[3] As a mat-

[93] Blaisdell v. Coe, 83 N.H. 167, 139 A. 758, 65 A.L.R. 626, 1923; Walker v. Waters, 118 Md. 203, 84 A. 466, 1912. But see Phillips v. Phillips, 213 Ala. 27, 104 So. 234, 1925; Lewis v. Thompson, 142 Ohio St. 338, 52 N.E. 2d 331, 1943—decided under statutes described in note 68 supra.

[94] Infra § 134.

[1] See infra note 3. As to the situation in absence of statutory provision, see Billington v. Jones, 108 Tenn. 234, 66 S.W. 1127, 56 L.R.A. 654, 91 Am. St.Rep. 751, 1901.

[2] Alabama, Connecticut, Florida, Illinois, Massachusetts, Michigan, Missouri, Nebraska, Nevada, New Jersey, North Carolina, Vermont, Washington, Wisconsin and Wyoming. See infra note 3.

[3] For a summary of the statutory provisions, see Bordwell, Statute Law of Wills, 14 Ia.L.R. 287–289. In general, see Evans, Testamentary Revocation by Act to the Document and Dependent Relative Revocation, 23 Ky.L.J. 559.

ter of fact, it makes no difference in most situations what particular forms of physical act are mentioned in the statute. For example, if a will is thrown in the fire and totally consumed, it is undoubtedly burned, and also destroyed, and very likely may be said to be obliterated. In case that the governing statute mentions any one of these three sorts of physical act, the act is sufficient for revocation. As there are few, if any, statutes which do not mention either burning, destroying or obliterating, the physical element of revocation is clearly present. However, in case the burning is only slight or partial, it could not be fairly said that the will was destroyed or obliterated. Then, unless the statute mentioned burning, it would seem that the will was not revoked.

It should be noted that certain of these words are directed toward the writing itself while others have reference to the paper upon which the writing appears. So far as the more specific forms of mutilation are concerned, such as burning, tearing, cutting, cancelling or obliterating, it is agreed that the instrument need not be entirely destroyed or rendered unrecognizable. The slightest singeing with the intent to destroy is a burning within the meaning of the statute.[4] However, there must be some visible effect, and if only the cover of the will is burned,[5] this is not enough. Any tearing of the paper upon which the will is written is sufficient tearing.[6] The will need not be torn into small bits. Tearing off of a seal, though a seal is not required, has been deemed sufficient tearing.[7] Cutting is tearing,[8] the use of a knife or shears not rendering it any the less so. Cutting off the signature is a sufficient mutilation—that being a favorite method of revocation by English testators.[9] Scratching off the

[4] White v. Casten, 46 N.C. 197, 59 Am.Dec. 585, 1853 (though no words were burned); Johnson v. Brailsford, 2 Nott. & McC.(S.C.) 272, 10 Am.Dec. 601, 1820; Bibb d. Mole v. Thomas, 2 W.Bl. 1043, 96 Eng.Rep. 613, 1775 (slight singeing and also slight tearing).

[5] Doe d. Reed v. Harris, 6 A. & E. 209, 112 Eng.Rep. 79, 1837. See supra, § 84 note 13 et seq.

[6] Crampton v. Osburn, 356 Mo. 125, 201 S.W.2d 336, 172 A.L.R. 344, 1947; Goods of Lewis, 1 Sw. & Tr. 31, 164 Eng.Rep. 615, 1858 (signature torn off).

[7] In re Thompason's Estate, 190 Misc. 760, 71 N.Y.S.2d 501, 1947 (reviewing the authorities).

[8] Burton v. Wylde, 261 Ill. 397, 103 N.E. 976, 1913; Hobbs v. Knight, 1 Curt. 768, 163 Eng.Rep. 267, 1838. And see Schnable v. Henderson, 152 S.W. 231, Tex.Civ.App.1912.

[9] Hobbs v. Knight, supra note 8; Goods of Lewis, 1 Sw. & Tr. 31, 164 Eng.Rep. 615, 1858. And see In re Nelson's Estate, 183 Minn. 295, 236 N.W. 459, 1931 (signature torn off); Sanders' Adm'r v. Babbitt, 106 Ky. 646, 51 S.W. 163, 1899. As to effect of retaining the part torn or the repair

signature is a form of lateral tearing and hence sufficient.[10] But the mere removal of a pin fastening the sheets of a will together is not sufficient tearing to work a revocation even if so intended.[11]

As used in the Statute of Frauds and the American statutes, the word obliterate may be satisfied though only a part of the words are affected,[12] and even these need not be entirely blotted out.[13] Erasing words is an obliteration.[14] The same is true of drawing lines through them.[15] The latter act would also amount to cancellation.[16] The English Wills Act, 1837,[17] does not recognize obliteration as a method of revocation unless the words of the will are no longer apparent. This legislation has given rise to some close and rather mechanized decisions,[18] and fortunately has not been adopted in the United States.

*Cancellation*

Cancellation is derived from a Latin word meaning lattice. Hence our ordinary concept of the verb cancel is to draw criss-cross lines across an instrument.[19] The entire will need not be so marked,[20] nor be rendered illegible thereby.[21] The drawing of

of the will, cf. In re Cabler's Estate, 124 Okl. 275, 257 P. 757, 1927; Sellards v. Kirby, 82 Kan. 291, 108 P. 73, 28 L.R.A.,N.S., 270, 136 Am.St.Rep. 110, 20 Ann.Cas. 214, 1910; Bell v. Fothergill, L.R. 2 P. & D. 148, 1870; Russell v. Tyler, 224 Ky. 511, 6 S.W. 2d 707, 1928, noted, 17 Ky.L.J. 176.

10 In re Morton, 12 Prob.Div. 141, 1887; Sanderson v. Norcross, 242 Mass. 43, 136 N.E. 170, 1931.

11 Woodruff v. Hundley, 127 Ala. 640, 29 So. 98, 85 Am.St.Rep. 145, 1900.

12 Townshend v. Howard, 86 Me. 285, 29 A. 1077, 1894; Michigan Trust Co. v. Fox, 192 Mich. 699, 159 N.W. 332, 1916; Matter of Kuntz's Will, 140 Misc. 598, 251 N.Y.S. 403, 1931; Evans' Appeal, 58 Pa. 238, 1868.

13 See authorities supra note 12; also Stuart v. McWhorter, 238 Ky. 82, 36 S.W.2d 842, 1931.

14 Cook v. Jeffett, 169 Ark. 62, 272 S.W. 873, 1925 (signature). But erasure of one item is not sufficient to revoke the entire will. Safe Deposit & Trust Co. v. Thom, 117 Md. 954, 83 A. 45, 1912; cf. Triplett's Ex'rs v. Triplett, 161 Va. 906, 172 S.E. 162, 1934, noted, 21 Va.L.R. 342.

15 See authorities, supra note 12.

16 See infra note 22.

17 7 Wm. IV & 1 Vict. c. 26, § 21.

18 Brasier's Estate, [1899] Prob. 36; Matter of Horsford, L.R. 3 P. & D. 211, 1874; Ffinch v. Combe, [1894] Prob. 191.

19 See Olmsted's Estate, 122 Cal. 224, 54 P. 745, 1898; Meredith v. Meredith, 5 W.W.Harr.(Del.) 35, 157 A. 202, 1931.

20 Hartz v. Sobel, 136 Ga. 565, 71 S.E. 995, 38 L.R.A.,N.S., 797, Ann. Cas.1912D, 165, 1911; In re Love's Will, 186 N.C. 714, 120 S.E. 479, 1923. See note 14 supra.

21 Cook v. Jeffett, supra note 14; In re Wikman's Estate, 148 Cal. 642,

vertical lines through the words of the will, or some of them, has been held to amount to cancellation.[22] However, marks on the margin or back of the will are not sufficient; some of the words, or the signature, must be touched thereby.[23] Cancellation may be done as effectively with a pencil,[24] as with a pen, though unexplained the former may be considered merely tentative, as in case of indicating the contents of a proposed new will.[25]

If, instead of using straight or crossed lines, the testator writes some words such as "cancelled," "void" or the like over material parts of the will, there seems to be sufficient cancellation.[26] The lines forming the letters and words are no less cancellation because they also communicate the intent to revoke. However, if the words are written on the margin or back of the will, there is no cancellation.[27] Such words are a mere unattested writing, not sufficient to work a revocation by physical act.[28]

It should be noticed that some statutes do not mention cancellation as a method of revocation. If cancellation is not a recognized method of revocation, there can be no revocation by crossing out words.[29] The latter acts cannot be regarded as destruction of the will,[30] unless possibly they have gone to the extent

84 P. 212, 1906; Noesen v. Erkenswick, 298 Ill. 231, 131 N.E. 622, 1921.

22 In re Kemper's Estate, 157 Kan. 727, 145 P.2d 103, 1944; Bigelow v. Gillot, 123 Mass. 102, 25 Am.Rep. 32, 1877; In re Frothingham's Will, 75 N.J.Eq. 205, 71 A. 695, 1909.

23 See infra note 27.

24 McIntyre v. McIntyre, 120 Ga. 67, 47 S.E. 501, 102 Am.St.Rep. 71, 1 Ann.Cas. 606, 1904; In re Fox's Estate, 192 Mich. 699, 159 N.W. 332, 1916; Hilyard v. Wood, 71 N.J.Eq. 214, 63 A. 7, 1906; In re Heller's Estate, 158 Pa.Super. 194, 44 A.2d 528, 1945 (smudge).

25 See Gardner v. Gardiner, 65 N.H. 230, 19 A. 651, 8 L.R.A. 383, 1889; Matter of Ridgway's Estate, 141 Misc. 582, 252 N.Y.S. 834, 1931; annotation, 62 A.L.R. 1375.

26 Franklin v. Bogue, 245 Ala. 379, 17 So.2d 405, 1944; Noesen v. Erkenswick, 298 Ill. 231, 131 N.E. 622, 1921; Matter of Barnes' Will, 76 Misc. 382, 136 N.Y.S. 940, 1912; Matter of Parson's Will, 119 Misc. 26, 195 N.Y.S. 742, 1922. See Battle, Revocation by Writing Across Face of Will, 9 Va.L.R. 98; note, 31 Yale L. J. 892; annotation, 3 A.L.R. 833.

27 Howard v. Hunter, 115 Ga. 357, 41 S.E. 638, 90 Am.St.Rep. 121, 1902; Dowling v. Gilliland, 286 Ill. 530, 122 N.E. 70, 3 A.L.R. 829, 1919; Yont v. Eads, 317 Mass. 232, 57 N.E.2d 531, 1944; Matter of Akers' Will, 74 App. Div. 461, 77 N.Y.S. 643, 1902; Thompson v. Royall, 163 Va. 492, 175 S.E. 748, 1934. But see Warner v. Warner's Estate, 37 Vt. 356, 1864.

28 See authorities supra note 27 and also infra § 87.

29 See Bordwell, Statute Law of Wills, 14 Ia.L.R. 289; also infra note 30.

30 Gay v. Gay, 60 Iowa 415, 14 N.W. 238, 46 Am.Rep. 78, 1882; Cheese

of rendering it illegible. On the other hand, tearing the will into small pieces has been regarded as destruction though the pieces may be fitted together.[31]

*Mutilation by Others*

The physical act to the instrument need not be done by the testator personally. The English and almost all American Statutes provide that it may be done by the testator or by another in his presence and at his direction.[32] If the acts are done by a stranger without authorization, the will should be probated as made.[33] When the acts of mutilation are done outside of the testator's presence, though by his direction, there is no effective revocation.[34] The weight of authority is that ratification of an unauthorized act of mutilation by another does not work a revocation.[35] This view may be justified on the ground that the will can only be revoked in the statutory manner. A few cases have recognized the possibility of revocation by the testator's ratification or adoption of unauthorized acts.[36] Theoretically it is difficult to justify the latter position, though as a practical matter it may seem a hardship that the testator is forced to make a new will to revoke a first will which has been destroyed by another.

v. Lovejoy, 2 Prob. 251, 1877. But see Johnson v. Brailsford, 2 Nott & McC.(11 S.C.L.) 272, 10 Am.Dec. 601, 1820; Tinsley v. Carevile, 212 Ind. 675, 10 N.E.2d 597, 1937, noted, 23 Corn.L.Q. 641.

31 See Evans' Appeal, 58 Pa. 238, 1868.

32 Bordwell, Statute Law of Wills, 14 Ia.L.R. 289, 290. In a number of jurisdictions however the direction and act must be proved by two witnesses under these circumstances. Ibid.

33 Cook v. Jeffett, 169 Ark. 62, 272 S.W. 873, 1925; Monroe v. Huddart, 79 Neb. 569, 113 N.W. 149, 14 L.R.A., N.S., 259, 1907; Stephens v. Leatherwood, 295 S.W. 236, Tex.Civ.App.1927.

34 Dower v. Seeds, 28 W.Va. 113, 57 Am.Rep. 646, 1886. See Matter of McGill's Will, 107 Misc. 109, 177 N.Y.S. 86, 1919. This has been held even if there is also a subsequent ratification by the testator. Miller v. Harrell, 175 Ky. 578, 194 S.W. 782, 1917. But if the statute does not require the destruction to be in testator's presence, the tearing of the will at testator's direction by the custodian who later reported the fact to testator is sufficient. In re Nish's Estate, 220 Iowa 45, 261 N.W. 521, 100 A.L.R. 1516, 1935, noted, 21 Ia.L.R. 819, 25 Ky.L.J. 92.

35 Mundy v. Mundy, 15 N.J.Eq. 290, 1858; Clingan v. Mitcheltree, 31 Pa. 25, 1857; Gill v. Gill, [1909] Prob. 157; In re Booth, [1926] Prob. 118 (destroyed by fire). See also Miller v. Harrell, supra note 34; In re Murphy's Estate, 217 Wis. 472, 259 N.W. 430, 99 A.L.R. 519, 1935.

36 Cutler v. Cutler, 130 N.C. 1, 40 S.E. 689, 57 L.R.A. 209, 89 Am.St.Rep. 854, 1902 (partially destroyed by vermin); Parsons v. Balson, 129 Wis. 311, 109 N.W. 136, 1906 (holding that the ratification prevents probate as a lost or destroyed will).

*Intent*

The testator's physical acts which comply with the statute do not by themselves constitute a revocation. In addition, there must be an intention to revoke.[37] Thus, if the testator has two wills and wishes to revoke one but by mistake tears the wrong instrument, it is not revoked because the act was not done for that purpose.[38] Of course, the other instrument is not revoked because no physical act has been done to it. Likewise if the testator is not mentally competent,[39] or is under undue influence,[40] there is no revocation as the required mental element is not present.

The intent requirement is carried into the cases when the testator changes his mind during the time that he is accomplishing the physical acts of destruction. While the slightest amount of tearing or burning may be enough if the acts done are all that testator intends to do,[41] if he relents during the process of destruction and does not complete all the mutilation that he originally intended, there is no revocation.[42] However, the fact that the testator was prevented by another from the complete destruction of his will as he had intended does not prevent a revocation where the testator did not change his intention and sufficiently mutilated the will to comply with the statutory requirements.[43] Moreover, a change of mind after the acts originally intended were fully completed, which change is manifested by a retention of the defaced instrument, does not affect the revocation or reinstate the will.[44]

Of course, intention to revoke must be established by proof. Probably all courts would admit declarations of the testator at

37 Porch v. Farmer, 158 Ga. 55, 122 S.E. 557, 1928; In re Bescher's Estate, 132 Misc. 625, 229 N.Y.S. 821, 1928; Giles v. Warren, L.R. 2 P. & D. 401, 1872.

38 Burns v. Burns, 4 Serg. & R.(Pa.) 295, 1818. See Burtenshaw v. Gilbert, Cowp. 52, 98 Eng.Rep. 961, 1774; Lord's Appeal, 106 Me. 51, 75 A. 286, 1909; Giles v. Warren, L.R. 2 P. & D. 401, 1872.

39 In re Burke's Will, 91 N.Y.S.2d 636, 1949 (intoxicated); cf. Simpson v. Neely, 221 S.W.2d 303, Tex.Civ. App.1949. See supra § 84.

40 Vaughn v. Vaughn, 217 Ala. 364, 116 So. 427, 1928; Rich v. Gilkey, 73 Me. 595, 1881.

41 See supra notes 4, 6.

42 Perkes v. Perkes, 3 B. & Ald. 489, 106 Eng.Rep. 740, 1820; see In re Burke's Will, supra note 39.

43 White v. Casten, 46 N.C. 197, 59 Am.Dec. 585, 1953; Bibb d. Mole v. Thomas, 2 W.Bl. 1043, 96 Eng.Rep. 613, 1775.

44 See authorities supra note 9.

the time of performing the acts of mutilation to the will.[45] In addition, most courts admit testator's prior or subsequent declarations as evidence of his state of mind at the later or earlier time.[46]

More often than not there is no direct evidence of the testator's intent, or even whether it was he who destroyed or mutilated the will. In this situation the courts usually apply a rebuttable presumption of revocation. When the mutilated will is found among the testator's effects the presumption is that the mutilation was done by the testator and within the intent to revoke.[47] The same presumption is indulged if the will had been last heard of in the testator's possession and is not found at his death.[48]

### *Duplicate Wills*

A will executed in duplicate is totally revoked by the testator's mutilation of one of the duplicates with the required intent.[49] This follows from the nature of duplicate wills, either copy being

[45] Burton v. Wylde, 261 Ill. 397, 103 N.E. 976, 1913; In re Ford's Estate, 301 Pa. 183, 151 A. 789, 1930.

[46] Law v. Law, 83 Ala. 432, 3 So. 752, 1887; Fletcher Trust Co. v. Morse, 97 N.E.2d 154, Ind.App.1951, noted, 26 Notre Dame Law 761, reversed on facts, 230 Ind. 44, 101 N.E. 2d 658, 1951; Stuart v. McWhorter, 238 Ky. 82, 36 S.W.2d 842, 1931; Behrens v. Behrens, 47 Ohio St. 323, 25 N.E. 209, 21 Am.St.Rep. 820, 1890; Jackson v. Hewlett, 114 Va. 573, 77 S.E. 518, 1913. And see Compton v. Dannenbauer, 120 Tex. 14, 35 S.W.2d 682, 79 A.L.R. 1488, 1931. Contra: In re Kennedy's Will, 167 N.Y. 163, 60 N.E. 442, 1901; Throckmorton v. Holt, 180 U.S. 552, 21 S.Ct. 474, 45 L.Ed. 663, 1900. See annotation, 79 A.L.R. 1493; Wigmore on Evidence, § 1737.

[47] In re Olmsted's Estate, 122 Cal. 224, 54 P. 745, 1898; Porch v. Farmer, supra note 37; In re Barrie's Will, 393 Ill. 111, 65 N.E.2d 433, 1946; Dawley v. Congdon, 42 R.I. 64, 105 A. 393, 1919. Cf. Lord's Appeal, supra note 38; In re Streeton's Estate, 183 Cal. 284, 191 P. 16, 1920. See annotation, 165 A.L.R. 1188; infra § 101.

[48] McDonald v. McDonald, 142 Ind. 55, 41 N.E. 336, 1895; Ferguson v. Billups, 244 Ky. 85, 50 S.W.2d 35, 1932; Coghlin v. White, 273 Mass. 53, 172 N.E. 786, 1930; In re Bates' Estate, 286 Pa. 583, 134 A. 513, 48 A. L.R. 294, 1926 (same in case of duplicate wills, one copy of which was in testator's possession). Cf. White v. Brennan, 307 Ky. 776, 212 S.W.2d 299, 3 A.L.R.2d 943, 1948; In re Morgan's Estate, 389 Ill. 484, 59 N.E.2d 800, 1945 (presumption rebutted by testator's declarations).

[49] In re Holmberg's Estate, 400 Ill. 366, 81 N.E.2d 188, 1948, noted, 27 Chi.Kent L.R. 174; Menzi v. White, 360 Mo. 319, 228 S.W.2d 700, 17 A.L. R.2d 796, 1950; Crossman v. Crossman, 95 N.Y. 145, 1884; In re Bates' Estate, 286 Pa. 583, 134 A. 513, 48 A. L.R. 294, 1926; Rickards v. Mumford, 2 Phill. 23, 161 Eng.Rep. 1066, 1812. Cf. Managle v. Parker, 75 N.H. 139, 71 A. 637, 24 L.R.A.,N.S., 180, Ann.Cas. 1912A, 269, 1908, where it was shown that testatrix did not have revocatory intent. And see Matter of Shields' Will, 117 Misc. 96, 190 N.Y.S. 562, 1921, noted, 35 Harv.L.R. 626.

regarded as the will so that revocation may be by physical act to either one of them. The presumption of revocation from the non-production of the will which was in testator's possession, or its production in a mutilated condition applies in the case of duplicate wills.[50] As a result all duplicate copies in the testator's possession must be produced intact, or the loss or mutilated condition explained, in order to obtain probate. Thus, the practice of executing wills in duplicate, often thought to be a safeguard against loss or fraudulent destruction, may prove to be a boomerang when the situation gives rise to the presumption of revocation and there is not sufficient evidence to overcome it.

*Mutilation of Will as Revoking Codicil and Vice Versa*

When the testator revokes his will by mutilation thereof, does this also revoke a codicil to the will? Even if the will and codicil are on separate sheets of paper it has been held that the codicil is revoked.[51] Some statutes declare that revocation of the will revokes the codicil in all cases.[52] In absence of statute, the separate codicil should not be regarded as revoked by reason of revocation of the will.[53] While the will and codicil are considered together for purposes of construction,[54] they are separate instruments for purposes of execution and revocation. As no physical act has been done to the codicil, it should not be considered revoked. While it may fail to have effect because of its dependence on the will, this would seem to be no objection to its probate.[55] Whether it may have effect is a question which arises upon construction. If the codicil is on the same paper as the mutilated will, a sufficient act of mutilation so far as the codicil is concerned plus an intent to revoke the codicil should be necessary to have that effect.[56]

50 See supra notes 47, 48, and infra § 101 at note 65.

51 Medlycott v. Assheton, 2 Add. 229, 162 Eng.Rep. 278, 1824; In re Pepper's Estate, 148 Pa. 5, 23 A. 1039, 1892.

52 Bordwell, Statute Law of Wills, 14 Ia.L.R. 284 (California, Idaho, Montana, North Dakota, Oklahoma, South Dakota and Utah).

53 Black v. Jobling, L.R. 1 P. & D. 685, 1869; In re Ayres' Will, 43 N.E.2d 918, Ohio App.1940, noted, 16 U. of Cin.L.R. 346.

54 Black v. Jobling, L.R. 1 P. & D. 685, 1869; Goods of Turner, L.R. 2 P. & D. 403, 1872; Gardiner v. Courthope, 12 Prob.Div. 14, 1886. Cf. Gelbke v. Gelbke, 88 Ala. 427, 6 So. 834, 1889.

55 See infra §§ 93, 96.

56 In Goods of Bleckley, 8 P.D. 169, 1883, both will and codicil were on the same paper, but only the signature of the will was cut off and the part containing the codicil was not defaced. Cf. Burton v. Wylde, supra note 45.

It is generally agreed that the destruction or mutilation of a codicil on a separate paper does not revoke the will even if the testator so intended.[57] If both instruments are on the same paper there must be a sufficient physical act to both will and codicil and also an intent to revoke each in order to revoke both.[58]

*Partial Revocation*

Both the Statute of Frauds and the present English statute provide that neither the will nor any clause or part thereof may be revoked except in the prescribed manner.[59] Most American statutes are framed in similar language.[60] This is deemed to warrant revocation of a part of the will by an act of mutilation to that part,[61] though a close study of the entire revocation section has led to the opposite result in some states.[62] In absence of some such statutory authorization, the prevailing view is that partial revocation by physical act is not permitted.[63] In these jurisdictions there is no revocation of either whole or part when the intention is merely to revoke a part.[64] On the other hand,

57 Osburn v. Rochester Trust & Safe Deposit Company, 209 N.Y. 54, 102 N.E. 571, 46 L.R.A.,N.S., 983, Ann.Cas. 1915A, 101, 1912 (will stands as modified by the revoked codicil); Malone's Adm'r v. Hobbs, 1 Rob.(Va.) 346, 39 Am.Dec. 263, 1842.

58 In Burton v. Wylde, supra note 45, the codicil was written on the back of the will. In cutting out portions of the codicil, testator also defaced the will. The court found an intention to revoke both. Held, both were revoked. But see In re Brookman, 11 Misc. 675, 33 N.Y.S. 575, 1895.

59 Bordwell, Statute Law of Wills, 14 Ia.L.R. 290.

60 Ibid.

61 Meredith v. Meredith, 5 W.W. Harr.(Del.) 35, 157 A. 202, 1931; Fletcher Trust Co. v. Morse, supra note 46; Gay v. Gay, 60 Iowa 415, 14 N.W. 238, 46 Am.Rep. 78, 1882; Home of the Aged v. Bantz, 107 Md. 543, 69 A. 376, 1908; In re Fox's Estate, 192 Mich. 699, 159 N.W. 332, 1916; In re Kirkpatrick's Will, 22 N.J.Eq. 463, 1871; Tomlinson's Estate, 133 Pa. 245, 19 A. 482, 19 Am.St.Rep. 637, 1890; In re Appleton's Estate, 163 Wash. 632, 2 P.2d 71, 1931; Swinton v. Bailey, 4 A.C. 70, 1878.

62 Lovell v. Quitman, 88 N.Y. 377, 42 Am.Rep. 254, 1882 (partial revocation not recognized); In re Johannes' Estate, 170 Kan. 407, 227 P.2d 148, 24 A.L.R.2d 507, 1951 (same). If no trace of the defaced portion can be found, the remainder has been probated, thus reaching the result of partial revocation. Matter of Enright's Estate, 139 Misc. 192, 248 N.Y.S. 707, 1931; but see In re Johannes' Estate, supra, holding that the entire will should be denied probate, unless the missing part is established.

63 Board of National Missions, etc. v. Sherry, 372 Ill. 272, 23 N.E.2d 730, 1939; In re Moerlin's Estate, 197 Misc. 715, 95 N.Y.S.2d 286, 1950; cf. note 62 supra.

64 Coghlin v. Coghlin, 79 Ohio St. 71, 85 N.E. 1058, 1908. But see Henry

partial revocation by cancellation or the like has been recognized in some states even when the statute is silent on the point.[65] The argument for this position is that since partial revocation is permitted by subsequent instrument, the intention of the testator should be recognized here as well. It is often necessary to enter into the subjective element of intention even where partial revocation is not allowed, since the court must always determine whether the testator intended to revoke the whole will or only part of it. However, the manner of mutilation often is indicative on that point.[66]

When partial revocation by mutilation is recognized, the beneficiary of the revoked part ordinarily gets nothing.[67] While there is some dispute, it is generally held that the residue may be swelled so as to catch the revoked gift without violation of the Statute of Wills.[68] Of course if another's name or a different subject matter is written in, the intended change cannot be effected as this would sustain an unattested testamentary disposition. Whether by the cancellation of certain words a devise or bequest can be increased would seem to depend on whether it is the *words* or the *provisions* of the will that may be revoked. Again there is some conflict, although it is perhaps orthodox to limit the revocation to provisions and hence hold that a beneficiary's specific share cannot be increased by partial revocation.[69]

v. Fraser, 58 App.D.C. 260, 29 F.2d 633, 62 A.L.R. 1364, 1928, and note, 27 Mich.L.R. 836.

65 Bigelow v. Gillott, 123 Mass. 102, 25 Am.Rep. 32, 1877. See Miles' Appeal, 68 Conn. 237, 36 A. 39, 36 L.R. A. 176, 1896.

66 Jeffett v. Cook, 175 Ark. 369, 299 S.W. 389, 1927; Olmsted's Estate, 122 Cal. 224, 54 P. 745, 1898; Worcester Bank & Trust Co. v. Ellis, 292 Mass. 88, 197 N.E. 637, 1935; Leonard v. Leonard [1902] Prob. 243.

67 Unless the doctrine of dependent relative revocation applies. See infra § 88.

68 Bigelow v. Gillott, 123 Mass. 102, 25 Am.Rep. 32, 1877; Barfield v. Carr, 169 N.C. 574, 86 S.E. 498, 1915; Brown v. Brown, 91 S.C. 101, 74 S.E. 135, 1912. Contra: Miles' Appeal, supra note 65.

69 Eschback v. Collins, 61 Md. 478, 48 Am.Rep. 123, 1883; Nelen v. Nelen, 52 R.I. 354, 161 A. 121, 1932; Pringle v. M'Pherson, 2 Brev.(S.C.) 279, 3 Am. Dec. 713, 1809; see Brown v. Brown, supra note 68. But see Fletcher Trust Co. v. Morse, supra note 46; Collard v. Collard, 67 A. 190, N.J. 1907, noted, 6 Mich.L.R. 272; Larkins v. Larkins, 3 Bos. & P. 16, 127 Eng. Rep. 10 (1802). See notes, 23 Harv. L.R. 558, 11 Can.Bar.R. 277, 22 Ibid. 542. Cf. Batt v. Vittum, 307 Mass. 488, 30 N.E.2d 394, 1940, and supra note 68.

## REVOCATION BY SUBSEQUENT INSTRUMENT

**87. A will may be revoked in whole or in part by a later will or codicil and, in most jurisdictions, by a subsequent instrument executed with the formalities required for a will, though it does not itself make disposition of testator's property.**

**An express clause of revocation in a duly attested instrument which declares a present intent to revoke is ordinarily conclusive as to the revocation of an earlier will and its codicils, but the mere designation of a subsequent will as the last is not regarded as an express revocation.**

**Even though there is no express revocation, a subsequent will of necessity revokes an earlier one to the extent that the respective provisions are entirely inconsistent. There may possibly be implied revocation if the later will indicates a different plan of disposition although the later will is not absolutely inconsistent with the first. When the later instrument is a codicil there is ordinarily revocation only to the extent that the codicil is absolutely inconsistent with the will.**

### *The Instrument of Revocation*

Prior to the Statute of Frauds a will might be revoked by mere oral declaration or unattested written statement.[1] That statute put an end to oral revocation of bequests of personalty unless reduced to writing on the testator's lifetime, and in the case of devises of land provided that there could be revocation only by the specified physical acts to the instrument or by a will or codicil or other writing attested in the manner required for execution of wills.[2] Quite generally American statutes provide that there can be revocation by subsequent instrument only if the latter is executed with the formalities required for a written will.[3] Accordingly, a nuncupative will cannot revoke a prior written will.[4]

Statutes in a few jurisdictions mention a will or codicil as the only instruments which may revoke an earlier will. Under provisions of this sort it has been decided that the revoking instru-

1 See supra § 84.

2 29 Car. II, c. 3, §§ 6, 22, 1677.

3 Bordwell, Statute Law of Wills, 14 Ia.L.R. 286. In general, see Evans, Testamentary Revocation by Subsequent Instrument, 22 Ky.L.J. 469.

4 In re Hadsell's Estate, 55 Ariz. 116, 99 P.2d 93, 1940; In re Grattan's Estate, 157 Kan. 116, 138 P.2d 497, 1943.

ment must be one making disposition of testator's property and that a document which merely declares a revocation is insufficient.[5] A preferable view is that taken by other courts that such a paper, if duly executed, is a "will" within the meaning of the statute.[6] In the great majority of jurisdictions,[7] any instrument executed with the formalities required for a will is sufficient to revoke a prior will, though it merely declares the revocation and makes no other testamentary provision.[8]

A duly attested revocation may be effective though written on the paper containing the revoked will. If attested words of revocation are written over the words of the will, this may be regarded either as revocation by subsequent instrument,[9] or as a cancellation.[10] An unattested indorsement of revocation can only operate as a cancellation and not as a revocation by subsequent instrument,[11] except in states recognizing holographic wills. In the latter jurisdictions an attested will may be revoked by a holographic instrument.[12] From this it seems that a statement on a will written, signed, and dated by the testator to the effect that the paper is void would work a revocation in these states.[13] When a holographic will is altered by the hand of the testator, this has been held to constitute both a revocation of the altered provisions and a valid disposition by the new provisions, the prior signature being adopted.[14]

5 Twilley v. Durkee, 72 Colo. 444, 211 P. 668, 1923.

6 Grotts v. Casburn, 295 Ill. 286, 129 N.E. 137, 14 A.L.R. 1015, 1920; In re Peirce's Estate, 63 Wash. 437, 115 P. 835, 1911. See supra § 1.

7 Supra note 3.

8 Derr v. Derr, 123 Kan. 681, 256 P. 800, 53 A.L.R. 515, 1927; In re Backus' Will, 49 App.Div. 410, 63 N.Y.S. 544, 1900 (here words of revocation were included in a deed). See In re Harrison's Estate, infra note 30.

9 Goods of Gosling, 11 Prob. 79, 1886.

10 See supra § 86.

11 Trotter v. Van Pelt, 144 Fla. 517, 198 So. 215, 131 A.L.R. 1018, 1940; In re Rinker's Estate, 158 Kan. 406, 147 P.2d 740, 1944; In re Williams' Estate, 336 Pa. 235, 9 A.2d 377, 1939.

12 In re Iburg's Estate, 196 Cal. 333, 238 P. 74, 1925, noted, 24 Mich.L.R. 319; Rabe v. McAllister, 177 Md. 97, 8 A.2d 922, 1939. Cf. In re Kelleher's Estate, 202 Cal. 124, 259 P. 437, 54 A.L.R. 913, 1927. But see McPherson v. McKay, 207 Ark. 546, 181 S.W.2d 685, 1944.

13 In re Cazaurang's Estate, 42 Cal. App. 796, 110 P.2d 138, 1941, noted, 40 Mich.L.R. 770.

14 La Rue v. Lee, 63 W.Va. 388, 60 S.E. 388, 14 L.R.A.,N.S., 968, 129 Am. St.Rep. 978, 1908. See In re Goodman's Will, 229 N.C. 444, 50 S.E.2d 34, 1948. The result might be different in most holographic will jurisdictions because of the requirement of dating. See In re Finkler's Estate, 21 P.2d 681, Cal.App.1933; also supra § 75.

*Words of Revocation*

When a valid second will expressly revokes a prior one, or revokes all previous wills, there is ordinarily no question but that there is a revocation.[15] Under exceptional circumstances, a clause revoking all former wills does not revoke a particular prior provision, when the court is convinced, after considering both the character of the original will and the later one, that the testator did not intend the revocation.[16] These are mainly cases in which it is established that the revocatory clause was included through mistake or inadvertence.[17] The revoking clause may, by its terms, be limited in operation to a part only of the prior will.[18] A revocation of all former wills extends to former codicils, since the "will" becomes the composite of the original instrument and its codicils.[19] The fact that a testator describes his will therein as "my last will and testament" does not amount to an express revocation.[20] The word "last" is not construed by the courts as "only"; rather it has reference to the element of time, and is regarded as a formal rather than substantial expression. However, a revocation may come about although the word "revoke" is not used, as in case that a testator, having made two prior wills, duly executes a document stating that he wishes the first to be in force.[21]

In general the words used must indicate a present intent to revoke.[22] There is a difference of opinion as to whether an attested

15 In re Webster's Estate, 43 Cal. App.2d 6, 110 P.2d 81, 1941; Puckett v. Brittain, 152 Okl. 184, 3 P.2d 876, 1931; In re Laege's Estate, 180 Wis. 32, 192 N.W. 373, 1923.

16 Allen v. Beemer, 372 Ill. 295, 23 N.E.2d 724, 125 A.L.R. 929, 1939; Owens v. Fahnestock, 110 S.C. 130, 96 S.E. 557, 1918, noted, 32 Harv.L.R. 183; and see Gelbke v. Gelbke, 88 Ala. 427, 6 So. 834, 1889; Watt's Estate, 168 Pa. 422, 32 A. 42, 1895; In re Smith's Wills, infra note 27. The execution of duplicate wills having revocatory clauses has no effect on either counterpart. Odenwaelder v. Schorr, 8 Mo.App. 458, 1880; cf. In re Woodley's Will, 73 N.Y.S.2d 141, 1947.

17 See infra, § 88.

18 Nelson's Estate, 147 Pa. 160, 23 A. 373, 1892; In re Freme's Estate, [1895] 2 Ch. 778.

19 Coffin v. Otis, 11 Metc.(Mass.) 156, 1846; Smith v. McChesney, 15 N.J.Eq. 359, 1867.

20 Fry v. Fry, 125 Iowa 424, 101 N.W. 144, 1904; Neibling v. Methodist Orphans' Home Ass'n, 315 Mo. 578, 286 S.W. 58, 51 A.L.R. 639, 1916; In re Wolfe's Will, 185 N.C. 563, 117 S.E. 804, 1923; Gordon v. Whitlock, 92 Va. 723, 24 S.E. 342, 1896; Simpson v. Foxon, [1907] Prob. 54.

21 Derr v. Derr, 123 Kan. 681, 256 P. 800, 53 A.L.R. 515, 1927. See infra notes 36 et seq.

22 Stratton v. Durham, 191 Miss. 420, 2 So.2d 551, 1941; Merritt v. Merritt, 158 S.W.2d 116, Tex.Civ.App.

direction for a third person to destroy a will is sufficient for revocation. Though English cases hold that the will is revoked,[23] our courts usually hold to the contrary because, while the testator wished to revoke, he did not intend that the paper which he executed should act as the revocation.[24] Even if the third party carries out the requested act of destruction, there would be no revocation by mutilation if the act was not done in the testator's presence.[25] One may not reserve power in a will to revoke or alter it in a manner not authorized by law.[26] Conversely, one may not, by express provision of his will, effectively prevent revocation of the same by the prescribed legal methods.[27] A will does not become irrevocable because the testator declares that it is not to be revoked.[28]

*Revocation by Lost Wills*

It is generally recognized that a lost will may be probated upon satisfactory proof of the execution thereof.[29] Proof that the lost will contained a revocation clause is sufficient to establish a revocation.[30] This seems to be true although the other provisions of

1942; cf. Luther v. Luther, 211 Ala. 352, 100 So. 497, 1924; Newboles v. Newboles, 169 Ark. 282, 273 S.W. 1026, 1925.

23 Walcott v. Ochterlony, 1 Curt. 580, 163 Eng.Rep. 203, 1837; Goods of Durance, L.R. 2 P. and D. 406, 1872. And see Bayley v. Bailey, 5 Cush. (Mass.) 245, 1849.

24 In re McGill's Will, 229 N.Y. 405, 128 N.E. 194, 1920, noted, 20 Col.L.R. 715, 18 Mich.L.R. 814, 19 Mich.L.R. 81, 29 Yale L.J. 941; see Harris v. McDonald, 152 Ga. 18, 108 S.E. 104, 1920.

25 See supra § 86. Cf. Harris v. McDonald, supra note 24, where the Georgia statute did not require that the destruction be in the testator's presence.

26 Hastings v. Bridge, 86 N.H. 172, 164 A. 906; s. c. 86 N.H. 247, 166 A. 273, 1933; Ragland v. Wagener, 142 Tex. 651, 180 S.W.2d 435, 152 A.L.R. 1232, 1944.

27 See In re Smith's Wills, 254 N.Y. 283, 172 N.E. 499, 72 A.L.R. 867, 1930, noted, 19 Cal.L.R. 97, 16 Corn.L.Q. 256, 25 Ill.L.R. 842, 16 Ia.L.R. 285, 79 U. of Pa.L.R. 241, where, however, the court looked to the contents of the first will to determine whether the printed revocation clause in the second was intended to revoke the first.

28 Bates v. Hacking, 28 R.I. 523, 68 A. 622, 14 L.R.A.,N.S., 937, 125 Am. St.Rep. 759, 1908.

29 On this subject generally, see infra § 97 at note 46; cf. infra § 92, note 26 et seq.

30 Giles v. Giles, 204 Mass. 383, 90 N.E. 595, 1910; In re Cunningham, 38 Minn. 169, 36 N.W. 269, 8 Am.St. Rep. 650, 1888; Williams v. Miles, 68 Neb. 463, 94 N.W. 705, 62 L.R.A. 383, 110 Am.St.Rep. 431, 4 Ann.Cas. 306, affirmed, on rehearing 68 Neb. 479, 96 N.W. 151, 1903 (opinion by Commissioner Pound). Melhase v. Melhase, 87 Or. 590, 171 P. 216, 1918; Brackenridge v. Roberts, 114 Tex. 418, 267 S.W. 244; Id., on rehearing, 114 Tex. 435, 270 S.W. 1001, 1924. See In re

the lost will are not shown.[31] In most jurisdictions it is not necessary to probate the lost will in order to establish the revocation.[32] Some courts, however, hold that probate is necessary upon the theory that a revocation takes effect only when the will of which it forms a part becomes effective at the testator's death.[33] The burden of proof that a lost will contained a clause of revocation is on the party asserting the revocation,[34] and generally there is no presumption that it did.[35]

*Implied Revocation*

Express revocation is not the only method of revocation by subsequent instrument. If the second will disposes of all the testator's property, it will necessarily nullify the effect of the first.[36] The testator's last will must be given effect, and if it disposes of his whole estate, there is nothing upon which the first will can operate. If the wills are entirely inconsistent, only the latter can stand. This result can be accounted for upon a mechanical basis, and it is not necessary to place the cases of total inconsistency upon the ground that the testator has demonstrated his intention to revoke the first will because of the provisions of the second.

Is the latter a tenable theory of revocation by subsequent instrument? Its validity will be tested in the cases where the actual inconsistency is only partial and the second instrument merely indicates a general scheme different from that of the

Laege's Estate, 180 Wis. 32, 192 N.W. 373, 1923, for a similar holding where the second will revoked the first by implication. But see In re Harrison's Estate, 316 Pa. 15, 173 A. 407, 94 A.L.R. 1019, 1934, noted, 29 Ill.L.R. 1092, 44 Yale L.J. 1263.

31 Giles v. Giles, Williams v. Miles, Melhase v. Melhase, all supra note 30. But see cases infra note 33.

32 Giles v. Giles and In re Cunningham, both supra note 30; Matter of Wear, 131 App.Div. 875, 116 N.Y.S. 304, 1909; In re Bassett's Estate, 196 Cal. 576, 238 P. 666, 1925; May v. Brown, 144 Tex. 350, 190 S.W.2d 715, 165 A.L.R. 1180, 1945.

33 Crooker v. McArdle, 332 Ill. 27, 163 N.E. 384, 1928, noted, 27 Mich. L.R. 595; Bates v. Hacking, supra note 28. And see In re Harrison's Estate, supra note 30.

34 Williams v. Miles, supra note 30; In re Rinker's Estate 158 Kan. 406, 147 P.2d 740, 1941; Grimes v. Nashville Trust Co., 176 Tenn. 366, 141 S.W.2d 890, 1940.

35 In re Dunahugh's Will, 130 Iowa 692, 107 N.W. 925, 1906; Connery v. Connery, 175 Mich. 544, 141 N.W. 615, 1913; Hellier v. Hellier, L.R. 9 P.D. 237, 1884. But see Melhase v. Melhase, supra note 30, where the will was drawn by an experienced lawyer.

36 In re Iburg's Estate, 196 Cal. 333, 238 P. 74, 1925; In re Mathews' Estate, 234 Iowa 188, 12 N.W.2d 162, 1944; see In re Wuppermann's Estate, 164 Misc. 900, 300 N.Y.S. 344, 1937, noted, 26 Geo.L.J. 786.

first. Thus, in case the first will disposes of certain specific property to A and the residue to B and the second will without a revocation clause gives other specific property to C and the residue to D, it is clear that B's gift is revoked. But is A's gift revoked? A categorical answer is scarcely possible; the problem is one of joint construction of the instruments, and this involves not only the exact language used but the situation surrounding the testator and possibly his declarations of intention. If the second instrument is a will as distinguished from a codicil the judicial tendency seems to be to construe the residuary clause on the second will as covering all property not disposed of in that instrument.[37] This tends to support the view that there can be revocation by the implication of the second will, which is not of necessity totally inconsistent with the first. Cases of other sorts do likewise.[38] However, there is plenty of judicial language to the effect that the revocation must either be express, or by a later will entirely inconsistent with the first, in order to work a total revocation.[39] This is particularly true if the testator denominates the second instrument as a codicil.[40] Choice of this term is an

[37] In re Danford Estate, 196 Cal. 339, 238 P. 76, 1925; Neibling v. Methodists Orphans' Home Ass'n, 315 Mo. 578, 286 S.W. 58, 51 A.L.R. 639, 1926, noted, 40 Harv.L.R. 329; see In re Reycraft's Estate, 260 Mich. 40, 244 N.W. 221, 1932. But see Adams v. Maris, 213 S.W.2d 622, Tex. Com.App.1919. As to whether declarations of the testator bearing on the intention to revoke are admissible, cf. Neibling case with In re Brown's Will, 143 Iowa 649, 120 N.W. 667, 1909. If parol evidence is relied upon, it must be clear and will be closely scrutinized. Williams v. Miles, supra note 30.

[38] Kearns v. Rousch, 106 W.Va. 663, 146 S.E. 729, 1929, noted, 15 Iowa L.R. 231 with which cf. Newcomb v. Webster, infra note 39; Gardner v. McNeal, 117 Md. 27, 82 A. 988, 40 L.R.A., N.S., 553, Ann.Cas.1914A 119, 1911; Dunsworth v. Dunsworth, 148 Kan. 347, 81 P.2d 9, 1938. In re Wawrzyniak's Estate, 297 Mich. 520, 298 N.W. 118, 1941; Wagner v. Wagner, 303 Ky. 140, 197 S.W.2d 86, 1946. See infra § 88, note 50 et seq.

[39] Whitney v. Hannington, 36 Colo. 407, 85 P. 84, 1906; Newcomb v. Webster, 113 N.Y. 191, 21 N.E. 77, 1899; Paully v. Crooks, 41 Ohio App. 1, 179 N.E. 364, 1931; Adams v. Maris, supra note 37.

[40] Driver v. Driver, 187 Ark. 875, 63 S.W.2d 274, 1933; Colonial Trust Co. v. Perry, 118 Conn. 357, 172 A. 857, 1934; Klein v. Gaines, 203 Miss. 871, 34 So.2d 488, 1948; In re Rainear's Estate, 304 Pa. 539, 156 A. 166, 1931; Eubank v. Moore, 15 S.W.2d 567, Tex.Com.App.1929, noted, 8 Tex. L.Rev. 164. See Bliss v. American Bible Society, 2 Allen (Mass.) 334, 1861; Succession of Berdon, 202 La. 621, 12 So.2d 654, 1943. As to whether codiciliary gifts to the same legatees are cumulative or substitutional, cf. Gould v. Chamberlain, 184 Mass. 115, 68 N.E. 39, 1903; Kemp v. Hutchinson, 110 S.W.2d 1126, Mo. App. 1937; and see Succession of Homan, 202 La. 591, 12 So.2d 649, 1943.

indication that the testator's second provision is only to modify and not to supersede the first.[41] Stated in another way an unambiguous disposition in a will is not revoked by doubtful expression in a codicil.[42] However, the whole question is one of intent, and a will may be entirely revoked by a "codicil." [43]

*Partial Revocation*

As already indicated,[44] the law is not uniform as to whether there may be partial revocation by act of mutilation in the absence of express statutory authorization. In the case of revocation by subsequent instrument, it is clear that a will may be revoked in part either by an express clause to that effect or by an inconsistent disposition of the second will.[45] Both instruments are regarded as the will of the testator—the earlier to be given effect except as altered by the provisions of the subsequent one.[46]

## DEPENDENT RELATIVE REVOCATION

**88. If the terms of a revocation are expressly conditional, the will is revoked if, and only if, the condition is fulfilled.**

**When a testator purports to revoke his will while laboring under a mistake of law or fact in connection therewith, the courts often declare that revocation is dependent upon the existence of the situation as believed by the testator and accordingly hold that the will is not revoked. Instead of this fiction of conditional revocation, it is more realistic to treat the problem as one of mistake, holding the revocation absolute or void in accordance with which position the individual testator would probably have preferred.**

Occasionally a revocation clause, by its terms, is dependent on a condition. The intention is not to revoke absolutely but only in

41 Matter of Mucklow's Will, 242 App.Div. 111, 272 N.Y.S. 776, 1934.

42 In re Dominci's Estate, 151 Cal. 181, 90 P. 448, 1907; Jackman v. Kasper, 393 Ill. 496, 66 N.E.2d 678, 1946; Lovering v. Balch, 210 Mass. 105, 96 N.E. 142, 1911; Creech v. McVaugh, 140 N.J.Eq. 272, 54 A.2d 443, 1947.

43 Kelly v. Richardson, 100 Ala. 584, 13 So. 785, 1893; Sturgis v. Work, 122 Ind. 134, 22 N.E. 996, 17 Am.St. Rep. 349, 1889.

44 Supra § 86.

45 In re Marx's Estate, 174 Cal. 762, 164 P. 640, L.R.A.1917F 234, 1917; In re Wolfe's Will, 185 N.C. 563, 117 S.E. 804, 1923; Adams v. Maris, supra note 37.

46 Wheat v. Wheat, 236 Ala. 52, 181 So. 243, 1938; In re Brodersen's Estate, 102 Cal.App.2d 896, 229 P.2d 38, 1951.

case that some future event happens. There should be no difficulty about this sort of provision. The revocation operates if the condition is fulfilled, but not if the contrary should prove to be the case.[1] Perhaps in a few cases of revocation by physical act the testator has a real conditional frame of mind, that is, he intends a revocation only upon a certain contingency.[2]

Few cases occur where there is actually a conditional frame of mind on the part of the testator in connection with a revocation. Far more frequent are the instances where the revocation was induced by some mistake of law or fact on the part of the testator. For example, he may be mistaken as to his ability to alter an executed will by crossing out some of its terms and inserting new ones,[3] or as to the validity of a new will,[4] or the effect of the intestate laws,[5] or whether a beneficiary under his will is still alive.[6] Typically the courts lump these cases of mistaken revocation with the infrequent examples of true condition under the classification of *dependent relative revocation.*[7] This term means, in substance, a conditional revocation; it presumes two acts: (1) one dependent (the act of revocation) (2) the other relative (the event upon which revocation depends). It was first applied to cases where the revocation was by physical act, but there is extensive current usage to employ it also in cases of revocation by subsequent instrument.[8] When the doctrine is employed in the mistake cases, either a condition is presumed con-

1 See Matter of Steiner's Will, 89 Misc. 66, 152 N.Y.S. 725, 1915; Matter of Decoster's Estate, 150 Misc. 807, 270 N.Y.S. 244, 1934. And see infra note 32. A future condition is not readily implied. Owen v. Busiel, 83 N.H. 345, 142 A. 692, 59 A.L.R. 1103, 1928, noted 27 Mich.L.R. 480.

2 In Dixon v. Solicitor to the Treasury, [1905] Prob. 42, the case was left to the jury upon the basis of a conditional state of mind of the testator. Yet, on analysis, the case seems to be one of mistake rather than condition. See infra note 23.

3 See infra notes 26–28.

4 See infra notes 47–52.

5 In the Estate of Southerden, [1925] Prob. 177, noted, 39 Harv.L.R. 405.

6 See infra notes 40, 41.

7 Appeal of Strong, 79 Conn. 123, 63 A. 1089, 6 L.R.A.,N.S., 1107, 118 Am.St.Rep. 138, 1906; Flanders v. White, 142 Or. 375, 18 P.2d 823, 1933; In re Marvin's Will, 172 Wis. 457, 179 N.W. 508, 1920; In re Lundquist's Will, 211 Wis. 541, 248 N.W. 410, 1937; In the Estate of Southerden, supra note 5. But see Townshend v. Howard, 86 Me. 285, 29 A. 1077, 1894; Semmes v. Semmes, 7 Har. & J.(Md.) 388, 1826; Sanderson v. Norcross, 242 Mass. 43, 136 N.E. 170, 1922; In re Estate of Nelson, 183 Minn. 295, 236 N.W. 459, 1931; Campbell v. French, 3 Ves.Jr. 321, 30 Eng.Rep. 1033, 1797; In re Churchill, [1917] 1 Ch. 206.

8 See infra note 49; cf. Evans, Book Review, 15 N.C.L.R. 441.

trary to the fact,[9] or else the jury is permitted to find a condition when there is no evidence thereof.[10] In the main the doctrine is a fictional process which consists of disregarding revocation brought about by mistake on the feigned ground that the revocation was conditional.

*Dependent Relative Revocation by Physical Act*

Here, there is good reason why the condition or mistake may be shown by parol evidence. Evidence of intent is freely received in all cases of revocation by act. If a testator is shown to have destroyed his will, parol evidence is admitted to show whether this was done accidentally, by mistake as to the identity of the instrument, or on the other hand with the true animus revocandi.[11] Similarly parol evidence is admissible to show that the revocation was intended as conditional only, or, as in the more usual case, to establish that the testator was mistaken as to matters which induced the revocation.[12]

Of course the further question remains: After the condition or mistake is shown, what should be done about it? In the condition cases, as has already been pointed out, there should be no difficulty in giving full effect to the condition. The mistake cases present more difficulty. For them, there are four possible solutions. The first is to disregard the mistake as in the ordinary case of mistake in the inducement of a will. Under this view the revocation, though caused by mistake, would be none the less final and absolute. This position has not been followed by the courts in general in cases of revocation by physical act.[13]

Another conceivable position is to regard the act of revocation made under mistake as ineffective revocation for the reason that

[9] See cases supra note 7.

[10] Dixon v. Solicitor to the Treasury, supra note 2.

[11] Appeal of Spencer, 77 Conn. 638, 60 A. 289, 1905; Giles v. Warren, L.R. 2 P. & D. 401, 1872. See also supra § 86.

[12] See In re Emernecker's Estate, 218 Pa. 369, 67 A. 701, 1907; Powell v. Powell, 1 P. & D. 209, 1886; Dixon v. Solicitor to the Treasury, supra note 2.

[13] See cases infra note 16. However in certain types of mistaken revocation cases, the courts refuse to give relief. See In re Emernecker's Estate, supra note 12; Sanderson v. Norcross, 242 Mass. 43, 136 N.E. 170, 1922. And see Goddard v. Orerend, [1911] 1 Ir. 469, where the court following the language of Theobald on Wills said: "The true view may be that a revocation grounded on an assumption of fact which is false takes effect unless as a matter of construction the truth of the fact is the condition of the revocation." For the treatment of mistake in the inducement of execution of the will, see supra § 59.

the animus revocandi is lacking on account of this error. This viewpoint has some support;[14] its weakness lies in the fact that the testator actually had an intention to revoke. From the subjective standpoint he has just as much mind to revoke as if he had not been in error regarding certain connected matters. The third possibility is to recognize that a revocation was intended but to disregard it because of the mistake. This really involves an exercise of equitable powers by the probate court, since the testator intended to revoke his will and the court is in effect setting aside the revocation on the ground of mistake. This view seems rather inconsistent with the general position refusing redress in the case of mistake in the inducement of the will.[15] Yet it seems plausible to give relief on the ground of mistake in cases of revocation by physical act while denying it in the execution cases. In the revocation cases we are always into the matter of the testator's state of mind in order to determine whether his acts were intended as a revocation. It is only going one step further to examine into the motivation behind an act intended as a revocation. Usually the courts accept the position that a revocation by physical act induced by mistake will not be given effect, though they do so under the guise of considering it a conditional or dependent relative revocation.[16]

The fourth possible viewpoint is to consider the wishes of the testator in determining whether or not the revocation should stand. This attitude is readily applied to cases of true conditional intent on the part of the testator. If an actual conditional state of mind is found, it is simply a question of determining whether the condition was fulfilled and admitting the will or rejecting it as revoked in accordance with these findings. In the case of revocation under mistake, the testator intends to annul

14 See generally Cornish, Dependent Relative Revocation, 5 So.Cal.L.R. 272, 293.

15 See supra § 59.

16 Appeal of Strong, 79 Conn. 123, 63 A. 1089, 6 L.R.A.,N.S., 1107, 118 Am.St.Rep. 138, 1906; Wolf v. Bollinger, 62 Ill. 368, 1872; Thomas v. Thomas, 76 Minn. 237, 79 N.W. 104, 77 Am.St.Rep. 639, 1899; Flanders v. White, 142 Or. 375, 18 P.2d 823, 1933; In re Marvin's Will, 172 Wis. 457, 179 N.W. 508, 1920; Onions v. Tyrer, 2 Vern. 742, 23 Eng.Rep. 1085, 1717 (leading case); Locke v. James, 11 M. & W. 901, 152 Eng.Rep. 1071, 1843; In re Goods of Horsford, L.R. 3 P. & D. 211, 1874; Dixon v. Solicitor to the Treasury, supra note 2; Powell v. Powell, supra note 12; In the Estate of Southerden, supra note 5. Cf. In re Estate of Nelson, 183 Minn. 295, 236 N.W. 459, 1931. It has been denied that the doctrine of dependent relative revocation exists in New York. Matter of McCaffrey, 174 Misc. 162, 20 N.Y.S.2d 178, 1940, noted 50 Yale L.J. 518. But see Matter of Macomber, infra note 21.

the will, believes erroneously that certain facts are true, and the idea of what he would have desired if he had known the true facts is never considered by him. It is highly unreal to delve into what he actually intended if it turned out that he was mistaken. However, it is possible to inquire into what he probably would have desired if he had known the true facts. This is a somewhat speculative undertaking, but the surrounding circumstances are often illuminating or even convincing.[17] Professor Joseph Warren[18] advocated this solution, and a considerable number of the cases[19] which take the third position would reach the same result under the fourth test. On the other hand, many cases follow the mechanical position of setting aside the revocation under mistake,[20] though the circumstances show that the testator would probably have preferred that the revocation should stand.

*The Same—Examples*

One of the most usual types of mistake is that in which the testator destroys his will under the belief that it has been superseded by another, which is invalid. The mistake is obviously concerning the validity of the second will. Here the courts generally apply the doctrine of dependent relative revocation, and declare that the testator intended to revoke the first will only if the second is valid.[21] Very seldom does a testator in fact have

17 See infra text at notes 30 and 55.

18 Dependent Relative Revocation, 33 Harv.L.R. 337. And see Evans, Dependent Relative Revocation, 16 Ky.L.J. 251; Evans, Testamentary Revocation by Act to the Document and Dependent Relative Revocation, 23 Ky.L.J. 561, and infra note 55. Cf. the treatment in Cornish, Dependent Relative Revocation, 5 So.Cal.L.R. 272, 393. Older writings on the subject are Dobie, Dependent Relative Revocation of Wills, 2 Va.L.R. 327; Roberts, Dependent Relative Revocation, 49 Am.L.Reg. 18.

19 Appeal of Strong, supra note 16; Flanders v. White, supra note 16; In re Lundquist's Will, 211 Wis. 541, 248 N.W. 410, 1933; Dixon v. Solicitor to the Treasury, supra note 2; In re Estate of Southerden, supra note 5; In the Estate of Zimmer, 40 Times L.R. 502. Ruel v. Hardy, 90 N.H. 240, 6 A.2d 753, 1939, expressly follows Professor Warren's position. See also In re Houghten's Estate, 310 Mich. 613, 17 N.W.2d 774, rehearing denied 310 Mich. 613, 18 N.W.2d 254, 1945, noted, 43 Mich.L.R. 1190; In re Dougan's Estate, 152 Or. 235, 53 P.2d 511, 1936.

20 Wolf v. Bollinger, supra note 16; Varnon v. Varnon, 67 Mo.App. 534, 1896; In re Knapen's Will, infra note 26; In re Marvin's Will, supra note 16.

21 Appeal of Strong, supra note 16; Estate of Nichels, 114 Me. 338, 96 A. 238, L.R.A.1918A, 911, 1916; Wilbourn v. Shell, 59 Miss. 205, 42 Am. Rep. 363, 1881; In re Lundquist's

this state of mind. On the contrary he may often have the intention to revoke the first will in any event. It would seem reasonable to assume such an intention if the second will is quite discordant from the first.[22] However, a conditional frame of mind is usually presumed in case of mistake as to the validity of the subsequent instrument.

Contrasting with the above cases are the ones in which the testator destroys his will with the intention of setting up a new testament at a later time. There is one case in which this destruction was regarded as conditional upon the execution of the later will.[23] Generally the revocation is held absolute,[24] a result which seems sound, for there is no mistake in such cases and the fact that testator evidently intended to be without a will for a while renders the existence of a conditional intent highly improbable.

In the jurisdictions which recognize the possibility of partial revocation by physical act to the instrument,[25] the doctrine of de-

Will, 211 Wis. 541, 248 N.W. 410, 1933; Onions v. Tyrer, supra note 16; Dancer v. Crabb, L.R. 3 P. & D. 98, 1873. And see Flanders v. White, 142 Or. 375, 18 P.2d 823, 1933, where testator attempted to set up an invalid book account instead of a second will; Casey v. Hogan, 344 Ill. 208, 176 N.E. 257, 1931, noted, 27 Ill.L.R. 327; In re Callahan's Estate, 251 Wis. 247, 29 N.W.2d 352, 1947 (second will destroyed to revive earlier will); Powell v. Powell, supra note 12 (same). See infra § 92, note 26 et seq.

22 Appeal of Strong, supra note 16; Banks v. Banks, 65 Mo. 432, 1877.

23 Dixon v. Solicitor to the Treasury, [1905] Prob. 42. This case is peculiar in that the court left the matter of conditional intent to be found by the jury, which was done. There seems to be no evidence of such an intention on testator's part. Another unusual feature of this case is that the testator was mistaken in his belief that mutilation of the old will was a necessary preliminary to the making of a new one.

24 In re Olmsted's Estate, 122 Cal. 224, 54 P. 745, 1898; McIntyre v. McIntyre, 120 Ga. 67, 47 S.E. 501, 102 Am.St.Rep. 71, 1 Ann.Cas. 606, 1904; Semmes v. Semmes, 7 Har. & J.(Md.) 388, 1826; Townshend v. Howard, 86 Me. 285, 29 A. 1077, 1894; In re Bonkowski's Estate, 266 Mich. 112, 253 N.W. 235, 1934; In re Emernecker's Estate, 218 Pa. 369, 67 A. 701, 1907; In re Dougan's Estate, supra note 19; In re Rauchfuss' Estate, 232 Wis. 266, 28 N.W. 173, 1939; In re De Lion's Estate, 28 Wash.2d 649, 183 P.2d 995, 1947. See also In re Kerckhof's Estate, 13 Wash.2d 469, 125 P.2d 284, 1942, noted, 18 Wash.L.R. 45 where there was also a mistake as to existence of relatives.

25 See supra, § 86. Of course, if partial revocation by physical act is not recognized in the jurisdiction, there is no revocation by means of striking out provisions and hence no occasion to apply the doctrine of dependent relative revocation. See Hartz v. Sobel, 136 Ga. 565, 71 S.E. 995, 38 L.R.A.,N.S., 797, Ann.Cas. 1912D 165, 1911.

pendent relative revocation is generally applied to cases where there is an attempt to alter a will after execution, by changing the name of a beneficiary,[26] the amount of a legacy,[27] or some other provision of the will.[28] Most cases proceed upon the premise that the testator did not intend to revoke unless the altered provision could be given effect, which is impossible of course unless there is a re-execution of the will in its altered form. A testator seldom has such a conditional frame of mind. Again, the actual situation is that he intends an absolute revocation but is mistaken as to the validity of the substituted provision. In cases of this type the courts also usually apply the doctrine of dependent relative revocation in mechanical fashion and with little heed to what would have been desired by the testator.[29] Clearly they should not disregard the revocation when the change is of such nature as to indicate that the testator would have preferred to have the revocation stand even if the substituted provision cannot be given effect.[30] Thus, it would seem reasonable to allow

26 Wolf v. Bollinger, 62 Ill. 368, 1872; In re Houghton's Estate, supra note 19; Thomas v. Thomas, 76 Minn. 237, 79 N.W. 104, 77 Am.St.Rep. 639, 1899; Gardner v. Gardiner, 65 N.H. 230, 19 A. 651, 8 L.R.A. 383, 1889; Smith v. Runkle, 86 N.J.Eq. 257, 98 A. 1086, 1916; In re Roeder's Estate, 44 N.M. 578, 106 P.2d 847, 1940; In re Knapen's Will, 75 Vt. 146, 53 A. 1003, 98 Am.St.Rep. 808, 1903; In re Marvin's Will, 172 Wis. 457, 179 N.W. 508, 1920; Goods of McCabe, 3 P. & D. 94, 1843. But see In re Goods of Horsford, 3 P. & D. 211, 1874; In the Estate of Zimmer, 40 Times Law Rep. 502; In re Bonkowski's Estate, 266 Mich. 112, 253 N.W. 235, 1934.

27 Gardner v. Gardiner, supra note 26; Locke v. James, 11 M. & W. 901, 152 Eng.Rep. 1071, 1843; In re Goods of Horsford, supra note 63 (refusing however to apply the doctrine to change of the name of the beneficiary); Ruel v. Hardy, supra note 19; In re Chacona's Estate, 80 F.Supp. 549, D.C.D.C.1948.

28 Varnon v. Varnon, 67 Mo.App. 534, 1896 (substitution of entire page); Pringle v. McPherson's Ex'rs, 2 Brev.(S.C.) 279, 3 Am.Dec. 713, 1809 (obliteration of exception in devise); Harris' Goods, 1 Sw. & Tr. 536, 164 Eng.Rep. 849, 1860 (substitution of executor); Greenwood's Goods, [1892] Prob. 7 (same); Rowley v. Merlin, 6 Jur.N.S. 1165, 1860 (change of word "absolutely" to "for his life" in devise). In Oklahoma, North and South Dakota, the principle established by the cases cited in notes 26–28 is enacted by statute. Bordwell, Statute Law of Wills, 14 Ia.L.R. 1, 290.

29 See cases cited supra notes 26–28; annotation, 62 A.L.R. 1401, 115 A.L.R. 721. In general it would seem that if testator attempts to change the beneficiary's name he would probably have desired an absolute revocation of the original gift. In re Goods of Horsford is in accord with this position, but has little following and has even been criticized upon this point. Warren, Dependent Relative Revocation, 33 Harv.L.R. 337, 345, note 32.

30 See In re Goods of Horsford, and Estate of Zimmer, both supra note 26.

the original bequest to stand if it had been increased by an unattested change, while if the bequest were decreased to much smaller amount cancellation of the former should normally work a revocation.[31] This is a rational approach, much preferred to the orthodox mechanical viewpoint, based on the fiction of conditional revocation.

*Dependent Relative Revocation by Subsequent Instrument*

Questions of dependent relative revocation are also involved in cases where the revocation is by subsequent instrument instead of by physical act. Many of the same observations may be made as with respect to the situation of revocation by physical act. Seldom is there an express conditional revocation, but if one is found it will be given effect.[32] Usually testator has made some mistake in connection with the revocation. There are also the same four possible positions which may be taken with respect to the mistake.[33] However, one vital distinction must be observed. In the cases of revocation by physical act, parol evidence is admitted freely to show the condition or the mistake.[34] If the revocation is by subsequent instrument however, the mistake must appear on the face of the latter.[35] Indeed, by analogy to the treatment of mistake in the inducement of the execution of a will,[36] it would seem that it should also appear from the revoking instrument what the testator would have done but for the mistake. The courts do not insist upon the latter requirement, but if it appears from the revoking instrument that the testator was induced to make the revocation upon a certain assumption, which is shown to be false, the court often disregards the revocation and probates the original will.[37] In some cases the courts put

31 See Ruel v. Hardy, supra note 19; but cf. In re Chacona's Estate, supra note 27.

32 In re Hamilton's Estate, 74 Pa. 69, 1873; Bradish v. McClellan, 100 Pa. 607, 1882; Goods of Hug, 2 P.D. 73, 1877; In re Bingaman's Estate, 281 Pa. 497, 127 A. 73, 1924. And see cases supra note 1. Cf. Dougherty v. Holscheider, 40 Tex.Civ.App. 31, 88 S.W. 1113, 1905.

33 See text supra after note 12 through note 31.

34 See note 12 supra.

35 In re Salmonski's Estate, 228 P. 2d 860, aff'd, 38 Cal.2d 199, 238 P.2d 966, 1951 (though first will was conditional); Dunham v. Averill, 45 Conn. 61, 29 Am.Rep. 642, 1877; see Gifford v. Dyer, 2 R.I. 99, 57 Am.Dec. 7.8, 1852; Skipwith v. Cabell's Ex'r, 19 Grat.(Va.) 758, 1870; Collins v. Elstone, [1893] Prob. 1.

36 See Gifford v. Dyer, supra note 35, and § 59 supra.

37 Gillespie v. Gillespie, 96 N.J Eq. 501, 126 A. 744, aff'd, 98 N.J.Eq. 413, 129 A. 922, 1924; Mordecai v. Boylan, 59 N.C. 365, 1863 (placed on

the decision upon the true ground of invalidating a revocation made by mistake, but in others the theory of dependent relative revocation is applied by presuming that testator intended to revoke only if his assumptions of law and fact were correct. While it has been doubted if relief should be given for mistake of law,[38] usually no distinction is made between errors of law and of fact.[39]

*The Same—Examples*

One class of cases where relief against revocation is given is that in which the revoking instrument states the reason for the revocation. When it appears that this reason is a mistaken one, the clause of revocation is usually declared to be without effect. Thus, in a leading case,[40] where a codicil revoked a legacy to certain relatives, "they being all dead," and the latter recital was untrue, there was held to be no revocation of the legacy. This case has been followed upon similar facts,[41] and in other cases where the erroneous reasons have been recited for a revocation.[42] There are, however, limitations upon this doctrine. If the court believes that the testator desired to revoke in any event and that the recited fact was not the principal inducement for the revocation, the latter will be given effect.[43] Accordingly, if the facts recited were peculiarly within the testator's knowledge, or in other words if he must have known that they were false, dependent relative revocation will not be applied.[44] In England

ground of mistake); Campbell v. French, 3 Ves.Jr. 321, 30 Eng.Rep. 1033, 1797; In re Bernard's Settlement, [1916] 1 Ch. 552.

38 In re Allen's Will, 88 N.J.Eq. 291, 102 A. 147, affirmed, 89 N.J.Eq. 208, 103 A. 1051, 1918.

39 Estate of Marx, 175 Cal. 762, 164 P. 640, L.R.A.1917F, 234, 1917; Appeal of Strong, 79 Conn. 123, 63 A. 1089, 6 L.R.A.,N.S., 1107, 118 Am.St. Rep. 138, 1906; Blackford v. Anderson, 226 Iowa 1138, 286 N.W. 735, 1939, noted, 24 Minn.L.R. 298, 5 Mo. L.R. 123. Onions v. Tyrer, 2 Vern. 742, 23 Eng.Rep. 1085, 1877; Ward v. Vander Loeff, [1924] A.C. 653; In re Estate of Southerden, [1925] Prob. 177.

40 Campbell v. French, supra note 37.

41 Gillespie v. Gillespie, supra note 37; Doe d. Evans v. Evans, 10 Ad. & El. 228, 113 Eng.Rep. 88, 1839.

42 Thomas v. Howell, L.R. 18 Eq. 198, 1874; Whitlock v. Vaun, 38 Ga. 562, 1868; Paris v. Erisman, 300 S.W. 487, Mo., 1927; Mordecai v. Boylan, 59 N.C. 365, 1863; In re Faris, [1911] 1 Ir.Ch. 469. But see In re Churchill, [1917] 1 Ch. 206.

43 In re Prevost's Estate, 264 Pa. 27, 107 A. 388, 1919; Skipwith v. Cabell's Ex'r, 19 Grat.(Va.) 758, 1870.

44 Giddings v. Giddings, 65 Conn. 149, 32 A. 334, 48 Am.St.Rep. 192, 1894; Hayes' Ex'rs v. Hayes, 21 N.J. Eq. 265, 1871; Mendinhall's Appeal, 124 Pa. 387, 16 A. 881, 10 Am.St.Rep. 591, 1889. Cf. Mordecai v. Boylan, supra note 42.

there is the doctrine that if a testator states that he revokes because he is advised of certain facts, the revocation is deemed absolute though the advice is erroneous.[45] The recital of the advice does not indicate that testator relied upon it—only that the facts may be as therein set forth.

There is another general type of situation where the doctrine of dependent relative revocation may be applied, viz., where an express clause of revocation is coupled with a gift of the same interest to others or in another manner, which latter provision is invalid for some reason. If this invalidity is due to a defect in execution, no question of dependent relative revocation arises for the clause of revocation would likewise be ineffective since the same formalities are required for a revoking as for a disposing instrument.[46]

However, the problem may arise when there is an express clause of revocation coupled with another disposition which fails for some reason other than external invalidity of the instrument. The failure may be due to incapacity of the beneficiary to take, to indefiniteness, violation of the rule against perpetuities, or because a charitable devise is excessive. In these cases the mistake of the testator usually appears on the face of the second will, for it is quite clear that he believed that the disposition of the second will was valid, or he would not have made it. In this he was in error and there is just as much reason why the court should relieve against the mistaken revocation as in the case of an invalid alteration of the terms of a will. Yet most courts refuse to give relief either on the ground of mistake or by denominating the revocation conditional upon the validity of the second disposition.[47] It is commonly said that, as there is an express revocation

45 Attorney General v. Lloyd, 1 Ves. Sr. 32, 27 Eng.Rep. 872, 1747; Attorney General v. Ward, 3 Ves.Jr. 327, 30 Eng.Rep. 1036, 1797. But see Thomas v. Howell, L.R. 18 Eq. 198, 1874, criticizing these cases.

46 See supra §§ 84, 87. The leading case of Onions v. Tyrer, supra note 16, was under the older law which permitted revocation by unattested writing. There the testator's second will was not duly executed but it expressly revoked all prior wills and testator also destroyed his first will. Hence, the case involved revocation both by physical act and by subsequent instrument.

47 Dudley v. Gates, 124 Mich. 440, 83 N.W. 97, 86 N.W. 959, 1901; Board of Com'rs of Rice County v. Scott, 88 Minn. 386, 93 N.W. 109, 1903; Ely v. Megie, 219 N.Y. 112, 113 N.E. 800, 1916; In re Melville's Estate, 245 Pa. 318, 91 A. 679, L.R.A. 1916C 98, 1914; Tupper v. Tupper, 1 Kay. & J. 665, 69 Eng.Rep. 627, 1855 (leading case). As to the application of the doctrine of dependent relative revocation to a lost will when nothing but the revocation clause can be

and as it did not appear what the testator would have done but for his error, the revocation must be given effect. Here most courts follow the general doctrine applied in the mistake in execution cases, though they generally refused to do so in most other revocation cases. In some cases the courts have refused to sustain the express revocation under these circumstances; they tend to place the decisions upon the true ground, that of mistake.[48] Recent cases have applied the doctrine of dependent relative revocation where there was an express revocation of charitable devises, and identical devises in the second will failed because testator did not survive for the statutory period after execution of the second will.[49] Here of course there is neither actual condition nor mistake but we can feel sure that in the circumstances testator would not have wished his first devise to be revoked.

There is yet another group of cases somewhat variant from the above in which there is no express clause of revocation, but there is an invalid disposition of the same property by the later instrument. Of course, if implied revocation can only result through necessity, there is no revocation [50] at all in such cases, and hence no need of discussing the application of the doctrine of dependent relative revocation. Some cases seem to recognize that there may be an implied revocation by a subsequent will which merely indicates an intention that the first will should not stand.[51] Under this view, if the second disposition is invalid there is an opportunity to apply the doctrine of dependent relative revocation. The tendency of the recent cases seems to be to hold the first will effective and unrevoked.[52] In most of such cases a sound result

established by proofs, cf. Luther v. Luther, 211 Ala. 352, 100 So. 497, 1924, with In re Thompson's Estate, 185 Cal. 763, 198 P. 795, 1921, and see annotation 94 A.L.R. 1029.

48 Security Co. v. Snow, 70 Conn. 288, 39 A. 153, 66 Am.St.Rep. 107, 1898; Charleston Library Soc. v. Citizens & Southern Nat. B., 200 S.C. 96, 20 S.E.2d 623, 1942; Bernard's Settlement, [1916] 1 Ch. 552. Cf. In goods of Irvine, 53 Ir.L.T.R. 143, noted, 33 Harv.L.R. 620.

49 Estate of Kaufman, 25 Cal.2d 854, 155 P.2d 831, 1945, noted, 33 Cal. L.R. 159; Linkins v. Protestant Episcopal Cathedral Fund, 187 F.2d 357, C.A.D.C.1950, noted in 39 Geo.L.J. 346, 64 Harv.L.R. 686, 37 W.Va.L.R. 461. Contra; Hoffner's Estate, 161 Pa. 331, 29 A. 33, 1894; cf. Sloan's Appeal, 168 Pa. 422, 32 A. 42, 47 Am. St.Rep. 889, 1895. See supra § 85, notes 12–15.

50 See supra § 87 at notes 37–39; also note 53 infra.

51 Owen v. Busiel, 83 N.H. 345, 142 A. 692, 59 A.L.R. 1103, 1928; Adams v. Cowan, 160 Va. 1, 168 S.E. 750, 1933; Kearns v. Roush, 106 W.Va. 663, 146 S.E. 729, 1929. And see supra § 87, notes 37, 38.

52 In re Marx's Estate, 175 Cal. 762, 164 P. 640, L.R.A.1917F, 234, 1917;

is reached though the decisions seem to conflict with the prevailing view in the situation where there is an express clause of revocation. Of course there is the other means of disposing of these cases, viz., to deny that there is any revocation unless the later inconsistent will is valid and effective.[53]

Concerning the whole matter of dependent relative revocation by subsequent instrument, the best solution is to uphold or disregard the revocation in accordance with what the testator would probably have intended had he known of the error. It would be more frank to treat the cases as instances of mistaken revocation rather than conditional or dependent revocation. What has already been said[54] along this line in connection with dependent relative revocation by physical act applies equally here. The subsequent instrument and the surrounding circumstances often give important clues to what testator would have desired. For instance, we can be fairly sure that if the later instrument made more or less similar dispositions to the same persons as did the first will, the testator would probably have desired the first will rather than intestacy. The converse is likewise true. Many,[55] if not most, of the cases will be found to have reached results in harmony with this position.

Austin v. Oakes, 117 N.Y. 577, 23 N.E. 193, 1890; In re Street's Estate, 138 Okl. 115, 280 P. 413, 1929; Ewell v. Sneed, 136 Tenn. 602, 191 S.W. 131, 5 A.L.R. 303, 1917; Ward v. Vander Loeff, [1924] A.C. 653, noted, 24 Col. L.R. 807; see Blackford v. Anderson, supra note 39. But see McGill v. Trust Co. of New Jersey, 94 N.J.Eq. 657, 121 A. 760, 1923; Carpenter v. Miller's Ex'rs, 3 W.Va. 174, 100 Am. Dec. 744, 1869.

53 United States Fidelity & Guaranty Co. v. Douglas' Trustee, 134 Ky. 374, 120 S.W. 328, 20 Ann.Cas. 993, 1909. And see In re Street's Estate, and In re Marx's Estate, supra note 52.

54 Text supra at notes 12 to 20.

55 Security Co. v. Snow, supra note 48; Board of Com'rs of Rice County v. Scott, supra note 47; Bernard's Settlement, supra note 48; Ward v. Vander Loeff, supra note 52; Goods of Horsford's supra note 26. But in the following cases the testator probably would not have desired the result: Price v. Maxwell, 28 Pa. 23, 1857; Tupper v. Tupper, supra note 47. For a suggested modification of this view, see Evans, Testamentary Revocation by Subsequent Instrument, 22 Ky.L.J. 469, 481–494.

## RE-EXECUTION

**89. Under modern statutes, in the absence of a subsequent instrument, an effective republication of an invalid or revoked will cannot be made except by re-execution of the will in the manner required for original execution of wills.**

The term republication, in so far as it suggests testator's second declaration of the instrument as his will, is inaccurate, for, as has been seen,[1] most jurisdictions do not require publication in this sense for the original execution of the will. Republication has been used to include the following: (1) The validation of a prior invalid will; (2) the revival of an instrument which has somehow lost its validity; (3) the reaffirmance or bringing down to date of a will by codicil or later will; (4) the restoration of a first will by the revocation of a second which had revoked the first. Strictly speaking there can be no republication in the first class of cases as the will was never validly executed. As pointed out by Dean Evans,[2] the latter situations are properly considered as cases of incorporation by reference. Yet it is usual and convenient to treat them with the other cases of republication.

Prior to the Statute of Frauds, a will, whether of personalty or realty, could be revived or republished by informal writing or even by oral declarations showing intent to revive.[3] Under that statute, republication of devises of lands was required to be in the same manner as necessary for the original execution of the instrument [4] though wills of personalty might be revived as before.[5] The Wills Act, 1837 [6] recognizes only formal re-execution, or codicils executed with the formalities required for wills, as means of revival of revoked wills, whether of realty or personalty.

Some American jurisdictions adopt the provisions of the latter statute,[7] and in almost all the others an oral or informal republi-

1 Supra § 68.

2 Testamentary Republican, 40 Harv.L.R. 71. See infra § 92. For a recent exhaustive study, see Zacharias and Maschinot, Revocation and Revival of Wills, 25 Chi-Kent L.R. 185, 271; 26 id. 107.

3 Braham v. Burchell, 3 Add.Eccl. 243, 162 Eng.Rep. 468, 1826 (personalty); Beckford v. Parnecott, Cro.Eliz. 493, 78 Eng.Rep. 744, 1596 (realty).

4 29 Car. II, c. 3, § 5, 1677. See Jackson v. Hurlock, Ambl. 487, 27 Eng.Rep. 318, 1764.

5 Miller v. Brown, 2 Hagg. 209, 162 Eng.Rep. 837, 1828.

6 7 Wm. IV & 1 Vict. c. 26, § 22. See infra § 92.

7 Bordwell, Statute Law of Wills, 14 Ia.L.R. 309. See also Zacharias & Maschinot, supra note 2.

cation is ineffective under the decisions.[8] In refusing to follow the English rulings as to personalty under the Statute of Frauds, the courts reason that the provisions requiring formalities for execution apply equally to re-execution.

Where a will is altered at testator's direction and in his presence and that of the original attesting witnesses, the will is not valid in its revised form,[9] but if the testator retraces his signature and the witnesses re-subscribe, there is effective republication.[10] The testator can adopt his signature upon a revoked will and if witnesses sign at his request, the instrument is republished.[11] But if the witnesses who sign merely attest to alterations in the will there is not sufficient republication of the altered instrument.[12] Where the testator alters his will and strikes off his signature and those of the witnesses and then all sign again in the presence of each other, there is clearly a republication.[13]

8 Barker v. Bell, 46 Ala. 216, 1871; Harwell v. Lively, 30 Ga. 315, 76 Am. Dec. 649, 1860; In re Penniman's Will, 20 Minn. 245 (Gil. 220) 18 Am. Rep. 368, 1873; Safe Deposit & Trust Co. of Baltimore v. Thom, 117 Md. 154, 83 A. 45, 1912 (attempted restoration of erased portion of will); Stickney's Will, 161 N.Y. 42, 55 N.E. 396, 76 Am.St.Rep. 246, 1899; Means v. Ury, 141 N.C. 248, 53 S.E. 850, 1906 (will revoked by operation of law); In re Baum's Estate, 269 Pa. 63, 112 A. 141, 1920; Brackenridge v. Roberts, 114 Tex. 418, 267 S.W. 244, rehearing denied 114 Tex. 418, 270 S.W. 1001, 1925. Cf. Cameron's Estate, 215 Iowa 63, 241 N.W. 458, 1932; Collins v. Collins, 110 Ohio St. 105, 143 N.E. 561, 38 A.L.R. 230, 1924 (statute). Of course this doctrine does not preclude republication by codicil (In re Engle's Estate, 129 Or. 77, 276 P. 270, 1929, and infra § 90), nor revival by revocation of a revoking will so far as that doctrine applies (infra § 92).

9 Hesterberg v. Clark, 166 Ill. 241, 46 N.E. 734, 57 Am.St.Rep. 135, 1900. Contra: Wright v. Wright, 5 Ind. 389, 1854. If the statutes regarding execution do not require subscribing witnesses but merely proving witnesses, the rewriting of the testator's signature after the first had been mutilated was sufficient republication. Re Brock's Estate, 247 Pa. 365, 93 A. 487, L.R.A.1915D, 1140, 1915. In case of holographic wills it has been held that there might be informal republication after alteration thereof. In re Cazaurang's Estate, 42 Cal.App.2d 796, 110 P.2d 138, 1941, noted, 40 Mich.L.R. 770; LaRue v. Lee, 63 W. Va. 388, 60 S.E. 388, 14 L.R.A.,N.S., 968, 129 Am.St.Rep. 978, 1908. But see Sawyer's Legatees v. Sawyer's Heirs, 52 N.C. 134, 1859 (holographic will revoked by marriage could not be republished orally), and Walker v. Hibbard, 185 Ky. 795, 215 S.W. 800, 11 A.L.R. 832, 1919 (statute).

10 Kohn's Estate, 172 Mich. 342, 137 N.W. 735, 1912.

11 P'Pool's Ex'r v. P'Pool's Ex'x, 121 Ky. 588, 89 S.W. 687, 1905. Cf. In re Moore's Estate, 166 Kan. 556, 203 P.2d 192, 1949 (under statute requiring publication for execution).

12 In re Penniman's Will, supra note 8. But see In re Flynn's Estate, 174 Misc. 565, 21 N.Y.S.2d 496, 1940.

13 In re Bissonnette's Will, 127 Misc. 215, 216 N.Y.S. 325, aff'd 217 App.Div. 809, 217 N.Y.S. 898, noted,

Plainly, oral declarations that the testator wishes his will to stand are not sufficient.[14] The foregoing principles apply not only to wills which have been revoked by acts of the testator, but also to instruments nullified by operation of law,[15] and contingent wills revoked by their own terms.[16]

## REPUBLICATION BY SUBSEQUENT INSTRUMENT

**90. A revoked will, which was once validly executed and never physically destroyed, may be republished by subsequent will, codicil or other instrument executed with the formalities required for wills. The same is said to be true of wills never duly executed, though here the doctrine of incorporation by reference must be applied to sustain the instrument.**

When a valid will has been revoked, it may be revived by a subsequent duly executed codicil,[1] or by a later instrument which is executed with the formalities of a will and which, by its terms, indicates that a revival is intended.[2] Re-execution is not required in these cases,[3] nor is it necessary that the will be present at the time the codicil is executed.[4]

27 Col.L.R. 103, though New York does not allow partial revocation by physical act. And see P'Pool's Ex'r v. P'Pool's Ex'x, supra note 11.

[14] Danley v. Jefferson, 150 Mich. 590, 114 N.W. 470, 121 Am.St.Rep. 640, 13 Ann.Cas. 242, 1908; In re Stickney's Will, supra note 8.

[15] Carey v. Baughn, 36 Iowa 540, 14 Am.Rep. 534, 1873; Means v. Ury, 141 N.C. 248, 53 S.E. 850, 1906; In re Baum's Estate, 269 Pa. 63, 112 A. 141, 1920. Nor will a change of the statutory ground of revocation revive a will so revoked. In re Berger's Estate, 198 Cal. 103, 243 P. 862, 1926.

[16] Walker v. Hibbard, supra note 9; Ferguson v. Ferguson, 288 S.W. 833, Tex.Civ.App.1927; French v. French, 14 W.Va. 458, 1878.

[1] Burge v. Hamilton, 72 Ga. 568, 1884; Farmers Bank & Trust Co. v. Harding, 209 Ky. 3, 272 S.W. 3, 1925; In re Hickman's Estate, 308 Pa. 230, 162 A. 168, 1932; Matter of Steele, L.R. 1 P. and D. 575, 1868. The foregoing cases are ones in which the revocation was by the testator's act. See note, 40 Mich.L.R. 770. Cf. In re Carr's Estate, 93 Cal.App.2d 750, 209 P.2d 956, 1949. The same principle applies if the revocation was by operation of law. In re Riddel's Estate, 104 Cal.App.2d 162, 230 P.2d 863, 1951; Brown v. Clark, 77 N.Y. 369, 1879; In re Coffield's Will, 216 N.C. 285, 4 S.E.2d 870, 1939; Gooch v. Gooch, 134 Va. 21, 113 S.E. 873, 1922.

[2] Derr v. Derr, 123 Kan. 681, 256 P. 800, 53 A.L.R. 515, 1927.

[3] Gooch v. Gooch, supra note 1.

[4] Wikoff's Appeal, 15 Pa. 281, 53 Am.Dec. 597, 1850. See Pope v. Pope, 95 Ga. 87, 22 S.E. 245, 1894.

Analytically, if the first will was never valid, the subsequent instrument cannot revive or republish the former. One cannot restore that which has never had life. Yet the courts often declare a revival in cases in which the first instrument was not an effective will because of incapacity,[5] undue influence,[6] or want of proper execution.[7] Properly speaking, these decisions can be justified only on the theory of incorporation by reference of the earlier paper.[8] Most jurisdictions recognize the latter doctrine,[9] and in these, the result of giving effect to the earlier instrument is justified though the terminology and the reasoning may be faulty.[10]

Jurisdictions which do not permit incorporation by reference should not allow validation of the ineffective instrument in this manner. New York, which in general does not recognize incorporation by reference,[11] allows a duly executed instrument to be validated by a subsequent codicil though the first was invalid because of the maker's unsound mind or undue influence practiced upon him.[12] When, however, the first instrument is not executed in due form, the courts of that state refuse to regard the first will as validated by a codicil, it being thought that this

5 Barnes v. Phillips, 184 Ind. 415, 111 N.E. 419, 1916; Stevens v. Myers, 62 Or. 372, 121 P. 434, 1912; Noble v. Phelps, 2 P. & D. 276, 1871. See, also, In re Campbell's Will, 170 N.Y. 84, 62 N.E. 1070, 1902; In re Engle's Estate, 129 Or. 77, 276 P. 270, 1929; In re Triebe's Will, 114 N.J.Eq. 227, 168 A. 404, 1933. Of course testator must be competent at time of execution of the codicil in order that the first instrument be validated by the codicil. Appeal of Rogers, 126 Me. 267, 138 A. 59, 1927.

6 Baird's Estate, 176 Cal. 381, 168 P. 561, 1917; Taft v. Stearns, 234 Mass. 273, 125 N.E. 570, 1920, noted, 33 Harv.L.R. 872; Kerr's Estate, 255 Pa. 399, 100 A. 127, 1917; see Sullivan v. Bond, 180 F.2d 47, C.A.D.C. 1950.

7 Rogers v. Agricola, 176 Ark. 287, 3 S.W.2d 26, 1928; Hurley v. Blankinship, 313 Ky. 49, 229 S.W.2d 963, 21 A.L.R.2d 817, 1950; Anderson v. Anderson, 13 Eq. 381, 1872, (bequest to attesting witnesses of first will); In re Ayres' Will, 43 N.E.2d 918, Ohio App.1942. But see In re Emmons' Will, infra note 13.

8 See Evans, Testamentary Republication, 40 Harv.L.R. 71; note, 33 Harv.L.R. 872; Hamlet v. Hamlet, 183 Va. 453, 32 S.E.2d 729, 1945.

9 Supra § 80.

10 Some of the cases proceed partially on the ground of incorporation by reference. See Taft v. Stearns, supra note 6; Rogers v. Agricola, supra note 7. Furthermore, cases where the "revived" instrument was once valid may be justified on the ground of incorporation by reference. See Derr v. Derr, supra note 2.

11 See supra § 80.

12 Cook v. White, 43 App.Div. 388, 60 N.Y.S. 153, affirmed 167 N.Y. 588, 60 N.E. 1109, 1901.

would be contrary to the New York holdings forbidding incorporation by reference.[13]

If the will attempted to be revived has been destroyed before the execution of the codicil, there can be no revival.[14] Obviously the theory of incorporation by reference cannot apply here because the instrument is not then in existence. On the revival theory, the instrument fails because it is not in writing at the time of the attempted validation. The ordinary cases of probate of lost wills [15] present no analogy because in them the instrument was in writing at the time when the necessary formalities of execution took place.

## CONSEQUENCES OF REPUBLICATION BY CODICIL

**91. The intention to republish is generally inferred from a mere reference in the codicil or second will to the first instrument, and this republication extends to prior codicils supplementary to the first, although not to instruments which revoke it.**

**When a will is republished by codicil, this had the effect of making the will speak as of the date of the codicil, though, according to the modern and better view, this doctrine should be applied only in the cases where a reasonable result in accordance with the testator's probable intention is reached thereby.**

*Intent to Republish*

The whole doctrine of republication or revival of a will by codicil should be based upon the intention to do so. In absence of indication of testator's intention to revive, there should be no revival.[1] This intention, however, is easily found. Reference to the earlier instrument, as "my will" is sufficient,[2] as is the fact

13 In re Emmons' Will, 110 App. Div. 701, 96 N.Y.S. 506, 1906; In re Lawler's Will, 195 App.Div. 27, 185 N.Y.S. 726, 1920. See note, 11 Col.L. R. 456.

14 Williams v. Miles, 68 Neb. 463, 94 N.W. 705, 96 N.W. 151, 62 L.R.A. 383, 110 Am.St.Rep. 431, 4 Ann.Cas. 306, 1903; Rogers v. Goodenough, 2 Sw. & Tr. 342, 164 Eng.Rep. 1028, 1862. See infra § 92, note 1.

15 See infra § 97.

1 Blackett v. Ziegler, 153 Iowa 344, 133 N.W. 901, 37 L.R.A.,N.S., 291, Ann.Cas.1913E 115, 1911 (no reference to earlier will). And see In re Pence's Estate, 117 Cal.App. 323, 4 P.2d 202, 1931.

2 Succession of Ledet, 170 La. 449, 128 So. 273, 1930; Taft v. Stearns, 234 Mass. 273, 125 N.E. 570, 1920, noted 33 Harv.L.Rev. 872; Gooch v. Gooch, 134 Va. 21, 113 S.E. 873, 1922 (statute). Statutes sometimes so de-

that the codicil was attached physically to the will and was described as the "first codicil." [3] Of course the intention to revive may appear more clearly from the specific language of the second will or codicil, but this, in general, is not necessary. The reviving codicil need not itself be dispositive.[4] A codicil expressly referring to a will revives it although the will referred to has been revoked by a later existing will and the effect of the revival is to displace the latter.[5]

*Extent of Republication*

As just indicated,[6] the republication of a first will does not carry with it later inconsistent or revoking wills, for the effect of that would be to hold that there was no republication of the first will. The same, is true of codicils which are repugnant to the first will: these are not revived.[7] However, the will with all its modifying and supplementary codicils is deemed republished, even where the last codicil refers merely to the first will by date and says nothing of the prior codicils.[8] Only valid codicils will be deemed republished when the reference is merely to the will.[9] Moreover, a testator may, by apt words, republish the will in its original terms, unaffected by intervening codicils.[10] The question of the extent of republication should depend upon the testator's intent in this regard.[11]

clare, as in California. Bordwell, Statute Law of Wills, 14 Iowa L.Rev. 308, 309; In re Seiler's Estate, 176 Cal. 771, 170 P. 1138, rehearing denied 176 Cal. 771, 179 P. 389, 1918.

3 Smith v. Runkle, 97 A. 296, affirmed 86 N.J.Eq. 257, 98 A. 1086, 1916. Cf. Blackett v. Ziegler, supra note 1.

4 Manship v. Stewart, 181 Ind. 299, 104 N.E. 505, 1914 (codicil merely appointing executor). And see Derr v. Derr, 123 Kan. 681, 256 P. 800, 53 A.L.R. 515, 1927.

5 In re Campbell's Will, 170 N.Y. 84, 62 N.E. 1070, 1902; In re Engle's Estate, 129 Or. 77, 276 P. 270, 1929; In re Knecht's Estate, 341 Pa. 292, 19 A.2d 111, 1941; Walpole v. Orford, 3 Ves. 402, 30 Eng.Rep. 1076, 1797. See infra § 92, note 14 et seq.

6 See supra note 5.

7 Freeman v. Hart, 61 Colo. 455, 158 P. 305, 1916. See Chichester v. Quatrefages, [1895] P. 186; Austin v. First Trust & Sav. Bank, 343 Ill. 406, 175 N.E. 554, 1931.

8 In re Dubois' Estate, 94 Cal.App. 2d 838, 211 P.2d 895, 1949, noted, 23 So.Cal.L.R. 427; Manship v. Stewart, 181 Ind. 299, 104 N.E. 505, 1914; Loveren v. Eaton, 80 N.H. 62, 113 A. 206, 1921; In re Van Ingen's Estate, 183 Misc. 281, 47 N.Y.S.2d 818, 1944; Third Nat. Bank v. Scribner, 175 Tenn. 14, 130 S.W.2d 126, 123 A.L.R. 1385, 1939; Green v. Tribe, 9 Ch.D. 231, 1878 (leading case).

9 Burton v. Newberry, 1 Ch.D. 234, 1875.

10 Lee's Estate, 16 Pa.Super. 627, 1901.

11 Manship v. Stewart, supra note 8; Wikoff's Appeal, 15 Pa. 281, 53

*Consequences of Republication*

Up to this point we have considered cases where it is a question of whether an invalid or revoked instrument is validated or revalidated by codicil. These are not the only cases where republication by codicil is important. Due to the doctrine that republication brings the will down to the date of the republishing as though originally executed at that time,[12] there are important consequences although the republished will was originally valid and never revoked.

The doctrine that a codicil republishes a will so as to make it speak from the time of the codicil had its first application in cases involving after-acquired lands. At common law such lands could not pass by a devise even though the latter was literally broad enough to cover such property. The courts applied the doctrine of republication by codicil to this situation so that realty acquired after the will and before the execution of the codicil passed under a general or residuary devise in the will.[13] Indeed, the courts seemed to apply the doctrine mechanically, regardless of whether the form of the codicil showed an intention to pass the after-acquired lands or not.[14] Of course there could be an effective republication as to after-acquired lands only if the expressions in the original will were broad enough to include them.[15] The doctrine of republication has little significance in cases of after-acquired lands at present, as a will may operate on after-acquired realty as well as personalty.

The principles first adopted in the after-acquired land cases were also applied to other situations. Thus, where testatrix bequeaths the residue of her property to the beneficiaries "heretofore named" and a codicil names other legatees, the codicil in effect republishes the will, making the codicillary legatees, "persons heretofore named," and hence entitled to a share of the residue.[16] Likewise a will which releases all debts operates in discharge of

Am.Dec. 597, 1950; Green v. Tribe, supra note 8.

12 See infra notes 13 to 33; also Revercomb's Estate, 315 Pa. 424, 172 A. 850, 1934; In re Campbell's Will, 170 N.Y. 84, 62 N.E. 1070, 1902.

13 Corr v. Porter, 33 Grat.(Va.) 278, 1880; Acherly v. Vernon, 1 Comyns 381, 92 Eng.Rep. 1121, 1724; Barnes v. Crow, 4 Bro.Ch. 2, 29 Eng.Rep. 747, 1792 (reviewing prior cases).

14 See cases supra note 13. But cf. Strathmore v. Bowes, 7 Tr. 482, 101 Eng.Rep. 1089, 1798.

15 Haven v. Foster, 14 Pick.(Mass.) 534, 1833.

16 Matter of Phelp's Will, 133 Misc. 450, 232 N.Y.S. 418, 1929. Cf. Alsop's Appeal, 9 Pa. 374, 1848, and see Evans, Testamentary Republication, 40 Harv.L.R. 71, 85–90; note, 31 Col.L.R. 128.

obligations incurred between the date of the will and a subsequent codicil, though the latter contains no express words of republication.[17] Where a codicil is executed after the passage of a statute giving the right of the spouse to claim a certain share of the estate against wills executed after the statute, the codicil was deemed to republish the will and to permit the spouse to elect.[18] Where testatrix makes a provision for the wife of one M, and the wife died prior to the execution of a codicil, the latter was held to republish the will so that M's second wife, whom he married after execution of the codicil, was entitled to the property.[19] There is reason to believe that this result is in accord with the intention of the testatrix, because she knew at the time of execution of the codicil that the first wife was dead and that the provision which she allowed to stand could only refer to a second wife. When testator willed his "present lease" to his daughter, which lease expired and a new one was taken and then a codicil was executed, the daughter took the second lease under the republished will.[20] Republication has even been applied with retroactive consequences, where a will described a document to be incorporated, which was not in existence at the time of the will, though it was at the time of the codicil.[21] A condition valid at the

[17] Coale v. Smith, 4 Pa. 376, 1846. Cf. In re Edward's Estate, 254 Pa. 159, 98 A. 879, 1916, where the will stated that testatrix had no large debts and that any indebtedness to her was canceled and thereafter she lent her son-in-law $32,000 on collateral security and afterward republished her will by codicil; held that this did not cancel the latter indebtedness.

[18] Re Greenberg's Estate, 261 N.Y. 474, 185 N.E. 704, 87 A.L.R. 833, 1933. And see Morse v. Ward, 92 Conn. 408, 103 A. 119, 1918 (devise void by statute when made was held valid where a codicil was executed after repeal of statute); In re Villard's Estate, 147 Misc. 472, 264 N.Y.S. 236, 1933.

[19] In re Hardyman, [1925] 1 Ch. 287. And see Perkins v. Micklethwaite, 1 P.Wms. 274, 24 Eng.Rep. 386, 1714. But see Bradley's Estate, 119 Misc. 2, 194 N.Y.S. 888, 1922; First Nat. Bank & Trust Co. v. Baker, 124 Conn. 577, 1 A.2d 283, 118 A.L.R. 339, 1938, noted, 24 Iowa L.R. 800. If there had been no codicil, the authorities are practically uniform that the second wife would not take. Although a will usually speaks as of the time of death, this is not so as to such restrictive words. Lavender v. Rosenheim, 110 Md. 150, 72 A. 669, 132 Am.St.Rep. 420, 1909; Gurley v. Wiggs, 192 N.C. 726, 135 S.E. 858, 1926; Garratt v. Niblock, 1 Russ. & M. 629, 39 Eng.Rep. 241, 1830.

[20] In re Reeves, [1928] 1 Ch. 351. But see Stilwell v. Mellersh, 20 L.J. Ch. 356, 1851, at 361, 362.

[21] Simon v. Grayson, 15 Cal.2d 531, 102 P.2d 1081, 1940, noted, 10 Brooklyn L.R. 217, 29 Cal.L.R. 94, 39 Mich. L.R. 1055, 15 Tulane L.R. 319; Lawrence v. Burnett, 109 S.C. 416, 96 S.E. 144, 1918; In re Goods of Truro, 1 P. and D. 201, 1866. But see Durham v. Northen, [1895] Prob. 66. Of course the other requisites for incor-

time of a will was deemed invalid because of change of conditions prior to republication by codicil.[22] Some cases hold that republication by codicil after a legatee has died makes the legacy void, being to a dead person and therefore preventing the operation of the anti-lapse statute.[23]

As seen from the foregoing examples, the doctrine that a codicil causes the will to be read as of the date of the codicil is applied in many situations. Sometimes this republication has the effect of increasing the scope of the provision of the original will; in other cases, the reverse is true. The doctrine has no particular importance with regard to devises and bequests describing property in general terms, as "all of my personalty," for these are construed to refer to the situation existing at the time of testator's death. Where the testamentary gifts are described with restrictive words, however, republication by codicil may be a matter of vital consequence.

Republication should be applied, "not as a rigid formula or technical rule, but as a useful and flexible instrument for effectuating a testator's intention." [24] Thus, where a legatee to a will witnesses the codicil, the republication by the latter does not have the effect of invalidating the legacies to this attester.[25] Likewise

poration by reference must be present, particularly the reference (though false at the time) in the original will to the document as then existing. See supra § 80.

[22] Hawke v. Euyart, 30 Neb. 149, 46 N.W. 422, 27 Am.St.Rep. 391, 1890.

[23] In re Matthews' Estate, 176 Cal. 576, 169 P. 233, 1917, noted, 6 Cal.L.R. 312, 31 Harv.L.R. 901, 16 Mich.L.R. 429, 27 Yale L.J. 852; In re Fraser, [1904] 1 Ch. 726. See note, 36 Mich.L.R. 520; infra § 140. But see Twitty v. Martin, 90 N.C. 643, 1884; Winter v. Winter, 5 Hare, 306, 67 Eng.Rep. 929, 1846.

[24] In re Moore, [1907] 1 Ir.R. 315. See also Massachusetts Audubon Soc. v. Ormond Village Imp. Ass'n, 152 Fla. 1, 10 So.2d 494, 1942.

[25] Kennedy v. Upshaw, 66 Tex. 442, 1 S.W. 308, 1886; Gurney v. Gurney, 3 Drew.Ch. 208, 61 Eng.Rep. 882, 1855; In re Trotter [1899] 1 Ch. 764. And see In re Shetter's Estate, 303 Pa. 193, 154 A. 288, 1931, noted, 80 U. of Pa.L.R. 467; note, 15 N.Y.U. L.R. 304; supra § 65. See Lougee v. Wilkie, 209 Mass. 184, 95 N.E. 221, 1911 (where the interest of a witness to the codicil was cut down by that instrument from what had been given by will); Historical Society of Dauphin County v. Kelker, 226 Pa. 16, 74 A. 619, 134 Am.St.Rep. 1010, 1909 (where witness to will became a legatee by a codicil, bequest held valid). Cf. Anderson v. Anderson, L. R. 13 Eq. 381, 1872 (where the bequest in the will, invalid because attested by legatee's wife, was republished by codicil with disinterested witnesses, bequest held good), with In re Kelly's Estate, 236 Pa. 54, 84 A. 593, 1912. And see generally, Evans, Testamentary Witnesses, 25 Mich.L.R. 238, 261–263.

in most cases where the bequests of the will have been satisfied before the execution of the codicil, they are not restored by the latter.[26] Here the will is deemed republished with the legacy satisfied. Moreover, under statutes invalidating charitable bequests if made within a certain number of days before testator's death, such testamentary gifts are effective if the will precedes the proscribed period although the codicil does not.[27] The approved modern viewpoint is to apply the doctrine of republication with good sense so that a reasonable result, in accordance with the testator's probable intention, will prevail.[28]

*Codicil to Qualified Gifts in Will*

There is still another manifestation of republication by codicil, though it is almost entirely a matter of construction of the two instruments. When a devise or bequest in the will is subject to certain incidents or conditions, a substituted or additional gift by codicil is normally deemed to be taken subject to the same incident or conditions.[29] But this does not apply when the codicilary gift is of a different nature,[30] or when the principle would violate the testator's intent.[31]

[26] Tanton v. Keller, 167 Ill. 129, 47 N.E. 376, 1897; Langdon v. Astor's Ex'rs, 16 N.Y. 9, 1857; Izard v. Hurst, Freem.Ch. 224, 22 Eng.Rep. 1173, 1698; see infra § 133. But if a second will, as distinguished from a codicil, repeats the gift after satisfaction, it will be deemed a new gift. Jaques v. Swasey, 153 Mass. 596, 27 N.E. 771, 13 L.R.A. 566, 1891.

[27] In re McCauley's Estate, 138 Cal. 432, 71 P. 512, 1873; In re Pence's Estate, 117 Cal.App. 323, 4 P.2d 202, 1931. Appeal of Carl, 106 Pa. 635, 1931. See supra § 35; § 88, note 49; infra § 140, note 9.

[28] In addition to the cases cited supra notes 24–27, see In re Edward's Estate, supra note 17. See also Evans, Testamentary Republication, 40 Harv.L.R. 71; note, 31 Col.L.R. 128.

[29] Equitable Trust Co. v. Banning, 17 Del.Ch. 95, 149 A. 432, 1930 (exemption of estate tax); Waterbury v. Munn, 159 Fla. 754, 32 So.2d 603, 174 A.L.R. 620, 1947 (spendthrift trust); Tilden v. Tilden, 13 Gray (Mass.) 103, 1859 (condition).

[30] Gilmore v. Doherty, 317 Mass. 188, 57 N.E.2d 564, 156 A.L.R. 788, 1944.

[31] De Campi v. Logan, 95 W.Va. 84, 120 S.E. 915, 1923.

## REVIVAL BY REVOCATION OF REVOKING WILL

**92. In the English common-law courts the revocation of a second instrument which revoked a prior will revived the first will, while in the ecclesiastical tribunals the prior will's revival depended upon the testator's intention to do so.**

**In absence of statute some American courts have adopted the common-law rule, others the ecclesiastical court doctrine, while still others declare there is no revival of the first will by revocation of the second, at least if the second will expressly revokes the first.**

**Statutes in England and in a number of our states now prevent revival of the first will by revocation of a later revoking instrument, except where the revocation of the second will is by a duly attested instrument declaring the revival or where the first will is re-executed.**

### *The English Law*

We come to the problem of whether a first will revoked by a second is revived by the revocation (usually by destruction or some physical act) of the latter instrument. It is clear that if the first will has been destroyed there can be no such revival.[1] In the absence of such destruction the rule of the common-law courts as to devises of land was that there was a revival of the first will.[2] The first will was revived regardless of testator's intention, and apparently it made no difference whether the second will expressly revoked the first or did so only because of inconsistency therewith. The cases proceeded upon the theory that, since the second will was ambulatory and could not take effect until death, its revocation prevented it from revoking the first will.

In the ecclestiastical courts, a different doctrine was maintained as to testaments of personalty. These tribunals made revival depend upon the testator's intention as gathered from all the circumstances of the case.[3] There was said to be no presumption

[1] Moore's Will, 72 N.J.Eq. 371, 65 A. 447, 1907; Burtenshaw v. Gilbert, 1 Cowp. 49, 98 Eng.Rep. 961, 1774. See supra § 90, note 14.

[2] Goodright d. Glazier v. Glazier, 4 Burr. 2512, 98 Eng.Rep. 317, 1770; Harwood v. Goodright, Cowp. 87, 98 Eng.Rep. 981, 1774. And see infra notes 4, 5.

[3] Wilson v. Wilson, 3 Phill. 543, 161 Eng.Rep. 1409, 1921. Cf. Usticke v. Bawden, 2 Add. 116, 162 Eng.Rep. 238, 1924. But see Helyar v. Helyar, 1 Lee, 472, 161 Eng Rep. 174, 1754 (presumption of intent not to revive?).

that the testator did or did not intend to restore the first will. Here also it seemed to make no difference whether there was an express clause of revocation in the second will, or whether the revocation was merely because the latter made a complete disposition of testator's property contrary to the provisions of his first will.

*American Rules*

In the absence of statute, there is great divergence of viewpoint among the American cases. No distinction is now made as to whether the instrument is a will of realty or a testament of personalty. Some jurisdictions follow the common-law rule in general, others that of the ecclesiastical courts, but often there are qualifications or variations of these two.

(1) There is a group of cases that hold that the earlier will is revived ipso facto, regardless of the intention of the testator. This is the common-law rule and the decisions adopt the same theory as the English cases.[4] At least some of these decisions follow this doctrine even in cases where the second will contained an express clause of revocation.[5] Of course the situation where the second will merely revokes the first by implication is an *a fortiori* case for revival of the first.

(2) A number of courts follow the ecclesiastical court rule, making revival dependent on intention and indulging in no presumption as to that fact.[6] The cases which assert that the earlier

4 Whitehill v. Halbing, 98 Conn. 21, 118 A. 454, 28 A.L.R. 895, 1922, noted, 32 Yale L.J. 70; Dawson v. Smith, 3 Houst.(Del.) 92, 1864; Stetson v. Stetson, 200 Ill. 601, 66 N.E. 262, 61 L.R.A. 258, 1903; Cheever v. North, 106 Mich. 390, 64 N.W. 455, 37 L.R.A. 561, 58 Am.St.Rep. 499, 1895, noted, 9 Harv.L.Rev. 364; Bates v. Hacking, 28 R.I. 523, 29 R.I. 1, 68 A. 622, 14 L.R.A.,N.S., 937, 125 Am.St.Rep. 759, 1907; Kollock v. Williams, 131 S.C. 352, 127 S.E. 444, 1925. See also Succession of Dambly, 191 La. 500, 186 So. 7, 1939.

5 So in Whitehill v. Halbing, Dawson v. Smith, Stetson v. Stetson, Bates v. Hacking, and Kollock v. Williams, all supra note 4. Cheever v. North, supra note 4, lays down the rule that if there is an express clause of revocation, this is final and destruction of the latter will does not revive the former without republication.

6 Blackett v. Ziegler, 153 Iowa 344, 133 N.W. 901, 37 L.R.A.,N.S., 291, Ann.Cas.1913E, 115, 1911, noted, 12 Col.L.R. 353, 21 Yale L.J. 672, (express revocation); In re Davis' Estate, 134 N.J.Eq. 393, 35 A.2d 880, 1944; Re Gould's Will, 72 Vt. 316, 47 A. 1082, 1900 (evidently implied revocation only). Cf. Williams v. Miles, 68 Neb. 463, 94 N.W. 705, rehearing denied 96 N.W. 151, 62 L.R.A. 383, 110 Am.St.Rep. 431, 4 Ann.Cas. 306, 1903; Ewell v. Rucker, 28 Tenn. App. 156, 187 S.W.2d 644, 1945.

will is not revived unless testator's intention of revival appears[7] can likewise be said to follow the ecclesiastical rule. Under the viewpoints described in this paragraph and the next, the testator's intention as to revival may be shown by oral evidence.[8]

(3) Another view has been expressed to the effect that the earlier will is revived unless testator intends not to do so.[9] Stated in another way, there is revival by the destruction of the second will unless it is shown that testator intended to die intestate. This is the ecclesiastical rule except that a presumption of intent to revive exists. Probably, however, the presumption is slight, and in practice this position does not differ materially from (2) above.

(4) A quite different position is that the earlier will is not revived by destruction of the second, and that revival can only come by republication. Most of the cases which so declare confine the holdings to situations where there was an express or general clause of revocation.[10] They hold that such clause in the second will is final, while admitting that if the revocation of the first will was merely by inconsistent provision there is possibility of revival. However, in a few jurisdictions[11] even an implied revocation has been held final.

It has been noted that some jurisdictions[12] hold that revocation by express or general clause of revocation contained in the

[7] Pickens v. Davis, 134 Mass. 252, 45 Am.Rep. 322, 1883; Lane v. Hill, 68 N.H. 275, 44 A. 393, 73 Am.St.Rep. 591, 1895. Reviewing the various positions and rejecting the above view is Tibbetts' Estate, 153 Minn. 53, 189 N.W. 401, 1922, noted, 8 Corn.L.Q. 183, 8 Ia.L.Bull. 52, 7 Minn.L.R. 158.

[8] Pickens v. Davis, supra note 7, and cases generally supra note 6 and infra note 9.

[9] Ford's Estate, 301 Pa. 183, 151 A. 789, 1930, noted, 26 Ill.L.R. 352, 29 Mich.L.R. 1031, 79 U. of Pa.L.R. 325, 6 Wis.L.R. 256; In re Burtt's Estate, 353 Pa. 217, 44 A.2d 670, 162 A.L.R. 1053, 1945, noted, 46 Col.L.R. 496, 94 U. of Pa.L.R. 257; Linginfetter v. Linginfetter, Hardin (Ky.) 119, 1807; Rabe v. McAllister, 177 Md. 97, 8 A.2d 922, 1939; see Ewell v. Rucker, supra note 6.

[10] James v. Marvin, 3 Conn. 576, 1821; (overruled by Whitehill v. Halbing, supra note 4); Danley v. Jefferson, 150 Mich. 590, 114 N.W. 470, 121 Am.St.Rep. 640, 13 Ann.Cas. 242, 1908, with which compare Cheever v. North, supra notes 4, 5; Brackenridge v. Roberts, 114 Tex. 418, 267 S.W. 244, 1924, (statute); Re Noon's Will, 115 Wis. 299, 91 N.W. 670, 95 Am.St.Rep. 944, 1902.

[11] Lively v. Harwell, 29 Ga. 509, affirmed, 30 Ga. 315, 76 Am.Dec. 649, 1859; but cf. Ga.Code, 1933, c. 113, §§ 403, 406; Bohanon v. Walcot, 1 How. (Miss.) 336, 29 Am.Dec. 631, 1836.

[12] See Cheever v. North, supra note 4; also authorities supra notes 5, 6, 10.

second will is final, while conceding that there may be revival if the second revokes the first only because of inconsistent provisions. The theory of this distinction is that the express clause of revocation should be considered apart from the second will and hence constitutes a statutory revocation at once, even if the second will is not effective at the testator's death; on the other hand, the second will, which revokes the first only because of inconsistency, is not deemed to do so until the revoking instrument is established at the testator's death. Most jurisdictions do not recognize this distinction and apply the same rule of revival regardless of whether or not there is an express clause of revocation in the second will.[13]

*Statutory Rules*

The various views taken by the courts have been subject to much criticism. On the one hand, the holding to the effect that the revocation of the second will revives the first regardless of testator's intention is subject to the objection that it is unreasonable to disregard testator's manifest desires. On the other hand, the courts which freely inquire into the testator's intention are criticized because this determines the matter by a dangerous sort of parol evidence.

Statutes have attempted to meet this dilemma in many jurisdictions. In England the Wills Act[14] provides that no revoked will or codicil shall be revived except by re-execution or by a codicil showing an intention to revive. Kentucky, Virginia and West Virginia have substantially similar statutes.[15] Under these it has been determined that there can be no revival by mere destruction of the revoking will,[16] even if the testator intended a revival.[17] Statutes of this type require re-execution or a codicil in order to restore a revoked will.

[13] In re Burtt's Estate, supra note 9; see note, 27 Ky.L.J. 227.

[14] 7 Wm. IV & 1 Vict. c. 26, § 22, 1837.

[15] Bordwell, Statute Law of Wills, 14 Ia.L.R. 309; Evans, Testamentary Revival, 16 Ky.L.J. 47; Farrier, Revival of a Revoked Will, 28 Cal.L.R. 265; Zacharias & Maschinot, Revocation and Revival of Will, 25 Chi-Kent L.R. 185, 208–215; see Model Probate Code § 41; 1948 Annual Surv. Am.L. 752.

[16] In Goods of Hodgkinson, [1893] Prob. 339 (partial implied revocation of first will by second which was destroyed; probate limited to so much of property as was not comprised by second will); Singleton v. Singleton, 269 Ky. 330, 107 S.W.2d 273, 1937.

[17] Rudisill's Ex'r v. Rodes, 29 Grat.(Va.) 147, 1877 (express revocation). See Clark v. Hugo, 130 Va. 99, 107 S.E. 730, 1921, semble accord

A number of other jurisdictions have statutes which provide that the revocation of the second will does not revive the first unless it appears by the terms of such revocation that there was intention to revive or unless the will is duly republished.[18] Under these statutes, if no intention to revive appears, clearly there is no revival.[19] The fact that testator expressed an intention to revive at some time after the revocation can have no effect in so doing.[20] Indeed, the prevailing view seems to be that the expression "by the terms of said revocation" refers only to a revocation by written and attested instrument.[21] Of course one revoking a will by later instrument may by the latter's provisions revive the first.[22]

The other possibility under these statutes, that of republication, seems to require that the testator re-sign or acknowledge his prior signature and have the witnesses sign again.[23] Mere taking of the original will by the testator before the original witnesses is not enough.[24] It has been held under such statutes that the revocation of a codicil which partially revokes a will does not restore the provision of the will which had been so revoked.[25] This portion of the testator's property passes under the intestate laws.

where the revocation of the first will was not express. See also Slaughter's Adm'r v. Wyman, 228 Ky. 226, 14 S.W.2d 777, 1929.

18 See Bordwell, supra note 15.

19 Beaumont v. Keim, 50 Mo. 28, 1872; Matter of Barnes' Will, 70 App.Div. 523, 75 N.Y.S. 373, 1902; In re Moore's Estate, 137 Misc. 522, 244 N.Y.S. 612, 1930; In re Ten Eyck's Estate, 155 Misc. 443, 279 N.Y.S. 436, 1935.

20 Barnett v. Bellows, 315 Mo. 1100, 287 S.W. 604, 1926 (here the will was revoked by testator's marriage).

21 Kern v. Kern, 154 Ind. 29, 55 N.E. 1004, 1900; In re Stickney's Will, 161 N.Y. 42, 55 N.E. 396, 76 Am.St.Rep. 246, 1899; Collins v. Collins, 110 Ohio St. 105, 143 N.E. 561, 38 A.L.R. 230, 1924. See also In re O'Donovan's Will, 168 Misc. 362, 6 N.Y.S.2d 456, 1938. But cf. Beaumont v. Keim, supra note 19.

22 Price v. Marshall, 255 Ala. 447, 52 So.2d 149, 1951; Derr v. Derr, 123 Kan. 681, 256 P. 800, 53 A.L.R. 515, 1927. See also § 91, notes 1–5.

23 See supra § 89.

24 In New York where publication, or oral declaration, that the instrument is the testator's will, is required for execution, it is possible that another oral declaration before the original witnesses, or even others, is all that the statute meant to require. Cf. In re Stickney's Will, supra note 21; Re Simpson, 56 How.Prac. 125, 1878; Re Kuntz's Will, 163 App.Div. 125, 148 N.Y.S. 382, 1914; Re Williams' Will, 121 Misc. 243, 201 N.Y.S. 205, 1923; Re Brewster's Will, 72 App.Div. 587, 76 N.Y.S. 283, 1902. Cf. Collins v. Collins, supra note 21, where publication is said to be necessary for revival by re-execution though publication is not necessary for original execution in Ohio.

25 Osburn v. Rochester Trust & Safe Deposit Co., 209 N.Y. 54, 102

*Probate of Revoked Will*

If, because of either statutory or non-statutory rules, the testator is unsuccessful in his attempt to revive his first will by revocation of the second, may the latter be probated? This is undoubtedly revocation under mistake, and it is not surprising that some cases have applied the doctrine of dependent relative revocation and have upheld the second will.[26] However, the latter doctrine should not be employed mechanically; it should be applied only if the circumstances show that the testator would have preferred his second will to intestacy. Probate of the second will can be granted where it has been merely cancelled. If the second will is totally destroyed, and there is a statute forbidding probate of a will lost or destroyed in testator's lifetime, probate of the second will must be denied.[27] Under the prevailing view, however, it is not necessary to probate the second will in order to show revocation of the first.[28] This may result in intestacy, which is the only reasonable solution in many of such cases; indeed the same is also often true where it is possible to probate the second will.

N.E. 571, 46 L.R.A.,N.S., 983, Ann. Cas.1915A, 101, 1913; Collins v. Collins, supra note 21. And see Goods of Hodgkinson, supra note 16. But see Estate of Schnoor, 4 Cal 2d 590, 51 P.2d 424, 1935; cf. Re Diament's Estate, 84 N.J.Eq. 135, 92 A. 952, affirmed 88 N.J.Eq. 552, 103 A. 199, 1918, holding that the entire will was restored in a jurisdiction having no statute.

26 See supra § 88 at note 21.

27 See infra § 97, note 11 et seq.

28 Rice v. Rice, 239 Mo.App. 739, 197 S.W.2d 994, 1946; In re Schmidt's Estate, 63 N.Y.S.2d 809, 1946. See infra § 97, note 46.

# CHAPTER 11

# PROBATE AND CONTEST OF WILLS

Sec.
93. Probate and Courts of Probate.
94. Limitations upon Probate.
95. Procedure in Probate of Will.
96. Effect and Necessity of Probate.
97. Probate of Lost or Destroyed Wills.
98. General Nature of Will Contests.
99. Parties to Will Contests.
100. Procedure and Evidence in Will Contests.
101. Burden of Proof and Presumptions.
102. Costs and Attorney Fees.

## PROBATE AND COURTS OF PROBATE

**93. Probate is the judicial establishment of an instrument as the last will of a competent testator, executed in the manner required by statute.**

**Wills may be probated only in the tribunals to which this jurisdiction is given by law and which are usually called probate courts.**

Having discussed most of the topics of the substantive law of intestacy and wills, it is convenient at this point to treat the procedural steps relating to succession, viz., the principles of probate of wills and the administration of estates. In the latter fields, general observations are often difficult to make, due to great diversities of the statutory law in the various jurisdictions. The yet untouched matters of substantive law will be given attention as they arise in the course of the administration proceedings.

### *Meaning of "Probate"*

The word "probate" comes from the Latin "probatio," meaning proof. As applied to the law of wills, it means the proof or establishment, before the appropriate tribunal, that the document produced is the valid last will of the deceased. It also has the related or subsidiary meaning of the certification of such court that the will was executed by a competent testator in the manner prescribed by law. As various rights of many persons—heirs, devisees, legatees, personal representatives and others—

depend upon the validity or invalidity of the will, it is extremely convenient that this fact should be established once and for all in a single proceeding, subject to appropriate review. Hence, it is desirable that the probate process should be in rem or effective against the whole world, and not, as in case of the determination of most questions of law and fact, binding merely upon the parties to the particular action. As a means of protection of the interested parties against the possible inconsistency of successive determinations of the will's validity and also as a time-saving device, one adjudication is generally made conclusive on every one.[1] This judicial determination is called the probate of the will.

*The English Practice*

So far as wills concerned devises of land, the English common-law practice did not require, nor even permit, probate in this in rem sense. A party who relied upon a will to establish his right to realty simply alleged and proved the existence and validity of the document in the action whenever the matter came into controversy, just as if the will was a deed.[2] The instrument was produced at the trial and its execution was proved by the attesting witnesses or proof of their signatures as it would be in case of a conveyance inter vivos. Other witnesses might be called as to the various issues concerning execution, revocation, testamentary capacity or the like. These questions were apt to arise in an action of ejectment wherein one of the parties relied upon the will as a muniment of title. The same will might be involved in several such actions. Unless the parties to the successive suits were the same so that the principles of res judicata applied, it was possible that in one action the will might be sustained while in the next proceeding it would be held invalid.[3] Successive actions

1 See infra note 12.

2 See Ash v. Calvert, 2 Camp. 387, 170 Eng.Rep. 1193, 1810; Simes, The Function of Will Contests, 44 Mich. L.R. 503, 506; references infra note 21; supra § 3 at notes 74–75, 79, 86–87.

3 This happened in New York, where the common-law method of proof of wills of realty was retained. "In the famous case of Stewart's Ex'r v. Lispenard, 26 Wend. 255, the Court of Errors held the testator competent to execute a will and the personalty passed under it, while in an action of ejectment a jury found that the testator was incompetent and the realty passed as in case of intestacy. See Delafield v. Parish, 25 N.Y. 9." In re Goldsticker's Will, 192 N.Y. 35, 84 N.E. 581, 18 L.R.A.,N.S., 99, 15 Ann. Cas. 66, 1908. In this state title to real estate passing by devise can be established either by probate of the will or by proof of the same in the manner permitted at common law. Bouton v. Fleharty, 215 App.Div. 180, 213 N.Y.S. 455, 1926.

at law or suits in equity might result in incongruous holdings as to the validity of a single will of land if different devises and parties were involved in the various proceedings. This was due to the fact that the evidence might be different in the various cases and, in addition, the same showing might not be equally persuasive to all courts and juries.

Testaments of personalty, on the other hand, were probated in the ecclesiastical courts which had jurisdiction over the deceased's chattels and originally supervised their distribution.[4] Here probate was of the in rem sort. It was an adjudication that the will was executed in the manner prescribed and by a testator who was competent and had not revoked the instrument. These matters could not be drawn into question later except in proceedings brought to review the order.

There were two forms of probate in early times. The first was called probate in common form, in which the executor or another person desiring to establish the will produced it and proved its execution by his own oath or such other witnesses as might be required, without giving notice to the other persons interested in establishing or defeating the instrument. The second method was the solemn form or probate per testes where the interested parties were given notice and opportunity to be heard and the witnesses were examined more thoroughly. When there was probate in solemn form there could be no re-examination except on appeal, but the common form might be called into question at any time within thirty years. and probate per testes required. The latter method was more expensive and time-consuming, and hence was used only where there was a suspicion regarding the validity of the will or where a caveat or protest was entered to probate in common form.[5]

Often the same will disposed of both lands and chattels. In this situation the ecclesiastical court would probate the instrument so far as it affected personalty. This action had no effect as to realty devised, and with respect to the latter the will would have to be proved as if it were a deed in each proceeding at law and in equity wherein it was necessary to establish title to lands

[4] See supra § 3. The ecclesiastical courts' jurisdiction regarding probate of testaments is very ancient, 3 Bl. Com. 96; see Setaro, A Prologue to a History of the English Ecclesiastical Law, 16 B.U.L.R. 358.

[5] Waters v. Stickney, 12 Allen (Mass.) 1, 90 Am.Dec. 122, 1866; Swinburne on Testaments and Wills VI, § 14; 2 Bl.Com. 508; Simes, The Function of Will Contests, 44 Mich. L.R. 502, 509.

formerly owned by the testator.[6] Since 1857, the English law[7] has permitted and indeed required all wills of both realty and personalty to be probated in the newly created court of probate. Thus, the general in rem procedure of the ecclesiastical court is now in effect as to all wills and testaments.

*American Courts and Methods of Probate*

In America there were never ecclesiastical courts with lay jurisdiction.[8] Here the probate power has always been vested in secular tribunals,[9] usually called probate courts though sometimes the name surrogate's, orphans', or prerogative court, or court of ordinary, has been used. There is generally one such court to each county. Sometimes probate jurisdiction is conferred upon the regular county court, or upon tribunals of general trial jurisdiction. Courts of chancery have no general probate powers,[10] though in some states they have jurisdiction in case of lost wills.[11]

Long before the step was taken in England, most states had adopted the in rem method of probate, regardless of whether the will disposed of realty or personalty or both.[12] Of course

[6] See Montgomery v. Clark, 2 Atk. 379, 26 Eng.Rep. 629, 1742.

[7] 20 & 21 Vict. c. 77, § 13. See supra § 3 at notes 86–87.

[8] Bordwell, An Introduction to Wills and Administration, 14 Minn. L.R. 1, 44; see Simes and Basye, The Organization of the Probate Court in America, 42 Mich.L.R. 965, 43 ibid. 113; supra § 4, note 41 et seq.

[9] See supra § 4, notes 41–46.

[10] Kaplan v. Coleman, 180 Ala. 267, 60 So. 885, 1912 (statute); Cousens v. Advent Church of City of Biddeford, 93 Me. 292, 45 A. 43, 1899; infra § 96, note 9. Cf. Sumner v. Staton, 151 N.C. 198, 65 S.E. 902, 18 Ann.Cas. 802, 1909; Alfred University v. Frace, 193 App.Div. 279, 184 N.Y.S. 216, 1920. As to the jurisdiction of Federal courts, see Atwood v. Rhode Island Hospital Trust Co., 34 F.2d 18, C.C.A.R.I., 1929; cf. Fakouri v. Cadais, 147 F.2d 667, C.C.A.La., 1945 and infra § 98, notes 9–12; § 107, notes 4, 5.

[11] See infra § 97, notes 4–6.

[12] This is the usual concept, though to the extent that notice is required and particularly if the notice must be personal, it is possible to say that the jurisdiction is quasi in rem, since for want of due notice probate may be set aside or even attacked collaterally. Though the view has been expressed that the will or testamentary status is the res, it is usually to regard the decedent's property within the jurisdiction as the res. Indeed, it is reasonable to regard all procedural steps from probate or grant of letters through final settlement as a single proceeding in rem for the purpose of jurisdiction. See Model Probate Code § 62; Simes, The Administration of a Decedent's Estate as a Proceeding in Rem, 43 Mich. L.R. 675; American Law of Property §§ 14.35, 14.37; infra §§ 94–96.

this is universal with regard to wills so far as they concern personalty. In all jurisdictions, wills of realty may now be established in the probate courts, though in a few a devisee may still prove the will without probate,[13] or the probate may not be conclusive as to devises of realty.[14] However, these qualifications are waning even in the few states in which they may still exist.

## LIMITATIONS UPON PROBATE

**94. Wills may not be probated, nor their validity adjudged, until after the testator's death.**

**In most jurisdictions there is no time limit within which a will may be probated. Statutes sometimes protect good faith purchasers from the heirs and some states prohibit probate after a designated number of years. The effect of provisions of the latter sort is to allow the property to pass under the intestate laws if the limitation period has expired.**

**The primary place of probate is in the state and county in which testator was domiciled at the time of his death. Afterward the will may be admitted to probate in other states where the deceased left property. Except for statutory modifications, domiciliary probate is conclusive everywhere so far as concerns personalty, but not with regard to lands in other jurisdictions.**

### *Probate Prior to Testator's Death*

As wills are revocable until death, they may not be finally set up as the testator's will until after his decease. There would be certain advantages in establishing, or at least preserving evidence of, the facts of execution, mental capacity,[1] absence of fraud and undue influence in the testator's lifetime when he might be sworn as a witness. Many unmerited will contests might be avoided by this procedure. A Michigan statute designed to make it possible for a testator to establish his will, except as to the possibility of subsequent revocation, was declared unconstitutional largely for the reason that the persons named as heirs

13 Bouton v. Fleharty, supra note 3.

14 McDevitt v. Deacon, 83 N.J.L. 712, 85 A. 186, 1912; see 5 Clapp, New Jersey Practice, Wills and Administration §§ 93, 95. See infra § 96, note 14.

1 See Hulbert, Probate Psychiatry—A Neuro-Psychiatric Examination of Testator from the Psychiatric Viewpoint, 25 Ill.L.R. 288; Stephens, Probate Psychiatry—Examination of Testamentary Capacity as a Subscribing Witness, 25 Ill.L.Rev. 276.

at law might not be so at testator's death when the will became effective.[2] The defects of this statute might be remedied.[3] It is possible that a proceeding under the declaratory judgment acts might be used for this purpose. The possibilities are little explored, however,[4] and we must await changes in legislation or judicial attitude before there will be ante-mortem probate.

Frequently it is provided by statute that a testator may deposit his will with the probate court, or officer thereof.[5] This legislation is designed to prevent loss of the will and to minimize claims of forgery or alteration thereof. Deposit by the testator under such statute is in no sense probate of the will, and after testator's death the usual formalities are required just as in case of wills not deposited. In the lifetime of the testator, no action will lie against a custodian of a will for cancellation of the same upon the ground that testator did not possess testamentary capacity.[6]

*Time Limitations on Probate*

Most jurisdictions have no statutory period within which a will may be established. The probate process is a "proceeding," as distinguished from an "action," so that the general Statute of Limitations is not usually held to apply.[7] In absence of legislation there is no time limit after testator's death within which a will may be probated.[8] Statutes often require the executor or

[2] Lloyd v. Wayne Circuit Judge, 56 Mich. 236, 23 N.W. 28, 56 Am.Rep. 378, 1885. See also Kellogg v. White, 103 Misc. 167, 169 N.Y.S. 989, modified 186 App.Div. 911, 172 N.Y.S. 548, 1918.

[3] See Cavers, Ante Mortem Probate, 1 U. of Chi.L.R. 440; Kutscher, Living Probate, 21 A.B.A.J. 427; Kutscher, Living Probate—Further Considerations, 70 U.S.L.R. 133; note by H. C. Lewis, 50 Am.L.R. 742; Redfearn, Ante-Mortem Probate, 38 Com. L.J. 571; 1948 Annual Surv.Am.L. 758.

[4] See American Law of Property § 14.2. Declaratory judgment laws are frequently used to obtain construction of probated wills. Ibid. § 14.42; infra § 145.

[5] See Model Probate Code § 59 and comment thereto.

[6] Pond v. Faust, 90 Wash. 117, 155 P. 776, Ann.Cas.1918A, 736, 1917.

[7] In re Hume's Estate, 179 Cal. 338, 176 P. 681, 1918; Barnhardt v. Morrison, 178 N.C. 563, 101 S.E. 218, 1919; Alsobrook v. Orr, 130 Tenn. 120, 169 S.W. 1165, Ann.Cas.1915B, 627, 1914. And see cases cited infra note 8. But see Gwinn v. Melvin, 9 Idaho 202, 72 P. 961, 108 Am.St Rep. 119, 2 Ann.Cas. 770, 1903; Thompson v. Penn, 149 Ky. 158, 148 S.W. 33, 1912; Bryan v. Seiffert, 185 Okl. 496, 94 P.2d 526, 1939.

[8] Cole v. Shelton, 169 Ark. 695, 276 S.W. 993, 43 A.L.R. 1008, 1925; Walden v. Mahnks, 178 Ga. 825, 174 S.E. 538, 95 A.L.R. 1101, 1934 (even after estate has been administered as if intestate); Peter v. Peter, 343 Ill. 493, 175 N.E. 846, 75 A.L.R. 890, 1931; Shumway v. Holbrook, 1 Pick.(Mass.)

the custodian to deliver the will to the probate court within a certain period after testator's death and impose a penalty or forfeiture for failure to do so.[9] These, however, do not prevent the probate of the will after this period.[10]

Bona fide purchasers from the heirs at law are often protected by statute if they purchase the land before probate of the will and more than a designated number of years after the testator's death.[11] Under this type of legislation the buyer may safely assume that the decedent died intestate when no will has been probated within the time limit. In absence of statutes of this type, such purchasers are not usually protected,[12] though the contrary has been held in at least one case.[13] The protection afforded these persons does not prevent the probate of the will. The will may be officially established, though this adjudication does not affect the rights of the innocent purchasers from the heirs at law. Where the parties interested in the probate of the will have been guilty of laches, or in other words where the case is one involving more than mere delay, probate has been denied.[14]

In a few jurisdictions there are statutes forbidding probate after a certain length of time. These will be given effect, and if the period has elapsed, the decedent's property will pass under the intestate laws as the instrument can no longer be established.[15]

114, 11 Am.Dec. 153, 1822; Haddock v. Boston & M. R. Co., 146 Mass. 155, 15 N.E. 495, 4 Am.St.Rep. 295, 1888 (after sixty-three years); Belt v. Adams, 125 Miss. 387, 87 So. 666, 1921. And see note 7 supra. But see Van Giesen v. Bridgford, 83 N.Y. 348, 1881, and cases infra note 14.

9 See Wohlfort v. Wohlfort, 123 Kan. 142, 254 P. 334, 1927 (loss of devise); Foote v. Foote, 61 Mich. 181, 28 N.W. 90, 1886. See infra § 95 at notes 4, 5.

10 In re Miller's Estate, 115 Cal. App. 109, 300 P. 975, 1931; Peter v. Peter, supra note 8; Moore v. Samuelson, 107 Kan. 744, 193 P. 369, 1920. But see Foote v. Foote, supra note 9, and infra § 95 at notes 4, 5, 11, 12.

11 Fox v. Fee, 167 N.Y. 44, 60 N.E. 281, 1901. Such a statute is not retroactive. Barnhardt v. Morrison, supra note 7.

12 Cole v. Shelton, supra note 8; Reid's Adm'r v. Benge, 112 Ky. 810, 66 S.W. 997, 57 L.R.A. 253, 99 Am.St. Rep. 334, 1902; Cooley v. Lee, 170 N.C. 18, 86 S.E. 720, 1915.

13 Wright v. Eakin, 151 Tenn. 681, 270 S.W. 992, 1924, noted, 10 Minn. L.R. 168. For cases where there has been a prior adjudication of intestacy, see infra § 96.

14 Allnutt v. Wood, 176 Ark. 537, 3 S.W.2d 298, 1928, (lost will); Hayes v. Simmons, 136 Okl. 206, 277 P. 213, 1929.

15 Gilbert v. Partain, 222 Ala. 459, 133 So. 2, 1931; State ex rel. Bier v. Bigger, 352 Mo. 502, 178 S.W.2d 347, 1944; cf. In re Smith, 144 Me. 235, 67 A.2d 529, 1949, noted, 48 Mich. L.R. 725 (lost will). And see Kentucky and Idaho cases cited supra note 7 and also note 18 infra.

Some of these statutes make an exception where there is an excuse for the delay; [16] others admit no exceptions.[17] Often statutes provide that nuncupative wills of personalty must be proved within six months after testator's death. This, of course, is a time limitation upon the probate of such wills and after the specified time the oral will cannot be established.[18]

*Territorial Jurisdiction*

Two sets of principles run parallel to a considerable degree to the law of territorial jurisdiction regarding probate of wills. One of these is the body of conflict of laws principles regarding administration of decedents' estates, which matter is discussed hereafter.[19] The other is the body of substantive law principles which determine what law governs testate and intestate succession when the decedent leaves property in more than one jurisdiction. The general common law of this matter is that the law of the decedent's domicile is applied to determine the rights of succession to his personalty, while the law of the situs of the property governs so far as his realty is concerned. For example, a will executed in accordance with the law of the testator's domicile is sufficient to pass his personalty located in another state or country, but realty will not pass under a will unless it was executed in accordance with the law of the situs of the land.[20] There are statutory deviations from this general rule. Thus, statutes commonly provide that a will is effective as to any local property if it is executed in accordance with either the local law, or the law of the testator's domicile, or of law of the place of execution.[21]

The primary place for probate of a will is in the jurisdiction wherein the testator was domiciled at the time of his death. Indeed a court in another jurisdiction may deny probate until there has been probate at the domicile, unless some good reason appears for absence of the latter.[22] Probate at the place of the last dom-

16 Owens v. Felty, 227 S.W.2d 379, Tex.Civ.App. 1950.

17 Gilbert v. Partain, supra note 15.

18 In re Brown's Estate, 101 Wash. 314, 172 P. 247, 1918. See generally supra § 76.

19 See infra § 106.

20 Restatement, Conflict of Laws, §§ 249, 306; Goodrich, Conflict of Laws, 3d Ed. §§ 166, 168. Indeed the law of the situs governs most of the matters of succession to land. See American Law of Property § 14.45.

21 See Hopkins, The Extraterritorial Effect of Probate Decrees, 53 Yale L.J. 221, 255; Model Probate Code § 50.

22 Davis v. Upson, 230 Ill. 327, 82 N.E. 824, 1907, noted, 2 Ill.L.R. 605; In re Corning's Estate, 159 Mich. 474, 124 N.W. 514, 1910; Rackemann v.

icile is usually held to be conclusive as to the validity of the bequests of personalty located elsewhere.[23] This means that nondomiciliary states will accept the domiciliary probate and will not permit a local contest. It has even been asserted that this recognition is necessary in case of sister states under the full faith and credit clause of the United States Constitution,[24] but this is probably an overstatement since the probate decree is not inter partes.

In absence of local statute a court is not concluded as to devises of land by probate in the foreign domiciliary jurisdiction.[25] This of course runs parallel to the principles governing the substantive common-law principles for execution of devises. Indeed even if a statute has provided for recognition of the substantive law of the domicile, probate by the domiciliary court need not be recognized and a local contest may be entertained.[26]

Statutes usually make provision for recording or probating of foreign wills.[27] Frequently a nonresident's will, probated in the state of his domicile, may be admitted to probate upon the production of a duly authenticated copy of the foreign probate, with-

Taylor, 204 Mass. 394, 90 N.E. 552, 1910; In re Holden's Estate, 110 Vt. 60, 1 A.2d 721, 119 A.L.R. 487, 1938.

In Parnell v. Thompson, 81 Kan. 119, 105 P. 502, 33 L.R.A.,N.S., 658, 1909, noted, 23 Harv.L.Rev. 467, where the testator, domiciled in England, left both an English and an American will, it was held that the latter could be probated in Kansas though it was not established in England. Cf. In the Estate of Todd, [1926] Prob. 173, 135 L.T.N.S. 381.

23 Goodman v. Winter, 64 Ala. 410, 38 Am.Rep. 13, 1879; Evansville Ice and Cold Storage Co. v. Winsor, 148 Ind. 682, 48 N.E. 592, 1897; In re Coppock's Estate, 72 Mont. 431, 234 P. 258, 39 A.L.R. 1152, 1925; Grignon v. Shope, 100 Or. 611, 197 P. 317, 1921; Martin v. Stovall, 103 Tenn. 1, 52 S.W. 296, 48 L.R.A. 130, 1899 (promissory notes secured by real estate mortgage); Ives v. Salisbury's Heirs, 56 Vt. 565, 1884. But see In re Gifford's Will, 279 N.Y. 470, 18 N.E.2d 663, 1939; Bowen v. Johnson, 5 R.I. 112, 73 Am.Dec. 49, 1858.

24 Evansville Ice & Cold Storage Co. v. Winsor, Ives v. Salisbury's Heirs, and Grignon v. Shope, all supra note 23.

25 Selle v. Rapp, 143 Ark. 192, 220 S.W. 662, 13 A.L.R. 494, 1920; Trotter v. Van Pelt, 141 Fla. 517, 198 So. 215, 131 A.L.R. 1018, 1940; Woodville v. Pizzati, 119 Miss. 442, 81 So. 127, 1919; Keith v. Keith, 97 Mo. 223, 10 S.W. 597, 1889; Kirkland v. Calhoun, 147 Tenn. 388, 248 S.W. 302, 1922. The full faith and credit clause does not apply, as the probate court has no jurisdiction as to foreign realty. Selle v. Rapp, Kirkland v. Calhoun, both supra. Contra: Bowen v. Johnson, 5 R.I. 112, 73 Am.Dec. 49, 1858; Holland v. Jackson, 121 Tex. 1, 37 S.W.2d 726, 1931, both holding domiciliary probate conclusive. See infra § 145, note 21 et seq.

26 See In re Gifford's Will, supra note 23; In re Barrie's Estate, infra note 29; Sternberg v. St. Louis Union Trust Co., infra note 28.

27 See Hopkins, supra note 21 at 258 et seq.; Carey, A Suggested

out other proof or notice. In other jurisdictions there must be notice to the persons interested. Under such statutes, the decisions are conflicting as to whether the will probated in another state may be contested so far as it concerns local realty.[28] Recently a revised Uniform Probate of Foreign Wills Act has been promulgated. It provides for recognition of the domiciliary probate of any written will, and likewise for recognition of the domiciliary rejection from probate unless the will was rejected upon grounds insufficient for rejection under the local law.[29]

Even though a court recognizes the domiciliary probate when personalty is involved, or because of statute provision in other cases, it is not bound by the prior determination of a court of another jurisdiction that the decedent died domiciled in the latter.[30] With regard to any property located within the local jurisdiction it is permissible to find that the testator was domiciled locally, and if this is done the contrary determination of domicile elsewhere and the consequent probate will be disregarded as to local property. The only important qualification to this is found in the cases where persons are precluded on principles of res judicata when they have already litigated the question of domicile in the other forum.[31]

Fundamental Basis of Jurisdiction with Special Emphasis on Judicial Proceedings Affecting Decedents' Estates, 24 Ill.L.R. 44, 53 et seq.

28 That it may be contested: Selle v. Rapp, supra note 25; Sternberg v. St. Louis Union Trust Co., 394 Ill. 452, 68 N.E.2d 892, 169 A.L.R. 545, 1946, noted, 25 Chi-Kent L.R. 353; Evansville Ice & Cold Storage Co. v. Winsor, supra, note 23; In re Gifford's Will, supra note 23 (unless all interested persons were made parties); In re Barrie's Estate, infra note 29. That the foreign probate is conclusive: Roach v. Jurchak, 182 Md. 646, 35 A.2d 817, 1944; State ex rel. Ruef v. District Court of Twelfth Judicial Dist., 34 Mont. 96, 85 P. 866, 6 L.R.A.,N.S., 617, 115 Am.St.Rep. 510, 9 Ann.Cas. 418, 1906; Simpson v. Cornish, 196 Wis. 125, 218 N.W. 193, 1928. See Stull v. Veatch, 236 Ill. 207, 86 N.E. 227, 1908, noted, 3 Ill. L.R. 534.

29 See In re Barrie's Estate, 240 Iowa 431, 35 N.W.2d 658, 9 A.L.R 2d 1399, 1949, dealing with rejection of probate at the domicile on account of revocation of the will.

30 Estate of Clark, 148 Cal. 108, 82 P. 760, 1 L.R.A.,N.S., 996, 113 Am.St. Rep. 197, 7 Ann.Cas. 306, 1905; In re Gifford's Will, supra note 23; McEwen v. McEwen, 50 N.D. 662, 197 N.W. 862, 1924; Holland v. Jackson, supra note 25. See Texas v. Florida, 306 U.S. 398, 59 S.Ct. 563, 83 L.Ed. 817, 121 A.L.R. 1179, 1939 (succession taxes); Riley v. New York Trust Co., 315 U.S. 343, 62 S.Ct. 608, 86 L.Ed. 885, 1942. Contra: Kurtz v. Stenger, 169 Md. 554, 182 A. 456, 1936.

31 Willett's Appeal, 50 Conn. 330, 1882; Lowenthal v. Mandell, 125 Fla. 685, 170 So. 169, 1936; cf. In re Fischer's Estate, 118 N.J.Eq. 599, 180 A. 633, 1936; In re Gifford's Will, supra note 23; Riley v. New York Trust Co., supra note 30. See infra § 107, notes 11, 12.

*County Venue*

Up to this point we have been concerned with the situation where the testator leaves property in one or more states or countries. There is properly only one probate in each state even though the decedent left property in two or more counties thereof. The proper county within the State for grant of probate is a matter of venue. In case of a resident of the state, under the statutory provisions generally probate should be in the county of the testator's domicile at the time of his death. There is considerable statutory divergence as to the county venue when the decedent was domiciled outside the state, although usually it is the county in which he left property or some designated kind or amount thereof.[32] According to the modern law probate by the first court wherein application is made or probate is granted precludes proceedings in other courts of the same state; [33] and determination of domicile is not jurisdictional as in case of interstate controversy over domicile.[34] This matter is more fully considered in connection with venue for grant of administration.[35] The problem is essentially the same.

32 See Basye, The Venue of Probate and Administration Proceedings, 43 Mich.L.R. 471, 476, 477.

33 Ibid. at 482 et seq. See Model Probate Code § 61; Bolton v. Schriever, 135 N.Y. 65, 31 N.E. 1001, 18 L.R.A. 242, 1892.

34 See supra note 30.

35 See infra § 107, note 6 et seq.

## PROCEDURE IN PROBATE OF WILL

**95. It is the duty of the one who has possession of the will at testator's death to produce it. The executor is the customary person to petition for its admission to probate, though if he does not do so the will may be propounded by any other interested person.**

**The petition for probate is usually in writing and should contain the jurisdictional allegations and other facts specified by statute.**

**Notice of the petition by personal service or publication is usually required to be made upon the interested parties, though many jurisdictions permit probate in common form without notice.**

**In an uncontested probate, the proponent should offer proof of notice of the hearing, if required by law, and also of the jurisdictional facts together with such evidence of due execution of the will as the local practice requires.**

**The duly executed will should be admitted to probate regardless of whether it consists of one or several instruments, or whether the provisions thereof are otherwise valid or invalid.**

### *Who should Produce and Propound the Will*

It is for the executor to produce the will if it is within his custody. He, as well as any other custodian of the instrument, is under a legal duty not to suppress the instrument.[1] Statutes often provide that interested persons may cause a citation to issue to parties suspected of concealing the will to show cause why it should not be produced.[2] Under some legislation the concealment or destruction of a will subjects the guilty party to criminal liability.[3] It is often provided that failure to produce a will within a certain time is reason for imposition of a penalty or

1 In re Hyde's Estate, 190 Wash. 88, 66 P.2d 856, 1937; In re Hawley's Estate, 118 W.Va. 144, 189 S.E. 305, 1937. Testator's attorney cannot assert a retaining lien for unpaid services. In re Croker's Will, 201 Misc. 264, 105 N.Y.S.2d 190, 1951, noted, 37 Corn.L.Q. 336, 27 N.Y.U.L.R. 342; In re French's Will, 115 N.Y.S.2d 289, 1952.

2 In re Hardy, 216 N.Y. 132, 110 N.E. 257, 1915. See Williams v. Bailey, 177 N.C. 37, 97 S.E. 721, 1919.

3 See Walch v. Orrell, 53 Colo. 361, 127 P. 141, 1912.

forfeiture,[4] though these provisions have been held not to apply to a mere casual possessor.[5]

The person named as executor is the logical person to petition for probate of the will.[6] He may do so even if he is not competent to act as personal representative, or is unwilling to accept the trust.[7] However, he is under no imperative legal duty to propound the will,[8] as distinguished from his obligation to produce it if it is in his custody.[9] Any other interested person may offer the will for probate, if the executor does not.[10] It is not necessary that the proponent benefit under the will; it is sufficient that he is interested in the estate and desires to start the proceeding for settlement along proper lines. Parties who would normally be interested persons in the establishment of the will may be estopped by their laches,[11] or other conduct,[12] from propounding it.

Some one must offer the will; the court will not ordinarily probate it on its own motion.[13] However, the propounder is not

4 Wohlfort v. Wohlfort, 123 Kan. 142, 254 P. 334, 1927 (forfeiture); Moore v. Smith, 5 Me. 490, 1830 (penalty); Foote v. Foote, 61 Mich. 181, 28 N.W. 90, 1886; Barron v. McCann, 25 Ohio App. 520, 159 N.E. 104, 1927 (forfeiture). For damage actions, see Scholen v. Guaranty Trust Co., 288 N.Y. 249, 43 N.E.2d 28, 141 A.L.R. 1273, 1942.

5 Barney v. Barney, 192 Mich. 45, 158 N.W. 101, 1916; Myers v. Exchange Nat. Bank, 96 Wash. 244, 164 P. 951, L.R.A.1918A 67, 1917. Cf. Britton v. Elk Valley Bank of Larimore, 54 N.D. 858, 211 N.W. 810, 50 A.L.R. 243, 1926. Nor does the statute apply to foreign wills. Oklahoma City University v. Baughman, 148 Kan. 510, 83 P.2d 681, 119 A.L.R. 1255, 1938.

6 Smith's Estate v. Davis, 168 Kan. 210, 212 P.2d 322, 1949; In re Gunderman's Estate, 102 Neb. 590, 168 N.W. 359, 1918.

7 Ratcliffe v. Seaboard Nat. Bank, 46 S.W.2d 750, Tex.Civ.App.1932.

8 Dodd v. Anderson, 197 N.Y. 466, 90 N.E. 1137, 27 L.R.A.,N.S., 336, 18 Ann.Cas. 738, 1910; note, 8 U. of Pitts.L.R. 146.

9 Supra note 1.

10 In re Witt's Will, 120 Kan. 200, 243 P. 296, 1926 (remainderman under will); Taylor v. Martin's Estate, 117 Tex. 302, 3 S.W.2d 408, 1928 (contingent legatee); In re Rankin's Estate, 164 Cal. 138, 127 P. 1034, 1912 (assignee of beneficiary); Matter of Tracy's Estate, 143 Misc. 800, 258 N.Y.S. 657, 1932 (spouse though not named in the will); Matter of Enright's Will, 109 Misc. 337, 179 N.Y.S. 757, 1919 (heir at law); In re Hyde's Estate, supra note 1 (creditor); Weaver v. Hughes, 26 Tenn.App. 436, 173 S.W.2d 159, 1943 (devisee of devisee). But see Logan v. Thomason, 146 Tex. 37, 202 S.W.2d 212, 1947 (creditor of testator).

11 Dowd v. Dowd, 62 Idaho 631, 115 P.2d 409, 135 A.L.R. 1213, 1941, noted, 90 U. of Pa.L.R. 373; Foote v. Foote, 61 Mich. 181, 28 N.W. 90, 1886.

12 In re Szalkiewicz's Will, 199 Misc. 262, 100 N.Y.S.2d 410, 1950.

13 Matter of Billet's Estate, 187 App.Div. 309, 175 N.Y.S. 482, 1919.

like the plaintiff in an ordinary civil action, for he may not withdraw the proceeding or take a nonsuit.[14] While some one must initiate the matter, there are strictly speaking no parties to the proceeding as it is in the nature of an action in rem for the benefit of all interested persons.[15]

*Petition for Probate*

Filing of the will has been held sufficient to initiate proceedings for probate,[16] but it is customary to file a petition for this purpose. Statutes are sometimes construed to require a written application,[17] and it is always desirable that this be done.[18] Frequently blank forms are provided by the court for this purpose, and when these exist, their use in drafting the petition is an aid to the keeping of records in the probate office. In absence of statute no particular form of petition is required and an objection to a petition for letters of administration on the ground that the testator died testate, accompanied by the alleged will, may be treated as an application for the probate of the latter.[19]

Statutes often enumerate the allegations which should be contained in the petition. The jurisdictional facts should be alleged, such as the testator's death,[20] and his domicile in the county at the time of his decease.[21] It is good practice to set forth the names, relationships, and residences of the heirs at law, and some states require this to be done if known.[22] It has been held that

Cf. Simmons v. Campbell, Tex.Civ. App., 213 S.W. 338, 1919 (statute). And see Woerner on Administration, 3d Ed., 701, 702.

14 In re Raymond's Estate, 38 Cal. App.2d 305, 100 P.2d 1085, 1940; In re Tresidder's Estate, 70 Wash. 15, 125 P. 1034, 1912. But see King v. Westervelt, 284 Ill. 401, 120 N.E. 241, 1918. In its discretion the court may allow withdrawal of the petition. In re Pynchon's Will, 115 Vt. 217, 55 A. 2d 519, 173 A.L.R. 957, 1947; see In re Lasak, 131 N.Y. 624, 30 N.E. 112, 1892.

15 In re Raymond's Estate, supra note 14; In re Hinton's Will, 180 N. C. 206, 104 S.E. 341, 1920.

16 In re Hermence's Estate, 235 Iowa 745, 15 N.W.2d 905, 1944. See In re Peirce's Estate, 63 Wash. 437, 115 P. 835, 1911 (where will was on file in probate court at testator's death).

17 Crossman v. Crossman, 95 N.Y. 145, 1884; In re Burke's Estate, 66 Or. 252, 134 P. 11, 1913.

18 In re Hermence's Estate, supra note 16.

19 Harris v. McDonald, 152 Ga. 18, 108 S.E. 448, 1921.

20 Bradshaw v. Roberts, 52 S.W. 574, Tex.Civ.App.1899 (but a reference to him as deceased is enough).

21 Alden v. Superior Court of Los Angeles County, 186 Cal. 309, 199 P. 29, 1921.

22 Matter of Clark's Estate, 144 Misc. 705, 259 N.Y.S. 377, 1932. See

testamentary capacity of the deceased need not be alleged in the petition.[23] In general, a petition need not contain anything except what the statute requires.[24] Normally the alleged will should accompany the petition.[25]

*Notice*

In more than a third of our states wills may be probated without giving notice to the heirs at law or other interested persons.[26] Here the probate is an ex parte proceeding, and in this respect similar to the probate in common form of the ecclesiastical courts.[27] No citation of any parties is necessary either by personal service or by publication of the notice. The court obtains jurisdiction to probate the will simply by reason of the fact that the executor or some other person presents the will together with a petition for its establishment.[28]

Most states, however, require some sort of notice to be given to interested parties.[29] Some of the statutes require personal service upon the persons who can be reached within the state,[30] but make notice by publication sufficient in other cases.[31] Other jurisdictions permit service by publication even as to parties who are residents.[32] Notice by publication is adapted to probate pro-

Bailey v. Gates, 52 Nev. 432, 53 id. 477, 290 P. 411, 1930 (where some of heirs were unknown.) But see infra note 24.

23 Hathway's Appeal, 46 Mich. 326, 9 N.W. 435, 1881; Lindemann v. Dobossy, 107 S.W. 111, Tex.Civ.App.1908. Cf. In re Strelow's Estate, 117 Neb. 168, 220 N.W. 251, 1928.

24 Shaffer v. Luby's Estate, 297 S.W. 582, Tex.Civ.App.1927 (names and residences of heirs); Brown v. Hawkins, 219 Ark. 239, 240 S.W.2d 863. 1951.

25 In re De Buck's Estate, 125 N.J. Eq. 80, 4 A.2d 309, 1939.

26 See Woerner on Administration, 3d Ed., 707–711; note, 43 Mich.L.R. 1153. Some question has been raised as to the validity of this procedure in the light of Mullane v. Central Hanover Bank & Trust Co., 339 U.S. 306, 70 S.Ct. 652, 94 L.Ed. 865, 1950. See Levy, Probate in Common Form in the United States: The Problem of Notice in Probate Proceedings, [1952] Wis.L.R. 420; cf. note, 50 Mich.L.R. 124; Model Probate Code §§ 14, 62, 66, 68–70, 73, 74.

27 See references supra note 26; also supra § 93 at note 4.

28 State ex rel. Mitchell v. Gideon, 215 Mo.App. 46, 237 S.W. 220, 1922. See Wells v. Odum, 205 N.C. 110, 170 S.E. 145, 1933. But one in military service may be entitled to relief, see infra § 96 at note 11.

29 See supra note 26.

30 In re Gahn's Will, 110 Misc. 96, 180 N.Y.S. 262, 1920; Matter of Bloss' Will, 130 Misc. 786, 226 N.Y.S. 441, 1928.

31 See Matter of Norwood's Estate, 111 Misc. 530, 181 N.Y.S. 494, 1920.

32 Renwick v. Macomber, 233 Mass. 530, 124 N.E. 670, 1919 (mailing of

ceedings as the latter are in rem for the judicial establishment of the will, and do not look toward a personal judgment. The persons notified are not regarded as defendants but only as possible objectors.

Where the required notice is entirely lacking, or is faulty in some essential particular, the court is sometimes said to be without jurisdiction to proceed with the probate.[33] Any interested person may have the probate set aside for failure to comply with the requirements of notice,[34] though if the applicant for nullification of the probate appeared at the hearing, want or insufficiency of the notice is not ground for vacation of the probate decree.[35] In the case of notice by publication it is said that there must be strict compliance with the statute.[36]

In many jurisdictions it is necessary to appoint a guardian ad litem if there is a minor or incompetent person interested in the estate, and indeed this may be true even if there is no will. The obligations of the guardian ad litem are real—he is under duty to see that the full rights of the ward are protected; but on the other hand he should not be compensated for raising fanciful objections in the alleged interests of the ward.

*Hearing of Uncontested Probate*

When there is no opposition to the probate of a will, the showing required to be made to the court is not a burdensome one. If the proceeding partakes of the nature of probate in solemn form, i. e., if notice is required of the petition, there should be proof of the service, whether it be personal or by publication.[37]

notice to interested persons is also required, but it is not necessary that copy reached the party); Shaffer v. Luby's Estate, 297 S.W. 582, Tex.Civ. App.1927. As to constitutionality, see supra note 26.

33 Travers v. Lavender, 81 A.2d 44, Md.1951; Scholl v. Scholl, 123 Ohio St. 1, 173 N.E. 305, 1930; In re Hegarty's Estate, 45 Nev. 145, 199 P. 81, 1921. But see In re Price's Estate, 230 Iowa 1228, 300 N.W. 542, 1941 (substantial compliance).

34 McGee v. Vandeventer, 326 Ill. 425, 158 N.E. 127, 1927; Young v. Guella, 67 Ohio App. 11, 35 N.E.2d 997, 1941. And see authorities cited infra note 33.

35 In re Ricks' Estate, 160 Cal. 467, 117 P. 539, 1911; Stead v. Curtis, 191 F. 529, C.C.A.Cal., 1911. See note, 18 So.Cal.L.R. 1315. As to the effect of sufficient notice as to some but not all, see American Law of Property § 14.37.

36 See authorities supra note 30; In re Hegarty's Estate, supra note 33. But see In re Price's Estate, supra note 33; Donnell v. Goss, 269 Mass. 214, 169 N.E. 150, 1930; Brown v. Hawkins, supra note 24.

37 In re Charlebois' Estate, 6 Mont. 373, 12 P. 775, 1887 (court has no authority to hear testimony without proof of notice); Heminway v. Reynolds, 98 Wis. 501, 74 N.W. 350, 1908

At the hearing some one cognizant of the facts should testify to the death of the testator,[38] and also to his domicile.[39] Then a showing should be made that the instrument offered is the testator's will, signed by him and due compliance had with the statutory requirements for the execution of wills.[40] Probably also proof may be required of the testator's mental capacity. Execution and capacity should ordinarily be shown by the attesting witnesses if they are available.[41]

Some statutes provide that a will may be admitted upon the testimony of one subscribing witness.[42] According to the old procedure for probate in common form, not even this was required for the will could be admitted merely upon the oath of the executor.[43] However, the statutes sometimes contemplate the examination of all living attesting witnesses.[44] If none of the attestors are available, the will may be established by proof of their signatures and such other evidence of execution as may be had.[45]

Naturally there is no great body of precedents as to the exact proof required in uncontested cases. The proponent of the will, having no opponent, need only satisfy the court.[46] The form and extent of the required proof varies from state to state and from court to court in the same jurisdiction. Unless one is familiar with the practice in the particular tribunal, he should be prepared at the hearing to offer a complete showing of the jurisdictional matters as well as the proper execution of the will, and

(proof required though no statutory provision therefor).

38 See Pond v. Faust, 90 Wash. 117, 155 P. 776, Ann.Cas.1918A 736, 1916. Cf. In re Sternkopf's Will, 72 N.J.Eq. 356, 65 A. 177, 1906 (proof of absence to satisfy statutory presumption of death is sufficient).

39 See Richards v. Huff, 146 Okl. 108, 293 P. 1028, 1931.

40 Gillis v. Gillis, 96 Ga. 1, 23 S.E. 107, 30 L.R.A. 143, 51 Am.St.Rep. 121, 1895. For example of testimony of a subscribing witness, see Deutsch and Balicer, How to Prove a Prima Facie Case, 145 et seq.

41 Gillis v. Gillis, supra note 40.

42 Polley v. Cline's Ex'r, 263 Ky. 659, 93 S.W.2d 363, 1936. See also Goodrich v. Hansom, 238 Mass. 313, 130 N.E. 675, 1921.

43 2 Bl.Com. 508.

44 See Hill v. Chicago Title & Trust Co., 322 Ill. 42, 152 N.E. 545, 1926; Cal.Prob.Code § 372; cf. N.Y.Surr.Ct. Act § 141 (two at least).

45 In re Blickensderfer's Will, 13 Ohio Supp. 93, 1944; In re Johnson's Will, 175 Wis. 1, 183 N.W. 888, 1921. For the effect of a proper attestation clause where direct evidence of execution is wanting, see supra § 72. For admissibility of evidence other than testimony of subscribing witnesses, see annotation, 63 A.L.R. 1195. And see infra, § 100, note 38.

46 See N.Y.Surr.Ct.Act § 144.

the competency of the testator. On the other hand, because of statutory provisions or the general attitude of probate courts toward wills, a proponent's burden may be considerably less onerous in that tribunal even when the will is opposed there, than in case of the trial of a will contest in the ordinary courts.[47]

*Libelous Matter*

Nondispositive parts of a will have been omitted from public probate records where they are scandalous or defamatory,[48] or contain military secrets.[49] There is no power in the probate court to expunge the objectionable words from the will itself,[50] relief being limited to their omission from the record.[51] Even the latter remedy should be granted sparingly,[52] and often it will be of very little benefit.[53]

*Invalidity of Provisions*

A portion of a will should not be rejected simply because it is invalid on account of violating the rule against perpetuities or of the incapacity of the beneficiary or the like.[54] Even if a will is totally ineffective, it should be admitted to probate if it is duly

47 See Ohio Gen.Code, §§ 10504–18, 10504–22; McWilliams v. Central Trust Co., 51 Ohio App. 246, 200 N.E. 532, 1935; note, 2 Ohio St.L.J. 292.

48 Matter of Bomar's Will, 18 N.Y.S. 214, 27 Abb.N.C. 425, 44 St.R. 304, 1892 (charge of illegitimacy clearly disproved); In re Croker's Will, 201 Misc. 264, 105 N.Y.S.2d 190, 1951 (no objection—reviews New York cases); In re Wartnaby, 1 Rob.Ecc. 423, 163 Eng.Rep. 1088, 1846; Marsh v. Marsh, 1 Sw. and Tr. 528, 161 Eng.Rep. 845, 1860 (by consent); In the Estate of White, [1914] Prob. 153; In the Goods of Bowker, [1932] Prob. 93. See notes, 17 B.U.L.R. 268, 35 Mich. L.R. 854.

49 In the Estate of Heywood, [1916] Prob. 47 (after taking advice of military authorities).

50 In the Estate of White, In re Croker's Will, both supra note 48.

51 In re Croker's Will, supra note 48 (original will sealed up).

52 In the Goods of Honywood, L.R. 2 P. & D. 251, 1871.

53 See Freifield, Libel by Will, 19 A.B.A.J. 301. It has been held that no action for libel survives against the testator's estate. Citizens & Southern Nat. Bank v. Hendricks, 176 Ga. 692, 168 S.E. 313, 87 A.L.R. 230, 1933; but see Brown v. Mack, 185 Misc. 368, 56 N.Y.S.2d 910, 1945, noted, 32 Va.L.R. 189. Cf. infra § 126, note 2. The executor, however, is privileged in presenting the will for probate. Nagle v. Nagle, 316 Pa. 507, 175 A. 487, 1934, noted, 48 Harv.L.R. 1028; Brown v. Mack, supra.

54 In re Plaut's Estate, 27 Cal.2d 424, 164 P.2d 765, 162 A.L.R. 837, 1945; Ireland v. Hudson, 92 Colo. 110, 18 P.2d 311, 1932; Taylor v. Hilton, 23 Okl. 354, 100 P. 537, 18 Ann.Cas. 385, 1909; In re Carson's Estate, 241 Pa. 117, 88 A. 311, 1913.

executed by a competent testator.[55] It is not ordinarily the business of the court to determine the effect of the will in proceedings for probate. Probate is not barred by testator's conveyance of all his property,[56] nor by his contract in his lifetime to dispose of the property contrary to the will.[57]

*Foreign Language Wills*

When a will is written in a foreign language, it should be probated in that tongue.[58] Proven translations may be placed upon the record,[59] but in case of dispute the will as executed by the testator must govern.[60]

*What is Included in Probate*

It is axiomatic that the will, the whole will and nothing but the will should be admitted to probate. If it consists of several instruments, all should be probated, even if they are somewhat inconsistent with each other, in which case the later instrument governs so far as there is inconsistency.[61] When a later will totally revokes an earlier one, only the subsequent instrument is probated.[62] In case of doubt as to whether the revocation is total, the court may either determine this matter on probate, or admit both instruments and leave the question of the extent of revocation for later determination upon construction. When a paper has been incorporated by reference it has been held proper

55 In re Davis' Will, 182 N.Y. 468, 75 N.E. 530, 1905; In re Murray's Will, 141 N.C. 588, 54 S.E. 435, 1906. Contra: Clearspring Township of Lagrange County v. Blough, 173 Ind. 15, 88 N.E. 511, 89 N.E. 369, 1909. Cf. In re Strelow's Estate, 117 Neb. 168, 220 N.W. 251, 1931.

56 Morey v. Sohier, 63 N.H. 507, 3 A. 636, 56 Am.Rep. 538, 1886.

57 Sumner v. Crane, 155 Mass. 483, 29 N.E. 1151, 15 L.R.A. 447, 1892. Cf. In re Carpentier's Estate, 104 Cal. App. 33, 285 P. 348, 1930. But see Walker v. Yarbrough, 200 Ala. 458, 76 So. 390, 1917. See also supra § 48, notes 61, 62

58 Walker v. Burtscher, 5 Ohio App. 388, 1916 (the original German will being lost and the translations of the various parties being at variance with each other, intestacy was decreed); In re Biondio's Will, 105 N.J.Eq. 281, 147 A. 479, 1929; L'Fit v. L'Batt, 1 P.Wms. 526, 24 Eng.Rep. 500, 1718. But see Caulfield v. Sullivan, 85 N.Y. 153, 1881.

59 See In re Cliff's Estate, [1892] 2 Ch. 229.

60 In re Cliff's Estate, supra note 59; L'Fit v. L'Batt, supra note 58. Contra: Caulfield v. Sullivan, supra note 58.

61 Wheat v. Wheat, 236 Ala. 52, 181 So. 243, 1938; In re Fischer's Estate, 283 Pa. 282, 128 A. 90, 1925.

62 Succession of Feital, 187 La. 596, 175 So. 72, 1937; In re Westfeld's Will, 188 N.C. 702, 125 S.E. 531, 1924; Brackenridge v. Roberts, 114 Tex.

to include the latter on the probate,[63] though this is not necessary in order to give testamentary effect to the paper.[64]

Of course alterations made after execution are not included in the probate, but the will should be set up in original form,[65] unless the changes result in partial revocation. The probate decree should be definite on the point.[66] When a part of the will is invalid because of undue influence this portion should be omitted and the remainder admitted.[67]

## EFFECT AND NECESSITY OF PROBATE

**96. A probated will is not subject to collateral attack on the ground of forgery, improper execution, lack of testamentary capacity or revocation. When a will has been discovered after probate of a prior will or adjudication of intestacy, it may be probated, and carried out, though parties relying upon the earlier decree will be protected.**

**A beneficiary under a will may not establish his title to the property unless the will is probated, except that in a few jurisdictions a devisee of land may establish the devise by proof of an unprobated will in any proceeding in which the title is involved.**

### *Matters Determined by Probate*

While the validity, effect or construction of the particular provisions of the will is not determined on probate,[1] the decree does adjudge matters of genuineness, due execution, capacity, and tes-

418, 267 S.W. 244, rehearing denied 114 Tex. 418, 270 S.W. 1001, 1924.

63 Shillaber's Estate, 74 Cal. 144, 15 P. 453, 5 Am.St.Rep. 433, 1887; Newton v. Seaman's Friend Soc., 130 Mass. 91, 39 Am.Rep. 433, 1881.

64 White v. Reading, 293 Mo. 347, 239 S.W. 90, 1922.

65 Hartz v. Sobel, 136 Ga. 565, 71 S.E. 995, 38 L.R.A.,N.S., 797, Ann.Cas. 1912D 165, 1911; Stuart v. Foutz, 185 Md. 401, 45 A.2d 98, 1945. Cf. Matter of Curtis' Will, 135 App.Div. 745, 119 N.Y.S. 1004, 1909 (probate denied in toto when original condition could not be shown); Triplett's Ex'r v. Triplett, 161 Va. 906, 172 S.E. 162, 1934 (alterations regarded as valid parts of holographic will).

66 Rockett's Will, 348 Pa. 445, 35 A.2d 303, 1944; see note, 20 Temple L.Q. 152.

67 Old Colony Trust Co. v. Bailey, 202 Mass. 283, 88 N.E. 898, 1909; In re Carothers' Estate, 300 Pa. 185, 150 A. 585, 69 A.L.R. 1127, 1930. But see Snyder v. Steele, 304 Ill. 387, 136 N.E. 649, 28 A.L.R. 1, 1922; McCarthy v. Fidelity Nat. Bank & Trust Co., 325 Mo. 727, 30 S.W.2d 19, 69 A.L.R. 1122, 1930. See supra § 61.

1 In re Osborn's Estate, 167 Kan. 656, 208 P.2d 257, 1949; Fisher v. Gear, 196 Okl. 18, 162 P.2d 182, 1945;

tamentary character of the instrument.[2] Except as hereafter qualified,[3] probate also establishes that the will has not been revoked.[4] After probate these matters can be questioned only in direct proceedings to set aside the probate or to contest the will.[5] If the time has elapsed for such direct attack, the probate is conclusive as to the external validity of the will for this is the subject of the adjudication by the probate. Although a few cases hold that probate is subject to collateral attack if the will itself or the record shows that the will was not properly admitted,[6] it is usually held that even an obvious error does not render the probate void.[7]

### *Setting Aside Probate*

A decree of probate may be set aside by showing of fraud or collusion upon the court in obtaining the order.[8] This is ordinarily granted by the probate court itself upon proper motion. But the fraud must be extrinsic or collateral to the matter tried.

Hembree v. Bolton, 132 S.C. 136, 128 S.E. 841, 1925. Cf. Reynolds v. Reynolds, 224 N.Y. 429, 121 N.E. 61, 1918 (statute). And see supra, § 95, notes 54, 55.

2 In re Holloway's Estate, 195 Cal. 711, 235 P. 1012, 1925; Barry v. Walker, 103 Fla. 533, 137 So. 711, 1931; Coleman v. Lindley, 115 Kan. 802, 224 P. 912, 1924; Midlow v. Ray's Adm'x, 302 Ky. 471, 194 S.W. 2d 847, 1946; In re Ford's Estate, 144 Minn. 454, 175 N.W. 913, 1920; State v. Nieuwenhuis, 43 S.D. 198, 178 N.W. 976, 1920; Cowan v. Cowan, 133 W.Va. 115, 54 S.E.2d 34, 1949, noted, 52 W.Va.L.R. 77. Cf. Coats v. Riley, 154 Okl. 291, 7 P.2d 644, 1931.

3 See infra note 14.

4 Estate of Parsons, 196 Cal. 294, 237 P. 744, 1925, (cancellation); Bowen v. Allen, 113 Ill. 53, 55 Am.Rep. 398, 1885 (by operation of law); Sebik's Estate, 300 Pa. 45, 150 A. 101, 1930.

5 In re Puett's Will, 229 N.C. 8, 47 S.E. 488, 1948; Sebik's Estate, supra note 4; Hardin v. Hardin, 66 S.W.2d 362, Tex.Civ.App.1934; Brown v. U. S., 65 F.2d 65, C.C.A.Cal., 1931. See In re Huston's Estate, 238 Iowa 297, 27 N.W.2d 26, 1947, refusing to allow heirs to object to distribution by the executor on grounds of testamentary incapacity and undue influence.

6 Leatherwood v. Sullivan, 81 Ala. 458, 1 So. 718, 1887; Thomas v. Williamson, 51 Fla. 332, 40 So. 831, 1906; Wall v. Wall, 28 Miss. 409, 1854 (testamentary character of instrument); Vanderpoel v. Van Valkenburgh, 6 N.Y. 190, 1852; Horton v. Barto, 57 Wash. 477, 107 P. 191, 135 Am.St.Rep. 999, 1910.

7 Blacksher Co. v. Northrup, 176 Ala. 190, 57 So. 743, 42 L.R.A.,N.S., 454, 1911; Gay v. Sanders, 101 Ga. 601, 28 S.E. 1019, 1897.

8 Caldwell v. Taylor, 218 Cal. 471, 23 P.2d 758, 88 A.L.R. 1194, 1933; In re Koellen's Estate, 167 Kan. 676, 208 P.2d 595, 1949. Cf. Weese v. Weese, 58 S.E.2d 801, W.Va.1950 (time limitation).

Probate will not be vacated on account of fraud which was actually in issue in the probate proceeding.[9]

Lack of the required citation or notice is ground for vacating the probate decree.[10] Failure to comply with the provisions of the Soldiers' and Sailors' Relief Act may result in a setting aside of the probate at the instance of one who was in military service.[11] Indeed this possibility exists with regard to almost any order or decree of a court of probate.[12] The order of probate may also be reopened upon ground of newly discovered evidence but the general limitations imposed upon motions for new trial apply to such applications.[13]

*Probate of After-Discovered Will*

Some cases have taken the position that a will which is discovered after probate of an earlier will cannot be probated on the ground that this constituted a collateral attack upon, or an unauthorized contest of, the first probate.[14] Most courts assert that the first probate could not have adjudicated upon the effect of a will which was not known to exist, and hence hold to the contrary.[15] Some of these jurisdictions hold that the first probate

[9] In re Broderick's Will, 88 U.S.(21 Wall.) 503, 22 L.Ed. 599, 1875; In re Crisler Estate, 83 Cal.App.2d 431, 188 P.2d 772, 1948; Blankenship v. Montgomery, 218 Ark. 864, 239 S.W.2d 272, 1951. Contrary to the English rule, revocation of probate is not ground of chancery jurisdiction, but must take place in the probate court. Sharp v. Sharp, 213 Ill. 332, 72 N.E. 1058, 1904; In re Broderick's Will, supra; cf. Seeds v. Seeds, 116 Ohio St. 144, 156 N.E. 193, 52 A.L.R. 761, 1927 (imposition of trust ex maleficio).

[10] Young v. Guella, 67 Ohio App. 11, 35 N.E.2d 997, 1941; and see supra § 95 at notes 33–36.

[11] See Kinsella v. Kinsella, 353 Mo. 661, 183 S.W.2d 905, 1944; In re Ehlke's Will, 247 Wis. 534, 19 N.W.2d 888, 1945; notes, 8 D.C.Bar Ass'n J. 398, 42 Mich.L.R. 480, 2 N.Y.U.Intermural L.R. 50.

[12] See Reed, Soldiers' and Sailors' Civil Relief Act of 1940, 28 Iowa L.R. 14; Stephens, Opening the Estate, [1951] Law Forum 376, 379, 382–383. Cf. Boone v. Lightner, 319 U.S. 561, 63 Sup.Ct. 1223, 87 L.Ed. 1587, 1943.

[13] Motions for new trial of a will contest are often denied. In re Trindle's Estate, 230 Iowa 165, 297 N.W. 317, 1941 (motion not timely); In re Schnack's Estate, 155 Kan. 861, 130 P.2d 591, 1942 (evidence cumulative); but see In re Noe's Estate, 241 Wis. 173, 5 N.W.2d 726, 1942; In re Lillibridge's Estate, 161 Kan. 93, 166 P.2d 720, 1946.

[14] In re Butt's Estate, 173 Mich. 504, 139 N.W. 244, 1913 (indicating there may be relief in equity); In re Baker's Estate, 244 Pa. 350, 90 A. 655, 1914. See supra note 4.

[15] In re Moore's Estate, 180 Cal. 570, 182 P. 285, 1919; Conzet v. Hibben, 272 Ill. 508, 112 N.E. 305, Ann. Cas.1918A 1197, 1916; Cousens v. Advent Church of City of Biddeford, 93 Me. 292, 45 A. 43, 1899; Waters v.

should be set aside before the second will can be probated,[16] but usually there is no such requirement.[17] The latter seems more desirable since if the attempt to probate the second will is unsuccessful there will be the waste motion in reprobating the first will; at any rate the point is not a substantial one.

The same general problem is presented when a will has been discovered after intestacy has been adjudged. Here the court is not concerned with the revocation of the former probate for there is none; it is rather a question of permitting the establishment of the will in the face of the order which appointed an administrator after finding that no will existed. Generally the courts allow a will to be probated under these circumstances,[18] even though there has been complete administration and distribution of the estate under the intestate laws.[19]

*Protection of Parties Relying on Former Decree*

Revocation of a probate court order is handled so as to result in as little injustice and inconvenience as possible. When the probate of a will is later set aside, bona fide purchasers from the devisees are protected.[20] Likewise testator's debtor who has paid

Stickney, 12 Allen (Mass.) 1, 90 Am. Dec. 122, 1866; Bowen v. Johnson, 5 R.I. 112, 73 Am.Dec. 49, 1858; Vance v. Upson, 64 Tex. 266, 1885; In re Elliott's Estate, 22 Wash.2d 334, 156 P.2d 427, 157 A.L.R. 1335, 1945; In Winzenrith's Estate, 133 W.Va. 267, 55 S.E.2d 897, 1949, noted, 1 Mercer L.R. 326. See annotations, 107 A.L.R. 249, 157 id. 1351; note, 48 Yale L.J. 1273; Model Probate Code § 81, appendix p. 275.

16 Conzet v. Hibben, supra note 15; see In re Puett's Will, 229 N.C. 8, 47 S.E.2d 488, 1948.

17 Waters v. Stickney, Cousens v. Advent Church of City of Biddeford, In re Moore's Estate, Vance v. Upson, all supra note 15. Of course if the second will is consistent with the first, the first probate should not be revoked. In re Marx's Estate, 174 Cal. 762, 164 P. 640, L.R.A.1917F 234, 1917.

18 In re Walker's Estate, 160 Cal. 547, 117 P. 510, 36 L.R.A.,N.S., 89, 1911; Walden v. Mahnks, 178 Ga. 825, 174 S.E. 538, 95 A.L.R. 1101, 1934; In re Broffee's Estate, 206 Mich. 107, 172 N.W. 541, 1919 (statute); In re Mear's Estate, 75 S.C. 482, 56 S.E. 7, 9 Ann.Cas. 960, 1906. Cf. Miller v. McNamara, 135 Conn. 489, 66 A.2d 359, 1949, noted, 34 Minn. L.R. 166.

19 In re Walker's Estate, supra note 18; Walden v. Mahnks, supra note 18.

20 Newbern v. Leigh, 184 N.C. 166, 113 S.E. 674, 26 A.L.R. 266, 1922; Reeves v. Hager, 101 Tenn. 712, 50 S. W. 760, 1899; Steele v. Renn, 50 Tex. 467, 468, 32 Am.Rep. 605, 1878; Foulke v. Zimmerman, 14 Wall. 113, 20 L. Ed. 785, 1871. But one may not become a bona fide purchaser during the period within which a will may be contested. Hughes v. Burriss, 85 Mo. 660, 1855. And cf. Fallon v. Chidester, 46 Iowa 588, 26 Am.Rep. 164, 1877.

an executor in good faith is not required to pay again to an administrator after the probate is revoked.[21] Conversely, where intestacy has been decreed, bona fide purchasers from the heirs are protected against devisees under a will subsequently probated.[22] However, purchasers from the heirs where there is no adjudication of intestacy are not entitled to the property against devisees under a will probated later,[23] unless they are somehow protected by a statute of limitation.[24] Even if the beneficiaries under the last adjudication of the court cannot pursue the property in the hands of bona fide purchasers, they can recover from the beneficiaries under the first proceeding to the extent that the latter have received the benefits.[25]

*Necessity of Probate*

Why is it necessary to probate a will? The answer is that the beneficiaries under the instrument cannot establish their rights without it. A testamentary instrument can be established only in probate court. Other tribunals accept the probate as proof of the will's execution by a competent testator but do not admit an unprobated will into evidence even when offered with proof of its genuineness and due execution. This has always been clear in the case of bequests of personalty.[26] Indeed, with regard to chattel interests, not only is probate necessary but the legatee cannot assert his right against third persons until after probate, and also assent to the legacy, or transfer to him of the property, by the executor. This is because the personal representative is re-

21 Allen v. Dundas, 3 T.R. 125, 100 Eng.Rep. 490, 1789. And see Schluter v. Bowery Savings Bank, 117 N.Y. 125, 22 N.E. 572, 5 L.R.A. 541, 15 Am. St.Rep. 494, 1899 (debtor paying administrator does not have to pay again to executor under will probated later).

22 Eckland v. Jankowski, 407 Ill. 263, 95 N.E.2d 342, 22 A.L.R.2d 1102, 1950, noted, 29 Chi-Kent L.R. 265, 40 Mich.L.R. 1089; Simpson v. Cornish, 196 Wis. 125, 218 N.W. 193, 1928, noted, 14 Ia.L.R. 111, 27 Mich.L.R. 118, 12 Minn.L.R. 768. See Hewson v. Shelley, [1914] 2 Ch. 13.

23 Cole v. Shelton, 169 Ark. 695, 276 S.W. 993, 43 A.L.R. 1008, 1925; Reid's Adm'r v. Benge, 112 Ky. 810, 66 S.W. 997, 57 L.R.A. 253, 99 Am.St. Rep. 334, 1937; Cooley v. Lee, 170 N. C. 18, 86 S.E. 720, 1915. Contra: Wright v. Eakin, 151 Tenn. 681, 270 S. W. 992, 1925, noted, 10 Minn.L.R. 168.

24 Fox v. Fee, 167 N.Y. 44, 60 N.E. 281, 1901. See note, 36 Mich.L.R. 120; supra § 94.

25 Thompson v. Samson, 64 Cal. 330, 30 P. 980, 1883. See In re West, [1909] 2 Ch. 180.

26 See Cousens v. Advent Church of City of Biddeford, 93 Me. 292, 45 A. 43, 1899; cf. Phoenix Mut. Life Ins. Co. v. Cummings, 67 F.Supp. 159, D.C. Mo.1946. See supra § 93.

garded as the necessary conduit of title to personalty from the deceased to his ultimate beneficiaries.

Likewise by the prevailing view a devisee cannot sustain his right to the land devised unless his title is proved by a probated will.[27] In absence of probate, the law generally regards the heirs at law as the owners of the land, so that if a devisee asserts title to land in an ejectment action, partition proceeding, or a suit to quiet title, he must show probate of the instrument under which he claims. A few jurisdictions still permit the devisee to prove the will as a deed in the common-law method in an action of ejectment or other proceeding in which title comes into controversy.[28] Most courts do not permit this manner of proof and in the case of personalty, probate is universally required in order for the legatee to assert his rights.

Where a defendant probated a forged will, he was held not liable in a suit to hold him as trustee ex maleficio brought by the beneficiary of a genuine, though unprobated, will.[29] In a similar case, from the same jurisdiction, it was held that the heir at law might recover.[30] The cases are distinguishable in that the heir does not have to rely upon an unprobated will to sustain his title to deceased's lands. However, in most jurisdictions a trust would be imposed in favor of a devisee under a suppressed will which could not be probated.[31] The legatee under an unprobated will may also recover damages from one who suppressed the instrument and prevented its probate.[32] Likewise, a beneficiary

[27] Collum v. Price, 185 Ala. 556, 64 So. 88, 1913; Roberts v. Roberts, 168 Cal. 307, 142 P. 1080, Ann.Cas.1916A 886, 1914; Barnett v. Barnett, 284 Ill. 580, 120 N.E. 532, 1918; Shumway v. Holbrook, 1 Pick.(Mass.) 114, 11 Am. Dec. 153, 1822; Graham v. Graham, 297 Mo. 290, 249 S.W. 37, 1923; Daniel v. Finley, 194 S.W. 955, Tex.Civ. App.1917; Cf. Mackey v. Mackey, 71 N.J.Eq. 686, 63 A. 984, 1906; Keyes v. Munroe, 266 Mo. 114, 180 S.W. 863, 1915 (unprobated will admitted without objection). And see Ohio Gen. Code, § 10504–29.

[28] Bouton v. Fleharty, 215 App.Div. 180, 213 N.Y.S. 455, 1926; see 5 Clapp, New Jersey Practice, Wills and Administration, §§ 93, 95; Hutton, Wills in Pennsylvania 316, 322; supra § 93, notes 13–14.

[29] Petitt v. Morton, 28 Ohio App. 227, 162 N.E. 627, 1928, noted, 14 Corn.L.Q. 108, 3 Cin.L.R. 107, 27 Mich.L.R. 453.

[30] Seeds v. Seeds, 116 Ohio St. 144, 156 N.E. 193, 52 A.L.R. 761, 1927; Gaines v. Chew, 2 How. 619, 11 L.Ed. 402, 1844. In both of these cases the plaintiff was legatee under the unprobated will as well as heir at law.

[31] See Miller v. McNamara, supra note 18; Adams' Heirs v. Adams, 22 Vt. 50, 1849.

[32] Creek v. Laski, 248 Mich. 425, 227 N.W. 817, 65 A.L.R. 1113, 1929, noted, 30 Col.L.R. 409; Dulin v. Bailey, 172 N.C. 608, 90 S.E. 689, L. R.A.1917B 556, 1916; Petitt v. Morton, 38 Ohio App. 348, 176 N.E. 494,

under a prior unprobated will may contest a later will.[33] Perhaps these exceptional cases are not contrary to the general rule announced, for in neither situation is the plaintiff relying on title to any specific property under the unprobated will,[34] and in both cases there is sufficient reason why the will has not been probated.

Probate of the will is not necessary to vest title in the devisee; it is merely vital in order to prove that title. Hence probate any time before the trial is sufficient to sustain the title of the devisee or one claiming under him.[35] Probate after commencement of an ejectment action by the devisee,[36] and even after the latter's death,[37] is sufficient to allow these rights under the will to be shown. Even probate taken after transfer of the land by the heirs to bona fide purchasers is sufficient to sustain the devisee's title,[38] provided no limitation period for the probate proceedings has run,[39] or the purchaser did not rely on an adjudication of intestacy.[40] It is sometimes said that probate of a devise relates back to the time of testator's death.[41] In a sense this is true, but this expression is somewhat misleading as probate is generally necessary only for proof, and not for the vesting, of title in the devisee.

affirmed 124 Ohio St. 241, 177 N.E. 591, 1931, noted in 9 N.Y.U.L.Q.R. 506. But it must be shown that probate is impossible. Allen v. Lovell's Adm'x, 303 Ky. 238, 197 S.W.2d 424, 1946, noted, 34 Corn.L.Q. 118, 45 Mich. L.R. 923.

33 Kennedy v. Walcutt, 118 Ohio St. 442, 161 N.E. 336, 1928; Cowan v. Walker, 117 Tenn. 135, 96 S.W. 967, 1906. See infra § 99, note 17.

34 See Petitt v. Morton, 38 Ohio App. 348, 176 N.E. 494, 1930. But cf. Petitt v. Morton, supra note 29. As to proof of a lost will to establish revocation of an earlier instrument, see infra § 97 at note 45 et seq.

35 Murphree v. Griffis, 215 Ala. 98, 109 So. 746, 48 A.L.R. 1032, 1926; Hausen v. Dahlquist, 232 Iowa 100, 5 N.W.2d 321, 141 A.L.R. 1304, 1942; Richards v. Pierce, 44 Mich. 444, 7 N.W. 54, 1880; Cooley v. Lee, 170 N. C. 18, 86 S.E. 720, 1915.

36 Murphree v. Griffis, supra note 35; Richards v. Pierce, supra note 35; Hausen v. Dahlquist, supra note 35 (partition).

37 Murphree v. Griffis, supra note 35; Tillson v. Holloway, 90 Neb. 481, 134 N.W. 232, Ann.Cas.1913B 78, 1912.

38 See authorities supra note 23.

39 Fox v. Fee, 167 N.Y. 44, 60 N.E. 281, 1901. See also Wohlfort v. Wohlfort, 123 Kan. 142, 254 P. 334, 1927. See supra § 94.

40 See authorities supra note 22.

41 See Barnard v. Bateman, 76 Mo. 414, 1882; annotation, 48 A.L.R. 1035.

## PROBATE OF LOST OR DESTROYED WILLS

**97. In the absence of statutory limitation, a will lost, or mutilated without intent thereby to revoke, may be admitted to probate upon satisfactory proofs of its contents and due execution.**

One can understand judicial reluctance to probate a will which is not produced before the court. In the first place the will may never have existed, or been validly executed. Then, too, there may be doubts as to the contents of the will, particularly if an exact copy is not offered. Finally, the situation is frequently one in which the testator himself may have destroyed the will with intent to revoke it. These considerations account for certain limitations imposed by the courts and the legislatures upon the power to establish a lost or destroyed will. However, subject to these, the jurisdiction is well recognized.[1]

At common law the ecclesiastical courts probated testaments which were lost or destroyed without being revoked,[2] while such wills could be established in chancery so far as they concerned realty.[3] Now the probate courts of our states generally have exclusive jurisdiction,[4] though in a few states the power is lodged in the equity court,[5] or there is concurrent jurisdiction in both tribunals.[6]

### *Testator's Knowledge of Destruction*

In absence of statute, it is immaterial whether the will was lost or destroyed before, or after, the death of the testator.[7] Some

[1] See generally Evans, The Probate of Lost Wills, 24 Neb.L.Rev. 283; Model Probate Code, appendix p. 298; annotation, 3 A.L.R.2d 950.

[2] Davis v. Davis, 2 Add. 223, 162 Eng.Rep. 275, 1824.

[3] Tucker v. Phipps, 3 Atk. 360, 26 Eng.Rep. 1008, 1746.

[4] Cousens v. Advent Church of City of Biddeford, 93 Me. 292, 45 A. 43, 1899; Aylward Coal Co. v. Luyckx, 261 Mich. 394, 246 N.W. 156, 1933; Hedgepeth's Will, 150 N.C. 245, 63 S.E. 1025, 1909; Valentine's Will, 93 Wis. 45, 67 N.W. 12, 1896.

[5] Bartlett v. Manor, 146 Ind. 621, 45 N.E. 1060, 1897 (statute); see Haven v. Wrinkle, 29 Tenn.App. 195, 195 S.W.2d 787, 1945; Simes, Cases and Material on Fiduciary Administration 34.

[6] Dorrity's Will, 118 Misc. 725, 194 N.Y.S.2d 573, 1922 (statute); Dower v. Seeds, 28 W.Va. 113, 57 Am.Rep. 646, 1886.

[7] Hodge v. Joy, 207 Ala. 198, 92 So. 171, 1921; Dickey v. Malechi, 6 Mo. 177, 34 Am.Dec. 130, 1839; Scoggins v. Turner, 98 N.C. 135, 3 S.E. 719, 1887; Tynan v. Paschal, 27 Tex. 286, 84 Am.Dec. 619, 1863.

cases declare that if the testator was aware of its destruction by another, the will is not entitled to probate.[8] This seems doubtful, for unless the will was destroyed at testator's request and in his presence, his mere knowledge or even acquiescence should not affect the question. Such knowledge and acquiescence do not constitute a revocation.[9] The instrument is testator's will and should be admitted to probate. To hold otherwise is practically to permit revocation in some other way than authorized by statute. Most of the cases [10] which declare that such wills are not entitled to probate may be explained on the ground that under the facts the testator must be presumed to have destroyed the will himself with revocatory intent.

*Effect of Statutes*

Statutes providing for the probate of lost wills are very common. Frequently they make no requirement as to the time when the will must have been lost or destroyed in order to entitle it to probate. Sometimes it is provided that a lost or destroyed will cannot be established unless it was in existence at the time of the testator's death or was fraudulently destroyed in his lifetime.[11] Under legislation of this type, where the will was destroyed in testator's lifetime, it is generally held that there must have been at least constructive fraud in the destruction in order to entitle the will to probate.[12] The authorities are conflicting as

8 Campbell v. Smullen, 96 N.J.Eq. 724, 125 A. 569, 926, 1923; Appeal of Deaves' Estate, 140 Pa. 242, 21 A. 395, 1895; Parsons v. Balson, 129 Wis. 311, 109 N.W. 136, 1906. And see Dawson v. Smith's Will, 3 Houst. (Del.) 335, 341, 1866. Most of the cases cited supra note 7, contain dicta to this effect.

9 See supra § 86, notes 32–36.

10 Parsons v. Balson, Campbell v. Smullen and Appeal of Deaves' Estate, all supra note 8, are cases of this nature.

11 So in California, Indiana, Minnesota, New York, Washington and elsewhere. See note, 8 Minn.L.R. 51; annotation, 34 A.L.R. 1304. The New York and Washington statutes require proof of contents by two witnesses. After the San Francisco earthquake a curative act was passed to permit probate of a will destroyed by public calamity in the testator's lifetime without his knowledge. See Patterson's Estate, 155 Cal. 626, 102 P. 941, 26 L.R.A.,N.S., 654, 132 Am. St.Rep. 116, 18 Ann.Cas. 625, 1909. For a discussion of measures to meet destruction due to bombings or other catastrophes, see Temey, 23 N.Y.S. Bar Bull. 47, 1951.

12 Estate of Kidder, 66 Cal. 487, 6 P. 326, 1885; Estate of Johnson, 134 Cal. 662, 66 P. 847, 1901; Kellogg v. Ridgely, 161 Ind. 110, 67 N.E. 929, 1903; In re Kennedy's Will, 167 N.Y. 163, 60 N.E. 442, 1901; In re Reiffeld's Will, 36 Misc. 472, 73 N.Y.S. 808, 1901. But see In re Havel's Estate, 156 Minn. 253, 194 N.W. 633, 34 A.L.R. 1300, 1923, noted, 8 Minn.L.R. 52, holding that existence in contem-

to whether destruction of a will without testator's knowledge or consent is fraud within the meaning of the statute where there is no actual fraudulent intent.[13] There is likewise a division of opinion as to whether existence of the will at the testator's death refers to physical or to legal existence, and as to whether a will destroyed without testator's authority is legally existing.[14] There is often a strong emotional pull to accept the latter construction, even though this makes hash out of the statutes. As a whole these statutory limitations are of doubtful wisdom.[15]

*Procedure*

Proceedings for the probate of a lost will are generally begun by a petition to the proper court, setting forth the substance of the will or a copy thereof, its due execution, and loss or destruction.[16] The execution, loss, and contents of a lost will are proved in much the same manner as those of any other instrument, except that, in view of the peculiar opportunities for fraud, the proof of the facts must be clear and convincing.[17] While the evi-

plation of law as an unrevoked instrument is all that is required under such statute.

13 Cf. In re Arbuckle's Estate, 98 Cal.App.2d 562, 220 P.2d 950, 23 A.L.R.2d 372, 1950; Schultz v. Schultz, 35 N.Y. 653, 91 Am.Dec. 88, 1866; Matter of Dorrity's Will, 118 Misc. 725, 194 N.Y.S. 573, 1922; cf. In re Breckwoldt's Will, 170 Misc. 883, 11 N.Y.S.2d 486, 1939, recognizing destruction without testator's consent as constructive fraud, with In re Reiffeld's Will, supra note 12 and In re Kerckhof's Estate, infra note 14, refusing to do so. See note, 39 Cal. L.R. 156.

14 Recognizing legal existence; In re Havel's Estate, supra note 12. Contra: In re Kerckhof's Estate, 13 Wash.2d 469, 125 P.2d 284, 1942, noted, 41 Mich.L.R. 358 and see other cases supra notes 12, 13. The Kerckhof case argues that recognition of "legal existence" nullifies the effect of the alternative of fraudulent destruction. Legal existence has been recognized under statutes which contain no such alternative. In re Eder's Estate, 94 Colo. 173, 29 P.2d 631, 1934; Rich v. Gilkey, 73 Me. 575, 1881.

15 Cf. Evans, supra note 1 at 296–297, 298–299, and note by Professor Ferrier, 32 Cal.L.R. 221.

16 Cf. Martin v. Wagner, 247 Ala. 591, 25 So.2d 409, 1946; Gfroerer v. Gfroerer, 173 Ind. 424, 90 N.E. 757, 1910; James v. Parker, 131 Md. 466, 102 A. 760, 1917; In re Herle's Will, 169 Misc. 197, 7 N.Y.S.2d 189, 1938.

17 Skeggs v. Horton, 82 Ala. 352, 2 So. 110, 1886; Coddington v. Jenner, 60 N.J.Eq. 447, 45 A. 1090, 1900; Scoggins v. Turner, 98 N.C. 135, 3 S.E. 719, 1887. Cf. Keil v. Wilson, 47 N.M. 43, 133 P.2d 705, 148 A.L.R. 397, 1942. For examples of insufficient showing, see Porter v. Sheffield, 212 Ark. 1015, 208 S.W.2d 999, 1948; McCarn v. Rundall, 111 Iowa 406, 82 N.W. 924, 1900; Matter of Purdy's Will, 46 App.Div. 33, 61 N.Y.S. 430, 1899; Apperson v. Dowdy, 82 Va. 776, 1 S.E. 105, 1887.

dence must be full and satisfactory, it need not be such as to remove all doubt.[18] Of course the burden upon these issues is upon the proponent.[19]

The party undertaking to establish a lost will must prove its due execution just as though the instrument itself was propounded for that purpose.[20] This proof must be effected by the attesting witnesses if they are available, the number required to be produced being determined by the local practice in regard to the probate of wills in general.[21] If the witnesses are dead, execution may be proved by secondary evidence,[22] as by proof of the handwriting of the witnesses by one who saw and recognized it,[23] or by otherwise showing the fact of attestation by the requisite number of persons.[24]

If a will was last known to be in the testator's possession and is not found upon his death, it is presumed to have been destroyed by him with intention to revoke.[25] The ordinary presumption

[18] Skeggs v. Horton, supra note 17; Goodale v. Murray, 227 Iowa 843, 289 N.W. 450, 126 A.L.R. 1121, 1940. The quantum of proof required does not differ from that necessary to prove a lost deed or other instrument. Jacques v. Horton, 76 Ala. 238, 1884.

[19] Newell v. Homer, 120 Mass. 277, 1876; Coddington v. Jenner, supra note 17; Collyer v. Collyer, 110 N.Y. 481, 18 N.E. 110, 6 Am.St.Rep. 405, 1888 (including proof that the instrument was not destroyed by the testator with intent to revoke). When proponent alleges incapacity of the testator to revoke a will destroyed by him, he must prove such incapacity. McIntosh v. Moore, 22 Tex.Civ.App. 22, 53 S.W. 611, 1899; Shacklett v. Roller, 97 Va. 639, 34 S.E. 492, 1899.

[20] Matter of Page, 118 Ill. 576, 8 N.E. 852, 59 Am.Rep. 395, 1886; Collyer v. Collyer, 4 Dem.(N.Y.) 53, 1886; Wright v. McDonald, 361 Mo. 1, 233 S.W.2d 19, 1950.

[21] Scott v. Maddox, 113 Ga. 795, 39 S.E. 500, 84 Am.St.Rep. 263, 1915. Execution may be shown by the testimony of one subscribing witness. Skeggs v. Horton, supra note 17; Chisholm's Heirs v. Ben, 7 B.Mon. (Ky.) 408, 1847. But see Allnutt v. Wood, 176 Ark. 537, 3 S.W.2d 298, 1928 (statute), holding that sole beneficiary of the lost will may not prove its execution.

[22] Bradway v. Thompson, 139 Ark. 542, 214 S.W. 27, 1919; Davis v. Sigourney, 8 Metc.(Mass.) 487, 1844.

[23] Tynan v. Paschal, 27 Tex. 286, 84 Am.Dec. 619, 1863.

[24] Preston v. Preston, 149 Md. 498, 132 A. 55, 1926; White v. Brennan's Adm'r, 307 Ky. 776, 212 S.W.2d 299, 3 A.L.R.2d 943, 1948 (testimony of scrivener who did not recall names of witnesses); In the Estate of Phibbs, [1917] P. 93.

[25] Scott v. Maddox, 113 Ga. 795, 39 S.E. 500, 84 Am.St.Rep. 263, 1915; Coghlin v. White, 273 Mass. 53, 172 N.E. 786, 1930; In re Kennedy's Will, 167 N.Y. 163, 60 N.E. 442, 1901; Behrens v. Behrens, 47 Ohio St. 323, 25 N.E. 209, 21 Am.St.Rep. 820, 1890; Gardner v. Gardner, 177 Pa. 218, 35 A. 558, 1896. The same rule applies to duplicate wills, one copy of which was in testator's possession. In re

can be rebutted by direct proof that the will was otherwise destroyed,[26] or through circumstantial evidence that it was not revoked.[27] No such presumption arises from the fact that the will cannot be found if it had been in the custody of another.[28]

Proof of a diligent and unsuccessful search for the will is sufficient to establish the element of loss so as to entitle the instrument to probate.[29] Proof of loss can also be made out by tracing it to a place which was destroyed by fire or public calamity.[30]

Of course if the contents of a lost will are to be proved, it must necessarily be done by secondary evidence. This may be accomplished by testimony of persons who had seen the will.[31] The rule of the ecclesiastical courts that the contents must be proved by two witnesses has been followed in the absence of statute by at least one American jurisdiction.[32] Some states have statutes to this effect.[33] In absence of statute most courts admit the will to probate upon the testimony of a single witness as to contents, if the showing is satisfactory.[34] This evidence must certainly be

Bates' Estate, 286 Pa. 583, 134 A. 513, 48 A.L.R. 294, 1926. See supra § 86 and infra § 101.

26 Foster's Appeal, 87 Pa. 67, 30 Am.Rep. 340, 1878. See note, 24 Wash.U.L.R. 105.

27 Spencer's Appeal, 77 Conn. 638, 639, 60 A. 289, 290, 1905; Gavitt v. Moulton, 119 Wis. 35, 96 N.W. 395, 1903; Gilbert v. Gaybrick, 195 Md. 297, 73 A.2d 482, 1950; see infra note 42.

28 Coddington v. Jenner, 57 N.J.Eq. 528, 41 A. 874, 1898; In re Gardner's Estate, 164 Pa. 420, 30 A. 300, 1894; In re Steinke's Will, 95 Wis. 121, 70 N.W. 61, 1897. Cf. Page v. Parks, 232 Iowa 879, 6 N.W.2d 298, 1942 (testator had access).

29 Gfroerer v. Gfroerer, supra note 16; Mann v. Balfour, 187 Mo. 290, 86 S.W. 103, 1905; Matter of Cosgrove's Will, 31 Misc. 422, 65 N.Y.S. 570, 1900.

30 Matter of Patterson's Estate, 155 Cal. 626, 102 P. 941, 26 L.R.A.,N.S., 654, 132 Am.St.Rep. 116, 18 Ann.Cas. 625, 1909; Matter of Reiffeld's Will, 36 Misc. 472, 73 N.Y.S. 808, 1901; In the Estate of Phibbs, supra note 24.

31 Hodge v. Joy, 207 Ala. 198, 92 So. 171, 1921; In re Thorman's Estate, 162 Iowa 237, 144 N.W. 7, Ann. Cas.1916B 484, 1887; Dickey v. Malechi, 6 Mo. 177, 34 Am.Dec. 130, 1839; In re Reynolds' Estate, 94 Cal.App. 2d 851, 211 P.2d 608, 1949 (beneficiary).

32 In re Fallon's Estate, 214 Pa. 584, 63 A. 889, 1906.

33 In re Camp's Estate, 134 Cal. 233, 66 P. 227, 1901 (but witnesses need not agree as to exact language of the will); Inlow v. Hughes, 38 Ind.App. 375, 76 N.E. 763, 1903; Fuentes v. Gaines, 25 La.Ann. 85, 1873 (holographic will); In re Needham's Estate, 70 Wash. 229, 126 P. 429, 1912. Cf. In re Guinasso's Estate, 13 Cal. App. 518, 110 P. 335, 1910 (where one witness had only heard the will read.) See supra note 11.

34 Skeggs v. Horton, 82 Ala. 352, 2 So. 110, 1886; In re Thorman's Estate, supra note 31; Harrell v. Harrell, 284 Mo. 218, 223 S.W. 919, 1920; In re Hedgepeth's Will, 150 N.C. 245, 63 S.E. 1025, 1909; Sugden v. Lord St. Leonards, 1 P.D. 154, 1876.

more than a dim recollection of the will's provisions.[35] Contents may also be shown by the production of a copy of the will and proof that it is such.[36] A draft of the will may be used for this purpose,[37] and also a memorandum of the provisions made by the testator.[38]

*Declarations of the Testator as Evidence*

Where there is other evidence with regard to the contents of a lost will, it is settled by the decided weight of authority that declarations of the testator, made before or after the execution of the will, may be received in corroborative proof of its contents.[39] Apparently the provisions of the will cannot be shown solely by such declarations.[40] They are also admissible in corroboration of other evidence as to the facts of due execution,[41] and to rebut the presumption of revocation.[42]

*Substance or Exact Words*

It is not necessary to prove the exact words used by the testator; only the substance of the will need be shown.[43] If this

35 McCarn v. Rundall, supra note 17; Apperson v. Dowdy, supra note 17, 1887; Harris v. Harris, 10 Wash. 555, 39 P. 148, 1895.

36 Forbing v. Weber, 99 Ind. 588, 1885.

37 Kearns v. Kearns, 4 Har.(Del.) 83, 1844 (with full proof and testimony of one witness of execution); Wyckoff v. Wyckoff, 16 N.J.Eq. 401, 1863.

38 Sugden v. Lord St. Leonards, supra note 34.

39 Schnee v. Schnee, 61 Kan. 643, 60 P. 738, 1900; Muller v. Muller, 108 Ky. 511, 56 S.W. 802, 1900; In re Lambie's Estate, 97 Mich. 49, 56 N.W. 223, 1893; Mann v. Balfour, 187 Mo. 290, 86 S.W. 103, 1905; Sugden v. Lord St. Leonards, supra note 34. But see Throckmorton v. Holt, 180 U.S. 552, 21 Sup.Ct. 474, 45 L.Ed. 663, 1901. Cf. note, 57 L.Q.R. 453.

40 Griffith v. Higinbotom, 262 Ill. 126, 104 N.E. 233, Ann.Cas.1915B, 250, 1914; Johnson v. Bruner, 203 Okl. 201, 219 P.2d 211, 1950; Woodward v. Goulstone, 11 App.Cas. 469, 1886.

41 Inlow v. Hughes, 38 Ind.App. 375, 76 N.E. 763, 1906; State v. Nieuwenhuis, 43 S.D. 198, 178 N.W. 976, 1920; McElroy v. Phink, 97 Tex. 147, 76 S.W. 753, 77 S.W. 1025, 1903.

42 Matter of Page, supra note 20; In re Miller's Will, 49 Or. 452, 90 P. 1002, 124 Am.St.Rep. 1051, 14 Ann. Cas. 277, 1907; Tunley v. Beall, 323 Mich. 108, 34 N.W.2d 477, 1948. See also White v. Brennan, 307 Ky. 776, 212 S.W.2d 299, 3 A.L.R.2d 943, 1948, where the will was not in testator's possession. Cf. Sparks, Admissibility of Oral Declarations of a Testator to Prove a Lost Will in Kentucky, 36 Ky.L.J. 431.

43 Allen v. Scruggs, 190 Ala. 654, 67 So. 301, 1914; In re Estate of Camp, 134 Cal. 233, 66 P. 227, 1901; Jones v. Casler, 139 Ind. 382, 38 N.E. 812, 47 Am.St.Rep. 274, 1894; Preston v. Preston, 149 Md. 498, 132 A. 55, 1926. Cf. Tucker v. Phipps, 3 Atk. 359, 26 Eng.Rep. 1008, 1746.

were not true it would usually be impossible to probate a lost will unless a copy could be produced. It is true that the rule allowing the witness to testify to the substance of the will may permit him, in effect, to construe the instrument. This is unavoidable and no difficulty is encountered in the case of simple provisions. To some extent this danger is guarded against by the rule requiring clear proof of the contents.[44]

### *Proof of Part of Lost Will*

It is commonly held that where the contents of a lost or destroyed will are not completely shown, probate will be granted to the extent to which they are proved.[45] Furthermore, a revocatory clause in a subsequent will may be proved to show the revocation of a prior will, though the remaining provisions of the later will are not shown and the subsequent will is not probated.[46] In some cases it has been held that to give effect to a lost will, its entire contents must be shown. This minority position is supported by good reason, at least where the unproved portions may qualify the devises and bequests proved,[47] or the establishment of a part of the will only may result in great inequality between the members of the testator's family.[48]

[44] See supra notes, 17–19, 34, 35.

[45] Skeggs v. Horton, 82 Ala. 352, 2 So. 110, 1887; Matter of Patterson's Estate, 155 Cal. 626, 102 P. 941, 26 L.R.A.,N.S., 654, 132 Am.St.Rep. 116, 18 Ann.Cas. 625, 1909; Jones v. Casler, 139 Ind. 382, 38 N.E. 812, 47 Am. St.Rep. 274, 1894; Tarbell v. Forbes, 177 Mass. 238, 58 N.E. 873, 1900; Sugden v. Lord St. Leonards, supra note 34.

[46] In re Estate of Bassett, 196 Cal. 576, 238 P. 666, 1925, noted, 15 Cal.L. R. 164; In re Cunningham, 38 Minn. 169, 36 N.W. 269, 8 Am.St.Rep. 650, 1888; Williams v. Miles, 68 Neb. 463, 96 N.W. 151, 62 L.R.A. 383, 110 Am. St.Rep. 431, 4 Ann.Cas. 306, 1903; May v. Brown, 144 Tex. 350, 190 S.W. 2d 715, 165 A.L.R. 1180, 1945; In re Laege's Estate, 180 Wis. 32, 192 N.W. 373, 1923. Contra: Reed v. Johnson, 200 Ark. 1075, 143 S.W.2d 32, 1940, noted, 26 Corn.L.Q. 742; Harrison's Estate, 316 Pa. 15, 173 A. 407, 94 A.L.R. 1019, 1934, noted, 29 Ill.L.R. 1092; see notes, 27 Mich.L.R. 594, 44 Yale L.J. 1263. Estate of Thompson, 185 Cal. 763, 198 P. 795, 1921, noted, 10 Cal.L.R. 257, 35 Harv.L.R. 348, applied the doctrine of dependent relative revocation when the contents of the second will was not shown; see also Bell v. Timmius, 190 Va. 648, 58 S.E.2d 55, 1950; but cf. In re Cunningham, supra. See supra § 87, notes 29–35, also § 92, note 26 et seq.

[47] Butler v. Butler, 5 Har.(Del.) 178, 1849. And see Tarbell v. Forbes, 177 Mass. 238, 58 N.E. 873, 1900, recognizing the majority rule in case of independent provisions. Cf. Preston v. Preston, 149 Md. 498, 132 A. 55, 1926. And see cases "contra", note 46 supra.

[48] Davis v. Sigourney, 8 Metc. (Mass.) 487, 1844. Quære: What if only the residuary clause was proved?

A similar problem is presented when a page or other part of a will is missing and the remainder is produced. The courts generally probate the part which is offered.[49] If the missing part cannot be shown and was in fact destroyed by the testator with intention to revoke, the case is one of partial revocation. Courts allowing partial revocation by act would apply this doctrine in this situation. Even in jurisdictions which do not expressly recognize partial revocation by act, some courts have, in effect, allowed it by probating the part produced when the contents of the remainder cannot be shown.[50]

*Wills Lost After Probate*

Probate of a lost or destroyed will is ordinarily just as necessary to sustain a claim thereunder as in case of a will which may be produced.[51] However, if a will has once been probated and subsequently destroyed, this does not apply. Under these circumstances formal evidence of its execution is not necessary before proof of its contents is admissible; [52] nor, when the record of probate has been destroyed by fire, does the refusal of the probate court to restore the record preclude claimants under the will from showing its probate.[53] When a will duly probated in another jurisdiction must remain at that place, foreign probate may be granted upon production of a duly authenticated copy.[54]

49 Burge v. Hamilton, 72 Ga. 568, 1884; Matter of Kent's Will, 169 App. Div. 388, 155 N.Y.S. 894, 1915, noted, 15 Col.L.R. 725. See supra § 86, note 62. But see In re Johannes' Estate, 170 Kan. 407, 227 P.2d 148, 24 A.L.R. 507, 1951.

50 See Matter of Kent's Will, supra note 49; supra § 86, note 62.

51 Aylward Coal Co. v. Luyckx, 261 Mich. 394, 246 N.W. 156, 1933, noted, 31 Mich.L.R. 1185. But see supra note 46.

52 Kotz v. Belz, 178 Ill. 434, 53 N.E. 367, 1899; Marshall v. Marshall, 42 S.C. 436, 20 S.E. 298, 1894.

53 McClaskey v. Barr, 47 F. 154, C. C.Ohio 1891. As to the manner of re-probate, see Kotz v. Belz, supra note 52. See supra note 11.

54 Drohan v. Avellar, 276 Mass. 441, 177 N.E. 583, 1931.

## GENERAL NATURE OF WILL CONTESTS

**98. Dependent upon statutory provisions in the individual jurisdiction, wills may be contested within the specified time in: (1) the probate court; (2) upon appeal from the order establishing the will or rejecting it from probate; (3) separate actions at law or in equity. While the interested parties must be given notice of the contest, no personal relief is asked against anyone and the ultimate issue is merely whether or not there is a validly executed will of a competent testator.**

The manner in which a will may be contested and the procedure in connection therewith varies greatly in the individual states. The three general methods are indicated in the black-letter text, although the matter is far more complicated than is there suggested. For example, some jurisdictions allow more than one method of contest, and what is far worse at least one allows successive contests without attaching the normal consequences of res judicata to the first.[1] It is natural that the procedure in the states allowing ex parte probate must follow somewhat different patterns than in states requiring notice before probate. However, some of the former permit the prospective proponent to file a caveat before probate, and if this is done the fundamental differences are not so great.

*Jurisdictions Where Wills are Probated without Notice*

In these states, contest before probate, while it may be theoretically possible even without a caveat, is not usual. In his signal study, Professor Lewis M. Simes[2] divides these jurisdictions into two groups. In the first, exemplified by Georgia, the contest is in the court of probate upon notice filed by interested parties after probate; this is substantially the ecclesiastical procedure of probate in solemn form.[3] The second, and Virginia is the original proponent, permits the contest in a higher court after probate, either by separate action or suit, or by appeal with trial de novo.[4]

1 Buerger v. Buerger, 317 Ill. 401, 148 N.E. 274, 1925; see Dyer, Will Contests, [1951] Univ. of Ill. Law Forum 416, 417, 437.

2 The Functions of Will Contests, 44 Mich.L.R. 503.

3 Ibid. 516–518.

4 Ibid. 518–524.

*Jurisdictions Which Require Notice Before Probate*

Professor Simes finds four major groups in these states. The first include the states in which contest is permitted only before probate, as in Massachusetts and New York.[5] Here, the contestants turn the probate proceedings into a contest by their objections, and if no objections are filed there is in substance probate by default. The contest is carried on in the court of probate. This presumes that the latter has a judge and other personnel qualified for the trial of the litigation and that a jury is available there. Of course this method is not suitable where there is ex parte probate, and will not be favored by those who believe that the requirement of notice before probate makes for unwarranted expense and delay.

California is the leader of a group of states which allow contest both before and after probate, though there are divergencies in these jurisdictions as to the manner and the forum in which contest after probate is conducted.[6] A third group, which includes Ohio, carry on the contest after probate and in a higher court.[7] Finally, there are some states in which there may be a contest before probate and also an appeal from probate with trial de novo.[8] In these it is probable that the serious contest will be on the appeal.

*Federal Court Jurisdiction*

The Federal courts have no general jurisdiction to probate wills, and they have diversity jurisdiction of will contests only if the contest is inter partes and is independent of the probate proceeding.[9] Where the contest is in the court of probate,[10] or is on appeal with trial de novo,[11] jurisdiction is denied on the ground that the contest is ancillary to probate. Probably even in most other states, will contests are also beyond the jurisdiction of the Federal courts.[12]

5 Ibid. 524–528.

6 Ibid. 528–535.

7 Ibid. 535–538.

8 Ibid. 638.

9 Fakouri v. Cadais, 147 F.2d 667, C.C.A.La.1947. See supra § 93, note 10.

10 Farrell v. O'Brien, 199 U.S. 89, 25 Sup.Ct. 727, 50 L.Ed. 101, 1905.

11 Sutton v. English, 246 U.S. 199, 38 Sup.Ct. 254, 62 L.Ed. 664, 1918.

12 See Simes, supra note 2 at 542–549.

*Nature of Contest*

As has been seen, the ordinary probate proceeding is an action in rem even though the statutes may require some sort of notice to the interested parties. A will contest likewise is generally regarded as a proceeding in rem.[13] This is true in the sense that it is an action to determine the issue of will or no will. Accordingly a contest successfully concluded by one heir should inure to the benefit of the other heirs, unless the latter are in some manner estopped.[14] Neither proponents nor contestants are seeking to recover any specific thing from the other. However, statutes ordinarily require notice of the contest to be given in some manner to the interested parties.[15] In some jurisdictions where the contest is carried on in a separate action it is said to partake somewhat of the nature of an inter partes proceeding.[16] Failure to notify the interested parties may be ground for dismissal of the contest, [17] even when raised for the first time in the appellate court.[18] Some courts have declared there is no jurisdiction to proceed with a will contest unless the interested persons are notified in the required manner.[19]

13 Ex parte Petty, 249 Ala. 393, 31 So.2d 575, 1947; In re Hesse's Estate, 62 Ariz. 273, 157 P.2d 347, 1945; Voyce v. Superior Court of City and County of San Francisco, 20 Cal.2d 479, 127 P.2d 536, 1942; Hogston v. Bell, 185 Ind. 536, 112 N.E. 883, 1916; Tatem v. Wright, 139 Md. 20, 114 A. 836, 1921 (all interested persons need not be made parties); In re Milner's Estate, 324 Mich. 269, 36 N.W 2d 914, 1949; Brissie v. Craig, 232 N.C. 701, 62 S.E.2d 330, 1950; Larus v. Bank of Commerce & Trust Co. 149 Tenn. 126, 257 S.W. 94, 1923. See also Campbell v. St. Louis Trust Co., 346 Mo. 200, 139 S.W.2d 935, 135 A.L.R. 316, 1940 (does not abate); In re Raymond's Estate, 38 Cal.App.2d 305, 100 P.2d 1085, 1940 (cannot dismiss).

14 In re Stewart's Estate, 358 Pa. 434, 58 A.2d 42, 1948; Larus v. Bank of Commerce & Trust Co., supra note 13. As to effect of estoppel, see Woerner on Administration, p. 724, and infra § 99, note 44 et seq.

15 In re Golden's Estate, 4 Cal.2d 300, 48 P.2d 962, 1935; cf. In re Redden's Will, 72 N.Y.S.2d 673, 1947.

16 Ex parte Walter, 202 Ala. 281, 80 So. 119, 1918: "But, clearly, not to such an extent as to affect its binding force as a proceeding in rem." See also In re Hesse's Estate and Voyce v. Superior Court of City and County of San Francisco, both supra note 13; Estate of Relph, 192 Cal. 451, 221 P. 361, 1923. And see infra cases cited notes 17–19.

17 See McDonald v. McDonald, 142 Ind. 55, 41 N.E. 336, 1895; Wells v. Wells, 144 Mo. 198, 45 S.W. 1095, 1908; In re Miller's Estate, 159 Pa. 562, 28 A. 441, 1894. See infra notes 18, 19.

18 Wells v. Wells, supra note 17.

19 Floto v. Floto, 213 Ill. 438, 72 N. E. 1092 (actual notice insufficient when notice was not served); Peters v. Moore, 154 Ohio St. 177, 93 N.E.2d 683, 1950.

*Time Limitations*

There are statutory time limitations, varying from twenty days to seven years, within which the contest must be commenced.[20] Some statutes extend the time in case of minors, incompetent persons, or those absent from the state. There is a legislative tendency to shorten the period. As a whole the time is noticeably longer on the jurisdictions which permit ex parte probate. Indeed in these states it would probably be unconstitutional to foreclose a contest unless several months were allowed in which to file it. Ordinarily a late contest is dismissed regardless of the equities of the case,[21] even when the heir died within the period,[22] or when an amendment passed after probate shortened the period.[23]

*Grounds of Contest*

Broadly speaking wills are contested upon the ground that the instrument offered for probate is not the will of the testator. More specifically a will may be contested upon the ground that it was not duly executed,[24] which objection may include failure to observe the statutory formalities of execution, alterations or additions after execution, or forgery of the instrument. The contest may also be based upon the grounds that the testator lacked testamentary capacity, that undue influence or fraud were practiced upon him, or that he was laboring under a mistake of the sort which invalidates the instrument.[25] A will may be contested upon the ground that it has been revoked.[26] The objection that the instrument was not intended as a will and did not possess testamentary character can likewise be ground of contest.[27]

The foregoing are objections which go to the external validity of the will. Objections to the will because of its internal inva-

20 See Simes, supra note 2 at 557–561.

21 McLaughlin v. McLaughlin, 186 Md. 165, 46 A.2d 307, 1946; Green v. Ferguson, 184 S.W.2d 790, Mo.App. 1945; Stitt v. Cox, 52 N.M. 24, 190 P.2d 434, 1948; Cowan v. Cowan, 133 W.Va. 115, 54 S.E.2d 34, 1949, noted, 52 W.Va.L.R. 77. See Mersch, Time Limits for Post-Probate Caveats in the District of Columbia, 31 Geo.L.J. 405, 426–430; noted, 20 U. of Cin. L.R. 305.

22 Mayweather v. Wallace, 195 Okl. 587, 159 P.2d 529, 1945; Kessler v. Martinson, 339 Ill.App. 207, 89 N.E. 2d 735, 1949, noted, 28 Chi-Kent L.R. 177.

23 McQueen v. Connor, 385 Ill. 455, 53 N.E.2d 435, 1944, noted, 22 Chi-Kent L.R. 302.

24 See generally c. 7 supra.

25 See generally, cc. 5, 6 supra.

26 See generally, c. 10, supra.

27 See generally, c. 4 supra.

lidity or effectiveness are not grounds of contest.[28] Such matters as violation of the law against charitable devises, the rule against perpetuities, the incapacity of the beneficiary to take, indefiniteness of the provisions, or testator's contract to dispose of his property in another manner are raised at some later stage of the administration when there is an attempt to carry the probated will into effect. The same is true of the assertion of the rights of the surviving spouse or the pretermitted child to take against the will, unless these rights are based upon statutes which declare that the events amount to a revocation.[29]

While will contests constitute one of the most important categories of litigation in the field of succession, only a small percentage of wills are contested and most of the contests are ultimately unsuccessful. Statistical studies indicate that less than one per cent of all wills are rejected.[30] Too often unmeritorious contests are initiated by disgruntled relatives for their nuisance value in hope of obtaining a compromise.[31] Members of the bar are faced with serious problems of practical wisdom and ethical considerations, not only regarding the decision to contest but also with respect to the conduct of the litigation if it is commenced.

## PARTIES TO WILL CONTESTS

**99. A will may be contested by the heirs at law or the beneficiaries under prior wills of the deceased, or in general by any one who will be directly benefited by a setting aside of the will.**

**One who would ordinarily be permitted to contest a will may be estopped to do so by receipt of benefits under the will or by his agreement not to contest.**

### *Who May Contest*

Statutes generally provide that "persons interested" or "aggrieved" may contest a will. This means two things: (1) That

28 See § 95 supra at notes 54–57. See In re Peterson's Estate, 230 Minn. 478, 42 N.W.2d 59, 18 A.L.R.2d 910, 1950 (will illegally drawn by layman). But see In re Denton's Estate, 166 Kan. 441, 201 P.2d 625, 1949 (imposition of trust).

29 See generally cc. 3, 10 supra; note, 19 So.Cal.L.R. 292.

30 See Taft, Comments on Will Contests in New York, 30 Yale L.J. 593, 599; Foley, Suggestions for Improvements in the Law of Estates, 7 Lectures on Legal Topics, 277, 281–282; Powell and Looker, Decedents' Estates, 30 Col.L.R. 919, 930–933; Grant, Law and the Family, 89; 1947 Annual Surv. Am.L. 931–932.

31 See 4 Mo.Bar J. 110.

all such persons are entitled to contest; (2) that no others may do so. Even if the statute provides for contest by any person, judicial construction has limited the right to those interested.[1] In general, one is interested if, and only if, it is to his pecuniary advantage that the will should be set aside.[2] When one takes a larger interest under the will, or when his interest is the same under the will as without it, he is not a proper contestant. While wills are ordinarily not construed upon probate, the tribunal before whom the contest takes place may render a tentative construction of the will for the purpose of determining the interest of the parties.[3] The question as to whether one is a proper contestant is sometimes one which must be determined as a matter preliminary to the actual trial of the contest.

*Heirs*

The heir or next of kin who would receive the property in case of intestacy is a proper contestant. Even if such person is excluded by a previous unprobated will, he may contest, for if the latter is afterward offered for probate, it also might be subject to contest.[4] When, however, there is a previous will disinheriting the heir which is admitted to be valid, the heir may not contest.[5] An alien heir who is not entitled to the property under the intestate laws is not a proper contestant for he has no legal interest in setting the will aside.[6] If the heir takes a larger share under

1 Crawfordsville Trust Co. v. Ramsey, 178 Ind. 258, 98 N.E. 177, 1912; In re Goldsberry's Estate, 95 Utah 379, 81 P.2d 1106, 117 A.L.R. 1444, 1938.

2 Ewart v. Dalby, 319 Mo. 108, 5 S.W.2d 428, 1928; Bloor v. Platt, 78 Ohio St. 46, 84 N.E. 604, 14 Ann.Cas. 332, 1908; Bowers v. McGavock, 114 Tenn. 438, 85 S.W. 893, 1905: "No one can question the validity of a will, or any provision in it, unless he stands in such relation to the testator that, in the event the provision is invalid, he will be entitled to an interest in the property involved in the controverted provision."

3 Ewart v. Dalby, supra note 2.

4 Lonas v. Betts, 160 F.2d 281, C.A. D.C. 1947; Marr v. Barnes, 126 Kan. 84, 267 P. 9, 1928; Stephens v. Brady, 73 S.E.2d 182, Ga. 1952; Hilfiker v. Fennig, 224 Ind. 594, 69 N.E.2d 743, 1947; In re Lent, 142 N.J.Eq. 21, 59 A.2d 7, 1948, noted, 49 Col.L.R. 275. Cf. Kane v. Hudson, 273 Ill. 350, 112 N.E. 683, 1916 (other children have no right to contest when testator had made a binding contract to leave property to the devisee); Succession of Feitel, 187 La. 596, 175 So. 72, 1937, noted, 12 Tulane L.R. 475 (proofs received of validity of former wills).

5 Wilcoxon v. Wilcoxon, 165 Ill. 454, 46 N.E. 369, 1896; Cowan v. Walker, 117 Tenn. 135, 96 S.W. 967, 1906. This is an exception to the rule that an unprobated will is not admissible in evidence. See supra § 96, and supra note 4.

6 Jele v. Lemberger, 163 Ill. 338, 45 N.E. 279, 1896.

the will than he would in case of intestacy he is not a proper contestant.[7] The contestant must be the present heir—it is not sufficient that he may at some future time succeed to the deceased's property. Thus a grandson of the deceased is not entitled to contest in the lifetime of the former's father who is the heir at law.[8] Nor may the spouse of a living heir contest on the basis of the right of dower or curtesy.[9]

Under modern statutes the widow is an heir of her husband.[10] Her rights are peculiar, however, and she is often entitled to take her full intestate share by simply electing not to take under the will.[11] In this situation it would seem that she is not a person aggrieved by the probate of the will since she can obtain as much without a contest as in case the will was set aside. The majority of cases so hold.[12] Of course, if the widow is entitled to more in case of intestacy of her husband than she would be by electing to take against the will, she is a proper contestant.[13] In any event, she may contest the will as guardian of the child of the deceased.[14]

[7] Biles v. Dean, 14 So. 536, Miss. 1893. The same rule applies where the heir would take the same amount under the will as by intestacy. In re Ballmann's Estate, 198 Misc. 916, 100 N.Y.S.2d 447, 1950; In re Adkins' Will, 179 Iowa 1025, 162 N.W. 193, 1917; Egbert v. Egbert, 186 Ky. 486, 217 S.W. 365, 1920 (widow). Cf. In re Benton's Estate, 131 Cal. 472, 63 P. 775, 1901 (uncertain as to which is the greater—heir is a proper contestant); In re Brindle's Will, infra note 8. A beneficiary under the will need not renounce the gift in order to contest. In re Purdy's Estate, 54 So. 2d 112, Fla. 1951.

[8] Gore v. Howard, 94 Tenn. 577, 30 S.W. 730, 1895. See Taff v. Hosmer, 14 Mich. 249, 1866; Braasch v. Worthington, 191 Ala. 210, 67 So. 1003, Ann.Cas.1917C, 903, 1915. Cf. Brindle's Will, 360 Pa. 53, 60 A.2d 1, 1948, noted, 53 Dick.L.R. 155, 62 Harv.L.R. 325, 34 Iowa L.R. 551, 97 U. of Pa.L.R. 447, 10 U. of Pitt.L.R. 380; In re Stoiber's Estate, 101 Colo. 192, 72 P.2d 276, 112 A.L.R. 1416, 1937 (person whom testator promised to adopt is proper contestant).

[9] Rogers v. Leahy, 296 Ky. 44, 176 S.W.2d 93, 149 A.L.R. 1267, 1944; and see Cain v. Burger, 219 Ala. 10, 121 So. 17, 1929.

[10] See supra § 15.

[11] See supra §§ 30, 33.

[12] In re Fallon's Will, 107 Iowa 120, 77 N.W. 575, 1908; Saunders v. Saunders, 310 Ill. 371, 141 N.E. 708, 1923; Eckert v. Givan, 298 Ky. 621, 183 S.W.2d 809, 1945; Jensen v. Hinderks, 338 Mo. 459, 92 S.W.2d 108, 1936; but see Dexter v. Codman, 148 Mass. 421, 19 N.E. 517, 1888.

[13] Freeman v. Freeman, 61 W.Va. 682, 57 S.E. 292, 11 Ann.Cas. 1013, 1907. And see In re Benton's Estate, 131 Cal. 472, 63 P. 775, 1901 ("possibility" that widow may take more under will does not defeat her right to contest).

[14] Hopkins et al. v. Taylor et al., 253 Ky. 142, 68 S.W.2d 787, 1934.

*Beneficiaries under Prior Wills*

Persons who are named as devisees or legatees under an earlier will have the right to contest a will which reduces their interest.[15] But if a beneficiary's interest is larger or the same under the second will, he may not contest.[16] It is not necessary that a contestant claiming under a prior will should show probate of that instrument.[17] Even if probate of the earlier will has been denied because it was revoked by the second, a beneficiary under the first may contest the second.[18] While such contestant need not show probate of the will under which he claims, he must at least prove the existence of the will and that it is apparently executed in due form.[19] In case there is controversy concerning both wills, they may be offered for probate separately and the contest of both may be united in a single trial.[20] Often this practice will be a great procedural convenience.

*Purchasers from the Heirs*

As has been seen, even one who purchases property in good faith from the heir is not protected against the claims of the devisee under a subsequently probated will, except by virtue of special statutes, or unless the purchaser relies upon an adjudication of intestacy.[21] In the excepted situations, the purchaser should not

15 In re Plaut's Estate, 27 Cal.2d 424, 164 P.2d 765, 162 A.L.R. 837, 1946 (contingent interest); Crowley v. Farley, 129 Minn. 460, 152 N.W. 872, 1915; Hamill v. Hamill, 162 Md. 159, 159 A. 247, 82 A.L.R. 878, 1932; Kennedy v. Walcutt, 118 Ohio St. 442, 161 N.E. 336, 1928. See annotation, Ann.Cas.1917C 905. Cf. In re Buffington's Estate, 249 Wis. 172, 23 N.W.2d 517, 1946. One who is an heir and also beneficiary under a prior will is not obliged to elect in which capacity he will contest. Hamil v. Hamil, supra.

16 In re Land's Estate, 166 Cal. 538, 137 P. 246, 1913. See also Best v. Burgess, 319 Mass. 67, 64 N.E.2d 444, 1946; Haines v. Little, 242 S.W. 266, Tex.Civ.App.1922; In re Rose's Estate, 185 Misc. 39, 57 N.Y.S.2d 289, 1945.

17 Crowley v. Farley, supra note 15; Morey v. Sohier, 63 N.H. 507, 3 A. 636, 56 Am.Rep. 538, 1886; Dower v. Church, 21 W.Va. 23, 1882. Cf. In re Zollikofer's Estate, 167 Cal. 196, 138 P. 995, 1914. See supra § 96, note 33.

18 Adams v. First M. E. Church of Irving Park, 251 Ill. 268, 96 N.E. 253, 1911. But cf. In re McCarty's Estate, 355 Pa. 103, 49 A.2d 386, 1946.

19 In re Wynn's Estate, 193 Mich. 223, 159 N.W. 492, 1916; Hahn v. Hammerstein, 272 Mo. 248, 198 S.W. 833, 1917 (will revoked). And see cases note 17, supra.

20 Lillard v. Tolliver, 154 Tenn. 304, 285 S.W. 576, 1925; Jones v. Wilherspoon, 182 Tenn. 498, 187 S.W.2d 788, 1945; see In re Kalskop's Will, 229 Wis. 356, 281 N.W. 646, 282 N.W. 587, 119 A.L.R. 1094, 1938. But see Smith v. Davis, 200 Ga. 317, 37 S.E.2d 182, 1946.

21 See supra §§ 94, 96.

be permitted to contest, for he is protected in spite of the will and has no interest in setting it aside. Where the purchaser is not so protected, most jurisdictions permit him to contest as he has acquired the interest of the heir.[22] In Illinois at least, one who purchases from the heir after probate of the will has no right to contest the will.[23]

*Personal Representatives*

There is a conflict of authority as to whether an administrator of deceased, or an executor under a prior will, may contest a will subsequently offered for probate. Such persons have an interest in the earning of their fees as personal representatives. In addition, there is a sort of a trust to preserve the interests of those who would be the ultimate beneficiaries according to the status under which the representative was appointed. This duty is more apparent in the case of an executor appointed by the testator under a prior will than in case of an administrator named by the court to administer the estate under the intestate laws upon the supposition that there was no valid will. Accordingly, more courts sustain the right of the executor to contest,[24] than allow the administrator to do so.[25] If a will is denied probate, the right

[22] Hooks v. Brown, 125 Ga. 122, 53 S.E. 583, 1906; Carthage Development Co. v. Cushman, 101 Misc. 57, 166 N.Y.S. 483, 1917; Savage v. Bowen, 103 Va. 540, 49 S.E. 668, 1905; Komorowski v. Jackowski, 164 Wis. 254, 159 N.W. 912, 1916. But one who purchases the expectancy in the testator's lifetime may not contest. Burk v. Morain, 223 Iowa 399, 272 N.W. 441, 112 A.L.R. 79, 1937, noted, 36 Mich.L.R. 869; see In re Vanden Bosch's Estate, 207 Mich. 89, 173 N.W. 332, 1919.

[23] McDonald v. White, 130 Ill. 493, 22 N.E. 599, 1889. But if the sale is prior to probate, the vendee may contest. Cassem v. Prindle, 258 Ill. 11, 101 N.E. 241, 1913.

[24] In re Monagahan's Estate, 60 Ariz. 346, 137 P.2d 390, 1943; In re Langley's Estate, 140 Cal. 126, 73 P. 824, 1903; Connelly v. Sullivan, 50 Ill.App. 627, 1893; In re Murphy's Estate, 153 Minn. 60, 189 N.W. 413, 1922. And see Boston v. Fox, 4 Sw. & Tr. 199, 164 Eng.Rep.1493, 1860. But the following cases have held that such an executor may not contest: In re Stewart's Estate, 107 Iowa 117, 77 N.W. 574, 1898; Helfrich v. Yockel, 143 Md. 371, 123 A. 360, 31 A.L.R. 323, 1923, with which compare Johnston v. Willis, 147 Md. 237, 127 A. 862, 1925; In re Meredith's Estate, 275 Mich. 278, 266 N.W. 351, 104 A.L.R. 348, 1936; In re O'Brien's Estate, 13 Wash.2d 581, 126 P.2d 47, 1942; State ex rel. Hill v. District Court, 242 P.2d 850, Mont. 1952, noted, 27 N.Y.U.L.R. 726. See note, 32 B.U.L.R. 126.

[25] That he may contest: In re Cornelius' Will, 14 Ark. 675, 1854; In re Davis' Will, 182 N.Y. 468, 75 N.E. 530, 1905. Contra: In re Miller's Estate, 54 Ariz. 58, 92 P.2d 335, 1939; Estate of Parsons, 65 Cal. 240, 3 P. 817, 1884; Cajoleas v. Attaya, 145 Miss. 436, 111 So. 359, 58 A.L.R. 1457, 1927, noted, 27 Col.L.Rev. 1012, 40

of an executor appointed under that will to seek its establishment upon appeal or other proceeding is fairly clear.[26] The cases are uniform that the testamentary trustee under a prior will may contest a later one.[27]

*Public Administrator and the State*

It is generally agreed that the mere right of the public administrator to earn his fees does not give him sufficient interest to contest a will.[28] However, the state may contest a will if the property would escheat for want of heirs in absence of will.[29] The mere possibility that the heirs may fail to appear has been held not to give the state a right to contest,[30] though on the other hand some cases sustain the state's right to contest as parens patria for heirs who may later appear.[31]

*Creditors*

The creditors of the deceased are not proper contestants of the will,[32] nor are they even proper parties to a contest proceed-

Harv.L.R. 1024; In re Sexton's Estate, 146 Nev. 618, 20 N.W.2d 871, 1946; In re Dong Ling Hing's Estate, 78 Utah 324, 2 P.2d 902, 1931. The following cases hold that the mere right to administer property in case of intestacy does not give the right to contest: In re Fallon's Will, 107 Iowa 120, 77 N.W. 575, 1898; Egbert v. Egbert, 186 Ky. 486, 217 S.W. 365, 1920; But see Watson v. Alderson, 146 Mo. 333, 48 S.W. 478, 69 Am.St. Rep. 615, 1898.

26 Quirk v. Pierson, 287 Ill. 176, 122 N.E. 518, 1919; Pryor v. Mizner, 79 Ky. 232, 1883; Cowans v. Beans, 155 Wis. 417, 144 N.W. 1129, 1914. See annotation, 88 A.L.R. 1170.

27 Johnston v. Willis, supra note 24; Reed v. Home National Bank, 297 Mass. 222, 8 N.E.2d 601, 112 A.L.R. 657, 1937, noted, 36 Mich.L.R. 685; see note, 25 Minn.L.R. 120.

28 In re Sanborn's Estate, 98 Cal. 103, 32 P. 865, 1893; State ex rel. Eakins v. District Court, 34 Mont. 226, 85 P. 1022, 1906; In re Neal's Will, 182 N.C. 405, 109 S.E. 70, 18 A.L.R. 77, 1921. But see In re Davis' Will, 182 N.Y. 468, 75 N.E. 530, 1905, allowing the public administrator to contest partly on the ground of his interest in the fees and partly to protect the interest of the heirs at law.

29 State ex rel. v. Rector, 134 Kan. 685, 8 P.2d 323, 1932; Warren v. Sidney's Estate, 183 Miss. 669, 184 So. 806, 1939; State v. Lancaster, 119 Tenn. 638, 105 S.W. 858, 14 L.R.A., N.S., 991, 14 Ann.Cas. 953, 1907. Cf. Hopf v. State, 72 Tex. 281, 10 S.W. 589, 1888; State v. Ames, 23 La.Ann. 69 (state not entitled to notice of probate). But see Matter of Leslie's Estate, 92 Misc. 663, 156 N.Y.S. 346, affirmed 175 App.Div. 108, 161 N.Y.S. 790, 1916.

30 State ex rel. Atty. Gen. v. Superior Court of Sacramento, 148 Cal. 55, 82 P. 672, 2 L.R.A.,N.S., 643, 1895.

31 State v. Rector, and Warren v. Sidney's Estate, both supra note 29; In re Davis' Will, supra note 28.

32 Montgomery v. Foster, 91 Ala. 613, 8 So. 349, 1890; Hooks v. Brown,

ing.[33] The same is true with regard to purchasers from the deceased in his lifetime.[34] These persons have the same rights and remedies in case of intestacy as under the will, so that it cannot be of any pecuniary interest to them whether the will is established or not.

The chief controversy centers around the right of the creditors of an heir to contest a will, or of the creditors of a legatee or devisee to resist its rejection. In the case of ordinary creditors it is generally agreed that they have no such right.[35] It is true that they have some interest in the establishment or rejection of the will, for if their debtor receives a benefit from the deceased's estate he will be more capable of paying the indebtedness, and the creditor may be able to reach this property in an action against his debtor. But to recognize it as sufficient might increase greatly the amount of litigation over the validity of wills. Serious controversy might arise as to whether the contestant has a valid claim; accordingly, most courts do not permit the ordinary creditor to contest.

When one is a judgment, attachment, or lien creditor of the heir or devisee, there is more of an argument to allow him to litigate the validity of the will of the debtor's ancestor. Such person has lien rights with respect to definite property if the will is overthrown. Probably most courts allow this sort of a creditor to contest,[36] though there are also contrary holdings.[37]

125 Ga. 122, 53 S.E. 583, 1906. The same is true of a debtor of the testator. In re Bily's Estate, 96 Cal.App. 2d 333, 215 P.2d 78, 15 A.L.R.2d 861, 1950.

33 Logan v. Thomason, 146 Tex. 37, 202 S.W.2d 212, 1947 (proponent); In re Jones, 68 Utah, 213, 249 P. 803, 1926.

34 Pena y Vidaurri's Estate v. Bruni, 156 S.W. 315, Tex.Civ.App. 1913.

35 San Diego Trust & Savings Bank v. Heustis, 121 Cal.App. 675, 10 P.2d 158, 1932; Smith v. Bradstreet, 16 Pick.(Mass.) 264, 1834; Shephard's Estate, 170 Pa. 323, 32 A. 1040, 1895. Contra: Brooks v. Paine's Ex'r, 123 Ky. 271, 90 S.W. 600, 1906.

36 In re Harootenian's Estate, 38 Cal.2d 242, 238 P.2d 992, 1951 noted, 4 Stanf.L.R. 607, 5 Vand.L.R. 857; In re Duffy's Estate, 228 Iowa 426, 292 N.W. 165, 128 A.L.R. 943, 1940, noted, 27 Iowa L.R. 443; Brooks v. Paine's Ex'r, supra note 35; Bloor v. Platt, 78 Ohio St. 46, 84 N.E. 604, 14 Ann.Cas. 332, 1908; Matter of Coryell's Will, 4 App.Div. 429, 39 N.Y.S. 508, 1896.

37 Lockard v. Stephenson, 120 Ala. 641, 24 So. 996, 74 Am.St.Rep. 63, 1898; Lee v. Keech, 151 Md. 34, 133 A. 835, 46 A.L.R. 1488, 1926, noted, 12 Corn.L.Q. 247, 36 Yale L.J. 150.

*Survival of Right to Contest*

When one entitled to contest a will dies before filing a contest, it is generally held that the right to contest survives to the heirs or personal representatives of the potential contestant.[38] This position seems sound because the proceeding is really one to vindicate a property right and there is usually survivorship with regard to proprietary claims. However, a few courts separate the property right from the remedy by way of contest and hold that the latter is personal and hence not subject to survival.[39] This is a narrow technical viewpoint. In case that one files a contest and dies pending the determination thereof, it would seem even clearer that the contest may be continued by the heir or personal representative of the original contestant.[40] This is true because the practice is generally more liberal in allowing a revival of a pending cause, than the survival of one not commenced in the lifetime of the owner.[41] Yet some courts deny that a contest or an appeal from probate may be revived.[42] In case that the contestant dies testate, his will should be probated before his successors may carry on the contest.[43]

*Estoppel to Contest*

The parties otherwise entitled to contest a will may be estopped from so doing. The most obvious case of this kind is when they have accepted benefits under the will. Many cases support the proposition that such persons are estopped under ordinary circumstances.[44] This has been held to apply even if the contestants

38 In re Field's Estate, 38 Cal.2d 151, 238 P.2d 578, 1951; Judson v. Staley, 163 App.Div. 62, 148 N.Y.S. 733, 1914; Chilcote v. Hoffman, 97 Ohio St. 98, 119 N.E. 364, L.R.A.1918D 575, 1918; In re Siebs' Estate, 70 Wash. 374, 126 P. 912, Ann.Cas.1913E 125, 1912. Cf. Ligon v. Hawkes, 110 Tenn. 514, 75 S.W. 1072, 1903.

39 Allen v. Pugh, 206 Ala. 10, 89 So. 470, 1921; Storrs v. St. Luke's Hospital, 180 Ill. 368, 54 N.E. 185, 72 Am. St.Rep. 211, 1899. And see infra note 42.

40 That they may continue the contest: In re Baker's Estate, 170 Cal. 578, 150 P. 989, 1915; Re Riggs' Estate, 120 Or. 38, 241 P. 70, 250 P. 753, 1925; Ingersoll v. Gourley, 78 Wash. 406, 139 P. 207, Ann.Cas.1915D 570, 1913, noted in 13 Col.L.R. 553. And see cases supra note 38.

41 See infra § 126.

42 Ex parte Liddon, 225 Ala. 683, 145 So. 144, 1932; Selden v. Illinois Trust & Savings Bank, 239 Ill. 67, 87 N.E. 860, 130 Am.St.Rep. 180, 1909; Glos v. Glos, 341 Ill. 447, 173 N.E. 604, 72 A.L.R. 1328, 1930; Braeuel v. Reuther, 270 Mo. 603, 193 S.W. 283, L.R.A.1918A 444, Ann.Cas.1918B 533, 1917.

43 In re Wiltsey's Will, 122 Iowa 423, 98 N.W. 294, 1904.

44 Madison v. Larmon, 170 Ill. 65, 48 N.E. 556, 62 Am.St.Rep. 356, 1897;

would have taken the whole estate under the intestate laws,[45] or if the acceptance was under protest that the will was invalid.[46] There is no estoppel however in case the person took under the will in ignorance of his right to contest, or was misled as to the facts, and has restored the property before entering upon the contest.[47] While not in accord with the general view, it has been held that an offer to return is sufficient under these circumstances,[48] and even an offer was not considered necessary if there was fraud.[49]

One may be estopped in other manners than by acceptance of benefits under the will. Thus, when an heir joined in the mortgage of land devised to his wife he is precluded from contesting the will.[50] One defending a will in a former contest may not start a later contest of his own.[51] Likewise a party to an action to construe a will in which its validity was alleged was held estopped to contest by his failure to question this allegation.[52]

One is not estopped to contest a will by reason of the fact that he was a party to the probate proceeding,[53] or, having knowledge of the proceedings, he made no objection.[54] Testifying upon pro-

Safe Deposit & Trust Co. v. Hanna, 159 Md. 452, 150 A. 870, 72 A.L.R. 1128, 1930; Utermehle v. Norment, 197 U.S. 40, 25 S.Ct. 291, 49 L.Ed. 655, 3 Ann.Cas. 520, 1905. Cf. University of Georgia v. Denmark, 141 Ga. 390, 81 S.E. 238, 1914; Christianson v. Talmage, 69 Or. 440, 138 P. 452, 1914.

45 In re Cummings' Estate, 153 Pa. 397, 25 A. 1125, 1893. But cf. Kostelecky v. Scherhart, 99 Iowa 120, 68 N.W. 591, 1896; Kelley v. Hazzard, 96 Ohio St. 19, 117 N.E. 182, 1917.

46 Stone v. Cook, 179 Mo. 534, 78 S.W. 801, 64 L.R.A. 287, 1904.

47 Hight v. Carr, 185 Ind. 39, 112 N.E. 881, 1916; Medill v. Snyder, 61 Kan. 15, 58 P. 962, 78 Am.St.Rep. 307, 1899; Holt v. Rice, 54 N.H. 398, 20 Am.Rep. 138, 1874; Miller's Estate, 159 Pa. 562, 28 A. 441, 1894.

48 Dreisback v. Spring, 93 Kan. 240, 144 P. 195, 1914; Schmidt v. Johnston, 154 Md. 125, 140 A. 87, 1928. But see Stone v. Cook, supra, note 46; In re Soule's Will, 1 Con. 18, 3 N.Y.S. 259, aff'd 57 Hun, 586, 11 N.Y.S. 949, 1890; Miller's Estate, supra note 47; Woodcock v. McDonald, 30 Ala. 411, 1857.

49 White v. Mayhall, 25 S.W. 881, 15 Ky.Law Rep. 830, 1894. But the majority of courts would require at least an offer to return under these circumstances. See supra, notes 47, 48.

50 Starkey v. Starkey, 166 Ind. 140, 76 N.E.2d 876, 1906; see also Stroup v. Imes, 185 Ga. 422, 195 S.E. 411, 1938.

51 Reichard v. Izer, 96 Md. 495, 54 A. 79, 1902.

52 Hodges v. Hale, 20 Tenn.App. 233, 97 S.W.2d 454, 1936. But see cases infra notes 53–56.

53 Gueydan v. Montagne, 109 La. 38, 33 So. 61, 1902; In re Soule's Will, supra note 48.

54 Foley v. O'Donaghue, 167 Ind. 134, 77 N.E. 352, 1906.

bate of the will does not work an estoppel.[55] Where no rights of third persons intervene it has even been held that consenting to the original probate does not preclude one from thereafter contesting the will upon after-discovered grounds.[56] In this case the fact that one has offered a will for probate does not necessarily estop him from contest.[57] No estoppel results from the suit of a disinherited heir to recover for services rendered to deceased, prosecuted to judgment against the executor,[58] nor does the fact that one qualifies as executor in ignorance of the grounds of contest.[59]

*Contracts with Deceased*

The fact that the contestant had dealt with testator as a person of lawful age does not prevent him from contesting the will on the ground of minority.[60] Contracts not to contest a will entered into between testator and heir at law are not against public policy.[61] If supported by good consideration, the heir's promise will estop him from contesting the will.[62] At least if the heir is the direct descendant the same result can be reached on the theory of release of the heir's expectancy.[63] It has been suggested that the contract theory is necessary, or at least preferable, in case the promisor is a collateral heir.[64]

55 Moore v. Martin, 273 S.W. 961, Tex.Civ.App.1925.

56 Bowen v. Howenstein, 39 App. D.C. 585, Ann.Cas.1913E 1179, 1913; Shea v. Bergen, 59 Misc. 294, 110 N.Y.S. 572, 1908; "Evidence which would support a contest of the will may not have been discovered until after probate." But see In re Wright's Estate, 103 Colo. 43, 82 P.2d 772, 1938.

57 In re Biehn's Estate, 41 Ariz. 403, 18 P.2d 1112, 1933; Succession of Gilmore, 157 La. 130, 102 So. 94, 1924 (where petitioner relied upon erroneous advice of brother who was a co-legatee).

58 Roberts v. Abbott, 127 Ind. 83, 26 N.E. 565, 1891.

59 Molander v. Anderson, 214 Ill. App. 446, 1919. But if the executor has knowledge at the time that he qualified he may not thereafter contest the will. Langhirt v. Hicks, 153 Md. 31, 137 A. 482, 1927.

60 Moore v. Moore, 23 Tex. 637, 1859.

61 In re Cook's Will, 244 N.Y. 63, 154 N.E. 823, 55 A.L.R. 806, 1926, noted, 27 Col.L.R. 758, 36 Yale L.J. 1029. And see cases cited infra note 62.

62 In re Garcelon's Estate, 104 Cal. 570, 38 P. 414, 32 L.R.A. 595, 43 Am. St.Rep. 134, 1894; In re Cook's Will, supra note 61. See also Gore v. Howard, 94 Tenn. 577, 30 S.W. 730, 1895 (release by children to father of all claim against his estate).

63 See infra § 130.

64 See Evans, Certain Evasive and Protective Devices Affecting Succession to Decedents' Estate, 32 Mich.L. R. 478, 498.

*Contracts between Heirs and Beneficiaries*

A contract not to contest a will entered into between the heirs and the beneficiaries under the will is not against public policy.[65] The law favors the settlement of disputes as to property matters. However, a particular agreement may be invalid because it interferes with the rights of others.[66]

The manner in which the agreement may be enforced by the proponent is not clear. It has been held that after such contract the beneficiary under the will may enjoin the prosecution of the contest.[67] In some jurisdictions the contract may be pleaded in bar of the contest by the executor who was not a party to the agreement.[68] In other states, the contract will have no effect upon the contest itself, relief to the beneficiaries being limited to a damage action if the heirs contest contrary to the agreement. When the beneficiary under the will does not fulfill his promise to the heir, an appropriate action lies,[69] though if the heir contests contrary to his agreement the beneficiary's duty to pay is terminated.[70] Unless the one to whom the legatee promised to pay is a party having the right of contest, the promise is without

[65] Warner v. Warner, 124 Conn. 625, 1 A.2d 911, 118 A.L.R. 1348, 1938; Callaghan v. Corbin, 255 N.Y. 401, 175 N.E. 109, 81 A.L.R. 1184, 1931; Cole v. Cole, 292 Ill. 154, 126 N.E. 752, 38 A.L.R. 719, 1920; Hutchinson v. Hattendorf, 216 Mich. 638, 185 N.W. 667, 1921; Grochowski v. Grochowski, 77 Neb. 506, 109 N.W. 742, 13 L.R.A.,N.S., 484, 15 Ann.Cas. 300, 1906; Ewing v. Waddington, 62 S.D. 166, 252 N.W. 28, 1934, noted, 32 Mich.L.R. 1174. Contra: Taylor v. Hoyt, 207 Wis. 520, 242 N.W. 141, 1932.

[66] Conklin v. Conklin, 165 Mich. 571, 131 N.W. 154, 1911; Ridenbaugh v. Young, 145 Mo. 274, 46 S.W. 959, 1898; Cook v. Morrison, 202 Okl. 693, 217 P.2d 810, 1950. See also Cochran v. Zachery, 137 Iowa 585, 115 N.W. 486, 16 L.R.A.,N.S., 235, 126 Am.St. Rep. 307, 15 Ann.Cas. 297, 1908 (agreement to contest a will in order to defeat interest of unborn person is void), and infra note 82.

[67] Ewing v. Waddington, supra note 65.

[68] Reichard v. Izer, 95 Md. 451, 52 A. 592, 1902. And see cases supra note 62. But see Staab's Estate, 166 Wis. 587, 166 N.W. 326, 1918; In re Vasgaard's Estate, 62 S.D. 421, 253 N.W. 453, 1934.

[69] Cole v. Cole, supra note 65 (specific performance); Greiner v. Greiner, 132 Kan. 507, 296 P. 349, 1931; Bartlett v. Slater, 182 Mass. 208, 65 N.E. 73, 1902; Blount v. Wheeler, 199 Mass. 330, 85 N.E. 477, 17 L.R.A.,N.S., 1036, 1908 (specific performance); Grochowski v. Grochowski, supra, note 65 (specific performance). Contra: Taylor v. Hoyt, 207 Wis. 520, 242 N.W. 141, 1932.

[70] In re Spinner's Estate, 252 Mich. 314, 233 N.W. 327, 1930; Wetherstein v. Gordon, 287 Pa. 436, 135 A. 116, 1926. But such agreement is not violated by bringing a suit to construe the will. Hansbarger v. Hansbarger 206 Mich. 281, 172 N.W. 577, 1919.

consideration and void.[71] Some courts insist that the heir should have reasonable ground for contest in order that the contract be valid,[72] though by the better view the heir need only show an intention in good faith to contest.[73]

There is little doubt but that a compromise of a will contest is valid, provided that all the persons interested are parties thereto and there is no fraud upon the rights of any one of them.[74] It is true that this may defeat the testator's intention and cause a different distribution of his property from that which he contemplated. But the living should not be ruled by the dead hand. As the beneficiaries could ultimately renounce their shares in the deceased's estate,[75] the testator's intention may be defeated in any event. Accordingly, there should be no objection to a fair settlement between the parties in order to avoid the expense and bad feeling of a will contest.

Concerning the part which the court of probate or of contest may take in carrying out the settlement, there is more doubt. We have just seen that the courts sometimes give direct recognition to an agreement not to contest a will and prevent the contracting heir from so doing.[76] Sometimes the parties desire instead that the will be rejected from probate and that the heirs pay the devisees or legatees something in settlement of their claims. Should the court reject the will upon a showing of such

71 House v. Callicott, 83 Miss. 506, 35 So. 761, 1904.

72 Crawford v. Engram, 157 Ala. 314, 47 So. 712, 1908; Cole v. Cole, supra note 65; Montgomery v. Grenier, 117 Minn. 416, 136 N.W. 9, 1912; Murphy v. Henry, 311 Ky. 799, 225 S.W.2d 662, 1949.

73 Blount v. Wheeler, 199 Mass. 330, 85 N.E. 477, 17 L.R.A.,N.S., 1036, 1908; Grochowski v. Grochowski, supra note 65; Warner v. Warner, supra note 65 (but there must be consideration).

74 Hodge v. Joy, 207 Ala. 198, 92 So. 171, 1921; Stipanowich v. Sleeth, 349 Ill. 98, 181 N.E. 632, 1932; Bakke v. Bakke, 242 Iowa 612, 47 N.W.2d 813, 1951 (though mutual mistake of law); Surratt v. Knight, 162 Md. 14, 158 A. 1, 1932; Callaghan v. Corbin, 255 N.Y. 401, 175 N.E. 109, 81 A.L.R. 1184, 1931; In re Stoffel's Estate, 295 Pa. 248, 145 A. 70, 1929; Peoples National Bank v. Rogers, 218 S.C. 11, 61 S.E.2d 391, 1950, noted, in 3 S.C.L.Q. 341 (minors represented by guardian); Moore v. Gregory, 146 Va. 504, 131 S.E. 692, 1925; Collins v. Collins, 151 Wash. 201, 275 P. 571, 1929. See supra notes 65, 66. But see Tator v. Valden, 124 Conn. 96, 198 A. 169, 117 A.L.R. 1243, 1938 (agreement to suppress will) and infra note 78. As to agreement to defeat a spendthrift trust, see Altmeier v. Harris, 403 Ill. 345, 86 N.E.2d 229, 1949, and infra note 82.

75 See Parker v. Broadus, 128 Miss. 699, 91 So. 394, 1922; Lehr v. Switzer, 213 Iowa 658, 239 N.W. 564, 1931. And see infra § 139.

76 See supra notes 62, 68.

agreement? Most courts would probably do so.[77] Yet the view is also taken that the probate court owes a duty to the testator to see that his will, if valid, is admitted to probate.[78]

*Distribution in Accordance with Compromise Agreement*

While the courts favor the fair compromise of will contests and most of them will admit or reject a will in accordance with the stipulation of the interested parties, it is more doubtful whether the probate court may be required to order distribution according to the terms of the compromise agreement. The position has been taken in some states that the tribunal must make its decree either entirely upon the basis of the will, or follow the intestate laws, in accordance with whether or not the will was admitted to probate.[79] This view requires that the adjustment between the heirs and beneficiaries be carried out independent of the probate proceedings. If the agreement is not carried out it may be sued upon like any other contract, but not in the probate court.[80] However, a number of liberal courts have permitted the probate court to recognize the agreement by ordering distribution in accordance therewith.[81] In some jurisdictions this power is expressly conferred by statute.[82]

77 Harris v. Harris, 211 Ala. 144, 99 So. 913, 1924; In re Murphy's Estate, 217 Iowa 1291, 252 N.W. 523, 1934, noted, 32 Mich.L.R. 1176; In re Swanson's Estate, 239 Iowa 294, 31 N.W.2d 385, 1948; Parker v. Broadhus, 128 Miss. 699, 91 So. 394, 1922, noted, 23 Col.L.R. 196; Stringfellow v. Early, 15 Tex.Civ.App. 597, 40 S.W. 871, 1897. See Henderson v. Bishop, 250 Pa. 484, 95 A. 663, 1915; Brakefield v. Baldwin, 249 Ky. 106, 60 S.W.2d 376, 1933. But an agreement between only a portion of the beneficiaries should not prevent probate. Connery v. Connery, 175 Mich. 544, 141 N.W. 615, 1913.

78 In re Dardis' Will, 135 Wis. 457, 115 N.W. 332, 23 L.R.A.,N.S. 783, 128 Am.St.Rep. 1033, 15 Ann.Cas. 740, 1908; Robertson v. Yager, 327 Ill. 346, 158 N.E. 709, 1927. Cf. Cole v. Cole, supra, note 65 (recognizing such agreements as valid in a suit on the agreement).

79 Cone v. Johnston, 202 Ga. 420, 43 S.E.2d 545, 1947; Rogers v. Benz, 136 Minn. 83, 161 N.W. 395, 1056, 1917; Shoen v. Wagner, 231 S.W.2d 269, Mo.App.1950; First Trust Co. v. Holden, 168 Wis. 1, 168 N.W. 402, 1918; In re Sipchen's Estate, 180 Wis. 504, 193 N.W. 385, 1923. See Bean v. Bean, 144 Mich. 599, 108 N.W. 369, 1906.

80 This is true even in Wisconsin, the state which has been most opposed to compromises of will contests. In re Sipchen's Estate, supra note 79. As to the validity of such agreements when made before testator's death, cf. Graef v. Kanouse, 205 Wis. 597, 238 N.W. 377, 1931, noted, 45 Harv.L.R. 1115, 30 Mich.L.R. 818, with Gadsby v. Gadsby, 275 Mass. 159, 175 N.E. 495, 74 A.L.R. 434, 1931, noted, 12 Bost.U.L.R. 516.

81 Byrkett v. Josephs, 149 Ark. 669, 233 S.W. 933, 1921; In re Noble's Es-

82 See Note 82 on following page.

## PROCEDURE AND EVIDENCE IN WILL CONTESTS

**100. The contestant must specify the grounds of the contest in writing, and in some jurisdictions the issues to be tried are raised by formal pleadings.**

**It is usually held that there is no constitutional right to jury trial in will contests. However, statutes generally provide for jury trial, although the right is sometimes qualified.**

**By the majority view the proponents of the will have the right to open and close the evidence and the argument, although in some jurisdictions this depends upon the ground of the contest, in others it is a matter of the trial court's discretion, and still others give the privilege to contestants.**

**The general rules relating to competency of witnesses and admissibility of evidence are applied to will contests. Where the issues of mental capacity and undue influence are litigated, the courts should, and usually do, determine questions of relevancy liberally in favor of the admissibility of evidence showing the testator's declarations, conduct and general situation, both at the time of the execution and within reasonable periods before and after.**

### *Raising the Issues*

The contestant must specify the grounds for his contest in the required manner. The form of objection is sometimes designated by statute, and of course is governed largely by the nature of the proceeding in which the contest takes place. Particularly if the contest is filed prior to probate a mere written objection to the will is contemplated.[1] When the contest is carried on by an appeal from probate, the appeal papers specify the grounds of con-

tate, 141 Kan. 432, 41 P.2d 1021, 97 A.L.R. 463, 1935. See White v. Roberts, 145 Md. 405, 125 A. 733, 1924; Fore v. McFadden, 276 S.W. 327, Tex. Civ.App.1925; In re Witte's Estate, 25 Wash.2d 487, 171 P.2d 183, 1946. As to inheritance tax in case of compromise, see In re Gartside's Estate, 357 Mo. 187, 207 S.W.2d 273, 1947.

82 These statutes permit judicial approval of almost any sort of a compromise with regard to a decedent's estate. Mass.Gen.Laws, 1932, c. 204, §§ 14–18; Mich.Ann.Laws, 1943, § 27.3178 (115–119); N.Y.Decedent Estate Law § 19; see Model Probate Code § 93. For typical applications see McDonagh v. Mulligan, 307 Mass. 464, 30 N.E.2d 385, 1941; Hay v. Le Bus, 317 Mich. 698, 27 N.W.2d 309, 1947, noted, 46 Mich.L.R. 580 (spendthrift trust and unborn heirs); In re Norris' Estate, 329 Pa. 483, 198 A. 142, 1938. See also Vaughan, Compromise Agreements Affecting Estates, 16 Fordham L.R. 37.

1 N.Y.Surr.Ct.Act § 147; see Model Probate Code § 72.

test. When the contest is initiated by separate action, formal pleadings by way of declaration, bill, complaint or petition are necessary. In whatever form the objections are set forth, the contestant is confined to the grounds alleged.[2] Particularly when the contest is in the nature of a separate action at law or suit in equity, the pleading must be drawn so as to withstand a demurrer.[3] The objections to the will should not be stated so generally as to amount to conclusions of law,[4] but on the other hand, they need not include the details of the evidence upon which the contestant relies.[5]

The contestant must set up the facts which show that he has sufficient interest to contest the will.[6] It has been held that a general allegation that he is the heir is insufficient.[7] It is clearly enough to show the relationship to the testator so that it will appear that contestant would be entitled to the property in case of intestacy.[8] When one contests as beneficiary under a prior will, it is sufficient to allege that the will under which he claims was duly executed.[9]

A charge that the testator was of unsound mind at the time of execution is a sufficient allegation of lack of testamentary capacity.[10] Stating that the will was not duly executed has been held a proper manner of asserting invalidity on this ground.[11] Undue influence may not be set up in general terms; the facts constituting the influence must be pleaded.[12] Even though un-

[2] In re Balk's Estate, 289 Mich. 703, 287 N.W. 251, 124 A.L.R. 431, 1939.

[3] Daggett v. Boomer, 210 Ala. 673, 99 So. 181, 1924; Gittings v. Jeffords, 292 Mo. 678, 239 S.W. 84, 1922.

[4] In re Streeton's Estate, 183 Cal. 284, 191 P. 16, 1920 (allegation that instrument is not the will of the testator is bad). Cf. Massey v. Reynolds, 213 Ala. 178, 104 So. 494, 1925 (statute).

[5] In re Bixler's Estate, 194 Cal. 585, 229 P. 704, 1924; Penniston v. Kerrigan, 159 Ga. 345, 125 S.E. 795, 1924.

[6] Smith v. Smith, 327 Mo. 632, 37 S.W.2d 902, 1931; Jackson v. Jackson, 84 W.Va. 100, 99 S.E. 259, 1919; In re Goldsberry's Estate, 95 Utah 379, 81 P.2d 1106, 117 A.L.R. 1444, 1938.

[7] Montgomery v. Foster, 91 Ala. 613, 8 So. 349, 1912.

[8] Jackson v. Jackson, supra note 6.

[9] Emhardt v. Collett, 191 Ind. 215, 131 N.E. 48, 1921.

[10] Batson v. Batson, 217 Ala. 450, 117 So. 10, 1928; Freeman v. Young, 147 Ga. 699, 95 S.E. 236, 1918. Cf. Peters v. Fekete, 329 Ill. 268, 160 N.E. 594, 1928 (presents issue of delusions); Ramseyer v. Dennis, 187 Ind. 420, 116 N.E. 417, 1917.

[11] Massey v. Reynolds, 213 Ala. 178, 104 So. 494, 1925 (statute); Wenning v. Teeple, 144 Ind. 189, 41 N.E. 600, 1895. Cf. Ater v. McClure, 329 Ill. 519, 161 N.E. 129, 1928.

[12] Peavey v. Crawford, 182 Ga. 782, 187 S.E. 13, 107 A.L.R. 828, 1936;

due influence is established by proof of confidential relationship between beneficiary and testator, it is not necessary to plead this relationship.[13] If the contestant claims that the will is revoked, he must specify the manner of the revocation.[14]

The contestant is not confined to a single ground of contest, but may set up as many as exist and is not required to elect between them.[15] Indeed, most contests, in their inception at least, are upon two or more grounds.

Under some procedures an answer to contestant's pleading is required,[16] although elsewhere the statutes contemplate the trial of a statutory issue without a responsive pleading by proponents.[17] If an answer is required and the proponent relies upon estoppel of the contestant, this should be pleaded.[18] In many states the contestant's pleading may be attacked by demurrer,[19] or parts of it may be stricken out on motion, if cause exists therefor.[20]

*Jury Trial*

Historically one was not entitled to jury trial upon questions of fact involved in the validity of a testament of personalty since the matter was determined by church tribunals, where there was no jury. On the other hand, there was jury trial of the issue of the external validity of a will devising real estate when that matter was determined in the common-law action of ejectment, or if chancery referred the matter to the law court to determine the issue of devisavit vel non. However, it seems that in the process of making all probate proceedings actions in rem to determine

Ryan v. Deneen, 375 Ill. 452, 31 N.E. 2d 582, 1941. Cf. Ross v. Washington, 233 Ala. 292, 171 So. 893, 1937.

13 Coghill v. Kennedy, 119 Ala. 641, 24 So. 459, 1898; Pirkl v. Ellenberger, 179 Iowa 1122, 162 N.W. 791, 1917.

14 In re Meyer's Estate, 69 S.D. 339, 10 N.W.2d 516, 1943.

15 In re Flaugher's Estate, 232 Iowa 520, 5 N.W.2d 821, 1942 (though inconsistent).

16 See Branstrator v. Crow, 162 Ind. 362, 69 N.E. 668, 1904, and authorities cited infra note 18.

17 Thompson v. Stonom, 57 N.E.2d 788, Ohio App.1944.

18 Wall's Ex'r v. Demmitt, 141 Ky. 715, 133 S.W. 768, 1911; Kelley v. Hazzard, 96 Ohio St. 19, 117 N.E. 182, 1917.

19 In re Goldsberry's Estate, 95 Utah 379, 81 P.2d 1106, 117 A.L.R. 1444, 1938; and see supra notes 3–5, 12, 13.

20 Skeeters v. Hodges, 270 S.W. 907, Tex.Civ.App.1925. Cf. Penniston v. Kerrigan, 159 Ga. 345, 125 S.E. 795, 1924 (improper to strike out evidentiary allegations of undue influence).

the validity of wills so far as they concern either realty or personalty, the legislature has created a right different from that asserted in the action of ejectment and hence the constitutional guarantee of trial by jury does not apply to will contests at the present time.[21]

However, statutes in the great majority of the states provide for jury trial in will contests,[22] though in some of them the right is restricted to a particular type of proceeding,[23] or is discretionary,[24] or the verdict is advisory only.[25] When the contest is carried on by action at law, the general provision for trial by jury in legal actions has been held to apply.[26] Professor Bade's study of the Minnesota cases indicated that the jury had a good record in trial of cases of capacity but is often reversed when the issue was undue influence.[27]

*Right to Open and Close*

There is difference of opinion as to whether the proponent or the contestant of the will has the right to open and close. Part of this divergence is due to statutory provisions, and part to the different manners in which a will is contested in the various jurisdictions. In addition, the privilege may vary in accordance with the ground of the contest and is awarded to the side having the burden of the proof. In some states it is discretionary with the trial court as to who has the right.[28] Elsewhere this has been

[21] In re Land's Estate, 166 Cal. 538, 137 P. 246, 1913; Crawfordsville Trust Co. v. Ramsey, 178 Ind. 258, 98 N.E. 177, 1912; Wills v. Lochnane, 72 Ky. (9 Bush.) 547, 1873; Cartwright v. Holcomb, 21 Okl. 548, 97 P. 385, 1908; Stevens v. Myers, 62 Or. 372, 121 P. 434, affirmed 62 Or. 372, 126 P. 29, 1912; Shaw v. Shaw, 28 S.D. 221, 133 N.W. 292, Ann.Cas.1914 B 554, 1911. Cf. Cockrill v. Cox, 65 Tex. 669, (under peculiar constitutional provision). But see Corley v. McElmeel, 149 N.Y. 228, 43 N.E. 628, 1896 (will of land); In re Barlow's Will, 180 App.Div. 860, 168 N.Y.S. 131, 1917.

[22] The statutes are collected in Simes, The Functions of Will Contests, 44 Mich.L.R. 503, 555.

[23] Ibid. Sometimes a jury can be obtained only upon appeal with trial de novo.

[24] Ibid. See Mitchell v. Hobart, 313 Mass. 776, 49 N.E.2d 725, 1943.

[25] Wainwright v. Bartlett, 51 Nev. 170, 271 P. 689, 62 A.L.R. 78, 1928; In re Weidman's Will, 189 Wis. 318, 207 N.W. 950, 1926.

[26] Garland v. Smith, 127 Mo. 567, 28 S.W. 191, 29 S.W. 836, 1895.

[27] Jury Trial in Will Cases in Minnesota, 22 Minn.L.R. 513.

[28] Bardell v. Brady, 172 Ill. 420, 50 N.E. 124, 1898 (will contested on ground of revocation); In re Brown's Will, 194 N.C. 583, 140 S.E. 192, 1921. See In re Cocklin's Estate, 232 Iowa 266, 5 N.W.2d 577, 1942 (wrong award is not reversible error).

flatly denied,[29] and it is surely not the prevailing attitude.[30] Perhaps the majority view is that the proponents have the right to open and close at least if the issues be as to due execution or mental capacity.[31] In other jurisdictions the contestant has the right to open and close.[32] Of course the privilege of the opening and closing argument follows the right to open and close the testimony.[33]

*Evidence in General*

The general rules regarding the competency of witnesses and the admissibility of evidence apply to will contests. While nowhere is a thorough knowledge of the law of evidence more necessary than on the trial of a will contest, and while some treatments of the latter subject deal at length with evidentiary matters,[34] considerations of space forbid extended treatment here. Only a brief indication of the problems is given below and the reader should seek further guidance from works on evidence.

*Witnesses*

While the dead man's statutes in some jurisdictions are held to prevent the legatee or the heir from testifying in a will contest, in most states they may testify at least as to some matters.[35] The statutory privilege against disclosure of communications made by the testator to his physician or his attorney are clearly waived if they were attesting witnesses, and even if they were not the privilege is not usually allowed in will contests.[36]

29 Mindler v. Crocker, 245 Ala. 578, 18 So.2d 278, 1944.

30 See infra notes 31, 34.

31 Mindler v. Crocker, supra note 29; Mottau v. Mottau, 243 Mass. 147, 137 N.E. 592, 1922; In re Mann's Estate, 219 Mich. 695, 189 N.W. 991, 1922; Morrow v. Board of Trustees of Park College, 353 Mo. 21, 181 S.W. 2d 945, 1944; Hall v. Hall, 181 Va. 67, 23 S.E.2d 810, 1943 (capacity). See In re Carpenter's Will, 171 Misc. 363, 12 N.Y.S.2d 724, 1934 (depends on issues).

32 Friberg v. Zeutschel, 379 Ill. 480, 41 N.E.2d 512, 1942; Schwarz v. Taeger, 44 Idaho 625, 258 P. 1082, 1927; In re Silver's Estate, 98 Mont. 141, 38 P.2d 277, 1935.

33 In re Mann's Estate, supra note 31; Mayes v. Mayes, 235 S.W. 100, Mo.1921.

34 See Welch, Will Contests, 89 Trusts & Estates 656; cf. Atkinson on Wills, 1st ed. § 195.

35 See annotations, 115 A.L.R. 1425, 173 id. 1282. See also In re Kenney's Will, 213 Iowa 360, 239 N.W. 44, 78 A.L.R. 1189, 1931. As to the effect of release or transfer of interest, cf. Snyder v. Steele, 304 Ill. 387, 136 N.E. 649, 28 A.L.R. 1, 19, 22, with May v. Brown, 144 Tex. 350, 190 S.W.2d 715, 165 A.L.R. 1180, 1945; and see note, 18 Tex.L.R. 111.

36 See Wigmore on Evidence §§ 2314–2315, 2391; annotation, 115 A.L. R. 1425.

*Evidence Regarding Execution*

On the issue of due execution, proponent is obliged to call the attesting witnesses if they are available.[37] However, proponent is not bound by their testimony and may show execution by other means.[38] Since the attesters are witnesses who must be called, the ordinary rule that one may not impeach his own witnesses does not apply.[39] While the attester's testimony that the will was not properly executed is admissible, the courts declare that this evidence is to be viewed with suspicion.[40] Particularly if there is a proper attestation clause, wills have been admitted in spite of the fact that the attesters swore that there had not been compliance with the essential formalities.[41]

*Evidence Regarding Mental Capacity*

Since attesters bear witness to the testator's capacity as well as to the facts of execution, their opinion as to capacity is always admissible in evidence; but if they had no previous acquaintance with the testator their testimony has no great weight.[42] As in case of an attester who denies due execution, the courts discredit the attester who asserts that the testator was mentally incompetent.[43]

Except in a few states, a non-expert witness who is not an attester may state his opinion as to this issue, based upon his observation of the testator.[44] Some jurisdictions require non-ex-

Counsel who gives material testimony violates the code of legal ethics by acting as an attorney at the trial or on appeal. In re Newman's Will, 187 Or. 641, 213 P.2d 137, 1950 (not permitted to present case in Supreme Court); In re Torstensen's Estate, 28 Wash.2d 837, 184 P.2d 255, 1947 (testimony discredited).

37 Gillis v. Gillis, 96 Ga. 1, 23 S.E. 107, 30 L.R.A. 143, 51 Am.St.Rep. 121, 1895. As to the number who must be called, see Wigmore on Evidence § 1304; In re Lanyon's Estate, 156 Neb. 21, 54 N.W.2d 262, 1952 (must call all).

38 Gillis v. Gillis, supra note 37; Tyson v. Utterback, 154 Miss. 381, 122 So. 496, 63 A.L.R. 1188, 1929.

39 Lott v. Lott, 174 Minn. 13, 218 N.W. 477, 1928, noted, 12 Minn.L.R. 661; Wigmore on Evidence, § 917.

40 In re Estate of Shaff, 125 Or. 288, 266 P. 630, 1928 (cum grano salis).

41 Lott v. Lott, supra note 39; cf. Poindexter's Adm'r v. Alexander, 277 Ky. 147, 125 S.W.2d 981, 1939 (no attestation clause).

42 See annotations, 93 A.L.R. 1049, 123 id. 88.

43 Stevens v. Leonard, 154 Ind. 67, 56 N.E. 27, 77 Am.St.Rep. 446, 1900.

44 See generally Green, Proof of Mental Incompetency and the Unexpressed Major Premise, 53 Yale L.J. 271, 282; Schuyler, Evidence of Testamentary Capacity in Illinois, 32 Ill. L.R. 921, 928; notes, 29 Cal.L.R. 430, 30 Ky.L.J. 425.

perts to relate the facts upon which their opinions are based before stating their opinions, although several of these make this requirement only if the witnesses testify to incapacity.[45] The preferred rule is to make no such requirement in any case since the opinions are often based upon absence of abnormal conduct, or upon myriads of facts which are difficult to recall and relate.[46]

There are countless quibbles as to the form of questions which should be put to these witnesses. They should not be asked whether the testator had mentality enough to make a will, since that calls for them to pass upon a question of law.[47] Probably the safest form of question is along the same lines as instructions to the jury on the issue, viz., whether in the witness' opinion the testator had the mental ability to realize the nature and extent of his property, the natural objects of his bounty, and the disposition made by his will.[48] Other types of interrogations are sometimes permitted.[49]

An expert may give his opinion as to the mental condition of the testator if he had an opportunity to observe the testator, or upon the whole evidence at the trial if it be not conflicting and he were present at the trial, or upon hypothetical questions based upon the facts in evidence.[50] In the latter case the question should relate the facts shown and the opinion should be based on those facts.[51] As in case of the non-expert the question should not require the expert to pass upon the legal test of testamentary capacity, though the courts are somewhat more liberal in allowing the latter to state his opinion in his own language.[52]

In addition to opinion evidence, a will contest may involve an investigation of almost the entire life history of the testator.[53] Of course his capacity at the time of execution of the will is the

45 Wigmore on Evidence § 1935.

46 Ibid. at § 1938.

47 In re Will of Lomax, 224 N.C. 459, 31 S.E.2d 369, 155 A.L.R. 278, 1944.

48 Walls v. Walls, 30 Ky.L.Rep. 948, 99 S.W. 969, 1907; Re Olson, 176 Minn. 300, 223 N.W. 677, 1929; but see Baddeley v. Watkins, 293 Ill. 394, 127 N.E. 725, 1920.

49 Houston v. Grigsby, 217 Ala. 506, 116 So. 686, 1928; Durant v. Whitcher, 97 Kan. 603, 156 P. 739, 1916.

50 Wigmore on Evidence § 674 et seq.

51 Ibid. § 676. See also Hulbert, Psychiatric Testimony v. Probate Proceedings, 2 Law & Contemporary Problems 448, 454; Rudersdorf v. Bowers, 112 S.W.2d 784, Tex.Civ.App. 1938 (question set forth in full).

52 Taft, Comment on Will Contest in New York, 30 Yale L.J. 593, 603, 604.

53 Taft, supra note 52 at 63; Welch, Will Contests, 89 Trust & Estates 656.

point in issue, but his conduct and declarations before and after are admissible if they bear upon this matter.[54] Usually the trial court has considerable discretion in either admitting this evidence or excluding it as too remote.[55] The testator's oral and written declarations are admissible, not for the purpose of showing the truth of the statements but as evidence of his state of mind.[56] Declarations of beneficiaries are frequently received as admissions of an unfavorable mental condition.[57]

Photographs of the testator [58] and specimens of his handwriting[59] may have some bearing upon his mental condition and are admissible upon this issue. Usually insanity in the testator's family can also be shown.[60] The provisions of the will alone are probably insufficient evidence of incapacity to submit the issue to the jury,[61] but if there is other proof the will may be considered in corroboration thereof.[62] An adjudication of insanity at or near the time of execution of the will may be shown,[63] but this is not conclusive since the adjudication was not on the question of testamentary capacity and usually the proponent was not a party to the guardianship proceeding.[64]

### *Evidence Regarding Undue Influence*

Undue influence is a subtle thing, almost always exercised in secret, and usually provable only by circumstantial evidence. A will cannot be rejected by mere proof of opportunity to exercise

54 In re Balk's Estate, 289 Mich. 703, 287 N.W. 351, 124 A.L.R. 431, 1939. As to declarations regarding testamentary intent, see annotation, 21 A.L.R.2d 319.

55 Ailes v. Ailes, 104 Ind.App. 302, 11 N.E.2d 73, 1937.

56 Wigmore on Evidence §§ 227–229, 1714–1715, 1739–1740.

57 In re Estate of Forsythe, 221 Minn. 303, 22 N.W.2d 19, 167 A.L.R. 1, 1946.

58 Brownlie v. Brownlie, 357 Ill. 117, 191 N.E. 268, 93 A.L.R. 1041, 1934.

59 Raymond v. Flint, 225 Mass. 521, 114 N.E. 811, 1917; see Gibbons v. Redmond, 142 Kan. 417, 49 P.2d 1035, 103 A.L.R. 893, 1935 (expert opinion based on handwriting).

60 Wigmore on Evidence § 232.

61 See Gay v. Gay, 183 Ky. 238, 209 S.W. 11, 1919; Kish v. Bakaysa, 330 Pa. 533, 199 A. 321, 1938.

62 See Ergang v. Anderson, 378 Ill. 312, 38 N.E.2d 26, 137 A.L.R. 984, 1941, and supra § 51, notes 1–4.

63 Holliday v. Shepherd, 269 Ill. 429, 109 N.E. 976, 7 A.L.R. 558, 1915; but see Lewandowski v. Zuzak, 305 Ill. 612, 137 N.E. 500, 1922, noted, 36 Harv.L.R. 756. See annotation, 68 A.L.R. 1309.

64 Duncan's Contested Will, 147 Pa. Super. 133, 23 A.2d 357, 1941; In re Bottger's Estate, 14 Wash.2d 676, 129 P.2d 518, 1942. See Green, supra note 44 at 286; also supra § 51, note 27.

undue influence.[65] A fourfold test of proof required, viz.: (1) a testator subject to such influence, (2) opportunity to exercise it, (3) disposition to exercise it, and (4) a result appearing to be the effect of the influence, originated in Wisconsin and appears to be gaining ground elsewhere.[66]

This catalog is suggestive of the type of evidence which is admissible generally upon the issue. Testator's declarations are admissible to indicate his state of mind but there must usually be other evidence to show the external fact that another exercised the influence.[67] As upon the issue of mental capacity, the will itself is admissible to show that the disposition was unjust or unnatural in the light of the surrounding circumstances, but here again this evidence by itself is not sufficient to sustain a finding against the will.[68] The operation of presumptions on account of the relationship of the beneficiary to the testator and of the beneficiary's activity in the making of the will, aids the contestant in many cases where the issue is undue influence.[69]

*Evidence Regarding Revocation*

To show revocation by physical act, two things must be proved: First, the testator's act of mutilation; second, his intention to revoke. It is orthodox to hold that the former may not be shown by testator's declarations,[70] although an increasing number of courts hold that his utterances may be used as evidence of the act of destruction.[71] When the will is not found, testator's dec-

65 Coulter v. Hardin, 274 Ky. 544, 119 S.W.2d 562, 1938; In re Mazanec's Estate, 204 Minn. 406, 283 N.W. 745, 1939.

66 Will of Leisch, 221 Wis. 641, 267 N.W. 268, 1936; In re Witte's Estate, 145 Neb. 295, 16 N.W.2d 203, 17 N.W. 2d 477, 1944; In re Rowland's Estate, 70 S.D. 419, 18 N.W.2d 290, 1945; Estate of Hull, 63 Cal.App.2d 135, 146 P. 2d 242, 1944. See notes, 30 Iowa L.R. 321, [1945] Wis.L.R. 633. Cf. supra § 55.

67 In re Wayne's Estate, 134 Or. 464, 291 P. 356, 79 A.L.R. 1427, 1930; cf. Welch's Adm'r v. Clifton, 294 Ky. 514, 172 S.W.2d 221, 148 A.L.R. 1220, 1943; In re Burton's Estate, 45 So. 2d 873, Fla.1950. As to beneficiaries declarations, see supra note 57.

68 See annotation, 66 A.L.R. 250; also supra notes 61, 62.

69 See supra § 55 and infra § 101.

70 Neibling v. Methodist Orphans' Home Association, 315 Mo. 578, 286 S.W. 58, 51 A.L.R. 639, 1926 (declaration of intent to revoke in future); In re Colbert's Estate, 31 Mont. 461, 78 P. 971, 80 P. 248, 107 Am.St.Rep. 439, 3 Ann.Cas. 952, 1904; In re Kennedy's Will, 167 N.Y. 163, 60 N.E. 442, 1901; In re Campbell's Will, 100 Vt. 395, 138 A. 725, 54 A.L.R. 1369, 1927; Throckmorton v. Holt, 180 U.S. 552, 21 S.Ct. 474, 45 L.Ed. 663, 1901. See also Brownfield v. Brownfield, 249 S. W.2d 389, Mo.1952 (subsequent instrument).

71 Ellis v. O'Neal, 175 Ga. 652, 165 S.E. 751, 1932; Stuart v. McWhorter,

larations are frequently admitted to strengthen or rebut the presumption of revocation arising from the will's disappearance while in his possession.[72] On the issue of intention to revoke, declarations at the time of the physical act are clearly admissible to show the animus revocandi.[73] In addition, prior and subsequent declarations are admissible to prove the intention at the time of the act, upon the theory that the earlier and later declarations are some evidence of the mental state at the time of the alleged revocation.[74]

When it is claimed that the will was revoked by testator's subsequent marriage, testimony is of course admissible as to matters of the fact and the validity of the alleged marriage.[75] In most jurisdictions parol evidence is not admissible to show testator's intention not to revoke his will by his subsequent marriage, since his intention is not material in case of revocation by operation of law.[76]

238 Ky. 82, 36 S.W.2d 842, 1931; Burton v. Wylde, 261 Ill. 397, 103 N.E. 976, 1913; In re Lambie's Estate, 97 Mich. 49, 56 N.W. 223, 1893 (in corroboration of other evidence); Compton v. Dannenbauer, 120 Tex. 14, 35 S.W.2d 682, 79 A.L.R. 1488, 1931; Wigmore on Evidence §§ 1736, 1737.

72 Bradway v. Thompson, 139 Ark. 542, 214 S.W. 27, 1919; White v. Brennan, 307 Ky. 776, 212 S.W.2d 299, 3 A.L.R.2d 943, 1948; In re Oswald's Will, 172 Wis. 345, 178 N.W. 462, 1920. But see In re Kennedy's Will and In re Colbert's Estate, both supra note 70. And see generally, § 86.

73 Burton v. Wylde, supra note 71; Pickens v. Davis, 134 Mass. 252, 45 Am.Rep. 322, 1883; Crampton v. Osborn, 356 Mo. 125, 201 S.W.2d 336, 172 A.L.R. 344, 1947.

74 Russell v. Tyler, 224 Ky. 511, 6 S.W.2d 707, 1928; Collagan v. Burns, 57 Me. 449, 458, 1867; Pickens v. Davis, 134 Mass. 252, 45 Am.Rep. 322, 1883; Wigmore on Evidence § 1737.

75 Research Hospital v. Continental Illinois Bank & Trust Co., 352 Ill. 510, 186 N.E. 170, 1933, noted, 28 Ill.L.R. 436.

76 See supra §§ 84, 85.

## BURDEN OF PROOF AND PRESUMPTIONS

**101. While the practice in some jurisdictions fixes the burden of going forward and even the risk of nonpersuasion upon the contestant, it is more usual to hold that the proponent must establish the due execution of the will by a preponderance of the evidence. According to the orthodox view the proponent has the burden of proof as to mental capacity, though a substantial number of courts place this burden on contestant. By the prevailing view the burden upon the issues of undue influence, fraud and revocation is upon contestant. Often, however, the party having the burden of proof is aided in establishment of his case by certain rebuttable presumptions and these have even been held to shift the ultimate burden to the opponent.**

These topics call for more extended treatment in the present work than that of the admissibility of evidence. This is because, for the most part, they are peculiar to will contests, and are complicated by statutes and by the nature and method of the contest.

*The Two Burdens of Proof—In General*

Any consideration of burden of proof should be prefaced by noticing the double sense in which the term is used by the courts.[1] First it may refer to the obligation of a party to so move the triers of fact that the particular issue may be regarded as established. Of course proof to an absolute conviction is not required in any case; in most civil issues, including those usually involved in will contests, establishment by a preponderance of the evidence is all that is required.[2] One party or the other must have this burden; otherwise there could be no decision in cases when the evidence places the triers' minds in equilibrium. This party may be said to have the risk of nonpersuasion, a term which is fairly descriptive of burden of proof in this first sense. According to orthodox theory this burden does not shift from one party to the other.[3] It becomes important when the court instructs the jury

1 For a general discussion, see Wigmore on Evidence § 2483 et seq.

2 Some courts require more than a mere preponderance of the evidence when the issues of fraud or undue influence are raised. See infra notes 39–43. As to lost wills, see supra § 97 at notes 17–19, and infra note 68.

3 Egbers v. Egbers, 177 Ill. 82, 52 N.E. 285, 1898; Miller v. Blumenshine, 343 Ill. 531, 175 N.E. 814, 76 A.L.R. 362, 1931; In re Mollan's Estate, 181 Minn. 217, 232 N.W. 1, 1930, noted, 15 Minn.L.R. 600 (undue influence); Goodfellow v. Shannon, 197 Mo. 271, 94 S.W. 979, 1906 (burden of proving facts of execution does not

that one party or the other must establish a particular issue by the preponderance of the evidence.

An entirely different meaning is also attributed to burden of proof. This is because the courts do not submit all issues of fact to the jury but only those in which the evidence is such that reasonable men might differ in their conclusions. If there is no fair controversy concerning a certain matter, the court directs the jury to find in accordance with the obvious state of the evidence and does not submit the matter for their determination. Burden of proof in this sense has to do with the quantum of the evidence necessary to have an issue submitted to the jury. It may shift from one party to the other and back and forth several times during the trial, dependent upon the character of the evidence already introduced at any given moment. It has been called burden of going forward with the evidence. The original burden of going forward is upon the party who has the risk of nonpersuasion, though the latter may satisfy it by the introduction of evidence which either establishes a prima facie case or which gives rise to a rebuttable presumption.[4] This burden becomes important when one party moves for a directed verdict or otherwise requests the court to remove a certain issue from the jury's consideration. Burden of proof in this sense should not be explained to the jury for they are not concerned with it except in the following of the judge's peremptory instruction, the reason for which they need not know.

It should be noticed that burden of proof in either sense refers to the burden on the various ultimate issues in the case. The risk of nonpersuasion may be on one party as to a certain issue and on his opponent as to other issues in the same case. Thus, the issue may be upon proponent to show due execution of the will, but if the instrument is also contested on the ground of undue influence, the contestant will probably have the burden as to the latter matter.[5] Burden of proof is not material with respect to the smaller evidential issues which go to make up the ultimate issues of execution, capacity, undue influence, and revo-

shift to contestant merely because proponent has introduced evidence sufficient to make out a prima facie case); Wigmore on Evidence § 2489. It has been shown that when certain rebuttable presumptions based upon some strong reason of public policy operate, the risk of nonpersuasion may shift to the party against whom the presumption operates. Bohlen, The Effect of Rebuttable Presumptions of Law upon the Burden of Proof, 68 U. of Pa.L.R. 307. See infra text at note 29.

4 See infra notes 24, 61.

5 See infra notes 8, 36.

cation. As it is not necessary for either side to prove its contentions by any particular evidence, the jury should be instructed as to risk of nonpersuasion only upon the main issues which have been raised by the pleadings and the evidence.

While in most jurisdictions the courts have placed the burden of proof (in either sense) upon proponents as to some issues and contestants as to others, legislation in some states has placed the burden on contestants as to all issues especially if the contest is after probate. Although this may relate only to the burden of going forward,[6] in some jurisdictions the risk of nonpersuasion is upon the contestants as to all issues.[7]

*Execution*

The majority of courts hold that in a will contest the risk of nonpersuasion is upon the proponent to prove due execution of the will.[8] This includes the element of genuineness of the instrument.[9] The proponent need only establish the facts of execution

6 See Morrow v. Board of Trustees of Park College, 353 Mo. 21, 181 S.W. 2d 945, 1944; In re Ash's Estate, 351 Pa. 317, 41 A.2d 620, 1945.

7 Tidholm v. Tidholm, 391 Ill. 19, 62 N.E.2d 473, 1945 (since 1941 revision of Supreme Court Rule 25); Meier v. Peirrano, 76 Ohio App. 9, 62 N.E.2d 920, 1945 (never shifts). In California the same rule applies to contests before probate. Estate of Relph, 192 Cal. 451, 221 P. 361, 1923, and see Simes, The Function of Will Contests, 44 Mich.L.R. 503, 552; annotations, Ann.Cas.1914C 535, L.R.A.1917E 533, and infra note 27.

8 Little v. Sugg, 243 Ala. 196, 8 So. 2d 866, 1942; Appeal of Jarboe, 91 Conn. 265, 99 A. 563, 1893; Wells v. Thompson, 140 Ga. 119, 78 S.E. 823, 47 L.R.A.,N.S., 722, Ann.Cas.1914C 898, 1913; Johnson v. Banker, 193 Ind. 16, 138 N.E. 505, 1923; Chambers v. Chambers, 297 Mo. 512, 249 S.W. 415, 1923; Murry v. Hennessey, 48 Neb. 608, 67 N.W. 470, 1896; In re Allen's Will, 282 N.Y. 492, 27 N.E.2d 22, 1940; In re Fuller's Will, 189 N.C. 509, 127 S.E. 549, 1925; In re Stover's Will, 104 Okl. 251, 231 P. 212, 1924. Contra: In re Hayes' Estate, 55 Colo. 340, 135 P. 449, Ann.Cas. 1914C 531, 1913; In re Latour's Estate, 140 Cal. 414, 73 P. 1070, 74 P. 441, 1903. Cf. supra § 73, note 8. Some expressions to the contrary indicate that the court was thinking of the shifting burden of the proof. Schrodt's Ex'r v. Schrodt, 189 Ky. 457, 225 S.W. 151, 1920; Isom v. Canedy, 128 Miss. 64, 88 So. 485, 1921; McElhinny v. Trinkle, 91 Okl. 259, 217 P. 179, 1923. Close examination of the latter three cases will indicate that they are not contrary to the text statement above. As has already been suggested, the proponent's burden may be somewhat less upon application for probate than in an actual will contest. See § 95, notes 46, 47.

9 Daggett v. Boomer, 210 Ala. 673, 99 So. 181, 1925; Dulin v. Dulin, 197 N.C. 215, 148 S.E. 175, 1929. But see Barger v. Barger, 221 Ind. 530, 48 N.E.2d 813, 1943. Cf. Lare's Will, 352 Pa. 323, 42 A.2d 801, 1945, noted, 50 Dick.L.R. 104, 51 id. 62; In re Pochron's Estate, 367 Pa. 306, 80 A.2d 794, 1951.

by a preponderance of the evidence;[10] but an instruction that if the evidence is equally balanced, the will should be upheld is erroneous.[11]

Even under this majority rule, if the will has been already admitted to probate, it is sometimes held that the contestant has the initial burden of going forward with evidence concerning execution.[12] Often, however, the proponent is aided in sustaining his burden by certain presumptions. Thus, while proponent has the ultimate risk of nonpersuasion upon the issue of whether alterations and additions were made before or after execution,[13] if the additions were in blank spaces or were necessary for the sense of the instrument there is a presumption that the words were inserted before execution.[14] Other presumptions sometimes aiding a proponent are that the required formalities were observed if a qualified lawyer supervised the execution of the instrument,[15] that the testator knew the contents of the document signed,[16] that the matters recited in the attestation clause are true,[17] that, upon proof of the signatures of absent attesting witnesses, compliance with the statute will be inferred in absence of proof to the contrary,[18] and that the will was executed on the date

10 Snider v. Burks, 84 Ala. 53, 4 So. 225, 1888; Pope v. Rogers, 93 Conn. 53, 104 A. 241, 1918; Brown v. Walker (Miss.) 11 So. 724, 1892.

11 But see Stuck v. Howard, 213 Ala. 184, 104 So. 500, 1925.

12 See supra note 6. Some jurisdictions hold that the risk of nonpersuasion is on the contestant. In re Choiniere's Estate, 117 Mont. 65, 156 P.2d 635, 1945 and see supra note 7.

13 Martin v. Martin, 334 Ill. 115, 165 N.E. 644, 67 A.L.R. 1127, 1929; Guerin v. Hunt, 118 S.C. 32, 110 S.E. 71, 1921; Cooper v. Bockett, 4 Moo.P.C. 419, 13 Eng.Rep. 365, 1846. Cf. Crossman v. Crossman, 95 N.Y. 145, 1884.

14 Martin v. Martin and Guerin v. Hunt, both supra note 13. This presumption does not apply to unexplained alterations of different nature than mentioned in the above text. In re Atkinson's Estate, 90 N.J.Eq. 139, 115 A. 370, 1921.

15 Matter of Caffrey's Will, 95 Misc. 466, 159 N.Y.S. 99, 1916; Hauer v. Hauer, 45 S.D. 103, 186 N.W. 566, 1922. Cf. In re Kindberg's Will, 207 N.Y. 220, 100 N.E. 789, 1912.

16 In re Lewman's Estate, 239 Iowa 563, 30 N.W.2d 737, 1948; In re Jenks's Estate, 164 Minn. 377, 205 N.W. 271, 1925; In re White's Estate, 262 Pa. 356, 105 A. 549, 1918. See supra § 58.

17 Moore v. Walton, 158 Ga. 408, 123 S.E. 812, 1924; Woodstock College of Baltimore County v. Hankey, 129 Md. 675, 99 A. 962, 1917; Burkland v. Starry, 361 Mo. 348, 234 S.W.2d 608, 1950; Fann v. Fann, 186 Tenn. 127, 208 S.W.2d 542, 1948; In re Maresh's Will, 177 Wis. 194, 187 N.W. 1009, 1922. See annotation, 76 A.L.R. 617; note, 23 Corn.L.Q. 588.

18 Mead v. Trustees of Presbyterian Church, 229 Ill. 526, 82 N.E. 371, 14 L.R.A.,N.S., 255, 11 Ann.Cas. 426, 1907; Leatherbee v. Leatherbee, 247

which it bears.[19] Of course all of these presumptions are rebuttable; and according to the orthodox view they do not shift the risk of nonpersuasion onto the contestant, although they require him to come forward with evidence under penalty of having a verdict directed against him.[20]

*Mental Capacity—Risk of Nonpersuasion*

By the orthodox view, the burden of proof, in the sense of risk of nonpersuasion, upon the issue of mental capacity, is on the proponent.[21] In other words, if and when the matter is submitted to the jury, they should be instructed that proponent must establish the testator's competency by a preponderance of the evidence, or the verdict should be against the will's validity.[22] It is true that the burden of going forward may be shifted to the contestant after introduction of proponent's evidence,[23] or by the

Mass. 138, 141 N.E. 669, 1923; German Evangelical Bethel Church of Concordia v. Reith, 327 Mo. 1098, 39 S.W.2d 1057, 76 A.L.R. 604, 1931. Cf. Cone v. Donovan, 275 Mo. 557, 204 S.W. 1073, 1918, where the instrument was in form of a letter.

19 Seaman v. Husband, 256 Pa. 571, 100 A. 941, 1917.

20 But see In re Warren's Estate, 138 Or. 283, 4 P.2d 635, 79 A.L.R. 389, 1931 (presumption due to attestation clause must be overcome by clear and convincing evidence); Van Meter v. Van Meter, 183 Md. 614, 39 A.2d 752, 1944 (same).

21 Roeber v. Cordray, 70 Colo. 196, 199 P. 481, 1921; Appeal of Wheeler, 91 Conn. 388, 100 A. 13, 1917; Wells v. Thompson, 140 Ga. 119, 78 S.E. 823, 47 L.R.A.,N.S., 722, Ann.Cas.1914C 898, 1913; Miller v. Blumenshine, 343 Ill. 531, 175 N.E. 814, 76 A.L.R. 362, 1931; Schrodt's Ex'r v. Schrodt, 189 Ky. 457, 225 S.W. 151, 1920; In re Loomis' Will, 133 Me. 81, 174 A. 38, 1934; Crowninshield v. Crowninshield, 2 Gray (Mass.) 524, 1854; In re Enyart's Estate, 180 Minn. 256, 230 N.W. 781, 1930; Fields v. Luck, 335 Mo. 765, 74 S.W.2d 35, 1934; In re Slattery's Estate, 125 Neb. 194, 249 N.W. 597, 1933; Matter of Chinsky's Will, 151 Misc. 129, 270 N.Y.S. 822, 1934; In re Knutson's Will, 149 Or. 467, 41 P.2d 793, 1935; Johnson v. Shaver, 41 S.D. 585, 172 N.W. 676, 1919; In re Harris v. Harris' Estate, 276 S.W. 964, Tex.Civ.App.1925; Williams v. Robinson, 42 Vt. 658, 1 Am. Rep. 359, 1870; Dickens v. Bonnewell, 160 Va. 194, 168 S.E. 610, 1933; Summers v. Summers, 107 W.Va. 38, 146 S.E. 894, 1929; Sutton v. Sadler, 3 C.B.(N.S.) 87, 140 Eng.Rep. 671, 1857. In Wigmore on Evidence § 2500, the above rule is said to be generally conceded, the only difference in the opinions being with respect to the burden of going forward with the evidence. But see cases infra, note 26. The position expressed in the text above is favored by Professor Warren in 33 Harv.L.R. 558, 559, and by most of the note writers. See 20 Ill.L.R. 313; 22 Ill.L.R. 785; 22 Mich.L.R. 70; 23 Mich.L.R. 422; 25 Mich.L.R. 925. Sometimes this result is demanded by the language of the statute. N.Y.Surr.Ct.Act, § 144.

22 Roeber v. Cordray, and Appeal of Wheeler, both supra note 21.

23 See infra notes 32, 34.

operation of the presumption of sanity which often comes into operation as soon as there is proof of execution of the will.[24] But the risk of nonpersuasion is not shifted by the state of the evidence or the operation of the presumption.[25] From the standpoint of logic, this view is supported upon the ground that testator's capacity as well as due execution are necessary for the validity of a will and that the proponent should prove both elements of his case. There is also the argument of policy that the law should favor the heirs at law and that he who seeks to defeat their interests should be handicapped by the burden of proof upon the issue of testamentary capacity.

Approximately an equal number of decisions declare that the burden of proof is upon the contestant on the issue of mental capacity.[26] As has been explained, this result is sometimes reached as a result of statutes which make contestant the plaintiff, or declare that probate of the will shall be prima facie evidence of the execution and validity of the will in case of a later contest. Such statutes have usually been construed as placing the risk of nonpersuasion upon the contestant in the later suit,[27]

24 See infra note 33.

25 Miller v. Blumenshine, Crowninshield v. Crowninshield, Roeber v. Cordray, and In re Enyart's Estate, all supra note 21. See annotation, 76 A.L.R. 373.

26 Tucker v. Houston, 216 Ala. 43, 112 So. 360, 1927; Emerich v. Arendt, 179 Ark. 186, 14 S.W.2d 547, 1929; In re Sexton's Will, 199 Cal. 759, 251 P. 778, 1926, noted, 25 Mich.L.R. 925; Myers v. Pleasant, 118 Fla. 715, 160 So. 204, 1927; Cooper v. Shannon, 165 Ga. 451, 141 S.E. 306, 1918; Millage v. Noble, 334 Ill. 315, 166 N.E. 50, 1929; In re Cooper's Estate, 196 Iowa 116, 194 N.W. 218, 1923, noted, 22 Mich.L.R. 70; Stoll v. Stoll's Ex'r, 213 Ky. 789, 281 S.W. 1028, 1926; Scheller v. Schindel, 153 Md. 547, 138 A. 415, 1927; Walker v. Hinckley, 270 Mich. 33, 258 N.W. 206, 1935, noted, 20 Corn.L.Q. 389 (statute); In re Triebe's Will, 114 N.J.Eq. 227, 168 A. 404, 1933; In re Brown's Will, 200 N.C. 440, 157 S.E. 420, 1931; Wood v. Wood, 168 Okl. 198, 32 P.2d 715, 1934; In re Lawrence's Estate, 286 Pa. 58, 132 A. 786, 1926; In re Bryan's Estate, 82 Utah 390, 25 P.2d 602, 1933; In re McKachney's Estate, 143 Wash. 28, 254 P. 455, 1927; Brosnan v. Brosnan, 263 U.S. 345, 44 S.Ct. 117, 68 L.Ed. 332, 1923, noted, 23 Mich.L.R. 422.

27 In re Latour's Estate, 140 Cal. 414, 73 P. 1070, 74 P. 441, 1903; Farleigh v. Kelley, 28 Mont. 421, 72 P. 756, 63 L.R.A. 319, 1905; Dobie v. Armstrong, 160 N.Y. 584, 55 N.E. 302, 1899; Mears v. Mears, 15 Ohio St. 90, 1864; Dickey v. Dickey, 66 Okl. 269, 168 P. 1018, 1917. Some jurisdictions hold, even in absence of statute, that the probate of the will places the burden of proof upon contestant. West v. Arrington, 200 Ala. 420, 76 So. 352, 1917; Stoll v. Stoll's Ex'r, supra note 26. And see Colman v. Lindley, 115 Kan. 802, 224 P. 912, 1924. In Michigan by statute passed in 1915 the burden of proof is placed upon contestant. Brereton v. Glazeby's Estate, 251 Mich. 234, 231 N.W. 566, 1930; Walker v. Hinckley, supra note 26. Prior to 1915 the Michigan

although it would be more reasonable to hold that they shift only the burden of going forward with the evidence. Other jurisdictions place the risk of nonpersuasion upon contestant because they regard the burden as shifted by the presumption of sanity.[28] This view runs contrary to the general principle that the risk of nonpersuasion does not shift, and this situation does not come within the exception that this burden may be shifted by the operation of certain presumptions which are based upon some strong reason of public policy.[29] The presumption of sanity is not of that nature, being founded merely upon mathematical probabilities. In addition, the presumption of sanity, having no particular logical core, should not remain as evidence and after the introduction of testimony on the issue should disappear from the case altogether.[30]

The only sound reason for placing the risk of nonpersuasion upon contestant is that a fair division of the burdens calls for regarding incapacity of testator as a matter of defense. After all, the matter is not one which can be solved on a mechanical basis. Ultimately the apportionment of the burden depends upon whether the court desires to favor the heirs, or the devisees and legatees. The court's intuitive judgment, rather than any logical principle, will be the determining factor. There is nothing inherently unsound in placing the burden upon the contestant if this conclusion is reached upon a frank recognition of a desire to favor testacy.

Many of the cases which declare that the burden of proof is on contestant refer merely to the burden of going forward with the evidence. In part, this will account for the apparently conflicting decisions in a single jurisdiction. Not all cases can be explained upon this basis. In some of the decisions the courts have confused the two burdens, and upon seeing that the burden of going forward has shifted by the operation of the presumption of sanity, have concluded that the risk of nonpersuasion does so also.[31] This reasoning is obviously erroneous.

court held the burden to be on proponent. Prentis v. Bates, 93 Mich. 234, 53 N.W. 153, 17 L.R.A. 494, 1892.

28 Millage v. Noble, 334 Ill. 315, 166 N.E. 50, 1929; Philpott v. Jones, 164 Iowa 730, 146 N.W. 859, 1914.

29 See supra note 3.

30 Appeal of Wheeler and Roeber v. Cordray, both supra note 21. See notes, 22 Ill.L.R. 785; 2 Ohio St.L.J. 292, 299. But see Scheller v. Schindel, supra note 26; Donovan v. St. Joseph's Home, 295 Ill. 125, 129 N.E. 1, 1920.

31 See Adams v. Cooper, 148 Ga. 339, 96 S.E. 858, 1918; Cooper v. Shannon, supra note 26. See 22 Mich. L.R. 70; 33 Harv.L.R. 559; 22 Ill. L.R. 785.

### *Mental Capacity—Burden of Going Forward*

No matter which party has the risk of nonpersuasion in the particular jurisdiction, it is agreed that the burden of going forward may shift from one side to the other.[32] In some jurisdictions all that is necessary for proponent's prima facie case as to mental capacity is proof of proper execution, whereupon he is entitled to the presumption of sanity.[33] In other states this does not make out a prima facie case for proponent, who is obliged to introduce at least some evidence on this point before he can rest without liability of having a verdict directed against him.[34] When the proponent has satisfied his burden of going forward and contestant makes no showing of incapacity, a verdict should usually be directed in favor of the will.[35] However, dependent upon the strength of proponent's evidence and upon whether he has the risk of nonpersuasion, this situation may merely call for submission of the issue to the jury.

### *Undue Influence—Risk of Nonpersuasion*

While only a minority of courts place this burden on contestants on the issues of execution and capacity, the risk of nonpersuasion upon the issues of fraud and undue influence is, by the great weight of authority, upon the contestant.[36] The latter mat-

[32] Schrodt's Ex'r v. Schrodt, 189 Ky. 457, 225 S.W. 151, 1920; McFadin v. Catron, 138 Mo. 197, 38 S.W. 932, 39 S.W. 771, 1896; In re Bayer's Estate, 119 Neb. 191, 227 N.W. 928, 1929, noted, 3 Dak.L.R. 222.

[33] Brosnan v. Brosnan, 263 U.S. 345, 44 Sup.Ct. 117, 68 L.Ed. 332, 1923, noted, 23 Mich. L.R. 422; Houston v. Grigsby, 217 Ala. 506, 116 So. 686, 1928; Van Meter v. Ritenour, 193 Ind. 615, 141 N.E. 329, 1923; Perkins v. Perkins, 39 N.H. 163, 1859; In re Morley's Estate, 138 Or. 75, 5 P.2d 92, 1931. Cf. Spradlin v. Adams, 182 Ky. 716, 207 S.W. 471, 1919 (burden discharged by showing rational nature of the will). See Wigmore on Evidence § 2500.

[34] Weaver v. Allison, 340 Mo. 815, 102 S.W.2d 884, 110 A.L.R. 672, 1937; In re Enyart's Estate, 180 Minn. 256, 230 N.W. 781, 1930; Tyson v. Utterback, 154 Miss. 381, 122 So. 496, 63 A.L.R. 1188, 1929; Matter of Schreiber's Will, 112 App.Div. 495, 98 N.Y.S. 483, 1906; In re Baldwin's Estate, 13 Wash. 666, 43 P. 934, 1896.

[35] In re Bayer's Estate, supra note 32.

[36] Martindale v. Bridgforth, 210 Ala. 565, 98 So. 800, 1924; Page v. Phelps, 108 Conn. 572, 143 A. 890, 1928; Michael v. Marshall, 201 Ill. 70, 66 N.E. 273, 1903; Mallow v. Walker, 115 Iowa 238, 88 N.W. 452, 91 Am.St. Rep. 158, 1901; Collis v. Walker, 272 Mass. 46, 172 N.E. 228, 1930; In re Loree's Estate, 158 Mich. 372, 122 N.W. 623, 1909, noted, 10 Col.L.R. 83; In re Keeley's Estate, 167 Minn. 120, 208 N.W. 535, 1926; In re Hagan's Estate, 143 Neb. 459, 9 N.W. 794, 154 A.L.R. 573, 1943; In re Schillinger's Will, 258 N.Y. 186, 179 N.E. 380, 1932; In re Bryan's Estate, 82 Utah 390, 25 P.2d 602, 1933. But see Breadheft v. Cleveland, 184 Ind. 130, 108 N.E. 5,

ters are usually looked upon as confession and avoidance and if the proofs stand in equipoise the proponent is entitled to win.[37] This position has been criticized on the ground that an uncoerced, as well as a sound, mind is necessary for an effective will.[38] However, the latter argument has no a priori validity, and for purely practical reasons the majority view seems sound. If undue influence or fraud existed they must have occurred in some particular manner. To hold that contestant should establish these by a preponderance of the evidence does not impose too great a burden upon him, bearing in mind that the proofs may be circumstantial. On the other hand, to require proponent to negative the various possibilities by a preponderance seems too great a handicap upon the establishment of wills.

*Undue Influence—Degree of Proof Required*

The prevailing view seems to be that the contestant need only establish undue influence by a preponderance of the evidence.[39] Hence it is not necessary to rebut all other hypotheses than that of undue influence.[40] nor even prove undue influence to the "satisfaction" of the jury.[41] Some courts, however, require a higher degree of proof than in ordinary civil issues,[42] and declare that undue influence should be established by clear or convincing evidence, upon the ground that the moral or even criminal stigma attached to such conduct calls for something more than the ordinary measure of proof.[43]

110 N.E. 662, 1915; Sheehan v. Kearney, 82 Miss. 688, 21 So. 41, 35 L.R.A. 102, 1896, discussed at length in note, 14 Miss.L.J. 103; Gaffney v. Coffey, 81 N.H. 300, 124 A. 788, 1924; Barry v. Butlin, 2 Moo.P.C. 480, 12 Eng. Rep. 1089, 1838. Cf. In re Ash's Estate, 351 Pa. 317, 41 A.2d 620, 1945.

37 In re Schillinger's Will, supra note 36.

38 See Gifford, Will or No Will?, 20 Col.L.R. 862, 878–880; Warren, The Progress of the Law, Wills and Administration, 33 Harv.L.R. 556, 558, 559; note, 10 Col.L.R. 83.

39 Compher v. Browning, 219 Ill. 429, 76 N.E. 678, 109 Am.St.Rep. 346, 1906; Cereghino v. Giannone, 247 Mass. 319, 142 N.E. 153, 1924; Bush v. Delano, 113 Mich. 321, 71 N.W. 628, 1897.

40 Bush v. Delano, supra note 39.

41 Miller v. Whittington, 202 Ala. 406, 80 So. 499, 1918, (reasonable satisfaction is enough).

42 In re Ball's Estate, 153 Wis. 27, 141 N.W. 8, 1913. And see In re Estate of Seiler, 176 Cal. 771, 170 P. 1138, 179 P. 389, 1917; Downey v. Guilfoile, 93 Conn. 630, 107 A. 562, 1919.

43 In re Ball's Estate, supra note 42.

*Undue Influence—Presumptions*

The whole matter of burden of proof regarding undue influence is complicated by the operation of certain presumptions in special cases. As has already been seen,[44] when the beneficiary sustained confidential relations with the testator and also drafted the instrument there is a presumption of undue influence, though in some jurisdictions this situation is said to merely raise an inference of undue influence or call for scrutiny. The principle is really broader than before indicated, and the consequences also attach when certain persons sustaining confidential relationships to the testator were active in procuring the will. No presumption exists, however, because the executor or testamentary trustee takes part in the execution of the will unless the latter obtained substantial benefits under the will.[45] Nor does the presumption ordinarily apply in case of the spouse procuring the instrument.[46] Only such relationships as those of attorney and client, clergyman and parishioner, physician and patient, or close business associates are sufficient to give rise to a presumption.[47] Moreover, by the majority rule the confidential relationship alone, unaccompanied by activity in procuring a will in favor of the attorney, clergyman, physician, or business associate does not raise a presumption of undue influence.[48] Some courts, however, apply the ordinary equity rule regarding gifts inter vivos to the wills' cases and presume undue influence from the mere fact of con-

44 Supra § 55, note 45 et seq. And see In re Lance's Estate, 216 Cal. 397, 14 P.2d 768, 1932, noted, 3 Idaho L.J. 170; In re Nutt's Estate, 181 Cal. 522, 185 P. 393, 1919, noted, 20 Col.L.R. 358; Boynton v. Simmons, 156 Minn. 144, 194 N.W. 330, 1923 (setting forth various views as to presumption, inference, case for scrutiny, etc.).

45 See supra § 55, note 44.

46 In re Thompson's Estate, 153 Neb. 375, 44 N.W.2d 814, 1950; In re Detsch's Estate, 191 Or. 161, 229 P.2d 264, 1951. See also Koppal v. Soules, 189 Md. 346, 56 A.2d 48, 1947.

47 See Gager v. Mathewson, 93 Conn. 539, 107 A. 1, 1919; In re Morrish's Estate, 156 Pa.Super. 394, 40 A.2d 907, 1945. But see In re Stewart's Estate, 354 Pa. 288, 47 A.2d 204, 1946.

48 McQueen v. Wilson, 131 Ala. 606, 31 So. 94, 1901; Hutcheson v. Bibb, 142 Ala. 586, 38 So. 754, 1905, noted, 6 Col.L.R. 57; In re Baird's Estate, 176 Cal. 381, 168 P. 561, 1917; Yess v. Yess, 255 Ill. 414, 99 N.E. 687, 1912; Goodbar v. Lidikey, 136 Ind. 1, 35 N.E. 691, 43 Am.St.Rep. 296, 1893; Liddle v. Salter, 180 Iowa 840, 163 N.W. 447, 1917; Buckner v. Tuggle, 356 Mo. 718, 203 S.W.2d 449, 1947; In re Llewellyn's Estate, 296 Pa. 74, 145 A. 810, 66 A.L.R. 222, 1929 (this jurisdiction requires also that testator should be of weak intellect, before presumption arises); Parfitt v. Lawless, L.R. 2 P. & D. 462, 1872. See also Wigmore on Evidence § 2503; notes, 7 Col.L.R. 439, 7 Mo.L.R. 188.

fidential relationship between testator and the beneficiary.[49] When the provision in the will is in favor of a close relative of the person in confidential relationship with the testator, undue influence is presumed if it would be presumed in case that person was the devisee or legatee.[50] It is usually held that there is no presumption merely on account of illicit relationship between testator and beneficiary,[51] or their membership in the same household,[52] or because there is inequality in the will's provisions in favor of the beneficiary.[53] While such facts are admissible, and may be taken into consideration in connection with other evidence,[54] they are not, by themselves, sufficient to submit the issue to the jury.

If the confidential relationship gives rise to a presumption rather than a mere inference or suspicion, the question remains as to the effect of presumption. Here there is the greatest confusion. Clearly the presumption is not conclusive, and proponent is entitled to introduce evidence to rebut it.[55] Moreover, the presumption should not shift the risk of nonpersuasion,[56] though some courts apparently hold that it does.[57] When a presumption

[49] Kirby's Appeal, 91 Conn. 40, 98 A. 349, 1916; Sittig v. Kersting, 284 Mo. 143, 223 S.W. 742, 1920.

[50] Yess v. Yess, supra note 48; In re Cooper's Will, 75 N.J.Eq. 177, 71 A. 676, 1909. Cf. Henry v. Hall, 106 Ala. 84, 17 So. 187, 54 Am.St.Rep. 22, 1894.

[51] Norton v. Clark, 253 Ill. 557, 97 N.E. 1079, 1912; Griffith v. Benzinger, 144 Md. 575, 125 A. 512, 1908; In re Gaddis' Will, 96 N.J.Eq. 668, 126 A. 287, 1924. Cf. Re Anna, 248 N.Y. 421, 162 N.E.2d 473, 1928.

[52] Downey v. Guilfoile, 93 Conn. 630, 107 A. 562, 1919.

[53] Burney v. Torrey, 100 Ala. 157, 14 So. 685, 46 Am.St.Rep. 33, 1893; In re Smith's Estate, 200 Cal. 152, 252 P. 325, 1926; Hegney v. Head, 126 Mo. 619, 29 S.W. 587, 1895. But see Gardiner v. Goertner, 110 Fla. 377, 149 So. 186, 1932; Johnson v. Shaver, 41 S.D. 585, 172 N.W. 676, 1919.

[54] Little v. Little, 209 Ala. 651, 96 So. 928, 1923; Norton v. Clark, supra note 51.

[55] Betz v. Lovell, 197 Ala. 239, 72 So. 500, 1916; In re Teller's Estate, 288 Mich. 193, 284 N.W. 696, 1939; Loveridge v. Brown, 98 N.J.Eq. 381, 129 A. 131, 1928; In re Anderson's Estate, 142 Okl. 197, 286 P. 17, 1929; In re Bryan's Estate, 82 Utah 390, 25 P.2d 602, 1933.

[56] Madden v. Keyser, 331 Ill. 643, 163 N.E. 424, 1928; Graham v. Courtright, 180 Iowa 394, 161 N.W. 774, 1917; Gay v. Gay, 308 Ky. 539, 215 S.W.2d 92, 1948; In re Mollan's Estate, 181 Minn. 217, 232 N.W. 1, 1930, noted, 15 Minn.L.R. 600; Munday v. Knox, 321 Mo. 168, 9 S.W.2d 960, 1928; In re Hagan's Estate, supra note 36; In re Kindberg's Will, 207 N.Y. 220, 100 N.E. 789, 1912; In re Schillinger's Will, 258 N.Y. 186, 179 N.E. 380, 1932. See notes, 3 Idaho L. J. 170, 20 Col.L.R. 358.

[57] Page v. Phelps, 108 Conn. 572, 143 A. 890, 1928, noted, 38 Yale L.J.

operates, the contestant has made out a prima facie case sufficient at least to submit the matter to the jury.[58] Whether the presumption is strong enough to require a verdict to be directed in favor of the contestant, in case the proponent offers no evidence in rebuttal is not clear; it would seem that it should be.[59] Finally, if the matter is submitted to the jury upon conflicting evidence it is questionable as to whether the court should inform the jury of the existence of the presumption,[60] though some courts apparently allow this.[61]

*Revocation—Risk of Nonpersuasion and Presumptions*

In general, at least where the will is produced, the burden of proof upon the issue of revocation is upon contestant.[62] Where contestant asserts revocation by a subsequent instrument, he must prove the latter by the same kind and measure of evidence as is required for the establishment of a will.[63]

831; In re Hollinger's Estate, 351 Pa. 364, 41 A.2d 554, 1945; cf. In re Palmer's Estate, 48 So.2d 732, Fla. 1950.

58 In re Lance's Estate, supra note 44. See also authorities infra note 59, and note, 12 Ia.L.R. 430.

59 See Gum v. Reep, 275 Ill. 503, 114 N.E. 271, 1916; Appeal of O'Brien, 100 Me. 156, 60 A. 880, 1905; In re Jernberg's Estate, 153 Minn. 458, 190 N.W. 990, 1922; In re Schillinger's Will, supra note 56; Leahy v. Timon, 204 S.W. 1029, Tex.Civ.App. 1918; Central Hanover Bank & Trust Co. v. Froment, 114 Vt. 523, 49 A.2d 111, 1946.

60 For a general discussion of this matter, see McCormick, Charges on Presumptions and Burden of Proof, 5 N.C.L.R. 291, 299 et seq.

61 See Pilstrand v. Swedish Methodist Church, 275 Ill. 46, 113 N.E. 958, 1916; Buerger v. Buerger, 317 Ill. 401, 148 N.E. 274, 1925; Graham v. Courtright, supra note 56. In Loehr v. Starke, 332 Mo. 131, 56 S.W.2d 772, 1933, it was said: "The presumption under consideration is not a mere legal fiction or procedural rule. It rests on a substantial basis of fact or inference. The presumption and fact, or inference, go hand in hand and really are the same thing. Hence, the presumption, with its underlying facts or inferences once being in the case never does or can disappear but raises an issue for the jury."

62 Cook v. Jeffett, 169 Ark. 62, 272 S.W. 873, 1925; Luther v. Luther, 211 Ala. 352, 100 So. 497, 1924; In re Rinker's Estate, 158 Kan. 406, 147 P. 2d 740, 1944; Aldrich v. Aldrich, 215 Mass. 164, 102 N.E. 487, Ann.Cas.1914 C 906, 1913; Cheever v. North, 106 Mich. 390, 64 N.W. 455, 37 L.R.A. 561, 58 Am.St.Rep. 499, 1895. Contra: Brackenridge v. Roberts, 114 Tex. 418, 270 S.W. 1001, 1924 (statute); May v. Brown, 144 Tex. 350, 190 S.W. 2d 715, 165 A.L.R. 1180, 1945. Cf. In re Thompson's Estate, 48 S.D. 474, 205 N.W. 47, 1925 (burden on proponent to show undue influence in connection with revocation); In re Marsden's Estate, 217 Minn. 1, 13 N. W.2d 765, 1944 (same).

63 In re Brown's Will, 143 Iowa 649, 120 N.W. 667, 1909; Minor v. Guthrie (Ky.) 4 S.W. 179, 1887 (revoking will lost); Williams v. Moorehead, 116 Miss. 653, 77 So. 658, 1917.

The matter of revocation by physical act is complicated by the operation of presumptions under certain circumstances. Thus, it is often held that where the will was in testator's possession and cannot be found at the time of his death, it will be presumed that the testator destroyed it with intent to revoke,[64] and the same has been held where a duplicate will in testator's possession cannot be found.[65] Indeed it is often said that the burden of proof is on the proponent under these circumstances.[66] There are several possible explanations of this language. Perhaps the courts may be here referring merely to the burden of going forward with the evidence and the ultimate burden may still be on the contestant to establish revocation by a preponderance of the evidence when, and if, the matter is submitted to the jury.[67] Assuming however that the risk of nonpersuasion is on the proponent in such cases, there may be two explanations of this position. First, it is conceivable that in actions to establish lost or mutilated wills, the burden may be upon the proponent to establish nonrevocation as well as execution.[68] Second, the presump-

[64] In re Crosby's Estate, 126 Neb. 509, 253 N.W. 652, 1934; In re Ladman's Estate, 128 Neb. 483, 259 N.W. 50, 1935, Cf. In re Smith's Estate, 140 Cal.App. 508, 35 P.2d 335, 1934; Thomas v. Thompson, 114 Fla. 833, 155 So. 321, 1934 (inference of fact only which is not required to be drawn); Coghlin v. White, 273 Mass. 53, 172 N.E. 786, 1930; McClellan v. Owens, 335 Mo. 884, 74 S.W.2d 570, 95 A.L.R. 711, 1934; In re Calef's Will, 111 N.J.Eq. 355, 162 A. 579, 1931; In re Staiger's Will, 243 N.Y. 468, 154 N.E. 312, 1927, noted, 23 Ill. L.R. 192; Flanders v. White, 142 Or. 375, 18 P.2d 823, 1933; Gardner v. Gardner, 177 Pa. 218, 35 A. 558, 1896; In re Robinson's Estate, 149 Wash. 307, 270 P. 1020, 1928. And see Wigmore on Evidence § 2523; supra § 86, notes 47, 48.

[65] Matter of McChesney's Will, 118 Misc. 545, 194 N.Y.S. 893, 1922; In re Bates' Estate, 286 Pa. 583, 134 A. 513, 48 A.L.R. 294, 1926. Cf. Menzi v. White, 360 Mo. 319, 228 S.W.2d 700, 17 A.L.R.2d 796, 1950 (inference). See supra § 86 at notes 49, 50. The presumption has been applied where both duplicates were in testator's possession but only one was found. In re Blackstone's Estate, 172 Misc. 479, 15 N.Y.S.2d 597, 1939; but see Phinizee v. Alexander, 210 Miss. 196, 49 So.2d 250, 1950, noted, 14 U. of Det.L.J. 161. Cf. Snider v. Burks, 84 Ala. 53, 4 So. 225, 1888; In re Mittelstaedt's Will, 278 App.Div. 231, 104 N.Y.S.2d 378, 1951. See note, 27 Chi-Kent L.R. 174.

[66] In re Smith's Estate, McClellan v. Owens, In re Crosby's Estate, all supra note 64; Shacklett v. Roller, 97 Va. 639, 34 S.E. 492, 1899; see In re Drake's Estate, 150 Neb. 568, 35 N.W. 2d 417, 1048, noted, 28 Neb.L.R. 620 (must be rebutted by more than preponderance); Langan v. Cheshire, 208 Ga. 107, 65 S.E.2d 415, 1951 (statute); In re Jensen's Estate, 141 N.J. Eq. 222, 56 A.2d 573, 1947.

[67] See Ferguson v. Billups, 244 Ky. 85, 50 S.W.2d 35, 1932; Thomas v. Thompson, supra note 64; note, 8 Tex.L.R. 408.

[68] See In re Smith's Estate, McClellan v. Owens, both supra note 64;

tion may actually have the effect of shifting the burden of proof in the cases in which it operates.[69]

Clearly the presumption is not a conclusive one.[70] It may be rebutted by proof that the will was destroyed without knowledge of the testator, or that he never intended revocation and died supposing the will to be in existence,[71] or that the testator's feelings toward the beneficiaries never changed, accompanied by proof that the will might have been lost or destroyed without his knowledge.[72] If the testator did not have access to the will after its execution, no presumption of revocation exists.[73] When the testator was insane during part of the time between execution of the will and his death, while it is presumed that it was destroyed by the testator if he had possession thereof, there is no presumption as to when it was destroyed and the party asserting its revocation must show it was destroyed by the testator during the period of sanity.[74]

Where a will has been duly executed and left with the testator, and upon his death it is found among his repositories, canceled or defaced, the testator is presumed to have done the act with intent to revoke.[75] A fortiori, if the testator is shown to have done the physical act of mutilation, this will be presumed to be with ani-

Schacklett v. Roller, supra note 66. See note, 24 St. John's L.R. 314, and supra § 97 at notes 17–19.

69 See supra text at notes 25, 28, 29.

70 In re Eder's Estate, 94 Colo. 173, 29 P.2d 631, 1934; In re Ladman's Estate, 128 Neb. 483, 259 N.W. 50, 1935; In re Auritt's Estate, 175 Wash. 303, 27 P.2d 713, 1934. See also Phinizee v. Alexander, In re Mittelstaedt's Will, both supra note 65. Cf. In re O'Connor's Estate, 191 Minn. 34, 253 N.W. 18, 1934 (statutory presumption of revocation due to change of circumstances is conclusive).

71 In re Eder's Estate, supra note 70; Foster's Appeal, 87 Pa. 67, 30 Am.Rep. 340, 1878; In re Auritt's Estate, supra note 70; In re Ronayne's Estate, 103 Cal.App.2d 852, 230 P.2d 423, 1951.

72 Patten v. Poulton, 1 Sw. & Tr. 55, 164 Eng.Rep. 626, 1858. And see In re Auritt's Estate, supra note 70.

73 In re Ross' Estate, 199 Cal. 641, 250 P. 676, 1926; White v. Brennan, 307 Ky. 776, 212 S.W.2d 299, 3 A.L.R. 2d 943, 1948; Schultz v. Schultz, 35 N.Y. 653, 91 Am.Dec. 88, 1866; McElroy v. Phink, 97 Tex. 147, 76 S.W. 753, 1903.

74 In re Will of Murray, 20 Ohio N.P.(N.S.) 305, 1917; Sprigge v. Sprigge, L.R. 1 P. & D. 608, 1868. But see Home of the Aged of the Methodist Episcopal Church v. Bantz, 107 Md. 543, 69 A. 376, 1908.

75 In re Fisher's Estate, 47 Idaho 668, 279 P. 291, 1929; Carrithers v. Jean's Ex'r, 249 Ky. 695, 61 S.W.2d 323, 1933; In re Hopkins' Will, 172 N.Y. 360, 65 N.E. 173, 65 L.R.A. 95, 92 Am.St.Rep. 746, 1902; Dawley v. Congdon, 42 R.I. 64, 105 A. 393, 1919. See supra § 86, notes 47, 48. As to

mus revocandi.[76] It has even been held that where the mutilation took place in the testator's lifetime, revocation will be presumed though others also had access to the will.[77] Usually, there is no such presumption in case the will did not come from the testator's custody.[78]

## COSTS AND ATTORNEY FEES

**102. The costs and attorney fees of an executor who proceeds in good faith to establish the will against opposition are usually allowed from the estate even if the will is not finally admitted to probate. The expenses of other persons should not be paid from the estate, though some courts permit such allowances to successful and even unsuccessful proponents and contestants when there was probable cause for their respective contentions.**

Many of the questions of costs which may arise in will contests are matters of general practice and, like the problems of new trials and appeals, have no place in the present work. However, the problem of the allowance of costs and attorney fees from the estate is of sufficient special nature to be treated here. In some states the questions in this connection are determined or influenced by statutes,[1] yet often the questions are not touched upon by legislative enactment.

The ordinary rule of general civil litigation that taxable costs of the prevailing party must be paid by the losing party is often altered in will contests, and the prevailing party's costs,[2] and

whether a total or partial revocation will be presumed depends on the nature of the mutilation, the instrument and other circumstances. In re Streeton's Estate, 183 Cal. 284, 191 P. 16, 1920; Burton v. Wylde, 261 Ill. 397, 103 N.E. 976, 1913. The presumption of course is not conclusive. Dawley v. Congdon, supra; Burton v. Wylde, supra; Flanders v. White, infra note 76; Russell v. Tyler, 224 Ky. 511, 6 S.W.2d 707, 1928. As to penciled marks, cf. Franklin v. McLean, 192 Va. 684, 66 S.E.2d 504, 1951, with In re Holcombe's Estate, 259 Wis. 642, 49 N.W.2d 914, 1951, noted, 35 Marq.L.R. 402.

76 Flanders v. White, 142 Or. 375, 18 P.2d 823, 1933.

77 Collyer v. Collyer, 110 N.Y. 481, 18 N.E. 110, 6 Am.St.Rep. 405, 1888; Lowe v. Fickling, 207 S.C. 442, 36 S.E.2d 293, 1945 (destruction).

78 Stevens v. Stevens, 72 N.H. 360, 56 A. 916, 1903; Throckmorton v. Holt, 180 U.S. 552, 21 S.Ct. 474, 45 L.Ed. 663, 1901.

1 See Matter of O'Brien's Estate, 146 Misc. 555, 263 N.Y.S. 877, 1933; also infra notes 4, 7, 11, 13.

2 In re Cobb's Estate, infra note 13; Hampden Trust Co. v. Leary, 186

sometimes even those of the losing party,[3] are paid from the funds of the estate. As in case of ordinary civil litigation, costs do not include the actual attorney fees, but only such items as docket, filing and witness fees and outlays for transcripts and printing.[4]

*Allowance to Personal Representatives*

The chief controversy has centered about the question of whether counsel fees, the principal item of the expense of the litigation, may be charged against the estate. As it is the executor's duty to uphold the will,[5] most cases declare that his costs and attorney fees in this connection should be charged against the estate.[6] Some courts so hold even if the executor is ultimately unsuccessful in his attempt to sustain the will,[7] and

Mass. 577, 72 N.E. 88, 1904; In re Morley's Will, 119 N.Y.S. 58, 1909. Cf. Cleveland v. Creed, 66 A.2d 195, N.J.Super.1949 (charged to unsuccessful contestant); McCrary v. Michael, 233 Mo.App. 797, 109 S.W.2d 50, 1937, noted, 3 Mo.L.R. 330 (same).

3 Harris v. Harris, 211 Ala. 144, 99 So. 913, 1924 (compromise—all costs); In re Hayer's Estate, 233 Iowa 1343, 11 N.W.2d 593, 1943 (executor); In re Winston, 172 N.C. 270, 90 S.E. 201, 1916 (all costs); In re Johnson's Estate, 100 Or. 142, 196 P. 1115, 1921 (all costs); McNaughton v. McGregor, 133 Wis. 494, 113 N.W. 956, 1907 (executor); In re Bilty's Will, 171 Wis. 20, 176 N.W. 220, 1920 (contestant).

4 In re Deehan's Will, 130 Me. 243, 154 A. 645, 1930; In re Doty's Estate, 231 Mich. 115, 203 N.W. 865, 1925. See Matter of Reimers, infra note 13, allowing costs but denying attorney fees to unsuccessful party. As to allowance of fees to expert witnesses, cf. In re Tipper's Estate, 88 N.J.Eq. 307, 102 A. 897, 1918, with In re Johnson's Estate, 170 Wis. 436, 175 N.W. 917, 1920. As in other litigation, small fixed statutory attorneys' fees may be allowed to the prevailing parties as part of the costs of will contests. The discussion of counsel fees in the present section does not relate to such items, but only to amounts which represent full or substantial compensation to counsel.

5 See supra § 95 and cases infra notes 6–9.

6 Powell v. Labry, 210 Ala. 248, 97 So. 707, 1923; McMillen's Ex'rs v. McElroy, 186 Ky. 644, 217 S.W. 927, 1920 ($2500 fee); In re Hentges' Estate, 86 Neb. 75, 124 N.W. 929, 26 L.R.A.,N.S., 757, 1910; In re Dickey's Estate, 87 Ohio App. 255, 94 N.E.2d 223, 20 A.L.R.2d 1220, 1949. See note, 70 Cent.L.J. 337. And see infra notes 7–10. But an attorney for executor has himself no standing to ask for allowance of his fees from the estate. Conley v. Fenelon, 266 Mass. 340, 165 N.E. 382, 1929.

7 Hutchins v. Hutchins, 48 App.D.C. 286, 1919; Medill v. McIntire, 136 Kan. 594, 16 P.2d 952, 1932 (allowance of $500 expense to person named as executor in forged will was within court's discretion though estate was only $1,300); Conley v. Fenelon, 266 Mass. 340, 165 N.E. 382, 1929 (statute); Butt v. Murden, 154 Va. 10, 152 S.E. 330, 69 A.L.R. 1048, 1930; In re Jolly, 3 Wash.2d 615, 101 P.2d 995, 128 A.L.R. 993, 1940; see Model Probate Code § 104. But see In re Austin's Estate, 194 Iowa 1217, 191 N.W.

though the contest occurred before probate,[8] and even if the executor would be the one chiefly benefited by sustaining of the will.[9] Other cases deny the right to charge the executor's expenses where one or more of the foregoing circumstances exist.[10] A few authorities indicate that the executor should ordinarily remain neutral and permit the interested parties to incur the necessary expenses.[11] Apparently all courts would deny the allowance if the executor carried on the litigation in bad faith.[12] Often the allowance is dependent upon the discretion of the trial or the probate court.[13]

An administrator who has been appointed upon the supposition that the estate was intestate should not be allowed his expense in attempting to prevent probate of a will subsequently presented,[14] even though the instrument is finally rejected.[15] This po-

73, 1922; Dodd v. Anderson, 197 N.Y. 466, 90 N.E. 1137, 27 L.R.A.,N.S., 336, 18 Ann.Cas. 738, 1910.

8 Hutchins v. Hutchins, supra note 7; Moushegian v. Sheppard, 279 Mass. 49, 180 N.E. 619, 1932 (statute). Contra: Lewis v. Mason, 156 Md. 32, 143 A. 585, 1928. And see Doan v. Herod, 56 Ind.App. 663, 104 N.E. 385, 1914 (executor's expense on contest before probate only permitted where will is ultimately established).

9 In re Jewe's Will, 201 Iowa 1154, 208 N.W. 723, 1926; Lassiter v. Travis, 98 Tenn. 330, 39 S.W. 226, 1896. Contra: Ellis v. Moss, 257 Ky. 168, 77 S.W.2d 377, 1934; In re Titlow's Estate, 163 Pa. 35, 29 A. 758, 1894; see also In re Charles' Estate, 123 Neb. 630, 243 N.W. 847, 1932.

10 See supra notes 7–9; infra note 11.

11 Dodd v. Anderson, supra note 7; Kelly v. Kennedy, 133 Minn. 278, 158 N.W. 395, L.R.A.1917A 448, Ann.Cas. 1918D 164, 1916; In re Vaughn's Estate, 149 Wash. 291, 270 P. 1030, 1928. And see Butt v. Murden, supra note 7, recognizing the ordinary rule, but holding that it had no application in case the bulk of the estate was left to pious or public uses. As to the rule in Pennsylvania, see In re Faust's Estate, 364 Pa. 529, 73 A.2d 369, 1950; notes, 41 Mich.L.R. 1180, 99 U. of Pa.L.R. 870.

12 In re Jones' Estate, 166 Cal. 147, 778, 135 P. 293, 1913; Smith v. Haire, 133 Tenn. 343, 181 S.W. 161, Ann.Cas. 1916D 529, 1915 (will procured by fraud of proponent executor); In re Graham's Estate, 156 Fla. 421, 23 So. 2d 485, 1945 (same); Deleglise v. Morrissey, 142 Wis. 234, 125 N.W. 452, 1910.

13 Estate of McKinney, 112 Cal. 447, 44 P. 743, 1896 (statute); Medill v. McIntire, supra note 7; In re Carroll's Estate, 59 Mont. 403, 196 P. 996, 1921 (statute); In re Coffield's Estate, 216 N.C. 285, 4 S.E.2d 870, 1939 (statute). See In re Limberg's Estate, 60 N.Y.S.2d 669, 1945 (denied when probate was denied for proponent's fraud); Matter of Reimers, 268 N.Y. 9, 196 N.E. 619, 1935, denying an allowance when the costs were eating up the entire estate. As to the amount of the fees allowed, see In re Cobb's Estate, 157 Fla. 590, 26 So. 2d 442, 1946; annotation, 143 A.L.R. 729.

14 Brown v. Eggleston, 53 Conn. 110, 2 A. 321, 1885; In re Dalton's Estate,

15 See Note 15 on following page.

sition is taken for the reason that it is the business of the heirs to conduct the contest as they, and not the estate, are interested in opposing the will. However, the legal expense of an unsuccessful guardian ad litem for a minor should be paid from estate funds,[16] as well as the fees of an attorney appointed by the court to represent absent legatees.[17]

*Allowance to Other Proponents*

Usually no allowance from the estate is made for the payment of the expenses of a devisee or legatee,[18] or their creditors,[19] in attempting to establish the will. This should be particularly true of the expenses of a beneficiary under the will when the executor also has employed counsel for the same purpose.[20] However, statutes sometimes permit the allowance to a proponent other than the executor.[21] Some decisions reach the same result in absence of legislation on the theory that, as the executor's expenses would be allowed from the estate, another who carries on the establishment of the will should be likewise reimbursed.[22] Such a

183 Iowa 1013, 168 N.W. 332, 1918; Edwards v. Ela, 5 Allen (Mass.) 87, 1862; In re Jones' Estate, 59 Utah 99, 202 P. 206, 1921 (special administrator). But see In re McLean, 180 App.Div. 269, 167 N.Y.S. 656, 1917.

15 Estate of Parsons, 65 Cal. 240, 3 P. 817, 1884.

16 Wright v. Upson, 303 Ill. 120, 135 N.E. 209, 1922; Enright v. Griffith, 165 Wis. 601, 163 N.W. 138, 1917 (discretionary). But see Lewis v. Mason, 156 Md. 32, 143 A. 585, 1928.

17 In re Roarke's Estate, 8 Ariz. 16, 68 P. 527, 1902; In re Otting's Estate, 62 S.D. 268, 252 N.W. 740, 1934 (but only fees and expense in probate court allowed where appeal was unreasonable). But see In re Genuchi's Estate, 104 Neb. 584, 178 N.W. 181, 1920.

18 In re Burgin's Estate, 191 Iowa 898, 183 N.W. 803, 1921; Wilson v. Wilson, 188 Ky. 53, 221 S.W. 874, 10 A.L.R. 780, 1920; In re Quinn's Estate, 179 Mich. 61, 146 N.W. 297, 1914; In re Doty's Estate, 231 Mich. 115, 203 N.W. 865, 1925; In re Baxter's Estate, 94 Mont. 257, 22 P.2d 182, 1933; Fox v. Martin, 108 Wis. 99, 84 N.W. 23, 1900. But the counsel fees may be charged against the proponent's share of the estate. In re Doty's Estate, supra; Smith's Estate, 165 Iowa 614, 146 N.W. 836, 1914.

19 Hamilton v. Shillington, 19 App. D.C. 268, 1902.

20 Henderson v. Simmons, 33 Ala. 291, 70 Am.Dec. 590, 1858; Atkinson v. May's Estate, 57 Neb. 137, 77 N.W. 343, 1898.

21 Bioren v. Nesler, 76 N.J.Eq. 576, 74 A. 791, 1909 (though will refused probate); In re Muellenschlader's Estate, 137 Wis. 32, 118 N.W. 209, 1908; see supra note 4 (attorney also employed by executor).

22 Boynton v. Laddy, 50 Hun 339, 3 N.Y.S. 93, 1888 (will named no executor); Wells v. Odum, 207 N.C. 226, 176 S.E. 563, 1934 (where executor's interest was identical with contestant's). And see In re Berry's Estate, 154 Iowa 301, 134 N.W. 867, 1912, where the expenses, however, were not allowed from the estate.

rule encourages litigation for the parties and their attorneys know that even if unsuccessful their legal expense will be paid from the estate. In the interest of preventing dissipation of estates, the courts should be conservative in making such allowances and statutory authority therefor should be narrowly construed.

*Allowance to Contestants*

Clearly a contestant should not be entitled to costs or attorney fees when the contest is without probable cause.[23] Allowances for counsel fees from the estate are sometimes made in case of successful,[24] or even unsuccessful, contestants.[25] The better view is to deny such recovery, even in case of successful contestants.[26] While the prevailing party would seem entitled to taxable costs against the opponent as in other civil cases and even be entitled to have these allowed from the estate if the unsuccessful proponent is the executor, the successful contestant should not obtain reimbursement for his attorney fees any more than the prevailing party in other types of litigation. To go to the extreme of allowing an unsuccessful contestant's fees to be paid from the estate, as some courts do, seems an unhealthy stimulation of will contests, even more serious than similar allowances to proponents. Attorney's fees are not usually awarded against an unsuccessful contestant.[27] This is in accord with the usual Ameri-

23 Sandusky v. Sandusky, 265 Mo. 219, 177 S.W. 390, 1915; In re Squier's Estate, 106 N.J.Eq. 267, 150 A. 430, 1930; In re De Lin's Estate, 135 Or. 8, 294 P. 600, 1930.

24 Everson v. Hurn, 89 Neb. 716, 131 N.W. 1130, 1911; Smith v. Haire, 138 Tenn. 255, 197 S.W. 678, 1917; In re Nachtsheim's Will, 166 Wis. 556, 164 N.W. 997, 1915 (statute). See note, 30 Ill.L.R. 81.

25 Seebrock v. Fedawa, 33 Neb. 413, 50 N.W. 270, 29 Am.St.Rep. 488, 1891; In re Story's Estate, 101 N.J.Eq. 716, 138 A. 199, 1927 (statute). And see In re Warrington's Will, 2 Boyce (Del.) 595, 81 A. 501, 1913 (recognizing that this might be done under exceptional circumstances). But see Greene v. Ballard, 45 Ga.App. 509, 165 S.E. 310, 1932; In re Gratton's Estate, 136 Or. 224, 298 P. 231, 79 A.L.R. 517, 1931; In re Simpson's Estate, 169 Wash. 419, 14 P.2d 1, 1932 (discretionary).

26 Taylor v. Minor, 90 Ky. 544, 14 S.W. 544, 1890. See In re Quinn's Estate, 179 Mich. 61, 146 N.W. 297, 1914; In re Titlow's Estate, 163 Pa. 35, 29 A. 758, 1894 (compromise). Cf. In re Faling's Estate, 113 Or. 6, 228 P. 821, modified 113 Or. 6, 231 P. 148, 1924. Different considerations are involved in suits for the construction of ambiguous wills, where costs and attorneys fees are commonly allowed from the estate, even to the unsuccessful party. See annotations, Ann. Cas.1915C 714, 79 A.L.R. 536, 142 A.L.R. 1470, 9 A.L.R.2d 1181; but cf. Kirkbride v. Hickok, 155 Ohio St. 165, 98 N.E.2d 4, 1951.

27 Re Simpson, 169 Wash. 419, 14 P.2d 1, 1932. But see Cleveland v. Creed, supra note 2.

can practice that the losing party is not liable for the counsel fees of his successful opponents.[28] Costs, however, may well be awarded against the losing party in favor of the prevailing party.

28 See Goodhart, Costs, 38 Yale L.J. 849; note, 21 Va.L.R. 920.

# CHAPTER 12

## GRANT OF ADMINISTRATION

Sec.
103. Functions and Necessity of Administration.
104. The Office of Personal Representative.
105. Joint Representatives.
106. Ancillary Representatives.
107. Jurisdiction over Administration.
108. Appointment of Executors.
109. Right to Administer.
110. Disqualifications for Office of Administrator.
111. Acceptance and Renunciation by Personal Representative.
112. Proceedings for Appointment.
113. Bond of Personal Representative.
114. Revocation of Letters, Removal, and Resignation.

## FUNCTIONS AND NECESSITY OF ADMINISTRATION

**103. The purposes of administration are to collect the personal assets of the decedent, pay the lawful claims against the estate, and distribute the balance to the legatees or distributees. For these reasons the title to the personalty passes to the personal representative rather than to the beneficiaries. If necessary in order to satisfy creditors' claims, the lands of the decedent may be sold by the personal representative.**

**Because of the desire to protect possible creditors against loss, the courts generally refuse to allow the beneficiaries to bring action for the recovery of the decedent's personal property or choses in action. If the beneficiaries can obtain the property without action and satisfy all unpaid creditors there is nothing to prevent a division of the property without official administration. Some courts have permitted the beneficiaries to recover the assets by action when they are convinced that creditors' rights will not be impaired thereby. Modern statutes often facilitate the recovery of wages, small bank accounts, or the entire estate if it is below a specific amount, by giving protection to the decedent's debtors who pay the heirs without administration.**

*Functions of Administration*

The purposes of administration of a decedent's property can be best grasped by inquiry into the functions of the personal representative whose business it is to carry on the administration. Upon his appointment the title to the decedent's chattels, both tangible and intangible, is said to pass to him.[1] His duties include the collection of the assets including choses in action which survive the deceased, payment of the deceased's creditors from the amount so realized and distribution of the balance to the persons entitled under the decedent's will or the intestate laws.[2] Administration is the means provided by law for the protection of the respective rights of creditors, debtors and beneficiaries, both as between these respective classes of interested persons and also as between different members of the same class. Of course, in a sense, it may be said that administration is necessary so that the legatees or distributees may ultimately receive title to the decedent's personalty. Viewed in a larger light the reason why title to chattels does not devolve directly upon legatees or distributees is that the law has deemed it advantageous that some one person should carry out these three functions, particularly that of seeing that decedent's creditors are satisfied before his property passes into the control of the beneficiaries of his estate.

This is the common-law concept of the devolution of personalty upon the owner's death. It is also the premise of the general statutory systems in force in most of our states. Louisiana, however, has the civil law system of universal succession wherein the heir may step into the place of the ancestor at once with the latter's full rights and liabilities and the additional obligations of paying legacies according to the latter's will.[3] If the civil law heir accepts unconditionally he must pay all debts even though

[1] Brown v. Copeland, 206 Ala. 124, 89 So. 274, 1921; Cunningham v. Rodgers, 50 App.D.C. 51, 267 F. 609, 1923; Denny v. Gardner, 149 Ga. 42, 99 S.E. 27, 1919; Lewis v. Lewis, 166 N.W. 107, Iowa, 1918; Garaventa v. Garaventa, 63 Nev. 304, 169 P.2d 540, 1946 (though no debts). See infra note 12. Under the statutory provisions in California and elsewhere both real and personal property passes to the heirs and devises but the personal representative must take possession of both. Cal.Prob.Code §§ 300, 573–575, 581, 582. Cf. Model Probate Code §§ 84, 124. These statutory provisions do not materially alter the above rule. Hall v. Alexander, 18 Cal.App.2d 660, 64 P.2d 767, 1937. Cf. note, 45 Mich.L.R. 898; and see Fountain v. Bank of America Nat. Trust & Savings Ass'n, 109 Cal.App.2d 90, 240 P.2d 414, 1952.

[2] Glidden v. Gutelius, 96 Fla. 834, 119 So. 140, 1928; Jones v. Peabody, 182 Wash. 148, 45 P.2d 915, 100 A.L.R. 64, 1935. And see generally c. 13.

[3] See La—LSA—arts. 976–1074; Jordan v. Smith, 206 La. 765, 20 So. 2d 17, 1944; Succession of Tullier, 218 La. 1005, 51 So.2d 606, 1951; Rheinstein, European Methods for Liquidation of the Debts of Deceased Persons, 20 Iowa L.R. 431. Rheinstein, The Model Probate Code: A Critique, 48 Col.L.R. 534, 537–542, 549.

they exceed the value of the estate. One may take, however, with benefit of inventory in which case there is administration practically as in a common-law jurisdiction and no liability to pay debts in excess of assets. An estate may also be placed under administration for cause shown at the instance of other interested persons. As a matter of fact, the great majority of estates in Louisiana are settled without official administration, and creditors rely on the personal liability of the heir.

*Realty*

At common law real property descended directly to the heirs or devisees without the intervention of a personal representative.[4] This rule was a reasonable one in early times because land was not liable for the deceased's general debts unless charged therewith by his will. Today, realty may be taken to pay the debts of the deceased owner in the absence of sufficient personalty to satisfy them. In spite of universal statutory provisions to this effect at the present time, the older rule that land passes directly to the heirs or devisees is still generally in effect.[5] It is possible to adhere to the earlier view of the descent of land because in most cases the personalty is sufficient to pay all lawful claims and in the remaining cases, the land, being incapable of being concealed or dissipated, may be followed into the hands of the heirs or devisees or their vendees. In cases where the land must be taken to pay debts, statutes give the personal representative a power, usually exercised by virtue of court order, to sell the land in order to raise the necessary funds. Until this power is exercised the heir or devisee is regarded as the owner of the realty and is entitled to the possession thereof. However, if such persons wish to be secure in the continued enjoyment of the property and particularly if they desire to offer a merchantable title to a purchaser, it will probably be necessary that administration should proceed, at least to the point of barring the claims of creditors.[6]

In many American states statutes give the personal representative rights of action and possession with regard to realty, and

4 Aubuchon v. Lory, 23 Mo. 99, 1856; see 2 Bl.Com. 201; American Law of Property § 14.6; supra §§ 3, 6, 96.

5 Aubuchon v. Lory, supra note 4; Stephens v. Comstock-Dexter Mines, 54 Ariz. 519, 97 P.2d 202, 1939; Wocet v. Seacat, 212 S.W.2d 449, Mo.App. 1948; In re Boyle's Estate, 133 N.J. Eq. 149, 30 A.2d 827, 1943; American Law of Property, § 14.7.

6 See Neuffer v. Hagelin, 369 Ill. 344, 16 N.E.2d 715, 1938; Rippe v. Weiters, 96 Kan. 738, 153 P. 536, 1915, and infra notes 49–53.

in some of these the provisions are so extensive that the immediate title of the heir or devisee is almost a hollow shell.[7] Of course the effect of this legislation is to increase the importance of administration with regard to land, and the same is true of statutes which contemplate distribution of land by decree of the probate court.[8]

*Effect of Will*

Most of the functions of administration apply equally to cases of testacy and intestacy. One cannot avoid administration by failing to make a will. Intestacy dispenses with probate of course, but not with official administration. Likewise one cannot provide effectively by will that administration of his estate may be dispensed with, for the law is solicitous for the protection of testator's creditors even if testator is not.[9] However, in a few jurisdictions a testator may stipulate for a minimum of official administration by apt provision in his will.[10]

In general, however, testacy is more apt to lead to a complete official administration than where there is no will.[11] This is for the reason that the establishment of a will is often necessary in order to provide a muniment of title. Also it is frequently a criminal offense to suppress a will. As probate exposes the existence of the estate to the court and is indeed an initiation of administration proceedings, the latter usually go forward in the normal manner in testate estates. Failure to do so might cause later embarrassment due to the hiatus that would appear from the probate court records. In addition, there might well be judicial pressure to cause the executor to proceed with the administration once the will is probated. Neither the will nor its probate vests title to the personalty in the legatees. Even the beneficiary of specific personal property under the will does not become the legal owner thereof until there has been assent or trans-

7 See supra note 1; American Law of Property §§ 14.7, 14.33, 14.34; note, 21 Iowa L.R. 793. Cf. Honsinger v. Stewart, 34 N.D. 513, 159 N.W. 12, 1916, with Hoffman v. Hoffman's Heirs, 73 N.D. 637, 17 N.W.2d 903, 1945.

8 See infra § 143; American Law of Property §§ 14.43, 14.44.

9 Sevier v. Woodson, 205 Mo. 202, 104 S.W. 1, 120 Am.St.Rep. 728, 1907.

10 See infra § 104 at notes 7 to 9.

11 See Robertson v. Yager, 327 Ill. 346, 158 N.E. 709, 1927; Seery v. Murray, 107 Iowa 384, 77 N.W. 1058, 1899; Wallace v. Dubose, 242 S.W. 351, Tex.Civ.App.1922.

fer by the personal representative.[12] This of course can be done only in the course of administration.

*Avoidance of Administration*

In spite of the fact that our law is so designed that official administration is the normal concomitant of succession, administration is avoided in many cases. The available figures show that there is about one administration for every four deaths.[13] Of course we must take into consideration infant deaths and adults who die penniless. Then too succession itself can be avoided to the extent that wealth is put in the form of life insurance, or jointly owned or trust estates.[14] Finally extra-legal or illegal devices such as indorsed securities or jointly owned safe deposit boxes are sometimes successful. But the average person does not and indeed cannot manipulate his affairs so that *none* of his

12 Strader v. Metropolitan Life Ins. Co., 128 Va. 238, 105 S.E. 74, 1920; Oulvey v. Converse, 326 Ill. 226, 157 N.E. 245, 1927. But see Skyes v. Hughes, 182 Md. 396, 35 A.2d 132, 150 A.L.R. 87, 1943. Cf. infra § 143. The formal transfer has been held necessary even when the sole beneficiary is also the executor and there has been complete administration. S. S. Pierce Co. v. Fiske, 237 Mass. 39, 129 N.E. 609, 1921. But cf. Cook v. Redfield, 103 Okl. 77, 229 P. 588, 1924.

13 In the period 1912–1923 there were a total of 184,958 adult deaths in 24 counties scattered through 13 states with only 43,512 administrations, or less than 24 per cent. Federal Trade Commission, National Wealth and Income, 1926, 58. Cf. 14 Studies in Income and Wealth, 160. In New York County, New York, there were a fraction over 30 per cent. of administrations resulting from the total number of adult deaths in the period 1914–1929, and counting all deaths, a fraction over 22 per cent. of administrations. Powell & Looker, Decedents' Estates, 30 Col.L.R. 919, 922, 923. For similar figures in other sections, see ibid., 928–930.

These data correspond with the researches of the author in certain counties of Kansas, Missouri and Michigan. The author's experience indicates that there are relatively more administrations to number of deaths in the rural than in the urban districts. This may be due to the greater percentage of decedents owning realty in rural communities coupled with a desire to clear the land from decedent's debts with a view to sale thereof.

In five typical years between 1929 and 1944 in Dane County, Wisconsin, about 42 estates per 100 adult deaths reached the probate court, though only about 37 estates per 100 adult deaths involved administrations. Ward & Beuscher, The Inheritance Process in Wisconsin [1950] Wis.L.R. 393, 396–399.

In the five year period 1934–1938 two-thirds of decedents in New Jersey left no estates reported to the probate court. Markle, Proposed Legislation Amending the Intestate Succession Laws of New Jersey, 5 Newark L.R. 1, 2.

14 See Oswald, Legal Efficacy of Attempting Methods of Avoiding Probate, 5 Wash.L.R. 1, and see generally supra c. 4.

property passes, or seems to pass, by succession. It is fair to conclude that administration is avoided in fully half of the cases in which the decedent died leaving more than a trifling amount of property passing by succession. The various means by which this is done will now be considered.

*Family Settlements*

Particularly if there is no will, and if there is no controversy as to who are the heirs at law, and they are all of full age and agreeable to a division of the decedent's property in a certain manner, and the deceased's property consists entirely of tangible personalty or money or other interests or claims which may be reduced to possession without legal action, and there are no claims against the deceased or the debts are satisfied by the heirs, and neither a public administrator nor any other person petitions for administration, there need not be official administration and the decedent's property can be informally divided.[15] No criminal offense is committed by so doing and as all interested parties are in agreement there is no one to insist upon the regular administration proceedings. The courts do not reach out to initiate official administration. Indeed the courts have declared that where the rights of creditors do not interfere, family settlements should be favored and enforced.[16]

If any one or more of the conditions favorable to informal settlements described in the preceding paragraph are absent, it is doubtful whether the heirs will be able to dispense with administration in the regular manner. However, there are a number

[15] See Murphy v. Freeman, 220 Ala. 634, 127 So. 199, 70 A.L.R. 381, 1930 (chancery); Love v. Rennie, 254 Ala. 382, 48 So.2d 458, 1950 (same—will); Pitts v. Pitts, 120 Fla. 363, 162 So. 708 (statute); Phillips v. Phillips, 163 Ga. 899, 137 S.E. 561, 1927 (statute allowing widow who is sole heir to succeed to her husband's property upon payment of debts); Martin v. Central Trust Co., 327 Ill. 622, 159 N.E. 312, 1927; In re Kuntz's Estate, 196 Wis. 344, 220 N.W. 206, 1928 (debts paid). See annotation, 70 A.L.R. 386.

Embarrassment may occur if the decedent left a car or other property registered in his name, though to some extent legislation has solved this difficulty. See Basye, infra note 17 at 405–408.

[16] Preston v. Ham, 156 Ga. 223, 119 S.E. 658, 1923; Riffe v. Walton, 105 Kan. 227, 182 P. 640, 6 A.L.R. 549, 1919; Engle v. Engle, 209 Mich. 275, 176 N.W. 547, 1920; Smith v. Williams, 141 S.C. 265, 139 S.E. 625, 54 A.L.R. 964, 1927. See infra note 45. These agreements, however, are a frequent source of litigation on account of alleged fraud upon the contracting parties or others. See Pfaff v. Clements, 213 Ark. 852, 213 S.W.2d 356, 1948; Moore v. Gregory, 146 Va. 504, 131 S.E. 692, 1925, noted, 10 Minn.L.R. 616; annotations, 6 A.L.R. 555, 38 A.L.R. 759, 54 A.L.R. 976.

of cases in which it is judicially determined that administration is not necessary though all of these factors do not exist.[17] Some of these decisions are due to statutory provisions,[18] while in others the solution has been reached upon a common-law basis. The results are often due to the peculiar facts of the individual case, and some decisions in a single jurisdiction are difficult to reconcile with each other. The problem involves many of the considerations treated below in this section.[19]

*Actions by Heirs Against Decedent's Debtors*

Perhaps the most usual case in which the general problem is presented is the one in which the heirs or their assignees bring suit on a chose in action owned by the deceased in his lifetime, or seek recovery of a specific chattel of the decedent or its value. In general such plaintiffs may not recover.[20] The legalistic reason frequently assigned is that as the administrator succeeds to the title he is the only one who can maintain the action. As the result of such holdings, a personal representative must be appointed to prosecute the suit. Looking behind this formal reasoning, it is apparent that the law refuses to allow the heirs to recover chiefly in order to protect the interests of possible unpaid creditors. Hence only the personal representative, who is charged with the duty of satisfying the latter, is permitted to give a lawful discharge to the estate's debtors. Accordingly no other person is a proper plaintiff in an action to recover the estate's assets.

In most jurisdictions the above difficulties cannot be avoided by allegation and proof in actions against the decedent's debtors

17 Braun v. Pettyjohn, 176 Ala. 592, 58 So. 907, 1912; Battey v. Meyerhardt, 157 Ga. 800, 122 S.E. 195, 1924. See Basye, Dispensing with Administration; 44 Mich.L.R. 329, 384–407; notes, 31 Mich.L.R. 734, 30 Va.L.R. 500, 44 Yale L.J. 478.

18 See Basye, supra note 17.

19 As the sub-titles indicate the problem is approached chiefly in the light of whether, in the absence of administration, a party may be successful in his assertion of rights concerning the estate.

20 Sowle v. Potter, 223 Ky. 136, 3 S.W.2d 174, 1928; Brobst v. Brobst, 190 Mich. 63, 155 N.W. 734, 1916; Champollion v. Corbin, 71 N.H. 78, 51 A. 674, 1901; Buchanan v. Buchanan, 75 N.J.Eq. 274, 71 A. 745, 22 L.R.A.,N.S., 454, 138 Am.St.Rep. 563, 20 Ann. Cas. 91, 1909; McBride v. Vance, 73 Ohio St. 258, 76 N.E. 938, 112 Am.St. Rep. 723, 4 Ann.Cas. 191, 1906; Mitchell v. Dreher, 150 S.C. 125, 147 S.E. 646, 1929 (statute); Mears v. Smith, 19 S.D. 79, 102 N.W. 295, 1905; McKenney v. Minahan, 119 Wis. 651, 97 N.W. 489, 1903. But the beneficiary may sue a debtor of the estate when personal representative is antagonistic to the estate. Gilchrist v. Gilchrist, 223 Ala. 562, 137 So. 406, 1931; Hatton v. Howard Braiding Co., 47 R.I. 47, 129 A. 805, 1925.

that the plaintiffs are the sole heirs and that there are no unpaid debts.[21] This position is sound, for neither other possible heirs nor unpaid creditors are parties to the suit and for that reason they would not be bound by the judgment therein. Either might appear later and secure the appointment of an administrator who, as the holder of the legal title of the personalty, would be entitled to recover again from the debtor in order that the property be subjected to administration. The only other alternative would be the unsatisfactory one of restricting the subsequently appointed representative to a recovery against the heirs who obtained the property from the decedent's debtor. These heirs might have dissipated the proceeds of their recovery and a judgment against them might be uncollectible. For this reason the orthodox position is to deny recovery by the heirs, thereby tending to subject the property to administration for the protection of respective claims of all interested persons.

Generally there is no question as to who are the lawful heirs,[22] but there is always a chance that unpaid creditors may appear. The existence, or possibility, of creditors is the main stumbling block to the avoidance of administration. An administration with due facilities for creditors to present their claims is the only certain way of determining that there are no unpaid claims.[23] Thus, we must usually have administration in order to establish the facts which render administration unnecessary.

Some cases have disposed of the possibility of existing creditors, so as to permit the heirs to sue their decedents' debtors. In some jurisdictions it is permissible for the heirs to allege and prove in the action that there are no creditors.[24] In other cases the plaintiff's allegation of no debts is deemed admitted by defendant's demurrer.[25] When the deceased was a minor, the

[21] In re McWhirter's Estate, 235 Ill. 607, 85 N.E. 918, 1928; In re Lindsay's Guardianship, 132 Iowa 119, 109 N.W. 473, 1906; Brobst v. Brobst, 190 Mich. 63, 155 N.W. 734, 1916; Weis v. Kundert, 172 Minn. 274, 215 N.W. 176, 1927. Cf. infra note 24 et seq.

[22] But see In re Railsback's Estate, 184 Wash. 42, 49 P.2d 934, 1935. And see Meyer v. Nischwitz, 198 Mo. App. 101, 199 S.W. 744, 1917 (administration necessary when heirs cannot agree as to distribution).

[23] Brobst v. Brobst and Weis v. Kundert, both supra note 21.

[24] Metropolitan Life Ins. Co. v. Fitzgerald, 137 Ark. 366, 209 S.W. 77, 1919. And see Business Men's Acc. Ass'n of America v. Green, 147 Ark. 199, 227 S.W. 388, 1921; Morris v. Arrington, 215 Ark. 564, 221 S.W. 2d 406, 1949. See also cases cited note 17, supra; cf. note 21 supra.

[25] Moore v. Brandenburg, 248 Ill. 232, 93 N.E. 733, 140 Am.St.Rep. 206, 1910.

Colorado court felt that there was no reasonable probability of debts and hence permitted his parents to recover his personalty.[26] Ordinary statutes of limitations give no relief because they do not run when there is no one to be sued, and the personal representative is the only proper defendant.[27] Moreover, the special nonclaim statutes requiring presentation of claims against decedent's estate within a designated time do not generally commence to run until a personal representative has been appointed or gives notice of his appointment.[28] In a few jurisdictions there are special statutes of limitations prohibiting the initiation of administration proceedings after a designated number of years.[29] After such time has lapsed, the possibility of creditors demanding administration is gone and the heirs have the full equitable right in the assets of the estate and should be able to discharge the estate's debtors and hence be able to recover from the latter. The same should be true where there has been administration down to the point of closing the estate against claims.[30] When the money or property sued for is exempt from creditor's claims the heirs should be permitted to sue in the absence of administration.[31] In some jurisdictions it is provided by statute that small bank accounts, or wage claims or even the entire proceeds of estates under a certain value may be recovered by the heirs.[32]

26 Graves v. Davenport, 45 Colo. 270, 100 P. 429, 1919. Cf. Drummond v. Hardaway, 21 Ga. 433, 1856 (idiot); Hargroves v. Thompson, 31 Miss. 211, 1856 (two months old child).

27 See infra § 127.

28 In re Collins' Estate, 102 Wash. 697, 173 P. 1016, 1918. And see infra § 127. But where the nonclaim statute commences to run upon decedent's death the heirs may sue after lapse of the period. Brown v. Baxter, 77 Kan. 97, 94 P. 155, 574, 1908; Glathart v. Madden, 122 Kan. 563, 253 P. 426, 1927; Granger v. Harriman, 89 Minn. 303, 94 N.W. 869, 1903.

29 See German v. Heath, 139 Iowa 52, 116 N.W. 1051, 1908; Tunnell v. Moore, 53 S.W.2d 324, Tex.Civ.App. 1932. It has even been held that the general statute of limitations applies to petitions for administration. Gwinn v. Melvin, 9 Idaho 202, 72 P. 961, 108 Am.St.Rep. 119, 2 Ann.Cas. 770, 1903.

30 Powell v. Pennock, 181 Mich. 588, 148 N.W. 430, 1914. Cf. Suit v. Crawford, 100 Ky. 355, 38 S.W. 500, 1897 (suit on note by distributee allowed because the estate was entirely administered). See note, 30 Va.L.R. 500. And see Nord v. Nord, 91 S.W.2d 223, Mo.App., 1936, noted, 1 Mo.L.R. 284 (residuary legatee may sue upon claim in favor of testator after administration was completed though this asset was not contained in inventory).

31 Williams v. Sykes, 170 Miss. 88, 154 So. 267, 1934; Evans v. Miller, 105 Okl. 289, 233 P. 199, 1925. See Hale v. Hannah, 56 S.W.2d 259, Tex. Civ.App.1933; Christie v. Chicago, R. I & P. R. Co., 104 Iowa 707, 74 N.W. 697, 1898. See supra § 34, especially at note 38.

32 See infra note 58.

*Voluntary Payments by Decedent's Debtors*

If the debtor of an estate feels certain that his payment is being made to all of the heirs and further is satisfied that the deceased had no unpaid debts, or that the heirs will reimburse him if he is required to pay again to a subsequently appointed administrator, he may be willing to pay the claim to the heirs. However, he cannot do so without risk,[33] and is both legally and morally justified in refusing to pay the heirs though he does not dispute the indebtedness to the deceased. If a debtor is inclined to oblige the heirs who are attempting to settle the estate without administration, he might conceivably pay his obligation at the request of the heirs in satisfaction of the deceased's funeral expenses with comparative safety. As these items are preferred claims against deceased's estate,[34] a court would not likely allow a subsequent recovery from the debtor who had discharged an obligation which was a first lien upon the estate's assets.[35]

*Creditor's Remedies*

Under the American procedure an unpaid creditor may petition for the appointment of a personal representative,[36] and indeed may qualify for the office himself.[37] During the process of the administration thus initiated, the creditor may present his claim and secure payment thereof from the assets of the estate. To obtain sufficient assets for this purpose, the personal representative so appointed may collect claims in favor of the deceased from the latter's debtors even if the debtors have already paid the indebtedness to the heirs. The administrator may look to the debtors rather than to the heirs who have received payment of the claim in the process of the informal settlement.[38]

At common law a creditor could recover from the heir who intermeddled with decedent's personalty, or indeed from any person

33 See Weis v. Kundert, supra note 21; Wood v. Weimar, 104 U.S. 786, 797, 26 L.Ed. 779, Mich.1881; In re Clary's Estate, 253 P. 778, Cal.App. 1927; Vail v. Anderson, 61 Minn. 552, 64 N.W. 47, 1895.

34 See infra § 128.

35 See Weingrad v. Lloyd, 56 N.Y.S. 2d 484, Sup.Ct.1945; cf. N.Y.Leg.Doc. (1951) 65M, 48.

36 See infra § 112. See opinion of Butler, J., in Rosenboom v. Cline, 90 Colo. 1, 6 P.2d 453, 1931 (inheritance tax).

37 See infra § 109.

38 In re Lindsay's Guardianship, 132 Iowa 119, 109 N.W. 473, 1906; Meyer's Adm'r v. Zoll, 119 Ky. 480, 84 S.W. 543, 1905; Bryson's Adm'r v. Biggs, 104 S.W. 982, Ky.1907. Cf. Baadte v. Walgenback, 185 Iowa 773, 171 N.W. 146, 1919 (no debts); Vail v. Anderson, supra note 33.

guilty of such conduct.[39] This recovery was based on the doctrine of executor de son tort, or that the law would consider that the intermeddler had assumed the liabilities of executor to the extent of value of the property taken. The doctrine and the name applied regardless of whether the decedent died testate or intestate, but it had no application to taking possession of land,[40] nor to intermeddling with personalty after the appointment of the personal representative.[41]

Of course the personal representative may recover from the intermeddler, regardless of whether the act took place before or after the plaintiff's appointment. Today in many states the doctrine of executor de son tort is expressly abolished by statute, and in others recovery by the creditor is deemed out of line with the statutory court supervision over presentment, allowance and payment of claims.[42] Here the creditor's course will be to secure the appointment of a personal representative whose duty will be to collect the purloined assets and pay claims in the regular course. In some jurisdictions, creditors can still proceed against the intermeddler by virtue of the ancient doctrine; [43] indeed

39 Read's Case, 5 Coke 32b, 77 Eng. Rep. 103, 1604; 2 Bl.Com. 507; Evans, The Intermeddler and the Fraudulent Transferee as Executor, 25 Geo.L.J. 78; Warren, Problems in Probate and Administration, 32 Harv.L.R. 317; see infra notes 43, 44. As to the right of a creditor to sue the heir on account of descent of land, see infra § 127.

40 King v. Lyman, 1 Root (Conn.) 104, 1785.

41 See Read's Case, supra note 41.

42 Andrew v. Dunn, 202 Iowa 364, 210 N.W. 425, 1926; Ventress v. Wallace, 111 Miss. 357, 71 So. 636, L.R.A. 1917A 971, 1916; Slate v. Henkle, 45 Or. 430, 78 P. 325, 1904; Blinn v. McDonald, 92 Tex. 604, 46 S.W. 787, 48 S.W. 571, 50 S.W. 931, 1899. And see Brown v. Drake, 103 Or. 607, 210 P. 710, 1922; Ryan v. Kelsey, 259 F. 945, 7 A.L.R. 234, C.C.A. 3d 1919. In Texas, a creditor can sue the heir if, and only if, there is no necessity for administration. See Pitts v. Thompson, 71 S.W.2d 368, Tex.Civ.App.1934. A creditor who obtains voluntary payment from the deceased's debtor may be required to refund the money at suit of the personal representative. Richardson v. Dreyfus, 64 Mo.App. 600, 1896.

See McGovney, Executor of His Own Wrong, 6 Ia.L.Bull. 65; note, 7 Ia.L.Bull. 40; Evans, supra note 39, at 91–92. As to the right of a contingent creditor to recover from distributees after distribution, see infra § 127. Cf. Westerfield v. Stout, 129 S.W.2d 478, Tex.Civ.App.1939.

43 Ebbinger v. Wightmen, 15 Colo. App. 439, 62 P. 963, 1900; Allen v. Hurst, 120 Ga. 763, 48 S.E. 341, 1905 (statute). It has been held that, under exceptional circumstances, a creditor may sue the heirs even when the doctrine of executor de son tort is not applicable. Hagan v. Lantry, 338 Mo. 161, 89 S.W.2d 522, 1935. And a creditor may sue if the personal representative refuses to do so. Mead Co. v. Doerfler, 146 Neb. 21, 18 N.W. 2d 524, 158 A.L.R. 724, 1945, noted, 45 Col.L.R. 953. See In re Watkins'

statutes sometimes preserve this right.[44] But even in these states the creditor can initiate an administration and secure payment of his claim in the course thereof.

*Denial of Administration*

If the heirs make voluntary distribution of the decedent's property and later one of them, becoming dissatisfied with the settlement, petitions for administration, this relief has been refused on the ground of estoppel.[45] Texas has a statute declaring that administration should be refused where there is no necessity therefor, and it has been liberally construed.[46] The courts which are liberal in allowing actions by the heirs to recover assets have often held that letters of administration need not be granted where it appears that there are no debts or other necessity for administration.[47] The orthodox doctrine is to grant administration even when opposed by the heirs who claim that there are no debts, for the reason that only through administration can this fact be determined.[48]

Estate, 114 Vt. 109, 41 A.2d 180, 157 A.L.R. 212, 1945, where an intermeddler attempted to evade liability for depreciation of assets by seeking appointment as administrator. The opinion deals at length with the doctrine of executor de son tort, though this seems unnecessary.

44 See Evans, supra note 39 at 91–92.

45 Faulkner v. Faulkner, 23 Ariz. 313, 203 P. 560, 1922; see also Holtan v. Fischer, 218 Minn. 81, 15 N.W.2d 206, 1944; Schoenwetter v. Schoenwetter, 164 Wis. 131, 159 N.W. 737, 1916. See supra note 16.

46 Rogers v. Barbee, 32 S.W.2d 666, Tex.Civ.App.1919.

47 Murphy v. Freeman, 220 Ala. 634, 127 So. 199, 70 A.L.R. 381, 1930; Chase v. Bartlett, 176 Ga. 40, 166 S.E. 832, 1932; In re Carter's Estate, 113 Okl. 182, 240 P. 727, 1925 (all property exempt); Murphy v. Murphy, 42 Wash. 142, 84 P. 646, 1906 (debts barred); State ex rel. Speckart v. Superior Court for Thurston County, 48 Wash. 141, 92 P. 942, 1906; In re Kuntz's Estate, 196 Wis. 344, 220 N.W. 206, 1928. See Hale v. Hannah, supra note 31. It is even held that after a personal representative has qualified, he cannot recover where it appears there is no necessity for administration. Christie v. Chicago, R. I. & P. R. Co., supra note 31 (settlement by heirs and entire estate exempt from creditors); Trent v. Griffy, 193 Ky. 124, 235 S.W. 22, 1921 (settlement by heirs and no debts); Richardson v. Cole, 160 Mo. 372, 61 S.W. 182, 83 Am.St.Rep. 479, 1901 (same—public administrator); Matter of Tangerman, 226 App.Div. 162, 235 N.Y.S. 213, 1929 (debts paid).

48 Rosenboom v. Cline, 90 Colo. 1, 6 P.2d 453, 1931; In re McWhirter's Estate, 235 Ill. 607, 85 N.E. 918, 1908; In re Railsback's Estate, 184 Wash. 42, 49 P.2d 934, 1935; Bush v. Reconstruction Finance Corporation, 79 Ga.App. 25, 52 S.E.2d 515, 1949; note, 9 K.C.L.R. 185.

*Protection of Land Against Sale for Debts*

Administration may be necessary or highly desirable even when the testator leaves only land. Though the title to realty passes directly to the heir or devisee, this is a defeasible title because the property may be sold in the course of administration to pay claims. One can never be certain that the land will not be sold unless the claims are paid or barred in the course of administration.[49] The statutes of limitations and nonclaim do not ordinarily run until an administrator has been appointed so that mere lapse of time does not give assurance that a creditor may not petition for administration.[50] Statutes sometimes declare that no lands shall be sold for the debts of the deceased owner after a designated number of years after his death.[51] Of course after this period has elapsed, there is no need of administration on account of the land and good title can be furnished to purchasers upon proof of the heirship of the grantors. If an immediate sale is desired such statutes are of no assistance. In absence of such legislation it is extremely doubtful whether the heirs can offer merchantable title in the absence of administration,[52] though in some jurisdictions the furnishing of an affidavit that the designated persons are the heirs of the deceased who died leaving no debts is sufficient.[53]

*Legislation*

Statutes are an increasingly important factor in permitting avoidance of administration of small estates. Professor Paul E.

[49] See supra note 6.

[50] See infra § 127.

[51] See Basye, supra note 17 at 392; cf. In re Levy's Estate, 335 Ill.App. 367, 82 N.E.2d 209, 1948 (seven year non-statutory period). See infra § 123, notes 24–26.

[52] Turner v. McDonald, 76 Cal. 177, 18 P. 262, 9 Am.St.Rep. 189, 1888; Siedel v. Snider, 241 Iowa 1227, 44 N.W.2d 687, 1950; Chauncey v. Leominster, 172 Mass. 340, 52 N.E. 719, 1899; Platt v. Newman, 71 Mich. 112, 38 N.W. 720, 1888; Dutton v. Buckley, 116 Or. 661, 242 P. 626, 1926. Cf. Coffey v. McEwen, 186 Tenn. 404, 210 S.W.2d 681, 1948 (heirs gave deed but price paid to executor).

[53] Schmidt v. Fontron Loan & Trust Co., 112 Kan. 535, 211 P. 630, 1923. And see Reed v. Reed, 46 Hun (N.Y.) 212, 1887. But cf. Campbell v. Harsh, 31 Okl. 436, 122 P. 127, 1912. See Lieberman, Are Affidavits a Cure for Unmarketable Title? 2 N.J.L.R. 48, 2 Current Legal Thought, 427. Affidavits have been regarded as sufficient if a number of years have elapsed since the death of the deceased owner. Perkins v. August, 109 Conn. 452, 146 A. 831, 1929; see Siedel v. Snider, supra note 52; Costigan, Problems Preliminary to Administration [1951] Univ. of Ill. Law Forum 357, 361

Basye's thorough study has classified the legislation.[54] Some of it has already been noticed above.[55] Other provisions include those similar to the Missouri pioneer statute which allows the court to make an order dispensing with administration and permits the surviving spouse or minor children to collect and sue for the property if it does not exceed the amount of statutory allowances, and also permits a creditor to obtain a similar order if no such relatives survive and the estate does not exceed $100 upon giving a bond to pay the debts in order of the statutory preference.[56] The constitutionality of a somewhat similar statute in Florida which renders administration unnecessary if the estate is less than $2000 has been upheld.[57] Many states have provision for the payment of bank accounts, wage claims or insurance, usually limited as to amount, to designated relations of the decedent.[58] In addition, there are provisions for the termination of administration when it appears that the estate does not exceed the amount of family allowances,[59] and for summary administration of estates below a certain size.[60]

Professor Max Rheinstein has suggested that by simply amending the section of the Model Probate Code so as to dispense with the requirement of a bond unless specially applied for by a creditor or other claimant, the parties would be in a position to wind up the estate without further cost and formalities.[61] If this be true the same result could probably be obtained by similar slight amendments of the probate codes of most of our states.

Something—and perhaps something quite extreme—must be done if the law is to keep pace with popular demand, unorganized

[54] Supra note 17. See also Dunbar, Some Advanced Probate Legislation, 24 Cas. & Com. 725; N.Y.Leg.Doc. (1951) No. 65 p. 55 et seq.

[55] Supra notes 15, 29, 44, 46, 51.

[56] Missouri—V.A.M.S. § 461.120; see Basye, supra note 17 at 357 et seq.

[57] Coral Gables First Nat. Bank v. Hart, 155 Fla. 482, 20 So.2d 647, 1945; see also Laramore v. Laramore, 49 So.2d 517, Fla., 1951; Broom v. Klein, 309 Ky. 224, 217 S.W.2d 206, 1949.

[58] See Basye, supra note 17 at 400 et seq.; N.Y.Leg.Doc.(1951) No. 65 M, pp. 60–62; N.Y.Decedent Estate Law § 130a, explained in N.Y.Leg.Doc. (1952) No. 65G. See also supra § 39, note 2.

[59] See Basye, supra note 17 at 337.

[60] See Basye, supra note 17 at 339, 355; Eagleton, The New Minnesota Probate Code, 20 Minn.L.R. 1, 4, 5; Fox, Summary Settlement of Small Estates, [1948] Wis. L.R. 453; Brooker, Small Estates, 23 Fla.L.J. 341; Staver, Administering Small Estates, 88 Trusts & Estate 553; notes, 19 Minn.L.R. 833, 20 ibid. 104, 21 ibid. 885; Merrill, The Proposed Model Small Estates Act, 5 Okl.L.R. 49, 1952.

[61] The Model Probate Code: A Critique, 48 Colo.L.R. 534, 541.

as this demand may be. The public is concerned about the expense of administration, although this element is probably exaggerated in the popular mind beyond the actual truth. Yet the figures show that a rather large percentage of the assets of small estates are consumed in charges.[62] Perhaps half of the estates which are administered are under $5,000,[63] and with these the time element is apt to be more important than the cost. Typically it takes more than a year to administer an estate.[64] When the decedent was the breadwinner and the family is in modest circumstances this is a great handicap to the survivors. It is no answer that the administration will prevent unwise spending of the heritage. That is as valid an argument for postponing the distribution for two, five, or ten years as it is for one. The dependents are generally faced immediately with the necessity of a financial readjustment. Capital, if available, can be used advantageously in order to provide special schooling or the establishment of a small business or other means of livelihood.

Of recent years many specific solutions have been offered.[65] There is more work to be done. Perhaps the most important conclusion to be gathered from current drafts and other writings is that the subject of avoiding and expediting administration is not one which can be considered in isolation. It is intimately tied in with such matters as the spouse's intestate and elective shares, family allowances, and whether certain transactions are to be regarded as testamentary. Furthermore, it cannot be divorced from the problems of simplifying and expediting the administration of decedents' estates generally.

62 It is said to average over 16 per cent. in estates under $5,000 and over 13 per cent. in estates under $10,000. Powell & Looker, supra, note 13 at p. 948. Cf. Ward & Beuscher, supra note 13 at p. 404.

63 Ward & Beuscher, supra note 13 at 399, show that 45% of administered estates were of less than $5,000. The earlier study of Powell and Looker, supra 13 at 933–938, has similar findings.

64 The nonclaim period here is the governing factor. As this is one year in the typical state at the present time (see infra § 127), and some time must be allowed for the qualification of the personal representative before the nonclaim period commences to run and a more or less similar period before the final account may be approved after the period has run, it would appear that in most jurisdictions thirteen or fourteen months is the minimum time for the settlement of an estate.

65 See Model Probate Code §§ 86–92; Model Administration of Small Estates Act; note, 49 Mich.L.R. 111; and supra notes 54, 60, 61.

## THE OFFICE OF PERSONAL REPRESENTATIVE

**104. If the personal representative is named by the testator, he is called the executor, while the representative of an intestate estate is denominated the administrator. When it is necessary to appoint some one in place of the executor, he is called administrator with the will annexed. If one representative administers an estate in part and then ceases to act, his successor is called administrator de bonis non, or, of the goods not administered.**

**Either by statute or at common law when necessity or convenience demands, courts are authorized to appoint special or temporary administrators whose authority is limited in time or to particular functions. Many jurisdictions have public administrators to administer estates, when there is no one else present, eligible and willing to do so.**

The office of personal representative, that is, executor or administrator, is of extreme importance in Anglo-American law. This is not only because he has important rights and duties in connection with the settlement of his decedent's affairs, but also for the reason that the estate is not recognized as a legal entity.[1] The representative is not regarded as an agent for the estate for, in legal contemplation, there is no such principal. He is regarded rather as the owner of the decedent's personal property though his ownership is not beneficial and will be terminated upon completion of the administration. He is also an officer of the court and as such vested with certain rights and burdened with certain duties. Though we often speak of claims against, or in favor of, the estate these expressions are apt to be misleading if taken too literally. The personal representative and not the estate is the one with whom the courts and third persons are concerned.

As has been previously pointed out [2] the personal representative named by the testator's will is called the executor. He is given this designation because he is the one who executes the will or carries it into effect. The office is an ancient one born out of the struggle of the ecclesiastical courts for their testamen-

[1] Ferrin v. Myrick, 41 N.Y. 315, 1869; A. L. Goetzmann Co. v. Gazett, 172 Minn. 68, 214 N.W. 895, 1927. See Barfield v. Miller, 70 S.W.2d 632, Tex. Civ.App.1934. But cf. Van Iperen v. Hays, 219 Iowa 715, 259 N.W. 448, 1935. In the early English law the executor was regarded as the absolute owner of the property, except for his obligation to satisfy the legatees. For the transitions from this viewpoint, see Holmes, Executors, 9 Harv.L.R. 42.

[2] See supra § 1.

tary jurisdiction.[3] The term executor is generally restricted to those representatives nominated by the testator.

The office of administrator, or the one who takes charge of the goods of an intestate, came later. It had its origin in a statute of 1357.[4] If the will names no executor, or if the one named dies, or is unable or unwilling to act, the court will appoint an administrator cum testamento annexo, c. t. a., or with the will annexed. If an executor ceases to act as such before completion of administration, the court appoints an administrator de bonis non cum testamento annexo, d. b. n. c. t. a., or, of goods not administered with the will annexed. Likewise if the original administrator ceases to act, his successor is called administrator de bonis non, d. b. n.[5]

Save for the fact that in case of testacy a personal representative makes distribution to the beneficiaries named in the will while the representative of an intestate estate turns over the remaining assets to the distributees enumerated by law, there are few major differences between the functions of administrators and executors. In some respects, statutes give larger powers to the executor than to the administrator, and by express testamentary provision the executor may have more extensive powers than a personal representative would otherwise possess.[6] With these exceptions the general powers and duties of the two officers are the same so that it is profitable to treat both together.

3 See Atkinson, Brief History of English Testamentary Jurisdiction, 8 Mo.L.R. 107; supra § 3. As to the executor de son tort, see supra § 103 at notes 39–44. It has been declared that there is no such legal entity as a literary executor. In re Bartlett's Estate, 198 Misc. 1000, 101 N.Y.S.2d 675, 1950; see N.Y.Times, Dec. 10, 1951, p. 26, col. 1.

4 31 Edw. III, st. 1, c. 11; see references note 3 supra.

5 At common law an administrator de bonis non could recover from his predecessor only such estate as remained in specie and not for goods wasted or converted, the latter right being in the legatees, distributees or creditors. Coleman v. M'Murdo, 5 Rand.(Va.) 51, 1827; annotation, 3 A.L.R. 1252. Frequently he may recover today by virtue of statutory changes. Cowan v. Perkins, 214 Ala. 155, 107 So. 63, 1926; Stapley v. Stapley, 29 Ariz. 187, 212 P. 1005, 1926 (action on bond); Woerner on Administration §§ 351, 352.

6 E. g. testamentary provision that executor may serve without bond, infra § 113; testamentary provision that executor may sell the real estate, infra § 123.

### *Independent Executors*

Under the Texas statute, the testator, by making his representative an independent executor, can limit the necessary steps to be taken in court to probate of the will and returns of an inventory, appraisement and list of creditors against the estate.[7] All else may be done without judicial action or supervision, though the independent executor's ultimate rights and duties to debtors, creditors, devisees and legatees are the same as in case of an ordinary executor.[8] A few other western states have statutes which permit a testator to provide for substantially the same freedom from court supervision as the Texas statute.[9]

### *Special Administrators—In General*

The ecclesiastical courts recognized the necessity of appointing special or temporary administrators in certain situations.[10] Statutes in most states authorize the probate courts to do likewise.[11] Even in the absence of pertinent legislative authorization, the courts may make a suitable appointment of a representative for a limited time or purpose in order to preserve the assets of the estate pending the qualification of the ordinary executor or administrator.[12] The court's authority to do so is found in the general power to make appointments of personal representatives.[13] Indeed, a court can probably appoint a representative for a limited purpose though the case did not come within the usual categories of appointments formerly made by the ecclesiastical courts.[14]

7 Tex Civ.Stat.Ann., 1939, arts. 3436–3437; See also arts. 3457–3465; Lovejoy v. Cockrell, 63 S.W.2d 1009, Tex.Com.App.1933.

8 Lovejoy v. Cockrell, supra note 7.

9 Ariz.Code Ann., 1939 § 38–1902; Idaho Laws Ann., 1943 §§ 15–237, 15–238; Washington Rev.Stat.Ann., 1932 §§ 1462, 1463. See In re Megrath's Estate, 142 Wash. 324, 253 P. 455, affirmed 142 Wash. 324, 256 P. 503, 1926; Basye, Dispensing with Administration, 44 Mich.L.R. 329, 351–355.

10 See 2 Bl.Com. 505.

11 Lanier v. Shonyo, 133 Ark. 396, 201 S.W. 108, 1918; Bruning v. Golden, 159 Ind. 199, 64 N.E. 657, 1902; Jones v. Minnesota Transfer R. Co., 108 Minn. 129, 121 N.W. 606, 1909; Matter of Belotti, 87 Misc. 81, 150 N.Y.S. 421, 1914. See Model Probate Code § 105.

12 Friedenwald v. Burke, 122 Md. 156, 89 A. 424, 1913; McArthur v. Scott, 113 U.S. 340, 5 S.Ct. 652, 28 L.Ed. 1015, 1885.

13 Authorities supra note 12. And see Martin v. Dry Dock, E. B. & B. Railroad Co., 92 N.Y. 70, 1883.

14 Pickering v. Weiting, 47 Iowa 242, 1877; Martin v. Dry Dock, E. B. & B. Railroad Co., supra note 13, holding that the surrogate could issue letters to prosecute a claim without authority to collect money thereon or compromise it.

*Pendente Lite*

When a will was contested, there was once some doubt as to the propriety of appointing a temporary administrator because there had been no adjudication of intestacy.[15] However, it became well established that an administrator pendente lite (pending the suit) could be appointed for preservation of the assets.[16] It has even been held that where the contest arises after appointment of the executor named in the will, his authority may be suspended and a temporary administrator appointed to serve until termination of the contest.[17] Of course, the authority of the administrator pendente lite ceases upon termination of the litigation.[18] The executor named in the will may be named for the temporary office,[19] but the court may name another in its discretion,[20] and probably should do so where the executor is charged with undue influence in procuring the will or is otherwise hostile to the estate.[21] An administrator pendente lite may also be appointed where there is a contest over who has the right to administer a testate,[22] or an intestate,[23] estate.

*Ad litem*

A special administrator is sometimes appointed for the purpose of supplying the necessary party to an action in which the decedent was, or his estate is, interested.[24] Ordinarily such an

15 Satterwhite v. Carson, 25 N.C. 549, 1843; Frederick v. Hook, Carth. 153, 90 Eng.Rep. 694, 1691.

16 Slade v. Washburn, 25 N.C. 557, 1843; State ex rel. Alderson v. Moehlenkamp, 133 Mo. 134, 34 S.W. 468, 1896; Barfield v. Miller, 70 S.W.2d 632, Tex.Civ.App.1934; Wills v. Rich, 2 Atk. 285, 26 Eng.Rep. 575, 1742.

17 State ex rel. Alderson v. Moehlenkamp, supra note 16. But see Steen v. Springfield, 91 Ark. 73, 120 S.W. 408, 1909.

18 State ex rel. Ashton v. Imel, 243 Mo. 180, 147 S.W. 989, 1912; Woolley v. Pemberton, 41 N.J.Eq. 394, 5 A. 139, 1886; Barfield v. Miller, supra note 16.

19 Renshaw v. Williams, 75 Md. 498, 23 A. 905, 1892; In re Williams' Estate, 55 Mont. 63, 173 P. 790, 1 A.L.R. 1639, 1918 (statute); Matter of Hilton's Will, 29 Misc. 532, 61 N.Y.S. 1073, 1899.

20 In re Shonts' Will, 191 App.Div. 427, 181 N.Y.S. 553, 1920.

21 O'Bryan v. Superior Court, 18 Cal.2d 490, 116 P.2d 49, 136 A.L.R. 595, 1941; Matter of Sterns, 2 Con. 272, 9 N.Y.S. 748, 1890. But cf. Matter of Hilton's Will, supra note 19.

22 In re Leland's Will, 175 App.Div. 58, 161 N.Y.S. 320, 1916.

23 Woods' Estate, 94 Cal. 566, 29 P. 1108, 1892. See Dekle v. McLeod, 144 Ga. 289, 86 S.E. 1082, 1915.

24 Keith v. McCord, 140 Ala. 402, 37 So. 267, 1904; In re Nugent's Estate, 77 Mich. 500, 43 N.W. 889, 1889; McKamy v. McNabb, 97 Tenn. 236, 36 S.W. 1091, 1896 (judgment binding on general administrator).

administrator ad litem will not be appointed where there is a general personal representative,[25] though if the latter is interested adversely to the estate, a special administrator may be appointed to conduct the litigation.[26] Of course the authority of an administrator ad litem is limited to the conduct or defense of the litigation; he has no other power even of a temporary sort.

*Other Types of Special Representatives*

The power to appoint a special or temporary administrator is not confined to the above mentioned cases. Thus, where the regular representative becomes incapacitated by temporary illness,[27] or absence,[28] a temporary administrator may be appointed to act during the period of incapacity. The same is true where the person named as executor or who would otherwise be entitled to administer is a minor,[29] although in the latter case the courts today, in absence of statutory provisions, would probably pass over the disqualified infant in favor of the one next in line.[30]

One of the most frequent occasions for the appointment of a special administrator is that in which the estate needs attention in the interval before the executor or administrator can be appointed.[31] This situation is not so apt to occur in the states where the executor or general administrator can be appointed immediately and without notice,[32] and it constitutes one of the best arguments for ex parte grant of letters since special administrations add to the total expense of the proceedings.

25 Grace v. Neel, 41 Ark. 165, 1883.

26 Phillips v. Duckett, 112 Ill.App. 587, 1903; Goodman v. Griffith, 155 Mo.App. 574, 134 S.W. 1051, 1911. Cf. Heinrich v. Harrigan, 288 Ill. 170, 123 N.E. 309, 1919.

27 In re Ponsonby, [1895] P. 287.

28 In re Estes' Estate, 65 Mo.App. 38, 1895 (statute); In re Suarez [1897] P. 82.

29 Woodruff v. Snoover, 45 A. 980, N.J.Prerog.1900; Blanck v. Morrison, 4 Dem.(N.Y.) 297, 1886; In re Blanck's Estate, 3 How.Prac.(N.S.) 58, 1886. Cf. West v. Willby, 3 Phill. 374, 161 Eng.Rep. 1357, 1820 (discretionary with court).

30 Rea v. Englesing, 56 Miss. 463, 1893; In re Nickals' Estate, 21 Nev. 462, 34 P. 250, 1893; Knox v. Nobel, 77 Hun. 230, 28 N.Y.S. 355, 1894.

31 Succession of Coco, 184 La. 144, 165 So. 646, 1936; Keegan's Estate v. Welch, 83 Neb. 166, 119 N.W. 252, 1909; In re Levine's Estate, 158 Misc. 116, 285 N.Y.S. 754, 1936. As to powers of the special administrator, see In re Palm's Estate, 210 Minn. 87, 297 N.W. 765, 1941; In re Holm's Estate, 141 Wash. 475, 252 P. 145, 1927; annotation, 148 A.L.R. 275.

32 See Model Probate Code § 105; infra § 112.

*Public Administrator*

In many states provision is made by statute for an officer whose duty is to collect and administer the estates of persons who leave no successors in the state and to represent the interests of the state in default of claimants to the property.[33] Sometimes the statutes provide that these duties should fall on another officer such as the county treasurer or sheriff.[34] The coroner has no right by virtue of his office to administer the goods of a person found dead in his county.[35] In absence of statutory provision, the office of public administrator is not recognized.[36]

In some jurisdictions the public administrator may undertake the handling of particular estates by virtue of his office;[37] elsewhere he must have especial grant from the court in each case.[38] Abuses sometimes arise in connection with the office, such as gross dissipation of estates through fees and charges,[39] neglect of unlucrative estates,[40] and administration for the primary purpose of earning fees and obtaining patronage for the incumbent.[41] It has been judicially declared that the statutes were not enacted for the benefit of the official but rather for the efficient administration of successions.[42] Perhaps the office is justified in large metropolitan centers, but elsewhere the slight convenience that is served is over-shadowed by the public vigilance necessary to guard against abuses.[43]

33 In re Graves' Estate, 8 Cal.App. 254, 96 P. 792, 1908; Estate of Munroe, 161 Cal. 10, 118 P. 242, Ann.Cas. 1913B 1161, 1911 (executor disqualified); In re McWhirter's Estate, 235 Ill. 607, 85 N.E. 918, 1908; Troll v. St. Louis Third Nat. Bank, 278 Mo. 74, 211 S.W. 545, 1919. In Wisconsin this officer administers only until those lawfully entitled to letters appear. Welsh v. Manwaring, 120 Wis. 377, 98 N.W. 214, 1904. Cf. Bailey v. McAlpin, 121 Ga. 111, 48 S.E. 699, 1904.

34 In re Rice, 12 Idaho 305, 85 P. 1109, 1906; Bridgman v. Bridgman, 30 W.Va. 212, 3 S.E. 580, 1887.

35 Jones v. Harbaugh, 93 Md. 269, 48 A. 827, 1901.

36 In re McClellan's Estate, 27 S.D. 109, 129 N.W. 1037, Ann.Cas.1913C 1029, 1911.

37 Elmore v. Bishop, 184 Ark. 243, 42 S.W.2d 399, 1931.

38 Whelan v. Bailey, 1 Cal.App.2d 334, 36 P.2d 769, 1934.

39 See Bossu's Succession, 115 La. 13, 38 So. 878, 1905; 2 Mo.L.R. 502, note 55.

40 See State ex rel. Russell v. Mueller, 332 Mo. 758, 60 S.W.2d 48, 91 A.L.R. 705, 1932.

41 See Richardson v. Cole, 160 Mo. 372, 61 S.W. 182, 83 Am.St.Rep. 479, 1900.

42 Bossu's Succession, supra note 39. See Richardson v. Cole, supra note 41.

43 Cf. Model Probate Code p. 20.

## JOINT REPRESENTATIVES

**105. Some wills provide for coexecutors and on occasions the courts will name coadministrators for an intestate estate. Such joint representatives must act jointly in the case of bringing actions and in certain other matters involving discretion, though any one of them has power to do ministerial acts in connection with the estate.**

In order to make administration less complicated, courts prefer a sole to a joint administration.[1] When there is a dispute as to who should be appointed administrator, it is usually unwise to appoint both claimants. Many wills, however, nominate two or more executors, and even in intestate estates the courts often have discretion to appoint two or more administrators.[2]

There has been much dispute and confusion as to whether the interests, powers and duties of corepresentatives are joint, several, joint and several, or joint or several; the matter is best approached by considering the various specific problems, without attempting to lay down an a priori concept of the relationship.[3] Ordinarily notice to one corepresentative is notice to all.[4] Each is entitled to the possession of the whole estate, and being so entitled, may retain that part which comes into his possession, even as against his coexecutors or coadministrators.[5] If one has possession he is deemed to hold, not for himself, but for all.[6]

When one of several corepresentatives dies the interest passes to the survivors.[7] The corepresentatives should all unite in ac-

[1] Brubaker's Appeal, 98 Pa. 21, 1881; Leggatt v. Leggatt, 1 Lee, 348, 161 Eng.Rep. 129, 1753.

[2] Copeland v. Shapley, 214 Mass. 132, 100 N.E. 1080, 1913; In re Drew's Estate, 183 Minn. 374, 236 N.W. 701, 1931; State ex rel. Gregory v. Henderson, 88 S.W.2d 893, Mo.App.1935; In re Meyers, 113 N.C. 545, 18 S.E. 689, 1893; Lethbridge v. Lauder, 13 Wyo. 9, 76 P. 682, 1904. Cf. Dorsey v. Dorsey, 140 Md. 167, 116 A. 915, 1922 (statute).

[3] See Evans, Powers and Relations of Co-Executors, 14 N.Y.U.L.Q.R. 127; note, 33 Mich.L.R. 99.

[4] Irwin v. Larson, 94 F.2d 187, 115 A.L.R. 386, C.C.A.Fla.1938.

[5] Burt v. Burt, 41 N.Y. 46, 1869; Smith v. Heyward, 115 S.C. 145, 105 S.E. 275, 1920.

[6] In re Appell, 199 App.Div. 580, 192 N.Y.S. 136, 1922. And see Burt v. Burt, supra note 5.

[7] Glidewell v. Pannell, 158 Miss. 249, 130 So. 288, 1930; Magie v. Kirkpatrick, 92 N.J.Eq. 386, 112 A. 725, 1921; Shepherd v. Darling, 120 Va. 586, 91 S.E. 737, 1917. The rule is often declared by statute. See Evans, supra note 3 at 159, and infra note 17. And see Acorn Wood Realty v.

tions with regard to the estate,[8] unless some valid reason exists for failure to join all.[9] This rule does not apply, however, to suits on contracts made by personal representatives after the deceased's death,[10] as these contracts do not bind the estate but only the executors or administrators personally.[11] A corepresentative who makes such an agreement may sue separately thereon.

One corepresentative may act for all with regard to matters which are ministerial or do not involve discretion. Thus, one may sell or assign a note payable to the decedent,[12] or release a debt due to the estate,[13] or make a sale of personalty belonging to the estate.[14] He may not, however, by borrowing money for the estate bind his corepresentatives.[15] In jurisdictions where a sole representative may compromise a claim against the estate or take a debt out of the Statute of Limitations, it has been held that a single corepresentative may also do so.[16]

In the case of certain important and discretionary matters, however, one corepresentative may not act alone. Such acts as the selling of realty,[17] the carrying on of the deceased's business,[18] the selection of counsel for the estate,[19] and the voting of stock owned by the deceased,[20] are examples of powers which

Old Colony Trust Co., 113 Fla. 320, 151 So. 533, 1933 (one executor disqualified, other may act as if he were survivor).

8 Smith's Ex'rs v. Chapman's Ex'r, 5 Conn. 14, 27, 1823; Judson v. Gibbons, 5 Wend.(N.Y.) 224, 1830.

9 Hattersley v. Bissett, 52 N.J.Eq. 693, 30 A. 86, 1894; In re Greims' Will, 140 N.J.Eq. 183, 54 A.2d 219, 1947 (appeal).

10 Sumner v. Williams, 8 Mass. 162, 5 Am.Dec. 83, 1811.

11 See infra § 119.

12 Wheeler v. Wheeler, 9 Cow.(N.Y.) 34, 1828. And see Mackay v. St. Mary's Church, 15 R.I. 121, 23 A. 108, 2 Am.St.Rep. 881, 1885 (note payable to two coadministrators).

13 Oldham's Trustee v. Boston Ins. Co., 189 Ky. 844, 226 S.W. 106, 16 A.L.R. 305, 1920.

14 Kershaw v. Hicks, 214 Ala. 605, 108 So. 513, 1926; Geyer v. Snyder, 140 N.Y. 394, 35 N.E. 784, 1893.

15 Rosenberg v. Rosenberg, 240 N.Y. 125, 147 N.E. 609, 1925.

16 Alerding v. Allison, 170 Ind. 252, 83 N.E. 1006, 127 Am.St.Rep. 363, 1908; Re Leopold's Estate, 259 N.Y. 274, 181 N.E. 570, 85 A.L.R. 197, 1932. But see Jordan v. Spiers, 113 N.C. 344, 18 S.E. 327, 1893.

17 Dingman v. Boyle, 285 Ill. 144, 120 N.E. 487, 1918; In re Simmons' Estate, 254 Pa. 231, 98 A. 871, 1916. As to power of those who accept when some renounce the office, see annotation, 36 A.L.R. 826.

18 Bank of Port Gibson v. Baugh, 9 Smedes & M.(Miss.) 290, 1848.

19 In re Estate of Dennett, 200 Wis. 84, 227 N.W. 280, 1929.

20 Sellers v. Joseph Bancroft & Sons Co., 25 Del.Ch. 268, 17 A.2d 831, 1941;

must be exercised by all. In some jurisdictions by statutory provision the majority of the coexecutors or coadministrators may make the decision in matters of this kind.[21] Sometimes the testator's will provides likewise as to the executors or their successors.[22] In most cases, however, a majority cannot act and this would be true in every situation if the representatives were equally divided in their views. Courts have refused to remove corepresentatives because of their failure to agree,[23] although as a result of a disagreement no steps can be taken, and it may be of vital consequence to the estate to act in some manner. Of course this question does not arise with respect to acts not involving discretion, as any one of the corepresentatives may act though the others object or dissent.

If corepresentatives give a joint bond each is liable for the other's maladministration as well as for his own.[24] Generally one is liable for the misfeasance of the other in which he concurs.[25] If one coexecutor obtains a secret profit or misapplies the property unknown to the other, the innocent representative is usually absolved from accounting for the sum.[26] It has been held that the ordinary rule that the release of one joint tort feasor releases all applies to case of misconduct of coexecutors and cotrustees.[27]

*Joint Administration of Two Estates*

A Utah statute provides for the joint administration of estates when one deceased person has descended from another, or where two or more deceased persons owned property in common.[28]

Highland v. Empire Nat. Bank of Clarksburg, 114 W.Va. 473, 172 S.E. 544, 1934.

21 See note, 33 Mich.L.R. 99, 103.

22 Oil City Nat. Bank v. McCalmont, 303 Pa. 306, 154 A. 497, 1931 (will provided that disputes were to be settled by a particular executor).

23 Smith v. Heyward, 115 S.C. 145, 105 S.E. 275, 1920. But see Highland v. Empire Nat. Bank of Clarksburg, supra note 20; In re Estate of Drew, 183 Minn. 374, 236 N.W. 701, 1931 (statute).

24 Lancaster v. Lewis, 93 Ga. 727, 21 S.E. 155, 1894; Hooper v. Hooper, 29 W.Va. 276, 1 S.E. 280, 1896.

25 In re Westfield Trust Co., 115 N.J.Eq. 611, 172 A. 212, 1934; Jose v. Lyman, 316 Mass. 271, 55 N.E.2d 433, 154 A.L.R. 190, 1944.

26 Spillos v. Papps, 288 Mass. 23, 192 N.E. 155, 1935; see Wlodarek v. Wlodarek, 167 Md. 556, 175 A. 455, 1934; Brown v. Fidelity Union Trust Co., 128 N.J.Eq. 197, 15 A.2d 788, 1940.

27 First & Merchants National Bank v. Bank of Waverly, 170 Va. 496, 197 S.E. 462, 116 A.L.R. 1156, 1938; cf. In re Sackman's Estate, 34 Wash.2d 864, 210 P.2d 682, 1949.

28 In re Martin's Estates, 109 Utah 131, 166 P.2d 197, 1946; see In re Cloward's Estate, 95 Utah 453, 82 P. 2d 336, 119 A.L.R. 123, 1938.

This has the merit of saving expense,[29] though it presents theoretical difficulties and has been narrowly construed.[30]

## ANCILLARY REPRESENTATIVES

**106. When the deceased leaves assets in a state other than that of his last domicile, it is frequently necessary that an ancillary administrator be appointed in the nondomiciliary jurisdiction in order to collect the assets therein. This representative has charge of the administration within his jurisdiction, and after local assets are collected and local creditors have received their just dues therefrom, the ancillary court will ordinarily order the remainder to be transmitted to the representative of the principal administration for distribution.**

### *Necessity of Ancillary Administration*

If there is to be but a single administration, it should be in the state of decedent's last domicile, since his personalty will usually pass under the laws of that state,[1] and also it is likely that the greater part of his property will be located there and that most of the debtors, creditors and others interested in the estate will reside there. However, in the interests of creditors or other interested parties administration will ordinarily also be granted in any nondomiciliary jurisdiction where the decedent left property and where some interested person applies.[2] The nondomiciliary administration is called ancillary as distinguished from the principal or domiciliary administration. Beale[3] has shown that the courts have played with three somewhat contradictory theories as to the domiciliary representative's powers in another state: (1) that the domiciliary representative is vested with the personal estate wherever located, (2) that the courts will protect local creditors whenever possible, (3) that various kinds of property are localized in some appropriate jurisdiction so that

29 Cf. Model Probate Code § 205 (guardianships).

30 In re Martin's Estates, supra note 28.

1 Restatement, Conflict of Laws § 303; Goodrich, Conflict of Laws, 3d ed. § 165. Cf. Caruso v. Caruso, 106 N.J.Eq. 130, 148 A. 882, 1929, noted, 42 Harv.L.R. 827, 28 Mich.L.R. 1045, 14 Minn.L.R. 810, 6 N.Y.U.L.Q.R. 456, 78 U. of Pa.L.R. 781.

2 Restatement, Conflict of Laws § 467; see infra § 107.

3 Beale, Conflict of Laws § 471.1; see also Hopkins, Conflict of Laws in Administration of Decedents' Intangibles, 28 Iowa L.R. 422.

it should be administered in that state. No one of these theories has been consistently followed through.

The first of the premises is obviously favorable to dispensing with ancillary administration, while the second is unfavorable since the courts may refuse to recognize payment by a local debtor or delivery of local property to the foreign domiciliary representative as a valid discharge of the obligation. The third theory may or may not be favorable, dependent on the nature of the assets and their location under the rules.

Many ancillary administrations are necessary because of the general rule that a foreign personal representative may not sue,[4] although it is usually held that this is merely a matter of lack of capacity rather than absence of title, and is therefore easily waivable.[5] In many jurisdictions there have been important legislative inroads upon the foreign representative's incapacity to sue.[6] Particularly if the claim is one for wrongful death which is not subject to the decedent's debts, the foreign representative may usually sue.[7] He can also sue upon, and exercise general power over: judgments obtained by him in his representative capacity,[8] choses in action created by transactions after his appointment,[9] and bearer negotiable instruments owned by the decedent in the representative's possession.[10] On the other hand, most

[4] Mansfield v. McFarland, 202 Pa. 173, 51 A. 763, 1902; Joy's Ex'r v. Swanton Sav. Bank & Trust Co., 111 Vt. 106, 10 A.2d 216, 1940; Restatement, Conflict of Laws § 507; Goodrich, Conflict of Laws 3d ed. § 185.

[5] Fort Fairfield Nash Co. v. Noltelmer, 135 Me. 84, 189 A. 415, 108 A.L.R. 1276, 1937.

[6] See Beale, Conflict of Laws § 507.2, showing that in more than half of the states the foreign representative may sue at least under some circumstances. In 1951, New York adopted Decedent Estate Law § 160 which permitted the foreign representative to sue under certain restrictions. For an interesting review of the history of New York, see 17th N.Y.Jud.Council Report 153–170.

[7] Ghilain v. Coulture, 84 N.H. 48, 146 A. 395, 65 A.L.R. 553, 1929, noted, 28 Mich.L.R. 938 (statute); Wiener v. Specific Pharmaceuticals, Inc., 298 N.Y. 346, 83 N.E.2d 673, 1949 (as statutory trustee); see Rose, Foreign Enforcement of Actions for Wrongful Death, 33 Mich.L.R. 545; note, 46 Col.L.R. 504.

[8] Talmadge v. Chapel, 16 Mass. 71, 1819; McCraw v. Simpson, 208 Ark. 471, 187 S.W.2d 536, 1945.

[9] De Paris v. Wilmington Trust Co., 7 Boyce (Del.) 178, 104 A. 691, 1 A.L.R. 1352, 1918 (purchase price of estate property); Beckham v. Wittkowski, 64 N.C. 464, 1870 (conversion of estate property).

[10] Sanford v. McCreedy, 28 Wis. 103, 1871. A general right to sue on any negotiable instrument belonging to decedent and in the possession of the plaintiff representative is asserted in Restatement, Conflict of Laws § 509, though this is doubtful, at least

courts hold that corporate stock is an asset in the jurisdiction where the corporation is organized, regardless of the presence of the stock certificate.[11] Though it is not too clear, the assignee of the domiciliary representative may probably sue in a nondomiciliary jurisdiction even upon an ordinary chose in action.[12]

A leading case [13] held that voluntary payment of a wage claim made to a foreign representative was a valid discharge when there was then no administration in the employer's state and when neither creditors or beneficiaries were prejudiced. Most courts would go that far.[14] However, such rulings do not help much in dispensing with ancillary administration since the debtor cannot be sure that there are no local creditors, or even that there is no local administration. It has been declared that payment to the domiciliary administrator should operate as a discharge whenever the debtor has received no notice of the appointment of an ancillary representative in the debtor's state,[15] but some authorities hold that the debtor is not absolved unless there was

in absence of statutory authority to sue. Pond v. Makepeace, 2 Metc. (Mass.) 114, 1840. However, there is a great deal of authority that the foreign representative in possession of a common-law or commercial specialty may discharge the obligation upon voluntary payment by the debtor, and that he may sue thereon if his incapacity to sue is removed by statute. See Goodrich, Conflict of Laws, 3d ed. § 182; Hopkins, Conflict of Laws in Administration of Decedents Intangibles, 28 Iowa L.R. 613; annotations, 114 A.L.R. 1461, 149 id. 1083.

11 See infra § 107, note 20; annotation, 72 A.L.R. 179; Pomerance, The 'Situs' of Stock. 17 Corn.L.Q. 43, 59–62. Cf. Restatement, Conflict of Laws §§ 477, 478.

12 Peterson v. The Chemical Bank, 32 N.Y. 21, 1865 (note); but cf. Thacker v. Lindahl, 48 S.W.2d 588, Tex.Com.App.1932 (assignment for collection.) Cf. Restatement, Conflict of Laws § 486 with Hopkins, supra note 3 at 440–445.

13 Wilkins v. Ellett, 76 U.S. 740, 9 Wall. 740, 19 L.Ed. 586, 1869; s. c., 108 U.S. 256, 2 Sup.Ct. 641, 27 L.Ed. 718, 1883.

14 In re William's Estate, 130 Iowa 553, 107 N.W. 608, 1906; Dexter v. Berge, 76 Minn. 216, 78 N.W. 1111, 1899, and see cases infra note 15. But see cases infra notes 16, 17.

15 Gray's Estate, 116 Pa. 256, 11 A. 66, 1887; cf. Maas v. German Savings Bank, 176 N.Y. 377, 68 N.E. 658, 98 Am.St.Rep. 689, 1903. See Restatement, Conflict of Laws § 482. The writers generally favor this rule. Mersch, Voluntary Payment to a Foreign Administrator, 18 Geo.L.J. 130; Hopkins, supra note 3 at 440; Goodrich, Conflict of Laws § 187; Lampke & Palmer, Voluntary Payment to a Foreign Fiduciary, 18 Legal Bull. of U. S. Svgs. & Loan League 18; Carey, A Suggested Fundamental Basis of Jurisdiction with Special Emphasis on Judicial Proceedings Affecting Decedents' Estates, 24 Ill.L.R. 44, 170. But see Buchanan & Myers, The Administration of Intangibles, 48 Harv. L.R. 911, 944.

actually no local ancillary representative at the time,[16] while others even deny protection as against an action by a subsequently appointed administrator unless no one is prejudiced by the voluntary payment to the domiciliary representative.[17]

Thus, it can be seen that while there are certainly theories and decisions which are favorable to dispensing with the need for ancillary administration, there are also rival theories and contrary decisions and some situations are clouded in doubt. Estate debtors in a nondomiciliary jurisdiction are often justified in refusing to pay the domiciliary representative because a local representative may be thereafter appointed and demand the debt. As a result it is often necessary to secure the appointment of an ancillary representative to discharge the local debtors, although no local creditors have applied for the ancillary representative. In most cases there are probably no creditors in the nondomiciliary jurisdiction, or, if they do exist, their right to payment from the domiciliary representative is sufficient protection of their interests. The Uniform Powers of Foreign Representatives Act has been promulgated to give security in the confused situation. It does not deal with the application for ancillary administration, but in absence thereof permits the domiciliary representative to exercise all the powers, including that of suit, which might be exercised by a local representative if appointed, and protects a debtor who has paid the domiciliary representative in absence of knowledge of a local administration or application therefor. This would dispense with many unnecessary ancillary administrations.[18] No state has adopted this act, though some recent piecemeal legislation is probably the result of its influence. The legislative inaction is probably due in part to conservatism, in part to an unjustified concern over the interests of local creditors, and in part to a feeling that it represents the existing law.[19] It is true that the act is largely declaratory and in accord with the best thought on the problem, but in most jurisdictions there are areas of uncertainty in the ap-

16 Grayson v. Robertson, 122 Ala. 330, 25 So. 229, 82 Am.St.Rep. 80, 1898; Reynolds v. McMullen, 55 Mich. 568, 22 N.W. 41, 54 Am.Rep. 386, 1885; Willard v. Hammond, 21 N.H. 382, 1850.

17 Ferguson v. Morris, 67 Ala. 389, 1880; Crohn v. Clay County State Bank, 137 Mo.App. 712, 118 S.W. 498, 1909; Richardson v. Neblett, 122 Miss. 723, 84 So. 695, 10 A.L.R. 272, 1920. See Beale, Voluntary Payment to a Foreign Administrator, 42 Harv. L.R. 596; Fizzell, Payment of Debt to Foreign Representatives or Heirs, 18 L.S.Mo.Bull. 3.

18 See Basye, Dispensing with Administration, 44 Mich.L.R. 331, 412, 414, 418–419, 424.

19 See report of Committee on Uniform State Laws, 21 Pa.B.Assn.Q. 366.

plicable law and as a result there must be two or more administrations of an estate when one should be ample.

*Jurisdiction to Appoint*

An ancillary administrator will usually be appointed if some interested person applies and shows the presence of assets within the jurisdiction.[20] Goods once in the possession of the domiciliary administrator are not deemed assets in another jurisdiction by reason of their removal to the latter.[21] The authorities are divided as to whether the bringing of chattels into a state after the decedent's death results in sufficient presence of assets.[22] Though ancillary letters normally follow domiciliary letters in point of time,[23] the former can be granted though there is no administration at the place of domicile.[24]

*Who May Be Appointed*

It is highly desirable that the estate wherever situated should be administered as a unit insofar as this is possible. The Uniform Ancillary Administration of Estates Act, adopted in Wisconsin,[25] is based on this premise. Accordingly, the act permits and indeed prefers the appointment of the domiciliary representative as local ancillary administrator. In other states it is usual to appoint the domiciliary representative if he applies,[26] though some jurisdictions forbid this by requiring all personal representatives to be residents of the state.[27] Often, a court may,

20 See infra § 107, notes 17–20; also supra notes 10, 11.

21 Hill v. Barton, 194 Mo.App. 325, 188 S.W. 1105, 1916. But goods never possessed by the domiciliary administrator and later removed may be properly taken by an ancillary administrator. Turner v. Campbell, 124 Mo. App. 133, 101 S.W. 119, 1907.

22 That it is sufficient to warrant local administration: Neal v. Boykin, 132 Ga. 400, 64 S.E. 480, 1909; Turner v. Campbell, 124 Mo.App. 133, 101 S.W. 119, 1907, noted, 7 Col.L.R. 119; In re Hughes, 95 N.Y. 55, 1884. To the contrary, see Christy v. Vest, 36 Iowa 285, 1873 (temporary purposes); Hoes v. New York, N. H. & H. R. Co., 173 N.Y. 435, 66 N.E. 119, 1903 (solely to serve as basis for grant of administration); Embry v. Millar, 1 A.K.Marsh.(Ky.) 300, 10 Am.Dec. 732, 1818.

23 Rackemann v. Taylor, 204 Mass. 394, 90 N.E. 552, 1910.

24 McCarron v. New York Cent. R. Co., 239 Mass. 64, 131 N.E. 478, 1921.

25 Wis.Laws, 1951, c. 252.

26 Purcell v. Cramton, 143 F.2d 22, Dist.Col.App.1944; Chadwick v. Stilphen, 105 Me. 242, 74 A. 50, 1909 (granted to one of two domiciliary executors); Babcock v. Collins, 60 Minn. 73, 61 N.W. 1020, 51 Am.St.Rep. 503, 1895.

27 Burkhim v. Pinkhussohn, 58 S. C. 469, 36 S.E. 908, 1900. And see infra § 110.

in its discretion, appoint someone other than the domiciliary representative.[28] As in case of letters generally,[29] the appointment is made upon petition of some interested person.[30]

*Relation to Local Assets and to Domiciliary Representative*

With respect to local assets, the ancillary administrator has generally the same powers and duties as any other personal representative.[31] He is an officer of the court appointing him.[32] He is regarded as having title to the local physical personalty,[33] and the right to sue the estate's debtors residing in his jurisdiction.[34] His rights in this regard normally exclude the domiciliary representative.[35] In no sense of the word are the domiciliary and local representatives regarded as corepresentatives.[36] Indeed it is said that there is no privity between them,[37] except when the same

28 Murdoch v. Murdoch, 81 Conn. 681, 72 A. 290, 129 Am.St.Rep. 231, 1909; Reed v. Bishop, 51 Ind.App. 187, 97 N.E. 1023, 1912.

29 See infra § 112.

30 Baldwin v. Rice, 183 N.Y. 55, 75 N.E. 1096, 1905. As to whether a nonresident creditor may make the application, see note, 79 U. of Pa.L.R. 352.

31 Except for matters of distribution of assets, see infra note 52.

32 Milner v. Hoag, 182 App.Div. 524, 169 N.Y.S. 755, 1918 (hence, suspension of the powers of the domiciliary executor does not interrupt the powers of the ancillary administrator); Keenan v. Toury, 91 N.H. 220, 16 A.2d 705, 132 A.L.R. 1362, 1940 (hence accountable only to the local court therefor, although he was also domiciliary representative).

33 McCully v. Cooper, 114 Cal. 258, 46 P. 82, 35 L.R.A. 492, 55 Am.St.Rep. 66, 1896 (against domiciliary administrator); Fox v. Carr, 16 Hun (N.Y.) 434, 1879 (money); Morrison v. Hass, 229 Mass. 514, 118 N.E. 893, 1918; Marden v. Jones, 165 Md. 450, 169 A. 309, 1933 (note). Cf. De Paris v. Wilmington Trust Co., 7 Boyce (Del.) 178, 104 A. 691, 1 A.L.R. 1352, 1918.

34 Hensley v. Rich, infra note 47 (though debtor resides in another county of the ancillary jurisdiction). But see Ellis v. Northwestern Mutual Life Ins. Co., 100 Tenn. 177, 43 S.W. 766, 1897 (insurance policy located in domiciliary jurisdiction).

35 McCully v. Cooper, supra note 33. Cf. Maas v. German Sav. Bank in City of New York, 176 N.Y. 377, 68 N.E. 658, 98 Am.St.Rep. 689, 1903, where ancillary representative was negligent in not collecting the claim and the payment to the domiciliary administrator was recognized as a good defense, in case there were no local creditors.

36 Merrill v. New England Mut. Life Insurance Co., 103 Mass. 245, 4 Am.Rep. 548, 1869; Bolton v. Barnett, 131 Miss. 802, 95 So. 721, 1923. And see Sherman v. Page, 85 N.Y. 126, 1881; Dolan v. Anthony, 51 R.I. 181, 152 A. 873, 1931. As to liability on the respective bonds when the same person is domiciliary and ancillary representative, see State ex rel. Lynch v. Whitehouse, 75 Conn. 410, 411, 53 A. 897, 1903; Adams' Heirs v. Adams' Adm'r, 11 B.Mon.(Ky.) 77, 1850.

37 De Paris v. Wilmington Trust Co., supra note 33; Baker v. Cooper,

person acts as executor in different states.[38] While a claim due decedent is merged in a judgment obtained thereon by the administrator in any state,[39] an action by another administrator is not barred when the judgment is for the defendant.[40] Nor is there res judicata on account of an action against a representative in another jurisdiction, regardless of the outcome of the first litigation.[41]

*Sale of Realty*

There is often statutory authority for the ancillary representative to sell local land upon the court's order for the purpose of paying creditors.[42] Usually the courts permit the sale if there is an insufficiency of local assets to pay local creditors, though the principal administration has sufficient assets to satisfy all.[43] Generally application may be granted in the ancillary administration to satisfy unpaid claims allowed in the domiciliary administration.[44] In some jurisdictions, the foreign domiciliary representative is entitled to procure an order for sale of land to pay debts in the absence of the appointment of an ancillary administrator;[45]

166 Md. 1, 170 A. 556, 1934; In re Sheley's Estate, 35 N.M. 358, 298 P. 942, 1931 (compromise not binding on other representative). Cf. Kenneson, The Relation to Each Other of Different Administrators of the Same Deceased, 6 Col.L.R. 15.

38 Carpenter v. Strange, 141 U.S. 87, 11 Sup.Ct. 960, 35 L.Ed. 640, 1891.

39 Louisville & N. R. Co. v. Jones' Adm'r, 215 Ky. 774, 286 S.W. 1071, 53 A.L.R. 1255, 1926 (death action); Restatement, Conflict of Laws § 505.

40 Ingersoll v. Coram, 211 U.S. 335, 29 Sup.Ct. 92, 53 L.Ed. 208, Mass. 1908; Restatement, Conflict of Laws § 506.

41 Brown v. Fletcher's Estate, 210 U.S. 82, 28 Sup.Ct. 702, 52 L.Ed. 966, 1906; Restatement Conflict of Laws §§ 510, 511. But see supra note 38. See Goodrich, Conflict of Laws, 3d ed. § 191. The Uniform Ancillary Administration of Estates Act, § 8, provides for privity and res judicata in all cases.

42 Hobson v. Payne, 45 Ill. 158, 1867; Comstock v. Crawford, 3 Wall. 396, 18 L.Ed. 34, 1865; Ohio Gen. Code, § 10511-15. And see authorities cited infra notes 43, 44. However the ancillary administrator may not exercise the testamentary power of sale given to the executor. In re Livingston's Estate, 91 Mont. 548, 9 P.2d 159, 90 A.L.R. 1036, 1932; Bacharach v. Spriggs, 173 Ark. 250, 292 S. W. 150, 1927.

43 Lawrence's Appeal, 49 Conn. 411, 1881; Cowden v. Jacobsen, 165 Mass. 240, 43 N.E. 98, 1896. But see Livermore v. Haven, 23 Pick.(Mass.) 116, 1839.

44 Dow v. Lillie, 26 N.D. 512, 144 N.W. 1082, L.R.A.1915D 754, 1914. And see Wolfe v. Lewisburg Trust & Safe Deposit Co., 305 Pa. 583, 158 A. 567, 81 A.L.R. 660, 1931. See note, 41 Harv.L.R. 922.

45 Mowry v. McQueen, 80 Minn. 385, 83 N.W. 348, 1900. See Uniform Powers of Foreign Representatives Act § 4.

but this authority is purely statutory and does not exist in absence of legislation.[46]

*Payment of Claims*

The chief object of the ancillary administration is said to be to secure the payment of the claims of local creditors from local assets without requiring them to present their claims in the principal administration.[47] Some jurisdictions seem to restrict the ancillary administrator to the satisfaction of local creditors,[48] though particularly if the estate is solvent, there is no reason why foreign creditors also may not be paid.[49] The courts should so administer the property of insolvent estates as to permit the local creditors to receive only the same percentage of their claims as creditors elsewhere obtain.[50] Both courts in the ancillary and in the domiciliary jurisdictions should strive to bring about equality in this regard. The court of the ancillary jurisdiction may command its representative to hold up transmission of the undisposed of assets until it is assured that the local creditors are treated as favorably as the others.[51]

46 Bank of Seneca v. Morrison, 200 Mo.App. 169, 204 S.W. 119, 1912; In re Robinson's Heirship, 119 Neb. 285, 295, 228 N.W. 852, 1930. See In re Diederichs' Estate, 255 Wis. 221, 38 N.W.2d 489, 1949. As to the right to possession and rents, see note, 23 Minn.L.R. 373.

47 Hensley v. Rich, 191 Ind. 294, 132 N.E. 632, 18 A.L.R. 1118, 1921.

48 Lewis v. Rutherford, 71 Ark. 218, 72 S.W. 373, 1879. And see Wedemann v. United States Trust Co. of New York, 258 N.Y. 315, 179 N.E. 712, 79 A.L.R. 1320, 1932. And see note, 79 U. of Pa.L.R. 352.

49 Rosenthal v. Renick, 44 Ill. 202, 1867. Goodall v. Marshall, 11 N.H. 88, 35 Am.Dec. 472, 1840. As to allowing a foreign creditor to prove his claim which is barred by the nonclaim statute in his own jurisdiction, see Toner v. Conqueror Trust Co., 131 Kan. 651, 293 P. 745, 72 A.L.R. 1018, 1930.

50 In re Gable's Estate, 79 Iowa 178, 44 N.W. 352, 9 L.R.A. 218, 1890; In re Hanreddy's Estate, 176 Wis. 570, 186 N.W. 744, 1922. And see Ramsay v. Ramsay, 196 Ill. 179, 63 N.E. 618, 1902. Some states have statutes to this effect. See In re Hirsch's Estate, 146 Ohio St. 393, 66 N.E.2d 636, 164 A.L.R. 761, 1946; Uniform Ancillary Administration of Estates Act § 11 and comment thereon in Nadelman, Insolvent Decedents' Estates, 49 Mich. L.R. 1129; Restatement, Conflict of Laws § 503. To prefer local creditors has been declared to be violative of the privileges and immunities clause of the United States Constitution. First. Nat. Bank of Appleton, Wis. v. Brauns' Estate, 276 Mich. 598, 268 N.W. 890, 106 A.L.R. 889, 1936, noted, 21 Minn.L.R. 331, 2 Mo.L.R. 103. But preferences based on the nature of the claim are granted in accordance with the law of the forum. Duehay v. Acacia Mut. Life Ins. Co., 70 App.D.C. 245, 105 F.2d 768, 124 A.L.R. 1268, 1939.

51 Dawes v. Head, 3 Pick.(Mass.) 128, 1926. And see Owsley v. Bow-

*Disposition of Remaining Assets*

As a general rule the court in the jurisdiction of the ancillary administration orders its officer to transmit the balance after payment of debts to the domiciliary representative.[52] This is reasonable since the personalty is distributed according to the law of the deceased's domicile. However, the ordinary practice of transmission is not an inflexible rule and the court may in its discretion order direct distribution by its representative to the persons entitled under the will or intestate laws.[53] Direct distribution has sometimes been ordered to protect the interest of a legatee,[54] or where the persons beneficially entitled are residents of the ancillary jurisdiction or neighboring states.[55]

den, 161 Ga. 884, 132 S.E. 70, 44 A.L.R. 795, 1926; First Nat. Bank of Appleton, Wis. v. Brauns' Estate, supra note 50.

52 Lawrence v. Kitteridge, 21 Conn. 577, 56 Am.Dec. 385, 1847; Dickson v. Fisher, 211 Ill.App. 45, 1918; Re Livingston's Estate, 91 Mont. 584, 9 P. 2d 159, 90 A.L.R. 1036, 1932; Todd v. Todd, 78 N.H. 386, 103 A. 17, 1917; Hopper v. Hopper, 125 N.Y. 400, 26 N.E. 457, 12 L.R.A. 237, 1891. When the assets are needed to pay creditors at the domicile, the property should be transmitted there. In re Gable's Estate, supra note 50.

53 In re Lane's Estate, 199 Iowa 520, 202 N.W. 244, 1925; Lawrence's Estate, 93 Vt. 424, 108 A. 387, 1919; Ohio Gen.Code, § 10511-25. But the property should be distributed according to the law of the domicile. See note 1 supra. Cf. In re Bruhns' Estate, 58 Mont. 526, 193 P. 1115, 1920.

54 In re Campbell's Estate, 53 Utah 487, 173 P. 688, 1918. See Hamilton v. Levy, 41 S.C. 374, 19 S.E. 610, 1894.

55 In re Welles' Estate, 161 Pa. 218, 28 A. 1116, 1895; In re Lorillard, [1922] 2 Ch. 638, 13 B.R.C. 560.

## JURISDICTION OVER ADMINISTRATION

**107. The probate court of the county in which the deceased was domiciled at the time of his death, or in case of ancillary administration, of the county in which he left assets, has jurisdiction to grant letters testamentary or of administration. Letters granted for the estate of a person who is not dead are ordinarily void, though many states have statutes authorizing absentees' estates to be administered with due provisions as to notice and preservation of the property for a reasonable time. Letters of administration should not be issued where there is a valid will nominating an executor. In some jurisdictions, letters must not be granted within a certain number of days after decedent's death, and other states have statutes forbidding the grant of administration more than a designated number of years after the death.**

### *What Court*

The granting letters of administration, like the matter of probate, was within the exclusive cognizance of the English ecclesiastical courts, which once also had jurisdiction over the subsequent administration steps, although in England the latter was largely taken over by equity through a creditors' bills when the estate was involved or controversies arose.[1] In America the grant of administration is by the court of probate, which also has jurisdiction over the administration of decedent's estates.[2] Administration in equity is obsolete or practically so in most American jurisdictions.[3]

The federal courts have no jurisdiction to administer estates of deceased persons by taking charge of the res itself.[4] However, if

1 See Atkinson, Brief History of Testamentary Jurisdiction, 8 Mo.L.R. 107, showing that the ecclesiatical courts, though their administration business receded with the growth of equity jurisdiction, retained the exclusive power to probate and grant letters and also substantial amount of administration litigation. For a description of the way that equity obtained jurisdiction over administration in England, see Langdell, A Brief Survey of Equity, Jurisdiction VI, VII—Creditors' Bills, 4 Harv.L.R. 99, 5 id. 101. See also infra § 127.

2 See infra § 4.

3 Sowle v. Potter, 223 Ky. 136, 3 S.W.2d 174, 1928; Perkins v. Warburton, 4 F.2d 742, D.C.Md., 1925. But see note, 29 Mich.L.R. 1057; Ex parte Cone, 226 Ala. 64, 145 So. 571, 1933. See generally 76 U. of Pa.L.R. 612; 4 Pomeroy, Equity Jurisprudence, 1941, § 1154.

4 Byers v. McAuley, 149 U.S. 608, 13 S.Ct. 906, 37 L.Ed. 867, 1893; In re McDonald's Estate, 42 F.2d 266, D.C.Minn.1930. Of course this limita-

the other elements of Federal jurisdiction are present, one may establish a debt against the estate in the federal court or his right to share in the estate as a distributee, provided this does not interfere with the possession of the state court holding through its officer, the personal representative.[5]

The grant of letters of administration by a court which has no jurisdiction to do so in any case is undoubtedly void and subject to collateral attack. When the court has general testamentary powers it should do so only in proper cases, but the grant of administration in improper cases should not go to the jurisdiction of the court. In other words the matters treated below in this section are not jurisdictional in this sense, although some of them are said or even held to be so.

*Domicile of Deceased*

The principal or domiciliary administration should be in the county where the deceased was domiciled at the time of his death.[6] While the statutes frequently use the term residence, this is interpreted as meaning technical domicile or the location that was decedent's fixed place of abode.[7] The place of death does not determine the place of residence at time of death, nor does it afford jurisdiction to grant letters.[8]

When letters have been granted in one county upon a finding of domicile there, the grant is not subject to collateral attack by a grant in another country.[9] There should be only one admin-

tion does not apply in the District of Columbia.

5 Yonley v. Lavender, 21 Wall.(88 U.S.) 276, 22 L.Ed. 536, Ark.1874; Hess v. Reynolds, 113 U.S. 73, 5 S.Ct. 377, 28 L.Ed. 927, Mich.1885; Waterman v. Canal-Louisiana Bank & Trust Co., 215 U.S. 33, 30 S.Ct. 10, 54 L.Ed. 80, 1909, noted, 10 Col.L.R. 100, 23 Harv.L.R. 225; United States v. Swanson, 75 F.Supp. 118, D.C.Neb. 1947. See generally, Woerner, Probate Jurisdiction of Federal Courts, 4 St.L.L.R. 69; notes, 43 Harv.L.R. 462, 41 Ill.L.R. 424; annotation, 158 A.L.R. 9. See also supra § 93.

6 In re Brady's Estate, 177 Cal. 537, 171 P. 303, 1918; In re Kladivo's Estate, 188 Iowa 471, 176 N.W. 262, 1920; In re Coppock's Estate, 72 Mont. 431, 234 P. 258, 39 A.L.R. 1152, 1925 (deceased domiciled in China). See Basye, The Venue of Probate and Administration Proceedings, 43 Mich. L.R. 471, 476.

7 In re Lassin's Estate, 33 Wash.2d 163, 204 P.2d 1071, 1949; In re Seymour, 107 Misc. 330, 177 N.Y.S. 702, 1919. Cf. Wilkinson v. Spiller, 143 Va. 267, 129 S.E. 235, 1925.

8 Tyer v. J. B. Blades Lumber Co., 188 N.C. 268, 124 S.E. 305, 1924; Henson v. Wolfe, 130 S.C. 273, 125 S.E. 293, 1924.

9 Bremer v. Lake Erie & W. R. Co., 318 Ill. 11, 148 N.E. 862, 41 A.L.R. 1345, 1925; Bolton v. Schriever, 135 N.Y. 65, 31 N.E. 1001, 18 L.R.A.,N.S., 242, 1892; Holmes v. Wharton, 194

istration in each state; the representative who is first properly appointed administers the decedent's entire estate found anywhere in that state. However, if the record shows that the deceased was domiciled in another county, the letters granted have been held void and subject to collateral attack.[10]

When letters are granted by the probate court of one state upon the basis of his domicile there, this does not prevent the court of another state from finding that the deceased died a resident within its own jurisdiction and therefore granting domiciliary letters.[11] The result of such conflicting adjudications of domicile is that each court administers such property as is within the jurisdiction and distributes the assets after payment of claims to the persons entitled under its own laws.[12]

N.C. 470, 140 S.E. 93, 1927; Sewell v. Christison, County Judge, 114 Okl. 177, 245 P. 632, 1926. Contra: Dresser v. Fourth Nat. Bank of Wichita, 101 Kan. 401, 168 P. 672, 1917. But see Kan.Gen.Stat.Ann., 1949, § 59-2203. See supra § 94, note 33.

When a petition for administration is pending in one county, a second court will ordinarily refuse to proceed until disposition of the first application. In re Daniels' Will, 140 Misc. 89, 249 N.Y.S. 436, 1931. Prohibition may issue to prevent the second court from proceeding. Hill v. Superior Court of San Luis Obispo County, 188 Cal. 352, 205 P. 430, 1922. When two counties have each granted letters some courts hold that the first grant prevails. Sewall v. Christison, County Judge, supra; Tilton v. O'Connor, 68 N.H. 215, 44 A. 303, 1894. Others hold that the grant of the first court wherein a petition is filed prevails. In re Greening's Estate, 232 Mo.App. 78, 89 S.W.2d 123, 1936, noted, 1 Mo.L.R. 192; see also note, 25 Corn.L.Q. 146. The latter position has the support of Basye, supra note 6 at 493 and Model Probate Code § 61, although the first view tends to expedite matters and is in accord with the rule in civil litigation generally. Under either view a court may entertain direct proceedings to revoke its own letters because of improper venue. In re Gingery's Estate, 103 Ohio St. 559, 134 N.E. 449, 1921. Cf. Pease v. Hudson, 195 Okl. 371, 157 P.2d 909, 1945.

10 Anderson v. Walter, 78 Kan. 781, 99 P. 270, 1908; Reynolds v. Lloyd Cotton Mills, 177 N.C. 412, 99 S.E. 240, 5 A.L.R. 284, 1919.

11 Colvin v. Jones, 194 Mich. 670, 161 N.W. 847, 1917; In re Crane's Estate, 205 Mich. 673, 172 N.W. 584, 1919; Baker v. Baker, Eccles Co., 242 U.S. 394, 37 S.Ct. 152, 61 L.Ed. 386, 1917, noted, 30 Harv.L.R. 486, 26 Yale L.J. 403. See annotation, 121 A.L.R. 1200; supra § 94, note 30 et seq.

12 See authorities cited supra note 11. It would seem that all parties who appeared personally in the first proceeding would be bound by the adjudication. See Riley v. New York Trust Co., 315 U.S. 343, 62 Sup.Ct. 608, 86 L.Ed. 885, 1942, and generally, Gavit, Jurisdiction of the Subject-Matter and Res Judicata, 80 U. of Pa.L.R. 386.

*Assets—Necessity of*

The presence of assets within the jurisdiction are not necessary for the appointment of a personal representative at the place of the decedent's last domicile.[13] While letters should be denied if there is no property anywhere and nothing for a representative to do,[14] the courts often grant administration upon showing of property of very little value.[15] Generally if the assets consist of an alleged cause of action, a prima facie showing of its validity is all that is required; the probate court does not determine the validity of the cause in order to ascertain whether administration should be granted.[16]

When the deceased was a nonresident of the state, or in other words when the administration is an ancillary one, there is no basis to grant letters unless there are assets within the state.[17] There need not be tangible assets; a claim against a resident debtor,[18] or a death claim against one who may be served with process there is sufficient.[19] For this purpose, corporate stock is

13 Watson v. Collins' Adm'r, 37 Ala. 587, 1861; Holburn v. Pfanmiller's Adm'r, 114 Ky. 831, 71 S.W. 940, 1903; Okfuskey v. Corbin, 170 Okl. 449, 40 P.2d 1064, 1935; Connors v. Cunard S. S. Co., 204 Mass. 310, 90 N.E. 601, 26 L.R.A.,N.S., 171, 134 Am. St.Rep. 662, 17 Ann.Cas. 1051, 1910; In re Barlass' Estate, 143 Wis. 497, 128 N.W. 58, 139 Am.St.Rep. 1111, 1910. But see Re Dickerson's Estate, 51 Nev. 69, 268 P. 769, 59 A.L.R. 84, 1928; Robinson v. Dana's Estate, 87 N.H. 114, 174 A. 772, 94 A.L.R. 1437, 1934. The difference of viewpoint is accounted for in part at least, by statutory language.

14 Wolf v. Gills, 96 Okl. 6, 219 P. 350, 1923; In re Barlass' Estate, supra note 13. An administrator may be appointed for the sole purpose of prosecuting a death claim. Pettibone v. Moore, 223 Ind. 232, 59 N.E.2d 114, 1945; see infra note 19.

15 In re Brasfield's Estate, 168 Kan. 376, 214 P.2d 305, 1950; Mitchell v. Dreher, 150 S.C. 125, 147 S.E. 646, 1929; In re Barlass' Estate, supra note 13.

16 In re Barlass' Estate, supra note 13; cf. In re Brasfield's Estate, supra note 15.

17 Flath v. Neal, 63 Ariz. 68, 159 P. 2d 617, 1945; Shirley's Estate v. Shirley, 334 Ill.App. 590, 80 N.E.2d 99, 1948; Liberty v. Kinney, 242 Iowa 656, 47 N.W.2d 835, 1951; Gregory v. Lansing, 115 Minn. 73, 131 N.W. 1010, 1911; In re Noyes' Estate, 182 Or. 1, 185 P.2d 555, 1947 (debt against United States). Cf. In re Tasanen, 25 Utah 396, 71 P. 984, 1903.

18 Hensley v. Rich, 191 Ind. 294, 132 N.E. 632, 18 A.L.R. 1118, 1921; Gregory v. Lansing, supra note 17; Liberty v. Kinney, supra note 17 (decedent's liability insurance); In re Nave's Estate, 344 Ill.App. 89, 100 N.E.2d 328, 1951 (same); Lund v. City of Seattle, 163 Wash. 254, 1 P.2d 301, 1931; cf. Flath v. Neal, supra note 17. See Carpenter, Jurisdiction over Debts, 31 Harv.L.R. 905; Buchanan & Myers, Administration of Intangibles, 48 Harv.L.R. 911, 937.

19 Hartford & N. H. R. R. v. Andrews, 36 Conn. 213, 1869; Findlay v. Chicago & G. T. Ry., 106 Mich. 700, 64

usually regarded as assets at the domicile of the corporation, or the place where it does business.[20]

Statutes commonly provide that the venue in case of a nonresident decedent is in the county where his property or some part of it is located.[21] If he left property in several counties of the ancillary jurisdiction the representative of the first court taking jurisdiction administers the property for the whole state since there should be only one administration for the entire state.[22]

*Death*

It is clear that a court should not grant ordinary letters of administration for one's estate unless he is shown to be dead. This has given rise to considerable difficulty in case of persons who have disappeared and are apparently dead though there is no positive proof. Courts frequently grant letters of administration upon a showing that one has been unheard of for seven years under circumstances that give rise to the presumption of death.[23] However, if after letters are granted upon the basis of this presumption or some other showing of death, the alleged decedent should return, then the letters and the entire administration pro-

N.W. 732, 1895; Hutchins v. St. Paul, M. & M. Ry. Co., 44 Minn. 5, 46 N.W. 79, 1890; Louisville & Nashville R. R. v. Herb, 125 Tenn. 408, 143 S.W. 1138, 1911; Berry v. Rutland R. Co., 103 Vt. 388, 154 A. 671, 1931. Contra: Mercer v. Dobbyn, 91 Ind.App. 682, 173 N.E. 338, 1930; Cox v. Kansas City, 86 Kan. 298, 120 P. 553, 554, 1912. In both of the last-mentioned cases, however, the clothes on the deceaseds' backs provided sufficient assets to appoint an administrator to sue upon the death claim. See note, 6 Ind.L.J. 506.

20 Nashville Trust Co. v. Cleage, 246 Ala. 513, 21 So.2d 441, 1945; Murphy v. Crouse, 135 Cal. 14, 66 P. 971, 87 Am.St.Rep. 90, 1901; Martin v. Central Trust Co., 327 Ill. 622, 159 N.E. 312, 1927; Black Eagle Mining Co. v. Conroy, 94 Okl. 199, 221 P. 425, 1923. But see In re Miller's Estate, 90 Kan. 819, 136 P. 255, L.R.A.1915D 856, Ann.Cas.1915B 699, 1913. Cf. Restatement, Conflict of Laws §§ 477, 478; Lohman v. Kansas City Southern R. Co., 326 Mo. 819, 33 S.W.2d 112, 72 A.L.R. 172, 1930. See note, 19 Va.L.R. 395 and supra § 106, notes 10, 11.

21 See Basye, supra note 6 at 477–48, where the statutes are analysed; Model Probate Code § 61.

22 Dungan v. Superior Court of Fresno County, 149 Cal. 98, 84 P. 767, 117 Am.St.Rep. 119, 1906.

23 Payne v. Home Sav. Bank, 193 Ga. 406, 18 S.E.2d 770, 140 A.L.R. 1397, 1942; Bornemann v. Ofsthun, 175 Minn. 493, 221 N.W. 876, 1928; Williams v. Hefner, 89 Mont. 361, 297 P. 492, 1931. And see Savings Bank of Baltimore v. Weeks, 110 Md. 78, 72 A. 475, 22 L.R.A.,N.S., 221, 1909, indicating that the full period of seven years need not have elapsed if there is other satisfactory proof of death.

ceedings are generally considered void. The owner can recover his property from the heirs or others who have possession thereof, his debts though the debtors have paid the personal representative, or even the value of the property from the administrator who has completely administered it and has been discharged.[24] The leading case upon this doctrine is Scott v. McNeal,[25] which decided that since there was no notice to the alleged deceased in the proceedings to grant administration, his property was taken without due process of law. It is undoubtedly true that the ordinary statutory procedure assumes that the property owner is dead and the notice contemplated is merely for the benefit of those interested in his estate, but if the statutes provide for adequate notice to him and for other reasonable safeguards of his interests, and there is compliance with these provisions, the court

In the somewhat analogous situation where two persons who might be heirs to each other have died in a common disaster and it would not be shown which survived, the civil law codes provide for certain presumptions based on age and sex of the parties. Succession of Langles, 105 La. 39, 29 So. 739, 1900. At common law there is no presumption of survival or that both perished at the same time. Carpenter v. Severin, 201 Iowa 969, 204 N.W. 448, 43 A.L.R. 1340, 1925. Most states have now adopted the Uniform Simultaneous Death Act, under which the property of each decedent passes as if he was the survivor. See Wigmore on Evidence, §§ 2532, 2532a, and pocket supplement; note, 1952 Wash.U.L.R. 400; annotation, 20 A.L.R.2d 235; infra § 140, note 25, and § 147, note 40. As to what evidence of survival is necessary to prevent this result, cf. Sauers v. Stolz, 121 Colo. 456, 218 P.2d 741, 1950, with In re Cruson's Estate, 189 Or. 537, 221 P.2d 892, 1951.

24 Bank of Jonesboro v. Wilson, 43 Ga.App. 839, 160 S.E. 653, 1913; Thomas v. People, to Use of Joiner, 107 Ill. 517, 47 Am.Rep. 458, 1883; Jochumsen v. Suffolk Savings Bank, 3 Allen (Mass.) 87, 1861; Beckwith v. Bates, 228 Mich. 400, 200 N.W. 151, 37 A.L.R. 819, 1924, noted, 5 Bost.U.L.R. 166, 9 Minn.L.R. 155 (suit against administrator who had administered the property); Fridley v. Farmers' & Mechanics' Savings Bank, 136 Minn. 333, 162 N.W. 454, L.R.A.1917E 544, 1916. Woerner on Administration § 208. But see Roderigas v. East River Savings Institution, 63 N.Y. 460, 20 Am.Rep. 555, 1875, which is probably overruled—see Matter of Killan's Estate, 172 N.Y. 547, 65 N.E. 561, 63 L.R.A. 95, 1902; Hamilton v. Orange Savings Bank, 99 N.J.Law, 503, 124 A. 62, 1924, noted, 19 Ill.L.R. 275, 34 Yale L.J. 97. As to the liability of the sureties on the bond of a personal representative when it appears that the owner was not dead, see Sligh v. Whitley, 41 Ga.App. 428, 153 S.E. 237, 1930, and National Surety Co. v. Wages, 48 Ga.App. 720, 173 S.E. 451, 1934. Articles on the subject are Redfield, 15 Am.L.Reg.N.S. 212; Redfield, 10 Am.L.R. 887; Hanna, Administration upon Estates of Persons Presumed to be Dead, 62 U. of Pa.L.R. 605; Lees, Property Rights of Persons Who Have Disappeared, 9 Minn.L.R. 89. And see note 26, infra.

25 154 U.S. 34, 14 S.Ct. 1108, 38 L Ed. 896, 1894.

should have power to determine the jurisdictional fact of death as well as that of domicile and this determination should not be subject to collateral attack.[26] However, the courts generally have contented themselves with declaring that the letters are absolutely void if the owner of the estate is not dead.[27] For this reason, they have been rather strict in requiring clear proof of death before granting letters of administration,[28] and have even refused to require the alleged decedent's debtor to pay an administrator when there is substantial doubt as to the fact of death.[29]

*Absentees' Estates*

Many jurisdictions have sought to deal with this problem by passing statutes for the administration of the estates of absentees. They provide for the giving of notice designed to reach the person if he is living, and permit the heirs or distributees to have possession of the estate after the giving of a bond to protect the absentee if he returns, or after the lapse of many years after the disappearance. Some statutes provide safeguards of both sorts. The existing legislation is usually conservative and has been sustained as being in accord with due process.[30] Even where these

[26] See Smith, The Validity of Administration upon the Estate of a Living Person, 14 Am.L.Rev. 337. This article was written prior to the decision in Scott v. McNeal. See also Model Probate Code §§ 69, 80, 81 and comments thereto; American Law of Property § 14.3; Hutton, Death as a Jurisdictional Fact Before the Register of Wills and the Orphans Court in Pennsylvania, 53 Dick.L.R. 108. But cf. cases infra note 27.

[27] See authorities supra note 24. Even if the statute purported to give the probate court authority to determine the death conclusively, it has been held that the due process clause is violated if the alleged deceased is alive. Clapp v. Houg, 12 N.D. 600, 98 N.W. 710, 65 L.R.A. 757, 102 Am.St. Rep. 589, 1904; Lavin v. Emigrant Industrial Sav. Bank, 1 F. 641, 1880. Moreover, even a provision for publication of notice to the alleged deceased does not seem to validate the finding. Carr v. Brown, 20 R.I. 215, 38 A. 9, 38 L.R.A. 294, 78 Am.St.Rep. 855, 1897. But cf. Hamilton v. Orange Savings Bank, supra note 24.

[28] See In re Wyllie's Estate, 134 Misc. 715, 236 N.Y.S. 370, 1929; In re Katz' Estate, 135 Misc. 861, 239 N.Y. S. 722, 1930. Cf. cases cited supra note 23; In re Nelson's Estate, 37 Wash.2d 397, 224 P.2d 347, 1951, noted, 27 Wash.L.R. 163.

[29] In re Goldstein's Estate, 299 N.Y. 43, 95 N.E.2d 425, 1949; cf. Payne v. Home Sav. Bank, supra note 23.

[30] Nelson v. Blinn, 197 Mass. 279, 83 N.E. 889, 15 L.R.A.,N.S., 651, 125 Am.St.Rep. 364, 14 Ann.Cas. 349, 1908; Cunnius v. Reading School District, 198 U.S. 458, 25 S.Ct. 721, 49 L. Ed. 1125, 3 Ann.Cas. 1121, 1905; Blinn v. Nelson, 222 U.S. 1, 32 S.Ct. 1, 56 L.Ed. 65, Ann.Cas.1913B 555, 1911; Chamberlain v. Anderson, 195 Iowa 855, 190 N.W. 501, 26 A.L.R. 957, 1922. See American Law of Property § 14.4; note, 43 Harv.L.R. 485, and articles cited supra note 24.

statutes exist, an estate may be administered under the regular procedure for estates of deceased persons and supplying the showing of death by circumstantial proof or the presumption of death after seven years absence,[31] although it is safer to proceed under the absentees' statutes.[32] However, the latter involve long delay or the giving of a bond which will continue in operation more or less indefinitely. It would be far better to permit a conclusive adjudication of death in the grant of administration under reasonable safeguards for the rights of the owner if he returns.[33]

### *Testacy or Intestacy*

The grant of ordinary letters of administration requires a determination of intestacy.[34] However, if a will is later discovered, it may be probated.[35] The letters of administration which have been issued in such cases are not void but merely voidable, and persons dealing with the administrator will be protected.[36] However, if general letters of administration are granted after a will is probated,[37] or while a contest is pending,[38] they have been declared to be void.

### *Time Limitations*

In some states, statutes provide that letters of administration should not be granted until a certain period after the decedent's death has expired.[39] Such legislation may either have the purpose of permitting a will to be offered for probate if one exists, or

31 Bornemann v. Ofsthun, supra note 23; Philpott v. Vesta Coal Co., 21 F.Supp. 37, D.C.Pa.1937, (production of body unnecessary); note, 1 Ohio St.L.J. 126. Cf. In re Nelson's Estate, supra note 28.

32 See in re Goldstein's Estate, supra note 29.

33 See Model Probate Code, § 81; American Law of Property §§ 14.3, 14.4.

34 In re Wedemeyer's Estate, 253 App.Div. 766, 300 N.Y.S. 1201, 1938; see also Estate of Danford, 196 Cal. 339, 238 P. 76, 1925; Hite's Adm'r v. Gibson, 251 Ky. 651, 65 S.W.2d 731, 1934.

35 See supra § 97.

36 Martin v. Dix, 134 Ga. 481, 68 S.E. 80, 1910; Schluter v. Bowery Sav. Bank, 117 N.Y. 125, 22 N.E. 572, 5 L.R.A. 541, 15 Am.St.Rep. 494, 1889.

37 Landers v. Stone, 45 Ind. 404, 1873; Ryno's Ex'r v. Ryno's Adm'r, 27 N.J.Eq. 522, 1875.

38 In re Edwards' Estate, 154 Cal. 91, 97 P. 23, 1908; In re Whitehouse's Estate, 223 Iowa 91, 272 N.W. 110, 1937; cf. In re Billet's Estate, 187 App.Div. 309, 175 N.Y.S. 482, 1919 (where will had been filed but was conceded to be invalid).

39 Ellwanger v. Ellwanger's Adm'r, 278 Ky. 584, 129 S.W.2d 127, 1939; see Dorsey v. Dorsey, 140 Md. 167, 116 A. 915, 1922.

allowing those primarily entitled to letters to demand them. A premature granting of letters is voidable rather than void.[40]

Many jurisdictions have statutes providing that letters of administration should not be granted after a certain length of time subsequent to the decedent's death.[41] Even in absence of such statutes, courts have sometimes denied application after an unreasonable lapse of time.[42] An appointment after the designated period should not be void so as to subject it to collateral attack.[43] If any one has initiated proceedings within the statutory time, he will not be permitted to dismiss them after that time to the prejudice of creditors.[44] Time limitations do not apply to the appointment of an administrator de bonis non.[45]

## APPOINTMENT OF EXECUTORS

**108. The testator's nomination of an executor can be either in express terms or by words showing a clear intention to do so. Court appointment is necessary but the selection of the testator is followed unless the person named is legally disqualified.**

### *Designation of Testator*

The testamentary power includes not only the selection of beneficiaries but also the designation of the executor. In order to nominate an executor it is not necessary that the testator should use the particular term executor. It is enough to name one "according to the tenor" if he is described as "administrator,"[1] or

40 Ellwanger v. Ellwanger's Adm'r, supra note 39; In re MacMullen's Estate, 117 Or. 505, 243 P. 89, 1926.

41 See infra notes 42–46. Cf. Ohio Gen.Code, § 10509–13.

42 Brewer v. Wilson, 185 Ark. 94, 46 S.W.2d 3, 1932 (eighteen years); In re Moore's Estate, 161 Kan. 603, 170 P.2d 838, 1946 (45 years); In re Foureman's Estate, 76 Ohio App. 74, 61 N.E.2d 730, 1945 (nineteen years—pending litigation over title in another court); State ex rel. Speckart v. Thurston County Superior Court, 48 Wash. 141, 92 P. 942, 1907 (thirteen years). But see Gorham v. Montfort, 137 Ga. 134, 72 S.E. 893, 1911 (twenty years); In re Wright's Estate, 170 Kan. 400, 227 P.2d 131, 1951 (petition by heirs, though creditor's rights barred by statute).

43 Nelson v. Bridge, 98 Tex. 523, 86 S.W. 7, 1905. And see Andrew v. Dunn, 202 Iowa 364, 210 N.W. 425, 1926. But see Rice v. Henly, 90 Tenn. 69, 15 S.W. 748, 1891.

44 In re Glover's Estate, 104 Neb. 151, 175 N.W. 1017, 1920.

45 Crossan v. McCrary, 37 Iowa 684, 1873.

1 Sauer v. Taylor's Ex'r, 184 Ky. 609, 212 S.W. 583, 1919.

as "trustee," [2] or the duties of the office are set forth in such way as to indicate that this was desired.[3] Whatever language indicates the person mentioned was intended by the testator to administer the estate is sufficient designation of the executor.

The designation, however, must be certain. The appointment of "one of my sisters" is on its face ambiguous and hence insufficient.[4] However, a will appointing the priest of testator's church is sufficient and will be interpreted as meaning the incumbent at the time of testator's death.[5] An appointment may be conditional,[6] and the testator may provide for successive,[7] as well as joint,[8] executors. Testator may also authorize and require his executors to appoint others to serve with them,[9] or may give the right of selection to some third person.[10]

A lawyer drafting a will should not insert a provision that he is to act as attorney for the estate. Quite aside from ethical considerations, there is no such office as attorney for the estate, although the term is sometimes used to indicate the attorney for the executor. Since the executor is charged with duties to creditors and others as well as to the beneficiaries and is responsible for his attorney's acts he must be free to select his own counsel and any attempted testamentary selection is not binding on him in most states.[11]

2 In re Johnson's Will, 233 N.C. 570, 65 S.E.2d 12, 1951; In re Kirby, [1902] P. 188.

3 In re Ringot's Estate, 124 Cal. 45, 56 P. 781, 1899 (statute); Equitable Trust Co. v. Coughlin, 148 Ky. 789, 147 S.W. 739, 1912. Cf. In re Leonard's Will, 218 N.C. 738, 12 S.E.2d 222, 1941.

4 In re Blackwell, 2 P.D. 72, 1877 (though only one sister survived the testator, when three were living at time of the will).

5 Lefort's Succession, 139 La. 51, 71 So. 215, Ann.Cas.1917E 769, 1916.

6 Butler University v. Danner, 114 Ind.App. 236, 51 N.E.2d 487, 1943.

7 Kinney v. Kepplinger, 172 Ill. 449, 50 N.E. 131, 1898; Cole v. Watertown, 119 Wis. 133, 96 N.W. 538, 1903. And see State ex rel. Lauridsen v. Superior Court for King County, 179 Wash. 198, 37 P.2d 209, 95 A.L.R. 819, 1934, noted, 19 Minn.L.R. 709.

8 See supra § 105.

9 Hutton v. Hutton, 41 N.J.Eq. 267, 3 A. 882, 1886.

10 Brown v. Just, 118 Mich. 678, 77 N.W. 263, 1898 (left to judge of probate); Hartnett v. Wandell, 60 N.Y. 346, 19 Am.Rep. 194, 1875; In re Effertz' Estate, 123 Mont. 45, 207 P.2d 1151, 11 A.L.R.2d 1278, 1949. See notes, 28 Chi-Kent L.R. 142, 30 Iowa L.R. 302.

11 Carton v. Borden, 8 N.J. 352, 85 A.2d 257, 1952; Matter of Caldwell, 188 N.Y. 115, 80 N.E. 663, 1907; In re Lachmund's Estate, 179 Or. 420, 170 P.2d 748, 166 A.L.R. 479, 1946; notes, 28 Can.B.R. 588, 31 Marq.L.R. 231, 123 N.Y.L.J. 284, 304, 2 Oh.St.L.J. 77, 10 U. of Cin.L.R. 184. But see Suc-

### *Source of Executor's Authority*

At common law it was said that the executor derives his office solely from the will and not from the probate which is only evidence of his right.[12] This is surely not the rule in the many jurisdictions where the executor can be required by the court to give bond. Even in the jurisdictions where no bond is required, the executor gets his authority from his official letters rather than from the will. The common-law doctrine is obsolete in most, if not all, states of this country.[13]

### *Disqualifications to Act*

The courts declare that they are not concerned with the wisdom of the testator's choice and that it to be their duty to appoint the person nominated by the testator if he is not disqualified.[14] Only a few states give the court discretion to disregard the testator's selection. Old age, bodily infirmities,[15] immorality,[16] poverty or lack of business experience,[17] inability to speak English,[18] or an interest adverse to the estate,[19] will not disqualify the testator's

cession of Martin, 56 So.2d 176, La. App.1952; In re Ogg's Estate, 262 Wis. 181, 54 N.W.2d 175, 1952.

12 Middleton's Case, 5 Co. 28b, 77 Eng.Rep. 93, 1603.

13 See In re Van Vleck's Estate, 123 Iowa 89, 98 N.W. 557, 1904; In re Miller's Estate, 216 Pa. 247, 65 A. 681, 1907. But cf. Hutchins v. Hutchins, 48 App.D.C. 286, 1919; Cavanaugh v. Dore, 358 Pa. 183, 56 A.2d 92, 1948, noted, 46 Mich.L.R. 1118.

14 In re Lawrence's Estate, 53 Ariz. 1, 85 P.2d 45, 1939; Smith's Appeal, 61 Conn. 420, 24 A. 273, 16 L.R.A. 538, 1892; In re Grattan's Estate, 155 Kan. 839, 130 P.2d 580, 1942; In re Leland's Will, 219 N.Y. 387, 114 N.E. 854, 1916, noted, 65 U. of Pa.L.R. 808; Trustees of House of the Angel Guardian, Boston v. Donovan, 71 R.I. 407, 46 A.2d 717, 1946, noted, 33 Va. L.R. 98; State ex rel. Lauridsen v. Superior Court for King County, supra note 7; Saxe v. Saxe, 119 Wis. 557, 97 N.W. 187, 1903. Cf. In re Schneider's Estate, 224 Iowa 598, 277 N.W. 567, 1938; In re Barck's Estate, 215 Minn. 625, 11 N.W.2d 149, 1943. See annotation, 95 A.L.R. 828. For an argument that the court should be given discretion to deny appointment to one although not disqualified on some statutory ground, see Horner, Proposed Revision of Administration, Conservator, and Guardian and Ward Acts, 2 Ill.L.Bull. 110, 111; Model Probate Code § 96 and comment thereto.

15 In re Leland's Will, supra note 14.

16 Clark v. Patterson, 214 Ill. 533, 73 N.E. 806, 105 Am.St.Rep. 127, 1905; Saxe v. Saxe, supra note 14. See note, 61 Cent.L.Jo. 106.

17 Smith's Appeal, supra note 14.

18 Li Po Tai's Estate, 108 Cal. 484, 41 P. 486, 1895.

19 In re Dolenty's Estate, 53 Mont. 33, 161 P. 524, 1916 (though possibly ground for later removal); In re Svacina's Estate, 239 Wis. 436, 1 N.W. 2d 780, 1942. Cf. Cogswell v. Hall, 183 Mass. 575, 67 N.E. 638, 1903; In re Barck's Estate, supra note 14.

choice. The court will be less apt to deny appointment to a person nominated as executor than it will to a person who has the preferred right to act as administrator.[20] But a court refused to appoint one executor of a large estate where both mind and body were impaired, though he was neither an imbecile nor a lunatic.[21] Of course persons falling in the latter classes will be refused letters.[22]

Nonresidence is not usually a disqualification.[23] However, some statutes disqualify nonresidents,[24] though even in these jurisdictions the person may qualify by becoming a resident after testator's death.[25] A corporation may act as executor in most states,[26] though often a foreign corporation cannot,[27] nor may one not authorized by its charter to act as a personal representative.[28]

20 See infra § 110; also supra note 14.

21 In re Leland's Will, supra note 14.

22 Kidd v. Bates, 120 Ala. 79, 23 So. 735, 41 L.R.A. 154, 74 Am.St.Rep. 17, 1898.

23 Brown's Estate, 80 Cal. 381, 22 P. 233, 1889; In re Connor's Estate, 16 Mont. 465, 41 P. 271, 1895; Stevens v. Cameron, 100 Tex. 515, 101 S.W. 791, 1907.

24 Nunn v. Hamilton, 233 Ky. 663, 26 S.W.2d 526, 1930; Re Cardoner's Estate, 27 N.M. 337, 201 P. 1051, 18 A.L.R. 575, 1921. Cf. Breen v. Kehoe, 142 Mich. 58, 105 N.W. 28, 1 L.R.A.,N.S., 349, 113 Am.St.Rep. 558, 1905; In Barck's Estate, supra note 14.

25 Nunn v. Hamilton and Re Cardoner's Estate, both supra note 24.

26 Equitable Trust Co. v. Plume, 92 Conn. 649, 103 A. 940, 1918; Minnesota Loan & Trust Co. v. Beebe, 40 Minn. 7, 41 N.W. 232, 2 L.R.A. 418, 1889; In re Rath's Estate, 107 Misc. 598, 176 N.Y.S. 887, 1919; In re McManus' Estate, 212 Pa. 267, 61 A. 892, 1905. See notes, 23 Ill.L.R. 614, 699, 49 Bankers L.J. 463.

27 Farmers' Loan & Trust Co. v. Smith, 74 Conn. 625, 51 A. 609, 1902; Matter of Avery's Will, 45 Misc. 529, 92 N.Y.S. 974, 1904. But see In re Lawrence's Estate, supra note 14. See annotation, 65 A.L.R. 1237. Cf. Re Wellings' Estate, 192 Cal. 506, 221 P. 628, 1923 (testamentary trustee).

28 German-American Bank of Baltimore v. Kopp, 132 Md. 422, 103 A. 1009, 1918.

## RIGHT TO ADMINISTER

**109. Under modern statutes the spouse usually has a preferred right to administer, then the next of kin, creditors and the public administrator in that order. However, there are often qualifications to the general rule, including a discretionary power to prefer one of several in the same class or even one over another of a prior class, and the right of the preferred person to nominate another to serve in his stead. In addition, superiority of interest in the estate sometimes overrides the general order of preference. This is usually true with regard to an appointment of an administrator with the will annexed, though some states follow the general statutory order even in this case.**

### *History*

By statute in 1357,[1] Parliament took the administration of intestate property out of the hands of the ordinary and gave it to "the next and most lawful friends of the dead person," appointed by the ordinary. In 1529,[2] the right to administer was given to the widow, or next of kin, or both, in the ordinary's discretion. Both by the legislation of 1357,[3] and by virtue of common-law principles,[4] the surviving husband had the right to administer his wife's property and this was confirmed by Parliament in 1677.[5]

### *Statutes—In General*

In America there are statutes in every jurisdiction announcing the rules under which the person who shall be granted letters of administration are to be determined and usually fixing a more or less definite order of persons to be given preference. While there are many local peculiarities and exceptions and often the court is given more or less discretion, the most usual order is: (1) surviving spouse; (2) next of kin; (3) creditors; (4) public administrator.

Some statutes place more or less emphasis on the interest of the applicant in the estate. Under these there may be departure

1 31 Edw. III, c. 11.

2 21 Hen. VIII, c. 5, §§ 3, 4.

3 Elliot v. Collier, 1 Wils.K.B. 168, 95 Eng.Rep. 554, 1747.

4 Watt v. Watt, 3 Ves.Jr. 244, 30 Eng.Rep. 992, 1796. Except for her separately settled property or that not reduced to the husband's possession, there was no occasion for administration of the wife's property, since her personalty became his on marriage. See supra § 7, note 3.

5 29 Car. II, c. 3, § 25.

from the normal order in case the spouse or other heirs have released or assigned their interest,[6] or where the appointment is of an administrator with the will annexed.[7] So far as the court is able to do so without violation of statute it grants administration to the person who will have the greatest interest in the final distribution of the property,[8] although in some cases positive statutory provisions require the appointment of one who has little or no interest as distributee of the estate.[9]

*Surviving Spouse*

The early English preference for the spouse is still justified today, not only on the basis of interest in the estate but also because commonly he or she aided in accumulating it and has the best knowledge about the property. Nevertheless some statutes permit the court in its discretion to appoint the children or next of kin.[10] Furthermore, the statutes sometimes deny letters to a spouse who has abandoned the decedent,[11] or to one who has released his interest in the estate.[12]

*Next of Kin*

When there is no spouse, the statutes usually provide for administration by the other relatives. If, as is sometimes the case, the law simply says "next of kin" this means one entitled to distribution under the intestate laws.[13] If he is ineligible, or if he renounces the right to administer, the cases are conflicting as to the right of the next closest relative who takes no share of the

6 In re Berner, 217 Mich. 612, 187 N.W. 377, 1922; In re Bartz' Estate, 207 Wis. 639, 242 N.W. 171, 1932, noted, 31 Mich.L.R. 577; Gooch v. Suhor, 121 Va. 35, 92 S.E. 843, 1917. See annotation, 114 A.L.R. 275.

7 See infra note 45 et seq.

8 State ex rel. Cowley v. Superior Court, 158 Wash. 546, 291 P. 481, 70 A.L.R. 1460, 1930.

9 Orear v. Crum, 135 Ill. 294, 25 N. E. 1097, 1890.

10 See Mullins v. Mullins, 307 Ky. 748, 212 S.W.2d 272, 1948.

11 In re Banaszak's Estate, 164 Misc. 829, 1 N.Y.S.2d 15, 1938.

12 See supra notes 6, 9.

13 Cooper v. Cooper, 43 Ind.App. 620, 88 N.E. 341, 1909; In re Wright's Estate, 210 Iowa 25, 230 N.W. 552, 1930; Gillespie v. Isbell, 51 S.W.2d 746, Tex.Civ.App.1932. And see Succession of McGee, 151 La. 225, 91 So. 716, 1922 (recognized illegitimate child); Redmond v. Wardrep, 149 Tenn. 35, 257 S.W. 394, 1932 (adopted child); In re Neukirchen's Estate, 186 N.Y.S. 240, 1921 (stepson entitled when he gets estate in default of all other relatives). A brother of the decedent has been preferred to the children of a deceased brother, though the latter share in the decedent's estate. Mobley v. Mobley, 149 Md. 401, 131 A. 770, 1926; Dawson v. Shave, 162 Ga. 126, 132 S.E. 912, 1926; but see In re Field's Estate, infra note 22.

estate.[14] Under statutes specifying the precise order of preference among relatives, it seems that the one highest on the list and willing to administer is entitled to letters even if he takes none of the property by intestate succession.[15]

*Several Applicants of Same Class*

If there are several persons in the preferred class of next of kin the court usually has discretion as to who should be appointed. While the court may appoint joint representatives, a sole administration is preferred.[16] Males are sometimes preferred to females,[17] the elder to the younger,[18] unmarried to married females,[19] residents to nonresidents,[20] and those who have no conflicting interests to those who have.[21] None of these matters is conclusive,[22] and it can be readily seen how the various considerations may conflict. Courts have broad discretion in such cases and unless this is clearly abused or some statutory preference is disregarded, the trial judge's appointment will not be disturbed on appeal.[23] Under some statutes the court may pass over the next of kin entirely if there is a dispute between them.[24]

*Guardian of Next of Kin*

It has been asserted that at common law the guardian of one, who but for his minority or other incapacity would be entitled

14 That he is entitled: Sanders v. Buenger, 311 Ill. 572, 143 N.E. 431, 1924; Murphy v. Karnes, 88 W.Va. 242, 106 S.E. 655, 1921. Contra: In re Weaver's Estate, 140 Iowa 615, 119 N.W. 69, 22 L.R.A.,N.S., 1161, 17 Ann. Cas. 947, 1909; Colbert v. Thornley, 71 A. 65, R.I.1914; State ex rel. Cowley v. Superior Court, 158 Wash. 546, 291 P. 481, 70 A.L.R. 1461, 1930.

15 See Sanders v. Buenger, supra note 14.

16 See supra § 105. Cf. Swart's Estate, 189 Pa. 71, 41 A. 1000, 1899.

17 Re Hill's Estate, 55 N.J.Eq. 764, 37 A. 952, 1897. But this must give way to the majority in interest rule. Iredale v. Ford, 1 Sw. & Tr. 305, 164 Eng.Rep. 740, 1859.

18 Levan's Appeal, 112 Pa. 294, 3 A. 804, 1886.

19 In re Curser, 89 N.Y. 401, 1882; Johnson v. Johnson, 15 R.I. 109, 23 A. 106, 1885.

20 O'Brien's Estate, 63 Iowa 622, 19 N.W. 797, 1884; Radford v. Radford, 5 Dana (Ky.) 156, 157, 1837.

21 Justice v. Wilkins, 251 Ill. 13, 95 N.E. 1025, 1911.

22 See Re Selling's Estate, 17 St.R. 833, 2 N.Y.S. 634, 1888 (sister preferred to brother with bad character); In re Field's Estate, 65 N.E.2d 70, Ohio App.1944 (resident grandson preferred to son in another county).

23 In re McMurray's Estate, 256 Pa. 233, 100 A. 798, 1 A.L.R. 1242, 1917; Langfelder v. Langfelder, 189 Md. 88, 54 A.2d 312, 1947.

24 In re Thomas' Estate, 167 Wash. 127, 8 P.2d 963, 80 A.L.R. 819, 1932.

to administration, should be granted letters.[25] This rule is frequently enacted by statute,[26] although some courts hold that silence on the subject in the statutory order of preference abolishes the guardian's right.[27]

*Right to Nominate Others*

In part by statute and in part by judicial decision, one entitled to administration is often given the right to nominate some other person in his stead.[28] Even where no such right is recognized, the court will often appoint the person so suggested, if no rule prevents.[29] Some jurisdictions allow the surviving spouse to nominate, but deny the right to others.[30] Some statutes require that the person who nominates another must be a resident of the state in order that his suggestion be binding.[31] Of course one who is insane may not nominate a person to serve in his stead,[32] nor may the representative who is removed from his office choose his successor, though he originally had the right to name another to act.[33]

25 Kinnick v. Coy, 40 Ind.App. 139, 81 N.E. 107, 1907; see In re Taylor's Estate, 61 Nev. 68, 114 P.2d 1086, 135 A.L.R. 580, 1941.

26 In re Turner's Estate, 143 Cal. 438, 77 P. 144, 1904; Anderson's Committee v. Anderson's Adm'r, 161 Ky. 18, 170 S.W. 213, L.R.A.1915C 581, 1914; In re Copperfield's Estate, 158 Okl. 40, 12 P.2d 490, 1932; Ex parte Frieson, 96 S.C. 34, 79 S.E. 791, 1913. As to the guardian's right when there are competent heirs in the same class, cf. In re Turner's Estate, supra, with Cottle v. Vanderheyden, 56 Barb.(N.Y.) 622, 1870.

27 McDonald v. O'Dea, 256 Mass. 177, 152 N.E. 341, 1926; In re Taylor's Estate, supra note 25; In re Golembiewski's Estate, 146 Ohio St. 551, 67 N.E.2d 328, 1903.

28 In re Rugh's Estate, 211 Iowa 722, 234 N.W. 278, 1931; In re Cameron's Estate, 86 Mont. 455, 284 P. 143, 1930; Thomas v. James, 69 Okl. 285, 171 P. 855, 1918; In re Martin's Estates, 109 Utah 131, 166 P.2d 197, 1946; Taylor v. Virginia-Pocahontas Coal Co., 78 W.Va. 455, 88 S.E. 1070, 1916. Cf. In re Gerard's Estate, 50 Ariz. 458, 72 P.2d 952, 113 A.L.R. 776, 1937; In re Rohkramer's Estate, 113 Mont. 545, 131 P.2d 967, 1942. As to appointment of an heir supported by the majority in interest, see Bell v. Bryan, 84 Ga.App. 104, 65 S.E.2d 628, 1951 (statute); Fortin v. Tanguay, 75 R.I. 102, 64 A.2d 188, 1949.

29 In re Waverley Trust Co., 268 Mass. 181, 167 N.E. 274, 1929; In re Alpaugh's Estate, 83 N.J.Eq. 616, 91 A. 588, 1914.

30 In re Utters' Estate, 112 Wash. 197, 191 P. 836, 1920. Cf. Commerce Union Bank v. Fox, 28 Tenn.App. 587, 192 S.W.2d 233, 1945.

31 In re Wise's Estate, 175 Cal. 196, 165 P. 531, 1917. But see In re Welscher's Estate, 77 Mont. 164, 250 P. 447, 1926.

32 O'Neill v. Read, 179 Iowa 1208, 162 N.W. 775, 1917.

33 In re Dolenty's Estate, 53 Mont. 33, 161 P. 524, 1916.

*Creditors*

Ordinarily if there is a spouse or kindred willing to serve, others have no right to appointment.[34] When there is no surviving spouse or next of kin, or these persons do not apply for administration, the statutes often declare that letters may be granted to a creditor of the deceased.[35] Indeed, it is sometimes intimated that in case of an insolvent estate creditors should be preferred to all others, since they are the only ones who are interested in the estate.[36] A claim against a distributee does not make one a creditor for this purpose.[37] If several claimants apply, some jurisdictions give preference to the largest creditor,[38] and others to the one first applying.[39]

*Public Administrators and Strangers*

In some jurisdictions the public administrator is preferred to creditors[40] and he is generally preferred to strangers.[41] When there is no office of public administrator, the court will not permit an estate to go unadministered for want of an interested representative and is authorized to grant letters to a proper person, who may be a total stranger to the estate.[42] As has already been seen a stranger is often permitted to serve upon the nomination

34 Loeb v. Callaway, 250 Ala. 524, 35 So.2d 198, 1948; State ex rel. Couch v. Kelso, 217 S.W.2d 596, Mo. App.1949; In re Wilcox's Estate, 122 Mont. 290, 201 P.2d 989, 1949; see annotation, 119 A.L.R. 143.

35 Lineback v. Howerton, 181 Ark. 433, 26 S.W.2d 74, 1930; In re Webb's Estate, 90 Colo. 470, 10 P.2d 947, 1932; Carson v. Blair, 32 Ga.App. 728, 124 S.E. 808, 1924; Bianco v. Piscopo, 263 Mass. 549, 161 N.E. 605, 1928; Lang v. Wilmer, 131 Md. 215, 101 A. 706, 2 A.L.R. 1698, 1917; In re Fellin's Estate, 108 Wash. 626, 185 P. 604, 1919.

36 In re Farrands, 1 P.D. 439, 1876. But see In re Dolenty's Estate, 53 Mont. 33, 161 P. 524, 1916; Loeb v. Callaway, supra note 34.

37 Murphy v. Freeman, 220 Ala. 634, 127 So. 199, 70 A.L.R. 381, 1930; Osmundson v. Leach, 139 Ill.App. 456, 1908. But see W. B. Smith & Co. v. Lowe, 16 La.App. 425, 134 So. 707, 1931.

As to whether the undertaker or the one paying his bill may apply, cf. Barton v. Tabler, 183 Md. 227, 37 A.2d 266, 1944, with Hildebrand v. Kinney, 172 Ind. 447, 87 N.E. 832, 19 Ann. Cas. 788, 1909.

38 Lang v. Wilmer, supra note 35; In re Sullivan's Estate, 25 Wash. 430, 65 P. 793, 1901.

39 In re Hawley's Estate, 37 Misc. 667, 76 N.Y.S. 461, 1902.

40 In re Morel's Estate, 103 Misc. 555, 171 N.Y.S. 759, 1918; see In re Ruane's Estate, 122 Mont. 387, 204 P. 2d 1037, 1949.

41 In re Moran's Estate, 176 Cal. 216, 168 P. 18, 1917; Matter of Printup's Estate, 121 App.Div. 322, 106 N.Y.S. 74, 1907.

42 In re Pollard's Estate, 105 Neb. 432, 181 N.W. 133, 1920; Matter of Paola, 36 Misc. 514, 73 N.Y.S. 1062, 1901.

of some interested person.[43] By treaty provisions, an alien's property may be administered by his foreign consul in certain cases.[44]

*Legatees*

When necessary to appoint an administrator with the will annexed, the common-law rule was that the letters should be granted to the residuary legatee or one of this class, or at least to one of the principal legatees.[45] These are the logical persons since they have the beneficial interest, residuary legatees being entitled to first preference because they have most to gain by an efficient administration of the estate.[46] Some statutes expressly adopt this rule.[47] Even if the only statutory provision is one preferring spouse and next of kin for letters of administration generally, the courts have often applied the foregoing principle in case of letters with the will annexed.[48] However, in some jurisdictions, it is held that the general statutory order must govern all cases, and hence the spouse or next of kin is entitled to letters regardless of who are the residuary or principal legatees.[49]

Under some statutes the personal representative of a deceased principal legatee is entitled to letters with the will annexed.[50] At common law the executor of an executor was always entitled to administer the estate of the first testator.[51] This right has now been abolished generally [52] and never extended to the administrator of an executor, nor to any representative of an administrator.[53]

43 Larson v. Union Pac. R. Co., 70 Neb. 261, 97 N.W. 313, 1903. See supra note 17 et seq.

44 Matter of D'Adamo's Estate, 212 N.Y. 214, 106 N.E. 81, L.R.A.1915D 373, 1914; cf. Lely v. Kalinoglu, 64 App.D.C. 213, 76 F.2d 983, 100 A.L.R. 1523, 1935; see Coudert, Rights of Consular Officers to Letters of Administration Under Treaties with Foreign Nations, 13 Col.L.R. 181.

45 Thomas v. Butler, 1 Vent. 217, 86 Eng.Rep. 146, 1672.

46 See Matter of Lasak's Estate, 55 Hun. 610, 8 N.Y.S. 740, 1890.

47 In re Bourquin's Estate, 84 Colo. 275, 269 P. 903, 1928 (nominee); Matter of Goggin's Estate, 43 Misc. 233, 88 N.Y.S. 557, 1904; In re Padelford's Estate, 189 Pa. 634, 42 A. 287, 1899. See annotation, 164 A.L.R. 844.

48 Kirkpatrick's Estate, 22 N.J.Eq. 463, 1871; In re Smith's Estate, 125 Okl. 104, 256 P. 725, 1927.

49 Long v. Christopher, 194 Minn. 238, 260 N.W. 314, 1935; see Phillips v. Clark, 176 Md. 578, 6 A.2d 220, 1939.

50 N.Y.Surr.Ct.Act § 133; In re Kessler's Estate, 213 Iowa 633, 239 N.W. 555, 1931.

51 2 Bl.Com. 506.

52 Petition of Davis, 237 Mass. 47, 129 N.E. 366, 1921, Woerner on Administration § 350.

53 2 Bl.Com. 506.

## DISQUALIFICATIONS FOR OFFICE OF ADMINISTRATOR

**110. One is ineligible to act as administrator by reason of being an infant, an insane person, or one clearly shown to lack ordinary integrity, and in many jurisdictions a nonresident. Modern statutes permit a corporation or a married woman to act. Illiteracy, lack of business experience, immorality, and adverse interest are not absolute disqualifications, although to the extent that the court has discretion in making the appointment these factors are ground for passing over a person otherwise entitled.**

Anyone disqualified to serve as executor [1] would likewise be disqualified for appointment as administrator. Under some statutes the grounds of disqualification are the same in both cases,[2] but many states impose added conditions in the case of administrators.[3]

### *Infants and Married Women*

A minor is not qualified to act as an administrator.[4] By the better view, however, the letters granted to an infant are not void; [5] and upon reaching majority before revocation he may continue under the original appointment.[6] Under modern statutes, a married woman is generally permitted to serve as if sole.[7]

### *Aliens and Nonresidents*

An alien was not disqualified at common law from acting as personal representative,[8] and this is the law in some of our states.[9] Statutes in other jurisdictions forbid persons who are not citizens of the United States from acting as administrator.[10]

1 See supra § 108.

2 N.Y.Surr.Ct.Act § 94.

3 See Ala.Code, 1940 §§ 61–69, 61–140 (residence); generally on disqualifications of personal representatives see note 26 Wash.U.L.Q. 106, 257.

4 Giglio v. Woollard, 126 Miss. 6, 88 So. 401, 14 A.L.R. 616, 1921; In re Winkhous, 157 Misc. 560, 284 N.Y.S. 52, 1936. See supra § 104.

5 Davis v. Miller, 106 Ala. 154, 17 So. 323, 1895; Giglio v. Woollard, supra note 4. But see Knox v. Nobel, 77 Hun 230, 28 N.Y.S. 355, 1894.

6 Davis v. Miller, supra note 5.

7 In re Dow's Estate, 132 Cal. 309, 64 P. 402, 1901; cf. Matter of Curser, 89 N.Y. 401, 1882; Allen v. Linger, 78 W.Va. 277, 88 S.E. 837, 1916.

8 Ex parte Barker, 2 Leigh (Va.) 719, 1830.

9 In re Rugh's Estate, 211 Iowa 722, 234 N.W. 278, 1931.

10 Livermore v. Ayres, 86 Kan. 50, 119 P. 549, 1911. In New York a resident alien is competent, but a nonresident alien is not. In re Kassam's Estate, 141 Misc. 366, 252 N.Y.S. 706, 1931.

Indeed, statutes in many states provide that a nonresident of the state,[11] or even of the county,[12] may not act as administrator. In some of these, a nonresident otherwise entitled to administer may nominate some resident person to act in his stead,[13] while in others he has no such privilege and the right to letters passes to the person next entitled under the statute.[14] However, residence is not required for any particular time,[15] and if bona fide it may be established after the decedent's death.[16] In absence of statutory provision on the subject, nonresidence is no disqualification for the office.[17]

*Mental and Moral Qualifications*

Insanity of course is a disqualification,[18] as is lack of ordinary intelligence.[19] Illiteracy by itself is no disqualification,[20] nor is lack of business experience.[21] Old age does not preclude one from obtaining letters,[22] and the same is true of physical disabilities.[23] Habitual drunkenness has been held to amount to disqualification,[24] though occasional intoxication does not.[25] Lack

11 Starlin v. Love, 237 Ala. 38, 185 So. 380, 1939; In re Barnes' Estate, 187 Cal. 566, 203 P. 100, 1921; Fishel v. Dixson, 212 Ky. 2, 278 S.W. 545, 1926.

12 Balfour v. Collins, 119 Tex. 122, 25 S.W.2d 804, 1930.

13 In re Welscher's Estate, 77 Mont. 164, 250 P. 447, 1926.

14 In re Davies' Estate, 201 Ill.App. 165, 1916.

15 Stevens v. Larwill, 110 Mo.App. 140, 84 S.W. 113, 1904.

16 In re Nix's Estate, 66 Mont. 559, 213 P. 1089, 1926.

17 Brown v. Brown, 204 Ala. 157, 85 So. 439, 1920; Faughnan v. Bashlor, 163 Ga. 525, 136 S.E. 545, 1927; Finnerty v. Shade, 210 Iowa 1338, 228 N.W. 886, 1930; Stubbs v. Ratliff, 202 S.C. 67, 24 S.E.2d 127, 1943.

18 O'Neill v. Read, 179 Iowa 1208, 162 N.W. 775, 1917; Mobley v. Mobley, 149 Md. 401, 131 A. 770, 1926.

19 Estate of Johnson, 182 Cal. 642, 189 P. 280, 1926. Cf. Matter of Ireland's Estate, 47 Misc. 545, 95 N.Y.S. 1079, 1905 (mere weakness of mind does not disqualify).

20 Bell v. Fulgham, 202 Ala. 217, 80 So. 39, 1918; Li Po Tai's Estate, 108 Cal. 484, 41 P. 486, 1895; Bowersox's Appeal, 100 Pa. 434, 45 Am.Rep. 387, 1882. Cf. In re Saville, 156 N.C. 172, 72 S.E. 220, 1911.

21 Griffin v. Irwin, 246 Ala. 631, 21 So.2d 668, 158 A.L.R. 288, 1945; Maddox v. Maddox, 27 Ga.App. 369, 108 S.E. 304, 1921; In re Rinio's Estate, 96 Mont. 344, 30 P.2d 803, 1934.

22 In re Wright's Estate, 177 Cal. 274, 170 P. 610, 1918 (ninety-two years).

23 Mobley v. Mobley, supra note 18 (paralysis); Griffin v. Irwin, supra note 21.

24 Nichols v. Smith, 186 Ala. 587, 65 So. 30, 1914.

25 Root v. Davis, 10 Mont. 228, 25 P. 105, 1890; Matter of Reichert's Estate, 34 Misc. 288, 69 N.Y.S. 644, 1901.

of chastity is not a bar to the appointment,[26] nor is conviction for illegal sale of liquor,[27] or of an unstated crime.[28] As a whole it may be said that one may be disqualified upon mental or moral grounds, but that the law does not demand a high standard in either respect.

In most states trust companies may now act as administrators either by virtue of express statutory declarations to this effect or of legislative authority to organize a corporation for this purpose.[29] Most statutes forbid a foreign corporation to act as administrator,[30] though there are exceptions to this rule.[31]

*Adverse Interest*

The fact that the applicant's interest is in some respects adverse to the estate is not per se a disqualification. In the case of one who is in the position of a creditor, this is clear, for the statutes generally give him the right to letters in the absence of application by relatives.[32] His claim may be so clear and fixed in amount as not to be open to question. Even if liability or the amount owing is disputed, an administrator ad litem may be appointed,[33] to represent the interests of the estate in this regard. At any rate the estate is protected against unfair dealing by the administrator's bond.

The interest of a debtor of the estate is not any more adverse than the interest of a creditor. The same arguments just set forth apply equally to the case of the debtor. Both claim against the estate, and the fact that one has the burden of proof while the other is on the defensive should not make any difference with regard to qualifications to act as administrator. While it is true that the statutes do not expressly authorize the appointment of a debtor, as they do in case of a creditor, it is well established

26 Barnett's Adm'r v. Pittman, 282 Ky. 162, 137 S.W.2d 1098, 1940 (30 years before).

27 In re Dunham's Estate, 181 Okl. 407, 74 P.2d 117, 1938.

28 In re Berry's Estate, 56 Cal.App. 2d 621, 132 P.2d 836, 1943; see note, 51 Harv.L.R. 552.

29 Petition of Worcester County Nat. Bank of Worcester, 263 Mass. 394, 161 N.E. 797, 1928; Mahoney v. McBirney, 184 Okl. 75, 84 P.2d 600, 1938. As to the common-law position, see 1 Bl.Com. 247.

30 Grunow v. Simonitsch, 21 N.D. 277, 130 N.W. 835, 1911. See supra § 108.

31 Re McGill's Estate, 52 Nev. 35, 280 P. 321, 65 A.L.R. 1232, 1929.

32 See supra § 109.

33 See supra § 104.

that the fact that the applicant is indebted to the estate does not preclude the grant of letters of administration to him.[34]

*The Court's Discretion*

The foregoing passages of this section have dealt with what are, and what are not, absolute disqualifications for the office of administrator. If the court finds some disqualifying matter to exist with respect to the applicant, the appointment should not be made. On the other hand, unless the court is given discretion it cannot refuse to appoint one who is given statutory preference and is not disqualified.[35] Discretion, as has already been seen,[36] exists in the case of several applicants each of whom are equally entitled to letters. It also exists expressly under some statutes, and under others which provide that the administrator must be a suitable or proper person. In these cases the court may upon finding certain objections to the applicant refuse to grant him letters.[37] Thus, while they are not absolute disqualifications, personal characteristics,[38] evidence of dishonesty,[39] adverse interest,[40] hostility to heirs,[41] and nonresidence,[42] have been held to

34 McFry v. Casey, 211 Ala. 649, 101 So. 449, 1924; In re Graham's Estate, 27 Ariz. 167, 231 P. 918, 1925; Dorsey v. Dorsey, 140 Md. 167, 116 A. 915, 1922. And see Marcus v. McKee, 227 Ala. 577, 151 So. 456, 1934, where the applicant claimed certain property also claimed by the deceased.

35 Calvert v. Beck, 240 Ala. 442, 199 So. 846, 1941; Vaught v. Struble, 63 Idaho 352, 120 P.2d 259, 1942; In re Taylor's Estate, 61 Nev. 68, 114 P.2d 1086, 135 A.L.R. 580, 1941. For an analysis of the statutes see note, 26 Wash.U.L.Q. 106, 118–120, and see supra § 109.

36 See supra § 109.

37 Woodruff v. Miller, 209 Ark. 759, 192 S.W.2d 527, 1946; State ex rel. Gentry v. O'Byrne, 221 Ind. 282, 46 N.E.2d 687, 1943; State ex rel. Gregory v. Henderson, 230 Mo.App. 1, 88 S.W.2d 893, 1936; Commerce Union Bank v. Fox, 28 Tenn.App. 587, 192 S.W.2d 233, 1946. But see Griffin v. Irwin, supra note 21. See notes, 1 Ala.L.R. 289, 23 Chi-Kent L.R. 266, 45 Mich.L.R. 203.

38 Martin v. Otis, 233 Mass. 491, 124 N.E. 294, 6 A.L.R. 1340, 1919.

39 In re Graff's Estate, 119 Mont. 311, 174 P.2d 216, 1946; In re Bredl's Estate, 117 Wash. 372, 201 P. 296, 1921.

40 Morgan v. Morgan, 267 Mass. 388, 166 N.E. 747, 1929 (deceased's trustee in bankruptcy); In re Elder's Estate, 160 Or. 111, 83 P.2d 477, 119 A.L.R. 802, 1943; Ex parte Tolbert, 206 S.C. 300, 34 S.E.2d 49, 1945 (deceased's partner); In re Watkins' Estate, 114 Vt. 109, 41 A.2d 180, 157 A.L.R. 212, 1945. Cf. Smith v. Harmer, 64 S.E.2d 481, W.Va., 1951.

41 Martin v. Otis, 233 Mass. 491, 124 N.E. 294, 6 A.L.R. 1340, 1919.

42 Eva's Appeal, 93 Conn. 38, 104 A. 238, 1918.

justify the court in rejecting the application. At least where there is discretion, it should be ground for refusal of appointment that there would be ground for removal if appointed.[43]

## ACCEPTANCE AND RENUNCIATION BY PERSONAL REPRESENTATIVE

**111. The executor named in the will or the person entitled by law to act as administrator may either accept or renounce the trust. By the prevailing view a renunciation may be withdrawn at any time prior to the granting of letters to another person.**

### *Executors*

The person named as executor may either accept or renounce the office. If such person proves the will,[1] accepts letters testamentary,[2] or takes the oath of,[3] or gives a bond as,[4] executor, he is deemed to have accepted and can no longer renounce but must resign before he can rid himself of the office.[5] The same is probably true of intermeddling with the estate.[6] But mere inaction does not ordinarily constitute either an acceptance or a renunciation.[7] A renunciation need not be in writing and it may be implied from conduct of the person named.[8] If necessary, the person named as executor may be cited into court to accept or reject the appointment.[9]

[43] Howd v. Clay, 312 Ky. 508, 228 S.W.2d 437, 18 A.L.R.2d 629, 1950, see infra § 114.

[1] Decker v. Fahrenholtz, 107 Md. 515, 68 A. 1048, 72 A. 339, 1908.

[2] Worth v. McAden, 21 N.C. 199, 1835.

[3] Seaman v. Jamison, 146 App.Div. 428, 131 N.Y.S. 155, 1911.

[4] Sears v. Dillingham, 12 Mass. 358, 1815.

[5] See Beacham v. Ross, 190 S.C. 219, 2 S.E.2d 690, 1939 and infra § 114.

[6] Decker v. Fahrenholtz, supra note 1. Cf. In re Ralston's Estate, 158 Pa. 645, 28 A. 139, 1893.

[7] In re Vernon's Estate, 182 Cal. 91, 187 P. 11, 1920; Donnelly v. Slaughter, 114 N.J.Eq. 302, 168 A. 762, affirmed 116 N.J.Eq. 542, 174 A. 507, 1933; Secrest v. Secrest, 146 Okl. 235, 294 P. 91, 1931; State ex rel. Laurisden v. Superior Court for King County, 179 Wash. 198, 37 P.2d 209, 95 A.L.R. 819, 1934. But see Abbott v. Appleton, 86 Ind.App. 607, 159 N.E. 167, 1928 (statute).

[8] In re Phillip's Estate, 202 Cal. 490, 261 P. 709, 1928; In re Howey's Estate, 216 Wis. 94, 256 N.W. 620, 1934. And see supra notes 1–4.

[9] See Stebbins v. Lathrop, 4 Pick. (Mass.) 33, 1826.

The effect of the renunciation is that letters may be granted to other persons named as joint executors in the will,[10] or in case of a single appointee by the will, letters of administration with the will annexed should be granted.[11] While probably one could confine his renunciation expressly to one jurisdiction, a general renunciation in the domiciliary court is also deemed to justify appointing another as ancillary representative.[12]

*Administrators*

It is desirable that renunciation by one entitled to appointment as administrator should be in writing,[13] though, in some jurisdictions at least, it may be oral.[14] Acquiescence in the appointment of another amounts to renunciation.[15] In many jurisdictions the one given a preferred right to administer must apply within a certain time, or letters can be granted to another.[16] Failure to apply within this period is not exactly the same as renunciation, for the preferred individual could still apply afterward if no one had been appointed meanwhile.[17] Nomination of another is a renunciation if the nominee is appointed,[18] but if not, the nominator can still ask for his own appointment.[19]

*Withdrawal of Renunciation*

There is some doubt as to whether one may retract a renunciation after it has once been made. Surely he cannot retract after another is appointed and is still acting.[20] However, by the prevailing rule one may withdraw his renunciation at any time

10 Briggs v. Probate Court, 23 R.I. 125, 50 A. 335, 1901.

11 Thornton v. Winston, 4 Leigh (Va.) 152, 1833. If the person named executor is also the one entitled to act as administrator, his renunciation as executor does not preclude him from acting as administrator. Briscoe's Devisees v. Widkliffe, 6 Dana (Ky.) 157, 1838.

12 State ex rel. Abercrombie v. Holtcamp, 267 Mo. 412, 185 S.W. 201, Ann. Cas.1918D 454, 1916.

13 Williams v. Neville, 108 N.C. 559, 13 S.E. 240, 1891; Arnold v. Sabin, 1 Cush.(Mass.) 525, 1848.

14 Rowell v. Adams, 83 S.C. 124, 65 S.E. 207, 1909.

15 Lee v. Earnest, 299 S.W. 931, Tex.Civ.App.1928.

16 Starlin v. Love, 237 Ala. 38, 185 So. 380, 1939.

17 In re Randall's Estate, 63 A. 806, R.I. 1904.

18 Bivin v. Millsap, 238 Ala. 136, 189 So. 770, 1939.

19 Matter of Haug's Estate, 29 Misc. 36, 60 N.Y.S. 382, 1899.

20 Vannoy v. Gibson, 102 S.W.2d 492, Tex.Civ.App.1937.

before letters are granted to another,[21] or after removal of the person who was appointed in his place.[22]

## PROCEEDINGS FOR APPOINTMENT

**112. Executors and administrators receive their letters of appointment in the course of regular proceedings which consist of:**

**(1) An application, usually in the form of a written petition containing the jurisdictional, and often other pertinent, facts;**

**(2) notice to the interested parties if required by statute;**

**(3) hearing of the petition and objections thereto by interested parties unless the appointment is ex parte;**

**(4) an order granting or denying the petition.**

As has been seen, the common-law doctrine that the executor derived his authority from the will is not the present American rule.[1] Court appointment has always been necessary to give the administrator authority to act. The court authority takes the form of letters testamentary in case of executor and letters of administration in case of administrators.

*Petition*

The application for letters may be made by any person interested in the estate, as a distributee or legatee,[2] creditor,[3] or others.[4] Persons not interested in the estate have no standing to file a petition,[5] though letters granted upon the petition of such person are not invalid except on direct attack.[6]

21 McCormick v. Brownell, 25 Idaho 11, 136 P. 613, 1913; Nunn v. Hamilton, 233 Ky. 663, 26 S.W.2d 526, 1930; In re McNichol's Estate, 282 Pa. 187, 127 A. 461, 1925. But see In re Blackburn's Estate, 48 Mont. 179, 137 P. 381, 1913.

22 Ross v. Pitcairn, 179 S.W.2d 35, 153 A.L.R. 215, Mo.1944.

1 See supra § 108.

2 In re Beghtel's Estate, 236 Iowa 953, 20 N.W.2d 421, 161 A.L.R. 1384, 1945 (distributee's next friend); Matter of Brown's Estate, 60 Misc. 628, 113 N.Y.S. 937, 1908.

3 Furst & Thomas v. Sanders, 134 Ark. 407, 204 S.W. 426, 1918; In re Miller's Estate, 130 Wash. 199, 226 P. 493, 1924.

4 Paperno v. Michigan Ry. Engineering Co., 202 Mich. 257, 168 N.W. 503, 1918 (foreign consul). But see In re Leskela's Estate, 176 Minn. 223, 223 N.W. 133, 1931 (creditor and assignee of heir).

5 Succession of Watkins, 156 La. 1000, 101 So. 395, 1924; Hancock's Estate v. Pyle, 187 Miss. 801, 193 So. 812, 1940; but see In re Pollard's Estate, 105 Neb. 432, 181 N.W. 133, 1920.

6 Mowry v. Latham, 20 R.I. 786, 40 A. 236, 341, 1898.

In some jurisdictions it is declared that a written application is not necessary.[7] A formal petition is usual, however, and is ordinarily made upon printed blank forms furnished by the probate office. The petition should show such facts as the death of the decedent,[8] his domicile within the county at the time of his death,[9] or assets within the county in the case of a nonresident,[10] and whether or not he left a will.[11] The interest of the applicant in the estate should also be set forth.[12] Many forms provide for additional data such as the date of the decedent's death, the value of his personalty and realty, and the names and residences of the heirs, distributees, legatees and devisees. Errors in the statements are not fatal to the jurisdiction of the court.[13] The petition ordinarily concludes with a prayer that the petitioner or some other person be granted letters testamentary or letters of administration. Where there is a will the same petition commonly prays for probate and for the issuance of letters.

*Notice*

In some states no notice of the petition need be given to the interested parties and the proceedings are entirely ex parte.[14] Where no notice was required an appointment on the day following the intestate's death was upheld.[15] Most states require notice although notice by publication is often sufficient.[16] The notice should state the time and place of the hearing.[17]

7 Savings Bank of Baltimore v. Weeks, 110 Md. 78, 72 A. 475, 22 L.R.A.,N.S., 221, 1909; Dallago v. Atlantic Coast Line R. Co., 165 N.C. 269, 81 S.E. 318, 1914.

8 Lee v. Allen, 100 Md. 7, 59 A. 184, 1904; Pleasants v. Dunkin, 47 Tex. 343, 1877.

9 Otero v. Otero, 11 Ariz. 260, 90 P. 601, 1907.

10 Tryon v. United States, 32 Ct.Cl. 425, 1897.

11 See Carson v. Blair, 32 Ga.App. 728, 124 S.E. 808, 1924.

12 Burkhalter v. Waters, 28 Ga.App. 296, 111 S.E. 73, 1922; Hancock's Estate v. Pyle, supra note 5.

13 Davis v. Miller, 106 Ala. 154, 17 So. 323, 1895 (date of death); Hilton v. Hopkins, 275 Mass. 59, 175 N.E. 162, 1931.

14 In the main these are the same states which do not require notice for probate. See supra § 95; note, 43 Mich.L.R. 1153.

15 Kaiser v. Ebersberger, 179 Md. 417, 19 A.2d 701, 133 A.L.R. 1479, 1941. See supra § 107, notes 39–40.

16 McDonald v. O'Dea, 256 Mass. 177, 152 N.E. 341, 1926; see In re Phillips' Estate, 86 Utah 358, 44 P.2d 699, 1935 (posting); note, 43 Mich. L.R. 1153.

17 Beckett v. Selover, 7 Cal. 215, 234, 68 Am.Dec. 237, 1857.

In case of failure to give the required notice, one interested in the estate may have the letters set aside.[18] However, administration granted without the required notice is not subject to collateral attack. For example, a debtor afterward sued by the executor or administrator cannot object because of failure to give notice in the statutory manner.[19] Official citation or publication may be dispensed with if all interested persons joined in the application or otherwise waive notice.[20]

*Hearing*

Before deciding the application the probate court should be convinced that facts support the petition and that notice, if required, has been given. In case there is no contest the court will act upon such proof as satisfies it of merit in the application. This would include a showing that no other person has the prior right to administer the estate.

When the petition is contested the petitioner is entitled to open and close.[21] Persons interested in the estate such as the husband of the decedent,[22] or the guardian of an infant heir,[23] or a creditor,[24] are entitled to object to the appointment, take part in the proceedings, and offer evidence. A mere debtor of the estate, however, has ordinarily no standing at the hearing.[25]

*Order*

After the hearing the order will take the form of granting or denying the petition. Letters are not ordinarily granted forthwith, for the reason that the person appointed must usually take an oath or furnish a bond before he has finally qualified for the office of executor or administrator.[26]

18 Dixon v. Clarke, 323 Mass. 85, 80 N.E.2d 37, 1948.

19 In re Upton's Estate, 199 Wash. 447, 92 P.2d 210, 123 A.L.R. 1220, 1939.

20 Dorsey v. Dorsey, 140 Md. 167, 116 A. 915, 1922; In re Rowe, 197 App.Div. 449, 189 N.Y.S. 395, 1921; Fischer v. Dolwig, 39 N.D. 161, 166 N.W. 793, 1918.

21 Weeks v. Sego, 9 Ga. 199, 1850.

22 Breen v. Pangborn, 51 Mich. 29, 16 N.W. 188, 1883.

23 In re Chase, 32 Hun (N.Y.) 318, 1884.

24 In re Bacher's Estate, 261 Ill. App. 547, 1932. See Carson v. Blair, 32 Ga.App. 728, 124 S.E. 808, 1924.

25 Lemmons v. Sims, 326 Ill.App. 97, 61 N.E.2d 764, 1945.

26 See infra § 113.

## BOND OF PERSONAL REPRESENTATIVE

**113. Administrators are required to give bond with sufficient sureties, usually in double the amount of the personalty in the estate, for the purpose of protecting interested parties against losses due to improper administration. Some jurisdictions require a similar bond of executors while others do not, and in a large number of states an executor must furnish bond unless the will directs otherwise.**

### *Administrators*

Early English statutes required administrators to give bond for the faithful administration of their trusts.[1] This is a general statutory requirement in the United States in case of administrators,[2] although commonly a corporate administrator need not give a bond [3] and there are occasionally other provisions for dispensing with the administrator's bond.[4]

### *Executors*

The English law did not require an executor to give bond because he was appointed by the testator and his authority was derived from the will rather than court appointment. Some American jurisdictions do not require a bond of an executor.[5] In the majority of our states a testator may by will dispense with the executor's bond, but in absence of such testamentary provision a bond will be required.[6] Statutes in still other jurisdictions re-

1 21 Hen. VIII, c. 5, § 3, 1529; 22 & 23 Car. II, c. 10, § 1, 1670.

2 "Administration bonds are for the benefit of creditors, and next of kin and to compel the administrator to perform the trust reposed in him and discharge the duties incumbent upon him." Vroom v. Smith Ex'rs, 14 N.J.L. 479, 483, 1834. As to what comes within the protection of the bond and actions thereon, see annotations, 76 A.L.R. 904, 104 id. 180, 109 id. 639, 119 id. 103, 144 id. 875; also infra § 116 note 66; § 117, note 29.

3 These exemptions apply to executors also. See States ex rel. North St. Louis Trust Co. v. Stahlhuth, 362 Mo. 67, 239 S.W.2d 515, 1951; Clippinger v. Wood, 98 N.E.2d 645, Ohio Com.Pl. 1950; Model Probate Code § 107 and appendix pp. 315–317.

4 See N.Y.Surr.Ct.Act §§ 106, 121; Model Probate Code § 107, for other methods of furnishing security.

5 Roberts v. Wilson, 198 Ga. 428, 31 S.E.2d 707, 1944; Evans v. Adams, 180 S.C. 214, 185 S.E. 57, 1936.

6 See N.Y.Surr.Ct.Act §§ 94, 97. Often it is discretionary with the court. In re Dennis' Estate, 146 Kan. 121, 68 P.2d 1083, 1937; In re Dillard's Estate, 184 Okl. 534, 88 P.2d 639, 121 A.L.R. 947, 1939 (court may dispense with bond after first requiring it).

quire a bond for both executors and administrators, and hence do not permit the testator to dispense with the bond in case of the former.[7] However, even if no bond is necessary in the ordinary case,[8] a bond may be required when the testator specifies one, or on account of nonresidence,[9] or insolvency of the executor,[10] or after partial administration when it appears that the estate is, or is about to be, prejudiced by the executor's misconduct.[11]

*Amount*

The amount of the bond is generally fixed by statute at twice the estimated value of the personal estate, though in some jurisdictions the amount is discretionary.[12] Statutes sometimes permit reduction of the amount in case the personal representative deposits the assets of the estate such as stocks and bonds with the court.[13] Usually the value of realty owned by the deceased does not increase the amount of the bond, as realty can be sold by the personal representative only by order of the court, and when this is necessary a special bond to protect the estate against loss of the proceeds is required.[14]

*Sureties*

Statutes in the United States usually require two or more sureties who are residents of the state.[15] In some jurisdictions the spouse,[16] or the attorney,[17] of the representative is not a competent surety. Corporate sureties who are authorized by their charters to act in this capacity are sufficient, and usually in this case, no cosurety is required.[18] According to the local statutes the

7 Chamberlain v. Husel, 178 Mich. 1, 144 N.W. 549, 1913.

8 See cases supra note 5.

9 Grigsby's Guardian v. Cocke's Ex'rs, 85 Ky. 314, 3 S.W. 418, 1887.

10 Dillen v. Fancher, 197 Ark. 995, 125 S.W.2d 110, 1939.

11 Naugher v. Hinson, 211 Ala. 278, 100 So. 221, 1924; Daniels v. Jones, 224 S.W. 476, Tex.Civ.App.1920.

12 For a summary of the statutes, see Model Probate Code, appendix pp. 310–315.

13 See supra note 4.

14 But where the representative has power to collect the rents, the bond should cover the annual rents. See Model Probate Code § 106, and appendix pp. 310–315.

15 Jones v. Smith, 120 Ga. 642, 48 S.E. 134, 1904.

16 Weeks' Succession, 104 La. 573, 29 So. 219, 1901.

17 Beresford v. American Coal Co., 124 Iowa 34, 98 N.W. 902, 70 L.R.A. 256, 1904. But the bond is not void on this account. Matter of Heinze's Estate, 97 Misc. 525, 163 N.Y.S. 415, 1917.

18 Barricklow v. Stewart, 31 Ind. App. 446, 68 N.E. 316, 1903 (foreign-

sureties as well as the form of the bond should be approved by the court or the clerk.[19]

*New Bond*

The court may require a new bond whenever the sureties appear to be insufficient,[20] or if for any other reason the bond is then inadequate protection.[21] In some jurisdictions the sureties may demand counter-security from the representative,[22] or upon finding themselves insecure may apply to the court for their discharge.[23] If the latter relief is granted the representative must furnish a new bond, though the old sureties will be liable for losses occurring prior to their discharge.[24]

*Effect of Failure to Give Bond*

Usually the giving of a bond, when the same is required, is a prerequisite to the granting of letters. Hence, if it should happen that letters were issued before the bond is furnished, the court is authorized to set aside the letters.[25] But the acts done by a personal representative before he has given bond are not void,[26] and the defect is cured upon his giving a bond later.[27]

corporation); Commonwealth v. Miller, 195 Pa. 230, 45 A. 921, 1900.

19 But lack of the court's approval does not affect validity of the bond, Cameron v. Cameron, 15 Wis. 1, 82 Am.Dec. 652, 1862, and is no defense to the surety, Linz v. Eastland County, 39 S.W.2d 599, 77 A.L.R. 1466, Tex.Com.App.1931.

20 Weeks' Succession, 104 La. 573, 29 So. 219, 1901

21 State ex rel. Homer v. Barrett, 121 Ind. 92, 22 N.E. 969, 1889. Weeks' Succession, supra note 20.

22 March v. Fidelity & Deposit Co., 79 Md. 309, 29 A. 521, 1894.

23 See Model Probate Code § 116 and comment thereto; infra note 24; also annotation, 118 A.L.R. 1261.

24 Century Indemnity Co. v. Maryland Cas. Co., 89 N.H. 121, 193 A. 221 (1937).

25 Stanley v. Stanley, 202 Ala. 661, 81 So. 617, 1919.

26 Ions v. Harbison, 112 Cal. 260, 44 P. 572, 1896; Sullivan v. Tioga R. Co., 112 N.Y. 643, 20 N.E. 569, 8 Am. St.Rep. 793, 1889.

27 In re Wiltsey's Will, 135 Iowa 430, 109 N.W. 776, 1907.

## REVOCATION OF LETTERS, REMOVAL, AND RESIGNATION

**114. The probate court may revoke letters which should not have been granted, or it may remove a representative because of his subsequent incapacity or maladministration of his trust. In most jurisdictions the court is authorized to accept the resignation of an executor or administrator.**

While the terminology is not always followed and is not vital, the expression "revocation of letters" is usually applied to the cases where they should not have been granted in the first place, and "removal of personal representative" is used where the original appointment was proper but subsequent misconduct or other circumstances have occurred.

### *Revocation of Letters*

Grounds for revocation include that the supposed decedent was living,[1] that his residence was elsewhere,[2] that he left a will and did not die intestate as was supposed,[3] that there was fraud in obtaining the letters,[4] that the deceased left no estate in the state,[5] that administration was unnecessary,[6] or was taken out in incorrect name,[7] that the court passed over one who has a prior right to administration,[8] or that the representative was not qual-

1 In re Paulsen's Estate, 35 Cal. App. 654, 170 P. 855, 1917; In re Clemens' Estate, 174 Misc. 1052, 22 N.Y.S.2d 168, 1940.

2 In re Gingery's Estate, 103 Ohio St. 559, 134 N.E. 449, 1921; In re Olson's Estate, 194 Wash. 219, 77 P. 2d 781, 1938.

3 Burgess v. Boswell, 139 Md. 669, 116 A. 457, 1922; In re Suskin's Estate, 214 N.C. 219, 198 S.E. 661, 1938. See supra § 107, notes 34–38.

4 O'Sullivan v. Palmer, 312 Mass. 240, 44 N.E.2d 958, 1942; In re Damsky's Estate, 164 Misc. 381, 298 N.Y.S. 937, 1937; Clancy v. Gay, 94 N.H. 33, 45 A.2d 658 (1946); In re Ober's Estate, 155 Ohio St. 279, 98 N.E.2d 805, 1951 (destruction of will); cf. Lefkoff v. Sicro, 189 Ga. 554, 6 S.E.2d 687, 133 A.L.R. 738, 1940 (set aside in equity).

5 McCoubrey v. Pure Oil Co., 179 Okl. 344, 66 P.2d 57, 1937; In re Olson's Estate, supra note 2; cf. McCool v. Old Nat. Bank in Evansville, 214 Ind. 679, 17 N.E.2d 820, 1939; In re Vilas' Estate, 166 Or. 115, 110 P.2d 940, 1941.

6 Murphy v. Freeman, 220 Ala. 634, 127 So. 199, 70 A.L.R. 381, 1930; Murphy v. Murphy, 42 Wash. 142, 84 P. 646, 1906.

7 Denson v. Crossley, 241 Ala. 445, 2 So.2d 916, 1941.

8 In re Sinclair's Estate, 231 Iowa 1320, 4 N.W.2d 237, 1942; In re Loflin's Estate, 224 N.C. 230, 29 S.E.2d 692, 1944; but cf. Starlin v. Love, 237 Ala. 38, 185 So. 380, 1939.

ified at the time of his appointment.[9] Letters will not be revoked on trifling or irrelevant grounds.[10]

*Removal*

The letters of a temporary administrator expire by their own terms when the general representative is appointed,[11] and it is not necessary either to revoke the former's letters or to formally remove him.[12] However, a general representative cannot be removed simply by appointing another to the office.[13]

A representative may be removed for habitual drunkenness,[14] and generally for insolvency,[15] but not for poverty.[16] Under many statutes when the representative becomes a nonresident of the state he may be removed,[17] but not upon merely changing his domicile to another county.[18] A mere change of state residence ipso facto does not work a removal.[19]

That an executor or administrator has a conflicting interest is not always sufficient ground for his removal,[20] though it may be if it appears that the matter cannot otherwise be settled or liti-

9 In re Allen's Estate, 30 F.Supp. 243, D.C.D.C.1940; Donelson's Estate v. Gorman, 192 S.W.2d 29, Mo.App. 1946. But cf. In re Sherman's Estate, 146 Fla. 643, 1 So.2d 727, 1941.

10 Robinson v. Robinson, 178 Md. 623, 16 A.2d 854, 1940 (preventing testator from marrying); In re Quinlan's Estate, 158 N.Y.S. 319, 1916 (failure to state exact value of estate).

11 Vaught v. Struble, 65 Idaho 26, 139 P.2d 456, 148 A.L.R. 269, 1943; Leahy v. Mercantile Trust Co., 296 Mo. 561, 247 S.W. 396, 1922.

12 In re Aquino's Will, 186 Misc. 15, 59 N.Y.S.2d 595, affirmed 270 App.Div. 994, 63 N.Y.S.2d 214, 1946.

13 Landrum v. Louisville & N. R. Co., 290 Ky. 724, 162 S.W.2d 543, 1942; cf. May v. Sansbery, 119 Ind. App. 523, 86 N.E.2d 88, 1949 (without notice). See infra note 19.

14 Gurley v. Butler, 83 Ind. 501, 1882.

15 Gibson v. Maxwell, 85 Ga. 235, 11 S.E. 615, 1890; In re Sharpless' Estate, 209 Pa. 69, 57 A. 1128, 1904; Bowen v. Phillips, [1897] 1 Ch. 174. But see In re Dolenty's Estate, 53 Mont. 33, 161 P. 524, 1916; In re Knowles' Estate, 148 N.C. 461, 62 S. E. 549, 1908.

16 Clark v. Patterson, 214 Ill. 533, 73 N.E. 806, 105 Am.St.Rep. 127, 1905; Gill v. Riley, 90 S.W. 2, Ky.1906. And see supra § 110.

17 Kelley's Estate, 122 Cal. 379, 55 P. 136, 1898; In re Rice's Estate, 158 Mich. 53, 122 N.W. 212, 1909; cf. In re Svancina's Estate, 239 Wis. 436, 1 N.W.2d 780, 1942.

18 Rieke's Adm'r v. Rieke, 183 Ky. 131, 208 S.W. 764, 1919.

19 Chicago, R. I. & P. Ry Co. v. Forrester, 72 Okl. 8, 177 P. 593, 8 A.L.R. 163, 1918; cf. Harber v. Kentucky Ridge Coal Co., 188 F.2d 62, C.C.A. Ky.1951 (removal without notice).

20 Trevathan v. Grogan, 210 Ky 694, 276 S.W. 556, 1925; In re Arduser's Estate, 226 Iowa 103, 283 N.W. 879, 1939.

gated satisfactorily.[21] Dishonesty connected with the estate is clearly ground of removal.[22] Failure to obey the court's order to file an account is sufficient cause for removal,[23] but the mere fact that an inventory,[24] or an account,[25] is not filed when lawfully due will not usually cause removal where there has been no prejudice therefrom. Where the estate is being wasted or mismanaged the representative should be removed.[26] However, the showing of the latter facts should be clear,[27] and the court was held justified in refusing to remove executors guilty of doing acts without support of law where there was no dishonesty.[28]

Statutes sometimes provide that certain matters are ground for removal.[29] These are largely declaratory of the rules at common law.[30] It is generally asserted that the statutory grounds are exclusive,[31] though a contrary view has also been declared.[32]

*Proceedings*

It is often said that only one interested in the estate may move for revocation of the letters or removal of the incumbent.[33]

21 Price's Adm'r v. Price, 291 Ky. 211, 163 S.W.2d 463, 1942; Quincy Trust Co. v. Taylor, 317 Mass. 195, 57 N.E.2d 573, 1944; In re Clawson's Estate, 3 Wash.2d 509, 101 P.2d 968, 1940.

22 In re Sullivan's Estate, 51 Ariz. 483, 78 P.2d 132, 1938 (fraud in account); Stewart v. Poinbeouf, 201 S.W. 1025, Tex.Civ.App.1918 (conversion).

23 Appeal of Senechal, 122 Me. 317, 119 A. 814, 1923.

24 Willoughby v. Willoughby, 203 Ala. 138, 82 So. 168, 1919; Jones v. Palmer, 215 N.C. 696, 2 S.E.2d 850, 1939.

25 Belt v. Hilgeman, Brundige Co., 138 Md. 129, 113 A. 721, 1921; In re Johnson's Estate, 178 Or. 214, 164 P.2d 884, 1946.

26 In re Busby's Estate, 288 Ill.App. 500, 62 N.E.2d 451, 1937; In re Herrmann's Estate, 130 N.J.Eq. 273, 22 A.2d 262, affirmed 132 N.J.Eq. 458, 28 A.2d 517, 1941.

27 In re Kaier's Estate, 264 Pa. 224, 107 A. 723, 1919; In re Hartman's Estate, 331 Pa. 422, 200 A. 49, 1938.

28 Hanssen v. Karbe, 234 Mo.App. 663, 115 S.W.2d 109, 1938; In re Hazeltine's Estate, 119 N.J.Eq. 308, 182 A. 357, affirmed 121 N.J.Eq. 49, 187 A. 177, 1936 (bad legal advice); In re Johnson's Estate, 178 Or. 214, 164 P.2d 886, 1946.

29 See Bocquin v. Theurer, 133 Ark. 448, 202 S.W. 845, 1918; In re Grover's Estate, 177 App.Div. 272, 164 N.Y.S. 209, 1917; In re Robison's Estate, 59 Utah 431, 204 P. 321, 1922. See Model Probate Code § 98 and notes 31, 32 infra.

30 Bruce v. Fogarty, 53 Ga.App. 443, 186 S.E. 463, 1936 (revocation of letters—"unfit"); Quincy Trust Co. v. Taylor, 317 Mass. 195, 57 N.E.2d 573, 1944 ("unsuitable").

31 Hawley v. Hawley, 72 App.D.C. 357, 114 F.2d 505, 1940; In re Hebblethwaite's Estate, 293 Ill.App. 493, 12 N.E.2d 923, 1938.

32 Koury v. Castillo, 13 N.M. 26, 79 P. 293, 1905.

33 Fowler v. Ball, 82 Ind.App. 167, 141 N.E. 64, 1923; In re Mack's Estate, 164 N.Y.S. 590, Sur.Ct.1917. But cf. In re Stutzman's Estate, 359 Pa. 502, 59 A.2d 694, 1948, and infra note 39.

Though there are some conflicting decisions, the courts tend to construe this broadly. One who claims the estate is in this category,[34] though it has been held that the nominee of a preferred claimant may not ask for revocation.[35] The public administrator [36] and creditors,[37] have been considered interested persons, but it is usually held that debtors are not.[38] According to some cases at least, the court may revoke letters of its own motion or upon the suggestion of an amicus curiæ.[39]

Laches or estoppel may take away the right to move to revoke letters.[40] Lapse of the time within which the moving party might apply for original letters has been held to preclude the motion.[41] A court may revoke letters although the term of court has expired.[42]

*Effect of Revocation of Letters or Removal*

When letters are revoked the authority to act as personal representative of course ceases.[43] However, acts already done in good faith by the representative before letters were revoked will be given effect.[44] The representative may be allowed his compensation and reasonable expenses incurred while his letters were

34 In re Gingery's Estate, 103 Ohio St. 559, 134 N.E. 449, 1921. But see Starlin v. Love, supra note 8.

35 In re Mintaberry's Estate, 183 Cal. 566, 191 P. 909, 1920.

36 In re Morland's Estate, 184 Misc. 435, 55 N.Y.S.2d 910, 1945.

37 Zipperer v. La Roche, 145 Ga. 829, 90 S.E. 40, 1916; see Knight v. Hamakar, 40 Or. 424, 67 P. 107, 1901. But see Kneeland v. Buzzell, 135 Me. 363, 197 A. 155, 1938.

38 Brinkley v. Allen, 200 Ark. 1147, 143 S.W.2d 187, 1940; In re Trost's Estate, 292 Ill.App. 60, 10 N.E.2d 857, 1937; In re Walsh's Estate, 131 N.J. Eq. 376, 25 A.2d 424, 1942. But see Reynolds v. Lloyd Cotton Mills, 177 N.C. 412, 99 S.E. 240, 5 A.L.R. 284, 1919.

39 Ashurt v. Union Bank & Trust Co., 200 Ala. 559, 76 So. 917, 1917; Brown v. Brown, 204 Ala. 157, 85 So. 439, 1920. See Wilkinson v. Nowers, 217 Ill.App. 314, 1920; Quincy Trust Co. v. Taylor, 317 Mass. 195, 57 N.E. 2d 573, 1944; In re Stutzman's Estate, supra note 33.

40 Garrett v. Harrison, 201 Ala. 186, 77 So. 712, 1918. And see McCowen v. Flanders, 155 Ga. 701, 118 S.E. 351, 1923.

41 Bowers v. Cook, 124 Md. 567, 93 A. 162, 1915.

42 Ross v. Pitcairn, 179 S.W.2d 35, 153 A.L.R. 215, Mo.1944.

43 Belden v. Belden, 118 App.Div. 296, 103 N.Y.S. 346, 1907; Rutenic v. Hamaker, 40 Or. 444, 67 P. 196, 1902.

44 State ex rel. Everette v. Petteway, 131 Fla. 516, 179 So. 666, 1938; Harrison v. Carter, 226 N.C. 36, 36 S.E.2d 700, 164 A.L.R. 697, 1946.

in force.[45] In case of either revocation of letters or removal, the displaced representative is obliged to render his account.[46]

*Resignation*

Statutes in many jurisdictions permit a personal representative to resign for good cause,[47] but the resignation is not effective until accepted by the court.[48] At common law it was held that the court had no authority to accept a resignation of one who had once undertaken administration,[49] but the modern tendency is to declare that this power is implied from the right to remove.[50] The latter view seems preferable, as otherwise a representative anxious to be relieved of his office might be tempted to commit acts justifying removal. It is unwise to force a representative to take such ends. Of course the resigning representative must settle his accounts and usually this is made a condition of the acceptance of the resignation.[51]

45 Justice v. Wilkins, 251 Ill. 13, 95 N.E. 1025, 1911; Brown v. McGee's Estate, 117 Wis. 389, 94 N.W. 363, 1903. And see Re Pedroli's Estate, 47 Nev. 313, 221 P. 241, 31 A.L.R. 841, 1923, holding that estate is even chargeable with the expenses of a representative incurred after his removal if they were for the protection of the property. See note, 20 N.D. Lawyer 53.

46 Middleton v. Carter, 73 N.J.Eq. 624, 68 A. 763, 1907. As to the liability of a former representative to his successor, see annotation, 3 A.L.R. 1252 and supra § 104.

47 Elmore v. Cunninghame, 208 Ala. 15, 93 So. 814, 1922; Macey v. Stark, 116 Mo. 481, 21 S.W. 1088, 1893.

48 Broadway's Succession, 114 La. 492, 38 So. 430, 1905. See Johnston v. Schwenck, 99 Ohio St. 59, 124 N.E. 61, 8 A.L.R. 170, 1918.

49 Haigood v. Wells, 1 Hill, Eq. (10 S.C.Eq.) 59, 1833; Sitzman v. Pacquette, 13 Wis. 291, 1907.

50 Thayer v. Homer, 11 Metc.(Mass.) 104, 1846; Balch v. Hooper, 32 Minn. 158, 20 N.W. 124, 1884; Ramp v. McDaniel, 12 Or. 108, 6 P. 456, 1885. As to resignation of a public administrator, see State ex rel. Sears, Roebuck & Co. v. Mueller, 332 Mo. 758, 60 S.W.2d 48, 91 A.L.R. 705, 1933.

51 Waterland v. Superior Court in and for Sacramento County, 15 Cal. 2d 34, 98 P.2d 211, 1940. Industrial Trust Co. v. Dean, 67 R.I. 504, 25 A. 2d 552, 1942.

# CHAPTER 13

## COLLECTION AND MANAGEMENT OF ESTATE

**Sec.**

115. Inventory and Appraisal.
116. Assets—What Are.
117. Collection and Care of Assets.
118. Torts of Personal Representatives.
119. Contracts of Personal Representatives.
120. Performance of Deceased's Contracts.
121. Continuation of Deceased's Business.
122. Sales of Personal Property.
123. Sales of Realty.
124. Investment of Assets.
125. Payment of Taxes.
126. Survival of Claims Against Estate.
127. Enforcement of Claims.
128. Priority of Claims in Insolvent Estates.

### INVENTORY AND APPRAISAL

**115. Within a certain period fixed by statute the personal representative is required to file a correct inventory of all the personalty owned by the deceased at the time of his death, and in many jurisdictions the realty must also be included in the inventory. Though not conclusive, the inventory is prima facie evidence of the extent of the assets of the estate.**

**When the inventory has been made, the various items are appraised by persons appointed by the court for this purpose. The value so fixed is regarded as presumptively correct for subsequent purposes, but it is not conclusive.**

As early as 1529, an English statute provided that the personal representative should make a "true and perfect inventory" of deceased's goods.[1] The later English legislation merely requires an inventory when the executor or administrator is called on to exhibit the same,[2] but in the United States the rule is practically uniform that an inventory is necessary in the first instance and indeed the filing of an inventory is usually one of the conditions

1 21 Hen. VIII, c. 15, § 4. See also 22 & 23 Car. II, c. 10, §§ 1 and 2, 1670.

2 20 & 21 Vict., c. 77, §§ 80, 81, 1857; 15 Geo. V, c. 23, § 25, 1925.

of the representative's bond.[3] In general the testator cannot authorize the representative to dispense with the inventory,[4] nor can the beneficiaries of the estate waive the filing of the same.[5]

There are two main reasons for the requirement of an inventory. The first is to serve as a basis of computation for the representative's intermediate and final accounts.[6] The second is to furnish information for the benefit of the beneficiaries, creditors and others interested in the estate.[7] If the personal representative neglects to file an inventory, the latter persons may move the court to order him to do so.[8]

*Time*

Statutes fix the time within which the executor or administrator must file his inventory. The period varies from one to three months after the representative has qualified.[9] Failure to file an inventory within the prescribed period may result in liability on the bond or other penalty,[10] though if no one is injured thereby

[3] In re McSpirit's Estate, 73 N.J.Eq. 613, 68 A. 755, 1907; Hayes v. Welling, 35 R.I. 76, 85 A. 630, 1913; In re Belt's Estate, 29 Wash. 535, 70 P. 74, 92 Am.St.Rep. 916, 1902. And see State ex rel. Daniels v. Rogers, 111 W.Va. 587, 163 S.E. 416, 1932. When a representative is entitled to the whole estate, he need not file an inventory unless ordered to do so upon the application of an interested party. In re Finkenzeller's Estate, 107 N.J. Eq. 180, 151 A. 905, 1929. In New York, in spite of directory language of the statute the court may decline to order an inventory. In re Erlanger's Estate, 159 Misc. 185, 287 N.Y.S. 263, 1936. In many counties of New York the filing of an inventory is rare; its place is supplied temporarily by the papers used in determination of the estate tax, and later by the representative's account.

[4] Naugher v. Hinson, 211 Ala. 278, 100 So. 221, 1924; Hayes v. Welling, 35 R.I. 76, 85 A. 630, 1913; see Black v. Morgan, 227 Ala. 327, 149 So. 845, 1933; cf. Darnell v. Tate, 177 Ga. 279, 170 S.E. 63, 1933 (appraisal); In re Doppes' Estate, infra note 12.

[5] Dant's Ex'rs v. Cooper, 123 Ky. 359, 96 S.W. 454, 1906.

[6] Lowry v. Crandale, 52 Ariz. 501, 83 P.2d 1003, 120 A.L.R. 271, 1938; Platt v. Jones, 149 Or. 246, 38 P.2d 703, 39 P.2d 955, 1935. See infra § 142.

[7] In re Brady's Estate, 6 Ohio Supp. 284, 1941; Lynch v. Skelly, 138 Conn. 376, 85 A.2d 251, 1951 (but not for debtor's benefit).

[8] Riebow v. Ensch, 220 Mich. 450, 190 N.W. 233, 1922; In re Seipel, 117 N.J.Eq. 239, 175 A. 626, 1935; In re Gillender's Estate, 98 Misc. 521, 162 N.Y.S. 955, 1917.

[9] See Woerner on Administration § 316.

[10] State v. French, 60 Conn. 478, 23 A. 153 (1891) (action on bond); Piersol v. Hays, 113 Ind.App. 214, 47 N.E. 2d 838, 1943 (damage action). As to loss of commissions, see annotation, 83 A.L.R. 732.

the breach is regarded merely as a technical one, without legal consequences.[11]

*What Should Be Included in Inventory*

The inventory should contain a list of all the personalty which belonged to the deceased, at the date of his death.[12] If there are profits or other additions accruing later, these should be shown in the representative's accounts rather than in the inventory.[13] The list should include property claimed to belong to the estate even if it is in the possession of another.[14] In case of doubt as to the ownership the item should be included,[15] and if it is later established that the property belongs to another, the matter can be adjusted by striking the item from the inventory, by filing an amended inventory, or by a proper indication in the subsequent accounts of the representative.

Choses in action should be included in the inventory.[16] If the chose is of doubtful collectability, it is well to indicate that it is a desperate item, for otherwise it might be appraised at its full value.

If there is to be only one administration, it is proper to include assets outside of the state in the inventory.[17] Generally, assets which will be administered in an ancillary administration need not be included in the inventory of the domiciliary representative.[18]

11 Phelan v. Smith, 100 Cal. 158, 34 P. 667, 1893 (inventory valid though filed late); McKim v. Harwood, 129 Mass. 75, 1880.

12 State to Use of Horsey v. Maryland Cas. Co., 164 Md. 69, 163 A. 856, 1933; In re Elliott's Estate, 113 Pa. Super. 350, 173 A. 880, 1934. Cf. In re Abddulah's Estate, 214 Wis. 336, 252 N.W. 158, 1934; In re Doppes' Estate, 70 Ohio App. 354, 42 N.E.2d 208, 1941 (notes given to evidence advancements).

13 Snodgrass v. Andrews, 30 Miss. 472, 64 Am.Dec. 169, 1855; In re Long's Estate, 143 Pa.Super. 176, 17 A.2d 686, 1941.

14 Succession of Carcagno (Succession of Saloy), 43 La.Ann. 1151, 10 So. 251, 1891; In re Boggs' Estate, 19 Cal.2d 324, 121 P.2d 678, 1942 (land).

15 Searle v. Crampton, 118 Conn. 42, 170 A. 480, 1934.

16 In re Love's Estate, 176 Tenn. 696, 145 S.W.2d 778, 1941 (though disputed); In re McSpirit's Estate, supra note 3.

17 Butler's Estate, 38 N.Y. 397, 1868.

18 In re Healey's Estate, 134 A. 684, 4 N.J.Misc. 785, 1926; Sherman v. Page, 85 N.Y. 123, 1881. But see Bridgeport Trust Co.'s Appeal, 77 Conn. 657, 60 A. 662, 1905 (on account of inheritance tax).

The various chattel interests should be set forth separately in the inventory and not combined in general categories.[19] This is required in order that the appraisers may perform their functions properly, and so that the inventory will be understandable to persons examining it.[20]

*Realty*

At common law the inventory did not include the deceased's lands,[21] since the personal representative had nothing to do with the realty and it could not be taken for the deceased's debts. In some states the statutes contemplate that only the personalty shall be included in the inventory,[22] but in most jurisdictions the realty also must be included.[23] This is reasonable since realty may now be sold to pay debts and if lands are included in the inventory, one may see at a glance what is available to creditors.

*Ordering Property to Be Included in the Inventory*

There is a difference of opinion as to whether the court may order a personal representative to include certain chattels in the inventory. This question becomes acute when the executor or administrator claims to own the property in question. It has been denied that the court has authority to compel the representative to inventory certain property claimed by him, such matters being properly disposed of on final account.[24] Most jurisdictions, however, recognize that the probate court may make such order,[25] though the general view is that the determination of the title is not final.[26] The reason assigned for the latter hold-

19 Poirier v. Burton-Swartz Cypress Co., 127 La. 936, 54 So. 292, 1911 (land); In re McConney's Estate, 72 Ohio App. 286, 51 N.E.2d 239, 1943. But excessive particularization is not required; a rule of reason should prevail.

20 See In re Rahauser's Estate, 52 York (Pa.) 37, 1938.

21 Prescott v. Tarbell, 1 Mass. 204, 1804. However, in Massachusetts the early colonial inventories usually included land. Atkinson, The Development of the Massachusetts Probate System, 42 Mich.L.R. 425, 428 and passim.

22 N.C.Gen.Stat., 1943, § 28–50; Tenn.Code, 1932, § 8189.

23 See Model Probate Code § 120 and comment thereto.

24 Matter of Goundry's Estate, 57 App.Div. 232, 68 N.Y.S. 155, 1901. And see Snodgrass v. Andrews, 30 Miss. 472, 64 Am.Dec. 169, 1855 (property claimed by third persons).

25 Heinrich v. Harrigan, 288 Ill. 170, 123 N.E. 309, 1919; Commonwealth v. Bullock, 178 Ky. 729, 200 S.W. 45, 1918; Linthicum v. Polk, 93 Md. 84, 48 A. 842, 1901; Barka v. Hopewell, 29 N.M. 166, 219 P. 799, 1923. Cf. In re Russell's Estate, 98 N.E.2d 592, Ohio Prob.1951.

26 Hartwig v. Flynn, 79 Kan. 595, 100 P. 642, 1909; Pratt v. Hill, 124

ings is that such matters are within the jurisdiction of the ordinary courts and not of the court of probate. If the right to trial by jury is preserved however, there is no reason why the probate courts cannot be given jurisdiction by statute to make binding determination as to the title after due notice of hearing. This power has not been given to most probate courts and their orders are merely incidental and tentative and not conclusive on anyone.

*Appraisal*

Statutes generally provide for the appointment of disinterested persons, usually two in number, to act as appraisers. These persons should evaluate separately the items of property appearing on the inventory at their market value,[27] on the date of the decedent's death.[28] If the estate consists entirely of money or claims for money against solvent debtors, there is no reason for an appraisal and the court should not require one even though the statutory provision makes no exception for this case.

*Effect of Inventory and Appraisal*

The inclusion of property of another in the inventory does not divest the title from its lawful owners.[29] The personal representative is not estopped to show that the property inventoried belongs to a third person,[30] or even to himself.[31] Likewise failure to include the property in the inventory is not a bar to its recovery for the benefit of the estate.[32] However, the inventory is

Md. 252, 92 A. 543, 1914; Gray v. Doubikin, 179 Mo.App. 240, 166 S.W. 1070, 1914. But see Brown v. Southern Ohio Savings Bank & Trust Co., 22 Ohio App. 324, 153 N.E. 864, 1926 (statute); Security-First Nat. Bank of Los Angeles v. King, 46 Wyo. 59, 23 P.2d 851, 90 A.L.R. 125, 1933; In re Bush's Estate, 155 Kan 556, 127 P.2d 455, 142 A.L.R. 518, 1942.

27 Matter of Shipman's Estate, 82 Hun 108, 31 N.Y.S. 571, 1894 (rather than face value of bonds); In re Matthews' Will, 174 Wis. 220, 182 N.W. 744, 1921: "Fair market value * * being that sum of money for which the thing could be exchanged in the open market under fair conditions." Cf. In re Crary, 31 Misc. 72, 64 N.Y.S. 566, 1900.

28 Matter of Bodman's Estate, 100 Misc. 390, 166 N.Y.S. 714, 1917.

29 Domby v. Heath, 327 Mich. 29, 41 N.W.2d 325, 1950; Brown v. Southern Ohio Savings Bank & Trust Co., supra note 26; Perry v. Perry, 67 Utah 45, 245 P. 695, 1926.

30 Hoover v. Miller, 51 N.C. (6 Jones) 79, 1858; Stewart's Estate, 137 Pa. 175, 20 A. 554, 1890.

31 Friedman v. Goodin, 53 Nev. 324, 299 P. 1017, 1931; In re Langenbach's Estate, 201 Wis. 336, 230 N.W. 141, 1930; nor is the inventory conclusive in the representative's favor. Weed v. Lermond, 33 Me. 492, 1851.

32 Lynch v. Skelly, supra note 7; Ewers v. White's Estate, 114 Mich. 266, 72 N.W. 184, 1897; Lewis v.

deemed prima facie to include all property belonging to the deceased and no other.[33]

The same presumption is indulged relative to the amount fixed by the appraisal. Prima facie the value is deemed correct,[34] and the appraisal has been held admissible in evidence in collateral proceedings.[35] The appraisal may be followed for the purpose of the inheritance tax in absence of any showing as to its incorrectness.[36] But the value fixed therein is not conclusive as to beneficiaries,[37] creditors,[38] or the personal representative.[39] Of course no one should be bound by the appraisal when he has no opportunity to object thereto. Even if a person may file objections, he is not precluded by his failure to do so.[40]

Lusk, 35 Miss. 696, 72 Am.Dec. 153, 1858; Murphy v. McMahon, 100 Vt. 86, 135 A. 3, 1926. But see Damron v. Allen, 102 W.Va. 537, 135 S.E. 600, 1926 (statute).

33 In re Wilson's Estate, 127 Misc. 518, 217 N.Y.S. 341, 1926; Moore v. Wooten, 280 S.W. 742, Tex.Com.App. 1926; see Model Probate Code § 123.

34 In re Williams' Estate, 133 Misc. 322, 232 N.Y.S. 521, 1929; see Model Probate Code § 123.

35 Jones v. Grindal, 121 Me. 348, 117 A. 308, 1922 (against a beneficiary of the estate). But see Harrison's Adm'r v. Harrison's Distributees, 39 Ala. 489, 1864. Cf. Morrison v. Burlington, C. R. & N. R. Co., 84 Iowa 663, 51 N.W. 75, 1892.

36 In re Matthews' Will, supra note 27.

37 Petition of Carlton, 79 N.H. 48, 104 A. 246, 1918; Platt v. Jones, 149 Or. 246, 38 P.2d 703, 39 P.2d 955, 1935. But see Mercantile Trust Co. v. Schloss, 165 Md. 18, 166 A. 599, 1933.

38 Willoughby v. McCluer, 2 Wend. (N.Y.) 608, 609, 1829; see In re Anastos' Estate, 100 N.E.2d 324, Ohio Prob.1944 (surviving partner).

39 Tompkins v. Tompkins, 18 S.C. 1, 1882.

40 See Brown v. Southern Ohio Savings Bank & Trust Co., supra note 26.

## ASSETS—WHAT ARE

**116. Tangible personal property and all choses in action which survive, including debts owed by the personal representative to the deceased, are assets for the payment of creditor's claims and distribution to legatees and distributees. In most jurisdictions interests in realty are not deemed assets in the hands of the personal representative as the heirs or devisees are entitled to possession thereof until the court orders a sale in order to satisfy creditors.**

**Property which the deceased has given away by gift causa mortis may be recovered by the personal representative for the benefit of creditors. The same is true in most jurisdictions of property which deceased transferred in fraud of creditors, though some courts require the creditors to bring the suit. In neither case can there be recovery if there are other assets sufficient to satisfy creditors, since legatees or distributees have no interest in the property in any event.**

The assets of an estate consist of the property which the personal representative is entitled to administer for the benefit of those interested in the estate.[1] Of course creditors, legatees and distributees are all persons falling in the latter category, and most assets are, or may be, of interest to any of these classes. This is not always true for property conveyed by the deceased in fraud of his creditors,[2] or chattels given away by gift causa mortis,[3] are recovered by the personal representative solely on behalf of the creditors and neither the legatees nor distributees are entitled to the proceeds of such recoveries. On the other hand, death claims are usually prosecuted by the personal representative solely for the benefit of the surviving family, and the proceeds are not liable for debts of the deceased.[4] Likewise in some jurisdictions life insurance payable to the estate is not liable for the insured's debts and hence is not assets.[5]

1 Formerly a distinction was made between legal assets (those things coming to the personal representative as such) and equitable assets (those things which are chargeable with debts but not falling within the description of legal assets, as land charged with debts or devised to pay debts). The latter were distributed to creditors without regard to priority. The distinction is now obsolete in England and in most at least of our states since statutes now provide the order and manner of subjecting property of decedents to pay debts. Titterington v. Hooker, 58 Mo. 593, 1875; Maitland, Equity, 1936, 254–257, 272; Woerner on Administration, 2d ed. § 313.

2 See infra notes 30–35.

3 See infra notes 36–40.

4 See infra notes 58–63.

5 See infra note 25.

In most states the heirs are entitled to the possession and enjoyment of the real estate to the exclusion of the personal representative.[6] Accordingly, lands are not technically assets for general purposes of administration even though the executor is given power of sale thereof.[7] While it is true that the land may be sold by order of the court in order to pay debts,[8] until this is done the heir or devisee is usually entitled to the possession and rents of the property.[9] In some jurisdictions, however, the personal representative is entitled to the rents and profits during administration,[10] so that these may become assets for the payment of debts.[11]

*Interests Concerning Realty and Personalty*

When a cause of action arises in connection with real property during the deceased's lifetime, such as for breach of covenants, trespass, or damages for condemnation, this right is a chose in action and passes to the personal representative.[12] On the other hand where the cause of action regarding realty accrues after deceased's death, the heirs are entitled to sue.[13] Likewise, rent due before the death passes to the executor or administrator,[14] while that due after the death goes to the devisee or heir.[15]

[6] Hewitt v. Sanborn, 103 Conn. 352, 130 A. 472, 1925; Kreise v. Cartledge, 262 Pa. 55, 104 A. 855, 1918; Madler v. Kersten, 170 Wis. 424, 175 N.W. 779, 1920. See supra § 103.

[7] Watts' Estate, 168 Pa. 431, 32 A. 25, 1925.

[8] See infra § 123.

[9] Ball v. First Nat. Bank of Covington, 80 Ky. 501, 1882; In re Boyle's Estate, 133 N.J.Eq. 149, 30 A. 2d 827, 1943; note, 48 Harv.L.R. 130.

[10] Haden v. Sims, 127 Ga. 717, 56 S. E. 989, 1907; Moody v. MaComber, 159 Mich. 657, 124 N.W. 549, 134 Am. St.Rep. 755, 1910. And see supra § 103.

[11] In re Pennock's Estate, 122 Iowa 622, 98 N.W. 480, 1904; In re Baker's Estate, 164 Misc. 92, 298 N.Y.S. 261, 1937; Nolan v. Mathis, 147 Okl. 155, 295 P. 801, 1931; cf. Hahn v. Verret, 143 Neb. 820, 11 N.W.2d 551, 1943.

[12] Prestwood v. McGowin, 128 Ala. 267, 29 So. 386, 86 Am.St.Rep. 136, 1900; Hamilton v. Wilson, 4 Johns. (N.Y.) 72, 4 Am.Dec. 253, 1809; O'Brien v. Pennsylvania S. V. R. Co., 119 Pa. 184, 13 A. 74, 1888. Cf. Raymond v. Fitch, 2 C.M. & R. 588, 150 Eng.Rep. 251, 1835.

[13] Aubuchon v. Lory, 23 Mo. 99, 1856. As to the right of action for fire insurance see Wyman v. Wyman, 26 N.Y. 253, 1863; Oldham's Trustee v. Boston Ins. Co., 189 Ky. 844, 226 S. W. 106, 16 A.L.R. 305, 1920; American Law of Property § 14.32.

[14] Ball v. First National Bank of Covington, supra note 9; Codman v. American Piano Co., 229 Mass. 285, 118 N.E. 344, 1918; Daniels v. Bishop, 79 W.Va. 240, 90 S.E. 828, 1916.

[15] Ball v. First National Bank, supra note 9; Codman v. American Piano Co., supra note 14; Owings v. Owings, 150 Mich. 609, 114 N.W. 393,

Upon the death of the lessee, the unexpired part of the lease passes to the personal representative, it being personalty,[16] and the same is true of an unforeclosed mortgage held by the deceased.[17] In case of a contract for the sale of land the vendor's interest for the unpaid purchase price is deemed personalty and goes to the executor or administrator,[18] while upon the vendee's death his interest is deemed to be land and passes to the heirs or devisees.[19] Fructus naturales, or the natural products of the soil, pass to the heirs or devisees if they were not severed from the land in the lifetime of the deceased owner.[20] Fructus industriales, or sown crops, go to the administrator of an intestate,[21] though if the land is devised some courts declare these pass to the devisee.[22] Fixtures or chattels which have been permanently affixed to the realty pass to the heirs or devisees rather than to the personal representatives.[23]

### *Ownership at Time of Death*

Upon the death of the first joint tenant the entire interest belongs to the surviving tenant, and no portion of it passes to the

1908; Staton v. Guillebeaux, 123 S.C. 363, 116 S.E. 443, 31 A.L.R. 1, 1923. But the rule is changed by statute in some states; see supra notes 10–11.

16 Allender v. Sussan, 33 Md. 11, 3 Am.Rep. 171, 1870 (though lease was for ninety-nine years and renewable forever); Lang v. Wilmer, 131 Md. 215, 101 A. 706, 2 A.L.R. 1698, 1917; Mills v. Connor, 104 Ohio St. 409, 135 N.E. 616, 1922; Doe ex dem. Shore v. Porter, 3 T.R. 13, 100 Eng.Rep. 429, 1789 (lease from year to year).

17 Williams v. Williams, 270 Ill. 552, 110 N.E. 876, 1915; Miller & Sons v. Blinn, 219 Mass. 266, 106 N.E. 985, 1914. But if mortgage is foreclosed the land goes to the heirs or devisees. Osborne v. Tunis, 25 N.J.Law 633, 1856. Of course the mortgagor's interest passes to his heirs as realty.

18 New York Cent. & H. R. R. Co. v. Cottle, 187 App.Div. 131, 175 N.Y.S. 178, 1919; Clapp v. Tower, 11 N.D. 556, 93 N.W. 862, 1903; In re Fields' Estate, 141 Wash. 526, 252 P. 534, 1927, noted, 2 Wash.L.R. 205. Cf. Stevens v. Flannagan, 131 Ind. 122, 30 N.E. 898, 1892, where contract provided that money should go to the heirs. As to the right to the land after foreclosure, see annotation, 110 A.L.R. 1397.

19 Baxter v. Robinson, 11 Mich. 520, 1863; Cutler v. Meeker, 71 Neb. 732, 99 N.W. 514, 8 Ann.Cas. 951, 1904; Palmer v. Morrison, 104 N.Y. 132, 10 N.E. 144, 1887.

20 Gee v. Young, 2 N.C. 17, 1792.

21 In re Ring's Estate, 132 Iowa 216, 109 N.W. 710, 1906.

22 In re Pope's Estate, 83 Neb. 723, 120 N.W. 191, 1909; Blum v. Frost, 234 Mo.App. 695, 116 S.W.2d 541, 1938. Contra: Kesler v. Heberling, 113 Kan. 571, 213 P. 639, 1923 (statute).

23 Pratt v. Baker, 92 Hun 331, 36 N.Y.S. 928, 1895 (furnace); Cunningham v. Cureton, 96 Ga. 489, 23 S.E. 420, 1895.

personal representative of the deceased.[24] Likewise an executor or administrator ordinarily has no interest in a life insurance policy payable to an individual beneficiary.[25] When a partner dies, the partnership personalty passes to the surviving partners for the purpose of closing the business including payment of partnership debts.[26] The share in the surplus of the partnership personalty after this settlement goes of course to the personal representative of the deceased, but by the prevailing rule the remaining partnership real property retains that character for purposes of distribution.[27] The deceased's share in the estate of another passes to his personal representative if the interest is personalty,[28] and to his heirs if it is realty.[29]

[24] See supra § 40.

[25] Cates v. Bankers' Health & Life Ins. Co., 27 Ga.App. 159, 107 S.E. 615, 1921; Wagner v. Thieriot, 203 App. Div. 757, 197 N.Y.S. 560, 1923. Cf. American Nat. Ins. Co. v. Wallace, 210 S.W. 859, Tex.Civ.App.1918 (beneficiary having no insurable interest). As to right to proceeds of an insurance policy when the insured was insolvent, see note, 28 Mich.L.R. 53; annotation, 106 A.L.R. 596. Usually if the policy is payable to the estate, it is assets and the personal representative may recover. Pope v. Carter, 210 Ala. 533, 98 So. 726, 1924; Succession of Le Blanc, 142 La. 27, 76 So. 223, L.R.A.1917F 1137, 1917. Cf. In re Will of Grilk, 210 Iowa 587, 231 N.W. 327, 1930; note, 1 La.L.R. 239 (statute providing such policies are not liable for debts); Lapland v. Stearns, 54 N.W.2d 748, N.D.1893 (same). An automobile liability policy has been held to be assets. Berry v. Smith, 85 Ga.App. 710, 70 S.E.2d 62, 1952. See supra § 107, note 18.

[26] DeCoe v. Johnson, 54 Cal.App. 592, 202 P. 362, 1921; Grigg v. Hanna, 283 Mich. 443, 278 N.W. 125, 1938. Legal title to firm realty passes as land to the heirs of the title holder, though subject to power in the surviving partners to contract to convey it if necessary to pay firm debts. Shanks v. Klein, 104 U.S. 18, 26 L.Ed. 635, Miss.1881. Cf. Strode v. Kramer, 293 Ky. 354, 169 S.W.2d 29, 1943. See American Law of Property § 14.16; Edmonds, Problems in Administration of Partnership Assets, [1951] U. of Ill.L.Forum 507.

By statute in a few states the personal representative of the deceased partner is entitled to administer the partnership estate upon giving a special bond. Woerner on Administration §§ 128, 129; annotation, 121 A.L.R. 860. But if such state later adopts the Uniform Partnership Act there is probably an implied repeal of this procedure and a restoration to the orthodox practice. Davis v. Hutchinson, 36 F.2d 309, C.C.A.Alaska 1929; note, 22 Wash.L.R. 35.

[27] Giddens v. Reddoch, 207 Ala. 297, 92 So. 848, 25 A.L.R. 381, 1921; see American Law of Property § 14.16, and supra note 26.

[28] Richardson v. Warfield, 252 Mass. 518, 148 N.E. 141, 1925; Alexander v. Fidelity Trust Co., 249 F. 1, C.C.A.Pa.1918.

[29] Oslund v. Peterson, 160 N.W. 899, Iowa 1917; Richardson v. Warfield, supra note 28.

### *Transfer in Fraud of Creditors*

When the deceased conveyed property in his lifetime in order to defraud his creditors, the transfer may be set aside for the benefit of the latter,[30] provided that there are not sufficient other assets to satisfy their claims.[31] However, the conveyance can only be set aside to the extent that it is necessary to pay the debts,[32] and the deceased's legatees, distributees, heirs or devisees are not allowed to share in the amount so recovered, as the deceased himself would not be permitted to do so.[33] Most jurisdictions allow the personal representative to prosecute the suit for the benefit of creditors,[34] though in some the action must be brought by the creditors themselves.[35] Assets of this nature may be used only for the satisfaction of creditors' claims and the surplus, if any, must be returned to the defendant, rather than distributed to the beneficiaries of the estate.

### *Gifts Causa Mortis*

A somewhat similar situation exists in the case of personal property disposed of by way of gift causa mortis, which is commonly said to be revocable at will.[36] A person is not permitted to give away his property in this manner to the prejudice of his creditors. In this respect the gift causa mortis is treated as if it were a legacy. The personal representative may recover such donations or their proceeds in the hands of the donee to the extent that they are necessary for the satisfaction of the claims of the deceased's creditors.[37] His recovery is limited to this amount

30 Chester County Trust Co. v. Pugh, 241 Pa. 124, 88 A. 319, 50 L.R.A.,N.S., 320, Ann.Cas.1915B, 211, 1913; Shears v. Rogers, 3 B. & Ad. 362, 110 Eng.Rep. 137, 1832. And see cases infra notes 34, 35.

31 Berryman v. Dore, 47 Idaho 582, 277 P. 565, 1929, noted, 14 Minn.L.R. 297.

32 Shiels v. Nathan, 12 Cal.App. 604, 108 P. 34, 1910; Berryman v. Dore, supra note 31.

33 Berryman v. Dore, supra note 31; Stierlin v. Teschemacher, 333 Mo. 1208, 64 S.W.2d 647, 91 A.L.R. 121, 1933. And see infra note 34, and annotation, 148 A.L.R. 230.

34 Morgan v. Catherwood, 95 Ind. App. 266, 167 N.E. 618, 1929 (statute); Howell v. Howell, 211 Iowa 70, 232 N.W. 816, 1930; In re McCluskey's Estate, 116 Me. 212, 100 A. 977, 1917; Chester County Trust Co. v. Pugh, supra note 30. See Evans, The Intermeddler and the Fraudulent Transferee as Executor, 25 Geo.L.J. 78; Model Probate Code § 125; note, 45 Yale L.J. 504, 510; annotations, 91 A.L.R. 133, 103 A.L.R. 555.

35 Bank of Willow Springs v. Lillibridge, 316 Mo. 968, 293 S.W. 116, 1927.

36 See note, 7 N.Y.U.Intermural L.R. 139.

37 Mitchell v. Pease, 7 Cush.(Mass.) 350, 1851; Rosenau v. Merchants'

and the next of kin are not interested in the recovery.[38] The subject-matter of the gift should not be taken to pay creditors if there are sufficient general assets for this purpose.[39] In such suits it is not necessary to show that the donor made the transfer to defraud creditors,[40] which is required in the case of the deceased's transfers described in the preceding paragraph.

*Property Obtained by Fraud Upon the Deceased*

If a transfer was obtained by fraud upon the deceased different considerations apply. Here the deceased had a right to recover the property and this passes to his personal representative as a general asset if the property obtained was personalty.[41] When realty was obtained through fraud on the deceased, generally the heirs or devisees should sue,[42] though the personal representative may recover in some jurisdictions by statute,[43] and also when he has been ordered to sell the property in order to pay debts.[44]

*Powers of Appointment*

A power of appointment is the power given to a person called the donee to designate, usually by his will, the persons who take the donor's property.[45] If the power is general,[46] that is if the donee can appoint anyone he pleases, it is usually held that if the

Nat. Bank of Dickinson, 56 N.D. 123, 216 N.W. 335, 60 A.L.R. 1040, 1927, noted 26 Mich.L.R. 700. See supra § 45. A similar rule applies to Totten Trusts. See supra § 41.

38 Seybold v. Grand Forks Nat. Bank, 5 N.D. 460, 67 N.W. 682, 1896.

39 See supra note 38.

40 See Rosenau v. Merchants' Nat. Bank of Dickinson, supra note 37; § 45 supra.

41 Combs v. Roark, 206 Ky. 454, 267 S.W. 210, 1924; Parker v. Simpson, 180 Mass. 334, 62 N.E. 401, 1902.

42 Feeney v. Runyan, 316 Ill. 246, 147 N.E. 114, 1925; Campbell v. Kuhn, 45 Mich. 513, 8 N.W. 523, 40 Am.Rep. 479, 1881; Neelen v. Holzhauer, 193 Wis. 196, 124 N.W. 497, 53 A.L.R. 359, 1927. See Parker v. Simpson, supra note 41. But the tort right of action for damages passes to the personal representative. Zartner v. Holzhauer, 204 Wis. 18, 234 N.W.2d 508, 76 A.L.R. 396, 1931.

43 Wheeler v. McKeon, 137 Minn. 92, 162 N.W. 1070, 1 A.L.R. 1514, 1917 (mental incapacity); Kashouty v. Deep, 75 App.D.C. 259, 126 F.2d 233, 1942.

44 McCully v. McCrary, 269 Pa. 581, 112 A. 755, 1921. And see Neelen v. Holzhauer, supra note 42.

45 Cf. Restatement, Property § 318. See supra § 81.

46 When the power is special, viz., can be only exercised in favor of a group not including the donee, creditors have no rights except to the extent that the creation of the power was in fraud of creditors. See Prescott v. Wordell, 319 Mass. 118, 65 N.E.2d 19, 1946; Restatement, Property § 326.

power is exercised by the donee's will [47] the property is subject to the claims of his creditors if his other property is insufficient to satisfy their demands.[48] This is on the theory that the donee must be just before he may be generous. Dependent on the intent indicated in the will, the donee's exercise of a general power may result in making the property available to pay his pecuniary legacies.[49] It thus appears that while the donee does not "own" the property, it may be in substance assets of his estate.

*Survival of Choses in Action*

Of course a chose in action which the decedent had in his lifetime is not assets of his estate unless it survives his death. While contract actions survived generally at common law,[50] a cause of action for breach of marriage did not, at least in absence of damage to the personal estate, since it fell within the principle of actio personalis moritur cum persona.[51] In recent years there has been a legislative tendency to increase the number of actions which survive and in some states all, or practically all, actions now survive.[52] In general, the answer to the question as to whether a certain type of action survives in favor of the personal

[47] Creditors have no rights if the power is not exercised. Gilman v. Bell, 99 Ill. 144, 1881. This restriction has been criticized and is said not to apply where the donor creates a trust with a life estate and general power in himself; statutes also sometimes alter the rule. See Restatement, Property §§ 327, 328. In some states at least, a power is deemed exercised by the ordinary residuary clause of the will. Slayton v. Fitch Home, 293 Mass. 574, 200 N.E. 357, 104 A.L.R. 669, 1936; see notes, 55 Harv.L.R. 1025, 46 Mich.L.R. 273.

[48] Shattuck v. Burrage, 229 Mass. 448, 118 N.E. 889, 1918; Restatement, Property § 329; annotations, 59 A.L. R. 1510, 97 id. 1071, 121 id. 803. See also Simes, The Devolution of Title to Appointed Property, 22 Ill.L.R. 480, 504; Gold, The Classification of Some Powers of Appointment, 40 Mich.L.R. 337, 365; note, 41 Mich.L.R. 289. But see St. Matthews Bank v. De Charette, 259 Ky. 802, 83 S.W.2d 471, 99 A.L.R. 1146, 1935

[49] Jackson's Estate, 337 Pa. 561, 12 A.2d 338, 129 A.L.R. 819, 1940, noted, 17 Temple U.L.Q. 186.

[50] Sleeper v. Union Insurance Co., 65 Me. 385, 20 Am.Rep. 706, 1876; Raymond v. Fitch, 2 C.M. & R. 588, 150 Eng.Rep. 251, 1835. Under the influence of early statutes, most proprietary actions survived. 4 Edw. III, c 7, 1330; 31 Edw. III, c. 11, 1357; see also 3 & 4 Wm. IV, c. 42, § 2, 1833. See generally, Evans, Survival of Claims for and against Executors and Administrators, 19 Ky.L.J. 195, and infra notes 55, 56.

[51] Chamberlain v. Williamson, 2 M. & S. 408, 105 Eng.Rep. 433, 1814; Hovey v. Paige, 55 Me. 142, 1867 (paternity); see note, 3 So.Cal.L.R. 346. Cf. Warner v. Benham, 126 Wash. 393, 218 P. 260, 34 A.L.R. 1358, 1923, noted, 8 Minn.L.R. 335.

[52] Evans, A Comparative Study of the Statutory Survival of Tort Claims for and against Executors and Administrators, 29 Mich.L.R. 969; Win-

representative so as to constitute assets is the same as the matter of whether a similar claim would survive against the representative so as to constitute a valid claim against the estate.[53] Hence the general problem is postponed and will be considered more fully in the latter connection.[54]

Actions involving wrongful death demand special attention at this point. At common law an action for personal injury did not survive the death of the injured party, regardless of whether or not injury caused the death,[55] but in many states the statutes provide that the action survives.[56] At common law neither one's personal representatives nor his dependents had a right of action for his wrongful death,[57] but in most jurisdictions a right is given by statutes, commonly called Lord Campbell's Acts after the parent English statute.[58] If both survival and death acts exist and there are no contrary provisions, it would seem that there are independent rights to recovery on both, and some cases so hold.[59] However, the prevailing judicial attitude seems to be that if the decedent's own claim for the injury was compromised,[60] reduced

field, Death as Affecting Liability in Tort, 29 Col.L.R. 239; note, 48 Harv. L.R. 1008.

53 Ibid. This is not always true in either the older or the modern law. See Russell's Case, 5 Co. 27a, 77 Eng. Rep. 91, 1565 (representative can bring trover); Hambly v. Trott, Cowp. 371, 98 Eng.Rep. 1136, 1776 (representative cannot be sued in trover but plaintiff may waive the tort and sue in contract). See also Evans, supra note 52 at 976.

54 See infra § 126.

55 Kelley v. Union Pac. Ry. Co., 16 Colo. 455, 27 P. 1058, 1891 (but allowing deceased passenger to recover in contract); see also Winfield, supra note 52.

56 See Evans, supra note 52; note, 44 Harv.L.R. 980.

57 Higgins v. Butcher, Yelv. 89, 80 Eng.Rep. 61, 1607. See Winfield, supra note 52.

58 See Schumacher, Rights of Action under Death and Survival Acts, 29 Mich.L.R. 114; note, 44 Harv.L.R. 980.

59 Kelley v. Union Pac. Ry. Co., supra note 55; St. Louis & S. F. R. Co. v. Goode, 42 Okl. 784, 142 P. 1185, L.R.A.1915E, 1141, 1914; May Coal Co. v. Robinette, 120 Ohio St. 110, 165 N.E. 576, 64 A.L.R. 441, 1929. But see Susemiehl v. Red River Lumber Co., 305 Ill.App. 473, 27 N.E. 285, affirmed 376 Ill. 138, 33 N.E.2d 211, 1941, noted, 35 Ill.L.R. 479, 19 Chi-Kent L.R. 110; Perry v. Louisville & Nashville R. Co., 199 Ky. 396, 251 S.W. 202, 39 A.L.R. 560, 1923; Olivier v. Houghton County St. Ry., 138 Mich. 242, 101 N.W. 530, 1904. See note, 15 St. John's L.R. 58.

60 Mellon v. Goodyear, 277 U.S. 335, 48 Sup.Ct. 541, 72 L.Ed. 906, 1928; Morton v. Georgia R. & E. Co., 145 Ga. 516, 89 S.E. 488, 1916. But see Rowe v. Richards, 35 S.D. 201, 151 N.W. 1001, L.R.A.1915E 1075, Ann. Cas.1918A, 294, 1915.

to judgment,[61] or barred by limitation [62] there can be no recovery under the death act. This position has been justified on the ground that it prevents double recovery, but in few states does recovery under either the survival or the death acts alone adequately compensate for the damages suffered by the decedent and his family.[63]

In a few states the dependents may sue upon a death claim in their own names,[64] but more frequently it is provided that the personal representative shall sue for their benefit.[65] Generally, however, the proceeds are not part of the general assets for satisfaction of creditors' claims,[66] and if there are no surviving beneficiaries the administrator cannot recover.[67] Under a few statutes the amount recovered is charged with the payment of certain debts.[68]

*Debts of Personal Representatives*

At common law if a testator appointed his debtor as executor the debt was deemed discharged as the executor could not sue himself.[69] An exception to this rule existed in case there were

61 Perry v. Louisville & Nashville Railroad Co., supra note 59. But see St. Louis & S. F. R. Co. v. Goode and May Coal Co. v. Robinette, both supra note 59.

62 Flynn v. New York, N. H. & H. R. Co., 283 U.S. 53, 51 S.Ct. 357, 75 L.Ed. 357, 72 A.L.R. 1311, 1931; Kelliher v. New York C. & H. R. R. Co., 212 N.Y. 207, 105 N.E. 824, L.R.A. 1915E 1178, 1914; Howard v. Bell Telephone Co., 306 Pa. 518, 160 A. 613, 1932. But see Dusek v. Pennsylvania, 68 F.2d 131, C.C.A.Ind., 1933 (not barred at decedent's death); annotations, 72 A.L.R. 1313; 99 id. 259.

63 See Oppenheim, The Survival of Tort Actions and the Action for Wrongful Death—A Survey and a Proposal, 16 Tulane L.R. 386; note, 44 Harv.L.R. 980.

64 Wettach, Wrongful Death and Contributory Negligence, 16 N.C.L.R. 211, 221. Even under the majority rule, the beneficiary may sue if the administrator fails to do so. Cudney v. United Power & L. Corp., 142 Kan. 613, 51 P.2d 28, 101 A.L.R. 835, 1935.

65 Treadway v. St. Louis, I. M. & S. R. Co., 127 Ark. 211, 191 S.W. 930, 1917; and see supra note 64.

66 Ellenberg v. Arthur, 178 S.C. 490, 183 S.E. 306, 103 A.L.R. 437, 1936; Beauvais v. Springfield Institute for Sav., 303 Mass. 136, 20 N.E.2d 957, 124 A.L.R. 611, 1939 (separate judgments for survival and death claims). But it has been held that the administrator's bond covers the proceeds of a death action. Boyd v. Richie, 159 S.C. 55, 155 S.E. 844, 1930, noted, 8 N.Y.U.L.Q.R. 691.

67 Wilder v. Charleston Transit V. Co., 120 W.Va. 319, 197 S.E. 814, 117 A.L.R. 948, 1938.

68 N.Y.Decedent Estate Law § 133 (medical and funeral expenses if included in action or settlement).

69 Wankford v. Wankford, 1 Salk. 299, 91 Eng.Rep. 265, 1795; Nedham's Case, 8 Coke, 135a, 77 Eng.Rep. 678,

not sufficient other assets to satisfy creditors.[70] When a debtor was appointed administrator this was deemed not to discharge the debt but only to suspend it, as the selection of the administrator was not the act of the deceased.[71] In equity the general rule as to executors was not followed, but his debt was deemed to be paid to the estate and he was obliged to include it in his accounts.[72] Either on account of statutes or through the adoption of the equity rule, the American courts now hold that the debt of the executor, like that of the administrator, is not discharged unless there is a will making express provision forgiving the debt.[73] The debt is deemed to be assets in the representative's hands; hence if he is individually solvent, his bondsmen are liable if he does not account for the debt,[74] though this should not be true if the representative is insolvent.[75]

1612. This rule has been recently applied in England so as to release all of several joint debtors, one of whom was named executor. Jenkins v. Jenkins, [1928] 2 K.B. 501, noted, 14 Corn.L.Q. 215.

70 Woodward v. Lord Darcy, Plowd. 184, 75 Eng.Rep. 282, 1557.

71 Ferrebee v. Doxey, 6 Ired.L.(N.C.) 448, 1846; Wankford v. Wankford, supra note 69.

72 Fleming v. Bolling, 3 Call.(Va.) 75, 1801; Ingle v. Richards, 28 Beav. 366, 54 Eng.Rep. 406, 1860.

73 In re Parker's Estate, 189 Iowa 1131, 179 N.W. 525, 1920; State v. Smith, 140 Me. 255, 37 A.2d 246, 1944; American Surety Co. v. Norton, 238 S.W. 1111, Tex.Com.App.1922; see note, 14 Corn.L.Q. 215, 217; Model Probate Code § 122.

74 Wachsmuth v. Penn Mut. Life Ins. Co., infra note 75 (if solvent at time of appointment); United States Fidelity & Guaranty Co. of Baltimore, Md., v. Jones, 22 Ohio App. 345, 153 N.E. 281, 1926. Cf. McCarty v. Frazer, 62 Mo. 263, 1876. See Sunderland, An Inroad on Fiduciary Integrity, 4 Mich.L.R. 349.

75 Wachsmuth v. Penn. Mut. Life Insurance Co., 241 Ill. 409, 89 N.E. 787, 26 L.R.A.,N.S., 411, 132 Am.St. Rep. 226, 1909; In re Hayer's Estate, 233 Iowa 1343, 11 N.W.2d 593, 1943; Baucus v. Barr, 107 N.Y. 624, 13 N.E. 939, 1887; Model Probate Code § 122. But see King v. Murray, 286 Mass. 492, 190 N.E. 526, 1934; American Surety Co. v. Norton, supra note 73; In re Howey's Estate, 216 Wis. 94, 256 N.W. 620, 1934.

## COLLECTION AND CARE OF ASSETS

**117. The personal representative is enjoined with the duty of exercising the care that a diligent person would take in the management of his own affairs to collect the tangible property and choses in action belonging to decedent. To this end he is authorized to commence appropriate actions or to compromise claims. Some jurisdictions require court approval of all compromises, and this is always desirable for the protection of the personal representative.**

**The executor or administrator is chargeable with the same degree of responsibility as indicated above with reference to the preservation and realization of the assets after they have been reduced to his possession.**

### *Collection of Assets*

The personal representative has the right and the duty to gather the assets of the estate. This includes the reduction of the tangible personalty to possession and the collection of choses in action. Of course if these things can be accomplished without suit this should be done; otherwise the representative should ordinarily bring suit for this purpose.

### *Discharge and Compromise of Debts*

The personal representative is authorized to receive full payment of an obligation in favor of the estate and to discharge the same.[1] If the representative extends the time of payment of a debt, he has been held liable for the losses occurring because of subsequent insolvency of the debtor.[2]

In absence of statute, an executor or administrator may compromise a debt without previous court sanction, provided this is advantageous to the estate.[3] The latter question is not ordinarily

1 Riley v. Moseley, 44 Miss. 37, 1870; In re Nolan's Trust Estate, 251 Pa. 309, 96 A. 714, 1916.

2 In re Gardner's Estate, 199 Pa. 524, 49 A. 346, 1901.

3 Walker v. Schertz, 201 Ill.App. 225, 1916; Jensen v. Murphy, 199 Iowa 524, 202 N.W. 232, 1925; Montgomery v. Mutual Life Ins. Co. of New York, 111 Miss. 6, 71 So. 162, 1916; Simes v. Ward, 78 N.H. 533, 103 A. 310, 1918. Under some statutes court approval is necessary for an effective compromise. Jones v. Gilliam, 109 Tex. 552, 212 S.W. 930, 1919. Other statutes for court approval do not abrogate the common-law power but simply give the representative added security that he acted judiciously. Wunderlich v. Bowen, 193 Ark. 284, 100 S.W.2d 80, 1937; In re Lucas' Estate, 23 Cal.2d 454, 144 P.2d 340, 1944.

passed upon until the presentation of the representative's accounts. Due to this fact the representative runs the risk that he may be charged with making an unwise settlement. Accordingly, it is advisable to secure court approval in advance before effecting a compromise, and statutes often provide for this procedure.[4] This court sanction will ordinarily protect the executor or administrator against subsequent claims that the settlement was not a prudent one.[5]

*Collection by Suit*

When a cause of action existed in the lifetime of the deceased, the personal representative should sue thereon in his official capacity.[6] If the cause of action came into being after the decedent's death, as by the conversion of the estate's property, the executor or administrator may proceed, at his option, in either his personal or his official capacity.[7] Of course in either event the recovery inures to the benefit of the estate. The authority of the personal representative relates back after his appointment to the date of the decedent's death, and he may sue on account of injuries to the decedent's estate occurring in the interim.[8]

*Courts—Discovery*

In absence of statutory provisions the representative should proceed against the estate's debtors in the court of law or of equity in which the case would normally have been commenced had it been prosecuted by the deceased in his lifetime.[9] The court of probate does not obtain jurisdiction over such proceed-

[4] Evans v. Tucker, 101 Fla. 688, 135 So. 305, 85 A.L.R. 170, 1931; see supra note 3.

[5] See supra notes 3, 4.

[6] Kent v. Bothwell, 152 Mass. 341, 25 N.E. 721, 9 L.R.A. 258, 1890; Evans v. Supreme Council of Royal Arcanum, 223 N.Y. 497, 120 N.E. 93, 1 A.L.R. 163, 1918. A creditor cannot ordinarily maintain an action to recover assets of the estate. Ryan v. Kelsey, 259 F. 945, 7 A.L.R. 234, C.C.A.N.J.1919. But he may if the representative neglects, or refuses to sue. Mead Co. v. Doerfler, 146 Neb. 21, 18 N.W.2d 524, 158 A.L.R. 724, 1945.

[7] Hanover Fire Ins. Co. v. Street, 234 Ala. 537, 176 So. 350, 1937; Thurmond v. Guyan Valley Coal Co., 85 W. Va. 501, 102 S.E. 221, 1920.

[8] Dempsey v. McNabb, 73 Md. 433, 21 A. 378, 1871; Brackett v. Hoitt, 20 N.H. 257, 1850; Brown v. Lewis, 9 R.I. 497, 1870; Y.B. 18 Hen. VI, 22 pt. 7. See Warren, Problems in Probate and Administration, 32 Harv.L. R. 315, 318, 319.

[9] McDonald v. First Nat. Bank, 58 N.D. 49, 224 N.W. 676, 1929; Johnson v. Nelson, 341 Ill. 119, 173 N.E. 77, 88 A.L.R. 849, 1930; In re Kallenbach's Estate, 184 Wis. 171, 199 N.W. 152, 1924. Cf. Gilleylen v. Hallman, 141 Ark. 52, 216 S.W. 15, 1919.

ings simply by virtue of the fact that the former owner has died and his estate is in the process of administration. In some states there are statutes authorizing summary proceedings in the probate courts to command persons concealing or withholding property of the estate to produce the same.[10] These statutes do not generally authorize the court to determine the disputed title to personalty or to give judgment for a debt.[11] The proceedings are primarily matters of discovery,[12] and in absence of such statutes discovery may be obtained in the equity courts.[13] However, there is nothing to prevent the legislature from permitting the probate court to try claims in favor of the estate as well as claims against it, subject to the preservation of the constitutional right to trial by jury in the probate court or upon appeal to a court of record.[14] When the representative claims the property as his own the court of probate may have jurisdiction to determine the title.[15]

*Liability for Failure to Collect*

Of course a representative is not obliged to bring suit to recover amounts which are uncollectible, such as bad debts.[16] Furthermore, he is not charged with the duty of obtaining satisfaction of every claim which might possibly have been collected.[17] He is liable only for losses of assets due to his bad faith or failure to take such steps as a prudent person would pursue with reference to his own property.[18]

10 See infra notes 11, 12.

11 Raymond v. Raymond, 134 Ark. 484, 204 S.W. 311, 1918; Vogel v. Wachtel, 99 Ind.App. 269, 189 N.E. 425, 1934; Farmers' Bank & Trust Co. v. Sheffler, 78 Okl. 44, 186 P. 479, 1920; Estate of Schaefer, 189 Wis. 395, 207 N.W. 690, 1926. Cf. Bowers v. Cook, 132 Md. 432, 104 A. 420, 1918; In re Leonard's Estate, 113 Misc. 205, 185 N.Y.S. 243, 1920. But see authorities cited infra note 14.

12 In re Heinze's Estate, 224 N.Y. 1, 120 N.E. 63, 1918.

13 Mitchell v. Weaver, 242 Mass. 331, 136 N.E. 166, 1922.

14 Matter of Akin, 248 N.Y. 202, 161 N.E. 471, 1928; Matter of Leary, 285 N.Y. 693, 34 N.E.2d 383, 1941; Vazis v. Zimmer, 209 S.W. 909, Mo.1919; cf. Matter of Schaefer, 294 N.Y. 24, 60 N.E.2d 193, 1945. See note, 27 Corn. L.R. 580; Model Probate Code § 130 and comment thereto.

15 Security-First Nat. Bank v. King, 46 Wyo. 59, 23 P.2d 851, 90 A.L.R. 125, 1933; cf. Hartwig v. Flynn, 79 Kan. 595, 100 P. 642, 1909. See supra § 115 note 24 et seq.

16 Tolly v. Champion, 191 Ky. 114, 229 S.W. 90, 1921; In re Baldwin's Estate, 311 Mich. 288, 18 N.W.2d 827, 1945.

17 Citizens' Nat. Bank v. Brewer, 253 Ky. 630, 60 S.W.2d 745, 1934; O'Shea v. Hurley, 248 Mass. 191, 142 N.E. 919, 1924.

18 McCallister's Adm'r v. Stanley, 186 Ky. 836, 218 S.W. 237, 1920; In re Dolenty's Estate, 53 Mont. 33, 161

*Waste*

The same measure of diligence is required in the care of the estate's property as in its collection. Thus, there may be liability for failure to withdraw funds from a bank known to be in failing circumstances.[19] An administratrix has been charged with the loss occasioned by neglecting to sell certain rights to purchase stock, although she was not aware that they had value.[20] This conclusion was reached because it was considered that a prudent person would have investigated the marketability of the rights. A representative is responsible for losses incurred in the sale of property which he knew or should know was below the market value.[21] On the other hand, a representative is not liable for failure to sell property, which later depreciated, if his judgment that the property would increase in value was reasonably held.[22]

A representative was held responsible for negligently permitting cattle belonging to the estate to stray and become lost.[23] Of course an executor or administrator is liable for his conversion of the assets of the estate; this is true even if the conversion was only technical and not for the benefit of the representative, as where the latter permitted the deceased's interest in a partnership to be used in the formation of a corporation.[24] A personal representative was held responsible for the theft by his agent to whom he had intrusted money to carry to the bank,[25] although he is not ordinarily liable for his attorney's embezzlement of funds collected for the estate.[26] A special administrator is not liable for

P. 524, 1917; In re Kramer's Estate, 255 Pa. 595, 100 A. 447, 1917; In re Rosenthal's Estate, 269 App.Div. 507, 54 N.Y.S.2d 507, 1945.

19 In re Jankes' Estate, 193 Minn. 201, 258 N.W. 311, 1935, noted, 35 Col. L.R. 610. See infra § 124.

20 In re Belcher's Estate, 129 Misc. 218, 221 N.Y.S. 711, 1927.

21 Young v. Ray, 193 S.W. 608, Mo. App.1917; In re Reilly's Estate, 77 Pa.Super. 178, 1921.

22 In re McDermid's Estate, 109 Or. 633, 222 P. 295, 1924; In re Borell's Estate, 256 Pa. 523, 100 A. 953, 1917; In re Johnston's Estate, 107 Wash. 25, 181 P. 209, 1919. And see In re Pettigrew's Estate, 116 N.J.Eq. 566, 174 A. 478, 1934.

23 In re Pedroli's Estate, 47 Nev. 322, 221 P. 244, 1923.

24 Heap v. Heap, 258 Mich. 250, 242 N.W. 252, 1932. And see Meyers' Adm'r v. Meyers, 244 Ky. 248, 50 S.W. 2d 81, 1932.

25 McElhinny v. Minor, 91 W.Va. 755, 114 S.E. 147, 1922.

26 In re Bender's Estate, 278 Pa. 199, 122 A. 283, 1923 (here there was no negligence in the employment of the attorney who had been vouched for by the testator). But the administrator was liable when he turned over the estate funds to an attorney and allowed him to have exclusive control. Kaufman v. Kaufman, 292 Ky. 351, 166 S.W.2d 860, 144 A.L.R. 866, 1942.

injuries to furniture intrusted to a caretaker where the damages were less than storage charges.[27] The foregoing are a few examples of the many holdings upon what is, and what is not, waste by the personal representative. Each case is decided upon the principle that the executor and administrator is charged with the duty of exercising good faith and reasonable care and diligence in the preservation of the estate's assets.

At common law the representative who committed waste could be sued by creditors, legatees or distributees on account of the devastavit.[28] However, the usual manner of treatment of such cases at the present time is to charge the executor or administrator with the amount of such losses upon his account. If he then neglects or refuses to reimburse the estate therefor, action may be brought upon the administration bond.[29]

## TORTS OF PERSONAL REPRESENTATIVES

**118. An executor or administrator is liable personally for his torts committed in the course of the administration, and only in exceptional instances may he be reimbursed from the estate on account of being required to pay tort judgments so rendered against him.**

As a general rule the estate is not liable for torts of the personal representative committed in the course of the administration.[1] The representative is not an agent, nor is the estate deemed the principal in this situation. Hence the representative should be sued in his individual capacity for such wrongs, and judgment should be rendered against him individually.[2] The substantial

27 In re Williams' Estate, 55 Mont. 63, 173 P. 790, 1 A.L.R. 1639, 1918.

28 Charlton v. Low, 3 P.Wms. 328, 24 Eng.Rep. 1087, 1734.

29 In re Delaney's Estate, 41 Nev. 384, 171 P. 383, L.R.A.1918D, 1022, 1918; Brown v. American Surety Co., 181 Or. 564, 182 P.2d 357, 1947 (by administrator d. b. n.). See supra § 113.

1 Stockmen's State Bank v. Merchants' & Stockgrowers' Bank, 22 Ariz. 354, 197 P. 888, 1921 (conversion); Toner v. Meussdorffer, 123 Cal. 462, 56 P. 39, 1899 (fraud); Evans v. Dickey, 50 Ga.App. 127, 177 S.E. 87, 1934 (personal injuries); Bannigan v. Woodbury, 158 Mich. 206, 122 N.W. 531, 133 Am.St.Rep. 371, 1909 (same); Miller v. Jacobs, 361 Pa. 492, 65 A.2d 362, 1949. But see Ernest G. Beaudry v. Freeman, 73 Ga.App. 736, 38 S.E.2d 40, 1946; Ewing v. Wm. L. Foley, Inc., infra note 7. See generally, Fulda & Pond, Tort Liability of Trust Estates, 41 Col.L.R. 1332; annotations 44 A.L.R. 637, 127 id. 687.

2 Johnston v. Long, 30 Cal.2d 54, 181 P.2d 645, 1947, noted, 35 Cal.L.R. 586, 47 Col.L.R. 1377, 21 So.Cal.L.R. 199, 33 Va.L.R. 775; Fisher v. McNeely, 110 Wash. 283, 188 P. 478, 14 A.L.R. 369, 1920. See also cases su-

difference between actions against the representative in his official capacity and in his personal capacity lies in the form and effect of the judgment. In the former case the judgment is de bonis testatoris (or intestati) and justifies execution against the assets of the estate, while the latter runs de bonis propriis and can be satisfied only out of the representative's own property.

The representative who is sued individually cannot ordinarily be reimbursed from the estate,[3] though he may if he is guilty of no negligence,[4] or wrong,[5] or where the estate has benefited from the conduct of the representative.[6] In these exceptional cases suit has sometimes been allowed against the executor or administrator in his representative capacity.[7] It should be noticed that this transfers the decision of whether the case comes within the excepted class from the probate court to the tribunal in which the tort action is prosecuted.

## CONTRACTS OF PERSONAL REPRESENTATIVES

**119. The contracts of a personal representative bind him individually though they are for the benefit of the estate, and the other contracting party cannot ordinarily file a claim against the estate or proceed against the representative in his official capacity with reference to these agreements.**

**The representative is entitled to be reimbursed from the estate for the reasonable expenses of the funeral and of administering and preserving the estate. Accordingly, if the representative is personally insolvent, the creditors of such obligations may proceed against the representative in his official capacity or directly against the estate for payment.**

With respect to contracts made by the decedent, the personal representative is sued in his official capacity, and under the modern probate procedure such claims are presented to the personal

pra note 1 and infra note 7; annotations, 7 A.L.R. 408, 123 id. 458.

3 George v. Bean, 30 Miss. 147, 1855; Re Yetter, 44 App.Div. 404, 61 N.Y.S. 175, 1899.

4 Keating v. Stevenson, 21 App.Div. 604, 47 N.Y.S. 847, 1897.

5 Havill v. Newton, 202 Ill.App. 15, 1916 (where representative claimed property in good faith for the estate).

6 Schmitt v. Jaques, 26 Tex.Civ. App. 125, 62 S.W. 956, 1901.

7 Ewing v. Wm. L. Foley, Inc., 115 Tex. 222, 280 S.W. 499, 44 A.L.R. 627, 1926. Contra: Kirchner v. Muller, 280 N.Y. 23, 19 N.E.2d 665, 127 A.L.R. 681, 1939.

representative and allowed by the court before payment.[1] These items are truly claims against the decedent and his estate.

*Promises of Personal Representatives*

However, promises by the personal representative, though made in connection with the administration of the estate, are deemed to be his contracts and he must be sued thereon in his individual capacity.[2] As already pointed out,[3] the estate is not an entity and the case is not like one in which the principal is bound by the agent's authorized act. Nevertheless if the representative voluntarily pays the indebtedness which he incurs, he is entitled to be reimbursed if the expenditure is reasonable in amount and for the benefit of the estate.[4] Still, except for statutory provisions, the obligation cannot be treated as a debt of the decedent so that it may be presented to the court for allowance before payment.[5] The representative must pay such claims and pray that the expenditure should be allowed as an item of his account.[6] Of course he runs the risk that the court may decide on the accounting that the disbursement was not a proper one, either in kind or amount.[7] There has been some remedial legislation in this connection, either by way of alteration of the fundamental theory of contracts of personal representatives, or by provision for court approval before payment is made.[8]

*Particular Contracts*

The doctrine that the contracts of the personal representative bind him only and not the estate has been applied to agreements

1 See infra § 127. So with decedent's open balances liquidated by agreement of the representative. Kingman v. Soule, 132 Mass. 285, 1882. So also with the representative's agreement to pay valid debt of decedent. Schmittler v. Simon, 101 N.Y. 554, 5 N.E. 452, 54 Am.Rep. 737, 1886.

2 Wilton v. Eaton, 127 Mass. 174, 1879 (promise of representative in return for new promise to him by decedent's creditor to forbear suit). See generally Evans, The Contractual Obligations and Transfers of Personal Representatives, 7 N.Y.U.L.Q.R. 17.

3 See supra §§ 104, 118. "An 'estate' cannot become a party to a contract, because neither a person or an artificial legal entity." Miller v. Phoenix Ins. Co., 191 Minn. 586, 254 N.W. 915, 1934.

4 See infra notes 24–37.

5 See infra notes 8–16.

6 See infra notes 24–37.

7 See infra notes 29, 35–37.

8 Probate courts are often given jurisdiction to pass on claims for expenses of administration. In re Murnan's Estate, 151 Ohio St. 529, 87 N.E.2d 84, 1949; see note, 13 Mo.L.R. 89; cf. Model Probate Code §§ 136, 143(b). See also notes 11–13 infra.

to pay funeral expenses,[9] or for tombstones,[10] to engage an attorney,[11] or others,[12] to look after the affairs of the estate, to borrow money,[13] or to obtain supplies or materials,[14] or a lease to carry on the business of the deceased.[15] It should be repeated for the sake of emphasis that even if the contract is one for a proper expense of administration for which the personal representative may obtain credit in his account,[16] the other contracting party normally must look to the representative personally for payment.

*Limitations upon Individual Liability*

When a contract is made after the decedent's death, the representative cannot absolve himself from personal liability by enter-

[9] This was the common law rule. Corner v. Shew, 3 M. & W. 350, 150 Eng.Rep. 1179, 1828; Green v. Salmon, 8 Ad. & E. 348 note, 112 Eng. Rep. 869, 870, 1838. And see Sweeney v. Muldoon, 139 Mass. 304, 306, 31 N.E. 720, 52 Am.Rep. 708, 1885. But the estate is liable if some other person ordered the funeral. Kingman v. Soule, 132 Mass. 285, 1882; Sweeney v. Muldoon, supra. Statutes frequently are interpreted to bind the estate for such expenses, regardless of who ordered the funeral. Probably a certain laxity in the practice has arisen because funeral expenses are a preferred charge to ordinary debts, and only in case that the estate or the personal representative is insolvent or the expenditures are excessive can it make any practical difference whether the representative is sued personally or in his official capacity. See Joseph S. Waterman & Sons v. Hook, 246 Mass. 522, 141 N.E. 596, 30 A.L.R. 440, 1923; Kelly v. Snow, 168 Minn. 298, 210 N.W. 105, 1926; Rocap v. Blackwell, 79 Ind.App. 232, 137 N.E. 726, 1926; In re Kelly's Estate, 183 Wis. 485, 198 N.W. 280, 1924.

[10] Call v. Garland, 124 Me. 27, 125 A. 225, 1924.

[11] Carpenter v. Hazel, 128 Ark. 416, 194 S.W. 225, 1922; Eaton v. Walker, 244 Mass. 23, 138 N.E. 798, 1923; In re Thiede's Estate, 102 Neb. 747, 169 N.W. 435, 1918. Cf. McMillen's Ex'rs v. McElroy, 186 Ky. 644, 217 S.W. 927, 1920 (can bind estate for attorney's services to sustain the will); Zagoren v. Superior Court, 117 Cal. App. 548, 4 P.2d 279, 1931 (statute absolves representative).

[12] E. A. Strout Farm Agency v. Worthen, 81 N.H. 95, 122 A. 327, 1923 (brokerage contract); Barrett v. King, 64 Pa.Super. 601, 1916. And see Jones v. Gilliam, 109 Tex. 552, 212 S.W. 930, 1919; cf. In re Rule's Estate, 25 Cal.App.2d 1, 152 P.2d 1003, 515 A.L.R. 1319, 1944 (statute).

[13] Exchange Nat. Bank v. Betts' Estate, 103 Kan. 807, 176 P. 660, 3 A.L.R. 1604, 1918, noted, 19 Col.L.R. 77, 3 Minn.L.R. 357 (estate not liable); Boyd v. Johnston, 89 Tenn. 284, 14 S.W. 804, 1890. Cf. Swanberg v. National Surety Co., 86 Mont. 340, 283 P. 761, 1930 (statute).

[14] Riedy v. Bidwell, 70 Cal.App. 552, 233 P. 995, 1925. But cf. Wilder Grain Co. v. Felker, 296 Mass. 177, 5 N.E.2d 207, 108 A.L.R. 385, 1936, noted, 36 Mich.L.R. 144 (feed for dececent's animals furnished before administrator was appointed).

[15] In re Thurber's Estate, 311 Ill. 211, 142 N.E. 493, 1921.

[16] See infra notes 24–37.

ing into the agreement, "as executor." [17] This expression is deemed to be merely descriptio personæ. Even if the contract is in the name of the estate "by" the personal representative, the courts are inclined to hold the latter is still bound personally because the estate cannot be held.[18] It is true that a representative may stipulate by express provision against his personal liability,[19] and in this case the promise has been interpreted as one by the executor to perform only in so far as assets and court approval permit.[20]

*Insolvency of Personal Representative*

The general rule that contracts of the personal representative subject him only to personal liability sometimes causes hardship. In certain instances the courts depart from the orthodox doctrine. Thus, in case of insolvency of the executor or administrator, suit has been permitted against him in his representative capacity upon contracts made after decedent's death.[21] The same is true of contracts made in accordance with the will of the decedent.[22] These decisions can be supported upon the equitable basis that as the expenditure, if reasonable, would be charged against the estate eventually, this should be done in the first instance if the other contracting party would otherwise be remediless. The orthodox position also works badly in the counterclaim cases, in which the plaintiff's claim is by or against the representative in one capacity while the counterclaim is in the other capacity. The courts generally deny the use of the counterclaim

17 Rittenhouse v. Ammerman, 64 Mo. 197, 27 Am.Rep. 215, 1876; Schmittler v. Simon, supra note 1; Dallas County v. Club Land & Cattle Co., 95 Tex. 200, 66 S.W. 294, 1902; Lovenskiold v. Nueces Hotel Co., 208 S.W. 759, Tex.Civ.App.1919.

18 Germania Bank v. Michaud, 62 Minn. 459, 65 N.W. 70, 30 L.R.A. 286, 54 Am.St.Rep. 653, 1895. See Call v. Garland, 124 Me. 27, 125 A. 225, 1924. But see Grafton National Bank v. Wing, 172 Mass. 513, 52 N.E. 1067, 43 L.R.A. 831, 70 Am.St.Rep. 303, 1887.

19 Jones Brewing Co. v. Flaherty, 80 N.H. 571, 120 A. 432, 1923; Grafton Nat. Bank v. Wing, supra note 18; Banking Co. v. Morehead, 116 N.C. 413, 21 S.E. 191, 1895; Beattie v. Latimer, 42 S.C. 313, 20 S.E. 53, 1894. See annotation, 138 A.L.R. 155.

20 See Call v. Garland, supra note 18.

21 In re Murray's Estate, 56 Or. 132, 107 P. 19, 1910; Willis v. Sharp, 113 N.Y. 586, 21 N.E. 705, 4 L.R.A. 493, 1889; Jones v. Peabody, infra note 39.

22 Wade v. Pope, 44 Ala. 690, 1870; Lund & Seamands v. Riggs, 174 Iowa 79, 156 N.W. 161, 1916.

in such cases,[23] although it would seem that they should consider the equitable instead of bare legal interests involved.

*Allowance of Expenses of Administration*

While expenditures by the personal representative may not be regarded as debts of the deceased, he may be allowed disbursements for reasonable costs and expenses of the administration. The items must be for proper purposes and must be reasonable in amount. Thus, expenditures for funeral expenses may be allowed, if reasonable.[24] The same is true of tombstones and markers,[25] and the amount paid for care of the cemetery lot, at least provided that the estate is solvent.[26] Travelling expenses incurred in preserving assets of the estate,[27] as well as the cost of the harvesting of fruit grown on the decedent's land,[28] are proper expenditures. Whether the representative, entitled to the rents of land by will or statute, is authorized to employ a real estate agent to collect them is dubious and may depend on the circumstances.[29]

In absence of statute the cost of the representative's official bond is deemed an expense of qualifying, rather than a cost of administration and must be borne by him personally.[30] At any rate, when the bond is continued for an unreasonable amount or

[23] Seaver v. Weston, 163 Mass. 202, 39 N.E. 1013, 1895; Patterson v. Patterson, 59 N.Y. 574, 17 Am.Rep. 384, 1875.

[24] Ward v. Wright, 197 Ky. 148, 246 S.W. 123, 1923; In re Kingston's Estate, 182 N.Y.S. 528, 1918. As to the reasonableness of various items, see Oster's Ex'r v. Ohlman, 187 Ky. 341, 219 S.W. 187, 1920, holding that the cost of a lunch for those participating in a wake was a proper item, though the cost of cards of thanks was not.

[25] Galloway v. Sewell, 162 Ark. 627, 258 S.W. 655, 1924; Gooch v. Beasley, 137 Tenn. 407, 193 S.W. 132, 1917; Richardson v. McCloskey, 276 S.W. 680, Tex.Com.App.1925; Holt v. Holt, 96 W.Va. 337, 123 S.E. 53, 1924 (but not for markers of other members of the family).

[26] Galloway v. Sewell and Gooch v. Beasley, both supra note 25. See infra § 128.

[27] Holland v. Doke, 135 Ark. 372, 205 S.W. 648, 1919 (in addition to commissions); In re Parker's Estate, 186 Cal. 668, 200 P. 619, 1921.

[28] Lamb Davis Lumber Co. v. Stowell, 96 Wash. 46, 164 P. 593, L.R.A. 1917E 966, 1917.

[29] Cf. Farley v. Davis, 10 Wash.2d 62, 116 P.2d 263, 155 A.L.R. 1302, 1941 (allowed) with In re Rodger's Estate, 147 Misc. 344, 264 N.Y.S. 624, 1933 (not allowed). See infra note 35.

[30] Eaker v. Husbands, 263 Ky. 283, 92 S.W.2d 43, 1936; In re Buck's Estate, 220 S.W. 714, Mo.App.1920; Jarvis v. Drew, 215 S.W. 970, Tex.Civ.App.1919. Cf. Floyd v. Thomason, 148 Ga. 208, 96 S.E. 175, 1918. But statutes now frequently make it part of the cost of administration. Eaker v. Husbands and In re Buck's Estate, both supra.

if there is delay in administering the estate, the excessive cost of the bond should not be borne by the estate.[31]

Reasonable attorney fees paid by the personal representative for services rendered on behalf of the estate may be allowed as proper expenses of administration.[32] The allowance lies in the sound discretion of the court upon the final accounting.[33] The fact that the representative has paid an unauthorized attorney fee is no reason why the payment should be credited to the executor.[34] If an attorney, or other person, is engaged to perform some part of the executorial function, this expense must be paid by the representative personally.[35] Usually legal expenses incurred by the heirs must be borne by them.[36] When the attorney represents the administrator's personal interest, the fees cannot be allowed from estate funds.[37]

An executor or administrator who is a lawyer is not expected to perform legal services for the estate gratis. He is justified in engaging a lawyer to perform this work and the expense is

31 In re Macky's Estate, 73 Colo. 1, 213 P. 131, 1923; In re Baldwin's Estate, 311 Mich. 288, 18 N.W.2d 827, 1945.

32 McKenzie v. Jensen, 212 Ala. 92, 101 So. 755, 1924 (though litigation was unsuccessful); In re Macky's Estate, supra note 31; Clements v. Fletcher, 161 Ga. 21, 129 S.E. 846, 1925; Stover v. Durfee, 219 Mich. 566, 189 N.W. 14, 1922. Cf. In re Read's Estate, 24 N.J.Misc. 305, 49 A. 2d 138, 1946 (foreign counsel). See supra § 102. But the representative who unsuccessfully claims that property belongs to the estate is not entitled to have his legal expenses paid from that property. McAdoo v. Dickson, 175 Tenn. 598, 136 S.W.2d 518, 126 A.L.R. 1345, 1940. As to expenses of one who was not properly appointed, see annotation, 4 A.L.R.2d 160.

33 In re Machado's Estate, 186 Cal. 246, 199 P. 505, 1921. Hence the probate court will not order the attorney to repay the excessive fees. Jackson v. Superior Court of Los Angeles County, 210 Cal. 59, 290 P. 448, 70 A. L.R. 475, 1930. But see note, 44 Yale L.J. 153.

34 In re O'Reilly's Estate, 27 Ariz. 222, 231 P. 916, 1925.

35 In re Parker's Estate, infra note 39 (watching stock market); Appeal of Larrabee, 98 N.J.Eq. 655, 130 A. 195, 1925 (making up account); In re Brodbeck's Estate, 123 Misc. 743, 206 N.Y.S. 142, 1924 (sale of realty). See supra note 29. Cf. Morris v. Morris, 210 Mich. 36, 177 N.W. 266, 1920.

36 In re Balke's Estate, 68 Ariz. 373, 206 P.2d 732, 1949 (foreign consul representing heirs); In re Ross' Estate, 179 Cal. 358, 182 P. 303, 1919; In re Colburn's Estate, 186 Iowa 590, 173 N.W. 35, 1919. But see In re Engebretson's Estate, 68 S.D. 255, 1 N.W. 2d 351, 1941.

37 In re Peterson's Estate, 38 Idaho 195, 220 P. 1086, 1923 (establishing representative's personal claim against estate); In re McClellan's Estate, 192 Iowa 384, 183 N.W. 398, 1921; Goode v. Reynolds, 208 Ky. 441, 271 S.W. 600, 63 A.L.R. 631, 1925.

properly credited to his account.[38] If the attorney-personal representative performs the legal services himself, by the orthodox view he is not entitled to compensation in addition to his commissions.[39] Likewise if the services are performed by a law partner of the executor or administrator or the law firm of which he is a member, no allowance is permitted.[40] The reason assigned for these holdings is that the representative's personal interest in the charges conflicts with his official duty to scrutinize the amount of the attorney's bill. This may be sound enough in theory; yet it tends to decrease the efficiency and increase the legal costs of the administration. The probate court, in its allowance or disallowance of the item, should be able to afford sufficient protection to other interested parties. The latter can obtain protection against exorbitant fees by objecting to items of the account for legal services performed by the personal representative.

38 In re Graham's Estate, 187 Cal. 222, 201 P. 456, 18 A.L.R. 631, 1921; Doss v. Stevens, 13 Colo.App. 535, 59 P. 67, 1899; In re Sternberg's Estate, 204 S.W.2d 761, Mo.1947 (trust company having lawyers in its employ).

39 In re Parker's Estate, 200 Cal. 132, 251 P. 907, 49 A.L.R. 1025, 1927, noted, 15 Cal.L.R. 339; Willard v. Bassett, 27 Ill. 37, 79 Am.Dec. 393, 1861; Needham v. Needham, 34 Idaho 193, 200 P. 346, 1921. Contra: Jones v. Peabody, 182 Wash. 148, 45 P.2d 915, 100 A.L.R. 64, 1935, noted, 49 Harv.L.R. 915. Cf. Holding v. Allen, 150 Tenn. 669, 266 S.W. 772, 36 A.L.R. 743, 1924 (holding executor's fees may be increased by his rendering of legal services). In some states express statutes permit the representative to be allowed fees for his legal services. Parker v. Wright, 103 N.J.Eq. 535, 143 A. 870, 1928; In re Hallock's Estate, 214 App.Div. 323, 212 N.Y.S. 82, 1925; see Model Probate Code § 103. In other jurisdictions statutes permitting a personal representative to be allowed fees for extraordinary services are sometimes interpreted as allowing them additional compensation for legal services. John v. Sharp, 148 Ala. 665, 41 So. 635, 1906; Davidson v. Story, 106 Ga. 799, 32 S.E. 867, 1899; Re Wilson's Estate, 83 Neb. 252, 119 N.W. 522, 1909; Sloan v. Duffy, 117 Wis. 480, 94 N.W. 342, 1903. But see Doss v. Stevens, supra note 38; Wisner v. Mabley's Estate, 70 Mich. 271, 38 N.W. 262, 1888.

40 In re Parker's Estate, supra note 39; Taylor v. Wright, 93 Ind. 121, 1884; Liles' Succession, 24 La.Ann. 490, 1872. Cf. Bendall's Distributees v. Bendall's Adm'r, 24 Ala. 295, 60 Am.Dec. 469, 1854. As to the possibility of double commissions as personal representative and also as trustee, see National City Bank v. Brennan, 259 N.Y. 497, 182 N.E. 153, 84 A.L.R. 662, 1932.

## PERFORMANCE OF DECEASED'S CONTRACTS

**120. The executor or administrator is liable upon all valid contracts of the deceased which are not of a personal character. If it represents good business judgment, the personal representative should perform these agreements and he is entitled to reimbursement for his reasonable expenses so incurred. If economically advantageous to the estate, however, he should refuse to complete the contract though he thereby becomes liable in his representative capacity for the consequences of the breach.**

### *Formal Transfer—Rescission*

The personal representative can be compelled to execute a formal assignment of personalty to complete the valid obligations of the decedent.[1] He may also deliver a deed executed by the deceased in accordance with the latter's inter vivos arrangements.[2] By will,[3] or by statute,[4] the executor is often given power to execute a deed or perfect a conveyance in accordance with the binding agreement of the decedent. In absence of such testamentary or statutory authority, the conveyance must come from the heirs or devisees.[5] An administrator may perform a contract for the purchase of land made by his intestate.[6] The representative can rescind contracts or transfers for fraud upon the decedent,[7] or on account of the latter's infancy.[8] His power of rescission on these grounds, however, is no greater than that of the deceased.[9]

1 In re Stockham's Estate, 193 Iowa 823, 186 N.W. 650, 22 A.L.R. 765, 1922.

2 Dettmer v. Behrens, 106 Iowa 585, 76 N.W. 853, 68 Am.St.Rep. 326, 1898; Loring v. Cunningham, 9 Cush.(Mass.) 87, 1851.

3 Griffith v. Stewart, 31 App.D.C. 29, 1908.

4 Gilbert v. Hanson, 49 S.D. 10, 205 N.W. 704, 1925; Clarke v. Johnson, 164 Wis. 461, 160 N.W. 180, 1916. See Model Probate Code § 132.

5 McQuitty v. Willhite, 218 Mo. 586, 117 S.W. 730, 131 Am.St.Rep. 561, 1909; Wollenberg v. Rose, 41 Or. 314, 68 P. 804, 1902.

6 In re Fulmer's Estate, 203 Cal. 693, 265 P. 920, 58 A.L.R. 430, 1928. See infra note 15.

7 Wilson v. Fahnestock, 44 Ind.App. 35, 86 N.E. 1037, 1909; Wheeler v. McKeon, 137 Minn. 92, 162 N.W. 1070, 1 A.L.R. 1514, 1917 (can maintain action for this purpose).

8 Tracy v. Gaudin, 104 Cal.App. 158, 285 P. 720, 1930 (without return of consideration); Bankers' Trust Co. v. Bank of Rockville Center Trust Co., 114 N.J.Eq. 391, 168 A. 733, 89 A.L.R. 697, 1933.

9 Gunther v. Thompson, 211 Cal. 631, 296 P. 611, 1931 (exchange of property).

### *Personal Contracts and Others*

If the deceased contracted to do something of a personal nature such as to paint a picture, write a book, or give a series of concerts, the promise is discharged by his death since performance of such agreements cannot be supplied adequately by another.[10] When the agreement is not of this nature, the personal representative is under a legal duty to perform his decedent's promise.[11] The representative is liable in an action for breach of contract brought by the promisee, in case of nonperformance of such contracts.[12] If the representative completes the contract he may sue the other party for the unpaid purchase price in his personal capacity, though part of the services or materials were furnished by the deceased.[13]

### *Breach or Performance by Personal Representative*

When the party contracting with the deceased demands performance of the latter's nonpersonal agreement, the personal representative has two conceivable courses of action. First, he may refuse to perform, thereby subjecting himself in his official capacity to an action for breach.[14] Again, he may perform the contract by incurring personal liability for labor and materials necessary for the completion, and thereafter claim allowance for these items in his official account.[15] If he abandons the contract, it may be claimed thereafter by the heirs that he should have performed rather than subjecting the estate to liability for nonperformance. On the other hand if he performs and a loss results, the heirs or creditors may object to the allowance of his expenses because the completion represented poor business judg-

[10] See Restatement, Contracts § 454; Evans, The Contractual Obligations and Transfers of Personal Representatives, 7 N.Y.U.L.Q.R. 16–22. As to survival of actions, see infra § 126.

[11] Janin v. Browne, 59 Cal. 37, 1881; Cummins v. Peed, 109 Ind. 71, 9 N.E. 603, 1886; In re Grooms' Estate, 204 Iowa 746, 216 N.W. 78, 1927; Wentworth v. Cock, 10 A. & E. 42, 113 Eng.Rep. 17, 1839.

[12] Mills v. Smith, 193 Mass. 11, 78 N.E. 765, 6 L.R.A.,N.S., 865, 1906. As to the right of the heir to require the representative to complete contracts made by decedent to improve real property, see Re Rushbrook's Will Trusts, [1948] 1 Ch. 421, 5 A.L.R.2d 1248.

[13] Marshall v. Broadhurst, 1 Cr. & J. 403, 148 Eng.Rep. 1480, 1831. And see In re Grooms' Estate, supra note 11.

[14] See cases supra note 12 and infra note 16.

[15] In re Burke's Estate, 198 Cal. 163, 244 P. 340, 44 A.L.R. 1341, 1926, noted, 14 Cal.L.R. 419; Clarke v. Johnson, 164 Wis. 461, 160 N.W. 180 1916.

ment.[16] In this dilemma it is advisable for the representative to obtain consent of those interested in the estate, or directions from the probate court, or possibly instructions from a court of equity.[17] Of course if a profit results from the transaction, the personal representative must account therefor; on the other hand, he should be entitled to allowance for expenditures even if a loss was incurred when good business judgment was exercised in the attempt to perform the decedent's contracts.

*Building Contracts*

A typical case is the one in which a contractor agrees to build a structure and dies before it is completed. Coke declared that the personal representative is obliged to complete the building,[18] and this is the prevailing view.[19] Though he is perilously near continuing the business of the deceased, which the representative ordinarily does at his own risk,[20] there is probably a distinction between the operation of the deceased's business merely to fulfill existing contracts and the general continuance of the business. At any rate, the representative has been allowed his reasonable expenses in completing the building, even though he did not obtain court permission for the venture.[21] However, persons furnishing services, materials or money after decedent's death cannot obtain repayment from the estate, but must look to the personal representative.[22]

16 Herman's Estate, 90 Pa.Super. 512, 1927. Here performance of the deceased's contract to pay for painting a building devised to the executor had not been commenced and the contract might have been terminated at little or no cost to the estate. And see In re Allam's Estate, 199 Pa. 573, 49 A. 252, 1901. Exchange Nat. Bank v. Betts' Estate, 103 Kan. 807, 176 P. 660, 3 A.L.R. 1604, 1918, noted, 19 Col. L.R. 77, 3 Minn.L.R. 357.

17 In re Burke's Estate, supra note 15 (but he may be allowed his reasonable disbursements for a contract carried out at a loss even if court permission is not obtained). See notes, 140 Law Times 255; 44 Yale L.J. 1433.

18 Quick v. Ludborrow, 3 Bulstr. 30, 81 Eng.Rep. 25, 1615.

19 Massey v. Doke, 123 Ark. 211, 185 S.W. 271, 1916; In re Burke's Estate, supra note 15; MacDonald v. O'Shea, 58 Wash. 169, 108 P. 436, Ann.Cas. 1912A 417, 1910. And see In re Allam's Estate, supra note 16. But cf. Exchange Nat. Bank v. Batts' Estate, supra note 16.

20 See infra § 121.

21 In re Burke's Estate, supra note 15.

22 Exchange Nat. Bank v. Betts' Estate, supra note 16. But see Bambrick v. Webster Groves Presbyterian Church Ass'n, 53 Mo.App. 225, 1893 (statute). If the representative were insolvent, it would seem that the person should have relief against the estate in equity. See supra § 119, and note, 19 Col.L.R. 77.

## CONTINUATION OF DECEASED'S BUSINESS

**121. A representative who continues the decedent's business without authority incurs personal obligation to those with whom he deals and is liable for all losses and must account to the estate for all profits.**

**Authority to operate the business of the deceased may exist temporarily to preserve the assets of the estate or to realize thereon and also by reason of:**

**(1) Express provision of testator's will, or,**

**(2) Consent of the interested parties, or,**

**(3) Order of the court (at least if the statute so provides).**

**The personal representative who is so authorized to conduct the business has the same liabilities as the unauthorized representative, except that he is not obliged to bear the losses, incurred in good faith.**

*Unauthorized Operation*

The cases described in the preceding section must be distinguished from those in which the executor or administrator attempts to carry on the business of the deceased generally. No authority exists for the latter activity unless the representative is given power by will, by consent of the interested parties, by statute, or possibly by court permission in absence of statute. If the representative carries on the business of the deceased without proper authority, the rule is clear. He binds himself personally for all expenditures which he makes in the course of operation of the business. He must account to the estate for all profits made, and if the venture results in a loss he must bear this loss personally.[1] No doubt he will be reimbursed for his expenses if a profit results and will be obliged to bear only the net losses, if some returns are realized but are exceeded by expenditures. Persons who have extended him credit must look to him and cannot recover from the estate.[2]

[1] Mayo v. Arkansas Valley Trust Co., 132 Ark. 64, 200 S.W. 505, 1917; Riedy v. Bidwell, 70 Cal.App. 552, 233 P. 995, noted, 13 Cal.L.R. 495, 1925; Schneeberger v. Frazer, 36 Idaho 737, 213 P. 568, 1923; In re Jennings' Estate, 74 Mont. 449, 241 P. 648, 1925; In re Moran's Estate, 261 Pa. 269, 104 A. 585, 1918. Cf. Joe Gouy Shong v. Joe Chew Shee, 254 Mass. 366, 150 N.E. 225, 1926 (illegal business); Gladstone v. Bank of Commerce & Trust Co., 281 Mass. 177, 183 N.E. 262, 1932.

[2] In re De Rome's Estate, 175 Cal. 399, 165 P. 919, 1917; Succession of

*Temporary Operation*

The fact that the deceased had leased the premises in which the business was conducted for a term which was unexpired at his death does not give the representative authority to carry on the business under guise of performing the unexpired lease.[3] On the other hand, a representative may be permitted, probably without special authority, to carry on the business temporarily to safeguard the assets of the estate. Thus the representative may, and probably should, complete the harvest of a crop,[4] and otherwise preserve the property of the estate or put it in saleable condition.[5] The same is true of operating a business so as to sell it as a going concern.[6] Likewise, as it is the duty of the representative to convert the tangible personalty into money for the purpose of paying debts or, at times, for distribution, it may be that he is authorized in selling the decedent's mercantile stock over the counter instead of arranging a sale in bulk.[7] But certainly the representative should not replenish the merchandise repeatedly and carry on the establishment under the claim that he is merely performing the executorial duty of sale of the personalty.[8]

*Authorized Operation*

Statutes are frequently found which permit the representative to carry on a business with leave of court.[9] In absence of such

Huxen, 149 La. 61, 88 So. 687, 1921; Hines v. Levers & Sargent Co., 226 Mass. 214, 115 N.E. 252, 1917; Multorpor Co. v. Reed, 122 Or. 605, 260 P. 203, 55 A.L.R. 504, 1927; Martin Bros. Co. v. Peterson, 38 S.D. 494, 162 N.W. 154, 1917 (executor allowed heir to carry on business). See supra § 119.

3 In re Thurber's Estate, 311 Ill. 211, 142 N.E. 493, 1924. As to liability of the estate for rent on an unexpired lease, see infra § 127, note 94.

4 C. L. Hardy & Co. v. Turnage, 204 N.C. 538, 168 S.E. 823, 1933; Smith v. Smith, 105 S.C. 393, 89 S.E. 1032, 1916.

5 In re Fernandez's Estate, 119 Cal. 579, 51 P. 851, 1898 (care of livestock); In re Linn's Estate, 124 N.J. 65, 199 A. 396, 1938; Allen v. Shanks, 90 Tenn. 359, 16 S.W. 715, 1891. See Evans, The Contractual Obligations and Transfers of Personal Representatives, 7 N.Y.U.L.Q.R. 17, 30, 31.

6 Merritt's Estate v. Merritt, 62 Mo. 150, 1876; In re Steeby's Estate, 143 Or. 501, 20 P.2d 1080, 1933.

7 See Harms v. Pohlmann, 222 Mo. App. 276, 297 S.W. 138, 1927; Shea v. Graves, 142 Or. 503, 19 P.2d 406, 1933. See infra § 122.

8 In re Thurber's Estate, supra note 3; Succession of Hawkins, 139 La. 228, 71 So. 492, 1916; Cf. C. W. Beggs, Sons & Co. v. Behrend's Estate, 156 Wis. 34, 145 N.W. 207, 1914.

9 Hewitt v. Beattie, 106 Conn. 602, 138 A. 795, 1927; Clark v. Tennessee Chemical Co., 167 Ga. 248, 145 S.E. 73, 1928; In re Harsh's Estate, 207 Iowa 84, 218 N.W. 537, 1928; Low v. First Nat. Bank & Trust Co. of Vicks-

legislation, it is doubtful if court authority is sufficient to justify the losses of the business being charged to the estate.[10] Clearly judicial leave to carry on the business for a specified time cannot warrant the operation for a longer period.[11]

A representative is often authorized to carry on the business with the consent of the interested parties.[12] However, if some of the beneficiaries of the estate are minors, their rights cannot be prejudiced though the others consent.[13] Furthermore, the consent of creditors is often difficult to obtain, and in absence of their consent, their interests cannot be impaired.[14]

While oral instructions of decedent do not serve as a license for the operation of his business after his death,[15] his partnership agreement,[16] or his will may authorize this to be done.[17] Testamentary directions must be clear in order to permit the continuation of the business,[18] and the authority is limited to that particularly given by the testator.[19] In absence of specific provision, only the assets engaged in the business may be employed in its

burg, 162 Miss. 53, 138 So. 586, 80 A.L.R. 112, 1932; Scott v. Taylor, 294 S.W. 227, Tex.Civ.App.1927; In re Austin's Estate, 37 Wyo. 313, 261 P. 130, 1927. See Abelman, The Power to Carry on the Business of a Decedent, 36 Mich.L.R. 185, 191; Model Probate Code § 131.

10 See Metzger v. Klanko, 98 Conn. 764, 120 A. 591, 1923; Alexander v. Herring, 99 Miss. 427, 55 So. 360, 1911; Multorpor Co. v. Reed, supra note 2. In other cases the probate court's power to authorize continuation of the deceased's business has been recognized. Fleming v. Kelly, Maus & Co., 18 Colo.App. 23, 69 P. 272, 1902; Smith v. Smith, 105 S.C. 393, 89 S.E. 1032, 1916.

11 Chicago Title & Trust Co. v. Corporation of Fine Arts Bldg., 288 Ill. 142, 123 N.E. 300, 1919; Glenn v. Worthy, 169 S.C. 263, 168 S.E. 705, 1933; In re Ennis' Estate, 96 Wash. 352, 165 P. 119, 1917.

12 Daniel v. Bank of West Point, 147 Ga. 695, 95 S.E. 255, 1918; Hicks v. Purvis, 208 N.C. 657, 182 S.E. 151, 1935; In re Ennis' Estate, 96 Wash. 352, 165 P. 119, 1917. Cf. Augustus v. New Amsterdam Casualty Co., 100 F.2d 581, C.C.A.Ill.1939 (estopped).

13 Hines v. Levers & Sargent Co., 226 Mass. 214, 115 N.E. 252, 1917.

14 See infra notes 22, 23.

15 In re Ennis' Estate, supra note 11.

16 Gaess v. Gaess, 132 Conn. 96, 42 A.2d 796, 160 A.L.R. 432, 1945.

17 Moore v. McFall, 263 Ill. 596, 105 N.E. 723, Ann.Cas.1915C 364, 1914; Mason v. Pomeroy, 151 Mass. 164, 24 N.E. 202, 7 L.R.A. 771, 1890; Willis v. Sharp, 113 N.Y. 586, 21 N.E. 705, 4 L.R.A. 493, 1889.

18 Pearce v. Pearce, 199 Ala. 491, 74 So. 952, 1917; Gould v. Gould, 126 Misc. 54, 213 N.Y.S. 286, 1926. See note, 140 Law Times, 255.

19 Haldeman v. Haldeman, 176 Ky. 635, 197 S.W. 376, 1917; In re Kohler, 231 N.Y. 353, 132 N.E. 114, 1921; In re Fleshman's Estate, 51 Idaho 312, 5 P.2d 727, 1932.

continuance,[20] though the testator may provide that his entire estate may be used for this purpose.[21]

Even in case that the operation of the business is authorized, the creditors of the deceased may object if their interests are being prejudiced.[22] They have ordinarily a prior claim to the assets over the persons extending credit to the executor,[23] though they may lose this by consent or estoppel,[24] or if the law considers business losses as an expense of the administration.[25] On orthodox theory post-mortem creditors have no claim against the estate or the representative in his official capacity,[26] except where the latter is insolvent.[27] They may look to the representative in his individual capacity,[28] and the latter when authorized to continue the business is entitled to reimbursement from the estate for his reasonable outlays though the business is conducted at a loss.[29] The difference between the case of the representative who

20 In re Kohler's Will, 193 App.Div. 8, 183 N.Y.S. 550, 1921; Hewitt v. Sanborn, 103 Conn. 352, 130 A. 472, 1925.

21 Willis v. Sharp, supra note 17.

22 See Willis v. Sharp, supra note 17; note 23 infra; Jacob, Trusts for Continuing a Decedent's Business, 18 Ia.L.R. 43, 55–57; note, 35 Va.L.R. 358.

23 In re Allen's Estate, 42 Cal.App. 2d 346, 108 P.2d 973, 1941; In re Ennis' Estate, supra note 11; Ex parte Garland, 10 Ves. 110, 32 Eng.Rep. 786, 1804; In re Oxley, [1914] 1 Ch. 604; 7 B.R.C. 504.

24 In re Ennis' Estate, supra note 11; In re Onstad's Estate, 224 Wis. 332, 271 N.W. 652, 109 A.L.R. 630, 1937; see Willis v. Sharp, supra note 17.

25 Cf. Hewitt v. Beattie, supra note 9. See also Adelman, supra note 9 at 213. Cf. Model Probate Code § 131.

26 Beneux v. Brown Shoe Co., 191 Ark. 579, 87 S.W.2d 28, 1935; Hewitt v. Beattie, supra note 9; supra § 118. But see Fleming v. Kelly, Maus & Co., supra note 10; Daniel v. Bank of West Point, supra note 12; Clark v. Tennessee Chemical Co., supra note 9 (statute); In re Bucks' Estate, 112 Pa.Super. 193, 170 A. 373, 1934; Holt v. Daniel Sons & Palmer Co., 8 F.2d 700, C.C.A.Ga.1926. See infra note 28.

27 Willis v. Sharp, supra note 17.

28 Beneux v. Brown Shoe Co., supra note 26; State Bank of Orlando & Trust Co. v. Cummer Lbr. Co., 105 Fla. 522, 141 So. 602, 1932; Willis v. Sharp, supra note 17. But cf. California Employment Stabilization Com'n v. Hansen, 69 Cal.App.2d 767, 160 P.2d 173, 1945 (statute); T. C. Fox & Sons v. Lampert, 12 N.J.Super. 1, 78 A.2d 721, 1951 (agreement). But even where authorized operation absolves the representative from personal liability for his contracts, his individual liability for tort remains. Johnston v. Long, 30 Cal.2d 54, 181 P. 2d 645, 1947. See notes, 35 Cal.L.R. 586, 33 Va.L.R. 775; supra § 118.

29 First Trust & Savings Bank v. Henderson, 101 Fla. 1437, 136 So. 370, 1931; Willis v. Sharp, supra note 17; Smith v. Smith, supra note 4; Hicks v. Purvis, supra note 12.

has authority to continue the decedent's business, and one who has no such right, is that the latter must bear these losses while the former need not.

## SALES OF PERSONAL PROPERTY

**122. A personal representative may, and sometimes must, sell the decedent's personalty but some jurisdictions require court approval of the sale. Sales to the personal representative himself are voidable at the election of persons interested in the estate.**

### *Power to Sell*

At common law the personal representative is deemed to be the owner of the property to the extent of being able to sell the chattel interests and pass good title to the purchaser.[1] In addition, he may pledge or mortgage the property for the benefit of the estate.[2] Furthermore, if the pledgee or mortgagee believes that the chattel is the individual property of the representative he will be protected,[3] but if he knows that it is estate property and that the loan is not for a proper purpose the contrary is true.[4]

In absence of statute today the common-law rule prevails and no court authority is necessary for sales of personalty. Statutes in many jurisdictions contemplate an order of the court authorizing all, or certain kinds of, sales. Some of this legislation is deemed merely for the protection of the personal representative, so that the claim will not afterward be made that the sale was at too low a price.[5] Under such statutes, a sale without court

1 In re Holt's Estate, 7 Alaska 630, 1928; Smith v. Steen, 20 N.M. 436, 150 P. 927, 1915; Matter of Heinze's Will, 224 N.Y. 1, 120 N.E. 63, 1918; Williams v. Ely, 13 Wis. 1, 1860; Nugent v. Gifford, 1 Atk. 463, 26 Eng. Rep. 294, 1738. It is often said that title to the object of a specific legacy is in the legatee. Sykes v. Hughes, 182 Md. 396, 35 A.2d 132, 150 A.L.R. 87, 1943; but see Strader v. Metropolitan Life Ins. Co., 128 Va. 238, 105 S.E. 74, 1920. Under the California statute title is in the legatees or distributees and the representative has only the rights of possession and of disposition under order of the court. Western P. R. Co. v. Godfrey, 166 Cal. 346, 136 P. 284, Ann.Cas.1915B 825, 1913.

2 Carter v. Manufacturers' Nat. Bank of Lewiston, 71 Me. 448, 36 Am. Rep. 338, 1880 (pledgee not responsible for appropriation by executor); Schell v. Deperven, 198 Pa. 591, 48 A. 815, 1901; McAuslan v. Union Trust Co., 46 R.I. 176, 125 A. 296, 1924.

3 Felton v. Felton, 213 N.C. 194, 195 S.E. 533, 1938.

4 Haley v. Austin, 74 Colo. 571, 223 P. 43, 1924; Goodell v. Munroe, 87 N.J.Eq. 328, 100 A. 238, 1917.

5 Phoenix Mut. Life Ins. Co. v. Harris, 45 App.D.C. 474, 1916; Flynn

authority passes good title to the purchaser, and subjects the representative to no liability in absence of fraud or bad business judgment. Other statutes absolutely require probate court approval for the sale and absence thereof invalidates the sale.[6] Such statutes generally cover sales of choses in action as well as of tangible property.[7] Often sales of crops or perishable property are excepted from the necessity of a court order.[8] In some jurisdictions private sales must be authorized by the court, though this is not necessary in the case of public or auction sales.[9] As a general rule an order of the court is not necessary when the testator has given power of sale to his executor.[10]

*Time and Manner of Sale*

A sale by one before letters are granted becomes valid upon his later appointment as executor or administrator according to the principle of relation back.[11] If the representative is under duty to sell he should do so within a reasonable time, and he is responsible for losses if he does not use reasonable prudence in this regard.[12] However, he is not liable for mere errors in judgment in regard to the time of sale,[13] nor for the price obtained.[14] He

v. Chicago Great Western R. Co., 159 Iowa 571, 141 N.W. 401, 45 L.R.A., N.S., 1098, 1913.

6 King v. Harford, 48 Cal.App. 405, 191 P. 998, 1920; Alexander v. Fidelity & Deposit Co., 108 Md. 541, 70 A. 209, 1908; Bowdry v. Stitzel-Weller Distillery, 200 Okl. 213, 192 P.2d 279, 1948; Shearn v. Fenton, 52 N.W.2d 830, S.D.1952.

7 Cummings v. Lowe, 52 Idaho 1, 10 P.2d 1059, 1932; Webb v. Reynolds (Tex.Com.App.) 207 S.W. 914, Tex.Civ.App.1919; Shearn v. Fenton, supra note 6. Contra: Grignon v. Shope, 100 Or. 611, 197 P. 317, 1921 (negotiable instrument).

8 See Levering v. Levering, 64 Md. 399, 2 A. 1, 1885; Baldwin v. Boaz, 34 Ga.App. 393, 129 S.E. 670, 1925. Cf. Ohio Gen.Code, §§ 10509–90, 10509–91 (both public and private sales subject to court approval).

9 Rossman v. Christenson, 117 Kan. 41, 230 P. 72, 1924.

10 Crenshaw v. Ware's Ex'r, 148 Ky. 196, 146 S.W. 426, 1912; Battey v. Battey, 94 Neb. 729, 144 N.W. 786, 1913. Cf. Koelling v. Citizens' Bank, 237 S.W. 176, Mo.App.1922. See infra note 17.

11 Outlaw v. Farmer, 71 N.C. 31, 1874; Shawnee Nat. Bank v. Van Zant, 84 Okl. 107, 202 P. 285, 26 A.L.R. 1349, 1921. But see Wilson v. Hudson, 4 Har.(Del.) 168, 1844.

12 Tyson's Estate, infra note 29; Beacham v. Ross, 187 N.C. 398, 197 S.E. 369, 1938. See infra note 26 et seq.

13 Matter of Lazar, 139 Misc. 261, 247 N.Y.S. 230, 1930; Commercial & Savings Bank of Winchester v. Burton, 183 Va. 133, 31 S.E.2d 289, 1944; see annotation, 92 A.L.R. 436.

14 In re Schleif's Estate, 169 N.Y.S. 814, 1918; Shupe v. Jenks, 195 Wis. 334, 218 N.W. 375, 1928. Cf. Park & Tilford Import Corporation v. Nash, 166 Me. 373, 171 A. 339, 1934 (sale set

cannot delegate the discretionary matters regarding the sale,[15] though he may employ an agent or an auctioneer.[16] In absence of statute a representative may sell either at auction or at private sale.[17] He can probably sell on credit provided he takes good security for the balance and he is not responsible on account of subsequent insolvency of the sureties.[18] Statutes sometimes regulate the matter of sales on credit.[19]

### *Sales to Personal Representative*

Following the general principle applicable to fiduciaries, an executor or administrator may not sell property to himself even at public sale.[20] Nor may he sell the property to his spouse,[21] or to a straw man who retransfers to the personal representative.[22] Sales to the representative are merely voidable, however, and they may be either avoided or ratified by the persons interested in the estate.[23] Furthermore, the representative may purchase the property with the consent of these parties.[24] Statutes in

aside for inadequacy of price); In re Bierbaum's Estate, 103 N.Y.S.2d 423, 1951 (executor surcharged).

15 Berger v. Duff, 4 Johns.Ch.(N.Y.) 368, 1820.

16 Lewis v. Reed, 11 Ind. 239, 1858; Landry v. Laplos, 113 La. 697, 37 So. 606, 1904.

17 Boyer v. Cole, 16 Del.Ch. 445, 143 A. 489, 1928; see supra note 9. As to testamentary power of sale authorizing private sale, see annotation, 11 A.L.R.2d 955.

18 Stewart's Adm'r v. Stewart's Heirs, 31 Ala. 207, 1857.

19 See Pierce v. Whipple, 123 Ark. 132, 184 S.W. 837, 1916; Leonard v. Leonard, 201 N.Y.S. 113, 1922; Model Probate Code § 154.

20 In re Pennewell, 12 Del.Ch. 408, 105 A. 377, 1918; Rossman v. Christenson, 117 Kan. 41, 230 P. 72, 1924 (sale to representative as agent for another, illegal); McFadden v. Jenkins, 40 N.D. 422, 169 N.W. 151, 1918 (sale to corporation in which representative was interested, illegal). See Meade v. Van de Voorde, 139 Neb. 827, 299 N.W. 175, 137 A.L.R. 554, 1941 (approval of final account no bar to objection); Jose v. Lyman, 316 Mass. 271, 55 N.E.2d 433, 154 A.L.R. 190, 1944 (executor was decedent's pledgee). As to representative's right to buy at sales brought about by another, see annotation, 77 A.L.R. 1513.

21 Lowery v. Idleson, 117 Ga. 778, 45 S.E. 51, 1903; but see In re Berry's Estate, 321 Ill.App. 365, 53 N.E.2d 149, 1944 (public sale approved by court).

22 See Comstock v. Bowles, 295 Mass. 250, 3 N.E.2d 817, 1936; supra note 20.

23 Ambruster v. Ambruster, 326 Mo. 51, 31 S.W.2d 28, 77 A.L.R. 782, 1930; Turk v. Grossman, 176 Md. 644, 6 A. 2d 639, 1939. See annotation, 111 A.L.R. 1362. Cf. Wells v. Wood, 125 Or. 38, 263 P. 54, 1928 (void by statute).

24 Tayloe v. Tayloe, 108 N.C. 69, 12 S.E. 836, 1891. See Ambruster v. Ambruster, supra note 23 (estoppel).

some jurisdictions allow the representative to buy subject to confirmation of the court.[25]

*Duty to Sell*

The personal representative is often under a positive duty to sell the personalty of the deceased. This is clearly the case with regard to perishable property.[26] Sometimes the will directs that the personalty be sold.[27] In addition, it is often necessary to convert tangible or intangible assets into money in order to pay the debts, costs of administration and legacies. In absence of this necessity, the object of a specific legacy ordinarily should not be sold.[28]

Where the nature of the property is such that distribution in kind cannot be arranged equitably, a sale is necessary.[29] On the other hand if the distributees agree on allotment in kind the representative should not sell the assets which are not necessary to pay debts.[30] Wills sometimes give the executor discretion as to whether to sell.[31] In the absence of any of these considerations the matter would seem to turn upon whether the executor or administrator is obliged to dispense in money or whether he may distribute in kind. The common-law practice seemed to contemplate distribution in money,[32] thus making a sale mandatory, but the present rule is sometimes affected by statutes and is often obscure.[33]

[25] See Oles v. Furlong, 134 Conn. 334, 57 A.2d 405, 1948; Model Probate Code § 155 and comment thereto.

[26] Griswold v. Chandler, 5 N.H. 492, 1831. But corporate stock is not perishable property requiring sale merely because it may fluctuate in value. In re Fisher's Estate, 128 Iowa 626, 104 N.W. 1023, 1905.

[27] Mewborn v. Moseley, 177 N.C. 110, 97 S.E. 711, 1919; Dunham v. Randall, 51 R.I. 55, 151 A. 193, 1930; Blackmon v. Blackmon, 113 S.C. 478, 101 S.E. 827, 1920.

[28] See State ex rel. Franklin v. Sullivan, 176 Tenn. 107, 138 S.W.2d 435, 127 A.L.R. 1067, 1940; but cf. Root v. Blackwood, 120 Ind.App. 545, 94 N.E.2d 489, 1950. See supra note 1 and generally infra §§ 136, 143.

[29] Tyson's Estate, 80 Pa.Super. 29, 1922 (diamond earrings).

[30] Fidelity Trust Co. v. Walton, 198 N.C. 790, 153 S.E. 401, 1930; see In re Stephen's Estate, 320 Pa. 97, 181 A. 559, 1935 (request to hold).

[31] Macy v. Mercantile Trust Co., 68 N.J.Eq. 235, 59 A. 586, 1904.

[32] Macy v. Mercantile Trust Co., supra note 31.

[33] See infra § 124, note 14 et seq.; infra § 143; Model Probate Code § 190.

## SALES OF REALTY

**123. A testator may give to his executor a general or limited power to sell and convey realty even though the property is devised to others by the will. Court authority is not necessary for the exercise of such powers.**

**Statutes provide that the court may empower the personal representative to sell decedent's land when necessary to pay the latter's debts, and in some states for other purposes as well. Detailed legislative provisions outline the procedure for such sales.**

Under the orthodox theory that the realty of the deceased passes directly to the heirs or devisees the personal representative cannot sell realty as he can personalty. To this rule there are two general exceptions: (1) When the will gives the executor power of sale; (2) where the personalty is insufficient to pay the debts of the decedent, in which case statutes provide that the court may authorize the executor or administrator to sell the realty in order to obtain the necessary funds.

*Testamentary Power of Sale*

The extent of an executor's power in this respect depends upon the language of the will. Authority to sell may be express, or it may be implied where otherwise it would be impossible to carry out the provisions of the will.[1] The executor is often commanded to sell,[2] or his power may be discretionary,[3] according to the terms of the instrument. He is sometimes given authority to sell for any and all ends,[4] or the power may be only for limited purposes such as to pay debts when the personalty is insufficient.[5] Usually if there is power of sale there is no necessity to obtain a court order for the sale,[6] though the will may direct that judicial approval be obtained.[7]

1 Hilles v. Hilles, 11 Del.Ch. 159, 98 A. 296, 1916; Broadhurst v. Mewborn, 171 N.C. 400, 88 S.E. 628, 1916; see annotations, 134 A.L.R. 378, 23 A.L.R.2d 1000. The power may extend to land not passing under the will. Hertz v. Burris, 289 Ky. 369, 158 S.W.2d 951, 139 A.L.R. 1138, 1942.

2 In re Backesto's Estate, 63 Cal. App. 265, 218 P. 597, 1923; Grove v. Willard, 280 Ill. 247, 117 N.E. 489, 1917.

3 New England Trust Co. v. Morse, 243 Mass. 39, 136 N.E. 835, 1922.

4 Mewborn v. Moseley, 177 N.C. 110, 97 S.E. 711, 1919.

5 Fies v. Feist, 145 Ark. 351, 224 S.W. 633, 1920; Kreise v. Cartledge, 262 Pa. 55, 104 A. 855, 1918.

6 Buckner v. Buckner's Ex'r, 185 Ky. 540, 215 S.W. 420, 1919; Justice

7 See Note 7 on following page.

The bare power of sale does not include the power to exchange lands,[8] especially where the executor is directed to invest the proceeds in personalty or to make distribution in cash.[9] But one which includes the right to reinvest in the other land gives, by inference, authority to exchange realty.[10] A mere power of sale does not give to the executor the right of possession,[11] for the donee of the power is in no sense the owner of the land.

A power given for purposes of distribution cannot be exercised after the devisees have sold the land.[12] Moreover, it is no bar to a partition suit between the devisees that a testamentary power of sale was given to the executor for the purpose of distribution, when the power had not been exercised at the time of the commencement of the action.[13] If land is sold under a testamentary power, the proceeds which are not necessary to pay debts or carry out some special provision of the will go to the persons who would have been entitled to the realty.[14]

Directions to sell realty within a certain time do not ordinarily prevent exercise of the power thereafter.[15] However, by express provision the power may be limited in duration.[16] This inter-

v. Soderlund, 225 Mass. 320, 114 N.E. 623, 1916. Cf. Wetmore & Morse Granite Co. v. Bertoli, 87 Vt. 257, 88 A. 898, 1913 (statute). Usually the executor may sell at private sale. See annotation, 11 A.L.R.2d 955.

7 McDermott v. Lingquist, 66 Colo. 88, 179 P. 147, 1919.

8 Tzeses v. Green, 105 N.J.Eq. 12, 146 A. 593, 1929; Trimboli v. Kinkel, 226 N.Y. 147, 123 N.E. 205, 5 A.L.R. 1385, 1919; see annotation, 63 A.L.R. 1003.

9 Ross v. Barr's Ex'r, 53 S.W. 658, 21 Ky.Law Rep. 974, 1899; Trimboli v. Kinkel, supra note 8.

10 Broaddus v. Centers, 116 S.W. 742, Ky.1909.

11 McCarty v. McCarty, 356 Ill. 559, 191 N.E. 68, 94 A.L.R. 1137, 1934; see Robertson v. Biernacka, 9 N.J. 591, 76 A.2d 47, 1950 (rents).

12 Van Norden Trust Co. v. O'Donohue, 122 App.Div. 51, 106 N.Y.S. 948, 1907.

13 Ruggles v. Powers, 201 Iowa 284, 207 N.W. 116, 1926. But see Weber v. Beales, 140 N.J.Eq. 423, 55 A.2d 67, 1947. Cf. Arlington State Bank v. Paulsen, 57 Neb. 717, 78 N.W. 303, 1899 (devise to executor to carry out will).

14 In re Raleigh's Estate, 206 Pa. 451, 55 A. 1119, 1903. See Bonded Bldg. & Loan Ass'n v. Konner, 118 N.J.Eq. 546, 180 A. 570, 1935, noted, 14 Tex.L.R. 265 (power of sale does not work equitable conversion of land into personalty). See note, 41 Mich. L.R. 332.

15 Hale v. Hale, 137 Mass. 168, 1884; Stork v. Merchant, 125 S.C. 377, 118 S.E. 530, 31 A.L.R. 1392, 1923; cf. Bryant v. Fingerlos, 138 Neb. 867, 295 N.W. 896, 132 A.L.R. 1467, 1941.

16 Pope v. Kitchell, 354 Ill. 248, 188 N.E. 451, 1933.

pretation is placed upon powers given for a particular purpose when that object can no longer be accomplished.[17]

According to the modern rule, the executors who qualify as such may exercise the power of sale though others named in the will renounce the office.[18] Formerly the power was deemed to be personal and did not extend to the administrator with the will annexed,[19] unless the will indicated that the authority was given to the representative simply by virtue of his office.[20] However, under modern statutes declaring that administrators with the will annexed may exercise the powers given to executors, it is usually held that such administrator may exercise a testamentary power of sale.[21]

*Sales by Order of the Court—In General*

In the absence of a testamentary power, it is necessary to rely upon statutory authority for the sale of land.[22] Except in Virginia,[23] statutes in every jurisdiction provide that land may be sold by order of the court in order to pay debts. This legislation outlines close judicial supervision for the sale and provides various safeguards against abuses.

[17] Conant v. Stone, 176 Mich. 654, 143 N.W. 39, 1913; Trask v. Sturges, 170 N.Y. 482, 63 N.E. 534, 1902.

[18] Clinefelter v. Ayres, 16 Ill. 329, 1855; Gray v. McCurdy, 114 Tex. 217, 266 S.W. 396, 36 A.L.R. 820, 1925. See Evans, The Survival of Powers of Joint Executors to Sell Land, 85 U. of Pa.L.R. 154.

[19] Lucas v. Price, 4 Ala. 679, 1843; Wills v. Cowper, 2 Ohio 124, 1825.

[20] Crouse v. Peterson, 130 Cal. 169, 62 P. 475, 615, 80 Am.St.Rep. 89, 1900 (declaring that doubtful language of the will should be so construed); Rollins v. Rice, 59 N.H. 493, 1880.

[21] Peters Mineral Land Co. v. Hooper, 208 Ala. 324, 94 So. 606, 1922; Vanhoose v. Brooks, 306 Ky. 639, 208 S.W.2d 963, 9 A.L.R.2d 1320, 1948. But cf. Snow v. Bray, 198 Ala. 398, 73 So. 542, 1916 (contrary intention in will).

[22] Swinehart v. Turner, 38 Idaho 602, 224 P. 74, 1924; Jones v. Gilliam, 199 S.W. 694, Tex.Civ.App.1918.

[23] In this state the only way in which land may be reached for satisfaction of creditors' claims is by action against the heir or devisee unless the will provides for payment out of land. Catron v. Bostic, 123 Va. 355, 96 S.E. 845, 1918. This is substantially the common-law procedure. See McCarthy v. Mullen, 82 N.J.L. 379, 82 A. 51, 39 L.R.A.,N.S., 688, 1912; American Law of Property §§ 14.6, 14.20. Statutes in some states preserve this as an alternative to sale by order of the court of probate. See N.Y.Decedent Estate Law §§ 176–178, 181, 182, and infra § 127.

Statutes in some states limit the time within which land may be sold to pay debts.[24] Elsewhere laches constitute a bar.[25] If administration has been closed it will scarcely be reopened for the purpose of selling the land.[26]

*Necessity of Debts*

When a statute merely authorizes a sale of land to pay the debts of the decedent, it is generally held that there is no power to sell for the purpose of paying legacies,[27] or expenses of the administration.[28] However, statutes often permit a sale for these purposes.[29]

To authorize the sale of realty to pay debts there must be valid and existing claims against the estate,[30] and in some jurisdictions the claims must have been allowed by the probate court.[31] Ordinarily the statutes do not authorize the sale of land unless there is a deficiency of personalty to pay the debts.[32]

24 N.Y.Surr.Ct.Act §§ 233, 245; see Johnson v. Barefoot, 208 N.C. 796, 182 S.E. 471, 1935; Cummings v. Lynn, 121 Iowa 344, 96 N.W. 857, 1903 (time limitation on grant of administration).

25 In re Neff's Estate, 389 Ill. 625, 60 N.E.2d 204, 1945; see American Law of Property § 14.21.

26 Cf. Abramson v. Rogers, 97 Ark. 189, 133 S.W. 836; Van Bibber v. Reese, 71 Md. 608, 18 A. 892, 6 L.R.A. 332, 1889.

27 Wattles v. Hyde, 9 Conn. 10, 1831; Baptist Female University of North Carolina v. Borden, 132 N.C. 476, 44 S.E. 47, 1007, 1903. But the land may be sold if charged with the legacy. In re More's Estate, 179 Mich. 237, 146 N.W. 319, 1914. Or power of sale may be given by the will for this purpose. See supra note 4.

28 First Trust & Sav. Bank v. Henderson, 109 Fla. 175, 147 So. 248, 1933; Howell v. Jump, 140 Mo. 441, 41 S.W. 976, 1897. But see Colyer v. Huntley, 179 Ga. 332, 175 S.E. 901, 95 A.L.R. 1140, 1934.

29 Ellyson v. Lord, 124 Iowa 125, 99 N.W. 582, 1904 (legacies); Falley v. Gribling, 128 Ind. 110, 26 N.E. 794, 1891 (expenses of administration); Ohio Gen.Code, § 10510–3. Often sales are authorized for the purpose of distribution. Oldham v. McElroy, 134 Ky. 454, 121 S.W. 414, 1909; Stout v. Stout, 82 Ohio St. 358, 92 N.E. 465, 137 Am.St.Rep. 785, 1910; In re Douty's Estate, 196 Pa. 432, 46 A. 483, 1900. See Model Probate Code § 152; note, 44 Col.L.R. 268, 270.

30 Townsend v. Beavers, 185 Miss. 312, 188 So. 1, 1939.

31 Cunniff's Estate, 272 N.Y. 89, 4 N.E.2d 946, 1936. See Pohlenz v. Panko, 106 Neb. 156, 182 N.W. 972, 1921 (formal order of allowance unnecessary in case of claims that are filed).

32 Dicus v. Scherer, 277 Ill. 168, 115 N.E. 161, 1917; Shaw's Guardian v. Grimes, 187 Ky. 250, 218 S.W. 447, 1919; George v. Brown, 84 W.Va. 359, 99 S.E. 509, 1919. In some jurisdictions the court has discretion to order a sale of realty although the personalty has not been exhausted. In re Pavert's Estate, 177 Cal. 353, 170 P. 827, 1918; Candee v. Candee,

*Interest to be Sold*

Any interest in realty which the deceased owned and which is not exempt from liability for his debts may be sold, including a reversionary,[33] or an undivided fractional,[34] interest. The homestead cannot be sold in the lifetime of those entitled to its benefits.[35] Ordinarily no more land should be sold than is necessary to obtain the money necessary to satisfy the debts.[36] But when a tract is indivisible it may be sold intact though it will produce more than enough to pay debts.[37]

*Jurisdiction*

As a general rule the probate court has exclusive jurisdiction to order and supervise the sale.[38] The jurisdiction of the court generally extends to sales of land located in any county of the state,[39] but not to lands outside of the state.[40]

*Who May Apply*

Application for leave to sell realty is ordinarily made by the personal representative. He is undoubtedly a proper petitioner for this purpose,[41] and in some jurisdictions he is the only one

87 Conn. 85, 86 A. 758, 1913. The executor has no standing to invoke rule that personalty must be exhausted, Tyler v. Reynolds, 121 W.Va. 475, 7 S.E.2d 22, 126 A.L.R. 901, 1939.

33 Kamerer v. Kamerer, 281 Ill. 587, 117 N.E. 1027, 1917.

34 Connell v. Harper, 202 Ky. 406, 259 S.W. 1017, 1924.

35 Patton v. Buxton, 238 S.W. 118, Mo.1922; Foltz v. Maxwell, 100 Neb. 713, 161 N.W. 254, 1916. And see Fritts v. Fritts, 298 Ill. 314, 131 N.E. 584, 1921, declaring that sales even subject to the homestead rights should not be made of such land. See generally supra § 34.

36 McKnelly v. Conley, 210 Ill.App. 609, 1918; Maulsby v. Citizens' Banking Co. of Modoc, 73 Ind.App. 502, 127 N.E. 821, 1920; Barry v. Fain's Adm'r, 172 Ky. 308, 189 S.W. 220, 1916.

37 Lindenberger v. Cornell, 190 Ky. 844, 229 S.W. 54, 1921. See also McGrady v. Clary, 247 S.W. 1099, Tex. Civ.App.1923.

38 Robinson v. Cogswell, 192 Mass. 79, 78 N.E. 389, 1906; Miskimins' Appeal, 114 Pa. 530, 6 A. 743, 1886; Lauraine v. Ashe, 109 Tex. 69, 191 S. W. 563, 196 S.W. 501, 1917. Cf. Neb. Rev.Stat., 1943 § 30–1101; Rucker v. Tennessee Coal, Iron & R. Co., 176 Ala. 456, 58 So. 464, 1912 (chancery).

39 Vail v. Rinehart, 105 Ind. 6, 4 N.E. 218, 1886; Reynolds v. Schmidt, 20 Wis. 374, 1866.

40 In re Robinson's Heirship, 119 Neb. 285, 228 N.W. 852, 1930; Wilkinson v. Leland, 2 Pet.(U.S.) 627, 7 L. Ed. 542, 1829.

41 Frackelton v. Masters, 249 Ill. 30, 94 N.E. 124, 1911; Tyndale v. Stanwood, 182 Mass. 534, 66 N.E. 23, 1903; Rheinfrank v. Hurr, 98 Ohio St. 439, 121 N.E. 645, 1918.

who may apply.[42] However, creditors are generally permitted to petition for the sale, at least if their claims have been allowed.[43]

*Petition*

The proceeding is commenced by the filing of a petition. This should be in writing,[44] contain the jurisdictional allegations of the purpose and necessity of the sale,[45] averments of who are the heirs or devisees,[46] and an exact description of the property to be sold.[47]

*Parties and Notice*

In some jurisdictions the proceeding is considered an adversary one and the heirs and devisees should be made parties.[48] Often, however, the proceeding is in rem or quasi in rem,[49] and does not require parties defendant, but notice must be given to the interested parties either personally or by publication as the statute directs.[50]

*Hearing*

The person applying for the order is ordinarily obliged to show to the court's satisfaction that unpaid debts exist,[51] and that there is insufficient personalty to pay them.[52] The heir is entitled to contest the validity of the claims alleged to be unsatisfied,[53] or

42 Rheinfrank v. Hurr, supra note 41. And see Barka v. Hopewell, 29 N.M. 166, 219 P. 799, 1923 (creditor's remedy is to obtain order of the court requiring personal representative to proceed with sale).

43 Trippe v. O'Cavanaugh, 203 Miss. 537, 36 So.2d 166, 1948; In re Baker's Estate, 164 Misc. 92, 298 N.Y.S. 261, 1937.

44 Townsend v. Steel, 85 Ala. 580, 5 So. 351, 1889.

45 Custer v. Beyer, 76 Ind.App. 303, 130 N.E. 834, 1921; In re Perkins' Estate, 122 Misc. 593, 204 N.Y.S. 667, 1924 (mere conclusion insufficient).

46 In re Levy's Estate, 141 Cal. 639, 75 P. 317, 1904.

47 Henley v. Johnston, 134 Ala. 646, 32 So. 1009, 92 Am.St.Rep. 48, 1902; Hazelton v. Bogardus, 8 Wash. 102, 35 P. 602, 1894.

48 Alward v. Borah, 381 Ill. 134, 44 N.E. 865, 1942 (old law); Graham v. Floyd, 214 N.C. 77, 197 S.E. 873, 1938.

49 Lamont v. Vinger, 61 Mont. 530, 202 P. 769, 1921.

50 Park v. Mullins, 124 Ga. 1072, 53 S.E. 568, 1906 (publication insufficient when statute requires personal service); Pohlenz v. Panko, 106 Neb. 156, 182 N.W. 972, 1921 (publication sufficient under statute). Cf. Ruff v. Baker, 146 Ohio 456, 66 N.E.2d 540, 1946 (contingent remainderman).

51 Howe v. Brown, 287 Ill. 532, 123 N.E. 46, 1919.

52 Howe v. Brown, supra note 51.

53 Timmons v. Gochenour, 69 Ind. App. 295, 117 N.E. 279, 1917; McNair

may prove that personalty is available for all necessary payments.[54] It is a defense to the application that the lands did not belong to the decedent at the time of his death.[55]

*Order of Sale*

After the hearing, the court should make the order, decree, or license of sale.[56] This should recite the finding of the jurisdictional facts,[57] and contain an accurate description of the property to be sold.[58] Some statutes require that the order should fix the time, terms and manner of the sale,[59] though if these matters are specifically pointed out by legislation it would seem that their repetition in the order is unnecessary. The effect of the order is ordinarily to vest in the personal representative a power to sell the decedent's realty as set forth therein and to pass title to the purchaser upon due compliance with the statutory procedure.[60]

*Oath, Bond and Appraisal*

Statutes often require the personal representative to take an oath to carry out the order of sale in the lawful manner.[61] Many states demand an additional bond for the faithful application of the proceeds of the sale,[62] though in some states the general administration bond also covers such funds and the special sale bond is merely additional security as to this money.[63] Statutes often require that the realty should be specially appraised before the sale.[64]

v. Cooper, 174 N.C. 566, 94 S.E. 98, 1917.

54 Cavitt v. Beall Hardware & Implement Co., 204 S.W. 798, Tex.Civ. App.1918.

55 Howe v. Brown, supra note 51; Myers v. Warrenfells, 153 Ga. 648, 113 S.E. 180, 1922.

56 Rudolph v. Smith, 148 S.W.2d 225, Tex.Civ.App.1941.

57 Linville v. Chenoweth, 115 Ind. App. 355, 59 N.E.2d 129, 1945.

58 Edwards v. Sands, 150 Ga. 11, 102 S.E. 426, 1920. Cf. Howe v. Brown, supra note 51.

59 See Alexander v. Hendricks, 201 Ky. 677, 258 S.W. 81, 1924; Jones v. Gilliam, 199 S.W. 694, Tex.Civ.App. 1918.

60 Humphrey v. Holland, 192 Ky. 168, 232 S.W. 642, 1921 (as to parties served).

61 See Hugo v. Miller, 50 Minn. 105, 52 N.W. 381, 1892.

62 Clark v. Hills, 134 Ind. 421, 34 N.E. 13, 1893; In re Snow, 96 Me. 570, 53 A. 116, 1902; Sharpley v. Plant, 79 Miss. 175, 28 So. 799, 89 Am.St.Rep. 588, 1900.

63 Durfee v. Joslyn, 92 Mich. 211, 52 N.W. 626, 1892; but see McKenzie v. Standard Accident Ins. Co., 189 S.C. 475, 1 S.E.2d 502, 1939; cf. Model Probate Code § 116; see annotation, 9 A.L.R. 943 (testamentary power).

64 Reed v. Brown, 215 Ind. 417, 19 N.E.2d 1015, 1939.

*The Sale*

The matters of notice of sale and of the time, place, terms and manner of sale are determined by statute or court order or both. Sales to the representative, or his close relatives are governed by the same considerations as in case of sales of personal property to these persons.[65] The probate rather than the equity court has jurisdiction to set aside fraudulent sales.[66]

*Report and Confirmation*

In most jurisdictions the representative is required to make report of his sale to the probate court and secure an order of confirmation.[67] On the hearing for confirmation, interested persons are entitled to object to the sale.[68] Usually the sale is not complete and the title does not pass until after confirmation by the court.[69] In some jurisdictions confirmation is not necessary or proper.[70]

*Rights of Purchasers*

Express warranties are not binding on the estate and none are implied.[71] The representative, however, may be liable personally upon his warranties.[72] If the decedent had no title to the land, the purchaser gets none.[73] This is likewise true if the proceed-

[65] See supra § 122; Clifton v. Guest, 216 Ark. 352, 226 S.W.2d 61, 1950 (wife); In re Denlinger's Estate, 98 Cal.App.2d 130, 219 P.2d 495, 1950 (allowed-statute); Wortham v. Marten, 354 Mo. 1, 188 S.W.2d 11, 1945 (straw men); Alburger v. Crane, 5 N.J. 573, 76 A.2d 812, 1950 (ratification); American Law of Property § 14.27.

[66] Farquhar v. New England Trust Co., 261 Mass. 209, 158 N.E. 836, 1927, noted, 76 U. of Pa.L.R. 612.

[67] Kulbeth v. Drew County Timber Co., 125 Ark. 291, 188 S.W. 810, 1916; Amundson v. Hanson, 150 Minn. 287, 185 N.W. 252, 1921; Jones v. Gilliam, supra note 59.

[68] In re Scott's Estate, 172 Cal. 485, 157 P. 242, 1916; In re Short's Estate, 13 Del.Ch. 428, 120 A. 484, 1922.

[69] Jones v. Temple, 126 Ark. 86, 189 S.W. 847, 1916; Amundson v. Hanson, supra note, 67; Farmers' Nat. Bank of Ponca City v. Cravens, 93 Okl. 58, 219 P. 138, 1923.

[70] Matter of Stewart, 71 Misc. 640, 130 N.Y.S. 1058, 1911; cf. In re Sturges' Estate, 36 N.Y.S.2d 141, 1942.

[71] Sumner v. Williams, 8 Mass. 162, 5 Am.Dec. 83, 1911; Hammert v. McKnight, 132 Okl. 14, 269 P. 289, 68 A.L.R. 649, 1928; Williams v. McDonald, 13 Tex. 322, 1855; Bauerle v. Long, 187 Ill. 475, 58 N.E. 458, 52 L.R.A. 643, 1900 (sale under testamentary power). But see Mains v. City Title Insurance Co., infra note 73.

[72] Sumner v. Williams, supra note 71; But cf. Ivey v. Vaughan, 93 S.C. 203, 76 S.E. 464, 43 L.R.A.,N.S., 377, Ann.Cas.1914D, 900, 1912.

[73] Gjerstadengen v. Van Duzen, 7 N.D. 612, 76 N.W. 233, 66 Am.St.Rep.

ings for the sale are so defective as to render them void.[74] However, at least in the latter case, the estate should not be allowed to retain the purchase money if the land is recovered from the purchaser.[75]

Execution and approval of the representative's deed creates the presumption that the statutory requirements have been complied with,[76] and even the deed alone containing recitals that the land was sold pursuant to court order makes a prima facie showing of due compliance with the law and orders of the court.[77] There are hundreds of cases passing on various grounds of invalidity of sale in various manners of attack.[78] After confirmation the sale should not be subject to collateral attack except for serious defects.[79]

679, 1898; Matson v. Johnson, 48 Wash. 256, 93 P. 324, 125 Am.St.Rep. 924, 1908; but see Mains v. City Title Ins. Co., 34 Cal.2d 580, 212 P.2d 873, 1949, noted, 23 So.Cal.L.R. 604, 2 Stanford L.R. 599. Some statutes have procedure for quieting title in the sale proceeding. See Model Probate Code § 162 and comment thereto; note, 18 Chi-Kent.L.R. 273.

74 Mumper v. Matthes, 186 Or. 357, 206 P.2d 82, 1949; see American Law of Property, § 14.27.

75 Hammert v. McKnight, 132 Okl. 14, 269 P. 289, 68 A.L.R. 649, 1928; Jarrell v. Farmers Nat. Bank of Opelika, 253 Ala. 119, 43 So.2d 116, 1949 (error corrected); see note, 44 Col. L.R. 268.

76 In re Jackson's Estate, 198 Iowa 680, 200 N.W. 310, 1924; Rust v. Rutherford, 101 Kan. 495, 167 P. 1056, 1917.

77 Pinnell v. Burroughs, 172 N.C. 182, 90 S.E. 218, 1916; Wilson v. Snow, 228 U.S. 217, 33 S.Ct. 487, 57 L.Ed. 807, 1913. See Ronken, Presumptions upon Sales of Land in Probate Court, 8 Minn.L.R. 514.

78 Cf. Skachenko v. Sweetman, 43 N.W.2d 683, N.D.1950, with Mumper v. Matthes, supra note 74; see cases infra note 79.

79 Lee v. Lee, 196 Ala. 522, 72 So. 24, 1916 (absence of notice); Wayne v. Brumley, 190 Ky. 488, 227 S.W. 996, 1921 (fraud); Amundson v. Hanson, 150 Minn. 287, 185 N.W. 252, 1921 (as to amendable defects); Mangold v. Grace, 110 Neb. 216, 193 N.W. 338, 1923 (inadequate price); Caddell v. Lufkin Land & Lumber Co., 225 S.W. 397, Tex.Com.App.1923 (failure to file statutory oath). But see Leininger v. Reichle, 317 Ill. 625, 148 N.E. 384, 1925 (as to remaindermen not made parties); Dennis v. Gorman, 289 Mo. 1, 233 S.W. 50, 1921 (sale of homestead); Magaw v. Emick, 167 Kan. 580, 207 P.2d 448, 1949 (jurisdiction). See supra note 50. As to conclusiveness of recitals in order of confirmation, see Hayes v. Betts, 227 Ala. 630, 151 So. 692, 95 A.L.R. 1484, 1933.

## INVESTMENT OF ASSETS

**124. Money belonging to the estate of deceased should ordinarily be deposited in a safe bank in the name of the estate. If the funds are to be kept for any length of time, they should be put at interest. Ordinarily it is not the function of an executor or administrator, as such, to invest the money even in land mortgages or government bonds, though this is authorized by statute in some jurisdictions and under certain circumstances would be proper even in absence of such legislation.**

### *General Considerations*

From the money or credits left by the deceased at the time of his death, the collection of the latter's choses in action, and the sales of his property, the personal representative usually acquires cash belonging to the estate. How should this money be kept by the personal representative? Should it be invested, and if so, in what manner? The answers to these questions will depend upon many circumstances, such as the terms of the will if one exists, the relative extent of the funds and the amounts of debts and expenses of administration, the probable duration of the administration, the manner of distribution contemplated, whether a testamentary trust will follow the administration and whether the representative is also the trustee of that trust, the wishes of persons interested in the estate, and finally the relative security afforded by available means of investment. The representative is expected to exercise good and conservative business judgment in the light of these and other surrounding factors.[1]

### *Deposit or Invest?*

The primary duty of the personal representative is to collect and distribute and not to invest. Hence in case of the small estate which will be administered promptly the estate funds should usually be deposited in a safe bank until distribution.[2] It has even been intimated that an executor is liable for losses due to his purchase of government bonds in a case of this nature.[3] If

[1] In re Macky's Estate, 73 Colo. 1, 213 P. 131, 1923; In re Wilmerding's Estate, 135 Misc. 674, 238 N.Y.S. 375, 1930 (here the will gave special powers regarding new investments and retention of old ones).

[2] Matter of Kruger, 139 Misc. 907, 249 N.Y.S. 772, 1931; Jones v. O'Brien, 58 S.D. 213, 235 N.W. 654, 1931; Model Probate Code § 134. See also Locke, The Care and Handling of Estates, 24 Conn.L.J. 414.

[3] See Walton v. Walton's Estate, 143 Miss. 666, 109 So. 707, 1926.

the estate is of some size or if distribution is to be delayed the funds should be put at interest.[4] This would not be regarded as a forbidden investment or loan, particularly if the money was subject to withdrawal on demand, although it has been held that a time deposit, or one subject to joint control of the representative and his bondsman is not authorized and the representative is subject to losses due to failure of the bank.[5] Wills and statutes sometimes authorize a representative to invest in designated types of securities or according to the general rule of prudence.[6] The representative acts as a trustee in making such investments.[7] Statutes are not readily construed as authorizing investments under all circumstances, but only as indicating the type of securities in case investment is proper at all.[8] The latter matter depends on the considerations enumerated in the first paragraph of this section. The statutes sometimes contemplate court approval of the investment.[9] Even in absence of testamentary or statutory authority investment in real estate mortgages and government securities has been approved under some circumstances,[10] but investment in land,[11] corporate stock [12] or unsecured loans is not proper.[13]

The subject of retention of securities owned by the deceased in his lifetime has already been touched upon.[14] The fact that the

[4] In re Jula's Estate, 3 N.J.Misc. 976, 130 A. 733, 1925; In re Reed v. Taliaferro, 37 Wyo. 107, 259 P. 815, 55 A.L.R. 941, 1927. Cf. O'Shea v. Barry, 252 Mass. 510, 147 N.E. 845, 1925 (executor not at fault in delaying administration is not liable for interest); McInnes v. Goldthwaite, 94 N.H. 331, 52 A.2d 795, 171 A.L.R. 1414, 1947. See Model Probate Code § 133.

[5] See Baer's Appeal, 127 Pa. 360, 18 A. 1, 4 L.R.A. 609, 1889; Jones v. O'Brien, supra note 2; cf. Model Probate Code § 108.

[6] See supra note 1 and infra notes 6–9; Model Probate Code § 133.

[7] In re Statz' Estate, 144 Neb. 154, 12 N.W.2d 829, 1944.

[8] See Robinson v. Georgia Sav. Bank & Trust Co., 185 Ga. 688, 196 S.E. 395, 1938.

[9] Paulk v. Roberts, 42 Ga.App. 79, 155 S.E. 55, 1930; cf. In re Krueger's Estate, 180 Wash. 165, 39 P.2d 381, 1935 (savings and loan association); see annotation, 126 A.L.R. 437.

[10] Tucker v. Tucker, 33 N.J.Eq. 235, 1880; Villard v. Villard, 219 N.Y. 482, 114 N.E. 789, 1916.

[11] In re Schummers' Estate, 210 App.Div. 296, 206 N.Y.S. 113, 1926; Hall v. Windsor Sav. Bank, 97 Vt. 125, 121 A. 582, 124 A. 593, 1924. Cf. Wilcox v. Hollar, 115 Kan. 27, 222 P. 758, 1924 (under will authorizing investment in land, executor may purchase realty in another state).

[12] Lovenskiold v. Nueces Hotel Co., 208 S.W. 759, Tex.Civ.App.1919.

[13] In re Wesley's Estate, 279 Ill. App. 349, 1935; see Jones v. O'Brien, supra note 2.

[14] See supra § 122.

securities are of the type authorized for trust investment is a strong argument for the right of retention.[15] Under some circumstances at least, it would be proper to retain when it would be improper for the representative to invest in the same securities.[16]

*Place and Form of Deposit*

The personal representative is charged with the duty of exercising due care in the choice of a depository for the estate's funds. If loss results from his failure to do so, he must bear the loss personally.[17] Moreover, the representative should deposit the funds in the name of the estate, or in his name as personal representative. If he deposits them in a personal account or mixes them with his own funds, he is liable for losses due to bank failure regardless of the care which he exercises in the selection of the depository.[18] But if he exercises reasonable care in the selection of the bank and designates the account as estate funds, he is not liable for loss due to failure of the bank.[19] The indication that the account belongs to the estate does not entitle the estate to a preference over other accounts in case of the bank's subsequent insolvency; such account being a general and not a special deposit.[20]

When the representative is to retain funds for any considerable length of time, his failure to put them at interest will result in charging him personally with the interest which might have been obtained.[21] If he uses estate money for his own purposes he is charged with interest at the legal rate and must also account to

15 Ibid.

16 See Matter of Kent, 146 Misc. 155, 261 N.Y.S. 698, 1932.

17 Harper v. Betts, 177 Ark. 977, 8 S.W.2d 464, 60 A.L.R. 484, 1928; Norwood v. Harness, 98 Ind. 134, 49 Am. Rep. 739, 1884; Officer v. Officer, 120 Iowa 389, 94 N.W. 947, 98 Am.St.Rep. 365, 1903.

18 In re Arguello, 97 Cal. 196, 31 P. 937, 1893; Gatewood v. Furlow, 19 Ga.App. 74, 90 S.E. 973, 1916 (description "adm'r" insufficient to absolve the administrator); Williams v. Williams, 55 Wis. 300, 12 N.W. 465, motion denied, 55 Wis. 300, 13 N.W. 274, 42 Am.Rep. 708, 1882 (though bank was informed of trust character and funds kept separate). As to putting estate investments in the representative's name, see annotations, 106 A.L.R. 271, 150 id. 805.

19 Officer v. Officer and Harper v. Betts, both supra note 17. Cf. supra note 5. If practical the deposits should be under the protection of the Federal Deposits Insurance Corporation—see 12 U.S.C.A. § 264.

20 Officer v. Officer, supra note 17. See annotation, 101 A.L.R. 602.

21 See supra note 4.

the estate for any additional profit made;[22] in addition he may be denied the commissions to which he would otherwise be entitled.[23]

## PAYMENT OF TAXES

**125. The personal representative should pay from the assets of the estate all taxes due at the time of decedent's death, personal property taxes assessed upon the property while administration is in progress, and the state and federal income and death taxes.**

The personal representative's duties regarding taxes are important. Of course the present work can deal only with the broad outlines of the matter and there are often difficult tax decisions which the representative must make. If the estate is large, Federal taxes demand careful attention.

### *Federal Income Taxes*

The representative should at once send a notice of his appointment together with a certified copy of his letters to the Commissioner of Internal Revenue so that notices regarding the income taxes of the decedent and his estate will be sent to the representative.[1] If the decedent died before filing his tax return for the previous year, this must be done by the representative. In addition, he must file a return for decedent's income during the fraction of the year in which the latter died if that income was $600 or more. Finally, if the estate income is $600 or more for the taxable year, a fiduciary return must be filed and likewise a return for subsequent years until the estate is closed. Of course the representative must also pay these respective taxes as well as those assessed against decedent for taxes for prior years. When the representative is discharged he should notify the Commissioner of Internal Revenue of that fact together with a certified copy of the discharge.

22 In re Jula's Estate, supra note 4. As to interest rate, see annotations, 37 A.L.R. 447, 55 id. 950, 112 id. 833, 156 id. 936. If the representative uses the money for his own purposes, the interest may be compounded. Russell v. Russell, 164 Miss. 335, 144 So. 542, 1932; cf. First Nat. Bank of Opp v. Weaver, 225 Ala. 160, 142 So. 420, 88 A.L.R. 201, 1932.

23 In re Jula's Estate, supra note 4; cf. In re Reed v. Taliaferro, supra note 4.

1 See generally Bailey & Stoel, The Executor, the Administrator, and the Tax Collector, 29 Or.L.R. 76; Miller, Federal Tax Problems of Attorneys for Estates, 35 Iowa L.R. 3; Bronston, Tax Problems in Administration [1951] U. of Ill.L.Forum 565; Collie, Tax Responsibilities of Executors, 90 Trusts & Estates 676.

*Federal Estate Taxes*

If the gross estate is expected to be over $60,000, the representative should file a notice of his appointment with the local collector of internal revenue within two months after qualification as representative.[2] The gross estate for this purpose includes not only the personalty and realty passing by succession, but also (1) marital interests such as dower passing to the surviving spouse, (2) property transferred by decedent in contemplation of death, to take effect on his death, or when he retains the power to amend or revoke the transfer, (3) property held by him jointly or in community, (4) life insurance on his life, (5) property over which he had at his death a power of appointment unless the appointees are limited to exempt corporations or certain close relatives of decedent or the creator of the power. From the gross estate, debts and administration and funeral expenses are deducted leaving the adjusted gross estate. Half of the latter constitutes the marital deduction, but the estate is entitled to this only and to the extent that the decedent's property passed absolutely to the surviving spouse. Charitable bequests are also deductible and finally there is a specific deduction of $60,000. Matters concerning computations and valuation demand close attention. The representative has fifteen months after decedent's death with which to file the return, although this time and the time within which payment must be made by the representative may be extended. When the representative is discharged he should send notice thereof to the Commissioner.

*Federal Gift Taxes*

If the decedent made a gift to any donee over $3,000 during the year in which he died and did not file a return the representative must file a return on his behalf. Likewise if the decedent received a gift over $3,000 during the year, the representative must file an information return if the decedent did not. Any unpaid gift taxes must be paid by the representative.[3]

*State Income and Inheritance Taxes*

Most states have income taxes and the representative's duties are similar to those in connection with the Federal taxes. This is likewise truc in states where there is an estate tax, though rates and usually exemptions are lower. Other jurisdictions have an inheritance tax, which is upon the privilege of receiving prop-

2 Ibid. See infra § 147, note 8 et seq.

3 See Miller, supra note 1 at 10.

erty by the beneficiaries, and here the representative is also under duty to make a report or return and to see that the amount of the tax is withheld and paid to the state.[4] A number of states also have gift taxes.[5]

*Property Taxes*

Usually unpaid taxes of all sorts—including various miscellaneous taxes—which were due in the lifetime of the decedent must be paid by the representative.[6] Taxes upon realty becoming due after the death must ordinarily be borne by the heirs,[7] though the contrary may be true by statute or testamentary provision.[8] Furthermore, the representative may pay current taxes if it is necessary to sell the land to pay debts.[9] The personal property may be taxed while administration is in progress and the representative must pay such taxes, and according to many statutes must make a return to the tax assessor showing the amount of the personalty in the estate.

*Personal Liability of Representative*

Of course the executor or administrator is allowed credit for payment of all taxes which he is required to pay.[10] Taxes are preferred to ordinary debts [11] and if the representative observes the correct order of payment and the statutory and regulatory provisions regarding return and assessment he is not personally liable for payment of taxes.[12] Otherwise he may incur personal liability to the taxing authorities.

4 See Bailey & Stoel, supra note 1 at 109. As to who must bear death taxes, see infra § 147 at note 13.

5 See Spangler v. Wisconsin Dep't of Taxation, 255 Wis. 51, 37 N.W.2d 857, 1949.

6 Brown v. Brown, 72 N.J.Eq. 667, 65 A. 739, 1907; see annotation, 163 A.L.R. 724.

7 In re Paradis' Estate, 134 Me. 333, 186 A. 672, 1936.

8 Hoffman v. Ness, 71 N.D. 283, 300 N.W. 428, 1941 (statute); Moore v. Bryant, 10 Tex.Civ.App. 131, 31 S.W. 223, 1895 (will).

9 Hogan v. Pigott, 60 W.Va. 541, 56 S.E. 189, 1906.

10 Davis v. Blumenberg, 107 Miss. 432, 65 So. 503, 1914; Kenyon v. Kenyon, 31 R.I. 270, 76 A. 798, 1910

11 See infra § 128.

12 See Miller, supra note 1 at 18; Bailey & Stoel, supra note 1 at 113.

## SURVIVAL OF CLAIMS AGAINST ESTATE

**126. At common law contract claims survived the death of the obligor, while tort claims usually did not survive. By statute the rule of survivorship has been generally extended to cases involving proprietary interests and in some jurisdictions to all causes of action though in many states the earlier view is still maintained as to claims based upon injuries to plaintiff in his person or feelings.**

At common law the general rule was that contract causes survived and might be enforced against the obligor's personal representative,[1] while tort claims did not and could not be so enforced.[2] Accordingly, it was held that trover would not lie against the personal representative of a converter although assumpsit could have been brought upon the same facts by waiving the tort.[3] It is doubtful if this distinction would be followed at the present time, since actions to vindicate property rights now usually survive regardless of the form in which they are cast.[4]

There are statutes in most jurisdictions announcing the rule as to what causes of action survive.[5] In the larger group of states

1 Troup v. Smith's Ex'rs, 20 John. (N.Y.) 33, 1809; see Raymond v. Fitch, 2 C.M. & R. 588, 150 Eng.Rep. 251, 1835; 3 Bl.Com. 302. However, if the injuries due to breach of contract were personal, they did not survive. Jenkins v. French, 58 N.H. 532, 1879; Stebbins v. Palmer, 1 Pick. (Mass.) 71, 11 Am.Dec. 146, 1822 (breach of marriage). See infra note 9. Cf. Quirk v. Thomas, [1916] 1 K.B. 516; Neal v. Haygood, 1 Ga. 514, 1846. And see note, 41 Harv.L.R. 913. As to survival of liability on joint obligations, see annotation, 67 A.L.R. 608.

2 Cravath v. Plympton, 13 Mass. 454, 1816; Coker v. Crozier, 5 Ala. 369, 1843 (case for fraud); Mellen v. Baldwin, 4 Mass. 480, 1808 (replevin); Hambly v. Trott, Cowp. 371, 98 Eng. Rep. 1136, 1776 (trover). As to personal injuries, see annotation, 78 A.L. R. 600. Cf. Harris v. Nashville Trust Co., 128 Tenn. 573, 162 S.W. 584, 49 L.R.A.,N.S., 897, Ann.Cas.1914C, 885, 1914 (action against executor for libel in testator's will may be maintained); cf. supra § 95, note 53. See Winfield, Death as Affecting Liability in Tort, 29 Col.L.R. 239.

3 Hambly v. Trott, supra note 2. However, this action survived in favor of a personal representative.

4 Raymond v. Bailey, 98 Conn. 201, 118 A. 915, 1922; Batty v. Greene, 206 Mass. 561, 92 N.E. 715, 138 Am. St.Rep. 407, 1910; Lee's Adm'r v. Hill, 87 Va. 497, 12 S.E. 1052, 24 Am. St.Rep. 666, 1891. But see Alexander v. Dean, 157 Ga. 280, 121 S.E. 238, 1924.

5 For a summary of the legislation, see Evans, A Comparative Study of the Statutory Survival of Tort Claims For and Against Executors and Administrators, 29 Mich.L.R. 969; Evans, Survival of Claims For and Against Executors and Administrators, 19 Ky.L.J. 792; note, 48 Harv. L.R. 1008.

the legislation enumerates the causes of action which are deemed to survive. Generally, the statutes in this group merely mentioned a few sorts of actions "in addition to those which survive at common law." A second group of statutes declare that all actions survive except certain enumerated ones. Naturally, such legislation tends to allow survival in more cases than statutes of the first type. In a few jurisdictions it is declared that all causes of action survive. At common law, and generally under the statutes, actions which survive the death of the injured person also survive the death of the obligor, and vice versa. Often the legislation declares that certain causes of action survive; these are generally interpreted as permitting the survival both for and against the personal representative. However, the rule of mutuality is not a universal one.[6]

Frequently statutes provide that actions for "injury to the person" survive, or do not survive. There is little doubt but that this expression includes actions for assault and physical injuries due to negligence; but whether or not it includes causes of action for death, for alienation of affections, loss of wife's services or society, or defamation, has given rise to much difficulty. In a broad sense, viewing the word "person" as a living entity, actions of these sorts fairly come within the statutory language of "injuries to the person." On the other hand, it is possible to regard the word "person" as meaning merely body, and to interpret the phrase as equivalent to physical injury. The courts often construe such provisions so as to follow the common-law rule denying survival of tort actions where the statute does not distinctly indicate the contrary.[7] This narrow interpretation is unfortunate. The common-law position was established at a time when ideas of compensatory relief were very much narrower than in present day society. In the earlier period, the position of the courts was that the tort-feasor owed a mere personal duty to re-

[6] See Clark v. Goodwin, 170 Cal. 527, 150 P. 357, L.R.A.1916A, 1142, 1915, noted, 4 Cal.L.R. 52; Mellen v. Baldwin, supra note 2. And see note 3 supra, and 8 infra. See also § 116 at note 50 et seq.

[7] Johnson v. Bradstreet Co., 87 Ga. 79, 13 S.E. 250, 1891; Gross' Adm'r v. Ledford, 190 Ky. 526, 228 S.W. 24, 14 A.L.R. 689, 1921; White v. Safe Deposit & Trust Co., 140 Md. 593, 118 A. 77, 24 A.L.R. 482, 1922 (alienation of affections); Hey v. Prime, 197 Mass. 474, 84 N.E. 141, 17 L.R.A.,N.S., 570, 1908; Forbes v. City of Omaha, 79 Neb. 6, 112 N.W. 326, 1907. See also note 9 infra. But see Waller v. First Savings & Trust Co. of Tampa, 103 Fla. 1025, 138 So. 780, 1931, noted, 80 U. of Pa.L.R. 1018; Ex parte Upton, 236 Ala. 264, 181 So. 905, 117 A.L.R. 572, 1938; note, 36 Mich.L.R. 833.

spond in damages, and that this personal obligation was ended by his death. We have outgrown this point of view and should look at the situation from the standpoint of the claimant, and hence deny that he should lose his right to compensation because of the death of the wrongdoer.

In early times the rule forbidding survival in tort actions could be justified on the ground that it provided some sort of a time limitation to the commencement of tort actions. With the passage of the Statute of Limitations applicable to personal actions in 1623, this reason ceased to exist, but the rule against survival of tort actions of a personal nature had long been established and was not altered except through express legislation. Statutes, as well as decisions, have often been illiberal. Even though by statute an action for personal injuries or death now generally may be brought by the personal representative of the victim, in many states it does not survive against the wrongdoer's representative.[8] The tendency to arrive at the same result regarding survival as would have been reached at common law is shown by decisions holding that actions for breach of marriage promises do not survive under statutes providing that "all actions founded on contract" survive.[9]

[8] Clark v. Goodwin, supra note 6; Wright v. Smith, 136 Kan. 205, 14 P. 2d 640, 1932; Brown v. Wightman, 47 Utah 31, 151 P. 366, L.R.A.1916A, 1140, 1915; Claussen v. Brothers, 148 S.C. 1, 145 S.E. 539, 61 A.L.R. 826, 1928. And see Severns v. California Highway Indemnity Exchange, 100 Cal.App. 384, 280 P. 213, 1928, noted, 18 Cal.L.R. 44 (personal injury action does not survive death of tort-feasor). But see Davis v. Nichols, 54 Ark. 358, 15 S.W. 880, 1891; Kahn v. Wolf, 151 Fla. 863, 10 So.2d 553, 1942; Hunt v. Authier, 28 Cal.2d 288, 169 P.2d 913, 171 A.L.R. 1379, 1946 (family's claim for support deemed a property right which survived tort-feasor's death); notes, 30 Minn.L.R. 127, 24 Cal.L.R. 716. Sometimes the right to sue depends on whether the plaintiff's decedent or the wrongdoer died first. Cf. Martinelli v. Burke, 298 Mass. 390, 10 N.E.2d 113, 112 A.L.R. 341, 1937, with White v. Cormier, 311 Mass. 537, 42 N.E.2d 256, 1942 and see notes, 40 Col.L.R. 702, 38 Mich.L.R. 907, 24 Tex.L.R. 214. See generally Wigmore, Death by Wrongful Act—Survival of Liability Upon Tort-feasor's Death, 4 Ill.L.R. 425; Killion, Wrongful Death Actions in California—Some Needed Amendments, 25 Cal.L.R. 170, 184–186.

[9] Warner v. Benham, 126 Wash. 393, 218 P. 260, 34 A.L.R. 1358, 1923. And see Bernstein v. Queens County Jockey Club, 222 App.Div. 191, 225 N.Y.S. 449, 1927, noted, 13 Corn.L.Q. 596, 41 Harv.L.R. 913 (action for implied warranty resulting in personal injuries to the plaintiff does not survive the death of defendant). Accord: Singley v. Bigelow, 108 Cal.App. 436, 291 P. 899, 1930, noted, 19 Cal.L.R. 289.

*Revival of Actions*

If the cause of action is one which does not survive, death of a sole defendant before judgment ordinarily ends the pending action and prevents the bringing of a new action against the personal representative.[10] In absence of statute even when the cause of action survived, a new action is necessary when either party dies.[11] By virtue of legislation in most jurisdictions the pending action, if it is upon a cause of action which survives, may be continued or revived after the death of the defendant without starting a new action.[12] Moreover, some statutes permit the continuance or revival of any pending action after death of a party, although the cause of action was not one which would have survived if no action had been commenced in the lifetime of the party.[13] The procedural details of revival are governed by statute, and generally consist of filing a pleading substituting the representative of the deceased party and giving notice thereof to the opponent.

[10] Neal v. Haygood, 1 Ga. 514, supra note 1; Olson v. Scully, 296 Ill. 418, 129 N.E. 841, 1921.

[11] See Green v. Watkins, 6 Wheat. (U.S.) 260, 5 L.Ed. 256, 1821.

[12] See annotation, 92 A.L.R. 956; Federal Rule of Civil Procedure 25a.

[13] Wright v. Smith, supra note 8; Levin v. Muser, 107 Neb. 230, 185 N.W. 431, 1921.

## ENFORCEMENT OF CLAIMS

**127. Under modern procedure the holder of a claim against a decedent must proceed upon it within the statutory period of nonclaim, typically one year or less. The tendency of the statutory systems is to permit, and indeed require, allowance of debt claims by the probate court though generally the ordinary courts still have jurisdiction over equitable and delictual claims against the decedent.**

**Unmatured, as well as matured, claims must be presented or filed within the period designated by law. The same is true of contingent claims in some states, though in others the latter may be asserted against the heirs if they do not become absolute before settlement of the estate.**

**Secured claims need not be presented in order for the creditor to obtain satisfaction out of the security. The heirs or specific legatees or devisees can usually insist that mortgage debts be paid from the general assets even though the creditor does not demand payment of the representative and relies instead upon the security.**

*The Older Practice*

The earlier method of payment of creditors from assets in the representative's hands was fraught with pitfalls for the representative and the enforcement procedure was often unsatisfactory so far as the creditor was concerned.[1] Modern probate systems have altered this practice to a marked degree, although something must be seen of the prior rules in order to deal with those which remain and to appreciate the legislative reforms.

Formerly the personal representative ordinarily paid the debts voluntarily and without court sanction. In doing so he ran the risk that the distributees or the residuary legatees would contend that the sums paid were not due or were excessive. Moreover, if there were not sufficient assets to satisfy all claims, judgments against the decedent had priority over specialty debts, which in turn were prior to other obligations. If the representative exhausted the assets in payment of debts of an inferior rank he was personally liable to pay creditors of a superior class even though he had no notice of the latter. However, by voluntary

1 Generally, see Adams, Equity, 8th ed. 1890, 248 et seq.; Langdell, Brief Survey of Equity Jurisdiction, 1905 cc. VI, VII; Maitland, Equity, 1936, 248–276; Rollison, Wills § 282: Woerner on Administration, 3d ed. c. XL

payment he could prefer certain creditors to others of the same class, and, although he lost this privilege against one who had commenced action, he could still prefer a creditor by confessing judgment in the latter's favor so as to give him a prior judgment.

If the creditor sued the representative at law the action determined not only whether there was a valid claim but also whether the defendant had estate assets out of which it was payable. To contest the latter, the representative was required to plead plene administravit—that he had fully administered all assets and none remained to satisfy the plaintiff's claim. If he failed to so plead or to sustain the plea by proof, sufficient assets were presumed to be in his hands and execution would go against his individual property.

Creditors were confronted with the difficulties that the common-law action did not afford an adequate means of proving what assets had come into the representative's hands, and that the judgment would not reach equitable assets, notably land which testator had charged with payment of his debts. Hence, creditors' suits were brought in equity to secure payment of their claims. If a bill was filed for the payment of all creditors the personal representative was obliged to pay the assets into the equity court which would then protect him by staying actions at law by other creditors who were thus forced to appear in the proceeding to secure payment of their claims. In making payment equity observed the common-law order of priority as to legal assets, but would marshal equitable assets so as to bring about equality between all creditors, regardless of rank, in so far as the equitable assets would permit.

Legatees and next of kin could also maintain bills for administration, and at least in later times so could the personal representative. An involved estate in England was apt to be plunged into equity where the superiority of the principles which were there applied was often offset by the delay and cost attendant upon the equity procedure.[2]

*Modern American Procedure—In General*

Early legislation in this country sought to improve upon the English system, and today in most states administration in equity is entirely or at least practically obsolete. This is due to the fact that our statutes have set up procedures for the establish-

[2] For modern English procedure, see Maitland, supra note 1.

ment and payment of claims under the jurisdiction of the court of probate so that resort to administration equity is unnecessary. The provisions in the various states are diverse but there is a somewhat common pattern which includes: (1) nonclaim limitation barring claims unless they are filed or presented within a stated short period, (2) the possibility of establishment of claims by the decree of the court of probate, (3) the principle that a creditor's judgment does not establish the presence of assets sufficient to satisfy his claim, nor enable him to get priority through execution, (4) denial of the representative's power to prefer one creditor over another or to retain assets for payment of his own debt.[3]

*Time Limitations on Prosecution of Claims*

There are now various sorts of time limits as to the prosecution of claims or actions against a decedent's estate. Among the common ones are: (1) The general Statute of Limitations; (2) the nonclaim statutes providing that claims must be presented to the personal representative or filed in the probate court within a designated period; (3) provisions that claims must be prosecuted within a certain time after being rejected for payment by the personal representative;[4] (4) provisions that actions may not be prosecuted against a personal representative until a certain time has elapsed.[5] All jurisdictions have limitations of the first two sorts; in some, limitations of all four kinds, and even additional ones, may be found.

*General Statute of Limitations*

As a rule if the general statute has commenced to run prior to the decedent's death, it is not interrupted by the latter event,[6] although, if the cause of action accrues after the death, the statute usually does not begin to run until a personal representative

3 For discussions of modern systems of handling claims against decedents' estates, see Wilson & McGehee, Probate Claims in Florida, 14 U. of Fla.L.R. 1; Kahn, Ascertainment and Payment of Claims, [1951] U. of Ill.L. Forum 533; see also Model Probate Code §§ 135–149.

4 Ohio Gen.Code, § 10509–133; see Levers v. Houston, 49 N.M. 169, 159 P.2d 761, 1945; Roberts v. Roberts, infra note 27.

5 See Eddy v. Adams, 145 Mass. 489, 14 N.E. 509, 1888.

6 Lang v. Wilmer, 131 Md. 215, 101 A. 706, 2 A.L.R. 1698, 1917 (judgment debt); In re Estate of Matson, 50 N. M. 155, 173 P.2d 484, 174 A.L.R. 1415, 1946. But see Robitaille v. Mumaugh, 167 Okl. 339, 29 P.2d 602, 1934. Cf. Collins v. Henry, 155 Ga. 886, 118 S.E. 729, 1923 (express statute). See note, 22 Iowa L.R. 557.

is appointed.[7] Naturally the Statute of Limitations is suspended during the period within which the personal representative may not be sued in accordance with provisions of the fourth type mentioned above.[8]

### *Nonclaim Statutes*

These statutes fix a definite time limit within which claims against decedents must be proceeded upon; their purpose is to provide relief against uncertainty in the late assertion of claims and to facilitate the speedy settlement of estates. It is clear that a claim may be barred by the nonclaim statute although the general Statute of Limitations has not run.[9] Some courts have held that a claim may be barred after death by the general statute although the nonclaim period has not expired,[10] although others hold that the claimant has the full nonclaim period within which to present his claim regardless of whether the general statute would have constituted a bar if the debtor had not died.[11]

The nonclaim statutes usually do not provide for extension of the time allowance because of absence, infancy, or incapacity of the claimant as in case of the general Statute of Limitations. The courts generally allow no extensions for disability or on other equitable grounds if the legislature makes none.[12] The nonclaim

7 Berger v. Jackson, 156 Fla. 251, 23 So.2d 265, 1945; In re Elwood's Estate, 309 Pa. 505, 164 A. 617, 1932.

8 Heckman v. Kassing, 76 Ind.App. 401, 132 N.E. 379, 1921; Walker v. Bennett, 209 Ky. 675, 273 S.W. 548, 1925.

9 Davis v. Shepard, 135 Wash. 124, 237 P. 21, 41 A.L.R. 163, 1925, noted, 35 Yale L.J. 504.

10 Brigham v. Garcelon, 254 Mass. 65, 149 N.E. 598, 1925; McKinzie v. Hill, 51 Mo. 303, 11 Am.Rep. 450, 1873; Gray Realty Co. v. Robinson, 111 Utah 521, 184 P.2d 237, 1947.

11 Briscoe v. Madden, 17 Ark. 533, 1856; In re Estate of Anderson, 200 Minn. 470, 274 N.W. 621, 112 A.L.R. 287, 1937. See notes, 36 Mich.L.R. 973, 22 Minn.L.R. 289; Model Probate Code § 135(c).

12 Lowe v. Jones, 192 Mass. 94, 78 N.E. 402, 6 L.R.A.,N.S., 487, 116 Am. St.Rep. 225, 7 Ann.Cas. 551, 1906; Davis v. Shepard, supra note 9; Morgan v. Hamlet, 113 U.S. 449, 5 S.Ct. 583, 28 L.Ed. 1043, 1884 (Arkansas statute). But see Sugar River Bank v. Fairbank, 49 N.H. 131, 1869 (nonclaim statute subject to principles of equity and estoppel just as general Statute of Limitations). Sometimes the court is authorized to grant relief in case of late claims. Chicago & N. W. R. Co. v. Moss, 210 Iowa, 491, 231 N.W. 344, 71 A.L.R. 936, 1930; Estabrook v. Moulton, 223 Mass. 359, 111 N.E. 859, 1916; Parkhurst v. Healy's Estate, 97 Vt. 295, 122 A. 895, 1914. See notes, 21 Ia.L.R. 152, 44 Harv.L. R. 649; annotation, 71 A.L.R. 940.

While there are still a few nonclaim statutes of the earlier type which barred claims only against the personal representative and permitted

statute has been held to bar a claim in favor of the state,[13] although it is now clear that a claim of the United States cannot be so barred.[14] Statutes sometimes provide certain exceptions to the running of nonclaim statute, and a few courts have given relief to claimants under disability without express statutory authority. However, in general the course of legislative and judicial thought has been that it is better policy to deny exceptions to the bar of the nonclaim statute rather than to impair its final effect by allowing exceptions, however meritorious.

The time when the nonclaim period commences to run is usually fixed by the terms of the statute. Sometimes the period starts with the appointment of the personal representative.[15] In other jurisdictions, the nonclaim statute commences to run when the personal representative publishes notice of his appointment or a notice to creditors to file or present their claims.[16] Where a statute of the latter type exists, it can be seen that if the personal representative does not publish an appropriate notice, the nonclaim statute will not run and the claim will not be barred except by the general Statute of Limitations.[17] In Kansas the statute formerly allowed a creditor to petition for the appointment of a personal representative fifty days after the death of the decedent in case no representative has been previously appointed. Because of the existence of this provision, the Kansas court held that the nonclaim statute commences to run as soon as a creditor could have petitioned for administration.[18] This

proceedings against heirs or distributees unless otherwise barred—see N. Y. Decedent Estate Law § 170 et seq. —— most statutes provide for a bar against everyone, see infra § 144, except in the case of contingent claims, see infra note 91.

13 In re Peers' Estate, 234 Iowa 403, 12 N.W.2d 894, 1944; State v. Evans, 143 Wash. 449, 255 P. 1035, 53 A.L.R. 564, 1927. Cf. In re Kuplen's Estate, 209 Wis. 178, 244 N.W. 623, 1932.

14 United States v. Summerlin, 310 U.S. 414, 60 Sup.Ct. 1019, 84 L.Ed. 1283, 1940. See notes, 29 Corn.L.Q. 258, 53 Harv.L.R. 1055.

15 Johnson v. Bain, 17 Ala.App. 71, 81 So. 849, 1919. See supra § 103, notes 27–31.

16 Inman v. Western Nat. Bank of Fort Worth, Tex., 83 Okl. 126, 200 P. 714, 1921.

17 Burr v. Goodwin, 126 Cal.App. 539, 14 P.2d 808, 1932, noted, 6 So.Cal. L.R. 174 (improper notice); McConaughy v. Wilsey, 115 Iowa 589, 88 N.W. 1101, 1902; Pratt v. Houghtaling, 45 Mich. 457, 8 N.W. 72, 1881. Cf. Thompson v. Owen, 249 Mass. 229, 144 N.E. 216, 1924.

18 Brown v. Baxter, 77 Kan. 97, 94 P. 155, 574, 1908; In re Hoover's Estate, 104 Kan. 635, 180 P. 275, 1919. The present Kansas nonclaim statute expressly starts to run from death. Gantz v. Bondurant, 159 Kan. 389, 155 P.2d 450, 1945.

holding had the desirable effect of barring claims of creditors who are not vigilant in the assertion of their rights and permitted the heirs to deal directly with the decedent's property after a period of fifty days plus the nonclaim period where no personal representative had been appointed. This result cannot be reached under typical nonclaim statutes, which do not commence to run until appointment of, or notice by, the personal representative.

In recent years there has been a marked tendency to shorten the nonclaim period and it is frequently as short as six months.[19] Probably the most usual period is one year. In those jurisdictions which have a period of time within which the personal representative may not be sued, this period is less (usually half of the nonclaim period).[20]

*Manner of Assertion of Claims*

In connection with nonclaim statutes, it should be noticed that there are two general types of provisions as to what the creditor must do before the nonclaim period has run. More frequently it is provided that the claimant must present his claim to the personal representative.[21] In case of such legislation it is held that a personal representative who has an individual claim in his favor need not present it for the reason that he already has notice of the matter.[22] However, if there are two personal representatives, the one asserting the claim should present it to his corepresentative.[23]

On the other hand, some jurisdictions require that the claim be filed with the probate court instead of presenting it to the personal representative.[24] This provision is often found in those jurisdictions in which the probate court has exclusive, or at least concurrent, jurisdiction to establish claims against the estate.[25]

19 George T. Webb & Co. v. Fogg, 134 Miss. 605, 99 So. 504, 1924. See note, 7 Ind.L.J. 129; Ohio Gen.Code § 10509–112 (four months). In Wisconsin the time for presenting claims is limited by order of the court which may fix the time at not less than four months nor more than one year. In re Walter's Estate, 183 Wis. 540, 198 N.W. 375, 1924.

20 See authorities supra notes 5, 8.

21 See Woerner on Administration, p 1246 et seq.; 24 C.J. 317; Am.Dig., tit. Executors and Administrators, 🔑 222.

22 In re Hoover's Estate, supra note 18.

23 Gallivan v. Jones, 102 F. 423, C.C.A.Cal.1900; see Winder v. Winder, 18 Cal.2d 123, 114 P.2d 347, 144 A.L.R. 935, 1941 (need not file with court).

24 Kowalski v. Guaranty Trust Co., 224 Mich. 122, 194 N.W. 581, 1923.

25 See infra note 110 et seq.

In such a statutory situation presentment of the claim to the personal representative is not enough; the claim must be actually filed in the court within the period allowed by the nonclaim statute.[26] Accordingly, it would seem that a personal representative must file his own individual claim.[27] Some statutes contemplate presentment of the claim to the representative and also filing the same with the court.[28]

The question may arise whether presentation of claim to the personal representative or filing of the claim with the court is a prerequisite to a suit upon the claim in the ordinary courts. Of course if the statute gives the probate court exclusive jurisdiction to determine claims of the particular nature,[29] this question can not arise. But where mere presentation to the personal representative is required, the commencement of action within the nonclaim period is sufficient presentation.[30] The suit papers can be deemed a notice of the claim.[31] Some statutes, however, require presentation as a condition to the commencement of the action. Under these, the creditor's declaration or complaint against the personal representative should show prior presentation to the representative or it does not state a cause of action.[32] However, if suit was started in the lifetime of the decedent it may be revived against the personal representative without presentation,[33] provided that the revival takes place before the nonclaim statute has run.[34]

26 Mayberry v. Moore, 137 Ill.App. 40, 1907; Fern v. Leuthold, 39 Minn. 212, 39 N.W. 399, 1888.

27 In re Ring's Estate, 132 Iowa 216, 109 N.W. 710, 1906; In re Charles' Estate, 159 Kan. 228, 154 P. 2d 117, 1944. Cf. Winder v. Winder, supra note 23; Roberts v. Roberts, 62 Wyo. 77, 162 P.2d 117, 1945.

28 Henn v. McGinnis, 182 Iowa 131, 165 N.W. 406, 1917; Keys v. Keys, 217 Mo. 48, 116 S.W. 537, 1909. And see Miller v. Bradburn, 106 Okl. 234, 233 P. 736, 1925 (creditor must present to representative and then either to the county judge or bring action upon the claim). For description of the unduly complicated system in Missouri, see note, 3 Mo.L.R. 66.

29 See infra notes 110, 112.

30 Hunley's Ex'x v. Shuford, 11 Ala. 203, 1847; Connecticut Life Ins. Co. v. Schurmeier, 117 Minn. 473, 136 N.W. 1, Ann.Cas.1913D 462, 1912; Clayton v. Dinwoodey, 33 Utah 251, 93 P. 723, 14 Ann.Cas. 926, 1908.

31 See Hunley's Ex'x v. Shuford, supra note 30.

32 Flynn v. Driscoll, 38 Idaho 545, 223 P. 524, 34 A.L.R. 352, 1924. But these statutes do not generally apply to noncontract or unliquidated claims. See infra note 114 et seq.

33 In re Lee's Estate, 240 Iowa 691, 37 N.W.2d 296, 1949; Milner v. First Nat. Bank of Minneapolis, 228 Minn. 324, 37 N.W.2d 450, 1949; Pull v. Nagle, 8 N.J.Misc. 653, 151 A. 385, 1930, noted, 29 Mich.L.R. 531; but see Cleage v. Jackson, 200 Okl. 375, 194 P.2d 843, 1948.

34 Bilby v. Hart-Parr Co., 102 Okl.

*Waiver of Limitations by Personal Representative*

In England the personal representative may ordinarily waive the general Statute of Limitations,[35] although there are some limitations upon his power to do so.[36] In some American jurisdictions there are express statutes, occasionally permitting,[37] more frequently forbidding,[38] waiver of the general Statute of Limitations by a personal representative. In the absence of such statutes there is great discrepancy in the holdings.[39] In some jurisdictions waiver is permitted in practically all cases.[40] Other states do not generally allow the representative to waive the statute,[41] though in some of these he may do so with reference to claims not barred at decedent's death,[42] and in still others he may start the statute running afresh if the debt is not already barred.[43] Where the personal representative is the creditor, the American courts are probably more apt to deny waiver than in case of other creditors' claims.[44] In most, though not in all, states, waiver affects the personal assets only.[45] Where waiver

53, 226 P. 360, 1934. As to limitation of revival under Federal Rules, see Anderson v. Yungkau, 329 U.S. 482, 67 Sup.Ct. 428, 91 L.Ed. 436, 1947. See also supra § 126, notes 10–13.

35 Hunter v. Baxter, 3 Giff. 214, 66 Eng.Rep. 388, 1861; Lowis v. Rumney, L.R. 4 Eq. 451, 1867; Hill v. Walker, 4 K. & J. 166, 70 Eng.Rep. 69, 1858 (representative's own debt).

36 Putnam v. Bates, 3 Russ. 188, 38 Eng.Rep. 547, 1826 (executor cannot keep debt alive so as to allow direct suit against the heir). See also Phillips v. Beal, 32 Beav. 26, 55 Eng.Rep. 11, 1863; Midgley v. Midgley, [1893] 3 Ch. 282.

37 Tsaraclis v. Characklis, 176 Md. 28, 3 A.2d 725, 1939.

38 See Elliott v. First Nat. Bank, 248 Ala. 360, 27 So.2d 623, 1946; but cf. Jones v. Baswell, 246 Ala. 410, 20 So.2d 715, 1945 (debt not barred at death). See annotation, 8 A.L.R.2d 660, 681.

39 See annotation, 8 A.L.R.2d 660.

40 Chambers v. Fennemore's Adm'r, 4 Har.(Del.) 368, 1846; McCoy's Adm'r v. McCoy (Ky.) 125 S.W. 177, 1910; Shreve v. Joyce, 36 N.J.Law 44, 13 Am.Rep. 417, 1872. Cf. McGowan v. Miles, 167 Tenn. 554, 72 S.W.2d 553, 1934, noted, 48 Harv.L.R. 337; Twiddy v. Mullen, 176 N.C. 16, 96 S.E. 653, 1918; Russell v. Hogan, 282 Ky. 764, 140 S.W.2d 615, 1940.

41 Abbott v. Johnston, 130 Ark. 1, 195 S.W. 676, 1917; Hammond v. Hammond, 150 Kan. 113, 91 P.2d 19, 1939; Schutz v. Morrette, 146 N.Y. 137, 40 N.E. 780, 1895; see infra notes 42–44.

42 Hunter v. Hunter, 63 S.C. 78, 41 S.E. 33, 90 Am.St.Rep. 663, 1902.

43 Holly v. Gibbons, 176 N.Y. 520, 68 N.E. 889, 98 Am.St.Rep. 694, 1903.

44 See Williams v. Williams, 79 Tenn. 652, 15 Lea (Tenn.) 438, 1885; McGowan v. Miles, 167 Tenn. 554, 72 S.W.2d 553, 1934 (claim of administrator's parent).

45 Houck v. Houck, 112 Md. 122, 76 A. 581, 1910; Bevers v. Park, 88 N.C. 456, 1883. Contra: Hodgdon v. White, 11 N.H. 208, 1840.

is not permitted, failure of the personal representative to assert the bar of the statute may permit the creditor to collect his barred claim,[46] but the representative will not be allowed credit on his final account for such payment.[47]

It is the general rule that a personal representative may not waive the nonclaim statute.[48] Moreover, even his fraudulent representations that the presentation of the claim is unnecessary will not excuse delay or failure to present the claim.[49] In the jurisdictions where claims are filed and allowed by the probate court, the court itself may, and probably should, of its own motion disallow claims filed too late. On the other hand, where mere presentation to the personal representative is required, it is within the power of the personal representative to pay the claim in spite of late presentation. However, in such case the personal representative paying a barred claim will not be entitled to credit for the payment.[50]

*Formal Sufficiency of Claim*

The notice which the creditor must present to the personal representative or the claim which he must file with the probate court need not be cast in any particular style.[51] Most statutes require, however, that it must be verified by affidavit,[52] but it is generally

46 But see Hammond v. Hammond, supra note 41 (court should disallow claim); In re Smith's Estate, 240 Iowa 499, 36 N.W.2d 815, 8 A.L.R.2d 640, 1949 (heirs may intervene and prevent sale of land).

47 See Van Winkle v. Blackford, 33 W.Va. 573, 11 S.E. 26, 1890; McGowan v. Miles, supra note 40.

48 Vanderpool v. Vanderpool, 48 Mont. 448, 138 P. 772, 1914; Henderson v. Tipton, 88 Tenn. 255, 14 S.W. 380, 1889.

49 State ex rel. Scherber v. Probate Court of Hennepin County, 145 Minn. 344, 177 N.W. 354, 11 A.L.R. 242, 1920, noted, 4 Minn.L.R. 536, 30 Yale L.J. 97; Harrison Machine Works v. Aufderheide, 222 Mo.App. 474, 280 S.W. 711, 1926. Cf. Anderson v. Storie, 208 Iowa 1172, 227 N.W. 93, 66 A.L.R. 1410, 1929. But see Burt v. Second Nat. Bank of Saginaw, 241 Mich. 216, 217 N.W. 71, 1928; Adams v. Hackensack Trust Co., 156 Fla. 20, 22 So. 2d 392, 1945.

50 Schneeberger v. Frazer, 36 Idaho 737, 213 P. 568, 1923; In re Lamberton's Estate, 10 Ohio Supp. 91, 1942.

51 Roth v. Ravich, 111 Conn. 649, 151 A. 179, 74 A.L.R. 364, 1930; People's Bank & Trust Co. v. Mills, 193 Ind. 131, 139 N.E. 145, 1923. And see infra note 53.

52 Ross v. Hull, 48 Ark. 304, 3 S.W. 190, 1887; Nevin-Frank Co. v. Hubert, 67 Mont. 50, 214 P. 959, 1923. But see Howe v. Gray, 119 Me. 465, 111 A. 756, 1920; Osborne v. Parker, 66 App.Div. 277, 72 N.Y.S. 894, 1901. And cf. Crist v. Tallman, 190 Iowa 1248, 179 N.W. 522, 1920 (verification may be filed after filing); Maupin v. Maupin, 261 Ky. 312, 87 S.W.2d 629, 1935 (verification waived).

agreed that it need not be in the form required of a pleading.[53] However, it must give the particulars of the claim,[54] even in the case of unmatured obligations.[55] The same is true of contingent claims when notice is required with reference to these claims.[56] Usually the probate courts furnish printed forms for claims against decedents' estates. Use of these blanks by creditors is desirable, though not ordinarily absolutely required. A claim may be amended,[57] even after the time limited for filing claims, if the amendment does not work a substantial change,[58] but a different cause of action may not be asserted after the nonclaim statute has run.[59]

*Nature of Claims Which Must Be Presented*

The statutes usually declare that all claims or demands should be presented or filed before the period of nonclaim has expired. There can be no doubt but that these provisions cover all past due liquidated money demands.[60] While presentment of a mort-

[53] Robinson v. Chapman, 98 Cal. App. 278, 276 P. 1081, 1929; In re Onstot's Estate, 224 Iowa 563, 277 N.W. 563, 1938; Rassieur v. Zimmer, 249 Mo. 175, 155 S.W. 24, 1913; Harwood v. Scott, 57 Mont. 83, 186 P. 693, 1920. And see supra note 51.

[54] In re West's Will, 246 Wis. 199, 16 N.W.2d 806, 1944. And see supra notes 51, 53. Cf. Pietrantonio v. Tonn's Estate, 278 Mich. 535, 270 N. W. 777, 1936 (waiver).

[55] Landis v. Woodman, 126 Cal. 454, 58 P. 857, 1899.

[56] See Barto v. Stewart, 21 Wash. 605, 59 P. 480, 1899.

[57] In re Davis' Estate, 142 Minn. 187, 171 N.W. 778, 1919; Smith v. Williams, 123 Mo.App. 479, 100 S.W. 55, 1907. See note, 27 Cal.L.R. 608.

[58] McCall v. Lee, 120 Ill. 261, 11 N. E. 522, 1887; In re Davis' Estate, supra note 57. See Weir v. Lake, 112 Ind.App. 318, 41 N.E.2d 828, 1942.

[59] State ex rel. Paramount Publix Corporation v. District Court of Seventh Judicial Dist. of State of Montana in and for Dawson County, 90 Mont. 281, 1 P.2d 335, 76 A.L.R. 1371, 1931; In re Boydston's Estate, 191 Or. 603, 232 P.2d 67, 1951; In re Mayer's Estate, 253 Wis. 32, 33 N. W.2d 213, 1948.

[60] Sanders v. Russell, 86 Cal. 119, 24 P. 852, 21 Am.St.Rep. 26, 1890 (judgment); Kittredge v. Nicholes, 162 Ill. 410, 44 N.E. 742, 1896; Crain v. Crain, 197 Ky. 813, 248 S.W. 176, 1923 (services rendered); Laupheimer v. Buck, 137 Kan. 935, 22 P.2d 949, 1933 (quantum meruit); Maine Cent. Institute v. Haskell, 71 Me. 487, 1880 (subscription); Marshall v. Perkins, 72 Me. 343, 1881 (note); Roddy v. Harrell, 40 S.W. 1064, Tex.Civ.App. 1897 (rent); Stitz v. Ryan, 192 Minn. 297, 256 N.W. 173, 94 A.L.R. 885, 1934 (award of workman's compensation). But presentment of a claim is not necessary to preserve a judgment lien on land in decedent's lifetime. Christerson v. French, 180 Cal. 523, 182 P. 27, 1919. Nor in case of a note already in executor's possession for collection. Gerhold v. Papathanasion, 130 Ohio St. 342, 199 N.E. 353, 103 A. L.R. 334, 1936. A claim for taxes

gage is not necessary in order to foreclose,[61] it is required in order to collect any deficiency from the estate.[62] The decisions are conflicting, however, as to whether the statutes apply in the case of unliquidated claims arising on contract,[63] and in case of tort actions for damages.[64] It is generally held that no presentment of claim is necessary in the following sorts of actions: ejectment,[65] replevin,[66] suit to quiet title,[67] specific performance,[68] or suit to impress a trust upon specific property.[69] It may well be argued that, as claims other than those which are based upon contract for a liquidated amount usually involve a lawsuit and

usually does not require presentation. See annotation, 109 A.L.R. 1370; notes, 12 Temple L.Q. 149, 21 Chi-Kent L.R. 119. See supra § 125.

61 Dake v. Woodcock, 181 Ark. 409, 26 S.W.2d 84, 1930; Savings Union Bank & Trust Co. v. Crowley, 176 Cal. 543, 169 P. 67, 1917 (pledge); Waughop v. Bartlett, 165 Ill. 124, 46 N.E. 197, 1897; Ross v. Lewis, 23 N.M. 524, 169 P. 468, 1917 (chattel mortgage); Pereles v. Leiser, 119 Wis. 347, 96 N.W. 799, 1903. But see State Bank of Orlando & Trust Co. v. Macy, 101 Fla. 140, 133 So. 876, 78 A.L.R. 1119, 1931.

62 Di Iorio v. Cantone, 49 R.I. 137, 140 A. 913, 1929; Pereles v. Leiser, supra note 61. The filing of a claim is not a waiver of the mortgage lien. Kendrick State Bank v. Barnum, 31 Idaho 562, 173 P. 1144, 2 A.L.R. 1129, 1918; see note, 43 Harv.L.R. 964. Cf. Storlie v. Sachse, 165 Wash. 291, 5 P.2d 342, 1931.

63 Presentment necessary: Flynn v. Driscoll, 38 Idaho 545, 223 P. 524, 34 A.L.R. 352, 1924; In re Bourke's Estate, 159 Kan. 553, 156 P.2d 501, 157 A.L.R. 1107, 1945 (partnership accounting). Contra: Boyd v. Applewhite, 121 Miss. 879, 84 So. 16, 1920.

64 Presentment necessary: Des Moines Transp. Co. v. Haring, 238 Iowa 395, 27 N.W.2d 210, 1947; Hackensack Trust Co. v. Van Den Berg, 92 N.J.L. 412, 105 A. 719, 1918; Randall v. Brayton, 26 R.I. 233, 58 A. 734, 1904; Pierce v. Johnson, 136 Ohio St. 95, 23 N.E.2d 993, 125 A.L.R. 867, 1939; Pinson v. Abbott, 93 F.Supp. 120, D.C.N.M., 1950; Lindsay v. Collins, 96 F.Supp. 994, D.C.Wyo.1951. Contra: National Automobile & Casualty Ins. Co. v. Ainge, 34 Cal.2d 806, 215 P.2d 13, 1950; Comstock v. Matthews, 55 Minn. 111, 56 N.W. 583, 1893; Feld v. Borodofski, 87 Miss. 727, 40 So. 816, 1906; Hornbeck v. Richards, 80 Mont. 27, 257 P. 1025, 1927; Clover v. Neely, 116 Okl. 155, 243 P. 758, 1926. Cf. Stitz v. Ryan, supra note 60.

65 Lamme v. Dodson, 4 Mont. 560, 2 P. 298, 1883.

66 Moore v. Moore, 141 Miss. 795, 105 So. 850, 1925; note, 24 Minn.L.R. 648. But cf. In re Del Paronto's Estate, 172 Kan. 7, 238 P.2d 464, 1951.

67 Maguire v. Cunningham, 64 Cal. App. 536, 222 P. 838, 1923.

68 Robinson v. McDonald's Widow & Heirs, 11 Tex. 385, 62 Am.Dec. 480, 1854; In re Bank's Estate, 80 Mont. 159, 260 P. 128, 1927. See Erwin v. Mark, 105 Mont. 361, 73 P.2d 537, 133 A.L.R. 1064, 1937 (contract to bequeath).

69 Elizalde v. Elizalde, 137 Cal. 634, 70 P. 861, 1902; McDonald v. Hartford Trust Co., 104 Conn. 169, 132 A. 902, 1926; Erwin v. Mark, supra note 68. But see Harvey v. Pocock, 92

will seldom be allowed by a personal representative, their presentment is a more or less idle act. Upon this hypothesis, claimants will merely be required to assert such claims before the various limitation periods have run, and before the estate has been closed and the personal representative discharged.

*The Same—Matured Claims*

Claims may be classified according to time of becoming due into four groups: (1) Those that were due at or before decedent's death; (2) claims which become due after the decedent's death but during the nonclaim period; (3) obligations which do not mature until after the nonclaim period has expired but which will become payable thereafter; (4) claims concerning which it cannot be ascertained whether they will ever become due. The first class and probably the second are called *matured* obligations, the third class are denominated *unmatured,* and the fourth, *contingent* claims.

No difficulty is encountered with reference to obligations of the first class. If the claims are of a nature requiring presentment, this must be done within the period of the nonclaim statute or the claim is barred, not only against the personal representative but usually against the heirs as well.[70] Claims which mature after the decedent's death but before the expiration of the nonclaim period should also be presented before the latter time,[71] although statutes sometimes permit this to be done within a certain time after maturity.[72] Claims which do not mature until after decedent's death must be distinguished from obligations which have no existence in his lifetime such as funeral expenses or costs of administration. The latter are claims against the personal representative rather than the estate. On orthodox theory the nonclaim statute has no application to them,[73] al-

Wash. 625, 159 P. 771, 1916; In re Grindrod's Estate, 158 Kan. 345, 148 P.2d 278, 1944.

70 Converse v. Nichols, 202 Mass. 270, 89 N.E. 135, 1909; Armstrong v. Loomis, 97 Mich. 577, 56 N.W. 938, 1893; Hancock v. Cochran, 126 Okl. 126, 258 P. 1046, 1927; Woods v. Ely, 7 S.D. 471, 64 N.W. 531, 1895. But see Home Brewing Co. v. Mahler, 92 N.J.Eq. 323, 112 A. 506, 1920 (statute); Durflinger v. Arnold, 329 Ill. 93, 160 N.E. 172, 1928 (heirs liable for realty devised). See supra note 12 and infra § 144.

71 See infra note 85.

72 See Michel Brewing Co. v. Wightman's Estate, 97 Wis. 657, 73 N.W. 316, 1897.

73 Lowry v. Crandall, 52 Ariz. 501, 83 P.2d 1003, 120 A.L.R. 271, 1938; Miller v. Monroe, 50 Idaho 726, 300 P. 362, 1931; Storlie v. Sachse, 165 Wash. 291, 5 P.2d 342, 1931; In re Kelly's Estate, 183 Wis. 485, 198 N.W.

though in some states the claimant can look directly to estate assets for payment in which case there must be compliance with the statute.[74]

*The Same—Unmatured Claims*

Unmatured claims which will certainly become due after the nonclaim statute has run must be presented within the nonclaim period under most statutes.[75] This is true when the statute provides that "all claims" must be presented.[76] No especial difficulty will be encountered in the preparation of an unmatured claim since the amount is ordinarily liquidated and the situation does not differ from one already due except as to the matter of maturity. There are several possible ways for handling the payment of unmatured claims. The amount which will be payable in the future may be discounted to its present value and the resultant sum paid at once to the creditor. As an alternative, the representative may retain in his hands a sum sufficient to discharge the obligation at maturity. On the other hand, distribution may be made to the heirs regardless of the obligation except that they are required to give bond for payment of the claim when it becomes due. Statutes often provide for dealing with unmatured claims in one or more of these manners,[77] and even in absence of legislation the courts have power to make use of these devices.[78] The creditors who have unmatured claims are given no special privileges. For example, they may not recover the amount of their claim from the legatees or distributees after settlement of the estate.[79] They should secure payment, or means of obtaining

280, 1924; City of Detroit v. Stafford, 320 Mich. 6, 30 N.W.2d 410, 1948 (taxes). See supra § 119.

[74] Butterworth v. Bredemeyer, 89 Wash. 677, 155 P. 152, 1916; Stults v. Forst, 135 Ind. 297, 34 N.E. 1125, 1893; In re Charles' Estate, supra note 27.

[75] Gross v. Thornson's Estate, 286 Ill. 185, 121 N.E. 600, 1919; Thompson v. Owen, 249 Mass. 229, 144 N.E. 216, 1924; In re Kleinschmidt's Estate, 167 Wis. 450, 167 N.W. 827, 1918.

[76] Watkins v. Parker, 97 Ark. 492, 134 S.W. 1187, 1911; Fillyau v. Laverty, 3 Fla. 72, 1850. But see Sampson v. Sampson, 63 Me. 328, 1874. An unmatured claim may be "justly due" within the meaning of the statute, Cassatt v. Vogel, 12 Mo.App. 323, 1882; or an "accrued" claim, Farris v. Stoutz, 78 Ala. 130, 1884.

[77] E. g. Ohio Gen.Code, § 10509–124; Model Probate Code § 138. For a discussion of the Massachusetts provisions, see Warren, Problems in Probate and Administration, 32 Harv.L.R. 315, 331.

[78] Petrie v. Voorhees' Ex'r, 18 N.J. Eq. 285, 1867; Bankers' Surety Co. v. Meyer, 205 N.Y. 219, 98 N.E. 399, Ann. Cas.1913D, 1218, 1912, noted, 12 Col. L.R. 172.

[79] Thompson v. Owen, 249 Mass. 229, 144 N.E. 216, 1924, noted, 23

payment, during the course of administration since the heirs generally take the property upon distribution free of all liability from claims which might have been established against the personal representative.

*The Same—Contingent Claims*

Legislation which merely provides that "all claims" shall be presented does not usually require that contingent claims shall be presented.[80] However, some statutes specifically require contingent, as well as other, claims to be presented.[81] In most jurisdictions having statutes of the latter type the claim must be presented although it is not liquidated in amount.[82] Some courts however hold that even under legislation of the latter sort, an unliquidated sum which may never become due is not even a contingent claim within the meaning of the statute.[83] A few statutes provide that claims may be presented within a certain period after becoming due. These do not require the presentment or filing of claims while they are in the contingent stage.[84] Even in jurisdictions where contingent claims are not required to be presented, if they become absolute during the nonclaim period, they must be duly presented or they are barred.[85] Furthermore if the claim becomes absolute after the nonclaim statute has run but before the personal representative has been discharged, the creditor may,[86] and indeed should,[87] proceed against the latter. However, if the executor or administrator has been discharged he is not

Mich.L.R. 185. See supra note 12, and infra § 144.

80 Union Trust Co. v. Shoemaker, 258 Ill. 564, 101 N.E. 1050, 1913; Sledge & Norfleet v. Dye, 140 Miss. 779, 106 So. 519, 1926; State ex rel. Patterson v. Tittmann, 134 Mo. 162, 35 S.W. 579, 1896; Pruett v. Caddigan, 42 Nev. 329, 176 P. 787, 1918; Logan v. Dixon, 73 Wis. 533, 41 N.W. 713, 1889.

81 See Warren, Problems in Probate and Administration, 32 Harv.L.R. 315, 331 n. 104; Model Probate Code §§ 135, 150.

82 Johnson v. Larson, 56 N.D. 207, 216 N.W. 895, 1927; Halloran-Judge Trust Co. v. Heath, 70 Utah 124, 258 P. 342, 64 A.L.R. 368, 1927; Barto v. Stewart, 21 Wash. 605, 59 P. 480, 1899.

83 Hantzch v. Massolt, 61 Minn. 361, 63 N.W. 1069, 1895; Nathan v. Freeman, 70 Mont. 259, 225 P. 1015, 41 A.L.R. 138, 1924; O'Neill v. Lauderdale, 80 Okl. 170, 195 P. 121, 1921.

84 Gay's Appeal, 61 Conn. 445, 23 A 829, 1892; Miller v. Shoaf, 110 N.C. 319, 14 S.E. 800, 1892.

85 Bennett v. Dawson, 18 Ark. 334, 1857. See Lytle v. Bond's Estate, 39 Vt. 388, 1867. But see Bates v. McGill, 223 Iowa 62, 272 N.W. 535, 1937, noted, 22 Iowa L.R. 764.

86 Oswald v. Pillsbury, 61 Minn. 520, 63 N.W. 1072, 1895.

87 Ebert v. Whitney, 170 Minn. 102, 212 N.W. 29, 51 A.L.R. 771, 1927.

ordinarily liable upon such claims,[88] though the contrary seems to be true in some of the cases of liability of stockholders of an insolvent bank.[89]

It is reasonable that a court should construe its statutes if possible so as not to require the presentment of purely contingent claims. Usually the devices to secure the payment of unmatured claims are unfitted for contingent claims.[90] It is unreasonable to postpone the final settlement of the estate until the contingency has occurred, for this may not happen until many years after decedent's death, or indeed may never take place. Moreover even a careful holder of a contingent claim might fail to present or file it in case it arises upon a warranty or bond, the breach of which has not yet occurred. Finally, if such claims are filed their number and tentative nature might cause perplexities in the adminis-

88 Zollickoffer v. Seth, 44 Md. 359, 1875. See Baker v. Baker, 220 Iowa 1216, 264 N.W. 116, 102 A.L.R. 995, 1935.

89 Considerable litigation has arisen out of the added liability attached to ownership of bank stock in case of the death of the stockholder. The estate is liable in case the insolvency occurred after the latter's death. Hirning v. Kurle, 54 S.D. 334, 223 N.W. 212, 1929; Farmers' State Bank v. Callahan, 123 Kan. 638, 256 P. 961, 1927. As to the liability of legatees and distributees, cf. Citizens' Bank v. Kasten, 54 S.D. 339, 223 N.W. 214, 1929, with Andrew v. Dunn, 202 Iowa 364, 210 N.W. 425, 1926; Seabury v. Green, 173 S.C. 235, 175 S.E. 639, 1934; Seabury v. Green, 294 U.S. 165, 55 S.Ct. 373, 79 L.Ed. 834, 96 A.L.R. 1463, 1935, noted, 44 Yale L.J. 1272 (minor legatees). When a receiver was appointed after decedent's death and before the nonclaim statute had run, but the assessment and claim were not made until after nonclaim statute had run, the action was not barred. Drain v. Stough, 61 F.2d 668, 87 A.L.R. 490, C.C.A. 9th, 1932. The same was held where the bank was not suspended and no claim filed until after the nonclaim statute had run. Baird v. McMillan, 53 N.D. 257, 205 N.W. 682, 41 A.L.R. 177, 1925; Tierney v. Shakespeare, 34 N.M. 501, 284 P. 1019, 1930, noted, 3 Dak.L.R. 220; In re Wilson's Estate, 127 Neb. 106, 254 N.W. 717, 1934, noted, 33 Mich. L.R. 638. Contra: Sanders v. Merchants' State Bank, 349 Ill. 547, 182 N.E. 897, 1932, noted, 19 Va.L.R. 645. But when liability becomes absolute before nonclaim statute has run, failure to file claim within the period is a bar. Ebert v. Whitney, supra note 87.

90 See note, 8 Mont.L.R. 30. But cf. Model Probate Code § 140. There is no possibility of reduction of a contingent claim to its present value as in case of an unmatured claim. Requiring the distributees to furnish a bond would often be a heavy burden on them. Some statutes permit the setting aside of a reserve fund; this may be feasible if only the amount of the debt is contingent. Cf. In re Reilly's Will, 175 Misc. 597, 24 N.Y.S. 2d 213, 1941, noted, 41 Col.L.R. 950, 27 Corn.L.Q. 111, 54 Harv.L.R. 1067. It has been held that where the reserved assets prove to be insufficient the contingent creditor may not recover the deficiency from the distributees. Dabney v. Dabney, 54 Cal.App. 2d 695, 129 P.2d 470, noted, 43 Col.L. R. 237, 41 Mich.L.R. 920.

tration without corresponding advantage. A much better practice is to omit the requirement of presenting or filing contingent claims but to permit suit upon the obligation against the heirs in case the contingency occurs after administration is completed. This remedy is often allowed either by statute or upon equitable principles.[91]

*Distinction Between Unmatured and Contingent Claims*

In those jurisdictions where one may proceed against the heirs on a contingent claim if the contingency occurs after discharge of the representative, it is important to distinguish between claims which are contingent and those which are merely unmatured. This is not always an easy matter. Usually a claim which is payable upon the death of a third person or a certain time thereafter is regarded as simply unmatured and not contingent and hence must be presented in due time.[92] Liability to pay a mortgage,[93] and usually rent under a lease,[94] not due until after decedent's death, is not contingent and hence presentment is required. There are conflicting decisions upon whether liability to pay an unpaid stock subscription upon call is contingent.[95] An absolute

[91] Baker v. Baker, supra note 88; Chitty v. Gillett, 46 Okl. 724, 148 P. 1048, L.R.A.1916A 1181, 1915; Logan v. Dixon, 73 Wis. 533, 41 N.W. 713, 1889. Cf. State ex rel. McClure v. Northrop, 93 Conn. 558, 106 A. 504, 7 A.L.R. 1014, 1919; Parks v. Murphy, 166 Ark. 564, 266 S.W. 673, 1924; Zollickoffer v. Seth, 44 Md. 339, 1875. See infra § 144.

[92] Farris v. Stoutz, 78 Ala. 130, 1884; McDaniel v. Putnam, 100 Kan. 550, 164 P. 1167, L.R.A.1917E 1100, 1917; In re Kleinschmidt's Estate, 167 Wis. 450, 167 N.W. 827, 1918. But see Tenny's Adm'r v. Lasley's Adm'rs, 80 Mo. 664, 1883. Cf. Minneapolis Trust Co. v. Birkholz, 172 Minn. 231, 215 N.W. 223, 1927.

[93] In re Fatland's Estate, 197 Iowa 1231, 198 N.W. 785, 1924; Schmidt v. Grenzow, 162 Wis. 301, 156 N.W. 143, Ann.Cas.1917B 163, 1916.

[94] Ray Estate Corp. v. Steelman, 90 N.J.L. 184, 100 A. 209, 1917. Obligation to pay rent is not terminated by tenant's death. Israel v. Beale, 270 Mass. 61, 169 N.E. 777, 68 A.L.R. 588, 1930. Claims for future rent have been held to require presentation. Lesser v. Pomin, 3 Cal.App.2d 117, 39 P.2d 451, 1934; Jewell v. MacFarland, 141 Kan. 40, 40 P.2d 330, 1935; James v. Corvin, 184 Wash. 356, 51 P.2d 689, 1935; cf. Nathan v. Freeman, 70 Mont. 259, 225 P. 1015, 41 A.L.R. 138, 1924. But see Chicago Title & Trust Co. v. Fine Arts Building, 288 Ill. 142, 123 N.E. 300, 1919; Estate of Wishnick, 199 Minn. 153, 271 N.W. 244, 1937. See generally, Bennett, The Modern Lease, 16 Tex. L.R. 47; notes, 26 Corn.L.Q. 702, 29 Ky.L.J. 301, 41 Mich.L.R. 121, 21 N.D.Lawyer 126, 49 Yale L.J. 151.

[95] Unmatured: Electric Welding Co. v. Simpkins, 215 Mass. 315, 102 N.E. 354, 1913. Contingent: South Milwaukee Co. v. Murphy, 112 Wis. 614, 88 N.W. 583, 58 L.R.A. 82, 1902. Where the statute requires presentment of contingent claims, such claims must be presented within the

guaranty of a note,[96] or an obligation to pay a sum not ascertained until the nonclaim period has run, are not contingent but merely unmature.[97] Nor is a tort claim contingent merely because the amount is unliquidated.[98] Liability as surety,[99] or upon covenants in a deed,[100] or for injuries occurring on leased property after decedent's death,[101] may be contingent. In case of doubt a prudent creditor will treat the obligation as if it were simply an unmatured claim.

*Duty to Defend—Compromise*

As has already been seen, the personal representative has ordinarily no right to waive the nonclaim statute, nor in many jurisdictions, the general Statute of Limitations.[102] Moreover, the executor or administrator is charged with the duty of contesting claims to which there is some other defense.[103] He has, however,

nonclaim period. Geary Street, P. & O. R. Co. v. Bradbury Estate Co., 179 Cal. 46, 175 P. 457, 1918. As to superadded liability of stockholders, see supra note 89.

96 State ex rel. First Minneapolis Trust Co. v. Fosseen, 192 Minn. 108, 255 N.W. 816, 94 A.L.R. 1149, 1934; Beebe v. Kirkpatrick, 321 Ill. 612, 152 N.E. 539, 47 A.L.R. 891, 1926; Nichols v. Harsh, 202 Iowa 117, 209 N.W. 297, 1926. Cf. Sledge & Norfleet Co. v. Dye, 140 Miss. 779, 106 So. 519, 1926 (liability as indorser of note is contingent). But see Dunningan v. Stevens, 122 Ill. 396, 13 N.E. 651, 3 Am. St.Rep. 496, 1887.

97 In re Walter's Estate, 183 Wis. 540, 198 N.W. 375, 1924. Cf. Barto v. Stewart, supra note 82, under statute requiring presentment of contingent claims.

98 Pierce v. Johnson, 136 Ohio St. 95, 23 N.E.2d 993, 125 A.L.R. 867, 1939.

99 Security Fire Ins. Co. v. Hansen, 104 Iowa 264, 73 N.W. 596, 1897; Savings, Bldg. & Loan Association v. Tart, 81 Miss. 276, 32 So. 115, 1902; Pruett v. Caddigan, 42 Nev. 329, 176 P. 787, 1918; Keifer v. Kissell, 83 Ohio App. 133, 75 N.E.2d 692, 1947.

100 Chambers' Adm'r v. Smith's Adm'r, 23 Mo. 174, 1856; Griswold v. Bigelow, 6 Conn. 258, 1826. But presentment is required in jurisdictions requiring presentment of contingent claims. Tropico Land & Improv. Co. v. Lambourn, 170 Cal. 33, 148 P. 206, 1915.

101 Ray Estate Corp. v. Steelman, supra, note 94. Presentment was not even required of such claim in a jurisdiction which required presentment of contingent claims. Nathan v. Freeman, 70 Mont. 259, 225 P. 1015, 41 A.L.R. 138, 1924. But see Verdier v. Roach, 96 Cal. 467, 31 P. 554, 1892.

102 See supra notes 40–48.

103 Winchell v. Sanger, 73 Conn. 399, 47 A. 706, 66 L.R.A. 935, 1900; Marshall v. Coleman, 187 Ill. 556, 58 N.E. 628, 1900; Gorham v. Gorham, 54 Ind.App. 408, 103 N.E. 16, 1913; In re Taylor's Estate, 251 N.Y. 257, 167 N.E. 434, 1929 (want of consideration). As to the representative's duty to insist upon the Statute of Frauds, see Smith v. Brennan, 62 Mich. 349, 28 N.W. 892, 4 Am.St.Rep. 867, 1886, and note, 44 Yale L.J. 1474.

no duty to seek to compel the creditor to accept less than is legally due.[104] At common law the representative has power to compromise claims against the estate,[105] but some statutes require court sanction for such settlements.[106] Of course if the compromise is in bad faith, or is not for the best interests of the estate, the representative will be denied credit in his account for the expenditure,[107] and the same is true in case of payment of a claim to which there is a valid defense.[108]

*Establishment of Claims in Probate Court*

At common law claims against a decedent's estate were not established in the court of probate. If the personal representative did not make voluntary payment, the creditors' remedy was to sue the personal representative in the common law or equity court. In absence of statute the old method of establishing claims prevails.[109] In many jurisdictions, however, the statutes contemplate the establishment of disputed claims in the probate court.[110] Naturally when this situation exists and the claims have been duly established, the personal representative is protected by payments in accordance with the allowances.[111] Sometimes the probate court is given exclusive jurisdiction to establish claims against the decedent, and actions in the ordinary courts will not lie in the first instance.[112] In such case it may be necessary to provide an appeal with trial de novo in the court of record

104 In re Pillsbury's Estate, 175 Cal. 454, 166 P. 11, 3 A.L.R. 1396, 1917.

105 In re Leopold's Estate, 259 N.Y. 274, 181 N.E. 570, 85 A.L.R. 197, 1932; Fender v. Phillips, 59 Ind.App. 85, 108 N.E. 971, 1915.

106 Jones v. Gilliam, 199 S.W. 694, Tex.Civ.App.1918; Trevathan's Ex'rs v. Dees' Ex'rs, 221 Ky. 396, 298 S.W. 975, 1927. Cf. In re Leopold's Estate, supra note 105, holding purpose of court authority is to protect the fiduciary. See also In re Lucas' Estate, 23 Cal.2d 454, 144 P.2d 340, 1943 and supra, § 117.

107 Trevathan's Ex'rs v. Dees' Ex'rs, supra note 106.

108 Marshall v. Coleman, supra 103.

109 Isaacs v. Stevens, 13 Conn. 499, 1840; Houck v. Houck, 112 Md. 122, 76 A. 581, 1910.

110 Buck v. Lockwood, 193 Mich. 242, 159 N.W. 509, 1916; Johnson v. Rutherford, 28 N.D. 87, 147 N.W. 390, 1914; In re Morgan's Estate, 46 Or. 233, 77 P. 608, 78 P. 1029, 1904; Barclay v. Barclay, 230 Pa. 467, 79 A. 667, 1911.

111 Merrill v. Regan, 117 Me. 182, 103 A. 155, 1918; Whittemore v. Coleman, 144 Ill.App. 109, 1908 (if no fraud); Houck v. Houck, supra note 109.

112 Johnson v. Rutherford, supra note 110; Ralston v. Stainbrook, 187 S.W. 413, Tex.Civ.App.1916. Cf. Buck v. Lockwood, supra note 110; McBeath v. Champion, 55 N.M. 114, 227 P.2d 625, 1951.

to preserve the constitutional right to trial by jury unless such trial is available in the court of probate.[113]

It is doubtful whether the exclusive jurisdiction of the probate court to establish claims and demands should be construed as extending to claims other than liquidated contract claims. Usually those claims which need not be presented to the personal representative, viz., those of delictual,[114] equitable,[115] or proprietary [116] nature, are cognizable only in the ordinary courts, for a probate court is not a suitable tribunal for the trial of these matters. In many jurisdictions the ordinary courts have authority to entertain actions for the establishment of contract claims which have been rejected by the personal representative or the probate court; [117] in other states the contract creditor may proceed initially in either court at his option.[118]

*Payment without Presentment or Allowance*

The question arises as to whether a personal representative should be allowed credit for a claim paid within the nonclaim period when presentment in the proper form has not been made by the creditor, or where the claim has not been allowed in the probate court as required by statute. There are decisions to the effect that he may not obtain credit for such payments even if the claim is a just one.[119] In other words, the heirs may object to an item in the personal representative's final account upon the sole ground that the claim was not presented or allowed by the pro-

113 In re Hiller's Estate, 171 Or. 428, 137 P.2d 828, 1943; cf. In re Boyle's Estate, 242 N.Y. 342, 151 N.E. 821, 1926. In some states jury trial of claims is discretionary. In re Blue's Estate, 67 Ohio App. 37, 32 N.E.2d 1941; In re Snyder's Estate, 368 Pa. 393, 84 A.2d 818, 1951; see Model Probate Code §§ 18, 143.

114 In re Thomas' Estate, 333 Ill. App. 238, 77 N.E.2d 426, 1948; In re Gilbert's Estate, 350 Pa. 13, 38 A.2d 277, 1944. But see Staniszewski v. Lane, 165 Mich. 585, 131 N.W. 180, 1911.

115 McNulty v. Hurd, 72 N.Y. 518, 1878; Barclay v. Barclay, 230 Pa. 467, 79 A. 667, 1911. But see State ex rel. Peterson v. Circuit Court, 177 Wis. 548, 188 N.W. 645, 1922 (statute).

116 Comstock v. Matthews, 55 Minn. 111, 56 N.W. 583, 1893 (statute).

117 Easley v. Rowe, 138 Ark. 58, 210 S.W. 145, 1919; Flynn v. Driscoll, 38 Idaho 545, 223 P. 524, 34 A.L.R. 352, 1924.

118 Howard v. Swift, 356 Ill. 80, 190 N.E. 102, 1934. See Model Probate Code § 136.

119 Ordway & Husted v. Phelps, 45 Iowa 279, 1876; Harper v. Lamb, 202 Ky. 771, 261 S.W. 280, 1924; Boyd's Estate v. Thomas, 162 Minn. 63, 202 N.W. 60, 1925; Thompson v. Thompson, 217 S.W. 863, Mo.App.1920; Converse & Co. v. Sorley, 39 Tex. 515, 1873. See note, 9 Mo.L.R. 274.

bate court. However, other courts indicate that the provisions regarding presentment and allowance of claims are merely for the protection of the personal representative.[120] They take the position that the personal representative may, if he chooses, take the risk of paying an unpresented or unallowed claim but should be reimbursed for all payments of valid obligations. This view provides a speedy means of satisfying creditors whose claims are small or indisputable, and relieves both the parties and the court from unnecessary proceedings.

If the will creates a trust for the payment of testator's debts, his executor may lawfully pay valid claims though they are not presented or filed in the manner prescribed by law.[121] However, a mere testamentary direction to pay debts does not create such a trust.[122] The language of many wills relative to the payment of debts has resulted in controversy on the question of whether a trust has been created for this purpose.[123] Likewise testamentary provisions as to particular debts are apt to give rise to question as to whether a legacy is intended or whether the claim requires presentation.[124]

*Exoneration from General Assets*

As has been seen,[125] the holder of a secured claim may either rely upon the security, or he may seek payment from the representative. Only in the latter case is he obliged to comply with the statutory provisions relative to the allowance or payment of claims. There are certain circumstances under which the personal representative may be obliged to pay secured claims from

120 In re Machado's Estate, 186 Cal. 246, 199 P. 505, 1921; In re Carpenter's Estate, 232 Iowa 95, 5 N.W.2d 172, 1942; Tolly v. Champion, 191 Ky. 114, 229 S.W. 90, 1921; Kinnan v. Wight, 39 N.J.Eq. 501, 1885; Trammell v. Blackburn, 116 Tex. 388, 292 S.W. 169, 1927; In re Hansen's Estate, 55 Utah 23, 184 P. 197, 1919; In re Hurley's Will, 193 Wis. 20, 213 N.W. 639, 1927 (to protect estate against mortgage lien). See Model Probate Code § 148.

121 Gordon's Adm'r v. McDougall, 84 Miss. 715, 37 So. 298, 5 L.R.A.,N.S., 355, 1904.

122 Peck v. Botsford, 7 Conn. 172, 18 Am.Dec. 92, 1828 (language used merely through custom); Collamore v. Wilder, 19 Kan. 67, 1877; Boyd's Estate v. Thomas, supra note 119. Such a provision does not revive a barred debt. Roosevelt v. Mark, 6 Johns.Ch.(N.Y.) 266, 1822.

123 See authorities supra note 122; also infra § 147, notes 52–55.

124 Cf. Fair v. Fair, 46 Ohio App. 51, 187 N.E. 727, 1933, with Devers v. Schreiber, 50 Ohio App. 442, 198 N.E. 601, 1935. See annotation, 65 A.L.R. 861. As to questions of election, see infra § 138.

125 See supra note 61.

the general assets, although the creditor has not presented or filed the same in the manner prescribed by law. First there are cases where the will clearly indicates that certain specific property is devised or bequeathed to beneficiaries, clear of encumbrances thereon.[126] Under these circumstances it is the representative's duty to discharge the encumbrance for the benefit of the legatees or devisees. In addition, there is the doctrine of exoneration of mortgage whereby the heir or devisee is entitled to discharge of the lien upon the property unless there is a will indicating that he takes the property subject to the mortgage.[127] Generally the doctrine does not apply unless the debt is a personal obligation of the decedent,[128] and some jurisdictions have abolished the entire rule by statute.[129] These statutes are in line with criticisms of the doctrine,[130] which often works injustice to the residuary legatees contrary to the decedent's intention. Most states, however, follow the common-law rule of exoneration and the beneficiaries may compel the representative to discharge the obligation.[131] It has been held that they may do so even though no claim has been presented and the nonclaim statute

[126] See Mann's Will, 179 Wis. 66, 190 N.W. 830, 1922. In Bank of Statesboro v. Simmons, 164 Ga. 885, 139 S.E. 661, 1927, noted, 6 N.C.L.R. 229, 76 U. of Pa.L.R. 471, it was held that the bequest of a business passed the business free of mercantile debts. Cf. Ryan v. Monast, 67 R.I. 377, 24 A. 2d 615, 139 A.L.R. 703, 1942, where the will expressly provided that the devisee should assume the mortgage; she was held liable although testator was not personally liable on the mortgage.

[127] Appeal of Beard, 78 Conn. 481, 62 A. 704, 1906; Brackey v. Jensen, 166 Iowa 109, 147 N.W. 188, 1914; Smith v. Kibbe, 104 Kan. 159, 178 P. 427, 5 A.L.R. 483, 1919; Hill v. Hill, 95 N.J.Eq. 233, 122 A. 818, 29 A.L.R. 1242, 1023. Cf. Fulenwider v. Birmingham Trust & Sav. Co., 222 Ala. 95, 130 So. 801, 72 A.L.R. 702, 1930, and Kellam's Ex'rs v. Jacob, 152 Va. 725, 148 S.E. 835, 1929, where rule of exoneration would defeat testator's testamentary scheme and hence was not applied. See Raines v. Shipley, 197 Ga. 448, 29 S.E.2d 588, 1944 (no exoneration from other property specifically devised); Currie v. Scott, 144 Tex. 1, 187 S.W.2d 551, 1945 (same); generally see § 137 infra.

[128] Barlow v. Cain, 146 Ark. 160, 225 S.W. 228, 1920 (taxes); Steiglitz v. Migatz, 182 Ind. 549, 105 N.E. 465, 1914; Marshall v. Middleton, 100 Or. 247, 191 P. 886, affirmed 100 Or. 247, 196 P. 830, 19 A.L.R. 1421, 1921, noted, 5 Minn.L.R. 240 (mortgage assumed by testator foreclosed in his lifetime, thus releasing him personally). See American Law of Property § 14.25.

[129] In re Black's Estate, 293 N.Y. 85, 56 N.E.2d 44, 1944; Hannibal Trust Co. v. Elzea, 315 Mo. 485, 286 S.W. 371, 1926, noted, 40 Harv.L.R. 630. See note, 16 St. John's L.R. 160. For similar changes in the modern English law, see Maitland, Equity, 1936, 267, 314.

[130] See note, 40 Harv.L.R. 630.

[131] See cases supra note 127.

has run,[132] and that the personal representative may pay the debt voluntarily although the mortgage creditor has not filed a claim.[133] There is some conflict about the latter holdings, and the prudent course for the heirs is to initiate their exoneration proceeding before the expiration of the nonclaim period. It would also be wise for the personal representative to secure court approval before payment of such debt if the creditor has not presented his claim.

## PRIORITY OF CLAIMS IN INSOLVENT ESTATES

**128. By statute certain classes of obligations are given priority over ordinary debts, viz., family allowances, funeral expenses, costs of administration, taxes, judgments, and sometimes others. These priorities become vital in case of insolvent estates, the rule being that the debts must be satisfied in the statutory order so far as assets permit and claims of the last class reached are paid pro rata. Liens are ordinarily prior to all other claims.**

The topical headings below show the classes of obligations which are given priority by legislation in their more usual order.[1] However, statutes in the various states are diverse. Frequently the legislation says nothing about some of these kinds of debts, in which case they rank only as debts of the last or general class.[2]

*Widow's or Family Allowances*

This matter has already been discussed.[3] Often the particular statute which lists the order of priority does not mention widow's allowances because these are not strictly debts of the decedent. However, by express provision of the statutes with reference to these allowances, they ordinarily take precedence over ordinary debts,[4] and often over expenses of administration and

132 In re De Bernal's Estate, 165 Cal. 223, 131 P. 375, Ann.Cas.1914D 26, 1913; In re Johnson's Estate, 66 S.D. 331, 283 N.W. 151, 120 A.L.R. 574, 1938; Brackey v. Jensen, supra note 127; Smith v. Kibbe, supra note 127. But see Boyd's Estate v. Thomas, supra note 119; Smith v. Wilson, 79 N.J.Eq. 310, 81 A. 851, 1911.

133 Appeal of Beard, supra note 127. And see In re Hurley's Will, supra note 120. But see In re Cardin, 132 Okl. 286, 270 P. 554, 1928.

1 Cf. Model Probate Code § 142.

2 In re Casserly, 170 N.Y.S. 841, 1918; Lehman v. Powe, 95 Miss. 446, 49 So. 622, 1909. See infra notes 15, 25, 33.

3 See supra § 34.

4 Grover v. Clover, 69 Colo. 72, 169 P. 578, 1918. But see Model Probate Code § 142, and infra note 5.

funeral expenses.[5] This is appropriate because the allowances are for the immediate support of the family and are payable long before ordinary debts are presented or allowed.

*Funeral Expenses*

Funeral expenses ordinarily come next after widow's allowances in the line of priority, and in some states the funeral expenses come first.[6] In some jurisdictions they are preferred to,[7] and in others come next after, expenses of administration.[8] Of course these expenses must be reasonable, especially when the estate is insolvent.[9] Because of the priority of funeral expenses, it is often ruled that the claimant can proceed at once for payment,[10] and that the personal representative may pay the claim without court approval.[11] Usually funeral claims need not be presented within the nonclaim period.[12]

In some states the expenses of the deceased's last illness rank with,[13] or directly after,[14] funeral expenses. In absence of statutory provision, such expenses are entitled to no preference over ordinary debts.[15]

5 Aiken v. Davidson, 146 Ga. 252, 91 S.E. 34, 1916; Barrett v. Heim, 152 Minn. 147, 188 N.W. 207, 1922; Brown v. Keen, 201 S.W. 621, Mo.App.1918; Loftis v. Loftis, 94 Tenn. 232, 28 S. W. 1091, 1895. Contra: O'Hara v. O'Hara's Adm'r, 182 Ky. 260, 206 S. W. 462, 1918. Cf. Eisenberry v. Reininger, 90 Colo. 511, 10 P.2d 945, 1931, noted, 9 Ry.Mt.L.R. 294. See supra § 123, note 35.

6 See supra note 5.

7 See In re Gage's Estate, 222 Ill. App. 258, 1921; Houts v. Fritz, 143 Kan. 367, 54 P.2d 920, 1936.

8 Elton v. Lamb, 33 N.D. 388, 157 N.W. 288, 1916; N.Y. Surrogate's Court Act. § 216.

9 Sullivan v. Horner, 41 N.J.Eq. 299, 7 A. 411, 1886. As to reasonableness of funeral expenses generally, see annotation, 4 A.L.R.2d 995.

10 Studley v. Willis, 134 Mass. 155, 1883.

11 Dampier v. Trust Co., 46 Minn. 526, 49 N.W. 286, 1891.

12 In re Kelly's Estate, 183 Wis. 485, 198 N.W. 280, 1924; Hildebrand v. Kinney, 172 Ind. 447, 87 N.E. 832, 19 Ann.Cas. 788, 1909. See supra § 127, note 73.

13 Iowa—I.C.A. § 635.65. As to what are expenses of the last illness, see Proto v. Chenoweth, 40 Ariz. 312, 11 P.2d 950, 1932; Long v. Northrup, 225 Iowa 132, 279 N.W. 104, 116 A. L.R. 1475, 1938.

14 Conn.Gen.Stat.1949, § 7014; Mich.Comp.Laws, 1948, § 708.10; Missouri—V.A.M.S. § 461.010.

15 Grace v. Smith, 14 Hawaii 144, 1902. But see Cunningham v. Lakin, 50 Wash. 394, 97 P. 447, 1908, indicating that they may possibly be considered as funeral expenses.

*Costs of Administration*

These expenses are preferred to ordinary debts of the decedent and in some jurisdictions even to funeral expenses.[16] The chief of these expenses is counsel fees, but they also include many other items.[17] When the representative has advanced his own funds in order to pay lawful expenses, he is entitled to reimbursement on a preferred basis.[18]

*Taxes and Public Debts*

By virtue of a federal statute, debts owing the United States have priority over other claims after funeral expenses, costs of administration and family allowances.[19] This does not give a lien upon the decedent's property,[20] but the representative is personally liable if he does not follow the law.[21] Being a matter of federal law, its efficacy is not dependent upon reenactment in the various states though many local statutes make due provision for this priority. There are generally state statutes preferring state taxes and public debts to ordinary debts.[22] However, taxes on realty due after deceased's death are not ordinarily payable by the representative at all.[23]

*Trust Funds Held by Deceased*

When trust moneys held by the decedent can be separated from his individual property they form no part of his estate.[24] If the separation is impossible, the cestuis are ordinarily entitled to no

[16] See supra note 8.

[17] Enscoe v. Fletcher, 1 Cal.App. 659, 82 P. 1075, 1905; Wilder Grain Co. v. Felker, 296 Mass. 177, 5 N.E. 2d 207, 108 A.L.R. 385, 1936, noted, 36 Mich.L.R. 144. See infra note 35.

[18] In re Shepherd's Estate, 220 Iowa 12, 261 N.W. 35, 1935; Miller's Ex'rs v. Miller's Heirs and Creditors, 172 Ky. 519, 189 S.W. 417, 1916; Perez v. Gil's Estate, 29 N.M. 313, 222 P. 907, 35 A.L.R. 43, 1924.

[19] 31 U.S.C.A. § 191; see U.S. v. Pate, 47 F.Supp. 965, D.C.Ark.1942, noted, 29 Corn.L.Q. 258; U. S. Dep't of Agriculture, Emergency Crop & Feed Loans v. Remund, 330 U.S. 539, 67 Sup.Ct. 891, 91 L.Ed. 1082, 1947, noted, 45 Mich.L.R. 640.

[20] Brent v. Bank of Washington, 10 Pet. 596, 9 L.Ed. 547, 1836. But it gives priority over an unperfected equitable lien in another's favor. In re Gruner, 295 N.Y. 510, 68 N.E.2d 514, 167 A.L.R. 628, 1946.

[21] 31 U.S.C.A. § 192; U. S. v. Duncan, Fed.Cas.No.15,003, 1850. See supra § 125.

[22] In re Morris' Estate, 37 Cal.App. 2d 155, 99 P.2d 294, 1940; see also In re Koehring's Estate, 230 Wis. 533, 284 N.W. 523, 1939; cf. In re Gruner, supra note 20.

[23] See supra § 125.

[24] Hubbard v. Alamo Irrigating & Mfg. Co., 53 Kan. 637, 36 P. 1053, 37 P 625, 1894.

preference and are mere ordinary creditors.[25] This hardship has led in some jurisdictions to the enactment of statutes giving these beneficiaries a priority over ordinary creditors.[26]

### *Judgment Debts*

In many states, statutes provide that a judgment obtained against the decedent in his lifetime is preferred to ordinary debts,[27] and sometimes such judgments are given priorities inter se according to their date.[28] Moreover, a judgment obtained in decedent's lifetime is usually a lien on his land entitled to satisfaction from the land in preference to all other claims.[29] A judgment rendered after decedent's death against his executor or administrator usually is not entitled to preference.[30]

### *Wages and Rent*

Wages are often given statutory preference over ordinary claims,[31] though sometimes only when earned in a certain period immediately prior to the decedent's death.[32] In absence of statutory provision there is no preference for wages.[33] Rent is also sometimes entitled to payment prior to ordinary debts,[34] but that

25 Crews v. U. S. Fidelity & Guaranty Co., 237 Ala. 14, 185 So. 370, 1939.

26 Chappell v. Neurath, 277 Ky. 87, 125 S.W.2d 1024, 1939; Morris v. Westerman, 79 W.Va. 502, 92 S.E. 567, 3 A.L.R. 1237, 1917.

27 Comer v. Light, 175 Ind. 367, 93 N.E. 660, rehearing denied 175 Ind. 367, 94 N.E. 325, 1911; Wright v. Wright, 70 N.J.Eq. 407, 62 A. 487, 1905; Weatherly v. Medlin, 141 S.C. 290, 139 S.E. 633, 1927.

28 Comer v. Light, supra note 27. But in absence of specific legislative provision all judgments share pro rata in the funds. McConnell v. Barnes, 142 S.C. 112, 140 S.E. 310, 57 A.L.R. 483, 1927.

29 Moore v. Jones, 226 N.C. 149, 36 S.E.2d 920, 1946; Poling v. Poling, 109 W.Va. 705, 156 S.E. 88, 1931; but see Dabney v. Continental Jewelry Co., 163 Miss. 1, 140 So. 338, 1932.

30 Benfield v. McMillan, 188 Ga. 52, 2 S.E.2d 600, 1939; Cook v. Jennings, 40 S.C. 204, 18 S.E. 640, 1893. But see In re Vandyke's Estate, 15 Del.Ch. 459, 136 A. 147, 1927. Cf. infra notes 68–70.

31 Chicago Title & Trust Co. v. McGlew, 193 Ill. 457, 61 N.E. 1018, 1901; International Harvester Co. v. Dyer's Adm'r, 297 Ky. 55, 178 S.E.2d 966, 1944; In re Ricciardi, 189 Misc. 174, 69 N.Y.S.2d 538, 1947.

32 In re Longstreet's Estate, 23 Erie (Pa.) 14, 1941; cf. International Harvester Co. v. Dyer's Adm'r, supra note 31.

33 Lehman v. Powe, 95 Miss. 446, 49 So. 622, 1909.

34 Wade v. Peacock, 121 Ga. 816, 49 S.E. 826, 1905. In New York rent may be given precedence if the surrogate believes it is for the good of the estate. Surrogate's Court Act § 212.

accruing after decedent's death upon a lease made by him is not entitled to preference as an expense of the administration.[35]

*Secured Debts*

Obviously the secured creditor does not lose his lien by reason of the death of his debtor.[36] The security gives the creditor a species of priority, which may be obtained without appealing to the probate court, for the filing of a claim is not a prerequisite of the right to foreclose.[37] The mortgagee of land may even obtain payment of the debt without taking any legal steps, as in case that the personal representative proceeds with his duty to exonerate the realty.[38] A secured creditor is not prevented from sharing in the general assets,[39] though he must file a claim if he wishes to recover the deficiency.[40] A mortgage or other lien claimant is entitled to no preference from the general assets.[41] Hence if a sale of the security is had and there is a deficiency, this is not preferred to other debts of the estate.[42] However, so far as the property secured is concerned, the mortgagee's claim is preferred to all others,[43] even to funeral expenses,[44] costs of administration,[45] and public debts.[46]

The manner of computing rights of a secured creditor of an insolvent estate has given rise to much difference of opinion. In absence of particular statutory provision there is no reason why

35 Brown's Ex'r v. United States Trust Co., 185 Ky. 747, 215 S.W. 815, 8 A.L.R. 1142, 1919.

36 Waughop v. Bartlett, 165 Ill. 124, 46 N.E. 197, 1896; Jones v. Null, 9 Neb. 57, 1 N.W. 867, 1879.

37 Supra § 127.

38 Ibid.

39 In re Jones' Estate, 275 Pa. 143, 118 A. 647, 1922.

40 See supra § 127.

41 Miller's Ex'rs v. Miller's Heirs & Creditors, 172 Ky. 519, 189 S.W. 417, 1916.

42 In re McDougald's Estate, 146 Cal. 196, 79 P. 875, 1905 (statute); Payne v. Johnson's Ex'rs, 95 Ky. 175, 24 S.W. 238, 1893; O'Brien Bros. v. Wilson, 86 Miss. 540, 38 So. 509, 1905.

43 First Nat. Bank of Hailey v. Glenn, 10 Idaho 224, 77 P. 623, 109 Am.St.Rep. 204, 1904; Iowa Loan & Trust Co. v. Holderbaum, 86 Iowa 1, 52 N.W. 550, 1892 (mortgage to pay debts); Wyatt v. Morse, 129 Tex. 199, 102 S.W.2d 396, 1937.

44 Ryker v. Vawter, 117 Ind. 425, 20 N.E. 294, 1889; Ray v. Honeycutt, 119 N.C. 510, 26 S.E. 127, 1896. But see Bauman v. Armbruster, 129 La. 191, 55 So. 760, 1911.

45 Ryker v. Vawter, supra note 44; Shepard v. Saltzman, 34 Or. 40, 54 P. 882, 1898.

46 Brent v. Washington Bank, 10 Pet. 596, 9 L.Ed. 547, 1836; In re Berger's Estate, 94 N.E.2d 248, Ohio Prob.1950, noted, 26 Notre Dame Lawyer 335. Cf. In re Gruner, supra note 20.

the rule should not be the same as in the case of insolvency of a living person.[47] There are two principal positions taken by the courts.[48] The first is the so-called chancery rule, under which the secured creditor is entitled to the full benefit of the security and also may prove the full amount of the claim and obtain his pro rata share thereof along with unsecured creditors.[49] Of course he is not permitted to recover more than the amount of his claim from these two sources. The second is the bankruptcy rule which allows the secured creditor to take advantage of his security and also be entitled to a pro rata share from the general assets on the difference between the amount of the debt and the sum realized from the security.[50] The chancery rule is upon the wane and is generally thought to operate unduly to the advantage of secured creditors.[51] A secured creditor may waive his security and proceed for a pro rata share of the general assets even though this works to the detriment of other creditors.[52]

### *Other Debts*

The common-law preference for specialty over ordinary debts has been abolished even in England.[53] All debts not given priority by legislation rank alike and are entitled to pro rata satisfaction if all cannot be paid. In some jurisdictions the statutes provide that claims presented within a certain period are given priority over claims presented later.[54] In case of insolvency, an ordinary creditor may under such a statute obtain nothing if he

47 See State v. Greenhaw, 50 Ariz. 436, 72 P.2d 950, 113 A.L.R. 398, 1937; Moore v. Jones, supra note 29.

48 For these and variations thereof, see Hanson, The Secured Creditor's Share of an Insolvent Estate, 34 Mich.L.R. 309; see also Maitland, Equity, 1936, 258 et seq.; note, 8 Minn.L.R. 232; annotation 94 A.L.R. 468.

49 Findlay v. Hosmer, 2 Conn. 350, 1817; Merrill v. National Bank of Jacksonville, 173 U.S. 131, 19 S.Ct. 360, 43 L.Ed. 640, 1898; West v. Bank of Rutland, 19 Vt. 403, 1847; Mason v. Bogg, 2 My. & Cr. 443, 40 Eng.Rep. 709, 1837.

50 Amory v. Francis, 16 Mass. 308, 1820; Gwynne v. Estes, 14 Lea (82 Tenn.) 662, 1885; Federal Trust Co. v Cohen, 116 N.J.Eq. 201, 172 A. 502, 1934; In re Baker's Estate, 47 D. & C.(Pa.) 444, 1943. See Model Probate Code § 139.

51 See Model Probate Code § 139 and comment thereto; Hanson, supra note 48.

52 In re Estate of Butterfield, 196 Iowa 633, 195 N.W. 188, 1923 (here the security was homestead property and hence not available to general creditors). Cf. Ivanhoe Building & Loan Assn. v. Orr, 295 U.S. 243, 55 Sup.Ct. 685, 79 L.Ed. 1419, 1935.

53 32 & 33 Vict.C. 46, 1869. Cf. Ga. Code Ann. § 113-1508. As to the common-law rule, see 2 Bl.Com. 511 and supra § 127.

54 See infra note 55.

fails to file his claim within the designated time. Probably the creditor who fails to file within the shorter period will also lose any other priority to which he would have been entitled.[55] This seems to follow, as the purpose of the statute is to permit immediate payment of all debts allowed during the shorter period. If these payments exhaust the estate, even the holder of a preferred claim has no remedy and must bear the consequences of his lack of vigilance.

*Retainer by Personal Representative*

As part of the common-law doctrine that a personal representative could prefer one creditor to another whose claim was of the same rank,[56] the representative could retain for his own debt,[57] except against obligations of a superior rank.[58] The right of retainer still exists in England,[59] but in America it is either expressly abolished by statute,[60] or is abridged by statutes requiring the representative's claim to be allowed by the probate court.[61] The securing of advantage by retainer is foreign to the spirit of American administration of decedent's estates and our courts today would probably be astute to find statutory provisions which, by inference at least, abolished this common-law privilege so far as it enabled the representative to obtain a preference for himself.

*Procedure of Paying Claims*

As already pointed out,[62] the executor or administrator at common law was faced with the twin hazards: (1) of exhausting the estate in payment of claims of an inferior class and therefore having to pay late claims of a superior class from his own pocket, and (2) being caught in the technicalities of pleading insufficiency of assets and thus be held liable to a creditor by way of a procedural penalty. Even if he submitted to administration in equity, the estate might not arrive in that court in time to avoid these pitfalls.

[55] Keith v. Parks, 31 Ark. 664, 1877; In re Youngquest's Estate, 102 Colo. 105, 76 P.2d 1117, 1938.

[56] See supra § 127.

[57] 2 Bl.Com. 511.

[58] Hancocke v. Prowd, 1 Saund. 328 (note 6), 85 Eng.Rep. 475, 1681.

[59] Administration of Estates Act, 1925 § 34(2).

[60] In re Magorty's Estate, 169 Cal. 163, 146 P. 430, 1915; Nelson v. Russell's Adm'rs, 15 Mo. 356, 1852; Lenoir v. Winn, 4 Desaus.(S.C.) 65, 6 Am.Dec. 597, 1809.

[61] Semmes v. Magruder, 10 Md. 242, 1856; Neilley v. Neilley, 89 N.Y. 352, 1882; see annotation, 144 A.L.R. 940.

[62] See supra § 127.

Today, however, the personal representative who follows the course outlined by law receives ample protection. In many jurisdictions he pays the debts only upon court order which will not be made until the time for proving claims has expired. In other jurisdictions provision is made for the special administration of insolvent estates. Upon the suggestion of insolvency by the personal representative or creditor the court investigates and if it so finds, declares the estate insolvent.[63] Commissioners are appointed to examine the claims,[64] and the period of nonclaim is often shortened from the one provided for estates in general.[65] Usually the claims are paid according to the statutory classification of priorities and prorated in case there are not sufficient assets to satisfy the creditors of the last class for which there are available assets.[66] In these jurisdictions if an administrator pays a claim in full before he has notice of the insolvency, he is liable to pay all other creditors their pro rata share even if he cannot recover from the overpaid creditor.[67] A personal representative runs considerable risk in paying ordinary claims before the nonclaim or the shorter priority period has expired. In jurisdictions where claims must be allowed by the court, the representative receives greater protection as the court will not order payment until the nonclaim or special priority statute has run, and at any rate the order to pay claims protects the personal representative.

A creditor today can obtain no priority by obtaining attachment, garnishment, or judgment after death of the debtor.[68] Furthermore such judgments, or claims established by the probate court, are not usually enforceable by execution,[69] at least without leave of the court of probate.[70]

63 Holliday v. McKinne, 22 Fla. 153, 1886; Powers v. Powers' Estate, 57 Vt. 49, 1885; Ohio Gen.Code, § 10509–130. See Robinson v. Hodge, infra note 69; Nadelmann, Insolvent Decedents' Estates, 49 Mich.L.R. 1129, 1138.

64 Shelton v. Hadlock, 62 Conn. 143, 25 A. 483, 1892; Agoos v. Cosmopolitan Trust Co., 241 Mass. 103, 134 N.E. 306, 1922.

65 Jellison v. Swan, 105 Me. 356, 74 A. 920, 1909.

66 Gish's Appeal, 31 Pa. 277, 1858; Gray v. Black, 267 S.W. 291, Tex.Civ.App.1925.

67 People's Bank & Trust Co. v. Seydel, 94 Conn. 526, 109 A. 861, 1920; see Reiley v. Healey, 122 Conn. 64, 187 A. 661, 1936; infra § 144.

68 Strouse v. Lawrence, 160 Pa. 421, 28 A. 930, 1894; Archer Blower & Pipe Co. v. Archer, 33 Wash.2d 317, 205 P.2d 595, 1949; see supra note 30.

69 Grife v. Equitable Life Assur. Soc. of U. S., 233 Iowa 83, 8 N.W.2d 584, 1943; see Pufahl v. Parks' Estate, 299 U.S. 217, 57 Sup.Ct. 151, 81 L.Ed. 133, 336 (Illinois Law); Model Probate Code § 145. But see Jackson v. Hubert, 234 S.W.2d 414, Tex.Sup. 1950; Robinson v. Hodge, 4 N.J. 397, 73 A.2d 158, 1950.

70 See N.Y.C.P.A. § 656.

# CHAPTER 14

# DISTRIBUTION AND SETTLEMENT OF ESTATE

**Sec.**

**129. Advancements.**
**130. Release of Expectancy.**
**131. Transfer of Expectancy.**
**132. Classes of Legacies and Devises.**
**133. Satisfaction.**
**134. Ademption.**
**135. Increase and Interest.**
**136. Abatement and Charges.**
**137. Exoneration.**
**138. Election.**
**139. Renunciation.**
**140. Lapse.**
**141. Retainer for Debts of Beneficiaries.**
**142. Accounting.**
**143. Decree of Distribution.**
**144. Refunding.**

## ADVANCEMENTS

**129. If an intestate transfers land or a substantial amount of personalty to one child, this will be presumed to be an advancement, and the value of the property so given will be deducted from the child's share upon distribution of the estate in order to equalize the shares of the other children or their descendants. The doctrine has no application where the ancestor dies wholly testate, nor, in most jurisdictions, to cases of partial intestacy.**

The English Statute of Distribution, 1670,[1] provided that any settlement of land, or advancement of personalty to a child,[2] by an intestate, should be taken into account in the distribution of the personalty so as to make the shares of all children "equal as near as can be estimated." In every state except New Mexico statutes recognize the doctrine of advancements, though some of this legislation deals very briefly with the subject.[3] In the ab-

1 22 & 23 Car. II, c. 10, § v.

2 On account of primogeniture, the statute provided that settlements of land on the heir at law did not reduce his share in the personalty.

3 See Model Probate Code § 29 and appendix pp. 253–256; 4 Vernier American Family Law 114–127; Elbert, Advancements I, 51 Mich.L.R. 665.

sence of legislation, or in case of its silence on particular points, the English statute or the pre-existing custom on which it was based will probably apply.[4] The basic idea of the doctrine of advancements is to bring about equality between the children when the parent has given some of them something by way of anticipation of inheritance.

Two simple illustrations will indicate the workings of the doctrine. Suppose that a father in his lifetime advanced $1,000 to his son John, $2,000 to his son Joseph and nothing to his son James, and then died intestate possessed of an estate of $12,000 leaving the three sons as his sole heirs. To compute the share of each son, one must add to the estate left by the decedent the sums which he has given by way of advancements. This would be $15,000. The share of each son would be $5,000, and this is the amount to which James is entitled, but as John and Joseph have received $1,000 and $2,000, respectively, their shares will be $4,000 and $3,000. The sums advanced are figuratively brought into hotchpot and then the amount given to each is deducted from what would have been the normal share if there had been no advancements.

Another example will illustrate a complication existent in some cases. Assume the case of a father who advanced $6,000 to his son Thomas, $1,000 to his son Timothy and nothing to his son Theodore, and died intestate leaving an estate of $2,000. A hasty calculation will show that Thomas has received by way of advancement more than his share of the estate on the basis of the preceding example. He is not obliged to return the excess, for an advancement is in this respect in the nature of a gift and not a loan.[5] Neither the father during his lifetime nor the other children after his death can recover any part of the advancement to Thomas due to the irrevocable character of the gift feature of advancements. Accordingly, Thomas and his advancement are disregarded in the calculation. After Timothy's $1,000 is brought into hotchpot there is a tentative total of $3,000, or $1,500 each

[4] In re Farmers Loan & Trust Co., 181 App.Div. 642, 168 N.Y.S. 952, 1918; see Grattan v. Grattan, 18 Ill. 167, 1856; Harper v. Harris, infra note 51 (New Mexico Law). For the history before the English statute, see American Law of Property § 14.10. For adjustment out of intestate land, see id. § 14.10, note 36, § 14.26, note 9, and infra § 141, notes 35–40.

[5] McPherson v. Black, 215 Ky. 92, 284 S.W. 413, 46 A.L.R. 1424, 1926; McCoy v. McCoy, 105 Va. 829, 54 S.E. 995, 1906; In re Sipchen's Estate, 180 Wis. 504, 193 N.W. 385, 1923 (express statute). Moreover bringing into hotchpot does not mean return to the estate in specie. Damron v. Bartley, 302 Ky. 83, 194 S.W.2d 73, 1946.

for Timothy and Theodore. As Timothy has already received $1,000, his share is $500, Theodore's is $1,500, and Thomas of course receives nothing.

*Advancements Distinguished from Other Transactions*

Not every transfer by a parent to a child is deemed an advancement. There are several other possibilities. The transaction may amount to an absolute gift, which will not be reckoned against the child's share in the distribution of the parent's intestate estate. There is nothing to prevent the latter from making such an unqualified donation to his child.[6] A second possibility is that the transfer to the child may be a loan. The loan like the advancement may be deducted from the child's share of the estate before payment of the latter to him,[7] but unlike the advancement, the heir can be obliged to repay the loan to the estate, if it exceeds his distributive share.[8] In the last example if the transaction had been a loan to Thomas the administrator would be entitled to recover $3,000 from Thomas, and Timothy and Theodore ultimately would receive $2,000 and $3,000, respectively. There is another distinction between a loan and an advancement, in that the Statute of Limitations runs against the former, but not upon the latter.[9] When physical property is transferred to the child, it is possible that the transaction may be regarded as a sale.[10] In the jurisdictions where a distributee's barred debts to the estate cannot be deducted from his distributive share,[11] a loan may thus prove to be a more favorable interpretation for the heir than an advancement. Except for this possibility, an advancement is more beneficial to the person receiving the money than a loan. Of course a gift construction of the transaction is the one most favorable to the recipient.

[6] However, in Kentucky the rule seems to be that all substantial gifts by an intestate parent to a child or grandchild are deemed advancements and the intention to make an absolute gift is of no avail. Sullivan v. Sullivan, 122 Ky. 707, 92 S.W. 966, 7 L.R.A.,N.S., 156, 13 Ann.Cas. 163, 1906; Day v. Grubbs, 235 Ky. 741, 32 S.W.2d 327, 72 A.L.R. 323, 1930; note, 24 Ky. L.J. 83.

[7] See infra § 141.

[8] Kinney v. Newbold, 115 Iowa 145, 88 N.W. 328, 1901.

[9] Hughes' Appeal, 57 Pa. 179, 1868.

[10] See Nobles v. Davenport, 183 N.C. 207, 111 S.E. 180, 26 A.L.R. 1086, 1922; Holland v. Bonner, 142 Ark. 214, 218 S.W. 665, 26 A.L.R. 1101, 1922. In re O'Hara's Estate, infra note 12.

[11] See infra § 141.

*Intent and Evidence Thereof*

Whether a certain transfer by a parent to a child is regarded as an advancement depends primarily upon the intention of the intestate,[12] regardless of the concurrence of the child.[13] If the parent intends to make a gift which was to be deducted from the child's distributive share, then the transaction is an advancement; otherwise not. Of course the determination of the subjective intent of a deceased person is not an easy matter. Express declarations of the parent are admissible for the purpose of discovering his intent,[14] as are his books of account.[15] The surrounding circumstances may also be considered.[16] The extent of the property given is a pertinent factor. If the subject-matter is land,[17] or money to purchase land,[18] or a large sum of money,[19] this is a strong indication that an advancement was intended. Trifling amounts of money or property are not normally regarded as advancements.[20]

The purpose for which the transfer was made is also important. Usually expenditures in discharge of parental duty are not

12 Holland v. Bonner, supra note 10; Ruch v. Biery, 110 Ind. 444, 11 N.E. 312, 1865; In re O'Hara's Estate, 204 Iowa 1331, 217 N.W. 245, 1928; Nobles v. Davenport, supra note 10; Miller's Appeal, 40 Pa. 57, 80 Am.Dec. 555, 1861; Trotman v. Trotman, 148 Va. 860, 139 S.E. 490, 1927.

13 Barron v. Barron, 181 Ga. 505, 182 S.E. 851, 1935. And see Fitts v. Morse, 103 Mass. 164, 1867 (agreement between children does not establish an advancement, without parent's approval). Cf. Higham v. Vanosdol, 125 Ind. 74, 25 N.E. 140, 1890 (secret intention of father to treat payment as a debt rather than an advancement cannot prevail).

14 Miller's Appeal, supra note 12; Rowe v. Rowe, 144 Va. 816, 130 S.E. 771, 1926; Gaylord v. Hope Natural Gas Co., 122 W.Va. 205, 8 S.E.2d 189, 1940. But see Chism v. Chism, 296 Ky. 73, 176 S.W.2d 101, 1944.

15 Greene v. Greene, 145 Miss. 87 110 So. 218, 49 A.L.R. 565, 1926.

16 Page v. Elwell, 81 Colo. 73, 253 P. 1059, 1927 (health and circumstances of child); Miller's Appeal, supra note 12; Trotman v. Trotman, supra note 12.

17 Pilkington v. Wheat, 330 Mo. 767, 51 S.W.2d 42, 1932; Grayton v. Phillips (Tex.Civ.App.) 297 S.W. 888, 1927. Where the child pays an inadequate consideration for the land, the excess value may be deemed an advancement. In re O'Hara's Estate, supra note 12.

18 Stacy v. Stacy, 175 Ark. 763, 300 S.W. 437, 1928; Hall v. Hall, 107 Mo. 101, 17 S.W. 811, 1891; Clary v. Spain, 119 Va. 58, 89 S.E. 130, 1916. And see Mott v. Iossa, 119 N.J.Eq. 185, 181 A. 689, 1935 (advancement or gift presumed rather than resulting trust).

19 Miller v. Richardson, 85 S.W.2d 41, Mo.1935, noted 1 Mo.L.R. 78.

20 Mitchell's Distributees v. Mitchell's Adm'r, 8 Ala. 414, 1845.

adjudged advancements,[21] though the older cases at least indicate that the expenses of a collegiate or professional education would be deemed advancements.[22] Laying out sums for the purpose of establishing the child in business or in life are usually considered advancements.[23] The distinction has been drawn between chattels given for the child's pleasure and those which can be employed for profit, the latter quality being an indication of an advancement.[24] Insurance policies on the parent's life in favor of the child have been held to constitute advancements although the child does not enjoy them until the parent's death, and the parent is entitled to change the beneficiary.[25]

Usually the evidence of an intent to make an advancement may be by parol,[26] though statutes in certain jurisdictions require that this be shown by written memoranda of the donor or acknowledgment in writing by the donee.[27] Of course under these statutes there is never a presumption of an advancement in the absence of written evidence; indeed, there is no possibility of an ad-

21 Brake v. Graham, 214 Ala. 10, 106 So. 188, 1925 (education); Page v. Elwell, supra note 16; Crain v. Mallone, 130 Ky. 125, 113 S.W. 67, 22 L.R.A.,N.S., 1165, 132 Am.St.Rep. 355, 1908; Matter of Denison's Estate, 157 Misc. 385, 284 N.Y.S. 705, 1935 (education); Greene v. Greene, 145 Miss. 87, 110 So. 218, 49 A.L.R. 565, 1926 (necessities); Douglass v. Hammel, 313 Mo. 514, 285 S.W. 433, 1926 (education).

22 Hill's Guardian v. Hill, 122 Ky. 681, 92 S.W. 924, 1906; Garrett v. Colvin, 77 Miss. 408, 26 So. 963, 1899; Robinson v. Robinson, Brayton (Vt.) 59, 1818.

23 Page v. Elwell, supra note 16; Bissell v. Bissell, 120 Iowa 127, 94 N.W. 465, 1903; Wenbert v. Lincoln Nat. Bank & Trust Co., 116 Ind.App. 31, 61 N.E.2d 466, 1945 (marriage portion).

24 Ison v. Ison, 5 Rich.Eq.(26 S.C. Eq.) 15, 1852 (horse which might be used as foal-getter).

25 Culberhouse v. Culberhouse, 68 Ark. 405, 59 S.W. 38, 1900; Thompson v. Latimer, 209 Ky. 491, 273 S.W. 65, 1925, noted, 14 Ky.L.J. 168, 24 Mich.L.R. 307; Rickenbacker v. Zimmerman, 10 S.C. 110, 30 Am.Rep. 37, 1877; Cazassa v. Cazassa, 92 Tenn. 573, 22 S.W. 560, 20 L.R.A. 178, 36 Am.St.Rep. 112, 1893. But see Vinson v. Vinson, 105 La. 30, 29 So. 701, 1896. Cf. Paschal v. Paschal, 197 N.C. 40, 147 S.E. 680, 1929 (mother's payments of premiums on policy taken by son on his own life are not advancements); Albers v. Young, 119 Colo. 37, 199 P.2d 890, 1948, noted, 48 Mich. L.R. 134 (joint bank account); Berry v. Berry, 208 Ga. 285, 66 S.E.2d 336, 1951, noted, 37 Va.L.R. 1154 (United States Savings Bonds in co-ownership).

26 Page v. Elwell, supra note 16. See supra notes 14, 16.

27 Cummings v. Bramhall, 120 Mass. 552, 1876; Olney v. Brown, 163 Mich. 125, 128 N.W. 241, 1910; Stark v. Stark, 128 Neb. 524, 259 N.W. 523, 1935; Liesse v. Fontaine, 181 Wis. 407, 195 N.W. 393, 1923. See McCall and Langston, A New Intestate Succession Statute for North Carolina, 11 N.C.L.R. 266, 297, 298.

vancement without such proof. In absence of legislative provision the courts usually declare that there is a presumption of an advancement in case of a substantial sum,[28] and that the burden of proof is on the child to show that a gift was intended.[29] The presumption of advancement may arise though the donor has declared that the thing given is a gift or a present, for an advancement is a gift, though of a peculiar nature.[30] The presumption of an advancement is not conclusive however.[31] If the child gives an interest-bearing note to his parent, he has the burden of proof to show that the transaction was an advancement and the presumption is that it was a loan.[32]

The intestate's intent at the time of the transaction is the pertinent factor.[33] Declarations of the intestate before or after that time may be admitted,[34] but only in order to determine the intention at the time. A change of the intention will not alter the effect to be given to the transfer if the consequences are more onerous to the donee. Thus an absolute gift may not be changed to an advancement,[35] unless the donee consents, nor may an advancement be shifted to a debt.[36] On the other hand, the donor may subsequently modify the transaction to the donee's advantage. An advancement can be changed to a gift.[37] Also a debt

28 Clements v. Hood, 57 Ala. 459, 1876; Johnson v. Mundy, 123 Va. 730, 97 S.E. 564, 1918. Cf. Holland v. Bonner, 142 Ark. 214, 218 S.W. 665, 26 A.L.R. 1101, 1920; Shaul v. Katzenstein, 172 Ark. 932, 290 S.W. 966, 1927 (presumption rebutted by child's repayment). Cf. Model Probate Code § 29.

29 Calhoun v. Taylor, 178 Iowa 56, 159 N.W. 600, 1916; Stephens v. Smith, 127 Mo.App. 18, 106 S.W. 533, 1907.

30 Miller v. Richardson, supra note 19.

31 Page v. Elwell, supra note 16; Packard v. Packard, 95 Kan. 644, 149 P. 404, 1915; Watkins v. Young, 31 Grat.(Va.) 84, 1878; Neil v. Flynn Lumber Co., 82 W.Va. 24, 95 S.E. 523, 1918.

32 In re Palmer's Estate, 194 Iowa 611, 190 N.W. 30, 26 A.L.R. 1097, 1922; Gibbs v. Gibbs, 254 Ky. 787, 72 S.W.2d 473, 1934. And see In re Grissinger's Estate, 104 Pa.Super. 184, 158 A. 582, 1932; Bowman's Adm'rs v. Bowman's Ex'r and Adm'r, 301 Ky. 694, 192 S.W.2d 955, 1946.

33 Nobles v. Davenport, supra note 10; Miller's Appeal, supra note 12; In re O'Hara's Estate, 204 Iowa 1331, 217 N.W. 245, 1928.

34 See supra note 14.

35 Elliott v. Western Coal & Mining Co., 243 Ill. 614, 90 N.E. 1104, 134 Am.St.Rep. 398, 17 Ann.Cas. 884, 1910.

36 Higham v. Vanosdol, 125 Ind. 74, 25 N.E. 140, 1890.

37 Wheeler v. Wheeler's Estate, 47 Vt. 637, 1874. But see Adams v. Adams, 82 W.Va. 244, 95 S.E. 859, 1918.

may be altered so as to constitute an advancement,[38] though not in case that the Statute of Limitations has run upon the debt.[39]

### *To Whom Doctrine Applies*

Most statutes provide for advancements to children or their descendants, though a number speak only of advancements to "children." [40] In the latter case a donation to a grandchild might be considered an advancement if it took place after the parent's death,[41] but transfers to grandchildren during their parent's lifetime are usually regarded as absolute gifts.[42] While a few statutes extend the doctrine of advancements to any heir, including the surviving spouse,[43] donations to the latter,[44] or to collateral relatives,[45] are not usually considered advancements. Since the doctrine of advancements is designed merely to secure equality between children and descendants, advancements to these will not generally be collated in the widow's favor in determining her distributive share.[46] Advancements made by one parent cannot be considered in the distribution of the other parent's estate.[47]

When a parent makes an advancement to a child who later dies leaving issue, the sum will be deducted from the share of the grandparent's estate, if other children of the latter survived

38 Baum v. Palmer, 165 Ind. 513, 76 N.E. 108, 1905; Jones v. Jones, 163 Tenn. 237, 43 S.W.2d 205, 1931. Cf. Farmers' Exchange Bank v. Moffett, 256 Ky. 160, 75 S.W.2d 1063, 1934 (by mutual agreement).

39 Melony's Appeal, 78 Conn. 334, 62 A. 151, 1905.

40 See supra note 3.

41 Wolfe v. Galloway, 211 N.C. 361, 190 S.E. 213, 1937.

42 Stevenson v. Martin, 11 Bush. (Ky.) 485, 1875. But see Ramsay v. Abrams, 58 Iowa 512, 12 N.W. 555, 1882. Cf. Weddle v. Waddle's Adm'r, 261 Ky. 208, 87 S.W.2d 383, 1935 (gift to grandchild deemed an advancement to latter's parent when the property was given for the benefit of the entire family).

43 See supra note 3.

44 In re Kennedy's Estate, 154 Iowa 460, 135 N.W. 53, 1912; In re Morgan, 104 N.Y. 74, 9 N.E. 861, 1887.

45 Johnson v. Antriken, 205 Mo. 244, 103 S.W. 936, 1907. And see Matter of Farmers' Loan & Trust Co., 181 App.Div. 642, 168 N.Y.S. 952, 1918.

46 Ruch v. Biery, 110 Ind. 444, 11 N.E. 312, 1886; Knight v. Oliver, 12 Grat.(Va.) 33, 1855. And see In re Denison's Estate, 157 Misc. 385, 284 N.Y.S. 705, 1936; Cochran v. Garth, 163 Tenn. 59, 40 S.W.2d 1023, 76 A.L.R. 1413, 1931. Contra: Klein v. Blackshere, 113 Kan. 539, 215 P. 315, 1923; Page v. Elwell, 81 Colo. 73, 253 P. 1059, 1927. Both of the latter decisions involved statutory construction as to whether the widow was an heir within the meaning of the advancement statute. Cf. In re Clark's Estate, 303 Pa. 538, 154 A. 919, 1931 (involving antenuptial agreement).

47 Oliver v. Crewdson's Adm'r, 256 Ky. 797, 77 S.W.2d 20, 1934.

him.[48] However, if none of the intestate's children survive, advancements to them are not material in determining the shares of the grandchildren when the latter take per capita and not in the right of their deceased parents.[49] Gifts to the husband or wife of a child have been considered advancements even in the absence of knowledge by the latter of the transaction.[50]

*Effect of Testacy*

The ordinary doctrine of advancements can have no application when the testator died wholly testate.[51] When the testator has made a complete distribution of his property, nothing remains with which to bring about equality; furthermore the will excludes prior transactions, and subsequent ones as well, except in so far as a payment in testator's lifetime may constitute satisfaction of a legacy given by the will.[52] Of course a testator may direct in his will that prior or subsequent advances should be deducted from the share otherwise given in the will.[53] Moreover, testamentary directions to deduct a certain sum claimed to have been advanced are to be given effect, regardless of whether or not the payment was actually made.[54]

48 Brown v. Taylor, 62 Ind. 295, 1878; In re Williams' Estate, 62 Mo. App. 339, 1895; Beebe v. Estabrook, 79 N.Y. 246, 1879; Mow v. Baker, 24 S.W.2d 1, 68 A.L.R. 405, Tex.Com.App. 1930; Coffman v. Coffman, 41 W.Va. 8, 23 S.E. 523, 1895; Proud v. Turner, 2 P.Wms. 560, 24 Eng.Rep. 862, 1729.

49 Skinner v. Wynne, 55 N.C. 41, 1854; Person's Appeal, 74 Pa. 121, 1873. And see Brown v. Taylor, supra note 48. But see Crump v. Faucett, 70 N.C. 345, 1874, where grandchildren were deemed to take per stirpes even if no children survived, and hence advancements to the children are considered in determining the shares of the grandchildren.

50 Ireland v. Dyer, 133 Ga. 851, 67 S.E. 195, 26 L.R.A.,N.S., 1050, 18 Ann. Cas. 544, 1910; Palmer v. Culbertson, 65 Hun 625, 20 N.Y.S. 391, 1892. And see Weddle v. Waddle's Adm'r, supra note 42.

51 In re Hayne's Estate, 165 Cal. 568, 133 P. 277, Ann.Cas.1915A 926, 1913, noted, 1 Cal.L.R. 532; In re Manatt's Trust, 214 Iowa 432, 239 N.W. 524, 1932 (but instrument which merely recited that testator did not make a will is not a will, thus giving rise to the possibility of advancements); Kragnes v. Kragnes, 125 Minn. 115, 145 N.W. 785, 1914; In re Gibson's Estate, 130 Neb. 762, 264 N.W. 762, 1936; Harper v. Harris, 294 F. 44, 32 A.L.R. 727, C.C.A. 8th 1923, noted, 8 Minn.L.R. 543.

52 See In re Bush's Estate, 155 Kan. 556, 127 P.2d 445, 142 A.L.R. 518, 1942, and infra § 132.

53 See In re Hayne's Estate, supra note 51; In re Laughlin's Estate, 354 Pa. 43, 46 A.2d 477, 165 A.L.R. 891, 1946.

54 Younce v. Flory, 77 Ohio St. 71, 83 N.E. 305, 1907; In re Eichelberger's Estate, 135 Pa. 160, 19 A. 1006, 1890; In re Estate of Wells, 184 Wis. 242, 199 N.W. 52, 1924; In re Kelsey, [1905] 2 Ch. 465. See supra § 59.

In most jurisdictions the doctrine of advancements does not apply to cases of partial intestacy, since as the doctrine relates only to the estate of an "intestate", and also a testator is presumed to have considered advancements in his calculations of the bequests.[55] The heirs are not obliged to bring into hotchpot, for the purpose of distribution of the intestate part, the portions which would have been considered advancements if the estate were entirely intestate. Advancements to other children have been disregarded in ascertaining the share of a pretermitted child who takes against the will.[56] A few statutes provide for the doctrine of advancements in cases of partial intestacy for the purpose of determining the shares of the intestate property.[57]

*Valuation*

The general rule is that advancements are valued as of the time the transfer was made.[58] Hence subsequent increases or decreases in value are immaterial for the purpose of ascertaining the distributive shares. However, for the purpose of valuation, an advancement is deemed to be made at the time that the donee obtains possession and enjoyment.[59] Thus, if the donor retains a life estate and remains in possession, the value should be taken as of the time of his death,[60] and insurance policies are usually valued at the amount payable upon the insured's death.[61] In a few jurisdictions by statute the advancement is valued as of the date of the donor's death, or at the time of distribution.[62] By

55 Gilmore v. Jenkins, 129 Iowa 686, 106 N.W. 193, 6 Ann.Cas. 1008, 1906; Bowron v. Kent, 190 N.Y. 422, 83 N.E. 472, 1908.

56 Gibson v. Johnson, 331 Mo. 1198, 56 S.W.2d 783, 88 A.L.R. 369, 1933. But see Sanford v. Sanford, 61 Barb. (N.Y.) 293, 1872.

57 Poff v. Poff, 128 Va. 62, 104 S.E. 719, 1920. See Gulley v. Lillard's Ex'r, 145 Ky. 746, 141 S.W. 58, 1911 (doctrine applied only as to intestate portion of estate).

58 Dicken v. Fairchild, 215 Ky. 496, 284 S.W. 1101, 1926 (plus improvements made by donor); Greene v. Greene, 145 Miss. 87, 110 So. 218, 49 A.L.R. 565, 1926; Oyster v. Oyster, 1 Serg. & R.(Pa.) 422, 1815; Ingram v. Ingram, 130 Va. 329, 107 S.E. 653, 26 A.L.R. 1175, 1921. It is the actual value and not the assessed value for taxation that controls. Miller v. Richardson, supra note 19. Cf. note, 12 Tulane L.R. 262.

59 Greene v. Greene, supra note 58; Keys v. Keys, 11 Heisk.(Tenn.) 425, 1872; Ingram v. Ingram, supra note 58; (land valued at time possession was given and not later when deed was made). But see Ward v. Johnson, 124 Ky. 1, 97 S.W. 1110, 1906.

60 Palmer v. Culbertson, 143 N.Y. 213, 38 N.E. 199, 1894.

61 Cazassa v. Cazassa, Culberhouse v. Culberhouse and Thompson v. Latimer, all supra note 25. Cf. Rickenbacker v. Zimmerman, supra note 25.

62 Eastwood v. Crane, 125 Iowa 707, 101 N.W. 481, 1904; Cain v. Cain,

agreement between the donor and donee the value of the land or chattel may be liquidated at a certain figure, and this will be binding upon the donee and the other heirs.[63] Interest is not ordinarily computed on advancements prior to the donor's death,[64] though it may be charged after the latter's death.[65]

## RELEASE OF EXPECTANCY

**130. A release by a child of his share of the parent's estate in return for fair consideration is binding upon the child and upon his issue if the releasing child should predecease his parent. The doctrine is best understood by regarding the consideration received as an advancement liquidated by agreement as the releasor's full share of the estate.**

By the prevailing view, an heir's release of his expectant share in his parent's estate during the latter's lifetime is effective if given for fair consideration.[1] This holding is adhered to though the statutes declare that an expectancy is not an interest, or is not transferable.[2] These decisions proceed upon the ground that such legislation was intended merely to declare the nonstatutory rule that the release is ineffective at law but enforceable in eq-

53 S.C. 350, 31 S.E. 278, 69 Am.St.Rep. 863, 1898.

63 Home Mixture Guano Co. v. McKoone, 168 Ga. 317, 147 S.E. 711, 1929 (liquidated as full share of the estate); Ladd v. Stephens, 147 Mo. 319, 48 S.W. 915, 1898; Ingram v. Ingram, supra note 58; N.Y. Decedent Estate Law, § 85. See infra § 130.

64 Taylor v. Everett, 60 Fla. 362, 52 So. 980, 1910; In re Pardee's Estate, 240 Wis. 19, 1 N.W.2d 803, 1942. But see Cline v. Cline, 215 Ky. 492, 284 S.W. 1110, 1926, distinguishing between ordinary and extraordinary advancements, interest being charged on the latter.

65 Cline v. Cline, supra note 64; Moore v. Burrow, 89 Tenn. 101, 17 S.W. 1035, 1872. Cf. In re Smith's Estate, 350 Pa. 418, 39 A.2d 513, 1944 (from time for settlement of estate).

1 Home Mixture Guano Co. v. McKoone, 168 Ga. 317, 147 S.E. 711, 1929; Mires v. Laubenheimer, 271 Ill. 296, 111 N.E. 106, 1916; Swigert v. Miles, 75 Ind.App. 85, 130 N.E. 130, 1921; Chidester v. Harlan, 180 Iowa 171, 159 N.W. 659, 1916: In re Simon's Appeal, 158 Mich. 256, 122 N.W. 544, 17 Ann.Cas. 723, 1909; Douglass v. Hammel, 313 Mo. 514, 285 S.W. 433, 1926; Riddell v. Riddell, 70 Neb. 472, 97 N.W. 609, 1903; Green v. Hathaway, 36 N.J.Eq. 471, 1883; Squires v. Squires, 65 W.Va. 611, 64 S.E. 911, 1909; Liesse v. Fontaine, 181 Wis. 407, 195 N.W. 393, 1923. See infra note 7 and generally Evans, Certain Evasive and Protective Devices Affecting Succession to Decedents' Estates, 32 Mich.L.R. 478, 491–498.

2 In re Garcelon's Estate, 104 Cal. 570, 38 P. 414, 32 L.R.A. 595, 43 Am. St.Rep. 134, 1894; Henrich v. Newell, 59 S.D. 372, 240 N.W. 327, 1932, noted, 31 Mich.L.R. 126.

uity. Of course in matters of this kind it is the equitable rule which governs the final result. The form of the release is not material. A receipt in full signed by the heir is sufficient,[3] as is the acceptance of a deed from the ancestor containing a recital that the property is received in satisfaction of the heir's share of the estate.[4] It would seem that the agreement may be entirely oral, though some cases deny this.[5]

*Nature of Consideration Required*

A fair consideration is one which would suffice in an action for specific performance. The acceptance of a smaller sum or property of lesser value presently is sufficient consideration for the relinquishment of a larger and uncertain amount in the future unless the discrepancy is very great.[6] A minority of courts refuse to recognize the release as such but give effect to the transaction only as an advancement of the sum actually received by the heir.[7]

*Theory Upon Which Doctrine Is Based*

While in most jurisdictions the release bars the heir from his share in the estate of the parent, or source, it is not clear upon what legal theory this result is reached. Some courts look upon the release as an extinguishment of the heir's right to take by descent.[8] A number of the decisions seem to proceed upon the

[3] Swigert v. Miles, supra note 1; Bennett v. Bennett, 50 App.Div. 127, 63 N.Y.S. 387, 1900; Liesse v. Fontaine, supra note 1; cf. In re Townsend's Estate, 229 Wis. 60, 281 N.W. 642, 1938.

[4] Bolin v. Bolin, 245 Ill. 613, 92 N.E. 530, 1910; Roberts v. Coleman, 37 W.Va. 143, 16 S.E. 482, 1892. Cf. Williams v. Swango, 365 Ill. 549, 7 N.E.2d 306, 1937.

[5] That an oral agreement is enough see Douglass v. Hammel, 313 Mo. 514, 285 S.W. 433, 1926; Mires v. Laubenheimer, supra note 1; see Patterson v. Volmar, 131 Ohio St. 48, 1 N.E.2d 323, 1936. Some jurisdictions hold that if land is involved there must be a writing to satisfy the Statute of Frauds. Riddell v. Riddell, supra note 1; Green v. Hathaway, 36 N.J. Eq. 471, 1883. In jurisdictions requiring written memorandum of advancements, it seems that the release should be in writing. See Liesse v. Fontaine, supra note 1.

[6] In re Simon's Appeal, supra note 1; Coffman v. Coffman, 41 W.Va. 8, 23 S.E. 523, 1895. See Klingensmith v. Klingensmith, infra note 10; In re McGillick's Estate, 67 S.D. 359, 293 N.W. 185, 1940; infra § 131, note 4.

[7] Weddington v. Adkins, 245 Ky. 747, 54 S.W.2d 331, 1932; Needles v. Needles, 7 Ohio St. 432, 70 Am.Dec. 85, 1857; Ferenbaugh v. Ferenbaugh, 104 Ohio St. 556, 136 N.E. 213, 1922, noted, 21 Mich.L.R. 219; Ratliff v. Meade, 184 Va. 328, 35 S.E.2d 114, 1945.

[8] Mires v. Laubenheimer, supra note 1. See Restatement, Property § 316.

theory that there is a valid contract which is enforceable in equity.[9] Other cases suggest the basis of equitable estoppel, in that the parent may have been induced to refrain from making a will.[10] Still other authorities speak of the transaction as an advancement, which is liquidated by agreement of the parties as the child's entire share.[11] In some of the opinions two or more of these theories may be mentioned by the court.

The liquidated advancement theory seems to be the best because it reaches results which are just and in accord with the normal understanding of the parties, and also because it may be applied to the holdings of certain decided cases which cannot be otherwise justified. Thus, where the only daughter released all her interest in the estate of her father, who died leaving no other relatives closer than brothers and sisters, the daughter took the entire estate in preference to the collaterals.[12] This seems fair, and any other result would seem to do violence to the intestate laws. An even stronger case may be stated for the application of this theory, viz., if at the time of the release the parent had another child, who however died without issue before his parent's death. To admit collateral relatives or the state in preference to the releasing child would seem strange indeed, as the obvious purpose of the release was to bring about approximate

9 Newsome v. Cogburn, 30 Ga. 291, 1860; Eissler v. Hoppel, 158 Ind. 82, 62 N.E. 692, 1901; Riddell v. Riddell, supra note 1.

10 In re Simon's Appeal, supra note 1; Green v. Hathaway, 36 N.J.Eq. 471, 1883; Coffman v. Coffman, supra note 6. See Klingensmith v. Klingensmith, 193 Iowa 350, 185 N.W. 75, 1921, recognizing the estoppel theory but insisting that there is none in case of receipt of $1,000 for a share worth $6,000.

11 Coffman v. Coffman, supra note 6; Liesse v. Fontaine, supra note 1; Home Mixture Guano Co. v. McKoone, supra note 1; Anderson v. Forbes, 169 Tenn. 223, 84 S.W.2d 104, 1935, noted, 14 Tenn.L.R. 115. And see Swigert v. Miles, supra note 1, indicating that a release in partial satisfaction of the child's share should be treated as an advancement. But see Douglass v. Hammel, supra note 1; Donough v. Garland, 269 Ill. 565, 109 N.E. 1015, Ann.Cas.1916E 1238, 1915.

12 Pylant v. Burns, 153 Ga. 529, 112 S.E. 455, 28 A.L.R. 423, 1922, noted, 21 Mich.L.R. 100. And see Cannon v. Nowell, 51 N.C. 436, 1859; Simonds v. Simonds' Estate, 96 Vt. 110, 117 A. 103, 28 A.L.R. 420, 1922, noted, 32 Yale L.J. 88; In re Knight's Estate, infra note 20. Cf. Squires v. Squires, 65 W.Va. 611, 64 S.E. 911, 1909; Pritchard v. Pritchard, 76 W.Va. 91, 85 S.E. 29, 1915. See also Evans, supra note 1 at 492 et seq. But see Restatement, Property § 316, Illustration 6. However, if the collateral heir was mentioned in the agreement, it might be possible to construe the release as a transfer of an expectancy to the collateral heir. See infra § 131.

equality between the two children, one of whom desired his share to be paid in the parent's lifetime.

*Who Is Bound by the Release*

When the source survives the releasing child, the latter's children are bound by the release if other children of the source survive.[13] This is in accord with the holdings regarding advancements.[14] It would seem that if the releasing child and all his brothers and sisters predecease the source, the shares of the grandchildren should not be affected by the release.[15] As the latter then take directly from the source and are not bound by simple advancements, the release should be disregarded in the distribution among the grandchildren. In case of the release of a share under a will the doctrine of ademption by satisfaction may be applied.[16] The only objection to the adoption of the theory of liquidated advancements as explanatory of the release cases is in case of release by collateral relatives. Transfers to the latter are not regarded as advancements,[17] but it would seem that they might be so regarded in case of positive agreement for the purpose in hand.[18] If a collateral heir, for consideration received, promises not to contest the promisee's will, the agreement is valid and enforceable.[19] However, if the releasor is the sole collateral heir on the ancestor's death, he should take in spite of the release, which should not be deemed to admit a new class of heirs in violation of the intestate laws.[20]

13 Simpson v. Simpson, 114 Ill. 603, 4 N.E. 137, 7 N.E. 287, 1885; Quarles v. Quarles, 4 Mass. 680, 1808; Coffman v. Coffman, supra note 6; Liesse v. Fontaine, supra note 1; Anderson v. Forbes, supra note 11. Contra: Mow v. Baker, 24 S.W.2d 1, 68 A.L.R. 405, Tex.Com.App.1930. And see Douglass v. Hammel, supra note 1.

14 See supra § 129.

15 There seem to be no cases, but the analogy of advancements seems to be in accord with the above statement. See supra § 129. Cf. Restatement, Property § 316, which takes the theory of absolute extinguishment of the entire line of the releasing child in all cases.

16 See infra § 133; Restatement, Property, §§ 315, 316. However, release of a devise is not usually permitted. Burnham v. Comfort, 108 N.Y. 535, 15 N.E. 710, 2 Am.St.Rep. 462, 1888; Graham v. Karr, 331 Mo. 1157, 55 S.W.2d 995, 1932; see American Law of Property § 14.12.

17 See supra § 129.

18 Cf. Leggett v. Martin, 203 Ark. 88, 156 S.W.2d 71, 1941.

19 In re Garcelon's Estate, supra note 2; In re Cook's Will, 244 N.Y. 63, 154 N.E. 823, 55 A.L.R. 806, 1927, noted, 27 Col.L.R. 758, 36 Yale L.J. 1029.

20 Cf. In re Knight's Estate, 155 Fla. 869, 22 So.2d 249, 1945 (spouse). See supra note 12.

## TRANSFER OF EXPECTANCY

**131. One who expects to inherit from another may assign this expectancy to a third person. If the transfer is based upon adequate consideration, it may be enforced as to any interest passing to the assignor by will or intestate laws upon death of the source. The assignment has no effect if the assignor predeceases the source or if the source disinherits the assignor by will.**

The expectation that one may succeed to another's property either by will or under the intestate laws is an uncertain one. It is subject to be defeated by later will disinheriting the expectant heir, or by death of the latter prior to the demise of the source. While such interests were not assignable at common law, they could be transferred in equity and the equitable rule prevails generally today,[1] even under statutes declaring that such interests are not assignable.[2] In order to be enforceable the transfer must be for adequate consideration.[3] Possibly the courts have insisted upon a more nearly equivalent consideration than in case of release to the ancestor who has no particular reason to overreach his expectant heir.[4] Some cases hold that the source should approve of the transfer,[5] but by the better and prevailing view his consent is not necessary.[6] The transfer of the expectancy

1 Bridge v. Kedon, 163 Cal. 493, 126 P. 149, 43 L.R.A.,N.S., 404, 1912; Donough v. Garland, 269 Ill. 565, 109 N.E. 1015, Ann.Cas.1916E 1238, 1915; Edler v. Frazier, 174 Iowa 46, 156 N.W. 182, 1916; Hite v. Hite, 120 Ohio St. 253, 166 N.E. 193, 1929, noted, 24 Ill. L.R. 717, 15 Ia.L.R. 91, 28 Mich.L.R. 1058, 16 Va.L.R. 74; Steele v. Frierson, 85 Tenn. 430, 3 S.W. 649, 1887; Hale v. Hollon, 90 Tex. 427, 39 S.W. 287, 36 L.R.A. 75, 59 Am.St.Rep. 819, 1897; Restatement, Property § 316. Contra: Hunt v. Smith, 191 Ky. 443, 230 S.W. 936, 17 A.L.R. 588, 1921; Snyder v. Snyder, 193 Ky. 233, 235 S. W. 743, 1921, noted, 31 Yale L.J. 662; Engle v. Walters, 282 Ky. 732, 140 S. W.2d 401, 1940 (devisee assigns).

2 Bridge v. Kedon, supra note 1; Bacon v. Bonham, 33 N.J.Eq. 614, 1881. See supra § 130, note 2.

3 Bridge v. Kedon, supra, note 1; Fidelity Union Trust Co. v. Reeves, 96 N.J.Eq. 490, 125 A. 582, 1924; Boles v. Caudle, 133 N.C. 528, 45 S.E. 835, 1903; In re Lennig's Estate, 182 Pa. 485, 38 A. 466, 38 L.R.A. 378, 61 Am.St.Rep. 725, 1897.

4 See Richey v. Richey, 189 Iowa 1300, 179 N.W. 830, 1920; In re Lennig's Estate, supra note 3; Boles v. Caudle, supra note 3.

5 McClure v. Raben, 133 Ind. 507, 33 N.E. 275, 36 Am.St.Rep. 558, 1890; Stevens v. Stevens, 181 Mich. 438, 148 N.W. 225, Ann.Cas.1916E 1259, 1914.

6 Betts v. Harding, 133 Iowa 7, 100 N.W. 1074, 1906; Gadsby v. Gadsby, 275 Mass. 157, 175 N.E. 495, 74 A.L.R. 434, 1931; Walker v. Walker, 67 Pa. 185, 1870. And see Fuller v. Parmenter, 72 Vt. 362, 47 A. 1079, 1900 (no-

may take any form. An agreement between prospective heirs in the lifetime of the source is sufficient.[7] However, an instrument will not be given the effect of an assignment unless it clearly manifests the intention to do so.[8]

Of course no analogy to advancements can be applied to transfers as distinguished from releases of an expectancy, for the reason that the prospective heir does not receive the consideration from the source but from a third person. Moreover, there is another important difference between release and transfer. While the former may operate to bar releasor's children in case of the releasor's predecease of the source, this is not true in the case of a transfer. When one conveys his expectancy in his parent's estate, and dies before the latter, the transferor's children inherit from their grandparent regardless of the assignment.[9] The transferee has no right of action against the estate of the source on account of the latter's subsequent disinheritance of the transferor,[10] nor does the transferee have sufficient interest to contest the will of the source.[11] These holdings indicate the speculative character of the interest obtained from the expectant heir or devisee. Yet the doctrine is well recognized in the situations in which it applies. An assignment made in good faith is valid against the assignor's creditor who had judgment before the assignment.[12]

tice to ancestor sufficient if even that is required); Hale v. Hollon, supra note 1 (consent not required in any event when ancestor is insane). But cf. with later case authorities cited supra note 5.

7 In re Wickersham's Estate, 153 Cal. 603, 96 P. 311, 1908; Gadsby v. Gadsby, supra note 6; Walker v. Walker, supra note 6. See Hofmeister v. Hunter, 230 Wis. 81, 283 N.W. 330, 121 A.L.R. 444, 1939.

8 Swan v. Pople, 118 W.Va. 538, 190 S.E. 902, 1937; Clark v. Gauntt, 138 Tex. 558, 161 S.W.2d 270, 1942. See Burnham v. Comfort, 108 N.Y. 535, 15 N.E. 710, 2 Am.St.Rep. 462, 1888 (will).

9 Donough v. Garland, supra note 1; Habig v. Dodge, 127 Ind. 31, 25 N.E. 182, 1890; Johnson v. Breeding, 136 Tenn. 528, 190 S.W. 545, L.R.A.1917C 266, 1916. But see Keys v. Keys, 148 Md. 397, 129 A. 504, 1925.

10 Casady v. Scott, 40 Idaho 137, 237 P. 415, 1925 (though transferor had a contract with the source which was later altered by agreement between them).

11 Burk v. Morain, 223 Iowa 399, 272 N.W. 441, 112 A.L.R. 79, 1937, noted, 36 Mich.L.R. 869.

12 Richey v. Rowland, 130 Iowa 523, 107 N.W. 423, 1906; Chatterton v. Clayton, 150 Kan. 525, 95 P.2d 340, 1939; annotation, 73 A.L.R. 1063.

## CLASSES OF LEGACIES AND DEVISES

**132. A "specific legacy" is a gift of some particular chattel interest capable of being designated and identified as part of the testator's estate.**

**A "general legacy" is one which is payable out of general assets of the estate and which does not require the delivery of any specific thing or satisfaction from any designated portion of testator's property. A simple pecuniary legacy is a typical case of general legacy.**

**A "demonstrative legacy" is one of a certain amount or quantity to be satisfied primarily out of a certain fund or particular property, but on failure of the latter, payable generally from the estate.**

**A "residuary legacy" is one which covers the remainder of testator's property after debts and specific and general legacies have been satisfied.**

**While it was once held that all devises of land were specific, it is now well recognized that devises may be general or residuary.**

At this point it is appropriate to discuss the various types of legacies and devises. This is for the reason that for centuries the courts have declared that various matters discussed in the subsequent sections turn upon whether a certain testamentary disposition is specific, demonstrative, general, or residuary. One may form his own conclusions as to how far this *should* be so, and as to whether the courts have in particular types of cases stretched the normal concept of some classifications so as to reach a desired result.[1] It is possible for the courts to hold that a type of legacy may be general if the problem is one of ademption but specific if abatement is involved.[2] This is certainly not orthodox, yet it may find some support upon realistic consideration of some of the cases.

The question of whether a legacy is specific, demonstrative, general, or residuary depends upon the intention of the testator

1 See Mechem, Specific Legacies of Unspecific Things—Ashburner v. Macguire Reconsidered, 87 U. of Pa.L.R. 546.

2 Cf. Estate of Woodworth, 31 Cal. 595, 601, 1867: "What is a specific bequest within the meaning of the [exoneration] rule?" And consider the case of the demonstrative legacy, infra note 31 et seq.; see also In re Davis' Will, 184 Misc. 952, 57 N.Y.S. 2d 356 1945; infra § 134, notes 29–32.

as disclosed by the language of his entire will,[3] the circumstances surrounding him,[4] and certain rules of construction applied by the courts.[5]

*Specific Legacies*

A specific legacy is a gift of some specific article or particular fund which the will distinguishes from all the rest of the testator's estate.[6] While it is usual to frame the definition in terms of some part of the testator's estate, no reason is apparent why the legacy would not also be specific if it were of a particular object owned by another, which the executor was required to procure for the legatee.[7]

When the testator intends that the legatee shall have a particular thing, the legacy is specific, as where particular notes owned by the testator are bequeathed,[8] or any other debt,[9] or a life insurance policy,[10] or the testator's interest in the estate of a deceased person.[11] A bequest of stock is specific if it appears from the will that the testator intended to pass particular designated shares.[12] Where the bequest is of "my" stock, this is a strong indication that the gift is specific,[13] and recent cases show

[3] Stifft v. W. B. Worthen Co., 177 Ark. 204, 6 S.W.2d 527, 1928; Spinney v. Eaton, 111 Me. 1, 87 A. 378, 46 L.R.A.,N.S., 535, 1913.

[4] Stifft v. W. B. Worthen Co., supra note 3; Leighton v. Leighton, 193 Iowa 1299, 188 N.W. 922, 1922; Patanska v. Kuznia, 102 N.J.Eq. 408, 141 A. 88, 1928.

[5] Patanska v. Kuznia, supra note 4 (presumed that he intended to dispose of whole estate to beneficiaries). And see infra notes 13, 40, and § 146.

[6] Goforth v. Goforth, 202 Ark. 1017, 154 S.W.2d 819, 1941; Lenzen v. Miller, 378 Ill. 170, 37 N.E.2d 833, 1941; In re Hartman's Estate, 233 Iowa 405, 9 N.W.2d 359, 1943; cf. Estate of Woodworth, supra note 2.

[7] Thus, a legacy of a certain picture "whether owned by me at the time of my death or not". Cf. Threlkeld's Ex'rs v. Synodical Presbyterian Orphanage of Anchorage, 307 Ky. 235, 210 S.W.2d 766, 1948; Avery v. Johnson, 108 Tex. 294, 192 S.W. 542, 1917; both to the effect that presumptively a devise or bequest is only of property which the testator owned. Cf. infra notes 16, 21–24, 47.

[8] In re Martin, 25 R.I. 1, 54 A. 589, 1903; O'Neil v. Cogswell, 223 Mass. 364, 111 N.E. 858, 1916.

[9] Hayes v. Hayes, 45 N.J.Eq. 461, 17 A. 634, 1889.

[10] Matter of Tailer, 147 App.Div. 741, 133 N.Y.S. 122, 1911.

[11] In re Goodfellow's Estate, 166 Cal. 409, 137 P. 12, 1913.

[12] Harvard Unitarian Society v. Tufts, 151 Mass. 76, 23 N.E. 1006, 7 L.R.A. 390, 1890; Gardner v. McNeal, 117 Md. 27, 82 A. 988, 40 L.R.A.,N.S., 553, Ann.Cas.1914A 119, 1911. See cases infra note 14.

[13] Kearns v. Kearns, 77 N.J.Eq. 453, 76 A. 1042, 140 Am.St.Rep. 575, 1910; Smith v. Smith, 192 N.C. 687, 135 S.E. 855, 1927; Walton v. Walton, 7 Johns.Ch.(N.Y.) 258, 1823.

a tendency to hold that a gift of stock may be specific even though there is no "my" or equivalent expression.[14] Gifts of "all my household goods," have been held to be specific.[15] If sufficiently described, a specific legacy may be made of property to be acquired by the testator after the execution of the will.[16]

A legacy of a certain sum of money to be paid only out of a particular fund or property is specific.[17] The same is true of a bequest of money to be realized from securities selected from testator's estate.[18]

*General Legacies*

A general legacy has been defined as a gift of personalty not amounting to a bequest of a particular thing, money, or fund.[19] Again, a general legacy is said to be one which may be satisfied out of the general assets of the estate without regard to any particular fund or thing.[20] While not entirely consistent with the above, bequests of all testator's personal property,[21] an aliquot part thereof,[22] of all property except certain things,[23] or the residue of testator's property [24] have been held to amount to general

14 In re Buck's Estate, 32 Cal.2d 372, 196 P.2d 769, 1948; In re Mandelle's Estate, 252 Mich. 375, 233 N.W. 230, 1930; In re Estate of Largue, 267 Mo. 104, 183 S.W. 608, 1915; Matter of Security Trust Co., 221 N.Y. 213, 116 N.E. 1006, 1917. See also Jewell & a., Ex'rs v. Appolonio, 75 N.H. 317, 74 A. 250, 1909. In the Buck and Security Trust Co. cases the stock was closely held. See infra note 27 and generally, infra §§ 134, 135. See also note, 36 Cal.L.R. 338.

15 Kearns v. Kearns, supra note 13; Weed v. Hoge, infra note 20. But see infra notes 21–24.

16 Kelly v. Richardson, 100 Ala. 584, 13 So. 785, 1893; Holcomb v. Mullin, 167 Ark. 622, 268 S.W. 32, 1925. See supra note 7; cf. infra notes 21–24, 47.

17 Gelbach v. Shively, 67 Md. 498, 10 A. 247, 1887; Waters v. Selleck, 201 Ind. 593, 170 N.E. 20, 1930, noted, 5 Ind.L.J. 583; Crawford v. McCarthy, 159 N.Y. 514, 54 N.E. 277, 1899. See infra § 134, note 33.

18 Allen v. Allen, 76 N.J.Eq. 245, 74 A. 274, 139 Am.St.Rep. 758, 1909.

19 Lenzen v. Miller, supra note 6.

20 Weed v. Hoge, 85 Conn. 490, 83 A. 636, Ann.Cas.1913C 543, 1912; Howe v. Howe's Ex'r, 287 Ky. 756, 155 S.W.2d 196, 1941; In re Weed's Will, 213 Wis. 574, 252 N.W. 294, 1934.

21 Estate of Woodworth, supra note 2; In re Hawgood's Estate, 37 S.D. 565, 159 N.W. 117, 1916; see Kaplan v. Leader, 297 Mass. 145, 8 N.E.2d 344, 1937.

22 Abila v. Burnett, 33 Cal. 658, 1867.

23 Kelly v. Richardson, 100 Ala. 584, 13 So. 785, 1893; In re Bernheimer's Estate, 352 Mo. 91, 176 S.W.2d 15, 1944.

24 Stanley v. Stanley, 108 Conn. 100, 142 A. 851, 1928; In re Hartman's Estate, supra note 6; Conway v. Shea, 282 Mass. 25, 183 N.E. 717, 88 A.L.R. 551, 1933. If these gifts or those de-

legacies. Doubtless the fact that the courts wish to prevent ademption or the operation of some other onerous principle leads them to construe doubtful cases as general legacies and indeed to allow this category to cover certain gifts fairly coming within the orthodox definition of specific legacies.[25]

Unless they are demonstrative, pecuniary legacies are usually general.[26] It is orthodox to consider that a legacy of a certain number of shares of a designated stock is general, in absence of any indication in the will that it is the testator's stock which is being given; [27] and the fact that the testator had, at the time of making the will, securities equal to or greater than the amount of those bequeathed does not in itself render the gift specific.[28] Bequests in different sums to various legatees of "my stocks and bonds at their par value," without further description, are general legacies,[29] as is also a gift of such an amount of securities as shall produce a certain income.[30]

*Demonstrative Legacies*

A demonstrative legacy is usually of money, made a charge on a particular fund and directed to be paid out of the latter, but payable at all events even if this fund fails, provided that the estate contains sufficient property which is not specifically de-

scribed in notes 21–23 supra are accompanied by other general or specific gifts, they would be usually considered residuary. Otherwise in strictness they seem to be specific. See supra note 15.

25 Maxim v. Maxim, infra note 34; Patanska v. Kuznia, supra note 4; In re Wilson's Estate, 260 Pa. 407, 103 A. 880, 6 A.L.R. 1349, 1918; Estate of Woodworth, supra note 2.

26 Kelly v. Richardson, 100 Ala. 584, 13 So. 785, 1893; Petition of Cain, 87 N.H. 318, 179 A. 347, 1935 (though given for a specific purpose); In re Doepke's Estate, 182 Wash. 556, 47 P. 2d 1009, 1935. See Gilmer's Legatees v. Gilmer's Executors, 42 Ala. 9, 1868.

27 Tifft v. Porter, 8 N.Y. 516, 1853; Bond v. Evans, 92 Colo. 1, 17 P.2d 311, 1932; In re McDougald's Estate, 149 Fla. 468, 6 So.2d 274, 1942; In re McFerren's Estate, 365 Pa. 490, 76 A.2d 759, 22 A.L.R.2d 451, 1950; In re Blomdahl's Will, 216 Wis. 590, 257 N. W. 152, 1934, noted, 2 U. of Chi.L.R. 490; Robinson v. Addison, 2 Beav. 515, 48 Eng.Rep. 1281, 1840. See Mersch, Is Tifft v. Porter Modified or Are Bequests of Closely-Held Stock an Exception to It?, 7 Fordham L.R. 364; note, 36 Cal.L.R. 338. But see cases cited supra note 14.

28 Capron v. Capron, 6 Mackey (D. C.) 340, 1887; Mecum v. Stoughton, 81 N.J.Eq. 319, 86 A. 52, 1913; and authorities supra note 27.

29 Canton's Succession, 144 La. 113, 80 So. 218, 1918; In re Hadden's Will, 1 Con. 306, 9 N.Y.S. 453, 1888.

30 Eggleston v. Merriam, 83 Minn. 98, 85 N.W. 937, modified 83 Minn. 98, 86 N.W. 444, 1901. And see Dugan v. Hollins, 11 Md. 41, 1857. Cf. Taylor v. Hull, 121 Kan. 102, 245 P. 1026, 1926. But see Jewell & a., Ex'rs v. Appolonio, supra note 14.

vised and bequeathed.[31] If it is payable only out of a specific fund or property, it is specific and not demonstrative.[32] A demonstrative legacy is a hybrid and partakes somewhat of the nature of a specific, and somewhat of the character of a general, legacy.[33]

In order to prevent ademption, the courts are inclined to construe legacies as demonstrative rather than specific.[34] Indeed, a demonstrative legacy is usually a fiction invented by the courts for this purpose, where the strict language of the will suggests either a general or a specific legacy.[35] A bequest of a certain amount to the legatee to be paid by turning over to him any of the testator's stocks or bonds at their market value, and in case these are not sufficient the balance to be paid in money, has been held to be a demonstrative legacy.[36] Here it is clear that the testator intended the full amount to be paid in any event, and the liberality of the decision consists in holding that there was sufficient designation of a particular fund in order to sustain the legacy as demonstrative. Where the testator provides a fund to furnish certain income to his widow, requiring it to be paid annually and that securities sufficient to that end be selected, the legacy was also held demonstrative.[37] Here there is no serious question concerning the indication of a particular fund and the court's liberality consists in finding that the testator intended the amount to be paid in any event.

31 Nusly v. Curtis, 36 Colo. 464, 85 P. 846, 7 L.R.A.,N.S., 592, 118 Am.St. Rep. 113, 10 Ann.Cas. 1134, 1906; Waters v. Selleck, supra note 17; In re Douglas' Estate, 149 Minn. 276, 183 N.W. 355, 1921; In re Wilson's Estate, 260 Pa. 407, 103 A. 880, 6 A.L.R. 1349, 1928; Maxim v. Maxim, 129 Me. 349, 152 A. 268, 73 A.L.R. 1244, 1930; In re Lewis' Estate, 148 Neb. 592, 28 N.W.2d 427, 1947, noted, 27 Neb.L.R. 462. See Mechem, supra note 1, at 561–566; notes, 4 N.Y.U.Intramural L.R. 146, 23 Iowa L.R. 435.

32 See supra note 17.

33 Nusly v. Curtis, supra note 31; Waters v. Selleck, supra note 17.

34 Maxim v. Maxim, 129 Me. 349, 152 A. 268, 73 A.L.R. 1244, 1930; Patanska v. Kuznia, supra note 4; In re Dieteman's Estate, 108 Colo. 508, 119 P.2d 611, 1941. See infra § 134, note 33. But see In re Lewis' Estate, supra note 31.

35 See In re Low's Will, 232 App. Div. 414, 250 N.Y.S. 192, 1931.

36 Baptist Female University of North Carolina v. Borden, 132 N.C. 476, 44 S.E. 47, 1007, 1903. See also Hibler v. Hibler, 104 Mich. 274, 62 N.W. 361, 1895.

37 Merriam v. Merriam, 80 Minn. 254, 83 N.W. 162, 1900. And see Maxim v. Maxim, 129 Me. 349, 152 A. 268, 73 A.L.R. 1244, 1930; White v. White, 73 S.C. 261, 53 S.E. 371, 1906. See annotation, 6 A.L.R. 1353.

*Residuary Legacies*

Like the ordinary specific legacy,[38] a residuary legacy is satisfied from the testator's estate in specie, but it is the rest and remainder of the estate not necessary to satisfy debt and other legacies instead of a designated thing contained in the estate. The amount and kind of property is unspecified in a residuary legacy, and in this sense it is more "general" than a pecuniary or other general legacy.[39] The enumeration of property included in a residuary bequest does not make a specific bequest of that property.[40] Usually the courts are liberal in construing doubtful residuary clauses as passing all property not necessary to satisfy debts or other legacies.[41] However, the use of the term "residue" or "remainder" is not conclusive indication of a residuary legacy. Thus, where the testator bequeathed $50,000 in trust and, after death of the life beneficiary, gave certain sums therefrom to various individuals, aggregating $41,000 and the remainder of the principal to A, the latter did not abate first as in case of an ordinary residuary bequest, because the principal sum was a fixed amount.[42]

*Devises*

It was once held that all devises were specific, due to the fact that after-acquired lands could not pass under the will.[43] With the disappearance of the latter rule, it is now generally held that the same tests apply as to kinds of legacies of personalty.[44] There can clearly be a residuary devise.[45] As in case of personalty, a residuary devise does not become specific merely because

38 See supra note 6.

39 See supra notes 21–24.

40 In re Kemp's Estate, 169 Mich. 578, 135 N.W. 270, Ann.Cas.1913D 1042, 1912; In re Crouse's Estate, 244 N.Y. 400, 155 N.E. 685, 1927; Williams v. Smith, 146 Tex. 269, 206 S.W.2d 208, 1947. See infra note 46.

41 Wood's Estate, 209 Pa. 16, 57 A. 1103; In re Hartwig's Estate, 70 Idaho 77, 211 P.2d 399, 1949; In re Bumsted's Estate, 1 N.J. 386, 64 A.2d 55, 1949.

42 Provident Trust Co. of Philadelphia v. Graff, 18 Del.Ch. 255, 157 A. 920, 1932, noted 80 U. of Pa.L.R. 1034.

43 McFadden v. Hefley, 28 S.C. 317, 5 S.E. 812, 13 Am.St.Rep. 675, 1887; Lancefield v. Iggulden, L.R. 10 Ch. App. 136, 1874. See supra § 85, note 82; American Law of Property §§ 14.9, 14.14.

44 In re Sutton's Estate, 11 Del.Ch. 460, 97 A. 624, 1915; Wilts v. Wilts, 151 Iowa 149, 130 N.W. 906, 1911; Matter of Gavey's Estate, 147 Misc. 332, 263 N.Y.S. 784, 1933. Cf. Kelly v. Richardson, 100 Ala. 584, 13 So. 785, 1893 (specific as to lands owned at time of execution; general as to after-acquired lands).

45 See Will of Kendrick, 210 Wis. 218, 246 N.W. 306, 1933; Daiss v. Hanes, infra note 46; In re Hartwig's Estate, supra note 41.

a particular parcel of land is mentioned as passing thereby.[46] Doubtless a devise of "160 acres of Adams County land" would be considered general, and it has been declared that a gift of all realty owned at the testator's death would be a general devise.[47] It has even been intimated that there may be a demonstrative devise.[48] A devise is specific if the realty to pass thereunder can be distinguished from other land owned by the testator. It is not necessary that the legal description be given in the will. A designation of the home of the testator is sufficient for a specific devise thereof.[49] Likewise a devise "of all my lands in S County",[50] or even of "all my real estate now owned by me," [51] is specific.

## SATISFACTION

**133. A general or residuary legacy may be satisfied in whole or in part by testator's inter vivos gift to the legatee after the execution of the will, if the testator so intends. When the testator stands in loco parentis to the legatee, his gift is presumed to be intended as satisfaction of the legacy. By the prevailing view the doctrine of satisfaction does not apply to devises of land.**

It is clear that if a testator makes a general pecuniary bequest and later gives an equal sum to the legatee, intending thereby to pay or satisfy the testamentary gift, the latter is considered satisfied,[1] and the legatee is not entitled to receive the amount under the will upon the testator's death. Indeed, if the testator is the parent of the legatee, the subsequent gift is presumed to be intended as satisfaction of the legacy,[2] though

46 Daiss v. Hanes, 85 Colo. 397, 277 P. 5, 1929. See supra note 40. But see Henderson v. First National Bank, 189 Ga. 175, 5 S.E.2d 636, 128 A.L.R. 816, 1939.

47 See Kaplan v. Leader, 297 Mass. 145, 8 N.E.2d 344, 1937. Cf. supra notes 15, 21–24.

48 Wheeler v. Hartshorn, 40 Wis. 83, 1876.

49 National Board of Christian Women's Board of Missions of Christian Church v. Fry, 293 Mo. 399, 239 S.W. 519, 1922.

50 Morisey v. Brown, 144 N.C. 154, 56 S.E. 704, 1907.

51 Kaplan v. Leader, supra note 47.

1 See generally, Barstow, Ademption by Satisfaction, 6 Wis.L.R. 217.

2 Paine v. Parsons, 14 Pick.(Mass.) 318, 1833; Carmichael v. Lathrop, 108 Mich. 473, 66 N.W. 350, 32 L.R.A. 232, 1896; Van Houten v. Post, 33 N.J.Eq. 344, 1880; Miner v. Atherton's Ex'r, 35 Pa. 528, 1860; Izard v. Hurst, Freem.C.C. 224, 22 Eng.Rep 1173, 1689. If, however, the gift is not of property of the same nature as the

this presumption may be rebutted by evidence showing a contrary intent.[3] However, the presumption will not operate against a child in favor of a stranger.[4] When the testator does not stand in loco parentis to the legatee, no such presumption exists;[5] but if intention to satisfy the legacy is shown, it will be deemed satisfied.[6] It is the testator's desire that is important,[7] and moreover his intention at the time of the subsequent gift.[8] When the legacy is for a certain purpose which is later accomplished by the testator in his lifetime, this is a strong indication that satisfaction was intended.[9] Payments to relatives of the legatee are not considered satisfaction of the legacy.[10]

Doubtless the basis of ademption by satisfaction is the same policy against double portions which is manifested with regard

legacy, no presumption arises. See infra note 19. In Kentucky, Virginia and West Virginia, statutes declare that there is no presumption of satisfaction on account of the testator standing in loco parentis to the legatee. Bordwell, Statute Law of Wills, 14 Ia.L.R. 433; Swinebroad v. Bright, 110 Ky. 616, 119 Ky. 684, 62 S.W. 484, 1901.

[3] Heileman v. Dakan, 211 Iowa 344, 233 N.W. 542, 1931; Grogan v. Ashe, 156 N.C. 286, 72 S.E. 372, 1911; Van Houten v. Post, 33 N.J.Eq. 344, 1880; Miner v. Atherton's Ex'r, 35 Pa. 528, 1860. See annotation, 94 A.L.R. 190–195. In California, Montana, North Dakota, Oklahoma, South Dakota and Utah, the intention to satisfy a legacy must be expressed in writing. Bordwell, Statute Law of Wills, 14 Ia.L. R. 434. And see Wickliffe v. Wickliffe, 206 Mo.App. 42, 226 S.W. 1035, 1920; cf. note 5 infra.

[4] In re Heather [1906] 2 Ch. 230.

[5] Heileman v. Dakan, 211 Iowa 344, 233 N.W. 542, 1931 (grandson not a member of testator's family); Selby v. Fidelity Trust Co., 188 Md. 192, 51 A.2d 822, 1947 (same); Latorraca v. Latorraca, 132 N.J.Eq. 40, 26 A.2d 522, 1942, affirmed, 133 N.J.Eq. 298, 31 A. 2d 819, 1943; In re Bernhardi's Estate, 151 Misc. 480, 273 N.Y.S. 250, 1934 (daughter-in-law); In re Will of Cramer, 183 Wis. 525, 198 N.W. 386, 1924. But an uncle may be shown to occupy the position of parent toward a niece so as to give rise to the presumption. Powys v. Mansfield, 3 Myl. & C. 359, 40 Eng.Rep. 964, 1837.

[6] Johnson v. McDowell, 154 Iowa 38, 134 N.W. 419, 38 L.R.A.,N.S., 588, 1912; Richards v. Humphreys, 14 Pick.(Mass.) 133, 1833. Cf. In re Shields, [1912] 1 Ch. 591; Selby v. Fidelity Trust Co., supra note 5.

[7] In re Mikkelsen's Estate, 202 Iowa 842, 211 N.W. 254, 1926; Richards v. Humphreys, supra note 6; Jones v. Mason, 26 Va.(5 Rand.) 577, 16 Am. Dec. 761, 1827. But see Wickliffe v. Wickliffe, supra note 3.

[8] Vincent v. Vincent, 241 Mich. 329, 217 N.W. 65, 1928; Kapiolani Maternity and Gynecological Hospital v. Wodehouse, 70 F.2d 793, C.C.A. 9th, 1934.

[9] Loyola College v. Dugan, 137 Md. 545, 113 A. 81, 1921; Grogan v. Ashe, 156 N.C. 286, 72 S.E. 372, 1911.

[10] Lake v. Harrington, 210 Miss. 74, 48 So.2d 845, 26 A.L.R.2d 1, 1950; Grogan v. Ashe, supra note 9.

to advancements in case of intestacy.[11] There is no occasion to resort to the theory of revocation in order to justify the doctrine of ademption by satisfaction, and none of the statutory methods of revocation are necessary for satisfaction of a legacy.[12] To give rise to satisfaction, the subsequent transaction must be in the nature of a complete gift.[13] The doctrine has no application where the gift preceded execution of the will.[14]

*Partial Satisfaction*

While there was formerly some doubt, it is now well settled that there may be a pro tanto as well as a total satisfaction of a legacy.[15] Thus a legacy of $2,000 may be partially satisfied by an inter vivos gift of $1,000 to the legatee if this result was intended by the testator. Some cases speak of total ademption of a legacy where the subsequent gift, though smaller in amount, was intended as a complete ademption. However, in all of these cases,[16] the legatee consented to the receipt of a smaller portion presently as an extinguishment of a larger testamentary provision, and in absence of the elements which will satisfy the requirements of release of expectancy, there is probably no total ademption.

11 In re Mikkelsen's Estate, supra note 7; In re Blundell, [1906] 2 Ch. 222. See Traughber v. King, 235 Ky. 658, 32 S.W.2d 8, 1930; In re Bush's Estate, 155 Kan. 556, 127 P.2d 455, 142 A.L.R. 518, 1942.

12 Jacobs v. Button, 79 Conn. 360, 65 A. 150, 1906; Carmichael v. Lathrop, supra note 2.

13 Meyerovitz v. Jacobovitz, 263 Mass. 47, 160 N.E. 331, 1928; In re Bernhardi's Estate, 151 Misc. 480, 273 N.Y.S. 250, 1934. Cf. In re Smith's Estate, 210 Iowa 563, 231 N.W. 468, 1930 (payment of son's debt is an ademption of legacy).

14 Marshall v. West, 18 Del.Ch. 341, 160 A. 637, 1932; Jaques v. Swasey, 153 Mass. 596, 27 N.E. 771, 13 L.R.A. 566, 1891; Lake v. Harrington, supra note 10.

15 Rogers v. Reinking, 205 Iowa 1311, 217 N.W. 441, 1928; Carmichael v. Lathrop, supra note 2; Vincent v. Vincent, supra note 8; In re French's Estate, 268 N.Y. 370, 197 N.E. 316, 1935 (no interest should be charged thereon); Watson v. Watson, 33 Beav. 574, 55 Eng.Rep. 491, 1864. But relatively small gifts are not considered even pro tanto satisfaction. State ex rel. Brown v. Crossley, 69 Ind. 203, 1879; Watson v. Watson, supra.

16 Heileman v. Dakan, 211 Iowa 344, 233 N.W. 542, 1931. Cf. Johnson v. McDowell, 154 Iowa 38, 134 N.W. 419, 38 L.R.A.,N.S., 588, 1912. See In re Crane's Estate, 6 Cal.2d 218, 57 P.2d 476, 104 A.L.R. 1101, 1936, dealing with settlements between husband and wife. And see supra § 130.

*Satisfaction of Specific Legacies*

It has been said that the doctrine of satisfaction applies only to pecuniary legacies.[17] When the subject of a specific legacy is given to the legatee in testator's lifetime there is ademption by extinction. It is sufficient reason for the legatee receiving nothing under the will that there is nothing to take, since the property is not included in the testator's estate at his death. However, it seems there may be satisfaction of specific legacies by the giving of other property of equal value if the intention to satisfy is clearly shown,[18] although here it may take concurrence of the legatee, making it substantially a case of release. The inter vivos payment or tender of money in place of an obligation to return a chattel is perhaps an analogy.

*Ejusdem Generis*

When the thing given is not of the same nature as the thing bequeathed, a presumption arises that an ademption by satisfaction was not intended.[19] This is the doctrine of ejusdem generis. However, this presumption is not conclusive and if the gift of other property is shown to have been intended as satisfaction of the pecuniary legacy, it may be so considered.[20] Thus, a legacy may be adeemed by conveyance of land if so intended.[21] However, here again, it is probable that there is no extinguishment unless there is substantially a release by the legatee.

*Satisfaction of Residuary Bequests*

Formerly it was held that there could be no total or partial ademption of an indefinite sum, thus preventing the ademption of a residuary legacy.[22] It is now settled that a residuary bequest may be satisfied at least pro tanto, by an inter vivos gift.[23]

17 Weston v. Johnson, 48 Ind. 1, 1874.

18 Jones v. Mason, supra note 7. See Roberts v. Wilson, 200 Ga. 201, 36 S.E.2d 758, 1946; Austin v. Austin, 147 Neb. 109, 22 N.W.2d 560, 1946.

19 In re Jaques, [1903] 1 Ch. 267. See Carmichael v. Lathrop, supra note 2.

20 Louisville Trust Co. v. Southern Baptist Theological Seminary, 148 Ky. 711, 147 S.W. 431, 1912; Carmichael v. Lathrop, supra note 2; Jones v. Mason, supra note 7.

21 Carmichael v. Lathrop, supra note 2; Vincent v. Vincent, supra note 8.

22 Farnham v. Phillips, 2 Atk. 215, 26 Eng.Rep. 533, 1741. Cf. Meyerovitz v. Jacobovitz, supra note 13.

23 Carmichael v. Lathrop, supra note 2; Vincent v. Vincent, supra note 8; Van Houten v. Post, supra note 2; Hayes v. Welling, 38 R.I. 553, 96 A. 843, 1916.

*Satisfaction of Devises*

While the doctrine of ademption by satisfaction is now broadly applied to legacies of personalty, the prevailing view is that devises cannot be satisfied either by gift of personalty or conveyances of other lands.[24] Formerly it could have been urged that satisfaction of a devise was really a species of revocation not permitted by the wills section of the Statute of Frauds.[25] Today the same formalities are required for revocation of devises as for legacies.[26] As legacies may be adeemed, without violation of the provisions regarding revocation, devises should also be capable of satisfaction by conveyance of other land, or a gift of personalty to the devisee. The minority position, which recognizes this possibility, seems sounder than the prevailing view.[27] However, to the extent that the devise is specific, the restrictions relative to satisfaction of specific legacies should apply.[28]

## ADEMPTION

**134. A testamentary gift of testator's specific real or personal property is adeemed, or fails completely, when the thing given does not exist as part of his estate at the time of his death. The doctrine now generally applies regardless of the intention of the testator, though if the change in the property is not substantial, there is no ademption.**

If a will makes a specific legacy and the testator subsequently disposes of the subject matter or it is destroyed, the courts could conceivably hold that the executor is obliged to procure the chattel or some similar one for the legatee or pay the latter its value.[1] By holding that the matter depended upon the inten-

24 Kemp v. Kemp, 92 Ind.App. 268, 154 N.E. 505, 1926, noted, 36 Yale L. J. 717; Graham v. Karr, 331 Mo. 1157, 55 S.W.2d 995, 1932; Burnham v. Comfort, 108 N.Y. 535, 15 N.E. 710, 2 Am.St.Rep. 462, 1888. And see cases note 25, infra.

25 See In re Brown's Estate, 139 Iowa 219, 117 N.W. 260, 1908; Burnham v. Comfort, supra note 24 (also because title to land should not be affected by informal transactions).

26 See supra ch. 10.

27 Hansbrough Ex'rs v. Hooe, 12 Leigh (39 Va.) 316, 37 Am.Dec. 659, 1841. See notes, 4 Ill.L.R. 350, 36 Yale L.J. 717. The statutes in Kentucky, Virginia and West Virginia provide that a devise may be satisfied. See Harrison's Executor v. Harrison's Administrator, 171 Va. 224, 198 S.E. 902, 1938; American Law of Property § 14.11.

28 See supra notes 17–21.

1 See Mechem, Specific Legacies of Unspecific Things—Ashburner v. Macguire Reconsidered, 87 U. of Pa.L.R. 546. But our courts refuse to do

tion [2] of the testator, the civil law accepted this position, and the early English decisions did likewise to a certain extent.[3] However, ever since the leading case of Ashburner v. Macguire,[4] the orthodox position has been that intent [5] has nothing to do with the matter, and that the sole question is whether the subject matter of the specific legacy is in the testator's estate at his death, and if it is not the legacy is adeemed, and the legatee gets nothing.[6] The doctrine of ademption does not apply to general legacies,[7] and hence when securities or other property are given it is often vital to determine whether the legacy is specific, part of the property owned by the testator, or general, that which may be satisfied from the general assets if nothing answering to the description is contained in the estate at the testator's death.[8]

this. See Owen v. Busiel, 83 N.H. 345, 142 A. 692, 59 A.L.R. 1103, 1928, noted, 27 Mich.L.R. 480, and cases infra note 6.

[2] This must refer to intent at the time of the disposition or destruction of the property. See infra note 5.

[3] See Mechem, supra note 1; Page, Ademption by Extinction, [1943] Wis. L.R. 11; Warren, History of Ademption, 25 Iowa L.R. 290.

[4] 2 Bro.C.C. 108, 29 Eng.Rep. 62, 1786.

[5] See supra note 2. However, the testator's intent or his presumed intent at the time of execution of the will is an important factor in avoiding the effect of ademption. See note 29 infra et seq.

[6] Lang v. Vaughn, 137 Ga. 671, 74 S.E. 270, 40 L.R.A.,N.S., 542, Ann. Cas.1913B, 52, 1912; Elwyn v. De Garmendia, 148 Md. 109, 128 A. 913, 40 A.L.R. 553, 1925, noted, 39 Harv. L.R. 404, 10 Minn.L.R. 75, 35 Yale L. J. 117; Moffatt v. Heon, 242 Mass. 201, 136 N.E. 123, 1922, noted, 4 Bost. U.L.R. 61; Welch v. Welch, 147 Miss. 728, 113 So. 197, 1927 (intention of testator that legatee of Packard car should take the Lincoln car which was exchanged therefor was immaterial); In re Tillinghast, 23 R.I. 121, 49 A. 634, 1901; Hill's Adm'rs v. Hill, 127 Va. 341, 103 S.E. 605, 1920 (parol evidence inadmissible). See also note 9 infra. In Humphreys v. Humphreys, 2 Cox Ch. 184, 30 Eng.Rep. 85, 1789, it was said by Lord Thurlow: "The only rule to be adhered to is to see whether the subject of the specific bequest remained in specie at the time of the testator's death, for if it did not, then there must be an end of the bequest; and the idea of discussing what were the particular motives and intention of the testator in destroying the subject of the bequest would be productive of endless uncertainty and confusion."

See Smith, Ademption by Extinction, 6 Wis.L.R. 229, 231 and articles supra notes 1, 3; note, 41 Yale L.J. 101; also infra notes 14–23; cf. infra notes 10, 39, 40; In re Cooper's Estate, infra note 37.

[7] In re Estate of McFerren, 365 Pa. 490, 76 A.2d 759, 22 A.L.R.2d 451, 1950, noted, 12 U. of Pitt.L.R. 465; In re Blomdahl's Will, 216 Wis. 590, 257 N.W. 152, 1934, noted, 2 Chi.L.R. 490; Partridge v. Partridge, Case, Temp. Talb. 226, 25 Eng.Rep. 749, 1736.

[8] See supra § 132.

The modern position is illustrated by the cases which hold that even if the subject of a specific devise or bequest is taken against the wishes of the testator, as in case of eminent domain, there is a fatal ademption.[9] However, a number of courts decline to hold that there may be an ademption by a disposition of the property by the guardian of a testator who becomes insane after execution of the will.[10] These are indeed hard cases, and it may be that the courts are here reverting to the older intention theory in order to alleviate the situation.

*Revocation Distinguished*

Formerly the testator's conveyance of devised land was said to revoke the devise, and even if the land was later reacquired by the testator it would not pass under the will.[11] This was due mainly to the common-law doctrine that a will could not operate upon land acquired after the will's execution. As a will can now operate upon after-acquired realty as well as personalty, the property described in either specific legacy or devise should pass by the will regardless of the fact that testator may not have continued as owner through all of the period since execution of his will.[12] If testator owned no such property at his death, there is an ademption, and in either case there is no occasion for thinking in terms of revocation.[13]

*Sale or Transfer by Testator*

When the subject-matter of a specific devise or bequest is sold by the testator, the gift is adeemed, and neither the proceeds, nor

9 Ametrano v. Downs, 170 N.Y. 388, 63 N.E. 340, 58 L.R.A. 719, 88 Am.St. Rep. 671, 1902. See also In re Dungan's Estate, 31 Del.Ch. 551, 73 A.2d 776, 1950, and Taylor v. Hull, 121 Kan. 102, 245 P. 1026, 1926, where securities were "called".

10 Lewis v. Hill, 287 Ill. 542, 56 N.E.2d 619, 1944, noted, 23 Chi-Kent L.R. 278; Buder v. Stocke, 343 Mo. 506, 121 S.W.2d 852, 1938; Duncan v. Bigelow, 96 N.H. 216, 72 A.2d 497, 1950; In re Cooper's Estate, 95 N.J. Eq. 210, 123 A. 45, 30 A.L.R. 673, noted, 37 Harv.L.R. 1141, 1923; Wilmerton v. Wilmerton, 176 F. 896, 28 L.R.A.,N.S., 401, C.C.A.Ill., 1910, noted, 11 Col.L.R. 72. Contra: Hoke v. Herman, 21 Pa. 301, 1853; In re Ireland's Estate, 257 N.Y. 155, 177 N.E. 405, 1931, noted, 16 Corn.L.Q. 623, 45 Harv.L.R. 710, 9 N.Y.U.L.Q.R. 506, 79 U. of Pa.L.R. 990, 17 Va.L.R. 584. The English Lunacy Act 1890 prevents ademption by the guardian. N.Y.C.P.A. § 1399 does likewise in the case of devises. See N.Y.Leg.Doc.1950, No. 65F; Model Probate Code § 231 and comment.

11 See supra § 85 at note 68 et seq.; American Law of Property §§ 14.9, 14.13.

12 Ibid.

13 See notes, 27 Mich.L.R. 480, 17 Ia.L.R. 552.

similar property purchased therewith, passes to the beneficiary.[14] If the will, however, gives the latter the proceeds of a specific fund, the legatee is entitled to this money if it can be traced.[15] When a debt or a mortgage is bequeathed, the bequest is adeemed by the debtor's payment to the testator in his lifetime.[16] When one devises real estate and later disposes of it taking a purchase-money mortgage thereon, the mortgage does not pass to the devisee but the devise is adeemed.[17] The converse is also true, as where the testator bequeaths a mortgage and later becomes the owner of the land itself.[18] The grant of a lease of devised lands passes the realty subject to the lease.[19] When the property bequeathed or devised has not been conveyed but only subjected to a contract of sale by the testator, the orthodox view is that the testamentary provision is adeemed and that the right

[14] Gardner v. McNeal, 117 Md. 27, 82 A. 988, 40 L.R.A.,N.S., 553, Ann. Cas.1914A 119, 1911; Harvard Unitarian Society v. Tufts, 151 Mass. 76, 23 N.E. 1006, 7 L.R.A. 390, 1890; Dunlap v. Hart, 274 Mo. 600, 204 S.W. 525, 3 A.L.R. 1493, 1918; May v. Sherrard's Legatees, 115 Va. 617, 79 S.E. 1026, Ann.Cas.1915B 1131, 1913. A partition of testator's undivided interest was held not to work an ademption. Brady v. Paine, 391 Ill. 596, 63 N.E.2d 721, 162 A.L.R. 138, 1945, noted, 24 Chi-Kent L.R. 367.

[15] Gist v. Craig, 142 S.C. 407, 141 S.E. 26, 1927; Georgia Infirmary for Relief and Protection of Aged and Afflicted Negroes v. Jones, 37 F. 750, C.C.N.Y. 1889; In re Frost's Estate, 354 Pa. 223, 47 A.2d 219, 165 A.L.R. 1030, 1946. And see Prendergast v. Walsh, 58 N.J.Eq. 149, 42 A. 1049, 1899; In re Bancroft, [1928] 1 Ch. 577; Gray v. McCausland, 314 Mass. 743, 51 N.E.2d 441, 149 A.L.R. 1059, 1943; also infra notes 20, 43. But if the money is invested in lands there is an ademption. Durham's Adm'r v. Clay, 142 Ky. 96, 134 S.W. 153, 1911.

[16] In re Estate of Jepson, 181 Cal. 745, 186 P. 352, 1919; Moffatt v. Heon, supra note 6; Wyckoff v. Perrine's Ex'rs, 37 N.J.Eq. 118, 1883; In re Bridle, 4 C.P.D. 336, 1879. But merely taking renewal notes does not work an ademption of a bequest of the notes. Ford v. Ford, 23 N.H. 212, 1851.

[17] Willoughby v. Watson, 114 Kan. 82, 216 P. 1095, 1923; Blaisdell v. Coe, 83 N.H. 167, 139 A. 758, 65 A.L.R. 626, 1927; Lewis v. Thompson, 142 Ohio St. 338, 52 N.E.2d 331, 1943, noted, 42 Mich.L.R. 1145. Cf. Phillips v. Phillips, 213 Ala. 27, 104 So. 234, 1925 (statute); Connecticut Trust & Safe Deposit Co. v. Chase, 75 Conn. 683, 55 A. 171, 1903 (here will directed payment of legacies from the proceeds of certain realty); Mee v. Cusineau, 213 Ark. 61, 209 S.W.2d 445, 1948, noted, 3 Ark.L.R. 111 (same, semble).

[18] Tolman v. Tolman, 85 Me. 317, 27 A. 184, 1893. And see Franck v. Franck, 72 S.W. 275, 24 Ky.Law Rep. 1790, 1903; Green v. Green, 231 N.C. 707, 58 S.E.2d 722, 1950. Contra: In re McLaughlin's Estate, 97 Cal.App. 485, 275 P. 875, 1929, criticized, 18 Cal.L.R. 711. See also note, 24 Iowa L.R. 617, and note 17 supra.

[19] Herrington v. Budd, 5 Denio (N. Y.) 321, 1848; In re Fuller's Estate, 71 Vt. 73, 42 A. 981, 1898 (grant of license). And see In re Evans' Estate, 145 Minn. 252, 177 N.W. 126, 8 A.L.R. 1631, 1920.

to enforce the contract and receive the proceeds does not pass to the legatee or devisee.[20] Some jurisdictions have statutes to the effect that an executory contract of sale does not work an ademption.[21]

*Destruction*

The death of animals bequeathed works an ademption.[22] Likewise when the subject of the bequest is lost at sea the legatee cannot recover the insurance.[23] However, when both the testatrix and her jewelry were lost in the same shipwreck, a legacy of the jewelry was not adeemed as the latter had existence at the death of the testatrix.[24] Acts of the executor after the testator's death do not work an ademption.[25]

*Pro Tanto Ademption*

An ademption by extinction may be pro tanto as well as of the entire gift. Though the portion of the thing devised or bequeathed not owned by the testator at the time of his death cannot go to the devisee or legatee, yet the part remaining in the testator's estate may pass under the will.[26] Thus, if the testator devises a tract of land and conveys a part of it, the rest passes to the devisee.[27] Likewise if the testator receives part payment of an obligation the unpaid portion thereof passes to the specific legatee of the debt.[28]

20 In re Bernhard's Estate, 134 Iowa 603, 112 N.W. 86, 12 L.R.A.,N.S., 1029, 1907; Walker v. Waters, 118 Md. 203, 84 A. 466, 1912; Newport Water Works v. Sisson, 18 R.I. 411, 28 A. 336, 1893. See supra § 85, note 91. Cf. In re Bancroft, [1928] 1 Ch. 577, where bequest of "rights" to a play was deemed to cover amounts due under testator's subsequent contract of sale of those rights. Most American authorities hold that testator's giving of an option does not work an ademption. See annotations 79 A.L.R. 268, 155 id. 571.

21 See Phillips v. Phillips, 213 Ala. 27, 104 So. 234, 1925; Lefebvre's Estate, 100 Wis. 192, 75 N.W. 971, 1898; also supra § 85, notes 90, 91; American Law of Property § 14.13.

22 Brady v. Brady, 78 Md. 461, 28 A. 515, 1894.

23 Durant v. Friend, 5 De G. & S. 343, 64 Eng.Rep. 1145, 1851.

24 In re Shymer's Estate, 136 Misc. 334, 242 N.Y.S. 234, 1930 (holding legatee entitled to recover damages for the loss).

25 In re Frahm's Estate, 120 Iowa 85, 94 N.W. 444, 1903; Thompson v. Ford, 145 Tenn. 335, 236 S.W. 2, 1921.

26 Taylor v. Hull, 121 Kan. 102, 245 P. 1026, 1926; King v. Sellers, 194 N.C. 533, 140 S.E. 91, 1927. And see authorities supra notes 19, 21.

27 Paris v. Erisman, 300 S.W. 487, Mo.1927. See also In re Henderson's Estate, 197 Misc. 468, 94 N.Y.S.2d 693, 1950, where part of the devised "farm" was turned into a filling station by testator.

28 Ashburner v. Macguire, 2 Bro. Ch. 108, 29 Eng.Rep. 62, 1786.

*Escape Devices—General or Demonstrative Legacy Construction*

There are a number of ways in which the courts may in certain cases avoid the rigor of the ademption principle. Formerly, at least, the courts often did so by adopting a general legacy construction in doubtful cases, *e. g.*, bequests which are not expressly of a specific part of the estate but which the testator probably thought of as of some particular property which he owned at the time of execution of the will.[29] However, some of the recent cases hold such legacies specific,[30] in order to give the legatee the advantages of increase after the testator's death [31] or of preference in the order of abatement.[32] These decisions, if consistently adhered to, will react to the legatee's disadvantage if the problem is one of ademption.

The demonstrative legacy construction also saves some legacies from annihilation by ademption. While, to the extent that the legacy is one of a particular fund, there is no possibility of its operation when the fund is gone, if it is demonstrative it can operate as a general legacy and be payable from general assets.[33]

*Same—Time of Death Construction*

Some legacies and devises can be saved from the effect of ademption by applying the testamentary expression of the gift to the situation as it exists at the time of the testator's death and thus passing the property then owned by him. Formerly this technique could not be applied to devises because of the rule regarding after-acquired land,[34] but the possibility now exists with respect to devises as well as bequests.[35] Most bequests in generic terms, such as "my linens" or "my household goods" are construed to pass the things owned at testator's death and which fairly fall in such categories.[36] There is more doubt as to whether this technique should be applied to such gifts as those of "my home", "my automobile", or "my diamond brooch." Here it is more likely that the testator was thinking of the thing owned by him at the time of the will. Yet many cases apply the time of

29 Supra § 132.

30 Ibid. at note 14.

31 Infra § 135.

32 Infra § 136.

33 See In re Cline's Estate, 67 Cal. App.2d 800, 155 P.2d 390, 1945; Bowen v. Dorrance, 12 R.I. 269, 1879. But see Tipton v. Tipton, 1 Coldw. (41 Tenn.) 252, 1860. Cf. Succession of Levy, 207 La. 1062, 22 So.2d 650, 1950. And see supra § 132, notes 34–37.

34 Supra notes 11–13.

35 Supra § 85.

36 Masters v. Masters, 1 P.Wms. 421, 24 Eng.Rep. 454, 1717. See note, 23 Iowa L.R. 380.

death construction to such gifts.[37] Of course this device is of no avail when the testator owns no property at his death which is capable of falling within the terms of the will, nor where the will expressly refers to objects which testator owned at the time of execution.

*Same—Changes of Form*

Changes of form, if not substantial, do not cause an ademption. Thus, where the testator bequeaths specific stock which is later split up into a larger number of shares of the same corporation, the legatee will take the amount of the new stock which represents the number of shares of the old which was bequeathed.[38] If, however, the stock is exchanged upon call for debentures of the corporation,[39] or for stock in a different company which succeeds the original company,[40] the change is more substantial and most courts hold that there is an ademption. Where the testator conveyed the devised realty to a corporation of which he was the sole stockholder, there was held to be an ademption.[41] A bequest of the money on deposit in a certain bank has been held not

37 Milton v. Milton, 193 Miss. 563, 10 So.2d 175, 1942; Lusk's Estate, 336 Pa. 465, 9 A.2d 363, 125 A.L.R. 787, 1939; Waldo v. Hayes, 90 App.Div. 454, 89 N.Y.S. 69, 1904; In re Cooper's Estate, 107 Cal.App.2d 592, 237 P.2d 699, 1951 (extreme case). But cf. In re Sikes, [1927] 1 Ch. 364. However, the time of death construction may operate to legatee's disadvantage. See Davis v. Price, infra note 38.

38 Fidelity Title & Trust Co. v. Young, 101 Conn. 359, 125 A. 871, 1924; Gorham v. Chadwick, 135 Me. 479, 200 A. 500, 117 A.L.R. 805, 1938 (reorganization); In re Mandelle's Estate, 252 Mich. 375, 233 N.W. 230, 1930; Adams v. Conqueror Trust Co., 358 Mo. 736, 217 S.W.2d 476, 7 A.L.R. 2d 268, 1949; In re Hinners' Will, 216 Wis. 294, 257 N.W. 148, 1930, noted, 10 Wis.L.R. 307; Re Leeming, [1912] 1 Ch. 828 (reincorporation). And see Johns Hopkins University v. Uhrig, 145 Md. 114, 125 A. 606, 1924 (mere change of name of corporation; note, 23 Minn.L.R. 553, and infra § 135, note 8 (stock dividends distinguished). But see Davis v. Price, 189 Tenn. 555, 226 S.W.2d 290, 1949.

39 Ademption: First National Bank of Boston v. Perkins Institute for Blind, 275 Mass. 498, 176 N.E. 532, 1931. Contra: Spinney v. Eaton, 111 Me. 1, 87 A. 378, 46 L.R.A.,N.S., 535, 1913 (intention theory applied).

40 Ademption: In re Horn's Estate, 317 Pa. 49, 175 A. 414, 97 A.L.R. 1029, 1934 (merger); Dean v. Tusculum, 195 F.2d 796, D.C.Cir.1952; Re Slater, [1907] 1 Ch. 665, 8 Ann.Cas. 141. Contra: Goode v. Reynolds, 208 Ky. 441, 271 S.W. 600, 63 A.L.R. 631, 1925 (consolidation of banks); Gardner v. Gardner, 72 N.H. 257, 56 A. 316, 1903 (intention theory applied); In re Peirce, 25 R.I. 34, 54 A. 588, 1903.

41 Schwartz v. Gertwagen Realty Corporation, 114 N.J.Eq. 428, 168 A. 820, 1933, noted, 82 U. of Pa.L.R. 404. Cf. Miles v. Odom, 3 N.J.Super. 376, 65 A.2d 754, 1949.

adeemed by withdrawal of the money and placing it in another bank.[42] Unless resort is made to the discarded intention theory, the decision can only be defended on the ground that the testator bequeathed the fund, similar to the proceeds cases already discussed.[43] Much depends upon the language of the will.

*Change of Location*

Where goods are aptly described in the will and their location is also given, a change of location will not work an ademption.[44] However, if the subject matter of the legacy is designated solely as the contents of a certain receptacle, a change of location has something of the effect of an ademption,[45] yet since the legacy can be increased by change of position, this general problem should be considered upon the broader basis already discussed of designation of the subject-matter by nontestamentary act.[46]

*Legislation*

There have been a few statutes designed to prevent ademption by acts of the testator's guardian.[47] Kentucky has an anti-ademption statute of broader import.[48] The suggestion [49] has been made that there should be general legislation in this field running roughly parallel to the statutes designed to prevent lapse.[50] This is a matter which deserves careful consideration, although the difficulties in framing a comprehensive statute are undoubtedly great.

42 Willis v. Barrow, 218 Ala. 549, 119 So. 678, 1929, noted, 42 Harv.L.R. 960. And see Prendergast v. Walsh, supra note 15.

43 E. g., the "proceeds" cases cited supra notes 15, 20; and see Elwyn v. DeGarmendia, supra note 6, where the testator gave one string of pearls to A and another to B and later had them all made into a single string; Gerlach Estate, 364 Pa. 207, 72 A.2d 271, 16 A.L.R.2d 1397, 1950 (bequest of interest in business which was later incorporated); Mitchell v. Mitchell, 208 Ark. 478, 187 S.W.2d 163, 1945 (change from corporate to personal ownership).

44 In re Chevalier's Estate, 167 Kan. 67, 204 P.2d 748, 1949; Wiggins v. Cheatham, 143 Tenn. 406, 225 S.W. 1040, 13 A.L.R. 169, 1920; Chapman v. Hart, 1 Ves. 271, 27 Eng.Rep. 1026, 1749.

45 Succession of Canton, 144 La. 113, 80 So. 218, 1918. And see Hastings v. Bridge, 86 N.H. 247, 166 A. 273, 1933.

46 See supra § 81. In addition the gift may not be specific—see supra § 132.

47 See supra note 10.

48 Ky.Rev.Stat.Ann. § 344.360. See also supra note 21 and American Law of Property § 14.13.

49 See Mechem, supra note 1; Page, supra note 3. Cf. Mechem, Why Not a Modern Wills Act, 33 Iowa L.R. 501, 504. See Model Probate Code p. 20–21.

50 See infra § 140.

## INCREASE AND INTEREST

**135. Specific legacies of debts or obligations ordinarily carry with them unpaid accrued interest, but bequests of stock do not pass cash or usually even stock dividends declared in testator's lifetime. A specific legatee or devisee is entitled to all accessions and accretions occurring after the testator's death.**

**General legacies usually bear interest at the legal rate after one year from testator's death, though in some jurisdictions by virtue of statutory provisions the interest does not begin to run until a certain time after the grant of letters or until the legacies are ordered paid by the court. The ordinary rule is subject to exceptions, as when the legacy is for the support of a minor child or is in payment of a debt, in which case interest runs from the death. Interest is borne by the residuary estate.**

### *Increase Before Testator's Death*

When a testator bequeaths securities or debts, there are often problems as to whether the legacy passes the accrued interest. Much depends on the language of the will. A legacy of a mortgage,[1] or of a debt,[2] owed to the testator passes the accrued unpaid interest, and a bequest of a bond has been held to pass the overdue interest coupon attached thereto.[3] But the legacy of a sum due upon a particular security does not pass interest in arrears.[4] Obviously interest which has been paid to the testator does not pass with the bequest of the debt or security.

A specific devise or bequest passes the thing given in its improved state at the time of the testator's death.[5] If the increased increment is not separable from the object the legatee has advantage of the increase.[6] But if dividends are declared on stock during the testator's lifetime, the dividends do not pass

1 Fleming v. Carr, 47 N.J.Eq. 549, 22 A. 197, 1891; Matter of Althaus' Will, 94 Misc. 43, 158 N.Y.S. 990, 1916.

2 Alford v. Bennett, 279 Ill. 375, 117 N.E. 89, 1917; Fleming v. Carr, supra note 1.

3 Ogden v. Pattee, 149 Mass. 82, 21 N.E. 227, 14 Am.St.Rep. 401, 1889.

4 Stultz v. Kiser, 37 N.C. 538, 1843.

5 Huard v. Hegarty, 122 Me. 206, 119 A. 609, 1923.

6 Re Bird [1952] Ont. 415, [1942] 3 D.L.R. 439. But see Smith v. Wheeler, 326 Mass. 223, 93 N.E.2d 544, 18 A.L.R.2d 516, 1950, where testator bequeathed "my" half interest in a business and later acquired the other half which was held to pass under the residuary clause.

to the legatee of the stock.[7] This is generally held even in case of stock dividends,[8] where it might be urged that the additional shares are really a part of the property represented by the original shares. Where the testator bequeathed thirty shares of stock of Standard Oil Company of New Jersey, which by order of the court was required to separate itself from its subsidiary corporations during testator's lifetime so that the testator thereafter owned the original thirty shares and in addition stock in the thirty-nine subsidiary companies, only the stock of the Standard Oil Company of New Jersey passed under this bequest.[9]

*Increase After Testator's Death*

Specific legacies, however, carry with them all accessions and accretions which accrue after testator's death.[10] Thus stock or cash dividends declared after that time pass to the specific legatee, though earned before the testator's death.[11] The same is true of royalties from oil leases.[12] Rent becoming due after testa-

[7] Perry v. Leslie, 124 Me. 93, 126 A. 340, 1924; In re Kernochan, 104 N.Y. 618, 11 N.E. 149, 1887.

[8] Griffith v. Adams, 106 Conn. 19, 137 A. 20, 1927; Hicks v. Kerr, 132 Md. 693, 104 A. 426, 10 A.L.R. 1323, 1918; First National Bank of Boston v. Union Hospital of Fall River, 281 Mass. 64, 183 N.E. 247, 89 A.L.R. 1125, 1932, noted, 13 Bost.U.L.R. 172, 42 Yale L.J. 973; Sherman v. Riley, 43 R.I. 202, 110 A. 629, 1920; see Davis v. Price, 189 Tenn. 555, 226 S.W.2d 290, 1950 (general legacy). Contra: Chase Nat. Bank v. Deichmiller, 107 N.J.Eq. 379, 152 A. 697, 1930; Butler v. Dobbins, 142 Me. 383, 53 A.2d 270, 172 A.L.R. 361, 1947; see Succession of Quintero, 209 La. 279, 24 So.2d 589, 162 A.L.R. 1150, 1945, noted, 3 Loyola L.R. 1916, 45 Mich.L.R. 245, 20 Tulane L.R. 647. Cf. Fidelity Title & Trust Co. v. Young, 101 Conn. 359, 125 A. 871, 1924, noted, 25 Col.L.R. 114, 38 Harv.L.R. 264 (stock split-up passes increased shares); In re Mandelle's Estate, 252 Mich. 375, 233 N.W. 230, 1930 (same); supra § 134, note 38. It is possible to distinguish between a stock dividend and a stock split-up on the ground that the former usually changes the capital structure by transfer of undivided profits into capital, while the capital structure is unchanged in case of a split-up.

[9] In re Brann, 219 N.Y. 263, 114 N.E. 404, L.R.A.1918B, 663, 1916, noted, 30 Harv.L.R. 523, 15 Mich.L.R. 604.

[10] In re Largue's Estate, 267 Mo. 104, 183 S.W. 608, 1916, noted, 14 Mich.LR. 696; Loring v. Woodward, 41 N.H. 391, 1860. See In re Mead's Estate, 227 Wis. 311, 279 N.W. 18, 116 A.L.R. 1127, 1938 (pecuniary legacy for satisfaction of which stock was set aside by executor). And see authorities infra notes 11–13. Cf. In re Jones' Estate, 314 Pa. 93, 171 A. 265, 1934 (general legacy of $5000 upon legatee's reaching age of 25 does not entitle him to income in the interim).

[11] Perry v. Leslie, supra note 7; Union Trust Co. of Springfield v. Nelen, 283 Mass. 144, 186 N.E. 66, 1933; Sherman v. Riley, 43 R.I. 202, 110 A. 629, 1920; In re Mandelle's Estate, supra note 8.

[12] Fisher v. Teter, 89 W.Va. 693, 109 S.E. 896, 1921.

tor's death goes to the devisees of the land, and they must bear the taxes thereon.[13]

*Interest*

Properly speaking specific legacies do not bear interest.[14] Such bequests carry the thing given and its increase after the testator's death and no more. If there is no income or interest so produced the specific legatee or devisee takes only the object given by the will. Residuary legacies also bear no interest,[15] because the amount is not ascertained and interest is not ordinarily computed on unliquidated sums, and also for the obvious reason that the residuum is the entire remainder of the estate so that there is nothing from which to pay interest thereon. As interest and income from the property not specifically bequeathed go into the residuary portion, those entitled thereto receive all the benefit of accumulations that they can possibly have. General legacies, however, bear interest; the ecclesiastical court rule being that it begins to run after one year from testator's death.[16]

The ecclesiastical rule is generally applied today to ordinary situations in the absence of contrary statutory or testamentary provisions.[17] It has been applied although the will was not probated immediately,[18] or more than a year was consumed in a will contest.[19] These holdings are defended on the ground that inter-

13 In re De Bernal's Estate, 165 Cal. 223, 131 P. 375, Ann.Cas.1914D, 26, 1913; In re Brickell's Estate, 4 Cal. App.2d 54, 40 P.2d 579, 1935 (rent of furniture specifically bequeathed); Freeth v. Rule, 117 N.J.Eq. 490, 176 A. 578, 1935 (land). See supra § 116. A legatee of specific personalty must bear the expense of its care and upkeep from the time of testator's death. In re Pearce, [1909] 1 Ch. 819.

14 Dennison v. Lilley, 83 N.H. 422, 144 A. 523, 1928.

15 Estate of Williams, 112 Cal. 521, 44 P. 808, 53 Am.St.Rep. 224, 1896. Cf. Matter of Gardner's Estate, 151 Misc. 342, 272 N.Y.S. 681, 1934 (residuary gift to charity transformed by statute into general legacy bears interest).

16 Hertford v. Lowther, 9 Beav. 266, 50 Eng.Rep. 345, 1846.

17 Cleary v. White's Estate, 134 Conn. 367, 58 A.2d 1, 1948; State Bank of Chicago v. Gross, infra note 19; Hamilton v. McQuillan, 82 Me. 204, 19 A. 167, 1889; Ogden v. Pattee, 149 Mass. 82, 21 N.E. 227, 14 Am.St. Rep. 401, 1889; Rowe v. Rowe, 113 N.J.Eq. 344, 167 A. 16, 1933; In re Taft's Estate, 114 Vt. 505, 49 A.2d 102, 1946; In re Forster's Will, 195 Wis. 58, 217 N.W. 740, 1928. See generally Evans, The Payment of Legacies, 2 Ida.L.J. 163; Kales, Do Legacies Bear Interest in Illinois? 2 Ill. L.R. 440; Lewis, When Does Interest Begin to Run on Legacies? 16 Minn. L.R. 226; note, 39 Yale L.J. 590.

18 Ogden v. Pattee, supra note 3.

19 State Bank of Chicago v. Gross, 344 Ill. 512, 176 N.E. 739, 75 A.L.R. 172, 1931; In re Woodward's Estate, 78 Vt. 254, 62 A. 718, 6 Ann.Cas. 524,

est is payable not by way of penalty for nonpayment, but because it is deemed to be in accordance with the testator's intention that interest should be paid after a reasonable period from his death.[20] Interest is payable although the general assets of the estate have not been productive.[21]

The normal rule is subject to many exceptions. For example, if the legacy is given for the support of a minor child, interest runs from the testator's death,[22] and the same is held in case of legacies given in satisfaction of a debt.[23] In some jurisdictions legacies given in lieu of dower carry interest from the death,[24] though the prevailing rule is that they bear interest only as ordinary legacies.[25] Annuities commence upon the death of the testator.[26] Of course all the rules are subject to alteration by provisions of the will itself.[27]

In some jurisdictions interest is deemed to begin only after a year from the grant of letters, because of statutes that declare that legacies are payable then.[28] However, some courts follow

1906 (though contest was by legatee). But see Goodman v. Palmer, 137 Tenn. 556, 195 S.W. 165, 1917 (interest allowed only from termination of contest).

20 State Bank of Chicago v. Gross, supra note 19; see Williams v. Smith, 146 Tex. 269, 206 S.W.2d 208, 1947. And see Kales, supra note 17. Cf. Matter of Stulman's Will, 146 Misc. 861, 263 N.Y.S. 197, 1933: "The principle upon which interest becomes payable in any case is that it is a species of damages for the withholding of a sum of money after the maturing of the obligation of the debtor to pay it to the creditor."

21 Matter of Bremer's Will, 156 Misc. 160, 281 N.Y.S. 264, 1935; Domestic & Foreign Missionary Soc. v. Crippled Children's Hospital, 163 Va. 114, 176 S.E. 193, 1934.

22 Welsh v. Brown, 43 N.J.Law, 37, 1881; Matter of Bremer's Will, supra note 21; In re Keech's Estate, 240 Pa. 491, 87 A. 623, 1913.

23 Landis v. Cumberland Trust Co. of Bridgeton, 92 N.J.Eq. 689, 116 A. 686, 1921.

24 Pollard v. Pollard, 1 Allen (Mass.) 490, 1861.

25 Howard v. Francis, 30 N.J.Eq. 444, 1879; Martin v. Martin, 6 Watts (Pa.) 67, 1837; In re Bignold, 45 Ch. Div. 496, 1890.

26 Willcox v. Willcox, 106 Va. 626, 56 S.E. 588, 1907. As to the right of annuitant to demand the principal sum, see infra § 138, note 3.

27 See Matter of Berbling, 134 Misc. 730, 236 N.Y.S. 367, 1929, noted, 39 Yale L.J. 590 (legacy payable in future); In re Jones' Estate, supra note 10.

28 Domestic & Foreign Missionary Soc. v. Crippled Children's Hospital, supra note 21; Matter of Bremer's Will, supra note 21 (now seven months after grant of letters); Redd's Adm'r v. Redd, 58 S.W. 428, 22 Ky. Law Rep. 505, 1900; In re Sharpless' Estate, 202 Iowa 386, 210 N.W. 528, 1926; Hallett v. Allen, 13 Ala. 554,

the ecclesiastical rule in spite of legislation of the latter type.[29] Other tribunals decline to follow the ecclesiastical rule because of statutes which declare that legacies are not due until their payment is ordered by the court, and they hold that interest runs only from that date.[30]

*Rate of Interest*

Unless there is some special testamentary or statutory provision regarding the rate of interest, it is computed at the legal rate.[31] Compound interest is allowed only under exceptional circumstances.[32]

*Interest Borne by Residuary Beneficiaries*

It remains to be seen who must bear the expense of paying interest on the legacies. As a general rule, this is borne by the residuary legatees and not by the executor personally.[33] This is because the testator has given the residuary legatees only what is left after payment of general legacies and their incidents. It is also just because the residuary legatees receive the benefit of income and accumulations on all except specific legacies. Where, however, the executor has unnecessarily delayed payment of the legacies, he may be surcharged with interest when the assets of the estate have not been productive.[34]

1848 (eighteen months after grant of letters); Stimson v. Rountree, 51 Ind. App. 207, 99 N.E. 439, 1912; Leonard v. Leonard, 107 N.C. 171, 12 S.E. 60, 1890 (two years after grant of letters); Gray v. Case School of Applied Science, 62 Ohio St. 1, 56 N. E. 484, 1900.

29 Davison v. Rake, 45 N.J.Eq. 767, 18 A. 752, 1888. See In re Woodward's Estate, 78 Vt. 254, 62 A. 718, 6 Ann.Cas. 524, 1906.

30 Cobb v. Stratton's Estate, 56 Colo. 278, 138 P. 35, Ann.Cas.1915C, 1166, 1913; Wiley v. Lockwood, 151 Minn. 372, 186 N.W. 699, 1922.

31 State Bank of Chicago v. Gross, supra note 19; Hutton v. Safe Deposit & Trust Co. of Baltimore, 150 Md. 539, 133 A. 308, 1926; In re Wadskier's Will, 88 N.J.Eq. 589, 103 A. 188, 1918; Matter of Bremer's Will, supra note 21; In re Brandon's Estate, 164 Wis. 387, 160 N.W. 177, 1916. Cf. In re Trescott's Estate, 199 Misc. 1087, 104 N.Y.S.2d 478, 1951 (4%).

32 Kent v. Dunham, 106 Mass. 586, 1871 (unless failure to pay was due to fault of the executor).

33 Ogden v. Pattee, supra note 3; Cleary v. White's Estate, supra note 17. See In re Kierstead's Estate, 128 Neb. 654, 259 N.W. 740, 1935.

34 In re Kierstead's Estate, supra note 33; In re Skeer's Estate, 253 Pa. 497, 98 A. 703, 1916. See Kales, supra note 17 at 446; American Jewish Joint Dis. Com. v. Eisenberg, 194 Md. 203, 70 A.2d 44, 18 A.L.R.2d 1380, 1949. Cf. Tilghman v. Fraser, — Md. —, 81 A.2d 627, 1951.

## ABATEMENT AND CHARGES

**136. "Abatement" is the reduction of legacies on account of the insufficiency of the estate to pay testator's debts and other legacies. Intestate property should be first applied for these purposes. In absence of testamentary indication as to order of abatement, legacies ordinarily abate in the following order: (1) Residuary legacies, (2) general legacies, (3) specific and demonstrative legacies, which give way together ratably.**

**General devises abate before specific devises and those in each class abate pro rata between others of the same group. Though there are still holdings that all legacies should give way before any devises, the modern and better view is that residuary devises and bequests should abate together in favor of general devises and legacies and these in turn should give way so as to prefer specific devises and bequests.**

It often happens that the property available for distribution among the beneficiaries under the will is insufficient to satisfy all in the manner contemplated by the testator. This may be due, (1) to the fact that his estate was depleted prior to his death, or (2) to the necessity of using a portion of the property to pay debts, or (3) to the exhaustion of assets in order to satisfy estate taxes, the share which the surviving spouse elects to take against the will, or the portion to which a pretermitted child is entitled.[1] The essential problem of abatement is that of what legacies must be paid first and which testamentary provisions must abate or give way to the payment of others or of the debts or other charges. The question of the abatement of devises is also frequently involved, but the matter will first be discussed upon the assumption that the estate consists entirely of personalty and thereafter the effect of the presence of realty will be considered.

[1] The order of abatement in case of election by the spouse or pretermitted child is frequently a matter of special statutory consideration; all other beneficiaries, regardless of the nature of their legacies, may be obliged to bear pro rata the burden of making up the elective shares. See supra §§ 33, 36. Cf. Model Probate Code § 184; 1948 Annual Surv.Am.L. 754.

In absence of statute the Federal Estate Tax falls on the residuary beneficiaries. Plunkett v. Old Colony Trust Co., 233 Mass. 471, 124 N.E. 265, 7 A.L.R. 696, 1919. Holdings of this kind led to statutes requiring apportionment of the tax among all beneficiaries; N.Y.Decedent Estate Law § 124 is the parent statute. See notes, 40 Col.L.R. 690, 62 Harv.L.R. 1022; infra § 147, note 13.

At the outset it should be observed that if the will expressly indicates the order of abatement of legacies, this provision must be given effect even if it departs from the normal order which the law has devised.[2] While the testator cannot prefer one creditor to another, he can provide the order in which his property shall be taken in payment of his debts, and thus prefer some beneficiaries over others. However, a direction that a legacy should be paid "in the first place," or the like, is generally deemed to indicate priority in time of payment and is not considered a command that other legacies abate in its favor.[3] The same is true of a testamentary direction that certain legacies should be paid upon the death of the testator or at a particular time after his death.[4] A legatee, who claims that the testator intended a preference regarding abatement other than that which the law normally assumes, has the burden of showing such intention.[5]

The general order of abatement of legacies is set forth in the black-letter text. While to some extent it can be argued that this orthodox rule is the one which the testator would have desired, it is largely arbitrary. This is shown by the rules in force in many jurisdictions, largely by reason of statutory provisions, to the effect that the burden of estate taxes and losses due to the elections of the spouse or pretermitted child are to be spread pro rata over the entire estate.

### *Intestate Property*

Property which does not pass by the will is the first fund to be applied to the payment of debts; this should be exhausted before resort to anything else.[6] Of course the most common case of partial intestacy is where there is no residuary clause.

[2] Benton v. Friar, 171 Miss. 361, 157 So. 356, 1934; In re Elmore's Estate, 292 Pa. 571, 141 A. 478, 1928; Quinn v. McDowell, 47 R.I. 314, 132 A. 888, 1926. And see Clement v. Whisnant, 208 N.C. 167, 179 S.E. 430, 101 A.L.R. 698, 1935; Bauer's Will, 289 N.Y. 326, 45 N.E.2d 897, 144 A.L.R. 543, 1942; Muse v. Muse, infra note 20.

[3] Swasey v. American Bible Soc., 57 Me. 523, 1869; Brown v. Allen, 1 Vern. 31, 23 Eng.Rep. 285, 1681.

[4] Rexford v. Bacon, 195 Ill. 70, 62 N.E. 936, 1902 (payable in installments as legatee may demand); Boston Safe Deposit & Trust Co. v. Plummer, 142 Mass. 257, 8 N.E. 51, 1886.

[5] Emery v. Batchelder, 78 Me. 233, 3 A. 733, 1886; In re Phillips' Estate, 18 Mont. 311, 45 P. 222, 1896; In re Weed's Will, 213 Wis. 574, 252 N.W. 204, 1934.

[6] In re Hall's Estate, 183 Cal. 61, 190 P. 364, 1920; Hays v. Jackson, 6 Mass. 149, 1809.

*Residuary Legacies*

Next, resort should be made to property covered by the residuary clause.[7] This is in accordance with the intention disclosed by the language of the average will. The residue or the rest or the remainder clearly means that which is left after payment of the debts, and the general and specific legacies. If there is no residue, ordinary residuary legatees receive nothing. However, the testator may, by apt provision of his will, provide for diminution of his other legacies in case that his estate shrinks in value, thus giving protection to the residuary legatees.[8]

*General Legacies*

If the residuum is exhausted, general legacies abate next, in favor of specific or demonstrative legacies.[9] General legacies normally abate pro rata between themselves.[10] In absence of special provision of the will this is true as between general legacies given by the will and those contained in a codicil,[11] and likewise as between legacies given to individuals and those given to charity.[12]

*Specific and Demonstrative Legacies*

As already seen, general legacies ordinarily abate in favor of specific legacies.[13] Demonstrative legacies are entitled to the same preference as specific legacies so far as they may be satisfied out of the particular property or fund designated for their payment.[14] However, if this property has disappeared from tes-

[7] In re Martin, 25 R.I. 1, 54 A. 589, 1903; Baker v. Farmer, L.R. 3 Ch. App. 537, 1868.

[8] In re Spencer, 16 R.I. 25, 12 A. 124, 1887. See supra note 1.

[9] In re Parsons' Estate, 150 Iowa 230, 129 N.W. 955, 1911; Rainey v. Rainey, 124 Miss. 780, 87 So. 128, 1921; Rowe v. Rowe, 113 N.J.Eq. 344, 167 A. 16, 1933; Petition of Cain, 87 N.H. 318, 179 A. 347, 1935. See infra note 13.

[10] Lewis v. Sedgwick, 223 Ill. 213, 79 N.E. 14, 1906; Matthews v. Targarona, 104 Md. 442, 65 A. 60, 10 Ann. Cas. 153, 1906; Rowe v. Rowe, supra note 9 (though some are given "absolutely"); In re Wilson's Estate, 260 Pa. 407, 103 A. 880, 6 A.L.R. 1349, 1918

[11] In re Wilson's Estate, supra note 10.

[12] Porter v. Howe, 173 Mass. 521, 54 N.E. 255, 1899.

[13] See supra note 9; also In re Woodworth's Estate, 31 Cal. 595, 1867; Baker v. Baker, 319 Ill. 320, 150 N.E. 284, 42 A.L.R. 1514, 1925, noted, 21 Ill.L.R. 294, 24 Mich.L.R. 738; Kaplan v. Leader, 297 Mass. 145, 8 N.E.2d 344, 1937.

[14] O'Day v. O'Day, 193 Mo. 62, 91 S.W. 921, 4 L.R.A.,N.S., 922, 1906; Baptist Female University of North Carolina v. Borden, 132 N.C. 476, 44 S.E. 47, 1007, 1903; Appeal of Arm-

tator's estate, demonstrative legacies rank with general bequests for purposes of abatement.[15] Demonstrative legacies combine the advantages of general and specific legacies. So far as abatement is concerned, they are as advantageous to the legatee as specific legacies; while as regards ademption, they have the qualities of general legacies, for they may be satisfied out of the general assets in case of failure of the designated fund from which they are primarily payable. When the assets are insufficient to satisy all specific or demonstrative legacies, these abate pro rata among themselves.

*Legacies for Maintenance and Value*

In most jurisdictions other general legacies abate in favor of provisions for the support or education of a near relative.[16] This exception is based upon the probable intention of the testator. A general legacy in payment of a debt is also entitled to preference over other general legacies.[17] The reason for this exception may be that the testator is assumed to so desire, but a better explanation is that, since the creditor-legatee could have proved his claim and thus come in with creditors and be preferred to all legatees, he should be given special consideration in the matter of abatement. At least if the debt is unliquidated as for services rendered, the fact that the legacy exceeds the amount of the obligation is no objection to preference of the entire legacy.[18] The testator is deemed to be the best judge of this matter. However, a general legacy for services rendered gratuitously is entitled to

strong, 63 Pa. 312, 1869; In re Hawgood's Estate, 37 S.D. 565, 159 N.W. 117, 1916.

15 Gelbach v. Shively, 67 Md. 498, 10 A. 247, 1887; Dunn's Ex'rs v. Renick, 40 W.Va. 349, 22 S.E. 66, 1895. See Matter of Collins' Estate, 156 Misc. 783, 282 N.Y.S. 728, 1935.

16 In re Nelson, 238 N.Y. 138, 144 N.E. 481, 34 A.L.R. 1245, 1924, noted, 3 Wis.L.R. 108 (if otherwise unprovided for); Towle v. Swasey, 106 Mass. 100, 1870 (until child becomes of age). See note, 36 Mich.L.R. 297. But the mere fact that the legatee is a close relative is not enough unless the legacy is given for support. In re Parsons' Estate, supra note 9; Chemical Bank & Trust Co. v. Barnett, 114 N.J.Eq. 4, 168 A. 173, 1933. Preference of a life interest does not necessarily mean preference of the remainder. In re Cameron's Estate, 278 N.Y. 352, 16 N.E.2d 362, 117 A.L.R. 1333, 1938, noted, 38 Col.L.R. 1312, 24 Corn.L.Q. 619, 24 Iowa L.R. 379; Towle v. Swasey, supra.

17 Matter of Schaaf's Estate, 120 Misc. 292, 199 N.Y.S. 284, 1923; Reynolds v. Reynolds, 27 R.I. 520, 63 A. 804, 1906. See Matthews v. Targarona, supra note 10.

18 Borden v. Jenks, 140 Mass. 562, 5 N.E. 623, 54 Am.Rep. 507, 1886. And see Matthews v. Targarona, supra note 10.

no preference.[19] Legacies given in lieu of dower present a particularly strong case for preference regarding abatement. Here the widow gives up a somewhat uncertain amount of dower interest, which, if claimed, would often upset the entire testamentary scheme. To encourage her to accept the general legacy instead, it should be preferred and most courts so hold.[20] In addition, the forced share which she gives up is prior to all legacies, and, if it is common-law dower, to debts as well. However, she is not entitled to preference if the testator left no estate from which she was entitled to dower.[21]

The question sometimes arises whether general legacies for maintenance or in lieu of debts or dower should also be preferred to specific legacies. Some courts hold that the latter must also abate in favor of the former,[22] while others declare the contrary.[23] On principle it would seem that the former view is sound in the debt and dower cases, since the claim which the legatee relinquishes would have priority to all legacies. This argument cannot be applied to legacies for support and hence general legacies for this purpose present a more doubtful case for preference over specific legacies. Still it can be contended with some force that most testators would have desired that such general legacies should be preferred to ordinary specific legacies.

How should the various categories of preferred legacies for support and for value be entitled inter se to preference in order of abatement? Authority is scanty, but it seems reasonable that they should abate in inverse order of priority over other inter-

19 Matthews v. Targarona, supra note 10; Towle v. Swasey, 106 Mass. 100, 1870.

20 Security Co. v. Bryant, 52 Conn. 311, 52 Am.Rep. 599, 1885; Moore v. Alden, 80 Me. 301, 14 A. 199, 6 Am.St. Rep. 203, 1888; Matthews v. Targarona, supra note 10; Davenhill v. Fletcher, Amb. 244, 27 Eng.Rep. 163, 1754; see Muse v. Muse, 186 Va. 914, 45 S.E.2d 158, 2 A.L.R.2d 603, 1947; In re Paulson's Estate, 208 Minn. 231, 293 N.W. 607, 1940. Contra: Clark v. Clark, 126 Miss. 455, 89 So. 4, 1921. Cf. In re Shepherd's Estate, 152 Or. 15, 49 P.2d 448, 1935, where bequest to widow was payable from the residuum. As to the respective preference of such legacies and those of creditors, cf. Dauel v. Arnold, 201 Ill. 570, 66 N.E. 846, 1903 (superior to creditors if not in excess of legal share); Tracy v. Murray, 44 Mich. 109, 6 N.W. 224 (takes pro rata with creditors); Howard v. Francis, 30 N.J.Eq. 444, 1879 (inferior to creditors). See infra note 24.

21 Perrine v. Perrine, 6 N.J.L. 133, 10 Am.Dec. 392, 1821.

22 Addison v. Addison, 44 Md. 182, 1876; Borden v. Jenks, 140 Mass. 562, 5 N.E. 623, 54 Am.Rep. 507, 1886. And see Davis v. Davis, 138 Va. 682, 123 S.E. 538, 1924.

23 Boykin v. Boykin, 21 S.C. 513, 1884.

ests, viz.: (1) legacies for support, (2) those to the spouse in lieu of an elective share which is subject to debts, (3) legacies to creditors, (4) legacies in lieu of common-law dower.[24]

*Devises*

With the fall of the concept that all devises are specific,[25] devises should abate inter se in the same order as do legacies, viz., residuary, general [26] and specific, subject to the contrary express or implied intent of the testator and to the exception of devises for value. While most cases are complicated by the presence of legacies as well as devises, the modern cases hold that residuary or general devises abate before specific devises,[27] and the latter abate ratably between themselves.[28]

*Abatement as Between Legacies and Devises*

Where the will contained both legacies and devises of the various types the problem of abatement was a complicated one at common law and there are still complications in the modern American law. This is no place to recount the older picture in detail.[29] It is sufficient to point to the early limited liability of land for the decedent's debts and the primary responsibility of the personalty therefor,[30] factors which were alleviated by a readiness of the courts to imply a testamentary charge upon the land for payment of debts and legacies.[31] In addition, the matter was much affected by the equitable principle of marshaling, under which in case one of two claimants has two funds which can be used to satisfy his claim and the other claimant can go directly against only one, the former is obliged to obtain satisfaction from his exclusive fund, or the latter will be entitled to claim it in place of the former. Thus, the legatee's common-law or initial right

24 See Farnum v. Bascom, 122 Mass. 282, 1877; note, 36 Mich.L.R. 297, 310; infra note 20. But it has been held that a legacy in lieu of dower is not preferred to creditors. Steele v. Steele, 64 Ala. 438, 38 Am.Rep. 15, 1879; cf. Hall's Case, 1 Bland Ch. (Md.) 203, 17 Am.Dec. 275, 1827.

25 See supra § 132.

26 Devises can doubtless be either residuary or general, although both are seldom met in the same will. See supra § 132.

27 In re McAllister's Estate, 191 Iowa 906, 183 N.W. 596, 1921; In re Nelson's Estate, 278 Pa. 416, 123 A. 326, 1924 (specific devise not destroyed by testamentary power of sale).

28 In re Sutton's Estate, 11 Del.Ch. 460, 97 A. 624, 1915; In re Glandon's Estate, 219 Iowa 1094, 260 N.W. 12, 1935.

29 See American Law of Property § 14.23.

30 See supra §§ 3, 123.

31 See infra note 49 et seq.

to satisfaction only out of the personalty was extended in equity to satisfaction from intestate land and from land charged with debts, from which creditors could obtain their payment as well as from the personal estate.[32] Finally, there was the matter of testamentary direction for the order of abatement; for example, it was early held that the making of specific legacies and devises in the same will indicated a desire for pro rata abatement between them.[33]

The whole matter was worked out in the Court of Chancery which had jurisdiction of the administration of estates. Maitland [34] states that a testator's property was taken in payment of debts in the following order:

1. Personalty not specifically bequeathed, retaining a fund sufficient to meet any pecuniary legacies.
2. Realty specifically appropriated for, or devised in trust for (and not merely charged with), payment of debts.
3. Realty that descends to the heir.
4. Realty charged with the payment of debts.
5. Fund (if any) retained to pay general pecuniary legacies.
6. Realty devised whether specifically or by general description and personalty specifically bequeathed *pro rata* and *pari passu.*
7. Property which did not belong to the dead man, but which is appointed by his will in exercise of any general power of appointment.

Some modern American statutes mention the common-law order of abatement,[35] and except in so far as the matter is governed by statutes we should start with the English principles. However, certain general changes affect the American law. The most important of these is that devises like legacies may be general or residuary as well as specific. The devise to pay debts is seldom met today, and the charge of debts on land is relatively unimportant in American law,[36] since statutes in effect do

[32] In re Salt, [1895] 2 Ch. 203; see supra note 29. The above statement assumes existence of liability of the land for debts, which was only partially realized under the early law.

[33] Long v. Short, 1 P.Wms. 403, 24 Eng.Rep. 445, 1717.

[34] Equity, 1936, 262–263.

[35] Vogel v. Saunders, 68 App.D.C. 81, 92 F.2d 984, 1937; Temple v. First Nat. Bank of Meridian, 202 Miss. 92, 30 So.2d 605, 1947.

[36] See infra notes 46–48.

this regardless of the will's provisions. These factors have led some courts to hold that there is no preference between realty and personalty in the order of abatement and that residuary realty and personalty abate together, then general devises and legacies and finally specific legacies and devises.[37] Of course a single case seldom passes on all of these phases. On the basis of presumed intent of the testator most cases hold that specific legacies and devises abate together.[38] Most of the American cases also hold that residuary land may be taken to pay pecuniary legacies, although this is usually done only upon a finding that the legacies were charged upon the land.[39]

However, in some jurisdictions the result is affected by statutory provisions that land can be sold only if the personalty is insufficient, thus preserving the old principle that personalty is the primary fund for the payment of debts.[40] This principle, sensible enough if the decedent died intestate, should be deemed to be overridden by the testator's implied direction when he includes both realty and personalty in the residue, and further makes general and specific devises and bequests. But some courts take the above statutes literally and hold that personalty must abate before realty within the respective classes of residuary, general and specific,[41] or even that all bequests must abate before any devises.[42]

Specific statutes govern the entire matter in some states. The best type is that included in the Model Probate Code [43] providing for abatement in the following order without preference to real

37 Kelly v. Richardson, 100 Ala. 584, 13 So. 785, 1892; O'Day v. O'Day, 193 Mo. 62, 91 S.W. 921, 4 L.R.A.,N.S., 922, 1906.

38 May v. Burns, 222 Ala. 68, 131 So. 232, 1931; Holcomb v. Mullin, 167 Ark. 622, 268 S.W. 32, 1925; Baker v. Baker, 319 Ill. 320, 150 N.E. 284, 42 A.L.R. 1514, 1925, noted, 21 Ill.L.R. 294, 24 Mich.L.R. 738; Farnum v. Bascom, 122 Mass. 282, 1877; Brant v. Brant, 40 Mo. 266, 1867; Armstrong's Appeal, 63 Pa. 312, 1869. And see supra note 33. Contra: Ballinger's Devisees v. Ballinger's Adm'r, 251 Ky. 405, 65 S.W.2d 49, 1933; Gordon v. James, 86 Miss. 719, 39 So. 18, 1 L.R.A.,N.S., 461, 1905; Rogers v. Rogers, 1 Paige (N.Y.) 188, 1828.

39 See infra note 49 et seq.

40 See infra notes 41, 42; Knox v. Stamper, 186 Md. 238, 46 A.2d 361, 1946; Gordon v. James, supra note 38. Cf. Temple v. First Nat. Bank of Meridian, 202 Miss. 92, 30 So.2d 605, 1947 (charge.)

41 Baptist Female University of North Carolina v. Borden, 132 N.C. 476, 44 S.E. 47, 1903; Gordon v. James, supra note 38.

42 Ballinger's Devisees v. Ballinger's Adm'r, supra note 38; Duck v. McGrath, 160 App.Div. 482, 145 N.Y.S. 1033, affirmed 212 N.Y. 600, 106 N.E. 1032, 1914; see also Warlick v. Boone, 120 Kan. 148, 242 P. 135, 1926.

43 Administration of Estates' Act,

over personal property: (1) intestate property, (2) the residuum, (3) general devise and bequests, (4) specific devises and bequests. Other statutes follow this order except that realty is preferred to personalty in the same classification.[44] In other states the statutory provisions are fragmentary or bear on the matter only in a general way. Here, the courts have sometimes favored the devisee over the legatee even to a greater extent than did the English courts of the nineteenth century.[45]

*Charge of Debts on Realty*

The readiness of the English Court of chancery to imply a charge of debts on the realty from a testamentary direction to pay debts goes back to the day when a non-specialty creditor could not reach the land and no creditor could hold the devisee liable for the debt. Such charge is now relatively unimportant to creditors since the land can always be sold for payment of debts.[46] Consequently the modern decisions impose a charge only when it is express or clearly implied from the will.[47] The subject is of some importance in modern American law, but relatively little as to the matter in hand.[48]

*Charge of Legacies on Realty*

This subject is of considerable current importance, particularly in those jurisdictions where the general doctrine prevails that all legacies abate before any devises. It has always been the law that devised realty must respond when it is expressly charged with the payment of legacies.[49] Moreover, when realty and personalty are blended indiscriminately in the residuary clause, as is usual, this is deemed sufficient to show an intent to charge the residuary realty as well as personalty with payment of the legacies, especially where there is also a general direction to pay testator's debts.[50] Modern courts are also apt to imply a charge

1925, 15 Geo. 5, § 34(1), and First Schedule; Cal.Prob.Code § 751.

44 The statutes are summarized in Model Probate Code, appendix 353–360.

45 See supra notes 33, 38.

46 See American Law of Property § 14.24.

47 In re Ritter's Estate, 239 Iowa 788, 32 N.W.2d 666, 2 A.L.R.2d 1301, 1948; Kelsey v. Warfield, 147 Kan. 445, 76 P.2d 777, 1938. But see In re Boyle's Estate, 133 N.J.Eq. 149, 30 A.2d 827, 1943.

48 Supra note 46.

49 Wilson v. Piper, 77 Ind. 437, 1881; Stringer v. Gamble, 155 Mich. 295, 118 N.W. 979, 30 L.R.A.,N.S., 815, 1909.

50 Michigan Trust Co. v. Driver, 270 Mich. 698, 259 N.W. 867, 1935; In re Roberts' Estate, 166 Minn. 315, 207

upon residuary realty when the testator made legacies which at the time of execution exceeded the value of his personalty.[51] In this situation it can well be argued that the testator must have intended a charge, for he clearly did not wish the legacies to fail.

The traditional remedy of a legatee in whose favor a charge was made was to pursue the charged property in an equity suit.[52] If the charge was express, he could probably also bring an action at law against the person who had accepted the charged land.[53] The common law gave no power to the executor to sell the land for payment of the legacy in absence of express testamentary provision to this effect.[54] This is purely a matter of remedy, and it would seem that the law should now imply such a power. Clearly the personal representative should be allowed to sell the realty under court order, where there is statutory power of sale to pay legacies as well as debts.[55] Some jurisdictions permit the court of probate to enforce the lien in favor of the legatees.[56] Even where the legatee must resort to his traditional remedy, the over-all result is often the same as under the modern rule of abatement under which legacies and devises abate pro rata and together, according to classification of residuary, general, and then specific.

N.W. 629, 1926; Marcy v. Graham, 142 Va. 285, 128 S.E. 550, 1925; Will of Kendrick, 210 Wis. 218, 246 N.W. 306, 1933. Cf. In re Estate of Schwartz, 275 Ill.App. 374, 1934. But see Lupton v. Lupton, 2 Johns. Ch. (N. Y.) 614, 1817, and the remedial statute, N.Y.Decedent Estate Law § 47d.

51 Bristol v. Stump, 136 Md. 236, 110 A. 470, 1920; Ely v. Megie, 219 N. Y. 112, 113 N.E. 800, 1916, noted, 26 Yale L.J. 333. Contra: Wentworth v. Read, 166 Ill. 139, 46 N.E. 777, 1897.

52 Miller v. Klossner, 135 Minn. 377, 160 N.W. 1025, 1917; Ditchey v. Lee, 167 Ind. 267, 78 N.E. 972, 1906; McFarland v. McFarland, 177 Ill. 208, 52 N.E. 281, 1898.

53 Selzer v. Selzer, 146 Kan. 273, 69 P.2d 708, 116 A.L.R. 1, 1937; Lundquist v. First Evangelical Lutheran Church of Battle Lake, 193 Minn. 474, 259 N.W. 9, 1935; Red v. Powers, 69 Miss. 242, 13 So. 586, 1891.

54 Wentworth v. Read, 61 Ill.App. 539, 1897; Robertson v. Broadbent, L. R. 8 App.Cas. 812, 1883.

55 Coulter v. Bradley, 163 Ind. 311, 71 N.E. 903, 1904; In re More's Estate, 179 Mich. 237, 146 N.W. 319, 1914; In re Temple's Estate, 211 Mo. App. 71, 245 S.W. 633, 1922; In re Strolberg's Estate, 106 Neb. 173, 183 N.W. 97, 26 A.L.R. 643, 1921. See In re Newcomb's Will, 98 Iowa 175, 67 N. W. 587, 1896 (testamentary power of sale). But see Hartzell's Estate, 178 Pa. 286, 35 A. 1051, 1896; St. John's German Evangelical Lutheran Church v. Dippoldsmann, 118 Md. 242, 84 A. 373, 1912. See supra § 123.

56 Brotzman v. Riehl, 119 Pa. 645, 13 A. 483, 1888; see St. John's German Evangelical Lutheran Church v. Dippoldsmann, supra note 55.

## EXONERATION

**137. In absence of statute or of testamentary directions to the contrary, mortgages and other liens upon the decedent's realty and upon the subject-matter of his specific bequests must be exonerated out of the general personal assets of the estate.**

As has been seen in connection with the payment of claims,[1] it is the personal representative's duty to apply the personal estate to exonerate the realty from liens even though no claim is presented by the lien holder. This principle obtains equally in favor of the heir in case of intestacy and the devisee where there is a will, even though the will does not provide for the exoneration.[2] The rule has been justified on the ground that, as the decedent's personal estate was benefited by the mortgage loan, the personalty should bear the burden of the obligation. This argument has no weight when a purchase-money mortgage is given, or a lien is incurred for the improvement or repair of the realty. Furthermore, it is very doubtful if many testators consider their realty and personalty as distinct categories or estates.[3]

Heirs or devisees are not entitled to exoneration unless the lien debt was the personal obligation of the decedent.[4] Hence, where the latter purchased the land subject to the mortgage there is no right to exoneration,[5] unless the decedent assumed the indebtedness and thereby became personally liable by this undertaking.[6] It has been held that when the testator was purchasing land on

[1] See § 127. See also In re Estate of Johnson, 66 S.D. 331, 283 N.W. 151, 120 A.L.R. 574, 1938. As to exoneration of a life insurance policy in favor of the beneficiary when the insured had borrowed against it, cf. In re Schwartz' Estate, 369 Pa. 574, 87 A.2d 270, 1952, with In re Stafford's Will, 98 N.Y.S.2d 714, Sur.Ct.1950.

[2] Jackson v. Bevins, 74 Conn. 96, 49 A. 899, 1901 (though land is described in will as subject to mortgage). See In re Morse's Estate, 95 Cal.App. 652, 273 P. 130, 1928.

[3] See American Law of Property § 14.25.

[4] Barlow v. Cain, 146 Ark. 160, 225 S.W. 228, 1920; Stieglitz v. Migatz, 182 Ind. 549, 105 N.E. 465, 1914; Marshall v. Middleton, 100 Or. 247, 191 P. 886, 19 A.L.R. 1421, 1921 (here the mortgage had been foreclosed before testator's death, thus relieving him from personal responsibility).

[5] Stieglitz v. Migatz, supra note 4; Tweddell v. Tweddell, 2 Bro.C.C. 101, 29 Eng.Rep. 58, 1787.

[6] Barlow v. Cain, supra note 4; Smith v. Kibbe, 104 Kan. 159, 178 P. 427, 5 A.L.R. 483, 1919; Owen v. Lee, 185 Va. 160, 37 S.E.2d 848, 1946. Cf. Creesy v. Willis, 159 Mass. 249, 34 N.E. 265, 1893.

contract and left all his real estate to his widow, she was entitled to his equity in the land under this devise, but not to payment of the unpaid purchase price from the personalty.[7]

The rule requiring exoneration has been abolished by statute in some states,[8] yet even in these jurisdictions the devisees are entitled to exoneration if the will so provides.[9] In cases of intestacy where different persons succeed to personalty and to realty, the rule is of importance,[10] though at present the doctrine would not usually be material where there is no will for the heirs and distributees are in most jurisdictions the same individuals. If there is a will, the matter is vital whenever the devisees and legatees are different persons, or when the beneficiaries take land and chattels in different proportions. The application of the rule is not affected by the presence or absence of a general testamentary direction to pay debts out of the estate,[11] though of course a testator may expressly or impliedly direct that his devisees shall take the land cum onere.[12]

### *Property Liable to Be Taken for Exoneration*

It is generally agreed that residuary personalty may be taken to discharge the mortgage or other liens.[13] On the other hand, the subject-matter of a specific legacy may not be used for this purpose,[14] unless this personalty is expressly charged with the

7 In re McNulta's Estate, 168 Wash. 397, 12 P.2d 389, 1932. But see In re Riegelman's Estate, 174 Pa. 476, 34 A. 120, 1896.

8 New York was the first common-law jurisdiction to provide that there should be no exoneration unless the will so provides. See American Law of Property, § 14.25; 21 St. John's L. R. 113; cf. Model Probate Code § 189. For more limited statutory changes, see In re Cline's Estate, 170 Kan. 496, 227 P.2d 157, 1951.

9 Peck v. Fillingham's Estate, 199 Mo.App. 277, 202 S.W. 465, 1918. But a mere direction to pay debts out of estate does not show an intention to exonerate the realty. Savings Trust Co. v. Beck, 73 S.W.2d 282, Mo.App. 1934.

10 Foster v. Foster, 219 Ala. 70, 121 So. 80, 1929. Cf. Campbell v. Campbell, 140 N.J.Eq. 144, 53 A.2d 630, 1947 (exoneration of dower).

11 Jackson v. Bevins, 74 Conn. 96, 49 A. 899, 1901; Hennegar v. Deadrick, 54 S.W. 138, Tenn.Ch.App.1899.

12 See Fulenwider v. Birmingham Trust & Sav. Co., 222 Ala. 95, 130 So. 801, 72 A.L.R. 702, 1930; Kellam's Ex'rs v. Jacob, 152 Va. 725, 148 S.E. 835, 1929.

13 Turner v. Laird, 68 Conn. 198, 35 A. 1124, 1896; In re Sutton's Estate, 11 Del.Ch. 460, 97 A. 624, 1915; Smith v. Kibbe, supra note 6.

14 Morgan v. Watkins, 214 Ala. 671, 108 So. 561, 1926; Currie v. Scott, 144 Tex. 1, 187 S.W.2d 551, 1945; Oneal v. Mead, 1 P.Wms. 693, 24 Eng. Rep. 574, 1720.

payment of such debts.[15] As to whether a general pecuniary legacy must abate in order to exonerate the land there is a well defined split of authority, some jurisdictions declaring that the general legacies must abate for this purpose,[16] while others hold that they do not.[17] The latter seems the preferable view, as the whole doctrine of exoneration is now considered undesirable and should be limited wherever possible.[18]

When there are assets available for the purpose of exoneration, the devisee is entitled to commence proceedings to compel the executor to pay the indebtedness if the latter fails to do so of his own initiative.[19] Personalty specifically bequeathed is also entitled to exoneration out of residuary property from incumbrances placed upon it by the testator, in absence of his manifest intent to the contrary.[20]

15 French v. Vradenburg, 105 Va. 16, 52 S.E. 695, 3 L.R.A.,N.S., 898, 115 Am.St.Rep. 838, 8 Ann.Cas. 590, 1906.

16 Brown v. Baron, 162 Mass. 56, 37 N.E. 772, 44 Am.St.Rep. 331, 1894; Todd v. McFall, 96 Va. 754, 32 S.E. 472, 1899.

17 Glass v. Dunn, 17 Ohio St. 413, 1867; Morris v. Higbie (N.J.Ch.) 27 A. 438, 1893; Smith v. Smith, [1899] 1 Ch. 365.

18 See note, 40 Harv.L.R. 630, and consider statutes mentioned supra note 8.

19 Smith v. Kibbe, supra note 6; Schade v. Connor, 84 Neb. 51, 120 N.W. 1012, 1909; Hill v. Hill, 95 N.J.Eq. 233, 122 A. 818, 29 A.L.R. 1242, 1923.

20 Lange v. Lange, 127 N.J.Eq. 315, 12 A.2d 840, 1940; cf. Model Probate Code § 189.

## ELECTION

**138. "Election" is the choice of a devisee or legatee between the provision made for him by the will and some inconsistent or alternative claim when there is an evident intention on the part of testator that both should not be enjoyed. Election is required in case the will makes a provision in lieu of the forced share of the surviving spouse; where the testator devises the property of one beneficiary to another devisee; or property is bequeathed to a creditor in satisfaction of a debt.**

**An election may be either express, or implied from the conduct of the person required to make the choice, and is irrevocable when made with full knowledge of the material factors involved.**

**If a person elects to take against the will, the court will ordinarily appropriate the testamentary benefits renounced so as to compensate the beneficiaries prejudiced by the election.**

Sometimes a will makes two provisions for a beneficiary and stipulates that he may only have one of them; here of course an election is required.[1] Other cases simply involve the problem as to whether a legatee has the right to select certain property under the will.[2] When the testator bequeaths a certain sum to be used for the purchase of an annuity, the common-law rule is that the legatee can demand the principal sum instead, since there would be nothing to prevent him from selling the annuity immediately.[3] Problems connected with the election of the surviving spouse have already been treated.[4] For the most part this section is concerned with questions as to whether other legatees or devisees must give up some interest to which they are otherwise entitled in order to take under the will.

1 In re Vanatta's Estate, 99 N.J.Eq. 339, 131 A. 515, 1926; Grindem v. Grindem, 89 Iowa 295, 56 N.W. 505, 1893.

2 See In re Connolly's Estate, 166 Pa.Super. 383, 71 A.2d 856, 1950, noted, 49 Mich.L.R. 776; note, 25 Cal.L.R. 126; supra § 60, note 34.

3 Parker v. Cobe, 208 Mass. 260, 94 N.E. 476, 33 L.R.A.,N.S., 978, 21 Ann.Cas. 1100, 1911; Barnes v. Rowley, 3 Ves. 305, 30 Eng.Rep. 1024, 1797. Contra: In re Johnson's Estate, 238 Iowa 1221, 30 N.W.2d 164, 1947, noted, 47 Mich.L.R. 139, 3 Wyo.L.J. 97. See also N.Y.Decedent Estate Law § 47 (b); note, 41 Mich.L.R. 276; Model Probate Code § 190b. Cf. American Bible Soc. v. Chase, 340 Ill.App. 548, 92 N.E.2d 332, 1950; Gilbert v. Findlay College, 74 A.2d 36, Md.1950; In re Maybaum's Will, 296 N.Y. 201, 71 N.E.2d 865, 169 A.L.R. 1357, 1947.

4 See supra § 33.

*By Beneficiary Whose Property Is Devised to Another*

An election is required when the testator purports to devise A's property to B and by the will also gives other property to A. Here A must decide whether he will accept the property given him by the will in which case he relinquishes his own property devised to B, or whether he, A, will claim his own property, thereby losing the testamentary gift in his favor.[5] It is not material whether testator was in error as to his ownership, or whether he knew he had no title thereto.[6] It is enough, if a reasonable interpretation of the will discloses a situation which should equitably put the beneficiary to an election; an express testamentary requirement of an election is not necessary.[7]

However, if the will, which is claimed to devise the property of another who is also a beneficiary, permits a reasonable construction not involving such disposition, that construction should prevail and the beneficiary should not be required to elect.[8] Thus, where the testator and the beneficiary are both interested in the property disposed of, the presumption is that the testator intended only to give what was his.[9] By the use of such expressions as "all my lands" or "all my estate," the testator is deemed to intend to pass only his interest in the property,[10] though it is otherwise if the testator owned a partial interest and devised the entire land by specific description.[11]

No election is required by reason of a purported devise of land owned by the spouse of devisee A to devisee B.[12] By the pre-

5 McDonald v. Shaw, 92 Ark. 15, 121 S.W. 935, 28 L.R.A.,N.S., 657, 1909; Moore v. Baker, 4 Ind.App. 115, 30 N.E. 629, 51 Am.St.Rep. 203, 1892; Drake v. Wild, 70 Vt. 52, 39 A. 248, 1907. Cf. Matter of Collins' Estate, 156 Misc. 783, 282 N.Y.S. 728, 1935, noted, 45 Yale L.J. 1147. See In re Schaech's Will, 252 Wis. 299, 31 N.W.2d 614, 1948, s. c., 254 Wis. 377, 36 N.W.2d 276, 1949, noted, 32 Marquette L.R. 230, [1949] Wis.L.R. 816 (T devised to B property which he owned jointly with B); Wachovia Bank & Trust Co. v. Burras, 230 N.C. 592, 55 S.E.2d 183, 1949 (same).

6 McDonald v. Shaw, supra note 5. Cf. infra notes 8–11.

7 Paulus v. Besch, 127 Mo.App. 255, 104 S.W. 1149, 1907.

8 Church v. Church, 57 Ohio St. 561, 49 N.E. 408, 1898; Lamb v. Lamb, 226 N.C. 662, 40 S.E.2d 29, 1946.

9 Witmer v. Witmer, 362 Pa. 119, 66 A.2d 241, 1949; Ragland v. Craig, 188 Tenn. 380, 219 S.W.2d 894, 1949.

10 La Tourette v. La Tourette, 15 Ariz. 200, 137 P. 426, Ann.Cas.1915B 70, 1914; Sherman v. Lewis, 44 Minn. 107, 46 N.W. 318, 1890. See Lewis v. Carver, infra note 11.

11 Penn v. Guggenheimer, 76 Va. 839, 1882 (devise of "home place"); Waggoner v. Waggoner, 111 Va. 325, 68 S.E. 990, 30 L.R.A.,N.S., 644, 1910; Lewis v. Carver, 140 Md. 121, 117 A. 108, 1922.

12 Bennett v. Harper, 36 W.Va. 546, 15 S.E. 143, 1892.

vailing view, when a testator conveys to A the land previously devised to B, A is not required to elect whether he will retain the land under the deed, or take other property given him by the will.[13]

*By Beneficiary of Insurance Policy Bequeathed to Another*

Another case requiring an election is that in which the testator, having an insurance policy upon his life payable to a beneficiary, purports to bequeath the policy to a third person and makes another testamentary disposition in favor of the beneficiary named in the policy. The latter may either claim the policy against the will, or he may accept the testamentary gift in his favor, but he is not entitled to both and must elect between them.[14]

*By Creditor Who Is Also Legatee*

An election is required if a testator makes a testamentary provision for a creditor intending this as satisfaction of the debt.[15] The creditor may either accept the legacy or proceed to recover his claim against the executor, but he cannot do both. Little controversy occurs when the will expressly states that the legacy is given in payment of a debt.[16] According to the orthodox view, when a testator gave a legacy to his creditor of an equal or greater amount than the debt, the legacy was presumed to be in satisfaction thereof.[17] This rule has been criticized,[18] and it is

13 Lansdale v. Dearing, 351 Mo. 356, 173 S.W.2d 25, 147 A.L.R. 728, 1943; Hattersley v. Bissett, 51 N.J.Eq. 597, 29 A. 187, 40 Am.St.Rep. 532, 1892. Contra: Flippin v. Banner, 55 N.C. 450, 1856. Cf. Allen v. Allen, 121 N.C. 328, 28 S.E. 513, 1897.

14 Van Schaack v. Leonard, 164 Ill. 602, 45 N.E. 982, 1897; Royal v. Moore, 187 N.C. 379, 121 S.E. 666, 1924. And see Wooten's Trustee v. Hardy, 221 Ky. 338, 298 S.W. 963, 1927, noted, 16 Ky.L.J. 277; In re Schaech's Will, supra note 5. Cf. Hartwig v. Schiefer, 147 Ind. 64, 46 N.E. 75, 1897; Commercial Nat. Bank of Charlotte v. Misenheimer, 211 N.C. 519, 191 S.E. 14, 110 A.L.R. 1310, 1937. See supra § 27, note 1.

15 Smith v. Furnish, 70 Cal. 424, 12 P. 392, 1886; Alexander v. Fidelity Trust Co., 249 F. 1, C.C.A. 3d, 1918.

16 See Rusling v. Rusling, 42 N.J. Eq. 594, 8 A. 534, 1887. As to testator's mistake regarding the amount of the debt, cf. Gofton v. Mill, 2 Vern. 141, 23 Eng.Rep. 698, 1690, with Shadbolt v. Vanderplank, 29 Beav. 405, 54 Eng.Rep. 684, 1861.

17 Allen v. Merwin, 121 Mass. 378, 1876; Fitzgerald v. National Bank, Ltd., [1929] W.N. 5 (Ont.). See Patsourakos v. Kolioutos, 132 N.J.Eq. 87, 26 A.2d 882, affirmed, 133 N.J.Eq. 37, 30 A.2d 27, 1942; In re Steinkraus' Estate, 233 Wis. 186, 288 N.W. 772, 1939; notes, 25 Minn.L.R. 122, 89 U. of Pa.L.R. 132.

18 Mulheran's Ex'rs v. Gillespie, 12 Wend.(N.Y.) 349, 1834; Fitzgerald v.

subject to a number of qualifications or exceptions. For example, it has been held that there is no such presumption when the testamentary provision is given for another express purpose,[19] or is contingent,[20] or is of specific chattels,[21] or realty,[22] or if there is a general direction for the payment of debts,[23] or where the indebtedness is unliquidated,[24] or incurred after the execution of the will,[25] or is smaller than the debt.[26] Parol evidence is not admissible to show that the legacy was intended as satisfaction of the debt,[27] but such testimony may be admitted to rebut the presumption of satisfaction which arises under the orthodox rule.[28] In all these ways the courts have undermined the general doctrine; and it has even been stated that the modern rule is that it should appear from the will that the legacy was intended as satisfaction of the debt and that no presumption to that effect should be indulged.[29] Of course, if the legacy is not deemed in satisfaction of the debt, the creditor-legatee may insist upon both and is not required to elect.

### *Cumulative and Substitutional Legacies*

The question of election does not arise in connection with determination of whether legacies to the same person are cumula-

National Bank, Ltd., supra note 17. And see infra note 29.

19 Strong v. Williams, 12 Mass. 391, 7 Am.Dec. 81, 1810.

20 Crompton v. Sale, 2 P Wms. 553, 24 Eng.Rep. 858, 1729.

21 Strong v. Williams, supra note 19.

22 Deichman v. Arndt, 49 N.J.Eq. 106, 22 A. 799, 1891.

23 Allen v. Etter, 92 Ind.App. 297, 175 N.E. 286, 1931; Shoberg v. Rock, 230 Iowa 832, 298 N.W. 834, 1941. But see Re Huish, L.R. 43 Ch.Div. 260, 1889.

24 Glover v. Patten, 165 U.S. 394, 17 S.Ct. 411, 41 L.Ed. 760, 1897. See White v. Deering, 38 Cal.App. 433, 177 P. 516, 1918, noted, 7 Cal.L.R. 289; In re Hill's Estate, 230 Iowa 189, 297 N.W. 278, 1941.

25 In re Hill's Estate, supra note 24.

26 Allen v. Etter, supra note 23, holding that a pro tanto satisfaction was not presumed. And see Strong v. Williams, supra note 19. But the fact that the debt carries interest, while the legacy does not, does not prevent a presumption of satisfaction. Fitzgerald v. National Bank, Ltd., supra note 17.

27 White v. Deering, supra note 24; Winner v. Shucart, 202 Mo.App. 176, 215 S.W. 905, 1919. Cf. Sharp v. Wightman, 205 Pa. 285, 54 A. 888, 1903.

28 Wallace v. Pomfret, 11 Ves.Jr. 542, 32 Eng.Rep. 1199, 1805.

29 White v. Deering, supra note 24; Card's Estate, 145 Misc. 686, 260 N.Y.S. 764, 1933; Rizzo v. Cunningham, 303 Mass. 16, 20 N.E.2d 471, 1939; Wilson v. Safe Deposit & T. Co., 183 Md. 245, 37 A.2d 321, 152 A.L.R. 892, 1944.

tive or substitutional. A cumulative legacy is one given in addition to a prior legacy to the same person. Legacies are generally considered cumulative when they are given by different instruments, as by will and codicil,[30] or are of different amounts or kinds of property,[31] or are made for different purposes.[32] Of course where the legacies are cumulative, the legatee is entitled to both and there is no occasion for an election. A substitutional legacy is one given in the place of a prior legacy. It will be presumed that a legacy is substitutional if it is given by the same instrument for the same amount, either generally,[33] or for the same express purpose.[34] There is likewise no necessity for an election in case of substitutional legacies—the latter provision alone is given effect.

### *What Constitutes an Election*

An election may be an express declaration showing the intention of electing, or it may be implied. In the latter situation the question turns upon the circumstances of each case. Election may be inferred from conduct of the party or from his acts, omissions and method of dealing with the property,[35] but to constitute an implied election the acts or conduct relied upon must be of an unequivocal character.[36] The taking and enjoyment of property to which the person has no right except under the will is usually an election of the benefits conferred by the will.[37] So, any assertion of title under the will, as by an action at law, in-

30 Wray v. Field, 6 Madd. 300, 56 Eng.Rep. 1105, 1822; In re Davies' Will, 192 Iowa 723, 185 N.W. 578, 1921; Kemp v. Hutchinson, 110 S.W. 2d 1126, Mo.App.1937, noted, 3 Mo.L. R. 328. But see Gould v. Chamberlain, 184 Mass. 115, 68 N.E. 39, 1903; and infra note 34.

31 Gordon v. Smith, 103 Md. 315, 63 A. 479, 1906; Curry v. Pile, 2 Br.Ch. 225, 29 Eng.Rep. 126, 1787.

32 Gregory v. Tompkins, 132 Mich. 205, 93 N.W. 245, 1903; Wildes v. Davies, 1 Sm. & G. 475, 65 Eng.Rep. 208, 1853; Curry v. Pile, supra note 31.

33 Thompson v. Betts, 74 Conn. 576, 51 A. 564, 92 Am.St.Rep. 235, 1902; In re Powell's Estate, 138 Pa. 322, 22 A. 92, 1890; Greenwood v. Greenwood, 1 Br.Ch. 31n, 28 Eng.Rep. 966, 1776.

34 Sears v. Hardy, 120 Mass. 524, 1876; In re Benson's Estate, 209 Pa. 108, 58 A. 135, 1904 (even if by different instruments).

35 King v. Skellie, 79 Ga. 147, 3 S.E. 614, 1887.

36 Wolfe v. Mueller, 46 Colo. 335, 104 P. 487, 1909; Bebout v. Quick, 81 Ohio St. 196, 90 N.E. 162, 1909. See Hahn v. Dunn, 211 Iowa 678, 234 N. W. 247, 82 A.L.R. 1503, 1931; Larivee v. Vanasse, 320 Mass. 213, 68 N.E.2d 688, 1946. See also infra note 42 et seq.

37 Crumpler v. Barfield & Wilson Co., 114 Ga. 570, 40 S.E. 808, 1902; Fry v. Morrison, 159 Ill. 244, 42 N.E.

dicates an election to take thereunder,[38] and an election against the interest conferred by the will may be indicated in like manner.[39] However, a petition for probate of the will,[40] or a motion for appointment of a trustee thereunder[41] does not necessarily constitute an election to take under the will.

To constitute an election the party's acts must be with full knowledge of his rights, and of all material facts which might influence the decision.[42] Thus, where all the acts of a devisee tending to show an election to take under the will occur before he knows that he has any other title to the land, no election is implied.[43] In order for any act to be binding upon a person, it must be done with the intention of constituting an election.[44]

*Time of Election*

There are generally no statutes governing the time for election except in case of the surviving spouse.[45] In other cases the person is given a reasonable period to elect, in view of the will's provisions, the interest of the various parties, and other circumstances.[46] A legatee cannot be compelled to elect until it has been determined whether he was the owner of property which the will purported to give to another.[47]

774, 1896; Hovey v. Hovey, 61 N.H. 599, 1882; Drake v. Wild, 70 Vt. 52, 39 A. 248, 1897; Alexander v. Fidelity Trust Co., 249 F. 1, C.C.A.3d, 1918. And see Wooten's Trustee v. Hardy, 221 Ky. 338, 298 S.W. 963, 1927, noted, 16 Ky.L.J. 277. But when the party has title to the land independent of the will, acts of ownership do not indicate an election. Mellen v. Mellen, 139 N.Y. 210, 34 N.E. 925, 1893.

38 Davis v. Badlam, 165 Mass. 248, 43 N.E. 91, 1896.

39 Smith v. Furnish, 70 Cal. 424, 12 P. 392, 1886 (suit for services rendered to testator is an election not to claim a legacy in payment of said services); In re Prerost's Estate, 40 S.D. 536, 168 N.W. 630, 1918.

40 Rives v. Caber, 213 Ala. 206, 104 So. 420, 1925. See note, 23 N.C.L.R. 380. Cf. Hardeman v. Ellis, 162 Ga. 664, 135 S.E. 195, 1926, noted, 40 Harv.L.R. 646; In re Schaech's Will, supra note 5.

41 In re Le Borius' Estate, 222 Minn. 31, 23 N.W.2d 1, 166 A.L.R. 313, 1946.

42 Watson v. Watson, 128 Mass. 152, 1880; Showalter's Ex'rs v. Showalter, 107 Va. 713, 60 S.E. 48, 1908.

43 Clark v. Hershy, 52 Ark. 473, 12 S.W. 1077, 1890.

44 Cobb v. MacFarland, 87 Neb. 408, 127 N.W. 377, 1910; Waggoner v. Waggoner, 111 Va. 325, 68 S.E. 990, 30 L.R.A.,N.S., 644, 1910; and see supra note 36.

45 See In re Schaech's Will, supra note 5.

46 Crumpler v. Barfield & Wilson Co., 114 Ga. 570, 40 S.E. 808, 1902; Soper v. Halsey, 85 Hun 464, 33 N.Y.S. 105, 1895 (here the will evidently gave an unlimited time to elect).

47 Lamar v. McLaren, 107 Ga. 591, 34 S.E. 116, 1899.

*Revocation of Election*

An election once made by a party bound to elect, acting with full knowledge of his rights and of all material circumstances, is irrevocable and binding upon the party and his privies.[48] While a court would doubtless set aside an election procured by fraud, it will not do so merely upon the ground that the thing elected was not a fair equivalent of the thing rejected.[49] The courts will usually permit an election to be set aside for mistake of fact but not for mistake of law.[50]

*Election by Infants and Incompetents*

The acceptance by an infant or incompetent person of the benefits under a will does not constitute an election in the will's favor.[51] Nor can his guardian make a binding election.[52] Where these disabilities exist, the election should be postponed until majority is reached or competency restored,[53] or, as is more usual, a court of equity should make the most advantageous election for the person under disability.[54] This may be done either at a judicial hearing approving the guardian's determination, or upon the independent decision of the court, or by reference of the entire matter to a master for investigation and report.

*Consequences of Election Upon Other Beneficiaries*

In general a renounced testamentary benefit will be conferred on the legatee or devisee who loses by the election. Usually the non-spouse cases present much simpler problems than elections

48 McQuerry v. Gilliland, 89 Ky. 434, 12 S.W. 1037, 7 L.R.A. 454, 1890; Job Haines Home for Aged People v. Keene, 87 N.J.Eq. 509, 101 A. 512, 1917; Penn v. Guggenheimer, 76 Va. 839, 1882; Alexander v. Fidelity Trust Co., 249 F. 1, C.C.A.3d, 1918.

49 Spofford v. Manning, 6 Paige (N. Y.) 383, 1837.

50 Waggoner v. Waggoner, 111 Va. 325, 68 S.E. 990, 30 L.R.A.,N.S., 644, 1910; Job Haines Home for Aged People v. Keene, 87 N.J.Eq. 509, 101 A. 512, 1917; Oglesby v. Springfield Marine Bank, 395 Ill. 37, 69 N.E.2d 269, 1946.

51 Brown v. Brown, 108 Mass. 386, 1871; Moorman v. Louisville Trust Co., 181 Ky. 566, 205 S.W. 564, 1918.

52 Van Steenwyck v. Washburn, 59 Wis. 483, 17 N.W. 289, 48 Am.Rep. 532, 1884.

53 Matter of Lyon, 173 App.Div. 473, 159 N.Y.S. 951, 1916; Streatfield v. Streatfield, Cas.t.Talb. 176, 25 Eng.Rep. 724, 1736.

54 Thom v. Thom, 101 Md. 444, 61 A. 193, 1905; McQueen v. McQueen, 2 Jones Eq. (55 N.C.) 16, 62 Am.Dec. 205, 1854 (referred to master); Ambrose v. Rugg, 123 Ohio St. 433, 175 N.E. 691, 74 A.L.R. 449, 1931 (court of probate—statute). See supra § 33.

by the spouse to take a dower or intestate portion, for in the latter, several specific and residuary devisees may be affected, and equitable adjustments between them are often delicate and difficult matters.[55] If a devisee or legatee elects to take his own property devised to another, the latter usually obtains the property given by the will to the former.[56] When a creditor proceeds upon his claim and renounces a legacy given in lieu thereof, the residuary legatee should take the renounced legacy, both because that is the normal effect of a residuary clause and on account of the equities of the situation.[57]

## RENUNCIATION

**139. A devisee or legatee may renounce a testamentary gift, even so as to defeat the inheritance tax which otherwise would be imposed upon the transfer, or so as to disappoint the creditors of the beneficiary. A renounced specific or general gift falls into the residue, while a rejected residuary portion becomes intestate property. An heir or distributee cannot renounce his interest in an intestate estate.**

At least if a testamentary gift is beneficial, the devisee or legatee will be presumed to have accepted the interest.[1] However, a person may renounce the gift, in which case it is deemed never to have passed to him.[2] There is nothing to compel a person to take under a will. A court is not inclined to regard

[55] See supra § 33.

[56] In re Shelley's Estate, 287 Pa. 105, 134 A. 468, 1926; Johnson v. Covington, 148 Tenn. 47, 251 S.W. 893, 1923. And see Farmington Sav. Bank v. Curran, 72 Conn. 342, 44 A. 473, 1899; In re Prerost's Estate, supra note 39.

[57] See Bradford v. Leake, 124 Tenn. 312, 137 S.W. 96, Ann.Cas.1912D, 1140, 1911, where a voluntary devisee renounced the devise because it was burdensome; the principle would seem to apply a fortiori in case of a renunciation by a creditor to whom property was willed in lieu of the debt.

[1] Lehr v. Switzer, 213 Iowa 658, 239 N.W. 564, 1931, noted, 17 Ia.L.R. 534, 31 Mich.L.R. 443; Chilcoat v. Reid, 154 Md. 378, 140 A. 100, 1928 (contra if burdensome); Bradford v. Leake, 124 Tenn. 312, 137 S.W. 96, Ann.Cas.1912D, 1140, 1911 (same); Brown v. Routzahn, 63 F.2d 914, C.C.A.6th, 1933.

[2] In re Murphy's Estate, 217 Iowa 1291, 252 N.W. 523, 1934; Bouse v. Hull, 168 Md. 1, 176 A. 645, 1935; In re Howe's Estate, 112 N.J.Eq. 17, 163 A. 234, 1932, noted, 81 U. of Pa. L.R. 645; Bradford v. Calhoun, 120 Tenn. 53, 109 S.W. 502, 19 L.R.A.,N.S., 595, 1907. Cf. Albany Hospital v. Albany Guardian Society and Home for Friendless, 214 N.Y. 435, 108 N.E. 812, Ann.Cas.1916D, 1195, 1915. As to the doctrine in Louisiana, see note, 26 Tulane L.R. 81.

doubtful words or acts as a renunciation;[3] but a renunciation once made is final and cannot be retracted.[4] Likewise where there has been an acceptance, the beneficiary is no longer in position to renounce.[5]

*Rejection of Part and Acceptance of Remainder*

Sometimes a beneficiary under a will may desire to accept certain provisions and reject others that are burdensome. This suggests the general matter of election; yet the problem is somewhat different as no choice between inconsistent things is involved.[6] Whether one may reject certain testamentary provisions for him and accept others in the same will is fundamentally a question of construction of the instrument. If the testator shows by the will that he desired the two provisions for a single person to be inseparable, one cannot be renounced without also surrendering all rights under the other.[7] On the other hand, if the language creates separate gifts, a renunciation of one and acceptance of the other is permitted.[8]

*Defeat of Tax or Creditors by Renunciation*

The motive of a devisee or legatee in rejecting the testamentary provision is immaterial. Thus, renunciation has been sustained though it was made in order to avoid the imposition of a succession tax upon the devise or bequest.[9] The interest fails to pass because of the renunciation; accordingly there is no transfer

[3] In re Howe's Estate, supra note 2; Blake v. Blake, 147 Or. 43, 31 P.2d 768, 1934.

[4] Bradford v. Leake, supra note 1. But a renouncement may be set aside for fraud. Miller v. Brode, 186 Cal. 409, 199 P. 531, 1921.

[5] Blake v. Blake, supra note 3. See Matter of Wilson, 298 N.Y. 398, 83 N.E.2d 852, 1949, noted, 15 Brooklyn L.R. 327, 35 Corn.L.Q. 227, 47 Mich. L.R. 866, 24 N.Y.U.L.Q.R. 634, 24 Notre Dame Lawyer 586, 1 Syracuse L.R. 323, 2 Vand.L.R. 720, 35 Va.L.R. 509.

[6] State Banking Co. v. Hinton, 178 Ga. 68, 172 S.E. 42, 91 A.L.R. 596, 1933.

[7] State Banking Co. v. Hinton, supra note 6 (gifts of realty and bank stock); Brown v. Routzahn, supra note 1.

[8] Foulkes v. Foulkes, 173 Ark. 188, 293 S.W. 1, 1927.

[9] People v. Flanagin, 331 Ill. 203, 162 N.E. 848, 60 A.L.R. 305, 1928; Bouse v. Hull, 168 Md. 1, 176 A. 645, 1935; Brown v. Routzahn, supra note 1. Generally see Rogers & Sterling, Post Mortem Estate Planning, 14 U. of Pitts.L.R. 224, 229; Roehner & Roehner, infra note 13. Cf. In re Howe's Estate, supra note 2. Under estate, as distinguished from inheritance, tax systems, the tax question is apt to involve the gift tax on the alleged transfer by the renouncer. See Hardenbergh v. Commissioner of Internal Revenue, infra note 12.

upon which to impose the tax. A devisee-debtor may even defeat his judgment creditors by renouncing the devise; [10] though the renunciation must come within a reasonable time after testator's death.[11] In case of intestacy the heir cannot renounce because title is deemed to pass instantly upon death and there is no other person to take.[12] This is extended, with less reason, to the distributee.[13] In the light of modern concepts the heir or distributee should be permitted to renounce as freely as the devisee or legatee, but this result apparently can be reached only through statutory change.[14]

*Effect of Renunciation*

When the beneficiary renounces the provisions of a will, the matter is treated as if the provisions had never been made.[15] A renounced devise or legacy ordinarily falls into the residue.[16] A renounced residuary portion passes as intestate property.[17]

10 Schoonover v. Osborne, 193 Iowa 474, 187 N.W. 20, 27 A.L.R. 465, 1922, noted, 36 Harv.L.R. 347; Lehr v. Switzer, supra note 1; Bradford v. Calhoun, supra note 2. And see note, 18 Cal.L.R. 298. But see In re Kalt's Estate, 16 Cal.2d 807, 108 P.2d 401, 133 A.L.R. 1424, 1941, noted, 29 Cal. L.R. 531, 25 Minn.L.R. 951, 18 N.Y.U. L.Q.R. 142, 27 Va.L.R. 936; also note, 43 Yale L.J. 1080; Model Probate Code § 58.

11 In the following cases the renunciation was held to come too late to defeat the devisee's creditors: Crumpler v. Barfield & Wilson Co., 114 Ga. 570, 40 S.E. 808, 1902 (thirteen years); Strom v. Wood, 100 Kan. 556, 164 P. 1100, 1917. And see In re Howe's Estate, supra note 2; Matter of Wilson supra note 5; cf. Ohio Nat. Bank v. Miller, 57 N.E.2d 747, Ohio App.1943 (will allowed six months to renounce).

12 Watson v. Watson, 13 Conn. 83, 1839; Coomes v. Finegan, 233 Iowa 448, 7 N.W.2d 729, 1943, noted, 28 Iowa L.R. 700, 92 U. of Pa.L.R. 105; Hardenbergh v. Commissioner of Internal Revenue, 198 F.2d 63, C.A.8th, 1952.

13 Bostian v. Milens, 239 Mo.App. 555, 193 S.W.2d 797, 170 A.L.R. 424, 1946, noted, 12 Mo.L.R. 67; Hardenbergh v. Commissioner of Internal Revenue, supra note 12. But see Roehner & Roehner, Renunciation as Taxable Gift—An Unconstitutional Federal Tax Decision, 8 Tax L.R. 289; Rogers & Sterling, supra note 9.

14 See Model Probate Code, § 58; N.Y.Law Rev.Com.Leg.Doc. (1950) No. 65 (J). Of course in any event a beneficiary who is not permitted to renounce may transfer his property to other heirs or devisees, but not so as to avoid creditors' claims or tax consequences. See cases supra notes 12, 13.

15 Greely v. Houston, 148 Miss. 799, 114 So. 740, 1927; Albany Hospital v. Albany Guardian Society and Home for Friendless, supra note 2; Model Probate Code § 58. Cf. In re Waring's Will, 293 N.Y. 186, 56 N.E.2d 543, 1944, noted, 45 Col.L.R. 285.

16 Myers v. Smith, 235 Iowa 385, 16 N.W.2d 628, 155 A.L.R. 1413, 1944; Albany Hospital v. Albany Guardian Society and Home for Friendless, su-

17 See Note 17 on following page.

## LAPSE

**140. When a legacy or devise cannot vest at testator's death by reason of the death of the beneficiary or his disability or unwillingness to take, the gift will lapse in absence of testamentary provision for other disposition of the subject-matter or appropriate statutory enactment substituting the issue or heirs of the original beneficiary in place of the latter.**

**When there is a lapse of a specific or general legacy or devise, the subject-matter of the gift passes under the residuary clause, but lapsed residuary portions generally become intestate property.**

**A void gift is one which from some circumstance could never have been effective even if the testator had died immediately after execution of the will. The same general rules govern the disposition of the subject-matter of void devises and bequests as in case of lapse.**

When the beneficiary named in the will becomes unable or unwilling to take at the time of testator's death, the gift must fall or lapse unless it is saved by appropriate testamentary or statutory provision. Death of the legatee or devisee during the testator's lifetime is the most usual cause of lapse. However, renunciation of a legacy may result in lapse,[1] as may the dissolution of a corporate devisee before the testator's death.[2] While a void gift is not exactly an example of lapse, the consequences of the invalidity are largely the same as true cases of lapse.[3]

pra note 2. As to whether a renounced life estate should accelerate the remainder, cf. Greely v. Houston, supra note 15, with Re Scott, [1911] 2 Ch. 374. The latter case is the subject of a series of interesting comments. 32 L.Q.R. 83, 392, 33 id. 132, 254.

17 Perkins v. Isley, 224 N.C. 703, 32 S.E.2d 588, 1945. See infra § 140, note 47 et seq.

1 See supra § 139. See also Sawyer v. Freeman, 161 Mass. 543, 37 N. E. 942, 1894.

2 Merrill v. Hayden, 86 Me. 133, 29 A. 949, 1893; National Bank of Greece v. Savarika, 167 Miss. 571, 148 So. 649, 1933. But the fact that a charitable corporation had voted to discontinue its functions and to direct its trustees to take steps for dissolution does not impair its right to receive a legacy. Old Colony Trust Co. v. Third Universalist Society of Cambridge, 285 Mass. 146, 188 N.E. 711, 91 A.L.R. 837, 1934.

3 See infra notes 53–58.

*Testamentary Provisions to Prevent Lapse*

Lapse is not prevented by a devise or legacy to one "and his heirs," the latter words being merely ones of limitation to indicate the extent of the interest which the beneficiary takes in the event of his surviving the testator.[4] However, if the gift is to one "or his heirs," the alternative is deemed a substitutional gift in case of the predecease of the designated person.[5] In this case the testator has by apt provision prevented a lapse by providing a substituted beneficiary. It is always open to a testator to provide for an alternative disposition in the event of the death of the first beneficiary.[6] Lapse can also be obviated by making a legacy or devise to several persons as joint tenants, or to a fluctuating class to be ascertained at the death of the testator, or at a subsequent time.[7] Extrinsic evidence is not ordinarily admissible to ascertain testator's intention regarding the matter of lapse. Certainly testator's oral declarations cannot be shown for this purpose.[8] Most cases hold that a codicil which has the effect of republishing the will does not prevent a lapse

[4] Morehouse v. Bridgeport City Trust Co., 137 Conn. 209, 75 A.2d 493, 1950; Bryson v. Holbrook, 159 Mass. 280, 34 N.E. 270, 1893; In re Spiers' Estate, 224 Mich. 658, 195 N.W. 430, 1923; McKiernan v. Beardslee, 72 N.J.Eq. 283, 73 A. 815, 1906; In re Wells, 113 N.Y. 396, 21 N.E. 137, 10 Am.St.Rep. 457, 1889; Evers v. Williams, 43 Ohio App. 555, 184 N.E. 19, 1932. See also In re Boyle's Estate, 121 Colo. 599, 221 P.2d 357, 1950, s. c., 123 Colo. 448, 231 P.2d 465, 1951 ("for herself, her heirs, personal representatives and assigns, forever").

[5] In re Simpson's Estate, 304 Pa. 396, 156 A. 91, 78 A.L.R. 989, 1931. See In re Gilmor's Estate, 154 Pa. 523, 26 A. 614, 35 Am.St.Rep. 855, 1893; In re Brunet's Estate, 34 Cal.2d 105, 207 P.2d 567, 11 A.L.R.2d 1382, 1949, noted, 63 Harv.L.R. 544, 23 So.Cal.L.R. 635 ("or his estate"); also notes, 3 Miami L.Q. 472, 43 Mich.L.R. 996.

[6] Rivers v. Rivers, 36 S.C. 302, 15 S.E. 137, 1892. And see Farnsworth v. Whiting, 102 Me. 296, 66 A. 831, 1906 (death of life tenant in testator's lifetime merely accelerates the time when the remainderman takes). Cf. note, 39 Ill.L.R. 287.

[7] Gordon v. Jackson, 58 N.J.Eq. 166, 43 A. 98, 1899; Rhode Island Hospital Trust Co. v. Calef, 43 R.I. 518, 112 A. 787, 1921. See generally Cooley, What Constitutes a Gift to a Class, 49 Harv.L.R. 903; also Corbett v. Skaggs, 111 Kan. 380, 207 P. 819, 28 A.L.R. 1230, 1922, noted, 36 Harv. L.R. 230, 21 Mich.L.R. 485; Worcester Trust Co. v. Turner, 210 Mass. 115, 96 N.E. 132, 1911; Viner v. Francis, 2 Cox Ch. 190, 30 Eng.Rep. 88, 1789; Succession of Lambert, 210 La. 636, 28 So.2d 1, 1946, noted, 7 La.L.R. 138, 4 Loyola L.R. 87, 21 Tulane L.R. 319.

[8] In re Pierce's Estate, 177 Wis. 104, 188 N.W. 78, 1922. And see Jackson v. Alsop, 67 Conn. 249, 34 A. 1106, 1896. Cf. Lenz v. Sens, 27 Tex.Civ.App. 442, 66 S.W. 110, 1901 (surrounding circumstances admissible when will is ambiguous). And see Gale v. Keyes, 45 Ohio App. 61, 186 N.E. 755, 1933.

of a legacy to one who died between the dates of the two instruments, since the mere republication is no indication of intent to pass the property to the legatee's heirs.[9]

*Statutes to Prevent Lapse*

Section 33 of the English Wills Act [10] provides that when any child or other issue of the testator is devisee or legatee and dies leaving issue during the testator's lifetime, the gift shall not lapse but shall take effect as if the death of such person had happened immediately after the death of the testator, unless a contrary intention is expressed in the will. In almost all states there are somewhat similar statutes designed to prevent lapse in certain cases.[11] This legislation has the purpose of effecting the probable intention of the average testator, if he had thought of the possibility of his surviving the legatee or devisee. Some of these statutes cover only the situation where the beneficiary is a child of the testator, others follow the English statute extending the class to all descendants, still others to all relatives, and some even to every beneficiary whether related to the testator or not. Most jurisdictions require that issue or descendants survive the predeceased legatee or devisee, though some jurisdictions provide that the portion may go to his heirs.

Many difficult problems arise in connection with these antilapse statutes.[12] First there are the questions as to who are included within the terms "relatives," "children," "issue," and the like. When the statute makes provision against lapse in case of a gift to a "relative," does this apply in case of the predecease of the testator's spouse who is a beneficiary under the will? It is held that the spouse is not a relative within the meaning of the legislation and that the gift will lapse, since a different interpretation would often divert the gift from testator's own kin to his spouse's relatives.[13] The same holding is made in case of gifts

9 First National Bank & T. Co. v. Baker, 124 Conn. 577, 1 A.2d 283, 118 A.L.R. 339, 1938; Rippel v. King, 126 N.J.Eq. 287, 8 A.2d 777, 1939. Contra: Re Gibbons, 192 Okla. 378, 137 P.2d 928, 146 A.L.R. 1361, 1943. See note, 30 Mich.L.R. 520; supra § 91, note 23.

10 7 Wm. IV & 1 Vict. c. 26, 1837.

11 See Bordwell, Statute Law of Wills, 14 Ia.L.R. 428.

12 For an able discussion, see Mechem, Problems under Anti-Lapse Statutes, 19 Ia.L.R. 1. See also note, 9 Mont.L.R. 120.

13 Farnsworth v. Whiting, 102 Me. 296, 66 A. 831, 1906; In re Spiers' Estate, 224 Mich. 658, 195 N.W. 430, 1923; In re Luckhardt's Estate, 131 Neb. 55, 277 N.W. 836, 115 A.L.R. 437, 1938. See Wilson v. Starbuck, 182 S.E. 539, 102 A.L.R. 485, W.Va., 1935, noted, 36 Col.L.R. 1013; note, 19 U. of Cin.L.R. 301.

to relatives of the spouse.[14] A sister, however, is a relative within the meaning of the statute though she is not the next of kin.[15]

The courts are in conflict as to whether the adopted child of a legatee comes within the term "issue," "lineal descent," or "child," who would be entitled to be substituted under the statute.[16] Indeed, it has even been held that the testator's own adopted child was not a "child," and that on the latter's predecease of the testator, the property does not go to the adopted child's issue.[17] The latter holding seems scarcely defensible, since a decedent's adopted child now universally inherits from the adoptive parent.[18]

Somewhat more than half of the states have a provision similar to the English expression "unless a contrary intention shall appear in the will," [19] and even in the jurisdictions which have no similar clause, the statute will not apply when the testator has indicated a different disposition.[20] A contrary intention is shown when the gift is to the legatee or devisee, "if he survives me." [21] Here it would be a manifest disregard of an express condition to permit the legatee's heirs to be substituted if the legatee predeceased the testator. An even clearer case is that in which there is a gift over to another if the legatee does not survive the

[14] In re Estate of Pfuelb, 48 Cal. 643, 1874; Bramell v. Adams, 146 Mo. 70, 47 S.W. 931, 1898.

[15] Rauch v. Metz, 212 S.W. 353, Mo. 1919.

[16] That the adopted child comes within such provision: Hoellinger v. Molzhon, 77 N.D. 108, 41 N.W.2d 217, 19 A.L.R.2d 1147, 1950 ("lineal descendants"); In re Walter's Estate, 270 N.Y. 201, 200 N.E. 786, 1936 ("child"); cf. Flynn v. Bredbeck, 147 Ohio St. 49, 68 N.E.2d 75, noted, 45 Mich.L.R. 649. Contra: Gammons v. Gammons, 212 Mass. 454, 99 N.E. 95, 1912 ("issue"); Rauch v. Metz, supra note 15 ("lineal descendants"); see notes, 21 Corn.L.Q. 346, 348, 38 Yale L.J. 441; 31 Col.L.R. 439; supra § 23, note 20.

[17] In re Phillips' Estate, 17 Pa. Super. 103, 1901.

[18] See supra § 23.

[19] See Bordwell, supra note 11 at 432.

[20] See Wallace v. Diehl, 202 N.Y. 156, 95 N.E. 646, 33 L.R.A.,N.S., 9, 1911.

[21] Wallace v. Diehl, supra note 20; Kunkel v. Kunkel, 267 Pa. 163, 110 A. 73, 1920. But see Gale v. Keyes, 45 Ohio App. 61, 186 N.E. 755, 1923. Cf. Schneller v. Schneller, 356 Ill. 89, 190 N.E. 121, 92 A.L.R. 838, 1934, where the testator gave his property to his three children or the survivor or survivors of them, they all being unmarried at the time of execution of the will—held: the anti-lapse statute applies. See also Union Trust Co. v. Richardson, 70 R.I. 151, 37 A.2d 777, 1944; Wetstein v. Shannon, 302 Ky. 371, 194 S.W.2d 830, 1946.

testator.[22] A more difficult instance is that in which the devise or bequest is "to X alone," or words of like import. Here also it would seem that the testator has expressed the desire that there should be no substitution, and hence the disposition should not be regarded as within the anti-lapse provision.[23] However, the statute has been applied to gifts under a will, which provides generally that all others not named as beneficiaries should be excluded from the testator's estate.[24]

When the legatee or devisee was dead at the time of the execution of the will, this is technically a case of a void rather than a lapsed gift, since the provision could never have been effective. However, by the prevailing view, the anti-lapse statute applies in such cases.[25] This seems sound, since the testator either was ignorant of the legatee's death, or must be deemed to have made the legacy with knowledge of the statute. There is a minority view to the contrary, found particularly in the jurisdictions where the term "lapse" appears in the statute.[26]

By the doctrine of "worthier title," a devisee who took the identical interest under the will that he would have taken by descent was deemed to succeed in the worthier capacity of heir. This ancient doctrine has been criticized in the light of modern theories and rules; [27] yet it has been applied by at least one court

22 In re Estate of Bennett, 134 Cal. 320, 66 P. 370, 1901; Leary v. Liberty Trust Co., 272 Mass. 1, 171 N.E. 828, 69 A.L.R. 1239, 1930.

23 See Mechem, supra note 12, at 11.

24 Sleeper v. Larrabee, 266 Mass. 320, 165 N.E. 121, 1929; Larwill's Ex'rs v. Ewing, 73 Ohio St. 177, 76 N.E. 503, 1905. And see Ryder v. Myers, 113 N.J.Eq. 360, 167 A. 22, 1933. The statute has been held to apply to a legacy placed in trust. Hester v. Sammons, 171 Va. 142, 198 S.E. 466, 118 A.L.R. 1938, noted 25 Va.L.R. 383.

25 Friederichs v. Friederichs, 205 Iowa 505, 218 N.W. 271, 1928; Lewis v. Corbin, 195 Mass. 520, 81 N.E. 248, 122 Am.St.Rep. 261, 1907; Lawnick v. Schultz, 325 Mo. 294, 28 S.W.2d 658, 1930; In re Force's Estate, 42 A.2d 302, N.J.Orphans Ct. 1945; Winsor v. Brown, 48 R.I. 200, 136 A. 434, 1927. See annotation, 3 A.L.R. 1682. Cf. infra note 34. As to whether the anti-lapse statute applies when it cannot be shown whether the testator or the legatee survived the other, cf. Carpenter v. Severin, 201 Iowa 969, 204 N.W. 448, 43 A.L.R. 1340, 1926, noted, 11 Iowa L.R. 93, with Matter of Macklin, 177 Misc. 432, 30 N.Y.S.2d 706, 1941, noted, 55 Harv.L.R. 691. See generally supra § 107, note 23, and infra § 147, note 40.

26 In re Estate of Matthews, 176 Cal. 576, 169 P. 233, 1917 (but see present Cal.Prob.Code § 92); Moss v. Helsley, 60 Tex. 426, 1883.

27 See Harper & Heckel, The Doctrine of Worthier Title, 24 Ill.L.R. 627. Cf. note, 46 Harv.L.R. 993.

so that upon the predecease of a devisee who was also the heir, the devise is considered a nullity and therefore the anti-lapse statute is inapplicable and cannot substitute the devisee's heirs.[28]

One of the most difficult problems is whether the anti-lapse statutes should apply to class gifts. The English,[29] and a minority of American authorities,[30] hold that this legislation has no application to class gifts. As a matter of logic this view is supported by the argument that, since the class is determined at the time of testator's death or at some subsequent period, there is no gift to persons who do not survive. However, this position sometimes reaches unjust and even absurd results.[31] A few statutes specifically provide that the rule covers class gifts.[32] Even in absence of such express provision, most American courts hold that the statute ordinarily applies to class gifts.[33] In other words

[28] Estate of Warren, 211 Iowa 940, 234 N.W. 835, 1931, noted, 16 Ia.L.R. 559. Cf. In re Finch's Estate, 239 Iowa 1069, 32 N.W.2d 819, 3 A.L.R.2d 1403, 1948; Beem v. Beem, 241 Iowa 247, 41 N.W.2d 107, 1950. Contra: McNeilly v. Wylie, 389 Ill. 391, 59 N.E.2d 811, 1945.

[29] Olney v. Bates, 3 Drew. 319, 61 Eng.Rep. 925, 1855; Re Harvey, [1893] 1 Ch. 567.

[30] Johns v. Citizens & Southern Nat. Bank, 206 Ga. 313, 57 S.E.2d 182, 1950; Stahl v. Emery, 147 Md. 123, 127 A. 760, 1925; Trenton Trust & Safe Deposit Co. v. Sibbits, 62 N.J.Eq. 131, 49 A. 530, 1901; Lacy v. Murdock, 147 Neb. 242, 22 N.W.2d 713, 1946.

[31] "Where, under the statute, a testator says 'my child' is taken to mean 'my child or his issue, if any, should he not survive me,' it becomes illogical and almost ridiculous to assume that under the same statute a testator who says 'my children' means 'only such of my children as shall survive me.' One of the anomalies of the English view is that even if all the members of the class die, leaving issue, the statute does not operate and there is a complete lapse." Mechem, supra note 12 at 16, 17.

[32] So in Kentucky, Maryland, Pennsylvania, Tennessee, Virginia and West Virginia. Bordwell, supra note 11 at 429, 430.

[33] Clifford v. Cronin, 97 Conn. 434, 117 A. 489, 1922; Rudolph v. Rudolph, 207 Ill. 266, 69 N.E. 834, 99 Am.St.Rep. 211, 1904; Howland v. Slade, 155 Mass. 415, 29 N.E. 631, 1892; Snow v. Ferril, 320 Mo. 543, 8 S.W.2d 1008, 1928; In re Mott's Estate, 137 Misc. 99, 244 N.Y.S. 187, 1930, noted, 44 Harv.L.R. 301; Gale v. Keyes, 45 Ohio App. 61, 186 N.E. 755, 1933; Williams v. Knight, 18 R.I. 333, 27 A. 210, 1893; Burch v. McMillin, 15 S.W.2d 86, Tex.Civ.App.1929. See Cooley, "Lapse Statutes" and Their Effect on Gifts to Class, 22 Va.L.R. 373, wherein, after a detailed consideration of the cases and a technical discussion of the statutes, it is concluded that the class gift should go to the surviving members of the group unless the lapse statute can achieve more beneficial results by giving the share to the issue of a predeceased member. See also Casner, Class Gifts—Effect of Failure of Class Members to Sur-

the anti-lapse statutes modify the concept of the class gift. However, the courts generally refuse to apply the statute in case of members of the class who were dead at the time of the execution of the will.[34]

Under the English act a gift which would lapse but for the statute goes to the estate of the original legatee and hence passes according to his will,[35] and is subject to his debts.[36] Most American statutes provide that the legacy passes to the substituted beneficiary or that the latter takes.[37] Hence the gift does not pass by the original legatee's will,[38] and is not subject to debts other than those of the testator.[39] Our courts are not uniform as to whether debts owing the testator by the original beneficiary may be deducted before payment to those who take in his place. The strict view is that they cannot, upon the theory that the gift is substitutional and direct from the testator, rather than derivative through the original legatee.[40] There is also strong authority to the contrary.[41] The analogy of advancements as well as the justice of the situation present good arguments for the latter position.[42]

vive the Testator, 60 Harv.L.R. 373; Restatement, Property § 298; notes, 22 So.Cal.L.R. 511, 13 U. of Detroit L.J. 140; 27 Cal.L.R. 579.

34 White v. Massachusetts Inst. of Technology, 171 Mass. 84, 50 N.E. 512, 1898; Pimel v. Betjemann, 183 N.Y. 194, 76 N.E. 157, 2 L.R.A.,N.S., 580, 5 Ann.Cas. 239, 1905; Almy v. Jones, 17 R.I. 265, 21 A. 616, 12 L.R.A. 414, 1891; In re Hutton's Estate, 106 Wash. 578, 180 P. 882, 3 A.L.R. 1673, 1919. Contra: Kehl v. Taylor, 275 Ill. 346, 114 N.E. 125, Ann.Cas. 1918D, 948, 1916; Zombro v. Moffett, 329 Mo. 137, 44 S.W.2d 149, 1931. Cf. Downing v. Nicholson, 115 Iowa 493, 88 N.W. 1064, 91 Am.St.Rep. 175, 1902 (testator's intent governs); Restatement, Property § 298b.

35 Mason's Will, 34 Beav. 494, 55 Eng.Rep. 726, 1865.

36 In re Pearson, [1920] 1 Ch. 247 (original legatee died insolvent).

37 See Bordwell, supra note 11, at 431, 432.

38 Halsey v. Convention of Protestant Episcopal Church, 75 Md. 275, 23 A. 781, 1892.

39 Wallace v. Du Bois, 65 Md. 153, 4 A. 402, 1885; Suydam v. Voorhees, 58 N.J.Eq. 157, 43 A. 4, 1899.

40 Hay v. Boling, 162 Ill.App. 55, 1911; Courtenay v. Courtenay, 138 Md. 204, 113 A. 717, 1921; Wattenbarger v. Payne, 162 Mo.App. 434, 145 S.W. 148, 1912.

41 Loehr v. Rueschenberg, 213 Iowa 639, 239 N.W. 529, 1931, noted, 32 Col.L.R. 541; Tilton v. Tilton, 196 Mass. 562, 82 N.E. 704, 1907; Baker v. Carpenter, 69 Ohio St. 15, 68 N.E. 577, 1903. See notes, 23 Minn.L.R. 398, 25 Va.L.R. 108; infra § 141.

42 See Mechem, supra note 12 at 22, 23.

*Effect of Lapse*

Anti-lapse legislation does not take care of all cases of lapse; hence, it remains to be seen what becomes of the ineffective legacies and devises not saved by statute. It is clear that a lapsed general or specific legacy passes to the general residuary legatees.[43] If, however, there is no residuary clause,[44] or the clause is not broad enough so as to fairly cover the subject-matter, the latter becomes intestate property.[45]

When the sole residuary legatee dies before the testator's death, the residue clearly becomes intestate property unless it is saved by the anti-lapse statute according to principles already noticed. If one of several residuary legatees predeceased the testator and the statute does not save the legacy, the orthodox view is that his portion becomes intestate property and does not go to the surviving residuary legatees.[46] It is commonly said that this is because there can be no residue of a residue, or, in other words, the residuary clause cannot "catch" property itself included in the residue. Some of the cases following this view do so reluctantly.[47] The law is changed in part at least by statute in a few jurisdictions.[48] Certain recent decisions that lapsed residuary

43 In re Boyle's Estate, supra note 4; English v. Cooper, 183 Ill. 203, 55 N.E. 687, 1899; In re Batchelder, 147 Mass. 465, 18 N.E. 225, 1888; Clark v. Mack, 161 Mich. 545, 126 N.W. 632, 28 L.R.A.,N.S., 479, 1910; Schoen v. Siegmund, 119 N.J.Eq. 524, 183 A. 292, 1936; Carter v. Board of Education of Presbyterian Church, 144 N.Y. 621, 39 N.E. 628, 1895; In re Powell's Estate, 138 Pa. 322, 22 A. 92, 1890; Rymer v. Stanfield, [1895] 1 Ch. 19.

44 Bill v. Payne, 62 Conn. 140, 25 A. 354, 1892; Magnuson v. Magnuson, 197 Ill. 496, 64 N.E. 371, 1902; Clark v. Cammann, 160 N.Y. 315, 54 N.E. 709, 1899.

45 Williams v. McKeand, 119 Mich. 507, 78 N.W. 553, 75 Am.St.Rep. 420, 1899; In re Kimball's Will, 20 R.I. 619, 40 A. 847, 1898. See annotation, 28 A.L.R. 1237.

46 Estate of Kelleher, 205 Cal. 757, 272 P. 1060, 1928 (residuum to two executors one of whom predeceased testator); In re Boyle's Estate, supra note 4; Lehr v. Switzer, 213 Iowa 658, 239 N.W. 564, noted, 17 Ia.L.R. 534, 1931 (renunciation by one of several residuary legatees); McLeod v. Andrews, 303 Ky. 46, 196 S.W.2d 473, 1946; Worcester Trust Co. v. Turner, 210 Mass. 115, 96 N.E. 132, 1911; Torre v. Chestnut, 159 S.C. 282, 156 S.E. 906, 74 A.L.R. 540, 1931; Ellet v. McCord, 41 S.W.2d 110, Tex.Civ.App.1931, noted, 18 Va. L.R. 333; Bagwell v. Dry, 1 P.Wms. 700, 24 Eng.Rep. 577 (1721). See annotations, 28 A.L.R. 1237, 139 id. 868; notes, 50 Harv.L.R. 366, 21 Miss.L.J. 423.

47 Aitken v. Sharp, 93 N.J.Eq. 336, 115 A. 912, 1922; Wright v. Wright, 225 N.Y. 329, 122 N.E. 213, 1919; In re Gray's Estate, 147 Pa. 67, 23 A. 205, 1892; In re Dunster, [1909] 1 Ch. 103. See Sands v. Ross, 89 N.E.2d 99, Ohio Prob.1949.

48 Ohio Gen. Code, § 10504–73; In re Verner's Estate, 358 Pa. 280, 56

portions go to the remaining residuary legatees have incited favorable comment.[49] While relatively few states take this position it has the obvious merit of observing the average testator's desires as manifested by his residuary clause which purports to pass his entire estate. Of course if the residuary legatees are joint tenants there is no lapse. The same is true when they are members of a class, for the interest of the predeceased member either passes under the anti-lapse statute, or the class gift is divided among the surviving members of the class.

*Lapsed Devises*

At common law the subject-matter of a lapsed devise of land did not pass into the residuum but became intestate property.[50] This was due to the fact that, as to devises, the residuary clause was deemed to speak as of the time of execution and not as of the time of death. In England and a number of our states, statutes now specifically provide that lapsed or void devises should be included in the residuary devise.[51] Even in absence of statutes of this type, it is generally held that, since after-acquired lands may now pass under a will, a lapsed devise will fall into the residuum.[52]

A.2d 667, 1948; Davis v. Crandall, 53 R.I. 33, 163 A. 227, 1932; note, 34 Va.L.R. 722.

49 Corbett v. Skaggs, supra note 7; Hedges v. Payne, 85 Ind.App. 394, 154 N.E. 293, 1926, noted 23 Ill.L.R. 300. And see Commerce Nat. Bank of Toledo v. Browning, 158 Ohio St. 54, 107 N.E.2d 120, 1952; In re Zimmermann's Estate, 122 Neb. 812, 241 N.W. 553, 1932, noted, 31 Mich.L.R. 585, 10 N.Y.U.L.Q.R. 97, 18 Va.L.R. 915. See also Snellings v. Downer, 193 Ga. 340, 18 S.E.2d 531, 139 A.L.R. 860, 1942; In re Clonney's Will, 189 Misc. 542, 71 N.Y.S.2d 587; In re Nielsen's Will, 256 Wis. 521, 41 N.W.2d 369, 1950.

50 Cox v. Harris, 17 Md. 23, 1860; Wright v. Hall, Fort. 182, 92 Eng.Rep. 810, 1736.

51 See Bordwell, Statute Law of Wills, 14 Ia.L.R. 187–190. And see note, 7 Minn.L.R. 392.

52 Galloway v. Darby, 105 Ark. 558, 151 S.W. 1014, 44 L.R.A.,N.S., 782, Ann.Cas.1914D, 712, 1912; Holbrook v. McCleary, 79 Ind. 167, 1881; Molineaux v. Raynolds, 55 N.J.Eq. 187, 36 A. 276, 1896; Cruikshank v. Home for the Friendless, 113 N.Y. 337, 21 N.E. 64, 4 L.R.A. 140, 1889. See Lee, The Devolution of Void and Lapsed Devises, 25 Col.L.R. 447; note, 19 Cal.L.R. 213. But see Rizer v. Perry, 58 Md. 112, 1881; Chrismer v. Allman, 302 Ky. 144, 194 S.W.2d 175, 1946 (statute). And see Bittner v. Bittner, 27 S.W.2d 852, Tex.Civ App. 1930, noted, 9 Tex.L.R. 265.

*Void Devises and Legacies*

A void legacy passes under the general residuary clause,[53] unless the invalid provision is itself a residuary bequest in which case the subject-matter generally becomes intestate property.[54] A special or restricted residuary clause may be so worded as not to include void bequests, so that the subject-matter is treated as intestate property.[55] At common law most of the cases held that a void devise, like one which lapsed, did not fall into the residuum but became intestate property.[56] The minority, though it would seem the more logical, view was that as nothing could ever have passed by the void devise, the subject-matter in effect went at once into the residuum; hence there was no violation of the spirit of the rule that wills of land speak as of the time of execution.[57] At present, under statutes permitting after-acquired land to be devised by will, the subject-matter of a void devise generally passes under an ordinary residuary clause.[58]

[53] Bridgeport Trust Co. v. Parker, 97 Conn. 245, 116 A. 182, 1922, noted, 6 Minn.L.R. 532; Crerar v. Williams, 145 Ill. 625, 34 N.E. 467, 21 L.R.A. 454, 1893; Dexter v. President, etc., of Harvard College, 176 Mass. 192, 57 N.E. 371, 1900; Milwaukee Protestant Home for the Aged v. Becher, 87 Wis. 409, 58 N.W. 774, 1894. See also Beardsley v. Merry, 136 Conn. 573, 72 A.2d 829, 1950.

[54] Powers v. Codwise, 172 Mass. 425, 52 N.E. 525, 1898; Booth v. Baptist Church of Christ, 126 N.Y. 215, 28 N.E. 238, 1891. See Davis v. Davis, 208 S.C. 182, 37 S.E.2d 530, 1946, and supra notes 46–49.

[55] Schumaker v. Grammer, 200 Ill. 48, 65 N.E. 722, 1902; Davis v. Davis, 62 Ohio St. 411, 57 N.E. 317, 78 Am.St.Rep. 725, 1900.

[56] Tongue's Lessee v. Nutwell, 13 Md. 415, 1858; Kelly v. Nichols, 18 R.I. 62, 25 A. 840, 19 L.R.A. 413, 1892; Stonestreet v. Doyle, 75 Va. 356, 40 Am.Rep. 731, 1881.

[57] Ferguson v. Hedges, 1 Har.(Del.) 524, 1835; Doe v. Underdown, Willes, 293, 125 Eng.Rep. 1179, 1741.

[58] Galloway v. Darby, 105 Ark. 558, 151 S.W. 1014, 44 L.R.A.,N.S., 782, Ann.Cas.1914D, 712, 1912; Kirkpatrick v. Kirkpatrick, 112 Kan. 314, 211 P. 146, 1922, noted, 7 Minn.L.R. 392; Milwaukee Protestant Home for the Aged v. Becher, supra note 53. And see statutes supra note 51. See generally Lee, The Devolution of Void and Lapsed Devises, 25 Col.L.R. 447. Contra: Bridgeport Trust Co. v. Parker, supra note 53.

## RETAINER FOR DEBTS OF BENEFICIARIES

**141. It is the privilege and the duty of the personal representative to retain from the distributive shares and pecuniary legacies for debts owing to the estate by the recipients, and in most states even though the claim is barred by the Statute of Limitations or is discharged in bankruptcy.**

**Some courts deny retainer in the case of land passing by descent or devise, although others in effect charge the land with a lien for the debts of heirs or devisees to their decedent.**

As here used,[1] retainer is the privilege of the personal representative in his official capacity to hold back a sufficient amount of the legacies or distributive shares to satisfy the debts which the legatees or distributees owe to the decedent's estate. Moreover, it is his duty to do so to the extent that the law permits. While the courts sometimes speak of retainer as in the nature of a set-off,[2] the doctrine should be put upon a broader basis,[3] analogous to the principle of equality secured by application of the law of advancements.[4] Otherwise difficulty will be encountered in reaching specific legacies or interests in land for satisfaction of the beneficiaries' debts to the decedent.[5]

### *Testamentary Directions for Deduction of Debts*

When a testator provides that debts owing by the beneficiaries shall be deducted from the property passing to them by the will, the question presented is essentially one of construction of the instrument and not that of the general law of retainer. It is clear that the testator may provide for the deduction of a barred debt.[6] The beneficiary is not permitted to question the validity

1 "Retainer" was also used to refer to the early practice whereby the personal representative applied estate funds in his hands to satisfaction of his own claims against the estate. See supra § 128, note 56 et seq.

2 Proctor v. Newhall, 17 Mass. 81, 1820; Oxsheer v. Nave, 90 Tex. 568, 40 S.W. 7, 37 L.R.A. 98, 1897.

3 Blackwood v. Blackwood, 120 Kan. 72, 242 P. 451, 1926; Webb v. Fuller, 85 Me. 443, 27 A. 346, 22 L.R.A. 177, 1893; Cherry v. Boultbee, 4 Myl. & C. 442, 41 Eng.Rep. 171, 1839. And see excellent comment, 34 Mich. L.R. 395; In re Smith's Estate, 179 Wash. 417, 38 P.2d 244, 1934; In re Jackson's Estate, 200 Wash. 116, 93 P.2d 349, 123 A.L.R. 1281, 1939 (executor's debt to be retained from his commissions).

4 In re Fussell's Estate, 129 Iowa 498, 105 N.W. 503, 1905; Stenson v. H. S. Halvorson Co., 28 N.D. 151, 147 N.W. 800, L.R.A.1915A, 1179, Ann.Cas. 1916D 1289, 1913. See supra § 129.

5 See infra notes 35–37.

6 Cummings v. Bramhall, 120 Mass. 552, 1876; Gillingham's Estate, 220

of the indebtedness which the will provides should be deducted, nor inquire into transactions between the parties prior to the execution of the will.[7] Payment subsequent to the date of the will may be shown, however.[8]

*Nature of Debt*

Independent of testamentary provision the right of retainer exists though the debt or claim did not arise until after testator's death, as loans of estate funds or sums for the purchase or rental of property from the estate,[9] or claims arising out of misapplication of assets of the estate,[10] or money paid by the estate to satisfy the beneficiaries' suretyship obligation.[11] However, the courts are divided as to whether the personal representative may retain for a debt not due at the time of distribution.[12] The fact that the indebtedness is also secured in another manner is no bar to the exercise of the privilege of retainer.[13] The doctrine has been applied where the beneficiary was one of two or more joint debtors of the estate,[14] but the debts of a husband cannot be deducted from the wife's share of the estate, unless the will so provides.[15] According to modern concepts of fiduciary powers

Pa. 353, 69 A. 809, 1908. In these jurisdictions a personal representative may not retain for a barred debt in the absence of testamentary provision. See infra note 20. See also Thompson v. McCune, 333 Mo. 758, 63 S.W.2d 41, 1933; In re Van Tassell's Will, 119 Misc. 478, 196 N.Y.S. 491, 1922 (though there was also a presumption of payment due to the lapse of twenty years); Avery Power Machinery Co. v. McAdams, 177 Ark. 518, 7 S.W.2d 770, 1928.

[7] Townsley v. Townsley, 167 Iowa 226, 149 N.W. 262, 1914; Nalle v. State Deposit & Trust Co., 120 Md. 187, 87 A. 770, 1913; Dunshee v. Dunshee, 243 Pa. 599, 90 A. 362, 1914. See supra § 59, note 2.

[8] Dunshee v. Dunshee, supra note 7.

[9] Parks v. Snyder, 126 Kan. 446, 268 P. 814, 1928; New v. New, 127 Ind. 576, 27 N.E. 154, 1890. And see Merritt v. Jenkins, 17 Fla. 593, 1880.

[10] Stanley v. United States Nat. Bank, 110 Or. 648, 224 P. 835, 1924; Small v. Usher, 77 S.C. 112, 57 S.E. 623, 1907.

[11] Harvey v. White, 46 R.I. 470, 129 A. 263, 1925; In re Monahan, 190 Iowa 578, 180 N.W. 644, 1920.

[12] Retainer allowed: Sproul's Appeal, 105 Pa. 442, 1884; Matter of Flint's Estate, 120 Misc. 230, 198 N.Y.S. 190, 1923. Contra: Hayes v. Hayes, 2 Del.Ch. 191, 73 Am.Dec. 709, 1879; Re Abrahams, 1908, 2 Ch. 69.

[13] Rice v. Bradley's Trustee, 159 Ky. 293, 166 S.W. 1013, 1914; Oxsheer v. Nave, supra note 2.

[14] Webb v. Fuller, supra note 3; Hemsley v. Hollingsworth, 119 Md. 431, 87 A. 506, 1913; Chafee v. Maker, 17 R.I. 739, 24 A. 773, 1892. But see Turner v. Turner, 1911, 1 Ch. 716 (partnership debt).

[15] Anderson v. Gregg, 44 Miss. 170, 1870; In re Braden's Estate, 122 Wash. 669, 211 P. 743, 1923. Former-

the personal representative should not retain for his own personal claim against the legatee or distributee.[16]

*Barred Debts*

There has been considerable controversy as to whether the personal representative may retain on account of a debt barred by the Statute of Limitations. Clearly the weight of authority holds that he can, the decisions usually being placed upon the ground that only the remedy and not the right is barred by the statute.[17] Behind this rationalization may lurk the idea that the privilege is somewhat in the nature of a lien which is not destroyed by the running of the statute. Additional reasons can be assigned, viz., the general equities of the situation, and in cases of testacy the probable intention of the decedent, as well as the analogy of advancements. It is somewhat doubtful whether claims barred at the time of execution of the will should be deductible,[18] though this point is seldom mentioned in the cases. In a jurisdiction which ordinarily follows the majority rule the court refused to allow the retainer where a presumption of payment existed because of a lapse of twenty years.[19] There is a general minority view that retainer cannot be exercised against a barred debt, because both right and remedy have been extinguished by the statute.[20] Even in these jurisdictions a barred

ly the contrary view was taken because the husband was entitled to his wife's personalty. McGee v. Ford, 5 Smedes & M.(Miss.) 769, 1846; Ranking v. Barnard, 5 Madd.Ch. 32, 56 Eng.Rep. 806, 1920.

16 Garner v. Garner, 84 Fla. 641, 95 So. 113, 1923; McLaughlin v. Barnes, 12 Wash. 373, 41 P. 62, 1895. Contra: Preston v. Davis' Ex'rs, 102 Va. 178, 45 S.E. 865, 1903; Hooper v. Hooper, 32 W.Va. 526, 9 S.E. 937, 1889.

17 Noble v. Tait, 140 Ala. 469, 37 So. 278, 1903; Holmes v. McPheeters, 149 Ind. 587, 49 N.E. 452, 1808; Holden v. Spier, 65 Kan. 412, 70 P. 348, 1902; In re Lindmeyer's Estate, 182 Minn. 607, 235 N.W. 377, 1931, noted, 27 Ill. L.R. 50, 30 Mich.L.R. 162, 15 Minn. L.R. 590, 80 U. of Pa.L.R. 140; Thompson v. McCune, supra note 6; In re Smith's Estate, 179 Wash. 417, 38 P.2d 244, 1934; In re Akerman, 1891, 3 Ch. 212. See notes 4 Br.R.C. 718, 28 Va.L.R. 551.

18 See In re Schaeffer's Estate, 53 Cal.App. 493, 200 P. 508, 1921, with which compare In re Clary's Estate, 253 P. 778, Cal.App.1927.

19 Sartor v. Beaty, 25 S.C. 293, 1866. Cf. In re Van Tassell's Will, supra note 6.

20 Holt v. Libby, 80 Me. 329, 14 A. 201, 1888; Allen v. Edwards, 136 Mass. 138, 1883; Greene v. Greene, 145 Miss. 87, 110 So. 218, 49 A.L.R. 565, 1926; Light's Estate, 136 Pa. 211, 20 A. 536, 537, 1890; In re Weidig's Will, 207 Wis. 107, 240 N.W. 832, 1937, noted, 31 Mich.L.R. 129, with

debt may be deducted if the testator so directs.[21]

The right of retainer may be exercised although the beneficiary's debt has been discharged in bankruptcy, regardless of whether the discharge took place in the lifetime of the decedent or thereafter.[22] However, it has been held that when the discharge was in testator's lifetime, the estate may retain only a pro rata share of the debt which the bankrupt's estate would pay.[23] The privilege of retainer may be asserted against the trustee in bankruptcy as well as against the legatee or distributee.[24]

*Against Whom Retainer May Be Asserted*

Regardless of notice, the privilege of retainer may be asserted against the beneficiary's assignee,[25] mortgagee,[26] and also general,[27] attaching,[28] and even judgment [29] creditors. By the weight of authority the personal representative may not retain against distributees taking in lieu of their predeceased ancestor who was indebted to the estate,[30] nor, as has been seen, against the pre-

which compare In re Mohr's Estate, 212 Wis. 198, 248 N.W. 143, 249 N.W. 517, 1933 (legatee's conduct held to estop him from asserting Statute of Limitations).

21 See supra note 6.

22 In re Fussell's Estate, 129 Iowa 498, 105 N.W. 503, 1905; Cucullu's Succession, 9 La.Ann. 96, 1854; Sartor v. Beaty, supra note 19; Leach v. Armstrong, 236 Mo.App. 382, 156 S.W. 2d 959, 1941, noted, 90 U. of Pa.L.R. 742. But see Parker v. Grant, 91 N.C. 338, 1884.

23 In re Orpen, 16 Ch.D. 202, 1880. And see Cherry v. Boultbee, 4 Myl. & C. 442, 41 Eng.Rep. 171, 1839.

24 Wick v. Hickey, 103 N.W. 469, Iowa 1905; Hoffman v. Armstrong, 90 Md. 123, 44 A. 1012, 1899.

25 Kinealy v. O'Reilly, 28 Ariz. 246, 236 P. 716, 1925; Stanley v. United States Nat. Bank, 110 Or. 648, 224 P. 835, 1924.

26 Traders' Nat. Bank v. Dennis' Estate, 221 S.W. 796, Mo.App.1920.

27 Armiger v. Reitz, 91 Md. 334, 46 A. 990, 1900. And see infra notes 28, 29.

28 Brown's Adm'r v. Mattingly, 91 Ky. 275, 15 S.W. 353, 1891; Sheppard's Estate, 180 Pa. 57, 36 A. 422, 1897.

29 Greenwood v. Greenwood, 178 Ga. 605, 173 S.E. 858, 1934; Blackwood v. Blackwood, 120 Kan. 72, 242 P. 451, 1926; Hornstra v. Avon State Bank, 55 S.D. 513, 226 N.W. 740, 1929. But see Bruce v. Farrar, 156 Va. 542, 158 S.E. 856, 75 A.L.R. 872, noted, 18 Va. L.R. 211, 1931.

30 Ellis v. Dumond, 259 Ill. 483, 102 N.E. 801, 1913; Barnum v. Barnum, 119 Mo. 63, 24 S.W. 780, 1893; Powers v. Morrison, 88 Tex. 133, 30 S.W. 851, 28 L.R.A. 521, 53 Am.St.Rep. 738, 1895. And see Rasor v. Rasor, 173 S.C. 365, 175 S.E. 545, 1934. Contra: Adams v. Yancy, 105 Miss. 233, 62 So. 229, 419, 47 L.R.A.,N.S, 1026, 1913; Martin v. Martin, 56 Ohio St. 333, 46 N.E. 981, 1897. See note, 55 Harv. L.R. 1013.

deceased legatee's issue who take under the anti-lapse statutes,[31] nor against an alternative legatee named by the will itself.[32]

*Property Against Which Retainer Is Proper*

There is no doubt but that the personal representative may retain against the share of a distributee of an intestate estate, or against a legatee who is given a general or residuary bequest. When a specific legacy is of money, the privilege of retainer ordinarily exists,[33] but the contrary has been held if the legacy is of a specific chattel.[34]

The few decisions on the latter point proceed on the basis that there can only be retainer where it is possible to deduct the debt. By itself this rejection of the lien theory of retainer would also prevent retainer out of intestate or devised lands; but here there are additional difficulties such as the doctrine that land passes at once to the heir or devisee, that the representative has nothing to do with land except to sell it for debts of the decedent, that the probate court lacks jurisdiction to sell land for distribution or to adjudge interests therein. For one or more of these reasons many courts have denied the right of retainer out of land,[35] but about an equal number have allowed it.[36] The latter holdings are apt to be found in states where the statutory powers of the probate court over land are extensive. The procedural and jurisdictional problems are much like those in connection with advancements.[37] Even in states which ordinarily refuse to allow

31 See supra § 140, notes 39–41.

32 Nicholson v. Serrill, 191 N.C. 96, 131 S.E. 377, 1926; Denise's Ex'rs v. Denise, 37 N.J.Eq. 163, 1883.

33 In re Gamble's Estate, 166 Cal. 253, 135 P. 970, 1916; Re Taylor, 1894, 1 Ch. 671.

34 Clarke v. Cotton, 17 N.C. 51, 1831; Re Savage, 1918, 2 Ch. 146.

35 Avery Power Machinery Co. v. McAdams, supra note 6; Meppen v. Meppen, 392 Ill. 30, 63 N.E.2d 755, 164 A.L.R. 712, 1945; Campbell v. Martin, 87 Ind. 577, 1882; Jones v. Treadwell, 169 Mass. 430, 48 N.E. 339, 1897; Broas v. Broas, 153 Mich. 310, 116 N.W. 1077, 1908; La Foy v. La Foy, 43 N.J.Eq. 206, 10 A. 266, 3 Am. St.Rep. 302, 1887; Bruce v. Farrar, supra note 29.

36 Streety v. McCurdy, 104 Ala. 493, 16 So. 686, 1894; In re Estate of Ferris, 234 Iowa 960, 14 N.W.2d 889, 1944; Loverett v. Veatch, 268 Ky. 797, 105 S.W.2d 1052, 1937; Wilson v. Chanell, 102 Kan. 793, 175 P. 95, 1 A.L.R. 987, 1918; Wright v. Green, 239 Mo. 449, 144 S.W. 437, 1912; Hornstra v. Avon State Bank, 55 S.D. 513, 226 N.W. 740, 1929. See notes, 24 Iowa L.R. 169, 22 Minn.L.R. 281. In Texas retainer is allowed against the heir— Oxsheer v. Nave, 90 Tex. 568, 40 S.W. 7, 37 L.R.A. 98, 1937—but denied against the devisee. Russell v. Adams, 299 S.W. 889, Tex.Civ.App. 1927.

37 See supra § 129, note 4.

retainer out of land, it has been permitted where the land is sold under testamentary power,[38] or where it has been sold to pay debts and money remains to which the indebted heir would otherwise be entitled.[39] In states where retainer out of land is generally denied, remedial legislation is called for, not only as a matter of convenience but also to prevent judgment creditors of the indebted heir or devisee from being preferred to the other heirs of the decedent.[40]

## ACCOUNTING

**142. American statutes require an accounting by the personal representative at stated intermediate periods and upon completion of the administration. Notice is given to the end that those interested in the estate may file objections to the account. The judicial settlement of the account is a conclusive adjudication which may be reversed or set aside only in the manner provided by law.**

The English courts of ordinary undertook to compel executors and administrators to render accounts of their administration,[1] but due to the limited powers of these courts the remedy was unsatisfactory.[2] Accounting was usually a voluntary matter, but if not forthcoming the usual practice was to proceed by bill in equity for an accounting.[3] In some American jurisdictions the equity courts still have certain concurrent jurisdiction to require an accounting.[4] Under the prevailing American statutory system the probate courts have jurisdiction, usually exclusive, over accounts of executors and administrators.[5] Unlike the common-law system where the representative did not account unless cited for this purpose, our statutes usually contemplate the filing of

[38] Koons v. Mellett, 121 Ind. 585, 23 N.E. 95, 7 L.R.A. 231, 1889.

[39] Fiscus v. Moore, 121 Ind. 547, 23 N.E. 362, 7 L.R.A. 235, 1890.

[40] See Model Probate Code § 189; American Law of Property § 14.26.

[1] Roberts v. Roberts, 2 Lee 399, 161 Eng.Rep. 383, 1757; Wainford v. Barker, 1 Ld.Raym. 232, 91 Eng.Rep. 1051, 1692.

[2] Greerside v. Benson, 3 Atk. 248, 26 Eng.Rep. 944, 1745; Brown v. Atkins, 2 Lee 1, 161 Eng.Rep. 243, 1754 (concluded by accountant's oath).

[3] Gibbons v. Dawley, 2 Chan.Cas. 198, 22 Eng.Rep. 909, 1674.

[4] See Hoffman v. Chester, 204 Ga. 296, 49 S.E.2d 760, 1948; Brown v. Fidelity Union Trust Co., 128 N.J.Eq. 197, 15 A.2d 788, 1940.

[5] Hayward v. Plant, 98 Conn. 374, 119 A. 341, 1923; In re Parker's Estate, 189 Iowa 1131, 179 N.W. 525, 1920; Loring v. Wise, 226 Mass. 231, 115 N.E. 302, 1917; Trumpler v. Royer, 95 Ohio St. 194, 115 N.E. 1018, 1917; In re Grollman's Estate, 273 Pa. 559, 117 A. 348, 1922.

intermediate accounts at stated intervals generally of six months or one year as well as a final accounting. Failure to render an account promptly subjects the personal representative to action upon his administration bond, revocation of letters, attachment, imprisonment, and loss of commissions.[6]

American statutes contemplate both a filing of the account and its allowance or settlement by the court. Partial settlements rendered on intermediate accounts generally have prima facie validity only,[7] though in some jurisdictions these are as conclusive as a final settlement.[8] If the required notice is given for the latter, it is ordinarily conclusive;[9] otherwise, none except those appearing at the settlement are bound.[10] Infants are not usually concluded unless a guardian ad litem is appointed to act in their behalf.[11] A settlement is not final as to anything which is not adjudicated.[12]

In some states the probate courts have jurisdiction to reopen final settlement under certain circumstances.[13] In others, equity

6 See Lane v. Tarver, 153 Ga. 570, 113 S.E. 452, 1922; In re Connolly's Estate, 73 Mont. 35, 235 P. 408, 1925; Woerner on Administration, § 501.

7 Holland v. Doke, 135 Ark. 372, 205 S.W. 648, 1918; Marshall v. Coleman, 187 Ill. 556, 58 N.E. 628, 1900; Glessner v. Clark, 140 Ind. 427, 39 N.E. 544, 1895; Parnham v. Weeks, 185 Iowa 455, 170 N.W. 750, 1919; McPike v. McPike, 111 Mo. 216, 20 S.W. 12, 1892; Jones v. Gilliam, 109 Tex. 552, 212 S.W. 930, 1919.

8 In re Ward's Estate, 152 Mich. 218, 116 N.W. 23, 1918 (in absence of fraud or mistake); In re Slater's Estate, 88 N.J.Eq. 296, 102 A. 384, 1917; In re Jarvis, 110 Misc. 5, 180 N.Y.S. 324, 1920.

9 Benning v. Superior Court of Sacramento County, 34 Cal.App. 296, 167 P. 291, 1917; First Trust & Savings Bank v. United States Fidelity & Guaranty Co., 156 Minn. 231, 194 N.W. 376, 1923; In re Hamilton's Estate, 351 Pa. 419, 41 A.2d 567, 1945; In re Everett's Estate, 114 Vt. 256, 44 A.2d 149, 1945.

10 Van Liew v. Barrett v. Barrett Beverage Co., 144 Mo. 509, 46 S.W. 202, 1898; Matter of Killan's Estate, 172 N.Y. 547, 65 N.E. 561, 63 L.R.A. 95, 1902; Simons v. Davenport, 66 Idaho 400, 160 P.2d 464, 1945; Crousore v. Allee, 118 Ind.App. 558, 82 N.E.2d 276, 1948; Bell v. Swift, 322 Mass. 145, 76 N.E.2d 133, 1947 (direct attack only).

11 Collins v. Collins, 140 Mass. 502, 5 N.E. 632, 1886; Butts v. Larison, 69 Okl. 150, 170 P. 500, 1918.

12 In re Ross' Estate, 179 Cal. 358, 182 P. 303, 1919; In re Enger's Estate, 225 Minn. 229, 30 N.W.2d 694, 1 A.L.R.2d 1048, 1948 (self dealing); Meade v. Vande Vorde, 139 Neb. 827, 299 N.W. 175, 137 A.L.R. 554, 1941; In re Linford's Estate, 207 P.2d 1033, Utah 1949 (concealed asset).

13 In re Mills' Estate, 158 Mich. 504, 122 N.W. 1080, 1909; In re Nelson's Estate, 26 S.D. 615, 129 N.W. 113, 1910. And see In re Hamilton's Estate, supra note 9; annotation, 132 A.L.R. 1522.

powers to set aside these decrees for fraud are vested in the probate courts.[14] The equitable right to set aside for fraud is limited, as in the case of ordinary judgments, to fraud which is collateral to the matter tried and to cases where the petitioner is not guilty of laches.[15]

*Form and Contents of the Account*

The inventory total should constitute the first item of debit of the account.[16] Other items of debit include gains in sales of personal property over the inventoried amounts, property discovered since the making of the inventory or not included therein for some other reason, interest or income collected from the assets, the proceeds of the sale of realty,[17] and any accretions to the estate's personalty. On the credit side the account shows the expenses of administration, the amounts paid for widow's allowances, losses upon the sale of personalty below their appraised value, losses due to uncollectible accounts, debts paid, legacies and distributive shares which may have been paid in whole or in part. Each item should be stated separately and specifically.[18] In addition, the account should show the balance of the money and property on hand.[19]

The foregoing is a brief description of the matters which would be included if only a single account was rendered. If there are intermediate accounts, the balance is ordinarily carried over from

[14] See Whittemore v. Coleman, 239 Ill. 450, 88 N.E. 228, 1909; In re Stafford's Estate, 146 Ohio St. 253, 65 N.E.2d 701, 1946.

[15] Bell v. Altheimer, 99 Ark. 529, 138 S.W. 993, 1911; Einstein v. Strother, 182 S.W. 122, Mo.App.1916; In re Macpherson's Estate, 260 Pa. 492, 103 A. 887, 1918. But see Candelaria v. Miera, 18 N.M. 107, 134 P. 829, 1913. Cf. Martinez v. Meyers, 167 Ala. 456, 52 So. 592, 1910. See infra § 143, notes 18–20.

[16] In re Osburn's Estate, 36 Or. 8, 58 P. 521, 1899. See supra § 115.

[17] Unless the will or a statute authorizes the personal representative to collect rents, he collects them as agent for the heirs and his fiduciary account need not include them. In re Moran's Estate, 261 Pa. 269, 104 A. 585, 1918. See also with reference to life insurance payable to a beneficiary, Stapley v. Stapley, 29 Ariz. 487, 242 P. 1005, 1926 (also no duty to include partnership account). As to duty to account for death claim, see annotation, 104 A.L.R. 181.

[18] In re Munger's Estate, 168 Iowa 372, 150 N.W. 447, Ann.Cas.1917B 213, 1915; In re Slater's Estate, 88 N.J. Eq. 296, 102 A. 384, 1917; In re Hammer, 94 Misc. 36, 158 N.Y.S. 981, 1916.

[19] In re Buck's Estate, 220 S.W. 714, Mo.App.1920; In re Dolenty's Estate, 53 Mont. 33, 161 P. 524, 1916. Cf. Estate of Bottoms, 156 Cal. 129, 103 P. 849, 1909 (not necessary in intermediate accounts).

the previous settlement, and only debits and credits occurring in the accounting period set forth.

According to the orthodox rule, a personal representative is not entitled to credit for expenses of administration, unless they have been actually paid.[20] Some liberal decisions permit the allowance to be made in advance of payment,[21] and statutes sometimes provide for judicial approval of expenses before they are paid.[22] This is a much needed rule, for if the personal representative has paid an attorney's fee which has not been allowed by the court, the representative may encounter both legal and practical difficulties in securing refund of the excess. Normally compensation of the personal representative is not fixed or payable until settlement of his final account.[23]

Usually the probate courts furnish blanks for the preparation of accounts. Receipts or vouchers of disbursements should be presented as proof that the payments have been made.[24]

*Objections to the Account*

Of course distributees or legatees may object to items of the account,[25] and so may undisputed assignees of such persons,[26] and creditors of the estate.[27] But the creditors of an heir may not,[28] nor the attorney for the administrator,[29] nor the heirs of

20 Bates v. Vary, 40 Ala. 421, 1867; In re Woods, 55 Misc. 181, 106 N.Y.S. 471, 1907.

21 In re Couts, 87 Cal. 480, 25 P. 685, 1891; Jackson v. Leech's Estate, 113 Mich. 391, 71 N.W. 846, 1897.

22 See N.Y.Surr.Ct.Act § 231a; Model Probate Code § 143b.

23 C. I. R. v. Cadwalader, 88 F.2d 274, C.C.A. 3d, 1937; In re Peterson's Estate, 12 Wash.2d 686, 123 P.2d 733, 1942. As to the amount of compensation, see Model Probate Code § 103 and comment thereto.

24 Ridgeway v. Jones, 125 Miss. 22, 87 So. 461, 1921; In re Oliver's Estate, 3 N.J.Misc. 453, 129 A. 434, 1925. Cf. In re Campbell's Estate, 98 Wash. 295, 167 P. 905, 1917 (canceled checks sufficient); In re Woods, supra note 20; Stapley v. Stapley, supra 17.

25 Hines v. Baldwin, 211 Ala. 322, 100 So. 466, 1924; In re Harrison's Estate, 103 Cal.App.2d 12, 228 P.2d 881, 1951; In re O'Neill's Estate, 266 Pa. 9, 109 A. 526, 1920. Cf. infra note 30. As to rights of non-objecting parties, see notes, 10 Brooklyn L.R. 378, 25 N.Y.U.L.R. 394.

26 In re Ross' Estate, 179 Cal. 358, 182 P. 303, 1919.

27 Taylor v. Bader, 117 Mo.App. 72, 98 S.W. 80, 1906; In re Mulligan's Estate, 60 S.D. 74, 243 N.W. 102, 1932.

28 Succession of Junqua, 123 La. 714, 49 So. 482, 1909; In re Linkins, 195 App.Div. 565, 186 N.Y.S. 904, 1921. But cf. In re Bennett's Estate, 13 Cal. 2d 354, 90 P.2d 84, 126 A.L.R. 771, 1939.

29 Ellsworth v. Struckmeyer, 27 Ariz. 484, 232 P. 56, 1924.

an estate which is hopelessly insolvent.[30] Statutes frequently require objections to the account to be in writing,[31] but in absence of legislative provision no particular form is required.[32] Exceptions should be to specific items and the court is justified in overruling a general objection to the account.[33]

## DECREE OF DISTRIBUTION

**143. Upon final settlement the probate court renders a decree finding the persons who are entitled to the remaining personalty according to the will or the intestate laws, and requiring the executor or administrator to make distribution accordingly. This order is conclusive as to the rights of the parties except for the possibility of appeal or relief for extrinsic fraud, and serves as protection to the personal representative who complies therewith. In some states the decree also adjudges the interests in decedent's lands.**

In most jurisdictions, the realty passes at once to the heirs or devisees, and no order of the court or act of the personal representative is required to vest those entitled thereto with possession and title.[1] However, the beneficiaries of the personal estate take from the personal representative.[2] Even in the case of a bequest of a specific chattel, the legatee at common law obtained neither possession nor title to the article until the executor assented to the legacy.[3] With the assent of the executor, the chattel specifically bequeathed became the property of the legatee.[4] Until assent no action at law would lie against the executor

30 In re Armstrong's Estate, 125 Cal. 603, 58 P. 183, 1890.

31 In re Marre's Estate, 127 Cal. 128, 59 P. 385, 1899 (but writing may be waived); Needham v. Needham, 34 Idaho 193, 200 P. 346, 1921; Von Hoven's Succession, 46 La.Ann. 911, 15 So. 391, 1894.

32 Ellsworth v. Struckmeyer, supra note 29; Needham v. Needham, supra note 31. But cf. In re Mills' Estate, infra note 33.

33 Russell v. Hogan, 282 Ky. 764, 140 S.W.2d 615, 1940; In re Mills' Estate, 349 Mo. 611, 162 S.W.2d 807, 1942.

1 Austin v. Austin, 147 Neb. 109, 22 N.W.2d 560, 1946; Jenks v. Liverpool & London & Globe Ins. Co., 206 Mass. 591, 92 N.E. 998, 1910; Satcher v. Grice, 53 S.C. 126, 31 S.E. 3, 1898. Cf. infra note 21.

2 In re Bauernschmidt's Estate, 97 Md. 35, 54 A. 637, 1903; Tourtelot v. Finke, 87 F. 840, 1898. See supra § 103.

3 Hayes v. Hayes, infra note 23; Strader v. Metropolitan Life Insurance Co., 128 Va. 238, 105 S.E. 74, 1928. But see Sykes v. Hughes, 182 Md. 396, 35 A.2d 132, 150 A.L.R. 87, 1943.

4 Buck v. Kelly, 108 Misc. 408, 178 N.Y.S. 676, 1919.

to recover a general legacy,[5] but equity would compel assent and order payment.[6] Equity would also require an administrator to distribute an intestate estate.[7]

*Decree of Distribution*

In some states the doctrine of assent, in form at least, still prevails.[8] However, most modern statutory systems contemplate that the executor or administrator will satisfy legacies and make distribution according to order of the probate court.[9] Such decree is not ordinarily given until it appears upon final settlement that the debts and superior charges have been paid.[10] If the representative makes distribution before that time without court authority he is personally liable to pay all lawful unsatisfied claims against the estate.[11] Some statutes permit a partial distribution upon order of the court, although they usually require the personal representative to take a refunding bond to guard against the contingency of unexpected debts or other charges which may appear later.[12] Often the representative makes voluntary payment before final settlement, but this may not be safe unless he takes a refunding bond.

The order of distribution serves the function of protecting the executor or administrator in case of payments in obedience to its terms.[13] It also acts as the procedural device by means of

5 Deeks v. Strutt, 5 T.R. 690, 101 Eng.Rep. 384, 1794.

6 Nelson's Adm'rs v. Cornwell, 52 Va.(11 Gratt.) 724, 1854.

7 Matthews v. Newby, 1 Vern. 133, 21 Eng.Rep. 955, 1682.

8 State ex rel. Franklin v. Sullivan, 176 Tenn. 107, 138 S.W.2d 435, 127 A.L.R. 1067, 1940; see also notes 3, 4 supra.

9 Hobbs v. Cunningham, 273 Mass. 529, 174 N.E. 181, 1930; Fitzpatrick v. Simonson Bros. Mfg. Co., 86 Minn. 140, 90 N.W. 378, 1902; Kenaday v. Sinnott, 179 U.S. 606, 21 S.Ct. 233, 45 L.Ed. 339, 1900. See Ladd & Brooke, Decree in Probate Proceedings Determining Heirs, Distributees & Distribution, 16 Ia.L.R. 195, 210.

10 In re Spreckels' Estate, 165 Cal. 597, 133 P. 289, 1913; Browne v. Doolittle, 151 Mass. 595, 25 N.E. 23, 1890; In re Lambie's Estate, 112 Mich. 118, 70 N.W. 442, 1897.

11 In re Craig's Estate, 101 Neb. 439, 163 N.W. 765, 1917; In re McFarlin's Estate, 267 Pa. 510, 111 A. 444, 1920. But he is not liable to creditors of the distributee. In re Bennett's Estate, 13 Cal.2d 354, 90 P.2d 84, 126 A.L.R. 771, 1939.

12 Parker v. Wilson, 98 Ark. 553, 136 S.W. 981, 1911; Chapell v. Shuec, 117 Ind. 481, 20 N.E. 417, 1889; In re Fleming's Estate, 38 Mont. 57, 98 P. 648, 1908. See note, 2 Ala.L.R. 397; infra § 144.

13 Shriver v. State, 65 Md. 278, 4 A. 679, 1886; Pierce v. Prescott, 128 Mass. 140, 1880; In re Coyne's Estate, 103 Okl. 279, 229 P. 630, 1924; Carter's Adm'r v. Skillman, 108 Va. 204, 60 S.E. 775, 1908. But a decree

which the beneficiaries may compel distribution at the proper time.[14] The latter may petition the court for the issuance of the order, and thus require the representative to pay legacies or make distribution without the necessity of an action at law or suit in equity which were formerly the only remedies.[15] The notice which the representative gives for his final settlement usually suffices also for the final decree of distribution.[16]

*Effect of Decree of Distribution*

The order of distribution finds the persons entitled to the personalty and their respective shares, following the will in case of testacy and the statute where there is no will. Upon principles of res judicata it is binding upon every one, even if the court has committed manifest error.[17] Relief against an erroneous order can be obtained only by appeal,[18] except when there has been extrinsic fraud in obtaining the order.[19] Courts are often liberal, however, in finding extrinsic fraud in order to vacate the de-

void because of insufficient notice does not protect the personal representative. Barber v. Chase, 101 Vt. 343, 143 A. 302, 1928, noted, 38 Yale L.J. 544. And see Welch v. Flory, 294 Mass. 138, 200 N.E. 900, 106 A.L.R. 813, 1936 (negligence). As to the formal discharge of the personal representative upon his compliance with the order of distribution, see Woerner on Administration §§ 570–573; Model Probate Code § 193.

[14] In re Bradford's Estate, 128 N.J. Eq. 372, 16 A.2d 268, 1940; Rondeau v. Miller, 314 Mass. 750, 51 N.E.2d 427, 1943; annotation, 134 A.L.R. 927.

[15] Packer v. Overton, 200 Iowa 620, 203 N.W. 307, 1925. Cf. Blake v. Blake, 92 W.Va. 663, 115 S.E. 794, 1923.

[16] Miller v. Pitman, 180 Cal. 540, 182 P. 50, 1919; In re Bradford's Estate, supra note 14; Crawford v. Le Fevre, 177 Okl. 508, 61 P.2d 196, 1936.

[17] Miller v. Pitman, supra note 16; In re Togneri's Estate, 296 Ill.App. 33, 15 N.E.2d 908, 1938; In re White's Estate, 256 Wis. 467, 41 N.W.2d 776, 1950; see annotation, 136 A.L.R. 1185; cf. Clark v. Capital Nat. Bank of Sacramento, 91 Cal.App.2d 865, 206 P.2d 16, 1949; Latham v. McClenny, 36 Ariz. 337, 285 P. 285, 1930. See also Ladd & Brooke, supra note 9. But see Flynn v. Stoutimore, 226 S.W. 591, Mo.App.1920. Cf. Parr v. Davison, 146 Wash. 354, 262 P. 959, 1928 (not binding as to property not owned by decedent).

[18] Lewis v. Woodrum, 76 Kan. 384, 92 P. 306, 1907; Cantillon v. Walker, 78 A.2d 785, Me.1951. Cf. Gorg v. Rutherford, 31 S.W.2d 585, Mo.App. 1930 (can set aside order during the term; thereafter there must be a showing of fraud in procuring the judgment).

[19] Sohler v. Sohler, 135 Cal. 323, 67 P. 282, 87 Am.St.Rep. 98, 1902; Hewitt v. Hewitt, 17 F.2d 716, C.C.A. 9th 1927; Miller v. Pitman, supra note 16; Pengelly v. Thomas, 151 Ohio St. 51, 84 N.E.2d 265, 1949, noted, 1 Mercer L.R. 121; In re Rice's Estate, 111 Utah 428, 182 P.2d 111, 1947; Gibson v. Gibson, 180 Or. 691, 178 P. 2d 702, 1947. See supra § 142, note 15.

cree.[20] By statute in a number of jurisdictions the order or decree of distribution adjudicates the title to realty by finding who are the heirs,[21] but the orthodox doctrine is that the order has no effect as to land.[22]

*Manner of Distribution*

A specific legacy is satisfied by delivery of the particular chattel.[23] Ordinary pecuniary legacies are payable in cash by the terms of the will.[24] Probably in absence of statute residuary legatees and distributees of an intestate estate may insist upon payment in cash. If this is true, the personal representative is under duty to convert the personal assets into money for this purpose.[25] Statutes frequently contemplate distribution in kind if this can be done equitably.[26] Sometimes the probate court is given discretion to order distribution in kind.[27] This manner of payment is always permissible if agreeable to the beneficiaries.[28]

20 Pickens v. Campbell, 98 Kan. 518, 159 P. 21, 1916. Cf. Davis v. Seavey, 95 Wash. 57, 163 P. 35, Ann.Cas.1918D 314, 1917; Pengelly v. Thomas, supra note 19; In re Gunderson's Estate, 251 Wis. 41, 27 N.W.2d 896, 1947. See note, 27 Wash.L.R. 167.

21 In re Wise's Estate, 34 Cal.2d 376, 210 P.2d 497, 1949; Thompson v. Lake Madison Chautauqua Ass'n of South Dakota, 41 S.D. 351, 170 N.W. 578, 1919; Ostlund's Estate, 57 Wash. 359, 106 P. 1116, 135 Am.St.Rep. 990, 1910; American Law of Property, § 14.43; Model Probate Code § 183, and appendix 349–350; cf. note [1948] Wis.L.R. 621.

22 Mosier v. Osborn, 284 Ill. 141, 119 N.E. 924, 1918.

23 Landis v. Eppstein, 82 Mo. 99, 1884; Hayes v. Hayes, 18 Stew.Eq.(N. J.) 461, 17 A. 634, affirmed, 47 N.J.Eq. 567, 21 A. 339, 1891.

24 See In re Jones' Estate, 314 Pa. 93, 171 A. 265, 1934; Villard v. Villard, 219 N.Y. 482, 114 N.E. 789, 1916.

25 See supra § 122, notes 29–33.

26 McClory v. Towne, 202 Ill.App. 185, 1916; Williams v. Taylor, 81 Conn. 90, 70 A. 643, 1908; Maynard v. Maynard's Adm'r, 251 Ky. 246, 64 S.W.2d 567, 91 A.L.R. 697, 1933. Often, however, such distribution is impossible or economically undesirable. Sartain v. Davis, 323 Ill. 269, 154 N.E. 101, 1926; Re Montgomery, 8 D.L.R. 699, 1912.

27 DuVall v. Faulkner, 113 Ohio St. 543, 149 N.E. 868, 1925; In re Dempster's Estate, 308 Pa. 153, 162 A. 447, 1932.

28 Cravens' Ex'r v. Cravens, 307 Ky. 83, 209 S.W.2d 827, 1948; Villard v. Villard, supra note 24.

## REFUNDING

**144. A personal representative who has overpaid legatees, distributees, or creditors may recover from them only if the deficiency of assets to provide for other creditors or beneficiaries resulted from factors unknown and unexpected at the time of the original payments. In most states a creditor can enforce his claim against the heirs, legatees, or distributees only when some circumstance prevented the operation of the nonclaim statute as a bar before closing of the estate.**

### *By Beneficiaries*

If the personal representative overpays a legatee or distributee, the former is obliged to restore the money to the estate out of his own pocket unless the payment was authorized by the court.[1] There is some conflict as to the right of the executor or administrator to recover back such sums from the beneficiary. Cases hold that he may recover against the overpaid beneficiary,[2] even if the latter has disposed of the original property,[3] and simple interest has been allowed.[4] However, recovery is permitted only if the personal representative has acted prudently, and the deficiency occurred as the result of unforeseen contingencies.[5]

1 In re Gavey's Estate, 147 Misc. 332, 263 N.Y.S. 784, 1933; In re Hawgood's Estate, 37 S.D. 565; 159 N.W. 117, 1916; Clegg v. Rowland, L.R. 3 Eq. 368, 1866.

2 Bidwell v. Beckwith, 86 Conn. 462, 85 A. 682, 1913; Clifton v. Clifton, 54 Fla. 535, 45 So. 458, 1907; Henderson v. First Trust & Savings Bank, 107 Fla. 212, 144 So. 415, 1932 (equity suit); Von Lingen v. Field, 154 Md. 638, 141 A. 390, 927, 1928 (against distributees of overpaid legatee); Liberty Title & Trust Co. v. Stevens, 115 N.J.Eq. 506, 171 A. 531, 1934; In re Strasenburgh's Estate, 148 Misc. 595, 266 N.Y.S. 634, 1933; Sprinkle v. Holton, 146 N.C. 258, 59 S.E. 680, 1907; Davis v. Davis, 8 Vin. Abr. 423 pl. 35, 1718. See generally, on this topic, Warren, Problems in Probate and Administration, 32 Harv. L.R. 315, 329; Smith, Debts and Legacies, 16 Juridical Rev. 235, 244.

3 In re Strasenburgh's Estate, supra note 2. Cf. In re Osnato's Will, 166 Misc. 618, 2 N.Y.S.2d 836, 1938.

4 Searles' Adm'r v. Gordon's Adm'r, 156 Va. 289, 157 S.E. 759, 1931; Gittins v. Steele, 1 Swanst. 199, 36 Eng. Rep. 356, 1818. Cf. Henderson v. First Trust & Savings Bank, supra note 2 (dividends accruing before demand of stock not returnable and executor cannot recover additional stock purchased through privilege attached to original shares).

5 Davis v. Newman, 2 Rob.(Va.) 664, 40 Am.Dec. 764, 1844; Orr v. Kaines, 2 Ves.Sr. 194, 28 Eng.Rep. 125, 1750; Clifton v. Clifton, 54 Fla. 535, 45 So. 458, 1907; Clark v. Truslow, 161 App. Div. 675, 146 N.Y.S. 750, 1914. And see authorities supra note 2.

By the orthodox view, payments made under mistake of law may not be recovered.[6] The failure of the personal representative to take a refunding bond in case of a partial distribution has been held to bar his recovery against the distributees.[7] Under modern statutes which provide that the personal representative shall not distribute until the nonclaim statute has run and then only under order of the court, overpayment of distributees will not occur as frequently as formerly. Furthermore, if the representative has disregarded the statute in making premature distribution, he has not acted prudently and should not be entitled to secure a refund from the overpaid beneficiaries.

*By Creditors*

The personal representative has been permitted to recover from a fully paid creditor when the remaining assets are not sufficient to satisfy other creditors.[8] Of course, such suits are subject to at least the same restrictions as in actions against overpaid legatees and distributees.[9] Probably the courts are even less favorably inclined toward such recoveries against creditors than toward actions against legatees or distributees who are mere volunteers. Moreover, overpayments of creditors are less excusable under modern probate procedure than formerly. Now creditors are not ordinarily paid until the nonclaim statute has run and the extent of the estate's liabilities for debts fully determined.[10]

*Liability of Heirs to Creditors*

After the personal representative has completed the administration and obtained his discharge, a creditor of the decedent cannot recover against him upon the claim.[11] Two reasons may

6 Northrop's Ex'rs v. Graves, 19 Conn. 548, 50 Am.Dec. 264, 1849; Harding v. Hewes, 87 N.H. 488, 179 A. 343, 1935. Cf. Prince de Bearn v. Winans, 111 Md. 434, 74 A. 626, 1909; In re Osnato's Estate, supra note 3; Moritz v. Horsman, 305 Mich. 627, 9 N.W.2d 863, 147 A.L.R. 117, 1943. See note, 25 Can.B.R. 640.

7 Montgomery's Appeal, 92 Pa. 202, 37 Am.Rep. 670, 1879. See American Bank & Trust Co. v. Douglass, 75 W. Va. 207, 83 S.E. 920, 1914. Cf. Henderson v. First Trust & Savings Bank, supra note 2. See supra § 143, note 12.

8 Wolf v. Beaird, 123 Ill. 585, 15 N.E. 161, 5 Am.St.Rep. 565, 1888; Woodruff v. H. B. Claflin Co., 198 N. Y. 470, 91 N.E. 1103, 28 L.R.A.,N.S., 440, 19 Ann.Cas. 791, 1910; Rogers v. Weaver, 5 Ohio 536, 1832. Contra: Findlay v. Trigg's Adm'r, 83 Va. 539, 3 S.E. 142, 1887.

9 See supra notes 5–7.

10 See supra § 127.

11 Zollickoffer v. Seth, 44 Md. 359, 1875. But see Parker v. Luehrmann, 126 Neb. 1, 252 N.W. 402, 1934.

be assigned for this position; first, the representative is protected by making distribution under order of the court, and in addition the claims will ordinarily be barred by the nonclaim statute. Generally, a creditor who might have asserted his claim against the executor or administrator has no remedy against heirs, devisees, legatees, or distributees after the completion of the administration of the estate.[12] Usually the nonclaim statute will have run under these circumstances and this will bar the creditor's rights against every one. However, if the nonclaim statute has not run for some reason such as the fact that the claim remained contingent during the entire course of the administration, the belated creditor may proceed against the beneficiaries of the estate to the extent that the latter have received assets.[13]

*Extent of Liability of Heirs*

The liability of the legatees and distributees to refund is not joint in most jurisdictions.[14] By the prevailing view, each is liable for the full amount of the plaintiff's claim if that much was received from the decedent's estate, and contribution from the others must be sought in a separate suit.[15] In a few states, the defendant is liable only for his proportionate share of the claim.[16] Perhaps the best view, however, is to require all beneficiaries,

12 Converse v. Nichols, 202 Mass. 270, 89 N.E. 135, 1909; Hunt v. Burns, 90 Minn. 172, 95 N.W. 1110, 1903; Beekman v. Richardson, 150 Mo. 430, 51 S.W. 689, 1899; Woods v. Ely, 7 S.D. 471, 64 N.W. 531, 1895. The nonclaim statute would also usually bar the creditor's right to sue distributees. See generally § 127; and Dabney v. Dabney, 54 Cal.App.2d 695, 129 P.2d 470, 1942, noted, 43 Col.L.R. 237, 41 Mich.L.R. 920. But in some states the nonclaim statute is merely for the protection of the personal representative. See supra § 127, note 12; cf. Fidelity Union Trust Co. v. Carter, 121 N.J.Eq. 78, 188 A. 696, 1937.

13 Baker v. Cooper, 166 Md. 1, 170 A. 556, 1934; City of Springfield v. Clement, 205 Mo.App. 114, 225 S.W. 120, 1922; Chitty v. Gillett, 46 Okl. 724, 148 P. 1048, L.R.A.1916A 1181, 1915; Clark v. Sloan, 215 Wis. 423, 254 N.W. 653, 1934. See supra § 127, note 91. But see Parker v. Luehrmann, supra note 11.

14 Rohrbaugh v. Hamblin, 57 Kan. 393, 46 P. 705, 57 Am.St.Rep. 334, 1896; Rubel v. Bushnell, 91 Ky. 251, 15 S.W. 520, 1891; South Milwaukee Co. v. Murphy, 112 Wis. 614, 88 N.W. 583, 58 L.R.A. 82, 1908. Contra: Cutright v. Stanford, 81 Ill. 240, 1876.

15 See authorities pro, supra note 14.

16 Cion v. Schupack, 102 Conn. 644, 129 A. 854, 1925; Cutright v. Stanford, supra note 14; Walker's Adm'r v. Deaver, 79 Mo. 664, 1883.

who may be served, to be joined as defendants and to decree that each solvent heir should be liable for his proportionate share of the indebtedness, in accordance with the amount of property received from the decedent.[17]

[17] Lewis v. Overby's Adm'r, 31 Grat. (Va.) 601, 1879. Cf. McClung v. Sieg, 54 W.Va. 467, 46 S.E. 210, 66 L.R.A. 884, 1903.

# CHAPTER 15

## CONSTRUCTION AND DRAFTING OF WILLS



### JURISDICTION OF COURTS

**145. A probate court has jurisdiction to make a binding construction of a will when it is necessary to interpret the instrument in the course of some step in administration procedure such as the settlement of accounts or the rendering of the decree of distribution. In absence of statute, probate courts have no further power to construe wills, but this is reserved for courts of law and equity in appropriate actions.**

*Probate Courts*

Courts of probate have jurisdiction to construe wills, whenever construction is necessarily involved in some proceeding which is within that court's function. Thus, upon probate the tribunal is obliged to pass on questions of whether the instrument is testamentary; hence if this question is raised the document must be examined for this purpose.[1] Likewise the court must often interpret a later will to ascertain whether it revokes prior wills, in order to decide whether the earlier one is entitled to probate.[2] Furthermore, probate courts are constantly called upon to construe wills in connection with questions arising on accounting or decree of distribution, for the rights of the parties must be ascertained from the will before settlements can be made or payments ordered.[3] However, probate courts pass only on such

1 In re Hughes' Estate, 140 Cal.App. 97, 35 P.2d 204, 1934; Reeves v. White, 136 Va. 443, 118 S.E. 103, 1923. Hence this matter is not open on suit to construe a probated will. Midlow v. Ray's Adm'x, 302 Ky. 471, 194 S.W. 2d 847, 1946. But the court does not determine upon probate the validity of the will's provisions. Dudley v. Gates, 124 Mich. 440, 83 N.W. 97, 86 N.W. 959, 1901; Taylor v. Hilton, 23 Okl. 354, 100 P. 537, 18 Ann.Cas. 385, 1909.

2 See Garner v. Garner, 167 Md. 423, 173 A. 386, 1934; American Law of Property §§ 14.35, 14.37, 14.42; notes, 58 L.Q.R. 27, 21 Va.L.R. 450.

3 Goad v. Montgomery, 119 Cal. 552, 51 P. 681, 63 Am.St.Rep. 145, 1898;

questions as to whom the executor must pay the funds, and do not adjudicate matters between the legatees themselves, as whether the legacy is absolute or for life only or subject to conditions.[4] When the probate court construes a will in the exercise of its ordinary powers, this construction is res judicata and conclusive except for reversal upon appeal.[5]

*Courts of Law and Equity*

In a few states, statutes give the probate courts general jurisdiction to construe wills.[6] In absence of such legislation, however, these tribunals may not entertain proceedings to construe a will except as incidental to the courts' general powers, as described in the preceding paragraph.[7] Except for the incidental or statutory constructions obtained in the probate courts, wills are usually construed by bills in equity brought for this purpose.[8] Wherever personalty is involved, an executor as a quasi trustee may bring a bill for instructions as to the execution of his trust,[9] or the legatees may seek a declaration of the trust relationship.[10] This ground of equity jurisdiction does not exist where realty is involved, and in these cases construction can generally only be had in an appropriate action at law,[11] unless there is an independ-

Bank of Saginaw v. Nason, 266 Mich. 595, 254 N.W. 217, 1934. See supra, §§ 142, 143.

4 Bramell v. Cole, 136 Mo. 201, 37 S.W. 924, 58 Am.St.Rep. 619, 1896; Northwestern Trust Co. v. Getz, 67 N.D. 15, 269 N.W. 53, 1936.

5 Goad v. Montgomery, supra note 3; Riebow v. Ensch, 220 Mich. 450, 190 N.W. 233, 1922. See annotation, 136 A.L.R. 1180; supra, § 143.

6 In re Hesse's Estate, 62 Ariz. 273, 157 P.2d 347, 1945; In re Kelly's Estate, 144 Misc. 330, 259 N.Y.S. 120, 1932; Ohio Gen.Code, § 10504–66 ("fiduciary" may ask construction). See Coster, The Equitable Jurisdiction of Surrogates' Courts in New York, 10 St. John's L.R. 199.

7 Jones v. Harsha, 225 Mich. 416, 196 N.W. 624, 1923; Skeif v. Bohall, 90 Ark. 339, 138 S.W. 461, 1911; Chadwick v. Chadwick, 6 Mont. 566, 13 P. 385, 1887; Washbon v. Cope, 144 N.Y. 287, 39 N.E. 388, 1895; Courtney v. Daniel, 124 Okl. 46, 253 P. 990, 1926.

8 See Cook, Equity Jurisdiction for the Construction of Wills, 21 Ia.L.R. 552. As to whether equity has jurisdiction to construe when the matter would be reached in normal course by the court of probate, cf. Strawn v. Trustees of Jacksonville Female Academy, 240 Ill. 111, 88 N.E. 460, 1909, with Bank of Saginaw v. Nason, 266 Mich. 595, 254 N.W. 217, 1934.

9 Parsons v. Millar, 189 Ill. 107, 59 N.E. 606, 1901; Hanscom v. Marston, 82 Me. 288, 19 A. 460, 1890.

10 Carroll v. Richardson, 87 Ala. 605, 6 So. 342, 1889; Read v. Williams, 125 N.Y. 560, 26 N.E. 730, 21 Am.St.Rep. 748, 1891 (next of kin opposing the will).

11 Strawn v. Trustees of Jacksonville Female Academy, 240 Ill. 111, 88 N.E. 460, 1909; Haugh v. Bokern, 325 Mo. 1143, 30 S.W.2d 47, 1930; Da-

ent ground of equitable jurisdiction such as partition, quieting title[12] or the administration of a trust concerning the land. There is a minority view that bills to construe wills constitute by themselves a separate branch of equity jurisdiction, and the fact that the suit is brought for construction is by itself sufficient basis for the suit.[13]

The decree rendered upon the executor's bill for instructions is really in the nature of a declaratory judgment allowed by the courts long before modern legislation on this subject.[14] Whether the general statutory declaratory judgment laws increase the power of courts to construe wills in absence of a prayer for coercive relief may be problematical.[15] However, this modern statutory procedural device is now employed frequently to obtain judicial construction of wills.[16]

*Construction by Executors and Others*

Testamentary provisions, similar to that contained in George Washington's will, that the executor or some other person shall have power to make a binding interpretation of the instrument, are usually upheld,[17] although some cases hold that the arbiter's decision may be questioned in a court,[18] and does not govern in case of an abuse of the power.[19] In any case the construction placed upon a will by the interested parties, while not conclusive, will be given consideration by the courts.[20]

vis v. Tremain, 205 N.Y. 236, 98 N.E. 383, 1912; Hart v. Darter, 107 Va. 310, 58 S.E. 590, 15 L.R.A.,N.S., 599, 13 Ann.Cas. 1, 1907. See note, 25 Ill. L.R. 78.

12 Bearss v. Corbett, 158 N.E. 299, Ind.App.1927. And see King v. King, 215 Ill. 100, 74 N.E. 89, 1905.

13 Hanna v. Prewitt, 153 Ky. 310, 155 S.W. 726, 1913; Wachovia Bank & T. Co. v. Lambeth, 213 N.C. 576, 197 S.E. 179, 117 A.L.R. 117, 1938.

14 Borchard, The Declaratory Judgment, (2d ed.) 144.

15 See Roberts v. Mosely, 100 Fla. 267, 129 So. 835, 1930, and dissenting opinion. Cf. Cook, supra note 8 at 564 et seq.

16 Cavin v. Little, 213 Ky. 482, 281 S.W. 480, 1926; Kariher's Petition, 284 Pa. 455, 131 A. 265, 1925; Miller v. Miller, 149 Tenn. 463, 261 S.W. 965, 1924; American Law Property § 14.42.

17 Wait v. Huntington, 40 Conn. 9, 1873; Nations v. Ulmer, 139 S.W.2d 352, Tex.Civ.App.1940; Moore v. Harper, 27 W.Va. 362, 1886.

18 Lydick v. Lydick, 147 Kan. 385, 76 P.2d 876, 1938.

19 Taylor v. McClave, 128 N.J.Eq. 109, 15 A.2d 213, 1940; see also Wait v. Huntington, supra note 17.

20 Pool v. Cross County Bank, 199 Ark. 144, 133 S.W.2d 19, 1939; Daly v. Rogers, 132 N.J.Eq. 200, 27 A.2d 885, 1942.

*Conflict of Laws*

A court of a state wherein devised land is situated has power to decline to follow the construction placed upon the devise by the court of another state,[21] and this power is often asserted.[22] Hence the courts do not ordinarily construe a devise of foreign land.[23] The construction placed upon a bequest of personalty by the court of the testator's domicile will be followed elsewhere,[24] though in absence of such construction, the court of the state wherein the personalty is located may take jurisdiction to construe.[25]

## CONSTRUCTION OF WILLS

**146. If possible, a will should be interpreted according to its terms viewed in the light of the general circumstances surrounding the testator in order to effectuate his intention. When the intention is not apparent from these sources, the will should be construed in accordance with the rules of construction adopted by the courts.**

**The rules of construction should be flexibly applied so as not to defeat such intention as may be manifested in the will, and in order to reach an equitable result in accordance with the policies of the law.**

After a will's external validity has been adjudged and the instrument has been admitted to probate, it is always necessary to determine what property of the testator passes, to whom, at what time, and subject to what conditions. This must be done primarily from the will itself, after consideration of the relevant objects and individuals in the physical world. No matter how clear the will may be, some one, either court or executor, must go through the process of giving meaning to the will in order that the estate should go to the proper persons in the manner outlined by the testamentary document. It cannot be said that this process

21 Clarke v. Clarke, 178 U.S. 186, 20 Sup.Ct. 873, 44 L.Ed. 1028, 1900. See supra § 94 note 20 et seq. as to what law governs.

22 Trotter v. Van Pelt, 144 Fla. 517, 198 So. 215, 131 A.L.R. 1018, 1940; McCartney v. Osburn, 118 Ill. 403, 9 N.E. 210, 1886; In re Hencke's Estate, 220 Minn. 414, 19 N.W.2d 718, 1945.

23 McNamara v. McNamara, 293 Ill. 54, 127 N.E. 130, 1920; cf. Zombro v. Moffett, 329 Mo. 137, 44 S.W.2d 149, 1931 (land in both states).

24 Smith v. Central Trust Co., 154 N.Y. 333, 48 N.E. 553, 1897.

25 United States Trust Co. v. Wood, 146 App.Div. 751, 131 N.Y.S. 427, 1912, affirmed, 205 N.Y. 564, 98 N.E. 1118; but see Gillette v. Stewart, 108 Conn. 611, 144 A. 461, 1929.

may be dispensed with simply because the job is an easy one. Of course if the will is well drawn and no unexpected intervening circumstances arise, no difficulty occurs and separate proceedings need not be brought for the construction of the instrument. Indeed, if the meaning of the will is clear, equity will refuse to entertain a suit to construe.[1]

*Strict and Liberal Construction*

As the late Albert R. Kales said, the expressions "strict" and "liberal", as applied to construction of wills, are often not much more than epithets provoked in the heat of controversy.[2] Yet there is a penumbra of meaning in the distinction. Strict construction places emphasis upon the written word, its usual and indeed its technical meaning. It stresses rules of construction and relies on decisions involving wills similar to the one in hand. Opinions taking this point of view are apt to declare that they cannot disturb the plain meaning of words [3] and that the meaning must be obtained from the four corners of the instrument.[4]

Liberal construction, on the other hand, emphasizes the element of the testator's intention, which is declared to be the polar star in the process of construction.[5] Consequently it is inclined to consider extrinsic evidence to determine the intent. It disparages the importance of rules or precedents [6] by insisting that no will has a brother, especially a twin,[7] and that we should not construe one man's nonsense by another man's nonsense.[8]

[1] Hoglan v. Moore, 219 Ala. 497, 122 So. 824, 1929; Baxter v. Baxter, 43 N.J.Eq. 82, 10 A. 814, 1887.

[2] Kales, Considerations Preliminary to the Practice of the Art of Interpreting Writings—More Especially Wills, 28 Yale L.J. 33, 49.

[3] This rule originated with Sir James Wigram. For criticism thereof, see Kales supra, note 2 at 40; Warren, Interpretation of Wills—Recent Developments, 46 Harv.L.R. 689. See supra § 60 at note 21 et seq.

[4] For the myriad of cases which so declare see American Digest System, tit. Wills § 440; 69 C.J. 59.

[5] Conlee v. Conlee, 300 Ky. 685, 190 S.W.2d 43, 1945; see West Digest System, tit. Wills § 439.

[6] Thurber v. Battey, 105 Mich. 718, 63 N.W. 995, 1895; Meeker v. Draffen, 201 N.Y. 205, 94 N.E. 626, 33 L.R.A.,N.S., 816, Ann.Cas.1912A, 930, 1911; Bennett v. Bradley, 149 Va. 746, 141 S.E. 756, 1928. Cf. Kales, Estates, Future Interests and Illegal Conditions and Restraints in Illinois, 1910, § 152.

[7] Conlee v. Conlee, supra note 5; In re King's Estate, 200 N.Y. 189, 93 N.E. 484, 34 L.R.A.,N.S., 945, 1910.

[8] Cf. Elphinstone, On the Limits of Rules of Construction, 1 L.Q.R. 466, 469; United States Trust Co. of New York v. Douglass, 143 Me. 150, 56 A.2d 633, 1948.

While it has been thought that the strict point of view is more apt to be taken in England and in the older states of this country, there are probably not two well defined camps—a court may take one approach in the first case, the other in a later controversy.[9]

Construction of the will in some phase accounts for the most important part of litigation in connection with decedents' estates. Many of the cases involving conditions, revocation by instrument, ademption, abatement, election, exoneration, and lapse are construction cases and the same is true in the field of future interests. In addition, there are many will construction problems which do not fit into any established category. It is natural that many judicial opinions should attempt to describe the technique and philosophy of construction and that the writers also should delve into the subject.[10]

*The Two Processes*

While the difference is not always recognized,[11] it is helpful to draw a distinction between interpretation and construction.[12] The former is the process of discovering the meaning or intention of the testator from permissible data. Construction, in its narrow sense,[13] consists of assigning meaning to the instrument

9 For a statistical appraisal, see Cahn, Testamentary Construction: The Psychological Approach, 29 Geo. L.J. 17, 27; see also Kales supra, note 2 at 50. Cf. Brown, Problems of Construction, 79 U. of Pa.L.R. 385, 389.

10 See supra notes 2, 3, 8, 9 and infra notes 11, 12. For more general discussions, see Chafee, The Disorderly Conduct of Words, 41 Col.L.R. 381; Schiller, Roman Interpretatio and Anglo-American Interpretation and Construction, 27 Va.L.R. 733.

11 See Restatement, Property § 241; Powell, Construction of Written Instruments, 14 Ind.L.J. 199, 202; Simes, Future Interests §§ 75, 76.

12 The distinction between interpretation and construction has been recognized in Woerner on Administration, pp. 1370, 1371, citing Lieber's Hermeneutics, c. I, § VIII, and c. III, § II; Cahn supra note 9; Schiller supra note 10. See also Heilman, Interpretation and Construction of Wills of Immovables in Conflict of Laws Cases Involving "Election," 25 Ill.L.R. 778; Cf. In re Wittner's Estate, 301 N.Y. 461, 95 N.E.2d 798, 1950; Holmes, The Theory of Interpretation, 12 Harv.L.R. 417; Thompson, Construction of Wills, 1928, § 2. And see Pound, Spurious Interpretation, 7 Col.L.R. 378, 381, 382, dealing with the interpretation of statutes. It is possible that text-writers on particular subjects do not in general make the distinction because they are principally interested in only one of the two processes. Thus, it would seem that writers on future interests are mainly dealing with problems of construction, while evidence is more largely concerned with interpretation.

13 Because of our word poverty, "construction" must sometimes include interpretation. However, the

when the testator's intention cannot be fully ascertained from proper sources. If interpretation answers all questions relative to disposition of the testator's property, there is no need of embarking upon the field of construction. In other words, construction is necessary only when interpretation fails.

*Interpretation*

This process can be best introduced by considering the sources of information available therein. Of course the principal source is the will itself; this is axiomatic. What else may be considered? The security of the executed will would be very largely overthrown if we admitted all sorts of evidence to contradict or supplement the instrument. On the other hand, it is practically agreed that the court is permitted to consider the circumstances surrounding the testator at the time of execution of the will to determine his meaning.[14] However strong the argument for an objective standard in case of contracts, the words of a will should be given the meaning that the testator gives them as distinguished from the usual or dictionary meaning. A court can never be confident as to testator's probable meaning unless it puts itself into the testator's armchair so as to see what he knew, liked, disliked and how he talked and wrote about the matters connected with his disposition. However, direct declarations of the testator's intent are not ordinarily admitted,[15] although even these are admissible to resolve an equivocation.[16]

latter is herein used solely to describe the process of determining the testator's actual intent.

14 Prall v. Prall, 204 Ark. 1074, 116 S.W.2d 1028, 1943; Waugh v. Poiron, 315 Ill.App. 78, 42 N.E.2d 138, 1942; Magill v. Magill, 317 Mass. 89, 56 N.E.2d 892, 154 A.L.R. 1406, 1944; Obetz v. Boatmen's Nat. Bank of St. Louis, 361 Mo. 221, 234 S.W.2d 618, 1950. And see In re Smith's Will, 254 N.Y. 283, 172 N.E. 499, 72 A.L.R. 867, 1930, noted, 79 U. of Pa.L.R. 241; Freifield, Factors in the Interpretation of Unambiguous Testamentary Dispositions, 8 U. of Cin.L.R. 174, Wigmore on Evidence § 2470; annotations, 94 A.L.R. 26, 215; 21 A.L.R. 2d 319. See also supra § 83, note 11.

15 Equitable Trust Co. v. Causey, 24 Del.Ch. 259, 9 A.2d 714, 1939; Calder v. Bryant, 282 Mass. 231, 184 N.E. 440, 94 A.L.R. 18, 1933; Raines v. Osborne, 184 N.C. 599, 114 S.E. 849, 1922; Miller v. Smith, 179 Or. 214, 170 P.2d 583, 1946. But see Shoemaker's Ex'r v. Consorti, 305 Ky. 866, 205 S.W.2d 697, 1947. See 9 Wigmore on Evidence § 2471; Restatement, Property § 242j; supra, § 60, note 12. Cf. re Lummis, 101 Misc. 258, 166 N.Y.S. 936, 1917, admitting declarations as to testator's likes and dislikes; Jones v. Holloway, 183 Md. 40, 36 A.2d 551, 152 A.L.R. 933, 1944. As to the admissibility of prior wills, see Orcutt v. Hoyt, 8 N.J.Super. 429, 73 A.2d 80, 1950; note, 46 Mich.L.R. 583.

16 Achelis v. Musgrove, 212 Ala. 47, 101 So. 670, 1924; In re Witwer's Estate, 253 Wis. 536, 34 N.W.2d 671, 1948; see supra § 60, notes 29, 30 and cf. § 60, notes 12, 20, 23, 26, 27; Wig-

Two qualifications must be noted at this point. If the testator employed a draftsman skilled in the use of technical words these must be given their technical meaning.[17] It is practically necessary that the testator's intent should be identified with that of the agent whom he employed to express the intent. Furthermore, to the extent that either a statute or established rule of decision attributes a certain meaning to particular words, that meaning must be accepted. Courts have so held despite clear indications that the testator's actual intention was otherwise,[18] although in absence of positive rule of law there is no excuse for refusing to give effect to the testator's intent when this appears from permissible sources.[19]

In determining the testator's intent, the whole instrument should be considered and effect given to all its parts if possible.[20] A will and a codicil should be interpreted together.[21] Where the general intent of the will is clear and it is impossible to effectuate all the language of the instrument, it is said that words expressing a special intent must yield to the general.[22] But this position is doubtful indeed if the special intent is clearly expressed. The ordinary meaning of non-technical language should prevail,[23] except when it appears that the testator has assigned

more on Evidence, §§ 2472, 2473; Warren, Interpretation of Wills—Recent Developments, 49 Harv.L.R. 689.

17 See In re Crosby's Will, 224 Minn. 173, 28 N.W.2d 175, 1947; Restatement, Property § 242e.

18 See Fox v. Snow, 6 N.J. 12, 76 A.2d 877, 1950, holding that giving of a bank account to husband with free power of disposition could not be cut down by a provision that niece was to have any money in the account at the husband's death. But see N.J.Laws 1951, c. 825; In re Keefer's Estate, 353 Pa. 281, 45 A.2d 31, 165 A.L.R. 1277, 1946; Smith v. Smith, 62 S.E. 2d 347, W.Va.1950.

19 See 1950 Annual Surv.Am.L. 694–695; 26 N.Y.U.L.R. 972.

20 Richmond v. Bass, 202 Miss. 386, 32 So.2d 136, 1947; Shearin v. Allen, 133 N.J.L. 276, 44 A.2d 210, 1945; In re Holland's Estate, 180 Or. 1, 175 P. 2d 156, 1946.

21 In re Thomas' Estate, 220 Iowa 50, 261 N.W. 622, 1935; Adams v. Legroo, 111 Me. 302, 89 A. 63, 1913; Ward v. Ward, 105 N.Y. 68, 11 N.E. 373, 1887.

22 Phelps v. Bates, 54 Conn. 11, 5 A. 301, 1 Am.St.Rep. 92, 1886; Brown v. Tuschoff, 235 Mo. 449, 138 S.W. 497, 1911; Aldrich v. Aldrich, 40 R.I. 324, 100 A. 882, 1917; Hill's Adm'rs v. Hill, 127 Va. 341, 103 S.E. 605, 1920. But see Rogers v. English, 130 Conn. 332, 33 A.2d 540, 147 A.L.R. 812, 1943; Dobson v. Smith, 213 S.C. 15, 48 S.E.2d 607, 1948, noted, 28 Tex.L.R. 123; Burney v. Burney, 145 Tex. 311, 197 S.W.2d 334, 1946.

23 In re Syverson's Estate, 239 Iowa 800, 32 N.W.2d 799, 1948 ("home farm"); Watterson v. Thompson, 404 Ill. 515, 89 N.E.2d 381, 14 A.L.R. 1239, 1950 ("children"); Lynn v. Strickler,

some unusual meaning thereto.[24] A will written by a layman ought to be interpreted as it would be understood by laymen in the circumstances.[25] When words are used in one part of a will in a certain sense, prima facie the same meaning is attributed to them in other portions of the instrument.[26] To effectuate a manifest intent a will may be read as if words were rejected,[27] supplied,[28] changed,[29] or transposed.[30] The court has thus certain power to rectify mistakes in the language adopted by the testator.[31] However, this power must be confined to those cases wherein the court is convinced from admissible data that there was a mistake and what was actually intended. Finally if the will gives rise to a necessary implication that a gift was intended,

213 S.W.2d 672, Mo.App. 1948 ("chattels"); Schaffer v. Oldak, 12 N.J. Super. 80, 78 A.2d 842, 1951 (end of war); Christ's Home v. Mattson, 140 N.J.Eq. 443, 55 A.2d 14, 173 A.L.R. 651, 1947 ("money"); In re Siemens' Estate, 346 Pa. 610, 31 A.2d 280, 153 A.L.R. 483, 1943 ("S.P.C.A."). As to contrasting meaning of "between" and "among", see Lefeavre v. Pennington, 217 Ark. 397, 230 S.W.2d 46, 1950; In re Moore's Estate, 157 Pa.Super. 296, 43 A.2d 359, 1945.

24 Briant v. Garrison, 150 Mo. 655, 52 S.W. 361, 1889; Kello v. Kello's Ex'rs, 127 Va. 368, 103 S.E. 633, 11 A.L.R. 322, 1920; In re Ehlers' Will, 155 Wis. 46, 143 N.W. 1050, 1913. See supra § 60.

25 In re MacPherson's Estate, 87 Cal.App.2d 1, 195 P.2d 807, 1948; Stockton v. State Bank of Rensselaer, 121 Ind.App. 7, 96 N.E.2d 910, 1951; Industrial Trust Co. v. Saunders, 71 R.I. 94, 42 A.2d 492, 1945 ("money"); Gilkey v. Chambers, 146 Tex. 355, 207 S.W.2d 70, 1948 ("personal property"); In re Hall's Will, 114 Vt. 400, 45 A.2d 574, 1946. See notes, 12 Fordham L.R. 202; 63 L.Q.R. 148, 64 id. 172, 183; 67 id. 161. Cf. supra note 17.

26 Bridgeport Trust Co. v. Parker, 97 Conn. 245, 116 A. 182, 1922; Stevenson v. Stevenson, 297 Ill. 338, 130 N.E. 771, 1921; Leighton v. Leighton, 193 Iowa 1299, 188 N.W. 922, 1922; Carr v. Smith, 25 App.Div. 214, 49 N.Y.S. 351, 1898; Carroll v. Herring, 180 N.C. 369, 104 S.E. 892, 1920.

27 In re Vismar's Estate, 117 Misc. 554, 191 N.Y.S. 752, 1921; In re Mills' Estate, 195 Misc. 104, 89 N.Y.S.2d 201, 1949 ("and/or"); Mason v. Willis, 326 Ill.App. 481, 62 N.E.2d 135, 1945.

28 Desmarteau v. Fortin, 326 Ill. 608, 158 N.E. 444, 1927, noted, 22 Ill. L.R. 761; In re Holland's Estate, 180 Or. 1, 175 P.2d 156, 1946.

29 In re Snell's Will, 154 Kan. 654, 121 P.2d 200, 1942 ("and" for "or"); In re Armstrong's Will, 63 N.Y.S.2d 255, 1946 ("prior" for "subsequent"); Williams v. Fundingsland, 74 Colo. 315, 221 P. 1084, 63 A.L.R. 77, 1923 ("widow" for "wife"). Cf. In re Lewis' Estate, 39 Nev. 445, 159 P. 961, 4 A.L.R. 241, 1916 ("devise"). See note, 66 L.Q.R. 24.

30 Renwick v. Macomber, 225 Mass. 380, 114 N.E. 720, 1917; Biles v. Biles, 281 Pa. 565, 127 A. 235, 1924. But see Watkins v. Bennett, 170 Ky. 464, 186 S.W. 182, 1916; Smith v. Ledsome, 95 W.Va. 429, 121 S.E. 484, 1924.

31 See supra § 60.

this intention will be effectuated although no gift was bestowed in express terms.[32] All these are reasonable manifestations of the process of interpretation, or ascertainment of the testator's intention.

When the intention fairly appears there is no need for attention to prior decisions or for the application of rules of construction. On the other hand, the court should give effect to the discovered intent, unless some positive rules of law, such as those designed for the protection of the spouse or relating to the legality of conditions or the rule against perpetuities,[33] prevent.

*Construction*

The foregoing process of interpretation is not always possible. Very often the court cannot come to any conclusion by this method of procedure. This may be either for the reasons: (1) that the testator never had an intention that was specific enough for legal purposes, or (2) he may have expressed his desires badly or incompletely, or (3) certain unforeseen circumstances may have occurred after the execution of the instrument, so that the testator never thought of the contingency with which the court is confronted. Obviously one cannot hope to find the testator's intention when this is unascertainable from available sources, or never existed in his own mind.[34] A conceivable solution would be that the provisions of such wills should fail for indefiniteness. Some wills or parts thereof are held nugatory on this ground,[35] but the courts are reluctant to reach this result.[36]

Instead, they bring to their assistance certain rules of construction. While some courts insist that they are merely continuing the quest for the testator's intention in the application

32 Phoenix State Bank & Trust Co. v. Johnson, 132 Conn. 259, 43 A.2d 738, 1945; Goodwin v. New England Trust Co., 321 Mass. 502, 73 N.E.2d 890, 1947; Brumfield v. Englesing, 202 Miss. 62, 30 So.2d 514, 1947; In re Latz's Estate, 95 N.Y.S.2d 584, 1950. Cf. Rawls v. Hewitt, 149 Neb. 161, 30 N.W.2d 623, 1948. As to the effect of a recital that something has been done, cf. In re Burkman's Estate, 71 S.D. 648, 28 N.W.2d 839, 1947 with Layton v. Tucker, 237 Iowa 623, 23 N.W.2d 297, 1946, noted, 45 Mich. L.R. 1069.

33 But see infra note 47.

34 See Gray, The Nature and Sources of the Law, 2d ed. 175.

35 Booe v. Vinson, 104 Ark. 439, 149 S.W. 524, 1912; In re Traylor, 81 Cal. 9, 22 P. 297, 15 Am.St.Rep. 17, 1889; In re Zilke's Estate, 115 Cal. App. 63, 1 P.2d 475, 1931, noted, 27 Ill.L.R. 98; Cope v. Cope, 45 Ohio St. 464, 15 N.E. 206, 1888. See Wigmore on Evidence, §§ 2407, 2473.

36 In re Northcutt's Estate, 16 Cal. 2d 683, 107 P.2d 607, 1941; Burke v. Crawfordsville Trust Co., 103 Ind. App. 1, 2 N.E.2d 817, 1936.

of these rules,[37] it is obvious that they are obliged to go beyond the testator's intention and into the realm of assigning meaning independent of sources diverging from the testator.[38] The court cannot complete its work from the language that the testator has left; it must hence go forward with the same data, now aided by the rules of construction. In the main these rules operate like rebuttable presumptions of the law of evidence; that is, the testator may indicate by the language and tenor of his will that he does not wish them to apply.

*Rules of Construction*

Jarman sets forth twenty-four rules of construction.[39] However, some of these, such as that mere negative words are not sufficient to disinherit the heir at law,[40] are positive legal rules and amount to more than mere presumptions.[41] In addition some of Jarman's rules are probably no more than descriptions of aspects of interpretation already noted.[42]

Rules of construction in the sense used in the present work can be stated in form of presumptions. Those most commonly met are the presumptions against intestacy,[43] in favor of the spouse and heirs,[44] for a just and reasonable construction,[45] in

37 Pontius v. Conrad, 317 Ill. 241, 148 N.E. 17, 1925; Coffman's Adm'r v. Coffman, 131 Va. 456, 109 S.E. 454, 1921; Peck v. Peck, 76 Wash. 548, 137 P. 137, 1913.

38 Matter of Lummis, 101 Misc. 258, 166 N.Y.S. 936, 1917.

39 Wills 8th ed. vol. III, pp. 2068–2072.

40 Ibid., vi. See supra § 36 at note 30 et seq.

41 In re Eason's Estate, 238 Iowa 98, 26 N.W.2d 103, 1947; Burpee v. Pickard, 94 N.H. 307, 52 A.2d 286, 1947; Powers v. Powers, 75 R.I. 461, 67 A.2d 837, 1949. See supra § 36, note 30. In Louisiana negative words may disinherit an heir and have the effect of disposing of the entire property to the other heirs. Allen's Succession, 49 La.Ann. 1096, 22 So. 319, 1897.

42 See supra text at notes 20–32.

43 In re Paulsen's Estate, 113 Colo. 373, 158 P.2d 186, 1945; Fass v. Blatz, 141 N.J.Eq. 32, 55 A.2d 458, 1947; Ferguson v. Ferguson, 225 N.C. 375, 35 S.E.2d 231, 1945; Petition of Maybaum, 270 App.Div. 1028, 63 N.Y.S.2d 85, 1946.

44 Luscher v. Luscher, 308 Ky. 677, 215 S.W.2d 581, 1948 (equality); Succession of Montegut, 217 La. 1023, 47 So.2d 898, 1950 (favoring same share as intestacy); In re Burke's Will, 298 N.Y. 450, 84 N.E.2d 631, 1949, noted, 48 Mich.L.R. 383 (same); Matter of Wittner, 301 N.Y. 461, 95 N.E.2d 798, 1950, noted, 2 Syracuse L.R. 376.

45 Luscher v. Luscher, supra note 44; Cross v. O'Cavanaugh, 198 Miss. 137, 21 So.2d 473, 1945.

favor of early vesting,[46] that a valid disposition is intended,[47] that the will speaks from death,[48] and that the last of two inconsistent provisions prevails.[49] This list is not exclusive; sometimes a court will in effect create a new rule of construction without so declaring.[50] Statutes sometimes enact rules of construction.[51]

Some rules of construction are based largely upon what it is thought that the typical testator would desire. Others have their basis primarily in some general policy which the law fosters. Both considerations are present in some cases, but some of the rules of construction in connection with future interests have neither, and are built upon artificial assignment of intent, or upon motivations of policy long since obsolete. Some rules of construction are thought to have more weight than others.[52] Thus, the preference of the last words of a will is said to be a rule of last resort.[53]

*Use of Rules of Construction*

In America the rules of construction are not slavishly followed,[54] though this has been regretted by some writers.[55] As

46 Fleshner v. Fleshner, 378 Ill. 536, 39 N.E.2d 9, 1942; Cramer v. Brown, 159 Kan. 423, 155 P.2d 468, 1945; see also In re Carmany's Estate, 357 Pa. 296, 53 A.2d 731, 174 A.L.R. 311, 1947.

47 Warren v. Duval, 124 Conn. 448, 200 A. 804, 1938; Goodloe's Trustee and Adm'r v. Goodloe, 292 Ky. 494, 166 S.W.2d 836, 1943; see Adams v. Simpson, 208 Mo. 168, 213 S.W.2d 908, 1948.

48 Henderson v. Henderson, 210 Ala. 73, 97 So. 353, 1923; McElroy v. Trigg, 296 Ky. 543, 177 S.W.2d 867, 151 A.L.R. 966, 1944; McComb v. McComb, 121 W.Va. 53, 200 S.E. 49, 1939. But it usually speaks of the date of execution as to specific legacies. Lansdale v. Dearing, 351 Mo. 356, 173 S.W.2d 25, 147 A.L.R. 728, 1943. So also as to identity of the beneficiary. In re Solms' Estate, 253 Pa. 293, 98 A. 596, 1916; cf. In re Hardyman [1925] 1 Ch. 287. See generally supra §§ 91, 132, 134.

49 Fraser v. Boone, 1 Hill Eq. (S.C.) 360, 27 Am.Dec. 422, 1833; cf. Weilmuenster v. Swanner, 404 Ill. 21, 87 N.E.2d 756, 1949; Kirk's Adm'rs v. Massie, 290 Ky. 960, 162 S.W.2d 783, 1942; Taylor v. Albree, 309 Mass. 248, 34 N.E.2d 601, 1941; In re Baylis' Will, 78 N.Y.S.2d 893, 1948; Frazier v. Wood, 219 Iowa 36, 255 N.W. 647, 1934.

50 See In re Upjohn's Will, 304 N.Y. 366, 107 N.E.2d 492, 1952.

51 Cal.Prob.Code §§ 102, 103. See also N.J.Laws 1952, c. 221; N.Y. Decedent Estate Law §§ 47a, 47c, 47d; In re Laughlin's Estate, 336 Pa. 529, 9 A.2d 383, 1939.

52 See Simes, Future Interests, § 77.

53 See cases cited supra note 49; Restatement Property § 246a.

54 Crapo v. Price, 190 Mass. 317, 76 N.E. 1043, 1906.

55 See Brown, Problems of Construction, 79 U. of Pa.L.R. 385. And see Gray, Nature and Sources of the

Professor Simes has said, they should be flexibly applied.[56] Indeed, it is impossible to do otherwise, for the individual rules themselves often lead to different conclusions. The rule disfavoring partial intestacy is not completely in harmony with the principle favoring the heirs at law.[57] There is no general hierarchy fixing an order of precedence for the rules of construction.[58] We have then competing principles, and there can be found in the rules of construction some plausible explanation of almost any result which it is desired to reach. As Professor Simes has also pointed out, it is often more desirable to consider the policies behind the rules than the rules themselves.[59] Precedents in similar cases cannot be strictly controlling; but they are of value, for unlike questions of pure interpretation, the courts are applying presumptions, which are rules of law.[60]

When we reach the process of construction, as distinguished from interpretation, we are usually not without some indication of testator's intention as shown by the will.[61] However, if the problem is one of true construction, the intention will be indicated incompletely or with confusion. The imperfect expression of intention should not be disregarded. Yet there is too much talk in these cases of arriving at the testator's true intention through the rules of construction. If the testator never had any relevant intention, or if this cannot be ascertained in its entirety, the process of attempting to find his intention is purely fictitious. Rather the process is the elastic application of the rules of construction to the incomplete data of the testator's intention in order to reach a fair and desirable result in accordance with the various policies behind the rules of construction.

Law, 2d ed. 175: "Now for cases in which a testator has not provided, it may be as well that there should be fixed rules, as there are for descent in cases of intestacy."

56 Law of Future Interests, 1936, § 310.

57 See In re Bresnehan's Will, 221 Wis. 51, 265 N.W. 93, 1936, noted, 84 U. of Pa.L.R. 1032.

58 Cf. notes 52, 53 supra.

59 Law of Future Interests, 1936, § 310. See In re Upjohn's Will, supra note 50.

60 Kales, Estates, Future Interests and Illegal Conditions and Restraints in Illinois, 1920, § 152. "Authority is especially valuable where the problem is one on which it is proper to assume the testator's mind never worked." And see Heilman, Interpretation and Construction of Wills of Immovables in Conflict of Laws Cases Involving "Election," 25 Ill.L.R. 778. That the rules of construction are legal is shown by the fact that they are often embodied in statute. See supra note 51.

61 It should be noticed how frequently the courts mention testator's intention in speaking of the rules of construction.

Rules of construction have a definite function when we cannot say what the testator's intention was. Application of the rules is unnecessary when the intention is discoverable without them, although it does no harm to bolster that intent by reference to the presumptions. However, a court should not put rules of construction into competition with an intent which is clearly and fully found. This would violate the primary principle of giving effect to the testator's intent.

## SUGGESTIONS REGARDING DRAFTING OF WILLS

**147. The preparation of a will calls for: (1) a sensible plan in accordance with testator's wishes and his family needs, and, in sizeable estates, due attention to the tax consequences; (2) full consideration of possible contingencies which may occur after execution of the will and which may be guarded against by apt provisions; (3) strict compliance with the rules concerning legality of the interests to be created; (4) clarity and certainty of expression.**

The drafting of a will, like the preparation of a contract or a statute, calls for both care and imagination. The testamentary instrument must not only be valid—it should be clear. One must try to detect the possible uncertainties and insufficiencies of the preliminary draft and clarify these in the final copy. Furthermore, it is not enough to anticipate the difficulties which might be encountered if the testator should die at once. He often lives for years after the execution of his will and neglects to supplant it by a later one though his situation has undergone marked alteration. While an attorney cannot guard against all future changes of conditions, much can be done in the preparation of the will to obviate the undesirable results which may come from such alterations of estate, family, and beneficiaries.

In England the art of testamentary draftsmanship has long been developed and precedents set down for almost every conceivable situation.[1] Many discussions, suggestions, and forms are available in American legal literature.[2] Some difficulties can

1 See Jarman on Wills, 8th Ed., Appendix A; Broughton, Reminders for Conveyancers, 163 L.T. 294, 316; Kales, The Will of an English Gentleman of Moderate Fortune, 19 Green Bag 214.

2 Shattuck, An Estate Planner's Handbook; Wormser, Theory and Practice of Estate Planning; Stephenson, Drafting Wills and Trust Agreements; Fingar and Bookstaver, New York Wills; Schwartzberg and Stocker, Drawing Wills (Practising Law Institute); Tweed and Parsons,

be avoided by putting in reverse the legal doctrines which may be found in the foregoing pages; in other words, undesired consequences of legal rules may often be avoided by specific testamentary provisions. Another group has to do simply with the avoidance of illegality. Still others deal with the economic and tax aspects of planning an estate. Writers and practitioners do not always seem to agree as to some matters of technique. Their apparent differences are accounted for in part because they have in mind somewhat different factual or legal situations. Quite aside from this, different considerations involved in the same problem may make its solution a debatable one. Often the choice of techniques is not a particularly vital one. The possibilities of discussion are almost limitless. Naturally only brief treatment can be indulged here.

*Interview with Testator*

If humanly possible, the draftsman should have a thorough interview with the prospective testator. A situation in which a third person communicates the provisions of the will is always unsatisfactory. If this third person is a beneficiary under the proposed instrument, or in some way interested in it, there is at least a cloud of suspicion regarding undue influence, and in some jurisdictions, a full presumption thereof.[3] In addition a conference with the client is necessary to obtain a complete knowledge of the extent and nature of the estate and the intended beneficiaries.[4] One should make certain, for example, that the prop-

Lifetime and Testamentary Estate Planning (American Law Institute); Trachtman, Estate Planning (Practising Law Institute); Leach, Planning and Drafting a Will, 27 B.U.L.R. 157; Thomas, Mechanics of Drafting a Will, [1950] U. of Ill.Law Forum, 325; Miller, Functions and Ethical Problems of the Lawyer in Drafting a Will, id. at 415; Ritchie, Drafting a Simple Will for a Moderate Sized Estate, 1952 Proceedings, Probate and Trust Law Divisions of American Bar Association 4, also printed in 91 Trusts and Estates 724; see infra note 66.

See also Gest, Practical Suggestions for Drawing Wills, 55 Am.L.Reg.(O. S.) 465; Remsen, A Plea for the Scientific Preparation of Wills, 77 Cent. L.J. 22; Remsen, The Post-Mortem Administration of Wealth, 19 Yale L. J. 36; Slater, Avoidance of Litigation with Regard to Wills, 13 A.B.A.J. 43.

3 See supra § 55. For a similar reason an attorney should refuse to prepare a will under which he is to be the recipient of anything but a most trifling remembrance. As a matter of self-interest, as well as professional ethics, the testator who is so disposed should be advised to see other counsel for the preparation of his will. See also supra § 100.

4 Check-lists or questionnaires have been formulated in order to acquire the information, including that necessary to formulate a tax plan. See infra text at note 8 et seq.

erty which the testator is about to bequeath or devise actually belongs to him and that he has power to dispose thereof. Thus, annoying questions of the necessity of an election between a beneficiary's own property which is devised to another and some other testamentary gift to the first beneficiary may be obviated.[5] Too many wills purport to devise property which testator owned jointly with another.

Deathbed wills should be avoided; this, however, is advice for testators rather than for attorneys. The latter are often called on to prepare such wills and they should not refuse to do so if the testator is competent. However, when a lawyer is required to draft such an instrument, it should be as simple as possible.

*Formal Parts of a Will*

Formerly wills usually commenced with the words "In the name of God amen." This is not customary today. A typical modern exordium reads "I, ———, of ———, declare this to be my last will, revoking all prior wills and codicils." The concluding phrase dispenses with a separate numbered provision of revocation. Words of express revocation are customary and advisable even if the instrument disposes of all of the testator's property.[6]

The recital of the testator's residence is not conclusive as to his domicile even at the time of the execution of the will, but it may have some practical effect in cases of disputed domicile. In addition, it may be relevant in connection with the validity or construction of the instrument.

Formerly the exordium often recited that the testator was of sound and disposing mind, and indeed also made declarations of the consciousness of death, etc. These are not usual today for they do no good, and conceivably may be seized upon as indicative that the draftsman considered that there might be some doubt about the matter of mental capacity.

5 See supra § 138.

6 It seems to be agreed that the old will should be removed from the testator's safe deposit box. Most writers favor its destruction by the testator; Professor Leach suggests that it first be photostated. 27 B.U.L.R. 157, 170. To the present writer the matter depends on what is most to be feared. Thus, if there may be an attempt to probate the old instrument as a lost will and the testator would prefer intestacy to the earlier will, it would seem better to preserve it after marking it well with cancellation marks, defacing the signatures and having the testator write "revoked" with his signature and the date. On the other hand if the last will is similar to the first and there is doubt as to present competency, the old will should be preserved intact so that it may be probated if the last will fails. See text infra at note 65.

An appropriate testimonium or concluding clause is "In witness whereof I have subscribed my name this ——— day of 19—," although "Witness my signature this ——— day of 19—" will do just as well. It is better to have the date appear here than at the commencement of the will. Of course every well drawn will concludes with an attestation clause.[7]

There may be variations from these suggestions, and indeed the formal parts can even be omitted. A certain degree of form has some utility, however. Quite aside from that, we are judged by appearances and the observation of usual forms is somewhat analogous to the matter of table manners.

*Tax Matters*

In days of high estate and income taxes it is well to first consider what if anything may be done to minimize these burdens in planning the disposition of the estate. Under the Revenue Act of 1948 there is no Federal estate tax if the decedent has a gross estate[8] of no more than $60,000, less funeral and administration expenses and debts. Of course there may be state estate or inheritance taxes, but in small estates these will not usually warrant much consideration about willing the property to someone else upon whom the burdens of taxation will not fall so heavily.

If the testator is married and his gross estate, less debts and expenses, is over $60,000 he will consider whether he wishes to take advantage of the federal marital deduction.[9] There is no tax on the amount given to the spouse up to a maximum of 50 percent of the gross estate after deducting debts and expenses but before deducting taxes or the $60,000 exemption. Thus, if a man has an estate of $120,000, and he leaves his wife $60,000, there is no estate tax, since the marital deduction and the $60,000 exemption together equal the entire estate. If she has no other property and dies the next day there would likewise be no federal tax on her estate since it also is entitled to the $60,000 exemption. From the tax standpoint the full marital deduction should be taken in this case. However, if the wife of this testator

7 See supra §§ 73, 74.

8 This includes, in addition to the estate passing by succession, property jointly held, revocable trusts, life insurance payable to an individual, etc. See supra § 125.

9 See Lefever, When and How To Take the Marital Deduction, 1950 Proceedings of Probate and Trust Law Divisions of the American Bar Association 4, also printed in 89 Trusts & Estates 644; Trachtman, supra note 2 at 12; Tweed & Parsons, supra note 2 at 37.

is worth $1,000,000, the total estates taxes payable on his death followed by hers may be increased if he takes the marital deduction since her estate will be in a much higher tax bracket. Her added income taxes must also be considered, and it would probably be desirable taxwise for the testator to leave all his property to his children. There are other factors to be considered, including her age, state of health, and probable expenditures in her living. Moreover, tax arithmetic is not the only matter involved in the decision of whether to take the marital deduction. If the testator feels that his wife may soon remarry, or may be imposed upon by her relatives or others, or if a closely held business is involved, the marital deduction may be a bad idea even if it will save taxes.

What the spouse receives in fee under the intestate laws or by virtue of an election to take against the will qualifies for the marital deduction as well as property given her by will. So also do interests obtained through survivorship estates, life insurance payable in a lump sum or with general power to appoint, or revocable inter vivos trusts. However, a life interest to the spouse does not qualify for the marital deduction, although a trust giving an unqualified life interest together with a general power to appoint the principal does so qualify.

At the time of this writing the marital deduction is the chief tax matter engaging the attention of estate planners. Sometimes interrelated with the marital deduction, and often quite apart from it, are the tax problems relating to jointly held property, income taxes of beneficiaries, state estate and inheritance taxes, the taxation of property passing under powers of appointment,[10] and the advisability of making inter vivos gifts to take advantage of the lower gift tax rates.[11] The best solution from the tax angle depends on many factors in the particular estate. Much has been written upon all these problems. Many of the older plans of estate disposition are still good enough for general purposes but recent legislation may have made them obsolete from the tax standpoint. In particular, the older suggestions must often be modified in the light of the marital deduction given by the Revenue Act of 1948, and the Federal Powers of Appoint-

10 See Turk, Powers of Appointment Act of 1951, 1951 Proceedings of Probate and Trust Law Divisions of the American Bar Association 52, also printed in 90 Trusts & Estates 428; Trachtman, supra note 2 at 161; Tweed & Parsons, supra note 2 at 47; Craven, Powers of Appointment Act of 1951, 65 Harv.L.R. 55.

11 See Trachtman, supra note 2 at 140; Tweed & Parsons, supra note 2 at 29; also supra § 125.

12 See supra notes 9, 11.

ment Act of 1951.[12] Taxes are important in planning an estate of any size, but it is often desirable to forego tax-saving devices, since the plans may result in loss of flexibility or other advantages.

*Apportionment of Taxes*

If there is a state inheritance tax the testator may desire to provide that the taxes on specific or pecuniary gifts should be payable out of the residue in order that the devisees or legatees will get the full interest free of tax obligation. In absence of statute federal and state estate taxes are usually payable out of the residue unless the will otherwise provides. Often the testator wishes to make a contrary provision, particularly if the specific and pecuniary gifts are substantial and the residuary beneficiaries are the chief objects of his solicitude. In a number of states there are apportionment statutes [13] providing that estate taxes are apportioned pro rata according to the benefits received by all beneficiaries after giving due allowance for any exemptions granted such as those in favor of charities, the spouse, or other relatives. These statutes permit the will to make a contrary provision, and in some cases testator desires to provide that some or all of the estate taxes should be paid from the residue. One important thing must not be overlooked, viz., the burden of estate taxes attributable to items of the gross estate which do not pass by succession. Under state tax apportionment laws this is usually borne by the beneficiaries of those interests unless the will otherwise directs. Frequently, the testator would desire that this be payable from the residue; if so, the will should specifically so provide.

*The General Testamentary Plan*

Sometimes it may be thought that no will is called for if the intestate laws place the property where the owner desires it to go. Even here a will may be desirable in order to appoint the person who will have charge of the administration and to dispense with his bond and the attendant expense.[14] Sometimes it may be desirable to set up an inter vivos trust,[15] or to transfer

[13] See Reidy, Problems of Apportionment of Estate Taxes under State Statutes, 1949 Proceedings of Real Property, Probate and Trust Law Section of American Bar Association 23; Reidy, Apportionment of Estate Taxes, 88 Trusts & Estates 623; Trachtman, supra note 2 at 49; Tweed & Parsons, supra note 2 at 68, 87, 120; also supra § 136, note 1.

[14] See infra text at note 58; also infra just prior to note 28.

[15] See supra § 42.

property into joint ownership,[16] but usually even in these cases there will be some property not included within the inter vivos transactions and upon which intestate succession will operate if there is no will.

If there is to be a will, the plan may be to pass all the property absolutely and unconditionally to one or more beneficiaries. This is particularly apt to be true in the case of small estates, and sometimes large fortunes are disposed of in this manner.[17]

*Future Interests and Trusts*

Even in modest estates it may be desirable to create life interests and remainders, and the larger the estate the greater is the probability that this is called for. The two common devices for this arrangement are the legal life estate and the testamentary trust. While there is no intention of "covering" herein the subjects of future interests and trusts, some mention must be made of certain phases of those fields.

It is neither difficult nor undesirable for a will to create a legal life estate in land in one taker with the remainder to another. However, the responsibilities for taxes, repairs, and waste should be clearly stated in the will. The legal life estate is the proper method of procedure when it is desired to provide for successive enjoyment of heirlooms such as portraits or jewelry. Future interest cannot be created in chattels consumable in their use,[18] although it is generally possible to create future legal interests in other chattels.[19] However, this is not ordinarily desirable; to mention only one objection the life tenant may be obliged to furnish a forthcoming bond, at least unless the

16 See supra § 40, notes 11–14.

17 The will of Edward H. Harriman, who died in 1909, passed vast estates and contained only ninety-nine words. It made no mention of the testator's children, and no attempt was made to exempt the widow from giving bond and was attested by only two witnesses. Except for the attestation clause it reads:

"I, Edward H. Harriman of Arden in the State of New York, do make, publish and declare this as and for my last will and testament that is to say:

"I give, devise and bequeath all of my property, real and personal of every kind and nature to my wife, Mary W. Harriman to be hers absolutely and forever and I do hereby nominate and appoint the said Mary W. Harriman to be executrix of this my will.

"In witness whereof, I have hereunto set my hand and seal this 8th day of June in the year 1903.

"Edward H. Harriman."

18 Seabrook v. Grimes, 107 Md. 410, 68 A. 883, 16 L.R.A.,N.S., 483, 1908 (printing presses); American Law of Property § 4.4.

19 Ibid.

will specifically excuses this. Even more objectionable are wills wherein property is given to a person outright with express or implied power to dispose of it for support or otherwise and with the provision that anything remaining on the beneficiary's death should go to another. It usually is not clear into what legal category this arrangement falls, and it often leads to trouble, litigation, and even defeat of the interest of the secondary beneficiary.[20]

When it is desired that the will should provide for life and subsequent interests in personalty the testamentary trust is usually a better device. Here the property, such as the residue of the estate or some specific sum, is devised and bequeathed to the trustee, "in trust never-the-less" for stated purposes. These usually include payment of the income to the life beneficiaries with provision for disposition upon their death. If, as is usually the case, the life beneficiary is the one in whose welfare the testator is primarily interested it is desirable to make some provision which also permits payments out of the principal to the life beneficiary to provide for personal emergencies and inflation. This may be in the sole discretion of the trustee on the one hand, or the life beneficiary may be given the unrestricted power to call on the latter for all or any part of the corpus. In between these extremes there may be limitations, such as the purposes for which the sum is to be used, or as to the amount in fixed sums or a proportion of the estate.[21]

Some wills contain provisions that the interest of any trust beneficiary shall not be subject to his anticipation by way of transfer, nor to interference by his creditors, until he actually receives the money or property. This is the "spendthrift clause". In some states this is valid as to both principal and income, in others effective only as to income, and in still others invalid altogether.[22] Statutes in some jurisdictions give limited protection without the clause. The law of the particular jurisdiction

[20] See Hanks v. McD ell, 307 Ky. 243, 210 S.W.2d 784, [illegible] A.L.R.2d 1, 1948, and supra § 146 at note 18.

[21] See Leach, supra note 2 at 180–185; Trachtman supra note 2 at 111; Tweed & Parsons, supra note 2 at 50, 85, 118. If a charity is the remainderman and it is desired to take advantage of the charitable deduction, it would be wise to put a definite limit on the extent to which principal may be invaded; at least some standard must be set up or the deduction will be lost. See Trachtman supra note 2 at 178. Generally, see Jacobs, Testamentary Trusts.

[22] See Bogert on Trusts, 3d ed. § 40; American Law of Property, § 26.88 et seq.; Griswold, Spendthrift Trusts, 2d ed. 1947.

must be consulted. The clause should not be included in all wills simply as a matter of routine.

A testamentary trust wherein the corpus is less than $10,000 is seldom advisable, since the expense of administration may be proportionately large and the life income relatively small. Indeed, trusts of even two or three times this amount are usually of marginal utility unless the beneficiaries are incompetent or lacking in ordinary business prudence.

*Powers of Appointment*

Sometimes flexibility is desired because the testator cannot foresee who will need or deserve his property at the death of the life tenant. For this or other reasons it may be desirable to give the latter power to appoint the secondary beneficiary.[23] This power may be general—to appoint anyone including the estate of the donee of the power—or special—to appoint only those of a designated class. In case of the latter the class must be clearly defined. In any event it should be provided how the appointment is to be exercised (usually by will of the donee of the power), and who should be entitled to property in absence of execution of the power by the donee.

In this connection it should be noticed that in some states the residuary clause of the will is deemed to exercise any general power of which the testator is the donee in favor of his residuary beneficiaries unless his will provides otherwise; in other jurisdictions this is not so. If there is any reasonable possibility that the testator may possess a power of appointment at his death, attention should be given to this matter in his will so as to effectuate his wishes.

*Rule against Perpetuities and Other Limitations*

According to the common-law rule against perpetuities no interest is good unless it must vest not later than twenty-one years after some life or lives in being at the creation of the interest. Most states preserve this rule, though there are statutory modifications in some. The most striking change is in New York where the statute is differently phrased and more restrictive. It forbids the suspension of the absolute power of alienation for a longer

23 Casner, Estate Planning—Powers of Appointment, 64 Harv.L.R. 185; Fleming, Provisions for Trusts and Powers of Appointment [1950] U. of Ill.Law Forum 341; Schuyler, Some Problems with Powers, 45 Ill.L.R. 57; see supra note 10; see generally, Simes, Future Interests, § 51 et seq.; American Law of Property, § 23.1 et seq.

period than *two* lives in being and there is no added period of years in gross.

The rules apply to vesting of beneficial interests under a trust as well as in legal life estates. A discussion of them falls outside the scope of this work.[24] The same is true of limitations upon accumulations.[25] Extreme care must be taken to avoid the many pitfalls, including those in connection with class gifts[26] and powers of appointment,[27] which involve these rules. There are also other pitfalls connected with the law of future interests which may lead to litigation and the defeat of the testator's intent. If the draftsman feels that he is not competent to frame a valid scheme along the desired lines he should consult one who is. There are plenty of such experts.

*Gifts to Minors*

If property is given to minors, this may necessitate the creation of a judicial guardianship with attendant trouble and expense. For this reason many men of modest estates with small children prefer to leave all the property outright to the spouse, relying upon her to care for the children to the best of her ability. Of course the children, including those who may be thereafter born or adopted, should be mentioned so that there will be no claim of forgotten or pretermitted heirs.[28] Under some circumstances it may be a good idea to mention grandchildren also.

Leaving everything to the widow runs the risk of her lack of business sagacity or fidelity to the interests of the children, but this consideration is often overshadowed by the inconvenience and expense of guardianships. When gifts of keepsakes or small pecuniary remembrances are made to infants, it is advisable to provide that delivery or payment of the legacy to one or both of his parents without the necessity of a bond will discharge the

[24] See Leach, Perpetuities in a Nutshell, 51 Harv.L.R. 638; Looker, The Rule against Perpetuities, 1951 Proceedings of Probate and Trust Law Divisions of the American Bar Association 7, also printed in 90 Trusts & Estates 653; Simes, Future Interests §§ 108–126; American Law of Property §§ 24.1 to 25.98.

[25] See American Law of Property §§ 24.65, 25.100 et seq.; Simes, Future Interests §§ 127–129.

[26] See Simes, Future Interests § 112; American Law of Property §§ 24.26–24.29. Gifts to the "children", or the "widow" of another may involve the rule against perpetuities. Id. 24.43–24.46.

[27] See Casner, supra note 23 at 198; American Law of Property §§ 24.30–24.36, 25.13; Simes, Future Interests § 113.

[28] See supra §§ 36, 85.

executor. Otherwise, except for special statutory provisions,[29] a guardianship may be necessary in order that the executor may obtain an acquittance from a competent person.[30]

In New York at least, substantial legacies are sometimes made to vest in a minor, with provision that it shall be retained by the executor who is empowered to apply it for the minor's benefit (power in trust). However, it is not certain that this avoids the necessity of guardianship and the entire device would be dubious indeed in many jurisdictions.

A trust is the best method of making substantial provisions for minors. Guardianship may be avoided by provision that the trustee may apply the income, and if desired also the principal, for the support and welfare of the infant. It is also often provided that the trustee may make payments to a parent without bond and that the trustee is not liable to see to the application of the funds so paid.[31]

*Protecting Interests of Chief Beneficiaries*

As a general rule it is advisable to avoid large specific or pecuniary gifts. There are two principal dangers in such dispositions. In the first place, if the specific devisee or legatee is a principal beneficiary, in whose welfare the testator is primarily interested, there is always a risk of ademption by extinction either with or without the voluntary act of the testator.[32] On the other hand, if the donee of the large specific devise or bequest is not the one whom the testator wishes particularly to benefit, but the latter is named merely as residuary beneficiary, a depletion of the testator's estate may divert the major share of the estate from the latter because of the principle that residuary bequests abate first.[33] For these reasons it is better to confine specific legacies to property and amounts of small value.

One desirable method of dealing with an estate is to make all substantial gifts proportionate shares of the residue. Another

29 E. g. N.Y.Surr.Ct.Act § 271 (up to $500.).

30 State ex rel. Lynch v. Whitehouse, 75 Conn. 410, 53 A. 897, 1902; McAdams v. Wilson, 164 S.W. 59, Tex. Civ.App.1914. Cf. In re Biederman's Estate, 186 Misc. 625, 57 N.Y.S.2d 560, 1945.

31 See Schwartzberg & Stocker supra note 2 at 53–54; Tweed & Parsons, supra note 2 at 67, 86, 192; Shattuck, A Practical Consideration of Some of the Legal and Tax Problems Inherent in Gifts to Minors, 31 B.U. L.R. 451.

32 See supra § 134.

33 See Leach, Lessons from the Depression in the Drafting of Wills and Trusts, 18 Minn.L.R. 27, 33–35; supra § 136.

device is to give the principal beneficiary a large specific or pecuniary gift and also make him the residuary beneficiary. When a demonstrative gift is possible this likewise overcomes many of the combined dangers of abatement and ademption.[34] It is always possible to provide a special order of abatement and this is often desirable where realty and personalty are devised to different persons.[35] If provisions are intended for support or in lieu of dower, this should be stated in order that these gifts will be given preference regarding abatement.[36] In addition, many family controversies will be avoided by a clear indication as to whether the share to the spouse is in lieu of or in addition to the forced share.[37]

*Survivorship Provisions*

To avoid disputes in case of gifts to several relatives, class gifts should be distinguished from those which are bequests to individuals. If the gift is to a class, the time at which the class is to be determined should be specifically stated and also whether the apportionment is to be per capita or per stirpes.[38]

In case of a legacy to an individual, it is quite common to add "if he survives me," and this is important if there is desire to avoid application of the anti-lapse statute when it would otherwise apply to the legacy. Where residuary gifts are made to two or more persons and would not be saved by the anti-lapse statute, it is important that appropriate provisions for survivorship be added. Otherwise the share of a predeceased residuary legatee becomes intestate property—a result which most testators would not desire.[39]

Most states have enacted the Uniform Simultaneous Death Act which declares that where "devolution depends on priority of death and there is no sufficient evidence that the persons have died otherwise than simultaneously, the property of each person shall be disposed of as if he had survived," unless the will provides otherwise. In these jurisdictions the act itself takes care

[34] See supra § 134. Beware a legacy simply payable "out of" a specified fund. If a specific legacy is intended, "only," or some equivalent expression, should be added. If a demonstrative legacy is desired, it should be stated that it is payable out of the general estate if the specified fund fails or to the extent that the fund proves insufficient.

[35] Clement v. Whisnant, 208 N.C. 167, 179 S.E. 430, 101 A.L.R. 698, 1935.

[36] See supra § 136.

[37] See supra §§ 33, 34.

[38] See annotation, 13 A.L.R.2d 1023 and supra note 26.

[39] See supra § 140.

of the most troublesome situations of death in common disaster. However, if there is any possibility that the will may be thought to provide otherwise, or if the state has not adopted the act, it will usually be advisable to frame a clause in the will to the same effect. Such expressions as death "in a common disaster" or "at or about the same time" should be avoided, for they are apt to lead to litigation. In some cases, such as those of childless or twice-married couples, it may be desirable to add that a person shall not be deemed to survive the testator if that person died within ——— days of the testator's death. The period cannot exceed six months if the provision for the spouse is to qualify for the marital deduction. There are other possibilities and complications in connection with such provisions. It is not profitable to spend too much time on them; their general utility is often exaggerated.[40]

*Tangible Personalty*

It is often desired to separate the personal and household effects from the residue and bequeath them to a certain person, frequently the surviving spouse. This sort of property is scarcely a fit subject to go into the corpus of a trust,[41] and moreover for reasons already seen it is undesirable to create a legal life estate therein. It should be given outright. The difficulty in so doing from the standpoint of draftsmanship is to designate, by words, all the property that it is to pass under such bequests without embracing other property not intended to be included. For example, the words "personal effects" may be broad enough under some circumstances to cover all personal property. If the goods are described as located on certain premises this might include money and securities found there. It is often desirable to except from such bequests money, securities, stock, evidences of indebtedness and documents of title.[42] The same result can be accomplished by restricting the personal property to that "which may be used in connection with my residence at the time of my death." It is usually desirable to avoid use of the expression "personal effects." "Tangible personal property" has now attained a certain currency. One should consider whether the phrase used will cover and is intended to cover such items as automobiles, boats, libraries, and stamp collections. The form-

40 See Trachtman, supra note 2 at 57; Tweed & Parsons, supra note 2 at 73, 93, 127; cf. Leach, supra note 2 at 191–193. See also supra § 107, note 23; § 140, note 25.

41 Cf. Ritchie, supra note 2.

42 See Kales, supra note 1 at 216; Gest, supra note 2 at 480.

books contain both good and bad examples of such clauses. These must be adapted to the situation and desires of the individual testator.

*Description of Property, Beneficiaries, and Purpose*

Care should be taken to describe accurately the property which is to be specifically devised or bequeathed. If a legal description of real property is used in the will, not only should every effort be made to obtain the correct one, but the land should also be referred to as "my land," "my farm," "my home" or the like so that if the description should prove erroneous, there may be some means of identifying the land.[43] Inquiry should be made as to whether land specifically devised is encumbered or is likely to be. If so, the testator's wishes as to whether the obligation should be discharged from the personal estate should be made explicit.[44]

In connection with legacies of shares of stock, whether specific or general, it is well to add a clause stating whether or not the testator desired to pass a proportionate interest in the corporation equivalent to the number of shares which he owned at time of execution of the will. This will guard against troublesome questions arising out of stock dividends and split-ups.

Pains should also be taken in the description of the beneficiaries. The residence of individuals should be stated if there is any chance of doubt. The exact corporate name of charitable beneficiaries should be ascertained. If a mistake is made in the name, two or more charities may claim the gift or the heirs or residuary legatees may contend that the gift should fail.[45] Sometimes such associations receive bequests in some other name than that by which they are ordinarily known, and improper designation may imperil the whole gift. It is often desirable for the attorney to confer with the officers of the charity. If this is not done, the organization may find it necessary to reject the gift because of restrictions or qualifications thereon. In this connection it is desirable so far as possible to persuade the testator to state the purposes for which the bequest may be used as generally as possible. Conditions change so that the need for a certain type of charitable endeavor may largely or even totally disappear.[46]

[43] See supra § 60.

[44] See supra § 137.

[45] See supra § 60. Cf. State v. American National Red Cross of Washington, D. C., 60 S.D. 608, 245 N.W. 399, 1932, noted, 19 Va.L.R. 650.

[46] See Gest, supra note 2, at 486, 487.

*Gifts to Creditors and Debtors of Testator*

Inquiry should be made into the financial relations of the testator with the beneficiaries. If the testator is indebted to them, does he wish the legacies or devises to be in satisfaction of these debts?[47] Perhaps more important, does he wish the provision to be in satisfaction of future obligations, such as those for care and support? It may be desirable to include a clause providing for a forfeiture of all testamentary gifts to any legatee or devisee who shall file a claim against the estate.[48] This is perhaps of even greater importance than a provision for forfeiture in case of will contest.[49] In either case a gift over to another should be made in case of forfeiture. While the general family situation usually does not warrant the inclusion of such clauses, sometimes it does.

Frequently the beneficiaries are, or may in the future be, indebted to the testator. Does the testator intend to forgive these debts, or are they to be deducted from the shares of the beneficiaries upon distribution? This should be made explicit, not only as to past but as to future debts.[50] The same should be done in the case of transactions which are not technically debts, but would be in the nature of advancements if there was no will. This is particularly true in case of advances before the execution of the will for these cannot be taken into account unless the will so provides.[51] It may be desirable that the amounts of past transactions should be specified, for these matters often lead to dispute.

*Directions to Pay Debts*

Formerly a direction to pay debts was a matter of some consequence. Now this is entirely unnecessary so far as the rights of creditors are concerned.[52] About the only benefit that may come from such directions in modern times is to indicate a proportionate order of abatement as between realty and personalty.[53] This result can be accomplished in a different and a better manner.[54] Usually it is better to omit entirely the clause directing payment of debts.[55]

47 See supra § 138, note 15 et seq.

48 See supra § 82.

49 Ibid.

50 See supra § 141.

51 See supra §§ 129, 141.

52 See supra § 127, especially at notes 121–124.

53 See supra § 136.

54 See supra text at notes 35, 36.

55 However, if the testator is a married woman, she may desire to pro-

*Choice of Executors and Trustees*

The choice of an executor is an important matter.[56] In small estates, the principal beneficiary, or one of the principal beneficiaries, is generally appointed. This is a good selection if the individual is physically able and of sufficient business experience to undertake the duties of the office. Often a business associate or a trust company is a better choice, particularly if the estate is of some size. A corporate fiduciary should be consulted before it is named, for it may be unwilling or even unable to act. Frequently it is wise for the testator to nominate his second choice in case that the first fails to qualify. Sometimes two or more executors are desirable, though generally this is confined to estates of considerable size. When a joint executorship is contemplated provision should be made for the possibility of a difference of opinion, either by stipulating for a majority rule or designating the persons whose views are to prevail in such case.[57] Provision should also be made in such cases as to whether the executors qualifying or surviving may act alone, and if not, as to the manner of selection of substitutes.

The custom varies as to the testamentary appointment of guardians for testator's minor children. In some states it is not ordinarily done. Elsewhere it is common to appoint a guardian of the person in case the spouse does not survive or dies without appointing a guardian. Often there is also appointment of the guardian of the estate. This seems incongruous with attempts of most testamentary plans to avoid guardianships if possible. Still it may be said that even if there is a testamentary nomination, no appointment need be made for guardian of the estate unless occasion for it arises. Testamentary appointment of a guardian is desirable if it appears that a guardian will be necessary or if family friction may arise on the death of both parents. Otherwise the local practice should be followed.

If a trust is created, a trustee or trustees should be designated. They are often the same persons who act as executors. However, they need not be, and in some cases the duties of the two offices

vide that her funeral expenses shall be borne by her estate rather than by her husband.

56 See Remsen, The Post-Mortem Administration of Wealth, 19 Yale L. J. 36; Cutter, What My Executor and Trustee Should Expect from Me and What I Should Expect from My Executor and Trustee, 23 Ill.L.R. 614; Blakeslee, Choosing an Executor, 23 Ill.L.R. 699; Mansfield, Executors and Trustees, [1950] Univ. of Ill.Law Forum 392. As to attempted testamentary appointment of attorney for estate, see supra § 108, note 11.

57 See supra § 105, notes 21–23.

are so different as to call for trustees who are not the same as the executors.

*Fiduciaries Bond*

When the statutes provide that the will may dispense with the executor's official bond, the testator's wishes in this regard should be consulted and careful consideration made of the premises.[58] Dispensing with the bond saves trouble and expense to the estate. It is particularly appropriate when the executor is the sole or principal beneficiary. The guardian of a minor's estate, and in some states the trustee, is obliged to give bond unless the will excuses it. This matter must also be duly considered. Practically everywhere a corporate fiduciary is excused by law from giving a bond.

*Powers of Executors and Trustees*

Considerable attention should be given to the problem of what special powers and authority it is desirable to give to executors and testamentary trustees. In the jurisdictions where independent executors and nonintervention wills are allowed by statute,[59] it is generally provided in wills that the executor may act without court supervision in so far as the law allows this. Of course the purpose here is to avoid red tape and legal expense. In fact, an attorney drafting a will in these states might be considered negligent for failure to include such provisions unless there is some special reason for its omission.

When there is any likelihood of a demand for an immediate sale of testator's realty, after his death, to pay debts or for any other reason, the executor should be given testamentary power of sale.[60] Otherwise it will be necessary either to incur the delay and expense of a sale by order of the court, or wait until the estate has been closed and the devisees are able to furnish a marketable title.

Dependent on the size and nature of the estate, power is frequently given to the executor to exchange, mortgage, and lease property, to lend and borrow money, and to compromise claims. Indeed extensive powers regarding investments, such as to retain existing securities, to reinvest in securities not authorized for trust funds, to vote stock and participate in reorganizations are often included in the enumeration of executorial powers. Ex-

58 See supra § 113.

59 See supra § 103.

60 See supra § 123.

press power is often given for the employment of agents, brokers, attorneys, accountants, and investment counsel. Power to distribute in cash or kind in the executor's discretion is often very desirable. In cases of express grant of powers it should be stated that the enumeration is to be deemed in addition to the common law and statutory powers.[61]

In some small estates the extensive grant of powers may be unnecessary and superfluous. When the estate is larger the desirability of considerable enumeration of powers increases. When a testamentary trust is created express powers in connection with investments are imperative. In most wills containing a trust the powers granted to the executors and trustees are identical. In theory this does not seem appropriate since the functions of the two fiduciaries are diverse. This blending may have a tendency to blur the distinction between the offices, especially when held by the same person. In practice little difficulty is encountered in this connection. However, it is sometimes desirable to grant different and more extensive powers to trustees, than to executors. The will should also provide whether or not the powers granted apply to successor fiduciaries; usually it is desirable to provide that they do.

If the testator is engaged in an individual business, it may be advisable to authorize the executor or trustee to continue the business.[62] If this is done, it is imperative to specify whether the entire funds of the estate or only the assets engaged in the business may be employed for this purpose.[63] Of course the answer to these problems will depend upon many factors of personality and economic risk.

61 Stephenson, supra note 2; Jacobs, Testamentary Trusts; Leach, supra 2 at 194–201; Schwartzberg & Stocker, supra note 2 at 65 et seq.; Tweed & Parsons, supra note 2 at 69–71, 87–90, 120–125; Trachtman, Administrative Provisions for Wills, 1950 Proceedings of Probate and Trust Law Section of American Bar Association 17, also printed in 89 Trusts & Estates 661. For brief forms, see Ritchie, supra note 2; 1948 Proceedings of Real Property, Probate and Trust Law Section 116–117; Trachtman, infra note 66.

62 See Trachtman, Executor's Problems with Closely Held Business, 1951 Proceedings of Probate and Trust Law Sections 18, also printed in 90 Trusts & Estates 668; Trachtman, supra note 2 at 176; Strickler, Estate Planning and the Sole Proprietor, 36 Minn.L.R. 874.

63 See supra § 121.

*Incorporation by Reference*

Incorporation into the will of another document by reference should be avoided if possible. Some jurisdictions do not permit this, and in others the extent to which the doctrine may be carried is in doubt.[64] There is always the chance of accidental or fraudulent destruction of the incorporated paper. When it seems necessary to incorporate a document by reference, it should be in existence, plainly referred to as being in existence and accurately described. It should be carefully explained to testators, and more particularly to testatrices, that they cannot effectively change the disposition of personal effects by leaving informal memoranda written after execution of the will.

*Codicils*

As a whole, codicils should be avoided since they may lead to difficulties in construing the various instruments together, as well as an additional burden of probate. It is better to prepare an entirely new instrument when a change of testamentary scheme is desired. At any rate, a codicil should never be prepared until the original will has been carefully studied and the effect of the codicil accurately forecast. The principal occasion for a codicil is when time does not permit the drafting of a complete new will. It has also been suggested that the codicil should be employed if there has been a change for the worse in testator's mental condition since execution of his prior will.[65]

*Conclusion*

Form-books containing clauses for almost every type of testamentary provision are numerous.[66] These works should be

[64] See supra, §§ 80–81. Particular care must be taken as to the validity and effect of an attempt to "pour over" into an amendable trust. If the theory employed is incorporation by reference the language of the will should sound quite different from that used under the theory of reference to non-testamentary act. See Matter of Rausch, 258 N.Y. 327, 179 N.E. 755, 80 A.L.R. 98, 1932.

[65] See Ritchie, supra note 2; Schwartzberg & Stocker, supra note 2 at 94; Tweed & Parsons, supra note 2 at 74; see also supra note 6.

[66] Gordon, Annotated Forms of Wills; Rollison, Will Clauses Annotated; Neuhoff, Standard Clauses for Wills, 82 Trusts & Estates, 285, 373, 479, 569; 83 id. 45, 131; see also references supra note 2. For forms of complete wills, see 1948 Proceedings of Real Property, Probate at Trust Law Section of American Bar Association 116; Ritchie, supra note 2; Leach, supra note 2; Stephenson, supra note 2 at 454; Schwartzberg & Stocker, supra note 2 at 99, 112 (sample will); Fingar & Bookstaver, supra note 2 at 812–899; Trachtman, The Warm Weather Special, P-H

consulted, especially by beginners in the art of drafting wills. However, they cannot be slavishly followed. Almost every specimen clause will require some adaptation to the needs and situation of the individual testator. In addition, some of the printed forms may be undesirable for any purpose. One should avoid the lack of clarity which may result from the joining together of isolated clauses from various sources. For the neophyte, the preparation of even a simple will may seem an arduous undertaking, but with a knowledge of the problems of the substantive law and the assistance of forms a creditable job can be done. Furthermore, with experience, drafting techniques will be developed, and, while every will has its special problems, many of the things which once seemed puzzling become practically matters of professional habit.

**Wills, Estates & Trusts Service ¶ 21, 314; also published in pamphlet form by Prentice-Hall; Proceedings of the Second Annual Institute of Estate Planning, Georgia, 1952, 45 et seq.**

# TABLE OF CASES

**Figures refer to pages**

## A


Abbey's Estate, In re, 324.
Abbott v. Appleton, 616.
Abbott v. Holway, 187.
Abbott v. Johnston, 694.
Abbott v. Lewis, 394, 400.
Abdale's Estate, In re, 74.
Abddulah's Estate, In re, 631.
Abila v. Burnett, 733, 734, 736.
Abila's Estate, In re, 152.
Abney v. Moore, 186.
Abraham, Re, 788.
Abraham v. Wilkins, 300.
Abrahams v. Abrahams, 102.
Abrahams v. Woolley, 232.
Abramson v. Horner, 183.
Abramson v. Rogers, 671.
Achelis v. Musgrove, 811.
Acherly v. Vernon, 470.
Ackerina, Matter of, 319.
Ackless v. Seekright, 309.
Acop v. Piraso, 296.
Acorn Wood Realty v. Old Colony Trust Co., 583.
Adam's Estate, In re, 326.
Adams, Matter of, 295.
Adams v. Adams, 84, 721.
Adams v. Conqueror Trust Co., 747.
Adams v. Cooper, 547.
Adams v. Cowan, 462.
Adams v. First M. E. Church of Irving Park, 521.
Adams v. Hackensack Trust Co., 695.
Adams v. Hagerott, 179.
Adams v. Legroo, 126, 811, 814.
Adams v. Maris, 208, 451, 452.
Adams v. Merced Stone Co., 203.
Adams v. Norris, 331.
Adams v. Simpson, 813, 815.
Adams v. Yancy, 790.
Adams' Ex'x v. Beaumont, 357.
Adams' Heirs v. Adams' Adm'r, 590.
Adams' Heirs v. Adams, 504.
Addington v. Allen, 268.
Addington v. Wilson, 246.
Addison v. Addison, 758.
Adkins' Estate, In re, 218, 224.
Adkins' Will, In re, 520.
Agoos v. Cosmopolitan Trust Co., 715.
Ahmann v. Elmore, 244, 246.
Ahnert v. Ahnert, 300, 301.
Aiken v. Davidson, 709.
Ailes v. Ailes, 538.
Ainsworth's Estate, In re, 314.
Aitken v. Sharp, 784.
Akerman, In re, 789.
Akers' Will, Matter of, 439.
Akin, Matter of, 647.
Albany Hospital v. Albany Guardian Soc. & Home for Friendless, 774, 776.
Albers v. Young, 720.
Albert Anderson Life Ins. Trust, In re, 163.
Alburger v. Crane, 675.
Alburger's Estate, 143.
Alden v. Superior Court of Los Angeles County, 493.
Aldrich v. Aldrich, 552, 811, 814.
Aldridge v. Aldridge, 187.
Alerding v. Allison, 583.
Alexander v. Dean, 683.
Alexander v. Fidelity Trust Co., 638, 769, 772, 773, 831.
Alexander v. Fidelity & Deposit Co., 665.
Alexander v. Hendricks, 674.
Alexander v. Herring, 662.
Alexander v. Johnston, 361, 383.
Alexander v. Lamar, 91.

Figures refer to pages

Alexander v. McAdams, 124.
Alexander v. Samuels, 88.
Alexander's Estate, In re, 323.
Alford v. Bennett, 749.
Alfred University v. Frace, 483.
Alger v. North End Sav. Bank, 175.
A. L. Goetzmann Co. v. Gazett, 576.
Allday v. Cage, 387, 392.
Allen v. Allen, 733, 769.
Allen v. Beemer, 448.
Allen v. Boomer, 389.
Allen v. Bromberg, 214.
Allen v. Dundas, 503.
Allen v. Edwards, 789.
Allen v. Etter, 770.
Allen v. Griffin, 338.
Allen v. Hendrick, 201, 204.
Allen v. Heron, 427.
Allen v. Heys, 254.
Allen v. Hurst, 571.
Allen v. Linger, 612.
Allen v. Lovell's Adm'x, 505.
Allen v. Maddock, 385, 387, 389, 391.
Allen v. Merwin, 769.
Allen v. M'Pherson, 270.
Allen v. Pugh, 525.
Allen v. Scruggs, 511.
Allen v. Shanks, 661.
Allen's Estate, In re, 427, 624, 659, 663.
Allen's Will, In re, 381, 460, 542, 543.
Allen's Succession, 814.
Allenbach v. Ridenour, 190, 390.
Allender v. Sussan, 637.
Allison v. Allison's Ex'rs, 142.
Allison's Ex'rs v. Allison, 314, 318.
Allman v. Malsbury, 243.
Allmon v. Pigg, 259.
Allnutt v. Wood, 486, 509.
Allred's Will, Re, 344.
Almy v. Jones, 783.
Alpaugh's Estate, In re, 609.
Alper v. Alper, 410, 413.
Alsobrook v. Orr, 485.
Alsop's Appeal, 470.
Alston v. Alston, 83.
Alston v. Davis, 208.
Alter's Appeal, 273.
Alter's Will, In re, 88.
Althaus' Will, Matter of, 749.
Altmeier v. Harris, 529.
Alvord's Estate, In re, 250.
Alward v. Borah, 673.
Ambrose v. Rugg, 120, 121, 773.
Ambruster v. Ambruster, 666.
American Bank & Trust Co. v. Douglass, 801.
American Bible Soc. v. Chase, 767.
American Jewish Joint Dis. Com. v. Eisenberg, 753.
American Nat. Bank v. Chapin, 124.
American Nat. Ins. Co. v. Wallace, 638.
American Surety Co. v. Norton, 644.
American Trust & Safe Deposit Co. v. Eckhardt, 223, 417.
American University v. Collins, 194.
American University v. Conover, 194.
Ametrano v. Downs, 743.
Amiss v. Hiteshew, 128.
Amory v. Francis, 713.
Amoskeag Trust Co. v. Haskell, 90.
Amundson v. Hanson, 675, 676.
Anastos' Estate, In re, 634.
Anderson, Estate of, In re, 690.
Anderson v. Anderson, 223, 467, 472.
Anderson v. Berkley, 266.
Anderson v. Crawford, 407.
Anderson v. Forbes, 727, 728.
Anderson v. French, 92.
Anderson v. Gregg, 788.
Anderson v. Larson, 190.
Anderson v. Miller, 229.
Anderson v. Storie, 695.
Anderson v. Walter, 596.
Anderson v. Yungkau, 694.
Anderson Nat. Bank v. Luckett, 98.
Anderson's Committee v. Anderson's Adm'r, 609.
Anderson's Estate, In re, 121, 241, 369, 371, 425, 551.
Andrew v. Dunn, 571, 602, 701.
Andrews v. Aikens, 219, 420.
Andrews' Estate, Matter of, 413.
Andrews' Will, In re, 303, 304.
Andros v. Flournoy, 131.
Angle, Matter of, 395, 396.
Ankeny's Estate, 289.
Anna, Re, 551.
Ansley v. Ansley, 87.
Anthony's Estate, In re, 360.
Appell, In re, 582.
Appenfelder's Estate, In re, 425.
Apperson v. Dowdy, 508, 511, 554.
Appleby v. Noble, 214.
Applehans v. Jurgenson, 241.

Appleton v. Rea, 284, 286.
Appleton's Estate, In re, 444.
Aquilini v. Chamblin, 329.
Aquino's Will, In re, 625.
Arbuckle's Estate, In re, 508.
Archambault's Estate, In re, 314.
Archer Blower & Pipe Co. v. Archer, 715.
Archer's Estate, In re, 152.
Arduser's Estate, In re, 625.
Arguello, In re, 679.
Arizona Land & Stock Co. v. Markus, 99.
Arland's Estate, In re, 220.
Arlington State Bank v. Paulsen, 669.
Armiger v. Reitz, 790.
Armington v. Armington, 79.
Armorer v. Case, 279.
Arms' Estate, In re, 125.
Armstrong, Appeal of, 756.
Armstrong v. Loomis, 698.
Armstrong v. Walton, 302.
Armstrong's Appeal, 761, 762.
Armstrong's Estate, In re, 796.
Armstrong's Ex'r v. Armstrong's Heirs, 302.
Armstrong's Will, In re, 812, 814.
Arneson's Will, 344.
Arnold v. O'Connor, 80.
Arnold v. Sabin, 617.
Arnold's Estate, In re, 256, 266, 431.
Arrington v. Brown, 390.
Arrington's Will, In re, 288.
Ash v. Calvert, 20, 481.
Ash's Estate, In re, 543, 549.
Ashburner v. Macguire, 742, 745.
Ashurt v. Union Bank & Trust Co., 627.
Asten v. Asten, 288.
Atchison v. Atchison's Ex'rs, 87.
Atchison v. Chamberlain, 111.
Aten v. Tobias, 421, 432.
Ater v. McClure, 432, 532.
Ater v. Moore, 266.
Atkins' Estate, In re, 84.
Atkinson, Estate of, 386.
Atkinson v. May's Estate, 558.
Atkinson v. Sutton, 119.
Atkinson's Estate, In re, 358, 544.
Atlantic Nat. Bank of Jacksonville v. St. Louis Union Trust Co., 179.
Attorney General v. Lloyd, 461.
Attorney General v. Parkin, 413.
Attorney General v. Vigor, 434.
Attorney General v. Ward, 461.
Atwood v. Rhode Island Hospital Trust Co., 393, 483.
Aubert v. Aubert, 240.
Aubuchon v. Lory, 563, 636.
Auerbach v. Continental Illinois Nat. B. & T. Co., 314.
Augustus v. New Amsterdam Casualty Co., 662.
Auritt's Estate, In re, 554.
Austin v. Austin, 740, 796.
Austin v. Central Sav. Bank of Baltimore, 173.
Austin v. First Trust & Sav. Bank, 469.
Austin v. Oakes, 463.
Austin's Estate, In re, 556, 557, 662.
Avery v. Brantley, 148.
Avery v. Chappel, 274.
Avery v. Everett, 96.
Avery v. Johnson, 732.
Avery Power Machinery Co. v. McAdams, 788, 790, 791.
Avery's Will, Matter of, 605.
Axcelrod, Estate of, 425, 427.
Axe v. Wilson, 270.
Ayers' Adm'r v. Ayers, 412.
Aylward Coal Co. v. Luyckx, 506, 513.
Ayres v. Ayres, 343.
Ayres' Will, In re, 443, 467.

# B

Baadte v. Walgenback, 570.
Babcock v. Collins, 589.
Bacharach v. Spriggs, 591.
Bacher's Estate, In re, 620.
Backesto's Estate, In re, 668.
Backham v. Wittkowski, 586.
Backus' Will, In re, 447.
Bacon v. Bonham, 729.
Baddeley v. Watkins, 537.
Baer's Appeal, 678.
Bagley v. Bagley, 212.
Bagnall v. Bagnall, 417.
Bagtas v. Paguio, 252.
Bagwell v. Dry, 784.
Bailey v. Bailey, 388.
Bailey v. Gates, 494.
Bailey v. McAlpin, 581.
Baird v. Baird, 364, 365.
Baird v. McMillan, 701.

Baird v. Yates, 91.
Baird's Estate, 467, 500.
Baker v. Baker, 131, 174, 306, 701, 702, 756, 761, 762.
Baker v. Baker, Eccles Co., 596.
Baker v. Baker's Estate, 303.
Baker v. Brown, 358.
Baker v. Carpenter, 783.
Baker v. Clowser, 90.
Baker v. Cooper, 590, 802.
Baker v. Farmer, 756.
Baker v. Heiskell, 76.
Baker v. Hendricks, 284.
Baker v. Hickman, 408.
Baker v. Moran, 203.
Baker v. Syfritt, 220.
Baker's Appeal, 304, 389, 391.
Baker's Estate, In re, 289, 501, 525, 636, 673, 713.
Bakke v. Bakke, 88, 529.
Bakke's Will, In re, 252, 275.
Balch v. Hooper, 628.
Baldwin v. Boaz, 665.
Baldwin v. Rice, 590.
Baldwin v. Spriggs, 423.
Baldwin's Estate, In re, 382, 545, 548, 647, 651, 652, 655.
Baldwin's Will, In re, 330, 336, 383.
Bales v. Elder, 83.
Balfour v. Collins, 613.
Balk's Estate, In re, 327, 532, 538, 651, 652, 655.
Ball v. Boston, 254.
Ball v. First Nat. Bank of Covington, 636.
Ball v. Mercantile Trust Co., 171.
Ball v. Miller, 293.
Ball v. Milliken, 102.
Ball's Estate, In re, 549.
Ballard v. Ballard, 112.
Ballesio's Estate, 383.
Ballinger v. Ballinger, 761.
Ballinger's Devisees v. Ballinger's Adm'r, 761, 762.
Ballmann's Estate, In re, 520.
Balme, Goods of, 385.
Bamberger v. Barbour, 302.
Bambrick v. Webster Groves Presbyterian Church Ass'n, 659.
Banaszak's Estate, In re, 607.
Banca D'Italia & Trust Co. v. Giordano, 177.
Bancroft, In re, 744, 745.
Bankers' Surety Co. v. Meyer, 699.
Bankers' Trust Co. v. Bank of Rockville Center Trust Co., 657.
Banking Co. v. Morehead, 653.
Bank of Jonesboro v. Wilson, 599.
Bank of Port Gibson v. Baugh, 583.
Bank of Saginaw v. Nason, 805.
Bank of Seneca v. Morrison, 592.
Bank of Statesboro v. Futch, 123.
Bank of Statesboro v. Simmons, 707.
Bank of Willow Springs v. Lillibridge, 639.
Banks v. Banks, 457.
Banks v. Goodfellow, 234, 237, 243.
Banks v. Sherrod, 231.
Bank's Estate, In re, 697.
Banks' Adm'r v. Marksberry, 184.
Bannigan v. Woodbury, 649.
Baptist Female University of North Carolina v. Borden, 671, 733, 735, 746, 756, 761.
Barbee v. Barbee, 258.
Barber v. Barber, 276, 416, 417, 418.
Barber v. Chase, 798.
Barber v. Henderson, 324.
Barber's Will, In re, 207.
Barck's Estate, In re, 604, 605.
Barclay v. Barclay, 693, 704, 705.
Bardell v. Brady, 534.
Bardsley v. Spencer, 185.
Barfield v. Carr, 445.
Barfield v. Miller, 576, 579.
Barger v. Barger, 543.
Barka v. Hopewell, 632, 673.
Barker, Ex parte, 612.
Barker v. Bell, 465.
Barker v. Comins, 278.
Barker v. Hinton, 292.
Barlass' Estate, In re, 597.
Barlow v. Cain, 707, 764.
Barlow's Will, In re, 534.
Barnard v. Bateman, 505.
Barnes, Goods of, 295.
Barnes v. Chase, 338.
Barnes v. Crow, 470.
Barnes v. Horne, 210, 362.
Barnes v. Phillips, 467.
Barnes v. Redmond, 70.
Barnes v. Rowley, 767.
Barnes' Estate, In re, 613.
Barnes' Will, Matter of, 439, 478.
Barnett v. Barnett, 113, 504.
Barnett v. Bellows, 427, 478.

Barnett v. Couey, 157.
Barnett's Adm'r v. Pittman, 614.
Barnewall v. Murrell, 207, 381.
Barney v. Barney, 492.
Barney's Will, In re, 140.
Barnhard v. Barnhard, 133.
Barnhardt v. Morrison, 485, 486.
Barnum v. Barnum, 790.
Barnum v. Mayor, etc., of City of Baltimore, 405.
Barr v. Sumner, 260.
Barrett v. Clark, 121.
Barrett v. Delmore, 93.
Barrett v. Heim, 709.
Barrett v. King, 651, 652.
Barricklow v. Stewart, 622.
Barrie's Estate, In re, 488, 489.
Barrie's Will, In re, 442.
Barron v. Barron, 719.
Barron v. McCann, 492.
Barry v. American Security & Trust Co., 409.
Barry v. Butlin, 549.
Barry v. Fain's Adm'r, 672.
Barry v. Walker, 500.
Barth v. Lines, 110.
Bartlett v. Manor, 506.
Bartlett v. Slater, 528.
Bartlett's Estate, In re, 431, 577.
Barto v. Stewart, 696, 700, 703.
Barton v. Robins, 252.
Barton v. Tabler, 610.
Bartram v. Holcomb, 89.
Bartz' Estate, In re, 607.
Basket v. Hassell, 201.
Baskin v. Baskin, 345.
Bassett, Estate of, In re, 512.
Bassett v. American Baptist Publication Soc., 212, 214.
Bassett's Estate, In re, 450.
Batchelder, In re, 784.
Bate v. Amhert, 399, 400.
Bates' Estate, In re, 553.
Bates v. Brown, 76.
Bates v. Hacking, 449, 450, 475.
Bates v. McGill, 698, 700.
Bates v. Vary, 795.
Bates v. Wilson, 156.
Bates' Estate, In re, 294, 442, 510.
Batson v. Batson, 244, 532.
Battey v. Meyerhardt, 567, 574.
Battis' Will, In re, 423, 431.
Batt v. Vittum, 445.
Battey v. Battey, 665.
Batty v. Greene, 683.
Baucus v. Barr, 644.
Bauerle v. Long, 675.
Bauernschmidt's Estate, In re, 796.
Bauer's Estate, In re, 358.
Bauer's Will, 755.
Baugh v. Howze, 200.
Baughman's Estate, In re, 315.
Baum v. Palmer, 722.
Bauman v. Armbruster, 712.
Baumann v. Kusian, 211, 212.
Baum's Estate, In re, 465, 466.
Baxter v. Bank of Belle of Belle Maries County, 331.
Baxter v. Baxter, 808.
Baxter v. Robinson, 637.
Baxter's Estate, In re, 558.
Bayer's Estate, In re, 545, 548.
Bayley v. Bailey, 449.
Baylis' Will, In re, 274, 815.
Beach v. Holland, 168, 170.
Beacham v. Ross, 616, 665.
Beals v. Croughwell, 402.
Bean v. Bean, 530.
Beane v. Yerby, 327.
Bear v. Millikin Trust Co., 179.
Beard, Appeal of, 707.
Beard v. Beard, 433, 743, 746.
Beardsley v. Merry, 786.
Bearss v. Corbett, 806.
Beattie v. Latimer, 653.
Beaty v. Richardson, 149.
Beaumont v. Keim, 478.
Beauvais v. Springfield Institute for Sav., 643.
Beaver v. Beaver, 173.
Beaver v. Crump, 211
Bebout v. Quick, 771.
Beck v. Belcher, 185.
Beck v. West Coast Life Ins. Co., 158.
Beck's Will, In re, 372, 373.
Beckett v. Selover, 619.
Beckford v. Parnecott, 464.
Beckwith v. Bates, 599.
Beddingfield v. Estill & Newman, 156, 157.
Bedirian v. Zorian, 168.
Bedlow, In re, 279.
Beebe v. Estabrook, 723.
Beebe v. Kirkpatrick, 703.
Beech, Estate of, 209, 372, 373.
Beekman v. Richardson, 802.

Beem v. Beem, 782.
Beggans' Will, In re, 342.
Beghtel's Estate, In re, 618.
Begovich v. Kruljac, 201, 202.
Behrens v. Behrens, 442, 509.
Beird, Succession of, 360.
Belcher's Estate, In re, 648.
Belden v. Belden, 627.
Bell v. Altheimer, 794.
Bell v. Bryan, 609.
Bell v. Fothergill, 438.
Bell v. Fulgham, 613.
Bell v. Mississippi Orphans Home, 135.
Bell v. Nealy, 148.
Bell v. Scammon, 78.
Bell v. Swift, 793.
Bell v. Timmius, 512.
Belotti, Matter of, 578.
Belshaw's Estate, In re, 78.
Belt v. Adams, 486.
Belt v. Hilgeman, Brundige Co., 626.
Belt's Estate, In re, 630.
Bemis v. Fletcher, 386, 392, 393.
Bendall's Distributees v. Bendall's Adm'r, 656.
Bender v. Bateman, 409, 410.
Bender's Estate, In re, 648.
Beneux v. Brown Shoe Co., 663.
Benfield v. McMillan, 711.
Bening v. Eischeid, 124, 125.
Benner's Estate, In re, 89.
Bennett, In re Estate of, 781.
Bennett v. Bennett, 726.
Bennett v. Bennett's Ex'x, 298.
Bennett v. Bradley, 808.
Bennett v. Brown, 432.
Bennett v. Dawson, 698, 700.
Bennett v. Harper, 768.
Bennett v. Hibbert, 244.
Bennett's Estate, In re, 795, 797.
Bennett's Will, In re, 208, 362.
Benning v. Superior Court of Sacramento County, 793.
Benolken's Estate, In re, 142, 143.
Benson's Estate, In re, 771.
Benton v. Friar, 755.
Benton Harbor Federation of Women's Clubs v. Nelson, 185, 187.
Benton's Estate, In re, 266, 520.
Berbling, Matter of, 752.
Berdon, Succession of, 451.
Beresford v. American Coal Co., 622.
Berg, In re, Estate of, 83.
Berger v. Duff, 666.
Berger v. Jackson, 690.
Berger's Estate, In re, 466, 712.
Bergland's Estate, Re, 412.
Bergren's Estate, In re, 122.
Berlin's Estate, 413.
Bernard's Estate, In re, 358.
Bernard's Settlement, In re, 460, 462, 463.
Berner, In re, 607.
Bernhardi's Estate, In re, 738, 739.
Bernhard's Estate, In re, 745.
Bernheimer v. First Nat. Bank of Kansas City, 84.
Bernheimer's Estate, In re, 733, 734, 736.
Bernstein v. Queens County Jockey Club, 685.
Berry v. Berry, 720.
Berry v. Berry's Estate, 224.
Berry v. Rutland R. Co., 598.
Berry v. Smith, 638.
Berry's Estate, In re, 558, 614, 666.
Berryman v. Dore, 639.
Besche v. Murphy, 91.
Bescher's Estate, In re, 441.
Best v. Burgess, 521.
Betts v. Harding, 729.
Betts v. Lonas, 323.
Betz v. Lovell, 551.
Bevelot v. Lestrade, 251.
Bevers v. Park, 694.
Beveridge v. Bailey, 226.
Beyschlag's Estate, In re, 195.
Bianco v. Piscopo, 610.
Bibb d. Mole v. Thomas, 437, 441.
Bidwell v. Beckwith, 800.
Biederman's Estate, In re, 827.
Biehn's Estate, In re, 92, 527.
Bierbaum's Estate, In re, 665.
Bierbrauer v. Moran, 156.
Bigelow v. Gillott, 438, 439, 445.
Bignold, In re, 752.
Bilby v. Hart-Parr Co., 693.
Bilderback v. Clark, 87.
Biles v. Biles, 812, 814.
Biles v. Dean, 520.
Bill v. Payne, 784.
Billet's Estate, In re, 601.
Billet's Estate, Matter of, 492.
Billings, Estate of, 359.
Billings v. Head, 88.

Billings v. Woody, 339.
Billington v. Jones, 436.
Billis' Will, In re, 209.
Bilty's Will, In re, 556.
Bily's Estate, In re, 524.
Bingaman's Estate, In re, 136, 459.
Binkley v. Switzer, 123.
Binns v. Dazey, 85.
Biondio's Will, In re, 498.
Bioren v. Nesler, 558.
Bird, Re, 749.
Birmingham v. Lesan, 404.
Birt, Goods of, In re, 304, 389.
Bishop v. Scharf, 237, 240, 241.
Bishop's Estate, In re, 257.
Bishop's Heirs v. Hampton, 75.
Bissell v. Bissell, 720.
Bissonnette's Will, In re, 465.
Bittner v. Bittner, 785.
Bivin v. Millsap, 617.
Bixler's Estate, In re, 532.
Bizzey v. Flight, 387.
Black v. Black, 167.
Black v. Herring, 412.
Black v. Jobling, 443.
Black v. Maxwell, 361.
Black v. Morgan, 630.
Black v. Smith, 266, 278, 289.
Black's Estate, In re, 707.
Blackborough v. Davis, 46, 47, 48.
Blackburn's Estate, In re, 618.
Black Eagle Mining Co. v. Conroy, 598.
Blacker v. Thatcher, 275.
Blackett v. Ziegler, 468, 469, 475.
Blackford v. Anderson, 460, 463.
Blackiston v. Russell, 189.
Blackmon v. Blackmon, 667.
Blacksher Co. v. Northrup, 500.
Blackstone's Estate, In re, 553.
Blackwell, In re, 603.
Blackwell v. Bowman, 85.
Blackwell v. Blackwell, 273.
Blackwood v. Blackwood, 787, 790.
Blades v. Szatai, 146.
Blair v. Kirchner, 203.
Blair's Will, In re, 306, 335.
Blaisdell v. Coe, 436, 744.
Blake v. Blake, 71, 775, 798.
Blake v. Rourke, 250.
Blanchard's Estate, In re, 431.
Blanck v. Morrison, 580.
Blanck's Estate, In re, 580.
Blankenship v. Blankenship, 358.
Blankenship v. Montgomery, 501.
Blanks v. Jiggetts, 156.
Blaydes' Estate, In re, 112.
Bleckley, Goods of, 443.
Blickensderfer's Will, In re, 496.
Blinn v. McDonald, 571.
Blinn v. Nelson, 600.
Bliss v. American Bible Soc., 451.
Bliss' Estate, In re, 139.
Bloechle v. Davis, 337, 338.
Blomdahl's Will, In re, 734, 742.
Bloomer v. Bloomer, 204.
Bloomfield v. Brown, 165.
Bloor v. Bloor, 191.
Bloor v. Platt, 519, 524.
Bloss' Will, Matter of, 494.
Blount v. Wheeler, 528, 529.
Blue's Estate, In re, 705.
Blum v. Frost, 637.
Blundell, In re, 739.
Boal v. Wood, 75.
Board of Com'rs of Rice County v. Scott, 461, 463.
Board of Nat. Missions, etc., v. Sherry, 444.
Bobblis v. Cupol, 402.
Bocquin v. Theurer, 626.
Boddington, Re, 431.
Bodine v. Bodine, 250.
Bodman v. American Tract Soc., 287.
Bodman's Estate, Matter of, 633.
Boehm, Goods of, 277.
Boehmer v. Silvestone, 386.
Boggess v. Crail, 403, 414.
Boggs' Estate, In re, 631.
Bohannon v. Trotman, 271.
Bohannon v. Wachovia Bank & Trust Co., 271.
Bohanon v. Walcot, 476.
Bohleber v. Rebstock, 421, 422.
Bohrmann's Estate, 243.
Boicelli v. Giannini, 190.
Boland v. Aycock, 260.
Boldwin v. Lay, 219.
Boles v. Caudle, 729.
Bolin v. Bolin, 726.
Bolles v. Toledo Trust Co., 115, 308, 396.
Bollinger v. Arkansas Valley Trust Co., 260.
Bolman v. Overall, 219, 220.
Bolton v. Barnett, 590.

Bolton v. Bolton, 336, 380.
Bolton v. Schriever, 490, 595.
Boman v. Boman, 142.
Bomar v. Wilkins, 119.
Bomar's Will, Matter of, 497.
Bond v. Evans, 734.
Bond v. Riley, 286.
Bond v. Seawell, 327, 381.
Bond's Estate, In re, 305, 421.
Bonded Bldg. & Loan Ass'n v. Konner, 669.
Bonkowski's Estate, In re, 457, 458.
Booe v. Vinson, 813.
Book's Will, In re, 430.
Boone v. Lewis, 309.
Boone v. Lightner, 501.
Booth, In re, 374, 440.
Booth, Will of, 302.
Booth v. Baptist Church of Christ, 388, 786.
Booth v. Oakland Bank of Sav., 175.
Borah v. Lincoln Hospital Assn., 285.
Borchers v. Borchers, 360.
Borden v. Jenks, 757, 758.
Borell's Estate, In re, 648.
Born v. Horstmann, 408.
Bornemann v. Ofsthun, 598, 601.
Boselly's Estate, In re, 134.
Bosserman v. Burton, 399, 400.
Bosse's Estate, In re, 129.
Bossu's Succession, 581.
Bostian v. Milens, 776.
Bostick v. Blades, 407, 408.
Boston v. Fox, 522.
Boston Safe Deposit & Trust Co. v. Plummer, 755.
Bottger's Estate, In re, 256, 266, 538.
Bottoms, Estate of, 794.
Bottrell v. Spengler, 390.
Boucher v. Lizotte, 142.
Boucher's Estate, In re, 193.
Bounds v. Johnson, 239.
Bourke's Estate, In re, 697.
Bourne v. Dorney, 88, 430.
Bourquin's Estate, In re, 611.
Bouse v. Hull, 774, 775.
Bouton v. Fleharty, 326, 481, 484, 504.
Bowdry v. Stitzel-Weller Distillery, 665.
Bowen v. Allen, 500.
Bowen v. Black, 128.
Bowen v. Bowen, 186.
Bowen v. Dorrance, 733, 746.
Bowen v. Howenstein, 527.
Bowen v. Johnson, 488, 502.
Bowen v. Morgillo, 293.
Bowen v. Phillips, 625.
Bowerman v. Burris, 279, 280.
Bower's Estate, In re, 358.
Bowers v. Cook, 627, 647.
Bowers v. Littlewood, 48.
Bowers v. McGavock, 519.
Bowersox's Appeal, 613.
Bowker, Goods of, 497.
Bowman v. Bowman, 721.
Bowman v. Howard, 85.
Bowman's Estate, In re, 256.
Bowron v. Kent, 724.
Box v. Lanier, 154.
Boyd v. Applewhite, 697.
Boyd v. Johnston, 651, 652.
Boyd v. Richie, 643.
Boyd's Estate, In re, 430.
Boyd's Estate v. Thomas, 705, 706, 708, 831.
Boydston's Estate, In re, 696.
Boyer v. Cole, 666.
Boyeus' Will, In re, 333.
Boykin v. Boykin, 758.
Boyle's Estate, In re, 563, 636, 705, 760, 762, 778, 784.
Boynton v. Laddy, 558.
Boynton v. Simmons, 550.
Bozarth v. Bozarth, 113.
Braasch v. Worthington, 520.
Brabrook v. Boston Five Cents Sav. Bank, 173.
Brackenbury v. Hodgkin, 217.
Brackenridge v. Roberts, 207, 449, 465, 476, 498, 552.
Brackenridge's Estate, In re, 293.
Brackett v. Hoitt, 646.
Brackey v. Jensen, 707, 708.
Braddock, Goods of, 335, 336.
Braden's Estate, In re, 788.
Bradford v. Blossom, 276.
Bradford v. Bradford, 410, 411.
Bradford v. Calhoun, 774, 776.
Bradford v. Culbreth, 406.
Bradford v. Eutaw Sav. Bank of Baltimore City, 177.
Bradford v. Leake, 774, 775.
Bradford's Estate, In re, 798.
Bradish v. McClellan, 459.
Bradley v. Onstott, 139.
Bradley's Estate, 471.

Bradley's Estate, In re, 89.
Bradshaw v. Roberts, 493.
Bradway v. Thompson, 509, 540.
Brady v. Brady, 435, 745.
Brady v. Cubitt, 422, 428, 429.
Brady v. Paine, 744.
Brady's Estate, In re, 595, 630.
Braeuel v. Reuther, 525.
Bragg's Estate, In re, 293, 325.
Braham v. Burchell, 464.
Brake v. Graham, 720.
Brakefield v. Baldwin, 530.
Bramell v. Adams, 780.
Bramell v. Cole, 805.
Brand, Succession of, 91.
Brandenburg v. Thorndike, 125.
Brandes v. Brandes, 216.
Brandon's Estate, In re, 753.
Brandow's Estate, In re, 361.
Branick's Estate, In re, 208.
Brann, In re, 750.
Branstrator v. Crow, 533.
Brant v. Brant, 761, 762.
Branther's Estate, In re, 260.
Brasfield's Estate, In re, 597.
Brasier's Estate, 438.
Bratt, Re, 412, 413.
Braun v. Brown, 201.
Braun v. Pettyjohn, 567, 574.
Braunstein's Will, In re, 131.
Brazil v. Silva, 422.
Breadheft v. Cleveland, 262, 548.
Breckwoldt's Will, In re, 508.
Bredl's Estate, In re, 615.
Breen v. Kehoe, 605.
Breen v. Pangborn, 620.
Bremer v. Lake Erie & W. R. Co., 595.
Bremer's Will, Matter of, 752, 753.
Brennan's Estate, In re, 240.
Brennen v. Derby, 221.
Brent v. Washington Bank, 710, 712.
Brereton v. Glazeby's Estate, 546.
Bresler's Estate, In re, 386, 387.
Bresnehan's Will, In re, 816.
Brewer v. Hamor, 84.
Brewer v. Wilson, 602.
Brewster's Will, Re, 478.
Briant v. Garrison, 812, 814.
Brickell's Estate, In re, 751.
Brickley v. Leonard, 220.
Brick's Estate, 26.
Bridge v. Abbot, 49.
Bridge v. Kedon, 729.
Bridgeport Trust Co. v. Parker, 786, 812, 814.
Bridgeport Trust Co.'s Appeal, 631.
Bridgman v. Bridgman, 581.
Bridle, In re, 744.
Briggs v. Probate Court, 617.
Brigham v. Garcelon, 690.
Brindle's Will, 520.
Brinkley v. Allen, 627.
Brisco v. Hamilton, 277.
Briscoe v. Madden, 690.
Briscoe's Devisees v. Widkliffe, 617.
Brissie v. Craig, 516.
Bristol v. Stump, 763.
Britt v. Darnell, 311, 320.
Brittingham v. Brittingham, 341, 342.
Britton v. Elk Valley Bank of Larimore, 492.
Brizendine v. American Trust & Sav. Bank, 408, 414.
Broaddus v. Centers, 669.
Broadhurst v. Mewborn, 668.
Broadway's Succession, 628.
Broas v. Broas, 791.
Brobst v. Brobst, 567, 568.
Brock's Estate, Re, 465.
Brodbeck's Estate, In re, 651, 652, 655.
Broderick's Will, 270.
Broderick's Will, In re, 501.
Brodersen's Estate, In re, 452.
Brodrick v. O'Connor, 167.
Broffee's Estate, In re, 502.
Brook v. Barker, 106.
Brook v. Kent, 399, 400.
Brooke v. Kent, 394, 400.
Brooke v. Ward, 420.
Brooker v. Brooker, 388.
Brookman, In re, 444.
Brooks v. Mitchell, 203.
Brooks v. Paine's Ex'r, 524.
Brooks' Estate, In re, 130, 361.
Broom v. Klein, 574.
Booth v. Baptist Church of Christ, 386.
Brosnan v. Brosnan, 542, 546, 548.
Brotzman v. Riehl, 763.
Broutin v. Vassant, 378.
Broward v. Broward, 71.
Brower v. Hunt, 80.
Brower's Will, In re, 249.
Brown v. Allen, 755.

Brown v. American Surety Co., 649.
Brown v. Atkins, 792.
Brown v. Avery, 206.
Brown v. Baron, 766.
Brown v. Baxter, 569, 691.
Brown v. Blesch, 92.
Brown v. Brown, 445, 613, 627, 682, 773.
Brown v. Clark, 466.
Brown v. Copeland, 562.
Brown v. Drake, 571.
Brown v. Eggleston, 557.
Brown v. Farndell, 42, 51.
Brown v. Fidelity Trust Co., 243, 584, 792.
Brown v. Fletcher's Estate, 591.
Brown v. Hawkins, 494, 495.
Brown v. Heller, 434, 743, 746.
Brown v. Just, 603.
Brown v. Kausche, 272.
Brown v. Keen, 709.
Brown v. Lewis, 646.
Brown v. Mack, 497.
Brown v. McGee's Estate, 628.
Brown v. Mercantile Trust & Deposit Co., 178.
Brown v. Navarre, 167.
Brown v. Parks, 151.
Brown v. Parry, Dick, 119.
Brown v. Peck, 414.
Brown v. Ray, 284.
Brown v. Riggin, 241.
Brown v. Routzahn, 774, 775.
Brown v. Scherrer, 424.
Brown v. Southern Ohio Sav. Bank & Trust Co., 633, 634.
Brown v. State, 364, 365.
Brown v. Taylor, 723.
Brown v. Tuschoff, 811, 814.
Brown v. United States, 367, 372, 500.
Brown v. Walker, 544.
Brown v. Webster, 221.
Brown v. Wightman, 685.
Brown's Adm'r v. Mattingly, 790.
Brown's Estate, In re. 161, 196, 250, 355, 487, 605, 741.
Brown's Estate, Matter of, 618.
Brown's Ex'r v. United States Trust Co., 712.
Brown's Will, In re. 451, 534, 546, 552.
Browne v. Doolittle, 797.
Brownfield v. Brownfield, 539.
Brownlie v. Brownlie, 538.
Broyles v. Magee, 110.
Brubaker's Appeal, 582.
Bruce v. Farrar, 790, 791.
Bruce v. Fogarty, 626.
Bruce v. Moon, 216.
Bruce v. Shuler, 316, 319.
Brucks v. Home Federal Sav. & Loan Ass'n, 176.
Bruer v. Johnson, 80.
Bruhns' Estate, In re, 593.
Brumfield v. Englesing, 813, 814.
Brunet's Estate, In re, 778.
Bruning v. Golden, 578.
Brunk v. Merchants Nat. Bank, 212.
Brunor, In re, 257.
Bruns v. Cope, 155.
Brush v. Wilkins, 422, 428, 429.
Brush's Will, In re, 248.
Bryan v. Batcheller, 149.
Bryan v. Bigelow, 397.
Bryan v. Harper, 407.
Bryan v. Seiffert, 485.
Bryan's Appeal, 388, 389.
Bryan's Estate, In re, 257, 546, 548, 551.
Bryant v. Bryant, 154, 157, 158.
Bryant v. Fingerlos, 669.
Bryant v. Thompson, 410.
Bryen's Estate, In re, 381.
Bryson v. Holbrook, 778.
Bryson's Adm'r v. Biggs, 570.
Buchanan v. Buchanan, 567.
Buchanan v. Pierie, 247.
Buchwald v. Buchwald, 394.
Buck, Succession of, 360.
Buck v. Kelly, 796.
Buck v. Lockwood, 693, 704.
Buck's Estate, In re, 651, 652, 654, 663, 733, 794.
Buckley v. Frasier, 87.
Buckner v. Buckner's Ex'r, 668.
Buckner v. Tuggle, 550.
Buder v. Stocke, 743, 748.
Budlong, Will of, In re, 266.
Budlong's Will, In re, 140.
Buehrer's Estate, In re, 364, 373.
Buehrle v. Buehrle, 210, 225.
Buerger v. Buerger, 514, 542, 552.
Buffington's Estate, In re, 521.
Bullard v. Village of Albion, 404.
Bullivant's Will, In re, 299.
Bullock v. Morehouse, 322, 323, 341.

Bumsted's Estate, In re, 736.
Bunce v. Bunce, 430.
Bunch v. Nicks, 184.
Bunker v. Bunker, 123.
Bunker v. Cooke, 20.
Burch v. McMillin, 782.
Burdick's Estate, 64.
Burdine v. Burdine's Ex'r, 219.
Burford v. Burford, 291.
Burgan v. Kinnick, 326, 340.
Burge v. Hamilton, 466, 513.
Burger v. Hill, 276, 277.
Burgess v. Belford, 250.
Burgess v. Boswell, 624.
Burgin's Estate, In re, 558.
Burk v. Morain, 522, 730.
Burke v. Central Trust Co., 282.
Burke v. Crawfordsville Trust Co., 813.
Burke's Estate, 419.
Burke's Estate, In re, 224, 493, 658, 659.
Burke's Will, In re, 441, 814.
Burkett v. Doty, 198.
Burkhalter v. Waters, 619.
Burkhart v. Gladish, 246.
Burkhart v. Rogers, 219.
Burkhim v. Pinhussohn, 589.
Burkland v. Starry, 544.
Burkman's Estate, In re, 813, 814.
Burnet v. Mann, 52.
Burney v. Allen, 342.
Burney v. Burney, 811, 814.
Burney v. Torrey, 551.
Burnham v. Comfort, 728, 730, 741.
Burnham v. Grant, 326.
Burnison's Estate, In re, 135.
Burns v. Burns, 427, 441.
Burns v. Nolette, 168, 170.
Burns v. Turnbull, 115.
Burns' Will, In re, 140.
Burpee v. Pickard, 814.
Burr v. Goodwin, 691.
Burr v. Sim, 79.
Burris v. Burgett, 82.
Burrows v. Burrows, 203.
Burt v. Burt, 582.
Burt v. McKibbin, 221.
Burt v. Second Nat. Bank of Saginaw, 695.
Burtenshaw v. Gilbert, 441, 474.
Burtman v. Butman, 409, 410.
Burton v. Newberry, 469.
Burton v. Wylde, 437, 442, 443, 444, 540, 555.
Burton's Estate, In re, 539.
Burtt's Estate, In re, 476, 477.
Busby's Estate, In re, 626.
Bush v. Delano, 549.
Bush v. Reconstruction Finance Corp., 573.
Bush's Estate, In re, 633, 723, 739.
Bush's Estate, Matter of, 434.
Bushell, Goods of, 274.
Business Men's Acc. Ass'n of America v. Green, 568.
Butcher v. Stapely, 220.
Butler v. Butler, 512.
Butler v. Dobbins, 750.
Butler v. Moulton, 304.
Butler v. Sherwood, 186, 200.
Butler University v. Danner, 603.
Butler's Estate, 631.
Butt v. Murden, 556, 557.
Butt's Estate, In re, 501.
Butterfield, Estate of, In re, 713.
Butterfield, Matter of, 71.
Butterworth v. Bredemyer, 699.
Button's Estate, In re, 297, 361, 362.
Butts v. Larison, 793.
Buzzell v. Fogg, 398.
Byars v. Smith, 238.
Bybee's Estate, In re, 181.
Bydalek v. Bydalek, 152.
Byers v. McAuley, 594.
Bynum v. Bynum, 343.
Byrd, In re, 334.
Byrne v. Fulkerson, 250.
Byrnes' Estate, In re, 120, 124, 125.

# C

Cabler's Estate, In re, 438.
Caddell v. Lufkin Land & Lumber Co., 676.
Cady's Estate, Matter of, 82.
Cadywold, In re Goods of, 425, 427.
Caesar v. Burgess, 311, 312, 317, 318.
Caffrey's Will, Matter of, 544.
Cain, Petition of, 734, 756.
Cain v. Barnwell, 123, 434, 743, 746.
Cain v. Burger, 520.
Cain v. Cain, 724.
Caines v. Marley, 184.
Cajoleas v. Attaya, 522.
Caldarone v. Caldarone, 256.

Calder v. Bryant, 810.
Caldicot v. Smith, 48.
Caldwell, Matter of, 603.
Caldwell v. Caldwell, 272.
Caldwell v. Cowan, 71.
Caldwell v. Miller, 83.
Caldwell v. Renfrew, 229.
Caldwell v. Taylor, 500.
Calef's Will, 553.
Calhoun v. Taylor, 721.
California Employment Stabilization Commission v. Hansen, 663.
California Trust Co. v. Bennett, 166.
Calkins v. Calkins, 339, 344.
Call v. Garland, 651, 652, 653.
Callaghan v. Corbin, 528, 529.
Callahan's Estate, In re, 457.
Calvert v. Beck, 615.
Calvert v. Calvert, 311, 313, 319.
Calvery v. Calvery, 409.
Calwell v. Black, 76.
Cameron v. Cameron, 622.
Cameron's Estate, 386, 465.
Cameron's Estate, In re, 83, 609, 757.
Camp, Estate of, In re, 511.
Camp's Estate, In re, 510.
Campbell v. Browder, 230.
Campbell v. Campbell, 126, 140, 188, 243, 276, 765.
Campbell v. Durrant, 405, 411.
Campbell v. French, 453, 460.
Campbell v. Harsh, 573.
Campbell v. Kuhn, 640.
Campbell v. Logan, 334.
Campbell v. Martin, 791.
Campbell v. Prater, 112.
Campbell v. St. Louis Trust Co., 516.
Campbell v. Smullen, 507.
Campbell's Estate, In re, 137, 203, 593, 795.
Campbell's Will, In re, 467, 469, 470, 539.
Campia's Estate, In re, 3.
Canada v. Ihmsen, 215, 226.
Cancilla v. Bondy, 114, 116.
Candee v. Candee, 671.
Candelaria v. Miera, 794.
Cannock's Will, In re, 341.
Cannon v. Nowell, 727.
Cannon v. Seybolt, 367.
Canterbury's Estate, In re, 298, 300.
Cantillon v. Walker, 411, 798.
Canton, Succession of, 748.
Canton's Succession, 734.
Capps v. Richardson, 416, 417.
Capra's Estate, In re, 82.
Capron v. Capron, 734.
Carcagno, Succession of, 631.
Card v. Alexander, 431.
Card's Estate, 770.
Cardin, In re, 708.
Cardoner's Estate, Re, 605.
Carey v. Baughn, 466.
Carey v. Carey, 146.
Carey's Estate, In re, 323, 422, 426.
Carl, Appeal of, 473.
Carlin v. Bacon, 214.
Carlson v. Layman, 132.
Carlton, Petition of, 634.
Carlton v. Carlton, 320.
Carmany's Estate, In re, 815.
Carmello's Estate, In re, 299.
Carmichael v. Lathrop, 737, 739, 740.
Carnahan v. Hamilton, 246.
Caro, Succession of, 359.
Caroleo's Estate, In re, 163.
Carother's Estate, In re, 127, 289, 499.
Carpenter v. Denoon, 347.
Carpenter v. Hazel, 651, 652.
Carpenter v. Miller's Ex'rs, 463.
Carpenter v. Severin, 599, 781.
Carpenter v. Strange, 591.
Carpenter's Estate, 153, 706.
Carpenter's Will, In re, 535.
Carpentier's Estate, In re, 498.
Carr v. Brown, 600.
Carr v. Smith, 812, 814.
Carr's Estate, 411.
Carr's Estate, In re, 466.
Carre, Succession of, 430.
Carrithers v. Jean's Ex'r, 554.
Carroll v. Carroll, 401, 403, 404.
Carroll v. Herring, 812, 814.
Carroll v. Richardson, 805.
Carroll's Estate, In re, 239, 557.
Carson v. Blair, 610, 619, 620.
Carson's Estate, In re, 267, 268, 269 279, 289, 497.
Carstairs v. Bomar, 220.
Carter v. Board of Education of Presbyterian Church, 784.
Carter v. Capshaw, 91.
Carter v. Crawley, 44, 45, 48.
Carter v. Madgwick, 184.

Carter v. Manufacturers' Nat. Bank of Lewiston, 664.
Carter v. Skillman, 797.
Carter v. Witherspoon, 217.
Carter's Estate, In re, 572
Carter's Heirs v. Carter's Adm'r, 414.
Carter's Will, In re, 249.
Carthage Development Co. v. Cushman, 522.
Carton v. Borden, 603.
Cartwright v. Cartwright, 297, 362, 416.
Cartwright v. Holcomb, 534.
Caruso v. Caruso, 585.
Casady v. Scott, 730.
Casey v. Hogan, 457.
Cassatt v. Vogel, 699.
Cassem v. Prindle, 522.
Casserly, In re, 708.
Casson v. Dade, 342.
Castle v. Persons, 200.
Caswell v. Lehrman, 261.
Cates v. Bankers' Health & Life Ins. Co., 638.
Catlett v. Catlett, 299, 302.
Catron v. Bostic, 25, 670.
Caulfield v. Sullivan, 296, 498.
Cavanaugh v. Dore, 604.
Cave v. Roberts, 50.
Cavin v. Little, 806.
Cavitt v. Beall Hardware & Implement Co., 674.
Caw v. Robertson, 319.
Cazallis v. Ingraham, 173, 174, 175
Cazassa v. Cazassa, 720.
Cazaurang's Estate, In re, 447, 465.
Cazier v. Hinchey, 151.
Center v. Kramer, 74.
Central Hanover Bank & Trust Co. v. Froment, 552.
Central Wright v. Eakin, 503.
Century Indemnity Co. v. Maryland Cas. Co., 623.
Cereghino v. Giannone, 549.
Chacona's Estate, In re, 458, 459.
Chaddick v. Haley, 260.
Chadwick v. Bristow, 224.
Chadwick v. Chadwick, 805.
Chadwick v. Stilphen, 589.
Chadwick v. Tatem, 435.
Chafee v. Maker, 788.
Challiner v. Smith, 250.
Chalmers v. Storil, 119.
Chambers v. Chambers, 542, 543.
Chambers v. Fennemore's Adm'r, 694.
Chambers v. Watson, 282.
Chambers' Adm'r v. Smith's Adm'r, 703.
Chambers' Estate, Re, 409.
Chamberlain v. Anderson, 600.
Chamberlain v. Husel, 622.
Chamberlain v. Williamson, 641.
Chamblee v. Wayman, 91.
Chambliss v. Bolton, 131.
Champollion v. Corbin, 567.
Chandler v. Chandler, 184.
Chandler v. Dockman, 304.
Chaney v. Baker, 238.
Channon's Estate, In re, 313.
Chapell v. Shuee, 797.
Chapin v. Cooke, 407.
Chaplin v. Chaplin, 187.
Chapman v. Hart, 748.
Chappell v. Neurath, 711.
Chapple's Estate, In re, 200.
Charch v. Charch, 768.
Charlebois' Estate, In re, 495.
Charles, Estate of, 312.
Charles' Estate, In re, 315, 557, 693, 699.
Charleston Library Soc. v. Citizens & Southern Nat. Bank, 462.
Charlton v. Low, 649.
Chase, In re, 620.
Chase v. Bartlett, 572.
Chase v. Kittredge, 344.
Chase v. Redding, 204.
Chase's Estate, In re, 303.
Chase Nat. Bank v. Deichmiller, 750.
Chatterton v. Clayton, 730.
Chauncey v. Leominster, 573.
Cheese v. Lovejoy, 439.
Cheever v. North, 475, 476, 552.
Chemical Bank & Trust Co. v. Barnett, 757.
Chenault v. Scott, 404.
Cheney v. Price, 250.
Cherry v. Boultbee, 787, 790.
Chester County Trust Co. v. Pugh, 639.
Chevalier's Estate, In re, 748.
Chevallier's Estate, Matter of, 359.
Chicago, R. I. & P. Ry. Co. v. Forrester, 625.
Chicago Title & Trust Co. v. Fine Arts Bldg., 662, 702.

Chicago Title & Trust Co. v. McGlew, 711.
Chicago & N. W. R. Co. v. Moss, 690.
Chichester v. Quatrefages, 469.
Chidester v. Harlan, 725.
Chilcoat v. Reid, 774.
Chilcote v. Hoffman, 525.
Chinsky's Will, In re, 254.
Chinsky's Will, Matter of, 545.
Chippendale v. North Adams Sav. Bank, 170.
Chisholm's Heirs v. Ben, 509.
Chism v. Chism, 719, 721.
Chitty v. Gillett, 702, 802.
Chochrel v. Robinson, 87.
Choiniere's Estate, 544.
Chongas' Estate, In re, 241.
Chrisman v. Chrisman, 251.
Chrismer v. Allman, 785.
Christerson v. French, 696.
Christian, Goods of, 333.
Christianson v. Talmage, 526.
Christie v. Chicago, R. I. & P. R. Co., 569, 572.
Christ's Home v. Mattson, 812, 814.
Christy v. Vest, 589.
Churchill, In re, 453, 460.
Churchill's Estate, In re, 305.
Church of Jesus Christ of Latter Day Saints v. Scarborough, 195.
Cion v. Schupack, 802.
C. I. R. v. Cadwalader, 795.
Cissna v. Beaton, 146.
Citizens' Bank v. Kasten, 701.
Citizens' Nat. Bank v. Brewer, 647.
Citizens' Nat. Bank v. Green, 129.
Citizens & Southern Nat. Bank v. Hendricks, 497.
City of. See under name of city.
Claflin's Will, In re, 345.
Clancy v. Gay, 624.
Clapp v. Houg, 600.
Clapp v. Tower, 637.
Clark, Estate of, 489.
Clark, In re, 300.
Clark v. Allen, 93.
Clark v. Berkeley, 433, 435.
Clark v. Boaler's Estate, 189.
Clark v. Bridges, 168.
Clark v. Cammann, 784.
Clark v. Capital Nat. Bank of Sacramento, 798.
Clark v. Carpenter, 307.
Clark v. Clark, 758.
Clark v. Commerce Trust Co., 260.
Clark v. Crandall, 326.
Clark v. Dennison, 386.
Clark v. Gauntt, 730.
Clark v. Goodwin, 684, 685.
Clark v. Hershy, 772.
Clark v. Hills, 674.
Clark v. Hugo, 206, 416, 477.
Clark v. Johnson, 314.
Clark v. Mack, 784.
Clark v. Patterson, 604, 6..
Clark v. Sloan, 802.
Clark v. Tennessee Chemical Co., 661, 663.
Clark v. Truslow, 800, 801.
Clark v. West, 216.
Clark's Estate, In re, 99, 349, 359.
Clark's Estate, In re, 722.
Clark's Estate, Matter of, 493.
Clarke v. Clarke, 806.
Clarke v. Commerce State & Sav. Bank, 161, 197.
Clarke v. Cotton, 791.
Clarke v. Johnson, 657, 658.
Clarke's Estate, 329.
Clarkson v. Bliley, 91, 92, 211.
Clarkson v. Kirtright, 342.
Clary v. Spain, 719.
Clary's Estate, In re, 570, 789.
Clausen v. Leary, 404, 411, 414.
Claussen v. Brothers, 685.
Clawson's Estate, In re, 626.
Clay v. Layton, 185.
Clayton v. Dinwoodey, 693.
Clayton v. Liverman, 223.
Clayton v. Lord Nugent, 297.
Cleage v. Jackson, 693.
Clearspring Township of Lagrange County v. Blough, 498.
Cleary v White's Estate, 751, 753.
Cleaver v. Mutual Reserve Fund Life Ass'n, 158.
Cleaves v. Kenney, 214.
Clegg v. Rowland, 800.
Clemenson v. Rebsamen, 405.
Clemens' Estate, In re, 624.
Clement v. Rainey, 239.
Clement v. Whisnant, 755, 828, 831.
Clements v. Fletcher, 651, 652, 655.
Clements v. Hood, 721.
Clere v. Brook, 38.
Cleveland v. Creed, 556, 559.

Cleveland Trust Co. v. Scobie, 169, 171.
Cleveland Trust Co. v. White, 178.
Clevidence v. Mercantile Home Bank & Trust Co., 167.
C. L. Hardy & Co. v. Turnage, 661.
Clifford v. Cronin, 782.
Clifford v. Kampfe, 113.
Cliff's Estate, In re, 498.
Cliff's Trusts, In re, 296.
Clifton v. Clifton, 238, 800, 801.
Clifton v. Guest, 675.
Clifton v. Murray, 252.
Cline v. Cline, 725.
Cline's Estate, In re, 733, 746, 765.
Clinefelter v. Ayres, 670.
Clingan v. Mitcheltree, 440.
Clippinger v. Wood, 621.
Clisby, Estate of, 360.
Clonney's Will, In re, 785.
Clover v. Neely, 697.
Cloward's Estate, In re, 584.
Coale v. Smith, 471.
Coats v. Riley, 500.
Cobb v. Hanford, 218.
Cobb v. MacFarland, 772.
Cobb v. Stratton's Estate, 753.
Cobb's Estate, In re, 555, 557.
Cochran v. Cochran, 116.
Cochran v. Garth, 722.
Cochran v. Zachery, 528.
Cocklin's Estate, In re, 409, 534.
Cockrill v. Cox, 534.
Coddington v. Jenner, 508, 509, 510, 554.
Codman v. American Piano Co., 636.
Codner v. Caldwell, 431.
Coffey v. McEwen, 573.
Coffield's Estate, In re, 557.
Coffield's Will, In re, 466.
Coffin v. Coffin, 329.
Coffin v. Otis, 448.
Coffman v. Coffman, 3, 723, 726, 727, 728.
Coffman v. Hedrick, 315.
Coffman's Adm'r v. Coffman, 814.
Coghill v. Kennedy, 533.
Coghlin v. Coghlin, 444.
Coghlin v. White, 442, 509, 553.
Cogswell v. Hall, 604.
Cogswell v. Tibbetts, 148.
Cohen v. Newton Sav. Bank, 174, 176.
Coker v. Coker, 152.
Coker v. Crozier, 683.
Colaci's Estate, In re, 112.
Colbert v. Thornley, 608.
Colbert's Estate, In re, 539, 540.
Colburn's Estate, In re, 651, 652, 655.
Colcord v. Conroy, 427.
Cole v. Cole, 528, 529, 530.
Cole v. Elfe, 132.
Cole v. Lewis, 75.
Cole v. Shelton, 485, 486, 503.
Cole v. Watertown, 603.
Cole v. Webb, 380, 381.
Coleman v. Lindley, 500.
Coleman v. M'Murdo, 577.
Coleman's Estate, In re, 136, 138.
Collagan v. Burns, 540.
Collamore v. Wilder, 706, 831.
Collard v. Collard, 445.
Collier v. Carter, 189.
Collier v. Collier's Ex'rs, 132.
Collier v. Rutledge, 219.
Collier v. Slaughter's Adm'r, 408.
Collingwood v. Pace, 54.
Collins v. Collins, 465, 478, 479, 529, 793.
Collins v. Elstone, 277, 459.
Collins v. Henry, 689.
Collins v. Long, 239, 249.
Collins v. Metropolitan Life Ins. Co., 95.
Collins v. Townley, 249.
Collins' Estate, In re, 244, 569.
Collins' Estate, Matter of, 757, 768.
Collis v. Walker, 252, 320, 548.
Collopy's Estate, 176.
Collum v. Price, 504.
Collyer v. Collyer, 509, 554, 555.
Colman, In re, 342.
Colman v. Lindley, 546.
Colonial Trust Co. v. Perry, 451.
Colonial Trust Co. v. Waldron, 404.
Colton v. Wade, 157, 158.
Columbia Trust Co. v. Christopher, 398.
Colvin v. Jones, 596.
Colyer v. Huntley, 671.
Combs v. Combs, 285.
Combs v. Roark, 640.
Comer v. Light, 711.
Commerce Nat. Bank of Toledo v. Browning, 785.
Commerce Union Bank v. Fox, 609, 615.

Commercial Bank of Augusta v. Burckhalter, 132.
Commercial Nat. Bank of Charlotte v. Misenheimer, 769.
Commercial Trust Co. v. White, 167.
Commercial & Sav. Bank of Winchester v. Burton, 665.
Commissioner v. Hart, 165.
Commonwealth v. Bullock, 632.
Commonwealth v. Miller, 622.
Commonwealth v. Nancrede, 88.
Commonwealth v. Stauffer, 407.
Compher v. Browning, 549.
Compton v. Dannenbauer, 442, 540.
Comstock v. Bowles, 666.
Comstock v. Crawford, 591.
Comstock v. Hadlyme Ecclesiastical Society, 276.
Comstock v. Matthews, 697, 705.
Conant v. Stone, 670.
Condit v. De Hart, 399.
Condry v. Coffey, 197.
Cone, Ex parte, 594.
Cone v. Donovan, 328, 545.
Cone v. Johnston, 530.
Conklin v. Conklin, 528.
Conlee v. Conlee, 808.
Conley v. Fenelon, 556, 557.
Connecticut Life Ins. Co. v. Schurmeier, 693.
Connecticut River Sav. Bank v. Albee's Estate, 173, 174.
Connecticut Transit & Safe Deposit Co. v. Chase, 744.
Connell v. Harper, 672.
Connelly v. Sullivan, 522.
Conners v. Murphy, 203.
Connery v. Connery, 450, 530.
Connolly's Estate, In re, 767, 793.
Connor v. Sheridan, 404.
Connors v. Cunard S. S. Co., 597.
Connor's Estate, In re, 605.
Conrad v. Long, 408, 413.
Conrades v. Heller, 313.
Conser v. Snowden, 204.
Continental Illinois Nat. Bank & Trust Co. of Chicago v. Art Institute, 394.
Converse v. Nichols, 698, 802.
Converse & Co. v. Sorley, 705.
Convey v. Murphy, 260.
Conway, In re, 304, 389.
Conway v. Shea, 733, 734, 736.
Conzet v. Hibben, 501, 502.
Coode, Goods of, 384.
Cook v. Catlin, 68.
Cook v. Hollyday, 261.
Cook v. Jeffett, 438, 440, 552.
Cook v. Jennings, 711.
Cook v. Morrison, 528.
Cook v. Morton, 255.
Cook v. Redfield, 565.
Cook v. Sink, 402, 405.
Cook v. White, 467.
Cook v. Winchester, 338, 342, 343, 344.
Cook's Estate, In re, 345, 380, 381, 417.
Cook's Will, In re, 527, 728.
Cooke v. Turner, 410.
Cookman v. Bateman, 250.
Cookson's Estate, In re, 258.
Cooley v. Lee, 486, 503, 505.
Cooley v. Powers, 87.
Coomes v. Finegan, 776.
Cooper, Goods of, 277.
Cooper v. Bockett, 338, 544.
Cooper v. Cooper, 607.
Cooper v. Remsen, 408.
Cooper v. Shannon, 546, 547.
Cooper's Estate, In re, 546, 742, 743, 747, 748.
Cooper's Will, In re, 289, 551.
Cope v. Cope, 813.
Copeland v. Shapley, 582.
Copenhaver v. Pendleton, 102.
Copperfield's Estate, In re, 609.
Coppock's Estate, In re, 488, 595.
Coral Gables First Nat. Bank v. Hart, 574.
Corbett v. Skaggs, 778, 785.
Corblis' Will, In re, 257.
Corby, Goods of, 371.
Corcoran v. Williams, 355.
Corley v. McElmeel, 534.
Cornelius' Will, In re, 522.
Corner v. Shew, 651, 652.
Cornett v. Hough, 80.
Corning's Estate, In re, 487.
Corr v. Porter, 470.
Cortte's Estate, In re, 111.
Coryell's Will, Matter of, 524.
Cosgrove's Estate, In re, 207, 326.
Cosgrove's Will, Matter of, 510.
Costello's Estate, Matter of, 81.
Coston v. Portland Trust Co., 183.

Cottle v. Vanderheyden, 609.
Couch v. Eastham, 276.
Coulter v. Bradley, 763.
Coulter v. Carter, 187.
Coulter v. Hardin, 539.
Councill v. Mayhew, 263.
Courtenay v. Courtenay, 783.
Courtney v. Daniel, 805.
Cousens v. Advent Church of City of Biddeford, 483, 501, 502, 503, 506.
Couts, In re, 795.
Cover v. Stem, 199.
Covington's Estate, In re, 381.
Cowan v. Cowan, 500, 517.
Cowan v. Perkins, 577.
Cowan v. Walker, 505, 519.
Cowans v. Beans, 523.
Cowden v. Jacobsen, 591.
Cowell's Estate, In re, 131.
Cowley v. Twombly, 408.
Cox, Appeal of, 313.
Cox v. Clark, 78.
Cox v. Cox, 65, 151.
Cox v. Harris, 785.
Cox v. Kansas, 598.
Cox v. Reed, 185, 187.
Cox' Will, In re, 299.
Coyne's Estate, In re, 304, 797.
Craig v. McVey, 208.
Craig v. Walthall, 121.
Craig v. Wismar, 344, 348.
Craig's Estate, In re, 797.
Crain v. Crain, 696.
Crain v. Mallone, 720.
Cramer, In re Will of, 738.
Cramer v. Brown, 815.
Cramer v. Hartford-Connecticut Trust Co., 178, 179.
Crampton v. Osburn, 437, 540.
Crane's Estate, In re, 111, 132, 134, 596, 739.
Crapo v. Price, 815.
Crary, In re, 633.
Cravath v. Plympton, 683.
Cravens v. Cravens, 799.
Crawford v. Engram, 529.
Crawford v. Le Fevre, 798.
Crawford v. McCarthy, 733, 735.
Crawford v. Thompson, 407.
Crawford v. Wilson, 92.
Crawford's Will, In re, 334.
Crawfordsville Trust Co. v. Ramsey, 204, 519, 534.
Crawley, In re, 283.
Crayton v. Phillips, 719.
Creamer v. Harris, 394.
Creech v. McVaugh, 452.
Creek v. Laski, 504.
Creesy v. Willis, 764.
Crenshaw v. Ware's Ex'r, 665.
Crerar v. Williams, 786.
Crews v. U. S. Fidelity & Guaranty Co., 711.
Creyts v. Creyts, 146.
Crisler Estate, In re, 501.
Crist v. Tallman, 695.
Crist's Estate, In re, 168.
Crocker v. Crocker, 124, 126.
Crocker v. Smith, 185.
Croft v. Snedow, 256.
Crohn v. Clay County State Bank, 588.
Croker's Will, In re, 491, 492, 497.
Croke's Estate, In re, 130.
Crompton v. Sale, 770.
Cronin v. Cronin, 405.
Cronin's Estate, Matter of, 412, 413.
Crooke v. Watt, 51.
Crooker v. McArdle, 450.
Crosby's Estate, In re, 553, 811.
Cross v. O'Cavanaugh, 814.
Crossan v. Crossan, 125.
Crossan v. McCrary, 602.
Crossman v. Crossman, 383, 442, 493, 544.
Crouse v. Peterson, 670.
Crouse's Estate, In re, 134, 736.
Crousore v. Allee, 793.
Crowell v. Tuttle, 313.
Crowley v. Farley, 521.
Crowley v. Nixon, 402.
Crowninshield v. Crowninshield, 545, 546, 554.
Crownover v. Crownover, 131.
Crozer's Estate, In re, 13.
Cruikshank v. Home for the Friendless, 785.
Crum v. Crum, 233, 234, 251.
Crumbaugh v. Owen, 247.
Crump v. Faucett, 65, 723.
Crumpler v. Barfield & Wilson Co., 771, 772, 776.
Cruson's Estate, In re, 599.
Cryan's Estate, In re, 90.
Cucullu's Succession, 790.

Cudney v. United Power & L. Corp., 643.
Culberhouse v. Culberhouse, 720.
Culley's Will, In re, 425.
Culp v. Culp, 142.
Culver v. Hess, 226.
Cummings v. Allen, 134.
Cummings v. Bramhall, 720, 787, 790.
Cummings v. Lowe, 665.
Cummings v. Lynn, 671.
Cummings' Estate, 329.
Cummings' Estate, In re, 326, 526.
Cummins v. Peed, 658.
Cunniff's Estate, 671.
Cunningham, In re, 449, 450, 512.
Cunningham, Succession of, 382, 431.
Cunningham v. Cunningham, 338, 343, 344.
Cunningham v. Cureton, 637.
Cunningham v. Davis, 186, 187.
Cunningham v. Edward, 271.
Cunningham v. Hallyburton, 294, 298, 347.
Cunningham v. Lakin, 709.
Cunningham v. Rodgers, 562.
Cunnius v. Reading School District, 600.
Curley v. Lynch, 399.
Currie v. Scott, 707, 765.
Curry v. Cotton, 226.
Curry v. Pile, 771.
Curry's Will, In re, 142.
Curser, In re, 608.
Curser, Matter of, 612.
Curtis v. Hewins, 83.
Curtis' Will, Matter of, 499.
Custer v. Beyer, 673.
Cutlar v. Cutlar, 76, 249, 339, 440.
Cutler v. Meeker, 637.
Cutler's Will, In re, 273.
Cutler's Will, Matter of, 2.
Cutright v. Stanford, 802.
C. W. Beggs, Sons & Co. v. Behrend's Estate, 661.
Byrkett v. Josephs, 530.

# D

Dabbs v. Richardson, 252.
Dabney v. Continental Jewelry Co., 711.
Dabney v. Dabney, 701, 802.
Daboll v. Moon, 408.
D'Adamo's Estate, Matter of, 611.
Daggett v. Boomer, 532, 543.
Dailey v. Dailey, 145.
Daintree v. Butcher and Fasulo, 324, 327.
Daiss v. Hanes, 736, 737.
Dalby v. Maxfield, 212.
Dale's Will, In re, 330.
Dallago v. Atlantic Coast Line R. Co., 619.
Dallas County v. Club Land & Cattle Co., 653.
Dallett v. Taggart, 231.
Dalton's Estate, In re, 557.
Daly v. Connolly, 80.
Daly v. Hussey, 241.
Daly v. Pacific Sav. & Loan Ass'n, 167.
Daly v. Rogers, 806.
Dambly, Succession of, 475
Dampier v. Trust Co., 709.
Damron v. Allen, 634.
Damron v. Bartley, 717.
Damsky's Estate, In re, 624.
Dancer v. Crabb, 457.
Danford Estate, In re, 451.
Danford, Estate of, 601.
Daniel v. Bank of West Point, 662, 663.
Daniel v. Finley, 504.
Daniel v. Tyler, 388.
Daniel v. Tyler's Executors, 395.
Daniels v. Benedict, 153.
Daniels v. Bishop, 636.
Daniels v. Jones, 622.
Daniels v. Taylor, 150.
Daniels' Estate, Matter of, 148.
Daniels' Will, In re, 596.
Danley v. Jefferson, 466, 476.
Dant's Ex'rs v. Cooper, 630.
D'Arcangelo v. D'Arcangelo, 144.
Dardis' Will, In re, 530.
Darling's Estate, In re, 89.
Darlington v. Pulteney, 223.
Darlington's Estate, In re, 136.
Darnaby v. Halley's Ex'r, 326, 332.
Darnell v. Tate, 630.
Darrough v. Davis, 84, 150, 151.
Darrow v. Darrow, 152.
Daub's Estate, In re, 122.
Dauel v. Arnold, 758.
Daugherty v. Preuitt, 195.

Daugherty v. State Sav., Loan & Trust Co., 249.
Davenhill v. Fletcher, 758.
Davenport, Matter of, 71.
Davers v. Dewes, 48.
Davidson v. Miners' & Mechanics' Sav. & Trust Co., 133.
Davidson v. Story, 656.
Davidson's Estate, In re, 138.
Davie v. Davie, 202.
Davies' Estate, In re, 613.
Davies' Will, In re, 771.
Davis, Estate of, 138.
Davis Estate, In re, 347.
Davis v. Aultman, 242, 245, 279, 280.
Davis v. Badlam, 772.
Davis v. Blumenberg, 682.
Davis v. Calvert, 266, 268.
Davis v. Crandall, 785.
Davis v. Davis, 293, 317, 506, 758, 786, 800.
Davis v. Davis' Estate, 149, 150.
Davis v. Fogle, 430.
Davis v. Hilliard, 124.
Davis v. Hutchinson, 638.
Davis v. John E. Brown College of Siloam Springs, Ark., 190, 192.
Davis v. Laning, 95.
Davis v. Mather, 123.
Davis v. Miller, 612, 619.
Davis v. Newman, 800, 801.
Davis v. Nichols, 685.
Davis v. Price, 747, 750.
Davis v. Rowe, 67, 71.
Davis v. Seavey, 799.
Davis v. Shepard, 690.
Davis v. Sigourney, 509, 512.
Davis v. Tremain, 805.
Davis v. Upson, 487.
Davis' Estate, In re, 324, 381, 475, 696.
Davis' Will, In re, 326, 498, 522, 523, 731.
Davison v. Rake, 753.
Davy v. Smith, 342.
Dawes v. Head, 592.
Dawkins v. Dawkins, 334.
Dawley v. Congdon, 442, 554, 555.
Dawley's Estate, In re, 325.
Dawson v. Corbett, 212.
Dawson v. Mays, 149.
Dawson v. Shave, 607.
Dawson v. Smith, 475.
Dawson v. Smith's Will, 507.
Dawson's Estate, In re, 383.
Day v. Day, 252.
Day v. Grubbs, 718.
Day v. Washburn, 214.
Deal v. Sexton, 75.
Dean v. Dickey, 357.
Dean v. Tusculum, 747.
Deans v. Deans, 140, 236.
Dearing v. Dearing, 380.
Deaves' Estate, Appeal of, 507.
De Bernal's Estate, In re, 707, 708, 751.
De Buck's Estate, In re, 494.
De Caccia's Estate, In re, 358.
De Campi v. Logan, 473.
Decker v. Decker, 125.
Decker v. Fahrenholtz, 616.
Decker v. Fowler, 172.
Decker v. Koenig, 258.
DeCoe v. Johnson, 638.
Decoster's Estate, Matter of, 453.
De Crow v. Harkness, 140.
Deeds v. Deeds, 137, 138.
Deehan's Will, In re, 556.
Deeks v. Strutt, 797.
Deem v. Millikin, 153.
Deery v. Hall, 251.
De France v. Johnson, 151, 152.
Deichman v. Arndt, 770.
Dekle v. McLeod, 579.
Delafield v. Parish, 234, 238, 481.
Delaney's Estate, In re, 649.
Delano v. Bruerton, 88.
De Lapp v. Anderson, 209.
Delavergne's Will, In re, 311, 320.
Delaware Trust Co. v. Fitzmaurice, 176, 405.
Deleglise v. Morrissey, 557.
Del Genovese's Will, 423.
De Lin's Estate, In re, 559.
De Lion's Estate, In re, 457.
Del Paronto's Estate, In re, 697.
Delprat's Will, In re, 330.
Demaris' Estate, In re, 341, 343.
De Mendoza, Appeal of, 429.
De Moulin's Estate, In re, 275, 285.
De Mouy v. Jepson, 287.
Dempsey v. McNabb, 646.
Dempster's Estate, In re, 799.
Denigan v. Hibernia Sav. & Loan Soc., 167.
Denise v. Denise, 791.

Denison v. Dawes, 111.
Denison's Estate, Matter of, 720, 722.
Denlinger's Estate, In re, 675.
Denmark v. Rushing, 366.
Dennett, Estate of, In re, 583.
Dennett v. Dennett, 184.
Dennis v. Gorman, 676.
Dennis v. Holsapple, 395, 399, 400.
Dennis' Estate, In re, 621.
Dennison v. Lilley, 751.
Denny v. Gardner, 562.
Denson v. Crossley, 624.
Denton v. Miller, 90.
Denton's Estate, In re, 518.
De Paris v. Wilmington Trust Co., 586, 590.
De Rome's Estate, In re, 660.
Derr v. Derr, 387, 447, 448, 466, 467, 469, 478.
Derruau's Estate, In re, 425.
Derusseau's Will, In re, 250.
Desmarteau v. Fortin, 812, 814.
Des Moines Transp. Co. v. Haring, 697.
Detroit, City of v. Stafford, 699.
Detsch's Estate, In re, 550.
Dettmer v. Behrens, 657.
Devers v. Schreiber, 706, 831.
Dexheimer's Estate, In re, 85.
Dexter v. Berge, 587.
Dexter v. Codman, 520.
Dexter v. President, etc., of Harvard College, 786.
Dexter v. Witte, 185.
Deyton's Will, In re, 342, 380, 383.
De Zotell v. Mutual Life Ins. of New Year Co., 154, 158.
Diament's Estate, Re, 479.
Dick v. Taylor, 122.
Dicken v. Fairchild, 724.
Dicken v. McKinlay, 215.
Dickens v. Bonnewell, 545.
Dickerson's Estate, Re, 597.
Dickey v. Dickey, 546.
Dickey v. Malechi, 506, 510.
Dickey's Estate, In re, 556.
Dickinson v. Dickinson, 318.
Dickman v. Birkhauser, 152.
Dickson v. Fisher, 593.
Dicus v. Scherer, 671.
Diederichs' Estate, In re, 592.
Dieteman's Estate, In re, 733, 735, 746.
Dietterich's Estate, In re, 304.
Diggs v. Smith, 269.
Di Iorio v. Cantone, 697.
Dillard's Estate, In re, 621.
Dillen v. Fancher, 622.
Dillon's Will, In re, 259.
Dimmitt, Estate of, In re, 209.
Dimmitt's Estate, In re, 390.
Dingman v. Boyle, 583.
Dinning v. Dinning, 361.
Di Persia's Estate, In re, 336.
Disston's Estate, 125.
Ditchey v. Lee, 402, 763.
Ditton v. Hart, 238.
Diver v. Fourth Nat. Bank of Wichita, 83.
Dixon v. Clarke, 620.
Dixon v. Solicitor to the Treasury, 453–457.
Doan v. Herod, 557.
Dobie v. Armstrong, 546.
Dobson v. Smith, 811, 814.
Dockum v. Robinson, 365.
Dodd v. Anderson, 492, 557.
Dodson v. Ward, 90.
Doe v. Redfern, 99.
Doe v. Underdown, Willes, 786.
Doe d. Allen v. Allen, 287.
Doe d. Evans v. Evans, 460.
Doe d. George Gord v. Needs, 288.
Doe d. Hiscocks v. Hiscocks, 282, 287.
Doe d. Perkes v. Perkes, 421.
Doe d. Reed v. Harris, 437.
Doe ex dem. Hubbard v. Hubbard, 283, 287.
Doe ex dem. Shore v. Porter, 637.
Doe ex dem. Small v. Allen, 265.
Doepke's Estate, In re, 734.
Doerfer, Estate of, 226.
Doherty v. Mangan, 369.
Dolan v. Anthony, 590.
Dolenty's Estate, In re, 604, 609, 610, 625, 647, 794.
Dombrovski v. Mayor and City Council of Baltimore, 97.
Dombrowski's Estate, In re, 301.
Domby v. Heath, 633.
Domestic & Foreign Missionary Soc. v. Crippled Children's Hospital, 752.
Dominci's Estate, In re, 452.
Donaldson, Estate of, 369.
Donaldson v. Hall, 423, 431.
Donegan v. Wade, 412.

Donelson's Estate v. Gorman, 625.
Dong Ling Hing's Estate, In re, 329, 523.
Donnell v. Goss, 495.
Donnelly, Estate of, In re, 96.
Donnelly v. Slaughter, 616.
Donnely's Will, In re, 267, 279.
Donough v. Garland, 727, 729, 730.
Donovan v. St. Joseph's Home, 547.
Doolittle's Estate, In re, 251.
Doppes' Estate, In re, 630, 631.
Dorrity's Will, 506.
Dorrity's Will, Matter of, 508.
Dorsey v. Dorsey, 582, 601, 615, 620.
Dorsey v. Georgia R. Bank & Trust Co., 134.
Doss v. Stevens, 656.
Doster's Estate, In re, 244.
Doty's Estate, In re, 556, 558.
Dougan's Estate, In re, 456, 457.
Dougherty v. Dougherty, 417.
Dougherty v. Holscheider, 459.
Dougherty's Estate, In re, 324.
Doughty's Will, In re, 435.
Douglas' Estate, In re, 3, 733, 735, 746.
Douglass v. Hammel, 720, 725–728.
Douglass v. Harkrender, 207.
Douty's Estate, In re, 671.
Dover Cooperative Bank v. Tobin's Estate, 168.
Dow v. Lillie, 591.
Dow's Estate, In re, 345, 612.
Dowd v. Dowd, 492.
Dowdey v. Palmer, 241.
Dowell v. Dowell, 126.
Dower v. Church, 521.
Dower v. Seeds, 440, 506.
Dowling v. Gilliland, 439.
Downey v. Guilfoile, 549, 551.
Downey v. Lawley, 260, 276.
Downing v. Maag, 220.
Downing v. Nicholson, 783.
Downings' Estates, In re, 70.
Doyle v. Brady, 316.
Doyle v. Fischer, 224, 419.
Drace v. Klinedinst, 413.
Drain v. Stough, 701.
Drake v. Drake, 282, 287.
Drake v. Knouff, 80.
Drake v. Rogers, 76.
Drake v. Security Trust Co., 202.
Drake v. Wild, 768, 772.
Drake's Estate, In re, 553.
Draper v. Draper, 70.
Dreisback v. Spring, 526.
Drennan v. Douglass, 213.
Dresser v. Fourth Nat. Bank of Wichita, 596.
Drew, Estate of, In re, 584.
Drew, Estate of, 832.
Drew's Estate, In re, 582.
Drewry v. Raleigh Sav. Bank & Trust Co., 134.
Dreyer v. Schrick, 89, 430.
Dreyfus, Estate of, 357.
Dries' Will, In re, 266.
Driver v. Driver, 451.
Droge's Will, In re, 323, 325, 326.
Drohan v. Avellar, 513.
Druen v. Hudson, 383.
Druey v. Druey, 110.
Drum v. Capps, 238.
Drummond v. Hardaway, 569.
Drummond v. Parish, 368, 369.
Drury v. King, 260.
Dubach v. Jolly, 340, 341.
Dubois' Estate, In re, 469.
Duck v. McGrath, 761.
Duckett v. Duckett, 257.
Dudley v. Gates, 461, 804.
Dudrow v. King, 80.
Duehay v. Acacia Mut. Life Ins. Co., 592.
Duffie v. Corridon, 337, 338.
Duffy v. Harris, 150.
Duffy's Estate, In re, 524.
Dugan v. Hollins, 734.
Duggins, Goods of, In re, 331, 332, 334.
Dulin v. Bailey, 504.
Dulin v. Dulin, 543.
Duling v. Duling's Estate, 167.
Dulles' Estate, In re, 125.
Dumas' Estate, In re, 382.
Dumont, Matter of, 370.
Dumont's Estate, In re, 369.
Dunahugh's Will, In re, 450.
Duncan v. Bigelow, 743, 748.
Duncan's Contested Will, 538.
Duncan's Estate, In re, 153.
Dungan v. Superior Court of Fresno County, 598.
Dungan's Estate, In re, 743.
Dunham v. Averill, 459.
Dunham v. Holmes, 238.

Dunham v. Randall, 667.
Dunham's Estate, In re, 614.
Dunkeson v. Williams, 310.
Dunlap v. Hart, 435, 744.
Dunlap v. Ingram, 413.
Dunlap v. Marnell, 191.
Dunlap's Will, In re, 336.
Dunn v. German-American Bank, 204.
Dunn v. Portsmouth Sav. Bank, 151.
Dunn v. Renick, 757.
Dunningan v. Stevens, 703.
Dunshee v. Dunshee, 788.
Dunster, In re, 784.
Dunsworth v. Dunsworth, 451.
Durance, Goods of, 449.
Durand v. Higgins, 187.
Durant v. Friend, 745.
Durant v. Prestwood, 48.
Durant v. Whitcher, 537.
Durfee v. Joslyn, 674.
Durfee v. Risch, 429.
Durflinger v. Arnold, 698.
Durham v. Clay, 744.
Durham v. Northen, 471.
Durkin, Succession of, 131.
Durlewanger, Estate of, 358, 359.
Dusbiber v. Melville, 408.
Dusek v. Pennsylvania, 643.
Dutcher's Estate, In re, 305.
Dutterer v. Logan, 409, 412.
Dutton v. Buckley, 573.
Dutton v. Donahue, 94, 98, 99.
Duvale v. Duvale, 217.
DuVall v. Faulkner, 799.
Dye v. Parker, 265, 271.
Dyke v. Walford, 56.
Dyste v. Farmers & Mechanics Sav. Bank, 169, 171, 176.

# E

Eaker v. Husbands, 651, 652, 654.
Eakins v. District Court, 523.
Earl v. Earl, 80.
Earl v. Mundy, 343.
Early v. Arnold, 209, 231.
Easley v. Rowe, 705.
Eason's Estate, In re, 814.
Eastman, Succession of, 349, 359.
E. A. Strout Farm Agency v. Worthen, 651, 652.
Eastwood v. Crane, 724.
Eaton v. Brown, 417, 418.
Eaton v. Walker, 651, 652.
Ebbinger v. Wightmen, 571.
Ebert v. Whitney, 700, 701.
Eckardt v. Osborne, 434.
Eckart v. Eckart, 430.
Eckert v. Givan, 120, 520.
Eckert v. Stewart, 192.
Eckland v. Jankowski, 503.
Edder's Estate, In re, 508.
Eddey's Appeal, 244.
Eddington v. Turner, 434, 734, 746.
Eddy v. Adams, 689.
Eddy v. Pinder, 190.
Eder's Estate, In re, 554.
Edgar v. Richardson, 151.
Edler v. Frazier, 729.
Edmundson's Estate, In re, 213.
Edwards v. Cuthbert, 152.
Edwards v. Ela, 558.
Edwards v. Fincham, 252.
Edwards v. Sands, 674.
Edward's Estate, In re, 471, 473, 601.
Effertz' Estate, In re, 603.
Egbert v. Egbert, 520, 523.
Eggers v. Eggers, 239.
Eggleston v. Merriam, 734.
Egley's Estate, In re, 89.
Egners v. Egbers, 541, 554.
Ehlers' Will, In re, 812, 814.
Ehle's Estate, In re, 140.
Ehlke's Will, In re, 501.
Eichelberger's Estate, In re, 723.
Eilbeck v. Wood, 433, 743, 746.
Einstein v. Strother, 794.
Eisenberg v. Reininger, 132, 709.
Eisenlohr's Estate, In re, 166, 198.
Eissler v. Hoppel, 727.
Eklund's Estate, In re, 252.
Ela v. Edwards, 381.
Elam v. Phariss, 277.
Elder's Estate, In re, 615.
Electric Welding Co. v. Simpkins, 702.
Elizalde v. Elizalde, 697.
Elkerton's Estate, In re, 327.
Elk Horn Coal Corp. v. Jacks Creek Coal Co., 283.
Ellenberg v. Arthur, 643.
Ellerson v. Westcott, 154, 155.
Ellet v. McCord, 784.
Ellicott v. Ellicott, 404.
Elliot v. Brent, 311, 316.
Elliot v. Collier, 606.
Elliott v. First Nat. Bank, 694.

Elliott v. Western Coal & Mining Co., 721.
Elliott's Estate, In re, 202, 502, 631.
Ellis v. Dumond, 790.
Ellis v. Moss, 557.
Ellis v. Northwestern Mutual Life Ins. Co., 590.
Ellis v. O'Neal, 539.
Ellis v. Smith, 323.
Ellis' Estate, In re, 82, 305.
Ellison v. Clayton, 208, 209.
Ellison v. Smoot's Adm'r, 416.
Ellsworth v. Struckmeyer, 795, 796.
Ellwanger v. Ellwanger's Adm'r, 601, 602.
Ellyson v. Lord, 671.
Elmore v. Bishop, 581.
Elmore v. Cunninghame, 628.
Elmore's Estate, In re, 755.
Elston v. Price, 332.
Elton v. Lamb, 709.
Elwood's Estate, In re, 690.
Elwyn v. De Garmendia, 742, 748.
Ely v. Megie, 461, 763.
Emart's Estate, In re, 345.
Embry v. Millar, 589.
Emden's Estate, In re, 329.
Emerich v. Arendt, 237, 546.
Emernecker's Estate, In re, 454, 457.
Emerson, Goods of, 298.
Emerson's Estate, In re, 156.
Emery, Appellant, 426.
Emery v. Batchelder, 755.
Emery v. Clough, 201, 202.
Emery v. Darling, 212.
Emery v. Emery, 258.
Emhardt v. Collett, 532.
Emmon's Will, In re, 467, 468.
Engelthaler v. Engelthaler, 288.
Enger's Estate, In re, 793.
England v. Fawbush, 262.
England's Estate, In re, 361.
Engebretson's Estate, In re, 651, 652, 655.
Engelbrecht v. Engelbrecht, 167.
Engelbrecht v. Herrington, 222.
Engle v. Engle, 566.
Engle v. Walters, 729.
Engle's Estate, In re, 218, 465, 467, 469.
English v. Cooper, 784.
Ennis' Estate, In re, 662, 663.
Enohin v. Wylie, 53.
Enright v. Griffith, 558.
Enright's Estate, Matter of, 444.
Enright's Will, Matter of, 492.
Enscoe v. Fletcher, 710.
Enyart, Estate of, In re, 87, 545, 546, 548, 554.
Epperson v. Bennett, 102.
Epperson v. White, 223.
Equitable Trust Co. v. Banning, 473.
Equitable Trust Co. v. Causey, 810.
Equitable Trust Co. v. Coughlin, 603.
Equitable Trust Co. v. Plume, 605.
Equitable & Central Trust Co. v. Zdziebko, 171.
Ergang v. Anderson, 538.
Erickson v. Lundgren, 140.
Erickson's Estate, In re, 260.
Erlanger's Estate, In re, 630.
Ernest G. Beaudry v. Freeman, 649.
Erwin v. Felter, 170.
Erwin v. Hammer, 367.
Erwin v. Mark, 697.
Eschback v. Collins, 445.
Eschen v. Steers, 204.
Eschmann v. Cawi, 386.
Escolle's Estate, In re, 202.
Eslick v. Wodicka, 345.
Estabrook v. Moulton, 690.
Estes v. Estes, 208, 209.
Estes v. Merrill, 150, 151.
Estes v. Nicholson, 73.
Estes' Estate, In re, 580.
Etheridge v. Doe ex dem. Malempre, 98.
Ettenheimer v. Heffernan, 99.
Eubank v. Moore, 451.
Evans' Appeal, 438, 440.
Evans, Goods of, 307.
Evans' Estate, In re, 435, 744.
Evans' Will, In re, 372.
Evans v. Adams, 621.
Evans v. Cole, 216.
Evans v. Dickey, 649.
Evans v. Evans, 188.
Evans v. Miller, 569.
Evans v. Supreme Council of Royal Arcanum, 646.
Evans v. Tucker, 646.
Evansville Ice & Cold Storage Co. v. Winsor, 488, 489.
Eva's Appeal, 615.
Evatt v. Miller, 84.
Eveleth's Will, In re, 243.

Evelyn v. Evelyn, 47.
Everett's Estate, In re, 793.
Evers v. Williams, 778.
Eversole v. Eversole, 153.
Everson v. Hurn, 559.
Ewart v. Dalby, 519.
Ewell v. Rucker, 475, 476.
Ewell v. Sneed, 463.
Ewers v. White's Estate, 633.
Ewing v. Waddington, 528.
Ewing v. Warner, 178.
Ewing v. Wm. L. Foley, Inc., 649, 650.
Exchange Nat. Bank v. Betts' Estate, 651, 652, 659.

# F

Fair v. Fair, 706, 831.
Fakouri v. Cadais, 376, 483, 515.
Faling's Estate, In re, 559.
Falley v. Gribling, 671.
Fallon v. Chidester, 502.
Fallon's Estate, In re, 510.
Fallon's Will, In re, 520, 523.
Fann v. Fann, 348, 544.
Faris, In re, 460.
Farleigh v. Kelley, 546.
Farley v. Davis, 651, 652, 654.
Farmer v. Davis, 245, 249.
Farmer's Estate, In re, 132.
Farmers Bank & Trust Co. v. Harding, 466.
Farmers' Bank & Trust Co. v. Sheffler, 647.
Farmers' Exchange Bank v. Moffett, 722.
Farmer's Ex'r v. Farmer's Ex'r, 326.
Farmers Loan & Trust Co., In re, 717, 791.
Farmers' Loan & Trust Co., Matter of, 722.
Farmers' Loan & Trust Co. v. McCarty, 123, 125.
Farmers' Loan & Trust Co. v. Smith, 605.
Farmers' Loan & Trust Co. of Columbia City v. Security Trust Co. of Indianapolis, 314.
Farmers' Nat. Bank of Ponca City v. Cravens, 675.
Farmers' State Bank v. Callahan, 701.
Farmington Sav. Bank v. Curran, 774.
Farnham v. Phillips, 740.
Farnsworth v. Whiting, 778, 779.
Farnum v. Bascom, 759, 761, 762.
Farquhar, In re, 371.
Farquhar v. New England Trust Co., 675.
Farr v. O'Neall, 258.
Farr v. Whitfield, 410.
Farrands, In re, 610.
Farrell, In re, 176.
Farrell v. O'Brien, 515.
Farrell v. Sullivan, 283, 286.
Farris v. Stoutz, 699, 702.
Fass v. Blatz, 814.
Fatland's Estate, In re, 702.
Faughnan v. Bashlor, 613.
Faulk's Will, In re, 256, 258.
Faulkes v. Brummett's Adm'r, 258.
Faulkner v. Faulkner, 572.
Faust's Estates, In re, 257, 557.
Fawcett v. Fawcett, 164, 195.
Fawcett's Estate, In re, 127.
Fay, In re Estate of, 360.
Fearn v. Postlethwaite, 317.
Federal Trust Co. v. Cohen, 713.
Fedi v. Ryan, 73.
Feeney v. Runyan, 640.
Feinson's Estate, In re, 411.
Feital, Succession of, 498, 519.
Felker v. Taylor, 367.
Fellin's Estate, In re, 610.
Fell's Estate, In re, 142, 143.
Felton v. Felton, 664.
Fender v. Foust, 201, 203.
Fender v. Phillips, 704.
Fennell v. Fennell, 123.
Ferenbaugh v. Ferenbaugh, 726.
Fergus v. Tomlinson, 93.
Ferguson v. Billups, 442, 553.
Ferguson v. Ferguson, 148, 186, 331, 332, 417, 466, 814.
Ferguson v. Hedges, 786.
Ferguson v. Mason, 184.
Ferguson v. Morris, 588.
Ferguson's Estate, In re, 294, 314, 319, 320.
Fern v. Leuthold, 693.
Fernandez's Estate, In re, 661.
Ferrin v. Myrick, 576.
Ferris, In re Estate of, 791.
Fertel, Succession of, 377.

Fesler v. Simpson, 387.
Ffinch v. Combe, 438.
Fickle v. Snepp, 386, 387.
Fidelity Title & Trust Co. v. Young, 747, 750.
Fidelity Trust Co. v. Union Nat. Bank of Pittsburgh, 163.
Fidelity Trust Co. v. Walton, 667, 799.
Fidelity Union Trust Co. v. Carter, 802.
Fidelity Union Trust Co. v. Reeves, 729.
Fiduciary Trust Co. v. Michou, 82.
Field v. Borodofski, 697.
Fields v. Luck, 545.
Fields v. Michael, 64.
Field's Estate, In re, 525, 607, 608, 637.
Field's Will, Matter of, 303.
Fies v. Feist, 668.
Fifth Third Union Trust Co. v. Wilenksy, 393.
Files v. Green, 148.
Fillyau v. Laverty, 699.
Filor's Will, In re, 119.
Finch's Estate, In re, 782.
Findlay v. Chicago & G. T. Ry., 597.
Findlay v. Hosmer, 713.
Findlay v. Trigg, 801.
Finkenzeller's Estate, In re, 630.
Finkler's Estate, In re, 447.
Finley v. Abner, 74.
Finnerty v. Shade, 613.
First Baptist Church in Exeter v. Soban, 285.
First Mechanic's Nat. Bank of Trenton v. Norris, 386.
First Nat. Bank v. Mulich, 168, 170.
First Nat. Bank of Appleton, Wis. v. Brauns' Estate, 592, 593.
First Nat. Bank of Birmingham v. Lawrence, 167, 170.
First Nat. Bank of Boston v. Perkins Institute for Blind, 747.
First Nat. Bank of Boston v. Union Hospital of Fall River, 750.
First Nat. Bank of Hailey v. Glenn, 712.
First Nat. Bank of Kansas City v. Schaake, 121.
First Nat. Bank of Opp v. Weaver, 680.
First Nat. Bank & Trust Co. v. Baker, 471, 779.
First State Bank of Milford v. Wallace, 165.
First Trust Co. v. Holden, 530.
First Trust & Sav. Bank v. Henderson, 663, 671.
First Trust & Sav. Bank v. United States Fidelity & Guaranty Co., 793.
First Wisconsin Nat. Bank of Milwaukee v. Schwab, 182.
First & Merchants National Bank v. Bank of Waverly, 584.
Fischer v. Dolwig, 620.
Fischer's Estate, In re, 489, 498.
Fiscus v. Moore, 792.
Fish v. Sawyer, 184.
Fishel v. Dixson, 613.
Fisher v. Fisher, 411.
Fisher v. Gear, 499.
Fisher v. McNeely, 649.
Fisher v. Teter, 750.
Fisher's Estate, In re, 71, 381, 554, 667.
Fisk v. Fisk, 67.
Fitts v. Morse, 719.
Fitzgerald v. National Bank, 769, 770.
Fitzhugh, Succession of, 360.
Fitzpatrick v. Simonson Bros. Mfg. Co., 797.
Flanders v. White, 453, 455–457, 553, 555.
Flanigon v. Smith, 258.
Flath v. Neal, 597.
Flaugher's Estate, In re, 533.
Fleck v. Baldwin, 174.
Fleck v. Harmstad, 4.
Fleetwood, In re, 314.
Fleming v. Bolling, 644.
Fleming v. Carr, 749.
Fleming v. Kelly, Maus & Co., 662, 663.
Fleming v. Morrison, 206.
Fleming's Estate, In re, 797.
Fleshman's Estate, In re, 131, 662.
Fleshner v. Fleshner, 815.
Fletcher Trust Co. v. Morse, 442, 444, 445.
Flint's Estate, Matter of, 788.
Flippin v. Banner, 769.
Flood v. Pragoff, 305.
Florey's Ex'rs v. Florey, 243.

Floto v. Floto, 516.
Floyd v. Thomason, 651, 652, 654.
Flynn v. Bredbeck, 780.
Flynn v. Chicago Great Western R. Co., 664.
Flynn v. Driscoll, 693, 697, 705.
Flynn v. Flynn, 348.
Flynn v. New York, N. H. & H. R. Co., 643.
Flynn v. Stoutimore, 798.
Flynn's Estate, In re, 465.
Foley v. O'Donaghue, 526.
Foltz v. Maxwell, 672.
Folwell v. Folwell, 103.
Fontaine v. Fontaine, 3, 306, 314.
Foote v. Foote, 486, 492.
Foraker v. Kocks, 170.
Forbes v. City of Omaha, 684.
Forbing v. Weber, 511.
Force's Estate, In re, 781.
Ford v. Ford, 134, 236, 421, 744.
Ford's Estate, In re, 139, 442, 476, 500.
Fore v. McFadden, 531.
Foreman Trust & Sav. Bank v. Seelenfreund, 125.
Forney v. Remey, 180.
Forney's Estate, In re, 85.
Forquer's Estate, In re, 418.
Forrest v. Turner, 361.
Forse v. Hembling, 426.
Forster's Will, In re, 751.
Forsyth v. Heward, 92.
Forsythe, Estate of, In re, 538.
Fort Fairfield Nash Co. v. Nolteimer, 586.
Fortin v. Tanguay, 609.
Foster, Re, 130.
Foster v. Foster, 765.
Foster v. Lee, 83.
Foster's Appeal, 510, 554.
Foulke v. Zimmerman, 502.
Foulkes v. Foulks, 775.
Fountain v. Bank of America Nat. Trust & Sav. Ass'n, 562.
Foureman's Estate, In re, 602.
Fowler v. Ball, 627.
Fowler v. Lowe, 211.
Fowler v. Stagner, 316, 338.
Fowles, Matter of, 386, 393.
Fox v. Carr, 590.
Fox v. Fee, 486, 503, 505.
Fox v. Martin, 259, 558.
Fox v. Snow, 811.
Fox's Estate, In re, 439, 444
Frackelton v. Masters, 672.
Frahm's Estate, In re, 745.
Frame v. Whitaker, 435.
France's Estate, In re, 125.
Francis, In re Estate of, 359.
Franck v. Franck, 744.
Franklin v. Bogue, 439.
Franklin v. McLean, 555.
Franklin Washington Trust Co. v. Beltram, 172.
Franks v. Chapman, 331, 335.
Franks' Ex'r v. Bates, 256.
Fransioli v. Podesta, 362
Fraser, In re, 472.
Fraser v. Boone, 815.
Fraser v. Jennison, 243.
Frazer v. Fulcher, 96.
Frazier, Estate of, In re, 91.
Frazier v. Frazier, 294.
Frazier v. Patterson, 225, 226.
Frazier v. Wood, 815.
Frederick v. Hook, 579.
Freeman v. Freeman, 520.
Freeman v. Hart, 469.
Freeman v. Young, 532.
Free's Estate, In re, 293.
Freeth v. Rule, 751.
Freme's Estate, In re, 448.
French v. French, 418, 466.
French v. Vradenburg, 766.
French's Estate, In re, 98, 99, 739.
French's Will, In re, 491, 492.
Fretheim's Estate, In re, 70.
Friberg v. Zeutschel, 535.
Fricke, In re, 250.
Frickey's Will, In re, 306.
Frick's Estate, In re, 131.
Fridley v. Farmers' & Mechanics' Savings Bank, 599.
Friedenwald v. Burke, 578.
Friederichs v. Friederichs, 781.
Frieders v. Estate of Frieders, 218.
Friedersdorf v. Lacy, 257.
Friedman v. Goodlin, 633.
Friend's Estate, 409.
Friese's Estate, In re, 111.
Frieson, Ex parte, 609.
Fritch's Estate, In re, 134.
Fritts v. Fritts, 672.
Fritze's Estate, In re, 145.
Fritz's Estate, In re, 383.
Frizzell's Estate, In re, 133.

Frost v. Frost, 198.
Frost's Estate, In re, 744.
Frothingham's Will, In re, 438, 439.
Fry v. Morrison, 771.
Fry v. Fry, 448.
Frye v. Frye, 140.
Fulbright v. Perry County, 246.
Fulenwider v. Birmingham Trust & Sav. Co., 707, 765.
Fulleck v. Allison, 246.
Fuller v. Fuller, 310.
Fuller v. Parmenter, 729.
Fuller v. Williams, 328, 332.
Fuller's Estate, In re, 744.
Fuller's Will, In re, 542, 543.
Fulmer's Estate, In re, 657.
Fulton v. Andrew, 275.
Fulton Trust Co. v. Trowbridge, 430.
Furst & Thomas v. Sanders, 618.
Fussell's Estate, In re, 787, 790.
Futentes v. Gaines, 510.

# G

Gable's Estate, In re, 592, 593.
Gaddis' Will, In re, 551.
Gadsby v. Gadsby, 530, 729, 730.
Gaess v. Gaess, 662.
Gaff v. Cornwallis, 394.
Gaffney v. Coffey, 549.
Gaffney's Estate, 173.
Gager v. Mathewson, 550.
Gage's Estate, In re, 709.
Gahn's Will, In re, 494.
Gaines v. California Trust Co., 112, 122.
Gaines v. Chew, 504.
Gaines' Estate, In re, 167.
Gainsburg v. Garbarsky, 146.
Gaither v. Gaither, 275.
Gale v. Gale, 435.
Gale v. Keyes, 778, 780, 782.
Galindo v. Garcia, 243.
Gallivan v. Jones, 692.
Gallmeier v. Kaiser, 243.
Galloway v. Darby, 785, 786.
Galloway v. Hogg, 232.
Galloway v. Sewell, 651, 652, 654.
Gambill's Adm'r v. Gambill, 249.
Gamble v. Butchee, 317.
Gamble v. Fulton, 128.
Gamble v. Rooney, 123.
Gamble's Estate, In re, 791.
Gammons v. Gammons, 780.
Gantz v. Bondurant, 691.
Ga Nun v. Palmer, 222.
Garard v. Yeager, 212.
Garaventa v. Garaventa, 562.
Garcelon's Estate, In re, 527, 725, 728, 729.
Garcia's Estate, In re, 85.
Gard v. Mason, 406.
Garde v. Goldsmith, 204, 208.
Gardiner v. Courthope, 443.
Gardiner v. Goertner, 256, 551.
Gardner v. Gardiner, 439, 458.
Gardner v. Gardner, 509, 553, 747.
Gardner v. Kern, 80.
Gardner v. McNeal, 135, 451, 732, 744.
Gardner's Estate, In re, 510, 645.
Gardner's Estate, Matter of, 751.
Garland, Ex parte, 663.
Garland v. Smith, 534.
Garland's Appeal, 168, 170
Garman v. Glass, 411.
Garner v. Garner, 789, 804.
Garner v. Phillips, 154, 156, 157.
Garner's Will, In re, 166.
Garratt v. Niblock, 471.
Garrett v. Bean, 68.
Garrett v. Colvin, 720.
Garrett v. Harrison, 627.
Garrett v. Kirtley, 153.
Gartside's Estate, In re, 531.
Garwols v. Bankers Trust Co., 154.
Gass' Heirs v. Gass' Ex'rs, 381.
Gatewood v. Furlow, 679.
Gattward v. Knee, 209, 369.
Gauthreaux, Succession of, 298.
Gavey's Estate, In re, 736, 800.
Gavitt v. Moulton, 510.
Gay v. Gay, 439, 444, 538, 551.
Gay v. Gillilan, 257.
Gay v. Sanders, 500.
Gaylord v. Hope Natural Gas Co., 719, 721.
Geale, Goods of, 252.
Geary Street, P. & O. R. Co. v. Bradbury Estate Co., 703.
Gee v. Young, 637.
Geffen's Estate, In re, 93.
Geisel v. Burg, 200.
Gelbach v. Shively, 733, 735, 757.
Gelbke v. Gelbke, 443, 448.
Gemmel v. Fletcher, 272.
Genschorck v. Blumer, 74.

Gensimore's Estate, In re, 434, 743, 746.
Genteman v. Sutter, 202.
Genuchi's Estate, In re, 558.
George v. Bean, 650.
George v. Brown, 671.
George v. Smith, 223.
George's Estate, In re, 260, 319, 360, 362.
George T. Webb & Co. v. Fogg, 692.
Georgia Infirmary for Relief & Protection of Aged and Afflicted Negroes v. Jones, 744.
Geraghty v. Kilroy, 314.
Gerard's Estate, In re, 609.
Gerety's Estate, In re, 285, 286.
Gerhold v. Papathanasion, 696.
Gerlach Estate, 748.
German v. Heath, 569, 574.
German-American Bank of Baltimore v. Kopp, 605.
German Evangelical Bethel Church of Concordia v. Reith, 347, 348, 545.
Germania Bank v. Michaud, 653.
Geske's Estate, In re, 256.
Geyer v. Snyder, 583.
Gfroerer v. Gfroerer, 508, 510.
Ghilain v. Coulture, 586.
Gibbons, In re, 779.
Gibbons v. Dawley, 792.
Gibbons v. Redmond, 538.
Gibbons' Estate, Matter of, 394.
Gibbs v. Gibbs, 721.
Gibson, Estate of, 369.
Gibson v. Gibson, 798.
Gibson v. Johnson, 724.
Gibson v. Maxwell, 625.
Gibson v. Nelson, 339.
Gibson v. Rikard, 84.
Gibson v. Van Syckle, 208.
Gibson v. Villines, 75.
Gibson's Estate, In re, 198, 723.
Giddens v. Reddoch, 638.
Giddings v. Giddings, 460.
Giddings v. Turgeon, 311, 317, 320.
Gidley v. Gidley, 259.
Giffith's Estate, In re, 305.
Gifford v. Dyer, 279, 459.
Gifford's Will, In re, 488, 489.
Giglio v. Woollard, 612.
Gilbert v. Findlay College, 767.
Gilbert v. Gaybrick, 510.
Gilbert v. Hanson, 657.
Gilbert v. Knox, 325, 329.
Gilbert v. Partain, 486, 487.
Gilbert v. Reynolds, 151.
Gilbert's Estate, In re, 705.
Gilchrist v. Gilchrist, 567.
Giles v. Giles, 449, 450.
Giles v. Warren, 441, 454.
Gilkey v. Chambers, 812, 814.
Gilkison v. Gore, 106.
Gill v. Gill, 440.
Gill v. Riley, 625.
Gillender's Estate, In re, 630.
Gillespie v. Gillespie, 459, 460.
Gillespie v. Isbell, 607.
Gillette v. Stewart, 807.
Gilleylen v. Hallman, 646.
Gilliken v. Norcom, 240.
Gillingham's Estate, 787, 790.
Gillis v. Gillis, 334, 496, 536.
Gillmann v. Dressler, 425.
Gilman v. Bell, 641.
Gilman v. McArdle, 178.
Gilmer's Legatees v. Gilmer's Executors, 734.
Gilmore, Succession of, 527.
Gilmore v. Doherty, 473.
Gilmore v. Jenkins, 282, 724.
Gilmor's Estate, In re, 778.
Gingery's Estate, In re, 596, 624, 627.
Ginter v. Ginter, 254, 256.
Girardot Buissieres v. Albert, 48.
Girard Trust Co. v. Schmitz, 405, 414.
Gish's Appeal, 715.
Gisler's Estate, In re, 287.
Gist v. Craig, 744.
Gittings v. Jeffords, 532.
Gittins v. Steele, 800.
Gjerstadengen v. Van Duzen, 675.
Gladstone v. Bank of Commerce & Trust Co., 660.
Glandon's Estate, In re, 759.
Glascott v. Bragg, 422, 428, 429.
Glasgow's Estate, 399, 400.
Glass v. Dunn, 766.
Glass v. Johnson, 407.
Glass' Estate, In re, 209.
Glathart v. Madden, 569.
Gleason v. Traynham, 132.
Glebus' Estate, In re, 365, 421.
Glenn v. Worthy, 662.
Glessner v. Clark, 793.
Glidden v. Gutelius, 562.

Glider v. Melinski, 258.
Glidewell v. Pannell, 582.
Glocksen v. Holmes, 188.
Glos v. Glos, 525.
Glover v. Glover, 133.
Glover v. Patten, 770.
Glover's Estate, In re, 602.
Gluckman's Will, In re, 275, 276, 277, 296.
Goad v. Montgomery, 804, 805.
Gockel v. Gockel, 254, 263, 265.
Godard v. Conrad, 364.
Goddard v. Orerend, 454.
Godden v. Long, 65.
Godfrey v. Smith, 364, 366.
Godman v. Godman, 372.
Godwin v. Godwin, 167, 171.
Goethe v. Browning, 380.
Goettel's Will, In re, 383.
Goff v. Goff, 142.
Goff v. Knight, 347.
Goffe v. Goffe, 406.
Goforth v. Goforth, 732, 736
Gofton v. Mill, 769.
Goggin's Estate, Matter of, 611.
Going, In re, 415.
Goist's Estate, In re, 258.
Goldberg, In re, 425.
Golden's Estate, In re, 516.
Golden's Will, In re, 304.
Golder's Estate, In re, 209.
Goldman v. Goldman, 182.
Goldsberry's Estate, In re, 519, 532, 533.
Goldsmith v. Gates, 252, 300.
Goldstein's Estate, In re, 600, 601.
Goldsticker's Will, In re, 481.
Golombiewski's Estate, In re, 609.
Gollnik v. Mengel, 153.
Golz's Will, In re, 139.
Gomez v. Higgins, 166.
Gonzales v. Gonzales, 296.
Gooch v. Beasley, 651, 652, 654.
Gooch v. Gooch, 206, 358, 392, 466, 468.
Gooch v. Suhor, 607.
Goodale v. Evans, 187.
Goodale v. Murray, 509, 554.
Goodall v. Marshall, 592.
Goodbar v. Lidikey, 550.
Goode v. Reynolds, 651, 652, 655, 747.
Goodell v. Munroe, 664.
Goodell v. Pike, 372.
Goodell v. Yezerski, 81.
Goodfellow v. Shannon, 541, 554.
Goodfellow's Estate, In re, 732.
Goodloe's Trustee and Adm'r v. Goodloe, 813, 815.
Goodman v. Goodman, 84, 85.
Goodman v. Griffith, 580.
Goodman v. Palmer, 752.
Goodman v. Winter, 488.
Goodman's Will, In re, 358, 447.
Goodrich v. City Nat. Bank & Trust Co. of Battle Creek, 179.
Goodrich v. Hansom, 496.
Goodright d. Glazier v. Glazier, 474.
Goodwin v. New England Trust Co., 813, 814.
Goof's Estate, In re, 143.
Goos v. Brocks, 94.
Gorden's Estate, In re, 119.
Gordon v. Burris, 266.
Gordon v. Jackson, 778.
Gordon v. James, 761, 762.
Gordon v. McDougall, 831.
Gordon v. Parker, 339.
Gordon v. Smith, 771.
Gordon v. Toler, 171.
Gordon v. Whitlock, 448.
Gordon's Adm'r v. McDougall, 706.
Gordon's Estate, In re, 329, 330.
Gore v. Clarke, 135.
Gore v. Dace, 317.
Gore v. Howard, 520, 527.
Gorg v. Rutherford, 798.
Gorham v. Chadwick, 747.
Gorham v. Daniels, 184.
Gorham v. Gorham, 703.
Gorham v. Montfort, 602.
Gosling, Goods of, 447.
Gossage, Estate of, 374.
Gostina v. Whitham, 198.
Gott v. Dennis, 140.
Gould v. Chamberlain. 451, 771.
Gould v. Gould, 662.
Gould v. Safford's Estate, 372.
Gould's Will, Re, 475.
Goundry's Estate, Matter of, 632.
Gowing v. Laing, 120.
Gowling v. Gowling, 124.
Grace v. Neel, 580.
Grace v. Smith, 709.
Gradwohl v. Campagna, 74.
Graef v. Kanouse, 530.
Graff's Estate, In re, 615.

Graffton's Estate, In re, 559.
Grafton Nat. Bank v. Wing, 653.
Graham v. Birch, 421, 434.
Graham v. Courtright, 261, 542, 551, 552.
Graham v. Deuterman, 250.
Graham v. Edwards, 303, 360, 361.
Graham v. Floyd, 673.
Graham v. Graham, 96, 270, 343, 504.
Graham v. Hoke, 199.
Graham v. Karr, 728, 741.
Graham v. Tucker, 305.
Graham's Estate, In re, 557, 615, 656.
Grand Rapids Trust Co. v. Bellows, 201
Granger v. Granger, 113.
Granger v. Harriman, 569.
Grant v. Bridger, 433, 743, 746.
Graser v. Graser, 226.
Grathwaite's Estate, In re, 137.
Grattan v. Grattan, 717, 791.
Grattan's Estate, In re, 367, 446, 604.
Grave v. Kittle, 425, 427.
Gravelin v. Porier, 216.
Graves v. Bowles, 300.
Graves v. Davenport, 569.
Graves' Estate, In re, 581.
Gray v. Black, 715.
Gray v. Case School of Applied Science, 753.
Gray v. Doubikin, 633.
Gray v. McCausland, 744.
Gray v. McCurdy, 670.
Gray v. Swerer, 79.
Gray v. Weatherford, 133.
Gray's Estate, 136, 587, 784.
Gray Realty Co. v. Robinson, 690.
Grayson v. Robertson, 588.
Greely v. Houston, 776, 777.
Green v. Davis, 322, 323, 342, 343.
Green v. Ferguson, 517.
Green v. Green, 744.
Green v. Hathaway, 725, 726, 727.
Green v. Old People's Home of Chicago, 411.
Green v. Pearson, 326.
Green v. Salmon, 651, 652.
Green v. Tribe, 469, 470.
Green v. Watkins, 686.
Green v. Whaley, 166.
Green's Estate, In re, 243.
Greenberg's Estate, Re, 471.
Greene v. Ballard, 559.
Greene v. Fitzpatrick, 91.
Greene v. Greene, 719, 720, 724, 789.
Greene v. Kirkwood, 407.
Greene's Estate, In re, 239, 245.
Greenhow v. James' Ex'x, 84.
Greening's Estate, In re, 596.
Greenlee v. Davis, 80.
Greenlees v. Allen, 258.
Greenough v. Greenough, 292.
Greenwich Trust Co. v. Tyson, 405.
Greenwood v. Greenwood, 771, 790.
Greenwood's Goods, 458.
Greerside v. Benson, 792.
Gregg v. Garvan, 95.
Gregg's Estate, In re, 95, 136.
Gregory v. Lansing, 434, 597, 743, 746.
Gregory v. Susong, 421.
Gregory v. Tompkins, 771
Gregson v. Taylor, 275, 276.
Greims' Will, In re, 583.
Greiner v. Greiner, 528.
Greves, In re Goods of, 388.
Gridley v. Gates, 2.
Gridley v. Home Ins. Co., 190.
Griesemer v. Boyer & Rex, 133.
Grife v. Equitable Life Assur. Soc. of U. S., 715.
Griffin v. Barrett, 256.
Griffin v. Irwin, 613, 615.
Griffin v. Sturges, 412.
Griffin v. Union Trust Co., 250.
Griffin's Will, In re, 142.
Griffith v. Adams, 750.
Griffith v. Benzinger, 551.
Griffith v. Higinbotom, 511.
Griffith v. Stewart, 657.
Griffiths v. Griffiths, 326, 331.
Grigg v. Hanna, 638.
Grignon v. Shope, 488, 665.
Grigonis' Estate, 203.
Grigsby's Guardian v. Cocke's Ex'rs, 622.
Griley v. Griley, 122.
Grilk, Will of, In re, 638.
Grimes v. Barndollar, 203.
Grimes v. Nashville Trust Co., 450.
Grimes Ex'rs v. Harmon, 282.
Grimm v. Tittman, 318.
Grindem v. Grindem, 767.
Grindrod's Estate, In re, 698.
Grissinger's Estate, In re, 721.
Griswold v. Bigelow, 703.
Griswold v. Chandler, 667.

Griswold's Estate, In re, 194.
Grober v. Clements, 149, 151.
Grobe's Estate, In re, 123, 124, 208.
Groce, In re Will of, 362.
Grochowski v. Grochowski, 528, 529.
Grogan v. Ashe, 738.
Grollman's Estate, In re, 792.
Grooms v. Thomas, 95, 96.
Grooms' Estate, In re, 658.
Grose v. Holland, 157.
Gross v. Thornson's Estate, 699.
Gross' Adm'r v. Ledford, 684.
Grotts v. Casburn, 447.
Grove v. Willard, 668.
Grover v. Clover, 708.
Grover's Estate, In re, 626.
Gruner, In re, 710, 712.
Grunow v. Simonitsch, 614.
Grymes v. Hone, 203.
Guaranty Trust Co. v. Catholic Charities, 285.
Gudewicz' Will, 218.
Guerin v. Hunt, 544.
Gueydan v. Montagne, 526.
Gugle v. Gugle, 167.
Guier v. Bridges, 79.
Guinasso's Estate, In re, 510.
Guiraud, Succession of, 382.
Gulley v. Lillard's Ex'r, 724.
Gum v. Reep, 552.
Gump v. Gowans, 318, 331.
Gunderman's Estate, In re, 140, 492.
Gunderson's Estate, In re, 799.
Gunther v. Thompson, 657.
Gurganus, Succession of, 416.
Gurley v. Butler, 625.
Gurley v. Park, 251.
Gurley v. Wiggs, 471.
Gurnet v. Mutual Life Ins. Co. of New York, 161.
Gurney v. Gurney, 472.
Gwin v. Wright, 365.
Gwin's Will, In re, 371.
Gwinn v. Melvin, 485, 569, 574.
Gwynne v. Estes, 713.

# H

Haber's Will, In re, 335, 338.
Habig v. Dodge, 730.
Hackensack Trust Co. v. Tracy, 106.
Hackensack Trust Co. v. Van Den Berg, 697.
Hacker v. Newborn, 258.
Hack's Estate, In re, 92.
Hadden's Will, In re, 734.
Haddock v. Boston & M. R. Co., 486.
Haddox v. Jordan, 283.
Haden v. Sims, 636.
Hadsell's Estate, In re, 446.
Hagan v. Cone, 153.
Hagan v. Lantry, 571.
Hagan's Estate, In re, 548, 551.
Hagar's Estate, In re, 92.
Hagedorn v. Reiser, 74.
Hagerty v. Union Guardian Trust Co., 153.
Hahn v. Dunn, 121, 771.
Hahn v. Hammerstein, 521.
Hahn v. Verret, 636.
Haight, Matter of, 414.
Haight, Re, 408.
Haigood v. Wells, 628.
Haile v. Hale, 153.
Haines, Estate of, 138.
Haines v. Hayden, 260.
Haines v. Little, 521.
Haldeman v. Haldeman, 662.
Hale, Goods of, 370, 371.
Hale v. Cox, 258.
Hale v. Hale, 176, 669.
Hale v. Hannah, 569, 572.
Hale v. Hollon, 729, 730.
Hale v. Wilmarth, 166.
Hale's Estate, 142.
Haley v. Austin, 664.
Hall, In re, 155.
Hall v. Alexander, 562.
Hall v. Brigstocke, 302, 360.
Hall v. Crook, 96.
Hall v. Dench, 433, 435.
Hall v. Gabbert, 83.
Hall v. Hall, 178, 251, 257, 258, 535, 719.
Hall v. Hancock, 75.
Hall v. Mercantile Trust Co., 244.
Hall v. Meriden Trust & Safe Deposit Co., 128.
Hall v. Mutual Life Ins. Co., 162.
Hall v. Williams, 282.
Hall v. Windsor Sav. Bank, 678.
Hall's Case, 759.
Hall's Estate, In re, 2, 425, 755.
Hall's Estate, Matter of, 89.
Hall's Will, In re, 812, 814.
Hallett v. Allen, 752.

Hallock's Estate, In re, 656.
Halloran-Judge Trust Co. v. Heath, 700.
Hallowell Sav. Inst. v. Titcomb, 174.
Halpern's Estate, In re, 115, 116, 176.
Halsey v. Convention of Protestant Episcopal Church, 783.
Halstead v. First Sav. Bank, 169.
Halston, In re, 283.
Halton's Estate, In re, 323, 325, 329, 330, 337.
Hamblin v. Marchant, 155.
Hambly v. Trott, 642, 683.
Hamill v. Hamill, 521.
Hamilton v. Levy, 593.
Hamilton v. McQuillan, 751.
Hamilton v. Orange Sav. Bank, 599, 600.
Hamilton v. Shillington, 558.
Hamilton v. Wilson, 636.
Hamilton's Estate, In re, 459, 793.
Hamlet v. Hamlet, 467.
Hammer, In re, 794.
Hammert v. McKnight, 675, 676.
Hammond v. Hammond, 694, 695.
Hampden Trust Co. v. Leary, 555.
Hampton, Bank of v. Smith, 132.
Hancock v. Cochran, 698.
Hancock's Estate v. Pyle, 618, 619.
Hancocke v. Prowd, 714.
Hani v. Germania Life Ins. Co., 203.
Hankins v. Young, 218.
Hanks v. McDanell, 824.
Hannibal Trust Co. v. Elzea, 707.
Hanover Fire Ins. Co. v. Street, 646.
Hanreddy's Estate, In re, 592.
Hansbarger v. Hansbarger, 528.
Hansbrough v. Hooe, 741.
Hanscom v. Marston, 805.
Hansen's Estate, In re, 706.
Hanson v. Fiesler, 219.
Hanson v. Hoffman, 229.
Hanson's Estate, In re, 247, 257, 259.
Hanssen v. Karbe, 626.
Hantzch v. Massolt, 700.
Hapgood v. Houghton, 413.
Haradon v. Clark, 412.
Harber v. Kentucky Ridge Coal Co., 625.
Harbison v. Beets, 242.
Hardeman v. Ellis, 772.
Hardenbergh v. Commissioner of Internal Revenue, 776.
Hardesty v. Mitchell, 84.
Hardin v. Hardin, 500.
Hardin v. Russell, 190.
Harding v. Hewes, 801.
Hardy, In re, 491.
Hardyman, In re, 471, 815.
Hargroves v. Thompson, 569.
Harlan v. Anderson's Ex'r, 207.
Harle v. Harle, 72, 88.
Harmening v. Harmening, 339.
Harmon v. Harmon, 201.
Harms v. Pohlmann, 661.
Harootenian's Estate, In re, 524.
Harp v. Parr, 381.
Harper v. Archer, 75.
Harper v. Betts, 679.
Harper v. Harris, 717, 723, 791.
Harper v. Lamb, 705.
Harrell v. Harrell, 510.
Harrell v. Hickman, 227.
Harrell v. Storey, 71.
Harriman v. Bunker, 201.
Harrington's Estate, In re, 89, 150.
Harris v. Harris, 115, 123, 220, 511, 530, 556.
Harris v. Harris' Estate, 545.
Harris v. McDonald, 449, 493.
Harris v. Morgan, 215.
Harris v. Nashville Trust Co., 683.
Harris' Estate, In re, 120, 361.
Harris' Goods, 458.
Harrison v. Axtell, 289.
Harrison v. Carter, 627.
Harrison v. Elvin, 334.
Harrison v. Harrison, 741.
Harrison v. Moncravie, 156.
Harrison's Adm'r v. Harrison's Distributees, 634.
Harrison's Estate, In re, 447, 450, 512, 795.
Harrison Machine Works v. Aufderheide, 695.
Harrod v. McComas, 178.
Harsh's Estate, In re, 661.
Hart v. Darter, 806.
Harter's Estate, In re, 324.
Hartford & N. H. R. R. v. Andrews, 597.
Hartman's Estate, In re, 626, 732, 733, 734, 736.
Hartnett v. Wandell, 603.
Hartwell v. Martin, 396.
Hartwig v. Flynn, 632, 647.

Hartwig v. Schiefel, 769.
Hartwig's Estate, In re, 736.
Hartz v. Sobel, 438, 457, 499.
Hartzell's Estate, 763.
Harvard Unitarian Society v. Tufts, 732, 744.
Harvey, Re, 782.
Harvey v. Pocock, 697.
Harvey v. Rackliffe, 172.
Harvey v. White, 788.
Harwell v. Lively, 465.
Harwood v. Goodright, 474.
Harwood v. Scott, 696.
Haskell v. Staples, 398.
Hastings v. Bridge, 395, 396, 449, 748.
Hastings v. Day, 426.
Hatchell v. Norton, 91, 92.
Hatcher v. Buford, 201, 204.
Hatfield v. Thorp, 309.
Hatfield's Estate, In re, 144, 427.
Hathaway v. Warren, 380, 381.
Hatheway v. Smith, 386, 393.
Hathway's Appeal, 494.
Hattersley v. Bissett, 583, 769.
Hatton, In re Goods of, 336, 383.
Hatton v. Howard Braiding Co., 567.
Hauer v. Hauer, 329, 544.
Haugh v. Bokern, 805.
Haug's Estate, Matter of, 617.
Haupt's Estate, In re, 314, 315.
Hausen v. Dahlquist, 505.
Havel's Estate, In re, 507, 508.
Haven v. Foster, 470.
Haven v. Wrinkle, 506.
Havens v. Mason, 238.
Havill v. Newton, 650.
Hawes v. Humphrey, 313.
Hawgood's Estate, In re, 733, 734, 736, 757, 800.
Hawke v. Euyart, 408, 414, 472.
Hawkins, Succession of, 661.
Hawkins v. Hawkins, 89.
Hawley v. Hawley, 626.
Hawley's Estate, In re, 491, 492, 610.
Hawn v. Stoler, 203.
Hay, Appeal of, 434, 743, 746.
Hay v. Boling, 783.
Hay v. Le Bus, 531.
Hayden v. Hayden, 312, 314, 317.
Hayer's Estate, In re, 556, 644.
Hayes v. Betts, 676.
Hayes v. Hayes, 732, 788, 796, 799.
Hayes v. Moffatt, 217.
Hayes v. Simmons, 486.
Hayes v. Welling, 630, 740.
Hayes' Adm'r v. Matlock, 72.
Hayes' Estate, In re, 542, 543.
Hayes' Ex'rs v. Hayes, 460.
Haynes v. Peterson, 95.
Hayne's Estate, In re, 723.
Hays v. Bowden, 254.
Hays v. Jackson, 755.
Hays v. Marschall, 383.
Hayward v. Plant, 792.
Hazeltine's Estate, In re, 626.
Hazelton v. Bogardus, 673.
Head v. Leak, 88.
Healey v. Bartlett, 343.
Healey's Estate, In re, 631.
Healy v. Healy, 211.
Heap v. Heap, 648.
Heaston v. Krieg, 189.
Heath v. White, 82.
Heather, In re, 738.
Heaton's Will, In re, 243.
Heavner v. Heavner, 345.
Hebblethwaite's Estate, In re, 626.
Hebb's Estate, In re, 88, 430.
Heckman v. Kassing, 690.
Hedderich v. Hedderich, 143.
Hedgepeth's Will, In re, 506, 510.
Hedges v. Payne, 785.
Hedin v. Westdala Lutheran Church, 238.
Hedlund v. Miner, 143.
Hegarty v. Curtis, 82.
Hegarty's Estate, In re, 495.
Hegney v. Head, 551.
Heileman v. Dakan, 738, 739.
Heim's Will, In re, 262.
Heinemann, Succession of, 358.
Heinrich v. Harrigan, 580, 632.
Heinrich v. Newell, 725, 729.
Heinze's Estate, In re, 647.
Heinze's Estate, Matter of, 622.
Heinze's Will, Matter of, 664.
Heitholt's Estate, In re, 262.
Helfrich v. Yockel, 522.
Heller's Will, In re, 326, 439.
Hellier v. Hellier, 450.
Helm v. Goin, 84.
Helyar v. Helyar, 474.
Hembree v. Bolton, 500.
Heminway v. Reynolds, 495.
Hemsley v. Hollingsworth, 788.
Henderson v. Bishop, 530.

Henderson v. First Nat. Bank, 737.
Henderson v. First Trust & Sav. Bank, 800, 801.
Henderson v. Henderson, 210, 815.
Henderson v. Jackson, 259.
Henderson v. Simmons, 558.
Henderson v. Tipton, 695.
Henderson's Estate, In re, 362, 745.
Henley v. Johnston, 673.
Henn v. McGinnis, 693.
Hennegar v. Deadrick, 765.
Henninger's Estate, 372.
Henning's Estate, In re, 208, 356.
Henry v. Fraser, 444.
Henry v. Hall, 551.
Henry's Estate, In re, 208.
Hensley v. Hilton, 219.
Hensley v. Rich, 590, 592, 597.
Henson v. Johnson, 84.
Henson v. Neumann, 217.
Henson v. Wolfe, 595.
Hentges' Estate, In re, 556.
Herd v. Chambers, 182.
Herle's Will, In re, 508.
Herman's Estate, 659.
Hermence's Estate, In re, 493.
Herren v. Herren, 187.
Herring v. Elliott, 130.
Herring's Will, In re, 326.
Herrington v. Budd, 744.
Herrmann's Estate, In re, 626.
Hertford v. Lowther, 751.
Hertrais v. Moore, 431.
Hertz v. Burris, 668.
Herzog v. Trust Co., 423, 424.
Heshy v. Clark, 223.
Heslop v. Heslop, 149.
Hess v. Renolds, 595.
Hesse's Estate, In re, 255, 516, 805.
Hessmer v. Edenborn, 386, 395, 400.
Hester v. Sammons, 781.
Hesterberg v. Clark, 465.
Hethrington v. Graham, 149.
Heuler's Estate, In re, 194, 210.
Heupel v. Heupel, 296.
Hewes v. Hewes, 392.
Hewett v. Gott, 153.
Hewitt v. Beattie, 661, 663.
Hewitt v. Hewitt, 798.
Hewitt v. Sanborn, 636, 663.
Hewson v. Shelley, 503.
Hey v. Prime, 684.
Heywood, Estate of, 497.
Hiatt v. McColley, 310, 311, 313.
Hibler v. Hibler, 733, 735, 746.
Hickey's Estate, Matter of, 372.
Hickman's Estate, In re, 306, 412, 466.
Hickox v. Johnston, 92.
Hicks v. Kerr, 750.
Hicks v. Purvis, 662, 663.
Higgins v. Butcher, 642.
Higgins v. Higgins, 80.
Higham v. Vanosdol, 719, 721.
Highland v. Empire Nat. Bank of Clarksburg, 584.
Hight v. Carr, 526.
Hildebrand v. Kinney, 610, 709.
Hildreth v. Hildreth, 289.
Hildreth v. Marshall, 265, 329.
Hilfiker v. Fennig, 519.
Hill, Matter of, 369.
Hill v. Barton, 589.
Hill v. Burger, 276.
Hill v. Chicago Title & Trust Co., 496
Hill v. Cornwall & Bro.'s Assignee 182.
Hill v. Davis, 328, 329.
Hill v. District Court, 522.
Hill v. Hill, 200, 432, 707, 720, 742, 766.
Hill v. Kalamazoo Probate Judge, 131.
Hill v. Superior Court of San Luis Obispo County, 596.
Hill v. Walker, 694.
Hill's Adm'rs v. Hill, 811, 814.
Hill's Estate, In re, 770.
Hill's Estate, Matter of, 210.
Hill's Estate, Re, 413, 608.
Hillaert's Estate, 426.
Hiller's Estate, In re, 705.
Hilles v. Hilles, 668.
Hillman v. McLeod, 126.
Hills v. Superior Court of Los Angeles County, 130.
Hills' Will, In re, 122.
Hilpire v. Claude, 430.
Hilt v. Ward, 131.
Hilton v. Hopkins, 619.
Hilton v. Johnson, 424.
Hilton's Will, Matter of, 579.
Hilyard v. Wood, 439.
Hindmarsh v. Charlton, 334, 338.
Hine v. Simon, 96.
Hines v. Baldwin, 795.

Hines v. Levers & Sargent Co., 661, 662.
Hinners' Will, In re, 747.
Hinton's Will, In re, 140, 257, 493.
Hirning v. Kurle, 701.
Hirsch v. Bucki, 398.
Hirsch's Estate, In re, 592.
Hirschberg v. Horowitz, 214, 219.
Hirshorn's Estate, In re, 394, 400.
Hiscock, Goods of, 369, 373.
Historical Society of Dauphin County v. Kelker, 472.
Hitchcock v. Shaw, 313.
Hite v. Hite, 729.
Hite's Adm'r v. Gibson, 601.
Hite's Estate, In re, 410, 412.
Hitner's Appeal, 153.
Hoagland's Estate, Matter of, 85.
Hoban v. Piquette, 233.
Hobart v. Hobart, 324.
Hobbs v. Cunningham, 797.
Hobbs v. Hobbs, 131.
Hobbs v. Knight, 437.
Hoblit v. Howser, 404.
Hobson v. Payne, 591.
Hoch v. Hoch, 87.
Hockaday v. Lynn, 86, 89.
Hockenberry v. Donovan, 110.
Hock's Will, In re, 254.
Hodgdon v. White, 694.
Hodge v. Joy, 506, 510, 529.
Hodges v. Hale, 526.
Hodgkinson, Goods of, 477, 479.
Hodgman v. Kittredge, 311, 312, 317, 318.
Hodgson v. Martin, 219.
Hodsden v. Lloyd, 422, 426.
Hoellinger v. Molzhon, 780.
Hoes v. New York, 589.
Hoff v. Hoff, 254.
Hoffman v. Armstrong, 790.
Hoffman v. Chester, 792.
Hoffman v. Hoffman, 292.
Hoffman v. Hoffman's Heirs, 564
Hoffman v. Ness, 682.
Hoffman v. Watson, 09, 70.
Hoffner's Estate, 462.
Hofmeister v. Hunter, 730.
Hogan v. Curtin, 408.
Hogan v. Pigott, 682.
Hogan v. Roche, 120.
Hogan v. Whittemore, 276.
Hogarth-Swann v. Steele, 174.
Hogg v. Whitham, 155.
Hoglan v. Moore, 808.
Hogston v. Bell, 516.
Hoitt v. Hoitt, 429.
Hoke v. Herman, 743, 748.
Hoks v. Wollenberg, 203, 204.
Holbrook v. McCleary, 785.
Holbrook's Estate, In re, 406, 407.
Holburn v. Pfanmiller's Adm'r, 597.
Holcomb v. Mullin, 733, 761, 762.
Holcombe's Estate, In re, 555.
Holden v. Spier, 789.
Holden's Estate, In re, 488.
Holdfast d. Anstey v. Dowsing, 309.
Holding v. Allen, 656.
Holiday v. McKinne, 715.
Holladay v. Holladay, 244, 245.
Holland v. Bonner, 718, 719, 721.
Holland v. Doke, 651, 652, 654, 793.
Holland v. Jackson, 488, 489.
Holland's Estate, In re, 811, 812, 814.
Holliday v. Shepherd, 538.
Holliday's Estate, In re, 372.
Hollinger's Estate, In re, 552.
Hollis' Estate, In re, 266, 289.
Holloway v. McCormick, 153.
Holloway's Estate, 500.
Holly v. Gibbons, 694.
Holmberg's Estate, In re, 442.
Holme v. Shinn, 80.
Holmes v. Campbell College, 237, 243.
Holmes v. Curl, 89.
Holmes v. King, 96.
Holmes v. McPheeters, 789.
Holmes v. Roddy, 284.
Holmes v. Wharton, 595.
Holmes' Estate, In re, 278, 289.
Holm's Estate, In re, 580.
Holsz v. Stephen, 215, 221.
Holt v. Bayles, 169.
Holt v. Daniel Sons & Palmer Co., 663.
Holt v. Holt, 651, 652, 654.
Holt v. Libby, 789.
Holt v. Rice, 526.
Holt's Estate, In re, 664.
Holt's Will, In re, 317.
Holtan v. Fischer, 572.
Holyoke Nat. Bank v. Bailey, 167, 169.
Holzman v. Wager, 230, 231.
Homan, Succession of, 451.
Home Brewing Co. v. Mahler, 698.

Home Mixture Guano Co. v. McKoone, 725, 727.
Home of the Aged of the Methodist Episcopal Church v. Bantz, 444, 554.
Honsinger v. Stewart, 564.
Honywood, Goods of, 497.
Hooker v. Bodine, 209.
Hooker v. Porter, 133.
Hooks v. Brown, 522, 523.
Hooper v. Hooper, 584, 789.
Hooper v. Stokes, 244.
Hooper's Estate, In re, 130.
Hoopeston Public Library v. Eaton, 214.
Hoover v. Keller, 327, 347.
Hoover v. Miller, 633.
Hoover's Estate, In re, 691, 692.
Hopf v. State, 523.
Hopkins v. Gifford, 88.
Hopkins v. Taylor, 520.
Hopkins' Will, In re, 554.
Hopper, In re Estate of, 386, 391.
Hopper v. Hopper, 593.
Hopper v. Sellers, 265, 266, 278, 279.
Hopper's Estate, 390.
Hoppe's Will, In re, 315.
Hops' Will, In re, 258.
Horn v. Horn, 189.
Horn's Estate, In re, 167, 747.
Horn's Estate v. Bartow, 339.
Hornbeck v. Richards, 697.
Horne v. Horne, 236.
Hornstra v. Avon State Bank, 790, 791.
Horsford, In re Goods of, 336, 438, 455, 458, 463.
Horst, Matter of, 143.
Horton v. Barto, 500.
Horton v. Johnson, 334.
Horton's Estate, In re, 261.
Hotsinpiller v. Hotsinpiller, 218.
Houck v. Anderson, 224.
Houck v. Houck, 694, 704.
Houghten's Estate, In re, 456, 458.
Houghton v. Dickinson, 83.
Houle v. McMillan, 171.
House v. Callicott, 529.
House v. Fowle, 112.
House of the Good Shepherd in Binghamton v. Rector, etc. of Church of Good Shepherd in City of Binghamton, 283.
Houston v. Grigsby, 537, 542, 546, 548.
Houston's Estate, In re, 134.
Houts v. Fritz, 709.
Hovey v. Hovey, 772.
Hovey v. Paige, 641.
Howard v. Bell Telephone Co., 643.
Howard v. Francis, 752, 758.
Howard v. Hunter, 439.
Howard v. Swift, 705.
Howard v. Williams, 204.
Howard's Estate, In re, 412.
Howd v. Clay, 616.
Howe v. Brown, 673, 674.
Howe v. Gray, 695.
Howe v. Howe, 733.
Howe v. Watson, 211.
Howe's Estate, In re, 195, 774, 775, 776.
Howell v. Howell, 639.
Howell v. Jump, 671.
Howell v. Moore, 356.
Howell v. Troutman, 267, 269.
Howey's Estate, In re, 616, 644.
Howland v. Slade, 782.
Howland's Adm'r v. Harr, 130.
Hoy v. Hoy, 424.
Hoyt v. Thomas, 220.
Huard v. Hegarty, 749.
Hubbard v. Alamo Irrigating & Mfg. Co., 710.
Hubbard v. Hubbard, 372, 373.
Hudemann v. Dodson, 190.
Hudson v. Flood, 311, 313, 316.
Hudson v. Hughan, 251.
Hudson Trust Co. v. Horwood, 277.
Huff v. Huff, 325.
Huffine v. Lincoln, 420.
Hug, Goods of, 459.
Hughes, In re, 589.
Hughes v. Bent, 387.
Hughes v. Burriss, 502.
Hughes v. Hughes, 428.
Hughes v. Merchants Nat. Bank of Mobile, 335.
Hughes v. Meredith, 262, 276.
Hughes' Estate, In re, 804.
Hughett v. Hughett, 74.
Hugo v. Miller, 674.
Huish, Re, 770.
Hulett v. Carey, 424.
Hull, Estate of, 539.
Hull v. Thoms, 214, 219, 221.
Hull's Estate, 386, 390.

Hull's Will, In re, 331, 345.
Hume's Estate, In re, 485.
Humiston's Estate, In re, 334.
Humphrey v. Holland, 674.
Humphrey v. Wallace, 325, 348.
Humphreys v. Humphreys, 742.
Humphrys v. Polak, 59.
Hunley's Ex'x v. Shuford, 693.
Hunsicker's Estate, In re, 89.
Hunt, Goods of, 273.
Hunt v. Authier, 685.
Hunt v. Burns, 802.
Hunt v. Furman, 383.
Hunt v. Hort, 288.
Hunt v. Hunt, 214.
Hunt v. Kingston, 25.
Hunt v. Smith, 729.
Hunt ex rel. City of Streator v. Evans, 390.
Hunter v. Hunter, 694.
Hurley v. Blankinship, 467.
Hurley's Will, In re, 706, 708.
Huston's Estate, In re, 500.
Hutcheson v. Bibb, 550.
Hutchins v. Hutchins, 556, 557, 604.
Hutchins v. St. Paul, M. & M. Ry. Co., 598.
Hutchinson v. Hattendorf, 528.
Hutton v. Hutton, 603.
Hutton v. Safe Deposit & Trust Co. of Baltimore, 753.
Hutton's Estate, In re, 783.
Huxen, Succession of, 661.
Huxley v. Security Trust Co., 123.
H. W. Wright Lumber Co. v. McCord, 151.
Hyde v. Hyde, 230.
Hyde's Estate, In re, 491, 492.
Hydrick v. Hydrick, 199.
Hyman v. Tarplee, 176.

# I

Ibey v. Ibey, 114.
Iburg's Estate, In re, 447, 450.
Iddings v. Iddings, 276.
Ihmsen's Estate, Matter of, 196.
Ijams v. Schapiro, 406.
Illinois Bankers Life Ass'n v. Collins, 158.
Imthurn v. Martin, 197.
Inda v. Inda, 115.
Inda's Estate, In re, 256.
Indianapolis Home, etc. v. Altenheim, 285, 286.
Industrial Trust Co. v. Dean, 132, 628.
Industrial Trust Co. v. Saunders, 812, 814.
Ingels' Estate, In re, 176.
Ingersoll v. Coram, 591.
Ingersoll v. Gourley, 248, 525.
Ingle v. Richards, 644.
Ingraham, Appeal of, 143.
Ingram v. Dowling, 132, 132.
Ingram v. Ingram, 724, 725.
Ingram v. Porter, 184.
Inlow v. Hughes, 510, 511.
Inman v. Western Nat. Bank of Fort Worth, Tex., 691.
Innes v. Potter, 199.
Innis v. Michigan Trust Co., 2.
International Harvester Co. v. Dyer's Adm'r, 711.
International Trust Co. v. Anthony, 330.
Ions v. Harbison, 623.
Iowa Loan & Trust Co. v. Holderbaum, 712.
Iredale v. Ford, 608.
Ireland v. Dyer, 723.
Ireland v. Hudson, 394, 400, 497.
Ireland v. Ireland, 112.
Ireland v. Jacobs, 226.
Ireland v. Terwilliger, 431.
Ireland's Estate, In re, 743, 748.
Ireland's Estate, Matter of, 613.
Irvine, Goods of, 462.
Irvine v. Irvine, 405.
Irvine's Estate, In re, 333, 338, 360.
Irving v. Irving, 429.
Irving Trust Co., In re, 405.
Irving Trust Co. v. Day, 31, 111.
Irwin v. Jacques, 304.
Irwin v. Larson, 582.
Irwin v. Lattin, 247.
Isaacs v. Manning, 90.
Isaacs v. Stevens, 704.
Isom v. Canedy, 542, 543.
Ison v. Halcomb, 188.
Ison v. Ison, 720.
Israel v. Arthur, 150.
Israel v. Beale, 702.
Israell v. Redon, 422, 428, 429.
Ivanhoe Building & Loan Assn. v. Orr, 713.

Iverson's Estate, In re, 297.
Ives v. Salisbury's Heirs, 488.
Ivey v. Vaughan, 675.
Izard v. Hurst, 473, 737.

## J

Jaaska's Estate, In re, 254.
Jackman v. Kasper, 452.
Jackman v. North, 244, 245.
Jackson, In re, 287.
Jackson v. Alsop, 778.
Jackson v. Bevins, 764, 765.
Jackson v. Hewlett, 442.
Jackson v. Hubert, 130, 715.
Jackson v. Hurlock, 464.
Jackson v. Jackson, 191, 338, 532.
Jackson v. Leech's Estate, 795.
Jackson v. Superior Court of Los Angeles County, 651, 652, 655.
Jackson v. Wilson, 133.
Jackson ex dem. Cooder v. Woods, 318.
Jackson ex dem. Van Dusen v. Van Dusen, 333.
Jackson's Adm'rs v. Moore, 84.
Jackson's Estate, 641.
Jackson's Estate, In re, 676, 787.
Jackson's Ex'r v. Semones, 255.
Jacobs v. Button, 739.
Jacobs' Will, In re, 334.
Jacoby v. Jacoby, 226.
Jacques v. Horton, 509, 554.
Jaggers v. Estes, 184.
Jahnke v. Selle, 70.
James v. Corvin, 702.
James v. Helmich, 88.
James v. James, 84.
James v. Marvin, 476.
James v. Parker, 508.
James White Memorial Home v. Haeg, 241.
Jamison's Estate, In re, 208.
Janes, In re, 266.
Janes, Matter of, 267, 269.
Janin v. Browne, 658.
Jankes' Estate, In re, 648.
Jaques, In re, 740.
Jaques v. Swasey, 473, 739.
Jarboe, Appeal of, 542, 543.
Jarnigan v. Jarnigan, 148.
Jarrell v. Farmers Nat. Bank of Opelika, 676.
Jarrett's Estate, In re, 130.
Jarvis, In re, 793.
Jarvis v. Drew, 651, 652, 654.
Jarvis' Will, In re, 305.
Jaster v. Spikings, 128.
Jefferson v. Simpson, 212, 218.
Jeffett v. Cook, 445.
Jele v. Lemberger, 519.
Jellison v. Swan, 715.
Jenkins v. French, 683.
Jenkins v. Gaisford, 298.
Jenkins v. Jenkins, 644.
Jenks v. Liverpool & London & Globe Ins. Co., 796.
Jenks's Estate, In re, 544.
Jenner v. Ffinch, 341.
Jennings v. Jennings, 187.
Jennings v. Reeson, 386.
Jennings' Estate, In re, 660.
Jensen v. Hinderks, 520.
Jensen v. Murphy, 645.
Jensen's Estate, In re, 208, 232, 553.
Jepson, In re Estate of, 744.
Jernberg's Estate, In re, 552.
Jesse v. Parker's Adm'rs, 334.
Jessop v. Watson, 52.
Jewell v. Appolonio, 733, 734.
Jewell v. MacFarland, 702.
Jewe's Will, In re, 557.
Job Haines Home for Aged People v. Keene, 773.
Jobson's Estate, In re, 91.
Jochumsen v. Suffolk Sav. Bank, 599.
Joe Gouy Shong v. Joe Chew Shee, 660.
Johannes' Estate, In re, 444, 513.
John v. Sharp, 656.
Johns v. Citizens & Southern Nat. Bank, 782.
Johns Hopkins University v. Uhrig, 747.
Johnson, Estate of, 507, 613.
Johnson, In re Estate of, 764.
Johnson v. Antriken, 722.
Johnson v. Bain, 691.
Johnson v. Banker, 542, 543.
Johnson v. Barefoot, 671.
Johnson v. Becker, 194.
Johnson v. Bradstreet Co., 684.
Johnson v. Brailsford, 437, 440.
Johnson v. Breeding, 730.
Johnson v. Bruner, 511.
Johnson v. Cooper, 190.

Johnson v. Covington, 774.
Johnson v. Farrell, 238.
Johnson v. Fleming, 190.
Johnson v. Grice, 200.
Johnson v. Hilliard, 205.
Johnson v. Hinton, 308.
Johnson v. Huntley, 72.
Johnson v. Jacob, 392.
Johnson v. Johnson, 608.
Johnson v. Larson, 700.
Johnson v. Lavene, 186.
Johnson v. McCue, 215.
Johnson v. McDowell, 738, 739.
Johnson v. Mundy, 721.
Johnson v. Nelson, 646.
Johnson v. Ramsey, 276.
Johnson v. Rutherford, 693, 704.
Johnson v. Shaver, 253, 545.
Johnson's Estate, In re, 168, 171, 213, 261, 301, 316, 326, 328, 347, 380, 556, 626, 708, 767.
Johnson's Will, 381.
Johnson's Will, In re, 496, 603.
Johnston v. City of Los Angeles, 102.
Johnston v. Glasscock, 366, 367.
Johnston v. King, 380.
Johnston v. Long, 649, 663.
Johnston v. Metropolitan Life Ins. Co., 153, 158.
Johnston v. Schwenck, 628.
Johnston v. Spicer, 110, 194.
Johnston v. Tomme, 215, 218.
Johnston v. Willis, 522, 523.
Johnston's Estate, In re, 416, 648.
Johnston's Will, In re, 324.
Jolly, In re, 556, 557.
Jones, In re, 524.
Jones, Matter of, 393, 396.
Jones v. Baswell, 694.
Jones v. Bean, 212.
Jones v. Brooks, 308.
Jones v. Camak, 288.
Jones v. Casler, 511, 512.
Jones v. Clifton, 182.
Jones v. Gilliam, 645, 651, 652, 670, 674, 675, 704, 793.
Jones v. Goodchild, 50.
Jones v. Grindal, 634.
Jones v. Grogan, 280.
Jones v. Guy, 92, 211.
Jones v. Habersham, 311, 312, 313.
Jones v. Harbaugh, 581.
Jones v. Harsha, 805.
Jones v. Holloway, 811.
Jones v. Hunter, 83.
Jones v. Hyndman, 84.
Jones v. James, 84.
Jones v. Jones, 77, 197, 413, 722.
Jones v. Kyle, 359, 360.
Jones v. Lewis, 102.
Jones v. Lingo, 186.
Jones v. McGonigle, 111.
Jones v. Mason, 738, 740.
Jones v. Minnesota Transfer R. Co., 578.
Jones v. Myers, 349, 359.
Jones v. Null, 712.
Jones v. O'Brien, 677, 678.
Jones v. Old Colony Trust Co., 175, 180.
Jones v. Palmer, 626.
Jones v. Peabody, 562, 653, 656.
Jones v. Robinson, 365.
Jones v. Smith, 622.
Jones v. Tebbetts, 319, 320.
Jones v. Temple, 675.
Jones v. Treadwell, 791.
Jones v. Tuck, 342, 343.
Jones v. Warren, 145.
Jones v. Witherspoon, 521.
Jones' Estate, In re, 130, 332, 342, 431, 557, 558, 712, 750, 752, 799.
Jones' Estate, Matter of, 338.
Jones' Will, In re, 278.
Jones Brewing Co. v. Flaherty, 653.
Jordan v. Smith, 562.
Jordan v. Spiers, 583.
Jordan's Estate, In re, 306.
Jorn v. Tallett, 244, 245.
Jose v. Lyman, 584, 666.
Jose Nadal, Will of, 276.
Joseph S. Waterman & Sons v. Hook, 651, 652.
Journeay's Will, In re, 241.
Joy's Ex'r v. Swanton Sav. Bank & Trust Co., 586.
Judson v. Gibbons, 583.
Judson v. Staley, 525.
Juhasz v. Juhasz, 111.
Jula's Estate, In re, 678, 679, 680.
Juneau v. Dethgens, 195.
Junqua, Succession of, 795.
Justice v. Soderlund, 668.
Justice v. Wilkins, 608, 628.

# K

Kaechelen v. Barringer, 232.
Kahl's Estate, In re, 338.
Kahn v. Wolf, 685.
Kaier's Estate, In re, 626.
Kaiser v. Ebersberger, 619.
Kaiser's Estate, 112.
Kallenbach's Estate, In re, 646.
Kalskop's Will, In re, 521.
Kalt's Estate, In re, 776.
Kamerer v. Kamerer, 672.
Kamorowski v. Jackowski, 522.
Kane v. Hudson, 519.
Kane's Estate, In re, 168.
Kansas City Life Ins. Co. v. Rainey, 162, 196.
Kantor v. Bloom, 152.
Kantor v. Cohn, 151.
Kapiolani Maternity & Gynecological Hospital v. Wodehouse, 738.
Kaplan v. Coleman, 483.
Kaplan v. Leader, 733, 734, 736, 737, 756.
Kapp's Will, In re, 370.
Kariher's Petition, 806.
Karolusson v. Paonessa, 137.
Karr v. Robinson, 427.
Karrer's Will, In re, 323, 338.
Kashouty v. Deep, 640.
Kassam's Estate, In re, 612.
Katz v. Greeninger, 176.
Katz' Estate, In re, 600.
Kaufman, Estate of, 462.
Kaufman v. Caughman, 337, 339.
Kaufman v. Kaufman, 648.
Kaufman v. Murray, 311, 313, 318.
Kauffman's Appeal, 132.
Kauffman's Estate, In re, 208.
Kaven's Estate, In re, 246.
Kayhart v. Whitehead, 412, 413.
Keal v. Rhydderck, 91.
Kearns v. Kearns, 511, 732, 733, 734.
Kearns v. Rousch, 451, 462.
Keating v. Augustine, 190.
Keating v. Stevenson, 650.
Keck v. McKinstry, 178, 179.
Keech's Estate, In re, 752.
Keefer's Estate, In re, 811.
Keefe's Will, In re, 324.
Keegan v. Geraghty, 92.
Keegan's Estate v. Welch, 580.
Keeler v. Keeler, 247.
Keeler v. Merchants' Loan & Trust Co., 388, 389.
Keeley's Estate, In re, 548.
Keely v. Moore, 331.
Keenan v. Tonry, 590.
Keenan's Will, Re, 409.
Kees' Estate, In re, 120.
Kehl v. Taylor, 783.
Kehl's Estate, In re, 299.
Keicher v. Mysinger, 148, 150.
Keifer v. Kissell, 703.
Keil v. Wilson, 508, 554.
Keith v. Keith, 488.
Keith v. McCord, 579.
Keith v. Parks, 714.
Kell v. Charner, 296.
Kellam's Ex'rs v. Jacob, 707, 765.
Kelleher, Estate of, 784.
Kelleher's Estate, In re, 208, 447.
Keller v. Keller, 111, 258.
Kelley v. Devin, 221.
Kelley v. Hazzard, 526, 533.
Kelley v. Union Pac. Ry. Co., 642.
Kelley's Estate, 625.
Kelliher v. New York C. & H. R. R. Co., 643.
Kellner v. Hagood, 365.
Kello v. Kello's Ex'rs, 812, 814.
Kellogg v. Ridgely, 507.
Kellogg v. White, 485.
Kelly v. Kennedy, 557.
Kelly v. Miller, 246.
Kelly v. Nichols, 786.
Kelly v. Richardson, 452, 733, 734, 736, 761.
Kelly v. Scott, 83.
Kelly v. Snow, 651, 652.
Kelly v. Stevenson, 426.
Kelly's Estate, In re, 300, 314, 422, 425, 426, 427, 472, 651, 652, 698, 709, 805.
Kelly's Will, In re, 326.
Kelsey, In re, 723.
Kelsey v. Warfield, 760, 762.
Kemp v. Hutchinson, 451, 771.
Kemp v. Kemp, 741.
Kemp v. Turnbull, 127.
Kemp's Estate, In re, 736.
Kemper's Estate, In re, 438, 439.
Kemph v. Belknap, 106.
Kemps's Will, In re, 207.
Kempthorne's Estate, In re, 276.
Kenaday v. Sinnott, 797.

Kendrick, Will of, 736, 763.
Kendrick State Bank v. Barnum, 697.
Kendrick's Estate, In re, 245.
Kenebel v. Scafton, 422, 428, 429.
Kenin's Trust Estate, In re, 162.
Kenlin's Estate, 198.
Kennedy v. Nelson, 200.
Kennedy v. Upshaw, 472.
Kennedy v. Walcutt, 505, 521.
Kennedy's Estate, In re, 112, 206, 722.
Kennedy's Will, In re, 442, 507, 509, 539, 540.
Kennell v. Abbott, 269.
Kennett v. Kidd, 313.
Kenney's Will, In re, 535.
Kent, Matter of, 679.
Kent v. Barker, 430.
Kent v. Bothwell, 646.
Kent v. Dunham, 753.
Kent v. Kent, 221.
Kent v. Mahaffey, 421, 422.
Kent's Will, Matter of, 513.
Kenyon v. Kenyon, 682.
Kenyon College v. Cleveland Trust Co., 126.
Keppelmann v. Keppelmann, 95.
Kerckhof's Estate, In re, 457, 508.
Kerens v. St. Louis Union Trust Co., 404.
Kern v. Kern, 478.
Kernochan, In re, 750.
Kerr's Estate, 467.
Kersey v. Lovell, 342.
Kershaw v. Hicks, 583.
Kerwin v. Donaghy, 114, 115.
Kesler v. Heberling, 637.
Kessinger v. Kessinger, 258.
Kessler v. Martinson, 517.
Kessler v. Olen, 213, 293.
Kessler's Estate, In re, 611.
Keyes v. Munroe, 504.
Keylway v. Keylway, 47.
Keys v. Keys, 693, 724, 730.
Keyser v. Calvary Brethren Church, 413.
Kidd v. Bates, 605.
Kidder, Estate of, 507.
Kielsmark's Will, 94.
Kierstead's Estate, 753.
Kihlken v. Kihlken, 80.
Killan's Estate, Matter of, 599, 793.
Kimball's Will, In re, 784.
Kimmel v. Williams, 83.
Kimmel's Estate, 297.
Kimmel's Estate, In re, 209.
Kindberg's Will, In re, 544, 551.
Kinealy v. O'Reilly, 790.
King, Ex parte, 275, 276.
King v. Harford, 665.
King v. King, 310, 806.
King v. Lyman, 571.
King v. Murray, 644.
King v. Sellers, 745.
King v. Skellie, 771.
King v. Westervelt, 493.
King's Estate, In re, 158, 808.
King's Ex'rs v. Hanna, 214.
Kingman v. Soule, 651, 652.
Kingston's Estate, In re, 651, 652, 654.
Kinnan v. Wight, 706.
Kinnear v. Langley, 142.
Kinnebrew's Distributees v. Kinnebrew's Adm'rs, 188.
Kinney v. Kepplinger, 603.
Kinney v. Newbold, 718.
Kinnick v. Coy, 609.
Kinsella v. Kinsella, 501.
Kirby, In re, 603.
Kirby v. Hulette, 192.
Kirby's Appeal, 551.
Kirchner v. Muller, 650.
Kirkbride v. Hickok, 409, 559.
Kirkendall's Estate, In re, 79.
Kirkholder's Estate, Re, 412.
Kirkland v. Calhoun, 488.
Kirkpatrick v. Kirkpatrick, 786.
Kirkpatrick's Estate, 611.
Kirkpatrick's Will, In re, 444.
Kirk's Adm'rs v. Massie, 815.
Kirkwood v. Smith, 190.
Kish v. Bakaysa, 538.
Kisner's Estate, In re, 313.
Kitby, Estate of, Re, 155.
Kitchell v. Bridgeman, 340, 343.
Kitchen's Estate, Re, 413.
Kittleson's Estate v. Kittleson, 296, 329, 347.
Kittredge v. Nicholes, 696.
Kladivo's Estate, In re, 595.
Klapp's Estate, In re, 89.
Klein v. Blackshere, 722.
Klein v. Gaines, 451.
Klein's Estate, In re, 244, 246, 347.
Kleinschmidt's Estate, In re, 699, 702.
Kling v. Bordner, 219.

Klingensmith v. Klingensmith, 726, 727.
Klingner v. Dugacki, 254.
Klink's Estate, In re, 257.
Knapen's Will, In re, 456, 458.
Knapp v. Knapp, 153.
Knapp v. Reilly, 297, 299.
Knapp's Estate, In re, 199.
Knapp's Will, In re, 315.
Knecht's Estate, In re, 469.
Kneeland v. Buzzell, 627.
Knight, Succession of, 356.
Knight v. Hamakar, 627.
Knight v. Knight, 185.
Knight v. Oliver, 722.
Knight's Estate, 372.
Knight's Estate, In re, 80, 727, 728.
Knights v. Knights, 113.
Knoll v. Hart, 197.
Knost v. Knost, 406, 407.
Knowles v. Knowles, 399, 400.
Knowles' Estate, In re, 625.
Knox v. Nobel, 580, 612.
Knox v. Perkins, 225, 263, 266, 268, 269.
Knox v. Richards, 365.
Knox v. Stamper, 761.
Knox's Estate, 208, 298, 303.
Knudson v. Knudson, 256.
Knutson's Estate, In re, 296, 316
Knutson's Will, In re, 545.
Koch's Estate, In re, 134.
Koehring's Estate, In re, 710.
Koellen's Estate, In re, 193, 500.
Koelling v. Citizens' Bank, 665.
Koelmel v. Kaelin, 284.
Koeninger v. Toledo Trust Co., 393.
Kofka v. Rosicky, 211.
Kohler, In re, 662.
Kohler v. Kohler, 111.
Kohler's Will, In re, 663.
Kohn's Estate, 465.
Kokomo Trust Co. v. Hiller, 192.
Koller's Estate, In re, 289.
Kollock v. Williams, 475.
Koll's Estate, In re, 249.
Koons v. Mellett, 792.
Koppal v. Soules, 550.
Koss' Estate, In re, 196.
Kostelecky v. Scherhart, 526.
Kotz v. Belz, 513.
Koury v. Castillo, 626.
Kowalski v. Guaranty Trust Co., 692.
Kragnes v. Kragnes, 723.
Kramer's Estate, In re, 648.
Kratli v. Booth, 116.
Krause v. Krause, 115.
Krause's Estate, In re, 212, 225, 293.
Kreise v. Cartledge, 636, 668.
Krell v. Codman, 198.
Kroff v. Amrhein, 88.
Krueger's Estate, In re, 678.
Kruger, Matter of, 677.
Kuehmsted v. Tunwall, 239.
Kuhn v. Kuhn, 156.
Kulbeth v. Drew County Timber Co., 675.
Kumpe v. Coons, 311, 313.
Kundinger v. Kundinger, 212.
Kunkel v. Kunkel, 780.
Kuntz's Estate, In re, 566, 572, 574.
Kuntz's Will, Re, 478.
Kuntz's Will, Matter of, 438.
Kuplen's Estate, In re, 691.
Kurtz v. De Johnson, 213.
Kurtz v. Hibner, 284.
Kurtz v. Kurtz, 391.
Kurtz v. Stenger, 489.
Kyle v. Jordan, 380, 381.

# L

Lacey v. Dobbs, 337.
La Chapelle v. Burpee, 96.
Lachmund's Estate, In re, 603.
Lacy v. Comstock, 187.
Lacy v. Murdock, 782.
Ladd v. Baptist Church of East Randolph, 124.
Ladd v. Stephens, 725.
Ladman's Estate, In re, 553, 554.
Ladner v. Ladner, 169.
Laege's Estate, 448.
Laege's Estate, In re, 450, 512.
Lafferty's Estate, 404.
La Foy v. La Foy, 791.
Lagershausen's Estate, 293.
Lake v. Harrington, 738, 739.
Lakemeyer's Estate, Matter of, 359.
Lakin v. Blum, 197, 198, 199.
Lakin v. Lakin, 149.
Lally v. Cronen, 225.
Lamar v. McLaren, 772.
Lamb v. Lamb, 768.
Lamb v. Parker, 433, 435.
Lambardo, Succession of, 378.

Lamb Davis Lumber Co. v. Stowell, 651, 652, 654.
Lambden v. West, 402.
Lambert, Succession of, 778.
Lambert's Estate, Re, 57.
Lamberton's Estate, In re, 695.
Lambie's Estate, In re, 511, 540, 797.
Lamme v. Dodson, 697.
Lamont v. Vinger, 673.
Lanart's Estate, In re, 356.
Lancaster v. Lewis, 584.
Lancefield v. Iggulden, 736.
Lance's Estate, In re, 550, 552.
Land v. Shipp, 111.
Land's Estate, In re, 521, 534.
Landers v. Stone, 601.
Landis v. Cumberland Trust Co. of Bridgeton, 752.
Landis v. Eppstein, 799.
Landis v. Woodman, 696.
Landreth v. Casey, 149.
Landrum v. Louisville & N. R. Co., 625.
Landry v. Laplos, 666.
Lane v. Hill, 476.
Lane v. Traver, 793.
Lane's Appeal, 292, 345.
Lane's Estate, In re, 320, 341, 343, 593.
Lang v. Vaughn, 435, 742.
Lang v. Wilmer, 610, 637, 689.
Langan v. Cheshire, 553.
Langdon v. Astor's Ex'rs, 396, 473.
Langdon v. Blackburn, 270.
Lange v. Lange, 766.
Lange v. Wiegand, 294.
Langehennig v. Hohmann, 207.
Langenbach's Estate, In re, 633.
Langfelder v. Langfelder, 608.
Langfitt v. Langfitt, 210.
Langhirt v. Hicks, 527.
Langles, Succession of, 599.
Langley v. Langley, 292.
Langley v. Mayhew, 131.
Langley's Estate, In re, 522.
Lanier v. Shonyo, 578.
Lansdale v. Dearing, 769, 815.
Lansing v. Haynes, 431.
Lanyon's Estate, In re, 536.
Lapland v. Stearns, 638.
Laramore v. Laramore, 574.
Lare's Will, 543.
Largrave v. Merle, 382.
Largue, In re Estate of, 733, 750.
Larivee v. Vanasse, 771.
Larkin v. Washington Loan & Trust Co., 94.
Larkins v. Larkins, 445.
Larrabee v. Porter, 226.
Larrabee, Appeal of, 651, 652, 655.
Larsen's Estate, In re, 425.
Larson v. Johnson, 192.
Larson v. Union Pac. R. Co., 611.
Larson's Estate, In re, 297, 341, 342.
LaRue v. Lee, 447, 465.
Larus v. Bank of Commerce & Trust Co., 516.
Larwill v. Ewing, 781.
Lasak, In re, 493.
Lasak's Estate, Matter of, 611.
Lasseigne, Succession of, 360.
Lassin's Estate, In re, 595.
Lassiter v. Travis, 557.
Latham v. Father Divine, 271, 422.
Latham v. McClenny, 798.
Latham v. Udell, 259.
Latimer v. Latimer, 184.
Latorraca v. Latorraca, 406, 407, 738.
La Tourette v. La Tourette, 768.
Latour's Estate, In re, 542, 543, 546.
Latrobe v. Carter, 78.
Latz's Estate, In re, 813, 814.
Lauck v. Logan, 185, 186.
Laudy's Will, Matter of, 305.
Laughlin's Estate, In re, 723, 815.
Laughnan v. Laughnan's Estate, 219.
Laundree, Application of, 172.
Laupheimer v. Buck, 696.
Laurain v. Ernst, 434, 743, 746.
Lauraine v. Ashe, 672.
Lavalleur v. Hahn, 254.
Lavender v. Rosenheim, 471.
Lavin v. Emigrant Industrial Sav. Bank, 600.
Law v. Law, 442.
Lawler's Will, In re, 468.
Lawless v. Lawless, 389.
Lawley v. Keyes, 73.
Lawman v. Murphy, 425.
Lawndale Nat. Bank of Chicago v. Kaspar American State Bank, 314, 315.
Lawnick v. Schultz, 781.
Lawrence v. Burnett, 471.
Lawrence v. Hebbard, 292.
Lawrence v. Kitteridge, 593.

Lawrence v. Scurry, 198.
Lawrence's Appeal, 591.
Lawrence's Estate, 593.
Lawrence's Estate, In re, 232, 546, 604, 605.
Lawson v. Mullinix, 216.
Layton v. Tucker, 813, 814.
Lazar, Matter of, 665.
Leach v. Alger, 249.
Leach v. Armstrong, 790.
Leach v. Burr, 434.
Leach v. Leach's Ex'r, 134.
Leahy v. Mercantile Trust Co., 625.
Leahy v. Old Colony Trust Co., 179.
Leahy v. Timon, 552.
Lear v. Manser, 399, 400.
Learned's Estate, 292.
Leary, Matter of, 647.
Leary v. Leary, 328.
Leary v. Liberty Trust Co., 781.
Leatherbee v. Leatherbee, 347, 544.
Leathers v. Greenacre, 369.
Leatherwood v. Sullivan, 500.
Le Blanc, Succession of, 638.
Le Blanc v. Coombes, 322.
Le Borius' Estate, In re, 772.
Le Collen's Will, In re, 395.
Ledbetter v. Ledbetter, 102.
Ledet, Succession of, 386, 468.
Lee v. Allen, 619.
Lee v. Barrow, 365.
Lee v. Bermingham, 88.
Lee v. Blewett, 426.
Lee v. Earnest, 617.
Lee v. Hunter, 135.
Lee v. Keech, 524.
Lee v. Kirby, 416.
Lee v. Lee, 676.
Lee's Adm'r v. Hill, 683.
Lee's Estate, 469.
Lee's Estate, In re, 336, 693.
Leedom Estate, 246.
Leeming, In re, 747.
Lefeavre v. Pennington, 812, 814.
Lefebvre's Estate, 745.
Leffler v. Leffler, 63, 139.
Lefkoff v. Sicro, 624.
Lefort's Succession, 603.
Leggatt v. Leggatt, 582.
Leggett v. Martin, 728.
Legrande v. Legrande, 163.
Lehman v. Lindenmeyer, 139.
Lehman v. Powe, 708, 711.
Lehr v. Switzer, 529, 774, 776, 784.
Leighton v. Leighton, 732, 812, 814.
Leininger v. Reichle, 676.
Leisch, Will of, 539.
Leitch v. Leitch, 312.
Leland's Will, In re, 579, 604.
Lely v. Kalinoglu, 611.
Lemayne v. Stanley, 302, 361.
Lemmons v. Sims, 620.
Lemp v. Lemp, 131.
Lennig's Estate, In re, 729.
Lenoir v. Winn, 714.
Lent, In re, 519.
Lenz v. Sens, 778.
Lenzen v. Miller, 732, 733, 736.
Leonard, Ex parte, 300, 320.
Leonard v. Leonard, 116, 186, 445, 666, 753.
Leonard v. Stanton, 265, 277.
Leonard's Estate, In re, 647.
Leonard's Will, In re, 603.
Leopold's Estate, Re, 583, 704.
Lepley's Estate, In re, 285.
Lepper v. Knox, 139.
Leskela's Estate, In re, 618.
Leslie's Estate, Matter of, 523.
Lesser v. Pomin, 702.
Le Strange v. Le Strange, 113.
Lethbridge v. Lauder, 582.
Levan's Appeal, 608.
Levering v. Levering, 665.
Levers v. Houston, 689.
Levin v. Muser, 686.
Levin v. Safe Deposit & Trust Co., 124.
Levine v. Ramler, 425.
Levine's Estate, In re, 580.
Levy, Estate of, In re, 128.
Levy, Succession of, 733, 746.
Levy's Estate, In re, 573, 574, 673.
Lewandowski v. Zuzak, 538.
Lewin v. Lewin, 46.
Lewis, Goods of, 437.
Lewis v. Carver, 768.
Lewis v. Corbin, 271, 781.
Lewis v. Hill, 743, 748.
Lewis v. Lewis, 220, 562.
Lewis v. Lusk, 633.
Lewis v. Mason, 557, 558.
Lewis v. Metropolitan Life Ins. Co., 163.
Lewis v. Overby's Adm'r, 803.
Lewis v. Reed, 660.

Lewis v. Rutherford, 592.
Lewis v. Sedgwick, 124, 756.
Lewis v. Thompson, 436, 744.
Lewis v. Woodrum, 798.
Lewis' Estate, In re, 195, 733, 735, 746, 812, 814.
Lewis' Will, In re, 424.
Lewman's Estate, In re, 544.
L'Fit v. L'Batt, 498.
Liberman, In re, 406, 408.
Liberty v. Kinney, 597.
Liberty Title & Trust Co. v. Stevens, 800.
Liddon, Ex parte, 525.
Lidle v. Salter, 550.
Lies v. DeDaiblar, 152.
Liesse v. Fontaine, 720, 725–728.
Lieurance's Estate, In re, 218.
Lightner's Appeal, 136.
Light's Estate, 789.
Ligon v. Hawkes, 525.
Likefield v. Likefield, 418.
Liles' Succession, 656.
Lillard v. Tolliver, 521.
Lillibridge's Estate, 328.
Lillibridge's Estate, In re, 326, 501.
Lim v. Chinco, 250.
Limbach v. Bolin, 337, 338.
Limberg's Estate, In re, 557.
Limond, In re, 370.
Lincoln v. Herndon, 80.
Lindemann v. Dobossy, 494.
Lindenberger v. Cornell, 672.
Lindewall, In re, 96.
Lindmeyer's Estate, In re, 789.
Lindquist's Estate, In re, 97.
Lindsay v. Collins, 697.
Lindsay's Guardianship, In re, 568, 570.
Lineback v. Howerton, 610.
Linford's Estate, In re, 793.
Linginfetter v. Linginfetter, 476.
Linkins, In re, 795.
Linkins v. Protestant Episcopal Cathedral Fund, 462.
Linn v. Linn, 191.
Linn's Estate, In re, 661.
Linney v. Cleveland Trust Co., 386.
Linthicum v. Polk, 632.
Linville v. Chenoweth, 674.
Linz v. Eastland County, 623.
Li Po Tai's Estate, 604, 613.
Lipphard v. Humphrey, 275.
Lippincott v. Wikoff, 317.
Lippold v. Lippold, 192.
Lister v. Smith, 206.
Little v. Little, 551.
Little v. Sugg, 259, 542, 543.
Little's Adm'r v. Sizemore, 199.
Littlefield v. Paul, 149.
Lively v. Harwell, 476.
Lively v. Paschal, 112.
Livermore v. Ayres, 612.
Livermore v. Haven, 591.
Livingston's Estate, In re, 591, 593.
Llewellyn's Estate, In re, 550.
Lloyd v. Tench, 48.
Lloyd v. Wayne Circuit Judge, 485.
Lloyd's Estate, In re, 197.
Lobb v. Brown, 411, 412.
Lobb's Will, In re, 262.
Lockard v. Stephenson, 524.
Locke v. James, 455, 458.
Lockyer v. Vade, 44.
Lodge's Estate, In re, 299.
Loeb v. Callaway, 610.
Loehr v. Rueschenberg, 783.
Loehr v. Starke, 542, 552.
Loeser v. Loeser, 112.
Loflin's Estate, In re, 624.
Loftis v. Loftis, 709.
Logan v. Dixon, 700, 702.
Logan v. Thomason, 492, 524.
Lohman v. Kansas City Southern R. Co., 598.
Lomax, Will of, In re, 537.
Lonas v. Betts, 519.
Lonergan's Estate, In re, 123, 124.
Long v. Christopher, 611.
Long v. Darks, 229.
Long v. Mickler, 327.
Long v. Northrup, 709.
Long v. Ryan, 191.
Long v. Short, 760, 762.
Long v. Zook, 291.
Long's Estate, In re, 631.
Longanecker v. Sowers, 255.
Longford v. Eyre, 341.
Longstreet's Estate, In re, 711.
Look, In re, 310, 319.
Look v. French, 255.
Loomis' Will, In re, 233, 545.
Loper v. Estate of Sheldon, 214.
Lord v. Lord, 310, 333, 334.
Lord v. Miller, 315.
Lord's Appeal, 441.

Lord Mansfield in Windham v. Chetwynd, 309.
Loree's Estate, In re, 548.
Lorillard, In re, 593.
Loring v. Cunningham, 657.
Loring v. Summer, 387.
Loring v. Wise, 792.
Loring v. Woodward, 750.
Lott v. Lott, 324, 348, 536.
Lougee v. Wilkie, 472.
Louisville Trust Co. v. Southern Baptist Theological Seminary, 740.
Louisville & Nashville R. Co. v. Herb, 598.
Louisville & Nashville R. Co. v. Jones' Adm'r, 591.
Love v. Gibbs, 326, 332, 334.
Love v. Rennie, 566, 574.
Love's Estate, In re, 383, 631.
Love's Will, In re, 438.
Lovejoy v. Cockrell, 578.
Lovell v. Quitman, 444.
Lovenskiold v. Nueces Hotel Co., 653, 678.
Loveren v. Eaton, 469.
Loverett v. Veatch, 791.
Loveridge v. Brown, 551.
Lovering v. Balch, 452.
Lovett v. Farnham, 178.
Lovett v. Lovett, 213, 217, 420.
Low v. First Nat. Bank & Trust Co. of Vicksburg, 661.
Low's Will, In re, 733, 735, 746.
Lowe v. Fickling, 555.
Lowe v. Jones, 690.
Lowe Foundation v. Northern Trust Co., 271.
Lowe's Estate, In re, 195.
Lowe's Will, In re, 259.
Lowenthal v. Mandell, 489.
Lowery v. Idleson, 666.
Lowis v. Rumney, 694.
Lowrance, Will of, 358.
Lowrance's Will, In re, 359.
Lowrimore v. First Sav. & Trust Co. of Tampa, 124.
Lowry v. Crandall, 630, 698.
Lowry v. Florida Nat. Bank of Jacksonville, 167.
Lowry v. Lowry, 188.
Loyd v. Spillet, 413.
Loyd, In re Estate of, 429.
Loyola College v. Dugan, 738.
Lucas v. Brown, 305.
Lucas v. Price, 670.
Lucas' Estate, In re, 645, 704.
Luckhardt's Estate, In re, 779.
Ludlow v. Ludlow, 330.
Lufkin's Estate, In re, 131.
Lugg v. Lugg, 428.
Lummis, Re, 811.
Lummis, Matter of, 814.
Lund v. City of Seattle, 597.
Lund & Seamands v. Riggs, 653.
Lundquist v. First Evangelical Lutheran Church of Battle Lake, 763.
Lundquist's Will, In re, 242, 453, 456.
Luper v. Werts, 325.
Lupton v. Lupton, 763.
Luscher v. Luscher, 814.
Lusk's Estate, 747.
Luther v. Luther, 449, 462, 552.
Lutostanski v. Lutostanski, 163.
Lutwich & Mitton, 743, 746.
Lux's Estate, In re, 134.
Lydick v. Lydick, 806.
Lyman's Will, In re, 326.
Lynch v. Melton, 413.
Lynch v. Skelly, 630, 633.
Lynch's Estate, In re, 80, 284.
Lynn v. Strickler, 811, 814.
Lyon, Matter of, 773.
Lyon v. Dada, 265.
Lyon v. Smith, 339.
Lyon v. Townsend, 240.
Lyons v. Lyons, 150.
Lysholm's Estate, In re, 155.
Lytle v. Bond's Estate, 698, 700.

# M

Maas v. German Sav. Bank in City of New York, 587, 590.
McAdams v. Wilson, 827.
McAdoo v. Dickson, 651, 652, 655.
McAlister v. Butterfield, 274.
McAlister v. Novenger, 149.
McAlister v. Pritchard, 188.
McAllister v. Fair, 153.
McAllister's Estate, In re, 759.
McArthur v. Scott, 578.
McAuslan v. Union Trust Co., 664.
McBeath v. Champion, 693, 704.
McBride v. Vance, 567.
McBurney, Succession of, 395.
McCabe, Goods of, 458.

McCaffrey, Matter of, 455.
McCahan's Estate, 412.
McCall v. Lee, 696.
McCall v. McCall, 283.
McCallister's Adm'r v. Stanley, 647.
McCarn v. Rundall, 508, 511, 554.
McCarron v. New York Cent. R. Co., 589.
McCarthy v. Fidelity Nat. Bank & Trust Co., 289, 499.
McCarthy v. Mullen, 670.
McCarthy v. Pieret, 195.
McCartney v. Osburn, 807.
McCarty v. Frazer, 644.
McCarty v. McCarty, 669.
McCarty's Estate, In re, 521.
McCary v. McCary, 91.
McCauley's Estate, In re, 473.
McChesney's Will, Matter of, 553.
McClain v. Adams, 364.
McClanahan v. McClanahan, 221, 225.
McClary v. Stull, 247.
McClaskey v. Barr, 513.
McClellan v. Owens, 553.
McClellan's Estate, In re, 111, 133, 364, 365, 367, 581, 651, 652, 655.
McClelland's Ex'r v. McClelland, 404.
McClory v. Towne, 799.
McCloskey v. Tierney, 197.
McClung v. Sieg, 803.
McClure v. Raben, 729.
McCluskey's Estate, In re, 639.
McColgan v. Walter Magee, Inc., 182.
McComb v. McComb, 815.
McConaughy v. Wilsey, 691.
McConihe's Estate, In re, 306.
McConnell v. Barnes, 711.
McConney's Estate, In re, 632.
McCool v. Old Nat. Bank in Evansville, 624.
McCormick v. Brownell, 618.
McCoubrey v. Pure Oil Co., 624.
McCowen v. Flanders, 627.
McCoy v. McCoy, 717.
McCoy v. Shawnee Bldg. & Loan Ass'n, 200, 204.
McCoy's Adm'r v. McCoy, 694.
McCrary v. Michael, 556.
McCraw v. Simpson, 586.
McCrocklin's Adm'r v. Lee, 247, 250.
McCue v. Turner, 305.
McCulloch, Appeal of, 430.
McCullough's Appeal, 406, 407.
McCully v. Cooper, 590.
McCully v. McCrary, 640.
McCune v. Oldham, 90.
McCune's Devisees v. House, 421.
McCurdy's Estate, In re, 390, 398.
McDaniel v. Putnam, 702.
McDermid's Estate, In re, 648.
McDermott v. Lingquist, 669.
McDevit v. Sponseller, 169.
McDevitt v. Deacon, 484.
McDole v. Thurm, 267.
McDole's Estate, In re, 136.
McDonald, Matter of, 371.
McDonald v. First Nat. Bank, 646.
McDonald v. Hartford Trust Co., 697.
McDonald v. McDonald, 254, 442, 516.
McDonald v. O'Dea, 609, 619.
MacDonald v. O'Shea, 659.
McDonald v. Shaw, 768.
McDonald v. White, 522.
McDonald's Estate, In re, 594.
McDonaugh v. Mulligan, 531.
McDonough, Matter of, 331.
McDougald's Estate, In re, 712, 734.
McDowell v. Addams, 69.
McDowell's Estate, In re, 243.
McEachin v. People's Nat. Bank, 121.
McElderry's Estate, In re, 323.
McElhinny v. Minor, 648.
McElhinny v. Trinkle, 542, 543.
McElroy v. Phink, 511, 554.
McElroy v. Rolston, 293, 360.
McElroy v. Trigg, 815.
McElwaine's Will, In re, 299.
McElwee v. McElwee, 80.
McEvoy v. Boston Five Cents Sav. Bank, 178.
McEwen v. McEwen, 489.
McFadden v. Hefley, 736.
McFadden v. Jenkins, 666.
McFadin v. Catron, 545, 548.
McFarland v. McFarland, 763.
McFarlin's Estate, In re, 797.
McFerren's Estate, In re, 734, 742.
McFry v. Casey, 615.
McGarry's Estate, In re, 369.
McGee, Succession of, 607.
McGee v. Ford, 789.
McGee v. Vandeventer, 495.
McGill v. Trust Co. of New Jersey, 468.
McGill's Estate, Re, 614.

McGill's Will, In re, 449.
McGill's Will, Matter of, 440.
McGillick's Estate, In re, 726.
McGillivray v. First Nat. Bank of Dickinson, 169, 180, 204.
McGinley's Estate, In re, 224, 420.
McGinn v. Gilroy, 226.
McGovern's Will, 246.
McGowan v. Miles, 694, 695.
McGrady v. Clary, 672.
McGraff's Estate, In re, 74.
McGraw's Estate, In re, 431.
McGuire v. Brown, 82.
McHale v. Toole, 202.
McIlhattan's Will, In re, 124.
McInnes v. Goldthwaite, 678, 679.
McIntosh v. Moore, 509, 554.
McIntosh's Estate, In re, 195.
McIntyre v. McIntyre, 439, 457.
McIntyre's Estate, In re, 257.
McKachney's Estate, In re, 546.
McKallip, In re Estate of, 398.
McKamy v. McNabb, 579.
McKean's Estate, In re, 209.
McKee v. McKee's Ex'r, 342.
McKellar v. Harkins, 81.
McKelway's Estate, In re, 172.
McKenna v. McKenna, 168.
McKenney v. Minahan, 567.
McKenzie v. Jensen, 651, 652, 655.
McKenzie v. Standard Accident Ins. Co., 674.
McKeown v. Morrow, 98.
McKiernan v. Beardslee, 778.
McKim v. Harwood, 631.
McKinley v. McKinley, 189.
McKinney, Estate of, 557.
McKinzie v. Hill, 690.
McKnelly v. Conley, 672.
McLain v. Garrison, 184.
McLaughlin v. Barnes, 789.
McLaughlin v. Cooper's Estate, 170, 172.
McLaughlin v. Green, 182.
McLaughlin v. McLaughlin, 517.
McLaughlin's Estate, In re, 744.
McLawhorn v. Smith, 112.
McLean, In re, 558.
McLean v. McAllum, 92.
McLean v. McLean, 142.
McLean's Estate, In re, 215, 219.
McLennan Estate, In re, 369.
McLeod v. Andrews, 784.
McLoughlin v. Sheehan, 237.
McMahon, In re Estate of, 361.
McManus' Estate, In re, 605.
MacMaster v. Fobes, 91.
McMerriman v. Schiel, 417.
McMichael's Heirs v. Bankston, 358.
MacMillan v. Knost, 258.
McMillan v. St. Louis Union Trust Co., 135.
McMillen's Ex'rs v. McElroy, 556, 651, 652.
MacMullen's Estate, In re, 602.
McMurdo's Goods, 371.
McMurray's Estate, In re, 608.
McNair v. Cooper, 673.
McNair's Estate, In re, 361.
McNair's Will, In re, 301.
McNamara v. McNamara, 807.
McNaughton v. McClure, 218.
McNaughton v. McGregor, 556.
McNeilly v. Wylie, 782.
McNichol's Estate, In re, 618.
McNulta's Estate, In re, 765.
McNulty v. Hurd, 705.
Macomber, Matter of, 455.
McPherson v. Black, 717.
McPherson v. McKay, 447.
Macpherson's Estate, In re, 794, 812, 814.
McPike v. McPike, 793.
McQueen v. Connor, 517.
McQueen v. McQueen, 773.
McQueen v. Wilson, 550.
McQuerry v. Gilliland, 773.
McQuitty v. Wilhite, 657.
McReynolds v. Smith, 247.
McSpirit's Estate, In re, 630, 631.
McWhirter's Estate, In re, 568, 572, 581.
McWilliams v. Central Trust Co., 497.
Macy v. Mercantile Trust Co., 667, 799.
Macey v. Stark, 628.
Mach v. Baranowski, 153.
Machado's Estate, In re, 651, 652, 655, 706.
Machir v. Funk, 398.
Mack v. Pairo, 150.
Mack's Estate, In re, 627.
Mackay v. Costigan, 262.
Mackay v. St. Mary's Church, 583.
Mackey v. Mackey, 504.

Macklin, Matter of, 781.
Macky's Estate, In re, 651, 652, 655, 677, 678.
Madansky's Estate, In re, 413.
Madden, Goods of, In re, 304.
Madden v. Keyser, 551.
Maddock, In re, 396.
Maddox v. Maddox, 407, 613.
Mader v. Apple, 305.
Madison v. Larmon, 525.
Madler v. Kersten, 636.
Magaw v. Emick, 676.
Magee v. McNeil, 417.
Magee's Estate, In re, 83.
Magie v. Kirkpatrick, 582.
Magill v. Magill, 810.
Maginn's Estate, Re, 380, 381, 382.
Magnus v. Magnus, 389.
Magnuson v. Magnuson, 784.
Magoohan, Appeal of, 208, 395.
Magorty's Estate, In re, 714.
Maguire v. City of Macomb, 411.
Maguire v. Cunningham, 697.
Maguire's Estate, In re, 360.
Mahlstedt's Estate, Matter of, 403, 404.
Mahoney v. Granger, 277.
Mahoney v. Grainer, 286.
Mahoney v. McBirney, 614.
Maine Cent. Institute v. Haskell, 696.
Mains v. City Title Insurance Co., 675, 676.
Major's Estate, In re, 208.
Malen, Goods of, In re, 304.
Male's Will, In re, 365, 367.
Mallery, Matter of, 370.
Mallett v. Grunke, 214.
Mallow v. Walker, 548.
Malone v. Cannon, 134.
Malone v. Sullivan, 170.
Malone's Adm'r v. Hobbs, 444.
Maloney v. Maloney, 214.
Managle v. Parker, 442.
Manatt's Trust, In re, 723.
Manchester v. Loomis, 212.
Manchester's Estate, In re, 293, 361.
Mandelle's Estate, In re, 733, 747, 750.
Mangold v. Grace, 676.
Mann v. Balfour, 510, 511.
Mann v. Jackson, 406.
Mann v. Land, 283, 284.
Mann's Estate, In re, 113, 535.
Mann's Will, 707.
Manners' Estate, In re, 325.
Manning v. Napp, 50.
Mansfield v. Hill, 146.
Mansfield v. McFarland, 586.
Mansfield v. Neff, 430.
Manship v. Stewart, 469.
Marble v. Treasurer & Receiver General, 172.
March v. Fidelity & Deposit Co., 623.
Marcus v. McKee, 615.
Marcy v. Graham, 763.
Marden v. Jones, 590.
Mardis v. Steen, 168.
Mares v. Martinez, 142.
Maresh's Will, In re, 544.
Markham v. Hufford, 404.
Markover v. Krauss, 87.
Maroncelli v. Starkweather, 139, 238.
Marr v. Barnes, 519.
Marre's Estate, In re, 796.
Marsden's Estate, In re, 420, 552.
Marsh v. Marsh, 497.
Marsh v. Rogers, 185.
Marshall v. Berry, 204.
Marshall v. Broadhurst, 658.
Marshall v. Coleman, 703, 704, 793.
Marshall v. Marshall, 143, 427, 513.
Marshall v. Mason, 338.
Marshall v. Middleton, 707, 764.
Marshall v. Perkins, 696.
Marshall v. West, 739.
Marshall's Estate, Re, 413.
Marshall & Ilsley Bank v. Voigt, 168, 171.
Marston, In re, 313.
Marston v. Churchill, 256.
Marston v. Fox, 422, 428, 429.
Marston v. Norton, 228.
Marston v. Roe, 423.
Martin, In re, 732, 756.
Martin, Matter of, 339.
Martin, Succession of, 604.
Martin v. Central Trust Co., 566, 574, 598.
Martin v. Dix, 601.
Martin v. Dry Dock, E. B. & B. Railroad Co., 578.
Martin v. Long, 95, 320.
Martin v. Martin, 113, 258, 405, 544, 752, 790.
Martin v. Otis, 615.
Martin v. Smith, 164.

Martin v. Stovall, 488.
Martin v. Wagner, 508.
Martin's Estate, In re, 65, 140, 431, 584, 585, 609.
Martin's Will, Matter of, 218.
Martin Bros. Co. v. Peterson, 661.
Martindale v. Bridgforth, 266, 274, 279, 548.
Martinelli v. Burke, 685.
Martinez v. De Martinez, 367.
Martinez v. Meyers, 794.
Martz' Estate, In re, 145.
Marvin's Will, In re, 453, 455, 456, 457.
Marx's Estate, In re, 452, 460, 462, 463, 502.
Mason v. Bogg, 713.
Mason v. Pomeroy, 662.
Mason v. Willis, 812, 814.
Mason's Guardian v. Soaper, 189.
Mason's Will, 783.
Mason's Will, Matter of, 372.
Massachusetts Audubon Soc. v. Ormond Village Imp. Ass'n, 472.
Massey v. Doke, 659.
Massey v. Reynolds, 323, 327, 532.
Massey's Estate, In re, 216, 220, 432.
Masters v. Masters, 746.
Matassa v. Matassa, 111, 112.
Matchette's Estate, In re, 410.
Matheson v. Matheson, 238.
Mathews, Succession of, 359.
Mathews v. Krisher, 123.
Mathews v. Tobias, 216.
Mathews' Estate, In re, 200, 450, 472.
Mathews' Will, In re, 91.
Matson v. Johnson, 676.
Matson, Estate of, In re, 689.
Matteote's Estate, In re, 425.
Matthew v. Moncrief, 103, 169.
Matthews, In re Estate of, 781.
Matthews v. Newby, 19, 797.
Matthews v. Targarona, 756, 757, 758.
Matthews' Will, In re, 633, 634.
Maud v. Catherwood, 65.
Maud v. Maud, 217.
Maudru v. Humphreys, 101.
Maulsby v. Citizens' Banking Co. of Modoc, 672.
Maupin v. Maupin, 695.
Maxey v. Queen, 209.
Maxim v. Maxim, 733, 734, 735, 746.
Maxwell v. Hill, 319.
May v. Brown, 450, 512, 535, 552.
May v. Burns, 761, 762.
May v. May, 372.
May v. Sansbery, 625.
May v. Sherrard's Legatees, 744.
Maybaum, Petition of, 814.
Mayberry v. Moore, 693.
Mayburn's Will, In re, 767.
May Coal Co. v. Robinette, 642, 643.
Mayer's Estate, In re, 696.
Mayer's Will, In re, 137.
Mayes v. Mayes, 535.
Mayfield v. Cook, 215.
Maynard v. Jacobs, 347.
Maynard v. Maynard, 799.
Maynard v. Tyler,
Maynard v. Vinton, 343.
Mayo v. Arkansas Valley Trust Co., 660.
Mays v. Burleson, 187.
Mays' Estate, In re, 133.
Mayweather v. Wallace, 517.
Mazanec's Estate, In re, 255, 539.
Mead v. Phillips, 120.
Mead v. Trustees of Presbyterian Church, 544.
Mead's Estate, In re, 402, 403, 750.
Mead Co. v. Doerfler, 571, 646.
Meade v. Vande Voorde, 666, 793.
Meads v. Earle, 302.
Means v. Ury, 465, 466.
Mears v. Mears, 546.
Mears v. Smith, 567.
Mear's Estate, In re, 502.
Mecum v. Stoughton, 734.
Mecutchen v. Gigous, 247.
Medaini, Re, 154, 155.
Medill v. McIntire, 556, 557.
Medill v. Snyder, 244, 526.
Medlycott v. Assheton, 443.
Mee v. Cusineau, 744.
Meech v. Grigsby, 152.
Meeker v. Draffen, 808.
Megit v. Johnson, 56.
Meglemry v. Meglemry, 286.
Megrath's Estate, In re, 578.
Me-hun-kah's Will, In re, 300, 347.
Meier v. Buchter, 255.
Meier's Will, In re, 330.
Meir v. Peirrano, 543.
Melhase v. Melhase, 449, 450.
Mellen v. Baldwin, 683, 684.
Mellen v. Mellen, 772.
Mellon v. Goodyear, 642.

Melony's Appeal, 722.
Melrose Avenue in Borough of the Bronx, In re, 99.
Melton v. Davidson, 75, 76.
Meluish v. Milton, 267, 268.
Melville's Estate, In re, 461.
Mendinhall's Appeal, 460.
Menke v. Duwe, 226, 419.
Mentney v. Petty, 45, 48.
Menzi v. White, 442, 553.
Meppen v. Meppen, 791.
Mercantile Trust Co. v. Schloss, 123, 634.
Mercer v. Dobbyn, 598.
Merchants Nat. Bank v. Hubbard, 112, 122.
Meredith v. Meredith, 438, 444.
Meredith's Estate, In re, 522.
Merigan v. McGonigle, 174.
Meriwether v. Fourth & First Bank & Trust Co., 88.
Merriam v. Merriam, 733, 735, 746.
Merrill v. Boal, 188, 385, 386, 393.
Merrill v. Hayden, 777.
Merrill v. National Bank of Jacksonville, 713.
Merrill v. New England Mut. Life Insurance Co., 590.
Merrill v. Regan, 704.
Merrill v. Winchester, 395, 399.
Merrill v. Wisconsin Female College, 404.
Merritt v. Jenkins, 788.
Merritt v. Merritt, 448.
Merritt's Estate v. Merritt, 661.
Mertes' Estate, In re, 156.
Mesecher v. Leir, 90.
Metcalf v. Sweeney, 394, 400.
Metcalf's Estate, In re, 133.
Metropolitan Life Ins. Co. v. Chappell, 163.
Metropolitan Life Ins. Co. v. Fitzgerald, 568.
Metzger v. Klanko, 662.
Meurer, Will of, 341.
Meutchen v. Gigous, 237.
Mewborn v. Moseley, 667, 668.
Meyer, Estate of, 273.
Meyer, Matter of, 3.
Meyer v. Nischwitz, 568.
Meyer's Adm'r v. Myers, 152, 648.
Meyer's Adm'r v. Zoll, 570.
Meyer's Estate, In re, 533.
Meyers, In re, 582.
Meyerovitz v. Jacobovitz, 434, 739, 740, 743, 746.
Mey's Estate, In re, 209.
Michael v. Marshall, 548.
Michel Brewing Co. v. Wightman's Estate, 698.
Michigan Trust Co. v. Driver, 762.
Michigan Trust Co. v. Fox, 438.
Middleton v. Carter, 628.
Middleton's Case, 604.
Midgley v. Midgley, 694.
Midlow v. Ray's Adm'x, 500, 804.
Mikkelsen's Estate, In re, 738, 739.
Milam v. Stanley, 208.
Milburn v. Milburn, 430.
Mildrum's Estate, In re, 166.
Mileham v. Montagne, 232.
Miles v. Odom, 747.
Miles' Appeal, 445.
Millage v. Noble, 546, 547, 554.
Millar's Estate, In re, 244, 245.
Miller, Estate of, 392.
Miller v. Allen, 195.
Miller v. Aven, 143.
Miller v. Blumenshine, 541, 545, 546, 554.
Miller v. Bower, 4.
Miller v. Bradburn, 693.
Miller v. Brode, 775.
Miller v. Brown, 464.
Miller v. Hammond, 119.
Miller v. Harrell, 440.
Miller v. Jacobs, 649.
Miller v. Klossner, 763.
Miller v. McClune, 198.
Miller v. McNamara, 502, 504.
Miller v. Miller, 101, 132, 146, 806.
Miller v. Monroe, 698.
Miller v. Pennington, 83.
Miller v. Phoenix Ins. Co., 651.
Miller v. Pitman, 798.
Miller v. Richardson, 719, 721, 724.
Miller v. Shoaf, 700.
Miller v. Smith, 811.
Miller v. Whittington, 549.
Miller's Appeal, 719, 721.
Miller's Estate, 520.
Miller's Estate, In re, 71, 131, 152, 320, 326, 364, 387, 486, 516, 522, 598, 604, 618.
Miller's Estate, Matter of, 88.
Miller's Estate, Re, 409.

Miller's Ex'rs v. Miller's Heirs & Creditors, 710, 712.
Miller's Will, In re, 370, 511.
Miller & Sons v. Blinn, 637.
Millis' Estate, 83.
Mills v. Connor, 637.
Mills v. Smith, 216, 658.
Mills' Estate, In re, 793, 796, 812, 814.
Millward v. Buswell, 304, 307.
Milner v. First Nat. Bank of Minneapolis, 693.
Milner v. Hoag, 590.
Milner's Estate, In re, 516.
Milroy v. Lord, 169.
Miltenberger v. Miltenberger, 296, 311, 312.
Milton v. Jeffers, 259.
Milton v. Milton, 747.
Milward, Goods of, 307.
Milwaukee Protestant Home for the Aged v. Becher, 786.
Mimey's Estate, In re, 320.
Mindler v. Crocker, 535.
Miner v. Atherton, 737, 738.
Minneapolis Trust Co. v. Birkholz, 702.
Minnesota Loan & Trust Co. v. Beebe, 605.
Minor v. Guthrie, 552.
Minor v. Rogers, 174.
Minot v. Harris, 70.
Mintaberry's Estate, In re, 627.
Minturn v. Conception Abbey, 257, 260.
Minuto v. Metropolitan Life Ins. Co., 163.
Mires v. Laubenheimer, 725, 726.
Miskimins' Appeal, 672.
Mississippi Valley Trust Co. v. Ruhland, 135.
Mississippi Valley Trust Co. v. Smith, 168.
Mississippi Valley Trust Co. v. Walsh, 89.
Mitchell v. Dreher, 567, 597.
Mitchell v. Hobart, 534.
Mitchell v. Mitchell, 259, 748.
Mitchell v. Pease, 639.
Mitchell v. Weaver, 161, 647.
Mitchell's Distributees v. Mitchell, 719.
Mittelsteadt's Will, 553.
Moale v. Cutting, 335.
Mobley v. Mobley, 607, 613.
Moerlin's Estate, In re, 444.
Moffatt v. Heon, 742, 744.
Moffet v. Cash, 90.
Mohr's Estate, In re, 790.
Moise v. Moise's Ex'r, 121.
Molander v. Anderson, 527.
Molineaux v. Raynolds, 785.
Mollan's Estate, In re, 541, 551, 554.
Moller's Will, In re, 307.
Monach v. Koslowski, 271.
Monagahan's Estate, In re, 522.
Monahan, In re, 788.
Moncrief's Will, In re, 84.
Moneyham v. Hamilton, 421, 422.
Monninger v. Koob, 225.
Monroe v. Huddart, 440.
Montague v. Jeoffereys, 433, 743, 746.
Montague v. Street, 360.
Montegut, Succession of, 814.
Montgomery, Re, 799.
Montgomery v. Blankenship, 393.
Montgomery v. Clark, 483.
Montgomery v. Dorion, 99.
Montgomery v. Foster, 523, 532.
Montgomery v. Grenier, 529.
Montgomery v. Mutual Life Ins. Co. of New York, 645.
Montgomery v. Perkins, 334.
Montgomery v. Willbanks, 267, 272.
Montgomery's Appeal, 801.
Montgomery's Estate, In re, 331.
Moody v. MaComber, 636.
Moon v. Morvell, 358.
Moore, In re, 472.
Moore, Re, 408.
Moore v. Alden, 758.
Moore v. Baker, 768.
Moore v. Brandenburg, 568.
Moore v. Bryant, 682.
Moore v. Burrow, 725.
Moore v. Dick, 4.
Moore v. Glover, 342, 345.
Moore v. Gregory, 529, 566.
Moore v. Harper, 806.
Moore v. Heineke, 267.
Moore v. Hoffman, 128.
Moore v. Horne, 253.
Moore v. Jones, 711, 713.
Moore v. Layton, 200.
Moore v. McFall, 662.
Moore v. Martin, 527.

Moore v. Moore, 85, 283, 425, 527, 697.
Moore v. Prudential Ins. Co. of America, 158.
Moore v. Robinson, 150.
Moore v. Samuelson, 486.
Moore v. Sanders, 325.
Moore v. Shifflett, 200.
Moore v. Smith, 492.
Moore v. Trott, 191.
Moore v. Walton, 347, 544.
Moore v. Wooten, 634.
Moore's Estate, In re, 135, 139, 146, 417, 465, 478, 501, 502, 602, 812, 814.
Moore's Ex'rs v. Blauvelt, 257.
Moore's Will, 474.
Moorman v. Louisville Trust Co., 410, 773.
Moos v. First State Bank, 310, 314.
Moran v. Moran, 412.
Moran v. Stewart, 87.
Moran's Estate, In re, 610, 660, 794.
Mordecai v. Boylan, 280, 459, 460.
Morecraft v. Felgenhauer, 244.
Morehouse v. Bridgeport City Trust Co., 778.
Morel's Estate, In re, 610.
Moreland v. Brady, 301.
Morello v. Cantalupo, 148.
More's Estate, In re, 671, 763.
Morey v. Sohier, 422, 428, 429, 434, 498, 521.
Morgan, In re, 722.
Morgan v. Catherwood, 639.
Morgan v. Hamlet, 690.
Morgan v. Ireland, 424.
Morgan v. Morgan, 615.
Morgan v. Sanborn, 213.
Morgan v. Watkins, 765.
Morgan's Estate, In re, 361, 442, 693, 704.
Morin v. Holiday, 85.
Morisey v. Brown, 737.
Moritz v. Horsman, 801.
Mork v. Mellett, 93, 94.
Morland's Estate, In re, 627.
Morley's Estate, In re, 243, 299, 542, 546, 548.
Morley's Will, In re, 556.
Moro's Estate, In re, 335, 336.
Morrell v. Morrell, 277.
Morris v. Arrington, 568.
Morris v. Burroughs, 410.
Morris v. First Nat. Bank of Atlanta, 73.
Morris v. Higbie, 766.
Morris v. Morris, 651, 652, 655.
Morris v. Mull, 411.
Morris v. Stokes, 289.
Morris v. Trotter, 92.
Morris v. Ward, 80.
Morris v. Westerman, 711.
Morris' Estate, In re, 710.
Morrish's Estate, In re, 550.
Morrison v. Burlington, C. R. & N. R. Co., 634.
Morrison v. Hass, 590.
Morrison v. Land, 218.
Morrison v. Reed, 412.
Morrison's Estate, In re, 349, 359, 383, 416, 417.
Morrow v. Board of Trustees of Park College, 535, 543.
Morrow v. Scott, 75.
Morrow's Estate, In re, 305.
Morse v. Slason, 192.
Morse v. Ward, 471.
Morse's Estate, In re, 764.
Mortgage Bond Corp. of New York v. Haney, 332.
Morton, In re, 438.
Morton v. Georgia R. & E. Co., 642.
Moseley v. Goodman, 286.
Moseley v. Harper, 134.
Mosely v. Mosely, 431, 432.
Mosier v. Osborn, 799.
Moskowitz v. Marrow, 171.
Moss v. Axford, 399, 400.
Moss v. Helsley, 781.
Mott v. Iossa, 719.
Mott v. National Bank of Commerce, 89.
Mott's Estate, In re, 782.
Mottau v. Mottau, 535.
Moultrie v. Hunt, 330.
Mountain Park Institute v. Lovill, 403, 404.
Moushegian v. Sheppard, 557.
Mow v. Baker, 723, 728.
Mowry v. Latham, 618.
Mowry v. McQueen, 591.
Moxley's Will, In re, 310.
Mucklow's Will, Matter of, 452.
Muellenschlader's Estate, In re, 558.
Mueller's Will, In re, 298.
Mug v. Ostendorg, 217.

Muldoon v. Moore, 20.
Mulheran's Ex'rs v. Gillespie, 769.
Mullan v. Bank of Pasco County, 128.
Mullane v. Central Hanover Bank & Trust Co., 494.
Muller v. Muller, 511.
Muller's Estate, In re, 95.
Mulligan v. Leonard, 367.
Mulligan's Estate, In re, 795.
Mullins v. Mullins, 607.
Mullin's Estate, In re, 299.
Mullis v. Phillips, 341.
Multorpor Co. v. Reed, 661, 662.
Mumper v. Matthes, 676.
Munday v. Knox, 551.
Mundy v. Mundy, 440.
Munger's Estate, In re, 794.
Munie v. Gruenewald, 90.
Munnikhuysen v. Magraw, 277.
Munroe, Estate of, 581.
Murchison v. Murchison, 153, 158.
Murdoch v. Murdoch, 590.
Murguiondo v. Nowland's Ex'r, 302.
Murnan's Estate, In re, 651.
Murphey v. C.I.T. Corporation, 182.
Murphree v. Griffis, 505.
Murphy v. Boling, 435.
Murphy v. Clancy, 381.
Murphy v. Crouse, 598.
Murphy v. Freeman, 566, 572, 574, 610, 624.
Murphy v. Henry, 529.
Murphy v. Karnes, 608.
Murphy v. McBride, 282.
Murphy v. McMahon, 634.
Murphy v. Markis, 431.
Murphy v. Moyle, 146.
Murphy v. Murphy, 572, 624.
Murphy v. Nett, 240.
Murphy's Estate, In re, 194, 335, 440, 522, 530, 774.
Murphy's Will, In re, 284, 295.
Murray, Goods of, 384.
Murray, Will of, In re, 554.
Murray v. Cazier, 194.
Murray v. Gadsen, 169.
Murray v. Lewis, 386.
Murray v. Murphy, 335.
Murray's Estate, In re, 653.
Murray's Estate, Matter of, 177.
Murray's Will, In re, 498.
Murry v. Hennessey, 299, 542, 543.
Muse v. Muse, 755, 758.
Musgrove v. Holt, 295, 305, 306, 307, 349.
Mushaw v. Mushaw, 114, 115.
Mutual Benefit Life Ins. Co. v. Ellis, 162.
Mutual Life Ins. Co. v. Armstrong, 158.
Myer's Estate, In re, 133.
Myers v. Exchange Nat. Bank, 492.
Myers v. Myers, 258.
Myers v. Pleasant, 546.
Myers v. Smith, 776.
Myers v. Vanderbelt, 295.
Myers v. Warrenfells, 674.

# N

Nachtsheim's Will, In re, 559.
Nagle v. Conard, 145.
Nagle v. Nagle, 497.
Nalle v. State Deposit & Trust Co., 788.
Nalley v. First Nat. Bank of Medford, 184, 187.
Nashville Trust Co. v. Cleage, 598.
Nathan v. Freeman, 700, 702, 703.
National Automobile & Casualty Ins. Co. v. Ainge, 697.
National Bank of Commerce of Charlestown v. Wehrle, 418.
National Bank of Greece v. Savarika, 777.
National Board of Christian Women's Board of Missions of Christian Church v. Fry, 737.
National City Bank v. Brennan, 656.
National Newark & Essex Banking Co. v. Rosahl, 178.
National Shawmut Bank v. Joy, 178, 179, 180.
National Society for the Prevention of Cruelty to Children v. Scottish National Society for the Prevention of Cruelty to Children, 285.
National Surety Co. v. Wages, 599.
Nations v. Ulmer, 806.
Natt, In re, 44.
Naugher v. Hinson, 622, 630.
Nave's Estate, In re, 597.
Neal v. Boykin, 589.
Neal v. Haygood, 683, 686.
Neal's Will, In re, 523.
Nedham's Case, 643.

Needham v. Needham, 656, 796.
Needham's Estate, In re, 510.
Needles v. Needles, 726.
Neelen v. Holzhauer, 640.
Neff's Estate, In re, 671.
Negus v. Negus, 427.
Neibling v. Methodist Orphans' Home Ass'n, 448, 451, 539.
Neil v. Flynn Lumber Co., 721.
Neil v. Neil, 342.
Neil's Estate, In re, 328.
Neill v. Brackett, 254.
Neilley v. Neilley, 714.
Neiman v. Hurff, 157, 158.
Nelen v. Nelen, 445.
Nelson, In re, 757.
Nelson, In re Estate of, 453, 455.
Nelson v. Blinn, 600.
Nelson v. Bridge, 602.
Nelson v. Cornwell, 797.
Nelson v. Nelson, 209.
Nelson v. Russell's Adm'rs, 714.
Nelson v. Schoonover, 420.
Nelson v. Spotts, 167.
Nelson's Estate, 448.
Nelson's Estate, In re, 133, 134, 437, 600, 601, 759, 793.
Nenaber's Estate, In re, 431.
Nera v. Rimando, 345.
Nesbitt v. Trindle, 80.
Neuffer v. Hagelin, 563, 573.
Neukirchen's Estate, In re, 607.
Nevin-Frank Co. v. Hubert, 695.
New v. New, 788.
Newbern v. Leigh, 502.
Newboles v. Newboles, 449.
Newburgh v. Newburgh, 283.
Newcomb v. Webster, 451.
Newcomb's Will, In re, 763.
Newell v. Homer, 509, 554.
Newell's Estate, In re, 143.
New England Trust Co. v. Morse, 668.
Newhall's Estate, In re, 254, 263, 264, 267, 269.
New Jersey Title Guarantee & Trust Co. v. Archibald, 170.
Newland v. Holland, 152.
Newland v. McNeill, 180.
Newlin's Estate, In re, 140.
Newman v. Dixon Bank & Trust Co., 245.
Newman v. Dore, 114, 180.
Newman v. Smith, 139, 243.
Newman v. Waterman, 144.
Newman's Estate, In re, 151.
Newman's Will, In re, 536.
Newport Water Works v. Sisson, 745.
Newsome v. Cogburn, 727.
Newton v. Clarke, 342.
Newton v. Seaman's Friend Society, 385, 387, 389, 499.
New York Cent. & H. R. R. Co. v. Cottle, 637.
Nichels, Estate of, 456.
Nicholas v. Adams, 201.
Nicholls, In re, 385.
Nichols, In re, 382.
Nichols v. Emery, 2.
Nichols v. Harsh, 703.
Nichols v. Nichols, 114.
Nichols v. Shephard, 67.
Nichols v. Smith, 613.
Nichols v. Wentz, 239, 240.
Nicholson v. Serrill, 791.
Nick v. Nick, 122.
Nickals' Estate, In re, 580.
Nicklas v. Parker, 173, 175, 176.
Nidy v. Rice, 130.
Nielsen's Will, In re, 785.
Nies' Will, In re, 335.
Nightingale v. Phillips, 398.
Nish's Estate, In re, 440.
Nix's Estate, In re, 613.
Nixon v. Armstrong, 318, 319.
Nixon's Will, In re, 262.
Noah v. Noah, 189.
Noble, In re, 310.
Noble v. Fickes, 185, 188, 189.
Noble v. Phelps, 467.
Noble v. Tait, 789.
Noble v. Teeple, 164.
Noble v. Tipton, 390.
Noble's Estate, In re, 123, 530.
Nobles v. Davenport, 718, 719, 721.
Nocholl v. Bergner, 287.
Nock v. Nock's Ex'rs, 343.
Noel v. Noel, 198.
Noe's Estate, In re, 501.
Noesen v. Erkenswick, 439.
Nolan v. Mathis, 636.
Nolan's Trust Estate, In re, 645.
Nolen v. Doss, 150, 151, 152.
Nols' Estate, In re, 201.
Noon's Will, Re, 476.
Nord v. Nord, 569.
Norris v. Bristow, 232, 237.

Norris' Estate, In re, 531.
Norswing's Estate, In re, 329.
Northcutt's Estate, In re, 813.
Northern California Conference Ass'n v. Smith, 190.
Northern Trust Co. v. Perry, 286, 287.
Northrop v. Graves, 801.
Northrop v. Hale, 81.
Northwestern Trust Co. v. Getz, 805.
Norton v. Bazett, 342.
Norton v. Clark, 551.
Norton v. Goodwine, 347.
Norton v. Jordan, 283, 286.
Norton v. Norton's Estate, 194.
Norton v. Tufts, 151.
Norton's Estate, In re, 156.
Norway Sav. Bank v. Merriam, 169.
Norwood v. Harness, 679.
Norwood's Estate, Matter of, 494.
Nosworthy, Goods of, 273.
Novak v. Reeson, 200.
Nowack v. Berger, 221.
Nowlin's Adm'r v. Scott, 364.
Noyes' Estate, In re, 209, 359, 597.
Nugent v. Gifford, 664.
Nugent's Estate, In re, 579.
Nunn v. Ehlert, 323, 324.
Nunn v. Hamilton, 605, 618.
Nunnemacher v. State, 31.
Nusly v. Curtis, 733, 735, 746.
Nutt v. Morse, 175.
Nutt v. Norton, 429.
Nutt's Estate, In re, 266, 550.
Nye v. Bradford, 224, 227.
Nye's Appeal, 152.

## O

Ober's Estate, In re, 624.
Obetz v. Boatmen's Nat. Bank of St. Louis, 810.
O'Brien, Appeal of, 552.
O'Brien v. Collins, 255.
O'Brien v. Pennsylvania S. V. R. Co., 636.
O'Brien v. Spalding, 238.
O'Brien's Estate, 608.
O'Brien's Estate, In re, 522.
O'Brien's Estate, Matter of, 555.
O'Brien Bros. v. Wilson, 712.
O'Bryan v. Superior Court, 579.
O'Connell v. Dow, 276, 320.
O'Connor, Matter of, 370.
O'Connor v. Immele, 226.
O'Connor's Estate, In re, 97, 98, 434, 554, 743, 746.
O'Day v. Meadows, 184.
O'Day v. O'Day, 756, 761.
O'Dell v. Goff, 247.
Odenbreit v. Utheim, 92, 221.
Odenwaelder v. Schorr, 448.
O'Donovan's Will, In re, 478.
Officer v. Officer, 679.
Offill's Estate, In re, 343.
Ogden v. Pattee, 749, 751, 753.
Ogg's Estate, In re, 604.
Ogle, Estate of, In re, 194.
Oglesby v. Springfield Marine Bank, 773.
O'Hara v. O'Hara's Adm'r, 709.
O'Hara's Estate, In re, 718, 719, 721.
Ohio Merchants' Trust Co. v. Conrad, 122.
Ohio Nat. Bank v. Miller, 776.
Ohlendiek v. Schuler, 214, 215.
Ohlsen's Estate, In re, 99.
Ohms v. Church of the Nazarene, 216.
Oil City Nat. Bank v. McCalmont, 584, 832.
Okfuskey v. Corbin, 597.
Oklahoma City University v. Baughman, 492.
Old Colony Trust Co. v. Bailey, 499.
Old Colony Trust Co. v. Cleveland, 393.
Old Colony Trust Co. v. Di Cola, 232.
Old Colony Trust Co. v. Hale, 395.
Old Colony Trust Co. v. Third Universalist Society of Cambridge, 777.
Old Colony Trust Co. v. Wolfman, 410.
Oldham v. McElroy, 671.
Oldham's Trustee v. Boston Ins. Co., 583, 636.
Oldhams' Estate, In re, 358.
Olding, Goods of, 338.
Old Ladies Home v. Cooper, 284.
O'Leary v. Lane, 386, 388.
Oleff v. Hodapp, 103, 157.
Oles v. Furlong, 667.
Oles v. Wilson, 212.
Oliffe v. Wells, 273.
Oliver v. Crewdson's Adm'r, 722.
Oliver's Estate, In re, 795.
Olivier v. Houghton County St. Ry., 642.

Olliver, In re, 333.
Olmsted's Estate, In re, 438, 442, 445, 457.
Olney v. Bates, 782.
Olney v. Brown, 720.
Olson, Re, 537.
Olson v. Larson, 314, 315.
Olson v. Scully, 686.
Olson's Estate, In re, 84, 624.
Olssen's Estate, In re, 359, 360.
Oneal v. Mead, 765.
O'Neal v. Miller, 152.
O'Neall v. Her, 143.
O'Neil v. Cogswell, 732.
O'Neil's Estate, In re, 245, 246.
O'Neil's Will, In re, 303.
O'Neill v. Lauderdale, 700.
O'Neill v. Read, 609, 613.
O'Neill's Estate, In re, 795.
Onions v. Tyrer, 455, 457, 460, 461.
Onofrey v. Wolliver, 168, 170.
Onstad's Estate, In re, 663.
Onstot's Estate, In re, 696.
Opdyke, Will of, 137.
Orchardson v. Cofield, 247, 257.
Orcutt v. Hoyt, 811.
Ordway & Husted v. Phelps, 705.
Orear v. Crum, 607.
O'Reilly's Estate, In re, 651, 652, 655.
Orndorff v. Hummer, 341.
Orpen, In re, 790.
Orr v. Kaines, 800, 801.
Orth v. Orth, 208.
Osborn v. Hoyt, 212.
Osborn's Estate, In re, 499.
Osborne v. Parker, 695.
Osborne v. Tunis, 637.
Osburn v. Rochester Trust & Safe Deposit Company, 444, 478.
Osburn's Estate, In re, 704.
O'Shea v. Barry, 678, 679.
O'Shea v. Hurley, 647.
O'Shea's Estate, In re, 132.
Oslund v. Peterson, 638.
Osmundson v. Leach, 610.
Osnato's Estate, 801.
Osnato's Will, In re, 800.
Oster's Ex'r v. Ohlman, 651, 652, 654.
Ostlund's Estate, 799.
Ostrander v. Davis, 435.
O'Sullivan v. Palmer, 624.
Oswald v. Nehls, 220.
Oswald v. Pillsbury, 700.
Oswald's Will, In re, 540.
Otero v. Otero, 619.
Otting's Estate, In re, 311, 313, 317, 558.
Oulvey v. Converse, 565.
Outlaw v. Farmer, 665.
Overbeck v. McHale, 113.
Overbury v. Overbury, 428.
Overton v. Heckathorn, 71.
Overton v. Lea, 407.
Owen, Matter of, 319.
Owen v. Busiel, 453, 462, 742.
Owen v. Crumbaugh, 247.
Owen v. Lee, 764.
Owens v. Bennett, 335.
Owens v. Fahnestock, 448.
Owens v. Felty, 487.
Owens v. McNally, 212.
Owens v. Owens, 153.
Owings v. Owings, 636.
Owsley v. Bowden, 592.
Owston, Goods of, 252.
Oxley, In re, 663.
Oxsheer v. Nave, 787, 788, 791.
Oyster v. Oyster, 724.

# P

Pace v. Eoff, 132.
Pace v. Klink, 88.
Pace v. Pace, 121.
Pacholder v. Rosenheim, 408, 411.
Packard v. Packard, 721.
Packer v. Overton, 798.
Packer v. Packer, 292.
Padden v. Padden, 192.
Padelford's Estate, In re, 611.
Padfield v. Padfield, 420.
Page, Matter of, 509, 511.
Page v. Elwell, 719, 720, 721, 722.
Page v. Parks, 510.
Page v. Phelps, 548, 551.
Pagel's Estate, In re, 209.
Paglia v. Messina, 295, 380.
Paine v. Paine, 197.
Paine v. Parsons, 737.
Palin v. Ponting, 389.
Palm's Estate, In re, 580.
Palmer v. Culbertson, 723, 724.
Palmer v. Garrard, 44.
Palmer v. Morrison, 637.
Palmer v. Owen, 381.
Palmer v. Riggs, 189.

Figures refer to pages


Palmer v. Treasurer & Receiver General, 165.
Palmer's Estate, In re, 552, 721.
Pancoast v. Eldridge, 218.
Paola, Matter of, 610.
Paperno v. Michigan Ry. Engineering Co., 618.
Paradis' Estate, In re, 682.
Paradis' Will, In re, 332.
Pardee v. Grubiss, 431.
Pardee's Estate, In re, 725.
Parfitt v. Lawless, 550.
Paris v. Erisman, 460, 745.
Park v. Mullins, 673.
Park & Tilford Import Corporation v. Nash, 665.
Parker v. Broadus, 529, 530.
Parker v. Cobe, 767.
Parker v. Foreman, 427.
Parker v. Grant, 790.
Parker v. Luehrmann, 801, 802.
Parker v. Potter, 154.
Parker v. Simpson, 640.
Parker v. Wilson, 797.
Parker v. Wright, 656.
Parker's Estate, In re, 644, 651, 652, 654, 655, 656, 792.
Parkhurst v. Healy's Estate, 690.
Parks v. Burney, 92.
Parks v. Murphy, 702.
Parks v. Snyder, 788.
Parmentier v. Pennsylvania Co. for the Ins. on Lives and Granting Annuities, 403.
Parnell v. Thompson, 384, 488.
Parnham v. Weeks, 793.
Parr v. Davison, 798.
Parramore v. Taylor, 250, 345.
Parrott v. Parrott's Adm'x, 207, 305, 307.
Parrott's Estate, In re, 143.
Parsons, Estate of, 500, 522, 558.
Parsons, In re Will of, 358.
Parsons, Will of, 359.
Parsons v. Balson, 440, 507.
Parsons v. Fitchett, 283.
Parsons v. Millar, 805.
Parsons' Estate, In re, 756, 757.
Parson's Will, Matter of, 439.
Partridge v. Partridge, 742.
Paschal v. Paschal, 720.
Pascucci v. Alsop, 422, 423, 428, 429.
Paskievitz' Estate, In re, 121.
Pass v. Stephens, 185.
Patanska v. Kuznia, 319, 732, 733, 734, 735, 746.
Patch v. Squires, 114.
Patch v. White, 284.
Paterson v. Patterson, 653.
Paterson's Estate, In re, 83.
Patsourakos v. Kolioutos, 769.
Patten v. Poulton, 554.
Patten v. Tallman, 320.
Patterson, Succession of, 295.
Patterson v. Brandon, 403.
Patterson v. Chapman, 198.
Patterson v. McClenathan, 178, 180.
Patterson v. Volmar, 726.
Patterson's Estate, 507.
Patterson's Estate, In re, 428, 430, 431.
Patterson's Estate, Matter of, 510, 512.
Patton v. Buxton, 672.
Patton v. Toronto General Trusts Corp., 414.
Paul v. Snyder, 222.
Paulk v. Roberts, 678.
Paully v. Crooks, 451.
Paulsen's Estate, In re, 624, 814.
Paulson's Estate, In re, 758.
Paulson's Will, In re, 111.
Paulus v. Besch, 768.
Pavert's Estate, In re, 671.
Pawtucket v. Ballou, 338, 344.
Pawtuxet Baptist Society v. Pawtuxet Baptist Church and Society, 286.
Payne v. Dotson, 149.
Payne v. Home Sav. Bank, 598, 600.
Payne v. Johnson's Ex'rs, 712.
Payne v. Payne, 152, 250.
Payne v. Tatem, 114.
Payne v. Tobacco Trading Corp., 200.
Peace v. Edwards, 294.
Pearce, In re, 751.
Pearce v. Pearce, 662.
Pearson, In re, 783.
Pease v. Allis, 318.
Pease v. Hudson, 596.
Peavey v. Crawford, 532.
Peck v. Botsford, 706, 831.
Peck v. Cary, 322.
Peck v. Fillingham's Estate, 765.
Peck v. Peck, 814.
Pedroli's Estate, In re, 628, 648.
Pedron v. Olds, 101.

Peebles' Estate, 132.
Peek v. Woman's Home Missionary Society, 411.
Peers' Estate, In re, 691.
Peiffer v. Old Nat. Bank & Union Trust Co., 432.
Peirce, In re, 747.
Peirce v. Graham, 25.
Peirce's Estate, In re, 3, 493, 447.
Pena y Vidaurri's Estate v. Bruni, 524.
Pence's Estate, In re, 89, 136, 468, 473.
Pendarvis v. Gibb, 239, 243, 245.
Pendergast v. Walsh, 744.
Pendock v. Mackender, 320.
Pengelly v. Thomas, 798, 799.
Pengelly's Estate, In re, 129.
Penick's Ex'r v. Walker, 280.
Penn v. Guggenheimer, 768, 773.
Pennewell, In re, 666.
Penniman Bro. v. Francisco, 80.
Penniman's Will, In re, 465.
Pennington's Estate, In re, 223.
Penniston v. Kerrigan, 532, 533.
Pennock's Estate, In re, 636.
Pentico v. Hays, 186.
People v. Flanagin, 775.
People's Bank & Trust Co. v. Mills, 695.
People's Bank & Trust Co. v. Seydel, 715.
Peoples Nat. Bank v. Rogers, 529.
Peoria Humane Soc. v. McMurtrie, 225.
Pepin's Estate, In re, 87.
Pepper's Estate, In re, 443.
Percival's Estate, In re, 98.
Pereles v. Leiser, 697.
Perera v. Perera, 241.
Perez v. Gil's Estate, 710.
Perkes v. Perkes, 441.
Perkins v. August, 573.
Perkins v. Isley, 777.
Perkins v. Micklethwaite, 471.
Perkins v. Perkins, 542, 546, 548.
Perkins v. Simonds, 78.
Perkins v. Warburton, 594.
Perkins' Estate, In re, 245, 673.
Perrine v. Perrine, 758.
Perry v. Leslie, 750.
Perry v. Louisville & Nashville R. Co., 642, 643.
Perry v. Perry, 412, 633.
Perry v. Rogers, 410, 413.
Perry v. Strawbridge, 154, 156.
Person's Appeal, 723.
Peter v. Peter, 485, 486.
Peters v. Clancy, 67.
Peters v. Fekete, 532.
Peters v. Moore, 516.
Peters Mineral Land Co. v. Hooper, 670.
Peterson, Estate of, In re, 143, 294.
Peterson v. The Chemical Bank, 587.
Peterson v. Weiner, 184.
Peterson's Estate, In re, 111, 285, 411, 518, 651, 652, 655, 795.
Petitt v. Morton, 270, 504, 505.
Petree v. Brotherton, 183.
Petrie v. Voorhees' Ex'r, 699.
Pett v. Pett, 45, 48.
Pettibone v. Moore, 597.
Pettigrew's Estate, In re, 648.
Petts, In re, 266.
Petty, Ex parte, 516.
Peugh v. McKinney, 131.
Pfaff v. Clements, 566.
Pfaffenberger v. Pfaffenberger, 311, 313.
Pfeifer v. Wright, 85.
Pflugar v. Pultz, 217.
Pfuelb, In re Estate of, 780.
Phalen v. United States Trust Co., 216.
Phelan v. Smith, 631.
Phelan's Estate, 302.
Phelps v. Bates, 811, 814.
Phelp's Will, Matter of, 470.
Phibbs, Estate of, 509, 510.
Phillippe v. Clevenger, 434.
Phillippi's Estate, In re, 144.
Phillips v. Beal, 694.
Phillips v. Clark, 611.
Phillips v. Duckett, 580.
Phillips v. Ferguson, 407, 412, 414.
Phillips v. Jones, 254.
Phillips v. McConica, 90.
Phillips v. Phillips, 436, 566, 574, 744, 745.
Phillips v. Townsend, 85.
Phillips v. Wiseman, 149.
Phillips' Estate, In re, 111, 143, 616, 619, 755, 780.
Phillips' Will, In re, 330.
Philpott v. Jones, 547, 554.

Philpott v. Vesta Coal Co., 601.
Phinizee v. Alexander, 553, 554.
Phipps v. Hale, 335.
Phoenix Mut. Life Ins. Co. v. Cummings, 373, 503.
Phoenix Mut. Life Ins. Co. v. Harris, 664.
Phoenix State Bank & Trust Co. v. Johnson, 813, 814.
Piatt's Estate, In re, 425.
Picard v. Succession of Picard, 360.
Pickens v. Campbell, 799.
Pickens v. Davis, 476, 540.
Pickering v. Weiting, 578.
Pickering v. Young, 392.
Pickett's Will, In re, 252.
Pierce v. Boston Five Cents Sav. Bank, 203.
Pierce v. Johnson, 697, 703.
Pierce v. Pierce, 372.
Pierce v. Prescott, 797.
Pierce v. Whipple, 666.
Pierce's Estate, In re, 778.
Piercy's Goods, 344.
Piersol v. Hays, 630.
Pietrantonio v. Tonn's Estate, 696.
Piffard, Matter of, 398.
Pilcher v. Pilcher, 362.
Pilkington v. Wheat, 719.
Pillsbury's Estate, In re, 89, 704.
Pilstrand v. Swedish Methodist Church, 542, 552.
Pimel v. Betjemann, 783.
Pindexter, In re Estate of, 68.
Pinkham v. Pinkham, 112.
Pinnell v. Burroughs, 676.
Pinson v. Abbott, 697.
Pirkl v. Ellenberger, 533.
Pitcairn's Estate, In re, 347.
Pitts, In re, 154.
Pitts v. Pitts, 566, 574.
Pitts v. Thompson, 571.
Plaster, Matter of, 137.
Plate's Estate, 299.
Platt v. Jones, 630, 634.
Platt v. Newman, 573.
Plaut's Estate, In re, 497, 521.
Playne v. Scriven, 344.
Plowden v. Plowden, 132.
Plumel's Estate, 392.
Plunkett v. Old Colony Trust Co., 754.
Plymale v. Keene, 191.
Pochron's Estate, In re, 543.
Poff v. Poff, 724.
Pohle v. Nelson, 92.
Pohlenz v. Panko, 671, 673.
Pohlman v. Untzellman, 218.
Pohlmann's Estate, In re, 254, 257, 260.
Poindexter, Estate of, 67.
Poindexter's Adm'r v. Alexander, 536.
Poirier v. Burton-Swartz Cypress Co., 632.
Poisson v. Pettaway, 80.
Poling v. Poling, 711.
Pollard v. Pollard, 752.
Pollard's Estate, In re, 610, 618.
Polley v. Cline's Ex'r, 496.
Pollock v. Glassell, 326, 332.
Polsey v. Newton, 283.
Pompal's Estate, In re, 132.
Pond v. Faust, 485, 496.
Pond v. Irwin, 78.
Pond v. Makepeace, 587.
Ponsonby, In re, 580.
Pontius v. Conrad, 814.
Pool v. Cross County Bank, 806.
Poole, In re, 389.
Poonarian's Will, In re, 417, 418.
Poore v. Poore, 188.
Pope, Appeal of, 324.
Pope v. Bain, 113.
Pope v. Carter, 638.
Pope v. Garrett, 271.
Pope v. Kitchell, 669.
Pope v. Pope, 466.
Pope v. Rogers, 328, 544.
Pope's Estate, In re, 637.
Pope's Will, In re, 334.
Popejoy v. Boynton, 211.
Porch v. Farmer, 441, 442.
Porter v. Howe, 756.
Porter v. Sheffield, 508, 554.
Porter v. Wolf, 294.
Porter's Appeal, 417.
Portland Nat. Bank v. Brooks, 171.
Portwood v. Hunter, 366.
Potter v. Jones, 244.
Potter v. Ritchardson, 301, 335.
Potter's Will, In re, 313.
Potter Title & Trust Co. v. Braum, 114, 204.
Potts v. House, 252.
Povey v. Povey, 124, 125, 126.

Powell v. Labry, 556.
Powell v. Pennock, 569.
Powell v. Powell, 454, 455, 457.
Powell v. Rawle, 411.
Powell's Estate, In re, 771, 784.
Power v. Overholt, 243
Powers v. Codwise, 317, 786.
Powers v. Morrison, 790.
Powers v. Powers, 814.
Powers v. Powers' Estate, 715.
Powers v. Scharling, 188.
Powers' Estate, In re, 239.
Powys v. Mansfield, 738.
Pozzuto's Estate, 177.
P'Pool's Ex'r v. P'Pool's Ex'x 465, 466.
Prall v. Prall, 810.
Pratt v. Baker, 637.
Pratt v. Hill, 632.
Pratt v. Houghtaling, 691.
Prendergast v. Walsh, 748.
Prentis v. Bates, 547.
Prerost's Estate, In ré, 772, 774.
Prescott v. Tarbell, 632.
Prescott v. Wordell, 640.
Prescott's Estate, 299.
President & Directors of Manhattan Co. v. Janowitz, 393, 394.
Preston v. Davis, 789.
Preston v. Ham, 566.
Preston v. Preston, 509, 511, 512.
Prestwood v. McGowin, 636.
Prevost's Estate, In re, 460.
Price, In re, 283.
Price v. Hitaffer, 154, 156.
Price v. Marshall, 478.
Price v. Maxwell, 463.
Price v. Price, 178.
Price v. Strange, 49.
Price's Adm'r v. Price, 626.
Price's Estate, In re, 495.
Priester v. Hohloch, 194.
Prince v. Prince, 91.
Prince de Bearn v. Winans, 801.
Pringle v. M'Pherson, 445, 458.
Printup's Estate, Matter of, 610.
Pritchard v. Pritchard, 318, 727.
Pritchard v. Thomas, 329.
Proctor v. Newhall, 787.
Proto v. Chenoweth, 709.
Proud v. Turner, 723.
Provenza v. Provenza, 267, 269.
Provident Trust Co. of Philadelphia v. Graff, 736.
Prudenzano's Will, In re, 111, 112.
Pruett v. Caddigan, 700, 703.
Pryor v. Coggin, 421.
Pryor v. Mizner, 523.
Puckett v. Brittain, 448.
Puckett's Estate, In re, 316.
Puckett's Ex'r v. Puckett, 425.
Puett's Will, In re, 500, 502.
Pufahl v. Parks' Estate, 715.
Puffer v. Clark, 102.
Pugsley's Estate, In re, 133, 134.
Pull v. Nagle, 693.
Pullen v. Placer County Bank, 203.
Pulley v. Cartwright, 293, 362.
Purcell v. Cramton, 589.
Purcell v. Sewell, 79, 80.
Purcell's Estate, In re, 208.
Purdy's Estate, In re, 520.
Purdy's Will, Matter of, 508, 554.
Purkert, Succession of, 377.
Pushcash v. Dry Dock Sav. Inst., 202.
Putbury v. Tervilian, 433, 743, 746.
Puterbaugh's Estate, In re, 90.
Putman's Will, In re, 261, 262.
Putnam v. Bates, 694.
Putnam's Estate, In re, 244.
Puukaiakea v. Hiaa, 184.
Puyoulet v. Gehrke, 99.
Pylant v. Burns, 727.
Pyle v. East, 199.
Pynchon's Will, In re, 493.

# Q

Quarles v. Fowlkes, 202.
Quarles v. Quarles, 728.
Quattlebaum v. Triplett, 130.
Quick v. Ludborrow, 659.
Quimby v. Greenhawk, 298.
Quincy Trust Co. v. Taylor, 626, 627.
Quinlan's Estate, In re, 625.
Quinn v. McDowell, 755.
Quinn's Estate, In re, 558, 559.
Quintero, Succession of, 750.
Quirk v. Pierson, 523.
Quirk v. Thomas, 683.

# R

Rabe v. McAllister, 447, 476.
Rackemann v. Taylor, 487, 589.

**Radford v. Radford, 608.**
**Ragland v. Craig, 768.**
**Ragland v. Wagener, 395, 397, 421.**
**Rahauser's Estate, In re, 632.**
**Rahn's Estate, In re, 94.**
**Railsback's Estate, In re, 568, 572.**
**Rainear's Estate, In re, 451.**
**Raines v. Osborne, 810.**
**Raines v. Shipley, 707.**
**Rainey v. Rainey, 756.**
**Raleigh v. Raleigh, 120, 121.**
**Raleigh's Estate, In re, 669.**
**Ralston v. Stainbrook, 693, 704.**
**Ralston's Estate, In re, 313, 616.**
**Ramp v. McDaniel, 628.**
**Ramsay v. Abrams, 722.**
**Ramsay v. Ramsay, 592.**
**Ramseyer v. Dennis, 532.**
**Rand's Will, In re, 299.**
**Randall, Estate of, 138.**
**Randall, In re, 247.**
**Randall v. Brayton, 697.**
**Randall's Estate, In re, 617.**
**Rankin's Estate, In re, 492.**
**Ranking v. Barnard, 789.**
**Ransdell v. Boston, 408.**
**Rapoport's Estate, In re, 98.**
**Rapp v. Reehling, 294.**
**Rash v. Bogart, 111, 112, 128.**
**Rash's Estate, In re, 130.**
**Rasor v. Rasor, 155, 790.**
**Rassieur v. Zimmer, 696.**
**Rastetter v. Hoenninger, 226.**
**Ratcliffe v. Seaboard Nat. Bank, 492.**
**Rathschek's Estate, In re, 152.**
**Rath's Estate, In re, 605.**
**Ratliff v. Meade, 726.**
**Rau v. Krepps, 122.**
**Rauch v. Metz, 780.**
**Rauchfuss' Estate, In re, 457.**
**Rausch, Matter of, 386, 388, 393, 396.**
**Rawls v. Hewitt, 813, 814.**
**Ray v. Hill, 344.**
**Ray v. Honeycutt, 712.**
**Ray v. Walker, 386, 388.**
**Ray's Estate, In re, 142.**
**Ray Estate Corp. v. Steelman, 702, 703.**
**Raymond v. Bailey, 683.**
**Raymond v. Fitch, 636, 641, 683.**
**Raymond v. Flint, 538.**
**Raymond v. Raymond, 647.**
**Raymond v. Wagner, 342.**
**Raymond's Estate, In re, 493, 516.**
**Raymond, Town of v. Goodrich, 122.**
**Rea v. Englesing, 580.**
**Read v. Williams, 805.**
**Read's Case, 571.**
**Read's Estate, In re, 651, 652, 655.**
**Reap v. Wyoming Valley Trust Co., 170.**
**Red v. Powers, 763.**
**Redd v. Redd, 752.**
**Redden's Will, In re, 516.**
**Reddy v. Graham, 178.**
**Reder v. Reder, 170, 171.**
**Redford v. Booker, 329.**
**Redmond v. Wardrep, 607.**
**Redway's Will, In re, 323, 325.**
**Redwood v. Howison, 432.**
**Reed v. Bishop, 590.**
**Reed v. Brown, 674.**
**Reed v. Geddes, 80.**
**Reed v. Hendrix's Ex'r, 300.**
**Reed v. Hollister, 265, 266.**
**Reed v. Home Nat. Bank, 523.**
**Reed v. Johnson, 512.**
**Reed v. Reed, 573.**
**Reed v. Roberts, 342, 343.**
**Reed v. Taliaferro, In re, 678, 679, 680.**
**Reed v. Watson, 338.**
**Reed v. Woodward, 295.**
**Reedy v. Kelley, 201.**
**Reel v. Elder, 148, 151, 152.**
**Rees' Estate, In re, 72.**
**Reese v. Stires, 104.**
**Reeves, In re, 471.**
**Reeves v. Duke, 3.**
**Reeves v. Hager, 502.**
**Reeves v. Hunter, 239.**
**Reeves v. White, 804.**
**Reformed Presbyterian Church of North America v. McMillan, 285.**
**Regland v. Wagener, 449.**
**Rehard's Estate, In re, 314.**
**Rehfeld's Estate, In re, 171.**
**Reh's Estate, In re, 202.**
**Reich's Estate, Matter of, 177.**
**Reichard v. Chicago, B. & Q. R. Co., 102.**
**Reichard v. Izer, 526, 528.**
**Reiche v. Williams, 247.**
**Reichert's Estate, Matter of, 613.**
**Reid v. State ex rel. Thompson, 98.**
**Reid's Adm'r v. Benge, 486, 503.**

Reid's Will, In re, 304.
Reidy's Will, In re, 278.
Reiffeld's Will, In re, 507, 508.
Reiffeld's Will, Matter of, 510.
Reilly's Estate, In re, 648.
Reilly, Succession of, 414.
Reilly's Will, In re, 304, 701.
Reil's Estate, In re, 67.
Reimers, Matter of, 556, 557.
Reinecke v. Northern Trust Co., 180.
Reinhardt v. Nehring, 256.
Reinheimer's Estate, 394, 400.
Reiter v. Carroll, 422.
Relph, Estate of, 516, 543.
Remmers v. Remmers, 430.
Rench v. Rench, 124.
Rendell's Estate, In re, 427, 430.
Renshaw v. Williams, 579.
Renwick v. Macomber, 311, 320, 494, 812, 814.
Repp's Estate, In re, 347, 348.
Repush's Will, In re, 366.
Research Hospital v. Continental Illinois Bank & Trust Co., 540.
Reuff v. Coleman, 407.
Revercomb's Estate, 470.
Rexford v. Bacon, 755.
Reycraft's Estate, In re, 345, 451.
Reynold's Estate, In re, 260.
Reynolds v. Balding, 189.
Reynolds v. Hitchcock, 82.
Reynolds v. Lloyd Cotton Mills, 596, 627.
Reynolds v. McMullen, 588.
Reynolds v. Massey, 338, 347.
Reynolds v. Reynolds, 149, 172, 176, 273, 500, 757.
Reynolds v. Schmidt, 672.
Reynold's Estate, In re, 260, 510.
Rheinfrank v. Hurr, 672, 673.
Rhode Island Hospital Trust Co. v. Calef, 778.
Rhodes' Estate, In re, 226.
Rice, In re, 581.
Rice, Will of, In re, 31.
Rice v. Andrews, 146.
Rice v. Bradley, 788.
Rice v. Freeland, 210, 373.
Rice v. Henly, 602.
Rice v. Rice, 479.
Rice's Estate, In re, 625, 798.
Rich v. Beaumont, 426.
Rich v. Gilkey, 441, 508.
Richards v. Huff, 496.
Richards v. Humphreys, 738.
Richards v. Piefer, 412.
Richards v. Pierce, 505.
Richards v. Richards, 166.
Richardson, Estate of, 209.
Richardson v. Byrd, 387, 390.
Richardson v. Cade, 211.
Richardson v. Cole, 572, 581.
Richardson v. Dreyfus, 571.
Richardson v. McCloskey, 651, 652, 654.
Richardson v. Neblett, 588.
Richardson v. Orth, 213, 324.
Richardson v. Warfield, 638.
Richardson's Estate, 152.
Richberg v. Robbins, 207.
Richey v. Richey, 729.
Richey v. Rowland, 730.
Richmond v. Bass, 811, 814.
Richmond v. Richmond, 223.
Rick's Estate, In re, 267, 495.
Rickards v. Mumford, 442.
Rickenbacker v. Zimmerman, 720.
Riddel's Estate, In re, 466.
Riddell v. Riddell, 725, 726, 727.
Ridenbaugh v. Young, 528.
Ridenour v. Callahan, 434.
Ridgeway v. Jones, 795.
Ridgway's Estate, In re, 142.
Ridgway's Estate, Matter of, 439.
Riebow v. Ensch, 630.
Riedlinger's Will, In re, 323.
Riedy v. Bidwell, 651, 652, 660.
Riegelman's Estate, In re, 765.
Rieke's Adm'r v. Rieke, 625.
Riffe v. Walton, 566.
Riggs v. Palmer, 155.
Riggs v. Riggs, 341, 342, 343, 344.
Riggs v. Safe Deposit & Trust Co., 275.
Riggs' Estate, In re, 233, 234, 525.
Right v. Price, 341.
Riley v. Allen, 212.
Riley v. Casey, 278.
Riley v. Collier, 143.
Riley v. Moseley, 645.
Riley v. New York Trust Co., 489, 596.
Riley v. Riley, 300, 334.
Rimes v. Graham, 132.
Ring's Estate, In re, 637, 693.
Ringot's Estate, In re, 603.

Rinio's Estate, In re, 613.
Rinker's Adm'r v. Simpson, 294.
Rinker's Estate, In re, 447, 450, 552.
Ripley v. Sutherland, 94.
Ripley v. Von Zedtwitz, 93, 94.
Rippe v. Weiters, 563, 573.
Rippel v. King, 779.
Rippon, In re, 369.
Rishton v. Cobb, 268.
Risley v. Dame Battinglass, 434.
Ritchey v. Jones, 326.
Rittenhouse v. Ammerman, 653.
Ritter's Estate, In re, 760, 762.
Rivers v. Rivers, 778.
Rives v. Caber, 772.
Rizer v. Perry, 785.
Rizzo v. Cunningham, 770.
Roach v. Jurchak, 489.
Roarke's Estate, In re, 558.
Robb v. Washington & Jefferson College, 180.
Robbins v. Fugit, 244.
Robbins v. Robbins, 329, 330.
Roberts v. Abbott, 527.
Roberts v. Coleman, 187, 199, 726.
Roberts v. Hardy, 153.
Roberts v. Johnson,
Roberts v. Mosely, 806.
Roberts v. Phillips, 335.
Roberts v. Roberts, 89, 504, 689, 693, 792.
Roberts v. Welch, 345.
Roberts v. Wilson, 621, 740.
Roberts' Estate, In re, 74, 97, 762.
Robertson, Succession of, 359.
Robertson v. Biernacka, 669.
Robertson v. Broadbent, 763.
Robertson v. Flynn, 283, 286.
Robertson v. Jones, 431.
Robertson v. Robertson, 324, 339.
Robertson v. Yager, 530, 564.
Robinson v. Addison, 734.
Robinson v. Chapman, 696.
Robinson v. Cogswell, 672.
Robinson v. Commissioner, 166, 823.
Robinson v. Dana's Estate, 597.
Robinson v. Georgia Sav. Bank & Trust Co., 678.
Robinson v. Hodge, 715.
Robinson v. Jones, 365, 367.
Robinson v. McDonald's Widow & Heirs, 697.
Robinson v. Robinson, 625, 720.
Robinson v. Schly, 188.
Robinson's Estate, 553.
Robinson's Estate, In re, 142, 626.
Robinson's Heirship, In re, 592, 672.
Robinson's Women's Apparel v. Union Bank & Trust Co., 196.
Robitaille v. Mumaugh, 689.
Robnett v. Ashlock, 417.
Robson, In re, 395.
Rocap v. Blackwell, 651, 652.
Roche v. Brickley, 178.
Rockafellow v. Rockafellow, 318.
Rockett's Will, 499.
Rockland Trust Co. v. Bixby, 313, 314.
Roco v. Green, 127.
Rodarmel v. Gwinnup, 286.
Roddy v. Harrell, 696.
Roderick's Estate, In re, 89.
Rodgers v. Fleming, 243.
Rodger's Estate, In re, 651, 652, 654.
Roderigas v. East River Savings Institution, 599.
Rodman v. Rodman, 221.
Rodney v. Burton, 243.
Roeber v. Cordray, 545, 546, 554.
Roeck's Estate, Matter of, 95.
Roeder's Estate, In re, 458.
Rogers, Appeal of, 238, 241, 467.
Rogers v. Agricola, 387, 392, 467.
Rogers v. Barbee, 572, 574.
Rogers v. Benz, 530.
Rogers v. English, 811, 814.
Rogers v. Goodenough, 468.
Rogers v. Hollister, 431.
Rogers v. Joughin, 214.
Rogers v. Law, 413.
Rogers v. Leahy, 520.
Rogers v. Reinking, 739.
Rogers v. Rogers, 761, 762.
Rogers v. Weaver, 801.
Rohkramer's Estate, In re, 609.
Rohrbaugh v. Hamblin, 802.
Roller v. Kling, 237.
Rollins v. Rice, 670.
Rolls v. Allen, 224, 226.
Rolls' Estate, In re, 419.
Rollwagen v. Rollwagen, 256.
Romaniw's Will, In re, 298.
Ronayne's Estate, In re, 554.
Rondeau v. Miller, 798.
Roosevelt v. Mark, 706, 831.
Root v. Blackwood, 667.
Rose v. Cunynghame, 396.

Rose v. Rose, 115, 125.
Rose v. Southern Michigan Nat. Bank of Coldwater, 224.
Rose's Estate, In re, 521.
Rosenau v. Merchants Bank, 202.
Rosenau v. Merchants' Nat. Bank of Dickinson, 204, 639, 640.
Rosenberg v. Rosenberg, 583.
Rosenblath's Estate, Matter of, 225.
Rosenboom v. Cline, 570, 572.
Rosenthal v. Renick, 592.
Rosenthal's Estate, In re, 131, 648.
Ross Estate, In re, 143.
Ross v. Barr's Ex'r, 669.
Ross v. Clore, 401.
Ross v. Ewer, 327.
Ross v. Huil, 695.
Ross v. Lewis, 697.
Ross v. Martin, 130.
Ross v. Pitcairn, 618, 627.
Ross v. Washington, 533.
Ross' Estate, In re, 554, 651, 652, 655, 793, 795.
Ross's Trusts, In re, 44.
Ross' Will, In re, 241.
Rossman v. Christenson, 665, 666.
Roth v. Ravich, 695.
Rothchild's Will, In re, 408.
Rothstein's Estate, In re, 332, 335.
Rountree v. Pursel, 79.
Rourke, Appeal of, 130.
Rowe, In re, 620.
Rowe v. Richards, 642.
Rowe v. Rowe, 719, 721, 751, 756.
Rowell v. Adams, 617.
Rowland's Estate, In re, 256, 276, 539.
Rowlett v. Moore, 292, 317.
Rowley v. Merlin, 458.
Roy v. Pos, 218.
Roy's Estate, In re, 266.
Royle v. Harris, 307.
Ruane's Estate, In re, 610.
Rubel v. Bushnell, 802.
Ruch v. Biery, 719, 722.
Rucker v. Tennessee Coal, Iron & R. Co., 672.
Rudersdorf v. Bowers, 537.
Rudisill's Ex'r v. Rodes, 477.
Rudd v. Searles, 409.
Rudolph v. Rudolph, 782.
Rudolph v. Smith, 674.
Rudolph's Estate, In re, 305.
Ruel v. Hardy, 456, 458, 459.
Ruff v. Baker, 673.
Ruff's Estate, In re, 85.
Ruffino's Estate, In re, 255.
Ruggles v. Powers, 669.
Rugh's Estate, In re, 609, 612.
Rule v. Fleming, 202.
Rule's Estate, In re, 651, 652.
Rumel v. Solomon, 4.
Ruple v. Hiram College, 136.
Rusha, Succession of, 282.
Rushbrook's Will Trusts, Re, 658.
Rusling v. Rusling, 769.
Russell v. Adams, 791.
Russell v. Agar, 211.
Russell v. Bulliner, 72.
Russell v. Hallett, 73.
Russell v. Hogan, 694, 796.
Russell v. Jordan, 90.
Russell v. Musson, 90.
Russell v. Pagan, 102.
Russell v. Russell, 680.
Russell v. Tyler, 438, 540, 555.
Russell v. Webster, 179.
Russell's Case, 642.
Russell's Estate, In re, 90, 246, 632.
Rust v. Rutherford, 191, 676.
Rutenic v. Hamaker, 627.
Rutherford v. Maule, 50.
Rutland v. Gleaves, 275.
Rutland v. Rutland, 49.
Ryan, Estate of, 79.
Ryan v. Andrews, 78.
Ryan v. Deneen, 533.
Ryan v. Kelsey, 571, 646.
Ryan v. Monast, 707.
Ryan v. Wachovia Bank & Trust Co., 409.
Ryan's Estate, In re, 119, 304, 425.
Rybolt v. Futrell, 293.
Ryder v. Myers, 781.
Ryker v. Vawter, 712.
Rymer v. Stanfield, 784.
Ryno's Ex'r v. Ryno's Adm'r, 601.

# S

Sackman's Estate, In re, 584.
Sadler v. Sadler, 283.
Safe Deposit & Trust Co. v. Hanna, 526.
Safe Deposit & Trust Co. v. Thom, 438, 465.

Sage's Will, In re, 324.
Saint v. Charity Hospital, 377.
St. John's German Evangelical Lutheran Church v. Dippoldsmann, 763.
St. Louis Union Trust Co. v. Hill, 87.
St. Louis & S. F. R. Co. v. Goode, 642, 643.
St. Matthews Bank v. De Charette, 641.
Salmons' Will, In re, 328, 329.
Salmonski's Estate, In re, 459.
Saloy, Succession of, 631.
Salt, In re, 760.
Saltzsieder v. Saltzsieder, 190.
Salyers v. Salyers, 314.
Salzwedel's Estate, In re, 197.
Sample v. Butler University, 227.
Sampson v. Sampson, 699.
Samson's Estate, In re, 130.
Samson's Will, In re, 71.
Sanborn's Estate, In re, 523.
Sanchez v. Torres, 83.
Sanderlin v. Sanderlin's Adm'r, 130.
Sanders v. Buenger, 608.
Sanders v. Merchants' State Bank, 701.
Sanders v. Russell, 696.
Sanders' Adm'r v. Babbitt, 437.
Sanderson v. Norcross, 438, 453, 454.
San Diego Trust & Sav. Bank v. Heustis, 524.
Sandlin's Adm'r v. Allen, 146.
Sandon v. Sandon, 88.
Sands v. Ross, 784.
Sandusky v. Sandusky, 559.
Sanford v. McCreedy, 586.
Sanford v. Sanford, 724.
Sanger v. McDonald, 266.
Sankey's Estate, In re, 75.
Sansona v. Laraia, 275.
Santourian's Estate, In re, 157.
Santovincenzo v. Egan, 94.
Sarasohn v. Kamaiky, 212.
Sargavak's Estate, In re, 209.
Sartain v. Davis, 799.
Sartor v. Beaty, 789, 790.
Satar's Estate, In re, 373.
Satcher v. Grice, 796.
Satterwhite v. Carson, 579.
Sauer v. Taylor's Ex'r, 602.
Sauer's Estate, In re, 89.
Sauers v. Stolz, 599.
Saunders v. Saunders, 185, 520.
Saunders v. Vautier, 58.
Saunders' Estate, In re, 247.
Savage, Re, 791.
Savage v. Bowen, 522.
Savage v. Lee, 184.
Saville, In re, 613.
Savings Bank of Baltimore v. Weeks, 598, 619.
Savings, Bldg. & Loan Ass'n v. Tart, 703.
Savings Trust Co. v. Beck, 765.
Savings Union Bank & Trust Co. v. Crowley, 697.
Sawyer v. Freeman, 777.
Sawyer's Legatees v. Sawyer's Heirs, 465.
Saxe v. Saxe, 604.
Sayre v. Weil, 174.
Scales v. Heirs at Law of Thornton, 365.
Scandurro v. Beto, 316.
Scanlon's Estate, 176.
Scarbrough v. Scarbrough, 435.
Scattergood v. Kirk, 309.
Schaaf's Estate, Matter of, 757.
Schacklett v. Roller, 554.
Schade v. Connor, 766.
Schaech's Will, In re, 121, 768, 769, 772
Schaefer, Estate of, 647.
Schaeffer's Estate, In re, 789.
Schaffenacker v. Beil, 121, 125.
Schaffer v. Oldak, 812, 814.
Schaffler v. Handwerker, 106.
Schauberger v. Tafel, 173.
Schell v. Deperven, 664.
Scheller v. Schindel, 546, 547.
Scherzinger v. Scherzinger, 202.
Schiffman's Estate, In re, 360.
Schillinger v. Bawek, 391.
Schillinger's Will, In re, 548, 549, 551, 552.
Schirmer v. Superior Court for Spokane County, 316.
Schleif's Estate, In re, 665.
Schlottman v. Hoffman, 288.
Schluter v. Bowery Sav. Bank, 503, 601.
Schmeizl v. Schmeizl, 148.
Schmetzer v. Broegler, 219.
Schmidt v. Fontron Loan & Trust Co., 573.

Schmidt v. Grenzow, 702.
Schmidt v. Johnston, 526.
Schmidt v. Northern Life Ass'n, 158.
Schmidt's Estate, In re, 92, 218, 479.
Schmitt v. Jaques, 650.
Schmitt's Estate, In re, 305.
Schmittler v. Simon, 651, 653.
Schmitz v. Summers, 364.
Schmneider's Will, In re, 323.
Schnable v. Henderson, 437.
Schnack's Estate, In re, 501.
Schnee v. Schnee, 334, 511.
Schneeberger v. Frazer, 660, 695.
Schneider v. Payne, 71.
Schneider v. Vosburgh, 232.
Schneider's Estate, In re, 604.
Schneller v. Schneller, 780.
Schnoor, Estate of, 479.
Schnur v. Dunker, 171.
Schoen v. Siegmund, 784.
Schoenwetter v. Schoenwetter, 572.
Schofield v. Cleveland Trust Co., 182, 183.
Scholen v. Guaranty Trust Co., 492.
Scholl v. Scholl, 495.
Schoonover v. Osborne, 776.
Schott, Goods of, 274.
Schreiber's Will, Matter of, 545, 548.
Schrodt's Ex'r v. Schrodt, 542, 543, 545, 548.
Schroeder's Will, In re, 304, 305.
Schultz v. Schultz, 508, 554.
Schultz's Estate, 91.
Schultze v. Schultze, 146.
Schumaker v. Grammer, 786.
Schummers' Estate, In re, 678.
Schutz v. Morrette, 694.
Schwartz, Estate of, In re, 763.
Schwartz v. Gertwagen Realty Corp., 434, 743, 746, 747.
Schwartz' Estate, In re, 764.
Schwarz v. Taeger, 535.
Schymer's Estate, In re, 745.
Scoggins v. Turner, 506, 508, 554.
Scott, Re 777.
Scott v. Gastright, 392.
Scott v. Harkness, 356.
Scott v. Keane, 182.
Scott v. McNeal, 599, 600.
Scott v. Maddox, 509.
Scott v. Nolan, 143.
Scott v. O'Connor-Couch, 311, 312, 314.
Scott v. Scott, 248.
Scott v. Taylor, 662.
Scott v. Union & Planters' Bank & Trust Co., 204.
Scott's Estate, 208.
Scott's Estate, In re, 675.
Scrogin v. Dickison, 165.
Seabrook v. Grimes, 823.
Seabury v. Green, 701.
Seaman, Estate of, In re, 305, 306.
Seaman v. Husband, 140, 545.
Seaman v. Jamison, 616.
Seaman's Estate, In re, 303, 336.
Seaman's Will, In re, 407.
Searle v. Crampton, 631.
Searles v. Gordon, 800.
Sears v. Dillingham, 616.
Sears v. Hardy, 771.
Sears v. Sears, 295, 305.
Seaton v. Seaton, 119.
Seattle's Estate, In re, 238.
Seaver v. Ransom, 213.
Seaver v. Weston, 653.
Seay v. Huggins, 185, 186.
Sebik's Estate, 500.
Secrest v. Secrest, 616.
Security Co. v. Bryant, 758.
Security Co. v. Snow, 462, 463.
Security Fire Ins. Co. v. Hansen, 703.
Security Trust Co., Matter of, 733.
Security-First Nat. Bank of Los Angeles v. King, 633, 647.
Seebrock v. Fedawa, 559.
Seeds v. Seeds, 270, 501, 504.
Seeley v. Curts, 191.
Seemes v. Magruder, 714.
Seery v. Murray, 564.
Seipel, Estate of, 413.
Seipel, In re, 630.
Seiler, Estate of, In re, 469, 549.
Seiter's Estate, In re, 305, 381.
Selby v. Fidelity Trust Co., 738.
Selby v. Smith, 190.
Selden v. Illinois Trust & Sav. Bank, 525.
Sellards v. Kirby, 304, 381, 438.
Selle v. Rapp, 488, 489.
Sellers v. Hayden, 339.
Sellers v. Joseph Bancroft & Sons Co., 583.
Sellick v. Sellick, 125, 126.
Selling's Estate, Re, 608.
Selzer v. Selzer, 763.

Semmes v. Semmes, 453, 457.
Senechal, Appeal of, 626.
Sense's Will, In re, 198.
Sergent v. North Cumberland Mfg. Co., 148.
Serveira's Will, In re, 306, 347.
Seuss v. Schukat, 111, 149.
Severance's Will, In re, 298.
Severns v. California Highway Indemnity Exchange, 685.
Sevier v. Woodson, 564.
Sewell v. Christison, 596.
Sewell v. Slingluff, 416.
Sexton's Estate, In re, 239, 240, 241, 523.
Sexton's Will, In re, 546.
Seybold v. Grand Forks Nat. Bank, 640.
Seymour, In re, 595.
Seymour's Will, In re, 3, 137, 381.
Shackelford v. Shackelford, 425.
Shacklett v. Roller, 509, 553, 554.
Shadbolt v. Vanderplank, 769.
Shafer's Estate, In re, 94.
Shaff, Estate of, In re, 345, 348, 536.
Shaffer v. Luby's Estate, 494, 495.
Shaffer v. Richarson's Adm'r, 149.
Shane v. Wooley, 336, 380.
Shanks v. Klein, 638.
Shanks' Will, In re, 243.
Shapley's Deed of Trust, In re, 178.
Shapter's Estate, Re, 339.
Sharp v. Hall, 185, 189.
Sharp v. Sharp, 501.
Sharp v. Wallace, 392.
Sharp v. Wightman, 770.
Sharp's Estate, In re, 206.
Sharpe v. Carson, 84.
Sharpe v. Sharpe, 202.
Sharpless' Estate, In re, 625, 752.
Sharpley v. Plant, 674.
Shattuck v. Burrage, 641.
Shaul v. Katzenstein, 721.
Shaull v. Shaull, 187.
Shaw v. Shaw, 534.
Shaw's Guardian v. Grimes, 131, 671.
Shawnee Nat. Bank v. Van Zant, 665.
Shay's Estate, In re, 249, 266.
Shea v. Bergen, 527.
Shea v. Graves, 661.
Shearin v. Allen, 811, 814.
Shearn v. Fenton, 665.
Shears v. Rogers, 639.
Sheehan v. Kearney, 549.
Sheldon v. Blackman, 198.
Sheley's Estate, In re, 591.
Shellenberger v. Ransom, 153.
Shelley's Estate, In re, 774.
Shelton v. Hadlock, 715.
Shepard v. Saltzman, 712.
Shephard's Estate, 524.
Shepherd v. Darling, 582.
Shepherd v. Murphy, 91.
Shepherd's Estate, In re, 427, 710, 758.
Sheppard's Estate, 790.
Sheridan's Estate, In re, 370.
Sherman v. American Congregational Ass'n, 404.
Sherman v. Flack, 124.
Sherman v. Goodson's Heirs, 420.
Sherman v. Lewis, 768.
Sherman v. Page, 590, 631.
Sherman v. Richmond Hose Co. No. 2, 411.
Sherman v. Riley, 750.
Sherman v. Sherman, 153.
Sherman v. Weber, 157, 158.
Sherman's Estate, In re, 625.
Sherrard v. Sloan, 403.
Sherwood v. Sherwood, 274, 276.
Shetter's Estate, In re, 472.
Shewmake v. Shewmake, 323, 324.
Shields' Will, Matter of, 442.
Shiels v. Nathan, 639.
Shiels v. Shiels, 206.
Shillaber's Estate, 390, 499.
Shipman's Estate, Matter of, 633.
Shires v. Glascock, 341, 342.
Shirley v. Ezell, 233.
Shirley's Estate v. Shirley, 597.
Shoberg v. Rock, 770.
Shoemaker v. Newman, 89.
Shoemaker's Estate, In re, 298.
Shoemaker's Ex'r v. Consorti, 811.
Shoen v. Wagner, 530.
Shonts' Will, In re, 579.
Shornick v. Shornick, 184.
Short v. Short, 298.
Short's Estate, In re, 675.
Shorten v. Judd, 422, 428, 429.
Showalter's Ex'rs v. Showalter, 772.
Shreve v. Joyce, 694.
Shriver v. Reister, 75.
Shriver v. State, 797.
Shriver's Estate, In re, 82.

Shroff v. Deaton, 164.
Shulsky v. Shulsky, 386, 389.
Shumway v. Holbrook, 485, 504.
Shupe v. Jenks, 665.
Shutz's Estate, 300.
Sickles' Will, In re, 257.
Sicourmat's Estate, 410.
Siebs' Estate, In re, 525.
Siedel v. Snider, 573.
Siegley v. Simpson, 286.
Siemens' Estate, In re, 812, 814.
Siemer's Estate, In re, 206.
Sigal v. Hartford Nat. Bank & Trust Co., 163.
Sigsworth, In re, 154.
Sikes, In re, 747.
Silva's Estate, In re, 339, 421.
Silver's Estate, In re, 326, 535.
Silverman's Will, In re, 300.
Silverthorn's Will, In re, 250.
Simes v. Ward, 645.
Simmons, In re, 90.
Simmons v. Campbell, 493.
Simmons v. Leonard, 334.
Simmons' Estate, In re, 261, 583.
Simon v. Grayson, 387, 390, 391, 471.
Simon's Appeal, In re, 725, 726, 727.
Simonds v. Simond's Estate, 727.
Simons v. Davenport, 793.
Simonton v. Edmunds, 69.
Simpkins v. Old Colony Trust Co., 200.
Simpson, Re, 478, 559.
Simpson v. Cornish, 489, 503.
Simpson v. Foxon, 448.
Simpson v. Heberlein, 203.
Simpson v. Neely, 441.
Simpson v. Simpson, 728.
Simpson's Estate, 559.
Simpson's Estate, In re, 778.
Sinclair's Estate, In re, 624.
Singer, In re, 336.
Singleton v. Singleton, 329, 477.
Singley v. Bigelow, 685.
Sipchen's Estate, In re, 530, 717.
Sisson v. Irish, 92.
Sisters of Charity of St. Vincent de Paul v. Kelly, 304, 306, 338.
Siter v. Hall, 196.
Sittig v. Kersting, 551.
Sitzman v. Pacquette, 628.
Sizer's Will, In re, 309.
Skachenko v. Sweetman, 676.
Skeer's Estate, In re, 753.
Skeeters v. Hodges, 533.
Skeggs v. Horton, 508, 509, 510, 512, 554.
Skeif v. Bohall, 805.
Skerrett's Estate, In re, 209, 382.
Skinner v. Rasche, 216.
Skinner v. Wynne, 723.
Skipwith v. Cabell's Ex'r, 459, 460.
Skyes v. Hughes, 565.
Slade v. Slade, 265, 327.
Slade v. Washburn, 579.
Slate v. Henkle, 571.
Slater, Re, 747.
Slater's Estate, In re, 793, 794.
Slattery's Estate, In re, 545.
Slaughter's Adm'r v. Wyman, 416, 478.
Slawson's Estate, In re, 121.
Slayton v. Fitch Home, 641.
Sledge v. Floyd, 89.
Sledge & Norfleet v. Dye, 700, 703.
Sleeper, Appeal of, 388, 390.
Sleeper, Re, 380, 381.
Sleeper v. Larrabee, 781.
Sleeper v. Union Ins. Co., 641.
Sleeper's Appeal, 388.
Sligh v. Whitley, 599.
Sliney v. Cormier, 196.
Sloan v. Duffy, 656.
Sloan v. Sloan, 330, 333.
Sloan's Appeal, 462.
Sloan's Estate, In re, 171.
Slocum v. Metropolitan Life Ins. Co., 154, 158.
Smith, Estate of, 78.
Smith, In re, 486.
Smith, In re Estate of, 392, 434, 743, 746.
Smith v. Bradstreet, 524.
Smith v. Brennan, 703.
Smith v. Buffum, 334.
Smith v. Burt, 284, 288.
Smith v. Central Trust Co., 807.
Smith v. Davis, 521.
Smith v. Diggs, 268, 269.
Smith v. Du Bose, 267.
Smith v. Ellis, 304.
Smith v. Eshelman, 205.
Smith v. Farrington, 111.
Smith v. Fay, 192.
Smith v. Fuller, 149, 151.
Smith v. Funk, 146.

Smith v. Furnish, 769, 772, 831.
Smith v. Goodell, 311, 312, 318.
Smith v. Gorham, 383.
Smith v. Haire, 557, 559.
Smith v. Harmer, 615.
Smith v. Heyward, 582, 584, 832.
Smith v. Jones, 318.
Smith v. Kibbe, 707, 708, 764, 765, 766.
Smith v. Ledsome, 812, 814.
Smith v. McChesney, 448.
Smith v. Northern Trust Co., 115.
Smith v. Ossipee Valley Ten Cents Sav. Bank, 174.
Smith v. Runkle, 458, 469.
Smith v. Shuppner, 232.
Smith v. Smith, 82, 139, 187, 207, 322, 532, 661, 662, 663, 732, 766, 811.
Smith v. Speer, 175.
Smith v. Steen, 664.
Smith v. Tebbitt, 248.
Smith v. Thompson, 213, 223, 420.
Smith v. Todd, 155, 158.
Smith v. Tracy, 51.
Smith v. Wheeler, 749.
Smith v. Williams, 566, 696.
Smith v. Wilson, 708.
Smith v. Young, 310.
Smith's Estate, 558.
Smith's Estate, In re, 192, 206, 348, 551, 553, 611, 695, 725, 739, 787, 789.
Smith's Estate v. Davis, 261, 492.
Smith's Ex'rs v. Chapman's Ex'r, 583.
Smith's Will, In re, 245, 420, 448, 449, 810.
Small v. Usher, 788.
Smalley v. Scotton, 287.
Smalley v. Smalley, 315.
Smallman, Matter of, 138.
Smallman v. Powell, 77.
Smallwood v. Brickhouse, 230.
Smart, In re Goods of, 391.
Smigell v. Brod, 113.
Smilie's Estate, In re, 209.
Smithsonian Institute v. Mead, 410.
Smithsonian Institution v. Meech, 412.
Smythe v. Irick, 326, 332.
Sneed v. Ewing, 429.
Sneed v. Reynolds, 209, 359.
Snelgrove v. Snelgrove, 326, 331.
Snell's Will, In re, 812, 814.
Snelling v. Darrell, 413.
Snelling's Estate, In re, 249, 365.
Snellings v. Downer, 785.
Snethun's Estate, In re, 83.
Snider v. Burks, 553, 554.
Snider's Estate, 132.
Snidow v. Brotherton, 203.
Snodgrass v. Andrews, 631, 632.
Snodgrass v. Bedell, 66, 69.
Snodgrass v. Snodgrass, 190.
Snorgrass v. Thomas, 415.
Snow v. Bray, 670.
Snow v. Ferril, 782.
Snow, In re, 674.
Snowden's Estate, Matter of, 2.
Snyder v. De Remer, 241.
Snyder v. French, 221.
Snyder v. Raymond, 277, 279.
Snyder v. Snyder, 729.
Snyder v. Steele, 260, 289, 499, 535.
Snyder's Estate, In re, 705.
Soher, In re, 388.
Sohler v. Sohler, 798.
Soho v. Wimbrough, 217.
Solms' Estate, In re, 815.
Somers v. Somers, 150.
Soper, Estate of, In re, 286.
Soper v. Halsey, 772.
Sorenson v. Churchill, 89.
Soules v. Silver, 294.
Soule's Will, In re, 526.
Southerden, Estate of, 453, 455.
Southerden, In re Estate of, 456, 460.
Southern v. Southern, 189.
Southern Mut. Life Ins. Ass'n v. Durdin, 198.
South Milwaukee Co. v. Murphy, 702, 802.
South Norwalk Trust Co. v. St. John, 409, 410, 412.
Sovell v. Lincoln County, 183.
Sowle v. Potter, 567, 594.
Spain, Estate of, In re, 292.
Spangler v. Bell, 348.
Spangler v. Vermillion, 178.
Spangler v. Wisconsin Dept. of Taxation, 682.
Spaniard v. Tantom, 143.
Sparhawk v. Sparhawk, 311, 312, 315.
Spark, In re Estate of, 369.
Sparks, Matter of, 154.
Sparks v. Bodensick, 73.
Speaks v. Speaks, 329.

Specht's Estate, In re, 194.
Speer v. Josenhans, 319.
Spencer, Appeal of, 454.
Spencer, In re, 245, 756.
Spencer's Appeal, 510.
Spencer's Estate, In re, 208.
Sperling, In re, 333.
Speroni v. Speroni, 431.
Spier v. Spier, 320, 328, 329.
Spiers' Estate, In re, 778, 779.
Spilios v. Papps, 584.
Spinks v. Rice, 210.
Spinner's Estate, In re, 528.
Spinney v. Eaton, 732, 747.
Splaine v. Morissey, 165.
Spofford v. Manning, 773.
Spofford v. Rose, 101.
Spradlin v. Adams, 542, 546, 548.
Spreckels' Estate, In re, 797.
Sprigge v. Sprigge, 554.
Springfield, City of v. Clement, 802.
Springvale Nat. Bank v. Ward, 175, 176.
Sprinkle v. Holton, 800.
Sproul's Appeal, 788.
Spurr v. Spurr, 257, 266.
Spyer v. Hyatt, 105.
Squier's Estate, In re, 559.
Squires v. Squires, 725, 727.
S. S. Pierce Co. v. Fiske, 565.
Staab's Estate, 528.
Stable, In re, 372, 373.
Stackpole v. Beaumont, 411.
Stacy v. Stacy, 719.
Stafford's Estate, In re, 794.
Stafford's Will, In re, 764.
Stagg v. Stagg, 201, 202.
Stahl v. Emery, 782.
Stahl v. Stevenson, 214.
Staiger's Will, In re, 553.
Stalting v. Stalting, 189, 190, 192.
Stanard v. Miller, 381.
Standard Oil Co. v. New Jersey, 98.
Standard Oil Co. of New Jersey v. Perkins, 99.
Stanforth v. Bailey, 191.
Staniszewski v. Lane, 705.
Stanley v. Chandler, 87.
Stanley v. Stanley, 47, 623, 733, 734, 736.
Stanley v. United States Nat. Bank, 788, 790.
Stapley v. Stapley, 577, 794, 795.
Stark v. Stark, 720.
Starke's Estate, In re, 300.
Starkey v. Starkey, 526.
Starks v. Lincoln, 2, 364, 365.
Starlin v. Love, 613, 617, 624, 627.
State v. American Nat. Red Cross of Washington, D. C., 830.
State v. Ames, 523.
State v. Chavez, 82, 85.
State v. Evans, 691.
State v. French, 630.
State v. Greenhaw, 713.
State v. Kearns, 98, 99.
State v. Lancaster, 523.
State v. Nieuwenhuis, 500, 511.
State v. Phoenix Mutual Life Ins. Co., 158.
State v. Reardon, 94.
State v. Smith, 644.
State v. Toop, 94.
State v. Unknown Heirs of Goldberg, 99.
State Bank of Chicago v. Gross, 751, 753.
State Bank of Orlando & Trust Co. v. Cummer Lbr. Co., 663.
State Bank of Orlando & Trust Co. v. Macy, 697.
State Banking Co. v. Hinton, 775.
State ex rel. Abercrombie v. Holtcamp, 617.
State ex rel. Alderson v. Moehlenkamp, 579.
State ex rel. Ashton v. Imel, 579.
State ex rel. Atty. Gen. v. Superior Court of Sacramento, 523.
State ex rel. Bier v. Bigger, 486.
State ex rel. Brown v. Crossley, 739.
State ex rel. Case v. Superior Court, 130.
State ex rel. Couch v. Kelso, 610.
State ex rel. Cowley v. Superior Court, 607, 608.
State ex rel. Daniels v. Rogers, 630.
State ex rel. Everette v. Petteway, 627.
State ex rel. First Minneapolis Trust Co. v. Fosseeen, 703.
State ex rel. Franklin v. Sullivan, 667, 797.
State ex rel. Gentry v. O'Byrne, 615.
State ex rel. Gregory v. Henderson, 582, 615.

State ex rel. Homer v. Barrett, 623.
State ex rel. Lauridsen v. Superior Court for King County, 603, 604, 616.
State ex rel. Lynch v. Whitehouse, 590, 827.
State ex rel. McClure v. Northrop, 702.
State ex rel. Mitchell v. Gideon, 494.
State ex rel. North St. Louis Trust Co. v. Stahlhuth, 621.
State ex rel. Paramount Publix Corp. v. District Court of Seventh Judicial Dist. of State of Montana in and for Dawson County, 696.
State ex rel. Patterson v. Tittmann, 700.
State ex rel. Peterson v. Circuit Court, 705.
State ex rel. Ruef v. District Court of Twelfth Judicial District, 489.
State ex rel. Russell v. Mueller, 581.
State ex rel. Scherber v. Probate Court of Hennepin County, 695.
State ex rel. Schirmer v. Superior Court for Spokane County, 314.
State ex rel. Sears, Roebuck & Co. v. Mueller, 628.
State ex rel. Smith v. Rector, 523.
State ex rel. Speckart v. Superior Court for Thurston County, 572, 602
State to Use of Horsey v. Maryland Cas. Co., 631.
Staton v. Guillebeaux, 637.
Statz's Estate, 678.
Stauffer's Estate, 133.
Stead v. Curtis, 495.
Stearns v. Stearns, 275, 285.
Stebbins v. Lathrop, 616.
Stebbins v. Palmer, 683.
Steeby's Estate, In re, 661.
Steele, Matter of, 466.
Steele v. Frierson, 729.
Steele v. Marble, 299.
Steele v. Renn, 502.
Steele v. Steele, 759.
Steen v. Springfield, 579.
Stege v. Stege's Trustee, 260.
Stegman's Estate, In re, 298.
Steiglitz v. Migatz, 707.
Stein's Will, Matter of, 373.
Steiner's Estate, In re, 293.
Steiner's Will, Matter of, 453.
Steinke's Will, In re, 510.
Steinkraus' Estate, In re, 769.
Steinkuehler v. Wempner, 247.
Stenson v. H. S. Halvorson Co., 787.
Stephan's Estate, In re, 145.
Stephen's Estate, In re, 667, 799.
Stephens v. Bonner, 246.
Stephens v. Brady, 519.
Stephens v. Comstock-Dexter Mines, 563.
Stephens v. Leatherwood, 440.
Stephens v. Rinehart, 190.
Stephens v. Smith, 721.
Stephenson's Estate, In re, 245.
Sternberg v. St. Louis Union Trust Co., 488, 489.
Sternberg's Estate, In re, 656.
Sternkopf's Will, In re, 496.
Sterns, Matter of, 579.
Stetson v. Stetson, 475.
Steuer v. Lang, 204.
Stevens v. Cameron, 605.
Stevens v. Flannagan, 637.
Stevens v. Larwill, 613.
Stevens v. Leonard, 250, 347, 348, 536.
Stevens v. Myers, 213, 224, 467, 534.
Stevens v. Stevens, 125, 555, 729.
Stevenson v. Earl, 196.
Stevenson v. Gray, 79.
Stevenson v. Martin, 722.
Stevenson v. Stevenson, 284, 812, 814.
Stewart, Matter of, 675.
Stewart v. Harriman, 314.
Stewart v. Mulholland, 422, 426.
Stewart v. Poinbeouf, 626.
Stewart's Adm'r v. Stewart's Heirs, 666.
Stewart's Estate, 633.
Stewart's Estate, In re, 516, 522, 550.
Stewart's Executor v. Lispenard, 234, 481.
Stewart's Will, Re, 412.
Stichler's Estate, In re, 218.
Stickney's Will, 465.
Stickney's Will, In re, 466, 478.
Stieglitz v. Migatz, 764.
Stierlin v. Teschemacher, 639.
Stifft v. W. B. Worthen Co., 732.
Stilley v. Folger, 110.
Stilwell v. Mellersh, 471.
Stimpson v. Murch, 404.
Stimson v. Rountree, 753.
Stinson's Estate, In re, 303, 304.

Stipanowish v. Sleeth, 529.
Stirk's Estate, In re, 266.
Stitt v. Cox, 517.
Stitz v. Ryan, 696, 697.
Stock v. Mitchell, 149.
Stockham's Estate, In re, 657.
Stockmen's State Bank v. Merchants' & Stockgrowers' Bank, 649.
Stockton v. State Bank of Rensselaer, 812, 814.
Stockwell v. Shalit, 191.
Stoddart's Estate, In re, 257.
Stoffel's Estate, In re, 529.
Stoiber's Estate, In re, 520.
Stoll v. Stoll's Ex'r, 546.
Stone v. Burgeson, 216, 217.
Stone v. Cook, 526.
Stone v. Daily, 191.
Stone v. Duffy, 146.
Stone v. Forbes, 398.
Stone v. Holden, 302.
Stonestreet v. Doyle, 786.
Stork v. Merchant, 669.
Storlie v. Sachse, 697, 698.
Storrs v. St. Luke's Hospital, 525.
Story v. Story, 144.
Story's Estate, In re, 559.
Stothers v. Flieger, 269.
Stout v. Stout, 671.
Stover v. Durfee, 651, 652, 655.
Stover's Will, In re, 330, 542, 543.
Stowe v. Stowe, 270.
Stradcutter v. Stradcutter, 201.
Strader v. Metropolitan Life Ins. Co., 564, 664, 796.
Strakosch v. Connecticut Trust & Safe Deposit Co., 218.
Strang v. Day, 434.
Strasenburgh's Estate, In re, 800.
Strathmore v. Bowes, 470.
Stratton v. Durham, 448.
Strauch v. Uhler, 133.
Straulina's Estate, In re, 209, 370.
Strawn v. Strawn, 130.
Strawn v. Trustees of Jacksonville Female Academy, 805.
Streatfield v. Streatfield, 773.
Streatley, Goods of, 335.
Street v. Street, 258.
Street's Estate, In re, 463.
Streeton's Estate, In re, 442, 532, 555.
Streety v. McCurdy, 791.
Strelow's Estate, In re, 432, 494, 498.
Stricker v. Groves, 299.
Stringer v. Gamble, 760, 761, 762.
Stringfellow v. Early, 530.
Strittmater's Estate, In re, 243.
Strode v. Kramer, 638.
Strolberg's Estate, 763.
Strom v. Wood, 776.
Strong, Appeal of, 453, 455, 456, 457, 460.
Strong v. Strong, 428.
Strong v. Williams, 770.
Stroup v. Imes, 526.
Strouse v. Lawrence, 715.
Strout v. Burgess, 167.
Struble v. Struble, 218.
Struth v. Decker, 259.
Strype v. Lewis, 272.
Stuart v. Foutz, 499.
Stuart v. McWhorter, 438, 442, 539.
Stuart v. Schoonover, 130.
Stuart's Estate, In re, 211.
Stubbs v. Ratliff, 613.
Stubbs v. Sargon, 394, 400.
Stuck v. Howard, 294, 295, 544.
Studley v. Willis, 709.
Stull v. Veatch, 489.
Stulman's Will, Matter of, 752.
Stults v. Forst, 699.
Stultz v. Kiser, 749.
Stump's Estate, In re, 250.
Sturdivant v. Birchett, 342.
Sturgeon's Adm'r v. McCorkle, 221.
Sturges' Estate, In re, 675.
Sturgis v. Citizens' Nat. Bank of Pocomoke, 169.
Sturgis v. Work, 452.
Sturmer's Estate, In re, 121.
Stutiville's Ex'rs v. Wheeler, 260.
Stutzman's Estate, In re, 627.
Stymus Will, In re, 285.
Suarez, In re, 580.
Sugar River Bank v. Fairbank, 690.
Sugden v. Lord St. Leonards, 510, 512.
Sughrue v. Barlow, 425.
Suit v. Crawford, 569.
Sullivan, Succession of, 378.
Sullivan v. Bond, 467.
Sullivan v. Brabason, 320.
Sullivan v. Horner, 709.
Sullivan v. Jones, 356.
Sullivan v. Prudential Ins. Co., 96.
Sullivan v. Sullivan, 317, 318, 718.

Sullivan v. Tioga R. Co., 623.
Sullivan's Estate, 610.
Sullivan's Estate, In re, 626.
Summers v. Summers, 545.
Sumner v. Crane, 217, 224, 498.
Sumner v. Staton, 289, 483.
Sumner v. Williams, 583, 675.
Surman v. Surman, 430.
Surratt v. Knight, 529.
Susemiehl v. Red River Lumber Co., 642.
Suskin's Estate, In re, 624.
Sutherland's Will, In re, 362.
Sutterlin's Will, In re, 345.
Sutton v. Chenault, 292.
Sutton v. English, 515.
Sutton v. Sadler, 545.
Sutton v. Sutton, 81, 83, 421.
Sutton's Estate, In re, 736, 759, 765.
Suydam v. Voorhees, 783.
Svacina's Estate, In re, 604.
Svanburg v. Fosseen, 211, 212.
Svancina's Estate, In re, 625.
Swaim's Will, In re, 381.
Swan v. Pople, 730.
Swan's Estate, In re, 293.
Swanberg v. National Surety Co., 651, 652.
Swann v. Housman, 187.
Swanson, Succession of, 360.
Swanson's Estate, In re, 530.
Swart's Estate, 608.
Swartz's Will, In re, 258.
Swasey v. American Bible Soc., 755.
Sweeney v. Muldoon, 651, 652.
Sweeney v. Vierbuchen, 254, 262.
Sweetland v. Sweetland, 307.
Sweitzer's Estate, In re, 191.
Swenson v. Lewison, 67.
Swenson's Estate, In re, 143.
Swetland v. Swetland, 386.
Swift v. Wiley, 337.
Swigert v. Miles, 725, 726, 727.
Swinebroad v. Bright, 738.
Swinehart v. Turner, 670.
Swinton v. Bailey, 444.
Swire's Estate, 303.
Swire's Estate, In re, 304.
Sykes v. Hughes, 664, 796.
Syverson's Estate, In re, 811, 814.
Szabo v. Speckman, 202.
Szalkiewicz's Will, In re, 492.
Szarat v. Schuerr, 348.

# T

Tabb v. Willis, 250.
Taff v. Hosmer, 520.
Taft v. Stearns, 387, 467, 468.
Taft v. Taft, 191.
Taft's Estate, In re, 751.
Tailer, Matter of, 732.
Talbot v. Talbot, 179.
Talbott v. Hamill, 402.
Taliaferro v. Rogers, 84, 85.
Talley v. Harris, 110.
Talley's Estate, In re, 89.
Tally v. Butterworth, 366.
Talmadge v. Chapel, 586.
Tangerman, Matter of, 572.
Tanton v. Keller, 473.
Tappenden v. Walsh, 229.
Tarbell v. Forbes, 512.
Tarlo's Estate, In re, 155.
Tart, In re, 202.
Tasanen, In re, 597.
Tate v. Camp, 409, 413.
Tate v. Hilbert, 203.
Tatem v. Wright, 516.
Tator v. Valden, 529.
Tayloe v. Tayloe, 666.
Taylor, Estate of, 382.
Taylor, Re, 791.
Taylor v. Albree, 815.
Taylor v. Bader, 795.
Taylor v. Bray, 69.
Taylor v. Coberly, 92.
Taylor v. Everett, 725.
Taylor v. Harmison, 200.
Taylor v. Hilton, 497, 804.
Taylor v. Hoyt, 528.
Taylor v. Hull, 734, 743, 745.
Taylor v. Johnson, 229.
Taylor v. McClave, 806.
Taylor v. Martin's Estate, 492.
Taylor v. Mason, 413.
Taylor v. Minor, 559.
Taylor v. Payne, 137.
Taylor v. Rains, 422, 426.
Taylor v. Virginia-Pocahontas Coal Co., 609.
Taylor v. Whitcomb, 132, 133.
Taylor v. Wilder, 188, 197.
Taylor v. Wright, 656.
Taylor Estate, 90.
Taylor's Estate, In re, 293, 307, 328, 329, 365, 609, 615, 703.

Taylor's Will, In re, 207.
Tays v. Robinson, 74.
T. C. Fox & Sons v. Lampert, 663.
Techt v. Hughes, 93, 94.
Teel's Estate, In re, 259.
Teller's Estate, In re, 551.
Telsrow's Estate, In re, 254.
Temple v. First Nat. Bank of Meridian, 760, 761.
Temple's Estate, In re, 763.
Ten Eyck's Estate, In re, 478.
Tennant v. John Tennant Memorial Home, 187.
Tenny's Adm'r v. Lasley's Adm'rs, 702.
Tensfield v. Magnolia Petroleum Co., 196.
Teopfer's Estate, In re, 423, 424, 427.
Terry's Appeal, 79.
Tetzloff v. May, 133.
Teuscher v. Gragg, 272.
Texada v. Spence, 135, 279.
Texas v. Florida, 489.
Thacker v. Lindahl, 587.
Thayer v. Homer, 628.
Thayer v. Thayer, 152.
Thiede's Estate, In re, 651, 652.
Third Nat. Bank v. Scribner, 469.
Thom v. Thom, 773.
Thomas v. Butler, 611.
Thomas v. Byrd, 195.
Thomas v. Conyers, 190.
Thomas v. Howell, 460, 461.
Thomas v. James, 609.
Thomas v. Marriott, 69.
Thomas v. People, to Use of Joiner, 599.
Thomas v. Stump, 250.
Thomas v. Thomas, 455, 458.
Thomas v. Thomas' Estate, 83.
Thomas v. Thompson, 553.
Thomas v. Timonds, 3.
Thomas v. Williams, 187.
Thomas v. Williamson, 500.
Thomas' Estate, In re, 301, 345, 608, 705, 811 814.
Thompason's Estate, In re, 437.
Thompkins v. Randall, 209.
Thompson, Estate of, 512.
Thompson, Ex parte, 370, 371.
Thompson v. Betts, 771.
Thompson v. Ford, 745.
Thompson v. Lake Madison Chautauqua Ass'n of South Dakota, 799.
Thompson v. Latimer, 720.
Thompson v. McCune, 788, 789, 790.
Thompson v. Owen, 691, 699.
Thompson v. Penn, 485.
Thompson v. Royall, 439.
Thompson v. Samson, 503.
Thompson v. Smith, 78.
Thompson v. Stevens, 211.
Thompson v. Stonom, 533.
Thompson v. Thompson, 326, 705.
Thompson v. Tucker-Osborn, 211.
Thompson v. Turner, 78.
Thompson's Estate, 403.
Thompson's Estate, Re, 404, 411, 462, 550, 552.
Thompson's Will, In re, 197, 292, 370.
Thomsen v. Thomsen, 124, 125.
Thomson v. Carruth, 301.
Thomson's Will, In re, 245.
Thorman's Estate, In re, 510.
Thorn, Estate of, 357.
Thornton v. Anderson, 88, 430.
Thornton v. Winston, 617.
Thorpe v. Bestwick, 311, 320.
Threlkeld v. Synodical Presbyterian Orphanage of Anchorage, 732.
Thrift Trust Co. v. White, 301.
Throckmorton v. Holt, 442, 511, 539, 555.
Thurber v. Battey, 808.
Thurber's Estate, In re, 651, 652, 661.
Thurmond v. Guyan Valley Coal Co., 646.
Thurston v. Tubbs, 189.
Thurston's Adm'r v. Prather, 208.
Tibbetts' Estate, 476.
Tibbetts' Estate, In re, 90.
Tidholm v. Tidholm, 543.
Tiemens' Estate, In re, 408.
Tierney v. Shakespeare, 701.
Tifft v. Porter, 734.
Tiger's Will, In re, 328, 329.
Tilden v. Tilden, 473.
Tilghman v. Fraser, 753.
Tillinghast, In re, 742.
Tillinghast v. Coggeshall, 79.
Tilson v. Holloway, 505.
Tilton v. American Bible Soc., 287.
Tilton v. Daniels, 331.
Tilton v. O'Connor, 596.
Tilton v. Tilton, 123, 783.

Figures refer to pages

Timmons v. Gochenour, 673.
Tinsley v. Carevile, 440.
Tinsley's Will, Re, 417.
Tipper's Estate, In re, 556.
Tipton v. Tipton, 733, 746.
Title Guarantee & Trust Co. v. Ebaugh, 398.
Titlow's Estate, In re, 557, 559.
Titterington v. Hooker, 635.
Tobin, Re, 343.
Tobin v. Nordness, 362.
Todd v. McFall, 766.
Todd v. Todd, 593.
Todd v. Williams' Adm'x, 197.
Toebbe v. Williams, 207.
Togneri's Estate, In re, 798.
Tolbert, Ex parte, 615.
Tollefson's Estate, In re, 208, 210.
Tolly v. Champion, 647, 706.
Tolman v. Tolman, 744.
Tomlinson's Estate, 295, 444.
Tompkins v. Tompkins, 634.
Tone's Will, In re, 137.
Toner v. Conqueror Trust Co., 592.
Toner v. Meussdorffer, 649.
Tongue's Lessee v. Nutwell, 786.
Tonnele v. Hall, 305.
Tonnelier v. Tonnelier, 420.
Tonneson's Estate, In re, 305.
Tood, Estate of, 488.
Toomer v. Van Antwerp Realty Corp., 144.
Toomey v. Turner, 69, 77.
Torlage, Succession of, 206.
Torre v. Chestnut, 784.
Torres Estate, In re, 152.
Torstensen's Estate, In re, 536.
Totten, Matter of, 176.
Toulouse v. New York Life Ins. Co., 162.
Tourtelot v. Finke, 796.
Tousey's Will, In re, 278, 280.
Towle, Estate of, 358.
Towle v. Swasey, 757, 758.
Town of. See under name of Town.
Townsend v. Beavers, 671.
Townsend v. Steel, 673.
Townsend's Estate, In re, 726.
Townshend v. Howard, 438, 453, 457.
Townsley v. Townsley, 788.
Tracy v. Gaudin, 657.
Tracy v. Murray, 758.
Tracy's Estate, In re, 341.
Tracy's Estate, Matter of, 492.
Traders' Nat. Bank v. Dennis' Estate, 790.
Trafton v. Trafton, 123.
Trammell v. Blackburn, 706.
Transylvania University v. Rees, 194.
Trask v. Sturges, 670.
Traughber v. King, 739.
Trautz v. Lemp, 166, 200.
Travers v. Lavender, 495.
Traylor, In re, 813.
Treadway v. St. Louis, I. M. & S. R. Co., 643.
Treadwell v. Putman, 411.
Tredick v. Bryant, 323, 324.
Trent v. Griffy, 572.
Trenton Sav. Fund Soc. v. Wythman, 196.
Trenton Trust & Safe Deposit Co. v. Sibbits, 782.
Trescott's Estate, In re, 753.
Tresidder's Estate, In re, 493.
Trevathan v. Grogan, 625.
Trevathan's Ex'rs v. Dees' Ex'rs, 704.
Tribe v. Tribe, 342.
Trice v. Shipton, 421, 422.
Trickett, In re, 143.
Triebe's Will, In re, 467, 546.
Trimboli v. Kinkel, 669.
Trindle v. Zimmerman, 226.
Trindle's Estate, In re, 501.
Trinitarian Congregational Church & Soc. of Castine, In re, 314, 318.
Triplett's Ex'r v. Triplett, 386, 438, 499.
Tripp v. Payne, 408.
Tripp's Estate, In re, 97.
Trippe v. O'Cavanaugh, 673.
Troll v. St. Louis Third Nat. Bank, 581.
Tropico Land & Improv. Co. v. Lambourn, 703.
Trost's Estate, In re, 627.
Trotman v. Trotman, 719.
Trotter, In re, 472.
Trotter v. Van Pelt, 447, 488, 807.
Troup v. Smith's Ex'rs, 683.
Truelove v. Truelove, 82.
Trumbauer v. Rust, 185, 187.
Trumbull v. Hale, 190.
Trumpler v. Royer, 792.
Truro, In re Goods of, 389, 390, 471.

Trust Co. of Georgia v. Ivey, 259.
Trustees of Epworth Memorial Methodist Church v. Overman, 244.
Trustees of House of the Angel Guardian, Boston v. Donovan, 604.
Trustees of Kenyon College v. Cleveland Trust Co., 125.
Trybom, Will of, 411.
Tryon v. United States, 619.
Tsaraclis v. Characklis, 694.
Tucker v. Houston, 546.
Tucker v. Phipps, 506, 511.
Tucker v. Simrow, 196.
Tucker v. Tucker, 678.
Tullier, Succession of, 562.
Tunley v. Beall, 511.
Tunnell v. Moore, 569, 574.
Tupper v. Tupper, 461, 463.
Turell's Will, In re, 355.
Turk v. Grossman, 666.
Turner, Goods of, 443.
Turner v. Campbell, 589.
Turner v. Cole, 150.
Turner v. Evans, 407.
Turner v. Laird, 765.
Turner v. McDonald, 573.
Turner v. Montgomery, 187, 189.
Turner v. Turner, 788.
Turner's Estate, In re, 609.
Turner's Trustee v. Washburn, 81.
Turner's Will, In re, 288.
Turton, In re, 414.
Tussey v. Owen, 216, 219.
Tuttle v. Berryman, 385, 391.
Tuttle v. Winchell, 216.
Tutunjian v. Vetzigian, 224, 225, 226.
Tweddell v. Tweddell, 764.
Twiddy v. Mullen, 694.
Twilley v. Durkee, 447.
Twitty v. Martin, 472.
Tyer v. J. B. Blades Lumbor Co., 595.
Tyler v. Reynolds, 672.
Tyler v. Tyler, 424.
Tyler's Estate, In re, 154.
Tylor's Estate, In re, 367.
Tynan v. Paschal, 506, 509.
Tyndale v. Stanwood, 672.
Tyrrell's Estate, In re, 361, 383.
Tyson v. Utterback, 327, 331, 536, 545, 548.
Tyson's Estate, 665, 667, 799.
Tzeses v. Green, 669.

# U

Underwood v. Rutan, 326, 328.
Union Trust Co. v. Hankins, 178, 179, 181.
Union Trust Co. v. Richardson, 780.
Union Trust Co. v. Rossi, 124.
Union Trust Co. v. Shoemaker, 700.
Union Trust Co. of Springfield v. Nelen, 750.
United States v. Burnison, 135.
United States v. Duncan, 710.
United States v. McCarty, 151.
United States v. Summerlin, 691.
United States v. Swanson, 595.
United States Dep't of Agriculture, Emergency Crop & Feed Loans v. Remund, 710.
United States Fidelity & Guaranty Co. v. Dempster, 98.
United States Fidelity & Guaranty Co. v. Douglas' Trustee, 463.
United States Fidelity & Guaranty Co. of Baltimore, Md., v. Jones, 644.
United States Nat. Bank v. Daniels, 119.
United States Trust Co. v. Wood, 807.
United States Trust Co. of New York, Matter of, 176.
United States Trust Co. of New York v. Douglass, 125, 801.
United States Trust Co. of Paterson v. Giveans, 195.
University of Georgia v. Denmark, 526.
University of Southern California v. Bryson, 198.
Updike v. Ten Broeck, 214.
Upington v. Corrigan, 102.
Upjohn's Will, In re, 90, 815, 816.
Upton, Ex parte, 684.
Upton's Estate, In re, 620.
Usticke v. Bawden, 474.
Utermehle v. Norment, 526.
Utters' Estate, In re, 609.

# V

Vail v. Anderson, 570.
Vail v. Rinehart, 672.
Valentine's Will, 506.
Van Alstyne v. Tuffy, 154, 157.

Vanatta's Estate, In re, 767.
Van Bibber v. Reese, 671.
Van Brunt v. Van Brunt, 399, 400.
Vance v. Grow, 272.
Vance v. Upson, 502.
Vance's Estate, 360.
Vance's Estate, In re, 167.
Vanden Bosch's Estate, In re, 522.
Vanderlinde v. Bankers Trust Co., 120.
Vanderpoel v. Van Valkenburgh, 500.
Vanderpool v. Vanderpool, 695.
Vandervort's Estate, Re, 413.
Vandeveer v. Higgins, 427.
Van Duyn's Estate, In re, 130.
Van Duzer v. Gordon's Estate, 370.
Vandyke's Estate, In re, 711.
Vanek v. Vanek, 424.
Van Giesen v. Bridgford, 486.
Van Guysling v. Van Kuren, 246.
Vanhoose v. Brooks, 670.
Van Houten v. Post, 737, 738, 740.
Van Ingen's Estate, In re, 469.
Van Iperen v. Hays, 576.
Van Liew v. Barrett & Barrett Beverage Co., 793.
Van Meter v. Norris, 217.
Van Meter v. Ritenour, 542, 546, 548.
Van Meter v. Van Meter, 320, 326, 332, 348, 545.
Van Natta v. Heywood, 221.
Van Ness' Will, In re, 260.
Van Norden Trust Co. v. O'Donohue, 669.
Vannoy v. Gibson, 617.
Van Schaack v. Leonard, 769.
Van Steenwyck v. Washburn, 773.
Van Tassell's Will, In re, 788, 789, 790.
Van Vleck's Estate, In re, 604.
Van Wert, Matter of, 200.
Van Winkle v. Balckford, 695.
Van Winkle v. Schoonmaker, 228.
Van Wormer's Estate, In re, 201.
Varley v. Sims, 202, 203.
Varnon v. Varnon, 381, 456, 458.
Vasgaard's Estate, In re, 528.
Vaughn v. Vaughn, 441.
Vaughn's Estate, 234.
Vaughn's Estate, In re, 326, 557.
Vaught v. Struble, 615, 625.
Vazis v. Zimmer, 647.
Veal v. Veal, 203.
Ventress v. Wallace, 571.
Verdier v. Roach, 703.
Vernon's Estate, In re, 616, 784.
Vernon v. Kirk, 300.
Vesper's Estate, In re, 251.
Vester v. Collins, 317.
Vestry of St. John's Parish v. Bostwick, 390.
Vicedomini's Estate, In re, 144.
Vickery v. Vickery, 206.
Vigil, Estate of, In re, 73.
Vilas' Estate, In re, 624.
Villard v. Villard, 678, 799.
Villard's Estate, In re, 471.
Vincent v. Vincent, 738, 739, 740.
Viner v. Francis, 778.
Vinson v. Vinson, 720.
Virgin v. Gaither, 201, 204.
Vismar's Estate, In re, 812, 814.
Vogel v. Lehritter, 336.
Vogel v. Saunders, 760.
Vogel v. Wachtel, 647.
Von Fell v. Spirling, 288.
Von Hoven's Succession, 796.
Von Koenneritz v. Hardcastle, 410.
Von Lingen v. Field, 800.
Voyce v. Superior Court of City and County of San Francisco, 516.
Vreeland's Ex'rs v. Ryno's Ex'r, 150.
Vroom v. Smith Ex'rs, 621.
Vrooman v. Powers, 311, 318, 320, 366.

# W

Wachovia Bank & Trust Co. v. Burras, 768.
Wachovia Bank & Trust Co. v. Lambeth, 806.
Wachsmuth v. Penn Mut. Life Ins. Co., 644.
Wade v. Peacock, 711.
Wade v. Pope, 653.
Wade v. Wade, 345.
Wadskier's Will, In re, 753.
Wadsworth v. Brigham, 143.
Waggoner v. Waggoner, 768, 772, 773.
Wagner v. Clauson, 273, 388.
Wagner v. Thieriot, 638.
Wagner v. Varner, 89.
Wagner v. Wagener, 451.
Wagstaff, In re, 267.
Wah-kon-tah-he-um-pah, Estate of, In re, 241.

Wainford v. Barker, 792.
Wainwright v. Bartlett, 534.
Wait v. Huntington, 806.
Waite v. Frisbie, 276, 299.
Walch v. Orrell, 491.
Walcott v. Ochterlony, 449.
Walden v. Mahnks, 485, 502.
Waldo v. Hayes, 747.
Walet v. Darby, 19, 139.
Walker v. Bennett, 690.
Walker v. Burtscher, 498.
Walker v. Case, 142.
Walker v. Deaver, 802.
Walker v. Fields, 367.
Walker v. Hibbard, 416, 465, 466.
Walker v. Hinckley, 546.
Walker v. Irby, 289.
Walker v. Matthews, 151.
Walker v. Schertz, 645.
Walker v. Walker, 342, 343, 729, 730.
Walker v. Waters, 436, 745.
Walker v. Yarbrough, 218, 498.
Walker's Estate, In re, 333, 502.
Wall v. McEnner's Estate, 92, 216.
Wall v. Pfanschmidt, 153.
Wall v. Wall, 184, 500.
Walls v. Walls, 537.
Wall's Ex'r v. Demmitt, 533.
Wallace, Ex parte, 83.
Wallace, Will of, 359.
Wallace v. Diehl, 780.
Wallace v. Du Bois, 783.
Wallace v. Dubose, 564.
Wallace v. Long, 221.
Wallace v. Pomfret, 770.
Wallace's Estate, In re, 84, 361.
Wallace's Will, In re, 259.
Wallahan v. Ingersoll, 99.
Waller v. Waller, 356, 362.
Wallis v. Hodson, 52.
Walpole v. Orford, 469.
Walsh v. Walsh, 48.
Walsh's Estate, In re, 627.
Walter, Ex parte, 516.
Walter's Estate, In re, 245, 692, 703, 780.
Walters, Matter of, 316, 317.
Walters v. Jordan, 149.
Walters v. Walters, 341.
Walton v. Walton, 434, 435, 732.
Walton v. Walton's Estate, 677.
Walton v. Yturria, 88.
Wampler v. Harrell, 233, 238.
Wamsley v. Snow, 96.
Wanger v. Marr, 225, 226.
Wankford v. Wankford, 643.
Wanstrath v. Kappel, 114, 116.
Ward v. Johnson, 724.
Ward v. Morton, 95.
Ward v. Pipkin, 427.
Ward v. Putnam, 306.
Ward v. Vander, 460, 463.
Ward v. Vander Loeff, 463.
Ward v. Ward, 811, 814.
Ward v. Wright, 651, 652, 654.
Ward's Estate, In re, 793.
Ward's Will, In re, 426.
Wardell's Estate, In re, 430.
Warden v. Hinds, 216, 217.
Wardrop, Estate of, 374.
Waring v. Waring, 234, 242.
Waring's Will, In re, 776.
Warlick v. Boone, 761.
Warneford v. Warneford, 298.
Warner v. Beach, 432.
Warner v. Benham, 641, 685.
Warner v. Burlington Federal Sav. & Loan Ass'n, 176.
Warner v. Warner, 528, 529.
Warner v. Warner's Estate, 439.
Warren, Estate of, 782.
Warren v. Baxter, 813.
Warren v. Duval, 813, 815.
Warren v. Harding, 370, 371, 373.
Warren v. Prescott, 90.
Warren v. Sidney's Estate, 523.
Warren v. Warren, 221, 222.
Warren's Estate, In re, 545.
Warrington's Will, In re, 559.
Warsco v. Oshkosh, 179.
Warsco v. Oshkosh Sav. & Trust Co., 178, 181, 187.
Wartnaby, In re, 497.
Warwick v. Zimmerman, 224, 225, 258, 259.
Washbon v. Cope, 805.
Washington Escrow Co. v. McKinnon, 435.
Wasmund v. Wasmund, 91, 92.
Wasserman's Estate, In re, 239.
Waterbury v. Munn, 473.
Waterland v. Superior Court In and for Sacramento County, 628.
Waterman v. Canal-Louisiana Bank & Trust Co., 595.
Waters v. Selleck, 733, 735, 746.

Waters v. Stickney, 482, 501, 502.
Watkins, Succession of, 618.
Watkins v. Bennett, 812, 814.
Watkins v. Covington Trust & Banking Co., 213.
Watkins v. Dean, 188.
Watkins v. Jones, 278, 280.
Watkins v. Parker, 699.
Watkins v. Watkins, 214, 417, 418.
Watkins v. Young, 721.
Watkins' Estate, In re, 206, 571, 615.
Watland, In re, 182.
Watson v. Alderson, 523.
Watson v. Collins' Adm'r, 597.
Watson v. Hinson, 386.
Watson v. Thompson, 79.
Watson v. Wagner, 132.
Watson v. Watson, 739, 772, 776.
Watson's Estate, Matter of, 402, 403.
Watson's Will, In re, 421.
Watt v. Watt, 606.
Watt's Estate, 448, 636.
Watt's Estate, In re, 209, 390, 392.
Wattenbarger v. Payne, 783.
Wattenbarger v. Wattenbarger, 354.
Watterson v. Thompson, 811, 814.
Wattles v. Hyde, 671.
Waugh v. Poiron, 810.
Waughop v. Bartlett, 697, 712.
Waverley Trust Co., In re, 609.
Wawrzyniak's Estate, In re, 451.
Wayman v. Miller, 207.
Wayne v. Brumley, 676.
Wayne's Estate, In re, 539.
W. B. Smith & Co. v. Lowe, 610.
Wear, Matter of, 450.
Weatherly v. Medlin, 711.
Weathers v. McFarland, 216, 266.
Weaver v. Allison, 545, 548.
Weaver v. Hollis, 154.
Weaver v. Hughes, 492.
Weaver's Estate, In re, 608.
Webb v. Fuller, 787, 788.
Webb v. Reynolds, 665.
Webb's Estate, In re, 88, 610.
Weber v. Beales, 669.
Weber v. Brak, 191.
Weber's Estate, In re, 238, 240.
Webster v. Yorty, 322.
Webster's Estate, In re, 448.
Weddington v. Adkins, 726.
Weddle v. Waddle, 722, 723.
Wedemann v. United States Trust Co. of New York, 592.
Wedemeyer's Estate, In re, 601.
Weed v. Hoge, 733, 734.
Weed v. Lermond, 633.
Weed's Will, In re, 733, 755.
Weedman's Estate, In re, 240.
Weeks v. Lund, 221.
Weeks v. Sego, 620.
Weeks' Succession, 622, 623.
Weels v. Wood, 666.
Weems v. Smith, 361.
Weems v. Weems, 241.
Weese v. Weese, 500.
Wehr's Will, In re, 424, 425.
Wehrkamp v. Burnett, 318, 347.
Weidig's Will, In re, 789.
Weidman's Will, In re, 534.
Weilmuenster v. Swanner, 815.
Weingrad v. Lloyd, 570.
Weir v. Chidester, 365.
Weir v. Lake, 696.
Weir's Estate, In re, 226.
Weis v. Kundert, 568, 570.
Weiss v. Fenwick, 201, 203.
Welch v. Flory, 798.
Welch v. Kirby, 299, 340, 344.
Welch v. Welch, 742.
Welch's Adm'r v. Clifton, 539.
Welles' Estate, In re, 593.
Wellings' Estate, Re, 605.
Wellington v. Apthorp, 214.
Wellman v. Carter, 258, 263.
Wells, In re, 778.
Wells, In re Estate of, 723.
Wells v. Lewis, 297.
Wells v. Menn, 410.
Wells v. Odum, 494, 558.
Wells v. Thompson, 149, 542, 543, 545.
Wells v. Wells, 516.
Welscher's Estate, In re, 609, 613.
Welsh v. Brown, 752.
Welsh v. Manwaring, 581.
Wenbert v. Lincoln Nat. Bank & Trust Co., 720.
Wendel's Estate, Matter of, 34.
Wenker v. Landon, 157.
Wenling, Succession of, 359.
Wenning v. Teeple, 269, 532.
Wentworth v. Cock, 658.
Wentworth v. Read, 763.
Wentworth v. Shibles, 202.
Wentworth's Will, In re, 218.

Wernher, In re, 371.
Wersich v. Phelps, 323, 324.
Wesley's Estate, In re, 678.
West v. Arrington, 546.
West v. Bank of Rutland, 713.
West v. Hardwick's Ex'r, 287.
West v. Sims, 221.
West v. West, 285, 318.
West v. Willby, 580.
West's Will, In re, 696.
Wester v. Wester, 366.
Westerfield v. Stout, 571.
Westerman's Will, In re, 297.
Western P. R. Co. v. Godfrey, 664.
Westfeld's Will, In re, 498.
Westfield Trust Co., In re, 584.
Weston v. Hanson, 140.
Weston v. Johnson, 740.
Wetherstein v. Gordon, 528.
Wetmore & Morse Granite Co. v. Bertoli, 669.
Wetstein v. Shannon, 780.
Wetter v. Habersham, 69–71.
Whaley v. Whaley, 120.
Wheat v. Wheat, 452, 498.
Wheatley's Estate, In re, 198, 208.
Wheeler, Appeal of, 545.
Wheeler v. Harshorn, 737.
Wheeler v. McKeon, 640, 657.
Wheeler v. Wheeler, 583, 721.
Wheeler & Roeber, Appeal of, v. Cordray, 547.
Whelan v. Bailey, 581.
White, In re, 276.
White, Estate of, 497.
White, Matter of, 279.
White v. Bower, 311, 317.
White v. Brennan, 442, 511, 540, 554.
White v. Brennan's Adm'r, 509.
White v. Casten, 437, 441.
White v. Cormier, 685.
White v. Deering, 770.
White v. McKnight, 215.
White v. Massachusetts Inst. of Technology, 783.
White v. Massee, 217.
White v. Mayhall, 526.
White v. Reading, 499.
White v. Repton, 369.
White v. Safe Deposit & Trust Co., 684.
White v. Smith, 187, 212.
White v. Trustees of British Museum, 323, 324.
White v. White, 135, 733, 735, 746.
White's Estate, In re, 544, 798.
White's Will, In re, 259.
Whitehead v. Tapp, 152.
Whitehill v. Halbing, 475, 476.
Whitehouse's Estate, In re, 601.
Whitlock v. Vaun, 460.
Whitlock v. Wardlaw, 274, 276.
Whitmarsh's Estate, In re, 240.
Whitmore v. First Congregational Parish, 402, 403.
Whitney v. Hanington, 383, 451.
Whitney v. Hay, 221.
Whitney v. Lott, 154, 155.
Whitney's Estate, In re, 131, 359.
Whitney's Will, In re, 303, 304, 389.
White v. Roberts, 531.
Whittemore v. Coleman, 704, 794.
Whitten v. Davis, 81.
Whittle v. Roper, 383.
Whitworth's Estate, In re, 233.
Whorff v. Johnson, 82.
Wick v. Hickey, 790.
Wickersham's Estate, In re, 730.
Wickliffe v. Wickliffe, 738.
Wides v. Wides' Ex'r, 220.
Wiechert v. Wiechert, 284.
Wiener v. Specific Pharmaceuticals, Inc., 586.
Wiese's Estate, In re, 311, 312, 313, 315.
Wiggins v. Cheatham, 748.
Wikoff's Appeal, 305, 306, 307, 349, 381, 466, 469.
Wikman's Estate, 438.
Wilbourn v. Shell, 456.
Wilbur v. Tobey, 99.
Wilcox v. Attorney-General, 391.
Wilcox v. Hollar, 678.
Wilcox v. Sams, 88.
Wilcox v. Wilcox, 185, 752.
Wilcox's Estate, In re, 610.
Wilcox's Will, In re, 301.
Wilcoxon v. Wilcoxon, 519.
Wilder v. Charleston Transit V. Co., 643.
Wilder v. Howard, 176.
Wilder Grain Co. v. Felker, 651, 652, 710.
Wildes v. Davies, 771.
Wilenou v. Handlon, 185.

Wiley v. Gordan, 316.
Wiley v. Lockwood, 753.
Wiley's Estate, In re, 365.
Wilkins v. Ellett, 587.
Wilkins' Estate, In re, 31, 155.
Wilkinson v. Joughlin, 267, 269.
Wilkinson v. Leland, 672.
Wilkinson v. Nowers, 627.
Wilkinson v. Spiller, 595.
Wilkinson v. Wilkinson, 408.
Willard v. Bassett, 656.
Willard v. Darrah, 287.
Willard v. Hammond, 588.
Willett's Appeal, 489.
Willey v. Lewis, 119.
Willey's Estate, In re, 385, 391.
Williams' Estate, In re, 317, 326, 328, 447, 579, 587, 634, 649, 723.
Williams, Estate of, 751.
Williams' Will, In re, 302, 329, 362, 478.
Williams v. Bailey, 491.
Williams v. Cordingly, 101.
Williams v. Daubner, 191.
Williams v. Ely, 664.
Williams v. Finnigan, 201.
Williams v. Fry, 405.
Williams v. Fundingsland, 812, 814.
Williams v. Hefner, 598.
Williams v. Kidd, 190.
Williams v. Knight, 782.
Williams v. Lambe, 113.
Williams v. Letton, 202.
Williams v. McDonald, 675.
Williams v. McKeand, 784.
Williams v. Miles, 449–451, 468, 475, 512.
Williams v. Moorehead, 552.
Williams v. Neville, 617.
Williams v. Noland, 3.
Williams v. Ragland, 262.
Williams v. Robinson, 545.
Williams v. Sechler, 122.
Williams v. Smith, 736, 752.
Williams v. Swango, 726.
Williams v. Sykes, 569.
Williams v. Taylor, 799.
Williams v. Trust Co. of Georgia, 68.
Williams v. Way, 316.
Williams v. Weber, 88.
Williams v. Williams, 224, 637, 679, 694.
Williamson v. Williamson, 142.
Williard v. Prudential Ins. Co. of America, 163.
Williford v. Phelan, 228.
Willis v. Barrow, 748.
Willis v. Fiveash, 186.
Willis v. Mott, 345.
Willis v. Sharp, 653, 662, 663.
Willoughby v. McCluer, 634.
Willoughby v. Watson, 744.
Willoughby v. Willoughby, 626.
Wills v. Cowper, 670.
Wills v. Lochnane, 534.
Wills v. Rich, 579.
Wilm's Estate, In re, 341.
Wilmerding's Estate, In re, 677, 678.
Wilmerton v. Wilmerton, 743, 748.
Wilmes v. Tiernay,
Wilmington Trust Co. v. Boden, 106.
Wilmington Trust Co. v. Houlehan, 407.
Wilson, Matter of, 775, 776.
Wilson v. Anderson, 92.
Wilson v. Bass, 83.
Wilson v. Carrico, 185, 186.
Wilson v. Chanell, 791.
Wilson v. Craig, 149, 300, 301.
Wilson v. Fahnestock, 657.
Wilson v. Findley, 116.
Wilson v. Fisher, 119.
Wilson v. Higgason, 416.
Wilson v. Hudson, 665.
Wilson v. Jones, 189.
Wilson v. Mitchell, 249, 252.
Wilson v. Piper, 760, 761, 762.
Wilson v. Randolph, 153.
Wilson v. Safe Deposit & T. Co., 770.
Wilson v. Snow, 676.
Wilson v. Starbuck, 779.
Wilson v. Wilson, 121, 194, 474, 558.
Wilson's Estate, In re, 166, 260, 261, 263, 634, 656, 701, 733, 734, 735, 746, 756.
Wilson's Estate, Matter of, 399, 400.
Wilson's Will, In re, 329.
Wilton v. Eaton, 651.
Wilts v. Wilts, 736.
Wiltsey's Will, In re, 525, 623.
Wimpey v. Ledford, 187.
Winchell v. Sanger, 703.
Winchelsea v. Norcliff, 47.
Winder v. Scholey, 272.
Winder v. Winder, 692, 693.
Windham v. Chetwynd, 327.

Windolph v. Girard Trust Co., 179.
Windsor v. Barnett, 125.
Wineland, Appeal of, 306.
Winfield v. Bowen, 222.
Wingrove v. Wingrove, 256.
Winkelmann v. Winkelmann, 92.
Winkhous, In re, 612.
Winkler v. Woodruff, 395.
Winn, Goods of, 417.
Winn v. Tabernacle Infirmary, 404, 414.
Winner v. Carroll, 171.
Winner v. Shucart, 770.
Winslow v. Kimball, 318.
Winsor v. Brown, 781.
Winston, In re, 556.
Winter v. Winter, 472.
Winterland v. Winterland, 414.
Winters Nat. Bank & Trust Co. of Dayton v. Cullen, 403.
Winters' Will, In re, 306, 421.
Winzenrith's Estate, 502.
Wirsig's Estate, In re, 275.
Wise v. Crandall, 407.
Wise's Estate, In re, 609, 799.
Wisehart v. Applegate, 311, 319, 320.
Wiseman v. Guernsey, 91.
Wiseman v. Wiseman, 152.
Wishnick, Estate of, 702.
Wisner v. Mabley's Estate, 656.
Wisner v. Wisner, 170.
Witham v. Witham, 390.
Witmer v. Witmer, 768.
Witt's Will, In re, 492.
Witte's Estate, In re, 531, 539.
Wittner, Matter of, 809, 814.
Witwer's Estate, In re, 811.
Wlodarek v. Wlodarek, 584.
Wnuk's Will, In re, 189.
Wocet v. Seacat, 563.
Woehrle's Will, In re, 421.
Wohleber's Estate, 166.
Wohlfort v. Wohlfort, 486, 492, 505.
Wolber v. Rose, 334.
Wolcott's Estate, In re, 358.
Wold v. Wold, 217, 222.
Wolf v. Bealrd, 801.
Wolf v. Bollinger, 455, 456, 458.
Wolf v. Gall, 84.
Wolf v. Gills, 597.
Wolfe v. Galloway, 722.
Wolfe v. Lewsburg Trust & Safe Deposit Co., 591.
Wolfe v. Mueller, 771.
Wolfe's Will, In re, 448, 452.
Wollenberg v. Rose, 657.
Wolverton Mortgaged Estate, In re, 287.
Wombacher v. Barthelme, 265.
Women's Foreign Missionary Soc. v. Mitchell, 285.
Wood v. Davis, 322, 323.
Wood v. Weimar, 570.
Wood v. Wood, 546.
Woodcock v. McDonald, 526.
Woodley's Will, In re, 448.
Woodroff v. Wicksworth, 48.
Woodruff v. H. B. Claflin Co., 801.
Woodruff v. Hundley, 438.
Woodruff v. Miller, 615.
Woodruff v. Snoover, 580.
Woodruff's Ex'r v. Woodruff, 248.
Woods, In re, 278, 795.
Woods Estate, 736.
Woods v. Dunn, 214, 215.
Woods v. Ely, 698, 802.
Woods v. Woods, 112.
Woods' Estate, 579.
Wood's Ex'rs v. Wood, 249.
Woodstock College of Baltimore County v. Farmers' & Mechanics' Nat. Bank of Frederick City, 326.
Woodstock College of Baltimore County v. Hankey, 328, 544.
Woodville v. Pizzati, 488.
Woodward v. Goulstone, 511.
Woodward v. Lord Darcy, 644.
Woodward's Estate, In re, 751, 753.
Woodworth, Estate of, 731, 732, 733, 734, 736, 756.
Woolery v. Woolery, 434.
Wooley v. Shell Petroleum Corp., 92.
Woolley v. Pemberton, 579.
Wooten's Trustee v. Hardy, 769, 772.
Worcester Bank & Trust Co. v. Ellis, 445.
Worcester County Nat. Bank of Worcester, Petition of, 614.
Worcester Trust Co. v. Turner, 778, 784.
Word v. Whipps, 297.
Worden v. Worden, 219, 221.
Workman v. Workman, 256.
World's Gospel Union v. Johnson, 432.
Wornall, Estate of, 239.

Worth v. McAden, 616.
Wortham v. Marten, 675.
Wray v. Field, 771.
Wren v. Coffey, 187.
Wright v. Cummins, 410, 413.
Wright v. Eakin, 486.
Wright v. Green, 215, 791.
Wright v. Hall, 20, 785.
Wright v. Jenks, 412.
Wright v. McDonald, 509.
Wright v. Smith, 685, 686.
Wright v. Upson, 558.
Wright v. Wakeford, 298.
Wright v. Wright, 225, 327, 465, 711, 784.
Wright's Estate, In re, 527, 602, 607, 613.
Wunderle's Estate, In re, 360.
Wunderlich v. Bowen, 645.
Wunderlich v. Buerger, 261.
Wuppermann's Estate, In re, 450.
Wurmbrand, In re, 144.
Wyatt v. Morse, 712.
Wyatt v. Wyatt, 278.
Wyckoff v. Perrine, 744.
Wyckoff v. Wyckoff, 51.
Wyllie's Estate, In re, 600.
Wyman v. Wyman, 636.
Wynn's Estate, In re, 521.

## Y

Yarnall's Will, In re, 366.
Yates v. Cole, 274.
Yates' Estate, In re, 91.
Yauch, Matter of, 171.
Yeates v. Yeates, 143.
Yerxa v. Youngman, 426.
Yess v. Yess, 550, 551.
Yetter, Re, 650.
Yonley v. Lavender, 595.
Yong's Estate, In re, 67.
Yont v. Eads, 439.
York v. York, 142.
York's Estate, In re, 393, 394, 396.
Yott v. Yott, 434.
Younce v. Flory, 723.
Young, Estate of, 391.
Young v. Bridges, 82.
Young v. Guella, 495, 501.
Young v. O'Donnell, 187.
Young v. Payne, 186.
Young v. Ray, 648.
Young v. Ridenbaugh, 238.
Young v. Stearns, 90.
Young's Estate, In re, 387, 417.
Youngblood v. Youngblood, 188.
Youngquest's Estate, In re, 714.
Yowell's Estate, In re, 358, 359.

## Z

Zagoren v. Superior Court, 651, 652.
Zaiac's Will, In re, 372.
Zakatoff's Estate, In re, 298.
Zalewski's Estate, In re, 120.
Zartner v. Holzhauer, 640.
Zaruba v. Schumaker, 298.
Zech's Estate, In re, 208.
Ziegler v. Brown, 298, 298, 300.
Zeigler v. Coffin, 261, 262, 289.
Zilke's Estate, In re, 813.
Zimmer, Estate of, 456, 458.
Zimmerman v. Hafer, 390.
Zimmermann's Estate, In re, 785.
Zipperer v. La Roche, 627.
Zollikofer's Estate, In re, 521.
Zollickoffer v. Seth, 701, 702, 801.
Zombro v. Moffett, 783, 807.
Zweig's Will, In re, 121.
Zych's Will, In re, 296.

# INDEX

**Figures refer to pages**

## A


**ABANDONMENT,**
See Unworthy Heirs.

**ABATEMENT, 754–763.**
See Devises, Legacies.

**ABSENTEES, 600–601.**

**ACCOUNTING,**
Allowance of expenses on, 652, 654–655, 658–659, 794–795.
Final, 793–795.
Finality of, 793–794.
Form of, 794, 795.
Fraud in, 794.
Intermediate, 793.
Inventory as basis of, 630, 794.
Objections to, 647, 649, 695, 705–706, 795–796.
See Assets; Decree of Distribution; Personal Representatives.

**ACCRETIONS, 749 et seq.**
See Legacies.

**ACKNOWLEDGMENT,**
See Execution of Wills.

**ACTIONS,**
Against,
Creditors who are overpaid, 801.
Debtors of deceased,
By heirs, 567–569.
By personal representative, 641, 643, 645–646.
Estate as entity, 649, 651, 652–653.
Heirs by creditors, 20–21, 24, 570–571, 702, 801–802.
Legatees who are overpaid, 802–803.
Personal representatives,
As executor de son tort, 570–572.
For contracts, 650–656, 658–659.
For obligations of deceased, see Claims.
For tort, 649–650.
For waste, 648–649.
Individual or representative capacity, 651 et seq., 663.
When insolvent, 653, 663.

**ACTIONS**—Continued
By,
Beneficiary under unprobated will, 503–504.
Creditors against,
Executor de son tort, 570–571.
Heirs, 567–569, 570–572, 702, 801–802.
Personal representative, see Claims.
Estate as entity, 649, 651, 652–653.
Foreign administrators, 585–589.
Heirs against deceased's debtors, 567–569.
Personal representative,
For instructions, 805–806.
In another jurisdiction, 585–589.
To recover assets, 639 et seq., 645, 646.
To recover from overpaid creditors and legatees, 801, 802.
For,
Death, 642–643.
Destruction of will, 504.
Fraud on deceased, 640.
Probating forged will, 504.
Procuring fraudulent omission from will, 271.
Transfer in fraud of creditors, 639.
On bond of personal representative, 649.
On contract not to revoke will, 419–420.
On contract to make will, 211–221, 224–227.
Revival of, 686.
Set-off by or against personal representative, 653–654.
Survival of, 641, 683–685.
See also, Ancillary Administration; Assets; Claims; Contest of Wills; Fraud; Refunding; Third Party Beneficiary; Trusts.

**ADEMPTION**, 741–748.
See Devises; Legacies; Revocation of Wills.

**ADMINISTRATION**,
Absentees' estates, 600–601.
Ancillary, see Ancillary Administration.
Application for, 618–619.
Attorneys fees, 654, 655–656, 710, 795.
Avoidance of,
By debtor paying funeral expenses, 570.
By direct suit of heir, 567–569.
By family settlement, 566–567.
By inter vivos transactions, see Substitutes for Wills.
By testamentary provision, 564.
By voluntary payment to heir, 570.
Causes of, 159, 160, 575.
Extent of, 166, 565–566, 563.
Legislation, 569, 572, 573–575.
Defined, 5.
Denial of, 572, 574.
Estate not an entity, 649, 651, 652–653.
Expenses of, 654–656, 710, 795.

**ADMINISTRATION**—Continued
Functions of, as to,
Personalty, 562–563.
Realty, 563–564.
Insolvent estates, 610, 714–715.
Jurisdiction for,
Assets, necessity of, 597–598.
Courts,
Ecclesiastical, see Ecclesiastical Courts.
Equity, 22–23, 688, 792.
Federal, 594–595.
Probate, 23–29, 494, 646–647, 687–689, 704–705, 714–715, 791, 792, 793, 799.
Death of deceased, 598–600.
Domicile of deceased, 595–596.
Time limitations, 569, 601–602.
Necessity of,
Determination of necessity, 572, 585.
Personalty, 562–563, 797.
Realty, 563–564, 796.
Termination of, 796–799.
Testate estates, 564.
Time limitations, 569, 601–602.
Venue, 595–596.
Who may demand,
Creditors, 570, 618.
Heirs, 572, 618.
Others, 618.
See also, Accounting; Actions; Administrators; Appraisal; Assets; Claims; Contest of Wills; Descent and Distribution; Executors; Inventory; Personal Representatives; Probate of Wills.

**ADMINISTRATORS,**
Acceptance of office, 616–617.
Acts binding though letters revoked, 503.
Ancillary, see Ancillary Administration.
Bond of, 621–623, 654, 674.
De bonis non, 5, 577, 670.
Defined, 5, 576–577.
Duties of, see Personal Representatives.
Exercise of power of sale under will, 670.
Joint, 582–584, 670.
Jurisdiction to appoint, see Administration.
Powers of, see Personal Representatives.
Proceedings for appointment,
Hearing, 620.
Notice, 619–620.
Order, 620.
Petition, 618–619.
Public, 523, 581, 610.
Qualification for office, 612–616.
Removal of, 624–628.
Renunciation of office, 616–618.

**ADMINISTRATORS**—Continued
Resignation of, 628.
Revocation of letters, 623–625, 627–628, 793.
Right to contest will, 522–523, 525.
Right to nominate, 609, 610–611, 617, 627.
Sales by, see Sales by Personal Representatives.
Special administrators, 578–580.
Ad litem, 579–580.
During absence, 580.
During minority, 580.
For collection of goods, 578.
In general, 576.
Pendente lite, 579.
With will annexed, 5, 577, 611, 670.
Who are entitled to act,
Children, 612.
Corporations, 614.
Creditors, 610, 614.
Debtors, 614–615.
Discretion of court, 615–616.
Legatees, 611.
Next of kin, 607–609.
Nonresidents, 589, 609, 612–613.
Public administrator, 523, 581, 610.
Spouse, 607.
Strangers, 610.
With will annexed, 5, 577, 611, 670.
See also, Accounting; Actions; Administration; Assets; Claims; Executors; Personal Representatives; Retainer.

**ADOPTION,**
See Children; Descent and Distribution; Lapse; Legacies; Revocation of Wills.

**ADULTERY,**
See Unworthy Heirs.

**ADVANCEMENTS,**
Alteration of nature of transfer, 721–722.
Application of doctrine,
Partial intestacy, 724.
Testacy, 723.
To transfers to what persons, 722–723.
Bringing into hotchpot, 717.
Distinguished from gift, loan and sale, 718.
Intention,
Evidence of, 719–721.
Requirement of writing, 720.
Of intestate or heirs, 719, 721.
Time of, 721.
Interest on, 725.
Origin of doctrine, 716.
Release as liquidated advancement, 727, 728.
Retainer of, 717n, 789.

**ADVANCEMENTS**—Continued
Valuation of, 724–725.
See Expectancy; Retainer.

**AFTER-ACQUIRED PROPERTY**, 2, 15, 18, 21–22, 433–434, 470, 786.
See Construction; Devises; Revocation of Wills.

**AFTER-BORN CHILDREN**,
See Children; Descent and Distribution; Legacies; Revocation of Wills.

**AGE**,
See Administrators; Descent and Distribution; Evidence; Execution of Wills; Executors; Testamentary Capacity.

**ALIENATION**,
See Conditions; Devises; Legacies; Revocation of Wills.

**ALIENS**,
See Administrators; Descent and Distribution; Escheat; Testamentary Capacity.

**ALLOWANCE**,
See Accounting; Claims; Family Allowance; Personal Representatives.

**ALTERATIONS**,
See Evidence; Execution of Wills; Probate of Wills; Revocation of Wills; Wills.

**AMBIGUITIES**,
See Construction; Mistake.

**ANCESTORS**,
See Advancements; Descent and Distribution; Expectancy; Unworthy Heirs.

**ANCESTRAL PROPERTY**, 39, 49, 77–81.

**ANCILLARY ADMINISTRATION**,
Disposition of assets in, 593.
Jurisdiction for, 589.
Necessity of, 585–588.
Payment of claims in, 592.
Privity with domiciliary administration, 590–591.
Sale of realty in, 591, 672.
Who may be appointed ancillary administrator, 589–590.
See Administration; Conflict of Laws; Probate of Wills.

**ANIMUS TESTANDI**,
See Execution of Wills; Testamentary Character; Testamentary Intent.

**ANNUITIES**, 752, 767.
See Conditions.

**ANTICIPATION**,
See Advancements; Devises; Expectancy; Legacies.

**APPEAL**,
From decree of distribution, 798.
From order allowing claims, 704–705.
From order for family allowance, 134.
See Contest of Wills.

APPOINTMENT,
See Administrators; Executors; Power of Appointment; Reference to Non-Testamentary Acts.

APPRAISAL,
As basis for accounts, 630, 794.
Effect of valuation in, 634.
On sale of realty by order of court, 674.
Procedure for, 633–634.
See Inventory.

ASSENT,
See Decree of Distribution; Election; Legacies.

ASSETS,
Care of,
Liability for acts of agents, 648.
Liability to dispose of stocks, etc., 648.
Tangible assets, 648–649.
Collection of,
By action, 646.
Compromise of debts, 645–646.
Discharge of debts, 645.
Discovery of, 632, 645.
Distribution of, 796–799.
Necessity of, for administration, 589, 597–599.
Waste, 648–649.
What are,
Choses in action,
For fraud on deceased, 640.
Survival in favor of personal representative, 641–642.
Crops, 637.
Death claims, 635, 642–643.
Debts owing by personal representative to deceased, 643–644.
Equitable interests, 101.
Estates for life, 103.
Estates tail, 103.
Fixtures, 637.
Future interests, 102, 103–104.
Joint interests of deceased and survivor, 103, 164–171, 637–638.
Life insurance, 638.
Partnership interests, 166, 638.
Property conveyed by deceased in fraud of creditor, 639.
Property given by gift causa mortis, 204, 639–640.
Realty, 636–637, 638.
See Accounting; Actions; Administration; Administrators; Ancillary Administration; Claims; Curtesy; Decree of Distribution; Dower; Executors; Personal Representatives; Power of Appointment; Sales by Personal Representatives.

ASSIGNMENT,
See Expectancy; Testamentary Character.

ATTESTATION,
See Execution of Wills.

**ATTORNEYS,**
As attesting witnesses, 261–262, 320, 352, 377.
Fees, 556–560, 654–656.
Personal representative as attorney for estate, 655–656.
Suggestions for drafting of wills, 817–836.
Suggestions for execution of wills, 348–354.
Will designating attorney for estate, 603.
See Administration; Contest of Wills; Evidence; Personal Representatives.

# B

**BANK ACCOUNTS,**
In trust for survivor, 173–177.
Joint accounts to survivor, 167–171.
Payable without administration, 574.
Tentative trust doctrine, 175–177.
See Personal Representatives.

**BASTARDS,**
See Children; Descent and Distribution; Evidence; Legacies; Revocation of Wills.

**BENEFICIARIES,**
See Conditions; Devises; Execution of Wills; Legacies; Mistake; Reference to Nontestamentary Acts.

**BEQUEST,**
Definition of, 4.
See Devises; Legacies.

**BIGAMY,**
See Fraud; Unworthy Heirs.

**BILLS AND NOTES,**
As substitutes for will, 198–199.

**BILLS OF SALE,**
As substitutes for will, 197.

**BLIND TESTATOR,**
Capacity to make will, 252.
Execution of will by, 252, 354.
Knowledge of contents of will, 252, 275.
Revocation by, 421.

**BONDS,**
Action on personal representative's bond, 649.
Administrators, 621–623.
Cost of, as expense of administration, 654–655.
Executors, 621–623, 833.
Filing inventory a condition of, 629–631.
On sale of realty, 674.

**BROTHERS,**
See Descent and Distribution.

**BURDEN OF PROOF,**
See Evidence.

## C

CANCELLATION,
See Revocation of Wills.

CANON LAW,
See Civil Law; Descent and Distribution; Ecclesiastical Courts.

CANONS OF DESCENT,
Stated and explained, 37–41, 60.
See Descent and Distribution.

CAPACITY,
See Administrators; Evidence; Executors; Testamentary Capacity.

CAPITA, PER,
Provision in will as to, 828.
See also, Descent and Distribution.

CAUSA MORTIS,
See Gifts Causa Mortis.

CHARGE,
See Conditions; Legacies; Renunciation.

CHARITABLE AND RELIGIOUS DEVISES,
Death-bed gifts curtailed, 135–136, 462.
Execution of, in Pennsylvania, 313n.
Limitation of amount, 135–137.
Prohibition of, 135–138.
Provisions for, 830.
Who may object to, 137–138.
See Testamentary Capacity.

CHECK,
As gift causa mortis, 203.
As nuncupative will, 365.
As substitute for will, 199, 365.

CHILDREN,
Adopted as heirs, 50, 59, 86–92, 440.
As administrator, 612.
As executor, 580.
As witnesses to will, 320, 377.
Illegitimates,
As heirs, 50, 59, 81–85.
Birth of as revoking will, 429–430.
Gifts to, 135n.
Litigation among, as undue influence, 257.
Prejudices against, as insane delusions, 245.
Protection of, against disinheritance by will,
After-born children, effect on will, 141–145, 427–428.
By forbidding charitable and religious devises and bequests, 135 et seq.
By limiting gifts to mistresses and illegitimate children, 135.
Claims against estate for support, 145–146.
Effect of failure to mention living children, 140–143, 754.
Express disinheritance without gift to another, 145.

**CHILDREN**—Continued
Protection of, against disinheritance by will—Continued
Legitime, 9–10, 15–16, 22, 35, 41, 92, 138–139.
Sympathetic verdicts in will contests, 139–140.
See Advancements; Charitable and Religious Devises and Bequests; Construction; Descent and Distribution; Disinheritance; Execution of Wills; Family Allowances; Forced Heirs; Legacies; Revocation of Wills; Testamentary Capacity.

**CHOSES IN ACTION,**
See Actions; Assets.

**CHURCH COURTS,**
See Ecclesiastical Courts.

**CIVIL DEATH,**
See Descent and Distribution; Escheat; Testamentary Capacity.

**CIVIL LAW,**
Ademption, 741.
Age capacity, 229.
Causation for fraud, 268n.
Concept of will, 2, 15.
Degree of kindred, 45–47, 69.
Gift causa mortis, 200n.
Influence in America, 26–27, 375–378.
Roman law, 8–10, 15, 18.
Universal succession, 562–563.

**CLAIMS,**
Appeal from order allowing or disallowing, 704–705.
Compromise of, 704.
Defeat of by transfer inter vivos, 182–183.
Defense to, 703–704.
Distinction between unmatured and contingent, 698, 702–703.
Establishment of claims,
Jurisdiction of courts, 595, 687–689, 692, 704–705, 714–715.
Necessity of, before payment, 705–706.
Filing of, 692–693.
For breach of contract not to revoke will, 224.
For breach of contract to make will, 217.
Forfeiture of legacies for presenting, 413, 831.
For obligations incurred by personal representatives, 650–655, 659–663.
Form of, 695–696.
Jury trial, 704–705.
Liability of heirs, 20–21, 24, 72, 570–572, 801–802.
Nonclaim statutes, 689–692, 693, 695, 698–700, 707–708, 802.
Notice to creditors, 691.
Payment of, by personal representative, 17, 704–708, 714–715.
Preferences, 708 et seq.
Presentment of claims,
Manner of, 692–693, 695–696.
Nature of claims requiring,
Contingent, 700–703.
Contractual, 697.
Delictual, 697, 703.

**CLAIMS—Continued**
Presentment of claims—Continued
Nature of claims requiring—Continued
Equitable, 697.
Matured, 696, 698.
Proprietary, 697.
Secured claims, 702, 706–708, 712–713.
Unliquidated, 697.
Unmatured, 698, 702.
Time limitations, 689 et seq., 802.
Waiver of, 694–695, 705–706.
Priority in insolvent estates,
Costs of administration, 710.
Family allowances, 133, 708.
Funeral expenses, 709.
General obligations, 713–714.
Judgments, 711.
Last illness expenses, 709.
Preferences, 713–714.
Rents, 711.
Retainer, 714.
Secured claims, 712–713.
Speciality, 713.
Statutes relating to, 708 et seq.
Taxes, 710.
Trust funds, 710–711.
Wages, 711.
Widows' allowances, 133, 708.
Procedure,
In general, 687–689, 692–693, 695–696.
Insolvent estates, 714–715.
Property liable for, 100–105, 127–129, 132–133, 164, 171, 177, 181–183, 204, 563, 573, 635–636, 639, 670.
Revival of actions, 686.
Secured claims,
Exoneration of, 706–708.
Foreclosure of, 697–698.
Presentment, 697–698.
Priority of, 712–713.
Survival of,
Against estate, 683.
In favor of estate, 641–642, 684–685.
Trusts for payment of, 706.
See Administration; Ancillary Administration; Assets; Exoneration; Refunding; Retainer.

**CLASS,**
See Construction; Descent and Distribution; Legacies.

**CODICIL,**
Capacity at time of, 241.
Construction with will, 811.
To be avoided if possible, 835.
Undue influence at time of, 260.

**CODICIL**—Continued
See Incorporation by Reference; Probate of Wills; Revival of Wills; Revocation of Wills; Wills.

**COLLATERAL ATTACK,**
See Administration; Construction; Decree of Distribution; Probate Courts; Probate of Wills; Sales by Personal Representatives.

**COMMISSIONS,**
Of personal representative, 630, 656, 680, 793, 795.

**COMMUNITY PROPERTY,** 26–27, 63–64, 108.

**COMPROMISE,**
See Assets; Claims; Contest of Wills.

**CONDITIONAL WILLS,**
Disfavored in construction, 416–417.
Distinguished from statement of inducement, 417–418.
In general, 416.

**CONDITIONS,**
Breach of, 410–413.
Distinguished from,
Charge, 402.
Reference to non-testamentary act, 401.
Statement of inducement, 402.
Illegal,
Effect of illegality, 413–415.
What are, 405–410.
Implied forfeiture for murder of testator, 155.
Impossibility of performance of, 413–415.
In deeds as affecting testamentary character, 184–188.
Particular conditions, affecting,
Marriage and matrimonial relations, 402, 404, 405–408, 431.
Miscellaneous matters, 404.
Payments to others, 402.
Right to contest will, 408–410, 412–413, 831.
Right to present claims, 413, 831.
Performance of, 410–411.
Precedent, 403–405, 414–415.
Requiring election, 118–120, 770.
Subsequent, 403–405, 414–415.
See Conditional Wills; Election; Renunciation; Revocation of Wills.

**CONFIDENTIAL RELATIONS,**
See Evidence; Undue Influence.

**CONFLICT OF LAWS,**
Administration, 596.
Adoption, 92.
Ancillary administration, 585–593, 672.
Construction, 807.
Election, 122n.
Execution, 487.
Partial wills, 383–384.
Power of sale of land, 591, 672.
Probate of wills, 384, 487–489.

CONSTRUCTION,
Ambiguities, 281 et seq., 810.
Charges on realty, 762–763.
Class gifts, 778, 782–783, 828.
Declaratory judgment for, 806.
Directions to pay debts, 706, 831.
"Four corners of instrument," 808.
Intention of testator, 281 et seq., 807 et seq.
Interpretation distinguished from construction, 809–810, 813.
Jurisdiction of courts to construe,
Equity, 281, 283, 805–806.
Law, 281, 805–806.
Probate, 281, 416, 497, 519, 804–805.
Territorial, 808.
Of conditions, see Conditions.
Of "personal effects," 829.
Of will as conditional, 416–418.
Of word "last" in will, 448.
On probate, 497–498, 500, 517–518, 519, 804–805.
Power of sale in will, 668–670.
Provision regarding abatement, 755, 757, 760, 761.
Provision regarding lapse, 778.
Reference to acts and facts, 400, 807.
Rules of construction,
Particular rules,
Disinheritance disfavored, 814, 816.
Early vesting favored, 815.
General intention governs, 811.
Gifts by implication, 812–813.
Intestacy disfavored, 814, 816.
Last words preferred, 815.
Ordinary meaning of words, 811.
Reasonable disposition preferred, 814.
Rejection, etc., of words, 812.
Technical meaning of words, 810, 811.
Valid construction preferred, 815.
Will construed as whole, 811.
Will speaks from death, 433–435, 470–473, 746, 815.
Use of rules, 815–817.
Trusts for payment of debts, 706.
Value of precedents, 808, 810, 816.
Who may demand, 805–806.
Wills republished by codicil, 470–473.
See also, Devises; Evidence; Legacies; Mistake; Revocation of Wills.

CONTEST OF WILLS,
Attorneys fees, 556–560.
Compromise of, 528–530.
Construction of will in, 519.
Contracts not to contest,
Between heirs and beneficiaries under will, 528–530.
With testator, 527.
Costs, 555–556, 560, 665.

**CONTEST OF WILLS**—Continued
Estoppel to contest, 525–527.
Evidence in, see Evidence.
Forfeiture provision for contests, 408–410, 412–413, 831.
Grounds of,
Contract to make different will, 218, 224.
Forgery, 517.
Fraud, 270, 517.
Improper execution, 517.
Innocent misrepresentation, 266.
Internal invalidity, 518.
Mental incapacity, 232 et seq., 517, 532.
Mistake, 273–281.
Revocation, 419, 517, 533.
Several grounds united, 253–254, 533.
Undue influence, 255 et seq., 531–532.
Jury trial in, 233, 237, 269, 533–534.
Nature of, as action in rem, 516.
Notice of, 514–515.
Of several wills at one trial, 521.
Parties to,
Beneficiaries under prior wills, 521.
Creditors, 523–524.
Heirs, 519.
Personal representatives, 522–523.
Purchasers from heirs, 521–522.
Spouse, 520.
State, 523.
Pleadings in, 531–533.
Proceedings, form of, 514–516.
Right to open and close, 534–535.
Survival of right to contest, 525.
What is, 412–413.
See also, Evidence; Probate of Wills.

**CONTINGENT CLAIMS,**
See Claims; Refunding.

**CONTINUATION OF BUSINESS**, 659–664.

**CONTRACTS,**
As substitutes for wills—testamentary character, 194–197, 822–823.
Not to revoke, 224, 419, 449, 498.
Of personal representative, 650–656.
Performance of deceased's, 657–659, 661.
Separation agreement, 112, 432.
To make will,
Action by third party beneficiary, 213.
Breach, 216–217.
Conditions, 216.
Consideration, 212–213.
Formalities, 213–215, 220–221.
In case of adopted child, 90–91.
Probate of, 210.
Remedies for breach, 217 et seq.

**CONTRACTS**—Continued
To make will—Continued
Statute of Limitations, 221–222.
Terms, definiteness of, 211, 223–227.
Writing, requirement of, 213–215, 220–221.
See Actions; Assets; Claims; Contest of Wills; Personal Representatives; Sales by Personal Representatives.

**CONTRIBUTION,**
See Election; Legacies; Refunding.

**CONVERSION,**
See Assets; Devises; Legacies.

**CONVEYANCE,**
See Assets; Deeds; Devises; Expectancy; Legacies.

**CONVICTS,**
See Descent and Distribution; Escheat; Execution of Wills; Testamentary Capacity.

**COSTS,** 555 et seq., 710.

**CORPORATIONS,**
As personal representative, 605, 614, 832, 833.
Devise to, 135.
Dissolution of, causing,
Ademption, 747, 750.
Lapse, 777.

**CREDITORS,**
As personal representatives, 610, 614, 832, 833.
As proponents of will, 523–524.
Consent to continue business of deceased, 662–663.
Defeat of by,
Bank account trust, 177.
Insurance, 161.
Joint bank account, 171.
Joint estate, 164–165.
Living trust, 181–182.
Of beneficiary, see Conditions; Contest of Wills; Renunciation.
Of decedent, see Actions; Claims.
Preferred to heirs and beneficiaries under will, 100, 562, 567–569.

**CREDITORS' BILLS,**
See Actions; Assets; Refunding.

**CRIMINALS,**
See Descent and Distribution; Escheat; Execution of Wills; Testamentary Capacity.

**CROPS,**
See Assets.

**CUMULATIVE LEGACIES,** 771.

**CURTESY,**
Abolished in England, 58.
Effect of adultery and elopement upon, 149, 152.
Election to take against will, 118 et seq.

**CURTESY—Continued**
Extent of interest, 62, 63.
Necessity of birth of issue, 105–106.
Statutory substitutes for, 62, 63, 107 et seq.
See Descent and Distribution; Dower; Election.

# D

**DATE,**
See Construction; Execution of Wills; Holographic Wills; Probate of Wills; Revival of Wills.

**DEAF AND DUMB TESTATORS,**
Execution of will by, 251.
Testamentary capacity, 251–252.

**DEATH,**
See Administration; Assets; Claims; Conditions; Deeds; Lapse; Probate of Wills; Survival.

**DE BONIS NON,**
See Administrators.

**DEBTS,**
See Actions; Administration; Administrators; Advancements; Assets; Claims; Insolvent Estates; Retainer.

**DECLARATIONS,**
See Evidence; Execution of Wills; Nuncupative Wills.

**DECLARATORY JUDGMENTS,**
See Construction; Probate of Wills.

**DECREE OF DISTRIBUTION,**
As to realty, 796, 799.
Conclusiveness of, 798–799.
Fraud in obtaining, 798.
In accordance with compromise agreement, 530.
In kind or cash, 799.
Notice required for, 798.
Protection of personal representative, 797.
See Accounting; Descent and Distribution; Devises; Legacies.

**DEEDS,**
As substitutes for wills—testamentary character,
Conditions expressed in deeds, 184 et seq.
Delivery upon death, 189 et seq.
Effect of revocability, 187–188.
Evidence of testamentary character, 185.
Of personal representative by order of court, 675–676.
Of property belonging to beneficiary as requiring election, 768–769.
Of realty as revocation, 433–435, 743.
Probate of, 188–189.
Setting aside deeds of decedent, 639, 640.
See Expectancy.

**DEFINITIONS, 1–5.**
See also, particular topics.

**DEGREES OF KIN,** 44–49, 68–72.

**DELIVERY,**
See Decree of Distribution; Deeds; Wills.

**DEMONSTRATIVE LEGACIES,**
See Legacies.

**DEPENDENT RELATIVE REVOCATION,**
Basis of doctrine, 453–456, 459–460.
By physical act, 454–459, 479.
By subsequent instrument, 459–463.
Conditional revocation, 452–453, 458, 479.
Intention of testator, 452–456, 459–460.
Mistaken revocation, 277, 453–456, 459, 463, 479.
See Mistake.

**DEPOSITS,**
See Assets; Bank Accounts; Personal Representatives.

**DESCENDANTS,**
See Advancements; Descent and Distribution; Expectancy; Lapse.

**DESCENT AND DISTRIBUTION,**
American law of, 33, 60–99.
Ancestral property doctrine, 39, 49, 77–81.
Canons of descent, 37–41, 60.
Corruption of blood, 54–55, 95–96.
Definitions of, 4.
Degrees of relationship, by, 45–49, 69–71.
English law of, 37–59.
Inheritance, by,
Adopted children, 50, 59, 86–92, 430.
Aliens, 53–54, 93–94.
Aunts, 39, 40, 48, 57, 62, 70, 73.
Bastards, 40, 59, 81–85, 429.
Brothers, 39, 40, 46–48, 58, 66–70.
Children, 33–35, 39, 42–44, 64–65.
Cousins, 48–49, 59, 72.
Grandchildren and more remote descendants, 39, 43–44, 65, 75.
Grandparents and more remote ancestors, 38, 48–49, 68, 72.
Half-blood, 39, 50–52, 58, 74, 78–79.
Illegitimates, 40, 59, 81–85, 429.
Murderer of intestate, 153–156.
Nephews, 48–49, 58–59, 67–68, 70–71.
Next of kin, 4, 16, 19, 44–49, 68–72.
Nieces, 48–49, 58–59, 67–68, 70–71.
Parents,
In general, 38–39, 46–47, 66–67, 72, 90–91.
Who have abandoned intestate children, 148.
Posthumous heirs, 52–53, 75, 76.
Relatives by marriage, 49, 73.
Sisters, 39, 40, 46–48, 58, 66–70.
Spouse,
In general, 40, 42, 58, 61–64.
Who is unfaithful to intestate spouse, 148 et seq.

**DESCENT AND DISTRIBUTION**—Continued
Inheritance, by—Continued
Uncles, 39, 40, 48, 57, 62, 70, 73.
Widow, 40, 42, 58, 61–62.
Widower, 40, 42, 58, 61–62.
Inheritance, from,
Adopted children, 59, 87, 90–91.
Aliens, 53–54, 93–95.
Bastards, 50, 59, 81–85.
Convicts, 54–55, 95–96.
Felons, 54–55, 95–96.
Illegitimates, 50, 59, 81–85.
Per capita, 42–43, 65, 67, 71–72.
Per stirpes, 42–43, 65, 67, 71–72.
Primogeniture, 11, 13, 22, 24, 25, 33, 38–40, 60, 64.
Representation of predeceased parent, 42–44, 47–48, 65, 69–72.
Sex, preference of male, see Primogeniture, above.
Shifting estates, 53, 76.
Worthier title, 781.
See Administration; Advancements; Children; Curtesy; Decree of Distribution; Dower; Escheat; Expectancy; History of Intestacy; Renunciation; Revocation of Wills.

**DESCRIPTION,**
See Construction; Incorporation by Reference; Mistake.

**DE SON TORT**, 570–572.
See Actions.

**DEVASTAVIT,**
See Assets; Personal Representatives.

**DEVISES,**
Abatement of, 759–763, 827–828.
Ademption of, 433–436, 743 et seq., 827–828.
After-acquired property, 2, 18, 21–22, 433–434, 470.
Charitable, see Charitable and Religious Devises and Bequests.
Classes of, 736–737.
Defined, 4.
Exoneration of lien claims, 706–709, 764–766.
From what assets, 765–766.
Forfeiture for breach of testamentary conditions, see Conditions.
Lapse of, see Lapse.
Religious, see Charitable and Religious Devises and Bequests.
Renunciation of, see Renunciation.
Revocation by alienation, 433–436, 743.
Revoked, passing under residuary clause, 445.
Rights to, under unprobated will, 504, 505.
Satisfaction of, 741.
By property settlement, 432.
Subject to charge to pay legacies, 762–763.
Void, as passing under residuary clause, 777, 786.
See also, Administration; Construction; Decree of Distribution; Evidence; Legacies; Retainer; Unworthy Heirs; Wills.

**DISCHARGE,**
See Assets; Decree of Distribution; Personal Representatives.

**DISCOVERY, 645–646.**
See Assets.

**DISINHERITANCE,**
Adopted children, 91, 92.
"Cutting off with shilling," 140.
Disfavored in construction of wills, 814.
Express word of, 143.
Showing mental incapacity or undue influence, 139, 140, 232, 255, 538, 539.
See Children; Curtesy; Dower; Family Allowances; Forced Heirs; Homestead; Revocation of Wills.

**DISTRIBUTEES,**
Defined, 4.
See also, Actions; Decree of Distribution; Descent and Distribution.

**DISTRIBUTION,**
See Administration; Ancillary Administration; Decree of Distribution; Descent and Distribution.

**DIVIDENDS,**
See Legacies.

**DIVORCE,**
See Conditions; Dower; Revocation of Wills; Unworthy Heirs.

**DOMICILE,**
See Administration; Administrators; Ancillary Administrators; Conflict of Laws; Executors; Probate of Wills.

**DOMICILIARY ADMINISTRATION,**
See Administration; Ancillary Administration; Probate of Wills.

**DOWER,**
Abolished in England, 58, 107.
Barred by divorce, 149.
Barred by elopement and living in adultery, 148 et seq.
Barred by jointure or settlement, 105, 110.
Election between will and dower, 118 et seq.
English common law, 40, 61–62, 104–105, 107.
Extent of interest, 104–105, 107.
Fraud on, 112–113, 204.
Liability for debts, 105.
Quarantine of dower, 128–129.
Statutory substitutes for, 62, 107 et seq.
See Curtesy; Descent and Distribution; Election; Legacies.

**DRUNKENNESS,**
See Administrators; Executors; Testamentary Capacity.

**DUPLICATE WILLS,**
See Revocation of Wills; Wills.

# E

**ECCLESIASTICAL COURTS,**
Jurisdiction of,
Abolished in England, 22, 483.
None in America, 23, 483.
To administer decedent's property, 15–19, 21, 22.
To appoint special administrators, 578.
To grant letters of administration, 594.
To probate lost wills, 506.
To probate wills, 482.
To require accounting, 792.
Rules of,
Computation of next of kin, 45–47, 69.
Interest on legacies, 751.
Revival by revocation of revoking will, 474–475.

**ECONOMIC BASES OF SUCCESSION,** 30–36.

**EDUCATION,**
See Administrators; Advancements; Executors; Legacies; Testamentary Capacity.

**ELECTION,**
Acceleration of remainder when life interest renounced, 124–126.
Between grounds of contest, 254, 533.
Between will and statutory allowances, 131–132.
By,
Attesting witness releasing interest, 318.
Beneficiary of insurance bequeathed to another, 769.
Beneficiary whose property is devised to another, 768–769.
Creditor who is also legatee, 769–770.
Infants and incompetents, 773.
Personal representative to complete decedent's contracts, 658–659.
Surviving spouse, 118–126.
Consequences of, 124–126, 767–770, 773–774.
Renounced interest, what becomes of, 122–126, 773–774.
Revocation of, 121–122, 773.
Testamentary provisions for, 118–119, 767, 769–770.
Time of, 120–122, 772.
What constitutes, 121, 526–527, 771–772.

**ELOPEMENT,**
See Unworthy Heirs.

**END OF WILL,** 303–307, 381–382.
See Execution of Wills; Integration of Wills.

**ENTIRETIES, ESTATE BY,** 165.

**EQUITABLE INTERESTS,**
See Assets.

**EQUITY,**
See Administration; Claims; Construction; Contracts; Probate of Wills; Trusts.

ESCHEAT,
For,
Alienage, 53–54, 93–95.
Felony, 54–55, 95–96.
Want of heirs, 33–34, 56, 59, 97–99, 523, 581.
Forfeiture distinguished, 54, 55.
Office found, 94, 98–99.
Proceedings in, 55, 94, 98–99.

ESCROW,
See Deeds.

ESTATE,
Entireties, 165.
Joint, 103, 164–166, 565, 637–638.
Life, 103, 823.
Not an entity, 576, 649, 651.
Tail, 103–104.

ESTATE TAX,
Apportionment, 681, 741n, 822.
Economics of, 31–32, 820–822.
Federal, 681, 820–832.
Joint interests, 165–166, 171–172, 681.
Life insurance, 161, 181–182, 681.
Living trusts, 181–182, 681, 821.
Marital deduction, 821.
Power of appointment, 681, 821–822.
Renunciation, effect, 775n.
Who must bear, 181–182, 741n, 822.
See Gift Tax; Inheritance Tax; Taxes.

ESTOPPEL,
See Administrators; Contest of Wills; Executors; Expectancy; Unworthy Heirs.

EVIDENCE,
As to,
Advancements, 719–721.
Conditional character of will, 416, 418.
Execution, 346–348, 352–353, 509, 536.
Incorporation by reference, 390–391.
Integration of will, 381.
Intent as to satisfaction, 737–738.
Intent of testator, 283, 286–289, 808 et seq.
Legitimacy, 85.
Lost wills, 449–450, 509–512.
Mental capacity, 139–140, 232 et seq., 351–352, 536–538.
Mistake in description, 281–288.
Revival, 475–477.
Revocation, 429, 441–442, 445, 459, 539–540.
Sham character of will, 205–207.
Testamentary character, 185, 351–352.
Undue influence, 139–140, 538–539.

**EVIDENCE**—Continued
Burden of proof,
Burden of going forward,
As to,
Execution, 544.
Mental capacity, 548.
Performance or breach of conditions, 410–411.
Revocation, 552.
Undue influence, 553.
Distinguished from risk of non-persuasion, 541–543.
Meaning of, 541–543.
Risk of non-persuasion.
As to,
Execution, 543.
Lost wills, 450, 508 et seq.
Mental capacity, 545–547.
Revocation, 450, 552–555.
Undue influence, 548–550.
Distinguished from burden of going forward, 541–543.
Character of will,
As to mental capacity, 139–140, 538.
As to undue influence, 139–140, 539.
Conduct of testator, 538.
Declaration of testator, upon issue of,
Intention of testator, 283, 286–289, 810.
Lost wills, 511.
Mental capacity, 538.
Mistake in description, 283, 286–289, 810.
Revival, 466, 476, 478.
Revocation, 441–442, 539–550.
Undue influence, 539.
Declarations of intestate as to advancements, 719, 721.
Facts surrounding testator, 810.
Guardianship, prior or subsequent, 538.
Heredity, 538.
Opinion as to mental capacity,
Experts, 537.
Laymen, 536–537.
Oral evidence of advancements, 720.
Parol evidence rule,
Conditional character of will, 416.
Interpretation of wills, 808, 810.
Mistake, 275–276, 287–288.
Revival, 466, 476, 478.
Revocation, 429, 454, 459.
Sham character of will, 206–207.
Specimen wills, 207.
Testamentary character, 185.
Presumptions, as to,
Acceptance of devise or bequest, 774.
Advancements, 719–721.
Against intestacy, 814.
Appraisal's correctness, 634.

**EVIDENCE—Continued**
Presumptions, as to—Continued
Execution,
Because of attestation clause, 347–348, 536, 544.
Upon proof of deceased attesters' signatures, 544.
Inventory's correctness, 633.
Knowledge of contents, 252, 274–277.
Revocation,
By lost wills, 450.
Duplicate wills, 443.
When will is defaced, 442, 443, 554–555.
When will is not found, 442, 443, 553, 554.
Sale of realty by personal representative, 676.
Sanity, 547.
Satisfaction of legacies, 737–738.
Undue influence when beneficiary drafts will, 261–262, 550–552, 818.
Remote, 537–538, 540.
Witnesses,
Attesters as, 350–352, 496, 509, 536.
Competency of, 309 et seq., 535.
Expert, 537.
Impeachment of attesters, 348, 535.
Privilege of, 535.
See Construction.

**EXECUTION OF WILLS,**
Alterations in will, 307, 349, 444–445, 499.
Attestation, 321 et seq.
Attestation clause, 346–348, 352–353.
Dating, 293–294, 820.
Delivery of will, 293.
Infirm testator, 252.
Interlineations, 307, 349, 499.
Language of will, 296–297, 498.
Moving picture wills, 296.
On Sunday, 294.
Order of signing, testator and witnesses, 337–339.
Phonographic wills, 296.
Practical hints regarding, 348–354.
Presence of testator, 339–344.
Publication of will, 327–330.
Request to witnesses, 325–326.
Sealing, 293, 298.
Signature of testator,
Acknowledgment of, to witnesses, 322 et seq.
After witnesses sign, 337–338.
At end, 303–307, 381–382.
By another, 299–301.
By mark, 298.
Incomplete, 299.
In presence of witnesses, 322 et seq.
Intention to sign, 299, 301, 302.
Place of, 301–307.

EXECUTION OF WILLS—Continued
Signature of testator—Continued
Seen by witnesses, 324.
What constitutes, 297–299
Statutes governing, 291, 292.
Witnesses,
Age of, 320.
Animus attestandi, 331–333.
Attestation by, 331–332.
Choice of, 351–352.
Competency of, 309 et seq.
Losing devises and bequests, 309, 315–317.
Mutual presence of, 344–345.
Number of, 308–309, 350–351.
Release of interest, 318.
Request of testator to,
Necessity of, 325.
Sufficiency of, 326.
Signature of,
Acknowledgment of, 344.
Before testator signs, 337–338.
By mark or proxy, 334.
In presence of each other, 344–345.
In presence of testator, 339 et seq.
When testator is blind, 344.
Necessity of, 333.
Place of, 335–336.
What constitutes, 333.
Supernumerary, 308–309, 319, 350–351.
Who may be,
Attorney drafting will, 320, 352, 377.
Convicts, 320, 377.
Creditors, 309, 315.
Devisees and legatees, 312 et seq., 377.
Executors and trustees, 314, 315.
Heirs of beneficiaries, 319.
Heirs of testator, 315, 377.
Minor, 320, 377.
Person writing testator's name, 320, 334.
Probate judge, 320.
Spouse of beneficiary, 317–319.
Spouse of testator, 318.
Writing, 294–296, 367, 372.
For execution of special types of wills, see Holographic Wills; Mystic Wills; Nuncupative Wills; Soldiers' and Sailors' Wills.
See also, Contest of Wills; Evidence; Probate of Wills; Revival of Wills; Wills.

EXECUTORS,
Acceptance of office, 616.
As attesting witnesses, 314, 315, 351.
As draftsmen of wills, 261–262, 550, 818n.
Assent to legacies, 503, 796–797.

**EXECUTORS**—Continued
Bond of, 621–623, 833.
Choice of, 832.
Construction of will by, 806.
Defined, 5, 576–577.
Designation by will, 5, 576, 602–603.
After testator's signature, 306.
De son tort, 570–572.
Duties of, see Personal Representatives.
Duty to present will for probate, 491–492.
Fees of, 656.
Independent executors, 564, 578, 833.
Joint, 582–584, 832.
Jurisdiction to appoint, see Administration.
Payment of debts to, when letters later revoked, 502–503.
Powers of, see Personal Representatives.
Powers of, designated in will, 602, 662–663, 668–670, 833–834.
Proceedings for appointment of, 618 et seq.
Qualifications for office of, 604–605.
Removal of, 624–628.
Renunciation of office, 616–617.
Resignation of, 628.
Revocation of letters, 624–625.
Right to contest wills, 522–523.
Sales by, see Sales by Personal Representatives.
Source of authority of, 604.
See also, Accounting; Actions; Administration; Administrators; Assets; Claims; Personal Representatives.

**EXEMPTION,**
See Claims; Family Allowances; Homestead.

**EXONERATION,**
From what assets, 765–766.
Intestate land, 706–709, 764, 765.
Land devised, 706–709, 764, 765.
Personalty, 766.
See Claims.

**EXPECTANCY,**
Release of,
By separation agreement, 110–112.
Requirements for,
Consideration, 726.
Writing, 726.
Theory of, 527, 726–727.
Validity of, 725.
Who are bound by, 728.
Transfer of,
Effect of, 730.
Form of, 729–730.
Requirements for,
Consent of source, 729.
Consideration, 729.

**EXPECTANCY**—Continued
Transfer of—Continued
Validity of, 729.
Who are bound by, 730.
See Advancements; Legacies.

# F

**FAMILY,**
See Children; Claims; Descent and Distribution; Disinheritance; Family Allowances; Forced Heirs; Homestead.

**FAMILY ALLOWANCES,**
Amount of, 133–134.
Barred by separation, 152–153.
Election in case of will, 131–132.
Exempt chattels, 132–133, 569, 574.
History and philosophy of, 35–36, 126–128.
Persons entitled to, 129–131, 152–153.
Priority, 132, 708–709.
Property subject to, 132–133.
See Children; Disinheritance; Homestead.

**FAMILY SETTLEMENT,**
Avoiding administration, 566.
Settling will contest, 528–530.

**FEDERAL COURTS,** 515, 594–595.

**FEES,**
See Administration; Contest of Wills; Personal Representatives.

**FELONS,**
See Descent and Distribution; Escheat; Execution of Wills; Testamentary Capacity.

**FINAL SETTLEMENTS,** 792–796.

**FIXTURES,**
See Assets.

**FORCED HEIRS,**
Defeated by living trust, 177–183.
Freedom of testation, 9, 14, 15–16, 19, 22, 34–36, 232.
In law of,
America, 138 et seq.
Anglo-Saxons, 12.
England, 14, 15–16, 19, 22, 138–140.
Rome, 9.
See also, Children; Construction; Curtesy; Disinheritance; Dower; Family Allowances; Homestead; Legacies; Revocation of Wills.

**FOREIGN ADMINISTRATORS,**
See Actions; Ancillary Administration.

**FOREIGN WILLS,** 383–384, 487–489, 807.
See also, Conflict of Laws; Probate of Wills.

**FORFEITURE,**
See Conditions; Election; Escheat; Renunciation; Unworthy Heirs.

**FORM,**
See Execution of Wills; Revocation of Wills; Testamentary Character; Wills.

**FRAUD,**
As causing the devise or bequest, 267–269.
As to bigamous marriage of beneficiary to testator, 267–269.
Distinguished from innocent misrepresentation and mistake, 254, 264, 266.
Intention of perpetrator, 267.
In the execution, 264–265.
In the inducement, 265–269.
In the revocation, 421–422.
Materiality of, 266.
Of witnesses in execution, 332.
On dower, 112–117.
Partial invalidity for, 289.
Relief for,
Constructive trust, 270–272, 421–423, 504.
Damage action, 271, 504.
Denial of probate, 270, 504.
See Accounting; Actions; Assets; Decree of Distribution; Evidence; Probate of Wills; Sales by Personal Representatives.

**FRAUDULENT CONVEYANCES,**
Fraud upon creditors,
In creating survivorship interest, 171.
In creating trust, 182.
Who may sue to set aside, 639.
Fraud upon deceased, who may sue for, 640, 657.
Fraud upon spouse, 112–117.

**FREEDOM OF TESTATION,**
See Children; Disinheritance; Forced Heirs.

**FUNERAL EXPENSES,**
See Administration; Claims; Personal Representatives.

**FUTURE INTERESTS,**
Acceleration of remainder after election, 124–126.
Creation of in wills, 823–824, 825–826.
Passing by succession, 102.

# G

**GENERAL DEVISES AND LEGACIES,**
See Devises; Legacies.

**GIFTS CAUSA MORTIS,**
Among Anglo-Saxons, 12.
As assets, 204, 639–640.
As substitute for will—testamentary character, 200–205.
Delivery, 202–203.
Last illness, 200–201.
Liability for donor's debts, 204, 639–640.
No writing required, 205.
Of chose in action, 203.

**GIFTS CAUSA MORTIS—Continued**
Of land, 12, 13–14, 201.
Property subject to, 201, 203, 205.
Revocability, 201, 204.

**GIFTS INTER VIVOS,**
As substitute for wills, 7, 8, 12–14, 199–200.
Creating survivorship interest, 167.
Death-bed, 201.
Not revocable, 199–200.
See Substitutes for Wills; Testamentary Character; Trusts.

**GIFT TAX,** 31, 199, 681, 682, 775n, 821.

**GRANDCHILDREN,**
See Advancements; Construction; Descent and Distribution; Expectancy.

**GRANDPARENTS,**
See Advancements; Descent and Distribution; Expectancy.

**GRAVESTONE,** 652, 654.
See Claims; Conditions; Personal Representatives.

**GUARDIAN,** 495, 608–609, 826–827, 832.
See Administrators; Evidence; Testamentary Capacity.

# H

**HALF-BLOOD,** 39, 50–52, 58, 74, 78–79.

**HEARING,**
See Accounting; Administration; Administrators; Claims; Decree of Distribution; Probate of Wills.

**HEIRS,**
Defined, 4.
See also, Actions; Administration; Advancements; Children; Construction; Contest of Wills; Descent and Distribution; Disinheritance; Escheat; Execution of Wills; Expectancy; Forced Heirs; Probate of Wills; Refunding; Renunciation; Retainer; Unworthy Heirs.

**HISTORY OF INTESTACY,**
American, 24, 60–61.
English,
Personalty, 16–17, 19, 22, 41–42, 606.
Realty, 13–14, 37–41.
See Descent and Distribution; Ecclesiastical Courts.

**HISTORY OF WILLS,**
Ancient world, in, 6–10.
Anglo-Saxon, 11–12.
Assyrian, 7.
Egyptian, 7.
English, 11–16, 18–20, 21–22, 309, 363, 368, 420, 481, 482.
Greek, 8.
Jewish, 7, 8.
Roman, 8–10, 368.

**HISTORY OF WILLS**—Continued
Teutonic, 11,
See particular topics.

**HOLOGRAPHIC WILLS,**
Alteration in, by testator, 447.
Capacity of testator, 356.
Execution,
Dating, necessity and sufficiency of, 359–360.
Entirely in testator's hand, 357–359.
Printed portion, effect of, 357–359.
Signature,
Place of, 360–361.
What constitutes, 362.
Integration of, 382–383.
Invalidly attested will good as, 359, 378.
Jurisdictions allowing, 27, 356.
Letters as, 207–209, 356, 362.
Place of deposit, 362.
Revocation of ordinary will by, 447.

**HOMESTEAD,**
As protection for family, 35, 127–128.
Not liable for debts, 127–128.
Who entitled to, 126–128, 152.

**HOMICIDE,**
See Claims; Unworthy Heirs.

**HUSBAND AND WIFE,**
See Administrators; Conditions; Contest of Wills; Curtesy; Descent and Distribution; Dower; Entireties; Execution of Wills; Family Allowances; Fraud; Legacies; Revocation of Wills; Testamentary Capacity; Undue Influence; Unworthy Heirs.

# I

**IDIOTS,**
See Administrators; Executors; Testamentary Capacity.

**ILLEGITIMATES,** 40, 59, 81–85, 429.
See Children; Evidence; Legacies; Revocation of Wills.

**ILLICIT RELATIONS,**
See Administrators; Conditions; Legacies; Undue Influence.

**ILLITERACY,**
See Administrators; Executors; Mistake; Testamentary Capacity.

**INCOME,**
See Assets; Interest; Legacies.

**INCOME TAX,** 680, 681, 821.

**INCONSISTENCY,**
See Construction; Mistake; Revocation of Wills.

**INCORPORATION BY REFERENCE,**
Distinguished from integration, 385.
Distinguished from reference to non-testamentary acts, 396.

**INCORPORATION BY REFERENCE—Continued**
Essentials of,
Identification of writing, 387–388, 835.
Intention to incorporate, 389–390.
Reference to writing as existing at time of execution, 388–389, 835.
Probate of document incorporated, 385, 498–499.
Proofs required,
Existence of writing, 390–391.
Identity of writing, 391.
What may be incorporated, 392–394.
Whether allowed, 385–386, 835.
See Integration; Reference to Nontestamentary Acts; Revival of Wills.

**INCREASE, 749–751.**

**INDIANS,**
See Testamentary Capacity.

**INFANTS,**
See Administrators; Children; Election; Execution of Wills; Executors; Legacies; Personal Representatives; Revocation of Wills; Soldiers' and Sailors' Wills; Testamentary Capacity.

**INHERITANCE,**
See Descent and Distribution; Disinheritance.

**INHERITANCE TAX,**
Attempts to reduce or avoid, by,
Adoption, 88.
Joint bank accounts, 171–172.
Joint estates, 165–166.
Joint safe deposit box, 161.
Life insurance, 161.
Renunciation of devise or bequest, 775–776.
Payment by personal representative, 681–682.
Validity of, 31, 32.
Who must bear, 681, 741n, 822.
Special provision in will, 822.
See Estate Tax; Gift Tax; Taxes.

**INSANITY,**
See Administrators; Contest of Wills; Election; Evidence; Executors; Legacies; Revocation of Wills; Testamentary Capacity.

**INSOLVENT ESTATES,**
Appointment of administrator for, 610.
Family allowances in, 132–134.
Fraudulent transfers as assets, 639–640.
Funeral expenses in, 710.
Gifts causa mortis as assets, 204, 639–640.
Priorities in, see Claims.
Procedure, 714–715.
Secured claims, right to share in general assets, 712–713.
See also, Refunding.

INSURANCE,
See Administration; Advancements; Election; Estate Tax; Legacies; Personal Representatives; Testamentary Character; Unworthy Heirs.

INTEGRATION OF WILLS,
Connection between pages, 350, 381.
Identification of pages, 350.
Of holographic wills, 382.
Presence of all pages at execution, 380–381.
Several pages permissible, 380.
Where will must be signed at end, 381–382.
See Duplicate Wills; Incorporation by Reference; Partial Wills.

INTENTION,
See Advancements; Construction; Evidence; Execution of Wills; Expectancy; Incorporation by Reference; Integration of Wills; Legacies; Revival of Wills; Revocation of Wills; Testamentary Character.

INTEREST, 749–753.
See Advancements; Legacies; Personal Representatives.

INTERLINEATIONS,
See Evidence; Execution of Wills; Probate of Wills; Wills.

INTERPRETATION,
See Construction.

INTER VIVOS,
See Gifts Inter Vivos; Substitutes for Wills; Trusts.

INTESTACY,
Adjudication of, 503, 601.
After-acquired realty, 433–436, 785.
Defined, 4.
Frequency of, 16, 159–160.
Partial,
Advancements, 724.
Forced share of spouse, 122–123.
Presumption against, 814.
See Administration; Descent and Distribution; Revocation of Wills.

INVENTORY,
As basis for accounting, 630, 633, 794.
Effect of including property in, 633.
Necessity of, 629–630.
Ordering property to be included in, 631–632.
Time of filing, 630–631.
What should be included in,
Personalty, 631–632.
Realty, 24, 633.
See Appraisal; Assets.

INVESTMENTS, 677–680, 833.
See Personal Representatives.

ISSUE,
See Conditions; Construction; Descent and Distribution.

## J

**JOINT ADMINISTRATORS AND EXECUTORS,**
See Administrators; Executors.

**JOINT AND MUTUAL WILLS,**
Contract not to revoke,
Effect of agreement, 224–226, 418–419, 498.
Proof of agreement, 225–226.
Remedy in case of breach, 224–226, 419.
Joint wills,
Defined, 222.
Probate of, 223, 224.
Validity of, 223.
Mutual wills,
Defined, 223.
Probate of, 224.
Probate of, 223–224.
Reciprocal will, 222, 223.
Revocability of, 224–226.

**JOINT ESTATES,**
See Estate; Substitutes for Wills.

**JUDGE,**
See Execution of Wills; Probate Courts.

**JUDGMENT,**
See Actions; Claims; Conflict of Laws; Decree of Distribution; Probate of Wills.

**JURISDICTION,**
See Accounting; Actions; Administration; Ancillary Administration; Claims; Conflict of Laws; Construction; Decree of Distribution; Mistake; Probate Courts; Probate of Wills; Sales by Personal Representatives.

**JURY,**
Instructions to, regarding,
Causation by fraud, 269.
Mental capacity, 232–234.
Undue influence, 255–256.
Right to,
Adjudications regarding claims, 705.
Will contests, 269, 533–534.
Sympathetic verdicts in will contests, 35, 139–140.
See Evidence.

## L

**LAND,**
See Administration; Advancements; After-Acquired Property; Assets; Claims; Decree of Distribution; Descent and Distribution; Devises; Exoneration; History of Wills; Probate of Wills; Retainer; Revocation of Wills; Sales by Personal Representatives.

LANGUAGE,
See Construction; Execution of Wills; Probate of Wills; Revocation of Wills.

LAPSE,
Causes of,
Death of beneficiary, 777.
Invalidity of devise or bequest, 777, 786.
Nonfulfillment of conditions, 777.
Renunciation, 774, 776, 777.
Class gifts, 778, 782–783.
Effect of, 783–785.
Residuary gifts, 784–785.
Statutes preventing, 143, 779–783.
Application to class gifts, 782–783.
Contrary provisions in will, 780–781.
Legacies to persons dead at execution of will, 781.
Legacies to what persons are saved, 779, 780.
Retainer for debts of original legatee, 783, 790–791.
Who gets legacy which would otherwise lapse, 87, 779.
Testamentary provisions regarding, 778–779, 780–781, 828–829.

LAST ILLNESS,
See Claims; Gifts Causa Mortis; Nuncupative Wills; Testamentary Capacity; Wills.

LEASES,
As assets, 636–637.
As substitute for will, 194.
Effect upon devised lands, 435.
Unexpired, performance by personal representative, 661, 702.

LEGACIES,
Abatement of,
Affected by charge on realty, 759–763.
By pretermitted child, 754n.
Order of,
Between legacies and devises, 759–761.
Fixed by will, 735, 755, 828.
In general, 754 et seq.
Legacies for support, 757.
Legacies for value, 757–759.
When necessary, 754.
Accretions to, 749–751.
Ademption of,
Application of doctrine to,
Demonstrative legacies, 735, 746.
General legacies, 742, 827.
Property taken without testator's consent, 742.
Specific legacies, 742–744, 827.
Testator insane at time, 743.
Distinguished from,
Revocation, 433, 743.
Satisfaction of legacies, 432, 740, 743.

**LEGACIES**—Continued
Ademption of—Continued
How accomplished,
Changes in location, 748.
Changes of form, 747–748.
Destruction, 745.
Sale or transfer by testator, 743–745.
Intention of testator as to, 742–743, 746.
Pro tanto, 745.
Annuities, 752, 767.
Assent to, 503, 792.
Charges of, upon realty, 759–763.
Charitable, see Charitable and Religious Devises and Bequests.
Classes of,
Demonstrative, 734–735.
General, 733.
Residuary, 736.
Specific, 732–733.
Cumulative, 771.
Defined, 4.
Dividends on bequeathed stock, 749–750, 830.
Exoneration of lien on bequeathed personalty, 766.
Forfeiture for breach of conditions, see Conditions.
Forgiving debts of legatee, 831.
Increase after testator's death, 750–751.
In satisfaction of debts due to legatee, 757, 769–770, 831.
Insurance on destroyed legacy, 745.
Interest upon,
Rate of interest, 753.
Time interest commences, 751–753.
What legacies bear interest, 751.
Who must bear, 753.
Lapse of, see Lapse.
Payment of, see Decree of Distribution.
Refunding of,
At suit of creditors, 801–802.
At suit of personal representative, 800–801.
Extent of liability, 802–803.
Religious, see Charitable and Religious Devises and Bequests.
Renunciation of, see Renunciation.
Revoked, passing under residuary clause, 445.
Right to, under unprobated will, 503.
Satisfaction of (ademption by satisfaction),
By property of different nature, 740.
By property settlement, 432.
Distinguished from,
Ademption by extinction, 434–436, 740.
Gift, 739.
General legacies, 737.
Intention,
Ejusdem generis, 740.
Presumptions as to, 737–739.

**LEGACIES**—Continued
Satisfaction of (ademption by satisfaction)—Continued
Intention—Continued
Testator's or legatee's, 738, 739, 740.
Time of, 738.
Partial satisfaction, 739.
Residuary legacies, 740.
Specific legacies, 740.
Substitutional, 771.
To,
Attesting witnesses, 309–313.
Draftsman of will, 261–262, 550–552, 818.
Illegitimate children, 135.
Minors, 826–827.
Mistresses, 135.
Murderer of testator, see Unworthy Heirs.
Void, as passing under residuary clause, 777, 786.
See also, Construction; Decree of Distribution; Devises; Evidence; Retainer; Revocation of Wills; Unworthy Heirs; Wills.

**LEGITIME,**
Among Anglo-Saxons, 11, 12.
In America, 35, 138–139.
In England, 15, 16, 19, 35, 59.
In Rome, 9, 10.
See Children; Disinheritance; Forced Heirs.

**LETTERS,**
See Administrators; Executors; Substitutes for Wills.

**LIBELOUS MATTER,**
See Probate of Wills.

**LIENS,**
See Claims; Conditions; Exoneration; Retainer.

**LIFE ESTATE,**
See Construction; Estate.

**LIFE INSURANCE,**
See Advancements; Assets; Election; Estate Tax; Testamentary Character; Unworthy Heirs.

**LIMITATIONS,**
See Administration; Claims; Conditions; Contracts; Probate of Wills; Retainer.

**LIVING TRUSTS,**
See Trusts.

**LOST WILLS,**
See Evidence; Probate of Wills; Revocation of Wills.

**LOUISIANA,**
Civil law, 35.
Legitime, 35, 139.
Mystic wills, 377–378.
Nuncupative wills, 376, 378.
Universal succession, 562–563.

**LUCID INTERVAL,**
See Testamentary Capacity.

# M

**MANAGEMENT,**
See Personal Representatives.

**MARINERS' WILLS,**
See Soldiers' and Sailors' Wills.

**MARRIAGE,**
See Administrators; Conditions; Curtesy; Descent and Distribution; Dower; Entireties; Execution of Wills; Family Allowances; Fraud; Legacies; Revocation of Wills; Testamentary Capacity; Undue Influence; Unworthy Heirs.

**MENTAL CAPACITY,** 232–248.
See Administrators; Executors; Revocation of Wills; Testamentary Capacity.

**MINORS,**
See Administrators; Children; Election; Execution of Wills; Executors; Legacies; Personal Representatives; Revocation of Wills; Soldiers' and Sailors' Wills; Testamentary Capacity.

**MISCONDUCT,** 147–158, 624–628.

**MISDESCRIPTION,**
See Construction; Mistake.

**MISREPRESENTATION,**
See Fraud; Mistake; Undue Influence.

**MISTAKE,**
As to,
Death of alleged decedent, 598–600.
Death of beneficiary, 453, 460, 781.
Disposition of assets by personal representative, 648.
Document mutilated for purpose of revocation, 441.
Effect of intestate laws, 453.
Validity of will, 456–457.
In revocation, see Dependent Relative Revocation.
In wills,
Ambiguities in description, 281–288, 830.
Courts where question is litigated, 274–275, 281 et seq.
Disregarding erroneous words, 283.
Distinguished from fraud and innocent misrepresentation, 254, 264.
Guarding against, 252, 830.
Ignorance of contents, 252.
Kinds of mistake, 273 et seq.
Partial invalidity for, 289.
Relief for mistake in,
Contents, 252, 274–277.
Description, 281 et seq., 812.
Document signed, 273–274.
Inducement, 277 et seq.

**MISTAKE**—Continued
In wills—Continued
Relief for mistake in—Continued
Legal effect, 277.
Revocation, see Dependent Relative Revocation.
Unusual personal word usage, 286, 811–812.
Wrong signature,
Of attesters, 333.
Of testator, 297.
See also, Construction; Dependent Relative Revocation; Evidence.

**MISTRESSES,**
See Conditions; Legacies; Undue Influence; Unworthy Heirs.

**MONEY,**
See Administration; Assets; Substitutes for Wills.

**MORAL DELINQUENCY,**
See Administrators; Conditions; Executors; Testamentary Capacity.

**MORTGAGES,**
See Ademption; Assets; Claims; Exoneration; Sales by Personal Representatives.

**MORTMAIN,**
See Charitable and Religious Devises.

**MURDER OF ANCESTOR,** 153–156.

**MUTILATION,**
See Revocation of Wills.

**MUTUAL PRESENCE OF WITNESSES,**
See Execution of Wills.

**MUTUAL WILLS,**
See Joint and Mutual Wills.

**MYSTIC WILLS,**
In Louisiana, 377.
See also, Civil Law; History of Wills.

# N

**NEGLIGENCE,**
See Assets; Claims; Personal Representatives.

**NEXT OF KIN,** 4, 16, 19, 44–49, 68–72.
See Administrators; Executors.

**NOMINATION,**
See Administrators; Executors.

**NONCLAIM,** 689 et seq.
See Administration; Claims; Refunding.

**NONRESIDENTS,**
See Administration; Administrators; Ancillary Administration; Probate of Wills.

**NONTESTAMENTARY ACT,**
See Reference to Nontestamentary Act.

**NOTICE,**
See Administrators; Claims; Contest of Wills; Decree of Distribution; Mutual Wills; Probate of Wills; Sales by Personal Representatives.

**NUNCUPATIVE WILLS,**
Execution of,
In last sickness, 364.
Place of making, 364.
Publication, 364–365.
Rogatio testium, 364–365.
Witnesses, 366.
Writing,
Reduction to, 367.
Requirement of, 363.
Louisiana, in, 376, 378.
Probate of, 367.
Property which may pass under,
Amount, 366.
Kind, 364.
Revocation of ordinary wills by, 367n, 446.
Statutes relating to, 20, 363–364.
Testamentary intent, 364–365.
See Soldiers' and Sailors' Wills.

## O

**OATH,**
Of personal representative, 620.
Upon sale of realty, 674.

**OLOGRAPHIC WILLS,**
See Holographic Wills.

**OMISSION,**
See Children; Disinheritance; Fraud; Mistake.

**ORAL WILLS,**
See History of Wills; Nuncupative Wills; Soldiers' and Sailors' Wills.

**ORDER,**
See Administrators; Claims; Decree of Distribution; Executors; Personal Representatives; Probate of Wills; Sales by Personal Representatives.

**ORDER OF SIGNING,**
See Execution of Wills.

**ORDINARIES,**
See Ecclesiastical Courts.

**ORPHANS' COURTS,**
See Probate Courts.

## P

**PARENTS,**
See Advancements; Descent and Distribution; Expectancy; Unworthy Heirs.

**PAROL EVIDENCE RULE,**
See Construction; Evidence.

**PARTIAL INVALIDITY,**
See Fraud; Mistake; Probate of Wills; Testamentary Capacity; Undue Influence.

**PARTIAL WILLS,**
Remaining part lost, 512–513.
Separate wills for different jurisdictions, 383–384.
Two or more instruments as single will, 498.

**PARTIES,**
See Accounting; Actions; Administration; Administrators; Claims; Contest of Wills; Decree of Distribution; Probate of Wills; Sales by Personal Representatives; Third Party Beneficiary.

**PARTITION,**
For distribution, 34, 35, 667, 677.
Revocation of devises by, 433–434.
See Legacies.

**PARTNERSHIP,**
Administration of property of, 638.
Agreements as substitute for will, 166, 195.
Assets, 638.
Continuing business of, 662.

**PAYMENT,**
See Administration; Assets; Claims; Conditions; Decree of Distribution; Personal Representatives; Refunding.

**PENDENTE LITE,**
See Administrators; Probate of Wills.

**PER CAPITA,**
Provision in will as to, 828.
See Descent and Distribution.

**PERPETUITIES, RULE AGAINST,** 461, 825–826.

**PERSONAL PROPERTY,**
See Administration; Assets; Decree of Distribution; Descent and Distribution; Exoneration; History of Wills; Legacies; Probate of Wills; Retainer; Sales by Personal Representatives.

**PERSONAL REPRESENTATIVES,**
Actions by and against, see Actions.
As attorney for estate, 655–656.
Bond of, 19, 42, 621–623, 654–655.
    On sale of realty, 674.
Compensation 630, 656, 680, 793, 795.
Continuation of deceased's business,
    By consent of interested parties, 662.
        When heirs are infants, 662.
    By court authority, 661.
    Statutory authority for, 661–662.
    Temporary, 661.

**PERSONAL REPRESENTATIVES—Continued**
- Continuation of deceased's business—Continued
  - Testamentary authority for, 662–663, 834.
  - Unauthorized, 660.
- Contracts of, 650–656.
  - Attorney's services, 652, 655–656.
  - Funeral expenses, 652, 654.
  - Preserving estate, 654, 661.
- Debts of, as assets, 643–644.
- Deposit of funds by, 677–679.
- Duties of, 4, 15, 17, 28, 561–564, 645–649, 657–659, 667, 677–679, 703–708.
- Individual liability of, 649–663, 682.
- Insolvency of, 644, 653–654.
- Investments by, 677–679.
- Joint, 582–584, 832.
- Liability for interest, 679, 753.
- Oath, 620.
- Performance of deceased's contracts, 657–659.
- Powers of, 24, 27–28, 561–564, 645–647, 657, 664, 668 et seq., 678–680, 806, 833–834.
- Preferences of creditors by, 687–689, 714–715.
- Protection of,
  - Allowance of claims, 704, 714–715, 801–802.
  - Court approval, 646, 651, 659, 661–662, 664–665.
  - Decree of distribution, 797.
- Retainer for own debts, 689, 692, 714.
- Retention of decedent's investments, 667, 679.
- Sales by, see Sales by Personal Representatives.
- Taxes,
  - Payment of,
    - Income, 680, 682.
    - Inheritance, 181, 182, 681, 682.
    - Property, 682, 751, 823.
  - Priority of, 710.
  - Right to recover trust property to pay, 181, 182.
- Torts of, 649.
- See also, Accounting; Administration; Administrators; Appraisal; Claims; Contest of Wills; Decree of Distribution; Executors; Inventory; Probate of Wills; Refunding; Retainer.

**PER STIRPES,**
- Provision in will as to, 828.
- See also, Descent and Distribution.

**PETITION,**
- Appointment of personal representative, 618–619.
- Decree of distribution, 798.
- Probate of will, 493–494, 619.
- Sale of realty, 673.

**PHYSICAL DISABILITY,**
- See Administrators; Executors; Testamentary Capacity.

PLACE,
See Administration; Ancillary Administration; Conflict of Laws; Execution of Wills; Nuncupative Wills; Partial Wills; Probate of Wills; Soldiers' and Sailors' Wills.

PLEADING,
See Actions; Claims; Contest of Wills; Probate of Wills.

PLEDGE,
See Sales by Personal Representatives.

PLENE ADMINISTRAVIT, 688.

POSSESSION,
See Administration; Assets; Personal Representatives.

POSTHUMOUS CHILD, 52–53, 75, 76.

POWER OF ALIENATION, 824, 825.

POWER OF APPOINTMENT,
As assets, 640–641.
Grant of, as valid nontestamentary act, 398–399.
Married woman's capacity to execute will exercising, 228–229.
Married woman's capacity to revoke will exercising, 426.
Provisions for, 825.
Taxation, 681, 821–822.

POWER OF SALE,
See Sales by Personal Representatives.

PREFERENCES,
See Claims.

PRESENCE OF TESTATOR,
See Execution of Wills; Revocation of Wills.

PRESENTATION AND ALLOWANCE OF CLAIMS,
See Claims.

PRESUMPTIONS,
See Evidence.

PRETERMITTED CHILDREN, 140–145.
See Children; Revocation of Wills.

PRIMOGENITURE, 11, 13, 22, 24, 25, 33, 38–40, 60, 64.

PRIORITIES,
See Claims.

PRIVATE SALES,
See Sales by Personal Representatives.

PRIVITY,
Between ancillary and domiciliary representatives, 590–591.

PROBATE COURTS,
American,
Early history of, 23–26.
In general, 483–484, 594–595.
English, 481–483, 594.
Judge of, as attesting witness, 320.

**PROBATE COURTS**—Continued
Jurisdiction, over,
Accounting, 792.
Claims against decedent, 689, 704–705, 714–715.
Claims in favor of deceased, 632–633, 646–647.
Construction of wills, 281 et seq., 497–498, 804–805.
Continuation of decedent's business, 662.
Decree of distribution, 757–759.
Determination of title to property, 632–633, 646–647.
Determination of whether will is conditional, 416–417.
Discovery of assets, 632–633, 646–647.
Family allowances, 133–134.
Grant of administration, 594–595.
Probate of wills, 217–218, 224, 481–484.
When will is lost, 506.
Questions of mistake, 273–274, 274–275, 277, 279, 281–282.
Retainer, 791.
Sale of realty, 670, 672.
Settlement of estates, 757–759.
Will contests, 514–515.
See Administration; Appeals; Ecclesiastical Courts; Probate of Wills.

**PROBATE OF WILLS,**
After adjudication of intestacy, 502, 601.
After probate of earlier will, 501–503.
Common form, 482, 484.
Conclusiveness of, 481–483, 499–500.
Conditional wills, 416.
Construction upon, 281, 416, 497, 519, 804–805.
Defined, 5, 479–480.
Destroyed wills, see Revocation of Wills.
Domiciliary, 487–489.
Duplicate wills, 383, 443.
Effect of, 22, 24, 481–483, 499–500.
English practice, 481–483.
Foreign wills, 383–384, 487–489.
Instruments which may be probated,
Conditional wills, 416.
Contracts to make wills, 217–218.
Deeds, 188–189.
Destroyed wills, see Revocation of Wills.
Documents incorporated by reference, 385, 498–499.
Foreign wills, 383–384, 487–489.
Invalid provisions, 497–498.
Joint and mutual wills, 223–224.
Lost wills, 506–511.
Partial wills, 289–291, 383, 512.
Portion above signature, 306–307.
Several instruments constituting single will, 383, 498.
Wills of personalty, 482.
Wills of realty, 481–482.
Wills revoked in violation of agreement, 217–218, 419–420.
Invalidity of provisions, 497–498.

PROBATE OF WILLS—Continued
Joint and mutual wills, 223–224.
Jurisdiction of courts to probate,
In America, 23–29, 483.
In England, 17, 19, 22, 23, 481–482.
Territorial jurisdiction, 383–384.
Language of will—translation, 296, 487–489, 498.
Libelous matter contained in will, 497.
Lost wills, 506–511.
Necessity of, 503–505.
Partial wills, 289, 383, 498, 512.
Prior to testator's death, 484–485.
Procedure,
Hearing, 495–497.
Notice, 494–495, 501.
Petition, 493–494.
Proofs necessary, 496–497.
Who should produce and offer for probate, 491–493.
Revocation of, 500 et seq.
Setting aside, 500–502.
Several instruments constituting single will, 383, 498.
Solemn form, 482, 494, 500.
Territorial jurisdiction, 383, 487–489.
Time limitations, 485–487, 501–503.
Venue, 490.
Who should produce and offer for probate, 491–493.
Wills of personalty, 18, 482, 503.
Wills of realty, 22, 24, 481, 504.
Wills revoked in violation of agreement, 217–218, 419.
See also, Actions; Contest of Wills; Evidence; Lost Wills; Testamentary Character.

PROPERTY,
See Administration; Assets; Descent and Distribution; Probate of Wills.

PUBLIC ADMINISTRATORS,
Office of, 581.
Right to contest wills, 523.
Right to demand administration, 566, 572n.

PUBLICATION,
See Administrators; Claims; Decree of Distribution; Execution of Wills; Probate of Wills; Sales by Personal Representatives.

PUBLIC SALES,
See Sales by Personal Representatives.

Q

QUALIFICATIONS,
See Personal Representatives.

# R

**REAL PROPERTY,**
See Administration; Advancements; After-Acquired Property; Assets; Claims; Decree of Distribution; Descent and Distribution; Devises; Exoneration; History of Wills; Probate of Wills; Retainer; Revocation of Wills; Sales by Personal Representatives.

**RECIPROCAL WILLS,**
See Joint and Mutual Wills.

**RE-EXECUTION,**
See Revival of Wills.

**REFERENCE TO NONTESTAMENTARY ACTS,**
Allowed as to acts having independent significance, 394 et seq.
Contents of room or receptacle, 394–395, 748, 829.
Distinguished from,
Conditions, 399, 401.
Incorporation by reference, 396.
Future acts,
Of beneficiary, 399.
Of testator, 394–397, 417.
Of third person, 398–399.
Of various persons in combination, 400.
Future lists, 396–397.
Past acts, 400.
Power of appointment, grant of, 398–399.
Will of another, 398.
See Conditions; Incorporation by Reference; Testamentary Character.

**REFUNDING, 800–803.**
See Actions; Legacies.

**RELATIONSHIP,**
See Construction; Descent and Distribution.

**RELEASE,**
As substitute for will—testamentary character, 197.
By attesting witness of legacy, 318.
Of expectancy, 112, 527, 725–728.

**RELIGIOUS DEVISES,**
See Charitable and Religious Devises.

**REMAINDERS,**
Passing under will, 102.

**REMEDIES,**
See Actions; Trusts.

**REMOVAL,**
See Administrators; Executors.

**RENTS, 563, 636–637, 702, 711–712, 750–751.**

**RENUNCIATION,**
By legatee-attester who is interested in provisions of will, 318.
By person who is also heir at law, 776.

**RENUNCIATION**—Continued
By separation agreement, 110–112.
Causing lapse, 774, 776, 777.
Effect of, 774, 777.
Of part and acceptance of remainder, 775.
Presumption of acceptance, 774.
Retraction of, 775.
To defeat creditors of legatee or devisee, 776.
To defeat taxes, 776.
See Administrators; Election; Executors.

**REPRESENTATION,**
See Advancements; Descent and Distribution; Expectancy.

**REPUBLICATION OF WILLS,**
See Revival of Wills.

**REQUEST THAT WITNESSES SIGN,**
See Execution of Wills.

**RESIDENCE,**
See Administration; Administrators; Ancillary Administration; Conflict of Laws; Executors; Probate of Wills.

**RESIDUARY CLAUSE,**
See Devises; Lapse; Legacies.

**RESIGNATION,** 628.

**RETAINER,**
By personal representative of his own debt against deceased, 694, 714.
For debts owing deceased by legatee or devisee,
Against whom right may be asserted, 783, 790–791.
Barred debts, 789.
Debt, nature of, 788–789.
Procedure, 787, 791–792.
Property against which retainer is proper,
Realty, 791–792.
Specific personalty, 791.
Testamentary directions, 787–788.

**REVALIDATION OF WILLS,**
See Revival of Wills.

**REVIVAL OF WILLS,**
Conditional wills, after non-happening of event, 418.
Destroyed wills, 468.
Re-execution, 464–465, 478.
Relation to incorporation by reference, 464, 467.
Republication,
By codicil, consequences of, 470–473.
Meanings of, 464.
Revalidation of revoked instrument, 464.
Revocation of revoking will,
American rules, 475 et seq.
Common law rule, 474.
Ecclesiastical court rule, 474–475.
Statutory rules, 477–478.

**REVIVAL OF WILLS**—Continued
Statutes relating to, 464, 477–478.
Validation of invalid instruments, 467.

**REVOCATION OF WILLS,**
Conditional, see Dependent Relative Revocation.
Contrary to agreement, 217–221, 224, 419–420, 449.
Definition of, 419.
Dependent relative revocation, see Dependent Relative Revocation.
Distinguished from ademption, 433–436, 743.
History of, 420.
Intention to revoke, 421, 423, 429, 433, 441–442, 444–445, 448–449, 450–452, 453, 458, 462.
Joint and mutual wills, 224.
Mental capacity for, 420, 432, 441.
Mistaken revocation, see Dependent Relative Revocation.
Operation of law,
Ademption distinguished, 433–436, 743.
Adoption of child, 430.
Alienation of property, 433–436, 743.
Birth of issue, 141, 427–428.
Adoption as, 430.
Illegitimate, 429–430.
Change of circumstances, 432.
Divorce, 431–432.
Marriage,
And birth of issue, 428–429.
Of female testator, 426–427.
Of male testator, 424–425.
Statutory authority for, 420, 422–429, 431–432, 435.
Testator's intention, 421, 423, 429, 433.
Physical act to instrument,
Cancellation, 438–440, 819.
Duplicate wills, 442–443.
Effect of, on other wills and codicils, 443–444.
Fraud of beneficiary as to, 421.
In presence of testator, 440, 449.
Intention to revoke, 441–442, 444–445, 479.
Mistake as to document mutilated, 441.
Mutilation by others, 440, 449.
Partial revocation, 444–445, 457–459.
Ratification of act of another, 440.
Sufficiency of act, 436 et seq., 441, 443.
Power of testator, 2, 183, 210, 217–218, 224, 419, 449.
In case of joint and mutual wills, 224.
Statutory manner of, 420, 422–429, 431–432, 435, 436–437, 446–447.
Subsequent instrument,
Codicil, 448, 451–452.
Formalities required, 439, 446–447.
Holographic will, 447.
Implied revocation, 450–452, 462.
Lost wills, 449–450.
Nuncupative will, 367n, 446.

**REVOCATION OF WILLS**—Continued
Subsequent instrument—Continued
Partial revocation, 452.
Soldiers' wills, 373–374.
When revoking instrument is lost, 449–450.
Words of revocation, 448–449, 819.
Written direction for another to destroy, 448–449.
Undue influence concerning, 420–421, 441.
Wills revoking former wills, see Revival of Wills.
See also, Dependent Relative Revocation; Evidence; Mistake; Probate of Wills; Revival of Wills.
**ROGATIO TESTIUM**, 364–365.

# S

**SAFE-DEPOSIT BOX**,
As devise for avoiding wills and administration, 160–161, 165–166, 565.
**SAILORS' WILLS**,
See Soldiers' and Sailors' Wills.
**SALES BY PERSONAL REPRESENTATIVES**,
Personalty,
Dependent on whether distribution is in kind, 667, 679.
Duty to sell, 667, 677.
Fraud in, 666.
Manner of sale, 666.
Power of sale, 664–665.
Power to pledge or mortgage, 664.
Time of sale, 665.
To self, 666–667.
Realty,
Order of court,
Fraud in, 676.
Interest to be sold, 672.
Jurisdiction of courts, 591, 672.
Necessity of debts, 671.
Procedure, 673–675.
Rights of purchasers, 675–676.
Statutory provisions for, 670 et seq.
Time limitations, 573.
To pay legacies, 671, 763.
Who may apply for, 672–673.
Who may buy, 675.
Testamentary power of sale,
Advisability of granting, 833.
Duty to sell, 668.
Language of will, 668.
Purpose of, 668–669.
Time of sale, 669–670.
Who may exercise, 670.
See Ancillary Administration.
**SATISFACTION**, 737–741.
See Advancements; Devises; Expectancy; Legacies.

**SAVINGS BANK ACCOUNTS,**
See Substitutes for Wills; Trusts.

**SEAL,**
See Claims; Execution of Wills.

**SENILE DEMENTIA,**
See Administrators; Executors; Testamentary Capacity.

**SEPARATE PROPERTY,**
See Community Property; Testamentary Capacity.

**SEPARATION,**
See Revocation of Wills; Unworthy Heirs.

**SET-OFF,**
See Actions; Retainer.

**SETTLEMENTS,**
See Accounting; Administration; Assets; Claims; Contest of Wills; Decree of Distribution; Dower.

**SHAM WILLS,**
Testamentary character of, 205–206.

**SICKNESS,**
See Claims; Testamentary Capacity; Wills.

**SIGNATURE,** 297 et seq., 360–362.
See Execution of Wills.

**SOCIAL BASES OF SUCCESSION,** 30–36.

**SOLDIERS' AND SAILORS' WILLS,**
Form—oral and written, 372–373.
History of, 20, 368.
How long valid, 373–374.
Letters as, 207–210, 373.
Property passing under, 372.
Revocation of ordinary wills by, 373.
When made, 369–371.
Where made, 369–371.
Who may make,
Mariners, 370–371.
Minors, 371.
Soldiers, 369.
See Nuncupative Wills.

**SOURCE OF INTESTATE'S TITLE,**
See Descent and Distribution.

**SPECIMEN WILLS,**
Forms, 819, 823n.
Testamentary character of, 207.

**SPIRITUALISM,**
See Testamentary Capacity; Undue Influence.

**SPOUSE,**
See Administrators; Conditions; Contest of Wills; Curtesy; Descent and Distribution; Dower; Election; Entireties; Estate Tax; Execution of Wills; Family Allowances; Fraud; Legacies; Revocation of Wills; Testamentary Capacity; Undue Influence; Unworthy Heirs.

**STATUTE OF FRAUDS,**
See Contracts; Execution of Wills; History of Wills; Revocation of Wills.

**STATUTE OF LIMITATIONS,**
See Administration; Claims; Contracts; Probate of Wills; Retainer.

**STEPCHILDREN,**
See Descent and Distribution; Lapse.

**STIRPES, PER,**
Provision in will as to, 828.
See, also, Descent and Distribution.

**STOCK,**
See Assets; Legacies; Personal Representatives.

**SUBSTITUTES FOR WILLS,**
Assignments, 197–198.
Bank accounts, 167–171, 173–177.
Bills and notes, 198–199.
Bills of sale, 197.
Checks, 199, 203, 365.
Contracts, 193 et seq.
Deeds,
By conditions expressed in deed, 184–189.
By manipulation of delivery, 189–192.
Gifts causa mortis, 200–205.
Gifts inter vivos, 199–200.
Joint estates, 163–172, 565, 637–638.
Leases, 193.
Letters, 207–208, 356, 373.
Life insurance, 161–162, 565, 638.
Partnership agreements, 166, 195.
Releases, 197.
Safe deposit box in joint names, 160–161, 166–167, 565.
Survivorship interests, 163–172, 565, 637–638.
Trusts,
Bank account, 173–177.
Life insurance, 162–163.
Living, 177–183.
Tentative, 175–177.
War Savings Bonds, 176.
See Administration.

**SUBSTITUTIONAL LEGACIES, 771.**

**SUCCESSION,**
See Administration; Assets; Descent and Distribution.

**SUCCESSION TAX,**
See Estate Tax; Inheritance Tax.

**SUNDAY,**
See Execution of Wills.

**SUPPORT,**
See Family Allowances; Legacies.

**SURCHARGE,**
See Accounting; Personal Representatives.

**SURROGATE COURTS,**
See Probate Courts.

**SURVIVAL, 641–643, 683–686, 828–829.**
See Assets; Claims; Lapse.

**SURVIVORSHIP, 598, 781, 828–829.**
See Assets; Entireties; Substitutes for Wills.

# T

**TAIL,**
See Estate.

**TAXES,**
Income, 680, 681, 821.
Personal liability of personal representative, 681–682, 710.
Priority over other debts, 710.
Property, 682, 710, 751, 833.
Renunciation to avoid, 775n, 776.
Testamentary directions as to, 754n, 823.
See Estate Tax; Gift Tax; Inheritance Tax.

**TEMPORARY ADMINISTRATORS,**
See Administrators.

**TENTATIVE TRUSTS, 173–177.**

**TERMINOLOGY, 1–6.**
See also, Construction.

**TESTAMENT,**
Distinguished from will, 3, 482.
See Probate of Wills.

**TESTAMENTARY CAPACITY,**
Aliens, 229.
Age for,
In general, 229–231.
Old persons, 249–250.
Soldiers' wills, 371.
Blind persons, 252, 344.
Convicts, 95–96, 229.
Deaf and dumb persons, 251.
Holographic wills, 356.
Illiterate persons, 249.
Indians, 229.

**TESTAMENTARY CAPACITY**—Continued
Married women, 228–229, 426.
Mental capacity,
Applied to particular will, 238.
Character of will itself, 232, 538.
Compared with capacity to do other acts, 240, 241.
Drugs, use of, 241.
Eccentricities, 244–245.
Evidence concerning, see Evidence.
Guardianship as affecting, 239, 538.
In general, 232 et seq.
Insane delusions, 242 et seq.
Insanity, ambiguity of term, 239.
Intoxicants, use of, 241.
Lucid intervals, 241.
Medical classifications, 235–236.
Monomania, 242.
Moral delinquency, 249.
Old persons, 233, 249–250.
Partial insanity, 234, 242–243.
Partial invalidity, 243.
Prejudices, 245–246.
Religious beliefs, 248.
Revocation, 420, 432, 441.
Special types of wills, in, 355–356.
Spiritualism, belief in, 246–247.
Test of capacity, 232 et seq.
Time of capacity, 241.
Witchcraft, belief in, 247.
Physical disability, 250–251.
Special types of wills, in, 355–356.
Time of, 231, 241.
See Contest of Wills; Evidence; Probate of Wills.

**TESTAMENTARY CHARACTER,**
Of particular instruments or transactions,
Assignments, 197–198.
Bank accounts,
Joint payable to survivor, 167–171.
Trust, for another, 173–177.
Bills and notes, 198–199, 356n.
Bills of sale, 197.
Checks, 199, 203, 365.
Contracts, 193 et seq.
Contracts to make wills, 210.
Deeds, 184 et seq.
Gifts causa mortis, 200–205.
Gifts inter vivos, 199–200.
Leases, 193.
Letters, 207–208, 356, 362, 373.
Life insurance policies, 161–162.
Partnership agreements, 166, 195.
Release, 197.

TESTAMENTARY CHARACTER—Continued
Of particular instruments or transactions—Continued
Safe deposit boxes in joint names, 160–161, 166–167, 565.
Survivorship interests, 163–172, 565, 637–638.
Trusts,
Bank account, 173–177.
Life insurance, 162–163.
Living, 177–183.
Tentative, 175–177.
See Reference to Nontestamentary Acts; Testamentary Intent.

TESTAMENTARY INTENT,
Holographic wills, 207–210.
Letters, 207–208, 356, 362, 373.
Nuncupative wills, 364–365.
Sham wills, 205–206.
Soldiers' and sailors' wills, 373.
Specimen wills, 207.
See Construction; Reference to Nontestamentary Acts; Testamentary Character.

TESTATOR,
See Administration; Construction; Contest of Wills; Devises; Evidence; Execution of Wills; Executors; Probate of Wills; Revival of Wills; Revocation of Wills; Testamentary Capacity.

THIRD PARTY BENEFICIARY,
Actions to recover bank accounts or bonds, 169–170, 172.
Actions to recover on contract for mutual wills, 223–224.
Actions to recover on contract to make wills, 213.
Actions to recover on insurance policies, 162, 163.

TIME,
See Administration; Advancements; After-Acquired Property; Charitable and Religious Devises; Claims; Construction; Decree of Distribution; Execution of Wills; Inventory; Probate of Wills; Testamentary Capacity; Undue Influence.

TITLE,
See Administration; Assets; Decree of Distribution; Descent and Distribution; Devises; Personal Representatives; Probate of Wills.

TORTS,
See Assets; Claims; Personal Representatives.

TOTTEN TRUSTS, 175–177.

TRANSFER,
See Expectancy.

TRANSFER TAX,
See Estate Tax; Inheritance Tax.

TRUSTS,
As substitutes for wills,
Bank account payable to survivor, 169.
Bank account trusts, 173–177.
Life insurance trusts, 162–163.

TRUSTS—Continued
As substitutes for wills—Continued
Living trusts, 177–183.
Control by settlor, 179–180.
Drafting of, 180–181.
Power of revocation, 178–179.
Tentative trust doctrine, 175–177.
Claims for—necessity of presentation, 706.
Constructive trust, for,
Forgery of will, 504.
Fraud "in effect", 272.
Fraud regarding revocation, 421–422.
Fraud regarding will, 270–271.
Murder of ancester or testator, 154–155.
Murder of joint tenant, 157–158.
Creation of in wills, 824–825, 827.
For continuation of business, 662.
For payment of claims, 706.
Incorporation or reference to living trusts, 388, 392–393, 396.
Priority of trust claims against deceased, 710–711.
Statutory trusts under Administration of Estates Act, 58.
Testamentary, 824–825, 827, 832, 834.
See Actions; Uses.

U

UNCERTAINTY,
See Construction; Mistake.
UNDUE INFLUENCE,
Advice as, 258.
As causing the devise or bequest, 260–261.
As to revocation, 420–421, 441.
Effect of, 255 et seq.
Husband's, 258.
Illicit relations, 258.
Meaning and nature of, 256 et seq.
Partial invalidity for, 289.
Person, exerting, 259.
Presumption in case of wills drawn by beneficiary, 261–262, 550–552, 818.
Relation to mental incapacity, fraud and mistake, 253–254, 263–264.
Spirit voices, 247.
Threats as, 257.
Time of, 260.
Unnatural wills, as showing, 255–256.
Wife's, 258.
See Evidence; Fraud; Probate of Wills; Testamentary Capacity.
UNITED STATES,
See Descent and Distribution; History of Intestacy; History of Wills; Probate Courts.
UNNATURAL WILLS, 139–140, 232, 538, 539.

UNWORTHY HEIRS,
Abandonment,
Of child, 148.
Of spouse, 152–153.
Denial of paternity of child, 148.
Murder,
Of ancestor, 153–156.
Of insured by beneficiary, 158.
Of one joint tenant by another tenant, 156–158.
Of testator, 154–155.
Unfaithful spouse,
Abandonment, 152–153.
Adultery, 148 et seq.
Bigamous marriage, 150, 152.
Elopement and living in adultery, 148 et seq.
Separation agreement, 112.
See Revocation of Wills.

USES,
Early substitutes for wills, 14, 18.
See Trusts.

## V

VALUE,
See Advancements; Appraisal; Assets; Lapse; Legacies; Sales by Personal Representatives.

VERDICT,
Sympathetic for children, 35, 139–140.
See Contest of Wills.

VOID LEGACIES,
See Legacies.

## W

WAIVER,
See Claims.

WAR,
See Descent and Distribution; Soldiers' and Sailors' Wills.

WASTE, 648–649.
See Personal Representatives.

WIDOW,
See Administrators; Conditions; Contest of Wills; Descent and Distribution; Dower; Election; Entireties; Estate Tax; Family Allowances; Fraud; Legacies; Undue Influence; Unworthy Heirs.

WIFE,
See Administrators; Conditions; Contest of Wills; Curtesy; Descent and Distribution; Dower; Election; Entireties; Execution of Wills; Family Allowances; Fraud; Legacies; Revocation of Wills; Testamentary Capacity; Undue Influence; Unworthy Heirs.

WILLS,
Alterations in, 307, 349, 444–445, 499.
Appointment of executor in, see Executors.
Codicil to, 448, 451–452, 466–473, 811, 835.

WILLS—Continued
Concealment of, 486, 491, 504.
Conditional wills, 416–418.
Construction of, see Construction.
Contest of, see Contest of Wills.
Custody of, 354, 374, 485, 491, 554.
Duplicate wills, 354, 442–443.
Holographic wills, 362.
Deathbed, 12, 16, 135, 136, 251, 364, 819.
Defined, 2–3.
Distinguished from other instruments, see Substitutes for Wills.
Drafting of, 817–836.
Duplicate wills,
Custody of, 354, 442–443.
Probate of, 383, 443.
Revocation of, 442–443, 553n.
Execution of, see Execution of Wills.
Existence of, as requiring administration, 564.
Foreign, 383–384, 487–489.
Form of,
Assignments, 197–198.
Bills and notes, 198–199.
Bills of sale, 197.
Checks, 199, 203, 365.
Contracts, 193 et seq.
Deeds, 188–189.
Letters, 207–208, 356, 362, 373.
Releases, 197.
Separate sheets, 380.
Trusts, 180–181.
Writing, 294–296, 367, 372.
History of, see History of Wills.
Holographic, see Holographic Wills.
Joint wills, see Joint and Mutual Wills.
Libelous matter in, 443, 444.
Lost wills, see Evidence; Probate of Wills; Revocation of Wills.
Moving picture wills, 296.
Mutual wills, see Joint and Mutual Wills.
Mystic wills, 377.
Nuncupative wills, see Louisiana; Nuncupative Wills.
Partial wills, 289–291, 383, 512.
Phonographic, 296.
Prejudice against making, 159–160.
Probate of, see Probate of Wills.
Reciprocal wills, see Joint and Mutual Wills.
Re-execution, see Revival of Wills.
Reference to acts in, see Reference to Nontestamentary Acts.
Reference to documents in, see Incorporation by Reference.
Republication, see Revival of Wills.
Revalidation, see Revival of Wills.
Revival of, see Revival of Wills.
Revocation of, see Revocation of Wills.
Sham wills, 205–206.

**WILLS**—Continued
Soldiers' and sailors' wills, see Soldiers' and Sailors' Wills.
Speak from what time, 2, 15, 18, 21–22, 433–436, 470, 815.
Specimen, 207.
Substitutes for, see Substitutes for Wills.
Sunday, 294.
Testament distinguished, 3, 482.
Unnatural, 139–140, 232, 255, 538, 539.
See also, Devises; Disinheritance; Forced Heirs; Legacies.

**WITNESSES,**
See Contest of Wills; Evidence; Execution of Wills; Probate of Wills.

**WOMEN,**
See Administrators; Revocation of Wills; Testamentary Capacity.

**WORDS,**
See Construction; Mistake; Revocation of Wills.

**WRITING,**
See Execution of Wills; Incorporation by Reference; Integration of Wills; Reference to Nontestamentary Acts; Revocation of Wills.

WEST PUBLISHING CO.